The Indo-European Puzzle Revisited

This book examines the impact of ancient DNA research and scientific evidence on our understanding of the emergence of the Indo-European languages in prehistory. Offering cutting-edge contributions from an international team of scholars, it considers the driving forces behind the Indo-European migrations during the third and second millennia BC. The volume explores the rise of the world's first pastoral nomads, the Yamnaya culture, in the Russian Pontic steppe, including their social organization, expansions, and the transition from nomadism to semi-sedentism when entering Europe. It also traces the chariot conquest in the late Bronze Age and its impact on the expansion of the Indo-Iranian languages into Central Asia. In the final section, the volume considers the development of hierarchical societies and the origins of slavery. A landmark synthesis of recent, exciting discoveries, the book also includes an extensive theoretical discussion regarding the integration of linguistics, genetics, and archaeology, and the importance of interdisciplinary research in the study of ancient migration.

Kristian Kristiansen is Professor of Archaeology at the Department of Historical Studies at the University of Gothenburg and Affiliated Professor at the Globe Institute, University of Copenhagen. He specializes in the Bronze Age of western Eurasia, archaeological theory, and cultural heritage studies.

Guus Kroonen is an Indo-Europeanist based at the Leiden University Centre for Linguistics. His specializations include Scandinavian, Germanic, and Indo-European linguistics. In addition, he is Professor with Special Responsibilities of Linguistic Prehistory at the Copenhagen University section of Indo-European Studies.

Eske Willerslev is Lundbeck Foundation Professor at the Globe Institute at the University of Copenhagen, and Prince Phillip Professor at the Department of Zoology at the University of Cambridge. He is an evolutionary geneticist, recognized for his studies on human evolution and environmental DNA.

The Indo-European Puzzle Revisited

Integrating Archaeology, Genetics, and Linguistics

Edited by

Kristian Kristiansen
Universities of Gothenburg and Copenhagen

Guus Kroonen
Universities of Leiden and Copenhagen

Eske Willerslev
Universities of Cambridge and Copenhagen

Shaftesbury Road, Cambridge CB2 8EA, United Kingdom

One Liberty Plaza, 20th Floor, New York, NY 10006, USA

477 Williamstown Road, Port Melbourne, VIC 3207, Australia

314–321, 3rd Floor, Plot 3, Splendor Forum, Jasola District Centre, New Delhi – 110025, India

103 Penang Road, #05–06/07, Visioncrest Commercial, Singapore 238467

Cambridge University Press is part of Cambridge University Press & Assessment, a department of the University of Cambridge.

We share the University's mission to contribute to society through the pursuit of education, learning and research at the highest international levels of excellence.

www.cambridge.org
Information on this title: www.cambridge.org/9781009261746

DOI: 10.1017/9781009261753

First published 2023

Printed in the United Kingdom by TJ Books Limited, Padstow Cornwall

A catalogue record for this publication is available from the British Library.

Library of Congress Cataloging-in-Publication Data
Names: Kristiansen, Kristian, 1948- editor. | Kroonen, Guus, 1979– editor. | Willerslev, Eske, editor.
Title: The Indo-European puzzle revisited : integrating archaeology, genetics, and linguistics / edited by Kristian Kristiansen, University of Gothenburg ; Guus Kroonen, University of Leiden ; Eske Willerslev, University of Copenhagen.
Description: Cambridge ; New York, NY : Cambridge University Press, 2023. | Includes bibliographical references and index.
Identifiers: LCCN 2022030552 (print) | LCCN 2022030553 (ebook) | ISBN 9781009261746 (Hardback) | ISBN 9781009261722 (Paperback) | ISBN 9781009261753 (epub)
Subjects: LCSH: Indo-European languages. | Indo-Europeans–Migrations. | DNA–Analysis. | Indo-European antiquities. | Historical linguistics. | BISAC: SOCIAL SCIENCE / Archaeology | LCGFT: Essays.
Classification: LCC P525 .I53 2023 (print) | LCC P525 (ebook) | DDC 417/.7–dc23/eng/20220720
LC record available at https://lccn.loc.gov/2022030552
LC ebook record available at https://lccn.loc.gov/2022030553

ISBN *978-1-009-26174-6 Hardback*

Contents

Figures

Tables

Contributors

Polina S. Ankusheva
South Ural Federal Research Center of Mineralogy and Geoecology, Ural Branch of the Russian Academy of Sciences, Miass, Russia

David W. Anthony
Hartwick College, USA

Quentin Bourgeois
Leiden University, The Netherlands

Igor V. Chechushkov
Institute of History and Archaeology, Ural Branch of the Russian Academy of Sciences, Yekaterinburg, Russia

Andrey V. Epimakhov
South Ural State University, Chelyabinsk, Russia

Ingo Feeser
University of Kiel, Germany

Morten Fischer Mortensen
The National Museum, Copenhagen, Denmark

Martin Furholt
University of Oslo, Norway

Wolfgang Haak
Max Planck Institute for Evolutionary Anthropology, Leipzig, Germany

Volker Heyd
University of Helsinki, Finland

Anthony Jakob
Leiden University, The Netherlands

Anders Richardt Jørgensen
University of Copenhagen, Denmark

Daria V. Kiseleva
Institute of Geology and Geochemistry, Ural Branch of the Russian Academy of Sciences, Yekaterinburg, Russia

Alwin Kloekhorst
Leiden University, The Netherlands

John T. Koch
University of Wales, Aberystwyth, UK

Kristian Kristiansen
University of Gothenburg, Sweden

Erik Kroon
Leiden University, The Netherlands

Guus Kroonen
1) Leiden University, The Netherlands; 2) University of Copenhagen, Denmark

Johan Ling
University of Gothenburg, Sweden

Alexander M. Lubotsky
Leiden University, The Netherlands

James P. Mallory
Queen's University Belfast, Ireland

Johannes Müller
University of Kiel, Germany

Anne Brigitte Nielsen
University of Lund, Sweden

Benedicte Nielsen Whitehead
University of Copenhagen, Denmark

William O'Brien
University College Cork, Ireland

Thomas Olander
University of Copenhagen, Denmark

Birgit Anette Olsen
University of Copenhagen, Denmark

Olga V. Orfinskaya
Centre for Egyptological Studies of the Russian Academy of Sciences, Moscow, Russia

Axel Palmér
Leiden University, The Netherlands

Luka Papac
Max Planck Institute for Evolutionary Anthropology, Leipzig, Germany

Tijmen Pronk
Leiden University, The Netherlands

Adam Ben Rohrlach
Max Planck Institute for Evolutionary Anthropology, Leipzig, Germany

Natalia I. Shishlina
Department of Archaeology, State History Museum, Moscow, Russia

Martin Sikora
University of Copenhagen, Denmark

Karl-Göran Sjögren
University of Gothenburg, Sweden

David Stifter
Maynooth University, Ireland

Philipp W. Stockhammer
1) Ludwig Maximilian University of Munich, Germany; 2) Max Planck Institute for Evolutionary Anthropology, Leipzig, Germany

Rasmus Thorsø
Leiden University, The Netherlands

Paulus van Sluis
Leiden University, The Netherlands

Andrew Wigman
Leiden University, The Netherlands

Eske Willerslev
1) Cambridge University, UK; 2) University of Copenhagen

Preface

From May 2 to 5, 2018, the editors of this volume hosted an international, interdisciplinary conference at Gothenburg University under the name "When Archaeology Meets Linguistics and Genetics." Thanks to a generous grant from Riksbankens Jubileumsfond in 2016, the three organizers had already become involved in multiple interdisciplinary research projects on European prehistory. It was our ambition also to bring together other scholars from the aforementioned fields, in particular those working to solve some of the central questions related to the puzzle of Indo-European origins. With this vision in mind, we invited some of the most active scholars from archaeology, linguistics, and genetics to come to Gothenburg, and to present the state of the art of their fields.

To make this a constructive interdisciplinary encounter, we decided to organize the conference around a number of themes, each with a contribution from archaeology, linguistics, and archaeogenetics, when possible. These are (1) early Indo-European and the origin of pastoralism, (2) migratory processes and linguistic dispersals between Yamnaya and the Corded Ware, (3) the cultural and linguistic significance of Bell Beakers along the Atlantic fringe, (4) the Bronze Age chariot and wool horizons, and (5) kinship systems, marriage, fosterage, free and unfree. It turned out to be a rewarding approach, we believe, even if some results were unexpected, surprising, or straight-out problematic. After all, it is only by identifying new problems that new explanations can be explored, and in the interdisciplinary arena of Indo-European studies, such identifications often only happen by combining all of the available data sets.

Now, we can present this volume as a lasting result of our ambition to unite scholars from our highly divergent but increasingly interdependent fields. We would like to express our deepest gratitude to all the participants for joining our meeting in Gothenburg, for presenting their ideas, and for participating in the discussions, and last but not least for reevaluating their results in the light of their experiences at the conference.

We further thank the authors for contributing one or sometimes even two papers, each of which can be considered pioneering studies in their corresponding areas of research. While we cannot claim to have solved all the problems concerning the dispersal of the Indo-European languages, we are confident that the papers presented in this book take important new steps toward understanding what lies at the heart of the formation of the Eurasian linguistic landscape, i.e., the Indo-European dispersal. Although the puzzle of the Indo-European origins is over a century old, there has hardly ever been a more fascinating time to study it. By addressing all the old and the new problems that this topic presents, fresh insights can be gained not only on this key question in European prehistory, but also on how to make new inroads into the development of interdisciplinary tools for addressing other such major questions concerned with our shared human past.

Finally, we thank Kristen de Joseph for her efforts in copy-editing all the contributions and Richard Potter for helping us prepare the manuscript for publication.

Introduction

1 RE-THEORIZING INTERDISCIPLINARITY, AND THE RELATION BETWEEN ARCHAEOLOGY, LINGUISTICS, AND GENETICS

KRISTIAN KRISTIANSEN AND GUUS KROONEN

1.1 Background: The Third Science Revolution

We are currently experiencing what could be called the "third science revolution" (Kristiansen 2014). The implications of this revolution are reshaping not only archaeological discourse, but – even more fundamentally – the nature and perception of interdisciplinarity (Stutz 2018). The current reconfiguration offers unique new opportunities for collaboration across the sciences and humanities, as we will show, but can also provoke a strong emotional response. This is apparent from the at times fierce debates about the role of science in archaeological, archaeogenetic, and perhaps especially archaeolinguistic interpretation (Gray, Atkinson, & Greenhill 2011 vs. Pereltsvaig & Lewis 2015; Ion 2017 and 2019; Ribeiro 2019; Sørensen 2016). We also see old debates about the role of historical linguistics in archaeology resurfacing (Hansen 2019). Common to all three revolutions – the Darwinian revolution, introducing the principles of stratification, deep time, and evolution to archaeology (1850–60); the environmental revolution and the C14 revolution, introducing absolute dating (1950–1960); and now the strontium/DNA revolution, introducing prehistoric population genomics and migrations (2010–2020) – is the transformation of previous relative knowledge to absolute knowledge.[1] In the process, each revolution freed intellectual resources to be spent on explaining change rather than describing and debating it. Thus, prior to the C14 revolution, most archaeological resources were poured into the classification and relative dating of prehistoric cultures. Beyond the safe dates of written sources, one had to project back in time the presumed length of time periods based on stratigraphy and typology. As we now know, all prehistoric periods earlier than the Bronze Age turned out to be much older than anticipated. Once the C14 revolution unfolded and thousands of dates established safe chronologies, intellectual resources could instead be spent on explaining change, leading to New Archaeology and what followed. Thus, these science revolutions were also intellectual revolutions, propelling archaeological theory and interpretation forward. However, these revolutions also exerted a deep impact on the other humanistic disciplines, especially linguistics. Historical linguistics was shaped during the same period of the mid nineteenth century, and while it developed its own methodology (Lehman 1992, chapter 2; Lehman 1993), it soon became apparent that timing the origin and expansion of the Indo-European languages demanded collaboration with archaeology, as well as environmental science, in order to establish secure dating. However, it was not until the second science revolution and the introduction of absolute dating that this collaboration could be based on safe chronological grounds. Unfortunately, this took place at a time when archaeology had lost interest in human migrations and diffusion, thus sidelining the question of the expansion of Indo-European languages – that is, until Colin Renfrew revitalized the debate with his controversial 1987 book *Archaeology and Language*.

However, the three science revolutions also expose a recurring dialectic between science-based and humanistic/historically based interpretations in archaeology, including historical linguistics. One might even call it a fight for interpretative dominance. Such debates are already unfolding during the third and present science revolution. It is reflected in a growing number of critical papers that, from various positions, opt for theoretical and interpretive renewal (Fuhrholt et al. 2018; Ion 2017; Ribeiro 2019), based in part on a critique of one-dimensional or deterministic interpretations (Arponen et al. 2020; Heyd 2017, response in Booth 2019; Kristiansen 2019), and problems with terminologies and their implicit implications for interpretation (Eisenman et al. 2019). We have already seen a number of responses from archaeogenetics that suggest a move toward a more holistic, systematic application of new interdisciplinary methods to integrate different

[1] This does not imply that there is no possible debate about the interpretation or improvement of methodologies. A good historical example is the calibration curve of C14; similarly, one can also discuss how aDNA data are analysed and presented using different statistical methods. However, the baseline is that certain types of questions can be answered with a high degree of probability, and that genetic base data are correct, if correctly sequenced. Importantly, genetic data are stored and made accessible for further reanalysis and testing in global public databases. To match this, archaeological data still have some way to go.

TABLE 1.1. Timeline of the historical disciplines. The first science revolution resulted from broad interdisciplinary interaction. The second and third were restricted to archaeology and genetics, respectively, but with huge long-term effects on the other disciplines. The fourth revolution will require breakthroughs in the development of qualitative rather than quantitative models in the field of computational comparative linguistics.

	historical linguistics	**prehistoric archaeology**	**evolutionary biology**
1850–1900	tree model sound laws protolanguages linguistic palaeontology	principles of stratigraphy technological evolution principles of typology dating and classification of cultures	Darwinism Mendelian inheritance phylogenetics
1900–1950	structuralism *double articulation*	culture-historical synthesis	"modern synthesis"
1950–2000		C14 dating	discovery of DNA
2000–	computational linguistics	bioarchaeology	palaeogenomics

strands and levels of evidence, which will allow high-resolution local studies to inform wider patterns of change (Iversen & Kroonen 2017; Kristiansen et al. 2017; Mittnik et al. 2019; Racimo & Sikora et al. 2020; Sjögren et al. 2020; Veeramah 2018). This may also include mechanisms behind language dispersals and shifts that are linked to social processes. It can be demonstrated through ethnographic-linguistic-genetic case studies that language expansion through a sedentary population is channeled along those patrilocal or matrilocal groups who stay in residence, as is also reflected in genetic admixture patterns (Lansing 2017). We may perhaps be witnessing here the first contours of a new interdisciplinary discourse (Racimo & Woodbridge et al. 2020) yet to unfold. Likewise, we have seen a move toward a redefinition of the results and position of Indo-European studies in archaeology (Kristiansen & Larsson 2005: chapters 6–7), as well as the increasingly prominent role of historical linguistics in general in formulating and contextualizing the research questions of archaeogenetics (Damgaard et al. 2018).

As of yet, there appear to be no predetermined rules for how cultural and genetic phenomena interact, and it is clear that there is no one-to-one relationship between the two. Thus, the Beaker package was transmitted and adopted with little or no genetic admixture (Olalde et al. 2018), while Corded Ware represented a new cultural and economic adaptation of Yamnaya steppe ancestry, which, however, shared rules of kinship and burial rituals (Fuhrholt 2019). The social mechanisms behind the rise of new archaeological complexes, such as the Corded Ware, can be integrated into models for local language transmission among genetically admixed groups (Kristiansen et al. 2017). Multifaceted approaches involving aDNA and stabile isotopes allow for the bioarchaeological reconstruction of local kinship systems and marital strategies, which additionally can be matched against their linguistically reconstructed equivalents (Mittnik et al. 2019; Sjögren et al. 2020). The new analytical techniques for the study of biomolecules thus promises not only to revolutionize the study of the human past by offering a new line of evidence, but also invites or perhaps even demands the unification of preexisting lines of evidence from archaeology, genetics, and linguistics into a single unified framework on human prehistory.

1.2 A Brief Research History

Historical linguistics and archaeology share a complicated and sometimes enigmatic interdisciplinarity relationship. In the postwar period, it unfolded most clearly in Colin Renfrew's now-classic reinterpretation of the dispersal of the Indo-European languages in his 1987 book *Language and Archaeology*. It was a rather fierce critique of some of the methodological foundations of historical linguistics, specifically the subfield of linguistic palaeontology, and it aimed to offer a new interpretation of the origin of the Indo-European languages as being located in Neolithic Anatolia. A counterresponse was soon delivered by Mallory (1989), who defended the steppe hypothesis, and criticized Renfrew for devaluing linguistic methods to serve his own purpose of reinterpreting the puzzle of Indo-European origins. Others criticized Renfrew for misrepresenting later prehistory by dooming post-Neolithic societies to immobility (Anthony 1990; Kristiansen 1989). However, Renfrew's approach did garner strong support among an archaeological community that adhered to an autonomous antimigration discourse for later European prehistory, based in part on a response to the political misuse of prehistoric migrations and their proposed ethnicities during the prewar era (Demoule 2014). On the negative side, Renfrew and many other archaeologists besides confounded critique of the purely linguistic study of Indo-European languages with critique of the social and religious structure of their society, as represented by George Dumezil, who was central in developing this comparative field of research (Dumezil 1995). The field was expanded and critically reevaluated by later generations (Garcia 1999; Lincoln 1999), and has increasingly been integrated with archaeological interpretation (Kristiansen & Larsson 2005). On the positive side, Renfrew's book mobilized a lot of new research, and also invited new methodological developments, even if debatable from a linguistic point of view (Gray & Atkinson 2003; Gray, Atkinson, & Greenhill 2011, response in Pereltsvaig & Lewis 2015).

However, Renfrew also denounced the concept of culture in archaeology, which he wanted to replace with polities, governed by theoretically informed, testable generalizations (Renfrew 1977). It was Ian Hodder who reintroduced culture as meaningfully constituted, and thus demanding theoretically informed interpretations. Inspired by the work of David Clarke (1968), he accepted the historical reality of culture and its role in demarcating various forms of identities, past and present (Hodder 1978, 1982). It was Oscar Montelius who had formulated the principles of typology that allowed for the classification and definition of archaeological cultures, universally adopted in archaeology by the late nineteenth century (Montelius 1903). His methodology was clearly inspired by Darwinian principles and has much in common with linguistic principles of language change, but its principles do not aspire to becoming laws. Nonetheless, today it is widely accepted that archaeological cultures are objective phenomena characteristic of human societies since the Palaeolithic. It is also clear that cultures are layered and not necessarily homogenous, just as one can apply different degrees of resolution in classifying and defining culture groups, producing both regional cultures such as the Nordic Bronze Age Culture or the Tumulus Culture, as well as local variants in the way of spoken dialects. David Clarke summarized much of what still today remains the theoretical and methodological basis of the "culture concept" in archaeology, amplified by quantitative methods, in his *Analytical Archaeology* (Clarke 1968). While the reality of culture cannot be questioned, its interpretation of course can be; this remains an underdeveloped field of research, due in part to oversimplified interpretations of the past. It therefore demands historical sensitivity to the way we employ cultural designations in archaeogenetic interpretation (Eisenman et al. 2018), but also to the way we designate linguistic and archaeological groups. However, the relation between culture, ethnicity, and language is clearly a potentially rewarding field of future research, when properly theorized (Hornborg 2014).

To linguists, the debates raging in archaeology can sometimes come across as otherworldly and bewilderingly overtheorized. Mobility is a ubiquitous factor in the expansion of languages in both the historic and modern periods, and the role it played in the shaping of the world's linguistic landscape is likewise assumed to have been fundamental (cf. recently Crevels & Muysken 2020). Thus, the antimigrationism that came to dominate mainstream archaeology in the latter half of the twentieth century implied an almost unimaginable violation of the uniformitarian principle and was never able to gain a foothold in historical linguistics. Archaeologists of the past decades have been correct to reject simplistic and essentialistic models that invoke large-scale mobility of ethnolinguistic monoliths as the default explanation of cultural and linguistic change (Adams, Von Gerven, & Levy 1978), and even today, historical linguists remain underinformed on average about the risks of overinterpreting archaeological evidence. By now it seems clear, however, that in the antimigrationist paradigm, human mobility was overproblematized to the extent that it acquired the characteristics of a taboo (Anthony 1990). While taboos are beneficial in that they may help us save energy on debating demonstrable misinterpretations, such as Holocaust denialism, the archaeological "ban on migration" appeared to be theoretically rather than empirically motivated. Moreover, it isolated archaeology from the other historical disciplines, and effectively put an embargo on interdisciplinary dialogue with linguistics, and initially also with palaeogenetics.

The same dialogue was further obstructed by yet another misunderstanding that appears to have been common among archaeologists, i.e., the assumption that the Indo-European language family is merely a "narrative" that can be replaced – almost interchangeably – with any other narrative, depending on which theoretical, political, or ideological perspective happens to be in vogue. From this "archaeocentric" interpretation of the linguistic data, it is perfectly understandable how some archaeologists appear to experience discomfort or even anxiety when confronted with the field of Indo-European studies, as it seems unclear why one would uphold what looks like an essentialistic, nineteenth-century interpretation of language and people (cf. most recently Hakenbeck 2019; Hansen 2019). The fact is that the Indo-European linguistic phylum is not an interpretative narrative that can be repurposed at will to suit any new ideological framework; rather, it is a mere taxonomic unit, directly inferred – by a universally accepted method – from the world's linguistic record, just like all other language families that have similarly been identified. Any answer to the puzzle of Indo-European origins will have to start from this basic, unalterable linguistic fact.

Over the past decades, several archaeologists have nevertheless attempted to come up with alternative narratives of the Indo-European origins. To linguists, many of these narratives appear "fact-free," or at least free of linguistic facts. Here we may recall the Anatolian Hypothesis, which was only able to thrive in non-linguistic research environments, as it questioned the culturally and temporally salient features, as they are captured in the reconstructed Proto-Indo-European lexicon, that are indicative of a Late Neolithic language community. We could also add more fanciful narratives. According to the Palaeolithic Continuity Theory (Alinei 1996, 2000; Ebbesen 2009; Otte 1999), Indo-European would have been spoken in Europe since the arrival of *Homo sapiens sapiens*, with no linguistic incursions having taken place ever since. Of late, a narrative has been created that calls the reality of the Indo-European language family itself into question (Demoule 2014). Such "post-factual" narratives from archaeology can be perplexing to the unsuspecting linguist, but what they seem to have in common is a shared aspiration to offer workarounds to the aforementioned archaeological taboo, i.e., the necessity of having to postulate prehistoric population movements.

The issue with such perspectives is, of course, that in the case of the Indo-European dispersal a Late Neolithic population movement is exactly what the linguistic data suggests, and has been shown to suggest since the late nineteenth century. The picture emerging from the breakthrough genetic studies of 2015 was that the detection of the massive gene flow from the Russian steppe to the Corded Ware complex (Allentoft et al. 2015; Haak et al. 2015; Malmström et al. 2020) ended a primarily archaeological controversy, i.e., the one between the Kurgan Hypothesis and the Anatolian Hypothesis. However, the idea that the Indo-European languages spread from the South Russian steppes does not itself hail from archaeology and was first developed in historical linguistics. Even before the discovery of Hittite and Tocharian and the decipherment of Linear B, the German Indo-Europeanist Otto Schrader (1883) was able to conclude as much on the basis of his cultural and environmental analysis of the reconstructed Proto-Indo-European lexicon.

Thus, the field of Indo-European linguistics was well prepared for the results of genetics, when they finally provided the proof that steppe migrations had fundamentally impacted the genetic composition of Europeans (Allentoft et al.; Haak et al. 2015; Olalde et al. 2018). It revealed the demographic vector that had been postulated on the basis of lexical evidence more than a century earlier and it was defended by linguistically informed archaeologists such as J. P. Mallory and D. W. Anthony. Perhaps more crucially, the revolutionary findings from genetics also offered an opportunity to overcome a decade-long stalemate on prehistoric mobility that had paralyzed the interdisciplinary dialogue between archaeology and linguistics.

The third science revolution has been unfolding since 2010, but its beginnings were much earlier. Ammerman & Cavalli-Sforza (1984) were among the first to take advantage of the initial genetic breakthrough of mitochondrial DNA in the early 1980s in an attempt to use modern genetic data to infer prehistoric migrations (discussed in Reich 2018: Introduction). Soon it became possible to extract mitochondrial DNA from ancient samples, which however, contains only a fraction of genetic evidence, linked to the female lineage. The first wave of optimism was soon replaced by pessimism, as it turned out that contamination from present-day human DNA was a nearly insolvable problem. It was only after the publication of the first full human genome in 2004 and the development of short-read sequencing technologies that ancient DNA genome research became a reality, with the first prehistoric genomes published by the Copenhagen team (Rasmussen et al. 2010) and the Max Planck team (Green et al. 2010) in 2010. Since then, we have seen a steep increase in new data, as well as new results that have changed the perception of prehistory globally (as summarized in popular books by Reich 2018 and Krause 2019). This has been followed by the extensive popular dissemination of results, sometimes in more sensational form than desired. On the other hand, this is nothing new for archaeology; the same happens when new excavations produce "sensational" results. Genetic results, however, are potentially more prone to ideological misuse. Often, new results will be published globally in more than one hundred news outlets within a week after publication, as happened with a paper on the earliest plague in the world (Rascovan et al. 2018). This demands an acute and critical understanding of the role of popular dissemination and its possible ideological use, for good and bad – a new field of research to be developed (for example in Källen et al. 2019).

In addition, modern DNA research raises fundamental questions about what it means to be human (Barrett 2014), what genetic variation means, what archaeological cultures mean (Roberts & Vander Linden 2011), and the prospects of such knowledge for ideological propaganda, whether racist/antiracist, nationalist or antinationalist (Frieman & Hofman 2018; Hakenbeck 2019). In short, it demands a stronger public engagement by archaeologists, scientists, and humanists, perhaps to a degree we are not used to. While archaeology has a long and sometimes glorious history of popularization, there is less experience in taking part in critical public debates, whether in newspapers, television, or on the web. Understanding the political and ideological impact of the past in the present is often best understood in critical retrospect (Diaz-Andreu & Champion 1996), which, however, may also serve as a warning in the present. Critical heritage studies present a new discourse to cope with these complex questions (Harrison 2013). Based on these observations, we shall discuss the impact and critical role of ideological misrepresentation.

1.3 The Danger of Ideological Misrepresentation

Many scholars researching the human past fear that the current revolution in the study of ancient DNA will again invite simplistic, racist equations of culture, people, and language as in the past. In the prewar period, the prehistoric spread of the Indo-European languages was increasingly attributed to the superiority of an alleged Indo-European-speaking ethnolinguistic unity, which, despite all linguistic evidence to the contrary, was claimed to have developed, since the Neolithic, in North Europe. Through the *Siedlungsarchäologie* of Gustaf Kossinna (1858–1931), the question of Indo-European linguistic origins was integrated into nationalist theories of German ethnic origins, which demanded a North European center of spread. But similar ethnic interpretations were widespread in both archaeology and ethnography. In his book *The Aryans* (1926), British archaeologist Gordon Childe proved himself reluctant to fully accept Schrader's South Russian homeland – because of a lack of archaeological data from that area, as he objects, but also, perhaps, because he had become convinced that the superiority of Indo-European-speaking groups ensued from "a more excellent language and the mentality it created." It is very well possible that future interdisciplinary studies will again lead to misinterpretations that are liable to political abuse. Here we should mention the rise of an "Out of India" model of Indo-European languages during the last generation, motivated primarily by Hindu nationalism. These are the same kind of forces that used the model of Gustaf Kossinna to support a Nazi racist ideology nearly one hundred years earlier. However, the Out of India model has been firmly refuted by recent aDNA results (Narasimhan et al. 2019), and it has little or no support in historical linguistic research (cf. Witzel 2012). However, it should serve as a warning example of the political impact of nationalism, even in the present (cf. also Schnirelman 2001).

The most obvious risks of ideological misrepresentation occur when such forces infiltrate the academic environment, as happened in Germany during the Nazi regime. But the risk of such abuse will likely only increase if relevant evidence is ignored rather than welcomed. If there is anything that the recent interdisciplinary biomolecular studies have shown, it must be that the once-dominant Eurocentric and supremacist perspectives on the Indo-European homeland are not supported by any genetic or linguistic evidence.

However, we must be aware of the huge popular interest in the new genetic results, and the need to constantly and critically debate their dissemination, also in the public domain (Kristiansen 2014: 25), where complex knowledge can sometimes be transformed into dangerous stereotypes (Frieman & Hoffman 2019; Heyd 2017). The past has always been exploited for political purposes, for good and bad (Diaz-Andreu 2007). One of the most destructive political misuses of the past has been in constructing nationalist narratives of exclusion (Kohl & Fawcett 1995). According to aDNA, all Europeans have been subject to the same genetic admixture processes, and thus there is no genetic support for such narratives. On the contrary, all Europeans belong to the same genetic stock or "family," a message that has been communicated in popular books by geneticists, science journalists, and others (Bojs 2017; Krause 2019; Reich 2018).

While some current researchers are concerned with the darker side of potential misuse (Hakenbeck 2019; Ion 2019), this should not lead us to introduce politically motivated restrictions on research and on academic freedom. Rather, we need to engage in the ways new results are disseminated (Källen et al. 2019), whether in writing popular books or articles or engaging with science journalists, whose articles reach a wide readership.

1.4 From Here On: Toward a New Interdisciplinarity?

Which theoretical developments and new forms of interdisciplinarity can we then expect of the future? First, we need to pay attention to the methodological and interpretative autonomy of the different research disciplines, whether in the sciences or the humanities – both when we criticize interpretations, and when we attempt to integrate interpretations. What are their commonalities and differences? How do we integrate different types of evidence from different disciplines – science, historical linguistics, and archaeology – into a unified interpretation respecting all three fields? In the words of Tim Flohr Sørensen, "we need to consider the potential that a question, an observation, an object, a fact, are not synonymous concepts in science and in the humanities. Why else would we apply different methods and theoretical perspectives?" (Sørensen 2017). While this may be correct, at least in part, the problems of interdisciplinary interpretation are of a more complex nature. No method can have priority over another method, as methods are inherent to a specific scientific tradition and cannot be questioned from the outside. But if Sørensen is correct, then neither can any interpretation of a specific set of data have priority over an interpretation of another set of data if they are confined within different discourses. Consequently, historical-archaeological interpretations are not inherently more correct than genetic or linguistic interpretations. In addition, there exists no genuine archaeological theory of human societies; what is inherently archaeological, besides excavation, is the repertoire of methods to describe changes in material culture. However, interpretation of that evidence can only be carried out by comparison between the known and unknown, that is through comparative analysis with ethnographically and historically documented societies. Archaeological theory is therefore based on shared, comparative theoretical models of human societies anchored in social and historical research traditions. So-called "middle-range theory" is an attempt to bridge the two – archaeological data and theory – in order to create a more robust middle ground, but it does not add up to a complete social theory (recent discussion in Arponen et al. 2018).

Likewise, with historical linguistics: this discipline shares certain basic methodological strategies, based on typology and regularities in language change, with archaeology and genetics. The spontaneous sound changes that occur randomly in languages are passed down the linguistic tree much in the same way that mutations accumulate in uniparental parts of the human genome (Comrie 2003). Famously, the taxonomic tree model itself was first developed and applied to languages by the linguist August Schleicher in 1861, after having read Darwin's *On the Origins of Species* and subsequently introduced to biology by Ernst Haeckel in 1866 (Aronoff 2017). However, unlike the random mutations of genomes, the sound changes by which languages evolve and diverge from each other can only be ordered, with the available linguistic methodology, in relative chronologies. For the absolute dating of protolanguages and their corresponding speech communities, historical linguistics depends on collaboration and comparative evidence from the other disciplines, most prominently archaeology: it is only through the linguistically reconstructed lexicon that prehistoric speech communities, i.e. linguistically defined population groups, can be approximated in space and time (cf. Mallory 2021). In the same way, aDNA results require archaeological evidence to be properly dated and contextualized, while their genetic interpretation depends on knowledge internal to the discipline. Their implications for archaeology, therefore, demands familiarity with the methodological and interpretative field of genetics, and vice versa (Booth 2019).

While historical linguistics, archaeology, and genetics have developed their own methodological repertoire – some shared, some not – both linguistics and genetics depend on archaeological historical dating and the correct interpretation of their contexts. Likewise, archaeology depends on linguistics and genetics for the correct interpretation of admixture processes and their implications for population genomics. With respect to linguistics, reconstructed protolanguages provide clues to the environmental context and stage of development of prehistoric groups – in the case of the Indo-European speech community, fundamental terminologies linked to technology (wagon and wheels, metals) social organization (kinship terminologies), and religion (names and functions of gods and rituals). Each of these knowledge domains is governed by analytical rules of proof and falsification internal to each discipline, but with implications for the other disciplines. Dating and correct historical interpretation depend on a proper source-critical understanding of the context of the archaeological source, and application of genetic and linguistic evidence in archaeological interpretation depends on a proper source-critical understanding of the genetic and linguistic contexts of the evidence. Otherwise, we may end up with circular reasoning based on flawed interpretations of the other disciplines. This imposes a demand for familiarity with the limits of interpretation internal to each discipline for interdisciplinary interpretations to be correct, or at least scientifically viable.

Thus, archaeology, historical linguistics, and genetics share the methodological demands of analytical systematics, statistical significance, and testable procedures in their basic repertoire. However, that does not produce a final interpretation; this demands a wider context, including comparative knowledge of results from other disciplines. And this inevitably reduces the number of researchers who are capable and willing to provide that extra investment of labor in a new field where such interpretations will remain debatable for the foreseeable future. Until now, the most productive way forward has been project teamwork where archaeologists, geneticists, and researchers from other relevant disciplines, such as environmental science, historical linguistics, and others, work together, from formulating research goals to final publication.

In the end, therefore, the real challenge is, how do we balance evidence from different disciplines in interpretation? As there is yet no methodological approach able to combine and statistically evaluate results from, say, environmental analysis, genetics, and archaeology, the task is a difficult one. One may be able to document statistical correlations between such different types of evidence, as has recently been done (Racimo & Woodbridge et al. 2020), but there is a giant step from correlation to explanation/interpretation. In the future, we may well see complex modeling that is able to handle the task of weighting qualitatively different types of data as to their relative impact in a historical process of change, but we are not yet there. It all comes down to the complexity of evidence that is anchored in different theoretical and methodological traditions, each of whose results have an impact on the interpretation of other types of data. In the end, the final interpretation will have to be presented in the form of an interpretative narrative, where documentation is either found in a supplementary, as is most common in science journals, or simply based on previous research (Kristiansen et al. 2017; Mittnik et al. 2019). Therefore, we need to develop the concept of interpretative narratives, which have long been debated in the discipline of history (White 1987). Perhaps it suffices, for the moment, to define them as platforms for the formulation of testable new hypotheses. We may then perceive scientific practice as a layered process, proceeding – through processes of proof and falsification – from basic information toward increasingly wider-ranging interpretations, ending in an interpretative narrative. This is irrespective of whether we are talking about large geographical regions or narrow, contextualized studies of single communities. The process remains the same, and the results should in the end be compatible. If not, a new interpretation is needed, and the process starts all over again.

This book is an attempt to establish such a new practice, where each discipline contributes knowledge to a common theme based on its own scientific premises, yet contributing to produce a new, integrated historical narrative. We hope it will inspire others to come up with new interpretations, whether critical or supporting. Being proven wrong is the first step toward getting it right. In that sense, Colin Renfrew's contribution to integrating language and archaeology in new ways, though since proven wrong, has been fundamental, since he propelled the research forward with new speed and intensity. From a theoretical point of view, his interpretative models rejuvenated the interdisciplinary field by providing a strong interpretative narrative. We are now starting the process anew.

References

Adams, W. Y., D. P. Von Gerven, & R. S. Levy. 1978. The retreat from migrationism. *Annual Review of Anthropology* 7: 483–532.

Alinei, M. 1996. *La teoria della continuità*. Bologna: Mulino.

2000. *Continuità dal Mesolitico all'età del Ferro nelle principali aree etnolinguistiche*. Bologna: Mulino.

Allentoft, M. E., et al. 2015. Population genomics of Bronze Age Eurasia. *Nature* 522(7555): 167–172.

Anthony, D. W. 1990. Migration in archaeology: The baby and the bathwater. *American Anthropologist* 92(4): 895–914.

2007. *The horse, the wheel, and language: How Bronze-Age riders from the Eurasian steppes shaped the modern world*. Princeton (NJ): Princeton University Press.

Aronoff, M. 2017. Darwinism tested by the science of language. In Claire Bowern, Laurence Horn, & Raffaella Zanuttini (ed.), *On looking into language: structures, relations, analyses*, 443–455. Berlin: Language Science Press.

Arponen, V. P. J., W. Dörfler, I. Feeser, S. Grimm, D. Groß, M. Hinz, D. Knitter, N. Müller-Scheesel, K. Ott, & A. Ribeiro. 2019a. Environmental determinism, and archaeology. Understanding and evaluating determinism in research design. *Archaeological Dialogues*, 1–11.

2019b. Two cultures in the times of interdisciplinary archaeology: A response to commentators. *Archaeological Dialogues* 26(1): 19–24.

Arponen, V. P. J., S. Grimm, L. Käppel, K. Ott, B. Thalheim, Y. Kropp, K. Kittig, J. Brinkmann, & A. Ribeiro. 2019c. Between natural and human sciences: On the role and character of theory in socio-environmental archaeology. *The Holocene* 29(10): 1671–1676.

Barrett, J. 2014. The material constitution of humanness. *Archaeological Dialogues* 21(1): 65–74.

Booth, T. J. 2019. A stranger in a strange land: A perspective on archaeological responses to the palaeogenetic revolution from an archaeologist working amongst palaeogeneticists. *World Archaeology* 51(4): 586–601.

Clarke, D. 1968. *Analytical archaeology*. London: Methuen & Co.

Comrie, B. Genetic and linguistic affinities between human populations in Eurasia and West Africa. *Human Biology* 75(3): 331–344.

Crevels, M. & P. Muysken. 2020. *Language dispersal, diversification, and contact*. Oxford: Oxford University Press.

Demoule, J. P. 2014. *Mais où sont passés les Indo-Européens? Le mythe d'origine de l'Occident*. Paris: Éditions du Seuil.

Diaz-Andreu, M. & T. Champion. 1996. *Nationalism and archaeology in Europe*. London: UCL Press.

Dumézil, G. 1995. *Mythe et Épopée I. II. III*. Paris: Quarto Gallimard.

Ebbesen, K. 2009. *The origins of the Indo-European languages. De Indoeuropæiske sprogs oprindelse*. Copenhagen: Attika.

Eisenmann, S., E. Bánffy, P. van Dommelen, K. P. Hofmann, J. Maran, I. Lazaridis, A. Mittnik, M. McCormick, J. Krause, D. Reich, & P. W. Stockhammer. 2018. Reconciling material cultures in archaeology with genetic data: The nomenclature of clusters emerging from archaeogenomic analysis. *Scientific Reports* 8: 13003.

Frieman, C. J. & D. Hofmann. 2019. Present pasts in the archaeology of genetics, identity, and migration in Europe: A critical essay. *World Archaeology* 51(4): 528–545.

Fuhrholt, M. 2018. Massive migrations? The impact of recent aDNA studies on our view of third millennium Europe. *European Journal of Archaeology* 21(2): 159–191.

2019. Re-integrating archaeology: A contribution to aDNA studies and the migration discourse on the 3rd millennium BC in Europe. *Proceedings of the Prehistoric Society* 85: 115–129.

Garcia Quintela, M. V. 2001. *Dumézil. Une Introduction. Suivie L'Affaire Dumezil*. Paris: Editions Armeline.

Gray, R. D. & Q. D. Atkinson. 2003. Language-tree divergence times support the Anatolian theory of Indo-European origin. *Nature* 426: 435–439.

Gray, R. D., Q. D. Atkinson, & S. J. Greenhill. 2011. Language evolution and human history: What a difference a date makes. *Philosophical Transactions of the Royal Society B* 366(1567): 1090–1100.

Green, R. E., et al. A draft sequence of the Neandertal genome. *Science* 328(5979): 710–722.

Haak, W., et al. 2015. Massive migration from the steppe was a source for Indo-European languages in Europe. *Nature* 522 (7555): 207–211.

Hakenbeck, S. 2019. Genetics, archaeology and the far right: An unholy Trinity. *World Archaeology* 51(4): 517–527.

Hansen, S. 2019. Noch einmal: Abschied von den Indogermanen. In S. Hansen, V. I. Molodin, & L. N. Mylnikova (ed.), *Mobility and migration: Concepts, methods, results*, 44–60. Novosibirsk: IAET SB RAS Publishing.

Harrison, R. 2013. *Heritage: Critical approaches*. London: Routledge.

Heyd, V. 2017. Kossina's smile. *Antiquity* 91(356): 348–359.

Hodder, I. (ed.). 1978. *The spatial organisation of culture*. London: Duckworth.

Hodder, I. 1982. *Symbols in action. Ethnoarchaeologial studies of material culture*. Cambridge: Cambridge University Press.

Hornborg, A. 2014. Political economy, ethnogenesis, and language dispersals in the prehispanic Andes: A world-system perspective. *American Anthropologist* 116(4): 810–823.

Ion, A. 2017. How interdisciplinary is interdisciplinarity? Revisiting the impact of aDNA research for the archaeology of human remains. *Current Swedish Archaeology* 25: 177–198.

2019. Who are we as historical beings? Shaping identities in the light of the archaeogenetics "revolution." *Current Swedish Archaeology* 27: 11–36.

Iversen, R. & G. Kroonen. 2017. Talking Neolithic: Linguistic and archaeological perspectives on how Indo-European was implemented in southern Scandinavia. *American Journal of Archaeology* 121(4): 511–525.

Källen, A., C. Mulcare, A. Nybom, & D. Strand. 2019. Archaeogenetics in popular media. Contemporary implications of ancient DNA. *Current Swedish Archaeology* 27: 69–91.

Knipper, C., A. Mittnik, K. Massy, C. Kociumaka, I. Kucukkalipci, M. Maus, F. Wittenborn, S. E. Metz, A. Staskiewicz, J. Krause, & P. W. Stockhammer. 2017. Female exogamy and gene pool diversification at the transition from the Final Neolithic to the Early Bronze Age in Central Europe. *PNAS* 114(38): 10083–10088.

Krause, J. (& T. Trappe). 2019. *Die Reise unserer Gene: Eine Geschichte über uns und unsere Vorfahren*. Berlin: Propyläen.

Kristiansen, K. 1991. Prehistoric migrations: The case of the Single Grave and Corded Ware cultures. *Journal of Danish Archaeology* 8(1): 211–225.

2014. Towards a new paradigm? The third science revolution and its possible consequences in archaeology. *Current Swedish Archaeology* 22: 11–34.

2017. The nature of archaeological knowledge and its ontological turns. *Norwegian Archaeological Review* 50: 120–123.

2019. Who is deterministic? On the nature of interdisciplinary research in archaeology. *Archaeological Dialogues* 26(1): 12–14.

2022. Towards a new prehistory: Re-theorising genes, culture and migratory expansions. In M. Daniels (ed.), *Homo migrans: Modelling mobility and migration in human history*, 31–54. (IEMA Distinguished Monograph Series). Albany: SUNY Press.

In press. A history of interdisciplinarity in archaeology: The three science revolutions, their implementation and impact. In M. Diaz-Andreu (ed.), *Handbook of the History of Archaeology*. Oxford: Oxford University Press.

Kristiansen, K., et al. 2017. Re-theorising mobility and the formation of culture and language among the Corded Ware culture in Europe. *Antiquity* 91(356): 334–347.

Lansing, J. S., et al. 2017. Kinship structures create persistent channels for language transmission. *PNAS* 114(49): 12910–12915.

Lehman, W. P. 1992. *Historical linguistics*. London: Routledge.

1993. *Theoretical bases of Indo-European linguistics*. London: Routledge.

Lincoln, B. 1999. *Theorizing myth. Narrative, ideology, and scholarship*. Chicago: University of Chicago Press.

Mallory, F. 2021. The case against linguistic palaeontology. *Topoi* 40: 273–284.

Mallory, J. P. & Douglas Q. Adams (ed.). 1997. *Encyclopedia of Indo-European culture*. London: Fitzroy Dearborn.

Mallory, J. P. 1989. *In search of the Indo-Europeans: Language, archaeology, and myth*. London: Thames & Hudson.

Mittnik, A., et al. 2019. Kinship-based social inequality in Bronze Age Europe. *Science* 366(6466): 731–734.

Montelius, O. 1903. Die typologische Methode. In O. Montelius, *Die älteren Kulturperioden im Orient und in Europa*. Stockholm.

Narasimhan, V., et al. 2019. The formation of human populations in South and Central Asia. *Science* 365(6457): eaat7487.

Nicholls, G. K. & R. D. Gray. 2008. Dated ancestral trees from binary trait data and their application to the diversification of languages. *Journal of the Royal Statistical Society: Series B (Statistical Methodology)* 70(3): 545–566.

Olander, T. 2018. Connecting the dots: The Indo-European family tree as a heuristic device. In David M. Goldstein, Stephanie W. Jamison, & Brent Vine (ed.), *Proceedings of the 29th Annual Indo-European Conference*, 181–202. Bremen: Hempen.

Otte, M. 1999. Did Indo-European languages spread before farming? *Current Anthropology* 40(1): 73–77.

Pereltsvaig, A. & M. W. Lewis. 2015. *The Indo-European controversy: Facts and fallacies in historical linguistics*. Cambridge: Cambridge University Press.

Racimo, F., M. Sikora, M. Vander Linden, H. Schroeder, & C. Lalueza-Fox. 2020. Beyond broad strokes: sociocultural insights from the study of ancient genomes. *Nature Reviews Genetics* 21: 355–366.

Racimo, F., J. Woodbridge, R. Fyffe, M. Sikora, K.-G. Sjögren, K. Kristiansen, & M. Vander Linden. 2020. The spatiotemporal spread and impact of human migrations during the European Holocene. *PNAS* 117(16): 8989–9000.

Rasmussen, M., et al. 2010. Ancient human genome sequence of an extinct Palaeo-Eskimo. *Nature* 463: 757–762.

Reich, D. 2018. *Who we are and how we got here: Ancient DNA and the new science of the human past*. Oxford: Oxford University Press.

Renfrew, C. 1973. *Before civilization: The radiocarbon revolution and prehistoric Europe*. London: Jonathan Cape.

1977. Space, time and polity. In J. Friedman & M. J. Rowlands (ed.), *The Evolution of Social Systems*, 89–114. London: Duckworth.

1987. *Archaeology and language: The puzzle of Indo-European origins*. New York: Cambridge University Press.

Ribeiro, A. 2019. Science, data, and case-studies under the third science revolution. Some theoretical considerations. *Current Swedish Archaeology* 27: 115–132.

Schrader, O. 1883. *Sprachvergleichung und Urgeschichte: Linguistisch-historische Beiträge zur Erforschung des indogermanischen Altertums*. Jena: Hermann Costenoble.

Shnirelman, V. A. 2001. *The value of the past: Myths, identity and politics in Transcaucasia. Senri Ethnological Studies 57.* Osaka: National Museum of Ethnology.

Sjögren, K.-G., T. D. Price, & K. Kristiansen. 2016. Diet and mobility in the Corded Ware of Central Europe. *PLoS ONE* 11(5): e0155083.

Sjögren, K.-G., I. Olalde, S. Carver, M. E. Allentoft, T. Knowles, G. Kroonen, A. W. G. Pike, P. Schröter, K. A. Brown, K. Robson-Brown, R. J. Harrison, F. Bertemes, D. Reich, K. Kristiansen, & V. Heyd. 2020. Kinship and social organization in Copper Age Europe: A cross-disciplinary analysis of archaeology, DNA, isotopes, and anthropology from two Bell Beaker cemeteries. *PLoS ONE* 15(11): e0241278.

Stutz, L. N. 2018. A future for archaeology: In defense of an intellectually engaged, collaborative and confident archaeology. *Norwegian Archaeological Review* 51(1/2): 48–56.

Sørensen, T. F. 2017. The two cultures and a world apart: Archaeology and science at a new crossroads. *Norwegian Archaeological Review* 50(2): 101–115.

2017. Archaeological paradigms: Pendulum or wrecking ball? *Norwegian Archaeological Review* 50(2): 130–134.

Veeramah, K. R. 2018. The importance of fine-scale studies for integrating paleogenomics and archaeology. *Current Opinion in Genetics & Development* 53: 83–89.

White, H. 1987. *The content of the form. Narrative discourses and historical representation*. Baltimore: Johns Hopkins University Press.

Witzel, M. 2012. The home of the Aryans. In A. Hinze & E. Tichy (ed.), *Anusantatyi: Festschrift fuer Johanna Narten zum 70. Geburtstag* (Münchener Studien zur Sprachwissenschaft, Beihefte NF 19), 283–338. Dettelbach: J. H. Roell.

Part I Early Indo-European and the Origin of Pastoralism

2 THE YAMNAYA CULTURE AND THE INVENTION OF NOMADIC PASTORALISM IN THE EURASIAN STEPPES

DAVID W. ANTHONY

Between 3000 and 2500 BCE, populations derived genetically from individuals assigned to the Yamnaya archaeological culture migrated out of their steppe homeland eastward to the Altai Mountains and westward into the Hungarian Plain and southeastern Europe, an east–west range of 5,000 km across the heart of the Eurasian continent (Allentoft et al. 2015; Narasimhan et al. 2019). In Europe, their descendants created the Corded Ware and Bell Beaker horizons (Haak et al. 2015; Frînculeasa et al. 2015; Olalde et al. 2018), establishing a large part of the genetic ancestry in modern Europeans and probably their linguistic ancestry in the Indo-European language family as well (Anthony 2007; Reich 2018). The Yamnaya archaeological culture (or "cultural-historical community," in Soviet archaeological jargon) has consequently become a focus of wide interest. One debated subject that is perhaps most relevant for understanding the outbreak of long-distance migrations is the nature of the Yamnaya pastoral economy – were they nomads? This essay addresses Yamnaya nomadism as an innovation that opened the Eurasian steppes to productive human exploitation. It does not consider nomadic pastoralism in other parts of the world. Because the Yamnaya culture is little known or understood by Western archaeologists, I begin with an overview of Yamnaya chronology and variability.

2.1 Yamnaya Chronology and Variability

The Yamnaya or Pit Grave[1] culture was first defined by V. A. Gorodtsov (1907). His excavations in kurgans around Kharkhov in the northern steppes of Ukraine established the stratigraphic sequence of three grave types (pit grave, catacomb grave, and timber grave) that still frame the Bronze Age in the Pontic–Caspian steppes. The Pit Grave (or Yamnaya) culture defined the Early Bronze Age (EBA); catacomb graves represented the Middle Bronze Age (MBA); and the Timber Grave (or Srubnaya) culture represented the Late Bronze Age (LBA). EBA pit graves were in simple roofed pits under kurgans, MBA catacomb graves were (usually) in a niche or catacomb dug into one wall of the pit, and LBA timber graves (often) were in pits roofed with wooden logs (or, in the treeless steppe, with bundles of *Phragmities* reeds mistaken for logs after decay). Both the chronological period assigned to Yamnaya and its absolute dates have shifted over the decades, but Gorodtsov's divisions of the steppe Bronze Age remain as a chronological framework.

By the 1950s, the paucity of metals in Yamnaya graves contrasted with the wealth of bronze weapons and tools in the emerging Bronze Age cultures of Europe, the Aegean, and even in Catacomb culture graves in the steppes. Two English-language syntheses of Soviet research of the 1950s and 1960s (Gimbutas 1956: 89–92; Sulimirski 1970: 127–136) described Yamnaya as Late Neolithic. The perception that Yamnaya was poor in metal persisted long after it was disproved. Hansen's (2013: Fig. 9.6) distribution map of copper and bronze daggers in EBA western Eurasia showed many daggers in Maikop contexts and many more in southeast Europe, but none in Yamnaya contexts in the Pontic–Caspian steppes. Meanwhile, in the Cyrillic literature, one regional survey of tanged metal daggers in Yamnaya graves counted fourteen examples in the Volga–Ural steppes (Morgunova 2014); another counted twenty in the lower Dnieper steppes (Ryndina and Degtyareva 2018: 322). Accumulating metal artifacts from Yamnaya graves like these, combined with radiocarbon dates and typological links with the late Maikop culture (Korenevskii 1980; Nechitailo 1991), prompted the gradual reassignment of the Yamnaya culture to the EBA by about 1990, returning to Gorodtsov's periodization (Anthony 2021 describes these shifts in more detail). However, as with any shifting debate, the return was incomplete: Some archaeologists retain the Eneolithic label for the earliest phase of Yamnaya (Rassamakin 2013) while most now regard the beginning of early Yamnaya as the start of the EBA (Telegin et al. 2003; Shishlina 2008; Morgunova 2014).

In the North Caucasus Mountains, bordering the steppes to the south, the EBA begins with the mid-fourth-millennium

[1] "Yamnaya" is the genitive plural of *yama*, the Russian word meaning "pit" in the nominative singular. The "culture *of the pits* [pit graves]" is *yamnaya kul'tura*, thus the use of the form *yamnaya* paired with English "culture."

BCE appearance of the Maikop culture and its impressive arsenical bronze metallurgy, the central culture of Chernykh's Circumpontic Metallurgical Province (Chernykh 1992: 67–83), in which Yamnaya was included. Maikop was the extreme northwestern frontier of sites displaying material and technological links with the "Uruk expansion" trade network of the West Asian EBA/Late Chalcolithic (Kohl 2007; Kohl and Trifonov 2014). Korenevskii (2016, 2020) has argued that Mesopotamian/Iranian symbols such as the goat on the tree of life (a cosmological symbol with deep roots in Mesopotamia/Iran) and paired bull-and-lion images (icons of Mesopotamian/Iranian kingship, displayed in a region without lions) found in the monumental kurgan graves of the Maikop elite indicate that Mesopotamian socio-religious ideologies were introduced to the North Caucasus piedmont and perhaps to the steppes by Maikop warrior-chiefs; their elevation was linked with those ideologies as well as with the gold, silver, carnelian, and turquoise ornaments and bronze weapons they displayed. According to Wang et al. (2019), the Maikop elite and ordinary people were genetically alike: local descendants of the Neolithic population that had migrated into the North Caucasus from Georgia about 4800 to 4700 BCE and remained connected genetically to Southern Caucasus/East Anatolian populations. Early Maikop material culture (ceramics, lithics, clay andirons) was deposited in two stratified Eneolithic settlements in the steppes of the lower Don River (Konstantinovka and Razdorskoe level VI), mixed with the late Sredni Stog material culture of the main occupation, probably in the mid-fourth millennium BCE. These sites testify to the occasional visits of early Maikop expeditions (in wagons?) as far north as the lower Don – without the luxury goods that distinguished Maikop chiefs. Maikop technologies, perhaps including wheeled vehicles (Reinhold et al. 2017), were then copied and diffused across the steppes, and these innovations were fundamental parts of the Yamnaya revolution. However, Maikop and Yamnaya mates were rarely exchanged, as these two populations, so deeply entangled in other ways, seemed to remain genetically largely apart (Wang et al. 2019).

Early Maikop, around 3700 to 3300 BCE, was pre-Yamnaya, but late Maikop, including the weapon-rich graves at Nalchik (Belinsky et al. 2017) and Klady (Wang et al. 2019), was contemporary with early Yamnaya, about 3300 to 3000 BCE. Yamnaya metalsmiths copied late Maikop bivalve-mold casting methods, their preference for arsenical bronze, and their weapon types, including cast-tanged daggers, flat axes with expanding blade edges, and single-bladed sleeved shaft-hole axes – new types that partly define the EBA in the steppes (Korenevskii 1980; Nechitailo 1991; Morgunova 2014; Ryndina and Degtyareva 2018; Klochko 2019). Metallurgical links to Maikop explain why Yamnaya is assigned to the EBA, and why the EBA begins in the steppes more than a millennium before the EBA in central and western Europe: The Bronze Age chronology of the Pontic–Caspian steppes was linked to the Bronze Age chronology of southwestern Asia (Anthony 2021), not to Europe. Consequently, Yamnaya migrants might begin their journey in the EBA, but as they moved west, they entered regions where their graves are assigned to the Late Eneolithic (in the Carpathian Basin) or the Late Neolithic (north of the Carpathians), a problem well reviewed by Heyd (2013).

I recently discussed the radiocarbon chronology of the early phase of the Yamnaya culture with the goal of defending a reasonable date for the beginning of Yamnaya (Anthony 2021). At least fifty radiocarbon dates on bones, teeth, or wood that are not contradicted by a second date on the same feature, from contexts assigned by the reporting archaeologist to the Yamnaya culture, fall into the ≥ 4350 BP (3000 cal BCE and older) category (Table 2.1). Seven of these early dates derive from three early Yamnaya settlements (Repin, Mikhailovka level II, and Generalka 2, phase 1) and forty-three early Yamnaya dates derive from human graves in twenty-seven kurgan cemeteries distributed from the east Carpathian piedmont to the Ural River steppes (Fig. 2.1). The calibrated averaged midpoint for these earliest Yamnaya settlements and cemeteries is between 3203 and 3107 BCE (Table 2.1). Early Yamnaya material culture and its associated kurgan cemeteries began as early as 3300 BCE, spreading rapidly across most of the Pontic–Caspian steppes in 3200 to 3100 BCE, and finally, in its late phase, beginning in 3000 BCE, saturated all the regions of the steppes as Yamnaya nomads penetrated into neighboring regions.

Early Yamnaya material culture, as known primarily from graves, included wheeled vehicles, tanged daggers, sleeved axes cast in bivalve molds, and silver or copper hair rings, all of which might have been copied from late Maikop models. There were also triangular flint projectile points with a concave base (dominant form, with several minor types), canine-tooth pendants, stone end-pestles, bone pins (several types), and a diverse range of late-fourth-millennium ceramics. Kurgan graves with elements of this package – classically with the dead in the "Yamnaya position" (supine with raised knees), but occasionally contracted on the side, and strewn with red ochre – began to appear across the Pontic–Caspian steppes about 3300 to 3200 BCE. The average Yamnaya grave was poor in material wealth, but the average Yamnaya kurgan was a large mound often made of turfs, 30 to 40 m in diameter, and it usually covered a single (occasionally double) central grave that contained an adult male in 70 to 80 percent of cases (the percentage of males varied regionally but was the majority everywhere).

Yamnaya material culture was not homogeneous regionally or chronologically. N. I. Merpert, director of the Russian Institute of Archaeology in Moscow, published the foundational synthesis of the Yamnaya culture (Merpert 1974, 1977). He divided Yamnaya into nine regional groups distinguished by variations in grave rituals, pottery, and funerary artifacts (Fig. 2.2). The variant in the lower Volga steppes (I) typified at Berezhnovka II represented his oldest Yamnaya phase, and later regional variants represented expansion to the west and south. His Berezhnovka II "early Yamnaya" graves have since been shown by radiocarbon dates to be Eneolithic, contemporary with Khvalynsk, a millennium before Yamnaya. Merpert's intuition, before Khvalynsk was discovered, that they were

TABLE 2.1. Radiocarbon dates of 4350 BP or older from three early Yamnaya settlements and twenty-seven graves: Sites with Repin-style ceramics are in italics. (from Anthony 2021).

Site name	Material	Lab #	Date BP	Calibrated date BCE	Midpoint of calibrated dates
Early Yamnaya Settlements					
Mikhailovka II	Bone tool - lower II 2m	Ki-8012	4710±80	3654–3346	3500
Mikhailovka II	Bone - upper II 1-1.2m	Ki-8186	4480±70	3362–2931	3146
Mikhailovka II	Bone - upper II 1–1.2m	Ki-8010	4570±80	3622–3025	3323
Generalka 2	Bone	OxA-23080	4366±28	3086–2907	2996
Repin Khutor	Cattle bone	Ki-15666	4380±90	3346–2881	3113
Repin Khutor	Horse bone	UCIAMS-218275	4400±30	3262–2917	3089
Repin Khutor	Horse bone	UCIAMS-223191	4375±15	3078–2919	2998
			Average of seven midpoints = 3167 BCE		
Later Yamnaya Phase					
Repin Khutor	Horse bone	Ki-15664	4070±60	2866–2473	2669
Repin Khutor	Horse bone	Ki-15665	4150±70	2896–2500	2698
Repin Khutor	Horse bone	Ki-15663	4180±80	2907–2577	2742
			Average of three midpoints = 2703 BCE		
Early Yamnaya Kurgan Cemeteries – Samara Region					
Grachevka II k.5 gr.2	Human bone	PSUAMS-4272	4410 ±25 BP	3282–2918	3100
Grachevka II k.7 gr.2 central	Human bone	AA-53808	4419±56	3335–2912	3213
Grachevka II k.7 gr.1 periph.	Human bone	AA-53807	4361±55	3317–2885	3101
Kutuluk kurgan 4 grave 1	Human bone	AA12570	4370±75	3335–2882	3108
Lebyazhinka V grave 8	Human bone	PSUAMS-4258	4355±20	3020–2909	2964
Lebyazhinka V grave 9	Human bone	PSUAMS-4257	4475±20	3335–3033	3148
Lopatino I k.31 gr.1	Human bone	AA-47804	4432±66	3339–2918	3128
Lopatino I k.31 gr.1, 2nd date	Human bone	Ki-7764	4560±80	3619–3020	3319
Lopatino I k.35 gr.1	Human bone	Beta-392489	4380±30	3090–2913	3001
Lopatino I k.1 gr.1	Human bone	Beta-392491	4420±30	3321–2921	3121
Nizhnaya Orlyanka 1 k.4 gr.2	Human bone	AA12573	4520±757	3360–3090	3225
Nizhnaya Orlyanka 1 k.4 gr.2, 2nd date	Human bone	PSUAMS-4158	4425±20	3307–2928	3117
Nizhnaya Orlyanka 1 k.1 gr.15	Human bone	OxA 4254	4510±75	3360–3090	3225
Nizhnaya Orlyanka 1 k.1 gr.5	Human bone	PSUAMS-4544	4370±20	3080–2914	2997
Utyevka V k.1 gr.1	Human bone	PSUAMS-5790	4430±25	3323–2928	3125
Podlesnoe k.1 gr.3	Human bone	PSUAMS-4412	4465±20	3331–3028	3179
			Average of sixteen midpoints = 3129 BCE		
Ural River steppes					
Gerasimovka II k.4 gr.2	Human bone	GrA 54389	4480±35	3390–3095	3242
Mustaevo V k.1 gr.1	Human bone	LE-6725	4460±110	3340–2930	3135
Mereke, kurgan 1, burial 4 - outlier	Human bone	PSUAMS-4944	4425±20	3307–2928	3117
			Average of three midpoints = 3165 BCE		
Lower Volga steppes					
Bykovo k.12 gr.7	Human bone	PSUAMS-7787	4350±35	3086–2896	2991 BCE
Panitskoe grave 1	Human bone	PSUAMS-4161	4505±20	3344–3102	3223 BCE
			Average of two midpoints = 3107 BCE		
North Caucasus steppes					
Sharakhalsun 6 k.2 gr.18 wagon grave	Wood from wheel	GIN-12401	4500±40	3336–3105	3220
Rasshevatskiy 1 k.21 gr.13	Human bone	MAMS-29181	4447±22	3308–3026	3221
Ostanii k.1 gr.160 wagon grave	Human bone	Le-2963	4440±40	3320–2930	3125
			Average of three midpoints = 3189 BCE		

Table 2.1. (*Cont.*)

Site name	Material	Lab #	Date BP	Calibrated date BCE	Midpoint of calibrated dates
Dnieper-Azov-lower Don steppes					
Vinogradnoe k.24 gr.20	Wood	Bln-4691	4371±36	3093–2905	2999
Obloy k.1 gr.7	Wood	Le-1508	4630±90	3632–3099	3365
Ozera	Human bone	Beta-432809	4390±30	3095–2915	3005
Bal'ki kurgan gr.57, wagon grave	Human bone	Ki-606	4370±120	3330–2880	3105
Volonterivka k.1 gr.3	Human bone	Ki-9917	4570±80	3622–3025	3323
Volonterivka k.1 gr.4	Human bone	Ki-9918	4535±80	3512–2937	3224
Volonterivka k.1 gr.5	Human bone	Ki-9919	4490±80	3482–2923	3202
Kremenivka k.6 gr.9	Human bone	Ki-7260	4465±60	3337–2905	3121
Kremenivka k.6 gr.8	Human bone	Ki-9898	4410±70	3560–3520	3540
Krivyansky IX k.4 gr.21A	Human tooth	PSUAMS-7979	4495±25	3345–3096	3221
Krivyansky IX k.1 gr.27	Human bone	PSUAMS-7867	4440+25	3330–2933	3131
			average of ten midpoints = 3203 BCE		
Dniester-Danube steppes					
Sarateni k.1 gr.5	Wood	Lu-2459	4360±30	3085–2903	2994
Sarateni k.1 gr.4	Wood, wagon parts	Lu-2476	4480±50	3361–2970	3166
Semenovka k.11 gr.6	Wood	Ki-1758	4400±50	3329–2804	3067
Semenovka k.14 gr.52	Wood	Ki-2126	4600±90	3627–3030	3329
Liman k.2 gr.2	Wood	Ki-2394	4490±90	3491–2914	3203
Novosil'ske k.19 gr.7, phase 1	Human bone	Ki-1219	4520±70	3360–3100	3230
Novosil'ske k.19 gr.15, phase 2	Human bone	Ki-1712	4350±70	3090–2880	2985
Prydnistryanske I, k.4, gr.4, level 2	Human bone	Poz-66230	4455±35	3323–3027	3175
			Average of eight midpoints = 3144 BCE		

typologically archaic was correct, but his date estimate was late. His chronology was based partly on stratified kurgans in the lower Volga steppes, such as Berezhnovka (Mallory 1977; Merpert 1977), and partly on two Yamnaya settlement sites, Mikhailovka in Ukraine and Repin in Russia (Anthony 2021).

Mikhailovka, a unique settlement overlooking a probable ford across the lower Dnieper River, had three stratified phases in about 2 m of cultural deposits: stratum I (about 1,000 m^2) was designated Late Eneolithic (ca. 3600–3300 BCE); II (about 1,500 m^2) was early Yamnaya (3300–3000 BCE), the *only* Eneolithic settlement in the Pontic–Caspian steppes to expand in size in early Yamnaya; and III (about 15,000 m^2 within fortification walls, not all occupied) was late Yamnaya (ca. 3000–2600 BCE). Merpert (1974: 116–117) regarded Mikhailovka II as the initial expansion into the Dnieper steppes of early Yamnaya pastoralists from his proposed homeland on the lower Volga. The site report (Lagodovskaya et al. 1959, 1962) agreed that Mikhailovka II was the earliest Yamnaya chronological phase in the North Pontic steppes, a conclusion maintained forty years later in an updated site monograph (Korobkova and Shaposhnikova 2005) and supported by radiocarbon dates (Table 2.1; Anthony 2021). The Mikhailovka II ceramic assemblage contained shell-tempered, cord-impressed, flat-based pots that show continuity with local Eneolithic Sredni Stog/Mikhailovka I pottery, as well as egg-shaped vessels that would become more typical of Yamnaya, and finally thick-bodied vessels of the Repin type, about 10 percent of all vessels, not found in I or III (Kotova and Spitsyna 2003).

The Repin style establishes a cultural-chronological link between the monotype Repin site (Kuznetsov 2013) on the lower Don (where the direct ancestors of modern domesticated horses were identified; see below) and Mikhailovka II, supported by radiocarbon dates from both sites of 3300/3400 to 3000/3100 BCE (Table 2.1; Anthony 2021). Most Yamnaya graves and the largest Yamnaya settlements do not date to this early Repin phase, but to late Yamnaya, after 3100 to 3000 BCE. Mikhailovka III enclosed a space ten times larger than Mikhailovka II, with stone fortification walls preserved to a height of 2.5 m in the 1950s. Similarly, the Yamnaya settlement at Generalka, 100 km north of Mikhailovka, was almost entirely late Yamnaya (typologically like Mikhailovka III) with one small early Yamnaya feature (Tuboltsev and Radchenko 2018; Kaiser et al. 2020). Late Yamnaya settlement components were thicker and larger in area than the few dated early Yamnaya settlements. The late Yamnaya period witnessed the rapid growth and expansion of people and sites that were culturally and/or genetically Yamnaya.

Individuals assigned to the Yamnaya culture by diverse archaeologists in the Pontic–Caspian steppes exhibit an unexpectedly narrow range of genetic variation (Wang et al. 2019), indicating that they shared ancestry in a small founding population. From a genetic perspective, the Yamnaya culture looks like a clan or sodality defined by shared paternal descent from a

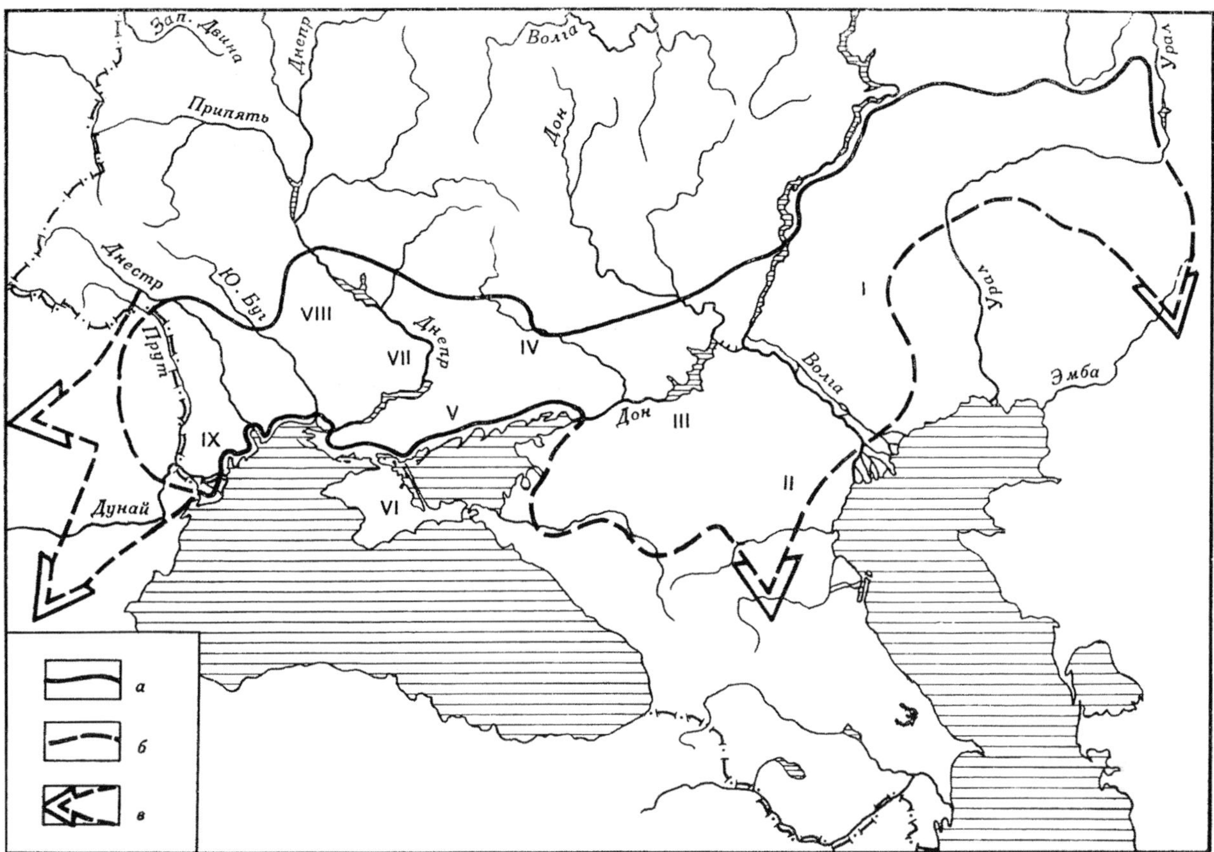

FIGURE 2.1. The nine regional groups (I–IX) of the Yamnaya culture defined by N. I. Merpert (1974). In his legend, a = a documented border of a culture region; b = a supposed border of a region; and c = the direction of invasion of other culture areas. He argued that the oldest Yamnaya phases were found in groups I, II, and III, the lower Volga, and the lower Don.

small set of male ancestors. How this homogeneous Yamnaya ancestry became established has not been adequately explained, but it contrasts with the variety shown in Yamnaya metals. Arsenical bronzes are more frequent in the North Pontic steppes (Klochko 2019), perhaps influenced by Maikop, versus "pure" copper tools and weapons in the Volga–Ural steppes, near the Yamnaya copper mines at Kargaly (Morgunova 2014: 305). Ceramics were even more variable, exhibiting continuity with preceding regional Eneolithic traditions: Khvalynsk on the Volga (Dremov and Yudin 1992), Repin on the Don, Mikhailovka I on the Dnieper, and Budzhak (Ivanova 2013) in the Danube steppes. For Ivanova (2006; Ivanova et al. 2018), the absence of a shared ceramic type meant that Yamnaya was not a proper archaeological culture (or cultural-historical community), but rather was an ideology or religion shared between distinct regional groups. Yamnaya was homogeneous in its genetic ancestry and funeral rituals but heterogeneous in its craft traditions in metal and ceramics, possibly suggesting that potters and metalworkers were local and genetically distinct from those buried under Yamnaya kurgans.

This summary establishes a brief foundation for understanding the Yamnaya economy. Important conclusions are that Yamnaya began in the late fourth millennium BCE almost everywhere in the Pontic–Caspian steppes at approximately the same time, an apparent rapid spread; the Maikop culture had a strong influence on early Yamnaya metals and weapon types and perhaps on politico-religious ideology, but the two communities remained genetically apart; Yamnaya kurgan graves contain a remarkably narrow range of human genetic variation, implying a small founding population that expanded rapidly; the largest and most numerous Yamnaya sites and the majority of radiocarbon dates come from the late phase, 3100/3000 to 2700/2600 BCE, implying significant growth in the Yamnaya population in its late phase, when it spread beyond the steppes; and Yamnaya homogeneity in genetics and funeral rituals contrasts with regional variability in ceramics and metals, perhaps suggesting that those buried under Yamnaya kurgans were an elite separate from local craftworkers.

But were they nomads? Recent specialist studies have made great progress in documenting the pastoral economy of the Yamnaya population.

2.2 Debates about Yamnaya Pastoralism

Nomadic pastoralism is the most mobile form of pastoralism, practiced in the Eurasian steppes by the Scythians, Huns, and Mongols, among many others. The people buried in Yamnaya

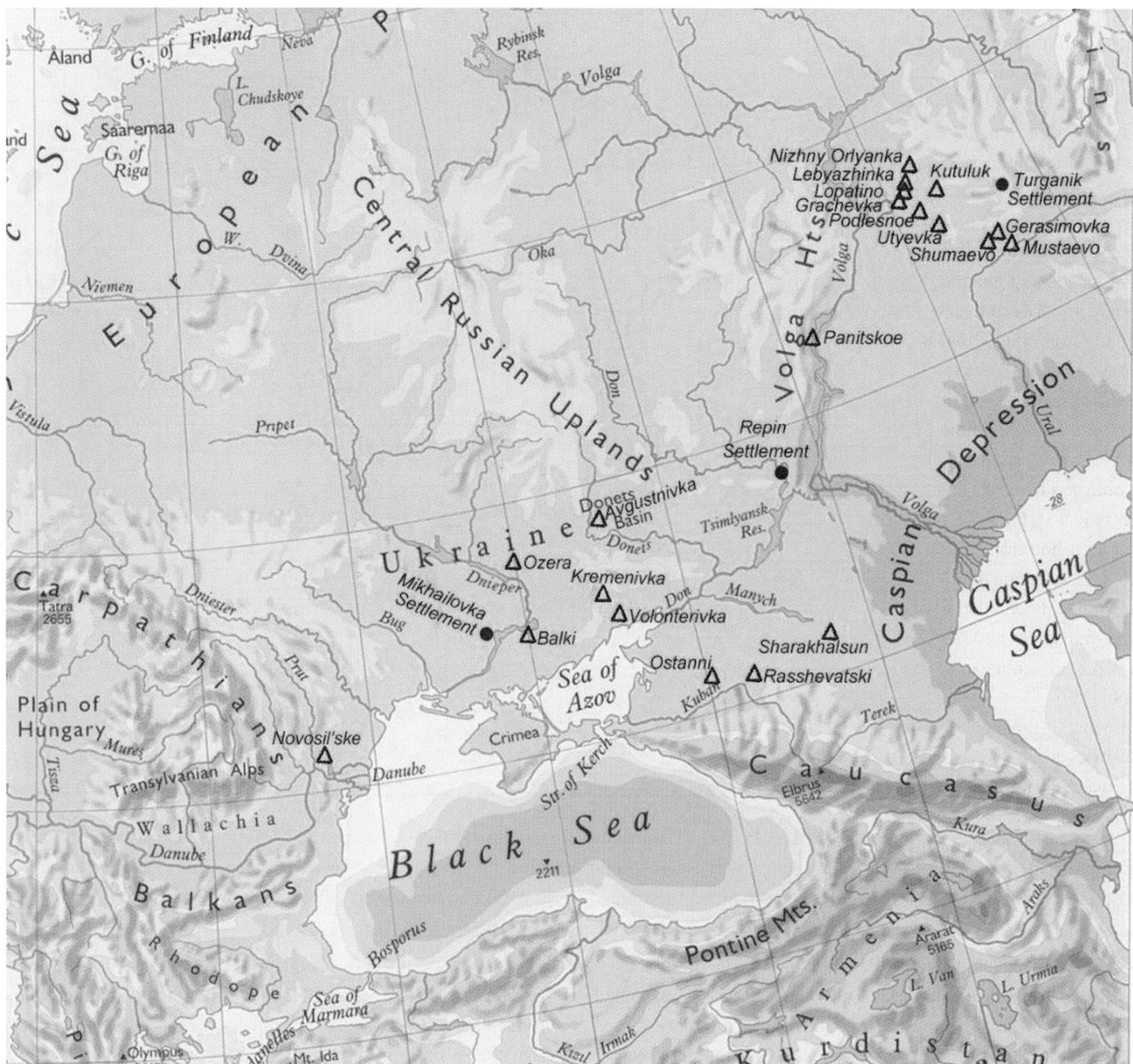

FIGURE 2.2. Early Yamnaya sites with radiocarbon dates ≥ 4350 BP. Circles: settlements, triangles: cemeteries. Non-Yamnaya sites of the same age are marked with a star. The concentration near Samara on the Volga reflects increased funding for dates from the Samara Valley Project, the Reich ancient DNA lab, and the Russian Academy of Sciences.

graves are described in the Cyrillic literature as 'stockbreeders' (*skotovody*), or pastoralists. But they were not the first people in the steppes to keep domesticated animals, so just how Yamnaya stockbreeding was different from Eneolithic stockbreeding is one debated question; the role of agriculture is another. Until recently, a respected body of theory insisted that nomadic pastoralism *could not* have existed in the Bronze Age, because the conditions necessary for its evolution were not yet present (Shnirelman 1980, 1992; Kuzmina 2008: 214–215; Khazanov 1994: 72–75). Häusler (2003) stated that Yamnaya nomads were a myth, and Spengler et al. (2021) extended that doubt even to the Iron Age nomads of Central Asia, who were described as dependent on agriculture. Kaiser (2010) claimed that cattle were the focus of Yamnaya pastoralism (but see below), noting that cattle are unsuitable for long-range nomads. Manzura (2005) argued that Yamnaya cattle were introduced by neighboring Cucuteni-Tripol'ye farmers, whose colonization of the steppes created the Yamnaya population and economy. Rassamakin (1999: 154) concluded that Yamnaya "... should not be described as nomadic, and even a semi-nomadic form of economy can only be proposed with reservations."

Other equally expert authorities described the Yamnaya economy as the earliest form of nomadic pastoralism in the Eurasian steppes, explicitly comparing it to the nomadic pastoralism of Iron Age and Medieval nomads (Gimbutas 1970, 1977; Merpert 1974; Shilov 1975, 1985; Dergachev 2007; Morgunova 2014: 276–293), but perhaps with shorter, more localized migration routes (Anthony 2007: 321–322; Shishlina 2008: 230–236). This debate about Yamnaya mobility complicates how we understand the pancontinental migrations that began about 3100 to 3000 BCE. If Yamnaya pastoralism was semisedentary, then the mobility associated with Yamnaya pastoralism was not so different from Eneolithic pastoralism, and Yamnaya migrations could not be even partly explained by the evolution of a new, higher-mobility way of life in the steppes.

If, however, the Yamnaya economy represented the first invention of nomadic pastoralism in the Eurasian steppes, then it was a revolutionary innovation. By specializing in the meat and milk of a few domesticated animals that converted grass into food, clothing, shelter, and transport, the first steppe nomads greatly simplified their diet and opened the steppe grasslands to human exploitation. The wild, unexploited steppe plateaus between the river valleys became named pastures. The annual migrations that define nomadic life required emerging pastoralists to develop social and political institutions that defined rights to claim and use new pastures, rights to move across pastures claimed by others, the maintenance of family and clan cohesion between mobile groups, the maintenance of political power among mobile constituents, and a variety of technical skills such as horse management (trickier than with modern horses; see below) and wagon repair. Once matured, this organization and its supporting skills and institutions could have facilitated other kinds of long-distance mobility, including migrations to new territories. But what could have caused people to embrace a new and extreme form of residential mobility?

Most of those who do support the nomadic interpretation of Yamnaya pastoralism attribute the innovation of nomadism to climate change, which created more arid conditions in the steppes in the late fourth millennium BCE (Merpert 1974; Shilov 1975; Gimbutas 1977). While there is some palynological evidence for increased aridity coinciding with pre-Yamnaya and early Yamnaya (Pashkevich 1992, 2003; Zakh et al. 2010), it was not a catastrophic change. In any case, nomadism was not an automatic response to increasing aridity, particularly among Eneolithic riverine steppe societies with complex diets including some domesticated cattle and sheep, hunted equids, deer and beaver, and abundant fish and shellfish (faunal lists in Dergachev 2007: 447–448; Anthony and Brown 2011; Vybornov et al. 2018, 2019).

I instead stress the introduction of wagon transport after about 3500 BCE, combined with horseback riding. Since Herodotus' account of the Scythians *c.* 450 BCE, the mobility of Eurasian steppe nomads has been described as based on two types of transport: horseback riding for rapid travel, herd control, and warfare, combined with ox-drawn wagons for the transport of heavy residential needs like tents, water, fuel, and food. The introduction of wagons (four wheels) and carts (two wheels) to the Pontic–Caspian steppes is well dated to about 3400/3300 BCE by parts of wagons and carts buried under hundreds of Yamnaya and Catacomb culture kurgans (Fansa and Burmeister 2004; Burmeister 2017). The oldest wheel in the steppes is currently from Sharakhalsun 2 in the North Caucasus steppes, dated 3336 to 3105 BCE (4500±40 BP/GIN-12401) (Reinhold et al. 2017). Wagons diffused across the steppes with the early Yamnaya expansion. Childe (1958: 137) and Piggott (1983: 241) have emphasized the status associated with the first vehicles rather than the changes in economy they made possible. Like them, Burmeister (2017:71) has argued that the adoption of wheeled vehicles was unrelated to transport, citing the mechanical inefficiency of early wagons (but see Rosenstock et al. 2019). Sherratt (1983, 2006) included wheeled vehicles in his secondary products revolution as part of a traction complex, including plows, that shifted his analysis toward the role of wagons in agriculture. But Bakker et al. (1999) and recently Reinhold et al. (2017) have accepted early wagons as revolutionary new functional tools that had profound economic effects, including involving humans in the breeding and maintenance of pairs of oxen for traction. In the words of Reinhold et al. (2017: 91), "The practical assets of the new vehicles are still the most plausible argument for the implementation of wheeled transport in steppe societies."

A mounted herder in Mongolia can manage three times more sheep than a pedestrian herder (Khazanov 1984: 32), so riding made it possible to triple herd sizes without increased labor. But horseback riding is difficult to identify in the archaeological record; therefore, riding is the more debated aspect of the riding-and-driving combination that seems to have been a necessary precursor of nomadic pastoralism in the Eurasian steppes (Shilov 1975, 1985; Shishlina 2008). New evidence has changed the debate about horse domestication and riding.

2.3 New Evidence: Horseback Riding, DNA, and Wheels

Horse domestication was inferred at Botai in northern Kazakhstan, 3500 to 3100 BCE, based on many indicators (Outram et al. 2009). Bit wear on horse lower premolar (P_2) teeth was the most direct indicator of horseback riding (Brown and Anthony 1998; Anthony, Brown and George 2006; Outram et al. 2009; Anthony and Brown 2011). A recent criticism (Taylor & Barrón-Ortiz 2021) of the evidence for bit wear at Botai focused on one kind of dental pathology (a vertical scar on the prow of the P_2) but ignored the second kind found at Botai (a beveled facet measuring at least 3 mm on the occlusal surface of the mesial or paraconid cusp of the P_2). The latter, the mesial occlusal wear facet, was the first bit-related dental pathology recognized in ancient horses (Clutton-Brock 1974) and is most studied, both by equine veterinarians (Clayton and Lee 1984; Cook 2011) and archaeologists (Azzaroli 1980; Brown and Anthony 1998; Bendrey 2007; Outram et al. 2009; Anthony and Brown 2011). At Botai, of nineteen P_2 teeth suitable for study, five had significant (3 mm or greater) mesial occlusal wear facets, not observed among the 105 wild and never-bitted adult horse P_2 teeth measured from Pleistocene, ancient, and modern contexts, excluding teeth aged 3≤ years and ≥20 years to avoid confusion with natural irregularities (Anthony, Brown, and George 2006). Mesial occlusal facets like those on the five Botai P_2 teeth were produced experimentally in horses ridden for 150 hours with rope bits (Brown and Anthony 1998; Anthony, Brown, and George 2006); the agent of wear was dirt trapped under the rope (see Sanson et al. 2007 for exogenous grit in dental microwear).

Other evidence for horse management at Botai included horse manure dumped in pits (waste management), putative corrals, and horse-milk residue in pots (Outram et al. 2009), the latter a certain indicator of domestication.

A millennium before Botai, at the Khvalynsk cemetery and related sites in the Volga steppes dated 4500 to 4000 BCE, Eneolithic riverine fisher-hunter-herders who already had domesticated cattle and sheep-goats, unlike Botai, began to behave differently toward horses in three new ways (Anthony and Brown 2011: 140–143; Anthony et al. 2022). At Khvalynsk, horse bones were included in human graves with cattle and sheep-goats in funerary sacrifices limited to these three mammals, excluding obviously wild mammals such as deer; also, horses were arranged in head-and-hoof deposits above the human graves at Eneolithic S'yezzhee, like the domesticated cattle and sheep head-and-hoof deposits at contemporary Khvalynsk; and new horse images were produced and included in Eneolithic graves, including stone maces shaped like horse heads (Dergachev 2007; Anthony et al. 2022). These new behaviors associated horses symbolically with humans, cattle, and sheep after 4500 BCE, the earliest signal that horses were moving away from the wild pole and toward the domesticated pole on the wild-domesticated continuum in the middle Volga steppes.

Tables 2.2 and 2.3 show that horse bones, usually just a phalange or carpal, appeared also in Yamnaya graves. But at the Tsa-Tsa cemetery in the Caspian steppes (Shilov 1985: 99–102), the central grave 5 in kurgan 1 contained an adult male with a copper tanged dagger, two small clay pots of early Catacomb types, and the skulls of forty horses. A single horse skull was placed in central grave 12 under kurgan 7, attributed to the Yamnaya culture. Horse-focused rituals like those conducted at Tsa-Tsa were not common in Yamnaya/Catacomb funerals, but their presence in human death rituals supports the idea that Yamnaya horses played important roles in life.

A recent groundbreaking study of ancient horse DNA (Librado et al. 2021) demonstrated that domesticated horses like those we have today (the lineage named DOM2) first appeared in fully modern genetic form about 2200 to 2100 BCE in the Don–Volga steppes, and that 95 percent of their ancestry was from earlier Don–Volga steppe horses, including a Yamnaya horse at Repin dated 3262 to 2917 BCE (Table 2.1) and a Yamnaya horse at Turganik dated 2889 to 2636 BCE. The horses of Botai and related sites in Kazakhstan (DOM1) were the ancestors of today's Przewalski horses and contributed little to DOM2 (Gaunitz et al. 2018). The DOM2 horses sacrificed in Sintashta chariot graves had mutations connected with a calmer mood that probably made them more tolerant of the violent sounds and motions of warfare than were Yamnaya horses, important in animals whose natural defenses included a quick startle-and-run reflex. DOM2 also had mutations affecting their lumbar vertebrae that probably made them more tolerant of long bouts of riding. DOM2 horses were so desirable that they rapidly replaced older equid genetic variants across Eurasia (including Europe) by about 1500 BCE, during the early era of chariot warfare.

Librado et al. (2021) found that the genetic admixture in the Repin horse (named C-PONT for Caspian–Pontic) was much closer to DOM2 than to NEO-CAS (for Neolithic Caspian) wild horses dated 5500 BCE, before domesticated animals appeared in the Don-Volga steppes. NEO-CAS was ancestral to C-PONT,

TABLE 2.2. Data on sacrificed animals found in Bronze Age graves located in the steppes between the lower Volga, the lower Don, and the North Caucasus. Multiple species can be present in one grave. Compiled and translated from Shilov 1985: Tables 2 & 4.

Culture name	Graves examined	Graves w/ fauna graves/%	With wild fauna graves/%	Sheep-goat graves/%	Cattle graves/%	Horse graves/%	Dog graves/%
YamnayaEBA	263	40 /15.2%	6 /2.3%	26 /65%	6 /15%	3 /7.5%	2 /5%
PoltavkaMBA	176	48 /27.3%	4 /2.3%	37 /77.1%	6 /12.5%	2 /4.6%	1 /2.1%
Pre-Caucasus/ CatacombMBA	604	152 /25.3%	8 /1.3%	106 /70%	21 /13.9%	11 /7.2%	1 /0.6%
SrubnayaLBA	1053	238 /22.6%	7 /0.7%	128 /53.8%	60 /25.2%	27 /11.3%	1 /0.8%
Bronze Age total/average	2096	22.6%	1.7%	66.5%	16.7%	7.7%	2.1%

TABLE 2.3. Data on sacrificed animals found in EBA and MBA graves located in the Samara and Orenburg steppes between the south Urals and the Volga. From Morgunova 2014: Table 22.

Culture name	Graves examined	Graves with fauna graves/%	Sheep-goat present	Cattle	Horse	Other fauna or unidentified
Yamnaya & Poltavka EBA & MBA	164	16 /10.0%	15 /94%	4 /25%	4 /25%	2 /13.5%

and C-PONT to DOM2. Horses contemporary with Khvalynsk in the late fifth millennium BCE, at Oroshaemoe in the lower Volga steppes and Semenovka I in Ukraine, showed intermediate ancestry (not given a separate acronym) between the sixth-millennium BCE wild steppe horses (NEO-CAS) and fourth-millennium Yamnaya steppe horses (C-PONT), forming a genetic continuum that documents a series of changes between wild horses (NEO-CAS) and those of Khvalynsk, Yamnaya (C-PONT), and Sintashta (DOM2).

Ancient DNA tells us when and where the fully modern DOM2 pattern of genetic ancestry first evolved among horses, but not when horse management began. No gene informs us if an equid was ridden or milked. The symbolic changes in the human treatment of horses seen archaeologically at Khvalynsk, S'yezzhe, and other Volga Eneolithic sites dated 4500 to 4000 BCE (Anthony and Brown 2011: 140–143; Anthony et al. 2022) signal the earliest shift in human attitudes toward horses within the pre-DOM2 population. The evidence from Botai follows in the mid-fourth millennium BCE with the DOM1 population. Osteologically, a Yamnaya individual from kurgan 1, grave 3 near Strejnicu, Romania had "rider's syndrome," a suite of skeletal pathologies consistent with riding, dated to 2822 to 2663 cal BCE, the first osteological evidence of a Yamnaya rider (Trautmann et al. 2021). Dairy peptides preserved in Yamnaya dental calculus from two individuals on the lower Don at the Krivyanskii IX kurgan cemetery (see below) show that they had *Equus* peptides in their teeth, the earliest peptide evidence for horse milking (Wilkin et al. 2021). And from zoology, larger horses attributed to steppe origins began to appear in central Europe during the early Yamnaya era (Kyselý & Peške 2016), although if they were C-PONT horses, they were later replaced by local European horses (Librado et al. 2021).

Yamnaya people rode horses, milked horses, sacrificed horses in graves, and selected horses for 95 percent of the genetic traits that would later define DOM2. But Yamnaya horses probably had less endurance as mounts than DOM2 and were more "skittish." In quiet activities such as travel or herding, Yamnaya horseback riding could have been an effective aid for light transport and the management of large herds, but Yamnaya riders might have dismounted to advance toward a predator or an aggressive human.

Horseback riding tripled the efficiency of herding, but by itself did not solve the problem of moving the herder's residence. The larger herds of cattle and sheep made *manageable* by horseback riding must be fed, and since fodder was not used among most Eurasian steppe pastoralists (Khazanov 1994: 72–74), a larger herd needed to move frequently to renew its pasture. *Maintaining* larger herds required increased residential mobility among the herders.

That problem was solved, and a new way of life made possible, when wheeled vehicles were invented in the middle of the fourth millennium BCE (Bakker et al. 1999; Fansa and Burmeister 2002; Burmeister 2017; Reinhold et al. 2017). They diffused across the Pontic–Caspian steppes beginning about 3400 to 3300 BCE, according to current radiocarbon dates (see Table 2.1 wagon graves). Wooden wheels and other vehicle parts were included in Yamnaya graves distributed geographically across the Yamnaya range, from Shumaevo in the Orenburg steppes, at the northeastern frontier of the Yamnaya culture area (Morgunova and Khokhlova 2013); to the Budzhak steppes near the Danube delta, at the southwestern frontier of the Yamnaya area (Ivanova and Tsimidanov 1993). The North Caucasus steppes, the southeastern Yamnaya frontier, had the largest concentration of wagon graves, with more than 300 known and the oldest radiocarbon dates (Gei 2000: 128; Reinhold et al. 2017). This might be where wheels were introduced to the steppes.

When people who rode horses to herd cattle and sheep began to construct large wooden machines that rolled on solid wooden wheels, capable of carrying 1 to 2 tons of cargo (Rosenstock et al. 2019: 1104), wagons became the first mobile homes. Oxen trained to pull weight became a valuable new human commodity (Sherratt 2006; Reinhold et al. 2018; Bogaard, Fochesato, and Bowles 2019). Permanent homes in the river valleys were abandoned, an event described below that partly defines the Yamnaya culture. The combination of slow, bulk transport in wagons and light, rapid transport on horseback made possible a new economy that combined extreme residential mobility with the production of a storable, movable economic surplus counted primarily in animals. The herders' diet was simplified to concentrate on meat and milk proteins from grazing animals. Surplus animals could be used for political purposes – feasts, gift-giving, public sacrifices, and the extension of loans.

In a cross-cultural study of nomadic pastoralists, Mulder et al. (2010) found that inherited differences in herd wealth tended to create relatively durable wealthy clans among nomads worldwide, so a degree of social inequality can be expected in any pastoral economy. Yamnaya kurgan graves and grave gifts do seem to indicate a persistent but weakly differentiated hierarchy consisting of very few richly equipped and many poorly equipped graves, consistent with this expectation (Merpert 1974; Dovchenko and Rychkov 1988). In addition to material wealth such as animal stock, weapons, and equipment, Mulder et al. (2010) found that differences in *relational* wealth – reputation, and social agreements providing access to extra labor – also were important in maintaining political inequality among nomads. Two aspects of reputation were the most important for nomadic chiefs generally: generosity, proven by hosting feasts and gifting animals; and being a reliable military ally, proven by successful military actions. Feasting and weaponry are two aspects of Yamnaya archaeology that might receive more attention from this perspective – *if* the Yamnaya pastoral economy can be described as nomadic.

I argue here that the Yamnaya pastoral economy in the Don–Volga–Ural steppes was the first and oldest form of nomadic pastoralism in the Eurasian steppes, in agreement with Shilov (1975, 1985), Merpert (1974), and Shishlina (2008). However, some archaeologists reject the term "nomadic pastoralism" for any Bronze Age steppe economy, and archaeologists have presented contrasting views of the Yamnaya economy in the Pontic–Caspian steppes. Below, I criticize dependency theory, present data from the Samara Valley Project on Yamnaya dietary isotopes and dental pathologies, review faunal evidence from three late-fourth-millennium settlements and from Yamnaya graves, and review new evidence of dairy peptides, including *Equus* milk, in the dental calculus of Yamnaya individuals.

2.4 Dependency Theory and the Evolution of Nomadic Pastoralism

Owen Lattimore captured the essence of nomadic dependency in a maxim usually rendered as "the only pure nomad is a poor nomad," although his exact words (Lattimore 1988 [1940]: 73–75) were "it is the poor nomad who is the pure nomad." Anatoly Khazanov's groundbreaking *Nomads and the Outside World* codified the dependency theory later expanded and elaborated by Barfield (1989). Pastoralism pursued as the sole source of subsistence was regarded as so unreliable in northern Eurasia that survival on that basis alone was a struggle. Nomadic pastoralism, the most mobile and specialized form of pastoralism, was interpreted as a complex parasitic economy that outsourced agriculture (and many other needs, such as metal-working) to China, Persia, and Greece in the form of trade or tribute, upon which the nomadic economy depended. Nomadic confederacies rose and fell with their hosts. They could not have evolved before the state-level societies that were uniquely able to produce the surpluses that nomads consumed.

An external source of cultivated grain was necessary, it was thought, because extreme winters recurred in the northern Eurasian steppes at intervals of five to ten years, causing the catastrophic deaths of many range animals (Khazanov 1984: 70–75). Steppe pastoralists must have a storable food or face recurring winter famines. In historic times, that food was bread. Prominent Russian and Ukrainian archaeologists cited Khazanov to argue that "true" nomadic pastoralism could not have evolved before the Iron Age, when states and their agricultural surpluses first appeared on the edges of the steppes (Shnirelman 1980, 1992; Bunyatyan 2003: 269; Koryakova and Epimakhov 2007: 210; reviewed in Anthony 2016). Spengler et al. (2021) criticized the word "nomad" as both too vague (underdefined) and too binary (overdefined), suggesting that "nomads" differed from other pastoral producers only in their degree of dependence on agriculture.

Archaeological discoveries in Central Asia seemed to support dependency theory by verifying that Iron Age and Medieval Eurasian steppe nomads ate and cultivated grain. Extensive dental caries indicating starchy cereal consumption was found in the teeth of nomadic Huns and Sarmatians in the Altai (Murphy 2003). Domesticated cereal remains were found at Iron Age and Medieval Golden Horde nomadic sites (Nedashkovskii 2010; Motuzaite-Matuzeviciute et al. 2012). Iron Age agricultural settlements were excavated on the edges of the steppes (Chang 2018). Bronze Age agropastoralist sites with stone-built houses in the Tien Shan had wheat and millet by 2500 BCE (Frachetti 2012: 15; Doumani et al. 2015). Steppe nomads living free from agriculture seemed to have been at best an aspirational ideal.

In the 1990s, several archaeological projects examined the role of agriculture in Bronze Age steppe economies in the Pontic–Caspian steppes, using systematic flotation and palynology (Chernykh 2004; Lebedeva 2005; Diaz del Rio 2006; Anthony et al. 2016). Two of these projects focused on Srubnaya sites of the early second millennium BCE, the LBA in the steppes, when EBA/MBA mobile pastoralists settled down and began to live in permanent homes that are rich sources of archaeological data. One question was why pastoral settlements appeared across the Eurasian steppes, Srubnaya to Andronovo, around 2000 to 1800 BCE, after more than a millennium of higher mobility. Was it because this was when they adopted agriculture?

The Samara Valley Project (Anthony et al. 2016) employed systematic flotation, palynology, and phytolith analyses to examine the role of agriculture at Krasnosamarskoe, a permanently occupied (all four seasons) LBA settlement of the Srubnaya culture, and two seasonal Srubnaya herding camps dated 1900 to 1700 BCE. We found no trace of agriculture. But we did find hundreds of charred seeds of *Chenopodium, Polygynum*, and *Amaranthus*, all nutritious wild seed species. Similar systematic flotation and extensive palynological sampling had the same negative result at the Srubnaya copper mining settlement at Gorny, but again, large numbers of charred *Chenopodium* seeds were recovered (Diaz del Rio et al. 2006). Systematic soil sampling and flotation conducted at two fortified settlements of the late MBA/early LBA Sintashta culture (2100–1800 BCE), east of the Urals, at Kammenyi Ambar and Stepnoe, recovered only wild seeds (including *Chenopodium*) (Rühl, Herbig, and Stobbe 2015; Hanks et al. 2018). Lebedeva (2005) conducted more limited soil coring at twelve Srubnaya settlements east of the Don River and analyzed her samples using flotation, finding no seeds of cultivated grain. Together, twelve LBA Srubnaya settlements and two MBA/LBA Sintashta settlements east of the Don River were analyzed with flotation and yielded no domesticated seeds. A few Srubnaya settlements west of the Don did have some agricultural seeds (Lebedeva 2005), showing the persistence, from the Yamnaya era, of economic differences east and west of the Don (see below). Surprisingly, settled LBA pastoralists in the Volga–Ural steppes yielded no trace of agricultural foods, while the nomads of the Iron Age were bread-eaters.

The viability of agriculture-free pastoralism in the Volga–Ural steppes is proven by the absence of cultivated grain in Srubnaya and Sintashta settlements. Hundreds of Srubnaya settlements with intact cultural strata are known in the Pontic–Caspian steppes, but they probably do not indicate a sudden increase in the LBA population, nor the introduction of agriculture. Rather, LBA settlements appeared because steppe nomads reduced their mobility, increasing their archaeological visibility, in reaction to a well-documented climatic shift to colder and drier winters in the late third millennium BCE, the 4.2 ka event, which eventually induced steppe herders to settle permanently near their most critical diminishing resource – rapidly shrinking *Phragmites* marshes – vital for domesticated animals' winter fodder (Anthony 2007: 389–91; Anthony et al. 2016). No new foods were introduced. Even the Srubnaya copper mine at Gorny thrived without agriculture through the mid-second millennium BCE (Diaz del Rio et al. 2006).

Dependency theory is therefore misleading for this region and period. Pastoralists in the Volga–Ural steppes did not need external sources of cultivated grain to succeed, thrive, and even conduct industrial-scale copper mining. Cultivated wheat and millet were choices, not necessities, and were widely consumed only in the Iron Age after agriculture was adopted in most of the ecological environments fringing the steppes, including the lower piedmont of the Tien Shan (Chang 2018) and the northern forest zone (Koryakova and Epimakhov 2007). During the early Yamnaya period, both environments were occupied by hunter-gatherers, as were the Kazakh steppes – the Botai people's only domesticates were horses and dogs. Yamnaya nomadic pastoralism was different from Iron Age nomadic pastoralism partly *because* agriculture remained absent in the Volga–Ural steppes as late as the LBA. Yamnaya pastoralists might have acquired cultivated grain from Tripol'ye C2 and late Maikop farmers on the western and southern frontiers of the Pontic–Caspian steppes, but these tribal societies did not have centralized storage for grain distribution or sufficient surpluses to maintain the Yamnaya diet.

2.5 The Abandonment of Eneolithic Settlements

Those who insist that Yamnaya pastoralists were semisedentary and limited to local territories must explain why the Yamnaya and Srubnaya settlement patterns were so different. No Yamnaya occupation site with an intact cultural layer has yet been found east of the Don River (Shilov 1975; Shishlina 2008: 230; Morgunova 2014: 26). *All* the excavated Yamnaya sites in the Volga–Caspian–Ural steppes (regions I, II, and III in Fig. 2.1) are kurgan cemeteries. Occasional scatters of flint tools and Yamnaya pottery sherds are reported in wind-deflated sites in the Caspian Depression (Merpert 1974: 100–101), attributed to Yamnaya herders' camps. Moreover, the Samara Valley Project used shovel testing to discover subsurface MBA (Poltavka culture in this region) sherd scatters, invisible on the ground surface, that had artifact densities of one small ceramic sherd per 4 to 8 m^2 (Anthony et al. 2016 and Fig. 2.3: 15–18), with no cultural level. One subsurface sherd per 2x2 m to 2x4 m unit is not recognizable as a site using normal archaeological methods. We found these ephemeral MBA sites only because the same favorable locations were later reused by semisedentary Srubnaya pastoralists who left much denser artifact deposits, among which we occasionally encountered an MBA sherd (but no Yamnaya sherds!). The dominance of temporary camps with vanishingly low artifact densities for at least one thousand years over this huge region implies a continuously mobile, nomadic mode of residence.

East of the Don River, Morgunova (2015: Fig. 2) and Shishlina (2008: Fig. 107) mapped eighty Neolithic and Eneolithic riverine settlements, none with a Yamnaya cultural level. Radiocarbon dates were from the late seventh to the mid-fourth millennia BCE. Radiocarbon dates on animal bones (excluding dates on organic crusts from pottery, which are centuries older) show that from about 4900 to 4700 BCE, riverine fisher-hunters began to keep some domesticated sheep and cattle (Vybornov et al. 2018, 2019). Their settlements contain stratified cultural levels in favorable locations and were riverine, near timber, deer, water, marshes, and fish. They were functionally varied, including some specialized camps in the arid Caspian steppes with more than 80 percent wild saiga antelope or steppe onager bones, and more diversified occupations in the middle Volga steppes (like Orashaemoe, with horses intermediate between NEO-CAS and C-PONT) containing the bones of red deer (*Cervus elaphus*) and elk (*Alces alces*), horses in a prominent dietary role, and fish, in addition to cattle, goats, and sheep (Morgunova 2015; Vybornov et al. 2018, 2019). The role of domesticated animals seems to have increased gradually during the fifth millennium BCE. All these Eneolithic settlement sites were abandoned after 3300 BCE.

West of the Don River, a handful of Eneolithic settlements have produced Yamnaya cultural levels, and two settlements, Mikhailovka and Repin, had dense artifact deposition including published fauna. Only Mikhailovka II and III and a late Yamnaya ritual site at Generalka on an island in the Dnieper Rapids (Kaiser et al. 2020; Tuboltsev and Radchenko 2018) had pits, postholes, house floors, and other built facilities. The other investigated Yamnaya settlements in the Dnieper and lower Don valleys, including Repin, Razdors'ke, Liventsovka, and a few others, lacked pits, postholes, or house floors. The absence of constructed facilities at most of the ten or so known Yamnaya settlements in the western part of the Yamnaya range suggests a reduction in settlement permanence and in anticipated length of stay (Kent and Vierich 1989; Kelly, Poyer, and Tucker 2005), compared with the Eneolithic occupations at the same places; but it also indicates some continuity between Eneolithic and Yamnaya settlement patterns. The western Yamnaya pastoral economy was tethered to a few habitual camps and one central settlement (Mikhailovka) in a landscape where more than 95 percent of Yamnaya sites were kurgan cemeteries. The eastern Yamnaya settlement pattern, east of the Don, lacked even these few occupation sites and seems to have been more mobile.

The abandonment of almost all riverine Eneolithic settlements across the Pontic–Caspian steppes after 3300 BCE is a hallmark of the beginning of the Yamnaya period. But it does not appear in most lists of Yamnaya traits. Both Morgunova and Rassamakin defined the Yamnaya culture typologically, by ceramic and grave types. If we define the beginning of the Yamnaya phenomenon by its economy and settlement pattern rather than by typology, then the abandonment of riverine settlements was a major defining trait. Morgunova (2014: 277) suggested that it was time to reexamine the analyses of V. P. Shilov (1975, 1985), whose

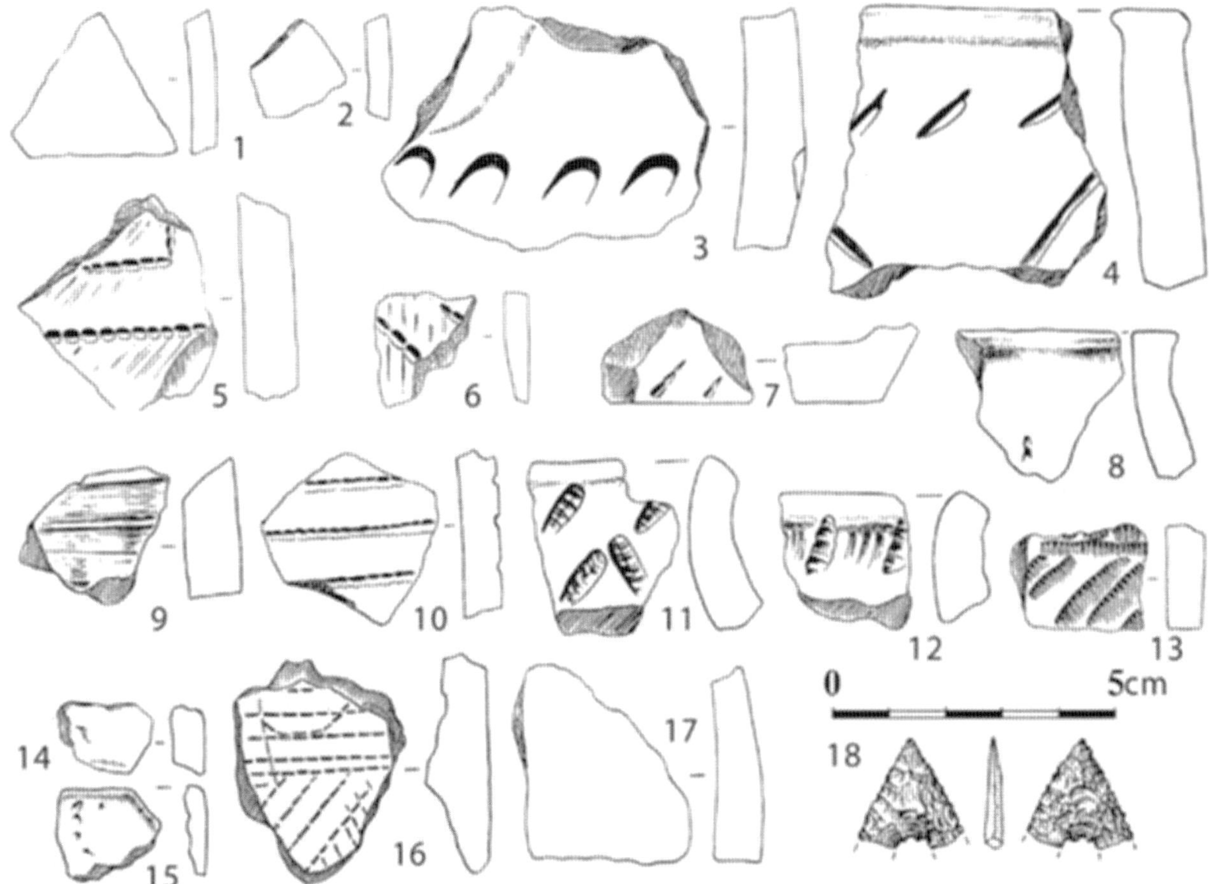

FIGURE 2.3. Seasonal herding camp artifacts from Peschanyi Dol 1, Samara Valley Project; 1–13, semisedentary LBA Srubnaya culture; 15–18, nomadic MBA Poltavka culture

theories about Yamnaya nomadism were submerged by Khazanov's dependency theory.

2.6 Yamnaya Nomadic Pastoralism: Sheep, Isotopes, and Dairy Peptides

V. P. Shilov's interpretation of the Yamnaya economy in the Don–Volga–Caspian steppes (regions I, II, and III in Fig. 2.2) included seven observations (by my count – he did not number them) indicating that Yamnaya pastoralists were nomadic (Shilov 1975, 1985). These were briefly reviewed and largely dismissed by Kaiser (2010: 23). They have not been described in English. In my view, they remain mostly valid today.

Shilov's seven arguments in favor of Yamnaya nomadism were: 1) the appearance of *wagons and horse bones* in Yamnaya graves indicated the presence of the kinds of transportation methods required by nomads (this states an important technological precondition for pastoral nomadism); 2) the *soils and rainfall* in much of the Don–Volga–Caspian steppe region were not suitable for rainfall agriculture; 3) *no carbonized grain* (and, we can now add, no caries from regularly eating grain) was found in hundreds of excavated Yamnaya graves; 4) the most frequently found sacrificed animals in Yamnaya graves were (in Russian terminology) "small horned cattle," or *sheep-goats, which are associated with more mobile pastoral economies* – not "large horned cattle," which need more water and are associated with more sedentary pastoral economies; 5) Yamnaya *settlements were completely absent* in the region, but dozens of large Yamnaya kurgan cemeteries appeared; 6) the *kurgan type of funerary monument*, visible from afar in a flat landscape, was typical of nomads, not settled farmers (this was the essentialist typological thinking of the 1960s, but many kurgans have since been shown (Borisova et al. 2019) to have been built from stacked squares of turf – literally pastures for the dead – which does suggest a pastoral economy); and 7) a few large Yamnaya kurgan cemeteries (Tsa-Tsa, Balkhin Khutor) appeared 30 to 90 km away from the major river valleys, and were the *first major monuments in the arid steppe plateaus* between the river valleys. This indicated a new economic exploitation of interior steppe grassland environments, suggestive of a nomadic economy.

Shilov's third and fourth points – the absence of cultivated grain and the dominance of sheep and goats over cattle – were about how to define and characterize the eastern Yamnaya diet.

Today we can examine the Yamnaya diet through the stable isotopes of ^{15}N and ^{13}C in Yamnaya skeletons, dental pathologies, animal bones from settlements, animals sacrificed in graves, and dairy peptides in dental calculus.

2.6.1 Dietary Stable Isotopes

During the Samara Valley Project, Schulting and Richards (2016) examined dietary stable isotopes in fifty-eight individuals chosen to represent a time series from the Eneolithic through the LBA, distributed across the Volga–Ural steppes around Samara, Saratov, and Orenburg (northern region I in Fig. 2.2). The sample included fourteen Eneolithic individuals from two cemeteries and nine Yamnaya individuals from six cemeteries (Fig. 2.4).

The clearest change through time was a marked difference between the Eneolithic and Yamnaya diets. The Eneolithic diet was distinguished by $\delta^{13}C$ values that were significantly more negative (Eneolithic –20.1 vs Yamnaya –19.1) than in Yamnaya (Mann-Whitney U test, Z = 4.43, p = 0.000); and also by $\delta^{15}N$ values (Eneolithic, c. 13.7‰; Yamnaya, c. 11.2‰) that were significantly higher (Z = 3.73, p =0.000) (Schulting and Richards 2016: 130, Table 7.2). This combination of relatively depleted $\delta^{13}C$ values and elevated $\delta^{15}N$ values can be attributed to an Eneolithic protein diet based largely on freshwater fish and forest game. The Yamnaya diet showed an isotopic shift from C3 resources derived from forests and rivers to a mixture of C3 and C4 resources typical of steppe-pastured grazing animals. In the North Caucasus, Knipper et al. (2020) found a similar contrast between C3 agricultural diets in the Eneolithic at Progress-2 and C3 and C4 in Yamnaya and later Bronze Age diets, as did Shishlina et al. (2009).

Yamnaya $\delta^{15}N$ remained higher than many prehistoric populations because high aridity raises the $\delta^{15}N$ in steppe plants. Bronze Age steppe ovicaprids showed a positive correlation between $\delta^{13}C$ and $\delta^{15}N$ values and also exhibited more elevated $\delta^{15}N$ values than cattle, and the Bronze Age Volga steppe human population showed the same two trends. The human isotopic results could be explained (Schulting and Richards 2016: 143) "if it is assumed that sheep milk and meat contributed the majority of the protein in Bronze Age human diets."

The shift from riverine to grassland resources, seen isotopically, was accompanied by the widespread abandonment of riverine Eneolithic residential sites (Shilov #5) and by the initial appearance of kurgan cemeteries in the inter-valley steppe plateaus (Shilov #7). This is what would be expected in a shift from a mixed riverine economy to grassland nomadic pastoralism.

2.6.2 Dental Pathologies

During the Samara Valley Project, Murphy and Khokhlov (2016: 169–171) examined 2,976 teeth from populations in the Volga–Ural steppes, Eneolithic, EBA, MBA, and LBA. Murphy recorded no caries in 256 teeth from 16 examined Yamnaya individuals and a continuing absence of caries in 1984 teeth from 175 MBA and LBA individuals. The absence of dental caries showed continuity between the Yamnaya (EBA) and Srubnaya (LBA) diets. All the Bronze Age pastoralists from the middle Volga steppes had teeth like hunter-

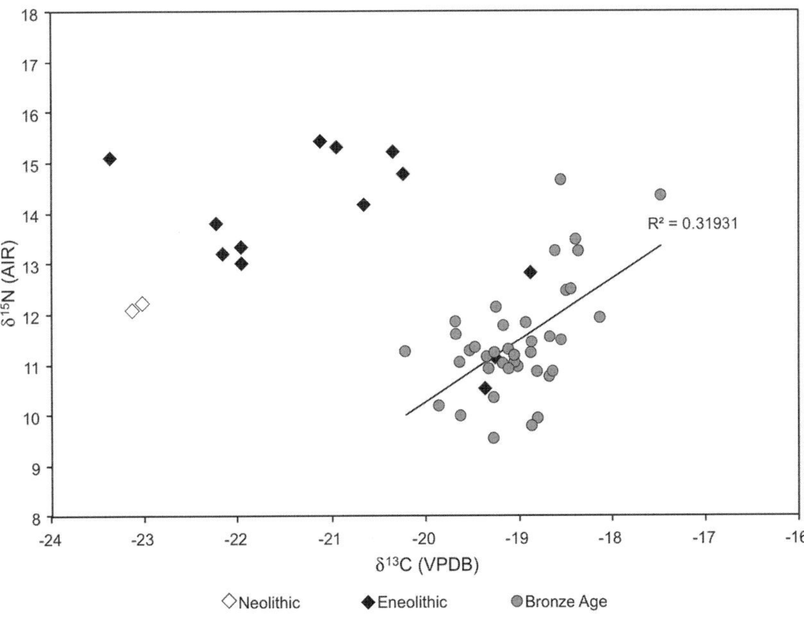

FIGURE 2.4. Bivariate plot of Eneolithic and Bronze Age stable dietary isotopes from humans in the middle Volga steppes. From Schulting and Richards 2016: Figure 7.2 Subsequent radiocarbon dating of these samples showed that the two anomalous "Eneolithic" individuals were actually dated to the Yamnaya period

gatherers, while Iron Age nomads from the Altai Mountains had extensive caries (Murphy 2003; Murphy and Khokhlov 2016: 169–171). The absence of caries (and by implication cultivated grain) in the teeth of Yamnaya pastoralists in the Volga steppes again distinguishes Yamnaya from Medieval nomadic pastoralism.

2.6.3 Faunal Evidence from Mikhailovka, Repin, and Usatovo

Two early Yamnaya settlements in the steppes have reported fauna: Mikhailovka II on the lower Dnieper and Repin on the lower Don. As described above, both had similar Repin-style pottery and radiocarbon dates (Table 2.1) and have traditionally been regarded as type sites for the early Yamnaya period, 3300 to 3000 BCE. Usatovo, a non-Yamnaya site, was another important settlement located near modern Odessa on the northwest coast of the Black Sea during the late fourth millennium BCE. Usatovo was not a Yamnaya culture site, but it had kurgan graves for its elite, and had a steppe-zone pastoral economy during the early Yamnaya period.

Eneolithic Mikhailovka I, dated 3600 to 3400 BCE, produced 1166 identifiable animal bone fragments, more than 95 percent from domesticated animals. Of the domesticated animals, 65 percent of the bones were from sheep-goats, 19 percent cattle, 10 percent horses, and less than 2 percent pigs (Tsalkin 1970: Table 51). Sheep-goats dominated the Mikhailovka I herds.

Mikhailovka II (early Yamnaya) and III (late Yamnaya mixed with early Catacomb) unfortunately were combined when the zoological remains were analyzed. Mikhailovka II–III together produced an unprecedented 51,151 animal bones, 44 times (!) more than the quantity recovered from Eneolithic Mikhailovka I (Shevchenko 1957; Tsalkin 1970: Table 51). This is more animal bones by an order of magnitude than any other Yamnaya site, and five times more than Usatovo (10,925). Cattle constituted 60 percent of domesticated animal bones and 45 percent of individuals MNI, followed by sheep-goats (30% bones/34% MNI) and horses (10% bones/18% MNI) (Tsalkin 1970; Shilov 1985; Dergachev 2007: 447). Wild hemiones (*Equus hemionus*) accounted for less than 1 percent of bones, but they were still hunted occasionally. Horse fats were detected on 37 percent of the ceramic sherds from Mikhailovka II analyzed for lipid residues (Mileto et al. 2018: 6), so horses might have been more important contributors to the diet than the bones suggest.

The dominance of cattle in the animal bones from Mikhailovka II–III could represent feasting activities, given the uniquely large quantity of cattle bones at this site. The difference in cattle between the piece count (60% of bone fragments) and the minimum number of individuals (45% of individuals) suggests that the cattle bones were more fragmented than other animals, thus dominating the piece count, consistent with intense butchering for cattle. The 30,538 cattle bone fragments from Mikhailovka II–III represented at least 1623 (MNI) consumed cattle (Tsalkin 1970: Table 51). If we assume a small adult body weight of 400 kg per cow or bull, with about 40 percent of that representing "retail" meat cuts, 1,623 cattle would produce 260,000 kg (!) of beef for a settlement that never had more than eight Yamnaya domestic structures. This quantity of beef suggests that guests from outside the settlement were feasted there.

At Repin, horses were counted as 55 percent of bones by V. Shilov (originally reported as 80% by Bibikova), cattle 18 percent, and sheep-goats only 9 percent, with the remainder (wild?) pigs and red deer (Shilov 1985: 29). A small reexcavation in 1989 obtained 142 additional animal bones and Repin-style pottery. Of 100 bones identifiable to species, 80 percent were horse (as in the original report by Bibikova), 8 percent were cattle, and 12 percent were sheep-goat (Kuznetsov 2013: 13). Horses were by far the species consumed most frequently at Repin, with cattle and sheep-goat a distant second or third. Some horse bones from Repin passed DNA screening and proved to be the direct ancestors of DOM2 horses (Librado et al. 2021). Repin was the last major settlement in the steppes to continue the equid-focused diet of Dereivka, Varfolomievka, and other Eneolithic sites (Anthony 2007: 174–186; Shishlina 2008: 222–230; Anthony and Brown 2011; Morgunova 2014). But even at Mikhailovka II, horse fats occurred on 37 percent of ceramic sherds analyzed.

The Usatovo settlement of 3 to 4 ha. was on the crest of a hill overlooking a bay on the northwest shore of the Black Sea, a marine-oriented site (Anthony 2007: 349–359). Usatovo was a coalescent culture, with cord-impressed coarse wares like late Cernavoda I in the steppes and painted Tripol'ye C2 fine pottery probably made in agricultural towns in the middle and upper Dniester valley. Coalescence between steppe and agricultural cultures, possibly in a patron–client relationship, also is suggested by two rich kurgan cemeteries near the settlement each of which was accompanied by a cemetery of poorer flat graves, without kurgans, similar to Tripol'ye C2 flat graves. The central graves under the kurgans contained riveted copper daggers with cast midribs, silver spiral temple ornaments, faience beads (the oldest in the steppes), and coral beads (*Gorgonarium*) from the Aegean Sea. Production and export of salt might explain its wealth (Ivanova 2010). Radiocarbon dates cluster between 3300 and 3000 BCE (Anthony 2007: Table 14.1), contemporary with Mikhailovka II, Repin, and late Maikop. The fauna recovered from Usatovo amounted to 10,925 identified bones from 892 individual animals (MNI). The dominant species was sheep-goat (62% of bones, 49% MNI), followed by cattle (24% of bones, 29% MNI), horses (13% of bones, 18% MNI), and pigs (0.5% of bones, 3% MNI) (Tsalkin 1970: Table 48). Horse images were incised on Usatovo pots.

Western archaeologists (Kohl 2007: 78, 162–164; Frachetti 2008, 2011; Kaiser 2010; Bendrey 2011) have asserted that cattle were the numerically dominant domesticated animal in the western Eurasian steppes during the Bronze Age. Kaiser

(2010) compiled faunal data that showed a shift, she asserted, from sheep-goat in the Eneolithic to cattle as the dominant herd species in EBA Yamnaya herds. She excluded from her EBA analysis the horse-dominant Repin site and assigned the ovicaprid-dominant Usatovo site to the Eneolithic, although both are shown by radiocarbon dates to have been contemporary with Mikhailovka II. Also excluded were the Caspian steppes south of the Volga, where Kaiser accepted the likelihood that Yamnaya herds probably had more sheep-goat than cattle for ecological reasons (Kaiser 2010: 31). The hypothesis that Yamnaya specialized in cattle leaned heavily on Mikhailovka II–III, a unique site. Other settlements with cattle-dominant fauna included the late Yamnaya (equivalent to Mikhailovkla III) ritual site at Generalka on an island in the Dnieper (Kaiser et al. 2020) or were Catacomb culture sites in the forest steppe, not relevant for steppe Yamnaya.

Steppe herd compositions varied from region to region during the EBA, according to the published faunas from three EBA settlements in the North Pontic steppes west of the Don River. Horse meat continued to play a prominent dietary role at Repin. Cattle seem to have been used as feasting animals at the unique residential center at Mikhailovka II–III and were dominant in the smaller faunal sample at the ritual site at Generalka. The sheep-dominant herds of the Usatovo culture, like the stable isotopes from Yamnaya skeletons in the middle Volga steppes, suggest a diet dominated by sheep-goat meat and dairy products. Yamnaya graves are much more numerous than settlements, and are distributed over the entire Yamnaya geographic range, unlike settlements. The animals sacrificed in graves therefore provide a wider window onto the animals herded by Yamnaya pastoralists.

2.6.4 Faunal Evidence from Graves

Shilov (1985) collected data on animal sacrifices in Yamnaya graves in the lower Don–lower Volga–Caucasus steppes (regions II, III, and the southern part of I in Fig. 2.2) and found that sheep-goat was the most frequent taxon sacrificed (Table 2.2). In 263 excavated Yamnaya graves from kurgans in this region, he found animal sacrifices in 40 graves, about 15% of the Yamnaya graves examined. Sheep-goat bones appeared in 65% of these graves, cattle in 15%, and horse bones in 7.5% (Table 2.2). Sheep-goat were in 70–77% of MBA graves with animal sacrifices, about the same as in EBA graves.

In the middle Volga–Ural steppes, the northeastern Yamnaya region (northern region I in Fig. 2.2), Morgunova compiled similar data from 164 excavated Yamnaya graves from 153 kurgans (Table 2.3). She came to the same conclusion as Shilov: graves with animal sacrifices were a distinct minority (10% of Yamnaya graves here), but in the graves with fauna, sheep-goats were by far the dominant taxon (appearing in 94% of the graves with fauna). Sheep-goats also were dominant in early Yamnaya graves in the Kuban steppes north of Maikop (Gei 2000: 128). Sheep-goats generally were the most frequent animals sacrificed in Yamnaya graves. A human diet dominated by sheep-goat proteins also explains the stable isotopes in Yamnaya individuals in the middle Volga steppes around Samara (Schulting and Richards 2016: 143), so the sheep-goat parts placed in Yamnaya graves might represent symbolic meals for the dead.

2.6.5 Peptides from Dairy

Wilkin et al. (2021) analyzed dairy peptides contained in dental calculus from eleven Eneolithic individuals with well-preserved proteomics from five cemeteries in the Volga steppes dated 4600 to 4000 BCE. Ten of the eleven contained no evidence for dairy consumption. One individual from the Khvalynsk cemetery (Khvalynsk II grave 1), dated 4500 to 4300 BCE, exhibited one bovine peptide (alpha-S1-casein), but lacked the most frequently recovered bovine peptide (beta-lactoglobulin [BLG]), so dairy consumption in this individual cannot be confirmed. Wilkin et al. also examined dental calculus in Yamnaya, Poltavka, and Sintashta individuals of the EBA, MBA, and MBA/LBA transition, 3300 to 1700 BCE. For the EBA individuals assigned to the Yamnaya culture, dairy peptides were recovered from fifteen of the sixteen individuals analyzed, a reversal of the Eneolithic pattern. All fifteen individuals with positive dairy results contained multiple peptide spectral matches to ruminant dairy proteins and some individuals also contained alpha S1-casein and alpha S2-caseins. *Ovis*, *Capra*, and *Bos* attributions were all made, with many individuals' calculus containing dairy peptides from multiple species. The Yamnaya people regularly consumed dairy products, probably in hard (cheese) or fermented (yogurt) forms, given the prevalence of lactose intolerance among them. This gives strong support to the hypothesis of a significant change in diet from the Eneolithic to the EBA. In an earlier study, Shishlina (2008: 232) examined human dental calculus from Yamnaya and Catacomb kurgan graves in the Kalmyk steppes south of the lower Volga dated 2800 to 2000 BCE, and found no cultivated seeds, cereal pollen, or cereal phytoliths in dental calculus.

Significantly, *Equus* milk peptides from the protein BLG I were identified in two Yamnaya individuals from Krivyanskiy IX. One of the Yamnaya individuals with *Equus* milk peptides in his dental calculus (kurgan 4, grave 21A) was dated 3345 to 3096 BCE (95%) (4495±25 BP, PSUAMS-7979), and the other (kurgan 2, grave 2) was dated 2881 to 2633 (95%) (4165±25 BP, PSUAMS-7978). This is the earliest *Equus* milk product in human dental calculus.

2.6.6 Stature

Yamnaya people in the Volga steppes were on average taller (male femoral length 466–480 mm, mean 472.1) and more robust than their Eneolithic ancestors (male femoral length 434–482 mm, mean 461.4), suggesting that the new diet led to taller, stronger people (Khokhlov 2010: 456, 476; Murphy and Khokhlov 2016: 162). They were also taller than European farmers in southeastern Europe (Mathieson et al. 2015: 502). The newly simplified diet seems to have been successful nutritionally.

2.7 Conclusion: The First Pastoral Nomads in the Steppes

The Eneolithic fisher-hunter-herders of the Volga steppes kept domesticated cattle and sheep-goats (and horses of uncertain status) and sacrificed them in human graves, but they apparently did not consume milk products. In contrast, dairy foods were ubiquitous in EBA Yamnaya dental calculus, clear evidence of a significant dietary change also indicated in dietary stable isotopes. The incidence of caries was like that found among hunter-gatherers, so starchy cereals were not a major part of the Yamnaya diet. The animals sacrificed in graves across the Yamnaya world were primarily sheep-goats, not cattle, and settlements of the early Yamnaya era (3300–3000 BCE) exhibited a variety of faunal compositions, each one probably more indicative of the site's function than of the Yamnaya diet in general. Mikhailovka was a special and central place, interpreted here as a kind of caravanserai where nomadic groups crossing the Dnieper paused to feast on beef and gather information. Other than Mikhailovka and a few additional settlements west of the Don, most Eneolithic riverine settlements were abandoned, replaced by kurgan cemeteries, some of which were the first large human monuments in the steppe plateaus between the river valleys. Wagons and carts were so important that they were included in hundreds of Yamnaya and Catacomb graves. Yamnaya people rode and milked horses, and Yamnaya horses from Repin and Turganik were among a small set of samples that contributed 95% of the ancestry of DOM2 horses. Together these observations support Shilov's argument that Yamnaya people were the first nomadic pastoralists in the Eurasian steppes.

The Yamnaya economic-ritual community enjoyed a decisive advantage because it was the first to fully commit to mobile herding using ox-drawn wagons and horse-mounted herders. Those who adopted the new economy were the first human groups to exploit the vast reserves of bioenergy stored in the Eurasian grasslands, converting that bioenergy into a simplified human diet focused on meat and milk proteins. This revolutionary economic adaptation spread across the steppes with a genetically homogeneous group of closely related people, perhaps an innovative elite, whose shared funeral ritual was accompanied by a shared set of religious beliefs and myths, as Ivanova (2006) suggested, expressed in a language that was probably late Proto-Indo-European. Comparative Indo-European mythology preserves traces of these beliefs (West 2007).

The new, productive nomadic pastoral economy opened a large, unexploited ecological zone to human exploitation, and at the same time the military advantages of mobility pushed and pulled the settled riverine population toward nomadic life. This process created a set of nomadic groups who became increasingly distinct from neighboring sedentary farming communities in southeastern Europe and the North Caucasus. The later Yamnaya migrations out of the Pontic–Caspian steppes and across 5000 km of Eurasia were facilitated by the development and maturation of the first pastoral nomadic economy in the steppes.

References

Allentoft, M. E., M. Sikora, K. G. Sjögren, S. Rasmussen, M. Rasmussen, J. Stenderup, P. B. Damgaard, H. Schroeder, T. Ahlström, L. Vinner, A.-S. Malaspinas, A. Margaryan, T. Higham, D. Chivall, N. Lynnerup, L. Harvig, J. Baron, P. Della Casa, P. Dąbrowski, P. R. Duffy, A. V. Ebel, A. Epimakhov, K. Frei, M. Furmanek, T. Gralak, A. Gromov, S. Gronkiewicz, G. Grupe, T. Hajdu, R. Jarysz, V. Khartanovich, A. Khokhlov, V. Kiss, J. Kolář, A. Kriiska, I. Lasak, C. Longhi, G. McGlynn, A. Merkevicius, I. Merkyte, M. Metspalu, R. Mkrtchyan, V. Moiseyev, L. Paja, G. Pálfi, D. Pokutta, Ł. Pospieszny, T. D. Price, L. Saag, M. Sablin, N. Shishlina, V. Smrčka, V. I. Soenov, V. Szeverényi, G. Tóth, S. V. Trifanova, L. Varul, M. Vicze, L. Yepiskoposyan, V. Zhitenev, L. Orlando, T. Sicheritz-Pontén, S. Brunak, R. Nielsen, K. Kristiansen, and E. Willerslev. 2015. Population genomics of Bronze Age Eurasia. *Nature* 522: 167–172.

Anthony, David W. 1986. The "Kurgan culture," Indo-European origins, and the domestication of the horse: A reconsideration. *Current Anthropology* 27(4): 291–313.

2007. *The horse, the wheel, and language: How Bronze Age riders from the Eurasian steppes shaped the modern world.* Princeton: Princeton University Press.

2016. The Samara Valley Project and the evolution of pastoral economies in the western Eurasian steppes. In: David W. Anthony, D. Brown, A. Khokhlov, P. Kuznetsov, and O. Mochalov (eds.), *A Bronze Age landscape in the Russian steppes: The Samara Valley Project* (Monumenta Archaeologica 37), 3–36. Los Angeles: Cotsen Institute of Archaeology Press.

2021. Early Yamnaya chronology and origins from an archaeological perspective. In: Volker Heyd, Gabriella Kulcsár, and Bianca Preda-Bălănică (eds.), *Yamnaya interactions: Proceedings of the international workshop held in Helsinki, 25–26th April 2019*. Vol. 2 of *The Yamnaya Impact on Prehistoric Europe*. Budapest: Archaeolingua.

Anthony, David W., and D. R. Brown. 2011. The secondary products revolution, horse-riding, and mounted warfare. *Journal of World Prehistory* 24(2): 131–160.

Anthony, David W., D. R. Brown, and C. George. 2006. Early horseback riding and warfare: The importance of the magpie around the neck. In Sandra Olsen, Susan Grant, Alice Choyke, and Laszlo Bartosiewicz (eds.), *Horses and humans: The evolution of the equine-human relationship* (British Archaeological Reports International Series 1560), 137–156. Oxford: Archaeopress.

Anthony, David W., D. R. Brown, A. Khokhlov, P. F. Kuznetsov, and O. Mochalov (eds.). 2016. *A Bronze Age landscape in the Russian steppes: The Samara Valley Project* (Monumenta Archaeologica 37). Los Angeles: Cotsen Institute of Archaeology Press.

Anthony, David W., A. A. Khokhlov, S. A. Agapov, D. S. Agapov, R. Schulting, I. Olalde, and D. Reich. 2022. The Eneolithic cemetery at Khvalynsk on the Volga River. *Praehistorische Zeitschrift* 97(1): 22–67.

Anthony, David W., and Don Ringe. 2015. The Indo-European homeland from linguistic and archaeological perspectives. *Annual Review of Linguistics* 1: 199–219.

Azzaroli, A. 1980. Venetic horses from Iron Age burials at Padova. *Rivista di Scienze Preistoriche* 35(1–2): 282–308.

Bakker, Jan Albert, Janusz Kruk, A. L. Lanting, and Sarunas Milisauskas 1999. The earliest evidence of wheeled vehicles in Europe and the Near East. *Antiquity* 73: 778–790.

Barfield, Thomas. 1989. *The perilous frontier.* Cambridge: Blackwell.

Belinskii, A., S. Hansen, and S. Reinhold. 2017. The great kurgan from Nalčik. A preliminary report. In: M. Tonussi and E. Rova (eds.), *Subartu XXXVIII: At the northern frontier of Near Eastern archaeology: Recent research on Caucasia and Anatolia in the Bronze Age*, 13–32. Turnhout: Brepols.

Bendrey, R. 2007. New methods for the identification of evidence for bitting on horse remains from archaeological sites. *Journal of Archaeological Science* 34: 1036–50.

2011. Some like it hot: Environmental determinism and the pastoral economies of the later prehistoric Eurasian steppe. *Pastoralism: Research, Policy and Practice* 1(8): 1–16.

Bogaard, Amy, M. Fochesato, and S. Bowles. 2019. The farming-inequality nexus: New insights from ancient Western Eurasia. *Antiquity* 93(371): 1129–1143.

Borisova, A. V., M. V. Krivosheev, R. A. Mimokhod, and M. V. El'tsov. 2019. "Sod blocks" in kurgan mounds: Historical and soil features of the technique of tumuli erection. *Journal of Archaeological Science: Reports* 24: 122–131.

Brown, D. R., and David W. Anthony. 1998. Bit wear, horseback riding, and the Botai site in Kazakstan. *Journal of Archaeological Science* 25: 331–347.

Bunyatyan, K. 2003. Correlations between agriculture and pastoralism in the North Pontic steppe area during the Bronze Age. In: M. Levine, C. Renfrew, and K. Boyle (eds.), *Prehistoric steppe adaptation and the horse*, 269–286. Cambridge: McDonald Institute.

Burmeister, Stefan. 2017. Early wagons in Eurasia: Disentangling an enigmatic innovation. In: Philipp W. Stockhammer and Joseph Maran (eds.), *Appropriating innovations: Entangled knowledge in Eurasia 5000–1500 BCE*, 69–77. Oxford: Oxbow Books.

Chang, Claudia. 2018. *Rethinking prehistoric Central Asia: Shepherds, farmers, and nomads*. London: Routledge.

Chernykh, E. N. 1992. *Ancient metallurgy in the USSR.* Cambridge: Cambridge University Press.

2004. Kargaly: The largest and most ancient metallurgical complex on the border of Europe and Asia. In: Katheryn M. Linduff (ed.), *Metallurgy in ancient eastern Eurasia from the Urals to the Yellow River* (Chinese Studies 31), 223–279. Lewiston: Edwin Mellen.

Childe, V. G. 1958. *The prehistory of European society.* London: Cassell.

Clayton, Hilary M., and R. Lee. 1984. A fluoroscopic study of the position and action of the jointed snaffle bit in the horse's mouth. *Equine Veterinary Science* 4(5): 193–196.

Clutton-Brock, Juliet. 1974. The Buhen horse. *Journal of Archaeological Science* 1: 89–100.

Cook, W. R. 2011. Damage by the bit to the equine interdental space. *Equine Veterinary Education* 23(7): 355–360.

Dergachev, Valentin A. 2007. *O Skipetrakh, O Loshadyakh, O Voine: Etiudy v zashchitu migrationnoi konseptsii M. Gimbutas*. Saint Petersburg: Nestor-Istoriya.

Di Cosmo, Nicola 1994. Ancient Inner Asian nomads: Their economic basis and its significance in Chinese history. *Journal of Asian Studies* 53(4): 1092–1126.

Diaz del Río, P., P. L. García, J. A. López Sáez, M. I. Martina Navarette, A. L. Rodrígues Alcalde, S. Rovira-Llorens, J. M. Vicent García, and I. de Zavala Morencos. 2006. Understanding the productive economy during the Bronze Age through archaeometallurgical and paleo-environmental research at Kargaly. In: D. L. Peterson, L. M. Popova, and A. T. Smith (eds.), *Beyond the steppe and the sown: Proceedings of the 2002 University of Chicago Conference on Eurasian Archaeology*, 343–357. Leiden: Brill.

Doumani, Paula N., M. D. Frachetti, R. Beardmore, T. M. Schmaus, R. N. Spengler, and A. N. Mar'yashev. 2015. Burial ritual, agriculture, and craft production among Bronze Age pastoralists at Tasbas (Kazakhstan). *Archaeological Research in Asia* 1/2: 17–32.

Dovchenko, N. D., and N. A. Rychkov. 1988. K probleme sotsial'noi stratigrafikatsii plemen Yamnoi kul'turno-istoricheskoi obshchnosti. In *Novye Pamyatniki Yamnoi Kul'tury Stepnoi Zony Ukrainy*, 27–40. Kiev: Naukova Dumka.

Dremov, I. I., and A. I. Yudin, 1992. Drevneishie podkurgannye zakhoroneniya stepnogo zaVolzh'ya. *Rossiskaya Arkheologiya* 4: 18–31.

Ewers, John C. 1955. *The horse in Blackfoot Indian culture.* Washington, DC: Smithsonian Institution Press.

Fansa, M., and S. Burmeister (eds.). 2004. *Rad und Wagen: Der Ursprung einer Innovation. Wagen im Vorderen Orient und Europa* (Archäologische Mitteilungen aus Nordwestdeutschland Beiheft 40). Mainz: Philipp von Zabern.

Frachetti, Michael D. 2008. *Pastoralist landscapes and social interaction in Bronze Age Eurasia*. Berkeley: University of California Press.

2011. Multiregional emergence of mobile pastoralism and non-uniform institutional complexity across Eurasia. *Current Anthropology* 53(1): 1–38.

Frînculeasa, Alin, Bianca Preda, and Volker Heyd. 2015. Pit-Graves, Yamnaya and kurgans along the Lower Danube: Disentangling IVth and IIIrd millennium BC burial customs, equipment and chronology. *Praehistorische Zeitschrift* 90(1/2): 1–69.

Furholt, Martin. 2014. Upending a "totality": Re-evaluating Corded Ware variability in Late Neolithic Europe. *Proceedings of the Prehistoric Society* 80: 67–86.

2018. Massive migrations? The impact of recent aDNA studies on our view of third millennium Europe. *European Journal of Archaeology* 21(2): 159–191.

Gaunitz, C., A. Fages, K. Hanghøj, A. Albrechtsen, N. Khan, M. Schubert, A. Seguin-Orlando, I. J. Owens, S. Felkel, O. Bignon-Lau, P. de Barros Damgaard, A. Mittnik, A. F. Mohaseb, H. Davoudi, S. Alquraishi, A. H. Alfarhan, K. A. S. Al-Rasheid, E. Crubézy, N. Benecke, Sandra Olsen, D. Brown, D. Anthony, K. Massy, V. Pitulko, A. Kasparov, G. Brem, M. Hofreiter, G. Mukhtarova, N. Baimukhanov, L. Lõugas, V. Onar, P. W. Stockhammer, J. Krause, B. Boldgiv, S. Undrakhbold, D. Erdenebaatar, S. Lepetz, M. Mashkour, A. Ludwig, B. Wallner, V. Merz, I. Merz, V. Zaibert, E. Willerslev, P. Librado, A. K. Outram, and Ludovic Orlando.

2018. Ancient genomes revisit the ancestry of domestic and Przewalski's horses. *Science* 360(6384): 111–114.

Gei, A. N. 2000. *Novotitorovskaya Kul'tura*. Moscow: Institut Arkheologii.

Gimbutas, Marija. 1956. *The prehistory of Eastern Europe* (American School of Prehistoric Research Bulletin 20). Cambridge, MA: Peabody Museum.

1970. Proto-Indo-European culture: The Kurgan culture during the fifth, fourth, and third millennia B.C. In: George Cardona, Henry Hoenigswald, and Alfred Senn (eds.), *Indo-European and the Indo-Europeans*, 155–198. Philadelphia: University of Pennsylvania Press.

1977. The first wave of European steppe pastoralists into Copper Age Europe. *Journal of Indo-European Studies* 5(4): 277–338.

Gorodtsov, V. A. 1907. Rezul'taty arkheologichekikh issledovanii v Bakhmutskom uezdie Ekaterinoslavskoi gubernii 1905g. *Trudy XIII A.S.* 1: 211–365. Moscow: State Historical Museum.

Haak, Wolfgang, I. Lazaridis, N. Patterson, N. Rohland, S. Mallick, B. Llamas, G. Brandt, S. Nordenfelt, E. Harney, K. Stewardson,Q. Fu, A. Mittnik, E. Bánffy, C. Economou, M. Francken, S. Friederich, R. G. Pena, F. Hallgren, V. Khartanovich, A. Khokhlov, M. Kunst, P. Kuznetsov, H. Meller, O. Mochalov, V. Moiseyev, N. Nicklisch, S. L. Pichler, R. Risch, M. A. R. Guerra, C. Roth, A. Szécsényi-Nagy, J. Wahl, M. Meyer, J. Krause, D. Brown, D. Anthony, A. Cooper, K. W. Alt, and D. Reich. 2015. Massive migration from the steppe was a source for Indo-European languages in Europe. *Nature* 522(7555): 207–211.

Hanks, Bryan, Alicia V. Miller, M. Judda, A. Epimakhovd, D. Razhevf, and Karen Privat. 2018. Bronze Age diet and economy: New stable isotope data from the Central Eurasian steppes (2100–1700 BC). *Journal of Archaeological Science* 97: 14–25.

Hansen, Sven 2013. The birth of the hero. The emergence of a social type in the 4th millennium BC. In: Elisabetta Starnini (ed.), *Unconformist archaeology: Papers in honour of Paolo Biagi*, 101–112. Oxford: Archaeopress.

Häusler, A. 2003. *Nomaden, Indogermanen, Invasionen. Zur Entstehung eines Mythos* (Orientwissenschaftliche Hefte 5). Halle: Orientwissenschaftliches Zentrum der Martin-Luther-Universität.

Hämäläinen, Pekka. 2008. *The Comanche Empire*. New Haven: Yale University Press.

Heyd, Volker. 2013. Europe at the dawn of the Bronze Age. In: Volker Heyd, G. Kulcsár, and V. Szeverényi (ed.), *Transitions to the Bronze Age: Interregional interaction and socio-cultural change in the third millennium BC Carpathian Basin and neighbouring regions*, 9–66. Budapest: Archaeolingua.

Ivanova, Svitlana V. 2006. Yamnaya kul'turno-istoricheskaya obshchnost': problemy formirovaniya v svete radiouglerodnogo datirovaniya. *Rossisskaya Arkheologiya* 2: 113–120.

2010. Prirodnye resursy i ekonomika drevnikh obshchestv. *Stratum plus* 2: 49–97.

Ivanova, Svitlana. 2013. Connections between the Budzhak culture and Central European groups of the Corded Ware culture. *Baltic-Pontic Studies* 18: 86–120.

Ivanova, S. V., A. G. Nikitin, and D. V. Kiusak. 2018. Mayatnikov'ye migratsii v tsirkum-Pontcheskoi i tsentral'noi Evrope v epokhu paleometalla i problema genesis a Yamnoi kul'tury. *Arkheologia Davnya Istoriya Ukraini* 1(26): 101–146.

Ivanova, Svitlana V., and V. V. Tsimidanov. 1993. O sotsiologicheskoi interpretatsii pogrebenii povozkami Yamnoi kul'turno-istoricheskoi obshchnosti. *Arkheologicheskii Al'manakh* 2: 23–34.

Kaiser, Elke 2010. Der Übergang zur Rinderzucht im nördlichen Schwarzmeerraum. *Godišnjak* 39: 23–34.

Kaiser, Elke, O. Tuboltsev, N. Benecke, R. P. Evershed, M. Hochmuth, S. Mileto, and M. Riesenberg. 2020. Der Fundplatz Generalka 2 der Jamnaja-Kultur in der Südukraine. Archäologische und naturwissenschaftliche Untersuchungen. *Praehistorische Zeitschrift*: aop.

Kelly, R. L., L. Poyer, and B. Tucker. 2005. An ethnoarchaeological study of mobility, architectural investment, and food sharing among Madagascar's Mikea. *American Anthropologist* 107: 403–416.

Kent, Susan, and Helga Vierich. 1989. The myth of ecological determinism: Anticipated mobility and site spatial organization. In: Susan Kent (ed.), *Farmers as hunters*, 96–130. Cambridge: Cambridge University Press.

Khazanov, Anatoly. 1994. *Nomads and the outside world*. Rev. ed. Madison: University of Wisconsin Press. First published 1984.

Khokhlov, A. A. 2010. Naselenie Khvalynskoi Eneoliticheskoi kul'tury po antropologicheckii materialam gruntovykh mogilnikov Khvalynsk I, Khvalynsk II, Khokhlov Bugor. In: S. A. Agapov (ed.), *Khvalynskie Eneoliticheskie Mogil'niki i Khvalynskaya Eneoliticheskaya Kul'tura: Issledovanija materialov*, 407–517. Samara: SROO IEKA "Povolzh'e."

Kiashko, A. V. 2017. Kul'turnei bronzy poseleniya Razdorskoe I na Nizhnem Donu. In: V. S. Bokcharyev and V. A. Alekshin (ed.), *Vneshnie I Vnutrennie Svyazi Stepnykh (Skorovodcheskikh) Kul'tur Vostochnoi Evropy v Eneolite I Bronzovom Veke (V-II tys. do n. e.)*, 84–88. Saint Petersburg.

Klochko, V. I. 2019. Metalevi sokiri rannogo etapu Yamnoi kulturi Ukraini. *Arkheologiya i Davnya Istoriya Ukraini* 2(31): 69–77.

Knipper, Corina, S. Reinhold, J. Gresky, N. Berezina, C. Gerling, S. L. Pichler, A. P. Buzhilova, A. R. Kantorovich, V. E. Maslov, V. G. Petrenko, S. V. Lyakhov, A. A. Kalmykov, A. B. Belinskiy, S. Hansen, K. W. Alt. 2020. Diet and subsistence in Bronze Age pastoral communities from the southern Russian steppes and the North Caucasus. *PLoS ONE* 15(10): e0239861.

Kohl, Philip K. 2007. *The making of Bronze Age Eurasia*. Cambridge: Cambridge University Press.

Kohl, Philip L., and V. Trifonov. 2014. The prehistory of the Caucasus: Internal developments and external interactions. In: Colin Renfrew (ed.), *Cambridge World Prehistory*, 1571–1595. Cambridge: Cambridge University Press.

Korenevskii, S. N. 1980. O metallicheskikh veshchakh i Utyevskogo mogil'nika. In: A. D. Pryakhin (ed.), *Arkheologiya Vostochno-Evropeiskoi Lesostepi*, 59–66. Voronezh: Vorenezhskogo Universiteta.

2016. Problemnye situatsii "post-Ubaidskogo perioda" v Predkavkaz'e (4500–3500 let do n.è.). *Stratum plus* 2: 1–26.

2020. Mif o dreve zhizni na poroge tsilivizatsii po dannym vaz iz Hafadzhi, Djirofta I nekropol Ura. In: M. T. Kashuba, S. E. Reinhold, and Y. Y. Piotrovskii (ed.), *Der Kaukasus zwischen Osteuropa und Vorderem Orient in der Bronze- und Eisenzeit: Dialog der Kulturen* (Kultur des Dialoges, Archäologie in Iran und Turan 19), 199–214. Berlin: Deutsches Archäologisches Institut Eurasien-Abteilung and Dietrich Reimer.

Korobkova, G. F., and O. G. Shaposhnikova. 2005. *Mikhailovka: Etalonni Pamiatnik Drevnei Yamnoi Kul'tury*. Saint Petersburg: Institut Istorii Material'noi Kul'tury RAN.

Koryakova, Ludmila, and Andrie Epimakhov. 2007. *The Urals and Western Siberia in the Bronze and Iron Ages*. Cambridge: Cambridge University Press.

Kotova, Nadezhda, and L. A. Spitsyna 2003. Radiocarbon chronology of the middle layer of the Mikhailivka settlement. *Baltic-Pontic Studies* 12: 121–131.

Kristiansen, Kristian, and T. B. Larsson. 2005. *The rise of Bronze Age society: Travels, transmissions, and transformations*. Cambridge: Cambridge University Press.

Kuzmina, Elena E. 2008. *The prehistory of the Silk Road*. Edited by V. Mair. Philadelphia: University of Pennsylvania Press.

Kuznetsov, P. F. 2013. Datirovka pamyatnika u Repina Khutora i khronologiya kul'turno-rodstvenniykh materialov epokhi Rannei Bronzy stepnoi zony vostochnoi Evropy. *Rossiiskaya Arkheologiya* 1: 13–21.

Kyselý, R., and L. Peške. 2016. Horse size and domestication: Early equid bones from the Czech Republic in the European context. *Anthropozoologica* 51(1): 15–39.

Lagodovskaya, E. F., O. G. Shaposhnikova, and M. L. Makarevich. 1959. Osnovnye itogi issledovaniya Mikhailovskogo poseleniya. *Kratkie Soobshcheniya Institut Arkheologii* 9: 21–28.

1962. *Mikhailovka Poseleniye*. Kiev: Naukova Dumka.

Lattimore, Owen. 1988. *Inner Asian frontiers of China*. Hong Kong: Oxford University Press. First published 1940 by the American Geographical Society (New York).

Lebedeva, E. Y. 2005. Archaeobotany and study of the Bronze Age agriculture in Eastern Europe. *Opus: Mezhdistsiplinarnye Issledovaniya v Arkheologii (Moscow)* 4: 50–68.

Librado, P., N. Khan, A. Fages, M. Kuslyi, T. Suchan, L. Tonasso-Calvière, S. Schiavinato, D. Alioglu, A. Fromentier, A. Perdereau, J. Aury, C. Gaunitz, L. Chauvey, A. Seguin-Orlando, C. Der Sarkissian, J. Southon, B. Shapiro, S. Alquraishi, A. H. Alfarhan, K. A. S. Al-Rasheid, T. Seregely, L. Klassen, R. Iversen, O. Bignon-Lau, P. Bodu, M. Olive, J-C. Castel, N. Alvarez, M. Germonpré, J. Wilczyński, E. Rannamäe, U. Saarma, L. Lõugas, R. Kyselý, L. Peške, A. Balasescu, D. Gerber, G. Kulcsár, E. Gál, R. Bendrey, M. Allentoft, H. Shephard, N. Tomadini, S. Grouard, V. Pitulko, G. Brem, B. Wallner, M. Keller, K. Kitagawa, A. Bessudnov, W. Taylor, J. Bayarsaikhan, D. Erdenebaatar, T. Kubatbeek, E. Mijiddorj, B. Boldgiv, T. Tsagaan, M. Pruvost, S. Olsen, C. Makarewicz, S. Valenzuela Lamas, S. Albizuri, A. N. Espinet, J. L. Garrido, N. Kotova, A. Pryor, P. Crabtree, R. Zhumatayev, T. Kuznetsova, D. Lordkipanize, M. Marzullo, O. Prato, G. Bagnasco, B. Clavel, S. Lepetz, H. Davoudi, M. Mashkour, P. Stockhammer, J. Krause, W. Haak, A. Morales, N. Benecke, M. Hofreiter, A. Ludwig, A. Graphodatsky, K. Yu. Kiryushin, G. Baryshnikov, E. Petrova, M. Sablin, A. Tishkin, E. Ananyevskaya, A. Logvin, V. Logvin, S. Kalieva, I. Kukushkin, I. Merz, V. Merz, S. Sakenov, I. Shevnina, V. Varfolomeyev, V. Zaibert, B. Arbuckle, S. Reinhold, S. Hansen, N. Roslyakova, P. Kosintsev, P. Kuznetsov, D. Anthony, G. J. Kroonen, K. Kristiansen, P. Wincker, A. Outram, and Ludovic Orlando. 2021. Genomic origins and spread of domestic horses from the Bronze Age Pontic-Caspian steppes. *Nature* 598: 634–640.

Mallory, J. P. 1977. The chronology of the early Kurgan tradition (part two). *Journal of Indo-European Studies* 5(4): 339–368.

Manzura, Igor. 2005. Steps to the steppe: Or, how the North Pontic region was colonized. *Oxford Journal of Archaeology* 24(4): 313–338.

Mathieson, Iain, I. Lazaridis, N. Rohland, S. Mallick, N. Patterson, S. A. Roodenberg, E. Harney, K. Stewardson, D. Fernandes, M. Novak, K. Sirak, C. Gamba, E. R. Jones, B. Llamas, S. Dryomov, J. Pickrell, J. Luís Arsuaga, J. M. Bermúdez de Castro, E. Carbonell, F. Gerritsen, A. Khokhlov, P. Kuznetsov, M. Lozano, H. Meller, O. Mochalov, V. Moiseyev, M. A. Rojo Guerra, J. Roodenberg, J. M. Vergès, J. Krause, A. Cooper, K. W. Alt, D. Brown, D. Anthony, C. Lalueza-Fox, W. Haak, R. Pinhasi, and David Reich. 2015. Genome-wide patterns of selection in 230 ancient Eurasians. *Nature* 528: 499–503.

Merpert, N. I. 1974. *Drevneishie Skotovody Volzhsko-Uralskogo Mezhdurechya*. Moscow: Nauka.

1977. Comments on "The chronology of the early Kurgan tradition." *Journal of Indo-European Studies* 5(4): 373–378.

Mileto, S., E. Kaiser, Y. Rassamakin, and R. P. Evershed. 2018. New insights into the subsistence economy of the Eneolithic Dereivka culture of the Ukrainian North-Pontic region through lipid residue analysis of pottery vessels. *Journal of Archaeological Science: Reports* 13: 67–74.

Morgunova, Nina L. 2014. *Pri-Uralskaya Gruppa Pamyatnikov v Sisteme Volzhsko-Ural'skogo Varianta Yamnoi Kul'turno-Istoricheskoi Oblasti*. Orenburg: OGPU.

2015. Pottery from the Volga area in the Samara and South Urals region from Eneolithic to Early Bronze Age. *Documenta Praehistorica* 42: 311–319.

Morgunova, Nina L., and O. S. Khokhlova. 2013. Chronology and periodization of the Pit-Grave culture in the region between the Volga and Ural Rivers based on radiocarbon dating and paleopedological research. *Radiocarbon* 55(2/3): 1286–1296.

Motuzaite-Matuzeviciute, Giedre, S. Telizhenko, and M. K. Jones 2012. Archaeobotanical investigation of two Scythian-Sarmatian period pits in eastern Ukraine: Implications for floodplain cereal cultivation. *Journal of Field Archaeology* 37(1): 51–61.

Mulder, Monique B., I. Fazzio, W. Irons, R. L. McElreath, S. Bowles, A. Bell, T. Hertz, and L. Hazzah. 2010. Pastoralism and wealth inequality: Revisiting an old question. *Current Anthropology* 51(1):35–48.

Murphy, E. M. 2003. *Iron Age archaeology and trauma from Aymyrlyg, South Siberia* (BAR International Series 1152). Oxford: Archaeopress.

Murphy, E. M., and A. A. Khokhlov. 2016. A bioarchaeological study of prehistoric populations from the Volga region. In: D. W. Anthony (ed.), *A Bronze Age landscape in the Russian steppes: The Samara Valley Project* (Monumenta Archaeologica 37), 147–214. Los Angeles: Cotsen Institute of Archaeology Press.

Narasimhan, Vagheesh M., N. Patterson, P. Moorjani, I. Lazaridis, M. Lipson, S. Mallick, N. Rohland, R. Bernardos, A. M. Kim, N. Nakatsuka, I. Olalde, A. Coppa, J. Mallory, V. Moiseyev, J. Monge, L. M. Olivieri, N. Adamski, N. Broomandkhoshbacht, F. Candilio, O. Cheronet, B. J. Culleton, M. Ferry, D. Fernandes, B. Gamarra, D. Gaudio, M. Hajdinjak, É. Harney, T. K. Harper, D. Keating, A. M. Lawson, M. Michell, M. Novak, J. Oppenheimer, N. Rai, K. Sirak, V. Slon, K. Stewardson, Z. Zhang, G. Akhatov, A. N. Bagashev, B. Baitanayev, G. L. Bonora, T. Chikisheva, A. Derevianko, E. Dmitry, K. Douka, N. Dubova, A. Epimakhov, S. Freilich, D. Fuller, A. Goryachev, A. Gromov, B. Hanks, M. Judd, E. Kazizov, A. Khokhlov, E. Kitov, E. Kupriyanova, P. Kuznetsov, D. Luiselli, F. Maksudov, C. Meiklejohn, D. Merrett, R. Micheli, O. Mochalov, Z. Muhammed, S. Mustafokulov, A. Nayak, R. M. Petrovna, D. Pettener, R. Potts, D. Razhev, S. Sarno, K. Sikhymbaeva, S. M.

Slepchenko, N. Stepanova, S. Svyatko, S. Vasilyev, M. Vidale, D. Voyakin, A. Yermolayeva, A. Zubova, V. S. Shinde, C. Lalueza-Fox, M. Meyer, D. Anthony, N. Boivin, K. Thangaraj, D. J. Kennett, M. Frachetti, R. Pinhasi, and David Reich. 2018. The formation of human populations in South and Central Asia. *Science* 365: 6457.

Nechitailo, A. P. 1991. *Svyazi Naseleniya Stepnoi Ukrainy i Severnogo Kavkaza v Epokhy Bronzy.* Kiev: Dumka.

Nedashkovskii, L. S. 2010. Economy of the Golden Horde population. *Anthropology and Archeology of Eurasia* 48(2): 35–50.

Olalde, Iñigo, S. Brace, M. E. Allentoft, I. Armit, K. Kristiansen, N. Rohland, S. Mallick, T. Booth, A. Szécsényi-Nagy, A. Mittnik, E. Altena, M. Lipson, I. Lazaridis, N. Patterson, N. Broomandkhoshbacht, Y. Diekmann, Z. Faltyskova, D. Fernandes, M. Ferry, E. Harney, P. de Knijff, M. Michel, J. Oppenheimer, K. Stewardson, A. Barclay, K. W. Alt, A. Avilés Fernández, E. Bánffy, M. Bernabò-Brea, D. Billoin, C. Blasco, C. Bonsall, L. Bonsall, T. Allen, L. Büster, S. Carver, L. Castells Navarro, O. E. Craig, G. T. Cook, B. Cunliffe, A. Denaire, K. E. Dinwiddy, N. Dodwell, M. Ernée, C. Evans, M. Kuchařík, J. F. Farré, H. Fokkens, C. Fowler, M. Gazenbeek, R. Garrido Pena, M. Haber-Uriarte, E. Haduch, G. Hey, N. Jowett, T. Knowles, K. Massy, S. Pfrengle, P. Lefranc, O. Lemercier, A. Lefebvre, J. Lomba Maurandi, T. Majó, J. I. McKinley, K. McSweeney, M. B. Gusztáv, A. Modi, G. Kulcsár, V. Kiss, A. Czene, R. Patay, A. Endrődi, K. Köhler, T. Hajdu, J. Luís Cardoso, C. Liesau, M. P. Pearson, P. Włodarczak, T. D. Price, P. Prieto, P.-J. Rey, P. Ríos, R. Risch, M. A. Rojo Guerra, A. Schmitt, J. Serralongue, A. M. Silva, V. Smrčka, L. Vergnaud, J. Zilhão, D. Caramelli, T. Higham, V. Heyd, A. Sheridan, K.-G. Sjögren, M. G. Thomas, P. W. Stockhammer, R. Pinhasi, J. Krause, W. Haak, I. Barnes, C. Lalueza-Fox, and D. Reich. 2018. The Beaker phenomenon and the genomic transformation of northwest Europe. *Nature* 555: 190–196.

Outram A. K., N. A. Stear, R. Bendrey, S. Olsen, A. Kasparov, V. Zaibert, N. Thorpe, and R. P. Evershed. 2009. The earliest horse harnessing and milking. *Science* 323: 1332–35.

Pashkevich, G. O. 1992. Do rekonstruktsii asortmentu kul'turnikh roslin epokhi Neolitu- Bronzi na teritorii Ukraini. In: S. V. Pan'kov and G. O. Voznesens'ka (ed.), *Starodavne Vibornitstvo na Teritorii Ukraini*, 179–194. Kiev: Naukovo Dumka.

2003. Paleoethnobotanical evidence of agriculture in the steppe and the forest-steppe of east Europe in the Late Neolithic and the Bronze Age. In: Marsha Levine, Colin Renfrew, and Katie Boyle (ed.), *Prehistoric steppe adaptation and the horse*, 287–297. Cambridge: McDonald Institute for Archaeological Research.

Piggott, Stuart. 1983. *The earliest wheeled transport: From the Atlantic Coast to the Caspian Sea.* New York: Cornell University Press

Rassamakin, Y. 1999. The Eneolithic of the Black Sea steppe: Dynamics of cultural and economic development 4500–2300 BC. In: Marsha Levine, Y. Rassamakin, A. Kislenko, and N. Tatarintseva (ed.), *Late prehistoric exploitation of the Eurasian steppe*, 59–182. Cambridge: McDonald Institute for Archaeological Research.

2013. From the Late Eneolithic period to the Early Bronze Age in the Black Sea steppe: What is the Pit Grave culture (late fourth to mid-third millennium BC)? In: Volker Heyd,G. Kulcsár, and V. Szeverényi (ed.), *Transitions to the Bronze Age: Interregional interaction and socio-cultural change in the third millennium BC Carpathian Basin and neighbouring regions*, 113–138. Budapest: Archaeolingua.

Reich, David. 2018. *Who we are and how we got here: Ancient DNA and the new science of the human past.* New York: Pantheon.

Reinhold, Sabine, J. Gresky, N. Berezina, A. R. Kantorovich, C. Knipper, V. E. Maslov, V. G. Petrenko, K. W. Alt, and Andrew B. Belinsky. 2017. Contextualising innovation. Cattle owners and wagon drivers in the North Caucasus and beyond. In: Philipp Stockhammer and Joseph Maran (ed.), *Appropriating innovations: Entangled knowledge in Eurasia, 5000–1500 BCE*, 78–97. Oxford: Oxbow.

Rosenstock, Eva, A. Masson, and B. Zich. 2019. Moraines, megaliths and moo: Putting the prehistoric tractor to work. In: J. Müller, M. Hinz, and M. Wunderlich (ed.), *Megaliths – Societies – Landscapes: Early monumentality and social differentiation in Neolithic Europe*, vol. 3, 1099–1110. Bonn: Dr. Rudolf Habelt GmbH.

Rühl, L., C. Herbig, and A. Stobbe. 2015. Archaeobotanical analysis of plant use at Kamennyi Ambar, a Bronze Age fortified settlement of the Sintashta culture in the southern Trans-Urals steppe, Russia. *Vegetation History and Archaeobotany* 24(3): 413–426.

Ryndina, N. V., and A. D. Degtyareva. 2018. Tsvetoi metal Yamnoi kulturno-istoricheskoi oblasti iz pamyatnikov Ukrainy: morfologiya I tekhnologiya izgotovleniya. *Stratum plus* 2: 317–346.

Sanson, G. D., S. A. Kerr, and K. A. Gross. 2007. Do silica phytoliths really wear mammalian teeth? *Journal of Archaeological Science* 34: 526–531.

Schulting, R. J., and Michael P. Richards. 2016. Stable isotope analysis of Neolithic to Late Bronze Age populations in the Samara Valley. In: David W. Anthony, Dorcas Brown, Aleksandr Khokhlov, Pavel Kuznetsov, and Oleg Mochalov (ed.), *A Bronze Age landscape in the Russian steppes: The Samara Valley Project* (Monumenta Archaeologica 37), 127–147. Los Angeles: Cotsen Institute Press, UCLA.

Secoy, R. F. 1953. *Changing military patterns of the Great Plains Indians*. Lincoln: University of Nebraska Press.

Sherratt, A. G. 1983. The secondary products revolution of animals in the Old World. *World Archaeology* 15: 90–104.

2006. La traction animale et la transformation de l'Europe néolithique. In: P. Pétrequin, R.-M. Arbogast, A.-M. Pétrequin, S. van Willigen, and M. Bailly (ed.), *Premiers chariots, premiers araires. La diffusion de la traction animale en Europe pendant les IVe et IIIe millénaires avant notre ère* (CRA Monograph 29), 329–60. Paris: CNRS.

Shevchenko, A. I. 1957. Fauna poseleniia epokhi bronzy v s. Mikhailovke na nizhnem Dnepre. *Kratkie Soobshcheniya Institut Arkheologii (Kiev)* 7: 36–37.

Shilov, V. P. 1975. Modeli skotovodcheskikh khozyaistv stepnykh oblastei Evrazii v epokhu eneolita i rannego bronzovogo veka. *Sovietskaya Arkheologiya* 1: 5–15.

1985. Problemy proiskhozhdeniya kochevogo skotovodstva v vostochnoi Evrope. In: K. N. Maksimov (ed.), *Drevnosti Kalmykii*, 23–33. Elista: Kalmytskii Nauchno-Issledovatel'skii Institut Istorii, Filogii i Ekonomiki.

Shishlina, N. I. 2008. *Reconstruction of the Bronze Age of the Caspian steppes: Life styles and life ways of pastoral nomads* (British Archaeological Reports International Series 1876). Oxford: Archaeopess.

Shishlina, N. I., E. P. Zazovskaya, J. van der Plicht, R. E. M. Hedges, V. S. Sevastyanov, and O. A. Chichagova. 2009. Paleoecology, subsistence, and ^{14}C chronology of the Eurasian Caspian steppe Bronze Age. *Radiocarbon* 51(2): 481–499.

Shnirelman, Victor A. 1980. *Proiskhozhdeni'e Skotovodstva*. Moscow: Nauka.

1992. The emergence of food-producing economy in the steppe and forest-steppe zones of Eastern Europe. *Journal of Indo-European Studies* 20: 123–43.

Spengler, Robert N., A. Ventresca Miller, T. Schmaus, G. Motuzaite-Matuzeviciute, B. K. Miller, S. Wilkin, W. T. T. Taylor, Y. Li, P. Roberts, and Nicole Boivin. 2021. An imagined past? Nomadic narratives in Central Asian archaeology. *Current Anthropology* 62(3): 251–286.

Sulimirski, T. 1970. *Prehistoric Russia: An outline*. London: John Baker.

Taylor, W. T. T., and C. Isabelle Barrón-Ortiz. 2021. Rethinking the evidence for early horse domestication at Botai. *Nature Scientific Reports* 11: 7440.

Telegin, D. Y., Sergei Z. Pustalov, and N. N. Kovalyukh. 2003. Relative and absolute chronology of Yamnaya and Catacomb monuments: The issue of co-existence. *Baltic-Pontic Studies* 12: 132–184.

Trautmann, M., A., Frînculeasa, B., Preda-Bălănică, M., Petruneac, M., Focşăneanu, S., Alexandrov, N., Atanassova, P., Włodarczak, P., Włodarczak, M., Podsiadło, J., Dani, S., Évinger, Z., Bereczki, T., Hajdu, R., Băjenaru, A., Ioniță, A., Măgureanu, D., Măgureanu, A., Popescu, D., Sârbu, G., Vasile, D., Anthony, V., Heyd. 2022. First Bio-Anthropological Evidence for Yamnaya Horsemanship. Science Advances (In review.)

Tsalkin, V. I. 1970. *Drevneishie Domashnie Zhivotnye Vostochnoi Evropy*. Moscow: Nauka.

Tuboltsev, Oleg V., and S. B. Radchenko. 2018. Generalka 2 "causewayed enclosures": primery otrazheniya polyarnogo mirovzzreniya drevnego naseleniya Evropy. *Stratum plus* 2: 119–148.

Vybornov, A. A., P. A. Kosintsev, M. A. Kulkova, N. S. Doga, and V. I. Platonov. 2019. Vremya poyavleniya proizvodyashego khozyaistva v Nizhnem PoVolzh'e. *Stratum plus* 2: 359–368.

Vybornov, A. A., M. Kulkova, P. Kosintsev, V. Platonov, S. Platonova, B. Philippsen, and L. Nesterova. 2018. Diet and chronology of the Neolithic-Eneolithic cultures (from 6500 to 4700 cal BC) in the lower Volga basin. *Radiocarbon* 60(5): 1–14.

Wang, C.-C., S. Reinhold, A. Kalmykov, A. Wissgott, G. Brandt, C. Jeong, O. Cheronet, M. Ferry, E. Harney, D. Keating, S. Mallick, N. Rohland, K. Stewardson, A. R. Kantorovich, V. E. Maslov, V. G. Petrenko, V. R. Erlikh, B. Ch. Atabiev, R. G. Magomedov, P. L. Kohl, K. W. Alt, S. L. Pichler, C. Gerling, H. Meller, B. Vardanyan, L. Yeganyan, A. D. Rezepkin, D. Mariaschk, N. Berezina, J. Gresky, K. Fuchs, C. Knipper, S. Schiffels, E. Balanovska, O. Balanovsky, I. Mathieson, T. Higham, Y. B. Berezin, A. Buzhilova, V. Trifonov, R. Pinhasi, A. B. Belinskij, D. Reich, S. Hansen, J. Krause, and Wolfgang Haak. 2019. Ancient human genome-wide data from a 3000-year interval in the Caucasus corresponds with eco-geographic regions. *Nature Communications* 10: 590.

West, M. L. 2009. *Indo-European poetry and myth*. Oxford: Oxford University Press.

Wilkin, Shevan, A. Ventresca Miller, R. Fernandes, R. Spengler, W. T. Taylor, D. R. Brown, D. Reich, D. Kennett, B. J. Culleton, L. Kunz, C. Fortes, A. Kitova, P. Kuznetsov, A. Epimakhov, A. K. Outram, E. Kitov, A. Khokhlov, D. Anthony, and Nicole Boivin. 2021. Dairying enabled Early Bronze Age Yamnaya steppe expansions. *Nature* 598: 629–633.

Zakh, Viktor A., N. E. Ryabogina, and J. Chlachula. 2010. Climate and environmental dynamics of the mid- to late Holocene settlement in the Tobol–Ishim forest-steppe region, West Siberia. *Quaternary International* 220: 95–101.

3 YAMNAYA PASTORALISTS IN THE EURASIAN DESERT STEPPE ZONE: NEW PERSPECTIVES ON MOBILITY

NATALIA I. SHISHLINA

3.1 Introduction

The Yamnaya culture of the Lower Don is a Bronze Age culture dated between 2900 and 2600 cal BC. Its population inhabited the Eurasian desert steppe belt, where their main subsistence activity was pastoralism. The Yamnaya population developed a distinctive economic model based on new principles of pasture rotation, landscape use, and individual mobility. The focus of this study is the analysis of the specific landscapes and geographical features of one of the Eurasian Steppe regions located between the Lower Don and Lower Volga regions, i.e. the Sal-Manych Ridge (Fig. 3.1); it includes the settlement pattern and economic model that the mobile Yamnaya pastoralists developed to adapt to this region, the resources of the steppes they exploited and the system of seasonal migration reflected in the mobility of individual Yamnaya groups.

This research is based on recent studies of the archaeological contexts of Yamnaya graves and kurgans in the pilot region, the reconstruction of their settlement pattern, modeling of the productivity of local pastures located near the Yamnaya sites, and the isotope study of collagen from human and animal bones (identification of $\delta^{15}N$ and $\delta^{13}C$ values), as well as variations in Sr isotopes.

3.2 Chronology and Archaeological Background of the Yamnaya Culture

Based on the available ^{14}C data (Shishlina 2008; Shishlina et al. 2011) (Table 3.1), the period of the Lower Don Yamnaya culture has been established to be between 2900 and 2600 cal BC.

The Yamnaya population buried its dead in kurgans, Bronze Age architectural structures that consist of a segment-shaped mound and a round or an oval ditch (Fig. 3.2a). Sometimes the upper part of the mound is flattened. The average diameter of primary kurgans is approximately 12 to 18 m, and their height is 0.65 to 1.10 m. Other structural details include stone mounds, stone walls, and stone rings (Fig. 3.2b. Many secondary graves were added to the primary Yamnaya kurgans (up to six or seven graves). Ritual areas with flint items, clay sherds, and bones of wild and domesticated animals are typical features of the Yamnaya kurgans.

The main grave construction is a simple rectangular pit, usually built for one deceased person; ledged pits are found only rarely. The pit was usually roofed. The burial normally contained many items: e.g., plant mats placed along the bottom, the walls, and the roof of the pit; details of wooden constructions; pillows stuffed with steppe plants; and wooden wagon walls or dwelling doors that were sometimes used as the pit roofing. A typical pose for the deceased is a contracted supine posture with extended arms (Fig. 3.2c); in some graves, the bodies are fully extended, prone or supine. The predominant orientation of the deceased in both primary and secondary graves is toward the east, though other orientations have been observed as well. Collective graves are only rarely recorded. The use of ochre is a characteristic feature of all local groups: ochre was used to sprinkle the skull, legs, hands, and funerary offerings, as well as the bottom of the pit; sometimes a piece of ochre was placed inside the grave as well.

The funerary assemblage usually contained lightly fired clay vessels tempered with chamotte, sand, and shell: e.g., egg-shaped, round-bottomed pots (Fig. 3.3 b), bowls, and amphorae (Fig. 3.3 a). Sets of hammer-headed bone pins and other amulets are very common (Fig. 3.3 c–d). Some of the graves contain round temple rings of metal and bone (Fig. 3.3 e), and sheep talus bones (Fig. 3.3 f). The Yamnaya graves are not rich in tools or weapons. The funerary assemblages sometimes include pestles and grinding stones, as well as bronze knives (Fig. 3.3 gh), usually placed under the head of the adult person. In several rare cases, the graves have yielded sets consisting of a bronze knife and an awl, and more rarely an axe.

Our study of more than 500 Yamnaya graves uncovered in both the Kalmyk Steppe and in the pilot region clearly reveals common features, such as the rectangular shape of the pits and their decoration, the position of the body and its orientation, and the use of ochre, as well as specific local differences in tradition. For example, stone rings around the graves are typical of the Middle Yergueni Hills and the Sal-Manych Ridge. These differences are important to note because, in our view, they suggest that this rather broad region between the Lower Volga and the Don was exploited by small family groups, each practicing its own funerary rite.

In our research, we have used this hypothesis as a basic assumption to establish the settlement pattern of the Yamnaya population in the pilot region and to discuss its mobility.

TABLE 3.1. ^{14}C data on the Lower Don Yamnaya; total probability (in parentheses) with estimated OxCal 4.3 (Bronk Ramsey 2009).

Unmodeled Sum calibrated age	Modeled Sum (within Phase) calibrated age	Modeled Sum (within Phase) (No Humans) calibrated age
2902–2582 BC (68%)	2910–2430 BC (95.4%)	2856–2700 BC (68%)
3010–2290 BC (95.4%)	2900–2449 BC (68%)	2904–2601 BC (95.4%)

3.3 The Settlement Pattern

To gain a better understanding of this settlement pattern, we examined a number of dry steppe river valleys (Russian *balkas*) with temporary or seasonal flows. These studies revealed numerous traces of the open steppe's occupation by prehistoric mobile pastoral groups in the pilot region (Shishlina et al. 2018b). Traces of Chalcolithic Yamnaya and Catacomb seasonal campsites were discovered in the middle reaches of meandering dry valleys with streams and well-defined terraces. We assume that almost all watershed plateaus and small steppe river valleys of the Sal-Manych Ridge were occupied and fully exploited by the Yamnaya population. Yamnaya clay sherds, a bronze knife (Fig. 3.3 g), and horse, sheep, and cattle bones were found at some campsites (Fig. 3.4). The presence of only small campsites and lack of large permanent settlements is therefore consistent with the assumption, mentioned earlier in the text, that during the Yamnaya period, small groups rather than large populations exploited the region in question. The economic potential of such groups not only allowed them to sustain themselves, but also to develop a special form of pastoral economy, as will be described further below.

New geomorphological, isotope, and pasture productivity data offer insight into the link between the Yamnaya economic model and their system of short- and long-term migrations.

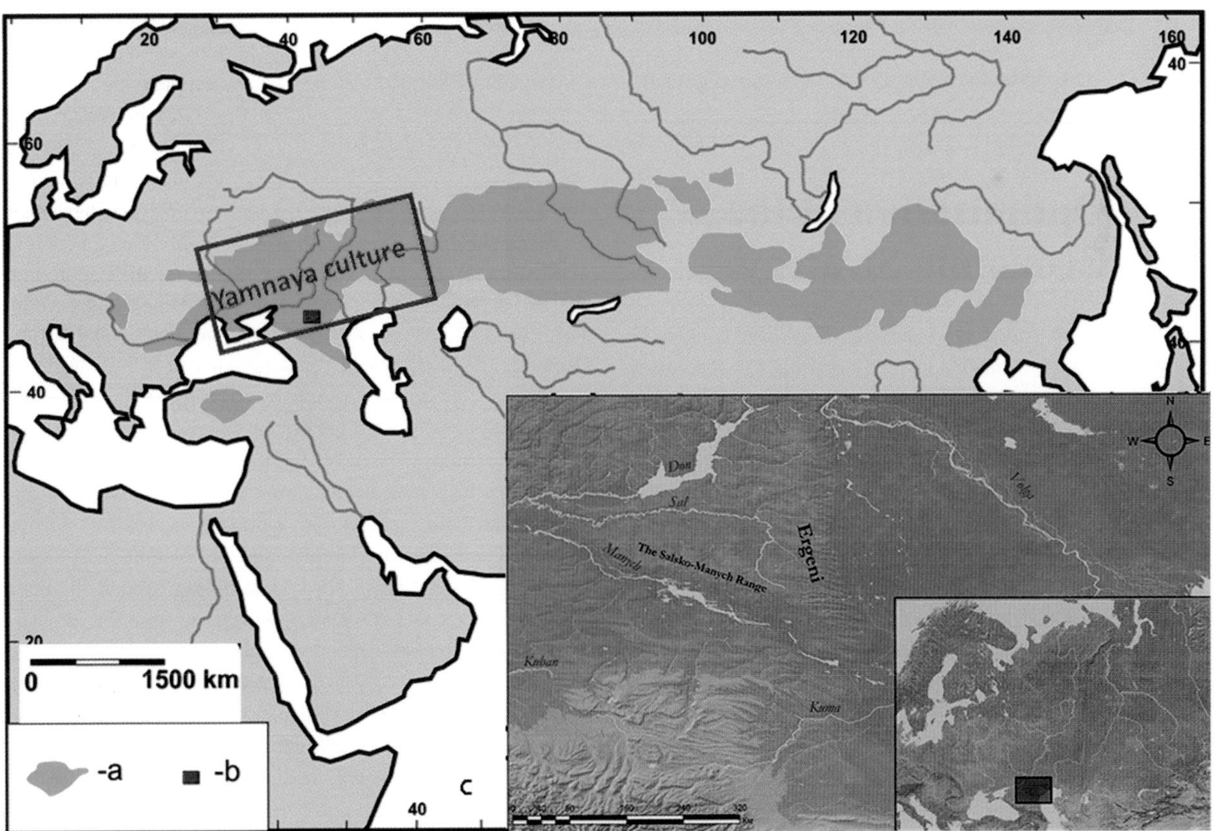

FIGURE 3.1. Pilot area of the research: a – Eurasian steppe belt, b Yamnaya culture, c Sal-Manych Ridge.

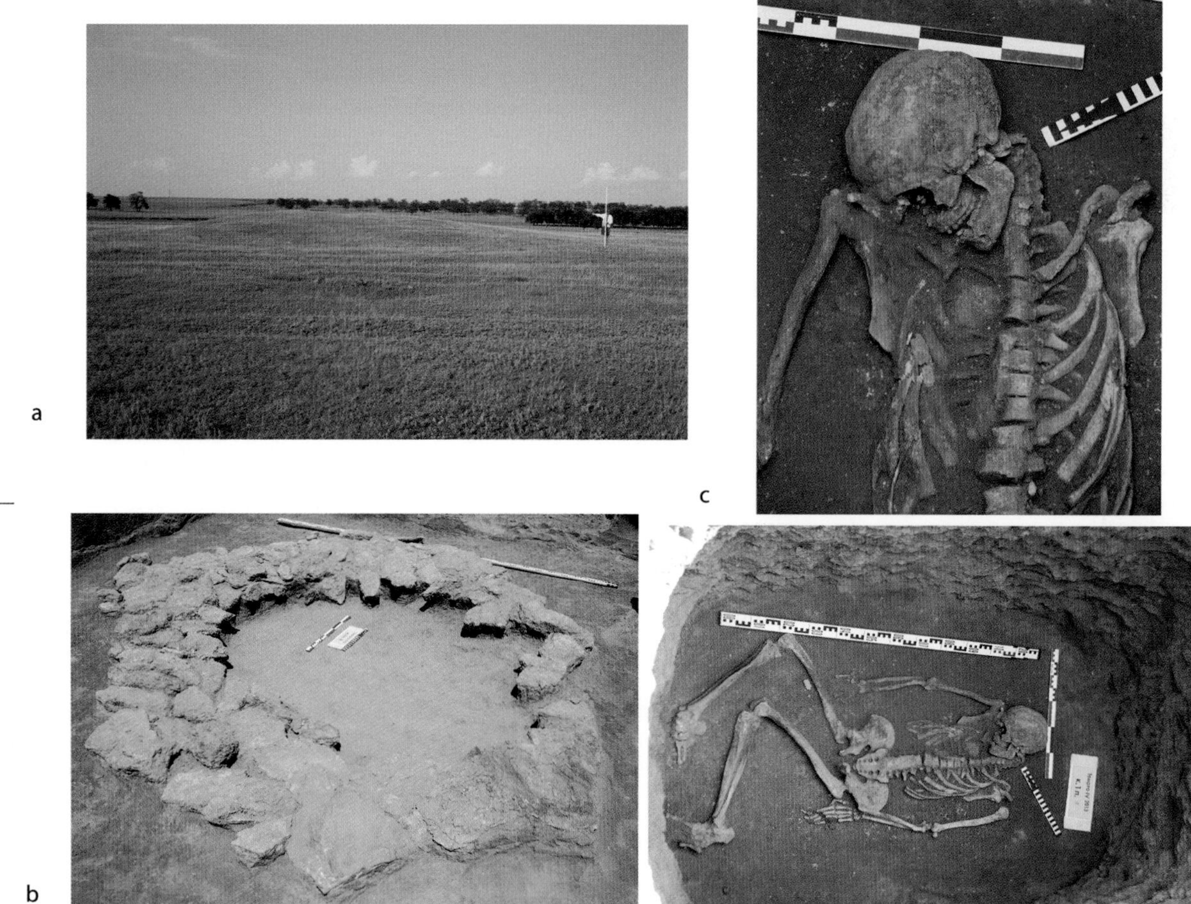

FIGURE 3.2. The Sal-Manych Ridge, Temrta IV burial ground: a Yamnaya culture kurgan, b stone ring around grave 9, c grave 9.

3.4 Optimization of the Economic Strategy

The Sal-Manych Ridge is characterized by severe climatic conditions: low temperatures in winter and high temperatures in summer; high wind speeds, especially in the cold period; and low precipitation, hence low productivity of ecosystems (Narodetskaya 1974). Life in a hot, dry climate forced prehistoric populations to develop rather sophisticated adaptation mechanisms for the harsh conditions. The pastoral economic strategy developed by the Yamnaya groups was stipulated by the specific features of pasture use in these desert areas, such as low forage yield, the seasonal nature of vegetation, and the difficulty or impossibility of procuring forage during the non-grazing period (Masanov 2000). The optimization of the seasonal economic cycle depended on the availability of winter pastures for animals. In order to optimize the herding economy, the population introduced pasture rotation. The height of snow cover, snow density, and presence of ice bands and crust in the snow, as well as the frequency of thaws, precipitation, and fog, are all factors that determine the quality of pastures in winter. When the snowfall is loose, goats and sheep cannot graze in snow cover of more than 25 to 30 cm; when the snow is dense, grazing is not possible at a snow height of 5 to 10 cm (Narodetskaya 1974). Snowfalls, blizzards, and the ice coverage of the land were taken into account when selecting winter pastures. The area of such pastures was determined by the distance that sheep could roam per day in winter. Animals would graze on winter pastures by roaming along a radius of 4–5 km, first away from the winter campsites, and then back toward the camps (Masanov 1995). Given the low forage yield of pastures in winter, herders were forced to move from one grazing area to another. In summer, successful grazing depended on the availability and accessibility of water sources. The duration of stays at campsites around the main watering places, as well as migrations away from the campsite into the open steppes, depended on the forage yield of summer pastures (Zhitetsky 1893; Masanov 1995; Smirnov 1999). When forage resources were depleted, people moved to other areas, and did not come back until the vegetation cover of the grasslands fully recovered. If a certain exploited ecological niche provided enough grass for the animals, most people would stay at the campsite longer, because the animals could graze outside the campsite during the day before being led back for the night.

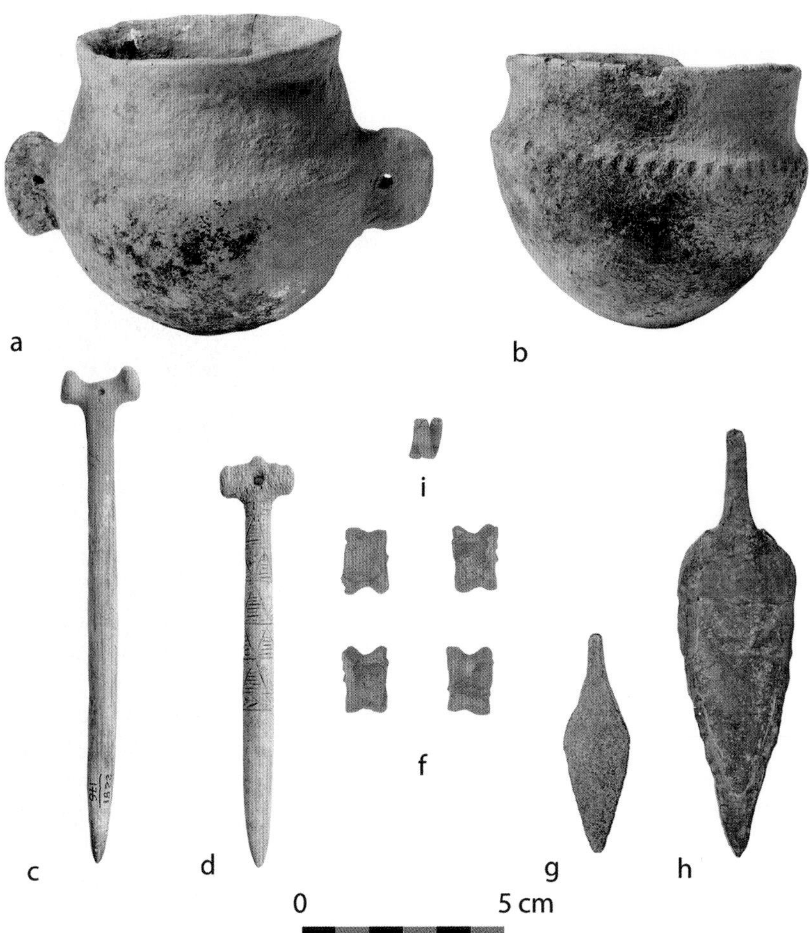

FIGURE 3.3. Yamnaya culture funerary goods: a, b clay vessels, Mu-Sharet 4, kurgan 1, grave 5; c hammer-headed bone pin, Zunda-Tolga 6, kurgan 2, grave 1; d hammer-headed bone pin, Chograisky V, kurgan 6, grave 4; e bone temple ring, Peschany IV, kurgan 13, grave 5; f sheep talus bones, Peschany IV, kurgan 13, grave 6; g bronze knife, Balka Chikalda; h bronze knife, Mandjikiny II, kurgan 11, grave 3.

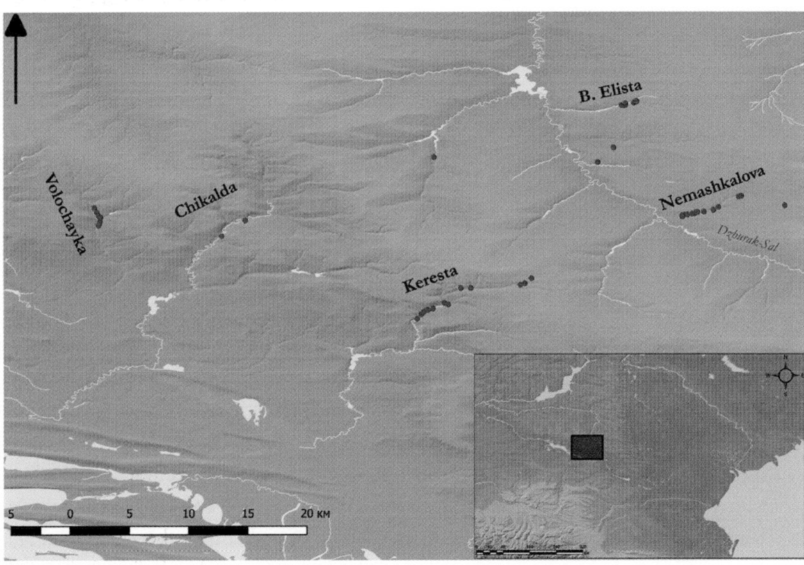

FIGURE 3.4. The Sal-Manych Ridge. Location of Bronze Age seasonal campsites.

The above-described model was probably the most viable for this region, with its harsh weather and sometimes scarce grassland resources. The region's use was reflected in the mobility of population groups that depended on the productivity of the grasslands, which also influenced the settlement pattern of the population that inhabited the pilot region. In order to obtain new information in support of our hypothesis, we conducted a number of studies.

3.5 Productivity of the Yamnaya Grasslands

The Sal-Manych Ridge, which encircles the Kuma-Manych Depression on the Kalmyk Steppe, extends to the Lower Don region in the north and merges with the Yergueni Hills in the east. This area is characterized by the presence of various small steppe river valleys with temporary flows (*balkas*), floodplain terraces, and larger river valleys. The small river valleys of the Manych River water system differ from the small river valleys that discharge waters into the Sal River. In contrast to the latter, the small river valleys of the Manych are deeply incised and have steep slopes. They are characterized by their sharp differentiation of geological formation conditions; that is why they are noted for their greater variety of valley structures. Small steppe river valleys with temporary flow are suitable for use as winter pastures, because the snow on their southern slopes does not form a continuous cover, or it melts quickly. For this reason, sheep and goats can graze in bad weather conditions when the high snow cover does not allow animals to graze in other landscape niches. At the same time, the vegetation growing on the steep, shadowy slopes with exposure to the north is not scorched in summer and persists even during the severe droughts of April and June. The area of these slopes can be used as winter and summer pastures (Fig. 3.5a).

The small river valleys of the Sal River system are usually less incised, and their slopes are gentler; these valleys have low relief and are used as pastures throughout the year, though no special grazing patterns have been identified here.

Nowadays, both smaller and larger river valleys have dikes; they do not have continuous flow. However, there are several natural springs in the small river valleys of the Kuma-Manych Depression. These are linked to the deep erosive dissection and tectonic differentiation of this area; that is why it is easy to tap groundwater reservoirs, and water is discharged easily into valley beds.

The method of determining Yamnaya pasture productivity is based on research into the productivity of contemporary pastures. Several pilot areas on the Sal-Manych Ridge have been used as references.

A comparative analysis of the forage yield of contemporary pastures in the Volochaika steppe river valley (Fig. 3.5b), near the Manych River, offered the opportunity to identify the seasonal forage yield of contemporary grasslands. This highlighted the objectively high forage value of these pastures, namely due to the native fescue-feather grass community growing on the gentle slope of the valley and the sedge and gramineous plant community growing in the lower floodplain, especially amid the gramineous plant regrowth of the spring period. It also underscored the generally low values and more noticeable contrast in seasonal values estimated for the forage yield of the Bolshaya Elista pastures (the Sal River basin).

We believe that the pastures located in the small river valleys of the steppe were seasonally exploited by the Yamnaya population, which moved from one pasture to another depending on pasture productivity. Isotope data provide additional evidence for this hypothesis.

3.6 Yamnaya Culture Isotope Data

The isotope data obtained for the Sal-Manych Yamnaya humans and animals confirm a high level of mobility among individual groups and flocks. Stable isotopes ($\delta^{15}N$ and $\delta^{13}C$) reveal differences in the components of individual human diets and animal fodder intake (Shishlina et al. 2012; 2014; 2018a).

The isotopic composition of the Yamnaya pasture-fed animals demonstrates that they primarily grazed on typical local C_3 pastures, though some isotopic variations have been identified (Shishlina et al. 2018a). The isotope study of sheep bones yielded several outliers, which means that some sheep or flocks of sheep grazed on pastures with stressed vegetation in more arid environments. The valleys of the East Manych and the Dzhurak-Sal – a tributary of the Sal River where many Yamnaya kurgans have been discovered, and where there are thickets of tall cane – meet the requirements for winter pastures, and these river valleys were most likely exploited in winter as well. The isotope composition of the cane used as contemporary winter feed is characterized by a high level of $\delta^{15}N$ values; the consumption of such plants could produce high nitrogen values in archaeological animal bones.

The sample of archaeological plants collected from the Yamnaya graves includes both typical C_3 and C_3-arid plants; the latter are characterized by high $\delta^{15}N$ values. Therefore, high values of $\delta^{15}N$ in the isotope composition of the Yamnaya animals can be attributed to high values in their fodder, due to both the aridity of the pastures as well as the specific isotope composition of winter fodder (Shishlina et al. 2018a). The variety of isotope composition in both archaeological plants and animal bones demonstrates that the exploited pastures were located in different ecological and geochemical environments, i.e., that herders moved across vast areas.

The isotope composition of individuals from the local Yamnaya steppe community also demonstrates large variations in $\delta^{15}N$ and $\delta^{13}C$ values compared to Yamnaya humans from other areas (Shishlina et al. 2012). These variations were caused by human diet, multicomponents of which originated from different places. Mobility caused people to consume various food components with different isotope values. The human diet was based on C_3 vegetation, sometimes with high $\delta^{15}N$ values (~13–15‰), and the meat and dairy of

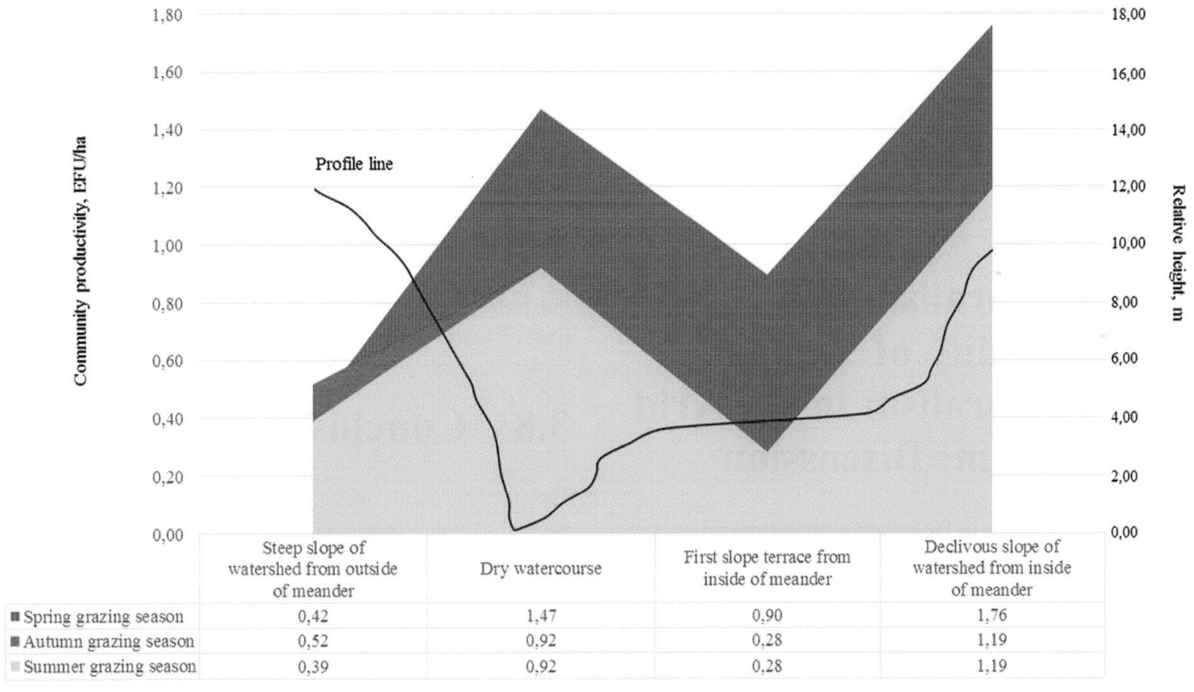

	Steep slope of watershed from outside of meander	Dry watercourse	First slope terrace from inside of meander	Declivous slope of watershed from inside of meander
Spring grazing season	0,42	1,47	0,90	1,76
Autumn grazing season	0,52	0,92	0,28	1,19
Summer grazing season	0,39	0,92	0,28	1,19

Figure 3.5. The Sal-Manych Ridge. Balka Volochaika: a – contemporary pastures; b – model of the seasonal productivity of the local pastures.

domesticated animals, but could also include aquatic components. Such food resources were probably also located in different geochemical environments.

We also studied variations in the strontium isotopes $^{87}Sr/^{86}Sr$ in human teeth, which can be used as an additional argument in support of population movements (Bentley et al. 2004; Eckardt et al. 2009) across the studied region of the Sal-Manych Ridge.

The variation in the strontium isotopes in the tooth enamel of individuals from Yamnaya burial grounds such as Peschany V,

Ulan-4, and Sukhaya Termista II is from 0.7090 to 0.7091. This correlates with the isotopic variations in the reference samples from the Dzhurak-Sal basin, the western slopes of the Middle Yergueni Hills, and the Don River basin from the middle reaches of the river, near the town of Volgodonsk, to the Lower Don valley (Shishlina and Larionova 2013). The variation in the strontium isotopes in the teeth of individuals from the Yamnaya burial grounds in the Southern Yergueni Hills and the Sarpa Plain, such as Mandjikiny and Kanukovo, is 0.7090. This also correlates with isotopic variations from the local reference samples of animal bones.

Generally speaking, the region with strontium isotopic variations from 0.7090 to 0.7091 encompasses several local steppe areas in the south of the Russian Plain. The likely place of birth of the local Yamnaya individuals examined is a geographical steppe area extending from the middle to the lower reaches of the Don River; it also includes the contiguous steppe areas of the western part of Kalmyk steppes.

However, there are some individual outliers in the strontium isotope variation of the tooth enamel: for example, that of the individual from Temrta IV, kurgan 16, grave 9 ($^{87}Sr/^{86}Sr$: 0.7094). These variations most likely mean that the buried male who is the outlier was a nonlocal, born in a geographical area to the south (Shishlina and Larionova 2013; Shishlina et al. 2016) but buried far from his birthplace. These outliers are not numerous.

Therefore, we may infer from this isotope data that almost all of the analyzed Yamnaya individuals inhabited the steppe and exploited only the steppe environment. The isotopic data also demonstrate that the migrations of the people and the animals took place only within the steppe, though in different ecological niches.

3.7 Pastoralism and Mobility of Yamnaya Pastoralism in the Arid System: Discussion

The landscape analysis of the contemporary grassland resource base reveals the potential for optimal organization of the seasonal economic cycle within the exploited steppe area. The resources within the steppe grazing systems are characterized by low forage yield, the seasonal nature of the vegetation, and the difficulty or impossibility of forage conservation and livestock stall-feeding (Narodetskaya 1974; Masanov 1999; Smirnov 1999). From the very start of exploiting steppe pastures, these factors made people move from place to place quite frequently, though their flock of domesticated animals was small.

It should be also noted that, basically, the composition of plant communities from the pilot region, i.e. the Sal-Manych Ridge, is suitable for grazing domesticated pasture-fed animals with low tolerance for water restrictions. Though the pasture yield perhaps varied depending on annual climatic fluctuations, the landscape resource base across seasons was not conducive to long-term stays.

This explains why the mobile economic cycle of the local Yamnaya pastoral economy evolved, and why the people involved in seasonal migrations within the exploited steppe landscape developed a mobile lifestyle. The place and the trajectory of the routes were determined by many reasons, e.g., economic, social, natural, and landscape-based; essentially, the principle of pasture rotation formed the basis of the new subsistence system and seasonal migrations.

The pastures thus began to be used throughout the year. The knowledge of pasture forage yield in the exploited pasture systems and the adaptive skills of domesticated animals stimulated the development of an expanded system of short- and long-distance routes, i.e., a special type of husbandry practice. As wagons appeared on the steppe, successful short-term moves were made possible by using bulls as pack animals, as evidenced by grave offerings. Interestingly, the examination of Yamnaya skeletons from the studied area reveals that the pastoralists walked a lot when they moved from place to place and suffered from osteochondrosis (S. Borutskaya and A. Khokhlov, personal communication).

The seasonality of this economy is consistent with the system of seasonal use of small steppe river valley pastures in the south of the Russian Plain as typical of the Kalmyks, the traditional nomads who roamed the Eurasian Steppe in the seventeenth to nineteenth centuries. As described by the mid-nineteenth-century missionary Parmen Smirnov, the small steppe river slopes and lowlands between the hillocks (hills) were the only grasslands that were humid and had vegetation in summer (Smirnov 1999). An average nomadic group with a herd of 50 to 100 horses, 70 to 100 cows, and a flock of up to 100 sheep would graze down a summer pasture in two to three weeks. Nomadic groups were able to return to the old pastures only after the rain, when grasslands recovered (ibid., 84, 90–91).

3.8 Conclusion

The economic model of the Yamnaya core groups encompassed various activities, such as raising domesticated animals, fishing, gathering, and the production of ceramic, tools, and implements, as well as weapons. Most likely, their economic success led to the formation of small mobile pastoral groups whose aim was to search for and exploit grasslands beyond the nearby areas. Basically, this was a new economic model based on the principle of pasture rotation, with short-term seasonal migrations resulting in a substantial increase in the exploited resource base, helping some groups in the mobile population to streamline their economic and production cycle and adapt to the severe conditions that prevailed in the desert steppe ecological niches in the south of the Russian Plain. Both the settlement pattern reconstructed for the pilot region, i.e., small seasonal campsites, as well as the isotope data provide additional testimony of the local pastoral groups' short-distance migrations across the exploited area.

Acknowledgments

This work was supported by RSF grant № 21-18-00026. I would like to thank I. Idrisov, T. Dyatlova, E. Azarov, J. van der Plicht, O. Kuznetsova, and V. Sevastyanov for participating in the settlement project; and P. Hommel for comments about the chronology.

References

Bentley, R. A., T. D. Price, & E. Stephan. 2004. Determining the local $^{87}Sr/^{86}Sr$ range for archaeological skeletons: A case study from Neolithic Europe. *Journal of Archaeological Sciences* 31: 365–375.

Bronk Ramsey, C. 2009. Dealing with outliers and offsets in radiocarbon dating. *Radiocarbon* 51(3): 1023–1045.

Eckardt, H., et al. 2009. Oxygen and strontium isotope evidence for mobility in Roman Winchester. *Journal of Archaeological Sciences* 36: 2816–2825.

Masanov, N. E. 1995. *Kochevaya tsivilizatsiya kazakhov (osnovy zhiznedeyatelnosti nomadnogo obshestva)* [Nomadic civilization of the Kazaks (the basis of the vital functions of nomadic society]. Almaty-Moscow: Sotsinvest-Gorizont. [in Russian].

2000. Osobennosti funktsionirovaniya traditsionnogo kochevogo obshestva kazakhov [Specific traits of the traditional nomadic society of the Kazakhs]. In: N. I. Shishlina (ed.), *Seasonality studies of the Bronze Age Northwest Caspian steppe*, 116–130. Moscow: State Historical Museum. [in Russian].

Narodetskaya, Sh. Sh. (ed.) 1974. Agroklimaticheskiye resursy. Kalmyskaya ASSR [Agroclimatic resources. Kalmyk ASSR]. Leningrad: Gidrometeoizdat. [in Russian].

Shishlina, N. I. 2008. Reconstruction of the Bronze Age of the Caspian steppes. Life styles and life ways of pastoral nomads (British Archaeological Reports international series 1876). Oxford: Archaeopress.

2009. Paleoecology, subsistence, and ^{14}C chronology of the Eurasian Caspian Steppe Bronze Age. *Radiocarbon* 51(2): 481–499.

Shishlina, N. I, J. van der Plicht, & E. Zazovskaya. 2011. Radiocarbon dating of the Bronze Age bone pins from Eurasian steppes. *Geochronometria* 38(2): 107–115.

Shishlina, N. I., & Yu. O. Larionova. 2013. Variatsii izotopnogo sostava strontsiya v obraztsakh sovremennykh ulitok yuga Rossii. In: A. B. Belinsky (ed.), *Materialy po izucheniyu istoriko-kulturnogo naslediya Severnogo Kavkaza XI*, 59–168. Stavropol: Naslediye. [in Russian].

2016. Variations in $^{87}Sr/^{86}Sr$ ratios in contemporary snail samples obtained from the Eastern Caucasus. *Arid Ecosystem* 6(2): 100–106.

Shishlina, N. I., V. Sevastyanov, & O. Kuznetsova. 2018a. Seasonal practices of prehistoric pastoralists from the south of the Russian plain based on the isotope data of modern and archaeological animal bones and plants. *Journal of Archaeological Science: Reports* 21: 1247–1258.

2018b. Innovatsionniye sezonniye migratsii I Sistema zhizneobespecheniya podvizhnykh skotovodov v pustynno-stepnoy zone Evrazii: rol sotsialnikh grup [The innovative seasonal migrations and subsistence system of the mobile pastoralists of the desert-steppe zone of Eurasia: The role of social groups]. *Stratum Plus* 2: 69–90. [in Russian].

Smirnov, P. 1999. Puteviye zapiski po Kakmytskim stepyam Astrakhanskoĭ gubernii. Elista: Kalmytskoe knizhnoe izdatel'stvo. [in Russian].

Zhitetsky, I. A. 1893. Ocherki byta astrakhanskikh kalmykov [Reports on the everyday life of the Astrakhan Kalmyks]. Astrakhan: Astrakhan Historical Society. [in Russian].

4 PROTO-INDO-ANATOLIAN, THE "ANATOLIAN SPLIT" AND THE "ANATOLIAN TREK": A COMPARATIVE LINGUISTIC PERSPECTIVE

ALWIN KLOEKHORST

Since the so-called "Ancient DNA Revolution" of the past decade, which has yielded many new insights into the genetic prehistory of Europe and large parts of Asia, it can no longer be doubted that the Indo-European languages spoken in Europe and Central and South Asia were brought there from the late fourth millennium BCE onward by population groups from the Pontic–Caspian steppes who had belonged to the archaeologically defined Yamnaya culture.[1] We may therefore assume that the population groups bearing the Yamnaya culture can practically be equated with the speakers of Proto-Indo-European, the reconstructed ancestor of the Indo-European languages of Europe and Asia, and that the spread of the Indo-European language family is a direct consequence of these migrations of Yamnaya individuals into Europe and Asia.

Moreover, the last few decades have seen the growing consensus, within Indo-European linguistics, that the Anatolian branch of the Indo-European language family occupies a special position: most scholars nowadays seem to accept the idea that the first split in the Indo-European language family was between Anatolian and the other, non-Anatolian branches (including Tocharian), which at that point still formed a single language community that, for some time after, continued to undergo common innovations not shared by Anatolian.[2] In the following, I will use the term Proto-Indo-Anatolian (PIA) for the language stage preceding the "Anatolian split," and the term "Classical Proto-Indo-European" (CPIE, sometimes also called "Core Proto-Indo-European," "Nuclear Proto-Indo-European," *vel sim.*) for the mother language of all the other, non-Anatolian, Indo-European branches; cf. Figure 4.1.[3]

As the first split of Classical Proto-Indo-European can be equated with the large Yamnaya migrations of the latter half of the fourth millennium BCE, the Anatolian split should be dated before that period. However, no consensus has yet been reached on the amount of time that must have passed between the Anatolian split and the breakup of Classical Proto-Indo-European.

It is the aim of the present chapter to shed light, from a comparative linguist's point of view, on the possible dating of the Anatolian split, as well as the possible route along which the Anatolian languages were brought to Anatolia (the "Anatolian trek").

4.1 Dating the "Anatolian Split"

Before we embark on discussing the possible date of the Anatolian split, it is important to mention the fact that comparative linguistics does not provide a tool with which prehistoric language stages can be dated with exact precision in an absolute way: all dating is, in principle, relative. However, there are some arguments we can rely on to make educated guesses about the absolute dating of reconstructed languages. The most important of these is the number of linguistic innovations one must postulate between a reconstructed pre-stage and its daughter language: the higher the number of these innovations, the further back in time the reconstructed stage must have been spoken. Note, however, that – since it is known that in some situations, languages change more rapidly than in others – the correlation between the number of reconstructed innovations and the length of the period in which these innovations have taken place is certainly not a constant. Nevertheless, on the basis of a broad comparison with the linguistic histories of, e.g., the Romance languages and the Indic languages (the mother languages of which are attested and can be historically dated), it should be possible to give relatively precise estimates for the dating of linguistic pre-stages based on the number and nature of the linguistic innovations that have taken place between these pre-stages and one or more daughter languages.

[1] Allentoft et al. 2015; Haak et al. 2015; Jones et al. 2015; Lazaridis et al. 2016.

[2] For recent discussions, see Kloekhorst (2008a: 7–11), Oettinger (2013/2014), Kloekhorst & Pronk (2019), Melchert (forthc.), and, more skeptically, Rieken (2009), Eichner (2015), and Adiego (2016).

[3] Cf. Kloekhorst & Pronk 2019.

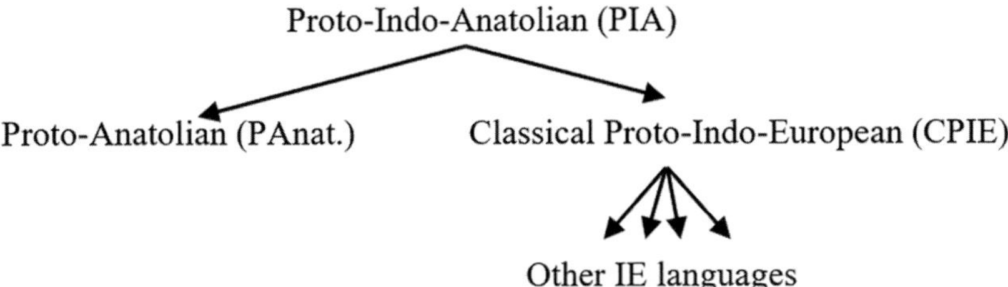

FIGURE 4.1. The family tree of Indo-European according to the Indo-Anatolian Hypothesis.

4.1.1 Dating Proto-Anatolian

Ten known languages are commonly regarded to belong to the Anatolian branch: Hittite,[4] Palaic,[5] Cuneiform Luwian,[6] Hieroglyphic Luwian,[7] Lydian,[8] Carian,[9] Lycian,[10] Milyan,[11] Sidetic,[12] and Pisidian.[13] Already in the very first documents written in ancient Anatolia (Old Assyrian clay tablets from the twentieth century BCE), we find references to Anatolian (Hittite) personal names, whereas the youngest attestations of an Anatolian language date to the second century CE (Pisidian grave inscriptions). It is commonly assumed that in the course of the first millennium CE, the entire Anatolian branch went extinct. In order to date the Proto-Anatolian mother language from which all these languages stem, we have to investigate the linguistic differentiation between them.

As noted above, the oldest attestations of an Anatolian language[14] are Hittite personal names attested in Old Assyrian documents, as discovered in Kültepe (ancient Kaniš/Nēša) and other sites and which date to ca. 1935 to 1715 BCE.[15] In Kloekhorst 2019, it is argued that these Hittite personal names, though unmistakably Hittite, display a distinct dialect when compared to the Hittite language as known from the later texts from Boğazköy (ancient Ḫattuša), which date to ca. 1650 to 1180 BCE. Moreover, this "Kanišite" Hittite dialect cannot be the ancestor of Ḫattuša Hittite, which means that the two varieties must linguistically be regarded as sisters, stemming from an earlier stage that may be called Proto-Hittite. Since the difference between the two Hittite dialects is small, not much time is needed to account for the diversification between the two, and it therefore seems safe to date Proto-Hittite to no more than a handful of generations before the earliest attestation of Kanišite Hittite, i.e., to ca. 2100 BCE.

The so-called Luwic languages (Cuneiform Luwian, Hieroglyphic Luwian, Lycian, and possibly Carian, Sidetic, and Pisidian)[16] form a distinct subbranch within Anatolian.[17] The two oldest attested languages within this group, Cuneiform Luwian (whose oldest texts date from the sixteenth century BC) and Hieroglyphic Luwian (attested from ca. 1400 BCE onward), are closely related dialects, and their common ancestor, Proto-Luwian, need not be much older than a handful of generations before the earliest Cuneiform Luwian attestations. It may thus be dated to the eighteenth or nineteenth century BCE. The third major Luwic language, Lycian, though attested considerably later (fifth to fourth century BCE), is, on the one hand, evidently closely related to the Luwian languages, but, on the other, also clearly distinct from them (especially with regard to the vowel system and certain morphological innovations).[18] Moreover, it is clear that Lycian cannot descend directly from Proto-Luwian. We therefore need to postulate a pre-stage of Proto-Luwian and Lycian, which we term Proto-Luwic. On the basis of the relatively small, but nevertheless clear linguistic distance between Lycian and the Luwian languages, we may assume that this stage preceded Proto-Luwian by a couple of centuries, and it therefore seems safe to assume that Proto-Luwic dates to the twenty-first to twentieth century BCE.

The status of the two remaining Anatolian languages, Palaic and Lydian, is somewhat debated,[19] though good arguments exist for assuming that they are more closely related to the Luwic branch, with Palaic sharing more common innovations with Proto-Luwic than Lydian does.[20] This means that we may view Palaic as a sister of Proto-Luwic, both deriving from an ancestor that can be called Proto-Luwo-Palaic. Lydian may thus be viewed as a sister of this latter language, both going back to a Proto-Luwo-Lydian ancestor language. However, since our knowledge of Palaic and Lydian is rudimentary, it is difficult to know the exact shapes of these ancestor languages. This also makes it difficult to give secure estimates of the lengths of the time gaps between Proto-Luwic, Proto-Luwo-Palaic, and Proto-Luwo-Lydian, respectively, although it seems reasonable to

4 Hoffner & Melchert 2008. 5 Carruba 1970.
6 Melchert 2003. 7 Payne 2010. 8 Gusmani 1964–1986.
9 Adiego 2007. 10 Melchert 2008. 11 Gusmani 1989/1990.
12 Orozco 2007. 13 Brixhe 1988.
14 Note that Kroonen, Barjamovic, & Peyrot (2018) have recently claimed that a number of personal names that are recorded in texts from Ebla dated to the 25th–24th centuries BCE (Bonecchi 1990), and which refer to individuals said to be from the state of Armi (a toponym that is further unknown), belong to one or more languages "that clearly fall within the Anatolian Indo-European family" (2018: 6). If correct, these names, which predate the Kanišite Hittite names from the Kültepe texts by half a millennium, would be the earliest attested witnesses of the Anatolian language branch. However, Kroonen, Barjamovic, & Peyrot do not offer a detailed analysis of this material, and at present, I would therefore regard the linguistic status of these names as too uncertain to make any broad claims.
15 Cf. Larsen 2015 for an introduction to Kültepe (Kaniš/Nēša) and the documents excavated there.

16 Since our knowledge of Carian, Sidetic, and Pisidian is only rudimentary, their classification as Luwic remains uncertain.
17 Rieken 2017: 299; Kloekhorst 2022a: 67–71.
18 Kloekhorst 2013. 19 Cf. Rieken 2017: 303.
20 Cf. Kloekhorst 2022a: 71–75, building on Oettinger 1978 and Yakubovich 2010: 6.

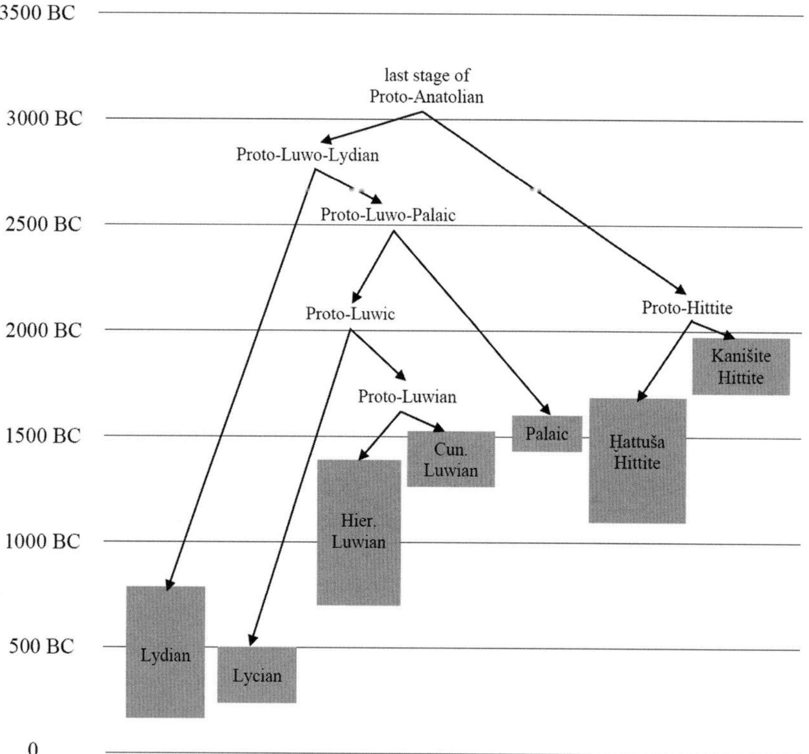

FIGURE 4.2. The phylogenetic composition of the Anatolian branch (gray blocks represent the period of attestation of that specific language stage).

assign several centuries to each of them. With Proto-Luwic probably dating to the twenty-first to twentieth century BCE, it seems plausible to date Proto-Luwo-Palaic to some point between the twenty-sixth and twenty-third century BCE, and Proto-Luwo-Lydian maximally to the twenty-ninth, minimally to the twenty-sixth century BCE.

Proto-Anatolian can now be defined as the ancestor language of, on the one hand, Proto-Luwo-Lydian (the ancestor of Lydian, Palaic, and the Luwic languages) and, on the other, Proto-Hittite. With Proto-Luwo-Lydian dating to the twenty-ninth to twenty-sixth century BCE, Proto-Anatolian must be dated before that time. This also applies when we compare the two language stages of the Anatolian branch whose shapes we can reconstruct relatively securely, namely Proto-Hittite and Proto-Luwic (which, as we saw above, seem to have been roughly contemporaneous, ca. 2100 BCE and the twentieth to twenty-first century BCE, respectively). If we look at the linguistic differences between these two languages, which is an indication of the distance from their pre-stage, we see that these differences are relatively sizable.[21] Proto-Luwic in particular seems to have undergone quite a number of phonological and morphological innovations vis-à-vis the reconstructable Proto-Anatolian stage: Čop's law, with later morphological restorations; the assibilation of the fortis palatovelar; the weakening of the lenis velars; the reduction of the vowel system; the massive spread of the so-called *i*-mutation paradigm; the grammaticalization of the genitival adjective; the reshaping of some nominal endings; etc. But Proto-Hittite too has undergone its share of linguistic innovations: the weakening of unaccented vowels; the assibilation of dental stop + *i̯; the almost complete elimination of paradigmatic alternations between fortis and lenis stops; the reshaping of some verbal endings; the transfer of many *mi*-verbs to the *ḫi*-conjugation; the spread of the *n*-stem in the word for 'earth'; etc. Not only the number of different innovations, especially of the Luwic subbranch, is telling, but also their nature. For instance, the massive spread of the *i*-mutation paradigm in Luwic is an innovation[22] that must have taken at least several generations, perhaps centuries. On the basis of the linguistic distance between Proto-Hittite and Proto-Luwic, I assume that the time gap between the two may have been approximately a millennium. This would mean that Proto-Anatolian should be dated to sometime around the thirty-first to thirtieth century BCE. This is in line with the observation that Proto-Anatolian must predate the Proto-Luwo-Lydian stage, which can be dated to the twenty-ninth to twenty-sixth century BCE. Moreover, it would mean that the first dissolution of Proto-Anatolian was not too far removed in time from the breakup of Classical Proto-Indo-European (from 3400 BCE onwards; cf. § 4.1.2.1), which would fit the Indo-Anatolian hypothesis.

All in all, we may schematize the phylogenetic composition of the Anatolian branch as presented in Figure 4.2.

[21] Cf. Kloekhorst 2022a for a discussion of the innovations of both Proto-Luwic and Proto-Hittite.

[22] Cf. Norbruis 2021: 9–50 for a detailed analysis of this innovation.

4.1.2 Dating Proto-Indo-Anatolian

From a comparative linguistic point of view, there are two approaches to evaluating the possibilities for the date of Proto-Indo-Anatolian: (1) assessing the possible length of the time gap between Proto-Indo-Anatolian and Classical Proto-Indo-European; and (2) assessing the possible length of the time gap between Proto-Indo-Anatolian and Proto-Anatolian.

In both cases, this assessment depends on making an inventory of all the innovations that have taken place between Proto-Indo-Anatolian and the respective daughter stage. This is a difficult task, however, since no consensus currently exists as to how Proto-Indo-Anatolian should be reconstructed. As a consequence, at present there is no commonly held view on the nature and number of innovations that distinguish Classical Proto-Indo-European and Proto-Anatolian, respectively, from their Proto-Indo-Anatolian mother language. The two paragraphs that follow therefore inevitably depend on my personal view of what the shape of Proto-Indo-Anatolian may have been, and which innovations may have taken place in the prehistories of Classical Proto-Indo-European and Proto-Anatolian.

4.1.2.1 The Gap between Proto-Indo-Anatolian and Classical Proto-Indo-European

As mentioned in the introduction of this chapter, the recent revolution in tracking prehistoric migrations on the basis of ancient DNA has erased all doubt that the speakers of Classical Proto-Indo-European can be equated with the bearers of the Yamnaya culture of the Early Bronze Age Pontic–Caspian steppes. The last phase of Classical Proto-Indo-European may be dated to the period directly prior to the migrations of the Yamnaya people to the east, into Central Asia, causing the rise of the Afanasievo culture (commencing ca. 3300 BCE),[23] which is generally seen as the ultimate ancestor of the Tocharian languages. The start of this migration, which we may term the "Tocharian split" and which constitutes the first breakup of Classical Proto-Indo-European,[24] may thus be dated a bit earlier than 3300 BCE, i.e. ca. 3400 BCE.

Recently, Tijmen Pronk and I have gathered a total of twenty-three examples that we regard as "good candidates" for possible linguistic innovations that have taken place between Proto-Indo-Anatolian and Classical Proto-Indo-European (Kloekhorst & Pronk 2019: 3–4). This list includes eight cases of semantic innovation (e.g. PIA **mer-* 'to disappear' > CPIE 'to die'),[25] ten morphological innovations (e.g. PIA **h₁eḱu-* > CPIE **h₁eḱu-o-* 'horse'),[26] three sound changes (e.g. PIA $*h_2$ = *[qː] > CPIE *[ħ] or *[ʕ]),[27] and two syntactic innovations (e.g. the marking of neuter agents).[28] Besides these twenty-three cases, we list another eleven examples that we regard as "promising, though perhaps less forceful" than the other ones, or as "requiring additional investigation before it can be decided whether we are genuinely dealing with an innovation of the 'classical' Indo-European languages" (ibid.: 4–5). Though it is possible that not every innovation on this list will ultimately be accepted by all specialists in the field, it seems unlikely that they will all be refuted. Moreover, some of the good candidates concern significant structural innovations (e.g. the rise of the feminine gender, including the creation of its morphological marking), which must have taken substantial time to develop. In Kloekhorst & Pronk 2019, we have therefore concluded that the time gap between Proto-Indo-Anatolian and Classical Proto-Indo-European (including Tocharian) may have been in the range of 800 to 1000 years. With the dating of Classical Proto-Indo-European to the period directly preceding the start of the "Tocharian split," i.e. ca. 3400 BCE, we would arrive at a date of ca. 4400 to 4200 BCE for the "Anatolian split," which means that the last stage of Proto-Indo-Anatolian must have been spoken before this date.

4.1.2.2 The Gap between Proto-Indo-Anatolian and Proto-Anatolian

In the period between Proto-Indo-Anatolian and Proto-Anatolian, linguistic innovations have taken place as well, but here, too, the same problem arises: there is no consensus on the exact shape of Proto-Indo-Anatolian; thus there is no generally accepted view on the nature and number of innovations that must have taken place in the period between these two stages.

Nevertheless, there are certain innovations in Proto-Anatolian that most scholars would agree on, namely with regard to the phonological system (the development of three consonantal series into two;[29] the "collapse" of the laryngeal system: the phonologization of coloring, partial merger of $*h_2$ and $*h_3$, and development of **VHC > V̄C*;[30] the creation of a new labialized laryngeal $*H^w$;[31] and lenition rules[32]) and especially the morphological system (a major reshuffling of the verbal system, including the loss of the optative and subjunctive categories, the loss of the present-aorist distinction, and probably the transformation of the perfect into the *ḫi*-conjugation,[33] but also the creation of sentence-initial particle chains).[34] The changes in the verbal system in particular seem to be innovations that would have needed considerable time to take place. We may therefore assume that the time gap between

[23] Anthony 2013: 10; Svyatko et al. 2017: 73.
[24] Cf. Peyrot 2019, who calls this stage "Proto-Indo-Tocharian."
[25] Kloekhorst 2008a: 8. [26] Kloekhorst 2008a: 10.
[27] Kloekhorst 2018. [28] Lopuhaä-Zwakenberg 2019.

[29] E.g., Melchert 1994: 60.
[30] Melchert 1994: 65–74; Kloekhorst 2006; Kloekhorst 2008a: 75–82.
[31] Kloekhorst 2006: 97–101; Melchert 2011: 129; Melchert 2020: 262.
[32] Eichner 1973: 79, 100[86]; Morpurgo Davies 1982/83; Kloekhorst 2014: 547–566.
[33] Oettinger 2017: 264–267, with references; Kloekhorst 2018.
[34] Luraghi 2017.

Proto-Indo-Anatolian and Proto-Anatolian may have been at least 1000 years, or perhaps even 1200 years.

If our dating of the last stage of Proto-Anatolian to around the thirty-first to thirtieth century BCE is correct, we would arrive at a date of around the forty-third to fortieth century BCE for Proto-Indo-Anatolian.

4.1.2.3 Combining the Two Approaches

We see that both approaches yield a comparable result: if we take Classical Proto-Indo-European as our point of departure, we arrive at ca. 4400 to 4200 BCE for Proto-Indo-Anatolian, and if we take Proto-Anatolian as our starting point, we arrive at ca. the forty-third to fortieth century BCE. The two approaches overlap in the period 4300 to 4200 BCE, with a margin ranging from ca. 4400 BCE to the fortieth century BCE. In the remainder of the chapter, I will therefore use 4300 to 4200 BCE as a shorthand for the date of the "Anatolian split," but we must bear in mind that the first dissolution of Proto-Indo-Anatolian could have taken place a bit earlier (up to ca. 4400 BCE) or a bit later (until ca. the fortieth century BCE).

4.2 Locating Proto-Indo-Anatolian

The question of where Proto-Indo-Anatolian must have been located ties in with two issues: (1) the Indo-European "homeland" question; and (2) the possible genetic relationships of Proto-Indo-Anatolian with one or more other languages or language families.

4.2.1 The Indo-European "Homeland" Question: Analyzing the Anatolian Lexicon

For decades, linguists and archaeologists have engaged in discussion as to where the Indo-European mother language was spoken, focusing on two scenarios: the steppe hypothesis, which states that the Indo-European languages originated in the Pontic–Caspian steppes and was spread throughout Europe and Asia by nomadic pastoralists in the late fourth millennium BCE,[35] and the Anatolian hypothesis, which assumes that the Indo-European mother language was spoken around 8000 to 7000 BCE in Anatolia by the first farmers, who, by gradually colonizing Europe and Asia, not only spread agriculture, but also their language.[36] Nowadays, since studies in ancient DNA have shown that in the latter part of the fourth millennium BCE, massive migrations must have taken place from the Pontic–Caspian steppes into the areas of Europe and Asia where later Indo-European languages are spoken,[37] no one can seriously uphold the Anatolian hypothesis for Classical Proto-Indo-European anymore.

However, since Proto-Indo-Anatolian must be dated substantially earlier than Classical Proto-Indo-European (cf. Section 4.1), one could theoretically argue that the Anatolian homeland hypothesis still applies to Proto-Indo-Anatolian. One would then have to assume that this protolanguage originated in Anatolia, and that after the "Anatolian split," the Anatolian branch in fact remained where it was, and that the other branch, which was to develop into Classical Proto-Indo-European, ended up in the Pontic–Caspian steppes in some way or another, from which it spread further into Europe and Asia. If this is true, Proto-Anatolian would be indigenous to Anatolia.

From a linguistic point of view, this hypothesis can be tested by analyzing the Anatolian lexicon. Unfortunately, we do not have enough lexical material for all the Anatolian languages at our disposal, so we cannot make such an analysis for the entire branch. Nevertheless, it is possible to perform such an investigation for Hittite and, as we will see, the results are robust enough to assume that we can apply them to the Anatolian branch as a whole.

We can approach the Hittite lexicon from two angles: (1) by assessing the semantics of its borrowed lexicon; and (2) by assessing the semantics of its inherited lexicon.

4.2.1.1 The Borrowed Lexicon of Hittite

The Hittite lexicon, as attested in the texts known to us, consists of some 1900 word stems whose meanings are clear (although the exact meaning of some of these words is less certain than others). With the use of the methods of comparative linguistics, it is possible to distinguish between two types of lexemes: (1) words that have a good Indo-European etymology, and can therefore be regarded as inherited words (i.e., they must already have been part of the pre-Hittite lexicon from the Proto-Indo-Anatolian stage onward); and (2) words that do not have a good etymology, and are therefore very likely borrowings (i.e. words that entered the Hittite lexicon through contact with other languages in the period between Anatolian splitting off from the Proto-Indo-Anatolian language stage and the period from which the Hittite texts stem).

In my etymological database of the entire Hittite lexicon (compiled in preparation for Kloekhorst 2008a), some 890 words (i.e., ca. 46% of the lexicon) are classified as "non-Indo-European," and can therefore be regarded as borrowings. These words fall into the following semantic categories:

1. Animals / pertaining to animals (63 words)
2. Body parts / medical (67 words)
3. Buildings / parts of buildings (44 words)
4. Celestial phenomena (4 words)
5. Cultic terms (115 words)
6. Foodstuffs (89 words)

[35] Gimbutas 1973; Mallory 1989; Anthony 2007, 2013.

[36] Renfrew 1987, 2000, 2003; Gray & Atkinson 2003; Bouckaert et al. 2012. See Pereltsvaig & Lewis 2015, however, for a devastating review of the latter two articles.

[37] Allentoft et al. 2015; Haak et al. 2015; Lazaridis et al. 2016.

7. Functionaries / professions (75 words)
8. Furniture (14 words)
9. Garments / clothing / wool (48 words)
10. Gems / materials (35 words)
11. Plants (80 words)
12. Royalty / rulership (18 words)
13. Tools / instruments (45 words)
14. Topographical features (34 words)
15. Vessels (58 words)
16. Other (101 words)

Several of these categories are interesting. Take, for instance, category 3 (buildings/parts of buildings): apart from the word *per / parn-* 'house', which may be of Indo-European origin, all other Hittite words for buildings are borrowings (*arkiu-*, *ḫištā-*, *kāškāštipa-*, *māk(kiz)ziịa-*, etc.). The same goes for words concerning royalty and rulership: although the Hittite words *ḫaššu-* 'king' and *ḫaššuššara-* 'queen' are built from Indo-European elements, all other words dealing with royalty are borrowings: the title of the king and queen (*labarna-*[38] and *tawannanna-*), the terms for 'crown prince' (*tuḫkanti-*),[39] 'throne' (*ḫalmašuitt-*), and 'palace' (*ḫalentiu-*), etc. The number of borrowings denoting vessels ('cup', 'bowl', 'basket', etc.) is impressive, and this also goes for the number of borrowings denoting cultic items and concepts.

In other words, almost all the Hittite terms referring to the "high culture" of the city-states characteristic of Middle/Late Chalcolithic and Early Bronze Age Anatolia are borrowings. This situation is not consistent with a scenario in which Proto-Anatolian (and therefore Hittite) was indigenous to Anatolia: in such a case, we would expect the Hittites to have indigenous words for all aspects of the high culture of Anatolia (and to find some of these words in the other Indo-European languages as well). On the contrary, this situation implies that the speakers of Proto-Anatolian/pre-Hittite were immigrants into Anatolia, having taken over the high cultures of population groups who spoke a language or languages different from theirs, and extensively borrowing words for all kinds of items and concepts that were new to them.

We can therefore safely reject the Anatolian hypothesis for the Proto-Indo-Anatolian stage. From a linguistic point of view, there can be no question that Proto-Indo-Anatolian was spoken outside of Anatolia. In view of its being the ancestor of Classical Proto-Indo-European, which was spoken in the Pontic–Caspian steppes, it seems best to assume that Proto-Indo-Anatolian was spoken somewhere near that region as well.

4.2.1.2 The Inherited Lexicon of Hittite

In order to pinpoint a more precise location for the Proto-Indo-Anatolian homeland, we have to look at the inherited lexicon of Hittite.[40] The inherited lexemes of Hittite, i.e., words that have good cognates in the other Indo-European languages, must have been passed down all the way from Proto-Indo-Anatolian, and can therefore be regarded as representatives of the Proto-Indo-Anatolian lexicon. Using the concept of linguistic palaeontology,[41] we can assume that the words used by the speakers of Proto-Indo-Anatolian represented concepts that were known to them. Since the Proto-Indo-Anatolian lexicon contains words for e.g. 'horse' (PIA *$*h_1$éḱu-*), 'cow' (PIA *$*g^w eh_3u$-*), 'sheep' (PIA *$*h_3$eui-*), 'yoke' (PIA **ieug-*), 'honey' (PIA **melit-*), and 'to pasture' (PIA **ues-*), which point to a pastoralist lifestyle, we may assume that the speakers of Proto-Indo-Anatolian were living in the steppes, just as their descendants, the speakers of Classical Proto-Indo-European, did. It should be noted that since the word for 'wheel' cannot be reconstructed for Proto-Indo-Anatolian (the Hittite word for 'wheel', *ḫurki-*, does not match the word for 'wheel' in the other Indo-European languages, which was *$*k^w ek^w lo$-*), the Proto-Indo-Anatolians may not have known the wheel. This is consistent with the dating of Proto-Indo-Anatolian before ca. 4300 to 4200 BCE, a period that predates the invention of the wheel by more than half a millennium.[42]

4.2.2 The Indo-Uralic Hypothesis

In order to pinpoint more precisely where in the steppes Proto-Indo-Anatolian may have been spoken, it may be fruitful to look further back in time to see whether we can identify one or more languages or language families that could have been relatives of Proto-Indo-Anatolian.

Throughout history, there have been many attempts to connect the Indo-European language family with other language families (see Kloekhorst and Pronk 2019: 9 for a selective overview), most of which are regarded with skepticism by Indo-Europeanists. One comparison stands out, however: namely, the one connecting Indo-European with Uralic.[43] The similarities between these two language families are mostly found in morphology (Kortlandt 2002 lists no fewer than twenty-seven morphemes of Indo-European and Uralic that are phonetically so similar to each other that he regards them as "definitely Indo-Uralic"), but there are also some matches both lexically and structurally.[44]

If this connection between Indo-European and Uralic, the so-called "Indo-Uralic hypothesis," is valid (and I regard this as highly likely), it would mean that Proto-Indo-Anatolian and Proto-Uralic would both stem from a common ancestor, Proto-Indo-Uralic. With Proto-Uralic being spoken somewhere near the Urals,[45] and Proto-Indo-Anatolian being the ancestor of Classical Proto-Indo-European, which was spoken in the Pontic–Caspian steppes, it stands to reason that Proto-Indo-Anatolian should be located in an intermediate region, i.e., the northeastern part of the Pontic–Caspian steppes, near the Ural Mountains.

[38] Kloekhorst 2008a: 520–521, *pace* Melchert 2003b.
[39] *Pace* Rieken 2016. [40] Cf. Kloekhorst 2008a.
[41] Cf. Olander 2017. [42] Anthony 2007: 63–76.
[43] E.g. Pedersen 1933; Collinder 1934, 1954; Čop 1975; Kortlandt 1989, 2002; Kloekhorst 2008b.
[44] Kortlandt 1989; Kloekhorst 2008b.
[45] E.g. Sammallahti 1988: 480; Carpelan & Parpola 2001: 78; Janhunen 2009.

4.3 Mapping the "Anatolian Trek"

In order to map, in time and space, the route by which the Anatolian branch may have been transferred from its presumed Proto-Indo-Anatolian homeland (northeast of the Pontic–Caspian steppes before 4300 to 4200 BCE) to the location where it is eventually attested (Anatolia, from ca. 2000 BCE onward) – which we may term the "Anatolian trek" – we have to answer two questions: (1) when did the Anatolian branch enter into Anatolia, and (2) via which point of entry did it do so?

4.3.1 The Date of Entry into Anatolia

The question of when the Anatolian branch was introduced into Anatolia ties in with the issue of whether Proto-Anatolian diverged inside Anatolia or rather outside of it. On linguistic grounds, this is not easy to answer with certainty at the moment. If we assume that Proto-Anatolian diverged outside of Anatolia, it would imply multiple, separate introductions of Anatolian-speaking population groups into Anatolia – for instance, speakers of (a pre-stage of) Proto-Hittite and those of (a pre-stage of) Proto-Luwo-Lydian. These immigrations would thus have taken place in the period after the first breakup of Proto-Anatolian (ca. the thirty-first to thirtieth century BCE) and the last stage of Proto-Luwo-Lydian (ca. the twenty-ninth to twenty-sixth century BCE).[46] However, simply because all known Anatolian languages were spoken in Anatolia, it is to my mind more economical to assume that the Anatolian languages arrived in Anatolia as a single group, which would mean that we are dealing with a single introduction, namely that of speakers of (a pre-stage of) Proto-Anatolian. This event should thus be dated before or to the thirty-first to thirtieth century BCE.

From a historical linguistic perspective, the "Anatolian trek" should thus have started around 4300 to 4200 BCE and would have transferred pre-Proto-Anatolian from the Proto-Indo-Anatolian homeland (the northeast of the Pontic–Caspian steppes) to Anatolia, where it was introduced at some time before the thirty-first to thirtieth century BCE.

4.3.2 The Point of Entry into Anatolia

There are, in theory, two routes leading from the Pontic–Caspian steppe region into Anatolia: one through the Balkan Peninsula, and one through the Caucasus.[47] From a linguistic point of view, it seems more probable that the Anatolian branch arrived in Anatolia from the west, i.e., via the Balkan route, than from the east, i.e., via the Caucasus route. This statement is based on the following four arguments.

4.3.2.1 The Western Location of the Anatolian Languages

In Figure 4.3, a reconstruction of the linguistic landscape of Anatolia at the beginning of the second millennium BCE is presented.

This map is based partly on information from contemporary sources,[48] as well as from later sources (both from the second and first millennium BCE). Some of the locations assigned to (pre-stages of) languages are based on a back projection of the later geolinguistic situation,[49] sometimes involving relatively complicated argumentation,[50] but the overall picture of the linguistic landscape of western, central, and southeastern Anatolia seems reasonably clear. Only for northeastern Anatolia do we have insufficient data to say anything about its linguistic make-up in this period.

It is striking that the Anatolian languages are found in west and south-central Anatolia, whereas the mid-central and eastern parts of Anatolia are occupied by non-Indo-European languages (Hattic, Hurrian), which to their south side are bordered by members of the Semitic family (Amorite, Babylonian, and Assyrian), which is non-Indo-European as well. This distribution, in which the Anatolian languages clearly cluster in the west whereas the rest of Anatolia is inhabited by non-Indo-European speaking groups, is best explained by assuming that the speakers of (pre-)Proto-Anatolian entered Anatolia from the west, via the Bosporus and/or Dardanelles. If they had entered Anatolia from the east, via the Caucasus, we would expect to find some traces of Anatolian languages from there all the way to western Anatolia. One could argue that since we do not have any solid evidence for the linguistic make-up of northeast Anatolia in this period, it cannot be excluded that some unknown Anatolian languages were spoken in this region. These would then form a trail from the Caucasus to the

[46] If Kroonen, Barjamovic, & Peyrot (2018) are right that Anatolian personal names are already recorded in Eblaite texts from the twenty-fifth to twenty-fourth century BCE (which, however, is difficult to assess; cf. footnote 14), this scenario, which implies that the speakers of Anatolian did not enter Anatolia until the first quarter of the third millennium BCE, becomes even more unattractive.

[47] A third route, namely going around the eastern coast of the Caspian Sea and then turning west through Iran, was probably taken by the speakers of Mittanni-Indic (showing up in Anatolia around 1600 BCE), but this is hardly an option for the Anatolians: the speakers of Mittanni-Indic possessed the horse-drawn chariot and were therefore much more mobile than the speakers of pre-Proto-Anatolian, who probably did not know the wheel, would have been.

[48] Cf. Kloekhorst 2019 for an analysis of the Old Assyrian and Old Hittite sources toward a reconstruction of the linguistic landscape of central Anatolia in the first half of the second millennium BCE.

[49] As in the case of pre-Caro-Lycian (the pre-stage of Carian, Lycian, Milyan, and possibly Sidetic), the location of which is based on a back projection of first-millennium Carian and Lycian.

[50] The location of pre-Lydian (the ancestor of Lydian, which was spoken in classical Lydia in the first millennium BCE) is based on the idea that the historical Lydians came from a more northerly region, namely the area that in Hittite times was called Māša. Cf. Beekes 2003: 10–24; Kloekhorst 2012: 49–50; 2022b: 208–9.

FIGURE 4.3. Reconstruction of the linguistic landscape of Anatolia at the beginning of the second millennium BCE. Names in small caps are Anatolian (Indo-European) languages; names in italics are non-Indo-European languages. The gray arrows indicate language spread in historic times (that of Luwian to southeast Anatolia and northern Syria and of Hittite into central Anatolia).

Anatolian language of the west; however, there is simply no evidence for such languages. Even from later sources (from the first millennium BCE and the first centuries CE), which do offer information on the linguistic landscape of northeast Anatolia in these periods, I know of no evidence that could be interpreted as pointing to an earlier presence, in this region, of languages that might have belonged to the Anatolian branch.[51]

4.3.2.2 The Kızıl Irmak River as a Linguistic Border

One of the clear landmarks of central Anatolia is the Kızıl Irmak river, which after rising in the eastern part of central Anatolia first runs westward, then veers off to the north, after which it runs back eastward in a northern direction before eventually flowing into the Black Sea (see Figure 4.3 for the Kızıl Irmak's typical bend). Moreover, the Kızıl Irmak is wide enough to form an obstacle when traveling through Anatolia: through time, it often even functioned as a boundary between regions and states.[52] At the beginning of the second millennium BCE, the area encompassed by the Kızıl Irmak bend, which was then called Ḫatti-land (the region centered around the city of Ḫattuša), was in essence Hattic-speaking.[53] Although Ḫattuša later became the capital of the Hittite kingdom, and the land of Ḫatti is traditionally seen as the Hittite heartland, it was in fact not until Anitta, king of Kaniš / Nēša, conquered Ḫattuša around 1730 BCE and Ḫattuša was later chosen as the capital of the Hittite royal family (ca. 1650 BCE) that speakers of Hittite may have settled in this region in large numbers. The presence of speakers of Hattic, a non-Indo-European language, within the Kızıl Irmak's bend contrasts with the presence of Anatolian (Indo-European) languages on the other side of the river: Palaic on its northwest side, Luwian on its southwest side, and Hittite on its south side. This distribution of Anatolian languages on all sides of the Kızıl Irmak's bend, while a non-Indo-European language was spoken inside the bend, strongly suggests that the speakers of these Anatolian languages came from the west, but that their migration was initially blocked by the Kızıl Irmak river, which they were not able to cross in large enough numbers to settle on its east side. Only later on, in historical times, were speakers of Hittite able to successfully cross the upper, southern course of the river with enough troops that they could eventually conquer the region inside the bend.

I therefore view the fact that the Kızıl Irmak seems to function as a linguistic border between Anatolian Indo-European languages, on the one hand, and a non-Indo-European one on the other as an argument in favor of assuming that the speakers of (pre-)Proto-Anatolian entered Anatolia from the west, i.e. via the Balkan route.

51 In this period, we do find evidence of Urartean, generally seen as a sister language of Hurrian, and of Armenian, an Indo-European language that forms its own branch, distinct from the Anatolian branch.

52 For instance, in the second millennium BCE, it functioned as the border of Ḫatti-land; in the first millennium BCE, as the border between the Lydian and the Persian empires (Bryce 2009: 281); and, later on, as the border between the Kingdom of Pontus and the Kingdom of Cappadocia.

53 Singer 1981: 120–125; Kloekhorst 2019: 246–247.

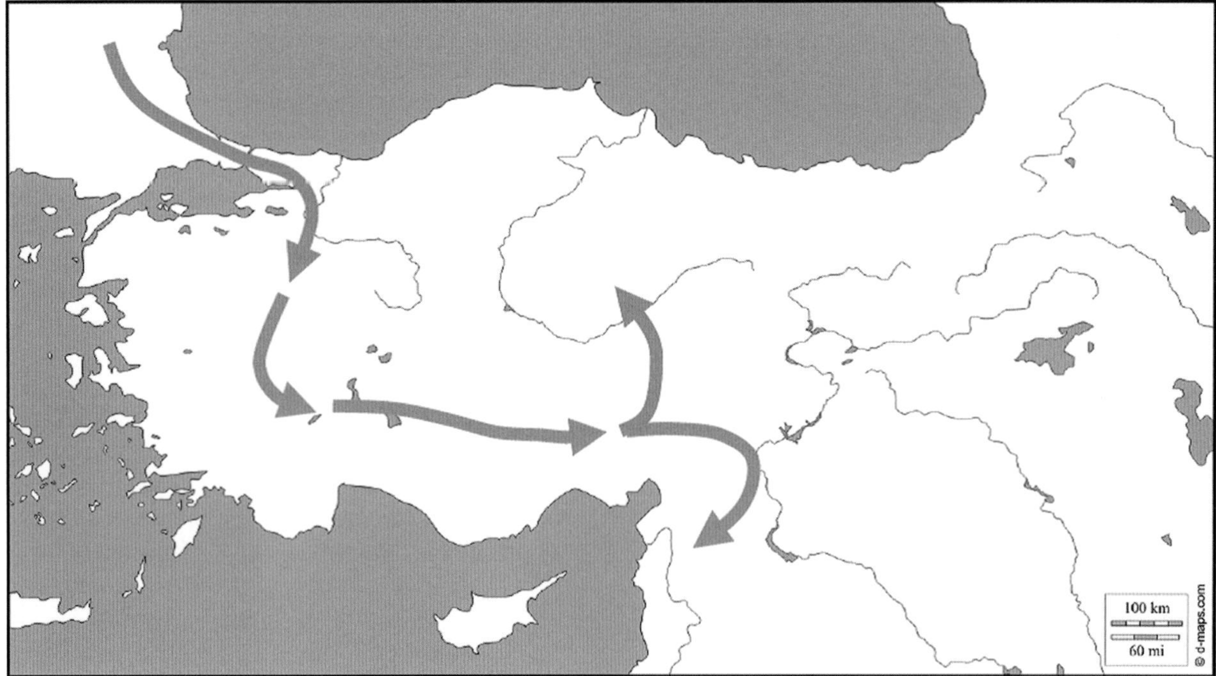

FIGURE 4.4. The route of the spread of (pre-stages of) Luwian within the Balkan scenario.

Within the scenario in which the Anatolian branch entered Anatolia from the east, i.e. via the Caucasus route, it is difficult to see how the distribution of languages on both sides of the Kızıl Irmak river could be explained in a natural way. We would then have to assume that in their move to the west, (the speakers of) (pre-)Proto-Anatolian did not enter the area to the north of the Kızıl Irmak, but instead took a route to its south, after which the Anatolian languages spread all over western Anatolia. But it is unclear why this would have been the case: what would have stopped these languages from spreading into the area north of the Kızıl Irmak river? Within the Caucasus scenario, I do not see any good explanation for this fact, whereas within the Balkan scenario, the initial absence of Anatolian languages inside the Kızıl Irmak bend can be linked to the shape of this river's course in a very natural way.

4.3.2.3 The "Drift" of the Anatolian Languages in Historic Times

Within the historical period, some Anatolian language spread into territories where they were not spoken previously. In Section 4.3.2.1, we saw that at the beginning of the second millennium BCE, Hittite was confined to the area south of the Kızıl Irmak River, but was able to spread to the north, into Ḫatti-land, in the eighteenth and seventeenth centuries BCE. Likewise, Luwian, which, at the beginning of the second millennium BCE, seems to have been at home in western Anatolia, is first attested in Kizzuwatna (present-day Adana province) (Luwian Kizzuwatnean ritual texts from the sixteenth century BCE), then spread to the Hittite heartland (influence on Hittite from ca. 1400 BCE onwards), and later moved eastward (all the way to the northern course of the Euphrates) and southward (into northern Syria) into areas where Semitic languages were originally spoken. It remained the dominant language there until the seventh century BCE.

This clear eastward drift of Luwian is particularly consistent with the Balkan scenario: we may thus see this movement to the east during the second and first millennium BCE as a mere continuation of the eastward movement that caused the initial entry of the Anatolian branch from the Balkan Peninsula into west Anatolia at the beginning of the third millennium BCE (cf. Figure 4.4).

Within the Caucasus scenario, we would have to assume that Proto-Anatolian first underwent a spread to the west, meanwhile diverging into different daughter languages, some of which ended up all the way in western Anatolia, and that, not much later on, one of these daughter languages, Luwian, started moving back all the way east again (cf. Figure 4.5). Although this may not be impossible, the scenario clearly seems less economical than the Balkan scenario.

4.3.2.4 Parallels from Later Times

The linguistic history of Anatolian is a rich one: throughout the past millennia, many different population groups have been able to settle in Anatolia from somewhere else, bringing their languages with them. Even nowadays, the modern state of Turkey is home to a dozen different languages. Some of these languages entered Anatolian through migrations from the west, via the Balkans. This is generally assumed to have been the case for Phrygian (entering Anatolia at the end of the second millennium BCE)[54] and Galatian (a Celtic language, entering in the third century BCE),[55] and likely applies to Armenian as

[54] Brixhe 2008: 69. [55] Darbyshire, Mitchell, & Vardar 2000.

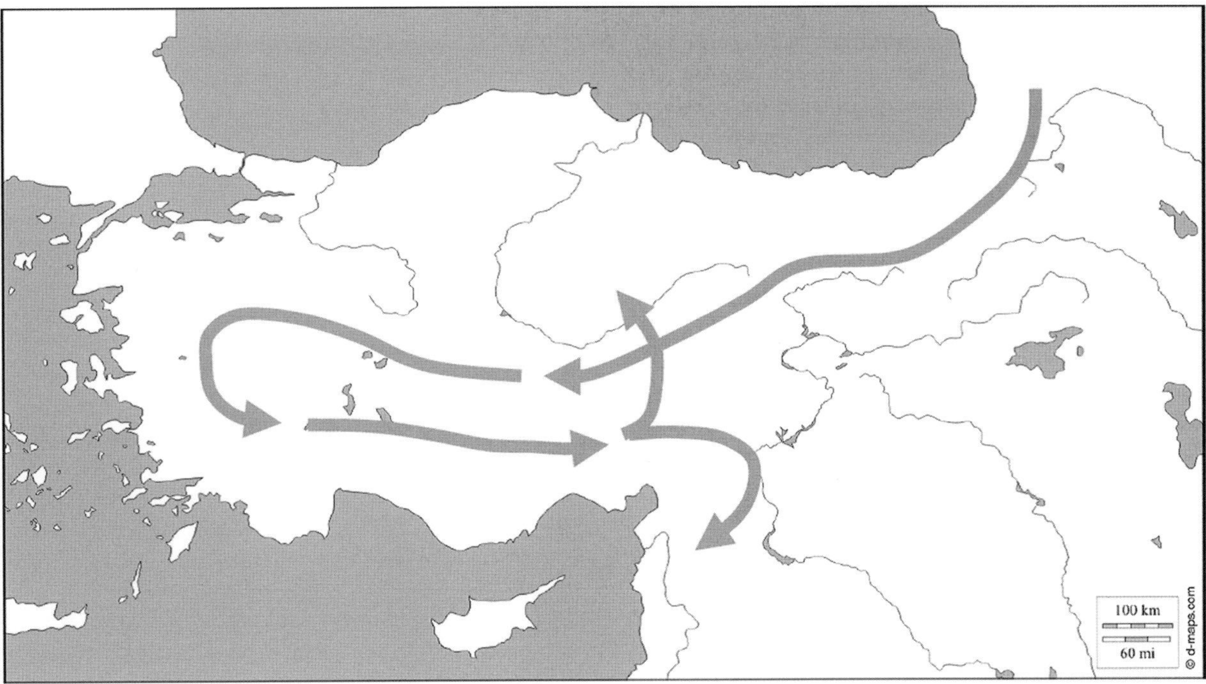

FIGURE 4.5. The route of the spread of (pre-stages of) Luwian within the Caucasus scenario.

well (entering together with Phrygian at the end of the second millennium BCE?).[56]

These cases therefore can serve as parallels to the arrival of the Anatolian languages in Anatolia, supporting the Balkan scenario.

Many other languages spoken in Anatolia in the past and present have come from the east, but in each case, these came either from the Levant or Mesopotamia (Phoenician, Aramaic, Arabic) or via the Iranian plateau (Mittanni-Indic, Kurdish, Zazaki, Turkish). It is true that there are some languages spoken in present-day Turkey that come from the Caucasus (Adygh, Laz), but these languages do not come from *beyond* the Caucasus, and therefore they cannot be used as parallels for a scenario in which the Anatolian languages spread from the steppes into Anatolia through the Caucasus.

It appears that there is no well-established parallel to the Caucasus scenario for the arrival of the Anatolian languages into Anatolia, whereas the Balkan scenario does have some clear parallels.

4.4 Conclusions on the Basis of Comparative Linguistic Arguments

Taking the identification of the speakers of Classical Proto-Indo-European with the bearers of the Yamnaya culture as an attractive working hypothesis, we arrive at the following reconstruction of the "Anatolian trek." First, the Anatolian branch must derive from Proto-Indo-Anatolian, which is the stage from which Classical Proto-Indo-European also derives. On the basis of the linguistic differences between Proto-Anatolian (which first diverged around 3100 to 3000 BCE) and Classical Proto-Indo-European (which first diverged around 3400 BCE, the time of the "Tocharian split"), it is estimated that Proto-Indo-Anatolian first diverged around 4300 to 4200 BCE. Because of its likely genetic relationship with Uralic, it must have been located to the northeast of the Yamnaya homeland. Moreover, since the Proto-Indo-Anatolian lexicon reflects a pastoralist lifestyle, the Proto-Indo-Anatolian homeland must have been in the steppes as well, probably the steppes near the Ural mountains. This is the location where, around 4300 to 4200 BCE, the "Anatolian trek" must have commenced.

On the basis of linguistic analyses of the Anatolian branch, it is likely that the Anatolian languages arrived in Anatolia before or around the thirty-first to thirtieth century BCE. On the basis of the geographical location of the Anatolian languages within Anatolia, their distribution along the Kızıl Irmak river, and their "drift" in historical times, taking into account historical parallels, it seems best to assume that their point of entry into Anatolia was the west, through the Bosporus and/or the Dardanelles. A hypothetical point of entry from the east, through the Caucasus, is very hard to reconcile with all these arguments.

With the northeast of the Pontic–Caspian steppes as the point of departure of the "Anatolian trek," and the west of Anatolia as its point of entry into Anatolia, the most economical assumption is that the intermediate route went through the Pontic–Caspian steppes and the east of the Balkan Peninsula, respectively. We can thus reconstruct the "Anatolian trek" as schematized in Figure 4.6. Note that this reconstruction is solely based on comparative linguistic arguments.

The dispersal of the Anatolian languages within Anatolia may be envisaged as indicated in Figure 4.7.

56 Diakonoff 1984.

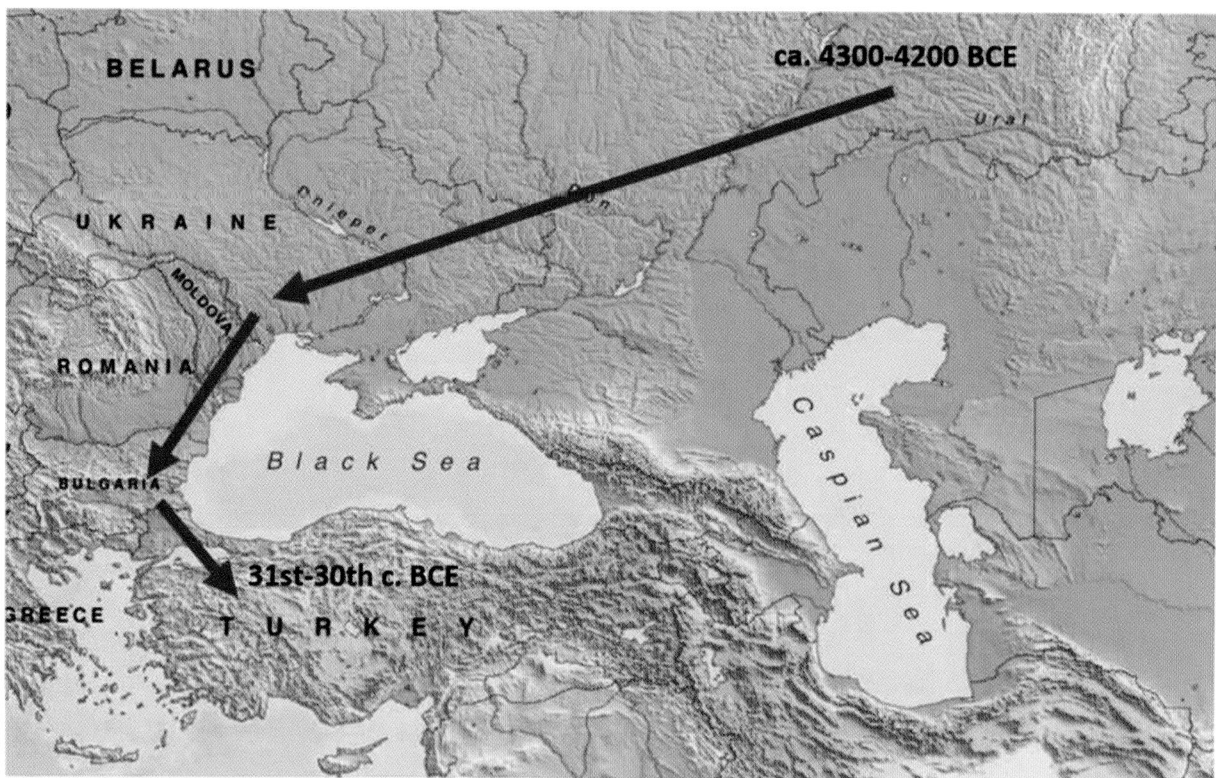

FIGURE 4.6. Schematic route of the "Anatolian trek."

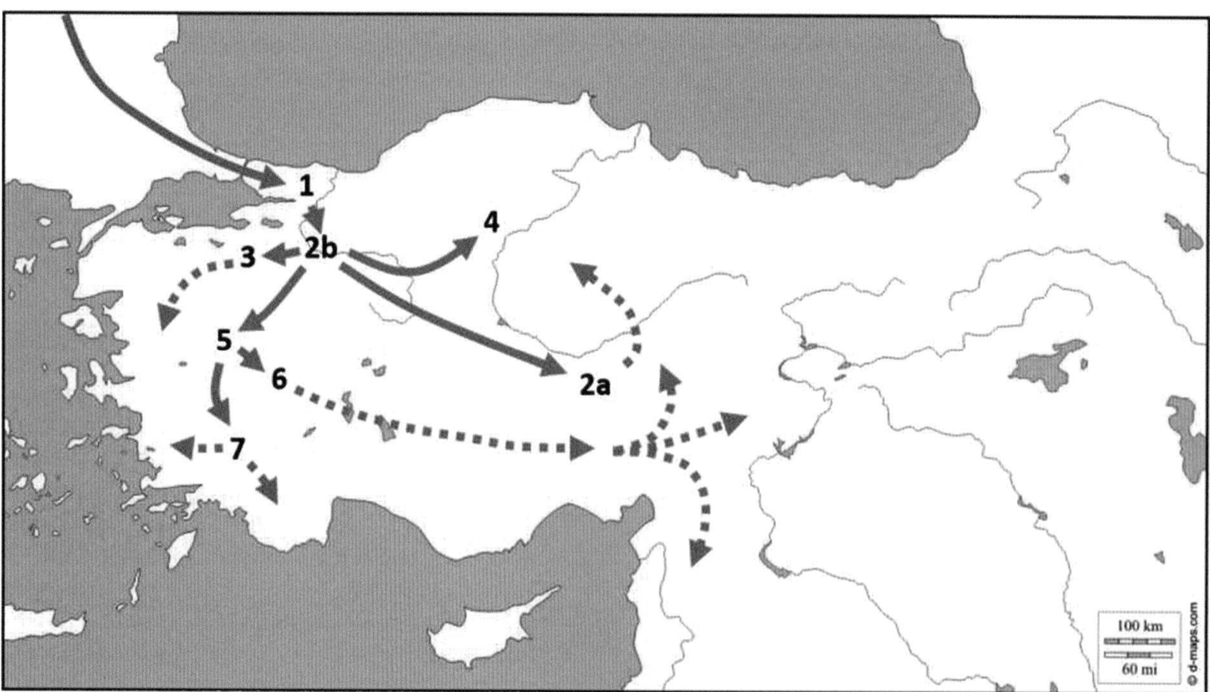

FIGURE 4.7. The dispersal of the Anatolian branch: 1. Proto-Anatolian (ca. 3100 BCE); 2a. Proto-Hittite (location around 2100 BCE, with northward drift in 18th and 17th c. BCE as a dashed line); 2b. Proto-Luwo-Lydian (ca. 2900–2600 BCE); 3. Pre-Lydian (location in 2nd. mill. BCE, with later drift into Classical Lydia after 1200 BCE as a dashed line); 4. Palaic (attested 16th c.); 5. Proto-Luwic (ca. 2200 BCE); 6. Proto-Luwian (ca. 19th c. BCE, with later eastward drift during the 2nd mill. BCE as dashed lines); 7. Proto-Caro-Lycian (ca. 1500 BCE?, with later drifts into Classical Caria and Lycia as dashed lines).

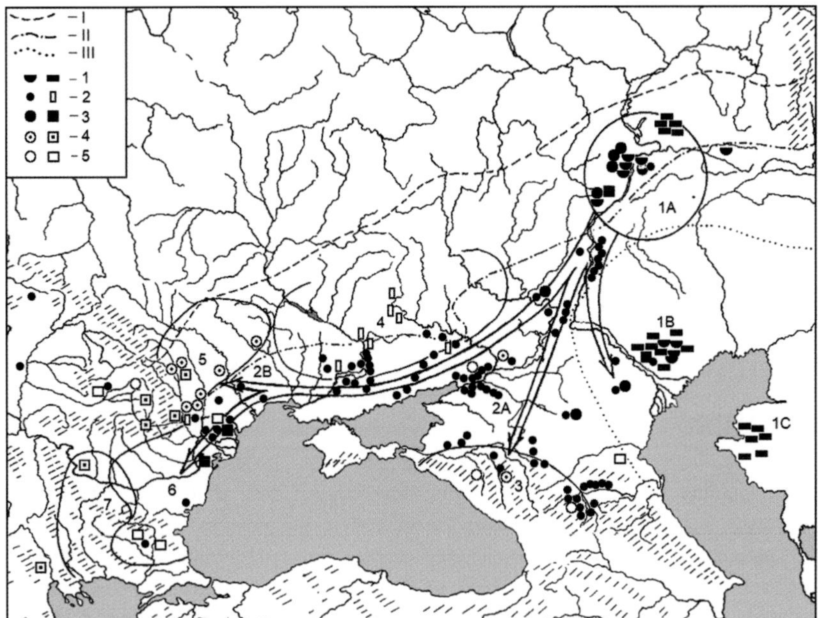

FIGURE 4.8. The spread of the stone horse-head maces in the Middle Eneolithic, (adapted from Dergačev 2007: 147). Ecoregions: I) southern border of forest-steppe; II) southern border of steppe; III) border of semidesert. Cultures: 1) burial complexes and settlements of Khvalynsk (1A – Middle Don; 1B – Northern Caspian; 1C – Western Caspian); 2) Burial complexes and remains of the Suvorovo-Novodanilovka type (2A – Eastern; 2B – Western); 3) Pre-Maikop; 4) Sredni Stog; 5) Cucuteni–Trypillia; 6) Bolgrad–Alden' – Gumelniţa–Karanovo VI; 7) Krivodol–Sălcuţa.

4.5 Mapping the "Anatolian Trek" onto Evidence from Archaeology

It goes beyond the scope of this chapter to discuss the entire archaeological side of the "Anatolian trek" question. It should be noted, however, that the reconstruction of the "Anatolian trek" as presented here – which, it must be stressed, is arrived at purely on the basis of comparative linguistic arguments – more or less fully coincides with Anthony's archaeological scenario for the spread of the Anatolian branch (Anthony 2007, 2013). My postulation of the Proto-Indo-Anatolian homeland in the northeastern part of the Pontic–Caspian steppes, near the Urals, before ca. 4300 to 4200 BCE would point to the Khvalynsk culture (4450–4350 BCE)[57] in the middle Volga region. My reconstruction of the first part of the "Anatolian trek," namely as commencing around 4300 to 4200 BCE and heading toward the Balkans, fits Anthony's description of how steppe herders spread into the lower Danube valley around 4200 to 4000 BCE, and "either caused or took advantage of the collapse of Old Europe" (2007: 133). According to Anthony (2007: 251), these herders, who formed the Suvorovo-Novodanilovka complex (ca. 4200–3900 BCE), "represent the chiefly elite within the Sredni Stog culture," which is situated in the middle Dnieper–lower Don area, i.e., in the western part of the Pontic–Caspian steppes. On the basis of Figure 4.8 (adapted from Dergačev 2007: 147), which depicts the spread of the stone horse-head maces that are one of the key attributes of the steppe herders who formed the Suvorovo-Novodanilovka complex (Anthony 2007: 234–235), it is likely that their origins go back to the Khvalynsk culture of the northeastern part of the Pontic–Caspian steppes.

We may therefore view this graph as a possible route map of the initial part of the "Anatolian trek."

The final part of the "Anatolian trek," i.e., the arrival of the Anatolian branch into Anatolia through the Bosporus and/or the Dardanelles, sometime before or around 3100 to 3000 BCE, is more difficult to trace archaeologically. A major factor in this is, as Bachhuber (2013: 279) observes, that archaeologists of Bronze Age Anatolia have for decades "struggled with [the concept of] large-scale population movements," and are hesitant to interpret changes in material culture as a signal of population spread. A notable exception is James Mellaart, who, in a series of articles, argued for interpreting archaeological facts as signaling the incoming of speakers of Indo-European into Anatolia from the west in the third millennium BCE.[58] However, cf. also Yakar 1981, who discusses archaeological data from sites like Demircihöyük (founded ca. 3000 BCE; ca. 30 km northwest of Eskişehir), which shows that, at the beginning of the third millennium BCE, there was "contact between the Danube, the Balkans, and Anatolia" (1981: 96). His conclusions – that "[t]he unmistakable southeast European

[57] Anthony et al. 2022.

[58] Cf. Bachhuber 2013 for an overview.

traits in the EBI cultures [ca. 3000–2700 BCE, AK] of the western, central and north-central regions point to the presence in Anatolia of displaced elements from the Balkans and Danube" (1981: 106) – would be consistent with the scenario of the arrival of the Anatolian branch into Anatolia as advocated in Section 4.3.2. However, a full assessment of such archaeological arguments is something I will have to leave to the specialists.

4.6 Mapping the "Anatolian Trek" onto Evidence from Palaeogenomics

In the case of the palaeogenomic literature regarding the "Anatolian trek" question, it is likewise the case that full coverage goes beyond the scope of the present paper. Nevertheless, some observations are in order.

When it comes to the initial part of the "Anatolian trek" as proposed here, i.e. as proceeding from the northeastern part of the Pontic–Caspian steppes to the Balkans from ca. 4300 to 4200 BCE onward, it is interesting that Mathieson et al. (2018), in their paper on the genomic history of southeastern Europe, state that they have found steppe ancestry in two individuals from the Copper Age Balkans, namely one from Varna (northeast Bulgaria, on the Black Sea coast), ANI163, dated to 4711–4550 BCE, and one from Smyadovo (some 100 km west of Varna), I2181, dated to 4550–4450 BCE. Interestingly, according to the figure showing the ADMIXTURE analyses of the samples they used in their study (2018: 207), steppe ancestry is also found in a third Copper Age sample from the Balkans, ANI152 (albeit clearly less than in the other two), which belongs to the individual found in Varna grave 43, who "was buried with more gold than is known from all other Neolithic and Copper Age burials, combined" (ibid.: 197).

At first sight, the presence of steppe ancestry in these three individuals from the Balkans dating to ca. 4700 to 4450 BCE may be viewed as too early to fit my reconstruction of the "Anatolian trek" above, which commenced with the "Anatolian split" ca. 4300 to 4200 BCE. However, it must be taken into account that a linguistic split is the final outcome of a longer process of separation of a population group from their home region, which usually includes an initial number of migrants who can operate as scouts, and a period of some early groups that may have moved back and forth (including return migration); cf. Anthony 1990: 902–905. During this initial period, when there was still relatively frequent contact between the migrants and their home region, their language would still share the innovations of the language of the home region. Only when the group of migrant speakers is large enough that a majority of speakers no longer has direct contact with speakers from the home region, or when such contact has been lost altogether, and linguistic innovations are no longer shared, can we speak of a real linguistic split. The steppe ancestry of the three Balkan individuals dating to ca. 4700–4450 BCE may therefore be seen as marking the initial phase of population movements from the Proto-Indo-Anatolian home region into the Balkans, which did not result in a full linguistic split (the "Anatolian split") until several generations later. The fact that one of these individuals was found in the richest burial known from this period is consistent with Anthony's reconstruction that these migrants formed a chiefly elite.

With regard to the final part of the "Anatolian trek" I have proposed, i.e., proceeding from the Balkans into Anatolia, where the Anatolian branch must have arrived around 3100 to 3000 BCE, Mathieson et al. (2018: 201) note that "although [they] find sporadic steppe-related ancestry in Balkan Copper and Bronze Age individuals, this ancestry is rare until the late Bronze Age," and they therefore state that there is "no evidence" that the Anatolian branch "was spread into Asia Minor by the movements of steppe people through the Balkan Peninsula during the Copper Age at around 4000 BC." Indeed, apart from the three samples mentioned, none of the other Copper Age samples analyzed by Mathieson et al. (dating 4700 to 3500 BCE) show steppe ancestry: only in samples dating to the Bronze Age (from 3200 BCE onward) do we see some steppe ancestry, but these samples are too late to be part of the "Anatolian trek" as proposed above. I therefore agree with Mathieson et al. that their data show that the spread of the Anatolian languages through the Balkans cannot have been the result of a massive migration. However, since the archaeological and palaeogenomic traces of the individuals who moved from the steppes into the Balkans indicate that they formed a wealthy upper class, to my mind it cannot be excluded that their language was taken over as an elite language, in accordance with the "elite dominance model" of language spread.[59] In such a situation, it was not necessary for the speakers of this language to have been present in large numbers and thus to have had a great impact on the genetic profile of the population group that eventually took over their language. Moreover, with the Suvorovo-Novodanilovka complex lasting until ca. 3900 BCE (see Section 4.5), we still have a period of some 800 years (ca. thirty-two generations) to bridge before the entry of this language into Anatolia may have taken place. This seems time enough for an initially relatively small influx of steppe genes to eventually be fully diluted away from the later population group's genetic profile. I therefore agree with Mathieson et al. (2018: 201) that "it remains possible that Indo-European languages were spread through southeastern Europe into Anatolia without large-scale population movement or admixture."

This point is important to take into account when assessing ancient DNA samples from Anatolia. In a recent paper by Damgaard et al. (2018), genetic samples of twelve ancient humans from central Anatolia have been analyzed, "including 5 individuals from presumed Hittite-speaking settlements." They report that these samples "do not genetically distinguish Hittite and other Bronze Age Anatolians from an earlier Copper Age sample," and thus seem to show "Anatolian/Early European farmer ancestry, but not steppe ancestry." This is

[59] Cf. Matasović 2009: 514.

interpreted as a demonstration that "the Anatolian IE language branch, including Hittite, did not derive from a substantial steppe migration into Anatolia."

First, we need to discuss the five samples that Damgaard et al. describe as coming "from presumed Hittite-speaking settlements." From the supplementary materials to this article, we learn that these samples were taken from the Kaman-Kalehöyük site (Kırşehir province, in the southwestern part of the Kızıl Irmak basin). Three of these (MA2205, MA2206, MA2208–2209) stem from stratum IIIc, "Middle Bronze Age ('Assyrian Colony Period') (~2000–1750 BCE)." As we have seen in Section 3.2.1, at the beginning of the second millennium BCE, the area within the Kızıl Irmak bend, where Kaman-Kalehöyük is situated, was probably home to speakers of Hattic, a non-Indo-European language. It may not have been until the time of Anitta, king of Nēša (reign ca. 1740–1725 BCE), that the first larger groups of Hittite speakers entered this area. Moreover, the establishment of a Hittite-speaking court at Ḫattuša took place only a century after the "Assyrian Colony Period" had ended, namely around 1650 BCE. The three individuals from Kaman-Kalehöyük stratum IIIc were therefore probably not speakers of an Anatolian language, and it is even dubious whether they could have been in (genetic) contact with people who were: the Kızıl Irmak River might not only have been a geographic obstacle that for a long time prevented language spread but might have blocked gene flows as well during this period. The other two samples from Kaman-Kalehöyük (MA2200–2201, MA2203–2204) stem from stratum IIIb, "Middle to Late Bronze Age ('Old Hittite period') (~1750–1500 BCE)." These individuals could thus indeed stem from the period in which Hittite was first introduced to the region inside the Kızıl Irmak bend and established as the elite language there. This depends, however, on whether these individuals stem from the earlier or latter part of this period. All in all, it may be clear that these five samples do not need to belong to speakers of an Anatolian language, and I think we should therefore be careful in using them to assess the palaeogenomic side of the "Anatolian trek."

The same goes for the three samples analyzed by Damgaard et al. (2018) that stem from outside the Kızıl Irmak bend, namely those from the site of Ovaören (Nevşehir province, 20 km south of the Kızıl Irmak river). These samples (MA2210, MA2212, MA2213) are taken from individuals dating to the Early Bronze Age II, which Damgaard et al. date to "~2200 BCE" (2018: 2). However, Yakar (2011: 68), for example, dates the Early Bronze Age II in Anatolia to 2600 to 2500 BCE. With the presumed dating of the arrival of the Anatolian languages into Anatolia around 3100 BCE (cf. Section 4.1.1), we may wonder whether they would have been able to fully disperse into the central part of Anatolia already by 2500 BCE. It seems quite possible to me that the arrival of the Anatolian languages into the Ovaören area postdates the period from which the three sampled Early Bronze Age individuals stem. If so, these samples would likewise be irrelevant for assessing the palaeogenomic side of the Anatolian trek.

What appears more relevant, however, are three samples analyzed by Lazaridis et al. (2017) that stem from the West Anatolian site of Göndürlü Höyük (Harmanören, ca. 150 km north of Antalya) and date to 2558 to 2295 BCE (I2495), 2836 to 2472 BCE (I2499), and 2500 to 1800 BCE (I2683), respectively (suppl. information, p. 24–25). The individuals from whom these samples are taken did live in a place and time where we may assume that speakers of one or more Anatolian languages were present. According to Lazaridis et al., these individuals genetically seem to be "a mixture of Neolithic Anatolians, Caucasus hunter-gatherers, and Levantine Neolithic" (suppl. information, p. 40), and thus show no steppe ancestry.[60] They therefore conclude that if the speakers of (pre-)Proto-Anatolian did come from the steppes, a "massive dilution of their steppe ancestry in the ensuing two millennia would be needed to account for its disappearance in the Bronze Age Anatolian sample" (suppl. information, p. 49). This is consistent with the rarity of steppe ancestry in the Copper Age samples from the Balkans (until 3500 BCE) as reported by Mathieson et al. 2018, and which was interpreted above as showcasing that the small influx of steppe genes onto the Balkans during the latter part of the fifth millennium BCE was, during the fourth millennium BCE, diluted away from the genetic profile of this population group, even though the language of these steppe herders, who formed an upper class in this area in the fifth millennium BCE, had been taken over as an elite language. We may thus assume that when the Anatolian languages spread into Anatolia at the end of the fourth millennium BCE, this was probably the result of a movement of speakers who no longer contained any traceable steppe ancestry.

Nevertheless, the absence of steppe ancestry in Anatolian Bronze Age samples has led some scholars to consider the possibility that the Anatolian branch was not originally spoken by a steppe population at all. Instead, the presence of Caucasian Hunter Gatherer (CHG) ancestry in these samples has led Damgaard et al. (2018: 8), for instance, to state that this would fit a "scenario in which the introduction of the Anatolian IE languages into Anatolia was coupled with the CHG-derived admixture before 3700 BCE." In the same vein, Kristiansen et al. (2018: 3) suggest that, possibly, "multiple groups moved into Anatolia from the Caucasus during the late fourth and third millennium BCE, including groups of [. . .] early IE Anatolian speakers."[61] Both Damgaard et al. and Kristiansen et al. do not make explicit, however, what their view on the location of the Proto-Indo-Anatolian homeland is, and how this relates to the

[60] Confusingly, in Mathieson et al. 2018: 207, these three samples are depicted as showing a considerable component of "Yamnaya from Samara" ancestry, namely some 30%. However, since in this depiction the admixture is constrained to show only four different components, namely Anatolian Neolithic, Yamnaya from Samara, EHG, and WHG, we may conclude that the ca. 32% CHG ancestry of these samples (as reported by Lazaridis et al. 2017) is forced here into the category of "Yamnaya of Samara" = steppe ancestry, even though they do not contain the necessary EHG component.

[61] Addendum: see now also Laziridis et al. 2022.

Classical Proto-Indo-European homeland in the steppes. More explicit in this regard are Wang et al. (2019), who suggest the possibility of a Proto-Indo-Anatolian homeland "south of the Caucasus" (2019: 10). The spread of the Anatolian languages into Anatolia would thus be genetically traceable by the spread of CHG ancestry into Anatolia. According to Wang et al., not only Anatolian could have this South Caucasian origin; they regard it "[g]eographically conceivable" that Armenian, Greek, and possibly even Indo-Iranian also derive from this homeland. The Indo-European language(s) that must have been spoken by the bearers of the Yamnaya culture on the Pontic–Caspian steppes, and which spread from there into Europe and Central Asia, would thus have arrived in the steppes as a result of population movements that are traceable as a "subtle gene-flow" of CHG ancestry from south to north through the Caucasus (ibid.). From a linguistic point of view, this scenario runs into insurmountable problems. First, it does not account for the fact that the reconstructed Proto-Indo-Anatolian lexicon points to a pastoralist lifestyle by its speakers, which means that they must have lived in a steppe region. Secondly, it does not account for the linguistic connection of Proto-Indo-Anatolian with the Uralic language family, which was spoken to the northeast of the Pontic–Caspian steppes. Third, it does not account for all the indications that the Anatolian branch entered Anatolia from the west, namely: (a) the geographic clustering of the Anatolian languages in the west of Anatolia; (b) the distribution of the Anatolian languages surrounding the course of the Kızıl Irmak river on its west bank, whereas on its east bank, a non-Indo-European language is spoken; (c) the historical eastward drift of the Anatolian languages; and (d) the parallels from history. Moreover, the scenario of Wang et al. fully ignores the fact that in the Caucasus, three distinct, non-Indo-European language families are spoken – Kartvelian, Northeast Caucasian, and Northwest Caucasian – which are unrelated to any other known language family,[62] and for which there is no indication whatsoever that they were not present in the Caucasus for at least several millennia. It is disappointing, therefore, that Wang et al. (2019) present a scenario involving prehistoric language spread through the Caucasus mountain range without even mentioning these indigenous Caucasian language families.[63]

[62] However, Northeast and Northwest Caucasian are sometimes regarded to be related to each other.

[63] It seems more likely to me that CHG ancestry may be linked to the speakers of Hurrian. In the historical records from the third and second millennium BCE, the Hurrian language shows a westward spread from northern Iraq and northeast Syria into central Anatolia (Wegner 2000: 15). Moreover, Hurrian may be related to the Northeast Caucasian language family (Wegner 2000: 29–30). If the east-to-west spread of Hurrian in the third and second millennium BCE is the continuation of earlier movements, we may assume that Hurrian originated from the Caucasus and moved into eastern Anatolia and northern Mesopotamia in the fourth and third millennium BCE, which may thus be genetically traceable in the spread of CHG ancestry.

4.7 Conclusions

We can conclude that from a comparative linguistic point of view, the Indo-European Anatolian language branch ended up in Anatolia in the following way. The Anatolian branch derives from a Proto-Indo-Anatolian ancestor language that was spoken in the northeastern part of the Pontic–Caspian steppes in the fifth millennium BCE, probably by bearers of the Khvalynsk culture. Sometime around ca. 4300 to 4200 BCE, a group of speakers of Proto-Indo-Anatolian lost contact with the language community in the Proto-Indo-Anatolian homeland because they had moved away to different regions (the "Anatolian split"). From that moment onward, the language of these speakers underwent specific innovations that, in the end, transformed it into Proto-Anatolian. During this period, this language spread to new regions (the "Anatolian trek"), first from the steppes into the Balkan Peninsula, after which it entered Anatolia from the west, through the Bosporus and/or the Dardanelles, before or in the thirty-first to thirtieth century BCE. The initial part of this "trek," from the steppes to the Balkans, is traceable in data from both archaeology and palaeogenomics. We find evidence for steppe herders, coming from the Khvalynsk area in the latter part of the fifth millennium BCE, who form a "chiefly elite" within the Suvorovo-Novodanilovka complex in the Balkans (ca. 4200 to 3900 BCE). Genetically, the three Copper Age individuals from the Balkan with steppe ancestry (dating to ca. 4700 to 4450 BCE) may be viewed as representing the very first waves of Proto-Indo-Anatolian-speaking people in this area before all contact with the PIA home region had been lost. However, the final part of this "trek," from the Balkans into Anatolia, cannot be traced in data from these fields thus far. In the case of archaeology, this may be due to the fact that for decades, archaeologists of Copper Age and Bronze Age Anatolia have been hesitant to interpret changes in material culture as signaling population movements, a situation that will hopefully change in the years to come. In the case of palaeogenomics, the absence of any steppe ancestry in the DNA of Bronze Age Anatolian samples may be explained by the possibility that pre-Proto-Anatolian entered the Balkans as a language of relatively few steppe immigrants who nevertheless formed an elite in Balkan society. If, during the last quarter of the fifth millennium BCE, their language was taken over by the local population (according to the "elite dominance model" of language spread), it is possible that in the millennium that followed, this language lived on, while the genetic profile of these steppe individuals was diluted away. When, later on, (pre-)Proto-Anatolian moved on and entered Anatolia, it would have been brought there by speakers whose genetic ancestry no longer contained any traceable steppe component. This scenario may be confirmed in the future when a more fine-grained picture of the palaeogenomic interactions between the Balkans and Anatolia is achieved by analyzing further samples from chronologically more multi-layered sites from these regions.

Due to the absence of steppe ancestry in Bronze Age Anatolian aDNA in some recent palaeogenomic papers, an alternative scenario for explaining the presence of the Anatolian languages in Anatolia has been suggested – namely one that sees the Anatolian branch as coming from the Caucasus, either because the "Anatolian trek" would have gone through the Caucasus, or because the Proto-Indo-Anatolian homeland would have been located in or near the Caucasus. This scenario must be rejected, however: it is at present difficult to see how it could be reconciled with the evidence from comparative linguistics.

References

Adiego, I. J. 2007. *The Carian language*. Leiden: Brill.

Allentoft, M. E., et al. 2015. Population genomics of Bronze Age Eurasia. *Nature* 522: 167–172.

Anthony, D. W. 1990. Migration in archaeology: The baby and the bathwater. *American Anthropologist* 92(4): 895–914.

Anthony, D.W. 2007. *The horse, the wheel, and language: How Bronze-Age riders from the Eurasian steppes shaped the modern world*. Princeton (NJ): Princeton University Press.

2013. Two IE phylogenies, three PIE migrations, and four kinds of steppe pastoralism. *Journal of Language Relationship (Вопросы языкового родства)* 9: 1–21.

Anthony, D. W., et al. 2022. The Eneolithic cemetery at Khvalynsk on the Volga River. *Prähistorische Zeitschrift* 97: 22–67.

Bachhuber, C., 2013. James Mellaart and the Luwians: A culture-(pre)history. In: A. Mouton, I. Rutherford, & I. Yakubovich (ed.), *Luwian identities. Culture, languages and religion between Anatolia and the Aegean*, 279–304. Leiden: Brill.

Beekes, R. S. P. 2003. *The origin of the Etruscans*. Amsterdam: KNAW.

Bonechi, M. 1990. Aleppo in età arcaica; a proposito di un'opera recente. *Studi Epigrafici e Linguistici sul Vicino Oriente Antico* 7: 15–37.

Bouckaert, R., et al. 2012. Mapping the origins and expansions of the Indo-European language family. *Science* 337: 957–960.

Brixhe, C. 1988. La langue des inscriptions épichoriques de Pisidie. In Y. L. Arbeitman (ed.), *A linguistic happening in memory of Ben Schwartz*, 131–155. Louvain-la-Neuve: Peeters.

2008. Phrygian. In R. D. Woodard (ed.), *The ancient languages of Asia Minor*, 69–80. Cambridge: Cambridge University Press.

Bryce, T. 2009. *The Routledge handbook of the peoples and places of ancient Western Asia*. London: Routledge.

Carpelan, C., & A. Parpola. 2001. Emergence, contacts and dispersal of Proto-Indo-European, Proto-Uralic and Proto-Aryan in archaeological perspective. In: Christian Carpelan, Asko Parpola, & Petteri Koskikallio (ed.), *Early contacts between Uralic and Indo-European: Linguistic and archaeological considerations*, 55–150. Helsinki: Suomalais-Ugrilainen Seura.

Carruba, O. 1970. *Das Palaische. Texte, Grammatik, Lexikon* (Studien zu den Boğazköy-Texten 10). Wiesbaden: Otto Harrassowitz.

Collinder, B. 1934. *Indo-uralisches Sprachgut: die Urverwandtschaft zwischen der indoeuropäischen und der uralischen (finnischugrisch-samojedischen) Sprachfamilie*. Uppsala: A.–B. Lundequistska.

1954. Zur indo-uralischen Frage. *Språkvetenskapliga Sällskapets i Uppsala Förhandlingar Jan. 1952–Dec. 1954*, 79–91.

Čop, B., 1975. *Die indogermanische Deklination im Lichte der indouralischen vergleichenden Grammatik*. Ljubljana: SAZU.

Damgaard, P. de B., et al. 2018. The first horse herders and the impact of early Bronze Age steppe expansions into Asia. *Science* 360: eaar7711.

Darbyshire, G., S. Mitchell, & L. Vardar. 2000. The Galatian settlement in Asia Minor. *Anatolian Studies* 50: 75–97.

Dergačev, V. A. 2007. *O skipetrax, o lošadjax, o vojne: etjudy v zaščity migracionnoj koncepcii M. Gimbutas*. St. Petersburg.

Diakonoff, I. M. 1984. *The pre-history of the Armenian people*. Delmar: Caravan.

Eichner, H. 1973. Die Etymologie von heth. *mehur, Münchener Studien zur Sprachwissenschaft* 31: 53–107.

Gimbutas, M. 1973. The beginning of the Bronze Age in Europe and the Indo-Europeans 3500–2500 B.C. *Journal of Indo-European Studies* 1: 163–214.

Gray, R. D., & Q. D. Atkinson. 2003. Language-tree divergence times support the Anatolian theory of Indo-European origin. *Nature* 426: 435–439.

Gusmani, R. 1964–1986. *Lydisches Wörterbuch. Mit grammatischer Skizze und Inschriftensammlung*. Heidelberg: Winter (1964). With Ergänzungsband Lfg. 1 (1980), Lfg. 2 (1982), Lfg. 3 (1986).

1989/1990. Lo stato delle ricerche sul milíaco. *Incontri linguistici* 13: 69–78.

Haak, W., et al. 2015. Massive migration from the steppe was a source for Indo-European languages in Europe. *Nature* 522: 207–211.

Hoffner, H. A. Jr., & H. C. Melchert. 2008. *A grammar of the Hittite language*. Winona Lake (Ind.): Eisenbrauns.

Janhunen, J. 2009. Proto-Uralic: What, where and when?. In: J. Ylikoski (ed.), *The quasquicentennial of the Finno-Ugrian Society*, 57–78. Helsinki: Tiedekirja.

Jones, E. R., et al. 2015. Upper Palaeolithic genomes reveal deep roots of modern Eurasians. *Nature Communications* 6: 8912.

Kloekhorst, A. 2006. Initial laryngeals in Anatolian. *Historische Sprachforschung* 119: 77–108.

2008a. *Etymological dictionary of the Hittite inherited lexicon* (Leiden Indo-European Etymological Dictionary Series 5). Leiden: Brill.

2008b. Some Indo-Uralic aspects of Hittite. *Journal of Indo-European Studies* 36: 88–95.

2012. The language of Troy. In: J. Kelder, G. Uslu, & Ö.F. Şerifoğlu (ed.), *Troy. City, Homer, Turkey*, 46–50. Amsterdam: Allard Pierson Museum.

2013. Ликийский язык [The Lycian language]. In: Y. B. Koryakov & A. A. Kibrik (ed.), *Языки мира: реликтовые индоевропейские языки Передней и Центральной Азии* [Languages of the World: Relict Indo-European languages of Western and Central Asia], 131–154. Moscow.

2014. *Accent in Hittite: A study in plene spelling, consonant gradation, clitics, and metrics* (Studien zu den Boğazköy-Texten 56). Wiesbaden: Harrassowitz.

2018. Anatolian evidence suggests that the Indo-European laryngeals $*h_2$ and $*h_3$ were uvular stops. *Indo-European Linguistics* 6: 69–94.

2018. The origin of the Hittite *ḫi*-conjugation. In: L. van Beek et al., *Farnah. Indo-Iranian and Indo-European Studies in*

Honor of Sasha Lubotsky, 89–106. Ann Arbor: Beech Stave Press.

2019. *Kanišite Hittite: The earliest attested record of Indo-European* (Handbuch der Orientalistik 1.132). Leiden: Brill.

2022a. Anatolian. In: T. Olander (ed.), *The Indo-European Language Family: A Phylogenetic Perspective*, 63–82. Cambridge: Cambridge University Press.

2022b. Luwians, Lydians, Etruscans, and Troy: the linguistic landscape of northwestern Anatolia in the pre-classical period. In: I. Hajnal et al. (edd.), *The political geography of western Anatolia in the Late Bronze Age. Proceedings of the EAA Conference, Bern, 7 September 2019*, 201–227. Budapest: Archaeolingua.

Kloekhorst, A., & T. C. Pronk. 2019. Introduction: Reconstructing Proto-Indo-Anatolian and Proto-Indo-Uralic. In: A. Kloekhorst & T. C. Pronk (ed.), *The precursors of Proto-Indo-European: The Indo-Anatolian and Indo-Uralic hypotheses* (Leiden Studies in Indo-European 21), 1–14. Leiden: Brill.

Kortlandt, F. 1989. Eight Indo-Uralic Verbs? *Münchener Studien zur Sprachwissenschaft* 50: 79–85.

2002. The Indo-Uralic verb. In: R. Blokland & C. Hasselblatt (ed.), *Finno-Ugrians and Indo-Europeans: Linguistic and literary contacts* (Studia Fenno-Ugrica Groningana 2), 217–227. Maastricht: Shaker.

Kristiansen, K. et al. 2018. Archaeological supplement A to Damgaard et al. 2018: Archaeology of the Caucasus, Anatolia, Central and South Asia 4000–1500 BCE.

Kroonen, G., G. Barjamovic, & M. Peyrot. 2018. Linguistic supplement to Damgaard et al. 2018: Early Indo-European languages, Anatolian, Tocharian and Indo-Iranian.

Larsen, M. T. 2015. *Ancient Kanesh. A merchant colony in Bronze Age Anatolia*. Cambridge: Cambridge University Press.

Lazaridis, I., et al. 2016. Genomic insights into the origin of farming in the ancient Near East. *Nature* 536: 419–424.

Laziridis, I., et al. 2017. Genetic origins of the Minoans and Mycenaeans. *Nature* 548: 214–218.

Lazaridis, I., et al. 2022. The genetic history of the Southern Arc: A bridge between West Asia and Europe. *Science* 377.

Lopuhaä, M. 2019. The Anatolian "ergative." In: A. Kloekhorst & T. C. Pronk (ed.), *The precursors of Proto-Indo-European: The Indo-Anatolian and Indo-Uralic hypotheses* (Leiden Studies in Indo-European 21), 131–150. Leiden: Brill.

Luraghi, S. 2017. The syntax of Anatolian: The simple sentence. In: J. Klein et al. (ed.), *Handbook of comparative and historical Indo-European linguistics* (Handbücher zur Sprach- und Kommunikationswissenschaft 41.1), 274–291. Berlin: De Gruyter Mouton.

Mallory, J. P. 1989. *In search of the Indo-Europeans: Languages, archaeology and myth*. London: Thames & Hudson.

Mallory, J. P., & D. Q. Adams (ed.). 1997. *Encyclopedia of Indo-European culture*, London: Fotzroy Dearborn.

Matasović, R. 2009. Historical evolution of the world's languages. In: V. Muhvic-Dimanovski & L. Socanac (ed.), *Linguistics* (Encyclopedia of Life Support Systems), 511–522.

Mathieson, I., et al. 2018. The genomic history of southeastern Europe. *Nature* 555: 197–203.

Melchert, H. C. 2003a. The dialectal position of Lydian and Lycian within Anatolian. In: Mauro Giorgieri, Mirjo Salvini, Marie-Claude Tremouille, & Pietro Vannicelli (ed.), *Licia e Lidia prima dell'ellenizzazione. Atti del Convegno internazionale, Roma, 11–12 ottobre 1999*, 265–272. Rome: Consiglio Nazionale delle Ricerche.

2003. Language. In: H. C. Melchert (ed.), *The Luwians* (Handbook of Oriental Studies, Section One, Near and Middle East Volume 68), 170–210. Leiden. Brill.

2003. Prehistory. In: H. C. Melchert (ed.), *The Luwians* (Handbook of Oriental Studies, Section One, Near and Middle East Volume 68), 8–26. Leiden: Brill.

2008. Lycian. In: R. D. Woodard (ed.), *The ancient languages of Asia Minor*, 46–55. Cambridge: Cambridge University Press.

2011. The PIE verb for "to pour" and medial *h_3 in Anatolian. In: S. Jamison et al. (ed.), *Proceedings of the 22nd UCLA Indo-European Conference*, 127–132. Bremen: Hempen.

2020. Hittite Historical Phonology after 100 Years (and after 20 years). In: R.I. Kim et al. (edd.), *Hrozný and Hittite: The First Hundred Years. Proceedings of the International Conference Held at Charles University, Prague, 11–14 November 2015*, 258–276. Leiden-Boston: Brill.

Forthcoming. The position of Anatolian. In: M. Weiss & A. Garrett (eds.), *Handbook of Indo-European Studies*. Oxford: Oxford University Press.

Morpurgo Davies, A. 1982/83. Dentals, rhotacism and verbal endings in the Luwian languages. *Zeitschrift für Vergleichende Sprachwissenschaft* 96: 245–270.

Norbruis, S. 2021. Indo-European *Origins of Anatolian Morphology and Semantics. Innovations and Archaisms in Hittite, Luwian and Lycian*. Amsterdam: LOT.

Oettinger, N. 2017. The morphology of Anatolian. In: J. Klein et al. (ed.), *Handbook of comparative and historical Indo-European linguistics* (Handbücher zur Sprach- und Kommunikationswissenschaft 41.1), 256–273. Berlin: De Gruyter Mouton.

Olander, T. 2017. Drinking beer, smoking tobacco and reconstructing prehistory. In: B. S. S. Hansen et al. (ed.), *Usque ad Radices. Indo-European studies in honour of Birgit Anette Olsen*, 605–618. Copenhagen: Musum Tusculanum.

Orozco, S. P. 2007. La lengua Sidética, Ensayo de síntesis. *Kadmos* 46: 125–142.

Payne, A. 2010. *Hieroglyphic Luwian. An introduction with original texts*. 2nd rev. ed. Wiesbaden: Harrassowitz.

Pedersen, H. 1933. Zur Frage nach der Urverwandtschaft des Indoeuropäischen mit dem Ugrofinnischen. *Liber Semisaecularis Societatis Fenno-Ugricae*, 308–325. Helsinki: Suomalais-Ugrilainen Seura.

Pereltsvaig, A., & M. W. Lewis. 2015. *The Indo-European controversy. Facts and fallacies in historical linguistics*. Cambridge: Cambridge University Press.

Peyrot, M. 2019. Indo-Uralic, Indo-Anatolian, Indo-Tocharian. In: A. Kloekhorst & T. C. Pronk (ed.), *The precursors of Proto-Indo-European: The Indo-Anatolian and Indo-Uralic hypotheses*. (= Leiden Studies in Indo-European 21), 186–202. Leiden: Brill.

Renfrew, C. 1987. *Archaeology and language. The puzzle of Indo-European origins*. London: Pimlico.

2000. 10,000 or 5000 years ago? Questions of time depth. In: C. Renfrew, A. McMahon, & L. Trask (ed.), *Time depth in historical linguistics*, 413–439. Cambridge: McDonald Institute for Archaeological Research.

2003. Time depth, convergence theory, and innovation in Proto-Indo-European: "Old Europe" as a PIE linguistic area. In: A. Bammesberger & T. Venneman (ed.), *Languages in prehistoric Europe*, 17–48. Heidelberg: Winter.

Rieken, E. 2016. Zum luwischen Ursprung von LÚta/uḫ(uk)kanti: "Kronprinz". In: H. Marquardt, S. Reichmuth, & J. V. García Trabazo (ed.), *Anatolica et Indogermanica. Studia linguistica in honorem Johannis Tischler septuagenarii dedicata* (Innsbrucker Beiträge zur Sprachwissenschaft, Band 155), 267–277. Innsbruck: Institut für Sprachen und Literaturen der Universität Innsbruck.

2017. The dialectology of Anatolian. In: J. Klein et al. (ed.), *Handbook of comparative and historical Indo-European linguistics* (Handbücher zur Sprach- und Kommunikationswissenschaft 41.1), 298–308. Berlin: De Gruyter Mouton.

Sammallahti, P. 1988. Historical phonology of the Uralic languages with special reference to Samoyed, Ugric and Permic. In: D. Sinor (ed.), *The Uralic languages: Description, history and foreign contacts*, 478–554. Leiden: Brill.

Singer, I. 1981. Hittites and Hattians in Anatolia at the beginning of the second millennium B.C. *Journal of Indo-European Studies* 9: 119–134.

Svyatko, S. V., et al. 2017. Stable isotope palaeodietary analysis of the Early Bronze Age Afanasyevo Culture in the Altai Mountains, Southern Siberia. *Journal of Archaeological Science: Reports* 14: 65–75.

Wang, C.-C., et al. 2019. Ancient human genome-wide data from a 3000-year interval in the Caucasus corresponds with eco-geographic regions. *Nature Communications* 10: 590.

Wegner, I. 2000. *Einführung in die hurritische Sprache*. Wiesbaden: Harrassowitz.

Yakar, J. 1981. The Indo-Europeans and their impact on Anatolian cultural development. *Journal of Indo-European Studies* 9: 94–112.

2011. Anatolian chronology and terminology. In: S. R. Steadman & G. McMahon (ed.), *The Oxford handbook of ancient Anatolia 10,000–323 B.C.E.*, 56–93. Oxford: Oxford University Press.

Part II Migratory Processes and Linguistic Dispersals between Yamnaya and the Corded Ware

5 THE CORDED WARE COMPLEX IN EUROPE IN LIGHT OF CURRENT ARCHAEOGENETIC AND ENVIRONMENTAL EVIDENCE

WOLFGANG HAAK, MARTIN FURHOLT, MARTIN SIKORA, ADAM BEN ROHRLACH, LUKA PAPAC, KARL-GÖRAN SJÖGREN, VOLKER HEYD, MORTEN FISCHER MORTENSEN, ANNE BRIGITTE NIELSEN, JOHANNES MÜLLER, INGO FEESER, GUUS KROONEN, AND KRISTIAN KRISTIANSEN

5.1 Introduction

Corded Ware is one of the main archaeological phenomena of the third millennium before the common era (BCE), with a wide geographic spread across much of central and northeastern Europe, from Denmark, the Rhineland, and Switzerland in the west to the Baltic and Western Russia in the east, and broadly restricted to the temperate, continental zones north of the Alps, the Carpathians, and the steppe/forest steppe border to the east (Glob 1944; Strahm and Buchvaldek 1991; Furholt 2014).

The Corded Ware complex is named after the characteristic cord imprints on its pottery, which is found as part of a relatively universal set of grave goods, and now commonly includes sub-units that were traditionally named Single Grave, Protruding Foot Beaker, Battle Axe, Boat Axe, and Fatyanovo/Balanovo culture. The archaeological unit is known chiefly from burials, mostly in single form (thus it is also termed "Single Grave culture" in Denmark and North Germany), while multiple burials also exist, and in predominantly sex-specific west-east or east-west orientation, with females on their left side and males on their right side in flexed position, both facing south (Figure 5.1) (Fischer 1958; Wentink 2020). The burial architecture varies from simple pits to wooden or stone cist construction, with or without burial mounds. In most areas with Corded Ware burials, settlement sites are largely unknown, with the exceptions of coastal areas in the Baltic and the Netherlands, some domestic sites in the Central European Mountain Range (Müller et al. 2009), lakeside dwellings in Switzerland (Furholt 2019), and, based on recent reports, the Mittelelbe-Saale region in Central Germany (Meller et al. 2019).

Given the relatively universal burial types and grave-good assemblages across a large geographic area, early scholars extrapolated the archaeological unit, which essentially represented a temporal expression of funerary rites, to a dogmatic belief in the concept of a culture (Müller 1898; Kossinna 1910; Glob 1944; Struve 1955) that was thought to represent a distinct group of people or "folk" who also spoke a common language (see e.g. Kossinna 1911 and his dogmatic concept of *settlement archaeology*). However, while this concept, which was largely misused as part of Nazi ideology in German archaeology, was soon abandoned after WWII (Veit 1989), it remained difficult to characterize and contextualize the Corded Ware horizon in the light of the archaeological evidence from the preceding Middle and Late Eneolithic and Neolithic periods (which varies according to local chronologies). As a consequence, the emergence of the Corded Ware continued to be the subject of ongoing scholarly debate, with some views that saw it as a symbolic or cultural "package" embedded in autochthonous traditions (Burgess and Shennan 1976; Strahm 2002; Furholt 2014); others supported the view that the Corded Ware represented a horizon of foreign elements that could only be explained by migration from regions further east (Kristiansen 1989; Harrison and Heyd 2007). The latter view was largely popularized by Marija Gimbutas's *kurgan hypothesis* in the 1960s and 1970s (Gimbutas 1979), which saw analogies to the large-scale burial architecture and prehistoric economies as found in the eastern European steppes. The hypothesis additionally built on the comparative linguistic reconstruction of an Indo-European protoculture, on the basis of which a population movement from the same area had been independently inferred in the late nineteenth century (Schrader 1883). This so-called Indo-European "homeland" on the North Pontic steppe was defended against alternative origins in Anatolia (Renfrew 1987) and the Caucasus (Gamkrelidze & Ivanov 1995) by Mallory (1989) and later updated by David Anthony (2007), who was able to draw on a better and more extended data set (Mallory 1989; Anthony 2007). The need to postulate an immigration wave from Eastern Europe was categorically rejected, however, by Alexander Häusler (Häusler 1996). In fact, the "steppe hypothesis" was originally challenged, in the early nineteenth century, by a similarly autochthonist view, according to which Indo-European developed as a local linguistic feature native to a Corded Ware ethnocultural unity (Kossinna 1911). Likewise, the link between the Corded Ware archaeological horizon and western Eurasian steppes was challenged by antimigrationist trends in the archaeological research of the 1960s to the early 2000s, which sought to find autochthonous roots for the Corded Ware in Europe (e.g., Lanting, Mook, & van der Waals 1973; Müller 2001; Hübner 2005; Furholt 2014). In contrast to the migration-based hypothesis,

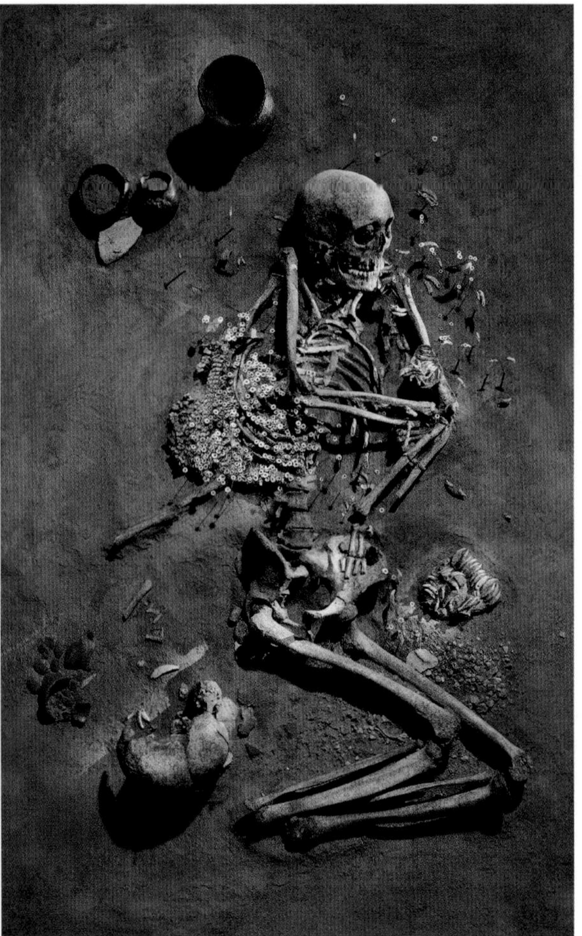

FIGURE 5.1. Double inhumation of an adult female and young boy with rich grave goods from the Late Neolithic Corded Ware at Karsdorf, Saxony-Anhalt, Germany. (Copyright: Juraj Lipták, Landesamt für Denkmalpflege und Archäologie Sachsen-Anhalt, Germany.)

alternative models were also explored; these integrated mobility patterns into a network concept in which different regions within the Corded Ware distribution had contributed to the formation of the Corded Ware phenomenon with different trajectories (Siemen 1997).

One issue that has to be taken into account is that Corded Ware, partly due to its wide area of distribution, is used to denote many different cultural traits, and many different forms of communities are also possibly subsumed under this one unified term (Furholt 2014). Depending on whether one prefers to emphasize the new burial rituals or the namesake Corded Ware pottery, different regions would stand out as more clearly impacted by Corded Ware. Therefore, it has been proposed, as a heuristic tool, to define the different variants of Corded Ware that predominate in different regions (Furholt 2019). Corded Ware Variant 1 (i.e., Jutland, Netherlands, Central and Southern Germany, Bohemia, Moravia, Lesser Poland, Baltic states), which is mostly characterized by the novel, gendered Single Grave burial ritual, is found in some regions where there are usually very few settlement sites with Corded Ware pottery. In other regions, such as Switzerland, the coastal Netherlands, and along the Baltic coast and Finland (Variants 2 and 3), settlement assemblages with Corded Ware pottery are abundant, but in turn the new burial rituals are not or only scarcely present.

On the basis of this long-standing debate, it is not surprising to note that the results of the genomic era (see below), thanks to methodological breakthroughs in recent years, provided a new quality of data for the archaeologists, anthropologists, and geneticists who had tackled these questions for many decades. It is precisely the large existing body of work and long history of research that is both an opportunity in the form of detailed factual knowledge and a burden in the form of ideological baggage (Heyd 2017), with political sensitivities on the one hand, but certainly a large number of preconceived ideas on the other, all of which need to be evaluated in the light of new genetic evidence (Bourgeois and Kroon 2017; Kristiansen et al. 2017; Furholt 2018; Frieman and Hofmann 2019).

Here, we present the first synthesis of the available genomic data from Corded Ware and associated individuals from a number of publications that have investigated individual aspects or regions, or in which Corded Ware had formed part of a large transect through time studies, but was never considered in a synthetic fashion. In addition, we present associated data from other lines of evidence, such as anthropological, isotope, and environmental studies.

5.2 Early Genetic Studies

The first ancient human genetic data from Corded Ware individuals became available in the form of short sequences of the hypervariable region of the mitochondrial DNA as part of an intrasite kinship and isotope study of the site Eulau, Germany (Haak et al. 2008). With the main emphasis on kinship, mobility, and palaeopathologies, and being based on a small number of individuals with very few ancient DNA data points to compare, insights into the population genetic structure were naturally limited. The mtDNA data was put into perspective five years later, when Brandt and colleagues presented a large-scale, mitochondrial, transect through time study from the Early Neolithic to the Early Bronze Age in Central Europe (Brandt et al. 2013, 2015). Here, the Corded Ware individuals (n=44) hinted at a second pulse of new lineages (I, T1, U2, U4) that had entered the region with the beginning of the Corded Ware horizon in Central Europe, roughly two thousand years after an almost complete replacement of the Mesolithic mtDNA diversity (U2, U5b, U5a, U8) by mtDNA lineages that were ascribed to early Neolithic farmers (e.g., T2, J, H, HV, V, K, U3, N1a, W, and X). The Corded Ware mtDNA and EBA Únětice groups (2200–1800 cal BCE) from Central Europe shared a common mtDNA diversity profile (enriched by Neolithic mtDNA lineages), which was temporally interspersed with individuals linked with the Bell Beaker phenomenon (2500–2200 cal BCE), who coexisted with the late Corded Ware individuals for roughly three hundred years and who predominantly carried haplogroup H (Brandt et al. 2015).

When compared with modern-day Europeans, it could also be shown that Eastern Europeans showed greater affinities with Corded Ware individuals, while south/southwestern Europeans more closely resembled Bell Beaker individuals. On the basis of this observation – and a fraction of mtDNA lineages among Corded Ware individuals that resembled the Mesolithic substratum of Eastern Europe, such as U2, U4, U5a – it was concluded that the Corded Ware groups represented an expansion from Eastern Europe that assimilated mtDNA variability from a distant geographic region during the Late Neolithic (Brandt et al. 2015; Juras et al. 2018).

5.3 Recent Genomic Studies

The first genome-wide data of Corded Ware-associated individuals was published in 2015 (Allentoft et al. 2015; Haak et al. 2015), with the surprising result that these individuals presented a marked shift in the genetic ancestry profile. Despite being sampled from the same geographic regions, individuals from the fifth and fourth millennia BCE shared the ancestry profile of the preceding European Early Neolithic farmers, while Corded Ware individuals from the third millennium BC in Central Europe revealed genetic affinities to individuals of Yamnaya steppe pastoralist communities. A follow-up study by Jones et al. 2015 also revealed that this – newly coined – "steppe ancestry" found in Yamnaya- and Corded Ware-associated individuals was formed in the eastern European steppe zones as a mixture of Eastern Hunter-Gatherer-like (EHG) ancestry, on one hand, and ancestry associated with Caucasus Hunter-Gatherers (CHG) on the other (Jones et al. 2015). Unlike the Yamnaya individuals from the Russian steppes in the Samara region and Kalmykia, the Corded Ware-associated individuals from Central Europe and the Baltic also carried a genetic component that was otherwise attributed to European Neolithic farmers, which pointed to the fact that gene flow into the Corded Ware groups must have occurred broadly around the appearance of the Corded Ware horizon in Central Europe or via earlier encounters in the eastern European contact zones at the easternmost extent of the farming world at the time.

To date, genome-wide data is available from ca. 80 individuals who are broadly associated with the Corded Ware, including individuals from the Scandinavian Battle Axe or Single Grave units or those that were originally assigned to non-Corded Ware units but do show a genetic profile and radiocarbon date characteristic of the Corded Ware range (Table 5.1. Excel spreadsheet, see www.cambridge.org/9781009261746/Appendix 1). Their geographic spread ranges from the Baltic region in northeastern Europe to Switzerland in the southwesternmost corner of the Corded Ware distribution (Figure 5.2). A recent preprint also offers insight into the genetic makeup of the associated Fatyanavo group in today's Western Russia (Saag et al. 2021, data not included here). However, it becomes clear that the

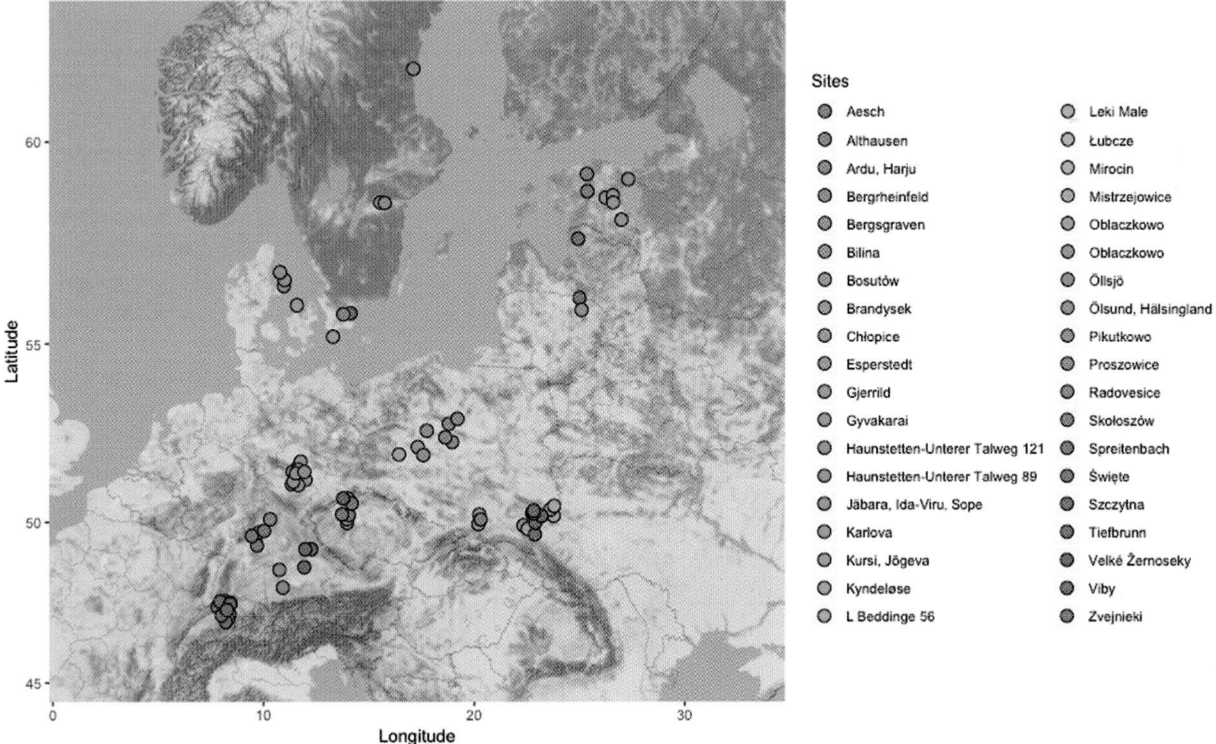

FIGURE 5.2. Geographic map of Corded Ware-associated individuals studied to date (random geographic jitter was used to prevent complete overlap of individuals per site). Individuals who were tested positive for *Y. pestis* were found at the sites Gyvakarai 1, Kunila 2, and Sope.

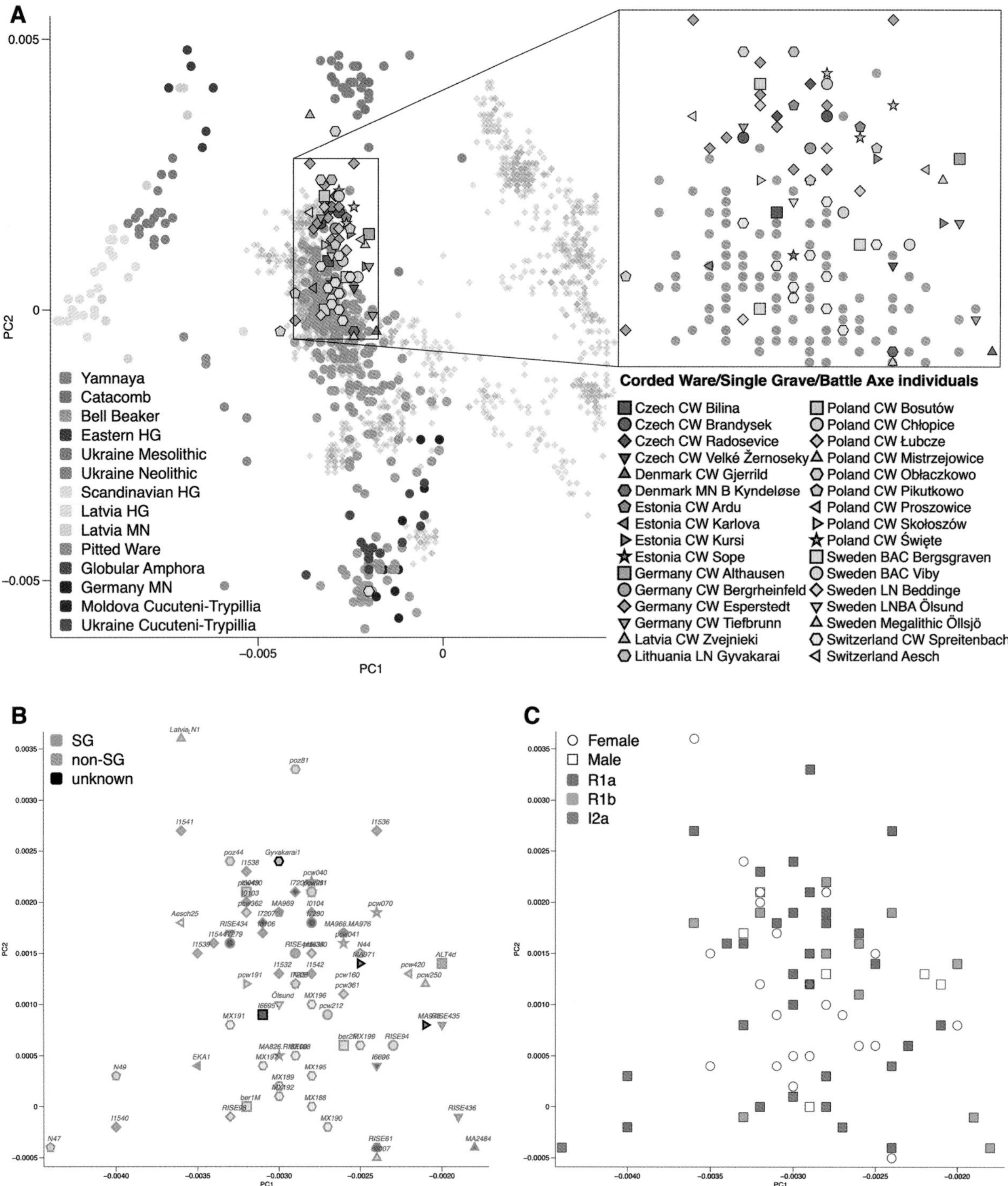

FIGURE 5.3. Principal component analysis plot highlighting published Corded Ware-associated individuals. Panel A shows a scaffold of modern-day West Eurasian individuals (grayed out in the background), on which Corded Ware individuals (filled symbols with black outlines) and relevant ancient groups (colored circles) are projected. The lower two panels each show a detail of the Corded Ware cloud with individuals labeled and assigned to a typical Late Neolithic/Early Bronze Age Single Grave (SG) or non-SG (B) type, and another detail in which individuals are sorted by genetic sex with respective Y chromosome lineages for males (C).

eastern European region in today's Belarus and Ukraine, which covers the critical contact zone between forest steppe and steppe as well as the formerly easternmost reach of farming groups, is currently undersampled or not represented at all.

The principal component analysis (PCA) plotted in Figure 5.3 presents a synthetic view of the currently available data, including around 80 Corded Ware-associated individuals that have never been jointly co-analyzed (Allentoft et al. 2015;

Haak et al. 2015; Mathieson et al. 2015, 2018; Jones et al. 2017; Saag et al. 2017; Fernandes et al. 2018; Mittnik et al. 2018, 2019; Olalde et al. 2018; Malmström et al. 2019; Narasimhan et al. 2019; Furtwängler et al. 2020; Linderholm et al. 2020). We excluded individuals with less than 20,000 variants on the Human Origins panel on which the ancient individuals are projected. Despite covering a large geographic region, the majority of Corded Ware individuals from the Baltic, Poland, Czech Republic, and Germany form a relatively tight cloud in PC space, which can be interpreted overall as a homogeneous metapopulation and corresponds to the position between the Baltic Meso- and Neolithic and Bronze Age and the actual "steppe ancestry" cluster, consisting of individuals assigned to Yamnaya, Afanasievo, and Catacomb cultural complexes. When grouped by site or geographic regions, the main body of these Corded Ware groups remains cladal with respect to other ancient populations. A recent study has argued for differential attraction to the putative sources of ancestry, here in particular Yamnaya versus Afanasievo (Linderholm et al. 2020). However, it remains unclear as to whether these subtleties arise from the use of different data types (shotgun vs. capture).

Several Corded Ware individuals carry very high amounts of "steppe ancestry," such as Latvia_LN1.SG/ZVEJ28, poz81 from Poland, and I1536 from Central Germany, and exhibit a genetic profile that is closer to Yamnaya steppe pastoralists in PCA (and ADMIXTURE) analyses. In contrast, other Corded Ware-associated individuals skew toward the major LNBA cloud that is mostly composed of individuals associated with the pan-western European Bell Beaker phenomenon. Many of these individuals come from sites in Denmark, Sweden, and Switzerland. A lower PC2 value equates to a higher contribution of Late Neolithic/Eneolithic farming ancestry, and thus might not seem too surprising given the geographic location in the south- and northwestern corners of the former distribution. At the same time, it should be noted that many of these individuals date to a later phase of the Corded Ware period, which means that time could also play a role in the increasing assimilation, with individuals carrying more "local," pre-Corded Ware ancestry profiles.

Of the individuals with a low PC2 value, i.e., higher "European Neolithic farmer" ancestry, we can distinguish three individuals (N47 and N49 from Pikutkowo in Poland, and I1540 from Esperstedt in Germany) who skew to the left on PC1 toward hunter-gatherer ancestry and are positioned midway between the "eastern" and "western" corners, as is often found in Scandinavian, Baltic, and Ukrainian hunter-gatherers.

The archaeological record indicates that Corded Ware burials that are 14C-dated to the earliest phase are predominantly male. With the statistical analysis of grave inventories and radiometric dating, Ralf Grossmann has presented a verified typochronological sequence for both Corded Ware and Bell Beakers for central areas of Germany (Grossmann 2016). Although the anthropologically sex-determined skeletons are low in numbers, especially in the older Corded Ware (ca. 2800–2620 BCE), the postulate of the extreme dominance of the male sex, which was put forward for Jutland on the basis of archaeological evidence (Hübner 2005; Kristiansen 2017), can be confirmed (Figure 5.4). Whether this trend holds true for other regions with Corded Ware burials is yet to be seen, but we can conclude that we have an emerging pattern. From the middle Corded Ware (ca. 2620–2480 BCE) onwards, the relationship between male and female gender in Corded Ware graves appears to have become more balanced. In contrast to the Corded Ware, observations from BB gender regulations in Germany and Northern France also suggest a more balanced gender ratio in the graves (Salanova 2011).

Unfortunately, there is hardly any overlap between the anthropological/archaeological and the genomic datasets, which preempts formal testing against the genetic data. Interestingly, the oldest genotyped individual to also have the highest PC2 value thus far is a female from Latvia (ZVEJ28, I4629). Indeed, at face value, a few of these early individuals for which genomic data are available do harbor higher amounts of steppe ancestry. We have therefore used PC2 as a proxy to explore whether there are any correlations between the amount of steppe ancestry and time, as well as geography (latitude/longitude). However, we find no statistical support for a correlation between time and steppe ancestry within the genomic Corded Ware data set, indicating that time is not a strong predictor of the amount of steppe ancestry (Figure 5.5), irrespective of the genetic sex of the individuals. We also do not find a correlation when plotting the PC2 values according to longitude or latitude (Figure 5.5). Even though PC2 appears to be weakly correlated with longitude ($p=0.031$), when we corrected for grave types, it was again uncorrelated for SG ($p=0.937$) and non-SG ($p=0.827$) individuals, suggesting that it is the grave type rather than the genetic ancestry that is driving this signal. Notably, while there seems to be a subtle signal of inclusion of Neolithic mitochondrial lineages into Corded Ware societies in a westward direction through time (Juras et al. 2018), this trend finds little support from the currently available autosomal data.

Until recently, the Y chromosome record of Corded Ware males displayed a seemingly simplistic pattern, with all lineages being attributed exclusively to R1a, while the majority of Yamnaya males could be assigned to R1b-Z2103 and those of the succeeding Bell Beaker to R1b-L51, and here in particular to the subgroup R1b-P312. However, the growing ancient DNA data set from Europe, including regionally differentiated groups in Poland, the Czech Republic, Jutland (Denmark), and SW Germany and Switzerland, now reveals a more complex picture for the male Corded Ware lineages. While R1a is the dominant lineage in Single Grave burials, other contexts also show a higher proportion of individuals with major Y lineages R1b and I2 (Figure 5.6). Phylogenetic placement of lineages observed in 41 higher coverage individuals reveals additional finer-scale structure in the geographic distribution of sublineages. Individuals carrying R1a-CTS4385 are predominantly found in SW Germany and the Czech Republic, whereas R1a-Z645 is more frequent in Poland, Scandinavia, and the Baltic. All R1b individuals belong to lineage R1b-L51, distinct from R1b-Z2103, which is the major lineage associated with individuals from Yamnaya burial contexts (Figure 5.6).

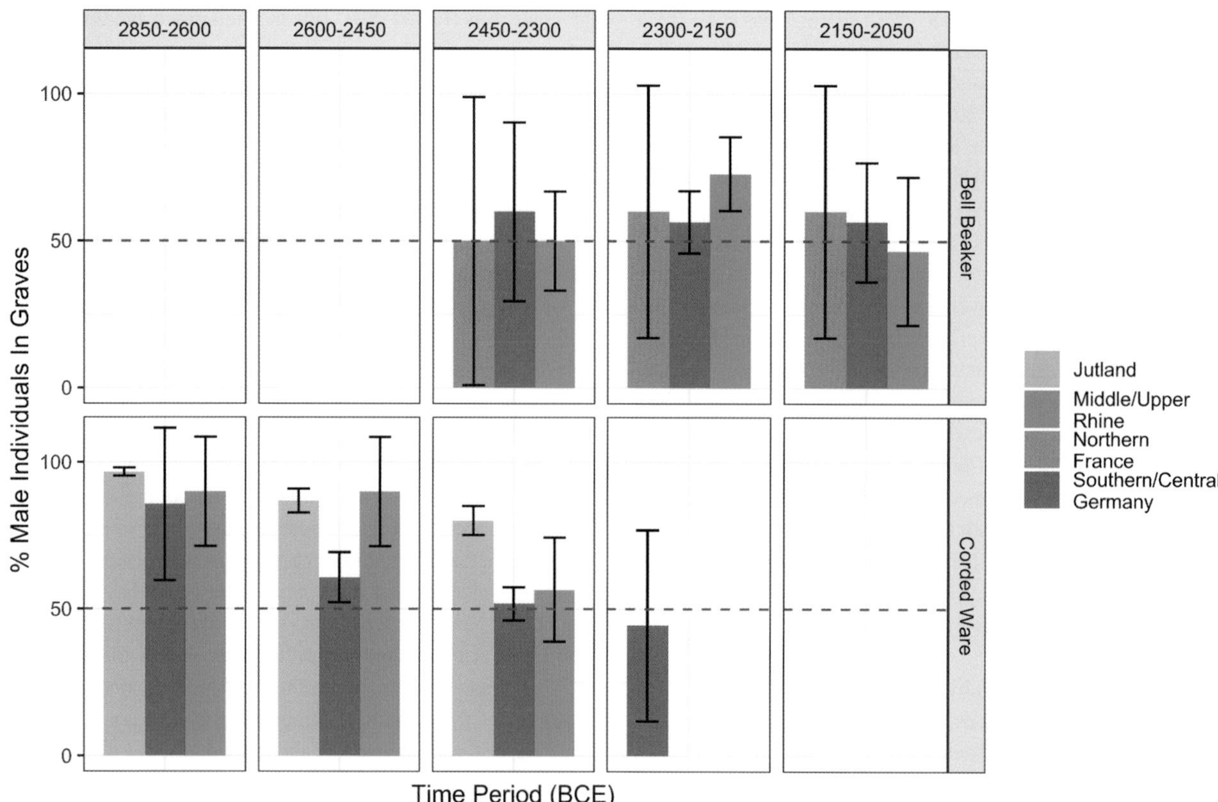

FIGURE 5.4. Percentage of male individuals in graves with 95% confidence intervals (black error bars) for Jutland (light blue), Middle/Upper Rhine (green), Northern France (pink), and Southern/Central Germany (green), split by time period (x-axis) and anthropological determinations of final Neolithic graves (y-axis). Chronological phasing based upon correspondence analyses of material culture in burials paired with 14C dates, derived from Hübner 2005; Ullrich 2008; Salanova 2011; Grossmann 2016. Sex determinations for Jutland are not based on anthropological determinations, but on archaeological estimations from burial items.

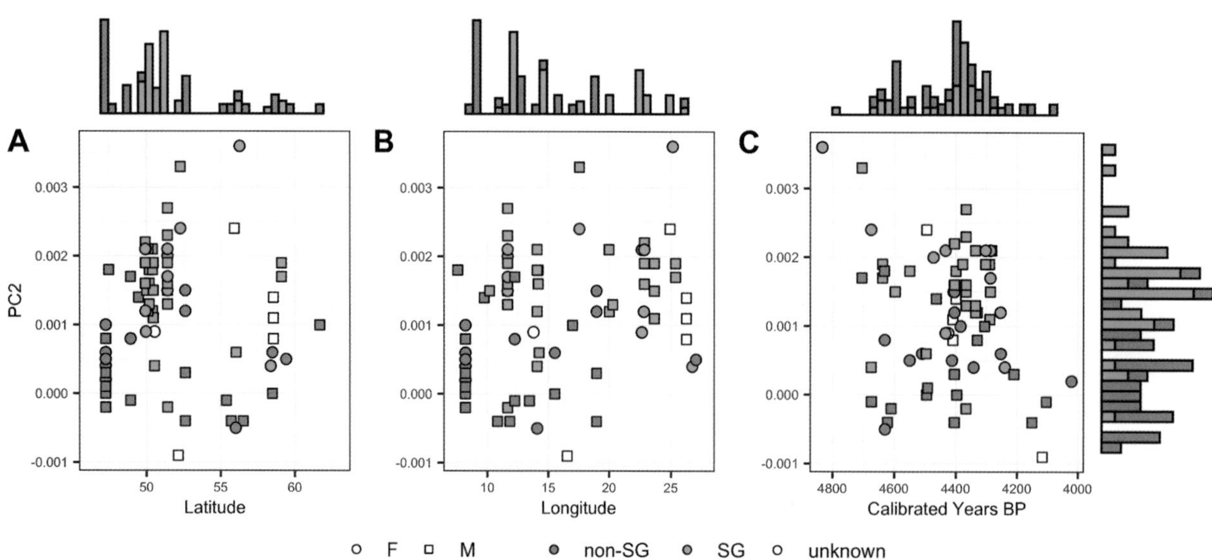

FIGURE 5.5. Testing correlations of PC2 as a proxy for steppe ancestry in published Corded Ware-associated individuals (female = circle, male = square; color-coded to Single Grave (SG) and non-SG context) with latitude, longitude, and time in averaged calibrated 14C dates. PC2 was uncorrelated with latitude ($p = 0.869$) and calibrated 14C date ($p = 0.471$). PC2 appears to be weakly correlated with longitude ($p = 0.031$), but when corrected for grave types was again uncorrelated for SG ($p = 0.937$) and non-SG ($p = 0.827$) individuals. Due to non-linearity, all correlations are Spearman correlations.

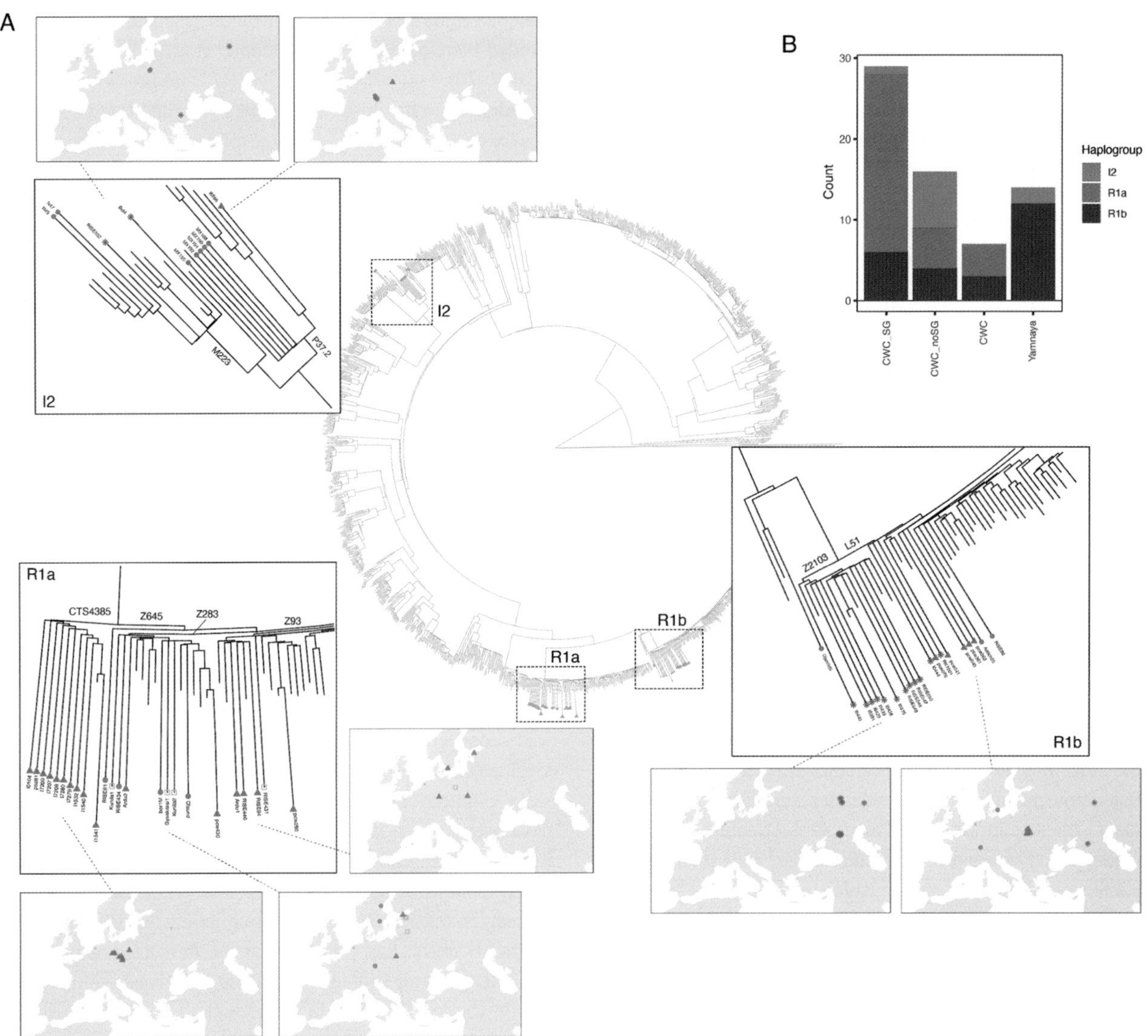

FIGURE 5.6. Y chromosome lineage diversity in Corded Ware-associated males. (A) Phylogenetic placement of Y chromosome sequences found in Corded Ware-associated males to date. A total of 41 individuals with higher coverage (> 2000 SNPs) were placed onto a reference tree of 1,244 present-day male individuals from the 1000 Genomes Project (center tree). Insets show detailed view of the placements for the three major lineages R1a, R1b, and I2a, together with the geographic distributions of individuals associated with major subclades. Burial context of Corded Ware males is distinguished into Single Grave (SG), non-SG, or unknown type using colored plot symbols. (B) Barplot showing the distribution of major lineages across all 55 Corded Ware-associated male individuals, stratified by burial context group. Data from 14 individuals associated with Yamnaya are included in (A) and (B) for context.

When the available genomic data is displayed according to the genetic sex and Y chromosome lineages (Figure 5.3C), it becomes apparent that all I2a lineages are found among individuals positioned more toward other LNBA/Bell Beaker individuals with less “steppe ancestry” and, in turn, more pre-Corded Ware “Neolithic ancestry.” Also, these lineages are overwhelmingly connected to individuals not buried according to the new Single Grave burial ritual, characteristic of the Type 1 Corded Ware introduced above. As discussed, many of these individuals also come from regions in the western Corded Ware distribution area. The I2a lineages are generally common in the European Mesolithic and the frequency of I2a also increases during the late phases of the Middle Neolithic (i.e. pre-Corded Ware) as part of the resurgence of HG ancestry in Europe (Haak et al. 2015; Lipson et al. 2017; Mathieson et al. 2018; Schroeder et al. 2019).

If one argues that the increase of Neolithic ancestry was driven by a westward expansion of the Corded Ware, and thus intensified contact with Middle and Late Neolithic and Eneolithic farming groups, it is important to note that such a contact likely included integration of males into the Corded Ware societies, which is interesting in light of the proposed sex bias seen in the autosomal DNA (Goldberg et al. 2017; Mittnik et al. 2019), but see also the response by Lazaridis and Reich 2017). Thus, it seems pertinent to consider alternative scenarios as well as to inspect contextual metadata in greater detail. Concerning the proposed sex bias by Goldberg et al. 2017, a signal of such form can arise from two scenarios: a) an imbalance of males/females in the expanding deme and balanced proportion in the sink deme (local population) or b) vice versa, i.e. a balanced male/female ratio in the expanding deme with a differential uptake of local males or females, which can vary by region. Evidence for both models exists in the genomic and uniparentally inherited data and, provided we identified all Corded Ware-associated individuals correctly as such, does not allow for a conclusion in support of one over the other. We can thus infer the inmarriage of Neolithic women due, on the one hand, to patrilocal and patrilineal social organization with female exogamy, and, on the other, to an influx of Neolithic males. However, there may also have been matrilocal marriage practices in which local women married foreign men.

While Neolithic kinship systems might have differed from the kinship and marriage systems that were connected with steppe migrants and first established in Central Europe in the context of Corded Ware (Schroeder et al. 2019), there is no reason to believe these differences were so fundamental that they were absolutely incompatible. Corded Ware communities might well have adopted some Neolithic principles with increasing degrees of cultural and genetic admixture, as suggested for Bell Beaker society (Sjögren et al. 2020), as well as the other way around. Various studies have argued and shown that patrilocal and patrilineal societies were likely the predominant structure in Western Eurasia since Neolithization (e.g., Wilkins and Marlowe 2006; Fortunato and Jordan 2010; Rasteiro and Chikhi 2013), which has been confirmed by ancient DNA data from Neolithic groups (Szécsényi-Nagy et al. 2015; Goude et al. 2019; Schroeder et al. 2019; Cassidy et al. 2020) and well-documented in Late Neolithic and Early Bronze Age groups (Knipper et al. 2017; Kristiansen et al. 2017; Sjögren et al. 2020). Based on the premise that there were no substantial differences in social organization between Neolithic groups and those bearing steppe ancestry (including Corded Ware), this might in part explain the genomic transformations that are so clearly visible in the genetic data of the third millennium BCE without having to evoke violent scenarios as the sole explanation (Kristiansen et al. 2017; Schroeder et al. 2019).

It is therefore pertinent to look more deeply into local processes of integration between Neolithic and Corded Ware communities. These aspects often fall by the wayside in mainly genetic publications, in which individuals should be analyzed primarily independently of archaeological labels or categories, i.e. free from preconceived ideas. However, it is important to note that it is critical to contextualize the genetic data in light of the existing archaeological metadata to reach new insights. For example, in the case of individuals from Spreitenbach, Switzerland, who show lower levels of steppe ancestry than contemporaneous Corded Ware groups and I2a male lineages, which generally places them in a position in PC space overlapping with Bell Beaker-associated individuals, the genomic data remains ambiguous, as is the archaeological attribution as well, which lacks clear, decisive elements of material culture or standards of burial characteristic of either Corded Ware or Bell Beaker (Doppler et al. 2012; Furtwängler et al. 2020).

Referring to the different variants of Corded Ware discussed above, our genetic analyses suggest that it is mostly the burial ritual, rather than the presence of Corded Ware pottery or tool types, that most consistently points to individuals with steppe ancestry. Outside of variant 1 regions (for example, in Switzerland), even when found in the context of Corded Ware material culture, directly or indirectly, buried individuals are neither deposited according to the new third-millennium burial customs, nor – with the exception of Aesch – do they display a similar level of steppe ancestry as most of the individuals buried according to the new Single Grave burial rite. Classifying the individuals according to their burial ritual shows that – although there is overlap – individuals buried in Single Grave burials in most cases show a higher amount of steppe ancestry (Figure 5.3B, Figure 5.5) and form a denser cluster than those individuals not associated with Single Grave burials, but instead classified as Corded Ware due to their association with the material culture or spatiotemporal context. Thus, a higher biological proximity to steppe lineages would have significantly enhanced the chance of being buried in a Single Grave burial. This could indicate that this new burial rite was connected with specific identities organized along kinship lines.

As pointed out above, the Corded Ware individuals that have been studied thus far from a wide geographic area form a rather coherent metapopulation that is clearly set apart from contemporaneous groups in the east (e.g. Catacomb and Yamnaya), but less so in succeeding groups in the west, such as Bell Beakers. It is possible that the formation of the characteristic genomic profile most clearly associated with individuals in Corded Ware single graves had arisen further east and expanded westward after a process of consolidation and/or homogenization. Given the current lack of early Corded Ware data from Eastern Europe, in particular from Ukraine, Belarus, Moldova, and Western Russia, such a scenario is not implausible and lends more weight to the developments of the (late) fourth-millennium BCE forest-steppe zone concomitant with and parallel to the emergence of the early Yamnaya horizon in the North Pontic steppe zone. Genome-wide data from the fifth- to fourth-millennium Eneolithic in the Samara region (Mathieson et al. 2015) and the North Caucasus (Wang et al. 2019) indicate that the main ancestry contributions to "steppe ancestry" were already widespread much earlier than the formation onset of the Yamnaya cultural complex. However, it is currently unclear how far north- and westward this proto-steppe ancestry was distributed, abutting the late hunter-gatherers with predominantly EHG-like ancestry in Northwest Russia and the Baltic, the Ukrainian Neolithic/Eneolithic with a blend of WHG/EHG ancestry to the west, as well as Late Neolithic farming groups such as the Globular Amphora, Cucuteni-Trypillia, and others interspersed throughout (Mathieson et al. 2015, 2018; Immel et al. 2020). How exactly the emergence and expansion of the Corded Ware are linked to the emergence and expansion of the Yamnaya horizon remains unclear. However, the Y chromosome record of both groups indicates that Corded Ware cannot be derived directly from the Yamnaya or late eastern farming groups sampled thus far, and is therefore likely to constitute a parallel development in the forest steppe and temperate forest zones of Eastern Europe. Even in Central Europe, the formation of the earliest regional Corded Ware identities was the result of local and regional social practices that resulted in the typical Corded Ware rite of passage.

In light of the above, it is noteworthy that the PCA plot also includes a few individuals associated with the Bell Beaker phenomenon who show comparably higher levels of steppe ancestry, which positions them within the Corded Ware variation or even at the extreme upper end of the PC2 distribution, such as male individual I2787 from the Felső-Ürge-hegyi-dűlő site in Szigetszentmiklós, Hungary, dated to 2458–2202 cal BCE (3840±35 BP, Poz-83640) (Olalde et al. 2018), or female individual UnTal58_68_Sk2 from Haunstetten-Unterer Talweg in southeast Germany, dated to 2470–2310 cal BCE (3910±20 BP, MAMS-18935) (Mittnik et al. 2019). Interestingly, male individual I2787 from Hungary also carries the Y chromosome lineage R1b-Z2103, which is very common in Yamnaya individuals (Figure 5.6), and while the 14C date is too late for a direct connection with Yamnaya groups, it can still be interpreted as a Yamnaya legacy in the Carpathian Basin.

5.4 Transformations of the Third Millennium BCE in Europe

5.4.1 Economy and Environmental Impact

Another way of gaining information about the nature of Corded Ware migrations is to study their environmental impact, i.e., how the landscape was altered, as evidenced, for example, by pollen diagrams. More recently, Racimo et al. were able to demonstrate significant differences between Neolithic societies and Corded Ware societies by linking genetic and environmental changes on a Europe-wide scale (Racimo et al. 2020). They postulated that the speed of migration was higher during Corded Ware than during Neolithic colonization, and also that it impacted the environment much more, in accordance with an economy with a stronger pastoral element. However, when contrasting this evidence with quantitative reconstructions of regional and local vegetation changes in Denmark, some variations can be demonstrated (Figure 5.7). Thus, there is a significant difference in environmental impact on the landscape in the primary area of Corded Ware/Single Grave colonization in Jutland, and the later, more gradual migrations into Neolithic territory in eastern Denmark.

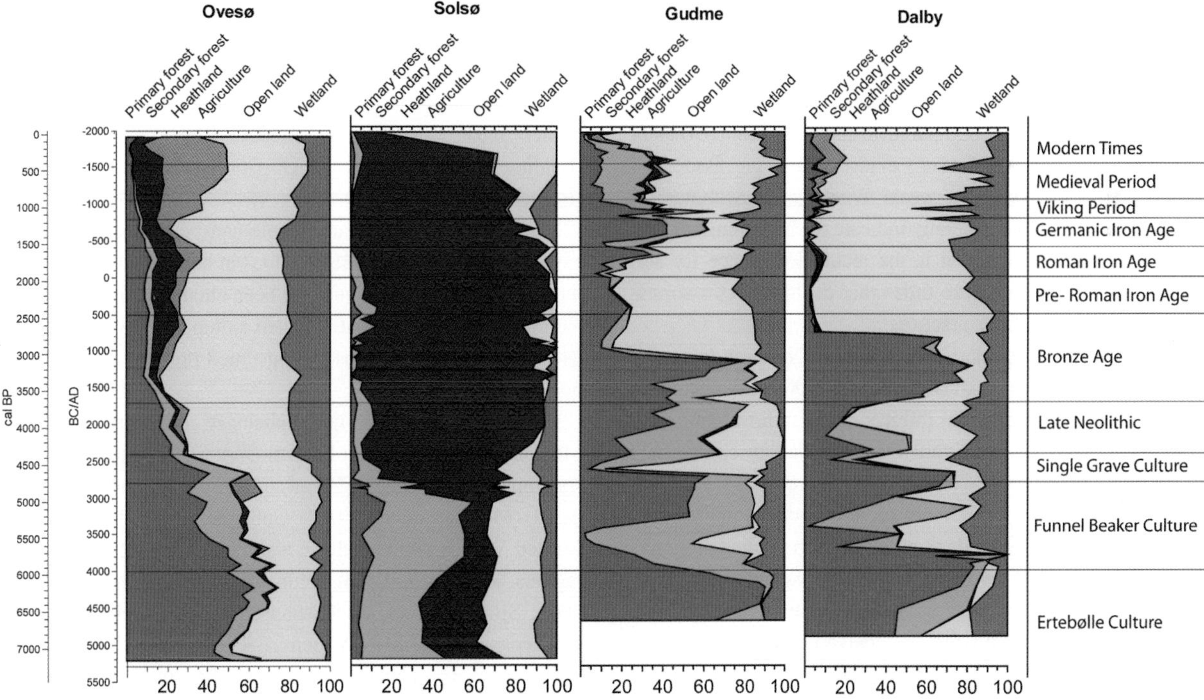

FIGURE 5.7. Landscape Reconstruction Algorithm (LRA) calibrated pollen diagrams (Sugita 2007a, 2007b; Theuerkauf and Couwenberg 2018) from Ove Sø (Andersen 1993), northwestern Jutland, Thy, Solsø (Odgaard 1994), western Jutland (note that the pollen sequence is not clear around 3000–2700 BCE), Gudme Sø (Rasmussen and Olsen 2009), Southeast Fyn, Dalby Sø, eastern Zealand (Mortensen, unpubl.). Ovesø was calibrated with the REVEALS model (Sugita 2007b; Theuerkauf and Couwenberg 2018), the remaining with the LOVE model (Sugita 2007a). Thus, the opening of landscape in western Jutland before the Single Grave culture can be linked to both the late TRB and the Single Grave culture.

Future archaeogenetic work in the form of a detailed time transect in this region could provide important parallels with respect to the model of incoming Corded Ware-related pastoralists as well as interactions with local late Funnel Beaker groups.

The initial migration into western and central Jutland shows a dramatic and rapid depletion of forests in the diagrams from Lake Ove in Thy and Solsø, western Jutland, leading to the formation of open grassland, as well as heath vegetation in the lighter soils of western Jutland. This steppe-like environment was maintained by regular burning, as demonstrated by pollen analyses from Single Grave barrows (Andersen, 1995), which stands in some opposition to the previous Neolithic economic strategy. There is no doubt that the settling and rapid formation of open lands in Jutland must have demanded a substantial influx of people and animals over a rather short period of time, also to maintain open lands once established. The start of the process could be associated with the appearance of late Globular Amphora material in Denmark around 3000 BCE, after which the Single Grave migration shortly followed (Johannsen and Laursen 2010). The Single Grave economy was dominantly pastoral, and so far, no house structures have been documented from the first two hundred years after migration (Nielsen 2020).

In Northern Germany, palynological evidence on a supraregional scale indicates that the degree of human impact on the environment was generally lower between ca. 2800 to 2500 BCE compared to ca. 4000 to 3100 BCE (Figure 5.8) (Brozio et al. 2019; Feeser et al. 2019). On a smaller geographical scale, however, we find regional variability: regions with comparatively higher agropastoral impact, such as Lauenburg and Altmark (Feeser et al. 2012; Diers et al. 2014; Diers and Fritsch 2019), and other regions, including Ostholstein (Feeser and Dörfler 2019), with comparatively lower human impact after around 2800 BCE compared to previous Funnel Beaker times (Figure 5.9). However, evidence for an associated stronger pastoral element is weak. Whereas archaeobotanical and palynological data generally indicate the remaining importance of cereal cultivation, it is the reduced evidence for soil erosion during Corded Ware times that could reflect a corresponding shift in land-use practices.

In contrast to Denmark, Corded Ware in Northern Germany follows a crisis phase between 3100 and 2900 BCE, characterized by Globular Amphorae influences and reforestation processes (Figure 5.8). Even until the Late Neolithic (ca. 2200 BCE), the variability of Corded Ware environments and subsistence activities does not reveal any sudden and distinct creation of larger grasslands as reflected in the pollen diagrams from western Jutland (Brozio et al. 2019; Feeser et al. 2019). In the Altmark and Lauenburg, the earliest Corded Ware (ca. 2800 BCE) is associated with the first palynological evidence of agricultural practices (Diers 2018). Therefore, the regional mosaic of Northern Germany supports the idea of more gradual processes of change, which can vary from region to region, with or without migrations. Moreover, in southern Sweden, pollen data suggest a slow and gradual opening of the landscape during the Neolithic, followed by regionally variable, large-scale deforestation in the late Bronze Age (Sjögren 2006; Hellman 2008; Zanon et al. 2018).

The later eastward influence of the Single Grave culture into eastern Jutland and the Danish islands, here represented by a diagram from Gudme on Fuenen, shows less impact on the forest (for eastern Schleswig-Holstein, see also Feeser et al. 2012). There is still a clear difference compared to the previous Neolithic economy; in some areas, more open land is established for subsistence activities, including cereal cultivation. This suggests a strategy of economic and perhaps genetic and cultural adaptation and admixture. Thus, the dominant burial ritual employs older megaliths, which suggests some integration with existing Neolithic populations and their rituals. However, we still need genetic evidence from passage graves to document what happened during this final period of Corded Ware expansion, even if the archaeology is well documented by now (Iversen 2015). Similar regional variations are probable in other parts of Europe. Thus, in Switzerland, the environmental impact is more similar to eastern Denmark (Doppler et al. 2017; Gerling et al. 2017).

5.4.2 Diet

From Neolithic to Bronze Age Central Europe, there is a general trend of increasing protein from higher trophic levels. This could be linked to a higher intake of protein from meat and milk products, even if increased levels of manuring could also contribute to such results. The data from Corded Ware individuals in this region fit this trend well and would suggest the rising importance of animals within a general economy of mixed agriculture (Sjögren, Price, & Kristiansen 2016; Münster et al. 2018). On a local scale, analyses from a multicultural site in Central Germany indicate a general trend of higher meat consumption already from ca. 3700 BCE (Baalberge) onwards, in which Corded Ware is integrated (Bergemann 2018).

The diet of Corded Ware people can be evaluated to some extent through $\delta^{13}C$ and $\delta^{15}N$ values in human collagen. As no modeling of the total diet has yet been attempted for this group, we must bear in mind that collagen isotope values mainly give us insight into the sources of consumed protein, not the composition of the total diet.

Currently, the most comprehensive data are from the Mittelelbe-Saale region in Eastern Germany, where individuals spanning a four-thousand-year time transect have been analyzed (Münster et al. 2018). Collagen isotope values from Corded Ware individuals have also been published from other regions, such as Southern Germany (Asam, Grupe, & Peters 2006; Sjögren, Price, & Kristiansen 2016), southeast Poland (Szczepanek et al. 2018; Werens, Szczepanek, & Jarosz 2018), Scandinavia (Fornander 2013), and the southeastern Baltic (Antanaitis-Jacobs, Daugnora, & Richards 2009; Piličiauskas et al. 2017, 2018, 2020).

The data from Mittelelbe-Saale show a clear trend of increasing $\delta^{15}N$ values over time, while no trend was seen in the $\delta^{13}C$ data, accommodating the recently postulated arrival of millet in Europe after 2000 BCE (Filipović et al. 2020). This trend could be observed in all time periods and archaeological

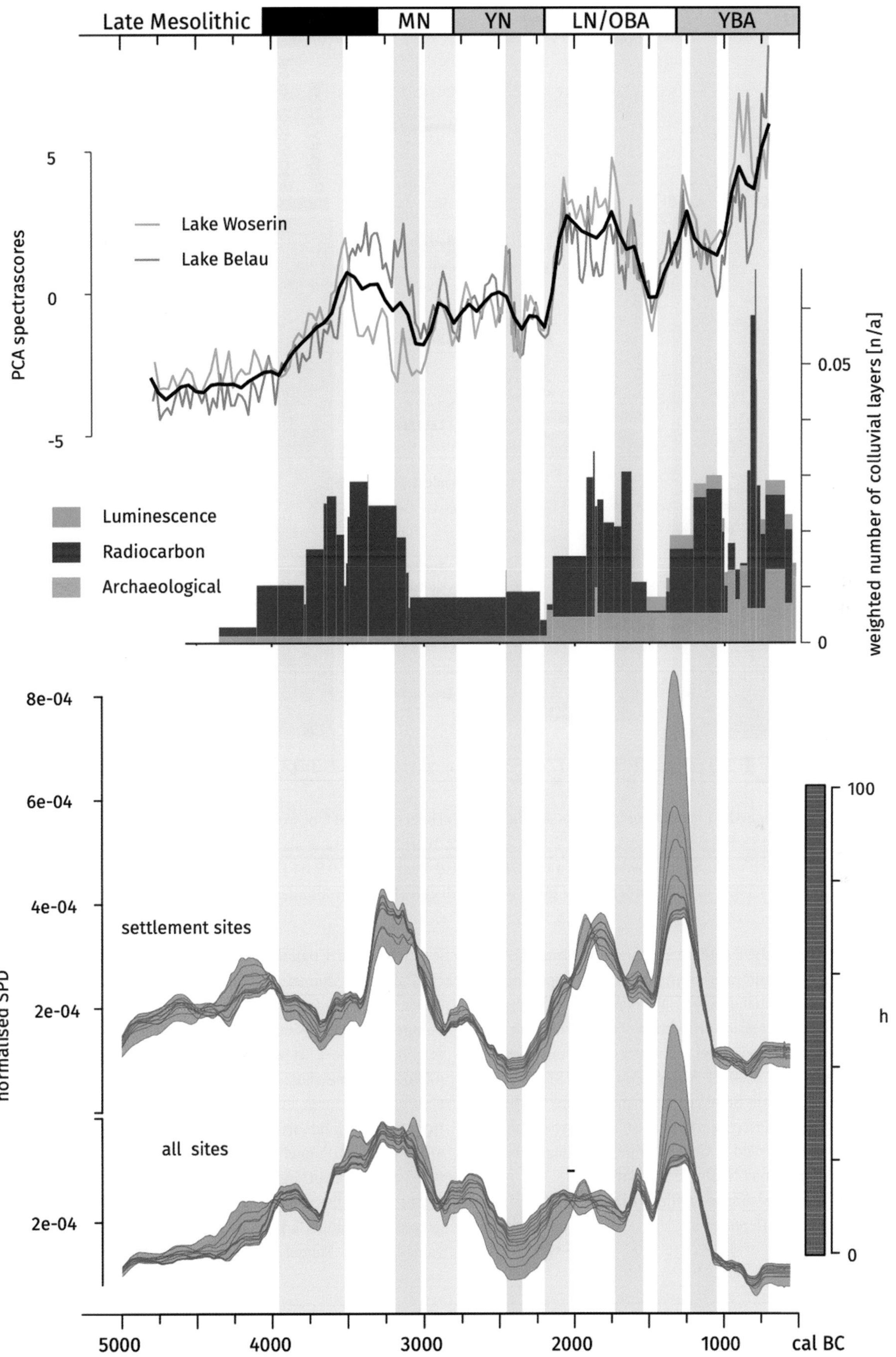

FIGURE 5.8. Land opening and reforestation are indicated by northern German palynological data (Feeser et al. 2019; Müller 2019). Colluvial layers support these observations by increasing and decreasing amounts of colluvial incidence (upper panel).

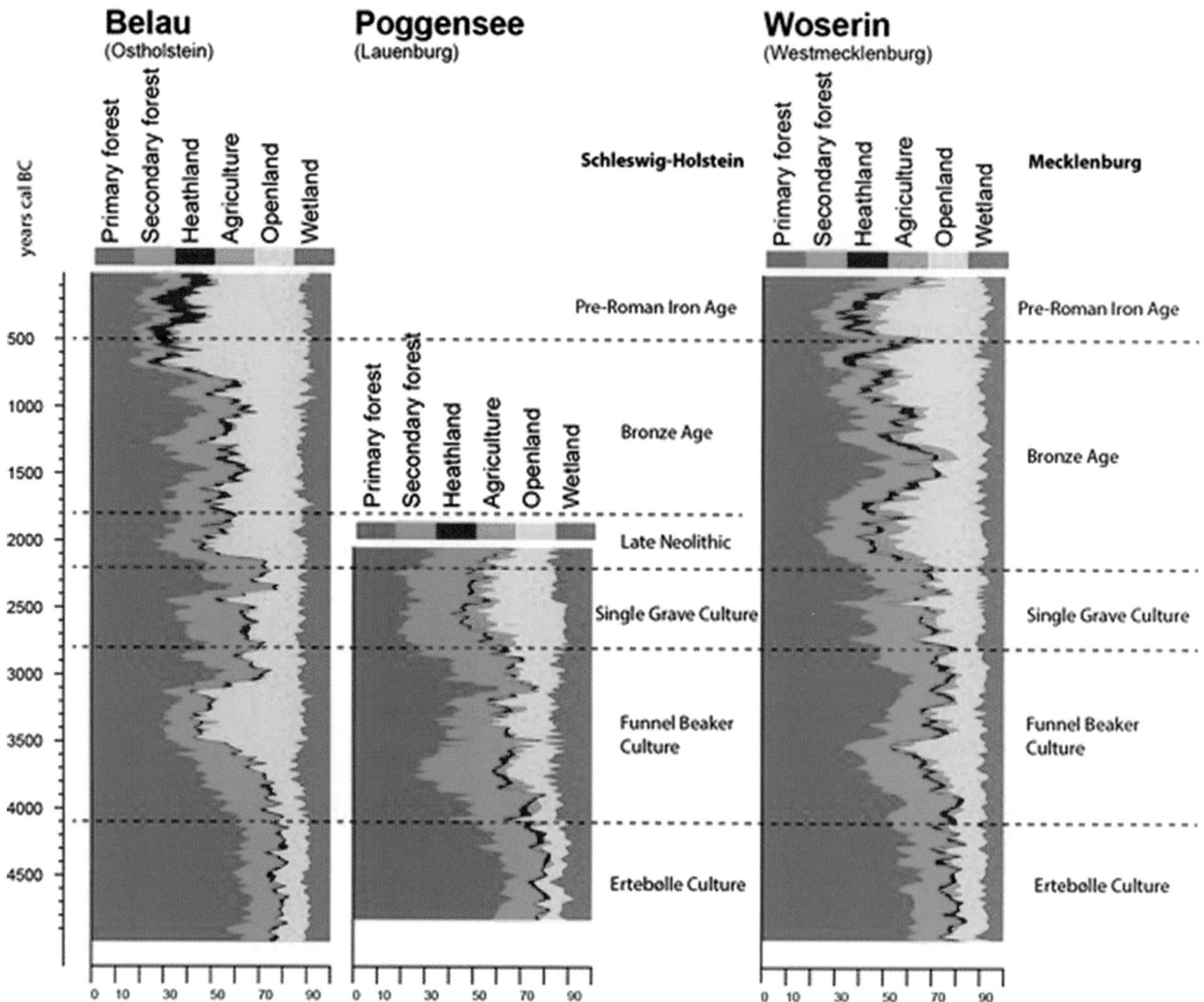

FIGURE 5.9. LRA calibrated pollen diagrams (Sugita 2007a, 2007b; Theuerkauf and Couwenberg 2018) from Lake Belau (Wiethold 1998; Dörfler et al. 2012), Poggensee (Feeser et al. 2012), and Lake Woserin (Feeser et al. 2016). The data was calibrated using the software R 3.6.3 and REVEALS as implemented in the DISQOVER Package ver.0.9.04 (Theuerkauf et al. 2016) with the default dispersal model (LSM) and the pollen productivity estimates for Mecklenburg-Vorpommern (PPE_MV2015).

cultures from the Early Neolithic to the Early Bronze Age. However, no such trend was seen in faunal isotope values, excluding increased manuring as the cause of this effect. Instead, a gradually increasing proportion of protein from animal sources was suggested and associated with a continuous opening of the landscape after 3700 BCE (Bergemann 2018). This fits partly with the data from Southern Germany (Asam, Grupe, & Peters 2006; Sjögren, Price, & Kristiansen 2016), where higher δ^{15}N values were observed in Corded Ware individuals than in individuals from previous Neolithic populations.

The Polish data are similar to those of Germany, but also show some regional differences in δ^{13}C values, probably due to environmental factors.

While these Continental European data support the notion of increased animal husbandry from around 3700 BCE onward, or perhaps even a pastorally dominated mixed agriculture in Corded Ware, as also inferred from land-use models (e.g. Lechterbeck et al. 2014), in Scandinavia, the isotopic picture is somewhat different. Data from the classic Single Grave culture area in western Jutland are lacking, but data from SGC individuals in Gjerrild, eastern Jutland, are similar to previous Funnel Beaker groups and show lower δ^{15}N values than in Germany (Friis-Holm Egfjord et al. 2021). In southern Sweden, values from Battle Axe culture graves show rather large individual variation, overlapping with values from Funnel Beaker groups. Further, δ^{13}C and

FIGURE 5.8. (*cont.*) Radiometric dating for settlement sites (and all sites) indicates a possible population variability including a decrease around 3100 BCE, which continued during the Corded Ware period (lower panel). Please note that the data in the lower panel might be affected by a regional preservation bias of organic material. PCA spectrascores represent the first eigenvector in the pollen PCA (human impact/landscape openness). SPD = summed probability density of archaeological 14C-dates.

$\delta^{15}N$ values are correlated, suggesting mixing of marine and terrestrial protein sources, and there are indications of regional variation (Fornander 2013).

Data from the southeastern Baltic and Finland again present a different scenario, and variable subsistence, including a significant aquatic contribution, has been suggested on the basis of both human collagen isotopes and analysis of biomarker lipid residues in pottery (Cramp et al. 2014; Heron et al. 2015; Piličiauskas et al. 2017, 2018, 2020; Robson et al. 2019). While "pure" Corded Ware contexts show more a terrestrial diet, including dairy lipids, it is the coastal "Rzucewo" group, with its significant Corded Ware contribution (Heron et al. 2015; Robson et al. 2019), that heralds the marine signal. Inland sites in the eastern Baltic show indications of a substantial freshwater fish intake (Piličiauskas et al. 2020). Even in East Holstein (Germany), a high degree of aquatic nutrition can be reconstructed (Knitter et al. 2019).

In summary, the data available at present suggest only minor differences between Corded Ware groups and other Neolithic populations, if any. Trends rather fall into overall trajectories along the timeline, while being variable according to region. Intensive research and innovative archaeometric approaches will be necessary to shed more light on the question of whether there exists a typical Corded Ware subsistence and dietary consumption pattern.

5.5 Mechanisms of Expansion and Their Possible Causes

5.5.1 Disease, Environment and Health

Here we briefly discuss evidence of a decline in Neolithic populations (Hinz et al. 2012; Shennan et al. 2013), and how it relates to environmental/economic changes and the arrival of new diseases, such as an early form of the plague (Rasmussen et al. 2015; Andrades Valtueña et al. 2017; Rascovan et al. 2019). To these observations, one could add changes in diet from a predominantly grain-based to a predominantly meat-based diet after 3000 BCE (Münster et al. 2018). Did the combined effect of such factors sum up to a selective advantage, or did steppe individuals expand opportunistically into territories that were successively abandoned by farming groups?

The generation of untargeted next-generation shotgun sequencing data from ancient specimens allows not only for the DNA analysis of the host organism (here the human individual) but also to assess the presence of infectious disease signatures in the individuals under study. Teeth are the preferred skeletal element to sample, as the desiccated blood of the tooth's pulp chamber is considered an optimal environment for preservation of blood-borne pathogens. It is therefore possible to trace pathogen DNA in the acute disease form, also in cases that would otherwise not leave visible traces on the skeleton to indicate the contraction of any infectious disease. To detect the potential pathogen DNA, the nonhuman DNA reads of the shotgun sequencing data are mapped against a candidate list of microbial taxa of interest, e.g., *Yersinia pestis*, the bacterial pathogen that is the causative agent of the Black Death pandemic in late medieval times.

Using this approach, Rasmussen and colleagues indeed found evidence of an early strain of *Y. pestis* by screening a large-scale Bronze Age data set (Allentoft et al. 2015; Rasmussen et al. 2015). A number of follow-up studies found further evidence of this early *Y. pestis* strain (Andrades Valtueña et al. 2017; Rascovan et al. 2019; Yu et al. 2020), which is known not to have caused the bubonic plague but nonetheless a deadly septicemic and/or pulmonary form of the disease (Spyrou et al. 2019). To date, almost a dozen *Y. pestis* genomes from the third and second millennium BCE have been reported, ranging from Central Europe in the west to the Altai and Lake Baikal in the east, and including two genomes from individuals associated with the Corded Ware (Gyvakarai1 from Lithuania and Kunila2 from Estonia). The oldest *Y. pestis* genomes are found in individuals associated with Yamnaya and Afanasievo, while a precursor form was reported from a late Funnel Beaker individual dated to the beginning of the third millennium BCE (Rascovan et al. 2019). This individual and two individuals from the Lake Baikal region are the only ones that do not carry steppe ancestry, which suggests that the genetic ancestry composition of a given population does not play a major role in susceptibility to this particular disease. In contrast, the topology of this early *Y. pestis* branch follows a strict molecular clock-like pattern, suggesting that the pathogen was either spread by mobile human groups or through continuously interconnected groups across a vast geographic region.

The disease etiology of this early form is still unclear. Even though there is considerable bias with respect to systematic screening of other regions and time periods, the current data suggests a heightened prevalence in groups that are linked in some form to (forest) steppe pastoralists. Interestingly, a more derived strain of *Y. pestis* that later gave rise to all modern forms, including the strains that led to the Plague of Justinian and the Black Death, has also been found in Bronze Age individuals of the Russian steppe zone (Spyrou et al. 2018, 2019).

Taken together, there is no evidence to suggest that steppe pastoralists were more immune to this and other infectious diseases, and as a consequence, models that consider pandemics as a unifactorial explanation for the decline of immunologically naive Late Neolithic farming groups and the concomitant rise and spread of steppe ancestry with eastern European pastoralist groups can be considered too simplistic. However, if we consider emerging infectious diseases to be a serious factor in late Neolithic and early Bronze Age societies, it is possible that the affected groups differed in their response and resilience to such outbreaks (including buffering capacities with respect to population densities and settlement sizes), which would thus have implications for the long-term stability of the social and economic power of the groups in question.

5.5.2 Social Institutions of Kinship and Inheritance

If we are to understand mechanisms and causes of expansion, we also need to gain a deeper insight into the social organization of third-millennium societies, such as those connected with Yamnaya and Corded Ware, not least their kinship systems. This again demands the possibility to genetically reconstruct kinship relations in local cemeteries/burial groups, which can then be combined with the evidence for diet and mobility from strontium analyses. So far, this has been done partially for Corded Ware (Haak et al. 2008; Sjögren, Price, & Kristiansen 2016; Monroy Kuhn, Jakobsson, & Günther 2018), but more extensively for Bell Beaker burial communities (Mittnik et al. 2019; Sjögren et al. 2020). While the evidence from these local case studies is still scarce, they point toward a rather similar kinship system, based on patrilineality, and patrilocality, with female exogamy, which on the surface might not appear to be radically or substantially different from the preceding or contemporaneous Neolithic groups. It is clear that detailed studies of both pre-Corded Ware and Corded Ware groups are needed.

Indeed, it might be possible that the similarities in social structure and demography did in fact facilitate the expansion of the Corded Ware complex. However, if we rule out all other factors, such as economic, epidemiological, or selective pressures, one question remains: what was the new twist?

Currently, the best evidence comes from what is most clearly expressed in the funerary practices. What we see is a new emphasis on certain ideological notions referring to a higher appreciation of some aspects of social organization that were already present during the preceding Neolithic period, but were less visible before the third millennium BCE. The new Single Grave burials (Furholt 2019) that emerge at the same time as Corded Ware material culture do highlight – to a much higher degree than before – the individual, binary gender roles (Robb and Harris 2018), and males bearing weapons. Their conspicuous display in the burial ritual points to changes in the social system, insofar as these aspects of social identity and status, which might have existed before, are now being deemed important, prominent characteristics (to be carried on and displayed in the afterlife), reflecting fundamental changes in the belief and value system. These can be connected with other changes that are less visible in the archaeological record. However, what seems to be clear now, thanks to genome-wide aDNA data, is that migrants with roots in Eastern Europe, probably the Eurasian steppe and forest steppe, were to a large degree involved in the formation of this new burial rite and worldview, including the associated social changes. In the Caucasus, the North Pontic, and regions to the north, some of the key elements, such as individual burials under earthen mounds (kurgans), stricter rules of body placement, the dominance of male burials, and the display of weapons, appear in the context of Eneolithic, (Steppe) Maykop, Usatovo, Sredny Stog, and Yamnaya (Ivanova 2013; Kaiser 2019), prior to the formation of Corded Ware. However, it should also be pointed out that those elements of burial rites were also not unknown in the European Neolithic (Heyd 2017; Krauß et al. 2017; Robb and Harris 2018). Further, the new data discussed here suggest that local Neolithic communities played a larger role in the formation of Corded Ware than the total replacement scenarios suggested in the light of the earlier aDNA evidence.

References

Allentoft, M. E., et al. 2015. Population genomics of Bronze Age Eurasia. *Nature* 522(7555): 167–172.

Andersen, S. T. 1993. History of vegetation and agriculture: At Hassing Huse Mose, Thy, Northwest Denmark, since the Ice Age. *Journal of Danish Archaeology* 11(1): 57–79.

1995. Pollen analytical investigations of barrows from the Funnel Beaker and Single Grave Cultures in the Vroue area, West Jutland, Denmark. *Journal of Danish Archaeology* 12 (1): 107–131.

Andrades Valtueña, A., et al. 2017. The Stone Age plague and its persistence in Eurasia. *Current Biology: CB* 27(23): 3683–3691.e8.

Antanaitis-Jacobs, I., L. Daugnora, & M. Richards. 2009. Diet in early Lithuanian prehistory and the new stable isotope evidence. *Archaeologia Baltica* 12: 12–30.

Anthony, D. W. 2007. The horse, the wheel, and language: How Bronze-Age riders from the Eurasian steppes shaped the modern world. Princeton: Princeton University Press.

Asam, T., G. Grupe, & J. Peters. 2006. Menschliche Subsistenzstrategien im Neolithikum: Eine Isotopenanalyse bayerischer Skelettfunde. *Anthropologischer Anzeiger; Bericht über die biologisch-anthropologische Literatur* 64 (1): 1–23.

Bergemann, S. 2018. *Zauschwitz (Landkreis Leipzig). Siedlungen und Gräber eines neolithischen Fundplatzes*. Bonn: Dr. Rudolf Habelt GmbH.

Bourgeois, Q., & E. Kroon. 2017. The impact of male burials on the construction of Corded Ware identity: Reconstructing networks of information in the 3rd millennium BC. *PLoS ONE* 12(10): e0185971.

Brandt, G., et al. 2013. Ancient DNA reveals key stages in the formation of Central European mitochondrial genetic diversity. *Science* 342(6155): 257–261.

2015. Human paleogenetics of Europe: The known knowns and the known unknowns. *Journal of Human Evolution* 79: 73–92.

Brozio, J. P., et al. 2019. Monuments and economies: What drove their variability in the middle-Holocene Neolithic? *The Holocene* 29(10): 1558–1571.

Burgess, C., & S. Shennan. 1976. *The Beaker phenomenon: Some suggestions*. British Archaeological Reports.

Cassidy, L. M., et al. 2020. A dynastic elite in monumental Neolithic society. *Nature* 582(7812): 384–388.

Cramp, L. J. E. et al. 2014. Neolithic dairy farming at the extreme of agriculture in Northern Europe. *Proceedings of the Royal Society B: Biological Sciences* 281(1791): 20140819.

Diers, S., et al. 2014. The Western Altmark versus Flintbek: Palaeoecological research on two megalithic regions. *Journal of Archaeological Science* 41: 185–198.

2018. *Mensch-Umweltbeziehungen zwischen 4000 und 2200 cal BC. Vegetationsgeschichtliche Untersuchungen an Mooren und trichterbecherzeitlichen Fundplätzen der Altmark*. Bonn: Dr. Rudolf Habelt GmbH.

Diers, S., & B. Fritsch. 2019. Changing environments in a megalithic landscape: The Altmark case. In: J. Müller, M. Hinz, & M. Wunderlich (ed.), *Megaliths – Societies – Landscapes. Early monumentality and social differentiation in Neolithic Europe*, 719–752. Bonn: Dr. Rudolf Habelt Verlag.

Doppler, T., et al. 2012. 14C-Datierung des endneolithischen Kollektivgrabes von Spreitenbach = Les datations radiocarbones de la sépulture collective de Spreitenbach. In: Thomas Doppler & Kurt W. Alt (ed.), *Spreitenbach-Moosweg (Aargau, Schweiz) : ein Kollektivgrab um 2500 v.Chr. = Spreitenbach-Moosweg (Argovie, Suisse) : une sépulture collective vers 2500 av. J.-C.*, 85–103. Basel: Archäologie Schweiz (Antiqua).

2017. Landscape opening and herding strategies: Carbon isotope analyses of herbivore bone collagen from the Neolithic and Bronze Age lakeshore site of Zurich-Mozartstrasse, Switzerland. *Quaternary International* 436: 18–28.

Dörfler, W., et al. 2012. A high-quality annually laminated sequence from Lake Belau, Northern Germany: Revised chronology and its implications for palynological and tephrochronological studies. *The Holocene* 22(12): 1413–1426.

Feeser, I., et al. 2012. New insight into regional and local land-use and vegetation patterns in eastern Schleswig-Holstein during the Neolithic. In: M. Hinz & J. Müller (ed.), *Siedlung, Grabenwerk, Grossteingrab. Studien zu Gesellschaft, Wirtschaft und Umwelt der Trichterbechergruppen im nördlichen Mitteleuropa. Frühe Monumentalität und Soziale Differenzierung*, 159–191. Bonn: Rudolf Habelt.

2016. A mid-Holocene annually laminated sediment sequence from Lake Woserin: The role of climate and environmental change for cultural development during the Neolithic in Northern Germany. *Holocene* 26(6): 947–963.

2019. Human impact and population dynamics in the Neolithic and Bronze Age: Multi-proxy evidence from north-western Central Europe. *The Holocene* 29(10): 1596–1606.

Feeser, I., & W. Dörfler. 2019. Land-use and environmental history at the Middle Neolithic settlement site Oldenburg-Dannau LA 77. *Journal of Neolithic Archaeology* 21: 157–207.

Fernandes, D. M., et al. 2018. A genomic Neolithic time transect of hunter-farmer admixture in central Poland. *Scientific Reports* 8(1): 14879.

Filipović, D., et al. 2020. New AMS 14C dates track the arrival and spread of broomcorn millet cultivation and agricultural change in prehistoric Europe. *Scientific Reports* 10(1): 13698.

Fischer, U. 1958. Mitteldeutschland und die Schnurkeramik. Ein kultursoziologischer Vergleich. *Jahresschrift für mitteldeutsche Vorgeschichte* 41/42: 254–298.

Fornander, E. 2013. Dietary diversity and moderate mobility: Isotope evidence from Scanian Battle Axe Culture burials. *Journal of Nordic Archaeological Science* 18: 13–29.

Fortunato, L., & F. Jordan. 2010. Your place or mine? A phylogenetic comparative analysis of marital residence in Indo-European and Austronesian societies. *Philosophical Transactions of the Royal Society of London. Series B, Biological Sciences* 365(1559): 3913–3922.

Frieman, C. J., & D. Hofmann. 2019. Present pasts in the archaeology of genetics, identity, and migration in Europe: A critical essay. *World Archaeology* 51(4): 528–545.

Friis-Holm Egfjord, A., et al. 2021. Genomic steppe ancestry in skeletons from the Neolithic Single Grave culture in Denmark. *PLoS ONE* 16(1): e0244872.

Furholt, M. 2014. Upending a "totality": Re-evaluating Corded Ware variability in Late Neolithic Europe. *Proceedings of the Prehistoric Society* 80: 67–86.

2018. Massive migrations? The impact of recent aDNA studies on our view of third millennium Europe. *European Journal of Archaeology* 21(2): 159–191.

2019. Re-integrating archaeology: A contribution to aDNA studies and the migration discourse on the 3rd millennium BC in Europe. *Proceedings of the Prehistoric Society* 85: 115–129.

Furtwängler, A., et al. 2020. Ancient genomes reveal social and genetic structure of Late Neolithic Switzerland. *Nature Communications* 11(1): 1915.

Gamkrelidze, T. V., & V. Ivanov. 1995. *Indo-European and the Indo-Europeans: A reconstruction and historical analysis of a proto-language and proto-culture*. Berlin: Mouton de Gruyter.

Gerling, C., et al. 2017. High-resolution isotopic evidence of specialised cattle herding in the European Neolithic. *PLoS ONE* 12(7): e0180164.

Gimbutas, M. 1979. The three waves of Kurgan people into Old Europe, 4500–2500 BC. *Archives Suisses d'anthropologie genérale* 43(2): 113–137.

Glob, P. V. 1944. Studier over den Jyske Enkeltgravskulturen. *Aarbøger* 1944: 1–283.

Goldberg, A., et al. 2017. Ancient X chromosomes reveal contrasting sex bias in Neolithic and Bronze Age Eurasian migrations. *Proceedings of the National Academy of Sciences of the United States of America* 114(10): 2657–2662.

Goude, G., et al. 2019. A multidisciplinary approach to Neolithic life reconstruction. *Journal of Archaeological Method and Theory* 26(2): 537–560.

Grossmann, R. 2016. *Das dialektische Verhältnis von Schnurkeramik und Glockenbecher zwischen Rhein und Saale*. Bonn: Verlag Dr. Rudolf Habelt GmbH.

Haak, W. et al. 2008. Ancient DNA, strontium isotopes, and osteological analyses shed light on social and kinship organization of the Later Stone Age. *Proceedings of the National Academy of Sciences of the United States of America* 105(47): 18226–18231.

2015. Massive migration from the steppe was a source for Indo-European languages in Europe. *Nature* 522(7555): 207–211.

Harrison, R. J., & V. Heyd. 2007. The transformation of Europe in the third millenium BC: The example of "Le Petit Chasseur I+III" (Sion, Valais, Switzerland). *Praehistorische Zeitschrift* 82: 129–214.

Häusler, A. 1996. Invasionen aus der nordpontischen Steppen nach Mitteleuropa im Neolithikum und in der Bronzezeit: Realität oder Phantasieprodukt? *Archäologische Informationen* 19: 75–88.

Hellman, S. 2008. *Validating and testing the landscape reconstruction algorithm in southern Sweden: Towards quantitative reconstruction of past vegetation*. Kalmar: School of Pure and Applied Natural Sciences, University of Kalmar.

Heron, C., et al. 2015. Cooking fish and drinking milk? Patterns in pottery use in the southeastern Baltic, 3300–2400 cal BC. *Journal of Archaeological Science* 63: 33–43.

Heyd, V. 2017. Kossinna's smile. *Antiquity* 91(356): 348–359.

Hinz, M., et al. 2012. Demography and the intensity of cultural activities: An evaluation of Funnel Beaker Societies (4200–2800 cal BC). *Journal of Archaeological Science* 39(10): 3331–3340.

Hübner, E. 2005. *Jungneolithische Gräber auf der jütischen Halbinsel. Typologische und chronologische Studien zur Einzelgrabkultur* (Nordiske Fortidsminder. Serie B). Copenhagen: Det Kongelige Oldskriftselskab.

Immel, A., et al. 2020. Gene-flow from steppe individuals into Cucuteni-Trypillia associated populations indicates long-standing contacts and gradual admixture. *Scientific Reports* 10(1): 4253.

Ivanova, M. 2013. *The Black Sea and the early civilizations of Europe, the Near East and Asia*. Cambridge: Cambridge University Press.

Iversen, R. 2015. Sen tragtbæger- og enkeltgravskultur på de danske øer i sen mellemneolitikum, ca. 2850–2350 f. Kr. *Strategi for yngre stenalders arkæologiske undersøgelser*, November 2015: 58–82. Kulturstyrelsen.

Johannsen, N., & S. Laursen. 2010. Routes and wheeled transport in late 4th–early 3rd millennium funerary customs of the Jutland peninsula: Regional evidence and European context. *Praehistorische Zeitschrift* 85(1): 15–58.

Jones, E. R., et al. 2015. Upper Palaeolithic genomes reveal deep roots of modern Eurasians. *Nature Communications* 6: 8912.

2017. The Neolithic transition in the Baltic was not driven by admixture with early European farmers. *Current Biology: CB* 27(4): 576–582.

Juras, A. et al. 2018. Mitochondrial genomes reveal an east to west cline of steppe ancestry in Corded Ware populations. *Scientific Reports* 8(1): 11603.

Kaiser, E. 2019. *Das dritte Jahrtausend im osteuropäischen Steppenraum: Kulturhistorische Studien zu prähistorischer Subsistenzwirtschaft und Interaktion mit benachbarten Räumen* (Berlin Studies of the Ancient World 37). Berlin: Edition Topoi.

Knipper, C., et al. 2017. Female exogamy and gene pool diversification at the transition from the Final Neolithic to the Early Bronze Age in central Europe. *Proceedings of the National Academy of Sciences of the United States of America* 114(38): 10083–10088.

Knitter, D., et al. 2019. Transformations and site locations from a landscape archaeological perspective: The case of Neolithic Wagrien, Schleswig-Holstein, Germany. *Land* 8(4): 68.

Kossinna, G. 1910. Der Ursprung der Urfinnen und Urindogermanen und ihre Ausbreitung nach Osten. *Mannus* 1/2: 225–245.

1911. *Die Herkunft der Germanen. Zur Methode der Siedlungsarchäologie*. Bonn: Mannus-Bibliothek.

Krauß, R., et al. 2017. Chronology and development of the Chalcolithic necropolis of Varna I. *Documenta Praehistorica* 44: 282–305.

Kristiansen, K. 1989. Prehistoric migrations: The case of the Single Grave and Corded Ware Culture. *Journal of Danish Archaeology* 8: 211–225.

2017. Re-theorising mobility and the formation of culture and language among the Corded Ware Culture in Europe. *Antiquity* 91(356): 334–347.

Lanting, J. N., W. G. Mook, & J. D. van der Waals. 1973. C14 chronology and the Beaker problem. *Helinium* 13: 38–58.

Lazaridis, I., & D. Reich. 2017. Failure to replicate a genetic signal for sex bias in the steppe migration into central Europe. *Proceedings of the National Academy of Sciences* 114(20): E3873–E3874.

Lechterbeck, J., et al. 2014. How was Bell Beaker economy related to Corded Ware and Early Bronze Age lifestyles? Archaeological, botanical and palynological evidence from the Hegau, Western Lake Constance region. *Environmental Archaeology* 19(2): 95–113.

Linderholm, A. et al. 2020. Corded Ware cultural complexity uncovered using genomic and isotopic analysis from south-eastern Poland. *Scientific Reports* 10(1): 6885.

Lipson, M. et al. 2017. Parallel palaeogenomic transects reveal complex genetic history of early European farmers. *Nature* 551(7680): 368–372.

Mallory, J. P. 1989. *In search of the Indo-Europeans: Language, archaeology and myth*. London: Thames & Hudson.

Malmström, H., et al. 2019. The genomic ancestry of the Scandinavian Battle Axe Culture people and their relation to the broader Corded Ware horizon. *Proceedings. Biological Sciences/The Royal Society* 286(1912): 20191528.

Mathieson, I., et al. 2015. Genome-wide patterns of selection in 230 ancient Eurasians. *Nature* 528(7583): 499–503.

2018. The genomic history of southeastern Europe. *Nature* 555: 197–203.

Meller, H., et al. (ed). 2019. *Late Neolithic and early Bronze Age settlement archaeology: 11th Archaeological Conference of Central Germany, October 18–20, 2018 in Halle (Saale)*. Halle: Landesamt für Denkmalpflege und Archäologie Sachsen-Anhalt, Landesmuseum für Vorgeschichte.

Mittnik, A., et al. 2018. The genetic prehistory of the Baltic Sea region. *Nature Communications* 9(1): 442.

2019. Kinship-based social inequality in Bronze Age Europe. *Science* 366(6466): 731–734.

Monroy Kuhn, J. M., M. Jakobsson, & T. Günther. 2018. Estimating genetic kin relationships in prehistoric populations. *PLoS ONE* 13(4): e0195491.

Müller, J. 2001. Zum Verhältnis von Schnurkeramik und jüngeren Trichterbechergruppen im Mittelelbe-Saale-Gebiet: Kontinuität oder Diskontinuität? In: T. H. Gohlisch & L. Reisch (ed.), *Die Stellung der endneolithischen Chamer Kultur in ihrem räumlichen und zeitlichen Kontext* (Kolloquien des Institutes für Ur- und Frühgeschichte Erlangen), 120–136. Erlangen: Dr. Faustus.

2009. A revision of Corded Ware settlement pattern: New results from the Central European Low Mountain Range. *Proceedings of the Prehistoric Society* 75: 125–142.

2019. Boom and bust, hierarchy and balance: From landscape to social meaning: Megaliths and societies in Northern Central Europe. In: J. Müller, M. Hinz, & M. Wunderlich (ed.), *Megaliths – Societies – Landscapes. Early monumentality and social differentiation in Neolithic Europe*, 29–74. Bonn: Dr. Rudolf Habelt GmbH.

Müller, S. 1898. De jydske Enkeltgrave fra Stenalderen. *Aarbøger* 1898: 157–282.

Münster, A., et al. 2018. 4000 years of human dietary evolution in central Germany, from the first farmers to the first elites. *PLoS ONE* 13(3): e0194862.

Narasimhan, V. M., et al. 2019. The formation of human populations in South and Central Asia. *Science* 365(6457).

Nielsen, P. O. 2020. The development of the two-aisled longhouse in the Neolithic and Early Bronze Age. In: L. Reedz-Sparrevohn, O. Thirup Kastholm, & P. O. Nielsen (ed.), *Houses for the living. Two-aisled houses from the Neolithic and Early Bronze Age in Denmark* (The Royal Society of Northern Antiquities), 9–51. Copenhagen: University Press of Southern Denmark.

Odgaard, B. V. 1994. The Holocene vegetation history of northern West Jutland, Denmark. *Nordic Journal of Botany* 14(5): 546–546.

Olalde, I., et al. 2018. The Beaker phenomenon and the genomic transformation of northwest Europe. *Nature* 555: 190–196.
Piličiauskas, G., et al. 2017. The transition from foraging to farming (7000–500 cal BC) in the SE Baltic: A re-evaluation of chronological and palaeodietary evidence from human remains. *Journal of Archaeological Science: Reports* 14: 530–542.
2018. The Corded Ware culture in the Eastern Baltic: New evidence on chronology, diet, beaker, bone and flint tool function. *Journal of Archaeological Science: Reports* 21: 538–552.
2020. Fishers of the Corded Ware culture in the Eastern Baltic. *Acta Archaeologica* 91(1): 95–120.
Racimo, F., et al. 2020. The spatiotemporal spread of human migrations during the European Holocene. *Proceedings of the National Academy of Sciences of the United States of America* 117(16): 8989–9000.
Rascovan, N., et al. 2019. Emergence and spread of basal lineages of Yersinia pestis during the Neolithic decline. *Cell* 176(1/2): 295–305.e10.
Rasmussen, P., & J. Olsen. 2009. Soil erosion and land-use change during the last six millennia recorded in lake sediments of Gudme Sø, Fyn, Denmark. *GEUS Bulletin* 17: 37–40.
Rasmussen, S., et al. 2015. Early divergent strains of Yersinia pestis in Eurasia 5,000 years ago. *Cell* 163(3): 571–582.
Rasteiro, R., & L. Chikhi. 2013. Female and male perspectives on the Neolithic transition in Europe: Clues from ancient and modern genetic data. *PLoS ONE* 8(4): e60944.
Renfrew, C. 1987. *Archaeology and language: The puzzle of Indo-European origins*. London: Pimlico.
Robb, J., & O. J. T. Harris. 2018. Becoming gendered in European prehistory: Was Neolithic gender fundamentally different? *American Antiquity* 83(1): 128–147.
Robson, H. K., et al. 2019. Diet, cuisine and consumption practices of the first farmers in the southeastern Baltic. *Archaeological and Anthropological Sciences* 11(8): 4011–4024.
Saag, L., et al. 2017. Extensive farming in Estonia started through a sex-biased migration from the steppe. *Current Biology: CB* 27 (14): 2185–2193.e6.
2021. Genetic ancestry changes in Stone to Bronze Age transition in the East European plain. *Science Advances* 7(4): eabd6535.
Salanova, L. 2011. Chronologie et facteurs d'évolution des sépultures individuelles campaniformes dans le Nord de la France. In: Laure Salanova and Yaramila Tcheremissinoff (ed.), *Les sépultures individuelles campaniformes en France*, 125–142. Paris: CNRS Éditions.
Schrader, O. 1883. *Sprachvergleichung und Urgeschichte: Linguistisch-historische Beiträge zur Erforschung des indogermanischen Altertums*. Jena.
Schroeder, H., et al. 2019. Unraveling ancestry, kinship, and violence in a Late Neolithic mass grave. *Proceedings of the National Academy of Sciences of the United States of America* 116(22): 10705–10710.
Shennan, S., et al. 2013. Regional population collapse followed initial agriculture booms in mid-Holocene Europe. *Nature Communications* 4: 2486.
Siemen, P. 1997. *Early Corded Ware culture. The A-horizon, fiction or fact? International symposium in Jutland, 2nd–7th May 1994* (Arkaeologiske Rapporter 2). Esbjerg: Esbjerg Museum.
Sjögren, K.-G. 2006. *Ecology and economy in Stone Age and Bronze Age Scania* (Skånska spår – Arkeologi längs Västkustbanan. National Heritage Board). Stockholm: Riksantikvarieämbetet.
2020. Kinship and social organization in Copper Age Europe. A cross-disciplinary analysis of archaeology, DNA, isotopes, and anthropology from two Bell Beaker cemeteries. *PLoS ONE* 15(11): e0241278.
Sjögren, K.-G., T. D. Price, & K. Kristiansen. 2016. Diet and mobility in the Corded Ware of Central Europe. *PLoS ONE* 11(5): e0155083.
Spyrou, M. A., et al. 2018. Analysis of 3800-year-old Yersinia pestis genomes suggests Bronze Age origin for bubonic plague. *Nature Communications* 9(1): 2234.
2019. Ancient pathogen genomics as an emerging tool for infectious disease research. *Nature Reviews. Genetics* 20(6): 323–340.
Strahm, C. 2002. Tradition und Wandel der sozialen Strukturen vom 3. zum 2. vorchristlichen Jahrtausend. In: J. Müller (ed.), *Vom Endneolithikum zur Frühbronzezeit: Muster sozialen Wandels? (Tagung Bamberg 14.–16. Juni 2001)* (Universitätsforschungen zur Prähistorischen Archäologie 90), 175–194. Bonn: Habelt.
Strahm, C., & M. Buchvaldek. 1991. *Die kontinentaleuropäischen Gruppen der Kultur mit Schnurkeramik*. Prague: Karolinum.
Struve, K. W. 1955. *Die Einzelgrabkultur in Schleswig-Holstein*. Neumünster: Offa-Bücher.
Sugita, S. 2007a. Theory of quantitative reconstruction of vegetation II: All you need is LOVE. *The Holocene* 17(2): 243–257.
2007b. Theory of quantitative reconstruction of vegetation I: Pollen from large sites REVEALS regional vegetation composition. *The Holocene* 17(2): 229–241.
Szczepanek, A., et al. 2018. Understanding Final Neolithic communities in south-eastern Poland: New insights on diet and mobility from isotopic data. *PLoS ONE* 13(12): e0207748.
Szécsényi-Nagy, A., et al. 2015. Tracing the genetic origin of Europe's first farmers reveals insights into their social organization. *Proceedings. Biological Sciences/The Royal Society* 282(1805).
Theuerkauf, M., et al. 2016. A matter of dispersal: REVEALSinR introduces state-of-the-art dispersal models to quantitative vegetation reconstruction. *Vegetation History and Archaeobotany* 25(6): 541–553.
Theuerkauf, M., & J. Couwenberg. 2018. ROPES reveals past land cover and PPEs from single pollen records. *Frontiers of Earth Science in China* 6(14).
Ullrich, M. 2008. *Endneolithische Siedlungskeramik aus Ergersheim, Mittelfranken. Untersuchungen zur Chronologie von Schnurkeramik- und Glockenbechern an Rhein, Main und Neckar* (Universitätsforschungen zur Prähistorischen Archäologie). Bonn: Habelt.
Veit, U. 1989. Ethnic concepts in German prehistory: A case study on the relationship between cultural identity and archaeological objectivity. In: S. Shennan (ed.), *Archaeological approaches to cultural identity*. London: Routledge.
Wang, C.-C., et al. 2019. Ancient human genome-wide data from a 3000-year interval in the Caucasus corresponds with ecogeographic regions. *Nature Communications* 10(1): 590.
Wentink, K. 2020. *Stereotype. The role of grave sets in Corded Ware and Bell Beaker funerary practices*. Leiden: Sidestone Press.
Werens, K., A. Szczepanek, & P. Jarosz. 2018. Light stable isotope analysis of diet in Corded Ware culture communities: Święte, Jarosław District, South-Eastern Poland. *Baltic-Pontic Studies*, 23(1): 229–245.

Wiethold, J. 1998. *Studien zur jüngeren postglazialen Vegetations- und Siedlungsgeschichte im östlichen Schleswig-Holstein* (Universitätsforschungen zur Prähistorischen Archäologie). Bonn: Habelt.

Wilkins, J. F., & F. W. Marlowe. 2006. Sex-biased migration in humans: What should we expect from genetic data? *BioEssays* 28(3): 290–300.

Yu, H., et al. 2020. Paleolithic to Bronze Age Siberians reveal connections with First Americans and across Eurasia. *Cell* 181(6): 1232–1245.e20.

Zanon, M., et al. 2018. European forest cover during the past 12,000 years: A palynological reconstruction based on modern analogs and remote sensing. *Frontiers in Plant Science* 9: 253–253.

6 EMERGENT PROPERTIES OF THE CORDED WARE CULTURE: AN INFORMATION APPROACH

QUENTIN BOURGEOIS AND ERIK KROON

6.1 Introduction

How do virtually identical burial rituals and worldviews emerge among widely dispersed communities? Five thousand years ago, preliterate Corded Ware communities throughout Europe achieved this remarkable feat. For half a millennium, these communities performed near-identical burial rituals in an area that extends from the Volga to the Rhine. What processes shaped such durable uniformity?

The emergence of the Corded Ware culture is a defining moment in European prehistory. It is hailed as the first pan-European network, which facilitated the spread of technologies such as the wheel and metallurgy. Furthermore, the advent of the Corded Ware culture is thought to mark the introduction of Indo-European languages into Western Europe (Kristiansen et al. 2017).

Following recent publications of aDNA (notably Allentoft et al. 2015; Haak et al. 2015; Olalde et al. 2018) and isotope analyses (Price et al. 2004; Sjögren et al. 2016), mobility has become a crucial factor in explaining the emergence of the Corded Ware culture, be it at the level of populations or individuals (cf. Furholt 2017; Vander Linden 2016). However, mobility in itself does not explain the emergence or upkeep of uniform practices. Therefore, we advocate a complementary approach to these issues: an archaeology of information exchange.

We argue that at the heart of the Corded Ware phenomenon is a distinct idea of a proper burial of the dead. The longevity and widespread distribution of Corded Ware practices result from the dissemination, agreement upon, and reiteration of this idea between past agents. The material legacy of this reiteration is recognizable to us in the archaeological record as the Corded Ware culture. In other words, the Corded Ware culture is an emergent property of an information-sharing system. Consequently, we argue that a study of information exchange is crucial to understanding the instigation and upkeep of the Corded Ware culture.

Our approach is based on two assumptions:

First, the more strongly two graves resemble each other in their dressing of the dead (i.e. which artifacts were placed in the grave in which positions relative to the dead), the more likely shared notions of the appropriate dressing of the dead existed among mourners.

Second, we assume that the similarity between graves is influenced by physical distance. The dissemination of information in the third millennium BC will have relied on human mobility. Therefore, the greater the distance between any two graves, the more effort would be needed for information to travel between the two events and therefore the less likely they are to be similar. Thus, the combination of similarity and distance reveals a core property of the Corded Ware culture.

Building on these assumptions, our analysis indicates that Corded Ware communities shared notions about the dressing of the dead within limited geographic ranges (ca. 200 km). Moreover, this pattern is strongly pronounced in left-flexed burials, but not in right-flexed burials, for which similarities frequently occur at ranges in excess of 400 km. This disparity suggests a social practice in which notions of dressing the male dead were shared efficiently across large distances.

Therefore, these results fit well with mounting evidence for a male gender bias in Corded Ware society and might be linked to social institutions such as *Männerbunde*: an initiation rite in which young men from various communities convened in roaming bands where they learned the cultural practices of Corded Ware society (Cf. Anthony & Brown 2017; Kershaw 2000; Kristiansen et al. 2017). The nature of these bands could make them a crucial means by which particular notions of burial rites spread, ultimately giving rise to the homogeneous cultural phenomenon we observe in the archaeological record.

6.2 Similarity and Death in the Corded Ware Culture

Understanding similarity in material culture has long been one of the crucial pursuits of archaeological research. Indeed, one of the core tools in the archaeologist's toolkit – typochronology, or simply typology – aims to create a culture-historical framework of the archaeological record through similarities in material culture and practices. And although this method is not without its problems, the fact that it often *works* is in and of itself revealing and informs us of critical social processes (Sørensen 2015).

With regard to the Corded Ware culture, its homogeneity is arguably most evident in the highly similar and far-flung Corded Ware burial ritual. This uniformity is such that almost identical burials can be found in, for example, the Netherlands, Denmark, and Poland (Fig. 6.1). As such, these uniform burials are also the defining element of the Corded Ware culture as an archaeological phenomenon (Furholt 2014; Kristiansen et al. 2017).

The similarity of Corded Ware burials involves three elements: specific funerary architecture, distinct semi-flexed positions of the dead, and a restricted set of grave gifts.

The first element of the uniform Corded Ware burial ritual is funerary architecture. Corded Ware burials commonly consist of grave pits intended for a single person. Above-ground elements created during the funerary ritual, such as a palisaded ditch surrounding a barrow covering the burial, were also shared across the vast distribution of the Corded Ware culture (Bourgeois 2013; Hübner 2005; Pospieszny et al. 2015; Smejda et al. 2006).

Secondly, the deceased are placed in specific positions inside the grave pit, with gender in a crucial role (Furholt 2014; Turek 2017). The bodies of the deceased were placed in a flexed position and oriented along cardinal directions. The majority of the men were placed on their right side, facing south and with the head pointing toward the west. By contrast, women were interred on their left side, head in an easterly direction, but also facing south. As such, men and women's graves feature the dead in mirrored positions. Note that the exact orientation may vary from region to region, but the dichotomy in orientation and gender opposition is generally maintained.

The third element in the uniformity of Corded Ware burials is the grave goods. The dead are provided with selections from a specific range of items, which are also stylistically similar throughout the distribution of the Corded Ware culture. This includes, among others, flint axes, battleaxes, beakers, amphorae, a range of ceramic vessels, flint blades/daggers, amber beads, and copper and amber ornaments (Furholt 2014).

Yet the similarity in Corded Ware burials extends beyond the abovementioned elements. As we have demonstrated previously, Corded Ware burials also exhibit strong preferential placement of the grave gifts within the burial pit (Bourgeois & Kroon 2017). This suggests that the uniformity of the Corded Ware culture cannot be reduced to the similarity in objects, but also entails conventions about the use of these objects in the burial ritual. Similar to the pose of the body, these conventions can be shown to relate to the gender of the deceased. For example, a persistent pattern in left-flexed burials is the placement of ceramic vessels behind the upper part of the body. Right-flexed burials may also exhibit this practice, but more commonly contain a flint dagger/blade in the pelvic area in combination with a battleax or flint ax in front of the body. We have previously argued that these distinct patterns are different

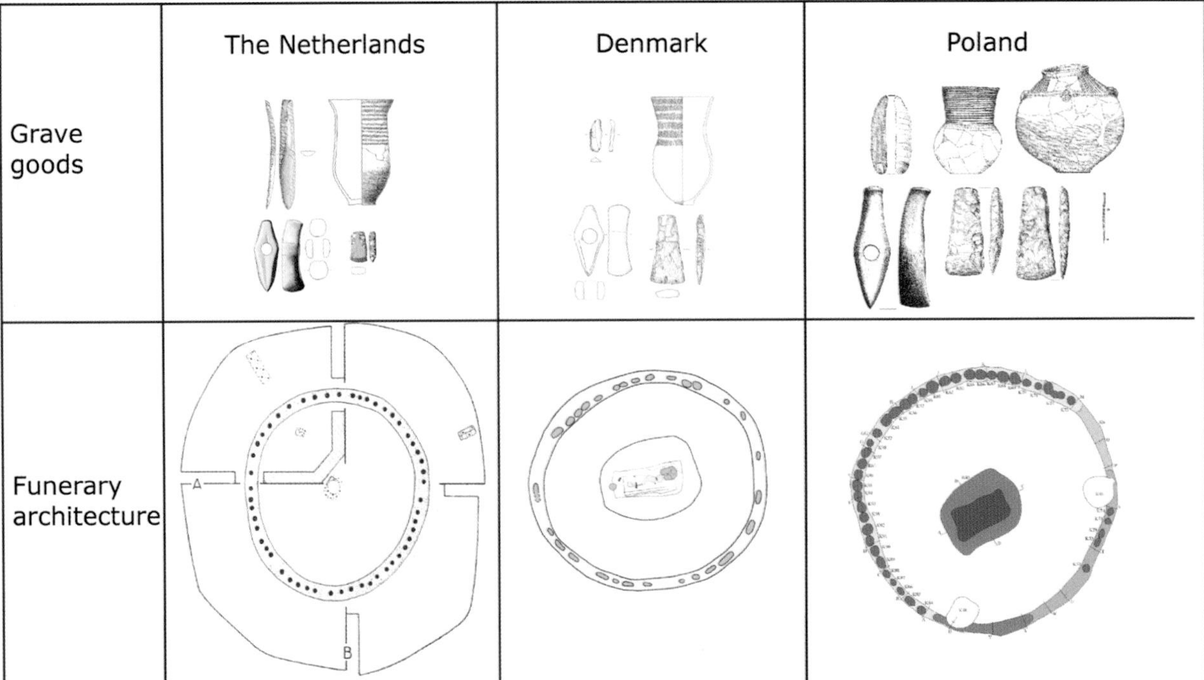

FIG. 6.1. Identical Corded Ware grave sets and graves from the Netherlands (Drenth & Lohof 2005; Van Giffen 1935), Denmark (Hübner 2005), and Poland (Pospieszny et al. 2015)(not to scale). Upper half: the grave sets include the eponymous Corded Ware culture beakers, as well as flint axes, battleaxes, and flint blades/daggers. Additionally, the grave from Poland features an amphora, a second flint ax, and a copper awl. Lower half: similarities in Corded Ware burials extend beyond the grave goods. The three graves from the same regions all feature a palisaded ditch surrounding a low mound, and a central grave pit.

ways in which specific Corded Ware communities dressed their dead for the afterlife (Bourgeois & Kroon 2017).

6.3 Understanding Corded Ware Similarities

The similarity of Corded Ware burials has been the subject of intensive debate. This debate essentially boils down to two questions. First, what process(es) gave rise to the Corded Ware culture? Second, how was such uniformity maintained over such a vast area and time span?

Early examples of the debate include the A-horizon hypothesis or *Einheitshorizont*. This hypothesis proposes that the Corded Ware culture started out as uniform and diversified over time as migrating communities slowly lost contact after a single migration event (e.g. Buchvaldek 1986; Furholt 2014).

The advent of new analytical techniques such as aDNA and isotope analysis has recently given the debate on the similarity of Corded Ware burials new impetus. Recently, two new positions have emerged in the debate about the homogeneity and emergence of Corded Ware culture. The first position revolves around aDNA analysis and population mobility. The second position emphasizes patterns of local variation and individual action. We argue that both explanations ultimately fall short of explaining these phenomena.

The first position related to the explanation of Corded Ware is largely based on recently published aDNA analyses (notably Allentoft et al. 2015; Haak et al. 2015; Olalde et al. 2018). These analyses demonstrate that Corded Ware (and later Bell Beaker) individuals exhibit stronger genetic links with Yamnaya culture individuals than individuals associated with earlier Neolithic cultures in Europe. Based on these findings, the Corded Ware culture is argued to be the product of a massive migration into Europe (Kristiansen et al. 2017).

In parallel (and slightly before the aDNA analyses), discussion of the nature of the Corded Ware culture has emphasized the dimension of local and individual variation within the Corded Ware culture (Furholt 2014; vander Linden 2004). Recently, the same authors expanded their position to include a critique on aDNA analyses (Furholt 2017; Heyd 2017; vander Linden 2016). They argue that Corded Ware culture should not be interpreted as a single entity, but rather that interpretations of this culture should emphasize the importance of individual mobility and its impact on local contexts, contrary to an invasion-like mass migration as a root cause for the Corded Ware culture.

Both approaches provide an interesting perspective on Corded Ware culture and there is clear-cut evidence backing arguments on both sides. On the one hand, the significant genetic change must have come about through a large-scale demographic event, regardless of whether it was caused by an actual mass-scale migration *sensu strictu* or by a more complex social phenomenon. On the other hand, focusing on individual and personal mobility clearly highlights the complexity of the Corded Ware phenomenon and its problematic, multifaceted nature.

Notwithstanding the validity of both perspectives, there is an underlying issue that remains unaddressed. Neither approach provides a mechanism by which the fundamental factors it proposes, be it individual actions or genetic change, result in the overarching phenomenon that we observe in the archaeological record: widespread and durable similarity in the shape of Corded Ware cultural practices. How does a migration lead to the instigation and, more importantly, the upkeep of similarity for several centuries? And, vice versa, why is the Corded Ware culture immediately recognizable as an entity if it consists of small-scale variability?

We argue below that we need to return to the most basic conceptualization of similarity in order to answer these questions. Similarity in the archaeological record results from past agents deciding to act in a similar fashion (Sørensen 2015). Returning to the Corded Ware burial ritual, we have argued that it is defined by a commonly shared idea of dressing the dead. Consequently, information on this idea must have circulated and – as is the nature of all information exchange – been modified through time and space. We argue that studying this information exchange and its properties is crucial to understanding the Corded Ware phenomenon.

Seen in this light, burials are ideal for reconstructing the transmission of information and comparing the flow of information between different regions. First, burials are closed events that represent discrete activities. Second, they are the material remnants of the acting out of (parts of) worldviews and ideas of the afterlife by mourners (Oestigaard & Goldhahn 2006). Third, burials result from conscious, emotionally charged choices and acts by mourners and can be considered fundamental rituals of society (Barraud & Platenkamp 1990) which are deeply rooted in worldviews (Metcalf & Huntington 1991). As a result, close resemblance in burials is therefore indicative of (particular elements of) shared worldviews. It is critical to emphasize that similarity in burials does not signify, *per se*, similar meanings attributed to these elements, but rather a similar conceptual framework in which these elements are employed.

Below, we detail this approach to Corded Ware culture that centers on information exchange and emergence. Furthermore, we argue that this approach can be a valuable complement to contemporary approaches such as aDNA analysis and small-scale processes.

6.4 Emergence and Information Sharing in the Corded Ware Culture

At the heart of the Corded Ware culture as an archaeological phenomenon are similar practices and material cultures. In the first place, these practices result from countless deliberate, informed choices by agents to act in a particular manner in the past (Sørensen 2015). These agents entered into meaningful negotiations with other agents on the proper course of action.

The outcomes of these negotiations contributed to the agent's own notions of proper action, which, in turn, were drawn from and reiterated in subsequent negotiations (cf. Lave & Wenger 1991; Wenger 1998). The uniformity observed in the archaeological record is the emergent outcome of countless such interactions in which information was shared, agreed upon, and put into practice (cf. Centola et al. 2007; Centola & Baronchelli 2015).

Returning to the Corded Ware culture itself, what we define as Corded Ware culture is an emergent property of countless events during which past agents shared information, agreed on a proper course of action, acted out this agreement, and ultimately left a material legacy in the archaeological record. As such, the properties of Corded Ware culture as a whole cannot be understood from the actions or the DNA of the individual agents alone, but rather require an understanding of the relations and of information sharing between these agents. These properties are systemic and are not recognizable at the level of agents.

This redefinition has an important corollary, as we explore in this article. Due to the central role attributed to interactions between agents in the distribution of information, one would expect the resulting agreements to be bound by distance. During the third millennium BC, the spatial distribution of information was strongly bound by the physical distance agents had to cross. Therefore, distance must have had a significant impact on the emergence and upkeep of Corded Ware culture. We refer to this corollary as "distance decay" and demonstrate its existence in Corded Ware burial ritual. Moreover, we show that right-flexed burials are less affected by distance decay than left-flexed burials.

6.5 Data and Method

This paper builds on the data set we presented previously (Bourgeois & Kroon 2017), which encompasses data on 1161 Corded Ware burials from the Netherlands, Denmark, Germany, and the Czech Republic (Fig. 6.2).

For each burial, we collected data on the orientation of the body, various categories of artifacts present (such as beakers, flint blades, and amphorae), and the position of these artifacts in the grave according to a predefined scheme (Bourgeois & Kroon 2017).

The number and position of artifacts were combined into a compound variable and attached to the graves as a string. Subsequently, we calculated the cosine similarity of each individual grave to every other grave in the data set. All input

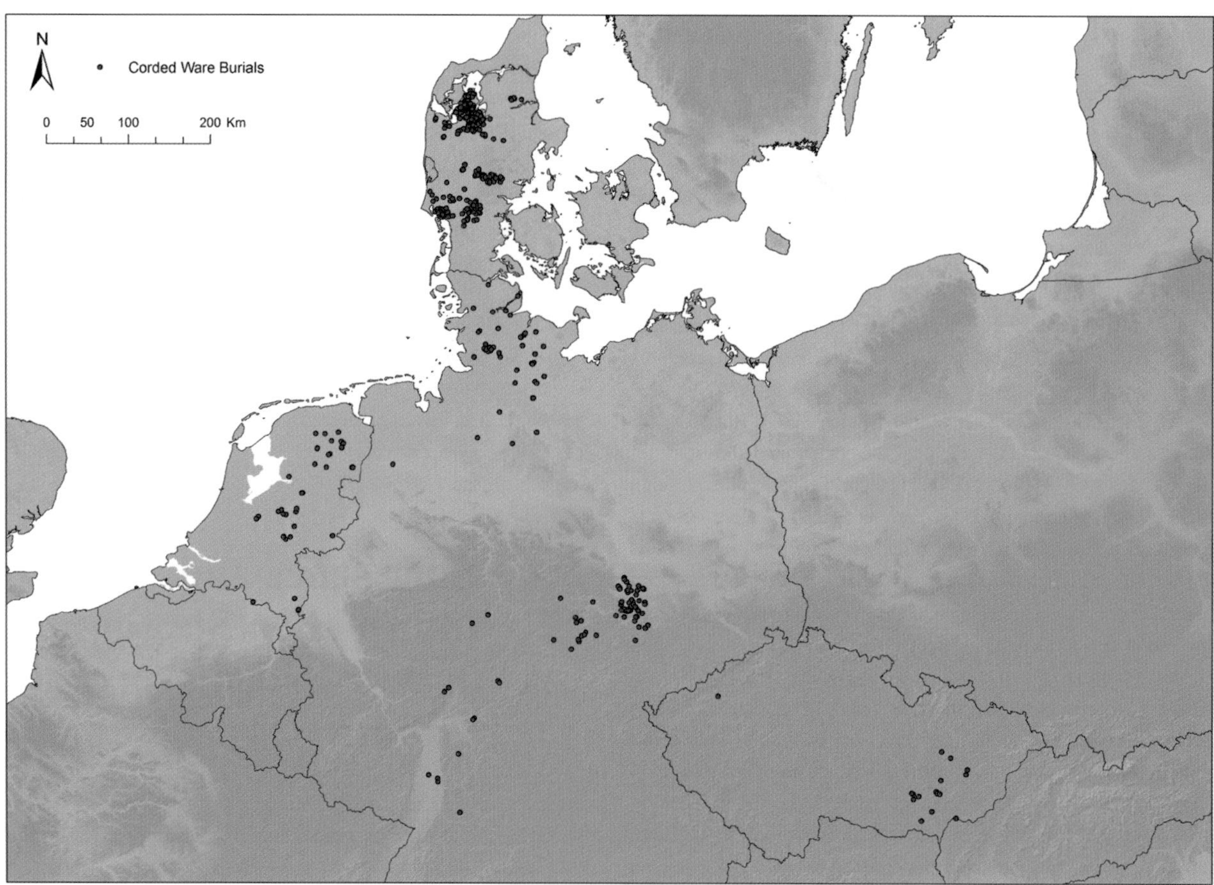

FIG. 6.2. Geographical distribution of Corded Ware (n = 1161) burials in the data set.

values were normalized prior to analysis to prevent a bias based on the number of objects. The cosine similarity index represents strings of variables as coordinates in a multidimensional space; the similarity of two strings is then calculated as the angle between lines from the origin to these coordinates (Salton & McGill 1983). For a more detailed discussion on the data and methodology, we refer to our previous work (Bourgeois & Kroon 2017).

In order to add a spatial dimension, we computed the distance (as the crow flies) between every possible pair of burials for the entire data set (n = 1161). Subsequently, we appended this data to a matrix with the similarity value for each pair of burials and removed all ties for which the similarity value equaled zero. The resulting data set contains 99,741 ties.

Each tie has four attributes: (1) the source burial for the comparison; (2) the target burial for the comparison; (3) the geographical distance separating these burials in kilometers; and (4) an expression of the similarity between source and target burials as a cosine similarity score between 0 and 1.

Among the 1161 burials in the entire data set, there are 281 burials in which skeletal remains were preserved and definitive observations about the orientation of the deceased can be made. This high-quality sub-data set contains 169 right-flexed and 112 left-flexed burials. We extracted all these burials and their ties to other burials in their respective group to compare patterns in the overarching data set to patterns in this high-quality data set.

6.6 Results

A preliminary analysis of the distances between target and source readily reveals a number of patterns, as well as a disparity between right- and left-flexed burials (see Fig. 6.3; Table 6.1). Fig. 6.3 shows the percentage of target nodes (i.e., similar burials) that fall within specific ranges of their sources.

The values derived from the entire data set show a clear drop-off beyond 200 km: nearly 65% of all similar graves can be found within 200 km of their sources. This number steadily increases to ca. 94% at ranges of 700 km.

However, the plots for connections among right-flexed and left-flexed burials differ in their relation toward this pattern for the entire data set. Among left-flexed burials, almost 86% of all similar burials can be found within 200 km of a burial. At ranges of 700 km, as much as 99.5% of all similar burials is accounted for. By contrast, right-flexed burials have close to half of their ties within a range of 200 km. This number steadily rises to roughly 92% at a range of 700 km.

It follows that uniformity in Corded Ware burial rituals is often found within a couple of hundred kilometers. This is particularly true for left-flexed burials, but not for right-flexed burials, for which similar targets frequently occur well beyond 400 and even 600 km. This finding corroborates the observation made previously, namely that right-flexed burials make an important contribution to the uniformity of the Corded Ware culture (cf. Bourgeois & Kroon 2017).

Fig. 6.3 captures the number of similar burials at given ranges but does not account for the actual similarity between these burials (all burials are presented as equally similar). Potentially, long-range targets could be significantly less similar than close-range targets (i.e. the further away two burials are from one another, the lower their similarity score). To compensate for the actual strength of the similarity between source and target, we summed the cosine similarity values (which are numeric values between 0 and 1) of all links within distance bins of 100 km and plotted a cumulative frequency distribution of the resulting values (see Fig. 6.4; Table 6.2). The numbers were converted to percentages to facilitate comparison between

TABLE 6.1. Background data for Fig. 6.3 From left to right: the upper boundaries of the distance bins, the number of targets in each bin for the entire data set, left- and right-flexed burials, and the cumulative percentage of targets by distance for the same categories.

Bins	**Count of target burials**			**Cumulative percentage of target burials**		
Upper boundaries	**All burials**	**Right-flexed burials**	**Left-flexed burials**	**All burials**	**Right-flexed burials**	**Left-flexed burials**
km	*N*	*N*	*N*	%	%	%
100	42072	1074	655	42,18	29,39	57,71
200	22604	680	320	64,84	48,00	85,90
300	4912	364	60	69,77	57,96	91,19
400	4054	264	26	73,83	65,19	93,48
500	5588	362	42	79,44	75,10	97,18
600	7226	376	13	86,68	85,39	98,33
700	7378	240	13	94,08	91,95	99,47
800	4178	140	1	98,27	95,79	99,56
900	816	82	2	99,09	98,03	99,74
1000	876	72	3	99,96	100,00	100,00
1100	36	0	0	100,00	100,00	100,00

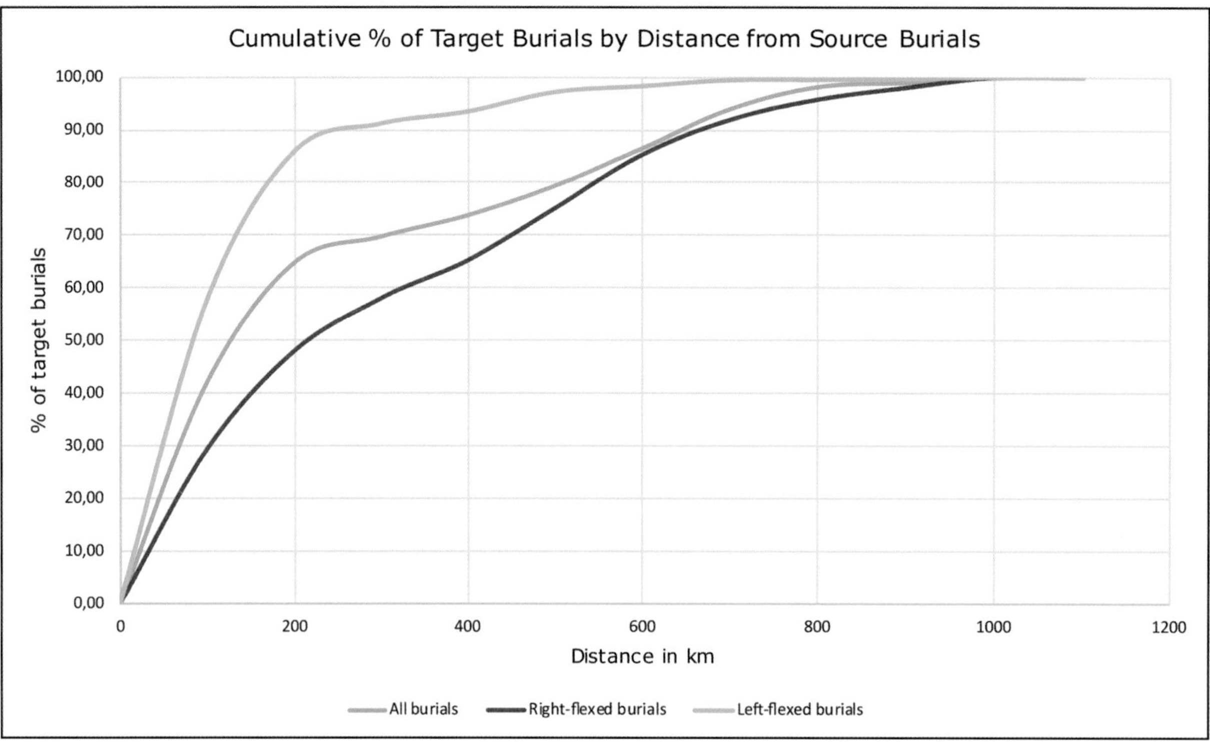

FIG. 6.3. Cumulative percentage of similar burials (i.e. target nodes) across all relations that occur within a specified distance (in km) of the source (see Table 1). The graph shows a steep decline in similar graves beyond 200 km for the entire data set and left-flexed burials in specific, while right-flexed burials feature a steady increase in the number of targets as distance increases.

all burials, and right-and left-flexed burials in particular. Note that Figs. 6.3 and 6.4 should be understood in conjunction, as Fig. 6.4 cannot distinguish between numerous targets with low similarity and single targets with high similarity (i.e. two burials with a similarity of 1 have the same weight as ten burials with a low value).

Fig. 6.4 effectively shows the percentage of the total similarity of all graves that occurs within specific ranges. It corroborates the trends initially observed in Fig. 6.3. For the entire data set, approximately 78% of the total similarity can be found within a range of 200 km, whereas ca. 97% of all similarity occurs within ranges of 700 km. The increase relative to the actual count of similar graves (65% to 78% respectively) further indicates that connections at short ranges represent more of the overall similarity than those at ranges beyond 200 km (i.e., the closer two burials are to each other in space, the more likely they are to be similar).

Fig. 6.4 also confirms the difference between left-flexed and right-flexed graves relative to the entire data set. The total similarity for left-flexed burials at a range of 200 km is almost 90% and shows an asymptotic increase toward 99.7% at 700 km (both values are close to the absolute counts in Fig. 6.3).

By contrast, right-flexed burials only exhibit ca. 54% of their total similarity at ranges below 200 km and gradually build toward 95% at ranges of 700 km. Contrary to the overall data set, these values are closer to the actual count of targets, which implies a more equal contribution of every target to the similarity overall. In other words, similarity is relatively unaffected by distance in right-flexed burials. A two-independent-sample Kolmogorov-Smirnov test confirms the significance of these differences between left- and right-flexed burials at 2sigma for a p-value smaller than 0.000.

The pattern for the entire data set demonstrates that the majority of similar graves in Corded Ware culture can be found at intervening distances of less than 200 km, but that significant similarities persist up to 700 km. Moreover, these graphs highlight the differences between left- and right-flexed burials. Left-flexed burials display this trend more extremely, with only 10% of similarity between graves at ranges in excess of 200 km. By contrast, the right-flexed burials are significantly less impacted by intervening distance.

6.6.1 A Network Perspective

To visualize the trends in similarity and distance visible in left- and right-flexed burials, we plotted both the right- and left-flexed data sets as networks (see Fig. 6.5 and 6.6). The distances between connected nodes (graves) in these networks are proportional to the geographical distance between these graves, whereas the strength of the ties is dependent upon the similarity between these graves (i.e., the color of the tie between them).

The network for left-flexed graves (Fig. 6.5) mirrors the patterns observed in Figs. 6.3 and 6.4. The strong ties in this network occur predominantly between burials with short intervening geographic distances. As a result, nodes cluster in groups that lie within the same or adjacent regions. A number of long-distance connections is also visible, but

TABLE 6.2. Total similarity by distance from Corded Ware source burials.

Bins	Summed similarity values of target burials			Cumulative percentage of similarity of target burials		
Upper boundary	All burials	Right-flexed burials	Left-flexed burials	All burials	Right-flexed burials	Left-flexed burials
km	*Similarity value*	*Similarity value*	*Similarity value*	%	%	%
100	24213,95	428,49	278,29	50,78	36,15	59,51
200	12893,83	212,90	137,54	77,82	54,12	88,92
300	1907,98	119,80	20,91	81,82	64,23	93,40
400	1294,18	78,15	9,49	84,53	70,82	95,43
500	1644,03	95,39	12,80	87,98	78,87	98,16
600	2017,68	104,39	4,52	92,21	87,68	99,13
700	2073,01	84,18	2,80	96,56	94,78	99,73
800	1129,87	29,56	0,15	98,93	97,28	99,76
900	249,71	20,27	0,76	99,45	98,99	99,92
1000	249,00	12,02	0,35	99,97	100,00	100,00
1100	13,70	0	0	100,00	100,00	100,00

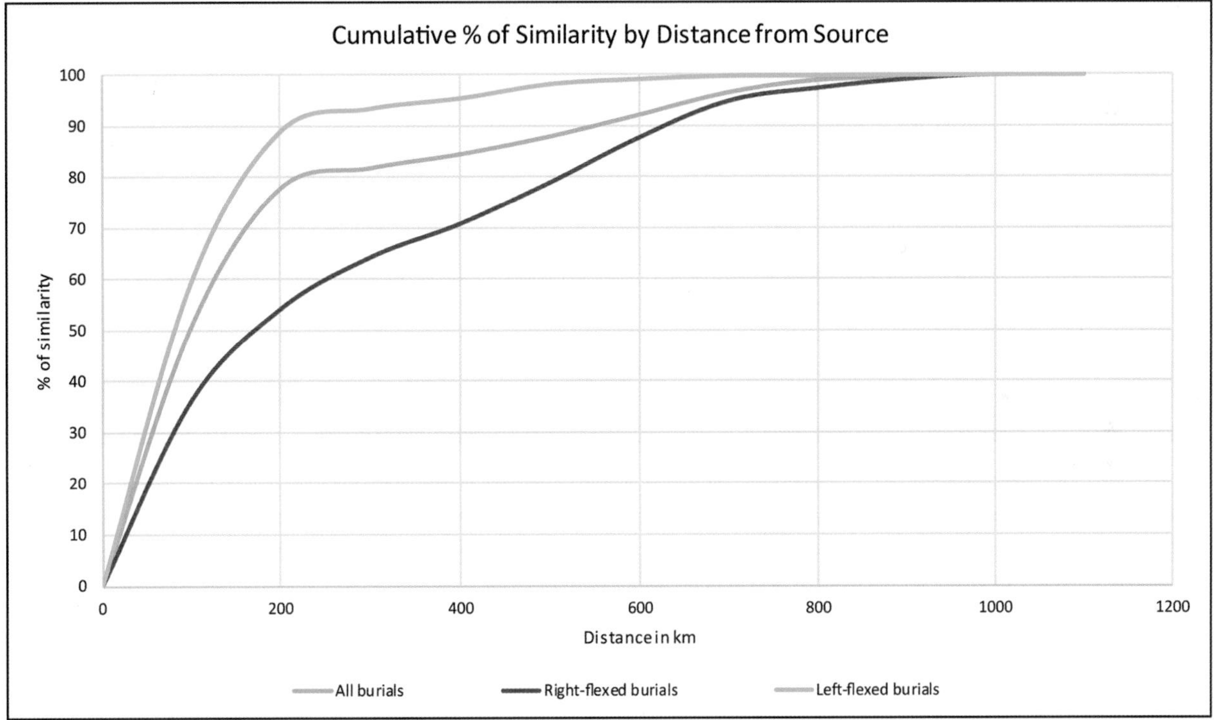

FIG. 6.4. Cumulative percentage curve of the total similarity within specified distances of the source for the entire data set, left-, and right-flexed burials. This graph shows the similarity between any two pairs of burials, summed by distance, and recalculated as percentages to facilitate comparisons (see Table 6.2). The entire data set exhibits a drop-off in similarity beyond 200km, followed by a steady increase toward 100%. However, left- and right-flexed burials show contrasting patterns. An asymptotic trend is visible for left-flexed graves: a sharp increase to 89% at a range of 200km, followed by minute increases toward 100%. By contrast, the curve for right-flexed burials exhibits a sharp increase to 36% at 100 km but follows a near-linear increase until 700 km (95%). A Kolmogorov-Smirnov Z test shows that the difference between these cumulative percentage distributions is significant at $p < 0.000$ for 2sigma.

these connections generally exhibit low similarity values (see, for example, the cluster of Danish burials at the bottom right).

When compared to Fig. 6.5, Fig. 6.6 shows a different pattern of overall connectivity for right-flexed graves. Graves from various regions are placed close together due to their small relative distances, but ties with high similarity values cut across these spatial separations, while strong internal connections are present as well.

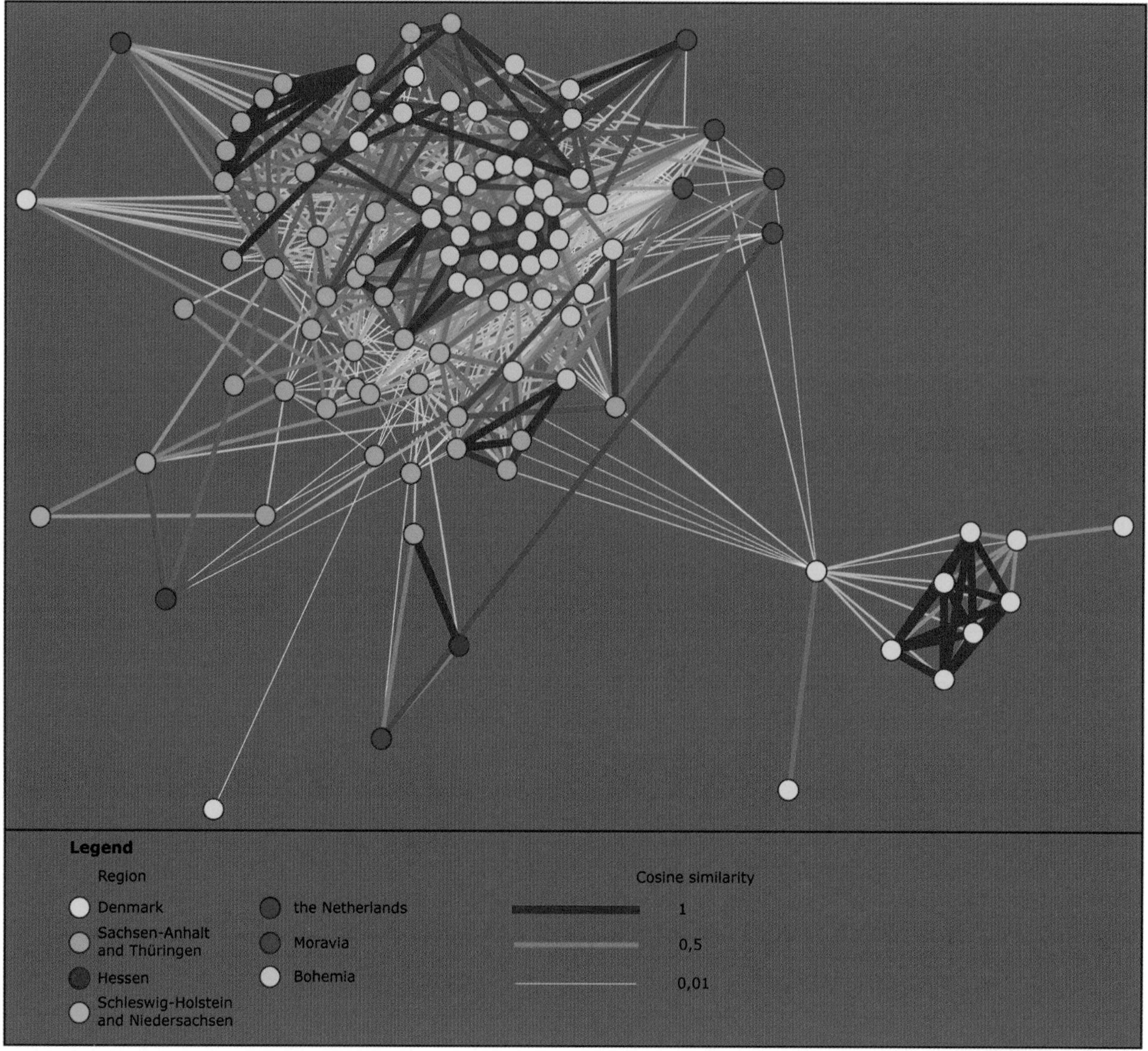

FIG. 6.5. Network representation of the distance and similarity between left-flexed burials in the data set. The similarity is indicated by the thickness and redness of the tie, whereas the length of the tie is proportional to the distance (as the crow flies) between the burials it connects. The strongest similarities in this graph are mostly found in graves within the same, or adjacent regions, resulting in several clusters of graves at short spatial distances.

6.7 Discussion

The results outlined above provide clear evidence for the existence of information decay within the Corded Ware culture. A general trend exists with regard to the occurrence of similar graves in which the number of similar graves and the relative similarity of graves decreases as distance increases. The basis for the observed similarities between graves is the presence and placement of objects in the burial pit with the deceased. These actions reflect deeply seated worldviews and are the outcomes of meaningful negotiations between mourners about the perceived proper way to dress the deceased for the afterlife.

6.7.1 Information Exchange in Corded Ware Culture

Our analysis of distance decay for the entire data set demonstrates a decline in similarity between burials at ranges of ca. 200 km. This pattern is emphasized in left-flexed burials, whereas it is less pronounced in right-flexed burials.

The 200 km range is grounded in the meaningful negotiations mourners undertook to determine the proper manner in which to bury deceased individuals in their communities: actions that are deeply rooted in the fundamental worldviews of societies. Therefore, the drop-off in similarity at ranges of 200 km suggests that such negotiations and interactions

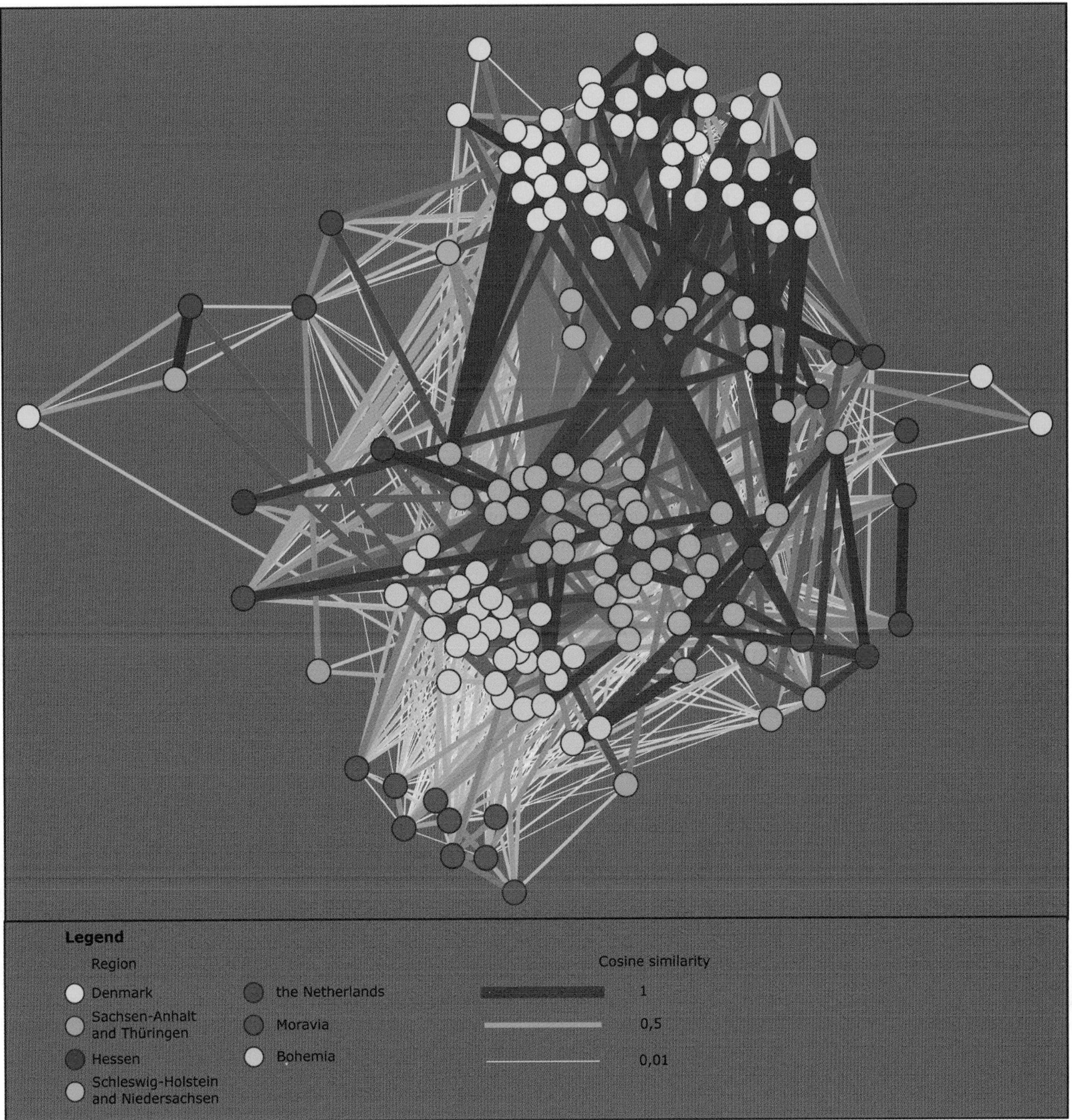

Fig. 6.6. Network visualization of the distances and similarities between right-flexed burials in the data set. Right-flexed burials show significantly more strong links across large distances when compared to left-flexed burials (Fig. 6.5), which is represented by the thick, dark red lines between regions. The strength of the ties is indicated by the thickness and redness of the lines. The length of a tie between two burials is proportional to the geographic distance (as the crow flies) between these burials.

themselves occurred at limited ranges. These ranges could be the boundaries of *communities of practice*: groups of people formed around a shared notion of the proper course of action (Lave & Wenger 1991; Wenger 1998). Following these inferences, the total distribution of the Corded Ware culture would be constituted by several such communities that represent the small-scale variability observed in Corded Ware culture (Cf. Furholt 2014). An interesting avenue of research would be to cross-reference such ranges in other practices, forms of material culture, or even dialects and mobility patterns.

If we accept the 200 km drop-off as the baseline distance for interactions within communities, then it is clear that right-flexed graves frequently cut across these communities. It should be noted that the same ranges do occur in left-flexed graves, but are less common. Therefore, right-flexed graves might constitute important connective events for different communities and as such have a profound impact on the spread of similar practices. In other words: these burials would have a crucial role in instigating and maintaining the overall similarities within Corded Ware culture (Centola & Baronchelli 2015).

6.7.2 Connections with aDNA, Isotope Analysis, and Linguistics

The exceptionally long-range similarities of right-flexed graves (sometimes well beyond 700 km) versus the tendency toward regionality in left-flexed burials highlight the important role of gender in the social conventions on dressing the dead. This outcome corroborates recurrent evidence for gender-related social phenomena visible in aDNA and isotope analysis.

Analyses of aDNA have pointed out substantial differences in continuity of sex-specific genetic material during the third millennium BC. These differences hint at a male sex bias in the migrations from the Pontic–Caspian steppes that is more pronounced in Western than in Eastern Europe (Brandt et al. 2013; Goldberg et al. 2017; Juras et al. 2018). Separately from aDNA analysis, isotope analyses have demonstrated high mobility in adolescent males of the Corded Ware culture, but strikingly also in females (Knipper et al. 2017; Sjögren et al. 2016).

The abovementioned aDNA and isotope evidence has been used to support linguistic evidence for the existence of so-called *Männerbunde* in which young men gathered and traveled around as a form of initiation (cf. Anthony & Brown 2017; Kershaw 2000; Kristiansen et al. 2017), as well as archaeological evidence for an exogamous marriage system among Corded Ware communities, in which wives were obtained from contemporary Neolithic groups (Kristiansen et al. 2017).

We argue that the observed differences in distance decay best fit a phenomenon such as the *Männerbunde* if considered against male sex bias in migration or an exogamous, patrilocal marriage system. The relatively small distance decay of right-flexed burials – of which the majority are male burials – as compared to left-flexed burials suggests that information on male burial practices traveled more widely. It seems unlikely that a male sex bias in migration alone gave rise to this pattern, as the differences are kept up over time. Simple movement of groups who take along burial practices is in itself insufficient to explain long-term homogeneity: such a feat requires continued interaction and negotiation of practices. Therefore, it is more likely that male mobility specifically occurred in a manner that facilitated the spread, and therefore homogenization, of practices of burial ritual. As such, the highly mobile and connective nature of *Männerbunde*, but also their role as "educative events," is an attractive hypothesis to explain the higher similarity in right-flexed burials. The coming and traveling together of young males from various areas in a social setting meant to transform them into adult members of society would be particularly suitable for the far-flung and diverse patterns of interaction required for the emergent uniformity of the Corded Ware culture.

Whereas isotope analysis also yields evidence for mobility in females, the homogenizing effect that mobility seems to have on male burial practices is absent in female burial practices. It is unclear why female mobility was not a vector for information on burial practices. We suggest that this is due to the nature of male vs. female mobility in the third millennium BC, which is possibly intertwined with conceptions of gendered mobility. An alternative explanation would be an exogamous patrilocal system in which women are integrated into male lineages and conform in terms of burial practices. However, we would argue that this was at least combined with an institution like *Männerbunde*, as it can be hypothesized that male burials would likely also develop localized practices in such a scenario (and the data does not bear this out). Apparently, notions of dressing the male dead were shared more efficiently over larger distances, suggesting a homogenizing social process that is absent in the female burial ritual.

Regardless, the differences we observe in distance decay between male and female burials as well as the results from aDNA and isotope analysis hint at a real-world social system in which information sharing was structured along gender. Corded Ware culture itself is an emergent property of this social system.

6.8 Concluding Remarks

How did preliterate Corded Ware communities initiate and maintain their strikingly uniform burial ritual for nearly five centuries, despite being dispersed across hundreds of kilometers of continental Europe?

We have argued that such similarities should be studied from the perspective of emergent social conventions and information exchange. These practices result from events in which agents shared, agreed upon, and put into practice information about the proper course of action. The Corded Ware culture is the emergent result of the material reflections of countless such events in the archaeological record.

We have studied the relation between intervening distance and the similarity of burials for a data set of 1161 Corded Ware burials. The similarities are grounded in the presence and placement of artifacts in the burial pit; factors that reflect meaningful decisions on the part of the mourners to dress their dead.

We have demonstrated that such notions exhibit distance decay: for the vast majority of graves, similar graves can be found within ranges of 200 km. We propose that this range reflects the baseline for interactions and is likely to be the limit of distinct communities of practice within Corded Ware culture. A patchwork of such communities constitutes the Corded Ware culture in its entirety and underlies its so-called multifaceted nature. The similarities of right-flexed graves frequently extend far beyond this 200 km range. Therefore, these burials may be events that bring together members of different communities of practice. As such, the meaningful negotiations among mourners for these particular burials contribute to the spread of highly similar notions of the proper manner to bury deceased individuals. Corded Ware culture as a whole encompasses several distinct communities organized around particular practices but connected through significant events.

References

Allentoft, M. E., M. Sikora, K.-G. Sjögren, ... & E. Willerslev. 2015. Population genomics of Bronze Age Eurasia. *Nature* 522(7555): 167–172.

Anthony, D. W., & D. R. Brown. 2017. The dogs of war: A Bronze Age initiation ritual in the Russian steppes. *Journal of Anthropological Archaeology* 48: 134–148.

Barraud, C., & J. D. M. Platenkamp. 1990. Rituals and the comparison of societies. *Bijdragen Tot Taal, Land En Volkenkunde KITLV* 146: 103–123.

Bourgeois, Q. P. J. 2013. *Monuments on the horizon: The formation of the barrow landscape throughout the 3rd and 2nd millennium BC.* Leiden: Sidestone Press.

Bourgeois, Q. P. J., & E. J. Kroon. 2017. The impact of male burials on the construction of Corded Ware identity: Reconstructing networks of information in the 3rd millennium BC. *PLoS ONE* 12(10): e0185971.

Brandt, G., W. Haak, C. J. Adler, & K. W. Alt. 2013. Ancient DNA reveals key stages in the formation of Central European mitochondrial genetic diversity. *Science* 342(6155): 257–261.

Buchvaldek, M. 1986. Zum gemeineuropäischen Horizont der Schnurkeramik. *Praehistorische Zeitschrift* 61(2): 129–151.

Centola, D., & A. Baronchelli. 2015. The spontaneous emergence of conventions: An experimental study of cultural evolution. *Proceedings of the National Academy of Sciences* 112(7): 201418838.

Centola, D., J. C. Gonzalez-Avella, V. M. Eguiluz, & M. San Miguel. 2007. Homophily, cultural drift, and the co-evolution of cultural groups. *Journal of Conflict Resolution* 51 (6): 905–929.

Drenth, E., & E. Lohof. 2005. Mounds for the dead: Funerary and burial ritual in Beaker period, Early and Middle Bronze Age. In L. P. Louwe Kooijmans, P. W. van den Broeke, H. Fokkens, & A. L. van Gijn (ed.), *The prehistory of the Netherlands*, 433–454. Amsterdam: Amsterdam University Press.

Furholt, M. 2014. Upending a "totality": Re-evaluating Corded Ware variability in Late Neolithic Europe. *Proceedings of the Prehistoric Society* 80: 1–20.

2017. Massive migrations? The impact of recent aDNA studies on our view of third millennium Europe. *European Journal of Archaeology* 21(2): 159–191.

Goldberg, A., T. Günther, N.A. Rosenberg, & M. Jakobsson. 2017. Ancient X chromosomes reveal contrasting sex bias in Neolithic and Bronze Age Eurasian migrations. *Proceedings of the National Academy of Sciences of the United States of America* 114(10): 2657–2662.

Haak, W., I. Lazaridis, N. Patterson, ... & D. Reich. 2015. Massive migration from the steppe was a source for Indo-European languages in Europe. *Nature* 522(7555): 207–211.

Heyd, V. 2017. Kossinna's smile. *Antiquity* 91(356): 348–359.

Hübner, E. 2005. *Jungneolithischen Gräber auf der Jütischen Halbinsel; Typologische und chronologische Studien zur Einzelgrabkultur.* Copenhagen: Det Kongeliche Nordiske Oldskriftselskab.

Juras, A., M. Chyleński, E. Ehler, ... & A. Kośko. 2018. Mitochondrial genomes reveal an east to west cline of steppe ancestry in Corded Ware populations. *Scientific Reports* 8(1): 11603.

Kershaw, K. 2000. *The one-eyed god: Odin and the (Indo-) Germanic Männerbund* (Journal of Indo-European Studies Monographs 36). Washington, DC: Institute for the Study of Man.

Knipper, C., A. Mittnik, K. Massy, ... & P. W. Stockhammer. 2017. Female exogamy and gene pool diversification at the transition from the Final Neolithic to the Early Bronze Age in central Europe. *Proceedings of the National Academy of Sciences* 114(38): 10083–10088.

Kristiansen, K., M. E. Allentoft, K. M. Frei, ... & E. Willerslev. 2017. Re-theorising mobility and the formation of culture and language among the Corded Ware Culture in Europe. *Antiquity* 91(356): 334–347.

Lave, J., & E. Wenger. 1991. *Situated learning: Legitimate peripheral participation.* Cambridge: Cambridge University Press.

Metcalf, P., & R. Huntington. 1991. *Celebrations of death: The anthropology of mortuary ritual.* Cambridge: Cambridge University Press.

Oestigaard, T., & J. Goldhahn. 2006. From the dead to the living: Death as transactions and re-negotiations. *Norwegian Archaeological Review* 39(1): 27–48.

Olalde, I., S. Brace, M. E. Allentoft, ... & D. Reich. 2018. The Beaker phenomenon and the genomic transformation of northwest Europe. *Nature* **555**(7695): 190–196.

Pospieszny, Ł., I. Sobkowiak-Tabaka, T. D. Price, ... & M. Winiarska-Kabacińska. 2015. Remains of a late Neolithic barrow at Kruszyn. A glimpse of ritual and everyday life in early Corded Ware societies of the Polish Lowland. *Praehistorisch Zeitschrift* **90**(1–2): 185–213.

Price, T. D., C. Knipper, G. Grupe, & V. Smrcka. 2004. Strontium isotopes and prehistoric human migration: The Bell Beaker period in Central Europe. *European Journal of Archaeology* **7** (1): 9–40.

Salton, G., & M. J. McGill. 1983. *Introduction to modern information retrieval.* New York: McGraw-Hill Book Company.

Sjögren, K.-G., T. D. Price, & K. Kristiansen. 2016. Diet and mobility in the Corded Ware of Central Europe. *PLoS ONE* **11**(5): e0155083.

Smejda, L., J. Turek, & H. Thrane. 2006. *Archaeology of burial mounds.* Plzen: University of West-Bohemia, Department of Archaeology.

Sørensen, M. L. S. 2015. "Paradigm lost": On the state of typology within archaeological theory. In K. Kristiansen, L. Šmejda, & J. Turek (ed.), *Paradigm found, archaeological theory present, past and future*, 84–94. Oxford: Oxbow Books.

Turek, J. 2017. Sex, transsexuality and archaeological perception of gender identities. *Archaeologies: Journal of the World Archaeological Congress* **12**(3): 340–358.

Van Giffen, A. E. 1935. Twee grafheuvels te Nieuw Roden, Gem. Roden. *Oudheidkundige Aantekeningen over Drenthse Vondsten* **2**: 117–8.

Vander Linden, M. 2004. Polythetic networks, coherent people: A new historical hypothesis for the Bell Beaker phenomenon. In J. Czebreszuk (ed.), *Similar but different; Bell Beakers in Europe*, 35–62. Leiden: Sidestone Press.

2016. Population history in third-millennium-BC Europe: Assessing the contribution of genetics. *World Archaeology* **48**(5): 714–728.

Wenger, E. 1998. *Communities of practice: Learning, meaning, and identity*. Cambridge: Cambridge University Press.

7 LINGUISTIC PHYLOGENETICS AND WORDS FOR METALS IN INDO-EUROPEAN

THOMAS OLANDER

7.1 Introduction

The prehistoric spread of Indo-European languages across Europe and Asia was a process with dramatic consequences that are still being felt in the modern world.[1] Today around half the world's population speak an Indo-European language; some of the most widely spoken are Spanish, English, Hindi, Portuguese, Bengali, and Russian. The Indo-European languages are grouped into ten major subgroups, or branches: Italic, Celtic, Germanic, Greek, Armenian, Albanian, Indo-Iranian, and Balto-Slavic, as well as Anatolian and Tocharian (both extinct). These branches all descend from a common ancestor, Proto-Indo-European.

When we set out to explore the dispersals of the Indo-European languages in prehistory, the fundamental task is to correlate the evidence of comparative–historical linguistics with the archaeological record. In correlating language and material culture, the main area of contention is that of chronology. While the field of archaeology has very precise methods of establishing both relative and absolute chronologies, linguistics is in a much less fortunate position: in many cases, only a relative chronology of linguistic changes can be established, whereas the absolute chronology can at best only be indirectly inferred from the data.

One way to draw inferences about absolute chronologies for a language family is linguistic palaeontology, i.e., the principle of analyzing the inherited vocabulary of two or more related languages and correlating the reconstructed lexical items with datable archaeological material (§ 7.2). Several caveats apply to this reasoning, one of them being the fact that if words are borrowed between closely related languages, they may not be detectable as loanwords. Therefore, the rule of thumb is: words occurring only in geographically neighboring subgroups cannot claim to have Proto-Indo-European status.

During the last couple of decades, it has become more widely accepted that the initial disintegration of the Indo-European language family did not take place as a sudden split into ten different subgroups, as was once commonly believed. Rather, the subgroups may have separated gradually from the main stem one at a time, resulting in a family tree whose higher-order subgrouping consists of binary splits (§ 7.3). This insight has led to a reinterpretation of several facts about Indo-European linguistics at the phonological, morphological, and lexical levels.

In discussions of linguistic palaeontology, however, with its implications for the correlation of linguistic and archaeological evidence, the purely linguistic insights into the early diversification of the Indo-European language family have so far only been exploited to a limited extent (§ 7.4). In this contribution, I put forward a suggestion for refining the methodology of linguistic palaeontology by exploring the phylogenetic approach. I will try to show that there are valuable insights to be gained about the question of the early dispersals of the Indo-European languages by using this approach.

To illustrate the implications of the phylogenetic approach to linguistic palaeontology, I examine the words used to refer to certain metals in the various Indo-European subgroups (§ 7.5).

I conclude that, contrary to what is usually stated, no words for metals can safely be reconstructed back to the earliest reconstructible stages of the Indo-European language family, including Proto-Indo-European (§ 7.6). The stage following the separation of Anatolian and then Tocharian, on the other hand, knew words for 'gold', 'silver', and 'copper or bronze'.

7.2 Linguistic Palaeontology

Linguistic palaeontology is based on the reasoning that if a certain word found in two or more related languages can be traced back to the common ancestor of these languages, then it is often also possible to infer the meaning of that word in the

[1] The initial work on this study was conducted within the framework of the project *The Homeland: In the Footprints of the Early Indo-Europeans* (2015–2018), supported by the Carlsberg Foundation. The final version was written as part of the research projects *Connecting the Dots: Reconfiguring the Indo-European Family Tree* (2019–2023), financed by the Independent Research Fund Denmark (project number 9037-00086B), and *LAMP: Languages and Myths of Prehistory* (2020–2025), financed by Riksbankens Jubileumsfond.

I am grateful to Jacob Engelbrecht, Benedicte Nielsen Whitehead, Birgit Anette Olsen, Lucas Poulsen de Sousa, and Esbern Thøgersen for their useful comments on earlier versions of the study.

ancestor language (for an introduction, see Hock & Joseph 2009: 477–509). An example is provided by the following list of words meaning 'daughter' in modern Germanic languages:

- English *daughter* 'daughter'
- German *Tochter* 'daughter'
- Yiddish *tokhter* 'daughter'
- Dutch *dochter* 'daughter'
- Swedish *dotter* 'daughter'
- Danish *datter* 'daughter'
- Norwegian (Nynorsk) *dotter* 'daughter'
- Icelandic *dóttir* 'daughter'
- Faroese *dóttir* 'daughter'

On the basis of the sounds constituting these words, we can establish that they have been inherited from the common ancestor of these languages, Proto-Germanic. Based on the fact that the word begins with *d* in almost all Germanic languages, we may reconstruct the initial sound of the word as Proto-Germanic **d* (the asterisk marks a form as reconstructed). The word begins with *t* in German and Yiddish, because there was a regular phonetic change of *d* to *t* at a pre-stage of these languages, also seen e.g., in German *Tür* 'door' and Yiddish *tir* 'door', corresponding to English *door*.

As for the meaning of the word in the common ancestor, it seems reasonable to assume that it was 'daughter'; anyone arguing that the original meaning was anything but 'daughter' will have to explain the change of meaning in all the attested daughter languages. Moreover, the hypothesis that the original meaning was 'daughter' receives support from the fact that in older Germanic languages, the meaning of the word was also 'daughter', e.g., Old English *dohtor*, Old High German *tohter*, Old Icelandic *dóttir*, and Gothic *dauhtar*, all meaning 'daughter'.

In the other Indo-European subgroups, we find similar words with the meaning 'daughter':

- Slavic: Old Church Slavonic *dŭšti* 'daughter'
- Baltic: Lithuanian *duktė̃* 'daughter'
- Iranian: Old Avestan *dugədar-* 'daughter'
- Indic: Vedic Sanskrit *duhitár-* 'daughter'
- Armenian: Armenian *dustr* 'daughter'
- Greek: Greek θυγάτηρ 'daughter'
- Celtic: Gaulish *duxtir* 'daughter'
- Italic: Oscan *futír* 'daughter'
- Tocharian: Tocharian B *tkācer* 'daughter'
- Anatolian: Lycian *kbatra* 'daughter'

Again, the phonetic shape of the words allows us to reconstruct an ancestor word in the proto-language of these languages, Proto-Indo-European: **d^{h}ugh$_2$tér-*. The correspondence between the initial *d* of Germanic, Baltic, and Slavic, the θ (*t^h*) of Greek, the *f* of Oscan, etc. is perfectly regular and recurs in other words. The attested words diverge from each other in form because of the phonetic developments that have affected each of the languages in the course of the millennia since the dissolution of their common ancestor.

It seems to be beyond any reasonable doubt that the basic meaning of this word in the common ancestor of these languages was 'daughter'. If we were to contest this and assume that the word had another meaning in Proto-Indo-European, say 'young girl', we would have to postulate several independent changes in the original meaning in the prehistories of the individual descendant languages, which is clearly a less economical solution.

Thus, using the comparative method, we can trace the above-listed words back to Proto-Indo-European, reconstructing its form, **d^{h}ugh$_2$tér-*, and a meaning, 'daughter'. Sometimes the original meaning of a reconstructed word is not obvious, but in other cases there can be no serious doubt about it. By applying the principle of linguistic palaeontology, then, we can infer that the speakers of Proto-Indo-European knew the concept of a daughter and talked about it.

Needless to say, it is not particularly interesting for our purposes that we are able to reconstruct the term 'daughter' for Proto-Indo-European: the term, and the concept it refers to, is not confined in space and time and so it does not allow us to infer anything about the location of the speakers of Proto-Indo-European. Other concepts, however, are much more interesting. Probably the most famous case is the terminology for wheeled vehicles in Indo-European languages. Since several subgroups (Tocharian, Germanic, Greek, and Indo-Iranian, but probably not Baltic; see Olander 2019a: 20–21) have a word meaning 'wheel' that can be traced back to an ancestral form, **k^{w}ék^{w}lo-*, the last common ancestor of these subgroups must have possessed a word with this particular phonetic shape. As with the words for 'daughter', by far the most economical, and thus most attractive, solution is to assume that the original meaning of the word was 'wheel', just like in the attested descendant languages, which simply retained the old meaning. This in turn implies that the speakers of the common ancestor of these languages must have known the concept of wheels, and since the invention of the wheel is datable with some degree of certainty to the middle of the fourth millennium BC (see the discussion in Anthony 2007: 59–82), this common ancestor cannot have dissolved prior to this period. Thus, linguistic palaeontology provides us with an absolute date for that language stage. We return to the wheel in § 7.4.

An important point that is often overlooked by nonlinguists (and some linguists; see Olander 2017) is that it is precisely these phonetic changes that allow historical linguists to assess whether a given word is inherited from a common ancestor, or if it has been borrowed at a later stage. In the word for 'daughter', the different shape of the word in the various subgroups makes it clear that the word was inherited from Proto-Indo-European: for example, the initial θ (*t^h*) of Greek would not be borrowed as *f* in Oscan, or vice versa. By enabling historical linguists to distinguish inherited words from loanwords, the comparative method in principle allows us to infer scenarios for relationships between languages, be they genealogical (by descent from a common ancestor) or the result of linguistic contact.

In practice, however, the methodology of linguistic reconstruction faces a problem that has proven difficult to solve: that of detecting loanwords across closely related languages. If one language has borrowed a word from another before any of the diagnostic sound changes have taken place, it cannot be distinguished from inherited linguistic material. This problem applies in particular to words of a certain phonetic shape; for instance, the word reconstructed as Proto-Indo-European **nu*/**nū* 'now' is very short, and the sounds it contains are among the more stable ones in linguistic evolution. Thus, even several millennia after the dissolution of Proto-Indo-European, the word would sound identical in several Indo-European languages, and so it would be difficult to see if it was borrowed from one language into another. Fortunately, however, cases like this one are relatively rare, and most words are longer and/or contain sounds that are more prone to change; however, the problem of undetected borrowing remains. Undetected borrowing is also a major problem for studies based on cognacy (§ 7.4; see e.g. Nakhleh, Ringe, & Warnow 2005: 386–388).

In order to circumvent the problem of undetected borrowing, a geographical principle can be applied based on the idea that direct borrowing can only take place if there is contact. Thus, Schrader (1907: 174–175) suggested that in order for a given word to be reconstructible for Proto-Indo-European, its reflexes must be represented (a) in Indo-Iranian and at least one European subgroup, (b) in at least one north Indo-European subgroup and a south Indo-European subgroup, or (c) in Greek and Latin. Similarly, Meillet (1903: 340) required reflexes across three non-contiguous subgroups in order for a word to be regarded as Proto-Indo-European. Mallory and Adams (2006: 109–110) have two different criteria for regarding a word as Proto-Indo-European. The first criterion is geographical: the word has to be attested in at least one European and in at least one Asian subgroup (Indo-Iranian and Tocharian). The other criterion is phylogenetic: the word has to be attested in an Anatolian language and a non-Anatolian language. The authors regard either of the criteria as sufficient for assuming that a given word existed in Proto-Indo-European. In this study, I am primarily concerned with the phylogenetic criterion. We shall briefly return to the geographical criterion in § 7.4.

7.3 Indo-European Linguistic Phylogenetics

Throughout most of the twentieth century, the generally perceived model of the Indo-European family tree was that the ten main subgroups – Anatolian, Tocharian, Italic, Celtic, Germanic, Greek, Armenian, Albanian, Indo-Iranian, and Balto-Slavic – descend from Proto-Indo-European in a nonhierarchical fashion (Fig. 7.1). In (relative) chronological terms, this implies that all the subgroups separated from the common ancestor at around the same time.

The last couple of decades, however, have witnessed a growing consensus that this model does not properly represent the evolution of the Indo-European language family. Most scholars nowadays agree that the Anatolian subgroup was the first one to separate from the remaining subgroups, implying that the remaining subgroups form a clade, which may be referred to as "Indo-Tocharian" (Peyrot 2019; Olander 2019b; see Fig. 7.2).

Perhaps as a consequence of recognizing the outgroup position of Anatolian, there has been a growing interest in the structure of the remainder of the Indo-European family tree: maybe the disintegration of the non-Anatolian half of the family also proceeded through a series of splits, not as a one-time event. Moreover, it has been stated that the traditional "big bang" view of the disintegration of Indo-European is typologically deviant: in most language families of a similar

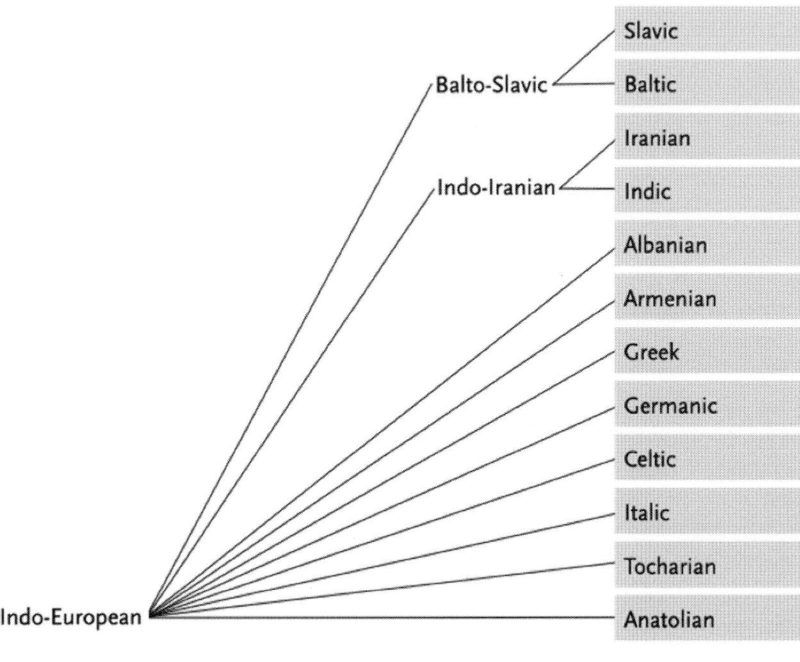

Fig. 7.1. Traditional model of the Indo-European language family.

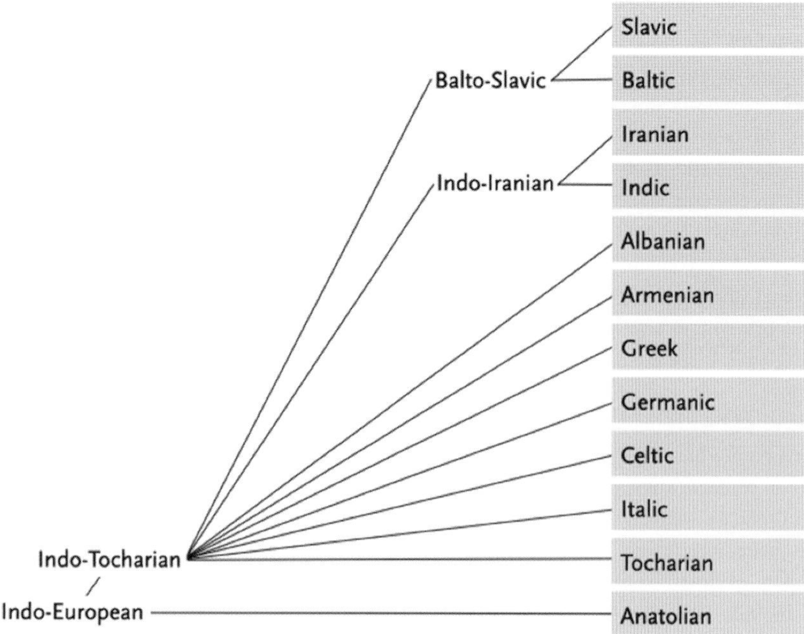

FIG. 7.2. The neo-traditional model of the Indo-European language family.

age as Indo-European, higher-order splits are usually binary (Nichols 1990: 489; 1997: 138). While this view needs further investigation (see the criticism in Campbell & Poser 2008: 316–318), it seems worthwhile to investigate the consequences of a binary-branching Indo-European family tree for the correlation of linguistics and archaeology.

Several different trees have been proposed, based on different datasets and methodologies, by individual researchers and research groups. Computational analyses of cognate words constitute the basis of Bayesian approaches (Gray & Atkinson 2003; Bouckaert et al. 2012; Chang et al. 2015; see Heggarty 2021 for an introduction; see also the overview in Holm 2007: 199–209). Other studies employ computational analyses of shared innovations in phonology and morphology combined with cognacy databases (Ringe, Warnow, & Taylor 2002; Nakhleh, Ringe, & Warnow 2005).

As there is a general consensus that shared innovations are the most reliable indicator of genealogical linguistic relationships, currently the most likely Indo-European family tree is that of Nakhleh, Ringe, & Warnow 2005. A modified version is presented in Fig. 7.3, employing the naming principles of Olander 2019b. In the remainder of this contribution, I assume – for the sake of the largely methodological arguments made here – that this tree is correct. It should be noted, however, that different models would lead to quite different results for the specific analyses in this study. The traditional tree, for example, if taken literally, implies that if cognate words are found in any two of the main subgroups, the ancestor of these words can be traced back to Proto-Indo-European. According to the tree proposed by Bouckaert et al. (2012: 959), an "Armeno-Tocharian" subgroup was the next to branch off after Anatolian, implying that if cognate words are found in Armenian or Tocharian plus any other non-Anatolian subgroup, these words may be traced back to the proto-language of the non-Anatolian subgroups – which makes the Armenian evidence much more important than in most other trees, where Armenian is deeply embedded (cf. Bouckaert et al. 2013: 1446, where Armenian has a different position in the tree).

The phylogenetic structure of the Indo-European language family has important consequences at all linguistic levels – phonology, morphology, syntax, lexicon – and should be taken into account in the reconstruction of prehistoric stages of the family (Ringe 1998; Olander 2018). In the next section, we examine a specific topic, namely the words for metals, in greater detail against the background of the structure of the Indo-European family tree.

7.4 From Relative to Absolute Chronologies

The nodes in the linguistic family trees presented in § 7.3 show relative chronologies; the branch lengths do not represent specific amounts of time. What we need in order to meaningfully correlate language stages with the archaeological evidence, however, are absolute chronologies: we have to make an attempt to ascribe approximate absolute dates to the nodes in the tree.

As with the attempts at establishing the phylogeny of the Indo-European language family mentioned in the preceding section, different methodologies have been employed in order to estimate the absolute age of the various nodes in the tree. One such approach is Bayesian inference, which, in its most widespread form, estimates the absolute dates of the nodes in a family tree on the basis of the rates of replacement of basic

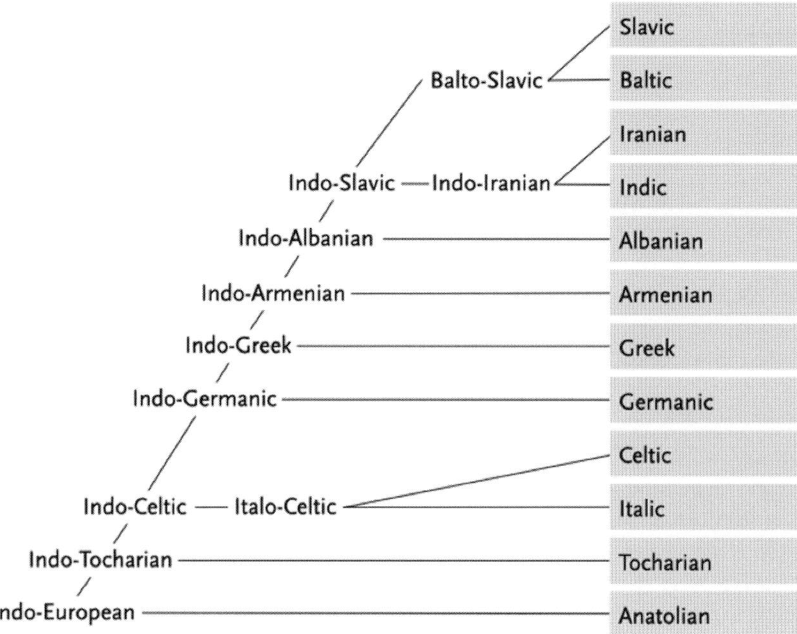

Fig. 7.3. A binary-branching model of the Indo-European language family (from Olander 2019b).

vocabulary items in the various lineages, with calibration points taken from known historical events (e.g. Gray & Atkinson 2003; Bouckaert et al. 2012; Chang et al. 2015; for an introduction to Bayesian linguistic phylogenetics, see Greenhill, Heggarty, & Gray 2021). Whether the results obtained by studies based on Bayesian inference are valid, however, is debatable: most historical linguists reject the methodology. In addition, the results so far have not matched particularly well with the observable facts (see the discussions in Pereltsvaig & Lewis 2015: 92–113; Ringe 2022).

Alternatively, the absolute dates of reconstructed language stages may be inferred by examining reconstructed lexical items referring to archaeologically datable concepts (linguistic palaeontology; see § 7.2). Cognates found in two or more subgroups may be reconstructed back to the common ancestor of these branches. It is important to note, however, that we cannot tell if an item was present or not at stages anterior to the last common ancestor, because vocabulary may be replaced without a trace for reasons unrecoverable to us.

Thus, we return to the word *k^wék^wlo- 'wheel', which, as mentioned in § 7.2, is present in four subgroups: Tocharian, Germanic, Greek, and Indo-Iranian. If we base our analysis on the family tree in Fig. 7.3, we see that the last common ancestor of these subgroups is the Indo-Tocharian stage. Since the word is not attested in the Anatolian subgroup, we cannot say if the ancestor of all the Indo-European languages, Proto-Indo-European, had the word or not; the word might have existed in Proto-Indo-European and have been lost at a pre-stage of Anatolian, or it might have been coined at a pre-stage of Indo-Tocharian. What we can positively conclude is that Proto-Indo-Tocharian had a word for 'wheel' and, accordingly, that that language stage cannot have dissolved before around 3500 BC, when the wheel was invented.

With the growing recognition of Anatolian as the first subgroup to split off, this reasoning has indeed been applied when establishing whether a given lexical item is reconstructible back to Proto-Indo-European or not (e.g. Mallory & Adams 2006: 109–110; Anthony 2007: 64–65). However, given that the structure of the remainder of the tree is still under debate, the principle is not usually applied to the non-Anatolian clade of Indo-European. I think this is a mistake, especially since we do have some understanding of at least the initial splits of the non-Anatolian part of the family.

The phylogenetic criterion does not make geographical criteria (§ 7.2) superfluous. Despite the difficulties in determining the geographical location of pre-stages of languages, which adds another dimension of uncertainty to geographical arguments, geography is still an important prerequisite, though not sufficient in itself for establishing the known age of a given word. Thus, for instance, a word with reflexes in Italic and/or Celtic as well as in Germanic cannot safely be reconstructed back to Proto-Indo-Celtic, for geographical reasons: it seems likely that the communities speaking Germanic, Italic, and Celtic were neighbors for an extended time period at a very early stage, and the possibility of undetected borrowing between the subgroups or from an unknown substrate is high. On the other hand, a word with reflexes in Anatolian and Greek should still be considered Proto-Indo-European, since it is likely that these subgroups only came into geographical contact at a relative late stage, after millennia of separation during which several independent phonological developments took place, making it possible to distinguish inherited items from loanwords.

In my opinion, the phylogenetic principle should take precedence over the geographical principle. I therefore do not accept the rule of thumb that Mallory and Adams mention as an alternative to the phylogenetic principle (see § 7.2), according to which "any word that shared cognates in a European language and an Asian language" may be regarded as Proto-Indo-European (Mallory & Adams 2006: 110; see also Mallory 2019). If geography were a sufficient criterion, we would assume that the 'wheel' word existed already at the Proto-Indo-European stage because it has cognates in European (Germanic, Greek) and in Asian (Tocharian, Indo-Iranian) subgroups. However, as it is not attested in Anatolian, reconstructing the word back to Proto-Indo-European contradicts the phylogenetic principle. My view is that, following the phylogenetic principle, the 'wheel' word may only be reconstructed back to Proto-Indo-Tocharian.

As this example shows, the implication of applying the phylogenetic principle for lexical reconstruction is that the requirements for reconstructing a given word and its meaning back to Proto-Indo-European are even stricter than before: a secure reconstruction of a word back to a given reconstructed stage demands that not only the geographical, but also the phylogenetic criterion is met. In the case of Indo-European, this means – if we use one of the trees in Fig. 7.2 or Fig. 7.3 as our point of departure – that a word with no cognates in the Anatolian subgroup cannot be shown to have existed in Proto-Indo-European, however well attested it is in the remaining subgroups. Moreover, using the tree in Fig. 7.3, a word not attested in Anatolian or Tocharian cannot be reconstructed further back than Proto-Indo-Celtic, and so on. On the plus side, the phylogenetic approach provides us with a more fine-grained picture of a gradually dissolving language community and allows us to infer the absolute dates of the internal nodes of the language family.

7.5 Metals in Early Indo-European

In order to illustrate the practical value of the methodological discussions thus far, in this section I give an example of how the phylogenetic approach may contribute to a better understanding of the question of which metals were known in the communities speaking the languages represented by the internal nodes and the root in the Indo-European family tree shown in Fig. 7.3. Note that Ehret (2015) takes a similar approach in an examination of the agricultural vocabulary of the putative Nilo-Saharan macro-family, which includes a useful methodological discussion (see also the discussion of words for 'pig' in early Indo-European languages in Olander 2018: 193–195; for the methodology, cf. Ringe & Eska 2013: 264–265; Mallory 2018).

There is extensive literature on metals in early Indo-European societies (e.g., on Indo-European words for metals in general: Huld & Mallory 1997b; Huld 2012; Mallory & Adams 2006: 241–242; on words for gold: Blažek 2017; on words for silver: Mallory & Huld 1984). In the following discussion, I aim to make relatively conservative evaluations of the evidence, in order not to arrive at conclusions that are too speculative.

Moreover, in presenting the linguistic evidence, I try to keep the discussion of details to a minimum; thus I do not systematically discuss terms that bear clear signs of not being inherited, i.e. later formations or loanwords. Furthermore, I do not discuss the archaeological evidence for metals in various regions at various times but hope that the patterns that emerge can be used by specialists in that field to link the linguistic layers to prehistorical material culture. Other contributions to this volume that deal with some of the same problems as this study, but from different perspectives, are: Thorsø et al.; O'Brien; Koch & Ling (pp. 310–311); van Sluis, Jørgensen & Kroonen (§ 13.3.2.6). With their different focuses and approaches to the problems, these studies complement each other in a way that hopefully will prove fruitful.

Note that in this section, for the sake of convenience, I use "Proto-Indo-European" (PIE) to mark reconstructions that, from a phonological and morphological perspective, might have existed in the Indo-European proto-language, regardless of whether a reconstruction is actually reconstructible that far back or not according to the phylogenetic principle. However, as the accompanying text and Fig. 7.4 should make clear how far back in time the specific reconstructions can be secured, this should not cause confusion.

7.5.1 Gold

In the early Indo-European languages, we find two groups of words meaning 'gold'. The first group points to a reconstruction PIE *$h_2$au̯so-, or perhaps rather *$h_2$au̯hso-, as indicated by Lithuanian (see below, and cf. the discussion in Thorsø et al. this volume, § 8.2.1). I do not find the connection with PIE *$h_2$eu̯s- 'dawn' compelling (cf. the discussion in Driessen 2003: 356–358, with diverging conclusions).

This word is represented in the Italic subgroup by Latin *aurum* 'gold', which was borrowed into Celtic and replaced the inherited Celtic word(s) (Prósper 2011: 62–63). Latin *aurum* may reflect either PIE *$h_2$au̯so- or, through *au̯aso- with syncope of the medial vowel, *$h_2$au̯hso- (for the syncope, cf. *au̯i-speks > Latin *auspex* 'bird-seer', and Archaic Latin IOVESAT > Latin *iūrat* 'swears'; see, slightly differently, Driessen 2003: 354–355).

In the Baltic group of the Balto-Slavic subgroup, Lithuanian *áuksas* 'gold' (Old Lithuanian *áusas*) and Old Prussian *ausis* 'gold' are cognate with Latin *aurum*. It is possible that the third Baltic language, Latvian, also preserves traces of it (Mühlenbach & Endzelīns 1923–1925: 231). The Lithuanian acute tone suggests the reconstruction of a medial laryngeal, viz. *$h_2$au̯hso-, with is compatible with the Latin evidence (see above).

With cognates in Italic and Balto-Slavic, we can reconstruct this word back at least to the Proto-Indo-Celtic stage (see Fig. 7.3), the last common ancestor of Italic and Balto-Slavic. Two other subgroups may preserve this word, but the evidence is difficult to interpret.

From a phylogenetic point of view, the alleged reflexes of PIE *$h_2$au̯hso- in Tocharian are potentially the most important

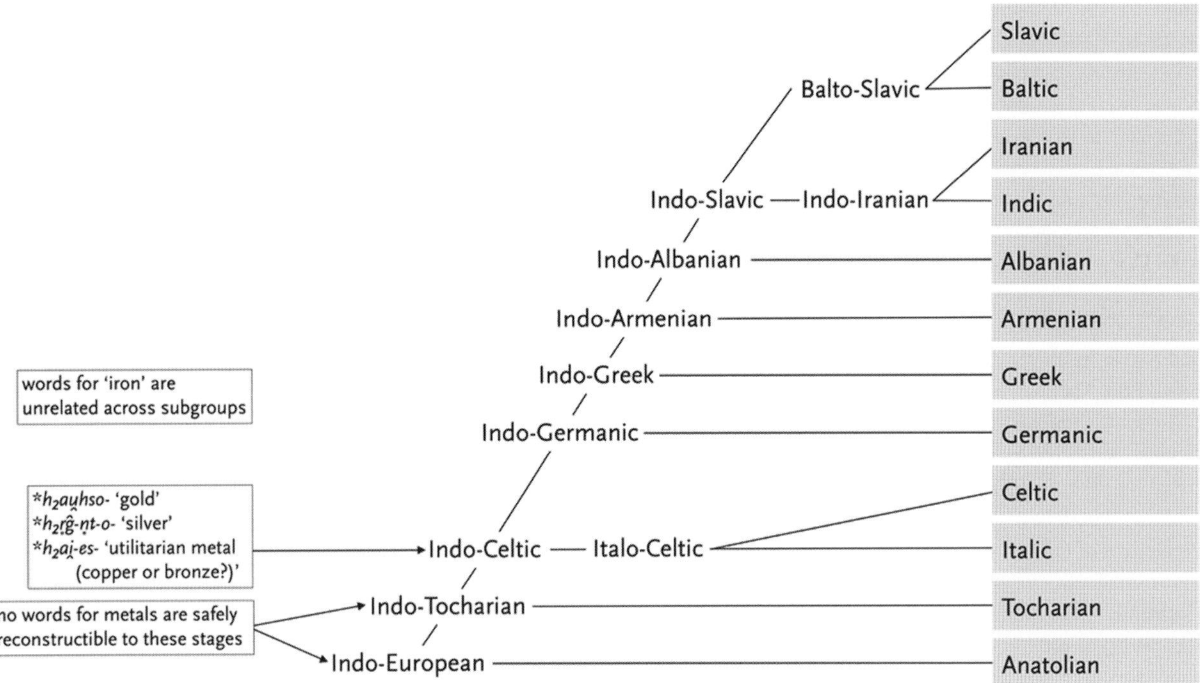

FIG. 7.4. Words for metals in a binary-branching model of the Indo-European language family.

ones, as they would push the existence of a word for 'gold' back to the Proto-Indo-Tocharian stage. Some authors assume that Tocharian B *yasa* 'gold' and Tocharian A *wäs* 'gold', from Proto-Tocharian **wi̯äsā*, reflect PIE "**h_2u̯esah$_2$*", an (irregular) variant of the **$h_2$au̯(h)so-* found elsewhere (e.g. Adams 2013: 525). Due to the irregular correspondence, however, it is uncertain whether the Tocharian words indeed belong together with the Italic and Baltic words. It has been suggested that they are instead loanwords from Samoyed (Schrijver 1991: 47; see also Driessen 2003: 348–350; Kallio 2004: 132–133), but the direction of borrowing may also have been the opposite, or the donor language may have been some unknown source (see the discussion in Joki 1973: 339–340). Given our present body of knowledge, it is difficult to decide which solution is correct, but it seems safest to conclude that the word can only be reconstructed back to Proto-Indo-Celtic, while keeping in mind that there are some indications that the word may have existed already in Proto-Indo-Tocharian (contrast this with e.g. Neumann 1975: 677: "An *Metallen* kannten die Idg. sicher *Gold* und *Silber* und wohl auch ein unedles Metall"; emphasis as in original).

The other subgroup with a dubious reflex of PIE **$h_2$au̯(h)so-* is Armenian, where the word for 'gold', *oski*, is usually connected with the Italic and Baltic (and possibly Tocharian) words (see e.g. Olsen 1999: 441; Martirosyan 2010: 532–533). However, due to phonological and derivational difficulties, it is uncertain whether Armenian *oski* is an actual cognate of the Italic and Baltic words. Since Armenian is relatively deeply embedded in the family tree, the status of *oski* is not crucial for our purposes, at least in the reference tree used in this contribution (Fig. 7.3); however, compare the tree in Bouckaert et al. 2012: 959, mentioned in § 7.3, where Armenian and Tocharian form the second group to split off (and cf. also the revised tree in Bouckaert et al. 2013: 1446).

Another set of related words meaning 'gold' can be traced back to a Proto-Indo-European root **ĝ^{h}elh$_3$-*, which also appears in words meaning 'yellow' and 'green' (cf. also the discussion in Thorsø et al. this volume, § 8.1.2). The meaning 'gold' is found in Germanic, Balto-Slavic, and Indo-Iranian. The Germanic attestations of the word are, e.g., Old English *gold* (and Modern English *gold*), Old High German *gold*, Old Icelandic *gull*, and Gothic *gulþ*. These words go back to Proto-Germanic **gulþa-* and **gulda-*, reflecting PIE **ĝ^{h}l̥h$_3$-to-*.

Vedic Sanskrit *híraṇya-* originally meant 'precious metal' and could be qualified with the adjectives *rajatá-* as 'silver' and *hárita-* or *suvárṇa-* as 'gold'. At a later stage, *rajatá-* was substantivized as 'silver', and *híraṇya-* came to mean 'gold' (Rau 1974: 18). Both *hárita-* and *híraṇya-* are formed from the Proto-Indo-European root **ĝ^{h}elh$_3$-*. In Iranian, Young Avestan *zaraṇiia-* 'gold' corresponds exactly to Vedic Sanskrit *híraṇya-*, reflecting Proto-Indo-Iranian **ǵ^{h}r̥han-*, probably meaning 'precious metal', apparently from PIE **ĝ^{h}l̥h$_3$-en-*. Vedic Sanskrit *hárita-*, on the other hand, seems to reflect **ĝ^{h}elh$_3$-to-* (technically, *hárita-* could also go back to PIE **ĝ^{h}olh$_3$-to-*, but such a form probably did not exist; see the following).

Within Baltic, Latvian has *zę̀lts* 'gold', apparently from PIE **ĝ^{h}elh$_3$-to-*, with the same suffix as in Germanic and Indic, but with an ablaut grade of the root that differs from that found in Germanic. Slavic (e.g., Russian *zóloto* 'gold' and Czech *zlato* 'gold'), on the other hand, points to PIE **ĝ^{h}ol-to-*, again with the suffix **-to-*, but with an ablaut grade of the root that differs from both Baltic and Germanic. The reason no laryngeal is reconstructed in the *o*-grade form **ĝ^{h}ol-to-* is the process known as the Saussure effect (see Rasmussen 1989: 175–197; Melchert 1994: 49–52; Yamazaki 2009), which probably took effect already at a pre-stage of Proto-Indo-European; note that Slavic itself does not indicate whether or not the proto-form contained a laryngeal. The Latvian falling tone in _zȩ̀lts_ is unexpected, since the root contained a laryngeal, but if we assume that Latvian originally possessed an _o_-grade formation without a laryngeal, the falling tone would be regular. We would then have to assume that Latvian introduced _e_-vocalism by analogy with other forms of the same root. If this explanation, which admittedly may be debated, is correct, the Latvian and Slavic forms may ultimately derive from the same proto-form, PBS *źalta-.

To sum it up, we are in a situation where Germanic, Indo-Iranian, and Balto-Slavic present slightly different formations based on the same root, *$\hat{g}^h elh_3$-, which probably meant 'yellow'. Possibly combined with a word for 'precious metal', derivatives of the root came to refer specifically to gold. Due to the formal differences between the words for 'gold' in Germanic, Indo-Iranian, and Balto-Slavic, it is difficult to reconstruct a proto-form for the common pre-stage of these subgroups, and it is likely that the nouns with meaning 'gold' are independent formations postdating the separation of these subgroups.

Moreover, even if such a proto-form could be reconstructed, the common pre-stage of the subgroups would be Proto-Indo-Germanic, a younger stage than Proto-Indo-Celtic, for which we just saw that another word for 'gold' is reconstructible. Accordingly, the reconstruction of a word based on *$\hat{g}^h elh_3$- for Proto-Indo-Germanic could simply mean that one word for 'gold' was being replaced by another in the period between these two stages, a scenario that would not have any dramatic consequences for the correlation of the linguistic and archaeological evidence.

7.5.2 Silver

An old word for 'silver' is reconstructible as PIE *h_2r̥ĝn̥to-, derived from a root *$h_2$erĝ-, meaning 'bright, shining', that is also found, e.g., in Hittite _ḫarki-_ 'white, bright', Tocharian B _ārkwi_ 'white', and Vedic Sanskrit _árjuna-_ 'shining, white' (cf. the discussions in Thorsø et al. this volume, § 8.2.1; Sluis, Jørgensen, & Kroonen this volume, § 13.3.2.6). The word has reflexes in Italic (e.g. Latin _argentum_ 'silver; money'; Oscan abl. sg. **aragetud** 'money'), Celtic (e.g. Old Irish _argat_, Old Welsh _argant_, and Breton _arc'hant_, all meaning 'silver'), Armenian (_arcatʿ_), and Iranian (e.g. Young Avestan _ərəzata-_, Old Persian _ardata-_, and related forms in later Iranian languages).

Some authors reconstruct an ablaut variant *$h_2$arĝn̥to- as the basis for the Italic and/or Celtic forms (e.g. Mallory & Huld 1984: 3 n. 3; Matasović 2009: 47). However, it is quite likely that *h_2r̥ĝn̥to- would directly yield the attested forms (Schrijver 1991: 67–68, 72; see also Weiss 2020: 57 n. 16). As the latter reconstruction is required for the Iranian forms, it is more economical and will be accepted here.

Armenian _arcatʿ_ 'silver' is often thought not to be directly traceable back to PIE *h_2r̥ĝn̥to- (or *$h_2$arĝn̥to-), which would presumably have yielded *arcan (Olsen 1999: 868; see also the discussion in Martirosyan 2010: 139 with copious references). It has been suggested that the word may owe its form, at least partly, to influence from early Iranian. However, Kümmel (2017: 445) has argued that Armenian _arcatʿ_ may indeed be the regular reflex of PIE *h_2r̥ĝn̥tó- (or *$h_2$arĝn̥tó-), if the *o was originally accented (followed by Thorsø et al. this volume, § 8.2.1 n. 13). Armenian thus seems to support the reconstruction of a word for 'silver' in Proto-Indo-Celtic.

Indic also has a related form represented by Vedic Sanskrit _rajatá-_, attested as an adjective meaning 'whitish, silver-colored, silvery' in the Rigveda and as a noun meaning 'silver' in the later Atharvaveda. The Indic form does not correspond exactly to the forms in the other subgroups, which would lead us to expect *r̥jatá-; the attested _rajatá-_, however, can probably be explained through internal Indic derivational processes (Mayrhofer 1996: 426; Mallory & Huld 1984: 4–5 and 1997c consider _rajatá-_ to be unrelated to the words for 'silver' in the other subgroups).

Albanian _argjend_, _argjand_, _ergjënd_ 'silver' is a recent borrowing from Latin (Orël 1998: 8, 89).

Although *h_2r̥ĝn̥to- is relatively easily understood as a derivation from *$h_2$erĝ- 'bright', and we might therefore suspect that it could have been created independently in the individual subgroups, the precise combination of the root *$h_2$erĝ- (when Indo-European languages are known for having an exceedingly high number of words for 'bright, shining') and the derivational suffix *-n̥to- (when there are several other suffixes that could have been used to create a new noun meaning 'silver') is unlikely to have taken place more than once in the individual subgroups. Thus, for instance, while the Greek word for 'silver', ἄργυρος, is derived from the same root, it has a different suffix.

It seems safe to conclude, on the basis of Italic, Celtic, Iranian, Armenian, and possibly Indic evidence, that Proto-Indo-Celtic had a word *h_2r̥ĝn̥to- meaning 'silver'. If we want to examine the possibility of tracing the word for 'silver' further back in time, we should look for evidence for it in Tocharian and Anatolian. Indeed, cognates of *h_2r̥ĝn̥to- have been proposed for both subgroups.

The Tocharian words for 'silver' are Tocharian B _ñkante_ and Tocharian A _nkiñc_. While the words are often thought to have been borrowed from Archaic Chinese, it has also been suggested that they derive from PIE *$h_2$reĝn̥tóm through assimilation of *r to _n_ (Witczak 1990; accepted by Adams 2013: 290). While it is certainly compelling to derive the Tocharian words for 'silver' from a well-known Indo-European formation, the problem with this explanation, apart from the assumption of an assimilation, is that the reconstruction *$h_2$reĝn̥tóm is based exclusively on the Vedic Sanskrit form, which is more likely to be secondary, since the base form of the root is *$h_2$erĝ- and not *$h_2$reĝ- (see above). We therefore cannot be certain that Tocharian attests reflexes of PIE *h_2r̥ĝn̥to-, and the Tocharian evidence does not allow us to reconstruct a word for 'silver' for Proto-Indo-Tocharian.

As for Anatolian, we do not have direct documentation of the word for 'silver' in Hittite because all attestations of the term use the Sumerogram KÙ.BABBAR (Kloekhorst 2008: 20). Interestingly, sometimes the word is spelled KÙ.BABBAR-*ant-*, which could represent **ḫarkant-* from PIE **h₂r̥ĝn̥to-* (or **h₂arĝn̥to-*) (Mallory & Huld 1984: 4; Puhvel 1991: 171; Kloekhorst 2008: 307), but this is very indirect evidence for the attestation of this word in Anatolian. Since my purpose here is to clarify what we know and to avoid speculation, I conclude that the Anatolian evidence, while highly interesting and potentially important, is too indirect to prove that there are reflexes of PIE **h₂r̥ĝn̥to-* in Anatolian.

Since neither Tocharian nor Anatolian provide sufficient evidence for an inherited word for 'silver' in these subgroups, we can conclude that Proto-Indo-Celtic had a word for 'silver', but we do not know if Proto-Indo-Tocharian or Proto-Indo-European had such a word. This conclusion differs from that of Huld and Mallory, who maintain that "[t]he distribution appears broad enough to suggest PIE status" (Huld & Mallory 1997c: 518; see also Huld 2012: 281, who mentions the existence of "a Proto-Indo-European word for 'silver' [...] the reconstruction of which is based on the discontiguous and far-flung geographical distribution [...] in at least four branches: Italic, Celtic, Armenian, and Iranian"; see also the quotation from Neumann 1975: 677 in § 7.5.1).

Another set of words for 'silver' deserves mention here, although they are clearly not inherited from a common ancestor. The set is attested in Celtic (Celtiberian *śilaPuŕ*), Germanic (e.g., Gothic *silubr*, Old Icelandic *silfr*, Old English *seolfor*), Baltic (Lithuanian *sidãbras*, Latvian *sidrabs*, *sudrabs*, Old Prussian acc. sg. *sirablan*), and Slavic (Old Church Slavonic *sьrebro*). While the words are superficially similar to each other, they cannot be reconstructed back to a common proto-form, and it is generally assumed that they have been borrowed from a non-Indo-European language (see, e.g., Vennemann 1997: 881–882, who considers the words to have been borrowed from Vasconic; Boutkan & Kossmann 2001; Kroonen 2013: 436; and Thorsø et al. this volume, § 8.2.2).

7.5.3 Copper/Bronze

Another interesting word is PIE **h₂ai̯es-*, which probably had the original meaning 'copper' or 'bronze' (or both) (cf. the discussion in Thorsø et al. this volume, § 8.3.1). It is well documented in Italic, where Latin *aes* 'copper; bronze; brass', Umbrian *ahesnes* (ablative plural) adj. 'made of bronze', and Oscan *aiznīō* (accusative plural) 'made of bronze' all testify to the presence of the word in Proto-Italic (see de Vaan 2008: 27–28 for the somewhat complicated phonetic development in Latin). In Germanic, we find Gotic *aiz* 'money', Old Icelandic *eir* 'ore; copper', and Old English *ǣr*, *ār* 'ore; brass; copper'. The word is also found in Indic as Vedic Sanskrit *áyas-*, which means 'utilitarian metal' (probably copper or bronze) in the oldest period; it is often glossed as 'iron', but this meaning only occurs in later texts (Rau 1974: 19–24; Witzel 2005: 342; see also Mayrhofer 1986: 104; cf. Chakrabarti 1979). In Iranian, Old Avestan *aiiah-* refers to a kind of metal, but while it is often glossed as 'iron', its precise meaning is not known (Skjærvø 1995: 168).

While the reconstruction of the word back to Proto-Indo-Celtic is uncontroversial, its meaning requires comment. The Italic and Germanic reflexes refer to 'copper; bronze', but the broader meaning 'utilitarian metal' found in Indo-Iranian suggests that the original meaning may have been simply that. However, since at the time of the dissolution of Proto-Indo-Celtic, the only known utilitarian metals were probably copper and bronze, the distinction between the meanings 'copper; bronze' on the one hand and 'utilitarian metal' on the other was perhaps not meaningful at that point.

What we can learn from this discussion is that in Proto-Indo-Celtic, there was a word for 'utilitarian metal' (probably copper and/or bronze), but due to the lack of cognates in the Tocharian and Anatolian subgroups, we cannot trace the word further back (cf. Bjørn 2017: 70: "The limited distribution makes a reconstruction to early PIE untenable"; but Huld & Mallory 1997b: 379: "The geographical distribution assures PIE status for this word"; Lehmann 1986: 22: "already in PIE").

7.5.4 Iron

Meteoric iron is very hard and difficult to process (Tylecote 1992: 3). To the extent that it was available to pre-Iron Age peoples, it probably did not play any significant cultural role (cf. Thorsø et al. this volume, § 8.4.1). Nonetheless, it may be interesting to examine the words for 'iron' in the Indo-European subgroups, as a sort of methodological test case: if our methodology leads us to reconstruct a word for 'iron' in, say, Proto-Indo-Tocharian, which dissolved long before the Iron Age started anywhere in Eurasia, we will have to reconsider our approach (cf. Thorsø et al. this volume, § 8.4).

The diverging words for 'iron' in the various subgroups show the expected outcome when a concept was not in use in a proto-language: several different terms are applied, and it is immediately obvious that these words are unrelated (see also Huld & Mallory 1997a: 314). This fact speaks against the often-repeated objection to the use of linguistic palaeontology in general and the reconstruction of the 'wheel' word in particular (e.g. in Coleman 1988: 450; Atkinson & Gray 2006: 293–294; and Heggarty 2015: 608–610), which presents a very different story. Thus, while the words for 'iron' are not interesting in and of themselves for the purposes of correlating linguistic and archaeological evidence, they serve as an important illustration of the validity of the methodological approach of linguistic palaeontology.

I shall not go into detailed analyses of the words for 'iron' in the various languages, but limit myself to an overview of the most important forms:

- Anatolian: Hittite *ḫapalki-* is probably a loanword from a non-Indo-European language (Vanséveren 2012: 204–208; cf. Puhvel 1991: 116–117).
- Tocharian: Tocharian B *eñcuwo* may be a loanword from Iranian; it has also been suggested that it is a native formation (with no reflexes in other subgroups), which, projected back to Proto-

Indo-European, would have the form *h_1n̥-ĝʰeu̯eh₂-n- 'what is poured in' (Adams 2013: 84–85).

- Italic: Latin *ferrum* is a loanword from a non-Indo-European language (Walde & Hofmann 1938: 485–486; de Vaan 2008: 214).
- Celtic: Old Irish *íarn* and related Celtic forms have no clear etymology (Matasović 2009: 172).
- Germanic: Gothic *eisarn*, Old Icelandic *éarn*, *járn*, Old English *īse(r)n*, *īren*, and related Germanic forms are loanwords from Celtic (Kroonen 2013: 271).
- Greek: σίδηρος has no clear etymology (Frisk 1970: 703–704; Beekes 2010: 1329). No word for 'iron' is attested in Mycenaean Greek – unsurprisingly, as the attestation of Mycenaean Greek predates the introduction of ironworking in Greece around 1000 BC (cf. Huld & Mallory 1997a: 313).
- Armenian: Armenian *erkatʿ* is sometimes regarded as an internal formation based on a word for 'dark', PIE *(h_1)regʷ- (see e.g. Huld 2012: 314), but this etymology presents formal difficulties (we would expect ***erek-*); the word may be a loanword from an unknown source.
- Albanian: Albanian *hekur* 'iron' is probably a loanword from Greek ἄγκυρα 'anchor' (Orël 1998: 144).
- Indo-Iranian: Vedic Sanskrit *áyas-* originally means 'copper' and/or 'bronze', whereas the precise meaning of the corresponding Avestan word, *aiiah-*, is unknown (§ 7.5.3).
- Balto-Slavic: The Baltic and Slavic words for 'iron' (e.g. Lithuanian *geležis*, Latvian *dzèls*; Old Church Slavonic *želězo*) are similar enough that they must be related, but they are difficult to reconcile formally; they are probably borrowed from an unknown source (Vasmer 1986: 42–43, but cf. Trubačëv's comment there).

As expected, no words for 'iron' in Indo-European subgroups seem to be inherited from a higher level. One might be tempted to conclude that the lack of inherited words for 'iron' proves that the early speakers of Indo-European did not know iron, but, as already mentioned in § 7.4, such *argumenta ex silentio* are not definitive (Dressler 1965: 35–36). For example, no word for 'finger' is reconstructible further back than the proto-languages of the individual subgroups; yet the early speakers of Indo-European certainly knew fingers and most probably also had a word for them (Ringe & Eska 2013: 264).

7.6 Conclusions

A summary of the results of the analyses carried out in § 7.5 are presented in Fig. 7.4 (cf. the discussion in Thorsø et al. this volume, § 8.7.1). On the basis of the purely linguistic evidence, we may conclude that the speakers of Proto-Indo-Celtic had words for 'gold', 'silver', and 'copper/bronze', although we do not know if they had a word for 'iron'. Moreover, it is uncertain whether the speakers of Proto-Indo-Tocharian and Proto-Indo-European had words for any metals. Again, while it is tempting to draw conclusions from the negative evidence – for instance, that the speakers of Proto-Indo-Tocharian knew gold, but not yet silver, bronze/copper, or iron – this should be avoided.

It should once again be emphasized that the conclusions from examining old Indo-European words for metals would be different if a different family tree had been used as the point of departure. For instance, as mentioned in § 7.3, if the tree in Bouckaert et al. 2012: 959 had been used, the evidence from Armenian would play a much more decisive role than in the present study. Similarly, in Holm's tree (2008: 635, based on Rix et al. 2001), where the initial split is between a northwestern subgroup (with Italo-Celtic, Germanic, and Balto-Slavic) and a southeastern subgroup (with Greek, Armenian, Albanian, Anatolian, Tocharian, and Indo-Iranian), the conclusions would also be different.

While the results from this investigation are preliminary and several details are open to different interpretations, I hope I have shown how the structure of the Indo-European family tree has important consequences for the reconstruction of the Proto-Indo-European lexicon and thus for the correlation of prehistoric linguistic stages of the Indo-European language family with the archaeological record.

References

Adams, Douglas Q. 2013. *A dictionary of Tocharian B*. 2nd ed., revised and greatly enlarged (Leiden Studies in Indo-European 10). Amsterdam & New York: Rodopi.

Anthony, David W. 2007. *The horse, the wheel, and language: How Bronze-Age riders from the Eurasian steppes shaped the modern world*. Princeton (NJ) & Oxford: Princeton University Press.

Atkinson, Quentin D., & Russell D. Gray. 2006. Are accurate dates an intractable problem for historical linguistics. In: C. P. Lipo (ed.), *Mapping our ancestors: Phylogenetic approaches in anthropology and prehistory*, 269–296. New Brunswick (NJ): Aldine Transaction.

Beekes, Robert S. P. 2010. *Etymological dictionary of Greek* (Leiden Indo-European Etymological Dictionary Series 10). Leiden & Boston: Brill.

Bjørn, Rasmus Gudmundsen. 2017. *Foreign elements in the Proto-Indo-European vocabulary: A comparative loanword study*. MA thesis, University of Copenhagen.

Blažek, Václav. 2017. Indo-European "gold" in time and space. *Journal of Indo-European Studies* 45(3/4): 267–311.

Bouckaert, Remco, Philippe Lemey, Michael Dunn, Simon J. Greenhill, Alexander V. Alekseyenko, Alexei J. Drummond, Russell D. Gray, Marc A. Suchard, & Quentin D. Atkinson. 2012. Mapping the origins and expansion of the Indo-European language family. *Science* 337: 957–960.

2013. Corrections and clarifications. *Science* 342: 1446.

Boutkan, Dirk, & M. Kossmann. 2001. On the etymology of "silver." *North-Western European Language Evolution* 50: 5–11.

Campbell, Lyle, & William J. Poser. 2008. *Language classification: History and method*. Cambridge: Cambridge University Press.

Chakrabarti, Dilip K. 1979. Iron in early Indian literature. *The Journal of the Royal Asiatic Society of Great Britain and Ireland* 1979(1): 22–30.

Chang, Will, Chundra Cathcart, David Hall, & Andrew Garrett. 2015. Ancestry-constrained phylogenetic analysis supports the Indo-European steppe hypothesis. *Language* 91(1): 194–244.

Coleman, Robert. 1988. Review of Colin Renfrew, *Archaeology and language: The puzzle of Indo-European origins* (New

York: Cambridge University Press, 1987). *Current Anthropology* 29(3): 449–453.

de Vaan, Michiel. 2008. *Etymological dictionary of Latin and the other Italic languages* (Leiden Indo-European Etymological Dictionary Series 7). Leiden & Boston: Brill.

Dressler, Wolfgang U. 1965. Methodische Vorfragen bei der Bestimmung der "Urheimat." *Die Sprache* 11(1/2): 25–60, 217.

Driessen, C. Michiel. 2003. *h_2é-$h_2$us-o-*, the Proto-Indo-European term for 'gold'. *Journal of Indo-European Studies* 31: 347–362.

Ehret, Christopher. 2015. Agricultural origins: What linguistic evidence reveals. In: Graeme Barker & C. Goucher (ed.), *The Cambridge world history. Vol. 2. A world with agriculture*, 55–92. Cambridge: Cambridge University Press.

Frisk, Hjalmar. 1970. *Griechisches etymologisches Wörterbuch*. Vol. 2. Κρ–Ω. Heidelberg: Winter.

Gray, Russell D., & Quentin D. Atkinson. 2003. Language-tree divergence times support the Anatolian theory of Indo-European origin. *Nature* 426: 435–439.

Greenhill, Simon J., Paul Heggarty, & Russell D. Gray. 2021. Bayesian phylolinguistics. In: Richard D. Janda, Brian D. Joseph, & Barbara S. Vance (ed.), *The handbook of historical linguistics*. Vol. 2, 226–253. Hoboken (NJ): John Wiley & Sons.

Heggarty, Paul. 2015. Prehistory through language and archaeology. In: Claire Bowern & Bethwyn Evans (ed.), *The Routledge handbook of historical linguistics*, 598–626. Oxford & New York: Routledge.

2021. Cognacy databases and phylogenetic research on Indo-European. *Annual Review of Linguistics* 7: 371–394.

Hock, Hans Henrich, & Brian D. Joseph. 2009. *Language history, language change, and language relationship: An introduction to historical and comparative linguistics*. 2nd. revised edition (Trends in Linguistics. Studies and Monographs 218). Berlin & New York: de Gruyter.

Holm, Hans J. 2008. The distribution of data in word lists and its impact on the subgrouping of languages. In: Christine Preisach, Hans Burkhardt, Lars Schmidt-Thieme, & Reinhold Decker (ed.), *Data analysis, machine learning and applications: Proceedings of the 31st Annual Conference of the Gesellschaft für Klassifikation e.V., Albert-Ludwigs-Universität Freiburg, March 7–9, 2007*, 629–636. Berlin & Heidelberg: Springer.

Huld, Martin E. 2012. Some observations on the development of Indo-European metallurgy. In: Martin E. Huld, Karlene Jones-Bley, & Dean Miller (ed.), *Archaeology and language: Indo-European studies presented to James P. Mallory* (Journal of Indo-European Studies, Monograph Series 60), 281–356. Washington, DC: Institute for the Study of Man.

Huld, Martin E., & James P. Mallory. 1997a. Iron. In: James P. Mallory & Douglas Q. Adams (ed.), *Encyclopedia of Indo-European culture*, 313–314. London & Chicago: Fitzroy Dearborn.

1997b. Metal. In: James P. Mallory & Douglas Q. Adams (ed.), *Encyclopedia of Indo-European culture*, 379–380. London & Chicago: Fitzroy Dearborn.

1997c. Silver. In: James P. Mallory & Douglas Q. Adams (ed.), *Encyclopedia of Indo-European culture*, 518–519. London & Chicago: Fitzroy Dearborn.

Joki, Aulis J. 1973. *Uralier und Indogermanen: die älteren Berührungen zwischen den uralischen und indogermanischen Sprachen*. Helsinki: Suomalais-Ugrilainen Seura.

Kallio, Petri. 2004. Tocharian loanwords in Samoyed? In: Irma Hyvärinen, Petri Kallio, & Jarmo Korhonen (ed.), *Etymologie, Entlehnungen und Entwicklungen: Festschrift für Jorma Koivulehto zum 70. Geburtstag* (Mémoires de la Société Néophilologique 63), 129–137. Helsinki: Société Néophilologique.

Kloekhorst, Alwin. 2008. *Etymological dictionary of the Hittite inherited lexicon* (Leiden Indo-European Etymological Dictionary Series 5). Leiden & Boston: Brill.

Kroonen, Guus. 2013. *Etymological dictionary of Proto-Germanic* (Leiden Indo-European Etymological Dictionary Series 11). Leiden & Boston: Brill.

Kümmel, Martin Joachim. 2017. Even more traces of the accent in Armenian? The development of tenues after sonorants. In: Bjarne Simmelkjær Sandgaard Hansen, Adam Hyllested, Anders Richardt Jørgensen, Guus Kroonen, Jenny Helena Larsson, Benedicte Nielsen Whitehead, Thomas Olander, & Tobias Mosbæk Søborg (ed.), *Usque ad radices: Indo-European studies in honour of Birgit Anette Olsen* (Copenhagen Studies in Indo-European), 439–452. Copenhagen: Museum Tusculanum.

Lehmann, Winfred P. 1986. *A Gothic etymological dictionary*. Leiden: Brill.

Mallory, James P. 2018. Linguistic palaeontology. Paper presented at Languages and Migrations in Prehistoric Europe: Roots of Europe Summer Seminar, National Museum of Denmark and the University of Copenhagen, August 7–12, 2018.

2019. Proto-Indo-European, Proto-Uralic, and Nostratic: A brief excursus into the comparative study of proto-languages. In: Birgit Anette Olsen, Thomas Olander, & Kristian Kristiansen (ed.), *Tracing the Indo-Europeans: New evidence from archaeology and historical linguistics*, 35–58. Oxford & Philadelphia: Oxbow.

Mallory, James P., & Douglas Q. Adams. 2006. *The Oxford introduction to Proto-Indo-European and the Proto-Indo-European world*. Oxford & New York: Oxford University Press.

Mallory, James P., & Martin E. Huld. 1984. Proto-Indo-European 'silver'. *Zeitschrift für vergleichende Sprachforschung* 97: 1–12.

Martirosyan, Hrach K. 2010. *Etymological dictionary of the Armenian inherited lexicon* (Leiden Indo-European Etymological Dictionary Series 8). Leiden & Boston: Brill.

Matasović, Ranko. 2009. *Etymological dictionary of Proto-Celtic* (Leiden Indo-European Etymological Dictionary Series 9). Leiden & Boston: Brill.

Mayrhofer, Manfred. 1986. *Etymologisches Wörterbuch des Altindoarischen*. Vol. 1. Heidelberg: Winter.

1996. *Etymologisches Wörterbuch des Altindoarischen*. Vol. 2. Heidelberg: Winter.

Meillet, Antoine. 1903. *Introduction à l'étude comparative des langues indo-européennes*. Paris: Hachette.

Melchert, H. Craig. 1994. *Anatolian historical phonology* (Leiden Studies in Indo-European 3). Amsterdam & Atlanta: Rodopi.

Mühlenbach, Karl, & Jānis Endzelīns. 1923–1925. *Lettisch-deutsches Wörterbuch. Redigiert, ergänzt und fortgesetzt von J. Endzelin*. Vol. 1. Riga: Izglītības ministrija; Kultūras fonds.

Nakhleh, Luay, Donald A. Ringe, & Tandy Warnow. 2005. Perfect phylogenetic networks: A new methodology for reconstructing the evolutionary history of natural languages. *Language* 81: 382–420.

Neumann, Günther. 1975. Frühe Indogermanen und benachbarte Sprachgruppen. In: Karl J. Narr (ed.), *Handbuch der Urgeschichte*. Vol. 2. Jüngere Steinzeit und Steinkupferzeit. Frühe Bodenbau- und Viehzuchtkulturen, 673–689. Bern & Munich: Francke.

Nichols, Johanna. 1990. Linguistic diversity and the first settlement of the New World. *Language* 66(3): 475–521.

1997. The epicentre of the Indo-European linguistic spread. In: Roger Blench & Matthew Spriggs (ed.), *Archaeology and language*. Vol. 1. Theoretical and methodological orientations (One World Archaeology 27), 122–148. London & New York: Routledge.

Olander, Thomas. 2017. Drinking beer, smoking tobacco and reconstructing prehistory. In: Bjarne Simmelkjær Sandgaard Hansen, Adam Hyllested, Anders Richardt Jørgensen, Guus Kroonen, Jenny Helena Larsson, Benedicte Nielsen Whitehead, Thomas Olander, & Tobias Mosbæk Søborg (ed.), *Usque ad radices: Indo-European studies in honour of Birgit Anette Olsen* (Copenhagen Studies in Indo-European 8), 605–618. Copenhagen: Museum Tusculanum.

2018. Connecting the dots: The Indo-European family tree as a heuristic device. In: David Goldstein, Stephanie Jamison, & Brent Vine (ed.), *Proceedings of the 29th UCLA Indo-European Conference*, 181–202. Bremen: Hempen.

2019a. The Indo-European homeland: Introducing the problem. In: Birgit Anette Olsen, Thomas Olander, & Kristian Kristiansen (ed.), *Tracing the Indo-Europeans: New evidence from archaeology and historical linguistics*, 7–34. Oxford & Philadelphia: Oxbow.

2019b. Indo-European cladistic nomenclature. *Indogermanische Forschungen* 124: 231–244.

Olsen, Birgit Anette. 1999. *The noun in Biblical Armenian: Origin and word-formation – with special emphasis on the Indo-European heritage* (Trends in Linguistics. Studies and Monographs 119). Berlin & New York: Mouton de Gruyter.

Orël, Vladimir E. 1998. *Albanian etymological dictionary*. Leiden, Boston, & Cologne: Brill.

Pereltsvaig, Asya, & Martin W. Lewis. 2015. *The Indo-European controversy: Facts and fallacies in historical linguistics*. Cambridge: Cambridge University Press.

Peyrot, Michaël. 2019. Indo-Uralic, Indo-Anatolian, Indo-Tocharian. In: Alwin Kloekhorst & Tijmen Pronk (ed.), *The precursors of Proto-Indo-European: The Indo-Anatolian and Indo-Uralic hypotheses* (Leiden Studies in Indo-European 21), 186–202. Leiden & Boston: Brill.

Prósper, Blanca María. 2011. The Hispano-Celtic divinity ILVRBEDA, gold mining in Western Hispania and the syntactic context of Celtiberian *arkatobezom* 'silver mine'. *Die Sprache* 49(1): 53–83.

Puhvel, Jaan. 1991. *Hittite etymological dictionary*. Vol. 3. Words beginning with H. Berlin & New York: Mouton de Gruyter.

Rasmussen, Jens Elmegård. 1989. *Studien zur Morphophonemik der indogermanischen Grundsprache* (Innsbrucker Beiträge zur Sprachwissenschaft 55). Innsbruck: Institut für Sprachwissenschaft der Universität Innsbruck.

Rau, Wilhelm. 1974. *Metalle und Metallgeräte im vedischen Indien* (Abhandlungen der Akademie der Wissenschaften und der Literatur. Geistes- und sozialwissenschaftliche Klasse, Jahrgang 1973, 8). Mainz: Akademie der Wissenschaften und der Literatur.

Ringe, Donald A. 1998. Some consequences of a new proposal for subgrouping the IE family. In: Benjamin K. Bergen, Madelaine C. Plauché, & Ashlee C. Bailey (ed.), *Proceedings of the Twenty-Fourth Annual Meeting of the Berkeley Linguistics Society, February 14–16, 1998. Special session on Indo-European subgrouping and internal relations*, 32–46. Berkeley: Berkeley Linguistics Society.

2022. What we can (and can't) learn from computational cladistics. In: Thomas Olander (ed.), *The Indo-European languages: A phylogenetic perspective*, 52–62. Cambridge: Cambridge University Press.

Ringe, Donald A., & Joseph F. Eska. 2013. *Historical linguistics: Toward a twenty-first century reintegration*. Cambridge etc.: Cambridge University Press.

Ringe, Donald A., Tandy Warnow, & Ann Taylor. 2002. Indo-European and computational linguistics. *Transactions of the Philological Society* 100(1): 59–129.

Rix, Helmut, Martin Kümmel, Thomas Zehnder, Reiner Lipp, & Brigitte Schirmer (ed.). 2001. *Lexikon der indogermanischen Verben*. 2nd expanded and improved edition. Wiesbaden: Reichert.

Schrader, Otto. 1890. *Sprachvergleichung und Urgeschichte: Linguistisch-historische Beiträge zur Erforschung des indogermanischen Altertums*. Dritte neubearbeitete Auflage. Jena: Costenoble.

Schrijver, Peter. 1991. *The reflexes of the Proto-Indo-European laryngeals in Latin* (Leiden Studies in Indo-European 2). Amsterdam & Atlanta: Rodopi.

Skjærvø, Prods Oktor. 1995. The Avesta as source for the early history of the Iranians. In: George Erdosy (ed.), *The Indo-Aryans of ancient South Asia: Language, material culture and ethnicity* (Indian Philology and South Asian Studies 1), 155–176. Berlin & New York: De Gruyter.

Tylecote, R. F. 1992. *A history of metallurgy*. 2nd ed. London: Maney.

Vanséveren, Sylvie. 2012. Noms de métaux dans les textes hittites. *Anatolica* 38: 203–219.

Vasmer, Max. 1986. *Ètimologičeskij slovar' russkogo jazyka* [*Etymological dictionary of the Russian language*]. Vol. 2. E–Muž. 2nd ed. Translated with additions by O. N. Trubačëv. Moskow: Progress.

Vennemann, Theo. 1997. Some West Indo-European words of uncertain origin. In: Raymond Hickey & Stanislav Puppe (ed.), *Language history and linguistic modelling. A Festschrift for Jacek Fisiak* (Trends in Linguistics. Studies and Monographs 101), 879–908. Berlin & New York: Mouton de Gruyter.

Walde, Alois, & J. B. Hofmann. 1938. *Lateinisches etymologisches Wörterbuch*. 3., neubearbeitete Auflage von J. B. Hofmann (Indogermanische Bibliothek, Abt. 1, Reihe 2, Band 1). Heidelberg: Winter.

Weiss, Michael. 2020. *Outline of the historical and comparative grammar of Latin*. 2nd ed. Ann Arbor (MI) & New York: Beech Stave.

Witczak, Krzysztof Tomasz. 1990. Tocharian A *nkiñc*, B *ñkante* 'silver'. *Tocharian and Indo-European Studies* 4: 47–48.

Witzel, Michael. 2005. Indocentrism: Autochthonous visions of ancient India. In: Edwin Bryant & Laurie L. Patton (ed.), *The Indo-Aryan controversy: Evidence and inference in Indian history*, 341–404. London & New York: Routledge.

Yamazaki, Yoko. 2009. The Saussure effect in Lithuanian. *The Journal of Indo-European Studies* 37(3): 430–461.

8 WORD MINING: METAL NAMES AND THE INDO-EUROPEAN DISPERSAL*

RASMUS THORSØ, ANDREW WIGMAN, ANTHONY JAKOB, AXEL I. PALMÉR, PAULUS VAN SLUIS, AND GUUS KROONEN

8.1 Introduction

The first use of metals in the production of objects among human societies was undoubtedly a defining event with a profound, irreversible impact on craftsmanship, agriculture, trade, warfare, and other cultural and political phenomena. The continuous refinement of metallurgical practice, including the introduction of new metals, has left behind some of the most conspicuous and important archaeological remains. Furthermore, the linguistic and archaeological evidence provided by metals can be combined to cast light on the relative placement of reconstructed languages in time and space through the use of linguistic palaeontology (cf. already Schrader 1883). For the study of the expansion of the Indo-European (IE) languages, examining the inventory of metallurgical vocabulary is thus highly relevant – not only for dating and locating the dissolution of each language, but also for determining the branching and spread of the successive daughter languages, and how they were influenced by foreign languages.

Here, we present and analyze IE linguistic material surrounding metallurgy, most of which is relevant to understanding the expansion of the IE languages. First of all, we ask which metals were known to the speakers of Proto-Indo-European (PIE) and which were adopted only after its dissolution. Furthermore, we aim to determine, where possible, where and when non-IE words for metals were adopted by the various daughter languages. A related question is which metals are the most relevant for such an analysis. Thus, in Sections 8.2 to 8.7, we analyze the most relevant lexemes according to their most dominant meaning in order to determine the earliest language stage for which they can be reconstructed and, where possible, their origin, either as inherited from PIE or adopted from a foreign source. This will provide the basis for a discussion (Section 8.8) where, by applying the principles of linguistic palaeontology, we seek to gain at least a rudimentary insight into the state of metallurgy in the IE branches, and the sources of metal trade and innovation. Here, special focus is placed on ironworking (8.8.2), which, by virtue of being a relatively late innovation compared to PIE, provides especially relevant information from the linguistic side. By identifying the earliest stage of a daughter branch that contained a word for iron, it should be possible to place this language stage in a material context and thus estimate the period and/or location of its existence. This is the principal aim of the present article.

* This study has received funding from the European Research Council under the European Union's Horizon 2020 research and innovation program (Grant N° 716732). It also received funding from the Dutch Research Council (grant n° PGW.19.022). We thank Agnes Korn, Cid Swanenvleugel, Maikel Kuijpers, and Michael Weiss for assistance and comments provided during the research for this paper. For more details and additional perspectives on the Proto-Indo-European metal terms, we refer the reader to Chapter 7 by Thomas Olander.

8.2 Gold

8.2.1 PIE *h_2eHus-

One likely IE word for 'gold' is found in Baltic (Lith. *áuksas* 3/1, Pr. (EV) *ausis*, (III) *ausin* acc.sg.) and Italic (Lat. *aurum*, Sabine [*Paul. ex Fest.*] *ausum*).[1] Traditionally, this word has been connected with the root *h_2*eus-* '(to) dawn, early' (cf. NIL 357–367; Blažek 2017: 272–276).[2] A simple thematic stem *h_2*eus-o-* cannot explain the acute accent in Baltic, however, and one would have to follow Driessen (2003) in reconstructing a reduplicated stem *h_2*é-*h_2*us-o-*. A reduplicated formation of this type would be rare and archaic, which, along with the exact match in Italic and Baltic, is good evidence that the formation would be of PIE date. On the other hand, it cannot be excluded that there is no link with the root 'to dawn', as several other reconstructions are possible (**HeHuso-* or **He/ouHso-*).

To approach a reconstruction of this word, the evidence of the Tocharian forms is crucial, but also problematic. ToA *wäs*, ToB *yasa* (gen.sg. *ysā[m̥]tse*) 'gold' reflect a PTo. **ẃəsā*. In order to establish direct cognacy with the aforementioned

[1] Blažek (2017: 284–285) adduces Luwian *wašḫa-* as cognate, but a meaning 'gold' for this word is not secure.

[2] A conceptual relation of 'sun' and 'gold' can be found in several South and Meso-American languages, e.g. Guaraní *kuarepoti-ju* lit. 'yellow sun faeces' (Bellamy 2018: 7).

forms, one can reconstruct **h*$_2$*ues-eh*$_2$*-* (cf. Adams 2013: 524–525), but this suffers from the extra assumption of *Schwebeablaut*. Alternatively, all of the 'gold' forms could reflect thematicizations of an ablauting *s*-stem **h*$_2$*éh*$_2$*u-s-* ~ **h*$_2$*h*$_2$*u-és-* (or **h*$_1$*eh*$_2$*u-*, **h*$_2$*eh*$_1$*u-*), of which the Tocharian form would continue the oblique stem **h*$_2$*h*$_2$*u-és-*.

However, the Tocharian word may not be inherited at all. Kallio (2004: 132–133) assumes that it is borrowed from Proto-Samoyed **wesä* 'metal, iron' (Nganasan *basa* 'metal, iron', Tundra Nenets *yesya*, Taz Selkup *kḛsi̯* 'iron'), in which case its potential reconcilability with the other IE forms would be due to chance. The Proto-Samoyed word can be compared to forms attested in the westernmost Uralic branches, including North Saami *veaiki* (< Proto-Saami **veaškē*) and Finnish *vaski* 'copper' (< Proto-Finnic **vaski*), reflecting a Proto-Uralic **wäśkä*. According to Kallio (l.c.), this represents the original Proto-Uralic situation, and irregularities in the central branches (Mordvin, Permic, and Hungarian) are due to later re-borrowing of the word.

There are problems with the native status of the words in the peripheral branches too, however. Aikio (2015: 43) points out that the Nganasan and Selkup forms with a back vowel can only be explained by positing a disharmonic Proto-Samoyed **wäsa*. Disharmonic roots are not typical of inherited Uralic vocabulary. Additionally, it is noteworthy that the Finnic word may not regularly reflect PU **wäśkä*, either. While the change **ä–ä* > **a–i* is regular in Finnic, it appears to have been blocked by a tautosyllabic palatal; cf. e.g. Fin. *päivä* 'day; the sun' (< **päjwä*), *nälkä* 'hunger' (< **ńälkä*), *hähnä* 'woodpecker' (< **śäśnä*) (Zhivlov 2014: 114–115; Aikio 2015: 40–41).[3] Therefore, the Uralic etymon as a whole is probably best treated as a *Wanderwort* of post-Proto-Uralic date (Aikio 2015: 43).

It is still quite remarkable that the Proto-Samoyed reconstruction provided here is essentially identical to Proto-Tocharian **wəsā*. Janhunen (1983: 119–121) argues that the borrowing went from Tocharian into Proto-Samoyed. However, while semantic arguments can be made in either direction ('gold' broadened to 'metal' or 'metal' narrowed to 'gold'), if the Samoyed and Tocharian forms indeed reflect this same *Wanderwort*, the direction of borrowing must have been from Samoyed to Tocharian; it is not appealing to detach the Proto-Samoyed word, which shows the regular simplification of *-*śk*- > *-*s*-, from the other Uralic forms, which cannot be explained as Tocharian borrowings. In conclusion, if the Samoyed and Tocharian words are connected, the Tocharian word was borrowed from Samoyed. Yet it remains theoretically possible that the Tocharian word is inherited from PIE, in which case its resemblance to the Samoyed word is a pure coincidence.

Armenian *oski* 'gold, golden' (GDA pl. *-eac*^{c}, inst.pl. *-wovk*^{c}) is another problematic comparandum. Unlike most other Armenian metal names, the substantive ('gold') and adjective ('golden') are not formally distinguished; cf. e.g., *arcat*^{c}*i* 'silvery' from *arcat*^{c} 'silver'. It is thus not immediately clear whether the final *-i* is originally part of the substantive stem or whether the adjectival form, where *-i* would be productive, was at some point generalized or substantivized. The difficulty of establishing an exact preform linking this word with the complex of 'gold' words covered above has led many to assume substrate origin or interference. None of these proposals is tenable, however.[4] Although it cannot be excluded that the word was borrowed from a completely obscure source, it can be furnished with a relatively convincing root etymology. Yet the stem formation is not very clear. Olsen (1999: 441) suggests **h*$_2$*ustu̯io-* 'leuchtungsfähig', a formation comparable to the isolated Skt. *kr̥-tvyá-* 'fit, capable'. There is, however, no need to project the clearly productive suffix *-i* all the way to the protolanguage. Thus, a formation **h*$_2$*ustu̯o-* (cf. Skt. *bhittvá-* 'splitting') is sufficient to produce **usk(o)-*.[5] With the addition of the suffix *-i*, the adjective **uski* would become *oski* through dissimilatory umlaut **u _ i* > *o _ i*,[6] after which, at a relatively late stage, the form of the substantive was replaced by that of the adjective. The motivation for this may have been the fact that virtually all other metal names are disyllabic. Among current proposals, a PIE formation **h*$_2$*us-t-u̯o-* remains the most likely reconstruction for Arm. *oski*, which would then represent the original adjective 'golden'. Yet, such a formation

[3] The Saami reflex may also be irregular, as the default outcome of PU **ä–ä* in Saami is **ā–ē*, e.g. Proto-Saami **ājmē* 'needle' (< PU **äjmä*). However, **ä–ä* sometimes yields **ea–ē*, particularly after labials; cf. **pealē* 'half' (< PU **pälä*), **peajvē* 'sun; day' (< PU **päjwä*); **weajē* 'be able' (< PU **wäjä*, cf. Finnish *voida*). In this case, **veaškē* 'copper' can also reflect **wäśkä*.

[4] A connection with Sum. *guškin* (Pedersen 1924: 219–220) must be abandoned, since this reading of the Sumerian logogram is now considered obsolete in favor of *ku*$_3$*sig*$_{17}$, a compound 'yellow precious metal'(Civil 1976; cf. the *Pennsylvania Sumerian Dictionary*). A borrowing from Uralic **wäśkä* (J̌ahowkyan 1987: 452) is unlikely for both geographic and phonological reasons. Schrader (1883: 243) suggests a connection with Kartvelian – cf. Georgian/Megrelian *okro*, Svan (*û*)*okûr* 'gold' – but it is difficult to understand phonetically and besides, these words may have been borrowed from Gk. ὠχρός 'pale (yellow), wan' (Klimov 1964: 151).

[5] Alternatively, a **h*$_2$*ustu̯o-* may represent a **u̯o*-derivation of the stem reflected in Hitt. *ḫust(i)-*, which perhaps means 'amber' (cf. HED 3: 411–413). This word is cautiously compared to the complex of 'gold' words by Blažek (2017: 281–283). Although the comparison with Armenian would be extremely shallow, it is perhaps morphologically more plausible. Blažek's (2017: 280, 294) own reconstruction for *oski*, an "appurtenance-formation" **h*$_2$*us-h*$_2$*u̯o-*, would probably not yield the correct outcome, as the medial laryngeal would vocalize in this environment; cf. *harawownk*^{c} 'fields' < **h*$_2$*erh*$_3$*m/u̯on-*. Martirosyan's (EDAIL 533) reconstruction **əu̯oskíya* is also difficult to understand, since laryngeals do not usually vocalize before **u̯*, and there seems to be no other obvious source for an initial schwa. The suggestion that *-*kV* represents a non-IE suffix (ibid.), reflected also in Uralic (**wäś-kä*), is not very convincing in view of its absence elsewhere in Armenian, and the already very weak evidence for its existence.

[6] Though it has not been met with broad acceptance, this rule is confirmed by transparent examples like *erko-k*^{c}*in* 'both' < *erkow* 'two' *Asori* 'Syrian' ← Gk. Ἀσσύριος (Olsen 1999: 803) and runs parallel with the change **i _ u* > *e _ u* recognized by Meillet (1936: 55).

would be isolated among the extant IE vocabulary in Armenian and thus cannot be established with full certainty.

8.2.2 PIE *ǵ^{h}elh$_3$-

The root *ǵ^{h}elh$_3$- 'green, yellow'[7] provides the basis for the words for 'gold' in Indo-Iranian, Phrygian, Balto-Slavic, and Germanic. In Balto-Slavic and Germanic, the formation is specifically a *-*to*- derivative of the root.

From this root derives the Proto-Indo-Iranian *n*-stem **jr̥Han*-, as reflected in YAv. *zaran-aēna-* 'golden'.[8] All other forms derive from a stem **jŕ̥Hania*-. These include Skt. *híraṇya*- 'precious metal, gold', OP *daraniya*-, Khot. *ysīrra*-, Sogd. *zyrn*, and Oss. *zærin*/*zærinæ* 'gold'.

Hungarian *arany* 'gold' and certain Ob-Ugric forms (Khanty *lorńə* ~ *ʟŏrńi̯* 'copper, brass', Mansi *tåreń* ~ *tariń* 'copper') can be combined under a reconstruction **sarńi* 'gold' (cf. Holopainen 2019: 232, with a different reconstruction).[9] Similar forms are found in other Uralic languages: Mari *šörtńö* ~ *šörtńi* (< **se̮rńV*?), Permic *zarńi* 'gold' (< **särńV*?), as well as Mordvin *si̯ŕńe* ~ *śiŕńä* 'gold' (< **serńä*?). Due to the numerous irregularities, it seems clear that the word spread through the Uralic languages as a *Wanderwort*, perhaps being adopted from several different Iranian sources (cf. Holopainen 2019: 234). Because of the initial **s*-, Uralic **sarńi* and the other forms were most likely borrowed from a post-Proto-Iranian source of the shape **zar(a)ni̯a*- (Häkkinen 2009: 23), as Proto-Indo-Iranian **j́* remained an affricate in Proto-Iranian (Cantera 2017: 492).

The Phrygian word for gold was almost certainly γλουρος. It is reported in the adjectival form γλούρεα by Hesychius and glossed as χρύσεα. Φρύγες 'golden things (among the Phrygians)' (EDG 277). An additional entry by Hesychius reads γλουρός· χρυσός and we can surmise that this too is a Phrygian word. The adjectival form γλούρεα is also attested in an undated inscription (W-11) from Dokimeion (Brixhe 2004: 17). The formation is cognate with Gk. χλωρός 'green, yellow, pale', reflecting PIE *ǵ^{h}l̥h$_3$-ro- (EDG 277).

In Northern Europe, there seems to be a general tendency to derive words for 'gold' from the root *ǵ^{h}elh$_3$- with the suffix *-*to*-. However, we find three different ablaut grades: the morphologically expected zero grade in Germanic **gulþa*- (Go. *gulþ*, OHG *gold*, OE *gold*) beside an *o*-grade in Slavic **zȍlto* (c) 'gold' (OCS *zlato*, Ru. *zóloto*, Cz. *zlato*, SCr. *zlâto*, Sln. *zlatộ*, etc.) and an *e*-grade in Latv. *zȩ̀lts*. It is therefore unclear to what extent these words represent a genuine isogloss. As the application of color terms for distinguishing metals is cross-linguistically common (cf. also 8.3.1), we may very well be faced with independently formed stems. The Latvian word, for instance, is likely an independent substantivization of the color adjective seen in Lith. *žel̃tas* 'yellowish, golden'. This is further supported by the fact that a different word for 'gold' can be reconstructed for Proto-East Baltic (see 8.2.1). A derivational base for the Slavic word is less forthcoming, but it may represent a fossilized derivative of the same Balto-Slavic adjective. Skt. *hárita*- 'yellow' and YAv. *zairita*- 'yellow' are independent Indo-Iranian derivations of PIIr **jarH-i*- rather than continuations of PIE *ǵ^{h}elh$_3$-to-, since a laryngeal would not vocalize in medial position in Avestan (Cantera 2017: 487).[10]

The morphological variation in this set of root comparanda strongly suggests that PIE *ǵ^{h}elh$_3$- was not lexicalized as 'gold' per se, but simply an adjective 'yellow-green', which, at most, could occasionally be applied as an epithet of gold. This use may even have arisen independently in the branches where it is attested.

8.2.3 Greek χρῡσός

Greek χρῡσός 'gold' has been attested since Myc. *ku-ru-so* (15th c. BCE) and is certainly a loan from Semitic; cf. Akk. *ḫurāṣu*, Ug. *ḫrṣ*, Phoen. *ḥrṣ*, and Hebr. *ḥāruṣ* (< **ḫrṣ*-) (Masson 1967: 37–38). The correspondence of Akk. *ḫ*, Ug. *ḫ*, and Hebr. *ḥ* demonstrates a Proto-Semitic **ḫ* (Militarev & Kogan 2000: LXVIII), and both *ḫ* and *ḥ* are borrowed as Greek χ (cf. Rosół 2013: 21). The word is considered most likely to have entered Greek from Phoenician (Masson 1967: 38).[11] Greek ῡ reflects Phoenician *ō* or *ū* from earlier *ā* (Akkadian preserves the inherited vocalism in *ḫurāṣu* [Militarev & Kogan 2000: CXXIV]), meaning that the Phoenician word, whose vocalism is otherwise hidden by orthographical conventions, was most likely *ḥurō*/*ūṣ* (Szemerényi 1964: 53–54).

[7] A close semantic parallel is the Semitic root YRQ; cf. Ugaritic *yrq* 'greenish yellow (of metals)', Aram. *yarq* 'herb, vegetables', Akk. (*w*)*arāq* 'to be yellowish-green, pale', etc. (Murtonen 1989: 222).

[8] OCS *zelenъ* 'green' is often compared to the YAv. *zaran*- (cf. Huld 2012: 308), but PSl. **zelenъ* is more likely an original past passive participle from an unattested verb **zelti* 'to make green(?)' (cf. Lith. *žélti* 'to grow green'). A similarly fossilized form is OCS *studenъ* 'cold', presumably from a verb **stusti*, 1sg. **studǫ* 'to cool' (compare Ru. *studít'* 'id.').

[9] The epenthesis of -*a*- in the cluster *-*rń*- in Hungarian is apparently not regular, at least judging by *horny* 'notch' (~ Finnish *kuurna* 'id.' < PU **kurńa*). On the other hand, a similar epenthesis is found in other words, e.g., *arasz* 'span' < **sorśi*. The Ob-Ugric forms appear to point to Khanty and Mansi **ă*.

[10] Skt. *hāṭaka*- 'gold, name of a country' is sometimes connected with the *-*to*- derivatives above (cf. Burrow 1972: 540) by attributing the retroflex to Fortunatov's Law, whereby **lt* > Skt. *ṭ* (Fortunatov 1881). However, due to the root final *-*h*$_3$, which should have yielded Skt. *i*, the proper condition for this sound law would not have arisen (unless one assumes that the laryngeal was lost because of the Saussure effect, the validity of which is debated; see Pronk 2011). According to KEWA (III: 589), *hāṭaka*- is unrelated to the words for 'gold' and the meaning is rather derived from the ethnogeographical designation, itself perhaps of non-IE origin.

[11] The emphatic sibilant *ṣ* is normally reflected in Greek as σσ, such as in βύσσος 'flax, linen' (cf. Akk. *būṣu*, Hebr. *būṣ*, etc.) (Masson 1967: 38), which led Belardi (1949: 309) to propose an original form *χρυσσός that was later simplified to χρῡσός. Another Semitic loan in Greek is κασία 'cassia' (cf. Hebr. *qəṣīʿā*), which also occurs rarely as κασσία (Rosół 2013: 21), so a form with a second σ is not necessary to reconstruct.

8.3 Silver

8.3.1 PIE *h_2(e)rǵ-nt-o-*

PIE *$*h_2$(e)rǵ-nt-o-* 'silver' is solidly attested across the IE languages: YAv. *ərəzata-*, Lat. *argentum*, OIr. *argat*, MW *aryant*.[12] In all likelihood, Arm. *arcatᶜ* also belongs here.[13] The latter seems to have been borrowed by a number of Daghestanian languages; cf. Godoberi *arci*, Lak *arcu*, Southern Akhvakh *arči*; perhaps also forms with **ars-*, e.g. Andi *orsi*, Botlikh, Archi *arsi*, all of which fail to show regular correspondences (Schultze 2013: 309–310). An Iranian source for these words is theoretically possible but less geographically obvious.

The stem *$*h_2$(e)rǵ-nt-o-* may be analyzed as a thematicized participle in **-nt-* built from the root *$*h_2$erǵ-* 'white, shining'; cf. Hitt. *ḫarki-*, ToA *ārki-* 'white'. A different and isolated formation is Gk. ἄργυρος, Myc. *a-ku-ro* 'silver' < *$*h_2$(e)rǵ-u-ro-*, based on a *u*-stem also seen in Ved. *árjuna-* 'white, bright, silver-colored', ToB *arkwi* 'white'. As the form based on the participle appears in noncontiguous IE dialects, the Greek form must represent a later innovation, a substantivization of an adjective combining the Caland-suffixes **-u-* and **-ro-* (note Skt. *r̥jrá-* 'shining, quick' and the *i*-stems in Hittite and Tocharian).

Although **ḫarkant-* 'silver' is not directly attested in Anatolian, its existence is suggested by the phonetic complement in Hitt. KÙ.BABBAR-*ant-* (HED 3: 171), showing that a formation *$*h_2$rǵ-ent-* 'silver' might have existed at the earliest stage of PIE. The later thematicization of this stem can thus be considered a Core IE innovation.[14]

[12] A more problematic form is Skt. *rajatá-* 'white, silvery', which seems to reflect *$*h_2$reǵ-nt-ó-*, with a different root shape. Although none of the words for 'silver' must reflect a form with root full grade, the reconstruction *$*h_2$reǵ-nt-ó-* is still in conflict with Skt. *árjuna-* 'bright, white, silvery', *árji-* 'bright-colored' (cf. Hitt. *ḫarki-*), which point to an original full grade *$*h_2$erǵ-*. Thus, *rajatá-* likely represents a secondary formation that may go back to older **r̥jatá-* or it reflects a different root altogether (cf. EWAia II: 426; Mallory & Huld 1984: 3).

[13] The Armenian reflex has been problematized on account of the final *-tᶜ*, as the commonly accepted reflex of **-nt-* is either *-n* or *-nd*. Thus, one expects a regular reflex **arcan(d)*. The traditional explanation is that *-tᶜ* results from contamination with *erkatᶜ* 'iron' or contains an identical suffix, of obscure origin (cf. Hübschmann 1897: 424; HAB I 318; EDAIL 131). However, this solution is not attractive as long as the *-tᶜ* of *erkatᶜ* is etymologically unexplained. Others have regarded the Armenian word as an early borrowing from an Iranian **ardzata* (Lamberterie 1978: 245–251; Olsen 1999: 868). Kümmel (2017: 444–446) seeks a regular explanation through a suggested development of pretonic **nt* > **nϑ* > *tᶜ* when not preceding a word boundary or single vowel; cf. *kitᶜ* 'milking, harvest'< **gem-tó/í-*. Thus, *$*h_2$(e)rǵ-nt-ó-* would yield **arcanϑ-* > *arcatᶜ*. This provides an attractive explanation for the final *-atᶜ*, which may later have been interpreted as a type of suffix and transferred to the word for 'iron' (see 8.5.7).

[14] For a similar thematicization, cf. Hitt *ḫuu̯ant-* < *$*h_2uh_1$-(e)nt-* vs. Skt. *vātá-*, W *gwynt*, Lat. *ventus* < *$*h_2ueh_1$-(e)nt-o-* 'wind' (cf. Pronk & Kloekhorst 2019: 4).

8.3.2 West European **sil(a)P(u)r*

Next to the aforementioned Indo-European word for silver, another, clearly non-IE, word is found in Europe and North Africa, namely PG **silubra-* (Go. *silubr*, ON *silfr* etc.), OCS *sъrebro*, Lith. *sidābras*, Pr. (III) *sirablan* (acc.sg.), (EV) *sira-plis*, and Celtiberian *śilaPuŕ*. These are all formally irreconcilable but show an undeniable similarity. Indeed, additional similar words are found in Basque *zil(h)ar* (< **zilpar?*), Berber **ẓrīp-/ẓrūp-*, and perhaps Proto-Semitic **ṣarp-* (Akk. *ṣarp-*, Arab. poet. *ṣarīf*).[15] This gives the impression of a *Wanderwort* that spread from the (Western?) Mediterranean to North Europe after the diversification and expansion of Indo-European languages.

8.4 Copper

8.4.1 PIE *$*h_2$eies-* 'metal, copper?'

Skt. *áyas-* 'metal, copper, iron', Av. *aiiah-* 'metal', Lat. *aes* n. (gen. *aeris*) 'ore, copper, bronze', Umb. **ahesnes** (dat. pl.), Go. *aiz* '(copper) coin, money',[16] and ON *eir* 'brass, copper' all support the reconstruction of a PIE neuter *s*-stem *$*h_2$eies-*. While this term is certainly associated with metals, it is not clear whether it is a generic designation applying to any metal, or if it originally refers to a specific one. It is noteworthy that the meaning 'copper' is attested in at least some languages in all of the branches where this word is continued, and the occasional meanings 'iron', 'bronze', 'brass', and 'ore' could easily be secondary developments. On the other hand, the absence of another candidate for a generic PIE word for 'metal' raises the possibility that *$*h_2$eies-* carried this meaning too. In fact, it is very likely that both the meanings 'copper' and 'metal' existed to some extent. Native copper is extremely common and due to its malleability, it could be worked cold even by Neolithic populations (cf. Forbes 1950: 291). As such, it is a metal par excellence and perhaps the only one that PIE speakers came across regularly (cf. Huld 2012: 299). By contrast, silver and gold are far more rare and unsuitable for practical use. Thus, *$*h_2$eies-* could be interpreted as 'workable metal or ore'. This stem cannot evidently be connected with a certain root, although a hypothetical *$*h_2$ei-* 'fire?' may underlie *$*h_2$eidʰ-* 'ignite' (Gk. αἴθω) if this is originally composed with *$*d^heh_1$-* 'to put'.[17]

[15] Boutkan & Kossmann (2001) do not accept the appurtenance of the Semitic word. The root is marginally attested with the meaning 'silver' and this use appears to be secondary from 'to burn, purify, refine'.

[16] A meaning 'copper' (or 'bronze') is suggested by the compound *aizasmiþa* (2 Tim. 4.14), which translates Gk. χαλκεύς 'coppersmith'. In the only attestation of the simplex *aiz*, acc.sg. (Mk. 6.8), it translates Gk. χαλκόν in the sense 'money'. One wonders if this is a calque of the Greek use of the word, whereby 'copper' can be considered the primary meaning in Gothic (cf. Huld 2012: 300).

[17] The old connection with Hitt *ā(i)-/i-* 'to be hot' should be abandoned, as this verb does not contain *$*h_2$* (EDHIL 200).

8.4.2 Sanskrit *lohá-*, Old Norse *rauði*, Old Church Slavonic *ruda*

The package of words containing PIIr. *$Hraud^ha$- (Skt. *lohá-* 'reddish metal, copper-colored, reddish, made of iron', MP/NP *rōy* 'copper, brass', and Bal. *rōd* 'copper')[18] as well as ON *rauði* 'bog iron ore' and OCS *ruda* 'ore, metal' can all be derived from the inherited root *h_1reud^h- 'red' (cf. Gk. ἐρυθρός). All forms can reflect an adjective *h_1roud^h-o- 'red', which also came to refer to 'copper' and/or 'ore', but as in the case of *$\acute{g}^helh_3$- for 'gold' (8.2.2), this may be an instance of similar yet independent semantic developments based on a natural description of copper as the 'red' metal. Despite their surface resemblance to Lat. *raudus, -eris* (8.4.3), the latter cannot be technically related (*pace* IEW 872–873), as *h_1reud^h-os- would have yielded ***rūbus*[19] (cf. the same root in *h_1rud^h-ro-, attested as Lat. *ruber* 'red').

8.4.3 Proto-Germanic **arut-* ~ Latin *raudus* ~ Sumerian *aruda*

A Proto-Germanic base **arut-* 'ore' can be reconstructed from the attestations ON *ørtog* 'type of weight' (< **aruti-tauga-*), Old Du. *arut*, OHG *aruz* 'ore' < **aruta-* and OHG *arizzi, erizzi*, MHG *erze*, G *Erz* n. 'id.' < **arutja-*. The underlying Pre-PG base **arud-* has of old been compared to Sum. *uruda, urudu* 'copper' (Schrader 1883: 62, 118). While the formal match has been criticized for being imperfect (Huld 2012: 305), the recent discovery of a regular development of *uruda* from Old Sumerian *aruda* (Jagersma 2010: 60–61) removes this objection. The traditional contextualization of this etymology is that a metal name spread from Mesopotamia to Europe where Indo-European languages could have adopted it after they had become established there (cf. Kauffmann 1913: 123 fn. 6). For geographic reasons, Sumerian cannot have been the direct donor language, however, and we may well be dealing with a *Wanderwort* that is nonnative in either language.

Another potential clue to the provenance of this loanword cluster is offered by Lat. *raudus* (var. *rōdus, rūdus*) 'piece of copper or brass (used as coin)', which has been adduced as a related Pre-Indo-European loan into Italic (Karsten 1928: 196). Although the appurtenance of this lexical item to the Germanic and Sumerian words is formally and semantically less evident (cf. Huld 2012: 304–305), the variation of Germanic and Sumerian **arud-* and Italic **raud-* falls within the relatively well-established pattern of lexical doublets with and without a non-Indo-European *a*-prefix in prehistoric loanwords in Europe (Schrijver 1997: 308; Iversen & Kroonen 2017: 518; Schrijver 2018: 363). Further evidence for a non-prefixed form might come from W *rhwd* 'rust, dirt', Old Breton *rod* glossing *erugi-nem uitalium* 'rust of the vital parts' < PC **rutu-*, which, if related, could be an independent imposition in view of **t* against **d* elsewhere (Koch 2020: 110).[20] If correctly applied, this pattern would associate the cluster with a specific stratum of the European Pre-Indo-European linguistic landscape, i.e. a single unclassified language (family) that mediated a term also found in Sumerian to Italic, Celtic, and Germanic.

8.4.4 Hittite *ku(wa)nna(n)-*

Hitt. *kuwannan-* (contracted variant *kunnan-* and later *a*-stem *kuwanna-*) is attested in the meanings 'copper' and, when preceded by the determinative NA_4, 'bead' or 'ornamental mineral'. Hom. κύανος 'dark blue (enamel), copper carbonate', later referring also to the color alone (cf. Eng. *cyan*), is probably an Anatolian loanword (Goetze 1947: 307–311); cf. also Myc. *ku-wa-no*, which refers to a blue decorative material, perhaps cobalt glass (Halleux 1969).

The ultimate source of the Hittite word is possibly Sum. *ku_3-an* 'a metal', which can be interpreted as a compound of *ku_3(.g)* 'precious metal' and *an* 'sky'. Thus it seems to refer to either a blue (i.e. sky-colored) metal or material, or a metal literally coming from the sky, i.e., meteoritic iron.[21] Determining which of the two meanings 'copper' and 'azurite (a blue copper ore)' is oldest is difficult and mostly relies on the exact interpretation of the ambiguous Sumerian compound (cf. Halleux 1969: 65–66). If this is indeed the source of the Hittite word, it is tempting to opt for the analysis of Sum. *ku_3-an* as 'blue (sky-colored) metal, copper carbonate'. This finds some support in the fact that Hurrian, which is a plausible vector for borrowing into Hittite (Halleux 1969: 65), appears to designate copper by the Sumerian *urud-* (cf. Richter 2012: 502).[22]

8.4.5 Greek χαλκός

Gk. χαλκός, Cretan καυχός, Myc. *ka-ko* 'copper, bronze' has no certain etymology, but cannot be inherited from PIE in view of

18 Arm. *aroyr* 'brass, bronze' must be borrowed from an Ir. **rauδ-*.

19 In fact, *h_1reud^h-os- does have a reflex in Latin, viz. *rōbus, -oris* 'red', but this seems to be a non-Roman form (Weiss 2020: 503), and in any case shows that *raudus* cannot be related.

20 W *rhwd* has alternatively been reconstructed to PC **ruddo-*, itself a compound of PIE *h_1reud^h- 'red' (8.4.2) and either *d^heh_1- 'to put' (Stifter 1998: 212–218) or **sed-* 'to sit' (Hill 2003: 196–202). Schaffner (2016/17: 114–115) alternatively reconstructs *h_2ru-ti- and connects *rhwd* to Irish *ruithen* 'ray, beam of light' and Lat. *rutilus* 'golden red; shining'. Finally, it is conceivable that W *rhwd* is borrowed from OE *rudu* 'redness'.

21 Giusfredi (2017) rejects the connection between the Sumerian and Hittite words on the basis that there is no Akkadian form that could have served as a vector of the borrowing. Any connection with Akk. *uqnû* 'blue, lapis lazuli' must be rejected, since it corresponds in texts with the sumerogram ^{NA4}ZA.GÌN. This circumstance is, however, entirely synchronic and does not exclude the possibility that Sum. *ku_3-an* was borrowed into the neighboring spoken languages, where it later lost its association with its original source.

22 Another suggested source is Hattic, where Puhvel (HED 4: 310) expects a hypothetical **kup(a)ro-* (underlying Gk. Κύπρος 'Cyprus' etc.; cf. 8.7.4) to alternate with **kuwano-*. This explanation has the clear downside that the relevant attestations are lacking in Hattic, where the usual word for 'copper' is *kinawar*. Further, there seems to be no basis for assuming an alternation of *r* and *n*.

the internal irregularity between the Homeric and Cretan forms, which respectively presuppose Proto-Greek **k*^{h}*alk*- and **k*$^{(h)}$*alk*^{h}-.[23] The traditional comparison with Lith. *geležìs* 'iron' etc. is difficult to maintain (cf. 8.5.5) and both of these etyma seem to represent relatively late borrowings in their respective branches. For the same reason, a direct relationship with Hitt. **ki/eklu(ba)*- 'iron, steel?', as per Blažek (2010: 28–29), is unlikely.

A clear candidate for a foreign source of χαλκός does not present itself. One such candidate may be the originally Hattic *ḫapalki* 'iron', which also entered Hittite and Hurrian (Pisani *apud* GEW II: 1071, EDG s.v.). However, unless this form was borrowed through an unknown medium or really features an archaic spelling for something like */ḫalki/, it is difficult to explain why the medial consonant *p* would not be reflected in any of the Greek forms.[24] The aforementioned Hitt. **ki/eklu(ba)*- seems too distant both formally and semantically. Slightly more promising is Dossin's suggestion (1948: 32 fn. 4, 1971: 9) of a connection with Sum. *kal(ag)ga* 'strong' (also 'a process involving silver'), which may have designated a 'strengthened copper', i.e., 'bronze' (the usual meaning in Homer). This would have been borrowed into Greek through some intermediary language(s) of Anatolia. For want of other attestations, this remains speculative.

In conclusion, although no etymology can be established, it is probably safe to say that χαλκός represents a non-IE loanword, most likely from a source in the East, adopted after Proto-Greek had begun to disintegrate.

[23] Assuming the possibility of earlier *χαλχ-, Tremblay (2004: 238) suggests that the Attic-Ionic form χαλκ- has preserved its initial aspirate due to association with e.g. χάλιξ 'pebble', χάλυψ 'steel', χαλεπός 'difficult, hard', whereas Cret. *καλχ- would be the regular outcome through Grassmann's Law. There are hardly any parallels for such a sporadic inverted dissimilation, and it seems we are dealing with independent adoptions of a foreign word. An anonymous reviewer points to a parallel for this in Gk. χίτων, Ionic/Doric κίθων 'chiton, tunic', which is probably from Semitic; cf. Phoen. *ktn*. In any case, the comparison with Balto-Slavic should probably be abandoned (cf. 8.5.5), leaving no external support for a stem **g*^{h}*l(e)ǵ*^{h}- vel sim.

[24] Note, however, that the common alternation of medial *p* and *w* in Hattic (Soysal 2004: 28) – cf. perhaps the toponym ^{URU}*Hawalkina* (Hoffner 1967: 184) – could reflect a phoneme (/f/?) that would have been lost in the Greek rendering of the word. Alternatively, Starostin (1985: 84–85) compares Hatt. *ḫapalki* to some West Caucasian forms, which he reconstructs as **ʁ́I*^{w}*ə-ƛ̣*^{w}*V* 'iron, lit. blue metal'(Adyghe *ǧ*^{w}*əç̣ə*, Abaza *jaç̣̌*^{w}*a* 'iron'), assuming a genetic relation between Hattic and West Caucasian. Although this relation is not well established (cf. Klinger 1995: 128–129), it is also possible to interpret this material in terms of borrowing. Leaving aside *ḫapalki*, the Proto-Circassian (and PWC?) compound **ǧ*^{w}*a-pλa* 'copper, lit. red metal'(Chirikba 1996: 400) could perhaps be considered an alternative, circuitous source of Gk. χαλκός; see Kas'jan 2010: 464–465, who also suggests that Hitt. **ki/eklu*- is a reflection of the West Caucasian word for 'iron'. These proposals are, unfortunately, impossible to verify. Witczak (2009) considers Hitt. *ḫa-palki* to be inherited from a putative (late) PIE "**pālaḱ*-" 'iron', but most of the comparisons involved are at odds with established sound laws. It seems clear that the word is originally Hattic (Vanséveren 2012: 204–206), though it remains possible to speculate on a horizontal relationship between this word and ToB *pilke* 'copper', and further perhaps West Germanic **blika*- 'sheet metal' (OHG *bleh*, G *Blech*, Middle Du. *blec*, *blic*, Du. *blik*).

8.4.6 Balto-Slavic Words for 'copper'

In East Baltic, we find a *ja*-stem **varja*- (Lith. *vãris*, obs. *vãrias*; Latv. *var̨š*), which corresponds to Pr. (EV) *wargien* 'copper'. The Prussian form can be interpreted as a neuter /warjan/ with the <g> reflecting a glide, as shown by *warene* /warinē/ 'brass pot'. This incidentally disproves the traditional comparison with Mari *würγeńe* 'copper' (Trautmann 1910: 458), whose initial *w*- may also be of secondary origin (see on this word 8.5.7). As no similar forms are found in neighboring languages, the only workable hypothesis appears to be an internal derivation from the root of Lith. *vìrti*, Latv. *varît* 'cook', PSl. **vьrěti* 'boil' (Ivanov 1977: 234), which may be cognate with Hitt. *ur*-$^{\bar{a}ri}$/*u̯ar*-$^{\bar{a}ri}$ 'burn', ToA *wrātk*- 'prepare (meat)' (< **uerh*$_{1}$-), referring to the process of its production.

In Slavic, a form **mȅdь* (a) 'copper, brass' is found (OCS *mědь*, Ru. *méd'*, Cz. *měď*, SCr. *mjȅd*, Sln. *mẹ̑d*). The acute accent can be attributed to Winter's Law, allowing a reconstruction **meid*-. Its etymology is disputed, but it seems possible to link it with the OIr. *méin*, MW *mwyn* 'ore, metal' through a reconstruction **meid-ni*- for Celtic. The Germanic forms Go. *maitan*, ON *meita*, OHG *meizan* 'to hew, cut' (IEW 697, with "?") have also been connected with the Celtic forms (Stokes & Bezzenberger 1979: 205). However, Kroonen (EDPG 349) considers the Germanic **t* to be of secondary origin, comparing ON *meiða* 'hurt, damage' < **maidjan*- (cf. LIV² 430 s.v. **mei̯th*$_{2}$-). This leaves only the Celtic and Slavic material as certain. In view of this limited distribution, it is uncertain whether **meid*- represents a PIE root.[25]

8.4.7 Celtic *omi-, *omiio-

PC **omiio*- is attested in OIr. *umae* 'copper, bronze, brass' and W *efydd* 'bronze, brass, copper'; PC **omi*- is found in OIr. *uim(m)* 'bronze'. A connection with PC **omo*- 'raw, crude, untreated' (OIr. *om*, W *of*, cf. Skt. *āmá*-, Gk. ὠμός, Arm. *howm* 'raw, uncooked' < **HoH-mó*- 'raw, uncooked') has been suggested, which may be understood as referring to the red color of the metal (Pedersen 1909: 166; Krogmann 1940; EDPC 298). The derivation may also be understood with reference to the secondary meanings of **omo*- as 'crude, untreated'; perhaps the derivatives **omiio*- and **omi*- originally meant 'untreated metal, ore' before the meaning narrowed to 'bronze'.[26] OIr. *umae* is neuter in the earliest Old Irish, just like other metal

[25] The comparison with Gk. μέταλλον 'mine, quarry', later 'mineral, metal' (van Windekens 1958: 135), is impossible in IE terms, but the word could perhaps be seen as a parallel loan from a Balkan source.

[26] The use of a single name for metal ores and their refined counterparts is rather common; cf. Huld (2012: 323 fn. 41) for parallels.

names. The shift from an adjective to a neuter noun implies an intermediate stage where **omiio-* was usually found as an adjective qualifying such a neuter noun denoting a metal. The original metal noun (**$h_2$eies-*?) was subsequently dropped, upon which **omiio-* was reinterpreted as denoting the metal and was nominalized to a neuter noun (Huld 2012: 345).

8.5 Iron

8.5.1 PIE **h_2eḱ-mon-* 'meteoritic iron?'

PIE **h_2eḱ-mon-*, which seems to be a **men*-derivation of the root **h_2eḱ-* 'sharp, pointy', is attested with two principal meanings. A meaning 'stone' is found in Ved. *áśman-*, Av. *asman-*; Lith. *akmuõ*, Latv. *akmens*, OCS *kamy*. In OP *asman-* and the remaining Iranian languages, the meaning is 'heaven, sky'. Gk. ἄκμων usually means 'anvil', but in a passage from Hesiod, it seems to mean 'meteorite' (*Th.* 722: χαλκεός ἄκμων οὐρανόθεν κατιών "a brazen ἄ. falling from the sky").[27] Hesychius offers the glosses ἄκμων· οὐρανός ἢ σίδηρον (heaven or iron) and Cypriot ἄκμονα· ἀλετρίβανον (pestle). These attestations could suggest that the older meaning in Greek is '(meteoritic) stone/ iron' (cf. LSJ). In most dialects, the meaning was extended from 'iron' to 'anvil' (also in Homer), but could have changed to 'heaven' in other dialects, if the testimony of Hesychius is to be trusted. It is tempting to connect this polysemy with that of Indo-Iranian, thus projecting the meaning 'meteorite, meteoritic iron' back to at least late PIE.

The semantic connection of 'stone' and 'heaven' is frequently interpreted in the context of PIE mythology, where the sky may have been considered to be a stony vault from which fragments could fall in the form of meteorites, or be thrown down by a thunder god (cf. Fortson 2010: 26), hence the later meaning '(divine) thunderbolt' in Sanskrit. The Greek material provides some tantalizing, albeit peripheral, evidence that meteorites were also associated with iron.

8.5.2 Proto-Germanic ~ Proto-Celtic **īsarn-*

Celtic and Germanic have an exclusive lexical correspondence in the word for 'iron': PC **ῑ̆sarno-* (Gaul. personal name *Isarnus*, OIr. *ïarn*, W *haearn*, B *houarn*) ~ PG **īsarna-* (Go. *eisarn*, ON *ísarn*, OE *īsern, īsen, īren*, OS, OHG *īsarn*). On the basis of the OE variant *īren* (MoE *iron*), a Verner variant **īzarna-* can technically be postulated for Proto-Germanic, but the limitation of this form to Old English would suggest some kind of secondary development.[28] On formal grounds, it is improbable that the word is native to Germanic: the voiceless sibilant shows that before the sound shifts, the stress would have been on the first syllable, Pre-Gm. **ī́sarno-*, but as *n* regularly assimilates to a preceding *r* in unstressed position, the regular outcome of this form should have been ***īsara-* in this scenario (through Pre-PG **īsarra-* by regular shortening of geminates in unstressed syllables). A more plausible scenario is therefore that Proto-Germanic borrowed the word from Celtic after the sound shifts had taken place. The timing of this borrowing event may thus coincide with the introduction of iron metallurgy itself to Northern Germany and Scandinavia from Central Europe around 500 BCE (cf. Brumlich 2005).

The etymology of PC **ῑ̆sarno-* is unclear. It has been suggested that the word was derived from the PIE word for 'blood'; cf. Hitt. *ēšḫar*, gen. *išḫanāš*, ToA *ysār*, B *yasar* (< PTo. **yəsar*), Gk. ἔαρ, gen. -ρος < **$h_1$esh$_2$-r/n-*, i.e. as a vṛddhi formation **h_1ēsh$_2$-r-no-* (Cowgill & Mayrhofer 1986: 86 fn. 10). However, there is no direct proof of the proposed semantic shift from 'blood' to 'iron' in Celtic. The derivational base is, in fact, not attested in this branch. Given the late arrival of iron metallurgy in Northwest Europe (see Fig. 8.1), i.e. roughly two millennia after the disintegration of the parent language, it seems a priori unlikely that an archaic PIE formation could be reconstructed for this word. It is possible that Celtic too acquired the word as foreign loan at the start of the Central European Iron Age.[29]

8.5.3 Latin *ferrum*

Lat. *ferrum* 'iron, steel' < PIt. **ferso-* (?) has been given a number of Indo-European etymologies, but none is satisfactory. An early connection was with the root **bʰers-*, then thought to mean 'fixate, solidify', but now better understood as meaning 'tip, end, bristle' (Vaniček 1881: 109; Fick I 1890: 94, 493). Recently, Garnier (2017: 252) has proposed a back-formation from a hypothetical **conferrātus* 're-welded', which he in turn derives from **fer-us, fer-er-is* 'firmness, stability' < **dʰér-e/os-*. Rather than assuming an Indo-European origin, it is more attractive to view Lat. *ferrum* as belonging to a cluster of *Wanderwörter* also including PG **brasa-* 'brass' (cf. OE *bræs* 'bronze, brass', OFri. *bress* 'copper', Middle Du. *bras-penninc*

[27] This interpretation is fully rejected by Beckwith (1998), however.

[28] A parallel development is seen in Eng. *our* < OE *ūre* < **unsr-*, on which see Schaffner (2001: 223).

[29] One possibility is to view PC **ῑ̆sarno-* within the context of several words in Latin exhibiting an *-rn-* (or perhaps *-r-n-*) suffix that are suggested to be loans from Etruscan. These include *alaternus* 'buckthorn', *clarnus* 'offering tray', *laburnum* 'broom (plant)', *santerna* 'borax from gold smelting', *vīburnum* 'arrowwood', etc. (Ernout 1946: 29–32; WH; EM; Breyer 1993). The strongest piece of evidence is probably Lat. *cisterna* 'tank, reservoir', which is ultimately from Gk. κιστή 'box, chest', but likely came through Etruscan, where *-rna* was added. It is speculative, but in view of this evidence, the word **ῑ̆sarno-* could have originated in the Etruscan spoken in the Villanovan culture (900–700 BCE) south of the Alps, which controlled several important iron mines in Tuscany and Elba (Pleiner 1996: 287–288). The alternation between *palaga* 'clot of gold' (*bal(l)ūx, bal(l)ūca*) and *palacurna* 'gold dust; ingot of gold' looks similar, but Pliny reports these words to be from Iberia (LS; WH I: 95; Witczak 2009: 297).

'(silver) coin'),[30] Svan (Kartvelian) _berež_ 'iron' (Furnée 1972: 232 fn. 13), and possibly also Ingush/Chechen _borza_ 'bronze'.[31] Widely acknowledged as belonging with _ferrum_ is also a Semitic cluster of words including Ug. _brḏl_, Hebr. _barzel_, Phoen. _brzl_, Aram. _przl_, Cl. Arab. _firzil_, etc. (Muller 1918: 148; Alessio 1941; Gerola 1942; WH; Breyer 1993; EDL 214). The Semitic forms were all borrowed from Akk. _parzillu-_ 'iron' (thus already Hommel 1881: 3386).

Recently, this Akkadian form has been proposed to originate in turn from Luw. *_parz-il(i)-_, an adjectival derivative of the nominal stem *_parza-_ 'iron ore' (Valério & Yakubovich 2010). However, only the forms _parzassa-_ 'made of _parza-_' and _parzagulliya-_ 'having loops made of _parza-_' are actually attested. As items described as being _parzassa_ include arrows, a leopard statue made of precious materials, and even 'times' (cf. the phrase 'hard times'), it seems doubtful that *_parza-_ could have meant a stone like hematite or magnetite. Given that arrows were made of it, it is more likely to have meant 'iron'. Additionally, in light of the Semitic forms being the only attestations containing an _l_-suffix, Luwian may not be the direct source after all. If the word passed through a Hurrian intermediary, we may assume that the Luwian stem vowel was replaced with the more frequent ending _-i_ and that the enclitic pronoun (3. pl.) _-l(la)_, which occasionally functions as a general plural marker (cf. Wegner 2000: 66), was added, here perhaps in a collective function.

Frequent contact with the Latin-speaking world could point to Phoen. _barzel_ (Muller 1918: 148) or more specifically its reflex in a Punic dialect (EDL 214) as being the source for the Latin word. Criticism of this connection has problematized (1) the fact that _ferrum_ shows no trace of the _l_ of the Semitic forms and (2) its initial _f_ (Georgiev 1936: 250; Huld 2012: 340). The _l_ cannot be expected to disappear by any regular sound change, but considering the vocalism in Hebrew (which helps elucidate the Phoenician vowels hidden by its consonant-only writing tradition), _ferrum_ could technically be a back-formation from *_ferzel-om_ reanalyzed as a diminutive *_ferz-elom_. However, given the additional non-Semitic comparanda mentioned above, it is more likely that a form closer to Luw. *_parza-_ without the _l_-suffix was in currency (and seemingly most likely with initial *_b_ or *b^h, the voiced nature of which could be hidden by Luwian spelling), and the Punic source does not easily explain the initial _f_.[32]

The initial _f_ has also been explained through Etruscan mediation (Alessio 1941: 552; Furnée 1972: 232; Breyer 1993: 444; WH), and the early cultural significance of the Etruscans on the Italian peninsula provides compelling circumstantial evidence for this; the earliest iron production on the Italian peninsula thus far is found in Etruria (Pleiner 1996: 287; Corretti & Benvenuti 2001). Etruscan has no phonemically voiced consonants and so could continue a _Wanderwort_ beginning with *$b^{(h)}$ as _p_, and some have claimed a tendency for _p_ to become _f_ in contact with _r_ (cf. Breyer 1993: 444). The phonological details of this do not stand up to close scrutiny, however.[33] While it cannot be ruled out that the _Wanderwort_ for 'iron' entered Etruscan in a form already with _f_ or _φ_, no such word is attested in the Etruscan corpus. Therefore, although it is clear that _ferrum_ arrived in Latin as a _Wanderwort_ whose ultimate origins lie between Anatolia and Mesopotamia, neither Phoenician/Punic nor (despite the archaeological evidence) Etruscan provides a satisfactory medium of transmission.

8.5.4 Iranian *_(ā̆)ću(a)n(i)ā̆-_ ~ Tocharian *_eñcə(u)wo-_

A widespread word for 'iron' in Iranian is reflected in Khot. _hīśśana-_ 'iron', Sogd. B _ʾspnʾyn_ /(ə)spanēn/ 'of iron', Khwar. _ʾspny_ /aspanī/ 'iron', Oss. _æfsæn_ 'plowshare (modern), iron (archaic)', Pashto _ōspana-_, _ōspīna-_ 'iron', Šu. _sipin_ 'iron', Wakhi _yišn_ 'iron', Munji _yūspən_, _yispən_, MP _ʾʾhwn_ /āhun/ 'iron', Parthian _ʾʾhwn_ /āsun/ 'iron', Bal. _āsin_ 'iron', etc. Although clearly related, the words cannot be regularly derived from a single Proto-Iranian form, and vary in the length of the initial vowel and in the shape of the "root", e.g. *_ćuan-_ (Oss.) : *_aćuan-_ (Khot.) : *_āćuan-_ (Pashto) : *_āćun-_ (MP), as well as in the form of the suffix, e.g. *_-ă-_ (Oss.), *_-ā-_ (Munji), *_-iā̆-_ (Pashto). Together, these forms will be referred to as *_(ā̆)ću(a)n(i)ā̆-_ 'iron'.

Several etymologies are at hand for this term (see Buyaner 2020). An Indo-European etymology derives the words from *_(H)ać-uan-_ < *h_2_eḱ-_ 'sharp' (Klingenschmitt 2000: 193

[30] Krogmann (1937: 268–269) connected the Latin and Proto-Germanic forms, albeit proposing an IE origin. He reconstructed an ablauting _s_-stem *b^h_er-s-_ ~ *b^h_r-os-_ of a now obsolete root *b^h_er-_, which he glossed as 'to shine; bright, brown' (cf. IEW 136-137, the examples of which are today generally understood to belong to several different roots).

[31] The appurtenance of Basque _burdina_ 'iron' (cf. Schuchardt 1913: 304–305) is less evident (Trask 2008: 148).

[32] Phoenician voiceless plosives were transcribed by speakers of Greek with voiceless aspirates (Segert 1967: 55), and Latino-Punic material (Punic written in the Latin alphabet) shows that its reflex of Proto-Semitic *_p_ was _f_. In Late Punic, non-initial /b/ and /w/ were undergoing a merger to /β/. There is even one possible example of /β/ > /f/ before /tʰ/ (Häberl n.d.). None of these phenomena explain how a Phoenician _b_ could become a Latin _f_, but there remains a possibility that some of the changes coincided with the development of PIE *b^h- > *p^h- > Lat. _f-_.

[33] The change from _p_ > _f_, presumably through φ, in contact with _r_/_l_, _m_/_n_, and _s_ in Etruscan is not entirely regular. It does not occur in Greek loans (cf. Προμᾱθεύς > _Prumaθe_), whereas τ and κ do occasionally become spirantized (Ἄτροπος > _Aθrpa_ but Πάτροκλος > _Patrucle_; Ἀρκάδιος > _Arχaza_ but Κίρκᾱ > _Cerca_).

In native Etruscan words, it occurs sporadically (_Hafure_ : _Hapre_, _Fufluna_ : _Pupuluna_, etc.) (de Simone 1970 II: 168–187). The simplest explanation is that it is a late, regional phenomenon (Pfiffig 1969: 38, 42). Additionally, for the change to occur, the _p_ must be in direct contact with the liquid/nasal/_s_. The only convincing cases of Gk. π > Etr. _φ_ that are not in direct contact with a triggering element and cannot be explained by anaptyxis or assimilation are _Φerśe_ ~ _Perse_ < Περσεύς and _Φulnice_ ~ _Pulunice_ < Πολυνείκης (de Simone 1970 II: 187). Note that neither of these demonstrate a change to _f_ in Etruscan. Romans treated voiceless aspirates as voiceless stops, so Etr. _φ_ is not expected to become Lat. _f_ unless it did so in Etruscan first.

fn. 7), in which case the variation within Iranian is due to independent thematicizations of an original athematic stem. This explanation fails to account for the forms with long *ā-, however,[34] and it is further complicated by YAv. *hao-safnaēna-* 'of steel' (lit. 'of good iron'?). Its apparent derivational base **safna-* is formally reminiscent of **(ă̄)ću(a)n(i)ă̄-* and Abaev (I 480–481) therefore argued that it could have arisen via metathesis from **spana-* < **ćuana-*. This scenario requires an additional, potentially ad hoc, change of **p* to **f*, however, and even if it can be maintained, it would merely add another variant to the already problematic array of irregular proto-forms. This variation is rather consistent with a post-Proto-Iranian *Wanderwort*.

ToA *añcwāṣi* 'in steel' and ToB *eñcuwo, iñcuwo* 'iron'[35] has been argued to be borrowed from an Old Sakan reflex of **(ă̄)ću(a)n(i)ă̄-* (Tremblay 2005: 424).[36,37] However, the **n* in the first syllable of this unattested Old Sakan **anču̯an-* remains difficult to substantiate without reverting to ad hoc explanations. The assumption of a borrowing in the converse direction, as proposed by Adams (2013: 85), similarly suffers from having to assume irregular loss of the nasal in Iranian. In addition, the proposed derivation of PTo. **eñcə(u)wo-* from **h_1n-ǵ^{h}eu-eh$_2$(-n)-* 'what is poured in' > 'cast (iron)' appears semantically uncompelling.

In conclusion, given the phonological and semantic similarity, it seems unlikely that Iranian **(ă̄)ću(a)n(i)ă̄-* and PTo. **eñcə(u)wo* are unconnected, but they cannot readily be explained as mutual borrowings and neither the Iranian nor Tocharian words can be given convincing Indo-European etymologies. This leaves the possibility of independent reflections of the same *Wanderwort* with an unclear path of transmission through Western and Central Asia.[38] Although **(ă̄)ću(a)n(i)ă̄-* displays significant variation, the regular outcomes of *-*ću*- in the attested forms shows that the word must have been present in the Iranian dialect area prior to the expected developments affecting this cluster in the emerging dialect groups (e.g., > *-*sp*-, Khot. -*śś*-), suggesting that Proto-Iranian began its dissolution shortly before the beginning of the Iron Age in the region.

8.5.5 Balto-Slavic **gele(ˀ)ź-*

Lith. *geležìs*, Latv. *dzèlzs* (dial. *dzelezs*), Pr. (EV) *gelso*, and OCS *želězo*, Ru. *želézo*, Pol. *żelazo*, and Sln. *želẹ́zọ* (< **želȅzo*) 'iron' have been traditionally been compared with Gk. χαλκός 'copper, bronze' (cf. REW I: 416). Ivanov (1977: 227), for instance, reconstructs IE **g^{h}el-eǵ^h-*. However, the comparison is phonologically problematic (**g^{h}l-ǵ^h-o-* would have yielded Gk. **κλαχός). If we are dealing with a *Wanderwort*, it is difficult to imagine how Greek -κ- or -χ- could correspond to Balto-Slavic *-*ź*- unless the borrowing was very early (i.e., predating Baltic satemization). An early time of borrowing into Proto-Balto-Slavic is contradicted, however, by the irregular internal correspondence: the long medial vowel with acute accentuation in Slavic suggest **g$^{(h)}$el-eǵ-*, while the Baltic terms suggest **g$^{(h)}$el-eǵ^h-*. Any connection with the Greek word should probably be abandoned.

The further comparison with Sino-Tibetan terms for 'iron' (e.g. Ivanov 1977: 229; EIEC 379) – cf. Old Chinese **l̥ˁik* (Baxter-Sagart 1256b) or Tibetan *lcags*, reconstructed by Chang (1972) as Proto-Sino-Tibetan **qhleks* – is difficult to substantiate, especially given the enormous geographical distance between the relevant languages. Huld (2012: 330) sees a potential bridge in Turkish *çelik* 'steel', but this word is unknown in other Turkic languages and may rather be from Slavic **ocělь* 'steel', of Romance origin (Menges apud Räsänen 1969: 104, cf. also Tietze 2002). Alternatively, it may be a native creation built on the root *çel-* (a front-vocalic variant of Proto-Turkic **çal-* 'strike, beat'; cf. Clauson 1972: 417). In any case, the word does not belong here. As a result, the Balto-Slavic term for 'iron' remains unetymologized, and it is probably best to simply follow Meillet (1923: 138) in assuming a loanword from an unknown source.

8.5.6 Greek σίδηρος

Gk. σίδηρος, Doric σίδᾱρος 'iron' represents an isolated word and has not been convincingly compared to other Indo-European words. The most plausible suggestion considers it to be an East Caucasian word (Tomaschek 1884; GEW II 703), of which the only surviving attestation would be Udi *zido* 'iron'; cf. Aghwan (Old Udi) *dai-zde* 'gold' with *dai*

[34] Explaining the forms with long **ā-* as vṛddhi derivatives is unsatisfactory.

[35] As well as Khwar. *hnč* 'tip of arrow or spear'.

[36] The alternative connection of Tocharian **eñcə(u)wo-* to Skt. *aṃśu-* 'soma plant' (Pinault 2006: 184–189) is difficult to defend due to the divergent semantics.

[37] Another group of words resembling the Tocharian forms are exemplified by Oss. *ændon* 'steel', a word that is also found in Permic (Komi *jendon*, Udmurt *andan*), Mansi *jēmtån* 'steel', and in Chechen-Ingush: Chechen *ondun* 'tough', Ingush *ondæ* 'steel' (Abaev I: 156–157). Abaev (l.c.) suggests a derivation from PIr. **han-dāna-*, corresponding to Skt. *saṃdhāna-* 'joining, uniting' with a semantic shift from 'steel plating' > 'steel'. Adams (2013: 84–85) traces these words, along with Persian *hundawāni*, back to **hindu-ān-*, designating the very popular Indian-produced wootz iron. Both suggestions thus consider Iranian to be the source of both the Permic and Chechen-Ingush words, implying that a semantic development to 'tough' took place independently in Chechen. Seeing that neither attempt at an Iranian etymology is fully convincing from the semantic side, it may be worth considering if, rather, Chechen-Ingush is the source of the Ossetic word, and thence the Uralic words. Dudarev (2004: 14) notes that Chechen *ondae ečīg* lit. 'tough iron' is still used as a designation for steel. OFr. *andaine* (Medieval Lat. *andena*) and the *ondan(i)que*, *undanique* used by Marco Polo to describe a type of iron or steel may have its source among this cluster as well.

[38] Blažek & Schwartz (2016: 53–54) suggest that the Tocharian word might be "an adaptation of the Chinese compound 暗鑄 *àn zhù* 'dark cast iron' < Middle Chinese **ʔʌm tɕuăh* < Han Chinese **ʔə̄mh tśo*." Such a compound is unattested and would not contain a word for 'iron', however. Their alternative suggestion of a borrowing from an unattested Lolo-Burmese **ʔaŋ-cu$^{(m)}$* or **ʔaŋ-cwo$^{(m)}$* is also speculative and largely based on archaeological considerations.

'yellow'. Since initial *z-* in Udi can reflect older **s-*, while the opposite is not the case in Greek, Schultze (2013: 302) considers it more likely that the Udi word is a Greek borrowing. However, there seems to be no clear explanation for Udi preserving only the first syllable of the Greek word. Obviously, the Greek word would not necessarily have been adopted from a direct ancestor of Udi, as it may simply be the last vestige of an old East Caucasian (or areal) word **sid-*. A significant problem remains the further derivation of the Greek word and the present confinement of this word to a single language. However, another possibly related word is Oss. *zdy* 'lead', to which the Udi word seems closer than the forms adduced by Abaev (IV 307–308). The semantic vacillation of 'iron' and 'lead' is paralleled in the geographically close Avar-Andic-Tsezic languages (cf. Schultze 2013: 303 and 8.7.4 fn. 55 below).

8.5.7 Armenian *erkatᶜ*

Arm. *erkatᶜ* (*o*-stem) 'iron' lacks an accepted etymology (HAB II 58–60; Olsen 1999: 949; Hübschmann 1897 *vacat*; EDAIL *vacat*). The suggestion (EIEC 314, Huld 2012: 314, 334) of a connection with *$*(h_1)reg^w$-es-* 'darkness' (cf. Arm. *erek* 'evening') should not be blankly rejected, but it is difficult to explain a root zero grade *$*(h_1)rg^w$-* if the term originates in an *s*-stem, while there is no certain reflex of an older adjective from the same root anywhere.

Attention may instead be drawn to similar words found in some neighboring languages of the Caucasus, viz. in Kartvelian – Old Georgian *rḳinay*, Georgian/Megrelian *rḳina*, *ḳina* (Schrader 1883: 287) – and in East Samur: Aghul/Tabasaran *ruq̇*, Lezgian *raq̇*, all 'iron' (HAB II 58). In the absence of any potential Indo-European cognates, Arm. *erkatᶜ* was probably borrowed from a Kartvelian or East Caucasian language.

Lezgian *raq̇* has the oblique stems *raq̇-u-*, *raq̇-uni-*; cf. also Tabasaran *ruq̇-an*. In Lezgian, the productive suffix *-uni-* is subject to the vowel harmonic alternation *-uni-/-üni-/-ini-* (Haspelmath 1993: 77). It seems possible, then, that the Georgian-Zan form, which is absent in Svan (cf. 8.5.3), was borrowed from a Lezgic form **ruq̇-ɨn(V)-* vel sim.[39]

Perhaps this stem was also the source for a set of Uralic words for 'copper', viz. Mansi *aryin* ~ *äryən* (< **äryən*), Mari *würyeńe* ~ *wəryeńə* (< **wŭ̈rgeńə*), Udmurt *i̮rgon*, and Komi *i̮rge̮n* (< **ürgän*), as originally suggested by Bugge (1893: 83). Some formal problems require attention, however. The reflection of **rVq̇-* as **Vrk-* can be understood as a result of the general avoidance of initial **r-* in Uralic. Note, however, also Oss. (Iron) *ærx°y*, (Digor) *ærxi* 'copper' which may likewise reflect a Lezgic borrowing. The Permic forms are possibly borrowed from Mari, as they did not undergo the (Pre-)Proto-Permic simplification of **-rk-* > **-r-*. The Mari and Mansi forms may both continue **ürkän(V)* vel sim. Perhaps, then, Mari *würgeńə* has initial *w-* due to the influence of **wŭ̈r* 'blood' (Viitso 2013: 192) and *ń* for **n* due to influence of the nominal suffix **-ńə* (UEW II 628).

As for the Armenian form, the final *-atᶜ* is hardly explicable as a borrowed element. The traditional assumption of a blend with *arcatᶜ* 'silver', or rather a reinterpretation of *-atᶜ* as a type of metal suffix, remains the best possible solution, especially as *arcatᶜ* may now be explained by regular sound change (cf. 8.3.1 fn. 13). It is difficult to decide whether the source of *erk-* is then a unsuffixed form like Lezgian *raq̇* or the Georgian-Zan *rḳina*.

Pisani (1959: 120) suggests connecting Alb. *hekur* with Arm. *erkatᶜ* by metathesis. Following Jokl, Orel (1998: 144) alternatively suggests borrowing from Gk. ἄγκῡρα 'anchor'. This is hardly possible, as it does not explain the first syllable of the Albanian word. At first sight, *hekur* looks like a participle from a root *hek-* (cf. perhaps *heq*, dial. *hek* 'draw, extract'). There are, however, formal problems, the most serious perhaps being that the expected Gheg form **hekun* does not appear to be attested. A connection between the Armenian and Albanian words (e.g., through a Balkan substrate connected to the Caucasus) remains within the sphere of possibility but cannot be confirmed.

8.6 Tin

8.6.1 Latin *stagnum*

Lat. *stagnum* occurs beside *stannum*, but there is little independent evidence for the authenticity of the latter form.[40] The word itself does not appear before Pliny or Suetonius, but the derived adjective *stagneus* is found in a Plautus fragment cited by Festus (LS), proving that it is quite old. In its earlier attestations, *stagnum* refers to a mixture of silver and lead.[41] Not until Late Latin (e.g., Isidore) does *stagnum* itself come to mean 'tin' (EM 646, WH II 585).

Attempts to etymologize *stagnum* as a native Italic term often involve a comparison with Gk. σταφύλη 'plumb bob', explained as a metaphorical extension of σταφυλή 'grape' (the original meaning, in light of the derivatives, which all generally have to do with grapes) based on similarity of shape (Boisacq 1938: 903–904; WH II 585; EDG 1391), but this does not work. Walde and Hofmann (WH II 585) reconstruct *$*stag^{wh}$-* for σταφυλή, but the implied *$*stag^{wh}$-no-* would not result in

[39] The word has been compared to Avar-Andic and Nakh words for 'key' or 'lock', e.g. Andi *reḳul* (NCED s.v. *rʕēnq̇wɨ), assuming a semantic shift in Lezgic (or at the latest in Eastern Samur); cf. the Lezgian plural *raq̇-ar* 'trap'. If this is accepted, the borrowing cannot have been older than the Lezgic protolanguage.

[40] The form *stagnum* is the only form attested in inscriptions and is the better attested form in manuscripts. It is also the form that survives into the Romance languages (Italian *stagno*, French *étain*, etc.) (EM 646; WH II 585; Flasdieck 1952: 14–15).

[41] In Pliny's *Nat. Hist.* (34, 160–163), it is a silver-colored metal used to coat bronze vessels. According to him, mock *stagnum* can be produced with a mixture of white copper and *plumbum album* 'white lead'. It is this *plumbum album* that most likely refers to tin (EM 646; WH II 585).

Latin *stagnum*[42] (EM; WH, *pace* Pedersen 1909: 103; and Flasdieck 1952: 16–17).

Pliny claims that the process of coating copper vessels in *plumbum album*, that is to say true tinning, originated in the Gallic provinces, leading some to suggest that it was borrowed from a Celtic language; cf. OIr. *stán*, W *ystaen*, B *staen*, Late Cornish *stean* 'tin' (Fick II 312; Boisacq 1938: 903–904; WH II 585; EM 646). While OIr. *stán* must itself be a borrowing, since inherited **st-* would have regularly surfaced as *s-* in Irish, inherited **st-* can regularly remain unchanged in Brittonic. Given the rich sources of tin in southwestern Britain and Brittany, which were exploited as early as the Bronze Age (Harding 2013: 374–375), it is tempting to propose that the Old Irish and Latin words are borrowings from Brittonic. However, there is no internal derivation that supports an ultimately Brittonic source for the Latin and the Irish. Furthermore, as the Celtic words exclusively mean 'tin', which is the later meaning in Latin, it is likely that all the Celtic forms are borrowed from Latin (cf. Deshayes 2003: 687).

A possible solution is offered by Gk. σταγών, -όνος 'drop' (cognate with OBret. *staer* 'river, brook' and Lat. *stāgnum* 'standing water'; cf. EDG 1388). Crucially, in one line of the *Timaeus Locrus*, σταγών follows gold, silver, copper, tin, and lead[43] in a list of metals. This means it too must be a metal, but almost certainly not one of those listed already. Hesychius, citing this line, defines it as 'pure iron' and a scholiast of the Timaeus text defines it as ὀρείχαλκος or ἄσπρον χάλκωμα (the latter meaning 'rough, newly minted/white copper'). Thus it seems that at some point, before falling into obscurity, σταγών referred to a metal alloy (Stéphanidès 1918), even if speakers at the time thought it was a homogeneous substance. This sounds very similar to the earliest conceptions of Lat. *stagnum*. The Latin could formally have developed by regular syncope from the Greek oblique stem σταγόν- through a proto-form **stagonom*, but the Greek cannot be derived from the Latin in such a way. Thus, despite the rich Cornish tin deposits, it seems more likely that Lat. *stagnum* was borrowed from Greek and further lent to the Celtic languages rather than the other way around.

8.6.2 Greek κασσίτερος

The Greek word for 'tin', Hom. κασσίτερος, Attic καττίτερος, is, judging from the geminate σσ/ττ, a word of nonnative origin.[44] The word spread from Greek to several other languages – cf. Lat. *cassiterum*, OCS *kositerъ*, Aram. *qsyṭr*, *qsṭyr*, Arab. *qaṣdīr*, Skt. *kastīra-* (lex.) 'tin' (GEW I 798; DELG 504) – but the source of the Greek word itself is obscure.[45]

It has been suggested that the Greek word reflects a derivation of Elamite *kassa-/kazza-* 'to forge' (cf. Hinz & Koch 1987: 409, 411, 447), e.g. by Freeman (1999). The name of the Kassites has long been connected by assuming an Elamite formation **kassi-ti-ra* 'from Kassi', which could have been borrowed independently as Skt. *kastīra-* (Hüsing 1907; WH I 178). Apart from the semantic issues that can be raised with this suggestion, it crucially does not provide an explanation for the geminate in Att. καττίτερος.

According to Loma (2005), the Greek word represents an early Iranian borrowing from **ka-ću̯iϑra-* 'tin', which contains **ću̯iϑra-* 'white, lead' (Kurdish *sīs* 'white, lead ore') < PIE **ḱuit-ro-*. Skt. *sīsa-* 'lead', *kāsīsa-*, *kāśīśa-* 'green vitriol' are assumed to be later borrowings of the same word.[46] The prefix *kă-* (cf. EWAia I 285; Loma 2005: 332–333) poses a problem, since it is not well attested in Iranian, where the safest example is YAv. *ka-mərəδa-* 'demonic head' against Skt. *mūrdhán-* 'head' (< **mlHdʰ-en-*; cf. OE *molda* 'top of the head').[47] On the other hand, the etymology provides a reasonable explanation for the variation -σσ-/-ττ- within Greek, as it could represent different reflections of Iranian **ć* or **ts*. However, the biggest phonological obstruction remains the unexpected reflection of Ir. **-ϑr-* as Gk. -τερ- (versus expected -θρ-/-τρ-). Anaptyxis could have been based on the desire to avoid three consecutive heavy syllables, but there seem to be no certain parallels for this.[48] In any case, this etymology seems more plausible than any alternative proposal.

[42] Nor is it likely the correct reconstruction for σταφυλή: Boisacq (1938: 903–904) and Beekes (EDG 1391) reconstruct **stm̥bʰ-* (the zero grade of a root shared with στέμφυλα 'squeezed olives or grapes' in the full grade), definitely precluding a relationship with *stagnum*.

[43] "χρυσός, ἄργυρος, χαλκός, κασσίτερος, μόλυβδος, σταγών" (*Timaeus Locrus* 99c).

[44] While the cluster is found in native words as a reflex of earlier **-ki̯-*, the implied sequence **-ki̯i-* cannot be IE. The presence of this geminate also renders impossible an identification with the root of Lat. *canus* 'gray' previously made in the framework of the defunct Pelasgian hypothesis (Georgiev 1941: 81). The same goes for the proposed link with κασίγνητος 'brother' and Arcadocypriot κας 'also, and' (e.g. Dossin 1971).

[45] An identification with the Gaulish *Cassi-*, attested in a number of proper nouns (cf. Delamarre 2003: 109–110) has been popular (e.g. d'Arbois de Jubainville 1902: 5), but the meaning of this word is uncertain, and the idea seems to hinge primarily on the assumption that the British Isles were an exclusive source for tin import in ancient Greece. First of all, it is difficult to understand the derivation in -τερος. D'Arbois de Jubainville (l.c.) considered it a comparative, but semantically this does not make much sense, and there does not seem to be any Celtic basis for this suffix. As for Gaulish *Cassi-*, an interpretation as 'hatred' and comparison with W *cas* 'hatred, hateful', OIr. *cais* 'love or hate' < **ḱh₂d-ti-*, or with OIr. *cas* 'curly-haired' (LEIA C-44), seems more plausible.

[46] However, the variant *kāśīśa-* in particular lacks an explanation. As there seems to be no basis for the palatal pronunciation, it seems likely, a priori, that *kāsīsa-* is based on folk-etymological association with *sīsa-*.

[47] According to Remmer (2006: 45 fn. 18), the **ka(m)-*prefix can be identified with the PIE particle **ko(m)* 'together, complete'; cf. Lat. *co(m/n)-*, PC **kom-*, PG **ga-*, Alb. *kë-*.

[48] Loma (2005: 334) considers the appearance of -τερ- to be based on the comparative suffix -τερο-, the replacement being motivated by the putative function of Iranian *kă-*. It is, however, highly unlikely that speakers of Greek would be familiar enough with this function to provoke analogical reshapement.

8.6.3 Proto-Germanic **tina-*

The Proto-Germanic word for 'tin' is **tina-* (ON *tin*, OE *tin*, OS *tin*, OHG *zin*). This form was borrowed into Saami. Cf. North Saami *datni* 'tin' < Proto-Saami **tẹnē*; the fact that it underwent the sound change Pre-Saami **i* > Proto-Saami **ẹ* (ultimately > *a*) reveals that the borrowing happened early, probably from Proto-Norse at the latest.

Within Germanic, **tina-* can be related to **taina-* 'twig' (Go. *tains* 'branch, shoot, twig', ON *teinn* 'twig; spit; stake', OE *tān* 'twig, sprout, shoot', OHG *zein* 'twig, stick, ruler, shaft, pipe, bar (of metal)'. The range of meanings in Germanic makes it possible to reconstruct a semantic shift 'branch, twig' > '(metal) rod' > 'tin' (see e.g. Schrader 1883: 305), but the limitation of the metallurgical connotation to High German casts doubt on the assumption that this shift dates back to the Proto-Germanic period. The alternative reconstruction as **dih₂-nó-*, by which the word is derived from the PIE root **deih₂-* 'to shine' (see Huld 2012: 337–338; LIV² s.v. **dei̯h₂-* 'aufleuchten'), is formally possible (by invoking Dybo's law of pretonic shortening), but remains semantically arbitrary. Furthermore, it presupposes a considerable age for the formation, which is not backed up by any certain cognates in the other IE branches. As with most other words for 'tin' found in the IE languages, we must therefore conclude that no compelling (Indo-European) etymology currently is at hand for this Germanic word.[49]

8.7 Lead

8.7.1 Greek μόλυβδος ~ Proto-Germanic **blīwa-*

Greek (Ionic-Attic) μόλυβδος 'lead' occurs in a wealth of variants (μόλιβδος, μόλυβος, μόλιβος, βόλυβδος, βόλιμος, βόλιβος; cf. GEW II: 251), clearly pointing to a non-IE origin. Myc. *mo-ri-wo-do* /moliwdos/ may be seen as a more primary form, which may account both for later -βδ- from the foreign sequence **-u̯d-* and for -β- via metathesized **-du̯-*, while the variants with -υ- for -ι- may be understood as an assimilation to the labial quality of the following consonant (Beekes 1999: 8–9).

The further origin of the Greek word is uncertain, but as already suggested by Pott (1833: 113), it is possibly connected with PG **blīwa-* 'lead' (ON *blý*, OS *blī*, OHG *blīo*), though not as an inherited word. The PG form would represent an independent borrowing from a related source. This form can reflect an earlier **mlīwo-* (EDPG 69). It thus becomes possible to conjecture the existence of a non-IE form **m(V)liw(d)-*. At the same time, this renders more uncertain the suggestion of Melchert (2008) that Gk. μόλυβδος is a borrowing from Lyd. *mariwda-* *'dark', attested as a theonym, which he reconstructs as PIE **morkʷ-i̯o-*.[50]

8.7.2 Latin *plumbum* ~ Proto-Celtic **(ɸ)loud(i)o-* ~ Berber **būldūn*

Proto-Celtic **(ɸ)loudio-* (Middle Irish *lúaide* 'lead') can be connected with Lat. *plumbum* 'lead', but the irregularity of the sound correspondences makes direct cognacy impossible. The Celtic form requires **ple/oud^(h)-* and the Italic **plo/uNdʰu̯-* (for the change **-Ndʰu̯-* > **-mb-*, cf. *lumbus* 'loin' < **londʰ-u̯o-*). While Huld (2012: 336) proposes that both are direct descendants from a formation **plou-dʰ(H)om* 'solder' < **pleu-* 'to flow, float', his explanations for the development of the nasal in Italic involve irregular changes. It is therefore more fruitful to consider the word a prehistoric *Wanderwort*, to which Berber **būldūn* may also be adduced (EDL 474).[51] A Celtic **(ɸ)loudo-* is the most likely source for Proto-(West-)Germanic **lauda-* (OE *lēad*, OFri. *lād*, Du. *lood* 'lead').

It is phonologically impossible for these forms to have directly been borrowed from Gk. μόλυβδος 'lead' (Beekes 1999: 10), but it seems plausible that this group of words is still ultimately related to the other group of prehistoric loanwords in 8.7.1, and so represent additional independent borrowings. Note the large internal variation of the Greek forms, where e.g., Attic (inscr.) βόλυβδος is not very far from the Italic reconstruction. Basque *berun* 'lead' appears likely to be related as well, because the sound law **-VlV-* > *-VrV-* and the restriction against clusters may explain its development from something like **bl(e)un(P)*. It is not entirely clear from which source it was borrowed and whether this was Romance (cf. Gascon *ploum*?) or not.

To all of these forms, Boutkan & Kossmann (1999: 92) tentatively add Proto-Romance **piltrum*,[52] which generally refers to a tin alloy. However, this form appears too formally distant to justify the assumption of a shared origin with Lat. *plumbum*. The limited distribution and lack of a defensible IE etymology could suggest substrate origin, but Flasdieck's (1952) suggestions of Ligurian, Etruscan, or Pelasgian origin are purely speculative (cf. Tripathi 1995: 163). W *elydn* 'brass, bronze, latten; copper; tin; pewter'

[49] The Proto-Germanic word has additionally been connected with OIr. *tinne* 'bar, rod of metal, ingot, mass of molten metal'. The meaning 'tin', however, is unattested for this word, which makes the connection doubtful. Since it can neither be excluded that the Irish form is a loan from the entirely unrelated OE *tinne* 'bar, rod' (cf. OHG *zinna* 'spike' < **tind-nō-*), the association with PG 'tin' is better abandoned. For an intra-Celtic etymology, see McManus (1991: 37).

[50] Note that the PIE root must be **mergʷ-* in view of the English form *murky* mentioned by Melchert (l.c.); cf. further ON *myrkr*, OE *mierce* 'dark' < **mrgʷ-io-*.

[51] Boutkan and Kossmann (1999: 92–93) reconstruct **βaldūn* ~ **βāldūn* ~ **būldūn* ~ **βaldūm* on the basis of Ahaggar Touareg *ăhâllun* 'tin, lead', Iwellemmeden Touareg *aldom* 'tin', Ghat Touareg *ahellum* 'lead', Kabyle *aldun* 'lead', Sous Berber *aldun* 'lead', Mzab *buldun* 'lead', etc. The "wild variation" shows that this word is foreign to Berber.

[52] Given as **peltyrum* by Walde and Hofmann (WH II 585 following Brüch 1914: 370–373), but emended to **piltrum* by Flasdieck (1952: 17–70) based on careful consideration of the Romance reflexes: Catalan, Spanish, Portuguese *peltre*, Italian, Tuscan *peltro*, Friulian *peltri*, Sicilian *piutru*, Old French *peautre*. Eng. *pewter*, Irish *péatar*, and Icelandic *pjátur* 'sheet metal' are borrowed from Romance.

and Middle Irish *elada*, *elatha* 'art, craft, skill' may continue PC *(ϕ)elotn-ī-*, *(ϕ)elotVn-* respectively; W *elydr* 'brass, bronze; copper; tin; pewter' can reflect a variant PC *(ϕ)elotr-ī-*. These forms come formally close to Proto-Romance *piltrum* and may reflect borrowings from a similar source.

8.7.3 Balto-Slavic *al(a)wa- 'lead/tin' and *św(e)in- 'lead'

In Slavic, one finds two competing words for 'lead'. PSl. *ȍlovo* (c) 'lead' (thus OCS *olovo*, ORu. *ólovo*, SCr. *ȍlovo*, Bulgarian dial. *élavo*) beside *ȍlovъ (Ru. dial. *lóv* ['tin'], OPl. *ołów*, Sln. dial. *olǫ́v*) is close to Pr. (EV) *alwis* 'lead'. Matching forms in East Baltic – Lith. obs. *álvas* and Latv. *al̃va*, *al̃vs* – have shifted to mean 'tin'. The same shift occurred in Ru. *ólovo* 'tin' as compared to ORu. 'lead'. Another ORu. word for lead, *svinьсь*, is the source of modern Ru. *svinéc* 'lead'. Although sparsely attested, the word must be Proto-Slavic in view of Sln. *svínəc* 'lead'. Such a peripheral distribution might support the idea that PSl. *svinь̀сь (b) is the original word for 'lead', which was replaced with *ȍlovo/ъ everywhere except the periphery. The shift to 'tin' in Baltic is perhaps no coincidence, considering that the Baltic word for 'lead' there, Lith. *švìnas*, Latv. *svins*, is cognate with PSl. *svinь̀сь.

Neither word has an acceptable etymology. The broken tone in Latv. *al̂va* probably means it cannot be syncopated from *alava*. The difference between the Baltic and Slavic forms could be resolved by reconstructing an ablauting *u*-stem *ál?-u-s* ~ *al?-éu-s* (cf. IEW 30–31). Perhaps a related form can also be identified in OHG *elo* 'pale yellow' (< *elwa-*), in view of the numerous parallels of color terms being used as designations for metals. The OHG word is usually compared with Skt. *aruṇa-* 'reddish-brown' (IEW 302), but it seems impossible to exclude the older theory that it was borrowed from Lat. *helvus* 'yellow' (AhdWb s.v.). As no entirely convincing comparanda are available, our word might as well not be of IE origin, as was concluded by e.g. Derksen (2015: 53–54).[53]

Baltic *švina- and Slavic *svinь̀сь could go back to an ablauting Balto-Slavic *świn-/*świn-. A root connection with PIE *ḱueit- 'white' (Skt. *śvéta-* 'white', Lith. *šviẽsti* 'to shine', etc.) has been proposed (Persson; Petersson *apud* LEW 1045); however, there is no evidence for an unextended root *ḱuei- (*pace* IEW 628, Lith. *šviesà* < *švait-sā-*), and the semantic connection between 'white' and 'lead' requires the extra assumption of an intermediate meaning 'tin'. Likewise, the old comparison with Gk. κύανος 'dark blue (enamel), copper carbonate' (see 8.4.4) is not possible in IE terms. Ivanov (1977: 231) assumes that the Greek and Balto-Slavic words are connected as a *Wanderwort*, attempting to explain the initial sibilant in Baltic as due to contamination with Hatt. *šiniti* 'copper'. This is quite implausible. Nor can we accept, as Trubachev does (1967: 33), a comparison with Iranian *(ă)ću (a)n(i)ă- (see 8.5.4). Both Fraenkel (LEW 1045) and Vasmer (REW 592) leave the word without etymology.

[53] In a non-IE context, Machek (1957: 413) compares Germanic *blīwa-* (see 6.1), but this is difficult to substantiate. Huld (2012: 343) asserts that the Balto-Slavic word is borrowed from PC *olHu̯o-* < PIE *polH-u̯o-* 'pale' (cf. Lith. *pal̃vas* 'light yellow'), which seems unfounded, because no such word is attested in Celtic.

8.7.4 Armenian *kapar*

Arm. *kapar* 'lead' has mostly been considered a Semitic or Hurrian loanword; cf. Akk. *abārum*, Syr. *ˀawārā*; Hur. *abari* 'lead' (see HAB II: 522 with references). The lack of an explanation for the initial *k-*, however, remains an insurmountable problem. The required assumption of a borrowing predating the Armenian sound shift is also problematic, as there seems to be no other Semitic borrowings from this period. It is possible that *kapar* is related to Hur. *kab(a)li*, Eblaite *kapalum* 'copper',[54] yet these forms are neither phonologically or semantically perfect matches. Unless we consider the possibility of contamination between Hur. *abari* 'lead' and *kab(a)li* 'copper', either in the Urartian reflex or in Armenian itself, the direct source of the word remains unknown.[55]

8.8 Discussion

8.8.1 Metals in PIE and the Daughter Branches

The metallurgical vocabulary reconstructible for PIE first of all allows us to reiterate the conclusions of earlier works like Schrader 1883 and Hirt 1905–1907: that this language was spoken before the introduction of iron and tin-bronze. Words for gold and silver are reconstructible at least for the non-Anatolian/Tocharian languages, as is *$h_2$eies-, which probably referred to a useful metal at a time when this could only have been copper. In contrast, words for tin, lead, and iron are all later innovations or, in particular, borrowings from non-IE languages.

Latin, Celtic, and especially Germanic probably borrowed a word for 'copper (ore)' from a European substrate language (8.4.3). The earliest copper use in Europe dates to the mid-sixth millennium BCE in Serbia. While it began with native copper, by the end of the millennium, slag finds suggest the earliest smelting also began in this area (Roberts 2009: 464–465). In Scandinavia, isolated copper finds are known from the late fifth

[54] These forms have also been compared with Greek Κύπρος 'Cyprus' (Neu 1995; Kas'jan 2010: 468–70), which was already mentioned by Ačaṙyan in relation to Arm. *kapar* (HAB II 522).

[55] Some similar forms in the Avar-Andic-Tsezic (East Caucasian) languages may be noted, e.g. Tsez *kebu*, Hunzib *kobo* 'lead', Andi *k:ub*, Chamalal *koba* 'iron' (Schultze 2013: 303). While these are semantically closer to the Armenian word, they lack the final *-r*. These forms are confined to the Avar-Andic-Tsezic group, so they may represent borrowings. Via the Caucasus, they seem to have entered Mordvinic as well; cf. Erzya *kivé*, Moksha *kiví* 'lead, tin'.

millennium BCE (Nørgaard et al. 2019), with the record growing exceptionally rich by the beginning of the Funnel Beaker culture, ca. 4000 BCE. Evidence of smelting is found at southern Neolithic Funnel Beaker sites beginning around 3800 BCE (Gebauer et al. 2020). When steppe groups settled in Europe, they may have adopted a non-IE word for copper from already present Neolithic societies. These steppe groups were coming from areas home to the Yamnaya/Pit Grave cultural horizon, which was already familiar with copper metallurgy in two traditions or "foci" and may have used the PIE word *$h_2$eies-*. The Pit Grave/Poltavka metallurgical focus attests tools cast or hammered from pure copper sourced from the Ural, Samara, and Belaya river basins, where they were likely mining it. The Lower Dniepr metallurgical focus attests alloyed arsenical bronze sourced from the Caucasus (Chernykh 1992: 83–91). The well-attested extensive copper trade relationship between Scandinavian Funnel Beaker sites and the Mondsee, Altheim, and Pfyn cultures of the Alpine region (Gebauer et al. 2020) might explain how a different word was borrowed from a common substrate into both Germanic and Italic.

Vocabulary surrounding the production of bronze and later alloys, like steel and brass, strikes us as exceedingly difficult to reconstruct. Prior to the spread of the word *bronze* itself, which is clearly an early modern event coinciding with the development of modern chemistry,[56] there seems to be no noteworthy linguistic distinction between copper and its derived alloys. This may suggest that for most of the Bronze Age, there was in fact no perceived distinction or awareness of the various elements composing a metal, but only a gradual distinction of different copper qualities. Nor did the introduction of tin mining leave a discernible imprint on the IE languages, as words for tin seem strikingly late and mostly have an unclear origin (especially 8.6.1, 8.7.3). Furthermore, frequent semantic vacillation between 'tin' and 'lead' suggests that these elements were frequently denoted by the same word (cf. also Lat. *plumbum album/nigrum*), probably due to having similar colors and melting points. It may however be noted that an Eastern (perhaps Iranian) source of the Greek (and by proxy Slavic) word for tin (8.6.2) has been suggested. Central Asia contains relatively large deposits of tin (Garner 2015). From the Bronze Age, there is evidence to suggest that most of the tin in the Mediterranean was imported from Cornwall (Berger et al. 2019), but the linguistic evidence does not necessarily mirror this.

As for the information about the expansion of the IE daughter languages that can be deduced from metal terminology, it is appropriate to begin with the Anatolian branch, which is usually regarded as the outlier among the IE languages (i.e. "the first to split off"); see most recently Pronk & Kloekhorst (2019). While metallurgical terminology does not provide direct evidence for this, the formation of the (inferred) word for silver (see 8.3.1) supports this scenario. Furthermore, there is no trace of the PIE word for 'gold' (8.2.1) or 'copper, metal' (8.4.1) in Anatolian. In fact, apart from the inferred existence of **ḫark(ant-)* 'silver', none of the extant metal vocabulary can be demonstrated to be of Proto-Indo-Anatolian origin, except in cases where this originates with color terms vel sim. (e.g. *parkui-* 'shining; bronze'). Central Anatolia became an important center of innovation with signs of early iron ore smelting during the second millennium BCE (Erb-Satullo 2019). Most of the metal terms in Hittite seem to originate with local languages of Anatolia/Mesopotamia, including *ku(wa)nna(n)-* 'copper' (8.4.4), and the Hattic borrowings *ḫapalki-* 'iron' and *arzili-* 'tin' (Vanséveren 2012: 215), which probably means that the language communities of Anatolia who were first to engage in metal production were non-IE speakers. This also speaks for the intrusive nature of the Anatolian IE languages and against a placement of PIE in the Anatolian region, which would probably have led to IE languages being dominant enough to have left some trace in the local metallurgical terminology.

Armenian preserves old IE terms only for 'silver' and perhaps 'gold', suggesting that its speakers always remained within the sphere of these precious metals. Other terms are clearly connected with the immediate north (Kartvelian, East Caucasian) or South (Hurrian/Urartian) in the case of 'iron' and 'lead', respectively; cf. further *anag* 'tin', which is clearly an adaptation of Akk. *annakum*, perhaps via Hurrian (Diakonoff 1985: 598–599). These are supplemented by later adoptions from Iranian (*płinj* 'copper, bronze', *aroyr* 'brass', *połovat* 'steel'). There is a conspicuous lack of influence from the languages of Anatolia on this part of the lexicon, which could suggest either a late arrival of Armenian (after ca. 1200 BCE) in the region or an arrival via the Caucasus. The word for 'iron' *erkatᶜ* has no certain etymology, but probably represents a borrowing from a Kartvelian or East Caucasian language. This coincides with the fact that the first iron finds in the Kura–Araxes valleys appear between ca. 1150 and 800 BCE, before the expansion of Urartians into this region (Erb-Satullo 2019).

Interestingly, Germanic and Balto-Slavic lost the PIE word for 'silver' (8.3.1) entirely, probably because their speakers migrated out of the silver sphere in the third millennium BCE. These branches appear to have readopted the metal along with the non-IE loanword **sil(a)P(u)r-* (8.3.2) when silver became known in Northern Europe from the second millennium BCE (Johannsen 2016). An Iberian center of spread is supported by linguistic evidence; cf. Celtiberian *śilaPuŕ* and Basque *zilhar* 'silver'. Silver circulated in the El Argar culture (ca. 2200–1550 BCE) from the start of the second millennium BCE and appears to have been an important status symbol (Lull et al. 2014).

The Greek metallurgical lexicon has a strikingly foreign provenance. Only 'silver' (8.3.1) reflects a PIE root but may be an independent derivation. While the origin of σίδηρος 'iron' cannot be identified with certainty, some limited evidence would connect it with the Caucasus (8.5.6). Material evidence for the Caucasus as an additional route of entry for iron objects into Europe from the thirteenth century BCE (Bebermeier et al. 2016) at least does not contradict this

[56] Eng. *bronze*, G *Bronze*, Ru. *brónza*, etc. can all be traced to Italian *bronzo* 'brass' (14th c. CE), whose origin remains uncertain (cf. Meyer-Lübke 1911: 79).

possibility. The word for 'gold' is clearly of Semitic origin (8.2.3), while an Eastern source seems plausible also for 'copper' (8.4.5) and 'tin' (8.6.2).

Meanwhile, the Greek word for 'lead' (8.7.1) represents a relatively late Pre-IE word shared with Germanic and perhaps also Italic and Celtic, clearly suggesting that this word was widespread in Europe. While lead, as a by-product of silver mining, becomes popular in the Near East and Mediterranean around 3000 BCE, where it is naturally available, it is rarer in Northern Europe, where the first lead objects appear from the beginning of the Bronze Age, during which it becomes more widespread. The relatively late adoption of a pervasive non-IE word could be speculated to coincide with the introduction of lead-alloyed copper, which appears in Wales around 1500 to 1300 BCE, then becomes widespread in western and southern Europe around 1000 BCE, and more sporadically in Scandinavia during the Late Bronze Age, 700 to 500 BCE (Johannsen 2016). The existence, in West Germanic languages, of a later borrowing of the Celtic word for lead (8.7.2) points to ongoing contact and trade.

8.8.2 Indo-European Languages at the Beginning of the Iron Age

More so than other metals, words for 'iron' provide highly relevant evidence for the prehistoric locations of the Indo-European daughter languages. As the introduction of iron in Europe probably postdates the dissolution of Proto-Indo-European by one to two millennia, the coupling of linguistic and material evidence can in some cases help narrow the time window for the emergence of the descendant protolanguages and for prehistoric linguistic contact. At the same time, evidence for linguistic contact can support material evidence in tracing the spread of ironworking.

The earliest remains of iron are meteoritic, found in Mesopotamia and Egypt, but soon Anatolia becomes very much involved in this use (see Figure 8.1). For PIE, an interesting polysemy can be reconstructed for PIE *h_2eḱ-men-*, whose cognates have meanings varying between 'stone' and 'heaven', with a marginal meaning 'iron' in Greek (8.5.1). It is therefore possible to imagine that this word was indeed

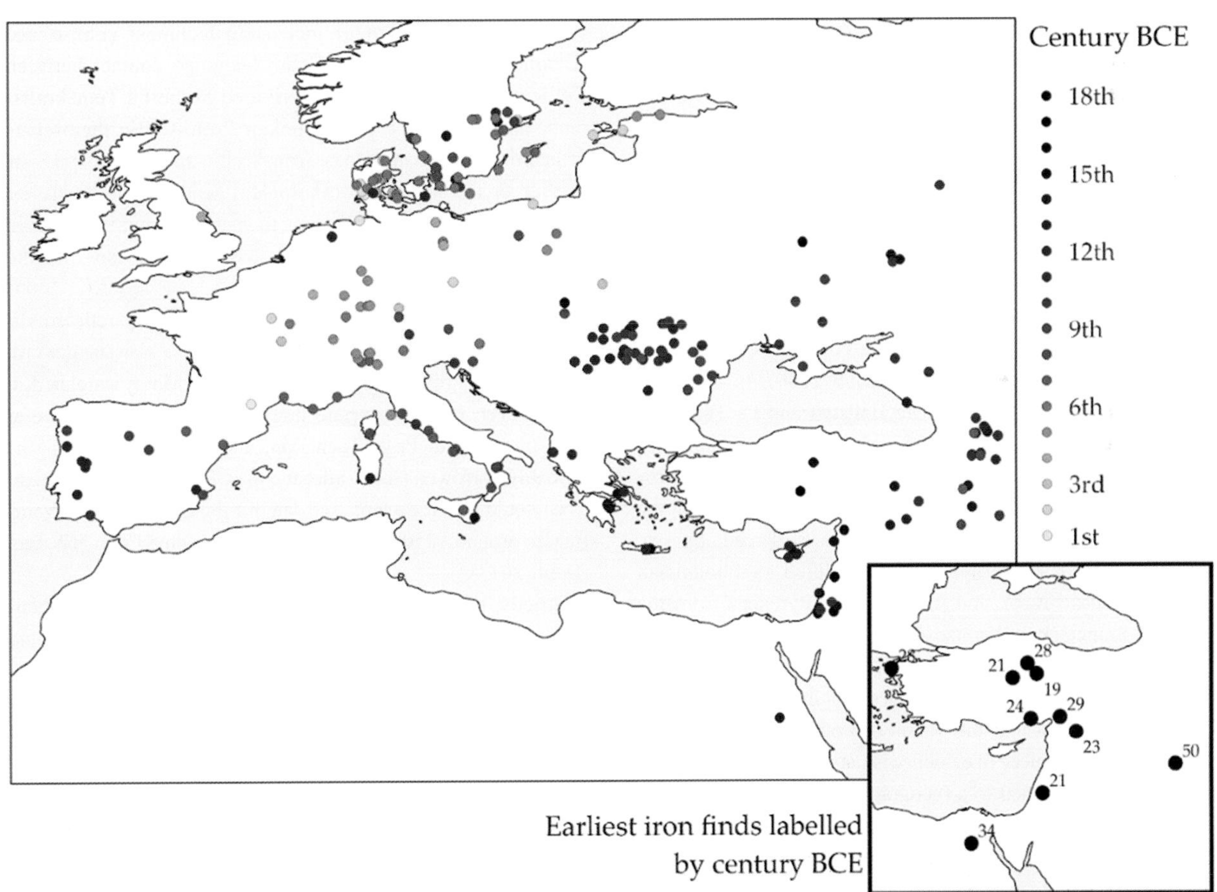

FIGURE 8.1. The spread of iron metallurgy in Europe.
The inset at the bottom right shows the earliest archaeological iron finds, many of which are of meteoritic iron. The main map shows selected sites from publications that specifically mention dated iron artifacts in the cultural assemblage, but is not exhaustive. (Compiled from Seyer 1982, Levinsen 1984, Boroffka 1991, Hjärthner-Holdar 1993 (with lit.), Pleiner 1996, Pigott 1999, Yalçın 1999, Giardino 2005, Bejko et al. 2006, Papadopoulos et al. 2007, Nieling 2009, Brumlich et al. 2012, Zapatero et al. 2012, Bebermeier et al. 2016, Foxhall 2018, Garcia 2018, Gimatzidis 2018, Lang 2018, Metzner-Nebelsick 2018, Nowakowski 2018, Teržan & de Marinis 2018, and Erb-Satullo 2019).

associated with knowledge of meteoritic iron among PIE speakers. This is supported by the unambiguous evidence for the processing of meteoritic iron in the Yamnaya and later Catacomb and Afanasievo cultures, where the rare metal appears to have been held in high regard (Koryakova et al. 2008: 112–127). This early tradition of processing meteorites appears to have been lost later and is unrelated to the later emergence of iron metallurgy (Terekhova 2008).

Generally speaking, iron ore acquisition and smelting are techniques associated with terms that are not shared between the IE languages. The IE subgroups apparently obtained them independently well after the disintegration of the original language community, which after all predates the Iron Age under the Steppe hypothesis. Iron smelting is attributed by the Ancient Greeks to the Chalybes (Bittarello 2016; Gnesin 2016), a group living inside the borders of the Hittite Empire in the early second millennium BCE, while the earliest certain remains of iron slag that clearly indicate smelting have been found at Kaman-Kalehöyük in Central Anatolia and date to the Old Assyrian Colony Period, ca. 1800 BCE (Akanuma 2007; see further Yalçın 1999).

With the continued early involvement of Anatolia and the Levant, true iron metallurgy emerges during the second millennium (Bebermeier et al. 2016). Greece is an early locus and the Balkans were likely a major inroad for iron into Europe (Pleiner 1996). The Caucasus and Carpathians are in this area, but surprisingly Etruria (Corretti & Benvenuti 2000) and the Iberian peninsula (Zapatero et al. 2012) take up iron metallurgy quite early (Pleiner 1996 generally). Here, the technology must have arrived by sea. In Italy, it spreads from the area of Tuscany and the Villanovan culture, but not necessarily rapidly. The exploitation of iron-rich Elba did not begin until relatively late. Meanwhile, the Greek colony at Pithekoussai already had iron (Corretti & Benvenuti 2000). In mainland Western Europe, e.g., in the Late Hallstatt and La Tène cultures, iron use begins only in the early first millennium BCE, and so we may expect more possible sources of iron words due to the longer traditions elsewhere in Europe. On the Iberian peninsula, there were two waves of spread: by sea, affecting the coast and being later amplified by Phoenician activity (Bronze Age), and then over the Pyrenees from the south of France (Late Bronze Age/Early Iron Age) (Zapatero et al. 2012).

Indeed, there is linguistic evidence supporting the spread of iron from Anatolia and the vicinity to other regions in West Eurasia. One such piece of evidence is Lat. *ferrum* (8.5.3), which can plausibly be traced to a (geographically) Anatolian source that additionally spread to Germanic, Svan (Kartvelian), and perhaps Nakh (East Caucasian). To this we may add a word for 'smith', Lat. *faber* (< PIt. **þabro-*), with which Arm. *darbin* 'smith, forger' has long been connected. In IE terms, this implies a root *d^hab^h- or d^hHb^h- (cf. HAB I 636, IEW 233–234). The traditional comparison to OCS *dobrъ* 'good', Lith. *dabà* 'character' is semantically arbitrary. Instead, it is tempting to see an origin in Hur. *tab/w-* 'cast metal', *taballi* 'smith', *ta/ibira/i* 'copper-worker' (Yakubovich *apud* Blažek 2010: 23), with additional reflexes in Ug. *tbl* 'blacksmith', Sum. *tibira*, and perhaps the Hebr. personal name *twblqyn* (DUL 845) showing the expansive spread of this word across the Middle East. While the Armenian word may have been a relatively late adaptation of an Urartian form (where the initial stop would be voiced), its presence in Italic suggests that it had spread widely by the first millennium BCE, perhaps together with the same stratum that brought the word for 'iron'.

In Proto-Germanic, the word for 'iron' is formally close to that of Proto-Celtic (8.5.2). This word has no convincing Indo-European etymology and can be analyzed as a Celtic loan into Proto-Germanic. This evidence for linguistic contact suggests that iron metallurgy was introduced to the Proto-Germanic language community by Proto-Celtic speakers. A potentially suitable archaeological context for such linguistic contact is found in the so-called *Schmiedegräber* in the core of the Jastorf culture and Nienburg group, where in the La Tène-period, burials appear with iron ore, slag, anvils, and complete sets of blacksmith tools (Brumlich et al. 2005). The appearance of these burials has been interpreted as a reflection of the rise of a latènisized "caste" of blacksmiths. Within La Tène there is also data showing an increasing use of hardened iron during the course of the period, agreeing with a general pattern of increasing technical competence (Champion 2018). If indeed the language contact between Celtic and Germanic can be attributed to the La Tène craftsmen, they may have either spoken Proto-Celtic themselves or acquired the terminology from Celtic-speaking specialists further to the south. Morphological features of the Celto-Germanic word further allow us to speculate that it may have been taken over from the pioneering Etruscans in the Italian peninsula.

The Tocharian and Iranian words for iron may reflect individual borrowings of the same West-Central Asian areal word, but it still cannot be excluded that they are entirely unrelated. It is, however, relevant to note that the Tocharian words are at least traceable to Proto-Tocharian, and the Iranian word was probably borrowed (soon) after the dissolution of Proto-Iranian. This would provide a tentative date for the dissolution of Proto-Iranian around 1250 BCE, when iron first spread into NW Iran (Danti 2013).

Strictly, no Proto-Balto-Slavic word for iron can be reconstructed. However, the clearly similar words in Proto-Baltic and Proto-Slavic seem to be borrowings from related sources. Assuming that the dissolution of the Balto-Slavic languages took place in the Baltic Sea region, we can thus tentatively place the protolanguage right before the final Bronze Age (800–500 BCE), when iron starts to appear in this region (Lang 2018). As in the case of 'tin/lead' (8.7.3), we may be faced with a loanword entering most of the Balto-Slavic language area, but from a different source than those found in the languages of Southern and Western Europe. This supports a relatively northern position for the Balto-Slavic languages at this point in time.

The development of the IE metal terms discussed in this paper, combined with the archaeological evidence for the timeline of Eurasian metallurgical development, is presented in Figure 8.2.

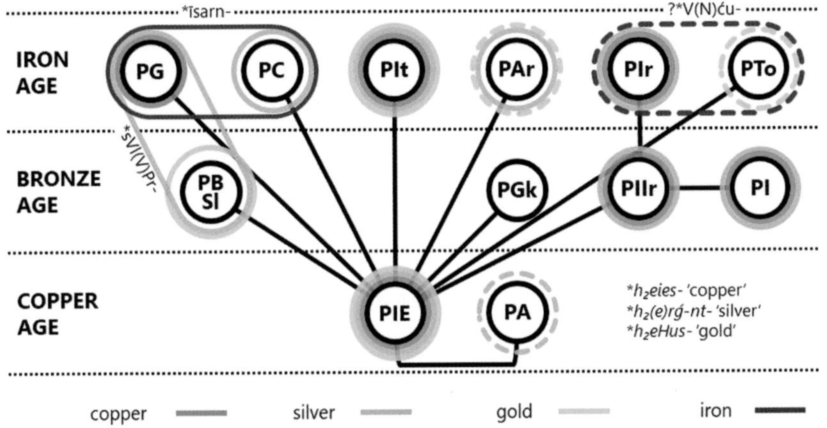

FIGURE 8.2. Schematic overview of the occurrence of the most important shared metal names in the Indo-European language family. Circles indicate terms inherited from PIE; dashed circles terms, whose IE etymology is uncertain or debated. Stadia represent areal terms that were absorbed locally after the IE dispersal.

List of Abbreviations

Akk. = Akkadian
Alb. = Albanian
Arab. = Arabic
Aram. = Aramaic
Arm. = Armenian
Av. = Avestan
B = Breton
Bal. = Balochi
Cz. = Czech
dial. = dialectal
Du. = Dutch
Eng. = English
EV = Elbing Vocabulary
G = German
Gaul. = Gaulish
Gk. = Greek
Go. = Gothic
Hatt. = Hattic
Hebr. = Hebrew
Hitt. = Hittite
Hom. = Homeric Greek
Hur. = Hurrian
Khot. = Khotanese
Khwar. = Khwarezmian
Lat. = Latin
Latv. = Latvian
Lith. = Lithuanian
Luw. = Luwian
MHG = Middle High German
MP = Middle Persian
NP = New Persian
MW = Middle Welsh
Myc. = Mycenaean Greek
OCS = Old Church Slavonic
OE = Old English
OFri. = Old Frisian
OHG = Old High German
OIr. = Old Irish
ON = Old Norse
OP = Old Persian
OPl. = Old Polish
ORu. = Old Russian
OS = Old Saxon
Oss. = Ossetic
PBSl. = Proto-Balto-Slavic
PC = Proto-Celtic
PG = Proto-Germanic
PGk. = Proto-Greek
Phoen. = Phoenician
PIE = Proto-Indo-European
PIIr. = Proto-Indo-Iranian
PIr. = Proto-Iranian
PIt. = Proto-Italic
Pr. = Old Prussian
PSl. = Proto-Slavic
PTo. = Proto-Tocharian
PU = Proto-Uralic
Ru. = Russian
SCr. = Serbo-Croatian
Skt. = Sanskrit
Sln. = Slovenian
Sogd. = Sogdian
Šu. = Šughni
Sum. = Sumerian
Syr. = Syriac
ToA = Tocharian A
ToB = Tocharian B
Ug. = Ugaritic
Umb. = Umbrian
Ved. = Vedic Sanskrit
W = Welsh
YAv. = Young Avestan

References

Abaev = V.I. Abaev. 1958–89. *Istoriko-etimologičeskij slovar' osetinskogo jazyka*. 4 vols. Leningrad: Nauka.

Adams, Douglas Q. 2013. *A dictionary of Tocharian B*. Amsterdam & New York: Rodopi.

Aikio, Ante. 2015. The Finnic 'secondary e-stems' and Proto-Uralic vocalism. *Journal de la Société Finno-Ougrienne* 95: 25–66.

Akanuma, Hideo. 2007. Analysis of iron and copper production activity in central Anatolia during the Assyrian colony period. *Anatolian Archaeological Studies* 16: 125–139.

Alessio, Giovanni. 1941. L'etrusco e due problemi etimologici latini. *Aevum* 15(4): 545–558.

d'Arbois de Jubainville, Henri. 1902. *Cours de litterature celtique XII: Principaux auteurs de l'antiquité à consulter sur l'histoire des Celtes depuis les temps les plus anciens jusqu'au règne de Theodose Ier*. Paris: Fontemoing.

Bailey, Harold W. 1979. *Dictionary of Khotan Saka*. Cambridge: Cambridge University Press.

Baxter-Sagart = William H. Baxter & Laurent Sagart. 2014–. List of Old Chinese reconstructions by Grammata Seria Recensa number. http://ocbaxtersagart.lsait.lsa.umich.edu/.

Bebermeier, Wiebke et al. 2016. The coming of iron in a comparative perspective. In: Gerd Graßhoff & Michael Meyer (ed.), *Space and knowledge: Topoi Research Group articles*, 152–189. Berlin: Excellence Cluster Topoi.

Beckwith, Miles. 1998. The 'Hanging of Hera' and the meaning of Greek ἄκμων. *Harvard Studies in Classical Philology* 98: 91–102.

Beekes, Robert S. P. 1999. The Greek word for 'lead'. *Münchener Beiträge zur Sprachwissenschaft* 59: 7–14.

2002. The prehistory of the Lydians, the origin of the Etruscans, Troy and Aeneas. *Bibliotheca Orientalis* 59: 205–241.

Bejko, Lorenc, Todd Fenton, & David Foran. 2006. Recent advances in Albanian mortuary archaeology, human osteology, and ancient DNA. In: Lorenc Bejko & Richard Hodges (ed.), *New directions in Albanian archaeology: Studies presented to Muzafer Korkuti*, 309–322. Tirana: International Centre for Albanian Archaeology.

Belardi, Walter. 1949. Review of *Traité de phonétique grecque* by Michel Lejeune (Paris: Klincksieck, 1947). *Maia* 2: 308–312.

Bellamy, Kate. 2018. Investigating interaction between South America and West Mexico through the lexicon of metallurgy. In: Rune Iversen & Guus Kroonen (ed.), *Digging for words: Archaeolinguistic case studies from the XV Nordic TAG Conference held at the University of Copenhagen, 16–18 April 2015*, 1–19. Oxford: BAR Publishing.

Benzing, Johannes. 1983. *Chwaresmischer Wortindex*. Wiesbaden: Harrassowitz.

Berger, D. et al. 2019. Isotope systematics and chemical composition of tin ingots from Mochlos (Crete) and other Late Bronze Age sites in the eastern Mediterranean Sea: An ultimate key to tin provenance? *PLoS ONE* 14(6): e0218326.

Blažek, Václav. 2010. *Indo-European "smith" and his divine colleagues* (JIES Monograph No. 58). Washington, DC: Institute for the Study of Man.

2017. Indo-European "gold" in time and space. *Journal of Indo-European Studies* 45(3/4): 267–311.

Blažek, Václav, & Michal Schwartz. 2016. *The early Indo-Europeans in Central Asia and China: Cultural relations reflected in language*. Innsbruck: IBK.

Boisacq, Emile. 1938. *Dictionnaire étymologique de la langue grecque*. Paris: Klincksieck.

Boroffka, Nikolaus. 1991. *Die Verwendung von Eisen in Rumänien von den Anfängen bis in das 8. Jahrhundert v. Chr.: Vortrag gehalten zu Ehren von John Alexander auf dem Symposium 'Europe in the 1st Millenium B.C.', New York, 3rd–4th April 1986, Institute of Archaeology Oxford*. Berlin: self-published.

Boutkan, Dirk, & Maarten Kossmann. 1999. Some Berber parallels of European substratum words. *Journal of Indo-European Studies* 27: 87–100.

2001. On the etymology of 'silver'. *NOWELE* 38: 3–15.

Breyer, Gertraud. 1993. *Etruskisches Sprachgut im Lateinischen unter Ausschluss des spezifisch onomastischen Bereiches*. Leuven: Peeters.

Brixhe, Claude. 2004. Corpus des Inscriptions Paléo-Phrygiennes. Supplément II. *Kadmos* 43: 1–130.

Brüch, Josef. 1914. Zwei ligurische Wörter im Lateinisch-Romanischen. *Zeitschrift für vergleichende Sprachforschung auf dem Gebiete der indogermanischen Sprachen* 46(4): 351–373.

Brumlich, Markolf, Michael Meyer, & Bernd Lychatz. 2012. Archäologische und archäometallurgische Untersuchungen zur latènezeitlichen Eisenverhüttung im nördlichen Mitteleuropa. *Praehistorische Zeitschrift* 87(2): 433–473.

Bugge, Sophus. 1893. Beiträge zur etymologischen erläuterung der armenischen sprache. *Zeitschrift für vergleichende Sprachforschung* 32(1): 1–87.

Burrow, T. 1972. A reconsideration of Fortunatov's law. *Bulletin of the School of Oriental and African Studies* 34: 538–559.

Buyaner, David B. On the etymology of the Old Iranian term for 'iron'. In: Shervin Farridnejad (ed.), *zaraθuštrōtəma. Zoroastrian and Iranian studies in honour of Philip G. Kreyenbroek*, 51–67. Leiden: Brill.

Cantera, Alberto. 2017. The phonology of Iranian. In: Jared Klein, Brian Joseph, & Matthias Fritz (ed.), *Handbook of comparative and historical Indo-European linguistics*, 481–503. Berlin: de Gruyter Mouton.

Champion, Timothy. 2018. Iron and iron technology. In: Colin Haselgrove, Katharina Rebay-Salisbury, & Peter S. Wells (ed.), *The Oxford handbook of the European Iron Age*.

Chang, Kun. 1972. Sino-Tibetan 'iron' *qhleks. *Journal of the American Oriental Society* 92(3): 436–446.

Chernykh, E. N. 1992. *Ancient metallurgy in the USSR: The early Metal Age*. Cambridge: Cambridge University Press.

Chirikba, Viacheslav A. 1996. *Common West Caucasian: The reconstruction of its phonological system and parts of its lexicon and morphology*. Leiden: CNWS.

Civil, Miguel. 1976. Notes on Sumerian lexicography III. *Journal of Cuneiform Studies* 28(3): 183–187.

Clauson, Gerard. 1972. *An etymological dictionary of pre-thirteenth-century Turkish*. Oxford: Clarendon Press.

Corretti, Alessandro, & Marco Benvenuti. 2001. The beginning of iron metallurgy in Tuscany with special reference to *Etruria Mineraria*. *Mediterranean Archaeology* 14: 127–145.

Cowgill, Warren C., & Manfred Mayrhofer. 1986. *Indo-Germanische Grammatik*. Vol. 1.1. Halbband. Heidelberg: Winter.

Danti, Michael D. 2013. Late Bronze and Early Iron Age in northwestern Iran. In: D.T. Potts (ed.), *Oxford handbook of ancient Iran*, 327–376. Oxford: Oxford University Press.

Delamarre, Xavier. 2003. *Dictionnaire de la langue gauloise*. 2nd ed. Paris: Editions Errance.

DELG = Pierre Chantraine. 1999. *Dictionaire étymologique de la langue grecque: histoire des mots*. 2nd ed. Paris: Klincksieck.

Derksen, Rick. 2007. *Etymological dictionary of the Slavic inherited lexicon*. Leiden & Boston: Brill.

2015. *Etymological dictionary of the Baltic inherited lexicon*. Leiden & Boston: Brill.

Deshayes, Albert. 2003. *Dictionnaire étymologique du breton*. Chasse-Marée: Douarnenez.

Diakonoff, Igor M. 1985. Hurro-Urartian borrowings in Old Armenian. *Journal of the American Oriental Society* 105(4): 597–603.

Dossin, Georges. 1948. Le vocabulaire de Nuzi SMN 2559. *Révue d'Assyriologie et d'archéologie orientale* 42(1/2): 21–34.

1971. Grèce et Orient. *Révue belge de Philologie et d'Historie* 49(1): 5–13.

Driessen, Michiel. 2003. *h_2é-$h_2$us-o-, the Proto-Indo-European term for 'gold'. *Journal of Indo-European Studies* 31: 347–362.

Dudarev, S. L. 2004. The mastering of iron-working by the peoples of the northern Caucasus in the Early Iron Age. *Ancient West and East* 3: 1–19.

DUL = Gregorio del Olmo Lete & Joaquín Sanmartín. 2015. *Dictionary of the Ugaritic language in the alphabetic tradition. 3rd ed.* Translated and edited by Wilfred G.E. Watson. Leiden & Boston: Brill.

EDAIL = Hrach Martirosyan. 2010. *Etymological dictionary of the Armenian inherited lexicon*. Leiden & Boston: Brill.

EDG = Robert S. P. Beekes 2010. *Etymological dictionary of Greek*. Leiden & Boston: Brill.

EDHIL = Alwin Kloekhorst. 2008. *Etymological dictionary of the Hittite inherited lexicon*. Leiden & Boston: Brill.

EDL = Michiel De Vaan. 2008. *Etymological dictionary of Latin and the other Italic languages*. Leiden & Boston: Brill.

EDPC = Ranko Matasović. 2009. *Etymological dictionary of Proto-Celtic*. Leiden & Boston: Brill.

EDPG = Guus Kroonen. 2013. *Etymological dictionary of Proto-Germanic*. Leiden & Boston: Brill.

EIEC = James P. Mallory & Douglas Q. Adams. 1997. *Encyclopedia of Indo-European culture*. London & Chicago: Fitzroy Dearborn.

EM = Alfred Ernout & Antoine Meillet. 2001. *Dictionnaire étymologique de la langue latine*. 4th ed. Paris: Klincksieck.

Erb-Satullo, Nathaniel L. 2019. The innovation and adoption of iron in the ancient Near East. *Journal of Archaeological Research* 27: 557–607.

Ernout, Alfred. 1946. *Philologica*. Vol. I. Paris: Klincksieck.

EWAia = Manfred Mayrhofer. 1992–1996. *Etymologisches Wörterbuch des Altindoarischen*. 2 vols. Heidelberg: Winter.

Fick = August Fick. 1890–1909. *Vergleichendes Wörterbuch der indogermanischen Sprachen*. 3 vols. Göttingen: Vandenhoeck & Rupprecht.

Flasdieck, Hermann M. 1952. *Zinn und Zink: Studien zur abendländischen Wortgeschichte*. Tübingen: Max Niemeyer Verlag.

Forbes, R. J. 1950. *Metallurgy in Antiquity: A notebook for archaeologists and technologists*. Leiden: Brill.

Fortunatov, Filipp F. 1881. L + dental im Altindischen. *Beiträge zur Kunde der indogermanischen Sprachen* 6: 215–219.

Foxhall, Lin. 2018. The central Mediterranean and the Aegean. In: Colin Haselgrove, Katharina Rebay-Salisbury, & Peter S. Wells (ed.), *The Oxford handbook of the European Iron Age*.

Freeman, Philip. 1999. Homeric κασσίτερος. *Glotta* 75(3/4): 222–225.

Furnée, Edzard J. 1972. *Die wichtigsten konsonantischen Erscheinungen des Vorgriechischen*. The Hague & Paris: De Gruyter Mouton.

Fortson, Benjamin W., IV. 2010. *Indo-European language and culture: An introduction*. 2nd ed. Malden (Mass).: Wiley-Blackwell.

Garcia, Dominique. 2018. Southern France. In: Colin Haselgrove, Katharina Rebay-Salisbury, & Peter S. Wells (ed.), *The Oxford handbook of the European Iron Age*.

Garner, Jennifer. 2015. Bronze Age tin mines in Central Asia. In Andreas Hauptmann & Diana Modarressi-Tehrani (ed.), *Archaeometallurgy in Europe III: Proceedings of the 3rd international conference, Deutsches Bergbau-Museum Bochum, June 29–July 1, 2011*, 135–143. Bochum: Vereinigung der Freunde von Kunst und Kultur im Bergbau.

Garnier, Romain. 2017. *La dérivation inverse en latin*. Innsbruck: IBS.

Gebauer, Anne Birgitte, Lasse Sørensen, Michelle Taube, & Daniel Wielandt. 2020. First metallurgy in Northern Europe: An Early Neolithic crucible and a possible tuyère from Lønt, Denmark. *European Journal of Archaeology*: 1–21.

Georgiev, Vladimir. 1936. Lat. ferrum, griech. χαλκός, abg. železo und Verwandtes. *Zeitschrift für vergleichende Sprachforschung auf dem Gebiete der indogermanischen Sprachen* 63(3/4): 250–256.

Gerola, B. 1942. Substrato mediterraneo e latino. *Studi Etruschi* 16: 345–368.

GEW = Hjalmar Frisk. 1960–1972. *Griechisches etymologisches Wörterbuch*. 3 vols. Heidelberg: Winter.

Giardino, Claudio. 2005. Metallurgy in Italy between the Late Bronze Age and the Early Iron Age: The coming of iron. In: Peter Attema, Albert Nijboer, & Andrea Zifferero (ed.), *Papers in Italian archaeology VI: Communities and settlements from the Neolithic to the Early Medieval period*, 491–505. Oxford: Archaeopress.

Gimatzidis, Stefanos. 2018. Northern Greece and the central Balkans. In: Colin Haselgrove, Katharina Rebay-Salisbury, & Peter S. Wells (ed.), *The Oxford handbook of the European Iron Age*.

Giusfredi, Federico. 2017. On Sumerian ku_3(.g)-an (a metal) and some allegedly derived words. *Mémoires de NABU*, March 2017: 13–15.

Goetze, Albrecht. 1947. Contributions to Hittite lexicography. *Journal of Cuneiform Studies* 1: 307–320.

HAB = Hračʿeay Ačaṙyan. 1971–1976. *Hayeren armatakan baṙaran*. 4 vols. 2nd ed. Yerevan: Erevani Hamalsaran.

Häberl, Charles. n.d. A question of orthography: The Latino-Punic inscriptions. Unpublished. https://www.academia.edu/19367013/A_Question_of_Orthography_the_Latino-Punic_Inscriptions.

Häkkinen, Jaakko. 2009. Kantauralin ajoitus ja paikannus: perustelut puntarissa. *Journal de la Société Finno-Ougrienne* 92: 9–56.

Halleux, Robert. 1969. Lapis-lazuli, azurite ou pâte de verre? À propos de *kuwano* et *kuwanowoko* dans les tablettes mycéniennes. *Studi micenei ed egeo-anatolici* 9: 45–63.

Harding, A. F. 2013. Trade and exchange. In: H. Fokkens & A.F. Harding (ed.), *The Oxford handbook of the European Bronze Age*, 370–381. Oxford: Oxford University Press.

Haspelmath, Martin. 1993. *A grammar of Lezgian*. Berlin & New York: Mouton de Gruyter.

HED = Jaan Puhvel. 1984–. *Hittite etymological dictionary*. Berlin & New York: Mouton de Gruyter.

Hill, Eugen. 2003. *Untersuchungen zum inneren Sandhi des Indogermanischen* (Münchner Forschungen zur historischen Sprachwissenschaft 1). Bremen: Hempen Verlag.

Hinz, Walther, & Heidemarie Koch. 1987. *Elamisches Wörterbuch.* Berlin: Reimer.

Hirt, Herman. 1905–1907. *Die Indogermanen: Ihre Verbreitung, ihre Urheimat und ihre Kultur.* 2 vols. Strassbourg: Trübner.

Hjärthner-Holdar, Eva. 1993. *Järnets och järnmetallurgins introduktion i Sverige.* Uppsala: Societas Archaeologica Upsaliensis.

Hoffmann, Karl, & Bernhard Forssman. 1996. *Avestische Laut- und Flexionslehre* (Innsbrucker Beiträge zur Sprachwissenschaft 84). Innsbruck: Institut für Sprachwissenschaft.

Hoffner, Harry A. 1967. Review of Die Kaškäer: Ein Beitrag zur Ethnographie des alten Kleinasien by E. von Schuler (Berlin: de Gruyter, 1965). *Journal of the American Oriental Society* 87(2): 179–185.

1968. A Hittite text in epic style about merchants. *Journal of Cuneiform Studies* 22(2): 34–45.

Holopainen, Sampsa. 2019. *Indo-Iranian borrowings in Uralic: Critical overview of the sound substitutions and distribution criterion.* PhD diss., University of Helsinki.

Hommel, Fritz. 1881. *Allgemeine Zeitung* 231 (August 19, 1881).

Hübschmann, Heinrich. 1897. *Armenische Grammatik.* 1. Teil: Armenische Etymologie. Leipzig: Breitkopf & Härtel.

Huld, Martin E. 2012. Some observations on the development of Indo-European metallurgy. In: M. E. Huld, K. Jones-Bley, & D. Miller (ed.), *Archaeology and language: Indo-European studies presented to James P. Mallory* (JIES Monograph No. 60), 281–356. Washington, DC: Institute for the Study of Man.

Hüsing, G. 1907. Miszellen. 4. Die Kassiteriden. *Orientalistische Litteraturzeitung*, January 1907, 1: 25–26.

IEW = Julius Pokorny. 1959. *Indogermanisches etymologisches Wörterbuch.* Bern: Francke.

Ivanov, Vjačeslav. 1977. O proisxoždenii nekotoryx baltijskix nazvanij metallov. *Baltistica* 13(1): 223–236.

Iversen, Rune, & Guus Kroonen 2017. Talking Neolithic: Linguistic and archaeological perspectives on how Indo-European was implemented in southern Scandinavia. *American Journal of Archaeology* 121(4): 511–525.

Jagersma, Abraham H. 2010. *A descriptive grammar of Sumerian.* PhD diss., Leiden University.

J̌ahowkyan, Gevorg B. 1987. *Hayocᶜ lezvi patmowtᶜyown: naxagrayin žamanakašrǰan.* Yerevan: Erevani Hamalsaran.

Janhunen, Juha. 1983. On early Indo-European-Samoyed contacts. In: J. Janhunen, A. Peräniitty, & S. Suhonen (ed.), *Symposium saeculare Societas Fenno-Ugricae*, 115–127. Helsinki: Société Finno-Ougrienne.

Johannsen, Jens Winther. 2016. Heavy metal: Lead in Bronze Age Scandinavia. *Fornvännen* 111: 153–161.

Kallio, Petri. 2004. Tocharian loanwords in Samoyed? In: Irma Hyvärinen, Petri Kallio, & Jarmo Korhonen (ed.), *Etymologie, Entlehnungen und Entwicklungen: Festschrift für Jorma Koivulehto zum 70. Geburtstag* (Mémoires de la Société Néophilologique de Helsinki 63), 129–137. Helsinki: Société Néophilologique.

Karsten, T. E. 1928. *Die Germanen: Eine Einführung in die Geschichte ihrer Sprache und Kultur.* Berlin & Leipzig: Walter de Gruyter & Co.

Kas'jan, A.C. 2010. Leksičeskie kontakty xattskogo jazyka. *Indoevropejskoe jazykoznanie i klassičeskaja filologija* 10 (1): 445–475.

Kauffmann, Friedrich. 1913. *Deutsche Altertumskunde.* 1. Hälfte: Von der Urzeit bis zur Völkerwanderung. Munich: Beck.

KEWA = Manfred Mayrhofer. 1953. *Kurzgefasstes etymologisches Wörterbuch des Altindischen.* 4 vols. Heidelberg: Winter.

Klimov, Georgij A. 1964. *Etimologičeskij slovar' kartvel'skix jazykov.* Moscow: Nauka.

Klingenschmitt, Gert. 2000. Mittelpersisch. In: Bernhard Forssman & Robert Plath (ed.), *Indoarisch, Iranisch und die Indogermanistik: Arbeitstagung der Indogermanischen Gesellschaft vom 2 bis 5 Oktober 1997 in Erlangen*, 191–229. Wiesbaden: Reichert Verlag.

Klinger, Jörg. 1995. Hattisch. In: M. P. Streck (ed.), *Sprachen des alten Orients*, 128–134. Darmstadt: WBG.

Koch, John T. 2020. *Celto-Germanic: Later prehistory and Post-Proto-Indo-European vocabulary in the north and west.* Aberystwyth: Canolfan Uwchefrydiau Cymreig a Cheltaidd Prifysgol Cymru.

Korn, Agnes. 2003. *Towards a historical grammar of Balochi: Studies in Balochi historical phonology and vocabulary.* PhD diss., Goethe University Frankfurt.

Koryakova, Ludmila, Sergei Kuzminykh & Galina Beltikova. 2008. The introduction of iron technology into Central-Northern Eurasia. In: Forenius, Svante, Eva Hjärthner-Holdar & Christina Risberg (ed.), *The introduction of iron in Eurasia: papers presented at the Uppsala Conference on October 4-8, 2001*, 112–127. Uppsala: Riksantikvarieämbetet.

Krogmann, Willy. 1937. Lat. ferrum. *Zeitschrift für vergleichende Sprachforschung auf dem Gebiete der indogermanischen Sprachen* 64(3/4): 267–269.

1940. Kelt. "*omii̯o-* „Erz, Kupfer". *Zeitschrift für Celtische Philologie* 21: 48–49.

Kümmel, Martin. 2017. Even more traces of the accent in Armenian? In: Bjarne S.S. Hansen et al. (ed.), *Usque ad Radices: Indo-European studies in honour of Birgit Anette Olsen*, 439–452. Copenhagen: Museum Tusculanum Press.

2018. The survival of laryngeals in Iranian. In: Lucien van Beek, Alwin Kloekhorst, Guus Kroonen, Michaël Peyrot, & Tijmen Pronk (ed.), *Farnah: Indo-Iranian and Indo-European studies in honor of Sasha Lubotsky*, 162–172. Ann Arbor & New York: Beech Stave Press.

de Lamberterie, Charles. 1978. Armeniaca I–VIII: Études lexicales. *Bulletin de la Société de Linguistique de Paris* 73: 243–283.

Lang, Valter. 2018. The eastern Baltic. In: Colin Haselgrove, Katharina Rebay-Salisbury, & Peter S. Wells (ed.), *The Oxford Handbook of the European Iron Age.*

LEIA = Joseph Vendryes, Édouard Bachallery, & Pierre-Yves Lambert. 1959–1996. *Lexique étymologique de l'irlandais ancien.* Dublin: Dublin Institute for Advanced Studies.

Levinsen, Karin. 1984. Jernets introduktion i Danmark. In: Poul Kjærum (ed.), *KUML 1982–1983: Årbog for Jysk Arkæologisk Selskab*, 153–168. Aarhus: Jysk Arkæologisk Selskab

LEW = Ernst Fraenkel. 1962–1965. *Litauisches etymologisches Wörterbuch.* 2 vols. Heidelberg: Winter.

LIV² = Helmut Rix, Martin Kümmel, Thomas Zehnder, Reiner Lipp, & Brigitte Schirmer (ed.). 2001. *Lexikon der indogermanischen Verben.* 2nd ed. Wiesbaden: Reichert.

Loma, Aleksandar. 2005. Zur Frage der frühesten griechisch-iranischen Sprachbeziehungen: Gr. κασσίτερος. In: Gerhard Meiser & Olaf Hackstein (eds.), *Sprachkontakt und Sprachwandel: Akten der XI. Fachtagung der*

Indogermanischen Gesellschaft, 17.–23. September 2000, Halle an der Saale, 332–340. Wiesbaden: Reichert.

LS = Charlton T. Lewis & Charles Short. 1897. *A Latin dictionary.* Oxford: Clarendon Press.

Lull, Vicente, Rafael Micó, Cristina Rihuete Herrada, & Roberto Risch. 2014. The social value of silver in El Argar. In: H. Meller, R. Risch & E. Pernicka (ed.), *Metalle der Macht: Frühes Gold und Silber: 6. Mitteldeutscher Archäologentag vom 17. bis 19. Oktober 2013 in Halle (Saale)*, 557–576. Halle (Saale): Landesmuseum für Vorgeschichte.

Machek, Václav. 1957. *Etymologický slovník jazyka českého a slovenského*. Prague: Nakladatelství Československé akademie věd.

Mallory, James P., & Martin E. Huld. 1984. Proto-Indo-European 'silver'. *Zeitschrift für vergleichende Sprachforschung* 97(1): 1–12.

McManus, Damian. 1991. *A guide to Ogam*. Maynooth: An Sagart.

Masson, Emilia. 1967. *Recherches sur les plus anciens emprunts sémitiques en grec*. Paris: Klincksieck.

Meillet, Antoine. 1923. Review of *Baltisch-slawisches Wörterbuch* by R. Trautmann (Göttingen: Vandenhoeck & Ruprecht, 1923). *Bulletin de la Société de Linguistique* 24(2): 135–139.

1936. *Esquisse d'une grammaire comparée de l'arménien classique*. 2nd ed. Vienna: Mekhitharistes.

Melchert, H. Craig. 2008. Greek *mólybdos* as a loanword from Lydian. In: B. J. Collins, M. R. Bachvarova, & I. C. Rutherford (ed.), *Anatolian interfaces: Hittites, Greeks and their neighbours*, 153–158. Oxford: Oxbow.

Metzner-Nebelsick, Carola. 2018. Central Europe. In: Colin Haselgrove, Katharina Rebay-Salisbury, & Peter S. Wells (ed.), *The Oxford Handbook of the European Iron Age*.

Meyer-Lübke, Wilhelm. 1911. *Romanisches etymologisches Wörterbuch*. Heidelberg: Winter.

Militarev, Alexander, & Leonid Kogan. 2000. *Semitic etymological dictionary.* Vol. I. Münster: Ugarit-Verlag.

Muller, F. 1918. Etymologiae Graecae. *Mnemosyne* 46(2): 135–155.

Murtonen, A. 1989. *Hebrew in its West Semitic setting*. Leiden & New York: Brill.

NCED = S. Nikolayev & S. L. Starostin. 1994. *A North Caucasian Etymological Dictionary.* Moscow: Asterisk.

Neu, Erich. 1995. Zur Herkunft des Inselnames Kypros. *Glotta* 73 (1): 1–7.

Nieling, Jens. 2009. *Die Einführung der Eisentechnologie in Südkaukasien und Ostanatolien während der Spätbronze- und Früheisenzeit*. Aarhus: Universitetsforlaget.

NIL = Dagmar S. Wodtko, Britta Irslinger, & Carolin Schneider. 2008. *Nomina im indogermanischen Lexikon*. Heidelberg: Winter.

Nørgaard, H. W., E. Pernicka, & H. Vandkilde. 2019. On the trail of Scandinavia's early metallurgy: Provenance, transfer and mixing. *PLoS ONE* 14(7): e0219574.

Nowakowski, Wojciech. 2018. Eastern Central Europe: Between the Elbe and the Dnieper. In: Colin Haselgrove, Katharina Rebay-Salisbury, & Peter S. Wells (ed.), *The Oxford Handbook of the European Iron Age*. https://doi.org/10.1093/oxfordhb/9780199696826.013.10.

Olsen, Birgit A. 1999. *The noun in biblical Armenian: origin and word-formation – with special emphasis on the Indo-European heritage*. Berlin & New York: Mouton de Gruyter.

Orel, Vladimir. 1998. *Albanian etymological dictionary.* Leiden, Boston, & Cologne: Brill.

Papadopoulos, John K., Lorenc Bejko, & Sarah P. Morris. 2007. Excavations at the prehistoric tumulus of Lofkënd in Albania: A preliminary report from the 2004–2005 seasons. *American Journal of Archaeology* 11(1): 105–147.

Pedersen, Holger. 1909. *Vergleichende Grammatik der keltischen Sprachen*. Bd. 1. Einleitung und Lautlehre. Göttingen: Vandenhoeck & Ruprecht.

1924. Armenier. B. Sprache. In Max Ebert (ed.), *Reallexikon der Vorgeschichte*, Vol. 1, 219–226. Berlin: de Gruyter.

Petr, V. J. 1898. Über den Wechsel der Laute *d* und *l* im Lateinischen. *Beiträge zur Kunde der indogermanischen Sprachen* 25: 127–158.

Peyrot, Michaël. 2018. Tocharian B *etswe* 'mule' and Eastern East Iranian. In Lucien van Beek, Alwin Kloekhorst, Guus Kroonen, & Tijmen Pronk (ed.), *Farnah: Indo-Iranian and Indo-European studies in honor of Sasha Lubotsky*, 270–283. Ann Arbor and New York: Beech Stave Press.

Pfiffig, Ambros Josef. 1969. *Die etruskische Sprache*. Graz: Akademische Druck- und Verlagsanstalt.

Pigott, Vincent C. 1999. *The archaeometallurgy of the Asian Old World*. Philadelphia: University of Pennsylvania Museum.

Pinault, Georges-Jean. 2006. Further links between the Indo-Iranian substratum and BMAC. In: Betil Tikkanen & Heinrich Hettrich (ed.), *Themes and tasks in Old Middle Indo-Aryan linguistics* (Papers of the 12th World Sanskrit Conference, vol. 5), 167–196. Delhi: Motilal Banarsidass Publishers.

Pisani, Vittore. 1959. *Saggi di linguistica storica*. Turin: Rosenberg & Sellier.

Pleiner, Radomír. 1996. Das frühe Eisen: Von den Kleinwaagemengen zu der ältesten Industrie. *Ethnographisch-Archäologische Zeitschrift* 37(3): 283–291.

Pott, August Friedrich. 1833. *Etymologische Forschungen auf dem Gebiete der indogermanischen Sprachen*. Lemgo: Meyer.

Pronk, Tijmen. 2011. The "Saussure effect" in Indo-European languages other than Greek. *Journal of Indo-European Studies* 39: 176–193.

Pronk, Tijmen, & Alwin Kloekhorst. 2019. Introduction: Reconstructing Proto-Indo-Anatolian and Proto-Indo-Uralic. In: T. Pronk & A. Kloekhorst (ed.), *The precursors of Proto-Indo-European: The Indo-Anatolian and Indo-Uralic hypotheses*, 1–14. Leiden & Boston: Brill.

Räsänen, Martti. 1969. *Versuch eines etymologischen Wörterbuchs der Türksprachen*. Vol. 1. Helsinki: Suomalais-Ugrilainen Seura.

Remmer, Ulla. 2006. *Frauennamen im Rigveda und im Avesta*. Vienna: Verlag der Österreichischen Akademie der Wissenschaften.

REW = Max Vasmer. 1953. *Russisches etymologisches Wörterbuch*. 2 vols. Heidelberg: Winter.

Richter, Thomas. 2012. *Bibliographisches Glossar des Hurritischen*. Wiesbaden: Harrassowitz.

Roberts, Benjamin W. 2009. Production networks and consumer choice in the earliest metal of Western Europe. *Journal of World Prehistory* 22: 461–81.

Rosół, Rafal. 2013. *Frühe semitische Lehnwörter im Griechischen*. Frankfurt am Main: Peter Lang.

Schaffner, Stefan. 2001. *Das Vernersche Gesetz und der innerparadigmatische Wechsel des urgermanischen im Nominalbereich*. Innsbruck: IBS.

2016/17. Lateinisch *rutilus*, rötlich, gelbrot, goldgelb', altirisch *ruithen*, Strahl, Glanz' und mittelkymrisch *rwt* 'Rost,

Korrosion.' *Die Sprache: Zeitschrift für Sprachwissenschaft* 52(1): 101–123.

Schrader, Otto. 1883. *Sprachvergleichung und Urgeschichte: Linguistisch-historische Beiträge zur Erforschung des indogermanischen Altertums*. Jena: Hermann Costenoble.

Schrijver, Peter. 1991. *The reflexes of the Proto-Indo-European laryngeals in Latin*. Amsterdam & Atlanta: Rodopi.

2018. Talking Neolithic: The case for Hatto-Minoan and its relationship to Sumerian. In: G. Kroonen, J. P. Mallory, & B. Comrie (ed.), *Talking Neolithic: Proceedings of the workshop on Indo-European origins held at the Max Planck Institute for Evolutionary Anthropology, Leipzig, December 2–3, 2013* (JIES Monograph No. 65), 336–374. Washington, DC: Institute for the Study of Man.

Schultze, Wolfgang. 2013. Historische und areale Aspekte der Bodenschatz-Terminologie in den ostkaukasischen Sprachen. *Iran and the Caucasus* 17: 295–320.

Schuchardt, Hugo. 1913. Baskisch-hamitische Wortvergleichungen. *Revista Internacional de Estudios Vascos/Revue International des Études Basques* 7: 289–340.

Segert, Stanislav. 1976. *A grammar of Phoenician and Punic*. Munich: C. H. Beck.

Seyer, Heinz. 1982. *Siedlung und archäologische Kulture der Germanen im Havel-Spree-Gebiet in den Jahrhunderten vor Beginn u.Z.* Berlin: Akademie Verlag.

De Simone, Carlo. 1970. *Die griechischen Entlehnungen im Etruskischen*. Wiesbaden: Harrassowitz.

Soysal, Oğuz. 2004. *Hattischer Wortschatz in hethitischer Textüberlieferung*. Leiden: Brill.

2006. Das hethitische Wort für 'Zinn'. *Historische Sprachforschung* 119: 109–116.

Starostin, Sergei. 1985. Kul'turnaja leksika v obščeseverokavkazskom slovarnom fonde. In: B.B. Piotrovskij, V.V. Ivanov, & V.G. Ardzinba (ed.), *Drevnjaja Anatolija*, 74–94. Moscow: Nauka.

Stéphanidès, Michel. 1918. Petites contributions à l'histoire des sciences. *Revue des Études Grecques* 31(142): 197–206.

Stifter, David. 1998. Study in red. *Die Sprache: Zeitschrift für Sprachwissenschaft* 40: 202–223.

Stokes, Whitley & Adalbert Bezzenberger. 1979. *Wortschatz der keltischen Spracheinheit*. 5th ed. Göttingen: Vandenhoeck & Ruprecht.

Szemerényi, Oswald. 1964. *Syncope in Greek and Indo-European and the nature of the Indo-European accent*. Naples: Instituto universitario orientale di Napoli.

Teržan, Biba, & Raffaele de Marinis. 2018. The northern Adriatic. In: Colin Haselgrove, Katharina Rebay-Salisbury, & Peter S. Wells (ed.), *The Oxford Handbook of the European Iron Age*. https://doi.org/10.1093/oxfordhb/9780199696826.013.10.

Tietze, Andreas. 2002. *Tarihi ve Etimolojik Türkiye Türkçesi sözlüğü*. Istanbul & Vienna: Simurg Kitapçılık, ÖAW.

Tomaschek, Wilhelm. 1884. Review of Schrader 1883. *Litteratur-Blatt für orientalische Philologie* 1 (Oct. 1883–Sept. 1884): 121–30.

Trask, R. L. 2008. *Etymological dictionary of Basque*. Edited for web publication by Max W. Wheeler. University of Sussex.

Trautmann, Reinhold. 1910. *Die altpreussischen Sprachdenkmäler*. Göttingen: Vandenhoeck und Ruprecht.

Tremblay, Xavier. 2004. Chalcographie: Sur χαλκός, lit *geležìs* et turc *qoruγžin*. *Historische Sprachforschung* 117(2): 238–248.

2005. Irano-Tocharica et Tocharo-Iranica. *Bulletin of SOAS* 68 (3): 421–449.

Tripathi, D. N. 1996. Tin in the ancient world: a literary study. In: Sarva Daman Singh (ed.), *Culture through the ages: Prof. B.N. Puri felicitation volume*, 161–167. Delhi: Agam Kala Prakashan.

Trubachev, Oleg N. 1967. Iz slavjano-iranskix leksičeskix otnošenij. *Ètimologija* 1965: 3–81.

UEW = Károly Rédei. 1986–1991. *Uralisches etymologisches Wörterbuch*. 3 vols. Budapest: Akadémiai Kiadó.

Valério, M., and I. Yakubovich. 2010. Semitic word for 'iron' as Anatolian loanword. In: T. M. Nikolaev (ed.), *Isseledovanija po lingvistike i semiotike: Sbornik statej k jubileju Vyač. Vs. Ivanova*, 108–116. Moscow: Jazyki slavjanskix kul'tur.

Vaniček, Alois. 1881. *Etymologisches Wörterbuch der lateinischen Sprache*. Leipzig: Teubner.

Vanséveren, Sylvie. 2012. Noms de métaux dans les textes hittites. *Anatolica* 38: 203–219.

Viitso, Tiit-Rein. 2013. Early metallurgy in language: The history of metal names in Finnic. In: Riho Grünthal & Petri Kallio (ed.), *A linguistic map of prehistoric Northern Europe*, 185–200. Helsinki: Suomalais-Ugrilainen Seura.

WH = Alois Walde & Johann Baptist Hofmann. 1965–1972. *Lateinisches Etymologische Wörterbuch*. Heidelberg: Winter.

Wegner, Ilse. 2000. *Einführung in die hurritische Sprache*. Wiesbaden: Harrassowitz.

Weiss, Michael. 2020. *Outline of the historical and comparative grammar of Latin*. 2nd ed. Ann Arbor & New York: Beech Stave Press.

Witczak, Krzysztof Tomasz. 2009. A wandering word for 'hardened iron, steel': A study in the history of concepts and words. *Studia Etymologica Cracoviensia* 14: 291–305.

van Windekens, Albert J. 1958. Pelasgisch und Westgermanisch: Neues Material. *Die Sprache* 4: 128–138.

Yalçın, Ünsal. 1999. Early iron metallurgy in Anatolia. *Anatolian Studies* 49: 177–187.

Zapatero, Gonzalo Ruiz, Manuel Fernández-Götz, & Jesús Álvarez-Sanchís. 2012. Die Ausbreitung der Eisenmetallurgie auf der Iberischen Halbinsel. In: Anton Kern et al. (ed.), *Technologieentwicklung und -transfer in der Hallstatt- und Latènezeit*, 149–166. Lagenweissbach: Beier & Beran.

Zhivlov, Mikhail. 2014. Studies in Uralic vocalism III. *Journal of Language Relationship* 12: 113–148.

Part III The Cultural and Linguistic Significance of Bell Beakers along the Atlantic Fringe

9 FROM THE STEPPE TO IRELAND: THE IMPACT OF aDNA RESEARCH

J. P. MALLORY*

"It has become almost a tradition to look for unknown origins in the 'mysterious' steppes of South Russia."
(Marija Gimbutas 1952: 604)

In 2015, the genetics laboratories of Harvard, Jena, and Copenhagen (Allentoft et al. 2015; Haak et al. 2015) published aDNA evidence for the extensive human migration that appeared to spread from the steppelands north of the Black and Caspian Seas, both eastward, as far as the Yenisei River and, ultimately, as far west as Britain (Olalde et al. 2018) and Ireland (Cassidy et al. 2016). The source of the expansion was credited to a population whose genomic signature emerged in the steppelands and was primarily comprised of an admixture of both a local Eastern Hunter Gatherer (EHG) origin and a more distant Caucasian Hunter Gatherer (CHG) origin, associated with populations from the area between the Caucasus and the Zagros region. This combination (EHG + CHG) typified the Yamnaya culture, an Eneolithic cultural horizon whose home territory extended from the Urals to the Danube and whose archaeological remains had been known to have spread westward, at least as far as Hungary (Ecsedy 1979). The genetic signature of the Yamnaya (or another culture with a similar genetic composition) was found among about 75% of the Corded Ware burials sampled in Germany, whose previous populations were exclusively represented by local Western Hunter Gatherer (WHG) and Anatolian Farmer (AF) genes. Samples of mtDNA recovered from both Yamnaya and Corded Ware burials also suggested an east-west cline of steppe ancestry, with its highest representation in eastern Corded Ware burials in Poland and the Czech Republic, while western Corded Ware females appeared to derive from local populations (Juras et al. 2018).

The derivation of the Corded Ware population from a steppe source provided significant support to the Steppe Model of Indo-European origins, which had argued that the Indo-European languages of Europe had spread from the Pontic–Caspian steppe before the formation of the Corded Ware culture. The latter was frequently regarded as the staging area of the formation and dispersion of the Baltic, Slavic, and Germanic languages, and – because Corded Ware was directly ancestral to (possibly) at least the northern half of the Beaker horizon and more certainly the Únětice and succeeding Bronze Age cultures of Central and Western Europe – also Celtic, Italic, and possibly other Indo-European languages (Mallory 1989: 108–109). The possibility that the Beaker culture and Celtic languages both derived from the same source, which had long been suggested on archaeological grounds (e.g., Gallay 2001), was enhanced when the steppe signature was clearly found in Beaker burials across Central and Western Europe, including Britain (Oldalde et al. 2017).

At present, archaeologists and linguists are only beginning to come to grips with interpreting this new evidence. As Philipp Stockhammer has quipped:

> Half the archaeologists think ancient DNA can solve everything. The other half think ancient DNA is the devil's work. (quoted in Callaway 2018)

And it is certainly difficult to disagree with Volker Heyd's (2017: 350) observation that "aDNA results force us to reconsider; to question our own evidence and the methodology we apply [. . .] and to re-focus our interpretations." In this chapter, I hope to review the background as to why the aDNA revolution has had such major repercussions by briefly surveying the history of research in support of the hypothesis that the Irish language ultimately owed its origins to a migration emanating from the Pontic–Caspian steppe.[1] This will be admittedly a

* With thanks to Dan Bradley who read an earlier draft of this paper.

[1] There are inevitably those who regard Irish traditional history, primarily narrated in the *Lebor Gabála Érenn* "Book of Takings of Ireland," as containing relic remembrances of Ireland's prehistoric past. So it is best to acknowledge outright that the traditional medieval account does trace the Irish language back to the descendants of Nemed, who led an attempt to colonize Ireland from the steppelands of Scythia ca. 2350 BCE (*LGE* 273), i.e. that the Irish originated in the steppelands and arrived in Ireland at the same time as the Beakers. It should be emphasized that this legend derives from the medieval narrative that all the peoples of Europe descended from Japhet, the son of Noah, whose staging area for European dispersals was Scythia. Hence, Scythia (Ukraine and southern Russia) in effect became the equivalent of the Indo-European homeland in discourse long before the "official" recognition of the Indo-European language

somewhat impressionistic *tour d'horizon*, in fact – a look at a whole series of horizons to establish our backstory – and it will be done from the viewpoint of a supporter of the Steppe Model who is, I hope, also painfully aware of its weaker points. The topic is most easily discussed in terms of a two-stage process. The first involves the evidence for an expansion from the Pontic–Caspian steppe westward to Central Europe and the formation of the Corded Ware culture, while the second concentrates on a continuation of the alleged migration process westward from the Corded Ware that carried the Beaker culture into Ireland. The principal focus of this chapter will be limited to how the evidence of aDNA has impacted on the archaeological narrative; the impact on linguistic models will be only very briefly addressed at the end of this chapter.

9.1 Before the Revolution: The Archaeological Models

9.1.1 Stage 1: Steppe to Corded Ware

Over the first half of the twentieth century, archaeologists (Childe 1926; Peake and Fleure 1928; Sulimirski 1933; Poisson 1934) began to construct an archaeological model to support the already existing linguistic hypothesis that the Indo-European homeland lay north of the Black Sea (Schrader 1907; Mallory in press). The model proposed an Indo-European homeland set in the steppelands of Ukraine and South Russia, and usually associated the earliest Indo-Europeans with the "Pit Grave" or Yamnaya culture, whose westward expansion brought into existence the Corded Ware culture as well as the languages of northern Europe, usually at least Germanic and Balto-Slavic but possibly also Italic and Celtic.

There were, of course, opponents to this model, and readers may well be surprised by the identity of the author of the following rather critical opinion:

> There is no archaeological support for the assumption that the culture of the "Pit graves" has been a very expansive culture which brought the so-called "Corded ware and battle-axe culture" to Northern Europe, as it was thought some time ago. (Gimbutas 1952: 604)

A little more than a decade later, however, the same author described a migration from the Russian steppes to Central Europe that initiated the collapse of the TRB culture and the emergence of the Corded Ware culture. She concluded that

> The thorough change, the "reorganization" of cultures in central and northern Europe is so convincing that the incursion of the steppe people has now become a universally acknowledged fact. (Gimbutas 1963: 825)

In many further publications, Marija Gimbutas elaborated on what became known as the Steppe or Kurgan Model of Indo-European origins, but the treatment of a steppe invasion into Central Europe and the creation of the Corded Ware culture was rarely dealt with in depth and usually relatively cautiously. According to her, the primary grounds for advocating a migration were a shift in burial practice and a new emphasis on pastoralism. In 1980, she very briefly implicated the Globular Amphora as a critical element in the formation of the Corded Ware culture (Gimbutas 1980: 302), and again referred to the similarities between Corded Ware, Globular Amphora, and Yamnaya burial practice in her final work on steppe expansions (Gimbutas 1994). More importantly, she briefly reviewed the evidence for the physical presence of steppe populations in the Corded Ware region, and while admitting a few steppe-type burials in (the former) Czechoslovakia and a steppe origin for some burials in Poland, she concluded: "Ansonsten war die Mehrheit der Bevölkerung von einheimischer, alteuropäischer Herkunft" (Gimbutas 1994: 107).

Others who supported a possible steppe origin were also circumspect about the validity of their case. Miroslav Buchvaldek, for example, could regard both the theory of autochthonous origin and a migration from the steppe as "justified," although he personally favored a migration perhaps from "somewhere between the Vistula and the Dnieper" (Buchvaldek 1980: 403). In 1987, the present author summarized his own wallow in the morass of Corded Ware origins by stating "It should be emphasized that there is no widely accepted solution to the problem of Corded Ware origins" (Mallory 1989: 247) and, after reviewing the pros and cons of deriving Corded Ware from the steppelands, concluded, "I would have to take it on intuition that some form of historical relationship between the Pontic and Central and Northern Europe will eventually be demonstrated, even if the evidence today is not convincing" (264). In a more recent account of the Steppe Model, David Anthony recognized that the material culture of the Corded Ware culture was largely local and the connections between the Corded Ware and Yamnaya largely behavioral, e.g., single burial under a mound and a pastoral economy (Anthony 2007: 367–368). As for the specific relationship between the two cultural worlds, Anthony wrote:

> The wide-ranging pattern of interaction that the Corded Ware horizon inaugurated across northern Europe provided an optimal medium for language spread. Late Proto-Indo-European languages penetrated the eastern end of this medium, either through the incorporation of Indo-European dialects in the TRB base population before the Corded Ware horizon evolved, or through Corded Ware-Yamnaya contacts later, or both. (Anthony 2007: 268)

In the decade preceding the aDNA revolution, much of the putative impact of the Yamnaya culture on Central Europe was regarded not so much the result of a population intrusion

family. The German polymath Leibnitz, for example, derived the Indo-European languages from Scythia. Moreover, the chronology adduced has nothing to do with the Beakers, but is a product of the synchronization of Irish prehistorical events against early world chronicles, calculated with respect to the creation of the world in the year 5199 BCE and the date of the Deluge.

beyond the Danube, where Yamnaya burials could be clearly seen as far as the Tisza River, but rather the impact of a Yamnaya socioeconomic "package." This was laid out in some detail by Harrison and Heyd (2007: 196–203), who noted parallels between Corded Ware and Yamnaya burial practice and economies, but emphasized that "[...] linking these elements together is not quite the same as accepting the old model that suggested the Corded Ware culture was a steppe intrusion"; rather, the transformation of the local cultures of Central Europe to one resembling the steppe was effected "under the impact of ideas originating in the Yamnaya culture" (Harrison and Heyd 2007: 201). Moreover, at a 2012 conference, Rune Iversen emphasized that "mass migration fails as a sole explanation for the occurrence of Corded Ware societies throughout its entire area of distribution" (2019: 90), and rather emphasized the important role of "contact networks" that had been established between Jutland and Central Europe prior to the arrival of the Corded Ware.

Naturally, for every supporter of an eastern origin of the Corded Ware culture, there have been its many critics, especially Alexander Häusler, a specialist in both the mortuary practice of the Yamnaya culture and Corded Ware: "Ockergrabkultur [= Yamnaya] und Schnurkeramik stellen sich uns also als zwei konträre, grundsätzlich unterschiedliche Kulturareale mit grundverschiedenen Strukturen dar" (Häusler 1992: 345). In their classic study of the European Bronze Age, Coles and Harding (1979: 6–8) argued that the Yamnaya culture appeared to be contemporary with the Corded Ware culture, so it could hardly be its antecedent, and that attempts to derive Corded Ware barrows from steppe kurgans failed because tumulus burial "is widespread in time and space and cannot possibly be taken as indicative of a unitary racial situation [=Kurgan migration; author's note]." Lothar Killian (2000: 116–117) drew up a comparative table of twenty-three "essential" cultural elements possessed by the Corded Ware and Yamnaya cultures to reveal that they shared only four of them (the use of cord ornaments, tumulus burials, perforated teeth ornaments, and supine flexed burials). Another long-time critic of the steppe theory, Evžen Neustupný, also found the theory of a steppe migration "highly improbable; East European archaeological finds are already well known and there are no culture groups there from which the Corded Ware culture could have emerged" (Neustupný 2013: 154).

In short, on the eve of the 2015 genetics papers, even the camp that supported some form of steppe origin, distant or otherwise, in the creation of the Corded Ware and later Central European Bronze Age cultures in no way envisaged that it was the product of a mass migration of steppe peoples into Central Europe. The archaeological evidence simply did not support such a model for the first stage of our journey. And for the critics of the steppe migration theory, such as Neustupný, while similarities between the Corded Ware and Globular Amphora and the Baden cultures have been cited, the "mechanism by which this culture [Corded Ware] emerged cannot yet be explained in greater detail."

9.1.2 Stage 2: Corded Ware to British/Irish Beakers

Our second stage involves the entry of the Beaker culture into Ireland. Until the mid-twentieth century, the Beaker culture was generally absent from archaeological discourse on Irish prehistory. Although the Beakers were well known across western Europe, including Britain, they were not believed to have reached Ireland, and by 1928, the only evidence that could be cited was a very old find (1832) of a Food Vessel, which had been misidentified as a Beaker and dismissed as the product of a female slave dragged off to Ireland (Macalister 1928: 52). But in the two decades that followed, evidence for Beakers had begun to increase, so much so that R. A. S. Macalister, both a senior archaeologist and a Celticist, reversed himself and penned what I once dismissed as a lurid assessment of the Beaker impact, but which now might seem (at least to geneticists) to have been remarkably prophetic. Macalister claimed that the Beaker Folk had

> exterminated the men, or at least reduced them to slavery. As for the women, they met the usual fate of women in warfare: "to every man a damsel or two," as the savage old Hebrew paean expresses it [...] it was the only catastrophe of ancient times, subversive enough to have effected such a complete change of language. (Macalister 1949: 87–88)

It could be argued that Macalister was merely keeping with the spirit of contemporary Beaker research, for two years earlier, Christopher and Jacquetta Hawkes had written about the arrival of the Beakers that

> several waves of energetic conquerors soon occupied the greater part of Britain, ruthlessly dispossessing the Neolithic communities of their best pastures, and also no doubt their herds, and sometimes their women. (Hawkes and Hawkes 1947: 54)

Although subsequent discussion did not generally provide such colorful descriptions of Beaker aggression, the concept of a Beaker migration was still very much regarded as a statement of fact. Peter Harbison, for example, described the Beakers as "the last large-scale 'invasion' of Ireland during the prehistoric period" (Harbison 1975: 113), and they were still coming into Ireland in strength enough to dominate the local inhabitants in Irish archaeological textbooks up to 1977 (Herity and Eogan 1977: 132).

But the last quarter of the twentieth century saw the rise of what Christopher Hawkes once dismissed as "immobilism," the concept that people rarely relocated in prehistory and the rise of a variety of attempts to explain the diffusion of cultural phenomena in terms of exchange, the emergence of interacting peer polities, emulation, or any other process that minimized the actual movement of people and focused on other explanations for the expansion of cultural phenomena. So at the end of one of the most detailed accounts of Beakers, Richard Harrison (1980: 166) concluded that the evidence

> Strongly suggests that the 'Beaker Folk' have no substance as a special population group. Seen in this way, the functional interpretations are far more plausible and coherent than fuzzy pictures of

peddlers and pastoralists making their way quickly all over Europe, bearing superior products, or an overlord economy.

Or, as Colin Renfrew could write:

> [. . .] peer-polity interactions were probably responsible for the development of the networks of contacts which facilitated the custom of using beaker drinking vessels as prestige objects around 2300 BC. This is seen today as a more acceptable explanation than migrations of "Beaker Folk," for which in reality there is no good evidence. (Renfrew 1987: 236)

Such interpretations continued to flourish in the present century. In his account of Scottish prehistory, Alistair Moffat remarked:

> It used to be thought that [the Beakers] heralded the arrival of a new culture, a wave of innovative immigrants known as the Beaker People. This interpretation is now largely discredited, but it is nevertheless true that the new pots had a direct stylistic link with earlier European beakers. (Moffat 2009: 155)

Further, Julian Heath, in his account of prehistoric warfare in Britain, concluded,

> the idea of a Beaker "invasion" is now rightly treated with scant respect, and today, the concept is largely defunct, with few if any, archaeologists continuing to believe in it. Nevertheless, evidence is increasing that there was small-scale immigration of "Beaker Folk". . .into Britain from the continent. (Heath 2009: 65)

Thus, by 1998, in the most authoritative textbook of Irish prehistory, John Waddell discussed how the old idea of a distinct Beaker ethnic group had been replaced, and that while this

> does not preclude the possibility that some users of Beaker pottery travelled from place to place, it does obviate the need to presuppose complex population movements to account for the European spread of "the Beaker assemblage." (Waddell 1998: 123)

Moreover, as for the subsequent period in Ireland, marked by single-grave burials accompanied by ceramics derived from the Beaker tradition (Food Vessels/Irish bowls):

> there is little evidence, apart from the presence of novel pot forms, to suggest large numbers of migrants arriving in Ireland from Britain. (MacSparron 2018: 312)

When I attempted to assess whether there was a serious case for a Beaker migration into Ireland, I found most lines of evidence either unable to shed much light on the problem, or not particularly supportive. Of the more than 219 Irish Beaker sites (Carlin 2018: 39), the largest category of site type was small pits with a few Beaker sherds, followed by "spreads" of Beaker sherds in soil, not clearly associated with any particular architectural remains. It is therefore difficult to associate the Beakers with the introduction of a new settlement type or domestic architecture. Classic Beaker burials involving inhumation accompanied by a distinctive Beaker kit (beaker, arrowheads, wrist bracer, copper dagger, ornaments) are entirely absent from Ireland, where Beaker burials are normally found in wedge tombs (here there is some association between a new tomb type and Beakers, but it is not a one-to-one association, as most excavated wedge tombs lack evidence of Beakers.) Moreover, Beaker sherds, possible votive offerings, are also found just as frequently inserted into earlier Neolithic megalithic tombs, especially court tombs, although in a context lacking a Beaker burial. If we review the evidence for ritual sites, there is also little evidence, other than interpreting Beaker sherds in pits as votive offerings and their residue in spreads as the result of selected deposition. What is striking is that Beakers were preceded by a horizon attributed to Grooved Ware (ca. 3000–2500 BCE), which did boast of the erection of some spectacular ritual structures, such as henges and timber circles (Carlin and Cooney 2017; Hartwell 2002; Sheridan 2004). Beaker-users settled on these and other, earlier ritual sites, but do not seem to have been the impetus for their initial construction. As for the economy, while it had been suggested that the Beakers introduced the domestic horse to Ireland (van Wijngaarden-Bakker 1986), the relevant evidence (the remains of a domestic horse presumed to have been associated with Beaker occupation at New Grange) has since been shown to date to the Late Bronze Age (Bendrey et al. 2013) and, so far at least, there is no secure evidence that the domestic horse was introduced into Ireland much before 1000 BCE. In terms of the Beaker kit, there is clear evidence for other Beaker-associated items (barbed and tanged arrowheads, stone "wrist bracers," gold ornaments), but all of these tend to occur as chance finds rather than in clear associations; it is almost as if the Beaker kit was deconstructed and the various items randomly distributed across the Irish landscape. The one area where there is a clear innovation associated with the Beakers is copper mining and metallurgy: Beakers are associated with Ireland's earliest copper mining at Ross Island (O'Brien 2015).

Attempting to wrestle some conclusions from the meager evidence available, I have tried to make a case for some migration on the basis of the following evidence (Mallory 2013a: 119–125):

1. Beaker ceramics: Beaker wares comprise all of the forms required for daily or ritual use, and they are the exclusive ceramic type after Grooved Ware. Their quality in Ireland suggests a domestic rather than a specialist craft and implies a significant number of female potters who were so numerous that they did not abandon their own ceramics for that of the (presumably) indigenous population (Grooved Ware).
2. Beaker metallurgy: The mining and processing of copper was seen to be so highly specialized that it would have required at least some migration of craftsmen competent to both mine and work metals.
3. Beaker network: Beaker finds such as lunulae, found in Ireland, Britain, and northern France, suggest an exchange system that might have echoed the migration stream that was established by Beaker immigrants.

This evidence was used to support a reluctantly tepid conclusion: "The mechanism for the spread of the Beaker culture to Ireland initially involved some immigration from both northern Britain and Atlantic Europe" (Mallory 2013a: 128).

In short, by the eve of the aDNA revolution, both stages of any trek from the steppelands to Ireland had been regarded as archaeologically unsupported. But material culture was not the only card the archaeologist had to play, and it is useful to consider the genetic evidence that was then available.

9.2 Before the Revolution: The "Pre-Molecular-Genetic" Models

9.2.1 Stage 1: Steppe to Corded Ware

One can easily ridicule the nineteenth- and early-twentieth-century attempts to reify the variations in the cephalic index (dolichocephalic vs brachycephalic) into fixed inherited physical types from which one could not only determine population groups and migrations, but also language and even intellectual capacity (Taylor 1921). Already by 1900, critics were despairing that "the human cranium will not bear the weight of any ethnological deductions" (Conway 1900: 78). This attitude became increasingly fossilized, at least in the Anglophone world, over the course of the twentieth century (e.g., Coles and Harding 1979: 5–6), despite the fact that – with greater numbers of apparently diagnostic measurements coupled with multivariate analysis and principal component mapping – it was becoming apparent that craniometrics was perhaps of greater validity than many archaeologists were willing to admit (Howells 1972). In terms of discerning migrations, the limiting factors were believed to be the size of the immigrating population with respect to the host population, and to what extent the newcomers were "different enough from the earlier population to change the body build and type structure in a measurable way" (Schwidetzky 1980). Schwidetzy's conclusions with reference to Yamnaya expansions were ambiguous: there was – on one measurement – a shortening of skull breadth from the east (Yamnaya) across the Globular Amphora culture that might have suggested an east-to-west genetic impact, but this was not apparent among the sample of Corded Ware skulls from Central Europe. Schwidetzky's sample was small, and a much more ambitious comparison was made by Roland Menk (1980), who employed twenty-six cranial measurements on an effective sample of 1,842 skulls, ranging from the steppelands west to Central Europe. Although Menk's grouping of physical types and cultures actually captured a respectable number of the correlations more recently verified by aDNA research (Mallory, Dybo, and Balanovsky 2019), on the critical question of whether there had been a Yamnaya (or other steppe culture) migration to account for the Corded Ware population, Menk concluded:

> Indo-Europeanization of northern Europe (i.e. of the Corded Ware culture [. . .]) cannot have taken place by a direct invasion of whatever extent of South Eurasian Kurgan people [=Yamnaya or related steppe population] [. . .] there are virtually no individuals within the whole sample of German Corded Ware people that would fit, statistically, into the South-Ukrainian Kurgan populations. (Menk 1980: 389)

Menk's principal component map had grouped his Corded Ware/Únětice samples with the earlier farming cultures of Central Europe, and not with the Yamnaya and other steppe cultures (although one might perhaps argue that they actually fell *between* the Yamnaya and Neolithic cultures).

In any event, even for those most in favor of deriving the Corded Ware culture from the steppelands, there was very little or no support from the evidence of physical anthropology.

9.2.2 Stage 2: Corded Ware to Irish Beakers

Craniometry has had a long though not particularly illustrious past in Ireland. By the middle of the nineteenth century, there had been attempts to devise tools capable of accurately measuring crania in Ireland (e.g., Grattan 1853). By the later part of the century, John Beddoe (1885: 270) could conclude that the Irish were a "cross of the Iberian with a long-faced, harsh-featured, red-haired race, who contributed the language and much of the character," and by 1891, Trinity College had established the Anthropometric Laboratory of Ireland. The ultimate survey was undertaken as part of the Harvard Mission to Ireland where, applying a typology usually employed in classifying American criminals, the largest Irish "subrace" was described as having dark hair, blue eyes, and long heads (Hooton and Dupertius 1955). But work on prehistoric populations and the possible evidence for migration was limited essentially to Cecil Martin's (1935) study of prehistoric assemblages, from which he discerned four cranial types, each associated with what he regarded as different immigrant populations. These comprised an Early Neolithic type with long and narrow high skulls and an Iberian type associated with megalithic burials, followed by a radical change with the Early Bronze Age Food Vessel population, and then an Iron Age population similar to the earlier megalithic type. The important thing to note here is that Martin, like many others, saw a major break between the Neolithic and the Early Bronze Age. This was repeated a half-century later, when Don Brothwell (1985) also saw a sharp break between Neolithic and Beaker skulls in Ireland, and similar results were seen in Neil Brodie's study of the Neolithic and Bronze Age transition in Britain (1994). In short, a break between the Neolithic and the Early Bronze Age, specifically the Beakers and, in an Irish context, Food Vessels, was already argued repeatedly but largely ignored by archaeologists who had lost faith in the results of the craniometrists.

9.3 Before the Revolution: Molecular-Genetic Models

9.3.1 Stage 1: Steppe to Corded Ware

Much of the initial application of molecular genetics to major archaeological and linguistic problems was associated with the work of Luca Cavalli-Sforza and his associates, which climaxed in his massive *The History and Geography of Human*

Genes (Cavalli-Sforza, Menozzi, and Piazza 1994) which employed a suite of classical markers to prepare principal component maps of potential migrations. Most relevant to the origins of the Corded Ware culture was his third PC for European populations that accounted for 10.6% of the total variance. Centered on the territory north of the Black Sea, with a gradient trending away to the west, this was regarded as a plausible expression of the Steppe Model that "should be given very serious consideration" (Cavalli-Sforza, Menozzi, and Piazza 1994: 293), but the authors recognized that the pattern might be accounted for by later expansions from the same general region (we could easily list Sarmatians, Alans, Huns, Avars, and Hungarians, for example, who would have carried "eastern" genes into Central Europe).

Genetic mapping continued, but with a shift to modern haplogroups, and for those promoting the Steppe Model, most attention centered on the distribution of R1a1a1 (M17), which was recognized by a number of geneticists, such as Spencer Wells et al. (2001: 10248), as "likely to represent traces of an ancient population originating in southern Russia/Ukraine, where M17 is found at high frequency (75%)." Stephen Oppenheimer (2007: 263–265), for example, investigated various haplotypes of R1a1 as potential evidence for the Steppe Model. It should be noted that at this time, R1b, anthropomorphized with the Basque male name Ruizko, was regarded as a relic of the postglacial colonization of western Europe.

9.3.2 Stage 2: Corded Ware to Irish Beaker

In *The Origins of the Irish* (2013), I attempted to assess the evidence for immigration into Ireland from its initial settlement in the Mesolithic until the appearance of a historically attested Irish-speaking population in the fifth century CE (Mallory 2013a). By 2013, there had been a number of attempts to interpret the course of past migrations through the patterns of modern genetic evidence (Mallory 2013a: 224–237). In terms of the Y-chromosome, the modern distribution of male haplogroups in Ireland appeared to separate into two divergent sources. Group 1 consisted of R1a, R1b, IJK, PN3, N3, I1a, I1b2, I1c, while Group 2 comprised E3b, G2a, J2. The first group was interpreted as the result of the initial postglacial migrations from southern France and Iberia, which reintroduced human settlement across Atlantic and Northern Europe after the retreat of the ice sheets. In terms of archaeological periods, their arrival would have been assigned largely to the Irish Mesolithic (ca. 8000–4000 BCE). Group 2 was assigned a Near Eastern origin and associated with the spread of agriculture and farmers in the Neolithic. Modern Irish males, who are overwhelmingly R1b, were then seen to reflect the earliest colonization of Ireland, while Near Eastern farmers added some new haplogroups, although they did not markedly alter the genetic make-up of the Irish. After the Neolithic, there was no clear genetic evidence for subsequent Bronze or Iron Age migrations.

On the basis of this evidence ca. 95% of the Irish male population was regarded as descendants of the earliest Mesolithic colonists of Ireland, who had made their way to Ireland from refuges in southern France and Iberia after the retreat of the glaciers (see, for example, Oppenheimer 2007: 222, where even the so-called Gaelic Modal Haplogroup, associated with Niall of the Nine Hostages, was believed to have entered Ireland before the Neolithic). Another ca. 5% were descendants of the earliest farmers who traced their origin back to the Near East. Other than historically attested migrations, e.g., the Norse and Anglo-Normans, there was minimal or no evidence for post-Neolithic immigrants to Ireland.

9.4 The Eve of the Revolution

On the eve of the aDNA revolution, then, anyone supporting the Steppe Model was faced with either conflicting or at best ambiguous evidence in its support. The archaeological evidence for the Stage 1 part of the migration was highly contested, and even those who supported it did not do so in terms of a mass migration, but rather as some form of socioeconomic emulation by native populations of Central and Eastern Europe, having come into contact with steppe societies. The evidence from craniometry, for those who were still paying attention, was not encouraging, and there was really no robust evidence for a migration of steppe tribes into Central Europe to form the Corded Ware culture. The new evidence gained from classical markers may have provided some minor evidence for a gene flow to the west, but that could be easily dismissed as temporally ambiguous, and it did not seem to be substantially represented. The evidence from the modern distribution of haplogroups gave some suggestion that variants of R1a may have indicated a migration from the steppelands, but, claims by some geneticists notwithstanding, there was no way to associate the evidence with the archaeological entities involved in the discussion.

As for Stage 2, there was an almost overbearing archaeological fashion to dismiss any evidence for migration, and so the presence of Beakers was explained away by any other vector than a substantial migration. The cranial evidence did appear to suggest that there was a substantial break between Neolithic and Early Bronze Age populations, but it was going to be a brave archaeologist indeed who was going to press the evidence of the skull-measurers over such pervasive archaeological fashion. The attempt to introduce molecular genetics was not going to convince anyone of a migration, because the dominant male haplogroup in both Britain and especially Ireland was R1b, which had been anchored to a population expansion from an Iberian refuge after the last glaciation.

9.5 The aDNA Revolution (2015–2018)

9.5.1 Stage 1: Steppe > Corded Ware

The aDNA revolution of 2015 had already been heralded several years earlier, when Brandt et al. (2013: 260–261) noted the appearance of mtDNA U2 in Corded Ware burials, where previously it was known only from Russia, suggestive of influence from an eastern steppe culture. Similarly, Jean Manco (2013: 145–146) noted that the patterns seen in the distribution of R1a1a and R1b, suspected of having some association with the spread of Indo-European languages from the steppelands, were now found in a Corded Ware (Haak et al. 2008) and Beaker (Lee et al. 2012) burial, respectively. But it was in 2015, with the publication of Haak et al. and Allentoft et al., that the weight of discourse shifted from the modern distributions of genetic data to an explosion in ancient DNA evidence. Both papers established that the primary components of their Yamnaya sample was an admixture of EHG (Eastern Hunter Gatherer) and CHG (Caucasian Hunter Gatherer) (Haak et al. 2015: 208; Allentoft et al. 2015: 168), and that this genetic signature, which first emerged on the steppe, appeared both earliest and as a significant admixture in their Corded Ware samples (Haak et al. 2015: 208–210; Allentoft et al. 2015: 168–169). In terms of the actual origin of the Corded Ware culture, Haak et al. (2015) argue that as the Corded Ware "are both the earliest and most strongly differentiated from the Middle Neolithic population," the genetic evidence indicates a "relatively sudden" migration rather than simply a continuous flow of genes westward. But the paper also cautions that their Yamnaya samples, extracted from burials in the Middle Volga region, might not be directly ancestral to Corded Ware, and that there may have been a "more western Yamnaya population" or an earlier steppe population "that migrated into central Europe." Allentoft et al. (2015) argue that the "admixture event resulted in the formation of peoples of the Corded Ware" and related cultures, including later downstream cultures such as Bell Beakers and Únětice.

Archaeological reaction was mixed, and there were several forms of criticism brought against the genetic evidence, as can be briefly noted:

1. The new migration model was built on the basis of an extremely limited number of samples from regional variants of vast archaeological "cultures," and then extrapolated into a broad explanatory narrative (Heyd 2017: 350).
2. The Corded Ware samples were from near the end of the culture's existence, and so could not be safely employed to establish its origins, nor be used to support a model that demanded a "massive migration" rather than some other process, especially as there were no samples from the latest periods of the preceding Neolithic culture (Furholt 2018: 165).
3. There were some traces of the so-called steppe aDNA in a few burials centuries before the Corded Ware culture emerged that could support processes of admixture before the putative expansion of the Yamnaya culture (Heyd 2017: 351; Furholt 2018: 166).
4. The monothetic model that concretizes Corded Ware, Bell-Beaker, and Yamnaya into disparate cultural units is far less sensitive and useful than a polythetic (*sensu* David Clarke) model that emphasizes the fluidity of social relations between diverse regional communities (Furholt 2019).
5. The genetic signature, especially of males, is different between the Yamnaya and Corded Ware populations; e.g., Yamnaya is largely R1b, while Corded Ware is R1a, and its R1b component differs from that found among the Yamnaya population (Balanovsky et al. 2017; Klejn 2018b: 199).
6. The strength of the steppe signature is found to be inversely proportional to its distance from the steppe, i.e., it was stronger in burials from Northern Europe than those from Central Europe (Ivanova et al. 2018: 130).

None of these criticisms is absolutely critical to the model of steppe expansions, and the broad conclusion that there was a population vector from the Pontic–Caspian region both eastward across Siberia and westward into Central and Western Europe is generally supported, even by those who have queried some of the aDNA interpretations. The specific genetic criticism, for example, indicated in point 4 above, can be mitigated by replacing Yamnaya with a "Yamnaya-related" population (Balanovsky 2019: 169) or "people with steppe ancestry" etc (Furholt 2019: 121), while the evidence of mtDNA does support an east-to-west cline (Juras et al. 2018).

9.5.2 Stage 2: Corded Ware > Irish Beaker

Although Beaker samples had exhibited the steppe signature in Allentoft et al. (2105), it was Cassidy et al. (2016) and Olalde et al. (2018) who demonstrated that this migration extended all the way to Ireland. First, aDNA was recovered from three Early Bronze Age Food Vessel (< Beaker) burials on Rathlin Island, Co Antrim (Cassidy et al. 2016), which carried the steppe signature, and then a much larger examination of Beaker and other remains across Atlantic Europe (Olalde et al. 2018) further cemented a new interpretive model.

The new evidence completely overturned the earlier models employed to explain the current male population of Ireland. Now one could argue that only ca. 12% (these percentages should not be taken too seriously) of the male population carried the genes of the Mesolithic colonists (which could also have been introduced as an admixture by later settlers). The evidence for farmers from the Near East was still relatively constrained, at ca. 4%, while about 84% of the male population was assigned to descendants of a Beaker migration ca. 2400 BCE. As to whether this influx of "steppe genes" was the result of a sudden change in the genetic structure of the population or the result of millennia of a migration stream from the east, Olalde et al. (2018) indicated that the genetic transformation of Britain, at least, was extremely rapid and could have been accomplished in a few centuries, and while there might be some evidence of "intermediates" in Ireland, the transition there was also very rapid and certainly thorough (Bradley, personal communication).

Irish archaeologists have reacted with some caution with respect to the evidence of aDNA. We should acknowledge (with Carlin 2018: 196–197) that while the attribution of a mass migration to Ireland during the Beaker period is probable, at the time of writing, it is not yet based on primary evidence, as we have no published aDNA from Irish Beaker burials. Rather, we have evidence from three Food Vessel burials, which are interpreted as cultural descendants of the Beakers. As mentioned above, the classic type of Beaker burials known in northwest Europe and Britain, single-grave burials under a barrow accompanied by the so-called "Beaker package," are unknown in Ireland (Carlin 2018), and the single-burial tradition only emerges (several centuries after the introduction of Beakers) with the Food Vessels, ca. 2200 BCE. As these are also known in Britain, one could entertain the remote possibility that the introduction of steppe genes was to be associated only later with an influx of people bearing the Food Vessel tradition into Ireland. Food Vessel origins is a complicated matter, but there is a tendency to regard the Irish bowls as the earliest exemplars and hence a distinctly, Beaker-derived, Irish innovation (Carlin 2018: 126). In any event, Food Vessels were a part of a network that also embraced Beakers (Wilkin 2013: 319–327), and does not markedly alter the case for a Beaker origin for steppe genes in Ireland.

9.6 The Challenges of aDNA to Archaeology

The results of recent aDNA research have brought a host of challenges to archaeologists, and here I would like to concentrate on a few aspects of the aDNA revolution that emerge in somewhat different forms in our two stages. In our discussion of the Steppe to Corded Ware transformation, we are confronted with a genetic model that appears to suggest that a "Yamnaya-like" population initiated the creation of the Corded Ware culture, a conclusion that we have seen is extraordinarily difficult to sustain purely on the basis of archaeological evidence. Witness, for example, Leo Klejn (2018a: 4): "I doubt that the discoveries in question reflect a direct migration from the Yamnaya to the Corded Ware cultures." Or (translated from the Russian), more forcefully: "from an archaeological point of view, neither a massive migration nor the origin of the Corded Ware from the Yamnaya is traceable" (Ivanova et al. 2018: 102). For this reason, archaeologists have understandably walked this conclusion back to how a "Yamnaya-like" genetic signal came to dominate the genome of Corded Ware males (at least those who have been sampled), since they still find it difficult if not impossible to demonstrate that the Yamnaya culture itself could have been *directly* responsible for the emergence of the Corded Ware.

Mechanisms have been sought to explain the genetic replacement of males who were primarily AF + WHG (e.g., TRB, Globular Amphora, Tisza, etc.) by those who had a similar balance of EHG + CHG as the Yamnaya. One suggestion is the possibility that the Corded Ware culture was organized into warbands and that the immigrants, largely males, engaged in bride abduction and, more certainly, exogamy (Kristiansen et al. 2017; see also Knipper et al. 2017). This appeal to a marriage network can get us only so far, as it still seems to imply that Yamnaya(-like) families, blessed with abundant abductable daughters, penetrated the marriage networks of the later Corded Ware to set this genetic transformation in motion. Unfortunately, the archaeological evidence does not indicate that the Yamnaya culture penetrated the subsequent territory of the Corded Ware, other than what would appear to be clearly defined and more recent contact zones where a later Corded Ware variant such as the Middle Dnieper culture came into direct contact with the Yamnaya culture (Telegin 2005). This has led to the search for an earlier vector that may have stimulated the rise of Corded Ware that also was genetically "Yamnaya-like." A few sites have produced pre-Yamnaya evidence of the steppe genetic signature, such as Varna and Smyadovo (Mathieson et al. 2017), but these take us no further than eastern Bulgaria, which is no one's starting point for the Corded Ware. Perhaps more promising is a steppe signature from a burial from the Tripolye cave site of Verteba, but the other sampled Tripolye skulls (ca. 3700–2700 BCE) lack this pattern. Archaeological evidence for steppe penetration further along the Danube, marked by graves of the Suvorovo–Novodanilovka group (Anthony 2007: 249–258; Furholt 2018: 166) are a plausible vector for earlier westward movement of the steppe genetic marker, but they do not even get us as far west as the later Yamnaya penetration (the Tisza River), so while they are suitably early, they do not provide a plausible geographical explanation for Corded Ware origins.

Within the framework of the classic steppe migration model of Marija Gimbutas, the relevant steppe predecessors of the Corded Ware culture would have derived from her second wave of migration (ca. 3400–3200 BCE), which would have resulted in the hybrid (local farming cultures + steppe intruders) Globular Amphora and Baden cultures (Gimbutas 1980). Gimbutas (and many others) have regarded the Globular Amphora culture as "a decisive factor in the formation of the succeeding Corded Ware culture" (Gimbutas 1980: 302; also 1991: 393). Unfortunately, none of the usual suspects have so far been very promising genetically, as the Globular Amphora culture (so far) lacks any evidence of the Yamnaya genetic signature (Fernandes et al. 2018; Haak 2018; Mathieson et al. 2017; Tassi et al. 2017). Although Fernandes et al. (2018) caution that all the Globular Amphora samples derive from the early period of the culture (which cannot exclude a later infiltration of a Yamnaya-like population), the genetic evidence certainly does nothing to support a steppe hybridization of the earlier TRB culture to produce the Globular Amphora, as expressed in a classic form of the Steppe Model (Gimbutas 1980: 291–302; 1994: 78–88). Another proposed steppe hybrid, the Baalberge culture (invoked as steppe-derived because of its very early tumulus burials [Gimbutas 1980: 291–292]), also reveals itself as essentially an AF and WHG admixture, at least with reference to the three burials sampled (Haak et al. 2015). Substantial pre-Yamnaya penetration along the Danube into Hungary, suggested again in Gimbutas's (1977: 285–291) proposals for a second Kurgan wave involving the hybridized creation of the Baden culture, is similarly unsupported by the existing evidence for aDNA (Lipson et al. 2017). Moreover, invoking some form of "pendular" migration/marriage network back along earlier migration paths from eastern Europe into the steppelands (Usatovo, Budzhak; Ivanova et al. 2018) remains to be demonstrated; however, as their putative source population might be expected to be very admixed itself (Late Tripolye + Yamnaya-like), it would be surprising if their steppe genetic signature were strong enough to supply the source for the extremely strong steppe signal found much further to the west in Corded Ware. Ivanova et al. (2018) themselves note that all Late Tripolye physical remains appear already to be divided into two physical types: Mediterranean (the AF of the geneticists) and Proto-Europoid (the EHG [± CHG?] of the geneticists). In short, explaining the massive steppe signature in the Corded Ware and later cultures remains a major problem, as most of the potential pre-Yamnaya suspects seem genetically unconvincing. The problem of identifying a suitable steppe source for the genetic cocktail found in the Corded Ware and later cultures is taking on the appearance of a hunt for a phantom archaeological culture carrying a very strong Yamnaya-like genetic signature.

So far, then, the various cultures traditionally described as the result of a process of archaeological admixture between steppe cultures and local Late Neolithic cultures reveal little or no evidence for genetic admixture. Obviously, one might hope that an archaeologically driven research project to widen sampling should eventually resolve the problem of the mystery culture or vector that introduced the steppe signature to the rest of Europe. But even when this source is identified, will archaeologists find themselves reinterpreting the evidence for our phantom culture's material remains to create a new narrative of Corded Ware origins?

Much more interesting, perhaps, is the failure of putative mixed archaeological entities or hybrids to be reflected in the genetic evidence (or the reverse situation). This emphasizes the accuracy of Anthony and Brown's (2017: 41) statement that we are in "uncharted territory" when it comes to matching the data sets generated by aDNA (marriage networks, migration) with archaeological interpretation. The larger cultural entities of the Eneolithic, Yamnaya, Corded Ware (Szmyt 1999: 207), and Beakers have all been interpreted as "packages," adopted by local populations. Only through the problem-focused application of aDNA are we likely to determine the mechanisms underlying our cultural entities (population replacement, marriage networks, socially limited exchange relationships) that archaeologists have speculated about since the existence of the discipline but have seldom been able to demonstrate confidently.

Another aspect, although present in our Stage 1 model, is best examined in Stage 2, and comprises the social mechanisms that resulted in the radical replacement of the (male) genome in Britain and Ireland during the Beaker period. We have already seen the discordance between the prevailing archaeological dismissals of any significant evidence of a Beaker immigration to Ireland and the evidence of aDNA, which suggests a major transformation of the Irish male genome, perhaps only over a period of several centuries. I doubt that there are many Irish archaeologists over the past three or four decades who would have predicted the type of population replacement suggested by recent aDNA studies. The lack of correlation between archaeological expectations and the aDNA evidence in Ireland is hardly unique, and after reviewing similar non-correlations, Stefan Burmeister suggested that it has become "obvious that archaeology has lost its previous methodological hold on investigating migration" (Burmeister 2016: 52).

Nevertheless, the rapid alteration of the Irish (primarily but by no means exclusively male) genome implies a massive replacement of the Late Neolithic (Grooved Ware in the context of Ireland) males by an intrusive Beaker-using population, and this requires an explanation (as does the replacement of native Neolithic populations in Central Europe by steppe populations). A variety of models can be suggested, although none as yet seem convincingly supported by archaeological evidence. Time and space will limit my discussion only to illustrating a few approaches that will require much deeper consideration.

The archaeological problem before us can briefly be stated as follows: *how did Beaker males suppress the native population and exclude the native males from the gene pool?*

We have already seen the sentiments voiced by R. A. S. Macalister; these have been largely repeated in terms of aDNA in the *Eupedia* account of Celtic expansions, which informs us that

> technologically superior Celtic warriors, equipped with Bronze weapons and riding on horses, massacred or enslaved indigenous men while taking their women, or they established a ruling elite that passed on more Y chromosomes through sustained polygamy over many centuries. (Hay 2016: 2.2)

So what is the actual evidence for these processes?

If one appeals to the military superiority of the Beakers over the native (Grooved Ware) population, in terms of technology, we find ourselves comparing the local petite-tranchet derivative (PTD) arrowheads of the Late Neolithic Grooved Ware (Heath 2009: 63; Woodman et al. 2006: 152–155) with barbed and tanged Beaker arrowheads (Heath 2009: 65–75). Whether PTDs were actually employed as arrowheads rather than as knives is a contested issue. Obviously, if the Grooved Ware population in Ireland totally lacked projectile weapons, we could credit the Beakers with a superior military technology. But as archery was clearly in evidence throughout the Early and Middle Neolithic, and transverse "arrowheads" are characteristic of the British Grooved Ware, it would seem strange indeed if the Grooved Ware population in Ireland had completely abandoned this technology. In his discussion of the British evidence, Heath (2009: 63) certainly treats PTDs as projectile heads and cites evidence from the French Late Neolithic of a PTD embedded in a human vertebra. If we assume the existence of Grooved Ware archery, it is difficult to give a major advantage to the Beakers in warfare unless they were also supplied with a far more effective bow, which is possible if they possessed a composite bow (Heath 2009: 71), and the Grooved Ware did not. All this remains to be demonstrated, however, and as Molloy (2017: 283) remarks about the Early Bronze Age in Ireland, "Without extant bows and dearth of arrow-shafts, little can be said about the role of archery on combat."

As for striking weapons, the Grooved Ware should have had access to both stone axes and probably mace-heads, while Beakers would have accessed stone and copper axes; any or all of these would have been effective weapons (Molloy 2017: 285–286). The only weapon that might have given the Beaker population a military advantage is probably the halberd, the "first artifact type in Ireland created for the purpose of fighting and killing people" (Molloy 2017: 285). Theoretically, the halberds could have been brought to Ireland by the earliest Beakers, but we lack sufficient contextual and chronological control to determine whether halberds were employed to reduce the existing male Grooved Ware population of Ireland, or simply a popular weapon for Beaker populations to kill and maim each other. Although the horse was once thought to be introduced into Ireland by the Beakers, we have already seen that there is no convincing evidence for the horse in Ireland much before 1000 BCE (Bendrey et al. 2013). In short, while the Beakers may have had some advantage in terms of military technology (composite bow? halberd?), it is difficult to credit the Beakers with such overwhelming technological superiority that could account for their genetic success over what we might presume to have been a far more numerous native Grooved Ware population.

Superior weaponry is not the only argument that might provide the Beakers with a major advantage over the Grooved Ware. Irrespective of the comparative effectiveness of the weapons, the important distinction may have been in social organization and the possibility that the Beaker community maintained the institution of the warband. The warband has been seen as a potential factor in stimulating language shift (Mallory 2016: 400) and, as we have already seen, it has been applied to the expansion of the Corded Ware culture, one of the major ancestral components of the Beaker horizon (Kristiansen et al. 2017: 339–340) in northern Europe. But as we have also seen, the classic association of an archery kit with a single-grave Beaker burial is not met in Ireland. There are seven Beaker arrowheads known from pits, but these are never accompanied by wrist bracers, axes, or daggers (Carlin 2018: 68), and only seven barbed and tanged arrowheads have been recovered from Wedge Tombs (Carlin 2018: 103). We might hope to find obvious warrior burials in the subsequent Single Grave tradition (2200–1600 BCE), but here again, the evidence is hardly substantial. In a data set of nearly 500 burials, McSparron (2018: 161) uncovered only three graves that were accompanied by arrowheads. From the same set, there were also eleven bronze daggers (2018: 163). In short, it is extremely difficult to propose a systematic association between male burials and weapons with the burial of military sodalities presumably associated with the introduction of steppe genes.

Another potential mechanism for change might be the introduction of a prestigious set of new rituals and beliefs. So far as we can see, when it comes to ritual structures, the Beakers were actually subtractive rather than adding to or replacing earlier forms. For example, in the previous Grooved Ware period, we have well over twenty presumably ritual timber structures, and probably the initiation of henge building in Ireland, i.e. evidence for the creation of central places and occasionally monumental architecture requiring large labor resources (Carlin and Cooney 2017: 42–46). As Carlin (2018: 201–203) argues, Beakers either maintained earlier traditions of the Late Neolithic – e.g., erection and depositions associated with timber circles, votive offerings before earlier megalithic tombs, copper distribution mapped on to earlier Neolithic exchange systems, and use of the same polished stone material for the manufacture of wrist guards – or were likely influenced by earlier local traditions, e.g. plain Beaker wares influenced by earlier plain Grooved Ware styles. In short, the evidence for social continuity between the Later Neolithic and the Beakers provides scant support that the relationship between the two populations was genocidal or involved the imposition of a prestigious Beaker ritual culture on simple natives. On the other hand, the evidence of aDNA certainly renders arguments for continuity highly perplexing. For example, Carlin writes that

> By placing Beaker-associated habitation materials into ancient monuments such as Early Neolithic court tombs, people may have been conducting exchanges with those they perceived as their ancestors or as founders of the group in a manner that celebrated the 'domestic,' but also demonstrated kinship and descent. (2018: 204)

The evidence of aDNA would suggest, however, no matter how much identity is a social construct, the earliest Beaker populations would be aware that their genetic ancestors lay elsewhere across the sea and not with the population that they were apparently extinguishing. On the other hand, we do know that throughout the Middle Ages, the early Irish did enjoy a long history of creative genealogy building (O'Rahilly 1946).

It might also be suggested that Beaker males were able to better spread their genes because Beaker immigrants made up a sizable addition to a population that had been seriously depressed either over the course of the Neolithic or because of diseases carried by the Beaker population. This has been argued for the transition to the Corded Ware culture in northern Europe on a number of occasions (Furholt 2018: 168), and evidence of the plague virus has recently been found in earlier contexts that have been associated with triggering a population decline in the Neolithic (Rascovan et al. 2019). With reference to Ireland, if one can utilize accumulative radiocarbon dates as proxy evidence for both the amount of human activity and the size of population (McLaughlin 2019; 2020), then we can see that here too there was a marked decrease in activity (population collapse?) in Neolithic Ireland ca. 3500 BCE, and the activity/population (?) remained relatively static until ca. 2700 BCE (McLaughlin 2020), when a slow rise began that accelerated rapidly after ca. 2400 BCE. (Fig. 9.1). This would place the introduction of the Beakers on a markedly rising population curve, although it is apparent that the increased activity (population?) may have already begun during the Grooved Ware period. Moreover, it might be argued that the presumption of a population collapse at ca. 3500 BCE does not provide an obvious fit with the major construction of passage tomb cemeteries such as Newgrange, Knowth, and Carrowkeel between ca. 3400 and 3000 BCE.

The result of this excursus into how well the archaeological evidence provides an explanation for the rapid genomic shift in

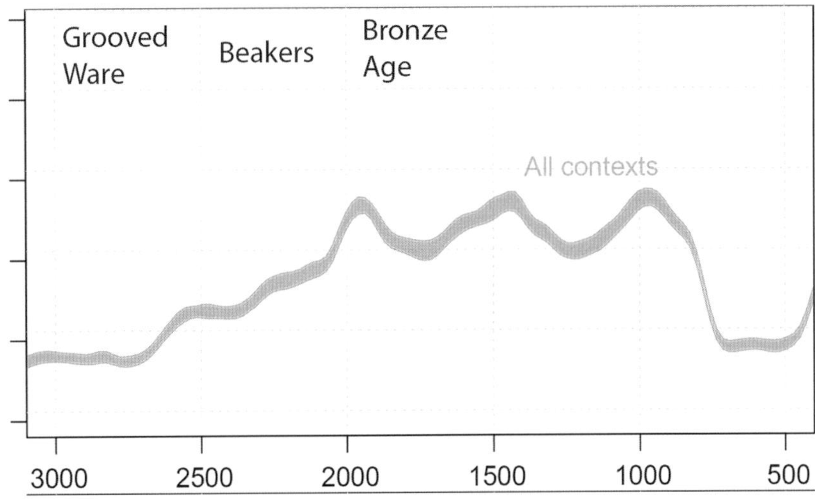

FIG. 9.1. Radiocarbon density (=population size?) indicating population growth from ca. 2700 BCE to end of Bronze Age. Based on McLaughlin 2020: 13, fig. 4.

Ireland has not been very promising. The categories reviewed – military superiority, social organization, religious institutions, and the evidence of palaeo-demography – have not displayed the type of evidence that an archaeologist, totally ignorant of the genetic evidence, would interpret as indicative of a catastrophic (at least for Late Neolithic males) change in population.

9.7 Conclusions

It seems obvious that recent work in aDNA has placed the subject of migrations back on the archaeological agenda and dampened the confidence of at least some archaeologists that they have the tools to discern migrations and their impact in the archaeological record. I would like to conclude by speculating on how we might turn some of these challenges into opportunities.

1. *Identifying migrations*. The genetic signatures associated, for example, with the steppe element in the Corded Ware culture has clearly stimulated reconsiderations of migrations in prehistory. What is needed at the outset is clarity as to what precisely is being envisaged by both geneticists and archaeologists and whether either has the equipment to justify their conclusions. We witness, for example, the dispute as to whether the steppe element in the Corded Ware is the result of a relatively sudden migration of a Yamnaya(-like) population into the earlier territory of Middle Neolithic Central Europeans, who were then to a large extent genetically absorbed by the immigrants, or whether the shift in the genetic signature was the result of the initiation of new marriage networks that, over time, favored the immigrants. Haak (2018: 179–180) provides the geneticists' justification for preferring a migration in his comments on Martin Furholt's paper (2018) by suggesting that a continuous and gradual genomic shift stimulated by new marriage networks would be expected to leave a genetic gradient (which, in the Corded Ware case, is not evident). Also, the mtDNA evidence of an east-west cline for the strength of the signal of Yamnaya-like females (Juras et al. 2018) may be more suggestive of a migration with Yamnaya(-like) males arriving with their families in the east, but gradually marrying local women the further west they advanced from their home base. But it would be all too easy to apply the "makes sense stopping rule," and I would be far more confident in such conclusions if all models were thoroughly tested. Archaeologists have concerned themselves with identifying how they might discern migrations in the archaeological record (e.g., Anthony 1997; Burmeister 2000, etc.), but what is needed is a more detailed explication of how geneticists reach their conclusions. As geneticists can access modern populations that have undergone migrations where we have good historical coverage, they should be able to move the level of discourse from plausible ("makes sense") but untested scenarios to more robust evidence-based predictions.
2. *Genetic processes*. We have seen a variety of models suggested to explain instances of major genomic shift. For example, a population collapse, be it Childe's Late Neolithic Crisis or more recently argued plague-induced depopulation, has been employed to explain the rapid spread of the steppe genetic signature over Central and Western Europe. Geneticists possess an arsenal of techniques for evaluating population sizes (total and effective, the existence of bottlenecks, etc.), and it will be interesting to see how these may eventually bear on some of the demographic models proposed by archaeologists. It should be noted that some of the techniques that have established the evidence for migration, such as SNP capture, may not be the best for resolving many of the demographic issues facing archaeologists, who may require more refined genetic methods, such as haplotype-based affinity or the recovery of rare variants.
3. *Cultural packages*. It is striking that the spread of the Yamnaya culture (outside of the steppe) (Harrison and Heyd 2007), Corded Ware (e.g. Szmyt 1999: 207) and Beakers (Burgess and Shennan 1976) have all been treated as "packages" adopted by local populations. Similarly, in the steppelands, we find taxonomic units greater than the single culture concept. A good example is the Andronovo culture, or more commonly in Russian literature, the "Andronovo archaeological community,"

and there are a considerable number of archaeologists who would view the level of variability in the Yamnaya culture and its successor, the Katakombnaya culture, at a similar taxonomic level. Geneticists may "unpack" some of these abstract concepts and provide archaeologists with the evidence of the mating networks that underlay and supported some of our cultural categories (Anthony and Brown 2017). Indeed, we already have a good start with respect to the recovery of the diverse genetic sources of Scythian populations that appeared to share the same material culture (Damgaard et al. 2018). Although one could easily say in hindsight that the fashion for "packaging" archaeological entities was merely a convenient strategy for archaeologists who were loath to be accused of invoking unfashionable narratives of migration, the archaeological arguments advanced were not without some merit. In short, it would be all too facile to presume that genetics has thoroughly exhausted the arsenal of social mechanisms that archaeologists have applied to explain culture change.

4. *Marriage networks*. The application of whole-genome analysis has opened up an enormous area for aDNA analysis to impact on archaeological interpretation. For example, from the area under discussion, we can begin with the Yamnaya culture and its frequently complex burial system. Often, on the steppe, we encounter a single burial under a kurgan that underwent periodic reuse, through both multiple enlargements of the mound and multiple secondary burials. Moreover, the kurgans themselves may be arranged in patterns. The frequent reuse of an initial Yamnaya burial is not restricted to the Yamnaya period but may run all the way up through the Middle Ages. The natural question – one that geneticists may obviously help to resolve – is to what extent are the patterns of reuse reflective of kinship units, or are they merely the random selection of preexisting burial monuments? We are already seeing studies that both confirm the genetic relationships of groups of individuals within a single burial complex (Corded Ware, Haak et al. 2008; Globular Amphora, Schroeder et al. 2019) or show instances where there is no obvious close genetic relationship (the Carrowkeel passage tomb cemetery, Kador et al. 2018) or relationships of the most incestuous sort (New Grange; Cassidy et al. 2020). While geneticists routinely supply assessments of the close familial relationships of their samples (siblings, mothers, fathers), it may be possible to establish more distant relationships that might bear on increasingly larger social units.
5. *Craniometrics*. While certain regions still place considerable value on the evidence of craniometrics, especially in Eastern Europe, many archaeologists have grown to either dismiss or ignore such evidence. aDNA now provides an excellent technique for testing the reliability of employing craniometrics to evaluate migrations or population admixture. While one might presume that aDNA research will simply obviate the need for employing craniometric data for evaluating migrations, the craniometric data set is so much larger than that of aDNA – which is not always obtainable from skeletal remains anyway – that craniometric data, perhaps calibrated against the evidence of aDNA, may still provide us with useful information (Mallory, Dybo, and Balanovsky 2019). And obviously, aDNA should be able to improve the selection of measurable cranial (or dental) traits that are primarily genetic and the level of precision that such measurements might attain. Or then, it may justify the traditional skepticism of archaeologists and finally settle the matter.

9.7.1 An eilifint sa seomra

Throughout this discussion of archaeology and genetics, there has, of course, been the spectral involvement of linguistics, specifically the problem of who introduced the direct ancestor of the Irish language into Ireland. From an archaeological perspective, the evidence of aDNA would, at least at first glance, appear to support R. A. S. Macalister's (and, in a more restrained echo, Peter Harbison's) conclusion that the arrival of the Beakers "was the only catastrophe of ancient times, subversive enough to have effected such a complete change of language" (Macalister 1949: 87–88). And there is little doubt that the spread of Beaker aDNA does provide a simple and clear model of Irish origins that does not require recourse to more recent and poorly (if at all) evidenced (e.g. Late Bronze Age, Hallstatt, La Tène) migrations or so far undemonstrated major changes in the genomic prehistory of Ireland. We have already seen that the new genetic evidence has been incorporated into narratives of Celtic dispersals, e.g. in the work of Manco (2015: 56–61), who identified the Beaker horizon with the period of Italo-Celtic unity prior to the evolution of Celtic and later Irish. For an archaeologist who has labored for some time on this problem (Mallory 1984, 1991, 2006, 2013a, 2013b, 2016; Mallory and Ó Donnabháin 1998), to query a straightforward Beaker solution to the problem of the origin of the Irish language would seem to be fashioning an unnecessarily heavy stick with which to beat oneself. On the other hand, I am reminded of a quote from the acerbic H. L. Mencken:

> For every complicated problem there is a solution that is simple, direct, understandable, and wrong. (H. L. Mencken)

There are (at least) two areas of concern regarding the acceptance that Irish Beakers equal the direct linguistic ancestor of Primitive or Ogam Irish, the earliest recorded form of Irish, ca. 400 CE. The first concerns the use of aDNA-reinforced archaeology to provide proxy dates for language dispersals. The "simple, direct, understandable" solution sets the split between the ancestor of Irish and the other Celtic languages (whatever cladistic model one embraces) to ca. 2400 BCE, the arrival of the Beakers in Ireland. The reason for skepticism that this is a plausible date is the degree of similarity between the Celtic languages when we first obtain sufficient written records (of course, if you prefer glottochronology, you can pick any date between ca. 3000 and 400 BCE; see Sims-Williams 2021: 518–519). For example, Peter Schrijver has argued that, excepting the treatment of the labiovelar (where $*k^w$ becomes *q* in Irish but *p* in Brittonic), during the first century CE, the ancestors of Irish and Welsh "were not just mutually comprehensible dialects, they were indistinguishable from one another" (Schrijver 2014: 80; see also Sims-Williams 2020: 518). Schrijver goes on to say:

> This is highly relevant to us if we wish to determine when Irish first arrived in Ireland. If Irish had been geographically isolated from British Celtic for any length of time before the first century AD, one would expect to find at least some early differences between them. (Schrijver 2014: 81)

TABLE 9.1. Comparison between words that appear in the earliest Celtic inscriptions (Ogam Irish and Gaulish) and their cognates in Germanic (Old English, Old Norse, Old High German and Gothic).

PROTO-CELTIC	OGAM	GAULISH	PROTO-GERMANIC	OLD ENGLISH	OLD NORSE	OLD HIGH GERMAN	GOTHIC
*dallo-	*dali*	*dallo*	*đwulaz	*dol*	*dul*	*tol*	–
*dubu-aidu-	*dovaidona*	*dovedōn*	*aiđaz	*ád*	–	*eit*	*iit*
*ek^{w}o-	*eqo-*	*epos*	*exwaz	*eoh*	*jór*	–	*aihva*
*genos-	*gena*	*genus*	*kunjan	*cyn*	*kyn*	*kunni*	*kuni*
*glano-	*glannani*	*glanis*	*gelwaz	*ȝeolu*	–	*gelo*	–
*gustu-	*-gusso(s)*	*gussu-*	*kustiz	*cyst*	*kostr*	*kust*	*-kusts*
*katu-	*cattu-*	*catu-*	*xaþuz	*heađu*	*hǫð*	*hadu*	–
*kunos	*cuna-*	*cuno-*	*xunđaz	*hund*	*hundr*	*hunt*	*hunds*
*maglo-	*magli*	*maglus*	*mekilaz	*micel*	*mikill*	*mihhil*	*mikils*
*medu	*meddo*	*medu*	*međuz	*meodu*	*mjǫðr*	*metu*	–
*olyo-	*ol-*	*ollos*	*allaz	*eall*	*allr*	*al*	*alls*
*rīg-	*rigas*	*rix*	*rīkjaz	*rice*	*ríkr*	*rīhhi*	*reikeis*
*rowdo-	*rod*	*roudius*	*rauđaz	*reád*	*rauðr*	*rōt*	*rauþs*
*trexsno-	*trena*	*trennus*	*þrakjaz	*đrece*	*þrekr*	–	–

Schrijver finds any date earlier than ca. 1000 BCE linguistically implausible and prefers a date closer to the first century CE.

One can gain an admittedly impressionistic glimmer of this issue if you compare cognates in the earliest Irish inscriptions (ca. 400–700 CE) and in the earlier Gaulish inscriptions and the logically deeper forms of Proto-Celtic. They are as similar to one another as the earliest attested Germanic languages, whose proto-language is usually dated to ca. 500 BCE (Table 9.1). In short, a Beaker origin for the separation of the Celtic languages suggests at least 2,500 years of language separation, which should have produced far more divergent languages than is evident from the earliest written evidence (Mallory 2013a: 261–262).

In addition, the reconstructed Proto-Celtic cultural vocabulary contains a number of items of material culture that seem either totally incongruent with a Beaker date, e.g., OIr *iarn(n)* < PC **isarno* 'iron,' or are, at least, far more comfortably set to the Irish Later Bronze Age or Iron Age than the Copper Age, e.g. 'fort' (OIr *dún* < PC **dūno-*); 'sword' (OIr *claideb* < PC **kladiwo-*), probably borrowed into Irish from Welsh (Kelly 1971) or the reverse (Matosović 2009, 205); 'sickle' (OIr *serr* < PC **serrā*); 'awl' (MIr *menad* < PC **menādo-*); 'auger' (OIr *tarathar* < PC **taratro-*); 'ring' (OIr *áinne* < PC * *āniyo-*); 'bracelet' (OIr *buinne* < PC **bondyo-*); and 'cauldron' (OIr *coire* < PC **kwaryo-*). To these we may add a rather extensive series of terms for social organization, a semantic field that usually experiences very poor retention over time (Schlerath 1987), e.g. 'king' (OIr *rí* < PC **rig-*); 'queen' (OIr *rígain* < PC **rigani*); 'lord' (OIr *tigern* < PC **tigerno-*), 'chief' (OIr *toísech* < PC **to-wissāko-*); and 'chief' (MIr *fál* < PC **walo-*). At the other end of the social spectrum, we have words for 'servant' (OIr *mug* < PC **mogu-*; OIr *foss* < PC **wasto-*); in addition, both Brittonic and Gaulish share another word for 'servant' (MW *amaeth*, Gaul *ambaktos* < PC **ambaxto-*). To these we might add various military terms for 'warrior' (OIr *caur* < PC **kawaro-*; OIr *cing* < PC **kenget*; OIr *ner* 'boar' < PC **nero* 'hero') and 'warbands' (MIr *cuire* < PC **koryo-*, OIr *slúag* < PC **slowgo-*; OIr *foirenn* < PC **worinā*). To these we could probably also add the word for 'horse' (OIr *ech* < PC **ek^{w}o-*), which does not appear in Ireland much before 1000 BCE.

While one could probably (but also laboriously) dispute every one of these reconstructions – e.g., meteoritic iron, the shift from stone to metal tool types (sickle, auger) and ceramic to metal (cauldron), and the name of a Beaker dagger evolving into a Bronze/Iron Age word for 'sword' – these late words do form a consistent image of what archaeologists either recover from later Bronze Age or Iron Age sites or the social roles we might have expected from the wealth-consuming military elites that we recover in the archaeological record of Late Bronze Age and Iron Age Europe.

The second problem has already been touched upon in the discussion of Beaker society. Unless we embrace the type of cataclysmic genocide suggested by Macalister, we must presume that the ancestor of Irish (and the Brittonic languages) involved some form of language shift. In an attempt to determine the likely type of archaeological evidence that might have indicated possible language shift, the most attractive horizons would seem to fall between ca. 1400 BCE and 100 BCE. The first of these is the horizon of hillforts (Mallory 2013a: 140–156), whose main floruit is ca. 1300 to 900 BCE (O'Brien and O'Driscoll 2017: 38). These would provide central places (O'Brien and O'Driscoll 2017; O'Driscoll 2017) that probably served a variety of functions and, therefore, could be regarded as potential vectors encouraging the rise of societal bilingualism and language shift (Mallory 2016: 402–403). In short, if there were a "hillfort language," it would certainly have made a plausible candidate for the prehistoric ancestor of Primitive Irish.

The second horizon is much smaller and marked by a series of so-called "royal sites" (Navan Fort, Knockaulin, Rathcroghan, Tara; see most recently Fenwick 2018) and other large-scale enclosures, e.g., Lismullin (O'Connell 2013), Co.

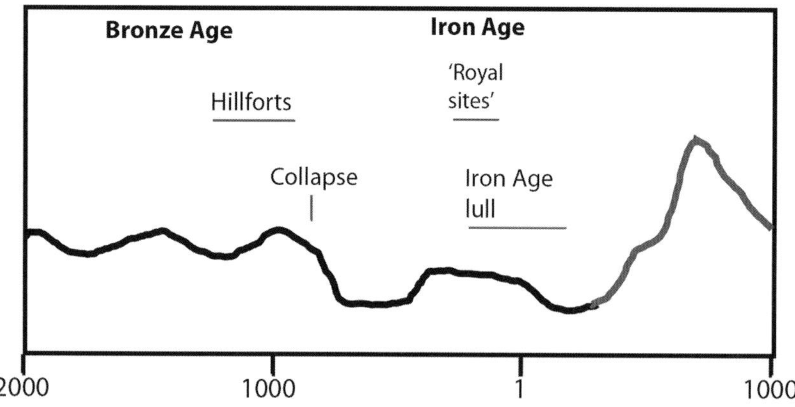

FIG. 9.2. Density of radiocarbon dates from the Bronze Age to the early medieval period indicating population collapse ca. 800 BCE and the "Iron Age lull" of ca. 200 BCE–200 CE.

Meath, dating to the first centuries BC and at a time when we see the marking out of large territories employing major linear earthworks (Ó Drisceoil and Walsh 2021) requiring exceptional appropriation of territorial labor.

In short, there are good reasons – both archaeological and linguistic – to seek the linguistic ancestors of the Irish between ca. 1400 and 100 BCE. From a genetic standpoint, these would not likely be substantively different from the earlier Beaker immigrants, and therefore would most likely bear some (perhaps diminished) evidence of the steppe genetic signature that spread to Atlantic Europe. For this reason, any differences would probably be far more subtle than those that allow us to distinguish between the North and Central European Beakers and the essentially WHG or AF populations that appeared earlier in the Mesolithic and Neolithic of Atlantic Europe. Now, to make matters even more "interesting," we are talking about periods where, if we accept some relationship between the density of radiocarbon dates and population size, we seem to move from a fairly high Late Bronze Age population to a (demographic?) crash ca. 800 BCE (Fig. 9.2), which may have produced a genetic bottleneck followed by a population rise, again ca. 450 BCE, that again descended into a decline (the so-called "Iron Age lull" of ca. 200 BCE–200 CE), and finally saw a remarkable rise through the early medieval period.

Unfortunately, even if there was a subtle change in the Irish genome over this period, it will be exceedingly challenging for us to recover it due to the overwhelming predominance of cremation burial over the relevant period. And even where we do recover samples from the minority of inhumations, there is always the possibility that social selection of burial form may obscure the genomic picture. In this case, we either may have to rely on the abundant evidence for early medieval (Christian) inhumations (Cassidy 2020: 49–50), or hope that Britain, which also adopted a Celtic language at approximately the same time (according to our model) and still maintained inhumation as a major burial strategy, might offer some evidence for immigration in the later prehistoric period.

The results of a more focused aDNA examination of the period between the Middle Bronze Age and the early medieval period should lead to one of two results. It may reveal that Macalister, Harbison, and others were absolutely correct in their evaluation of the Beakers as the last major prehistoric immigration in Ireland. If so, many linguists will be forced to reconsider a model of Irish origins that they had presumed was linguistically implausible. Or, the results may indicate that there was a potentially more recent source for the Irish language in the later Bronze Age or Iron Age, which would force them to consider the mechanics and evidence of how one Indo-European (Later Bronze Age or Iron Age Celtic) language so thoroughly replaced a presumably earlier Indo-European Beaker language in Ireland.

In short, it seems that the geneticists have gifted not only archaeologists, but also linguists with the opportunity of living in "interesting times."

References

Allentoft M. E., et al. 2015. Population genomics of Bronze Age Eurasia. *Nature* 522(7555): 167–172.

Anthony, David W. 1997. Prehistoric migration as social process. In: John Chapman and Helena Hamerow (ed.), *Migrations and invasions in archaeological explanation* (British Archaeological Reports International Series 664) 21–32. Oxford: Archeopress.

2007. *The horse, the wheel, and language: How Bronze Age riders from the Eurasian steppes shaped the modern world.* Princeton: Princeton University Press.

Anthony, David W., and Dorcas R. Brown. 2017. Molecular archaeology and Indo-European linguistics: Impressions from new data. In: Bjarne Simmelkjaer Sandgaard Hansen et al. (ed.), *Usque ad radices: Indo-European studies in honour of Birgit Anette Olsen*, 25–54. Copenhagen: Museum Tusculanum Press.

Balanovsky, Oleg. 2019. Comments on the Caucasian Substrate hypothesis. *Journal of Indo-European Studies* 47: 166–174.

Balanovsky, Oleg, et al. 2017. Genetic differentiation between upland and lowland populations shapes the Y-chromosomal landscape of West Asia. *Human Genetics* 136: 437–450.

Beddoe, John. 1885. *The races of Britain.* Bristol: Arrowsmith.

Bendrey, Robin, et al. 2013. The origins of domestic horses in North-west Europe: New direct dates on the horses of Newgrange, Ireland. *Proceedings of the Prehistoric Society* 79: 91–103.

Brandt, G., et al. 2013. Ancient DNA reveals key stages in the formation of central European mitochondrial genetic diversity. *Science* 342: 257–261.

Brodie, N. 1994. *The Neolithic-Bronze Age transition in Britain* (British Archaeological Reports 238). Oxford: BAR.

Brothwell, D. 1985. Variation in early Irish populations: A brief survey. *Ulster Journal of Archaeology* 48: 5–9.

Buchvaldek, Miroslav. 1980. Corded Pottery complex in Central Europe. *Journal of Indo-European Studies* 8: 393–406.

Burgess, C. B. and S. Shennan. 1976. The beaker phenomenon: Some suggestions. In: C. B. Burgess and R. Miket (ed.), *Settlement and economy in the third and second millennia B. C.* (British Archaeological Reports 33), 309–326. Oxford: BAR.

Burmeister, Stefan. 2000. Archaeology and migration: Approaches to an archaeological proof of migration. *Current Anthropology* 41: 539–567.

2016. Archaeological research on migration as a multidisciplinary challenge. *Medieval Worlds* 4: 42–64.

Callaway, Ewen. 2018. Divided by DNA: The uneasy relationship between archaeology and ancient genomics. *Nature* 555: 573–576.

Carlin, Neil. 2018. *The Beaker phenomenon? Understanding the character and context of social practices in Ireland 2500–2000 BC*. Leiden: Sidestone Press.

Carlin, Neil and Gabriel Cooney. 2017. Transforming our understanding of Neolithic and Chalcolithic society (4000–2200 BC) in Ireland. In: Michael Stanley, Rónán Swan, and Aidan O'Sullivan (ed.), *Stories of Ireland's past* (TII Heritage 5), 23–56. Dublin: Transport Infrastructure Ireland.

Cassidy, Lara M. 2020. Sizing it up: A commentary on "An archaeology of Ireland for the information age." *Emania* 25: 45–52.

Cassidy, Lara et al. 2016. Neolithic and Bronze Age migration to Ireland and the establishment of the insular Atlantic genome. *Proceedings of the National Academy of Sciences* 113(2): 368–373.

Cassidy, Lara et al. 2020. A dynastic elite in monumental Neolithic society. *Nature* 582: 384–388.

Cavalli-Sforza, L. L., P. Menozzi, and A. Piazza. 1994. *The history and geography of human genes*. Princeton: Princeton University Press.

Childe, V. Gordon. 1926. *The Aryans*. London: Keagan Paul.

Coles, J. M. and A. F. Harding. 1979. *The Bronze Age in Europe*. New York: St Martin's Press.

Conway, R. S. 1900. The riddle of the nations. *Current Review* 77: 74–81.

Damgaard, P., et al. 2018. 137 ancient human genomes from across the Eurasian steppes. *Nature* 557: 369–374.

Ecsedy, István. 1979. *The people of the Pit-Grave kurgans in eastern Hungary*. Budapest: Akadémiai Kiadó.

Fernandes, D. M., et al. 2018. A genomic Neolithic time transect of hunter-farmer admixture in central Poland. *Science Reports* 8: 14879.

Furholt, Martin. 2018. Massive migrations? The impact of recent aDNA studies on our view of Third Millennium Europe. *European Journal of Archaeology* 21: 159–191.

2019. Re-integrating archaeology: A contribution to aDNA studies and the migration discourse on the 3rd millennium BC in Europe. *Proceedings of the Prehistoric Society* 85: 115–129.

Gallay, Alain. 2001. L'énigme campaniforme. In: F. Nicholis (ed.), *Bell Beakers today: Pottery, people, culture, symbols in prehistoric Europe*, vol. 1, 41–57. Trento: Servizio Beni Culturali.

Gimbutas, Marija. 1952. On the origin of North Indo-Europeans. *American Anthropologist* 54: 602–611.

1963. The Indo-Europeans: Archaeological problems. *American Anthropologist* 65: 815–836.

1977. The 1st wave of Eurasian steppe pastoralists into Copper Age Europe. *Journal of Indo-European Studies* 5: 277–338.

1980. The Kurgan wave #2 (*c.* 3400–3200 B.C.) into Europe and the following transformation of culture. *Journal of Indo-European Studies* 8: 273–315.

1991. *The civilization of the goddess*. San Francisco: Harper.

1994. *Das Ende Alteuropas: Der Einfall von Steppennomaden aus Südrussland und die Indogermanisierung Mitteleuropas*. Budapest: Archaeolingua Alapítvány.

Grattan, John. 1853. On the importance, to the archaeologist and ethnologist, of an accurate mode of measuring human crania, and of recording the results; with a description of a new craniometer. *Ulster Journal of Archaeology* 1: 198–208.

Günther, Torsten, and Mattias Jakobsson. 2016. Genes mirror migrations and cultures in prehistoric Europe: A population genomic perspective. *Science Direct* 41: 115–123.

Haak, Wolfgang. 2018. Comments on Furholt's *Massive migrations? European Journal of Archaeology* 21: 178–181.

Haak, Wolfgang et al. 2008. Ancient DNA, strontium isotopes, and osteological analyses shed light on social and kinship organization of the Later Stone Age. *PNAS* 105: 47.

Haak, Wolfgang et al. 2015. Massive migration from the steppe was a source for Indo-European languages in Europe. *Nature* 522: 207–211.

Harbison, Peter. 1975. The coming of the Indo-Europeans to Ireland: An archaeological assessment. *Journal of Indo-European Studies* 3: 101–119.

Harrison, Richard J. 1980. *The Beaker folk: Copper Age archaeology in Western Europe*. London: Thames and Hudson.

Harrison, Richard, and Volker Heyd. 2007. The transformation of Europe in the third millennium BC: The example of "Le Petit-Chasseur I + II" (Sion, Valais, Switzerland). *Prähistorische Zeitschrift* 82: 129–214.

Hartwell, B. N. 2002. A Neolithic ceremonial timber complex at Ballynahatty, Co. Down. *Antiquity* 76: 526–532.

Häusler, Alexander. 1992. Zum Verhältnis von Ockergrabkultur und Schnurkeramik. *Praehistorica* 19: 341–348.

Hawkes, Christopher, and Jacquetta Hawkes. 1947. *Prehistoric Britain*. London: Chatto and Windus.

Hay, Maciamo. 2016. Genetic history of the British and the Irish. *Eupedia*. Updated October 2016. https://www.eupedia.com/genetics/britain_ireland_dna.shtml.

2017. Haplogroup R1b (Y-DNA). *Eupedia*. https://www.eupedia.com/europe/Haplogroup_R1b_Y-DNA.shtml.

Heath, Julian. 2009. *Warfare in prehistoric Britain*. Amberly: Stroud.

Herity, Michael, and George Eogan. 1977. *Ireland in prehistory*. London: Routledge and Kegan Paul.

Heyd, Volker. 2017. Kossinna's smile. *Antiquity* 91: 348–359.

Hooton, E. A., and C. W. Dupertius. 1955. *The physical anthropology of Ireland*. Cambridge (MA): Peabody Museum of Archaeology and Ethnology, Harvard University.

Howells, W. W. 1972. Analyses of patterns of variation in crania of recent man. In: Russel Tuttle (ed.), *The functional and evolutionary biology of primates*, 123–151. Chicago and New York: Routledge.

Ivanova, S. V., A. G. Nikitin, and D. V. Kiosak. 2018. Mayatnikovye migratsii v tsirkum-pontiyskoy stepi i tsentral'-noy Evrope v epokhu palaeometalla i problems genezisa yamnoy kul'tury. *Arkheolohiya i davnya istoriya Ukraïny* 1: 101–146.

Iversen, Rune. 2019. On the emergence of the Corded Ware societies in Northern Europe: Reconsidering the migration hypothesis. In: Birgit Olsen, Thomas Olander, and Kristian Kristiansen (ed.), *Tracing the Indo-Europeans*, 73–96. Oxford: Oxbow.

Juras, Anna, et al. 2018. Mitochondrial genomes reveal an east to west cline of steppe ancestry in Corded Ware populations. *Nature* 8: 11603.

Kador, T. L., et al. 2018. Rites of passage: Mortuary practice, population dynamics, and chronology at the Carrowkeel passage tomb complex, Co. Sligo, Ireland. *Proceedings of the Prehistoric Society* 84: 225–255.

Kelly, Fergus. 1971. OI *claideb* and its cognates. *Ériu* 22: 192–196.

Kilian, Lothar. 2000. *De l'origine des Indo-Européens*. Paris: Labyrinthe. Translated by Felicitas Schuler. First published 1983 as *Zum Ursprung der Indo-Germanen*.

Klejn, Leo S., et al. 2018a. Discussion: Are the origins of Indo-European languages explained by the migration of the Yamnaya culture to the West? *European Journal of Archaeology* 21: 1, 3–17.

2018b. The steppe hypothesis of Indo-European origins remains to be proven. *Acta Archaeologia* 88: 193–204.

Knipper, C., A. Mittnik, et al. 2017. Female exogamy and gene pool diversification at the transition from the Final Neolithic to the Early Bronze Age in Central Europe. *PNAS* 114(38), 10083–10088.

Kristiansen, Kristian, et al. 2017. Re-theorising mobility and the formation of culture and language among the Corded Ware culture in Europe. *Antiquity* 91: 334–347.

Lee, E. J. *et al.* 2012. Emerging genetic patterns of the European Neolithic: Perspectives from a late neolithic Bell Beaker site in Germany. *American Journal of Physical Anthropology* 148: 4, 571–579.

Lemercier, Olivier. 2011. Le guerrier dans l'Europe du 3e millénaire avant notre ère. In: Luc Baray et al. (ed.), *L'armement et l'image du guerrier dans les sociétés anciennes: de l'object à la tombe*, 121–151. Dijon: Éditions Universitaires de Dijion.

LGE = *Lebor Gabála Érenn*

Macalister, R. A. Stewart. 1940. *Lebor Gabála Érenn, part III.* Dublin: Irish Texts Society.

Lipson, M., et al. 2017. Parallel paleogenomic transects reveal complex genetic history of early European farmers. *Nature* 551: 368–372.

Macalister, R. A. S. 1928. *The archaeology of Ireland*. London: Methuen.

1949. *The archaeology of Ireland*. 2nd and rev. ed. London: Methuen.

Mallory, J. P. 1984. The origins of the Irish. *Journal of Irish Archaeology* 2: 65–69.

1989. *In search of the Indo-Europeans*. London: Thames and Hudson.

1991. Two perspectives on Irish origins. *Emania* 9: 53–58.

2006. Irish origins: The archaeological, linguistic and genetic evidence. In: B. S. Turner (ed.), *Migration and Myth: Ulster's Revolving Door*, 97–111. Downpatrick: Ulster Local History Trust.

2013a. *The origins of the Irish*. Thames and Hudson: London.

2013b. The Indo-Europeanization of Atlantic Europe. In: John T. Koch and B. Cunliffe (ed.), *Celtic from the west 2: Rethinking the Bronze Age and the arrival of Indo-European in Atlantic Europe*, 17–39. Oxford and Oakville: Oxbow.

2016. Archaeology and language shift in Atlantic Europe. In: John T. Koch and Barry Cunliffe (ed.), *Celtic from the west 3*, 387–406. Oxford: Oxbow.

(In press.) The evolution of the steppe model of Indo-European origins. *From Palaeolithic to Cossack Ukraine: Telehin Centenary Conference*. Kiev: Institute of Archaeology.

Mallory, J. P. and Barra Ó Donnabháin. 1998. The origins of the population of Ireland: A survey of putative immigrations in Irish prehistory and history. *Emania* 17: 47–81.

Mallory, J. P. et al. 2019. The impact of genetics research on archaeology and linguistics in Eurasia. *Russian Journal of Genetics* 12: 1472–1487.

Manco, Jean. 2013. *Ancestral journeys: The peopling of Europe from the first venturers to the Vikings*. London: Thames and Hudson.

2015. *Blood of the Celts*. London: Thames and Hudson.

Martin, C. A. 1935. *Prehistoric man in Ireland*. London: Macmillan.

Matasović, Ranko. 2009. *Etymological dictionary of Proto-Celtic*. Leiden and Boston: Brill.

McLaughlin, T. Rowan. 2019. On applications of space-time modeling with open-source 14C age calibration. *Journal of Archaeological Method and Theory* 26(2): 479–501.

McSparron, Cormac. 2018. *Statistical analysis of the Single Burial tradition in Early Bronze Age Ireland and some implications for social structure*. PhD diss., Queen's University Belfast.

2020. An archaeology of Ireland for the information age. *Emania* 25: 7–29.

Menk, Roland. 1980. A synopsis of the physical anthropology of the Corded Ware complex on the background of the expansion of the Kurgan Culture. *Journal of Indo-European Studies* 8: 361–392.

Moffat, Alistair. 2009. *Before Scotland: The story of Scotland before history*. London: Thames and Hudson.

Molloy, Barry P. C. 2017. Hunting warriors: The transformation of weapons, combat practices and society during the Bronze Age in Ireland. *European Journal of Archaeology* 20: 280–316.

Neustupný, Evžen. 2013. The Corded Ware culture. In: Evžen Neustupný et al. (ed.), *The prehistory of Bohemia 3: The Eneolithic*, 130–154. Prague: Archeologický ústav AV ČR.

O'Brien, William. 2015. *Prehistoric copper mining in Europe*, 5500–500 BC. Oxford: Oxford University Press.

O'Brien, William and James O' Driscoll. 2017. *Hillforts, warfare and society in Bronze Age Ireland*. Oxford: Archaeopress.

O'Connell, Aidan. 2013. Harvesting the stars: A pagan temple at Lismullin, Co. Meath. Dublin: National Roads Authority.

Ó Drisceoil, Cóilín, and Aidan Walsh. 2021. *Materialising power: The archaeology of the Black Pig's Dyke, Co. Monaghan*. Dublin: Wordwell.

O'Driscoll, James. 2017. Hillforts in prehistoric Ireland: A costly display of power? *World Archaeology* 49: 506–525.

Olalde, Iñigo, et al. 2018. The Beaker phenomenon and the genomic transformation of Northwest Europe. *Nature* 555: 190–196.

Oppenheimer, Stephen. 2007. *The origins of the British*. London: Robinson.

O'Rahilly, Thomas. 1946. *Early Irish history and mythology*. Dublin: Institute for Advanced Studies.

Peaker, Harold and Herbert John Fleure. 1928. *The steppe and the sown*. Oxford: Clarendon Press.

Poisson, Georges. 1934. *Les Aryens: Étude linguistique, ethnologique et préhistorique*. Paris: Payot.

Rascovan, N. et al. 2019. Emergence and spread of basal lineages of *Yersina pestis* during the Neolithic decline. *Cell* 176: 295–305.

Renfrew, Colin 1987. *Archaeology and language: The puzzle of Indo-European origins*. London: Jonathan Cape.

Schlerath, Bernfried. 1987. Können wir die urindogermanische Sozialstruktur rekonstruieren? In: Wolfgang Meid (ed.), *Studien zur indogermanische Wortschatz*, 249–264. Innsbruck: Institut für Sprachwissenschaft der Universität.

Schrader, Otto. 1907. *Sprachvergleichung und Urgeschichte*, 3rd ed. Jena: Hermann Costenoble.

Schrijver, Peter. 2014. *Language contact and the origin of the Germanic languages*. Oxford: Routledge.

Schroeder, H., et al. 2019. Unraveling ancestry, kinship, and violence in a Late Neolithic mass grave. *PNAS* 116: 22, 10705–10710.

Schwidetzky, Ilse. 1980. The influence of the Steppe People based on the physical anthropological data in special consideration to the Corded-Battle Axe culture. *Journal of Indo-European Studies* 8: 345–360.

Sheridan, A. 2004. Going around in circles? Understanding the Irish Grooved Ware "complex" in its wider context. In: H. Roche et al. (ed.), *From megalith to metals: Essays in honour of George Eogan*, 26–37. Oxford: Oxbow.

Sims-Williams, Patrick. 2020. An alternative to "Celtic from the east" and "Celtic from the west." *Cambridge Archaeological Journal* 30: 511–529.

Sulimirski, Tadeusz. 1933. Die schnurkeramischen Kulturen und das indoeuropäische Problem. *La Pologne au VIIe Congrès International des Sciences Historiques*, vol. 1, 287–308. Warsaw: Société Polonaise d'histoire.

Szmyt, Marzena. 1999. *Between West and East: People of the Globular Amphora culture in Eastern Europe: 2950–2350 BC* (Baltic-Pontic Studies 8). Poznań: Adam Mickiewicz University.

Tassi, F. et al. 2017. Genome diversity in the Neolithic Globular Amphorae culture and the spread of Indo-European languages. *Proceedings of the Royal Society B* 284: 20171540.

Taylor, Griffith. 1921. The evolution and distribution of race, culture, and language. *Geographical Review* 11: 54–119.

Telegin, D. Ya. 2005. The Yamna Culture and the Indo-European homeland problem. *Journal of Indo-European Studies* 33: 339–357.

Van Wijngaarden-Bakker, L. H. 1986. The animal remains from the Beaker settlement at Newgrange, Co. Meath: Final report. *Proceedings of the Royal Irish Academy* 86C: 17–111.

Waddell, J. 1998. *The prehistoric archaeology of Ireland*. Galway: Galway University Press.

Wells, R. Spencer, et al. 2001. The Eurasian heartland: A continental perspective on Y-chromosome diversity. *PNAS* 98(18): 10244–10249.

Wilkin, Neil C. A. 2013. *Food Vessel pottery from Early Bronze Age funerary contexts in northern England: A typological and contextual study*. PhD diss., University of Birmingham.

Woodman, Peter, Finlay, Nyree, and Anderson, Elizabeth. 2006. *The archaeology of a collection: The Keiller-Knowles collection of the National Museum of Ireland*. Wordwell: Bray.

10 BEAKER CULTURE METAL AND MOBILITY IN ATLANTIC EUROPE: SOME IMPLICATIONS FOR GENETIC AND LANGUAGE ORIGINS

WILLIAM O'BRIEN

The importance of metal for an understanding of the international Beaker culture is well established, whether as a driver of trade connections and other forms of exchange, or as a material expression of ethnicity, ideology, or social relations. While copper and gold were used in earlier times in Europe, Beaker groups can be associated with a spread of metallurgical knowledge across the Atlantic zone during the later third millennium BC. This chapter will consider long-distance networks of metal production and supply in relation to the mobility of the Beaker culture. The nature of those connections will be explored, whether they involved migration of ethnic groups or the small-scale movement of specialists, their ideas and material culture, through trade and other forms of exchange. The implications for genetic and language origins will be considered, with a focus on connections between Iberia, France, and Ireland in that period.

10.1 The Atlantic Seaways

There is a long tradition of research into the importance of early maritime connections across the different regions of Atlantic Europe. Such ideas have been brought together in a seminal work by Barry Cunliffe (2001), which examines how the peoples of the Atlantic lands have shared a maritime identity over the past ten thousand years. Ireland is an obvious example, where seaborne contacts lie at the center of origin legends recounted in the eleventh-century *Lebor Gábála Erenn* ('Book of Invasions of Ireland'), the ninth-century *Historia Brittonum*, and earlier works. The medieval sources record a succession of foreign invasions that originated in Spain, from where the name of Ireland supposedly derived. The last and most significant of those settlements was the arrival of the Gael, the Sons of Míl, who it is said introduced the earliest form of the Irish language.

That pseudohistory has been deconstructed by scholars in the modern era, who attribute such legends to sources used by medieval monks to establish a Biblical pedigree for the ancient Irish. As one authority puts it, the idea of Spanish origins was "the fruit of a medieval imagination rather than a dim recollection of a prehistoric past" (Carey 2001, 2005; see also Ní Lionaín 2012). While this is a literary invention, there can be no doubt that seaborne connections were significant for this island at different times in prehistory. That subject has been explored many times in search of archaeological connections across the Atlantic seaways (e.g. Forde 1930; MacWhite 1951; Bowen 1972; Waddell 1992; Almagro-Gorbea 1995; Gibson 2013). In some cases, there is evidence of direct links over long distances, though it is more usual to find commonalities in styles of material culture, art, and monuments that speak to patterns of indirect contact involving intermediary regions. An example of this fusion of "similar but different" in exchange networks is a recent study of Beaker culture gold in Atlantic Europe (FitzPatrick et al. 2016).

There have also been attempts to trace Atlantic connections through the physical ancestry of the Irish, using skeletal, blood, and genetic markers. The notion of "Atlantean peoples" dates back to Beddoe's (1885) assertion of an Irish racial type of Spanish origin (see Quinn 2005 for controversial views on early Irish connections with Iberia and North Africa). While such ideas of racial origins are now rejected, scientific analysis of modern Irish and British populations points to a significant gene flow into both islands in prehistory (see Oppenheimer 2007; Mallory 2013). Those studies indicate the earliest settlement of Ireland was part of a wider move of human groups into northwest Europe, coming from glacial refugia in southern France and northern Spain at the end of the Ice Age.

Atlantic seaway connections are also relevant to gene flows at the beginning of the Neolithic in Ireland. While modern Irish populations have a small percentage of Middle Eastern genetic ancestry (Chapter 9), archaeological evidence points strongly to an immigrant population bringing agriculture to Ireland. The most likely origin is southern Britain, based on similarities in the type of houses, material culture, and technology of the Early Neolithic on both islands. Recent studies indicate the genetic background of the first farmers in Britain is connected with the spread of agriculture across the Mediterranean from the Middle East (Brace et al. 2019). A similar genetic signature is likely for the onward spread of agriculture to Ireland ca. 3800 to 3700 BC, particularly as the indigenous Mesolithic contribution to the establishment of farming here seems minimal. This is supported by the (admittedly) few aDNA analyses of

Neolithic burials in Ireland, starting with the Ballynahatty woman (3343–3020 BC), who had a genome of predominantly Near Eastern origin (Cassidy et al. 2016).

The contrast between the genetic profile of Irish farmers of the fourth millennium BC and Irish populations today may be explained by large-scale replacement with Yamnaya steppe ancestry at the beginning of the Bronze Age. The results from aDNA analysis of three Early Bronze Age burials from Rathlin Island, Co. Antrim, point in this direction (Cassidy et al. 2016). While more data is required, it does seem likely Ireland was caught up in the same genomic transformation that occurred across western Europe around 2000 BC (Olalde et al. 2018). Whether that was connected with migrations of Beaker people to Britain and Ireland in the later third millennium BC, or to a process of genetic drift through prolonged cultural exchange with the continent, remains to be resolved (Armit and Reisch 2021).

These maritime connections also have important implications for language transmission. This is highlighted by the Celts from the West project, which explored the possibility the Celtic family of languages originated in Atlantic Europe, from where they spread to the north Alpine region during the late Chalcolithic or Bronze Age (Koch and Cunliffe 2010; 2013; 2016). This is a challenge to the long-accepted view that those languages evolved in Hallstatt and La Tène culture networks in central Europe during the Iron Age, from where they spread west through the migration of Celtic peoples to eventually reach Britain and Ireland. The deeper origins of Celtic as an Indo-European language are controversial, with debate centered on two major "homeland" models. The first is that Indo-European originated in Anatolia, from where it dispersed into Europe with the Neolithic farming package, reaching Iberia in the fifth millennium BC through Cardial culture connections across the Mediterranean (Renfrew 1987; 2013). The second, and much older, interpretation is that Indo-European originated in the south Russian steppes, from where it spread into northern Europe, connected with the mobility of Beaker or Bronze Age cultures (see Mallory 1989 and this volume, Chapter 9).

Both models have major implications for gene flow into Atlantic Europe in prehistory. What precisely Pontic steppe or Anatolian genetic ancestry means for language, culture, and identity during later periods in the Atlantic zone is unclear. Various models of language displacement have been advanced, from large-scale migration, systems collapse, and elite dominance to a population movement connected with technological innovations such as farming or metallurgy (Renfrew 1987). The spread of a Celtic language to the islands of Britain and Ireland was probably different from what occurred in mainland Europe, with little evidence of mass migration ("coming of the Celts") and other types of contact-induced change. Taking Ireland as an example, models of elite dominance, initially Hallstatt and La Tène arrivals (Raftery 1994), and more recently Late Bronze Age hillfort builders (Mallory 2013: 286), have been questioned (O'Brien 2016; see also Mallory 2016: 389), and are unlikely on their own to explain language transmission.

Other possibilities in terms of language shift include a *lingua franca* connected with trade networks across Atlantic Europe (Waddell and Conroy 1999). Mallory (2016: 391–392) has questioned whether that on its own was enough to displace a language in Britain or Ireland, and also whether early forms of Celtic have linguistic elements consistent with such origins. Trade aside, there has also been much discussion on the role that major technological innovations such as farming or metallurgy played in the spread of Indo-European languages across Europe. This paper will examine some of those questions by considering the significance of mining networks and metal exchange for language transmission in Atlantic Europe during the later third millennium BC. Understanding the origins and spread of metallurgical knowledge provides an archaeological context for exploring these wider issues of language as well as genetics.

10.2 Metal as Knowledge

> Language is a vehicle for the expression or exchange of thoughts, concepts, knowledge, and information as well as the fixing and transmission of experience and knowledge (Bussmann 1996).

The communication of technological knowledge was fundamental to the successful initiation of copper metallurgy in Neolithic societies. This was often preceded by some exposure to copper objects from external metal-using cultures, which in turn stimulated interest in the new technology. Where local geology was favourable, that curiosity might lead to the discovery of copper minerals, with experimentation and incipient metallurgy informed by external knowledge obtained through trade or other contacts. Occasionally, fully or partly developed technological processes were transmitted directly from one cultural group to another, in exchanges of mutual benefit connected with the circulation of the ensuing metal. This may have required the participation of outside specialists with the requisite knowledge: Childe's vision of prospectors voyaging in search of metal sources or traveling smiths plying their trade. Such specialists may have cooperated with native populations who controlled access to sources of metal, supplying the requisite knowledge of metal prospecting, production, and fabrication. That could have involved full-fledged mining expeditions in core/periphery relations, coercive or otherwise. In other instances, a mutually beneficial arrangement may have been agreed on with indigenous groups who adopted the new technology with this outside assistance.

These contact scenarios have important implications for language and communication between early metal-using cultures in Europe. While often presented in opposition, external influences and local initiative may have combined in the inception of metal use and metallurgy, as part of a complex web of cultural and economic exchange. A free flow of information should not be envisaged, as knowledge of the new technology was carefully controlled by early metal-producing cultures. This is one reason why metallurgy spread slowly across the continent, from early origins in the Balkans during the sixth millennium BC to its introduction to Ireland and Britain in the mid-third millennium BC. A restricted access to this knowledge, together with geological factors limiting the supply of copper resources that could be exploited with available technology, explains the slow advance of copper metallurgy when compared to the circulation of finished objects. These constraints created a basis for monopoly-type production, evident in the emergence of large mining centers that dominated copper supply over long periods. That stated, the stylistic similarity of early metal artifacts across Europe indicates such developments did not occur in isolation. The circulation of copper and gold objects eventually led to a wider dissemination of technological information. For Britain and Ireland, this occurred through participation in the Beaker exchange network, which played a central role in the diffusion of metallurgical knowledge in Atlantic Europe.

10.3 Beakers in Britain and Ireland

The production and exchange of metal (copper and gold, and the earliest bronze) was an important element of the Beaker culture, one of several factors that explain its wide connectivity in the Atlantic zone during the third millennium BC. Insight into those exchange networks continues to be hampered by uncertainty around the cultural significance of this material (pots or people?) and its transregional variability. The history of Beaker research began with an emphasis on race and ethnicity, with models of migration and trade central to culture-historical interpretations in the twentieth century. This was replaced in modern times by more socially informed interpretations that emphasize ideological aspects of Beaker culture in different contexts. The wheel has turned in recent years as scientific studies (aDNA and stable isotopes) place renewed emphasis on mobility.

The earliest use of metal in Britain and Ireland probably occurred during the twenty-fifth century BC, closely connected with the arrival of Beaker culture from the European mainland. The two islands differ significantly in their response to that external influence. For Britain, early studies of the funerary record and its pottery, from Abercromby (1912) to Clarke (1970), proposed migrations of "Beaker Folk" from the European mainland. Though unfashionable for many years, this perspective has been reinvigorated by a number of high-profile scientific studies. These include isotope analysis of the Amesbury Archer burial from near Stonehenge. The discovery that this man had spent much of his youth in mainland Europe created a new appreciation of the mobility of the Beaker culture (FitzPatrick 2009). This is supported by recent aDNA studies, the most important being that of the Harvard team who demonstrated that the Beaker culture introduced high levels of steppe-related ancestry to Britain, leading to the replacement of approximately 90% of Britain's gene pool within a few hundred years (Olalde et al. 2018, fig. 3; see also Parker Pearson et al. 2019). While perhaps controversial, this genetic data does resonate with archaeological evidence of funerary traditions, technology, and material culture introduced to Britain in the same period from mainland Europe.

Though there are common elements, Beaker material culture in Ireland has important differences from that in Britain. The Irish record includes a range of ceramic styles (Case 1995; Brindley 2004; Grogan and Roche 2010, fig. 7), as well as items of archery equipment, dress ornament, and copper and gold metalwork that are part of the so-called Beaker set or "international assemblage" (FitzPatrick 2013). The pottery has an early Atlantic component, resulting from contacts with early Beaker groups in western France and possibly Iberia. These may have been particularly significant during the earliest phase of Beaker contacts. That is overtaken by a stronger influence from Britain, ultimately connected with Beaker cultures in northern Europe. As elsewhere, distinctive local characteristics developed in Irish Beaker pottery (Case 1995: 20), the use of which was relatively short-lived before it was replaced by food vessel ceramics ca. 2100 BC.

Irish beakers are typically found in settlement sites and in older monument types, such as megalithic tombs, in what is generally characterized as an Atlantic tradition of deposition extending from Iberia to northern France. British beakers, on the other hand, fall into a north-central European pattern of deposition, with an emphasis on funerary display in single grave contexts. While this distinction was eventually blurred through close contacts between Beaker groups in Britain and Ireland, created in part by a flow of metal between both islands and the existence of an important "fusion zone" in northern France (Needham 2005, fig. 3), it derives ultimately from different origins and ethnic contexts for the use of this material culture. Colin Burgess was one of the first to argue that the Irish tradition had dual origins, beginning with an early Atlantic influence followed by an assimilation of Beaker elements from Britain. He concluded that a good case can be made for an initial Atlantic source for Irish metallurgy, which was later modified by northwest European influences transmitted via Britain (Burgess 1980: 65).

While the British record indicates a major cultural intrusion, almost certainly involving migrant populations, the evidence from Ireland points to more selective assimilation of Beaker influences leading to the acculturation of indigenous Neolithic societies. Beaker pottery in Ireland is commonly found in sites with an older Neolithic association, such as the Boyne Valley passage tomb cemetery or the Lough Gur settlement landscape (see Waddell 2010). Though not overlapping to any extent, Beaker pottery is found with Late Neolithic Grooved Ware at several sites, including a number of henges. This, together with similar patterns of deposition in other contexts, emphasizes a continuity of indigenous settlement during the third millennium BC (Carlin and Brück 2012; Carlin 2018). There are also important elements of change, such as the Beaker association with the first use of metal, and a new monument type, the wedge tomb.

The assimilation of Beaker culture influences into indigenous Late Neolithic societies, through trade and other external contacts, does not rule out the arrival of small groups of specialists from the European mainland into different parts of Ireland. It is difficult to assess the absorption of those external influences using genetic information, as there is presently only limited aDNA data from Ireland. The results of the aforementioned Rathlin Island study (Cassidy et al. 2016) provide some evidence of new arrivals at the beginning of the Bronze Age, but this needs to be assessed further. The availability of human bone samples for aDNA analysis is a challenge, in a part of Europe where Neolithic funerary practice was dominated by cremation and where unburnt Beaker-associated burials are relatively few.

Whether future genetic studies will confirm Beaker migration to Ireland on a significant scale, comparable to the proposed displacement of native Neolithic populations in Britain, remains to be established. Elsewhere, I have argued that external Beaker influences had a transformative effect during a short-lived Chalcolithic, ca. 2450 to 2100 BC (O'Brien 2012). It is likely those interactions with Britain and mainland Europe did not involve a significant movement of population to Ireland, but rather small-scale movements of metalworkers, traders, and other specialists. The ability of genetic and isotope studies to detect movements on that scale is a challenge for future scientific research.

10.4 Beaker Networks and the Transmission of Metallurgical Knowledge

The demand for metal continues to be relevant, though perhaps not central, to different interpretations of the international Beaker culture, in both its ideological aspects and as an important driver of mobility during the later third millennium BC. The spread of metallurgical knowledge across northwest Europe at that time was closely connected with those exchange networks. In a period before metal was commodified as an essential raw material, demand for copper was driven in part by the emergence of elites interested in prestige goods as signifiers of rank and power. Some of those individuals were able to exploit a desire for new material innovations through control of production and exchange networks. At a time of intensive lithic production across western Europe, the knowledge of metallurgy did not spread because of a shortage of efficient work tools. This occurred because new social conditions made the exchange of metal desirable in terms of elite aggrandizement, a desire that quickly became a new type of economic power. The exchange of high-quality objects, be it pottery, lithics, copper, or gold, eventually led to a flow of technological information as to their manufacture. As Burgess (1980: 63) has observed, Beaker pots represent a high level of ceramic technology and the wide dissemination of this expertise, confirmed by petrological studies that suggest it was the ideas and not the pots that traveled, may have gone hand in hand with diffusion of metallurgical knowledge. While this pottery was fashionable in terms of design and quality, for indigenous Neolithic societies with long-established ceramic traditions, the acquisition of metal was a significant feature of contact with the Beaker world in mainland Europe.

The earliest use of copper in Britain ca. 2500 to 2400 BC is recorded from Beaker single burials, of which the Amesbury Archer is a notable example. The first daggers and wire ornaments were made with copper brought into Britain from mainland Europe (Northover 1999; Needham 2002). That required long-distance journeys of the type undertaken by the Archer in his youth, some of which FitzPatrick (2009) believes were connected with metal prospecting in the Irish Sea zone. There is no evidence of indigenous production in Britain until the twenty-second century BC, when the development of bronze based on the tin resources of Cornwall triggers a wave of copper prospecting in Wales and the English Midlands (see Timberlake 2016).

The situation in Ireland at the onset of metal use was different, with the discovery, by a Beaker culture group ca. 2400 BC, of a major source of fahlore copper at Ross Island, Co. Kerry (Fig. 10.1; O'Brien 2001; 2004). That single mine would control supply for several centuries, with significant flows of arsenicated copper into Britain (Northover 1999; 2004), and possibly, to a lesser extent, western France (Gandois et al. 2019). Production there was based on a distinctive Beaker metallurgy that involved the smelting of high-grade fahlore (tennantite) ore using a primitive low-temperature furnace technology (see Merkl 2010). The presence of tennantite in large amounts is a unique feature of Ross Island, and accounts for the consistent impurity pattern (As>Sb>Ag) of the resulting metal over the approximately five-century working life of that mine (Northover 2004; see also Bray and Pollard 2012 for recycling of Ross Island copper). That metal circulated widely within a short period, with the likely emergence of secondary production and distribution centers across Ireland, together with a strong exchange of this metal into western Britain.

This first metalworking in Ireland did not rely on imports of copper from mainland Europe, but that does seem to be where the metallurgical knowledge came from. The evidence points to the arrival of external specialists who somehow discovered the fahlores at Ross Island. The discovery of that exceptional resource enabled metal production to begin in Ireland at the same technological level then practiced in Atlantic Europe. This greatly stimulated the adoption of metallurgy in Ireland, most visible in large-scale production of copper axe-heads. The background to these developments must lie in mainland Europe, as there is no evidence of fahlore smelting in Britain in the third millennium BC. The closest centers of fahlore metallurgy lie in Iberia and southern France, while the use of arsenical copper is also a strong feature of Beaker cultures in Atlantic France (Ambert 2001).

10.5 Atlantic Mining Networks

There is abundant evidence of copper mining and metallurgy in Iberia and southern France during the third millennium BC (O'Brien 2015). The production of arsenical copper is recorded in southeast Spain (Montero Ruiz 1994), and from Beaker

FIGURE 10.1. Chalcolithic/Beaker culture copper mines at Ross Island, southwest Ireland (photograph: author).

metalworking centers such as Zambujal and Leceia in Portuguese Estremadura (Cardoso 1989; Muller et al. 2007), among many others (see Gibson 2013: 74–76). Copper mines contemporary with the Ross Island production in Ireland are recorded at El Aramo and El Milagro in Asturias, and La Profunda in León (Blas Cortina 1998; 1999). The most detailed studies have been undertaken at El Aramo, where a complex network of mining tunnels dated between 2500 and 1500 BC extends to a depth of 150 m (Fig. 10.2; Blas Cortina and Suárez Fernández 2010). The mining technology is similar to that of Ross Island, using a combination of fire setting, stone, bone, and wooden tools. Recent excavations conducted close to the mine workings on this mountain uncovered evidence of copper smelting in direct association with Maritime Beaker pottery, dated between 2700 and 2460 BC (Blas Cortina 2015, 168, fig. 1). There are obvious comparisons with Ross Island, in respect of the furnace types and the association with Beaker pottery.

Fahlore mining and metallurgy are recorded in the same period at Cabrières in the Languedoc region of southern France (Fig. 10.3; Ambert 1995). This production began ca. 3100 BC and continued through the third millennium BC, overlapping with mining at Ross Island. Mine workings are recorded at a number of sites (Fig. 10.4), including Pioch Farrus IV, antimony-bearing tetrahedrite ores were extracted for smelting in adjacent settlements such as Roque Fenestre and La Capitelle du Broum. Though not directly associated with Beaker pottery, the discovery of Palmela Points in the Cabrières district (Ambert 1998) suggests connections with Beaker metalworking in Iberia. The spread of this antimonial copper from the Languedoc region to Atlantic regions of France can be traced from the mid-third millennium BC (Ambert et al. 1996, fig. 35).

There are other indications of fahlore metallurgy in Atlantic France during the same period. A review undertaken by Paul Ambert recorded a large number of daggers, Palmela points, swords, awls, and other items with a distinctive arsenical composition, probably derived from the smelting of tennantite ore from unconfirmed source(s). He drew attention to the prevalence of Beaker metalworking using arsenicated copper in Atlantic France, from Normandy and Brittany to the Saintonge region (Ambert 2001). Numerous flat copper axeheads are known from Beaker and pre-Beaker contexts in this region, while finds of copper daggers, Palmela Points, and other objects can be directly connected with Beaker metalworking (see Briard and Roussot-Larroque 2012; Labaune 2013). Beaker pottery has been found at a number of sites with evidence of copper metallurgy in Atlantic France. These include Passe de l'Ècuissière in Charente-Maritime (Querré 2009), La République in Talmont-Saint-Hillaire in the Vendée (Gandois and Le Carlier 2015), Crec'h Choupot, Tredarzer, and ZAC des Gabrielles, Bédee, in Brittany (Nicolas 2014), and Les Florentins, Val-de-Rueil, in Normandy (Billard et al. 1991).

FIGURE 10.2. Entrance to Chalcolithic copper mines at El Aramo, Asturias (photograph: author).

This Beaker metalworking in Atlantic France was part of a wider spread of arsenic copper metallurgy that eventually reached Ireland. The arsenicated copper produced from tennantite ore at Ross Island can be connected with the same Beaker metallurgical tradition of the mid-third millennium BC. That copper was produced using a low-temperature, oxidizing, and non-slagging process in furnace pits such as those used to smelt fahlore at Cabrières and Ross Island, and oxidized ores at El Aramo (Blas Cortina 2015). When the analytical and technological evidence is considered, along with broad similarities in the style of metalwork in general circulation, the origins of the Ross Island technology are seen to lie in contacts with Beaker metallurgists in Atlantic France in the twenty-fifth century BC, who in turn had connections with counterparts in the Languedoc and Cantabrian Spain.

10.6 First Encounters with Metal

How did the knowledge of metal/metallurgy spread to Ireland? What were the implications for language and communication, mobility and gene flow? These important questions may be addressed in three ways:

First, the knowledge of metal was acquired through the initiative of the Late Neolithic inhabitants of Ireland, in the course of journeys to the European mainland ca. 2500 BC. That interest could have been stimulated by contact with early Beaker groups in southern Britain using copper imported from the continent. The Irish groups may have taken this further by forming contacts with primary metal producers, the nearest at that time being in southern France and Cantabrian Spain, where mining of fahlore and oxidized mineralization were well established. This, in turn, could have led to the communication of technological information, either directly to the traveling Irish or a situation in which Beaker specialists were invited to Ireland.

The difficulty with this model is that there is very little evidence for contact with the European mainland during the Irish Late Neolithic (ca. 3000–2500 BC). Earlier patterns of contact did exist in Atlantic Europe during the fourth millennium BC, established by the spread of farming and expressed in the exchange of certain types of material culture, and by connected belief systems such as the passage-tomb tradition. Those networks seem to have broken down in a significant way after 3000 BC, when Britain and Ireland participated closely in a largely closed network marked by the use of Grooved Ware and henges. In the centuries that followed, Irish material culture is notably absent in mainland Europe, while French or Spanish material is similarly lacking in Ireland.

A second approach is to consider older ideas of Beaker culture migration or invasion, which are now being reassessed in light of recent scientific research. This is where knowledge of metal and metallurgy was brought to Britain and Ireland by Beaker-using populations moving, peacefully or otherwise, from the European mainland. It is uncertain whether the scale of any such movements was enough to create significant gene flow and language displacement. Whereas recent aDNA and isotope research on Beaker burials in Britain points in that direction (FitzPatrick 2009; Olalde et al. 2018), the scientific evidence from Ireland is more equivocal. As already noted, the contextual evidence from Ireland is more indicative of Beaker acculturation of indigenous Neolithic societies than migration on any significant scale.

A third scenario allows for more limited population movement, where specialists with the requisite knowledge introduced the new technology to Britain and Ireland. Those individuals and groups may have acted independently as traders or prospectors, but are more likely to have been connected to wider Beaker culture populations in mainland Europe. Case (1995: 26) considered these cultural contacts in terms of seasonal movements

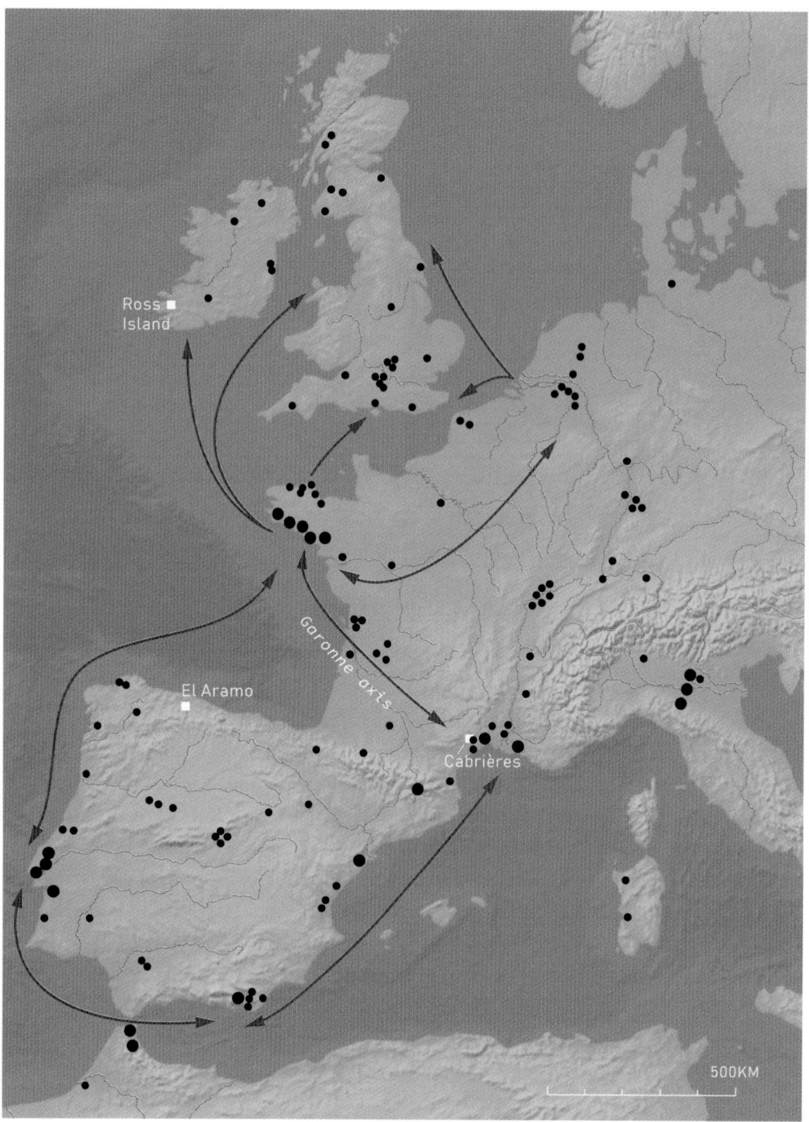

FIGURE 10.3. Beaker culture networks in Atlantic Europe, showing location of Chalcolithic copper mines at El Aramo, Cabrières, and Ross Island. Black dots represent finds of Maritime Beaker pottery (re-drawn from Cunliffe 2008, with additions).

by small groups seeking exchanges and resources. The incentive may have been a search for new sources of copper, in particular fahlore deposits, as well as gold, undertaken at a time of growing demand in Atlantic Europe. None of this required large-scale movement of people to Ireland, as the presence of even a few foreign specialists might have been sufficient to initiate metal-working activity in Ireland. This is plausible as it now seems that early expertise in mining and metal production was concentrated at one location. The discovery of a major fahlore source at Ross Island allowed metal production to begin in Ireland at the same technological level that existed at that time in France and Spain.

In this model, the Irish Sea is an important zone of interaction for Beaker specialists engaged in metal circulation across Atlantic Europe. That situation continued over several centuries, driven by a flow of Ross Island copper into Britain, and possibly back to Atlantic France (Gandois et al. 2019), exchanges that were also stimulated by a demand for Irish and Cornish gold (Standish et al. 2015). Those connections extended into the beginning of the Bronze Age, ca. 2200 to 2000 BC, when the discovery of Cornish tin through gold prospecting stimulated the mining of non-fahlore copper deposits in Wales, with the likely involvement, in both cases, of late Beaker groups prospecting in the Irish Sea zone (see Timberlake 2016).

How did Beaker metallurgists from Atlantic France find Ross Island mine? This is an important question in respect of contact and communication between the new arrivals and the indigenous population. While Ross Island is located in a part of Ireland closest to France, this is a lacustrine setting with limited access, approximately 25 km from the coast. Rich fahlore deposits that have this surface exposure are rare in Ireland, with perhaps one other example in the southwest region. The discovery of the Ross Island mineralization must have followed a sustained search with some level of support from the local Neolithic population. The language implications are considerable, in

FIGURE 10.4. Chalcolithic copper mines at Les Neuf Boches, Cabrières (photograph: author).

terms of communicating intent and local knowledge, securing access, and establishing a settlement base in the Killarney area. It is difficult to examine those interactions as there is only limited knowledge of Late Neolithic settlement in southwest Ireland. The absence of a local Neolithic component in the ceramics from Ross Island does support the idea of an intrusive Beaker group. It may also be significant that pollen studies indicate the first significant farming in the Killarney area occurred around the time of this Beaker copper mining (Mitchell and Cooney 2004).

10.7 Conclusions: Metal, Genes, and Memes

It is proposed that the transmission of metallurgical knowledge to south-west Ireland required a movement of specialist metalworkers or some small-scale migration of metal-using groups from mainland Europe. The technological processes involved in metal production were too complex to be transmitted orally or by familiarity with the finished objects, though the latter would certainly have sparked the initial interest. The earliest metallurgy in Ireland was established against a background of sustained contact within an Atlantic zone of Beaker metallurgy. The technological background of Ross Island mine must lie in Beaker culture metallurgy in France and Spain. From earlier Iberian origins, Beaker metallurgy was established in Spain, Portugal, and southeast France, spreading west along the Garonne-Gironde corridor to reach Atlantic France by 2500 BC. The transmission of this knowledge to Ireland may have occurred through maritime contacts with the Brittany–Loire region (Cunliffe 2001, figs 2.24 and 2.26), where a hybridization of Atlantic and Middle Rhine Beaker influences took place that partly explains the mixed nature of the Irish Beaker culture.

As copper metallurgy was introduced to Ireland as part of the expanding Beaker network of contacts across Atlantic Europe ca. 2500 BC, what are the implications in terms of language? The existence of those Beaker networks (Fig. 10.3) may have promoted a lingua franca for trade between regions with different native languages. The linguistic implications are likely to be much deeper given the permanent nature of Beaker culture settlement in Britain and Ireland. A lingua franca in trade would only have developed over time, whereas there must have been a high degree of mutual intelligibility to explain the peaceful reception of Beaker metallurgists to Ireland in the twenty-fifth century BC. This is emphasized by the likelihood that knowledge of metal and metallurgy was introduced to Ireland within a single generation, by small groups of specialists able to communicate with the indigenous population. That suggests a common language base in Atlantic Europe, where speakers of different but related varieties could understand each other (Salanovo 2016: 34). For reasons explained above, the derivation of that language base is unlikely to lie in British or Irish contacts with the European mainland during the Late Neolithic. Instead, the origin of what may be a Late Indo-European language in Atlantic Europe may lie in Neolithic cultures of the fourth millennium BC, connected with the fusion of non-Indo-European and early Indo-European languages in northwest France. Whether that language was a form of Proto-Celtic remains to be established, but its existence is supported by archaeological evidence for an exchange of ideas, cosmology, and material culture across Atlantic Europe during the fourth and third millennia BC. This evidence includes similarities in megalithic tomb design and art extending from Iberia to Atlantic France to the Irish Sea zone.

Different genetic and linguistic inputs are also likely through Beaker culture networks in northern Europe entering Ireland through Britain. This is supported by stylistic influences on Irish Beaker pottery (Case 1995; Brindley 2004), and by new aDNA results (Cassidy et al. 2016), though it is too early to draw conclusions from the limited genetic data in Ireland. Those connections do not explain the introduction of metallurgy to Ireland; as outlined above, there is no evidence of primary copper production in Britain for at least two centuries after Ross Island mine was established. The different character and origins of British Beaker culture are also relevant. This pushes the focus back on Irish connections with the Atlantic zone, particularly western France from Brittany to the Gironde, where Beaker metallurgists ca. 2500 BC were using significant amounts of arsenical copper in an environment lacking primary sources of that metal. That alone may have been an incentive to prospect widely through the developing Beaker network of exchanges, leading to contacts with Ireland and the eventual discovery of Ross Island mine. While that "French connection" was most important, contact with metal producers of the Beaker culture in Cantabrian Spain cannot be ruled out as another source for the diffusion of the new technology to Ireland.

References

Abercromby, J. 1912. *A study of the Bronze Age pottery of Great Britain and Ireland*. Oxford: Clarendon Press.

Almagro-Gorbea, M. 1995. Ireland and Spain in the Bronze Age. In: J. Waddell & E. Shee Twohig (ed.), *Ireland in the Bronze Age*, 136–148. Dublin: Stationery Office.

Ambert, P. 1995. Les mines préhistoriques de Cabrières (Herault): quinze ans de recherches. Etat de la question. *Bulletin de la Société Préhistorique Française* 92(4): 499–508.

1998. Importance de la métallurgie campaniforme en France. In: L'Enigmatique Civilisation Campaniforme, *Archéologia* 9: 36–41.

2001. La place de la métallurgie campaniforme dans la première métallurgie française. In: R. Harrison et al. (ed.), *Bell beakers today*, 577–588. Trento: Proceedings of the 1998 Riva del Garda conference.

Ambert, P., L. Carozza, B. Lecholon, & N. Houles. 1996. De la mine au metal au sud du Massif Central au Chalcolithique. *Archéologie en Languedoc* 20: 35–42.

Armit, I., & D. Reich. 2021 The return of the Beaker Folk: Rethinking migration and population change in British Prehistory. *Antiquity* 95(384): 1464–1477.

Beddoe, J. 1885. *The races of Britain*. Bristol: Arrowsmith.

Billard, C. 1991. L'habitat des Florentins à Val-de-Reuil (Eure). *Gallia Prehistoire* 33: 140–171.

Billard, C., J. R. Bourhis, Y. Desfossés, J. Evin, M. F. Hault, D. Lefèbvre, & M. A. Paulet-Locard. 1991. L'habitat de Florentins à Val-de-Reuil (Eure). *Gallia Préhistorie* 33: 140–171.

Blas Cortina, M. A. De 1998. Producción e intercambio de metal: la singularidad de las minas de cobre prehistóricas del Aramo y El Milagro (Asturias). In: G. Delibes de Castro, A. Ramos Millán, et al., *Minerales y metales en la prehistoria reciente* (Studia Archaeologica 88), 71–103. Valladolid: Universidad de Valladolid y Fundación Duques de Soria.

1999. Asturias y Cantabria. In: G. Delibes de Castro & I. Montero Ruiz (ed.), *Las primeras etapas metalúrgicas en la península Ibérica: II estudios regionals*, 41–62. Madrid: Instituto Universitario Ortega y Gasset y Ministerio de Educación y Cultura.

2015. La cuestión canpaniforme en el Cantábrico Central y las minas de cobre prehistóricas de la sierra del Aramo. *CuPauam (Cuadernos de Prehistoria y Arqueología)* 41: 165–179.

Blas Cortina, M. A. De & M. Suárez Fernández. 2010. La minería subterránea del cobre en Asturias: un capítulo esencial en la prehistoria reciente del norte de Espana. In: M. A. De Blas Cortina, G. Delibes de Castro, A. Villa Valdes, & M. Suárez Fernández (ed.), *Cobre y Oro. Minería y Metalurgia en la Asturias Prehistórica y Antigua*, 43–82. Oviedo: Real Instituto de Estudios Asturianos.

Bowen, E. G. 1972. *Britain and the western seaways*. London: Thames and Hudson.

Brace, S. et al. 2019. Ancient genomes indicate population replacement in Early Neolithic Britain. *Nature Ecology and Evolution* 3: 765–771.

Bray, P. & A. M. Pollard. 2012. A new interpretative approach to the chemistry of copper-alloy objects: Source, recycling and technology. *Antiquity* 86: 853–867.

Briard, J. & J. Roussot-Larroque. 2012. Les débuts de la métallurgie das la France Atlantique. In: M. Bartelheim, E. Pernicka, & R. Krause, (ed.), *The beginnings of metallurgy in the Old World*, 135–160. Rahden: Verlag Marie Leidorf.

Brindley, A. 2004. Prehistoric pottery. In: W. O'Brien, *Ross Island: Mining, metal and society in early Ireland* (Bronze Age Studies 6), 316–338. Galway: National University of Ireland Galway.

Burgess, C. 1980. *The age of Stonehenge*. London: Dent.

Bussmann, H. 1996. *Routledge dictionary of language and linguistics*. London: Routledge.

Cardoso, J. 1989. *Leceia: Resultados das escavações efectuadas 1983–8*. Oeiras: Câmara Municipal de Oeiras.

Carey, J. 2001. Did the Irish come from Spain? *History Ireland* 9 (3): 8–11.

2005. Lebor Gabála and the legendary history of Ireland. In: H. Fulton (ed.), *Medieval Celtic literature and society*, 32–48. Dublin: Four Courts Press.

Carlin, N. 2018. *The Beaker phenomenon? Understanding the character and context of social practices in Ireland 2500–2000 BC*. Leiden: Sidestone Press.

Carlin, N. & J. Brück. 2012. Searching for the Chalcolithic: Continuity and change in the Irish Final Neolithic/Early Bronze Age. In: M. J. Allen, J. Gardiner, & A. Sheridan, (ed.), *Is there a British Chalcolithic?* (Prehistoric Society Research Paper 4), 193–210. Oxford: Oxbow Books.

Case, H. J. 1995. Irish Beakers in their European context. In: J. Waddell & E. Shee Twohig (ed.), *Ireland in the Bronze Age*, 14–29. Dublin: Stationery Office.

Cassidy, L., R. Martiniano, E. Murphy, M. Teasdale, J. Mallory, B. Hartwell, & D. Bradley. 2016. Neolithic and Bronze age migration to Ireland and establishment of the insular Atlantic genome. *Proceedings of the National Academy of Sciences of the United States of America* 113(2): 368–373.

Clarke, D. L. 1970. *Beaker pottery of Great Britain and Ireland*. Cambridge: Cambridge University Press.

Cunliffe, B. 2001. *Facing the ocean: The Atlantic and its peoples*. Oxford: Oxford University Press.

2008. *Europe between the oceans 9000 BC – AD 1000*. New Haven: Yale University Press.

FitzPatrick, A. 2009. In his hands and in his head: The Amesbury Archer as metalworker. In: P. Clark (ed.), *Bronze Age connections: Cultural contact in prehistoric Europe*, 176–188. Oxford: Oxbow Books.

2013. The arrival of the Beaker set in Britain and Ireland. In: J. Koch, & B. Cunliffe (ed.), *Celtic from the West 2*, 41–70. Oxford: Oxbow Books.

FitzPatrick, A., G. Delibes de Castro, E. Guerra Doce, & J. Velasco Vázquez. 2016. Bell Beaker connections along the Atlantic façade: the gold ornaments from Tablada del Rudrón, Burgos, Spain. In: E. Guerra Doce & C. L. Von Lettow-Vorbeck (ed.), *The economic foundations supporting the social supremacy of the Beaker groups*, 37–54. Oxford: Archaeopress.

Forde, C. D. 1930. Early cultures of Atlantic Europe. *American anthropologist* 32(1): 19–100.

Gandois, H. & C. Le Carlier. 2015. Quid des traces d'activités métallurgiques sur le site de l'anse de la République à Talmont-Saint-Hilaire (Vendée)?. In: S. Boulet-Gazo (ed.), *Le campaniforme et l'âge du bronze dans les Pays de la Loire*, 146–157. Project Collectif de Recerche Rapport d'activité-Année 2014.

Gandois, H., A. Burlot, B. Mille, & C. Le Carlier de Veslud. 2019. Early Bronze Age axe-ingots from Brittany: Evidence for connections with southwest Ireland? *Proceedings of the Royal Irish Academy* 119: 1–36.

Gibson, C. 2013. Beakers into bronze: Tracing connections between western Iberia and the British Isles 2800–800 BC. In: J. Koch & B. Cunliffe (ed.), *Celtic from the West 2*, 71–99. Oxford: Oxbow Books.

Grogan, E. & H. Roche. 2010. Clay and fire: The development and distribution of pottery traditions in prehistoric Ireland. In: M. Stanley, E. Danaher, & J. Eogan (ed.), *Creative minds: Production, manufacturing and invention in ancient Ireland*, 27–45. Dublin: National Roads Authority.

Koch, J. & B. Cunliffe (ed.). 2010. *Celtic from the West 1*. Oxford: Oxbow Books.

(ed.), 2013. *Celtic from the West 2*. Oxford: Oxbow Books.

(ed.), 2016. *Celtic from the West 3*. Oxford: Oxbow Books.

Labaune, M. 2013. Bell Beaker metal and metallurgy in Western Europe. In: M. Pilar Prieto Martínez & L. Salanova (ed.), *Current researches on Bell Beakers. Proceedings of the 15th international Bell Beaker conference: From Atlantic to Ural*, 177–188. Santiago de Compostela: Copynino.

MacWhite, E. 1951. *Estudios sobre las relaciones Atlánticas de la Península Ibérica en la Edad del Bronze*. Madrid: Seminario de historia primitiva.

Mallory, J. P. 1989. *In search of the Indo-Europeans: Language, archaeology and myth*. London: Thames and Hudson.

2013. *The origins of the Irish*. London: Thames and Hudson.

2016. Archaeology and language shift in Atlantic Europe. In: J. Koch & B. Cunliffe (ed.), *Celtic from the West 3*, 387–406. Oxford: Oxbow Books.

Merkl, M. B. 2010. Bell Beaker metallurgy and the emergence of fahlore-copper use in Central Europe. *Interdisciplinaria archaeologica* 1(1): 19–27.

Mitchell, F. & T. Cooney. 2004. Vegetation history in the Killarney valley. In: W. O'Brien, *Ross Island: Mining, metal and society in Early Ireland*. Bronze Age Studies 6, 481–493. Galway: National University of Ireland Galway.

Montero Ruiz, I. 1994. *El origen de la metalurgia en el sureste Peninsular*. Almeria: Instituto de Estudios Almerienses.

Muller, R., G. Goldenberg, M. Bartleheim, M. Kunst, & E. Pernicka. 2007. Zambujal and the beginnings of metallurgy in southern Portugal. In: S. La Niece, D. Hook, & P. Craddock (ed.), *Metal and mines: Studies in archaeometallurgy*, 15–26. London: Archetype.

Needham, S. P. 2002. Analytical implications for Beaker metallurgy in north-west Europe. In: M. Bartelheim, E. Pernicka, & R. Krause (ed.), *Die anfänge der metallurgie in der alten welt*, 99–133. Freiberg: Forschungen zur Archäometrie und Altertumswissenschaf 1.

2005. Transforming Beaker culture in north-west Europe: Processes of fusion and fission. *Proceedings of the Prehistoric Society* 71: 171–217.

Nicolas, T. 2014. Les lingotières De Trédarzec (Crec'h Choupet; Côtes-d'Armor) et de Bédee (ZAC de Gabrielles, Ille-et-Vilaine). Des indices de métallurgie de la fin du IIIme millenaire AV. J.-C. en Bretagne. *Bulletin de l'APRAB* 12: 134–136.

Ni Lionain, C. 2012. *Lebor Gábála Erenn*: The use and appropriation of an Irish origin legend in identity construction at home and abroad. *Archaeological review from Cambridge* 27(2): 13–51.

Northover, J. P. 1999. The earliest metalwork in southern Britain. In: A. Hauptmann (ed.), *The Beginnings of Metallurgy: Proceedings of the international conference*, 211–226. Bochum: Der Anschitt, Beiheft 9.

2004. Ross Island and the physical metallurgy of the earliest Irish copper. In: W. O'Brien, *Ross Island: Mining, metal and society in early Ireland* (Bronze Age Studies 6), 525–538. Galway: National University of Ireland Galway.

O'Brien, W. 2001. New light on Beaker metallurgy in Ireland. In: R. Harrison et al. (ed.), *Bell Beakers Today*, 144–160. Trento: Proceedings of the Riva del Garda conference, May 1998.

2004. *Ross Island: Mining, metal and society in early Ireland* (Bronze Age Studies 6). Galway: National University of Ireland Galway.

2012. The Chalcolithic in Ireland: A chronological and cultural framework. In: M. J. Allen, J. Gardiner, & A. Sheridan (ed.), *Is there a British Chalcolithic?* (Prehistoric Society Research Paper 4), 211–225. Oxford: Oxbow Books.

2015. *Prehistoric copper mining in Europe 5500–500 BC*. Oxford: Oxford University Press.

2016. Language shift and political context in Bronze Age Ireland: Some implications of hillfort chronology. In: J. Koch & B. Cunliffe (ed.), 2016. *Celtic from the West 3*, 219–246. Oxford: Oxbow Books, Oxford.

Olalde, I. et al. 2018. The Beaker phenomenon and the genomic transformation of northwest Europe. *Nature* 555: 190–196.

Oppenheimer, S. 2007. *The origins of the British: The new prehistory of Britain and Ireland from Ice-Age hunter-gatherers to the Vikings as revealed by DNA analysis*. London: Constable.

Parker Pearson, M., A. Sheridan, M. Jay, A. Chamberlain, M. Richards, & J. Evans (ed.). 2019. *The Beaker people: Isotopes, mobility and diet in prehistoric Britain* (Prehistoric Society Research Paper 7). Oxford: Oxbow Books.

Querré, G. 2009. Métallurgie et hautes températures Campaniforme et Artenac. In: L. Laporte (ed.), *Des premiers paysans aux premiers métallurgistes su la caçade Atlantique de la France (3500–2000 av. J.-C.)*, 540–541. Chauvigny: Mémoire 33 de L'Association des Publications Chauvinoises.

Quinn, B. 2005. *The Atlantean Irish: Ireland's oriental and maritime heritage*. Dublin: Lilliput Press.

Raftery, B. 1994. *Pagan Celtic Ireland: the enigma of the Irish Iron Age*. London: Thames and Hudson.

Renfrew, C. 1987. *Archaeology and language. The puzzle of Indo-European origins*. London: Jonathan Cape.

2013. Early Celtic in the West: The Indo-European context. In: J. Koch & B. Cunliffe (ed.), *Celtic from the West 2*, 207–217. Oxford: Oxbow Books.

Salanova L. 2016. Bell Beakers and identities in Atlantic Europe (3rd millennium BC). In: J. Koch & B. Cunliffe (ed.), *Celtic from the West 3*, 13–39. Oxford: Oxbow.

Standish, C., B. Dhuime, C. Hawkesworth, & A. Pike. 2015. A non-local source of Irish Chalcolithic and Early Bronze Age gold. *Proceedings of the Prehistoric Society* 81: 149–177.

Timberlake, S. 2016. Copper mining, prospection and the Beaker phenomenon in Wales: The significance of the Banc y Tynddol gold disc. In: J. Koch & B. Cunliffe (ed.), *Celtic from the West 3*, 111–138. Oxford: Oxbow.

Waddell, J. 1992. The Irish Sea in prehistory. *The Journal of Irish Archaeology* 6: 29–40.

2010. *The prehistoric archaeology of Ireland*. Dublin: Wordwell.

Waddell, J. & J. Conroy. 1999. Celts: Maritime contacts and linguistic change. In: R. Blench & M. Spriggs (ed.), *Archaeology and language IV*, 127–138. London: Routledge.

11 "FROM THE ENDS OF THE EARTH": A CROSS-DISCIPLINARY APPROACH TO LONG-DISTANCE CONTACT IN BRONZE AGE ATLANTIC EUROPE

JOHN T. KOCH AND JOHAN LING

11.1 Introduction

Recent chemical and isotopic sourcing of copper alloys, mostly from Scandinavia but some also from Britain (Ling et al. 2013; 2014; Melheim et al. 2018; Radivojević et al. 2018), point to a production–distribution–consumption system that connected the South with the North along the Atlantic façade during the period 1400/1300 to 700 BC. Up to now, Scandinavia has not been directly related to the Atlantic Bronze Age of this time. Parallel to these discoveries, aDNA evidence has revealed a bidirectional north–south genetic flow at nearly the same time, 1300 to 800 BC, as early European farmer (EEF) ancestry rose in southern Britain and fell in the Iberian Peninsula, accompanied there by a converse rise in steppe ancestry (Patterson et al. 2021). It appears, therefore, that people as well as metals were on the move during a period of intensified contacts across Europe's westernmost lands in the Middle and Late Bronze Age. Thus, there arose a network comparable to that established earlier in connection with the Beaker phenomenon, one coinciding with a comparably significant transformation of the region's populations (Olalde et al. 2018; Koch & Fernández 2019).

These are startlingly unexpected discoveries, challenging earlier thinking about Bronze Age networks and leading to new questions about the social basis of production, transport technology, exchange, consumption, and interrelationships of the regional economies and societies. What was the volume of this trade? When and why did it begin and end? How was it related to episodes of migration, as cause or effect? How were the societies organized in order to enter long-distance exchange of metals? Who were the primary agents in the system? Was this exchange mostly long-distance or staged with transshipment hubs (in e.g., Galicia, Brittany, Ireland, Britain)? Especially if the former, who filled the labor gaps in the annual food-production cycle created by lengthy trading-raiding expeditions? Slaves? And, if so, to what extent was slave trade a factor in the detected gene flow? Do the recent finds of Baltic amber in the ore-bearing regions of Southwest Iberia (Murillo-Barroso, M. & M. Martinón-Torres 2012; Odriozola et al. 2017) indicate a system of copper-for-amber exchange? And what are the implications for the Indo-Europeanization of the region and for the post-Proto-Indo-European diversification and interaction of its dialects on their paths to the early attested languages?

A preliminary look at (1) rock-art motifs shared by these regions at this time (Koch 2013a, 111–114; Ling & Uhnér 2015, 31–35) and (2) the earliest layer of vocabulary shared by Germanic and Celtic, but not Indo-European as a whole (Hyllested 2010; Koch 2019; 2020; cf. Matasović 2009; Kroonen 2013), leads to the hypothesis that seafaring warriors were the primary agents of this trade. Key elements of this "trader-raider" socioeconomic system can be seen to anticipate the Viking Age two thousand years later, as formulated in the "Maritime Mode of Production" (MMP) model (Ling et al. 2018). The MMP sociopolitical organization was realized by the fusion of two key economic sectors: (1) a land-based agrarian sector, which entailed ownership of intensified farms that regularly produced surpluses and (2) a sea-based sector, in which the agricultural surpluses were invested in seaworthy vessels with professional crews specialized to undertake long-distance exchange and slave raiding. A system prototypically anticipating the MMP can be discerned in the rapid spread by sea of the Beaker phenomenon, but then became fully realized when groups in Bronze Age Scandinavia refocused their activities on long-distance exchange (Ling et al. 2018). This working hypothesis leads to further research questions. What was the role of rock art – as both cause and effect – in the formation of this warrior-led maritime exchange network? To what extent is shared iconography and shared inherited vocabulary consistent with our "Proto-Viking" interpretation of this episode of long-distance Bronze Age contact? Were "secret societies" responsible for the creation of rock art in Scandinavia and Iberia during the Bronze Age (Hayden 2018; Ling & Chacon 2018), i.e. socio-ritual sodalities that controlled ritual, politics, and surplus production, as well as long-distance exchange, warfare, and contacts between regional cultures?

To pursue these questions, we have embarked on a four-year cross-disciplinary project funded by the Swedish Research Council (Vetenskapsrådet) and entitled Rock Art, Atlantic Europe, Words & Warriors (RAW). This research initiative combines two methodological strategies: (1) high-resolution comparisons of martial motifs in rock art and (2) an in-depth reexamination of vocabulary shared by Celtic and Germanic (with special focus on martial, maritime, and ideological semantic fields) as possible witnesses to this network. In particular, we aim much more fully to investigate the parallels thus far recognized between Scandinavian rock art and Europe's Atlantic façade, the British Isles, Galicia, north Portugal, and most especially the metal-rich southwestern Iberian Peninsula. A first step will be to identify the sources of shared motifs as they reflect Bronze Age artifacts, e.g. shields, swords, wheeled vehicles, jewelry, seaworthy vessels, and representations of these in other media.

11.2 Theoretical Background

An integrating system of exchange emerged in Bronze Age Europe and created the comparative advantage of one region over another in the production and distribution of essential raw materials, such as copper, amber, tin, and gold. The European regions benefited in moving from self-sufficiency, being reliant on resources within one region, to specialization (Ling & Rowlands 2013). A new, complex pattern of flows of raw materials and finished forms emerged in the Bronze Age, to be understood in terms of the values, ideology, economy, and cosmology of that age.

In considering long-distance exchange, two perspectives have tended to dominate Bronze Age studies: one is a top-down approach that emphasizes elite-controlled exchange within a world system (e.g. Kristiansen 1998; Sherratt 1998) another is based on a bottom-up perspective, emphasizing heterarchical and agent-based aspects of trade, focusing on materiality and down-the-line trade (e.g. Harding 2000; 2013; Kienlin 2012). Lately, however, most scholars have strived to integrate these "grand narratives" so as to synthesize both macro- and microeconomic analysis, hierarchical and heterarchical social organization, and agent-based materiality studies and quantitative perspectives (Kristiansen 2018).

Although several researchers have argued for a Bronze Age world system (A. Sherratt 1999; S. Sherratt 2003; 2009; Vandkilde 2016), Iberian evidence remains a conspicuous gap, tending to be de-emphasized or ignored. Thus, there has been insufficient recognition of the roles of Scandinavia and Iberia as terminus zones in an integrated Atlantic sea route between 1300 and 900 BC, and the dual role of the Iberian Peninsula in the Late Bronze Age as both an extraordinarily metal-rich country and the sole maritime junction of the Atlantic and Mediterranean networks. In short, our view is that there could not have been a European world system in the Bronze Age excluding Iberia and that the understanding of European prehistory will be advanced through a fuller appreciation of this fact.

Cultural connectivity and movement along the Atlantic façade can be traced back to the spread of the megalith phenomenon, about 4000 BC (Cunliffe 2001; 2010; 2019; Schulz Paulsson 2017; 2019). A renewed process of interaction over Atlantic seaways starts about 2600/2500 BC with the expansion of the Bell Beaker Complex north- and eastwards, out of Iberia (Harrison & Heyd 2007; Van der Linden 2007; Cleary & Gibson 2019).

The demand for wealth such as copper and amber can be seen among the drivers behind this movement. For instance, Beaker groups initiated the first mining of copper in Ireland at Ross Island ca. 2400 BC (O'Brien 2004) and soon after in Wales (Timberlake 2016). Secondly, early Beaker groups, as an Atlantic-facing culture spreading from a formative area on the Tagus estuary in central Portugal, held a decisive advantage in maritime know-how. This factor facilitated their rapid expansion, as shown by the maritime distribution of Beaker Complex finds across Western Europe (Fitzpatrick 2013). This advanced technology is reflected in finds of plank-built boats from Early Bronze Age Britain, as early as ca. 2000 BC (Van de Noort 2006; 2011). Based on the distribution of settlements, Beaker groups were probably the first Europeans to use boats for large-scale trade.

Between 2000 and 1300 BC, there is evidence of continued interaction along the Atlantic façade (Brandherm 2007), but also of a partial lull or hiatus in some parts, and "post-Beaker" regional fragmentation; the connections are less pronounced than in the preceding phase. From 2000 to 1700 BC, first copper halberds, then bronze ones are widely distributed (Horn 2014; cf. Needham 2016), and depictions of halberds on rock occur from south Portugal to southern Scandinavia. Moreover, the fact that outside the British Isles, Scandinavia is the area with the most numerous finds of typical British and Irish Early Bronze Age copper-alloy axes indicates that well-established maritime trade routes were maintained between these distant regions.

Some artifacts of the Scandinavian Early Bronze Age (Late Neolithic through Period II) indicate copper sources from the mines in Ceredigion, Mid Wales (Nørgaard et al. 2019). By 1600 BC, Scandinavia is getting copper from the Great Orme mine in North Wales: several swords from Denmark were made with copper consistent with that source (Melheim et al. 2018).

Toward the beginning of the Late Bronze Age, a renewed cycle of economic activity began in Atlantic Europe, visible in the increased exchange of metals, coinciding with a restrengthened ideological commitment evident in rock art (Almagro Basch 1966; Koch 2013a; Vandkilde 2013; Ling et al. 2014; Ling & Uhnér 2015). The rise of advanced seafaring and long-distance exchange along the Atlantic façade are essential components of this post-Beaker reintegration of Western Europe (Earle et al. 2015).

Recent research suggests that Ireland, like Scandinavia, had to import most of its copper and tin in the period between 1300 and 900 BC. This coincided with a significant decline in insular copper mining, due to the depletion of surface-oxidized mineralization and a technological barrier to the extraction of copper-iron sulfide ores. There are indications of growing reliance on imported metal supplies after 1400 BC, details of which have yet to be clarified by scientific analysis of Irish metalwork. The organization of this complex overseas trade required a strong political context, provided by the emerging chiefdom structures of the Middle to Late Bronze Age.

Hillforts, as the central places of these Irish chiefdoms, were important nodes of production, consumption, and redistribution in a prestige-goods economy where access to bronze, as well as exotic materials used to make sumptuary goods, was limited by social convention (O'Brien 2016). The use of this material culture was political, whether it concerned the bronze weapons central to warrior identity, or the prestige objects used in social transactions and ritual deposition, essential for the maintenance of chiefdoms (O'Brien & O'Driscoll 2017). Hillforts were probably multifunctional: a military response to seaborne raids, competitive prestige, and control of wealth, answering the immediate challenges posed by increasingly advanced vessels traveling greater distances with increasingly valuable cargoes and well-armed crews.

Ireland may have been a pivotal intermediary for the movement of metal and other goods between Iberia and Scandinavia. This included the supply of bronze from sources in Spain and Portugal, as well as the strong demand for Baltic amber that emerged in Ireland in this period (Eogan 1995). The wider context of these exchanges has long been presented as the "Atlantic Bronze Age," a zone of trade and other cultural interaction between western Iberia and the British Isles ca. 1300 to 900 BC. Those seaborne connections are most evident through stylistic influences on metalwork, with many similar ornament and weapon traditions across the Atlantic seaboard, as well as common elements of feasting ritual, hoard deposition, funerary practice, and hillfort construction.

Especially concrete evidence of interaction between groups from the British Isles, Iberia, and Scandinavia comes from Cliffs End on the Isle of Thanet, at Britain's southeastern extremity (McKinley et al. 2013; 2015). Cliffs End has been interpreted as an important Late Bronze Age and Early Iron Age trading center, as evidenced by finds such as bun ingots and Baltic amber. The site's most dramatic finds are strontium and oxygen isotope data from human bone. Besides several local people from Kent, some of the analyzed individuals show signatures consistent with Scandinavian geology, while others point to the Western Mediterranean.

An important milestone in the intensification of north–south links in metallurgy at this time was the standardization of tin bronze, to the exclusion of other copper alloys, in SW Iberia by 1300 BC, an innovation that began in the British Isles 2300/2000 BC (Needham 1996; Pare 2000; Koch 2013a). Although tin bronze occurs in southern Iberia as early as 1700 BC, artifacts made from arsenic copper remained the norm throughout the Iberian Middle Bronze Age.

11.3 New Perspectives on an Ancient Keynote

Between 450 and 430 BC, Herodotus wrote:

> About the far west of Europe I have no definite information, for I cannot accept the story of a river called by non-Greek peoples the *Eridanus*, which flows into the northern sea, where amber is supposed to come from; nor do I know anything of the existence of islands called the Tin Islands [Κασσιτερίδες], whence we get our tin . . . [I]n spite of my efforts to do so, I have never found anyone who could give me first-hand information of the existence of a sea beyond Europe to the north and west. Yet it cannot be disputed that tin and amber do come to us from what one might call the ends of the earth. It is clear that it is the northern parts of Europe which are richest in gold, but how it is procured is another mystery . . . In any case it does seem to be true that the countries which lie on the circumference of the inhabited world produce the things which we believe to be most rare and beautiful. (Herodotus III, 115–116; trans. de Sélincourt 1972)

Easily recognized in this passage are economic and aesthetic values going back a thousand years further, to a Bronze Age world system encompassing Western Eurasia and North Africa (cf. Sherratt 1993; Sherratt 2009). This system arose through widespread demand for wealth items, most essentially standardized tin bronze, gold, and amber (Pare 2000; Vandkilde 2013; Kristiansen & Suchowska-Ducke 2015).

Literal geographical distance was an obvious factor in this value system. At its apex, its triad of exotica came from "the ends of the earth." As implied in the passage, it was not only spatial distance that made goods exotic and valuable, but also linguistic and conceptual distance. Herodotus' mental map is disk-shaped, with the Aegean at its center, and the most rare and beautiful raw materials arrived from the Ocean Stream, encompassing the world's semi-mythical outer edge. As *Hellenes*, Herodotus and his readers inhabited a world whose limits were those of the Greek language. (Cf. Wittgenstein, *Tractatus Logico-Philosophicus* 5.6: "Die Grenzen meiner Sprache bedeuten die Grenzen meiner Welt.") Coming from barbarian (i.e. non-Greek) languages, information about the sources of amber, tin, and gold could not be fully understood or trusted. The resulting mystification of the margins of the known world enhanced the value of these commodities.

Amber, gold, and bronze – raw materials regarded as most precious – were shades of luminous yellow (Maran 2004; 2016). Amid the ideological and cosmological associations of colors, these shades suited solar symbolism, as so often suggested by the finished forms given them. They were thus tied into a wider constellation of sun symbols manifested by numerous monuments, artifacts, and images in the Bronze Age (Kaul 2013). Semantic and early poetic connections in the Celtic languages suggest that these associations extended to honey and mead, e.g. Welsh *mêl* 'honey', *melyn* 'yellow', and the high hero's reward of *medd o eur* 'mead from gold' (cf. Enright 1996).

11.4 Rising Social Complexity against Declining Mutual Intelligibility and Some Implications of Archaeogenetics

It has long been known that the prehistoric languages reconstructed by philologists – such as Proto-Indo-European,

Proto-Celtic, Proto-Germanic, etc. – must belong to the same times and places studied by prehistoric archaeology. But to determine how, where, and when these protolanguages coincided specifically with archaeological cultures has presented a formidable challenge. The breakthrough of the past few years thanks to the archaeogenetic revolution is a game changer. Genome-wide sequencing of ancient DNA has revealed the massive gene flow from present-day Ukraine and South Russia into Central, Northern, and Western Europe during the third millennium BC. These advances in archaeogenetics have made two propositions concerning the linguistic prehistory of Western Eurasia highly probable: (1) in almost no area did the First Farmers of the Neolithic period speak Indo-European; (2) during the third millennium BC, mass migrations originating in the Pontic–Caspian steppe introduced early Indo-European speech to extensive regions – from the Siberian Altai in the east, to Ireland and Britain in the west (Anthony & Ringe 2015; Cassidy et al. 2016; Damgaard et al. 2018; Olalde et al. 2018; Narasimhan et al. 2019). In other words, genome-wide sequencing of aDNA has provided support for the Steppe Hypothesis of the Indo-European homeland (Allentoft et al. 2015; Haak et al. 2015; Anthony & Brown 2017; Kristiansen et al. 2017), at least as far as the later or post-Anatolian stage of Proto-Indo-European is concerned (Damgaard et al. 2018; Lazaridis 2018). Strontium and oxygen isotope data from human bone have added evidence for the mobility of individuals (Fitzpatrick 2013; McKinley et al. 2013). It therefore appears that mass migrations probably resulted in a continuum of shallowly differentiated post-Anatolian Proto-Indo-European dialects, widely distributed across Western Eurasia and retaining a high level of mutual intelligibility, along the lines anticipated by Garrett (2006; cf. Koch 2013a). Regarding our research area, it now appears that Scandinavia and Atlantic Europe were initially “Indo-Europeanized” in the age of Corded Ware and the Beaker Phenomenon, i.e. the Neolithic–Bronze Age Transition.

Therefore, the situation during, and in the immediate wake of, these migrations differed fundamentally from the world described by Herodotus. In the latter, the Indo-European branches had fully crystallized and presented serious barriers to the majority of individuals who lived their lives within only one of them. Unlike the early generations of the Indo-European founders, long-distance exchange over the course of the Bronze Age increasingly became the province of specialists who had learned to operate between local societies whose languages had declining mutual intelligibility.

The period when Iberian copper was traded to Scandinavia was about a thousand years after the age when an undifferentiated post-Anatolian Indo-European was diffused amid the migrations from the steppe homeland, and well into the subsequent epoch of the widely extended Indo-European branches. What was the impact of rising linguistic differences on long-distance exchange? Was it only an impediment or did it stimulate the rise of classes of mobile specialists moving rare, high-value raw materials (copper, tin, amber, and gold) between diverging linguistic worlds? Was long-distance interaction in the Late Bronze Age intense enough and did it involve enough individuals to become a significant counterweight to natural tendencies for dialects to evolve apart?

The episode of Iberian–Scandinavian contact can be pinpointed in absolute chronology, as well as by synchronizing regional archaeological cultures, and as belonging to a particular stage of linguistic evolution. The Old Indic of Mitanni and Mycenaean Greek, both found in writing by 1400 BC, show these Indo-European languages were no longer similar enough to be mutually intelligible (cf. Ventris & Chadwick 2008; Witzel 2019). The Indo-European dialect continuum formed by mass migration in the third millennium BC had given way to discrete linguistic branches. Any viable Indo-European family tree might therefore be seen as implying that, when Greek and Indic had become separate languages, Germanic and Celtic had done likewise (see Fig. 11.1). If so, the Late Bronze Age maritime travelers who brought Iberian copper to Scandinavia and Baltic amber to Iberia would not have been operating within a milieu of undifferentiated or shallowly differentiated late post-Anatolian Indo-European, but crossing between the separate languages, such as those that became the Celtic and Germanic of historical times, as well as passing through or around non-Indo-European languages, including the forerunners of Basque and Iberian. Alternatively, we might consider that the key factor in sustaining mutual intelligibility was not the proximity of Proto-Celtic and Proto-Germanic (compared to, say, Proto-Greek and Proto-Indo-Iranian) on the tree model, but their geographic proximity and sustained or renewed interaction during the Bronze Age. Would they have continued to understand each other because they had more occasion to talk to each other (Koch 2020)? Could the intensified contact between the West and North in the Middle to Late Bronze Age be the key to the problematical dialect position of Germanic identified in Ringe et al. 2002 (Fig. 11.1), i.e. an earlier proximity to the forerunners of Balto-Slavic and Indo-Iranian followed by a reorientation toward Italo-Celtic?

11.5 North-West Indo-European and Celto-Germanic

Subsets of vocabulary limited only to geographical neighbors within the Indo-European world reveal key chapters in the story of Proto-Indo-European’s diffusion into branches. In some cases, the languages sharing words with restricted distributions are not even close relatives on the Indo-European family tree (see Fig. 11.1). In such cases, the shared vocabulary can be explained as the result of contacts between the separating branches after they had left the Indo-European homeland, but before the languages are attested in writing or had evolved enough for transferred vocabulary to be identifiable as loanwords.

The Celto-Germanic (CG) vocabulary is one such subset. It falls within broader groupings of words that can be found in

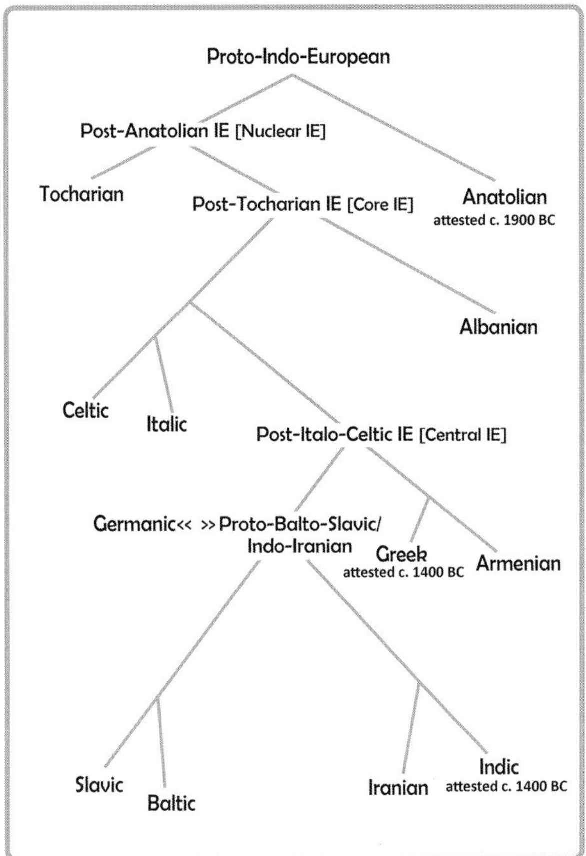

FIGURE 11.1. *First-order subgroups of Indo-European: simplified Indo-European family tree of Ringe, Warnow, and Taylor (2002), indicating the close association of Italic and Celtic and the anomalous position of Germanic.*

languages along the northwestern edge of the Indo-European world, but are absent from Anatolian, Albanian, Greek, Armenian, Tocharian, and Indo-Iranian. Thus, there is a significant body of Italo-Celtic/Germanic (ICG) vocabulary, words found also in Latin and/or other Ancient Italic languages (such as Oscan or Venetic), as well as Celtic and Germanic. Because Celtic and Italic have long been recognized as sharing many common features, and many linguists see them as descending from a common Proto-Italo-Celtic ancestral node (going back to Schleicher 1861/1862; Fig. 11.2 here; more recently, e.g., Ringe et al. 2002, fig. 7; Schrijver 2016); this is hardly surprising and does not necessarily indicate a stage of contact separate from that reflected in the Celto-Germanic vocabulary. More broadly still, there are words that occur throughout Northwest Indo-European (NW), i.e. Italo-Celtic, Germanic, and Balto-Slavic (Mallory & Adams 2006, 109–110, 130). With any individual inherited word, it may appear in only some Indo-European languages because it has died out in the others through the regular process of lexical attrition over centuries. In other words, there may be a skewed geographic distribution for a single word as a random occurrence. However, as sizable classes of words, these subsets can be understood as reflecting successive post-Proto-Indo-European stages: first NW, then ICG, then CG. At least some of the numerous CG words reflect a stage after Italic and Celtic had separated, but Germanic and Celtic had come (back) into close contact. With Latin so fully attested in ancient sources, it probably is significant that much of the inherited vocabulary shared by Celtic and Germanic is not found in the Italic branch.

Another significant pattern is that many of the Celto-Germanic words are attested in Old Norse and Early Irish. It is usually easy with this group to screen out borrowings from the Viking Age, which postdate such linguistic changes as Grimm's Law in Germanic. Had the contact taken place mainly in the Late Iron Age in Central Europe, we would expect the shared words to be more concentrated in Old High German and Gaulish.

More early (i.e. pre-Grimm's Law) Celto-Germanicisms that can be identified as originating in one branch and spreading to the other are those from Celtic to Germanic (Hyllested 2010). This observation leads to the working hypothesis that the predominant interregional language of elite trade in Bronze Age Atlantic Europe was an idiom on the evolutionary path to the attested Celtic languages. Much of the semantic content of this vocabulary, especially the items that can be plausibly lined up with motifs common to Iberian and Scandinavian rock art, can be correlated with this episode of interregional contact in the Bronze Age (Koch 2019a).

Rock art provides key evidence for three post-Proto-Indo-European innovations linking Scandinavia and the Atlantic West: (1) the generalization of tin bronze as the material of weapons, ornaments, and tools (Pare 2000); (2) the horse-and-chariot package; and (3) advanced seafaring (Koch 2013a). For example, **ark*^{w}*o-* 'bow and arrow' is confined to Italo-Celtic and Germanic. Bows and arrows are represented with similar conventions in Scandinavian and Iberian Late Bronze Age rock art (Koch 2016; 2020). The Early Iron Age "Ameixial 2" inscription begins **aark^{u}uio**, which is probably the earliest attestation of the common Hispano-Celtic personal name ARQVIVS 'archer', feminine ARCEA (Koch 2013b; 2020). **gaiso-* 'spear' is another example of a CG word corresponding to a centrally important element of rock-carving imagery in Iberia and Scandinavia, as well as in the inventory of Bronze Age artifacts. Some Celtic and Germanic words have different etymologies, but both referred to the same thing and sounded so much alike as to rule out coincidence: for example, Proto-Celtic **skeito-* and Pre-Germanic **skeltu-*, both meaning 'shield' an object central to, and similarly represented in Nordic rock art and Iberian warrior stelae, as discussed below. Other Celto-Germanicisms can be related to the organization of warrior societies: e.g. Celtic *ambaxtos* 'man acting for a leader' < 'one sent back and forth', whence Gothic *andbahts* 'servant, minister', Old English *ambiht* 'office, service, commission, command, attendant, messenger, officer', Old High German *ambaht* 'servant, employee, official, messenger', Modern *Amt*, Old Norse feminine form *ambátt* 'bondwoman, concubine'. It is also the most common Hispano-Celtic name, *Ambatos*, first attested as **anb^{a}at^{i}ia** 'daughter of Amba(x)tos' on an Early Iron Age stela (Koch 2016; 2019b).

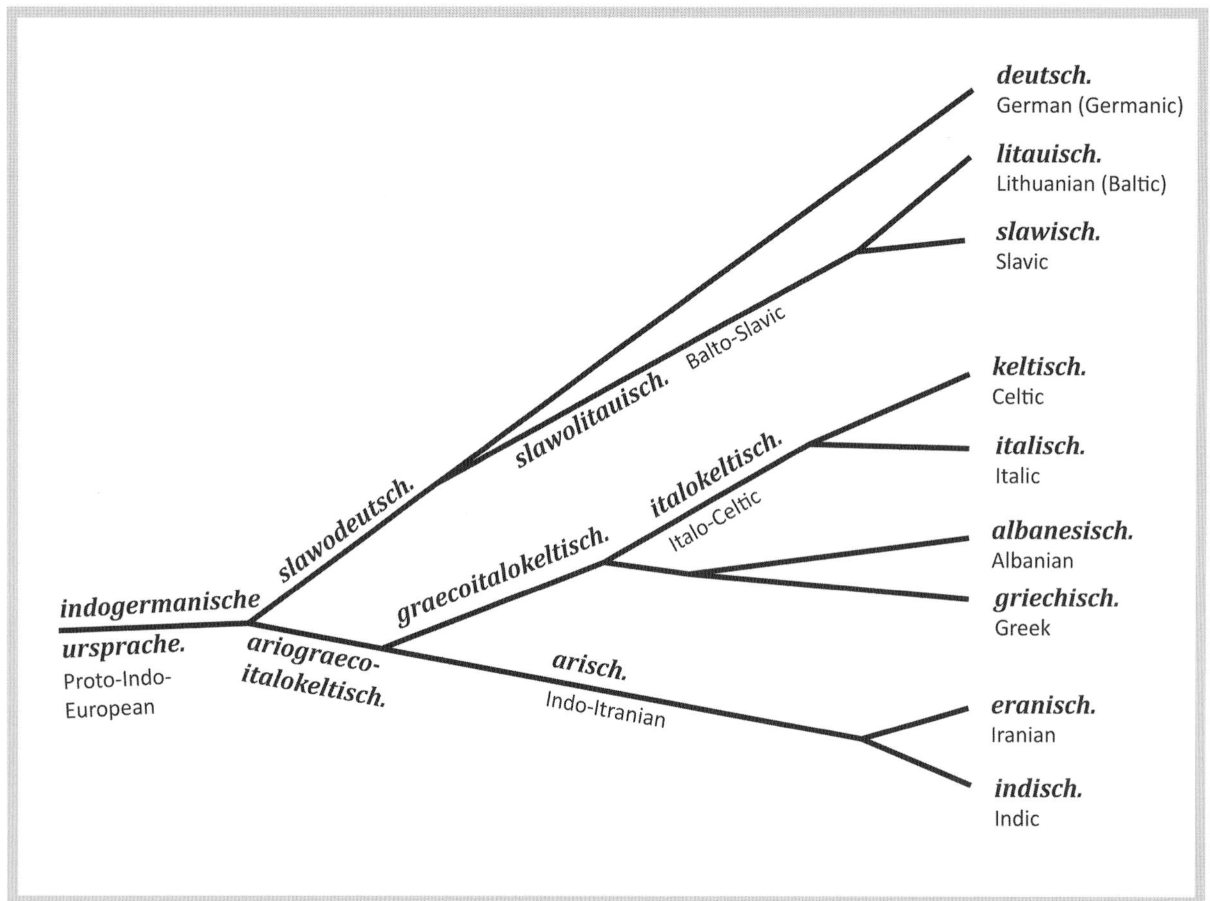

Figure 11.2. *The Indo-European family tree published by August Schleicher in 1861 anticipated groupings universally accepted (Balto-Slavic and Indo-Iranian) or widely accepted (Italo-Celtic) today. At the time, Anatolian and Tocharian had not yet been discovered.*

11.6 Language and Metal Cultures

About 2000 to 1700/1600 BC, distinct regional metal cultures arose in Europe. In earlier work, metal cultures have been understood on the basis of the material and forms of artifacts, without considering language. Following recent breakthroughs with aDNA, the separation of languages and the rise of distinct regional metal cultures during the Bronze Age can be understood as parallel processes, interacting with each other in forming identities across Western Eurasia. For two reasons, we suspect that the Indo-European branches in our research area are generally coterminous with the major typological regions of Bronze Age metalwork: (1) the complexities and subtleties of evolving casting styles and techniques could be transmitted effectively only between masters and apprentices, artisans and patrons, who could communicate with native or near-native competence through a shared language; (2) the geographical boundaries of metalwork typologies of Atlantic Europe correspond closely to the territories of pre-Roman languages, strongly suggesting that these two were parallel developments in the formation of post-Proto-Indo-European regional identities.

Our innovative approach recognizes the interplay between material culture and language to understand what shaped, then transformed the distinct metal cultures, their boundaries, and the interaction between them. In the period from 1300 to 900 BC (continuing another century outside Iberia), two major metal cultures faced the Atlantic: the so-called Atlantic Bronze Age (Burgess & O'Connor 2008; Milcent 2012), which embraced western Iberia, parts of France, Belgium, Ireland, and Britain, and the Nordic Bronze Age, stretching from Scandinavia in the north to the Netherlands in the south (Kristiansen 1998). The Rhine formed a border between them.

The Atlantic Bronze Age itself was discontinuous: there was little or no metalwork of an "Atlantic" type around the Bay of Biscay, from the Gironde to western Cantabria (Milcent 2012). The linguistic map of pre-Roman Europe presents a closely similar pattern: Celtic languages from west of the lower Rhine to Atlantic Iberia, Germanic east of the Rhine, and non-Indo-European languages around the Bay of Biscay and Pyrenees (Koch et al. 2007; Koch 2016); in the linguistic sphere, the Gironde again defined a sharp frontier. Pioneering provenance studies of metals and amber now show that raw materials, such as copper and tin, transgressed these cultural borders (Murillo-Barroso & Martinón-Torres 2012; Ling et al. 2014; Odriozola et al. 2017).

Our theory adapts Lévi-Strauss's duality of "the raw and the cooked" (*Le cru et le cuit*) (1964). Raw and unworked metals and amber moved across linguistic barriers and became "cooked" in a recognizable regional style by speakers of a particular language, and then used as artifacts within the monoglot linguistic culture of that region. A highly mobile minority of traders, warriors, etc., moved these raw materials across vast distances. Their shared cultural codes, with implications for a lingua franca, are evident in rock art in Scandinavia and Iberia.

11.7 Bronze Age Warriors and Long-Distance Trade

Many scholars argue that warfare and warriors became institutionalized and semi-professional during the Bronze Age (Harrison 2004; Kristiansen & Larsson 2006; Vandkilde et al. 2006; Kristiansen 2018). Thus, warfare and warriorhood became pan-European phenomena in the Bronze Age, from the Aegean in the east to Iberia in the west and Scandinavia in the north. However, it is important to stress that warfare and warriorhood were articulated on different scales and magnitudes due to different societal structures (centralized or decentralized societies) and different levels of social stratification (Kristiansen 2007). Even so, "classic" professional weapons, such as swords, armor, and chariots – used for fighting, not for hunting, nor doubling as tools – are introduced to most regions of Europe for the first time in the Bronze Age.

The shift from the Neolithic to the Bronze Age was a profound structural transformation based on a changing political economy (Kristiansen & Earle 2015). Large-scale trade in metals and other forms of wealth across Europe developed in the Bronze Age. In simple terms, the Bronze Age witnessed an emergence of social stratification based on elite control over long-distance trade (Earle 2002). Fundamental to this transformation was the investment in long-distance trade and advantages of maritime interaction and exchange. These created, in turn: the comparative advantage for maritime chiefdoms based on specialized boat building and knowledge; strategic locations for controlling trade; and warriors to protect shipping (Ling & Rowlands 2013). As both cause and effect, Bronze Age violence can be related to these societies' investments in long-distance trade of metals, and both were also linked to rising social complexity and inequality (Earle et al. 2015). There is, interestingly, no war-related figurative rock from the Neolithic era in Scandinavia (4300–1700 BC) or Iberia (5500–3000 BC). In the light of widespread evidence of violence during the Bronze Age, it is not surprising to find rock art illustrating diverse scenes of conflict and fighting, ranging from ritualistic to more realistic. These characteristics are pronounced in both Scandinavian and Iberian Bronze Age rock art; the former displays action scenes, while the conventions of the latter are more static and abstract. It is important to stress that this war-related figurative rock art appears and vanishes with the Bronze Age.

In this context, we argue that rock art was made by Bronze Age ritual sodalities, secret societies (Hayden 2018), in accordance with exclusive socio-ritual manifestations and initiations to social events such as long-distance exchange voyages, warfare, and practices associated with death manifested in the form of boats, weapons, and warriors and the occurrence of some of the rock art in funeral contexts. Moreover, certain rock art images depict anthropomorphic beings that appear to be wearing masks or headgear – a practice found in many secret societies. We also argue that Bronze Age Scandinavian rock art could be associated with the transmission of knowledge relating to navigation, boat construction, watercraft maintenance, warfare, religion, and cosmopolitan affairs. Thus, we posit that the presence of secret societies facilitated long-distance exchange and that these ritual sodalities were responsible for the creation of rock art in Scandinavia during the Bronze Age (Ling et al. 2018).

Our hypothesis takes on more depth as we synthesize recent archaeogenetic evidence. Before full-genome sequencing of ancient DNA became possible, many researchers were already convinced that the Steppe Hypothesis of Proto-Indo-European homeland was the strongest alternative purely on the linguistic and archaeological evidence (Gimbutas 1970; Mallory 1989; Anthony 2007). The archaeogenetic evidence now appears to confirm that model (Allentoft et al. 2015; Haak et al. 2015; Anthony & Brown 2017), at least for post-Anatolian Indo-European (Damgaard et al. 2018; Lazaridis 2018). Other studies show that steppe ancestry – probably bringing Indo-European speech with it – had transformed populations over wide regions of Atlantic Europe by 2000 BC, replacing the paternal ancestries that had predominated in these areas in the Neolithic (Martiniano et al. 2017; Olalde et al. 2018; 2019; Valdiosera 2018). Previously, alternative chronologies could not be ruled out: that Proto-Indo-European had already spread widely and formed branches in the Neolithic *or* first reached Western Europe as late as 1000 BC or later.

At the present moment in intellectual history, the great question posed by genome-wide sequencing of aDNA is how to map languages onto populations and archaeological cultures for the period between the mass migrations from the steppe and the earliest attested Indo-European languages. Bronze Age Europe can no longer be treated as mute prehistory. Rather, it occupies a post-Proto-Indo-European interval, between the expansion of post-Anatolian Indo-European from the Pontic–Caspian steppe in the third millennium BC and the appearance of diverse written Indo-European languages.

A less dramatic but equally important archaeogenetic finding is that Northern and Western Europe underwent no subsequent turnover of population so stark after 2000 BC. It would not be until the European colonial expansion of early modern times that we would see a comparable large-scale and abrupt mingling of populations previously isolated for thousands of years. On the other hand, what did occur in Middle to Late Bronze Age Atlantic Europe were rising proportions of early European farmer (EEF) ancestry in the North (i.e. southern Britain) and steppe ancestry in the South, pointing to intense interaction and bidirectional movement of people throughout the region, trailing off at the Bronze-Iron Transition, ca. 800 BC (Patterson et al. 2021). For now, the combined evidence remains consistent with the working hypothesis that it was during the post-Proto-Indo-European interval that Germanic evolved *in situ* in Northern Europe and Celtic in the West. And thus, the visible division at the Rhine between Nordic and Atlantic Bronze Age metal cultures may anticipate emerging Germanic and Celtic linguistic spheres.

11.8 Rock Art as Evidence of Long-Distance Exchange

To recap, it is only recently that chemical and isotopic sourcing has revealed copper from the Iberian Peninsula in the Atlantic North and Baltic amber in metal-rich Southwest Iberia, both in the period from 1400/1300 to 900 BC, the Middle to Late Bronze Age (Ling et al. 2014; Ling & Uhnér 2015; Melheim et al. 2018; Radivojević et al. 2018; see also Fig. 11.3). It is at precisely this time that a new close dating and detailed study of Iberian "warrior" stelae and Scandinavian rock art come to show an extensive repertory of shared motifs – swords, shields, spears, horned warriors, chariots, mirrors, bows, and arrows – often represented following similar, unnaturalistic artistic conventions. We will discuss this in greater detail below. This evidence leads to our basic hypothesis that when the production–distribution–consumption system arose, its primary agents were seafaring specialists, whose shared warrior ideology is reflected in the rock art. Their cultural influence was especially strong in the Scandinavian and Iberian terminus regions of this Atlantic network. This observation can be seen as most consistent with directional, rather than down-the-line, exchange.

Two early scholars argued for the idea of long-distance exchange between Scandinavia and Iberia: Arthur Nordén, on the basis of metal and broad similarities between the Iberian and Scandinavian rock art (1925), and later, one of the most prominent twentieth-century archaeologists, Gordon Childe, inferring from metalwork typology (1939). Nordén argued for and favored a model of long-distance exchange reflected in cultural connections, as could be supported by the find of a

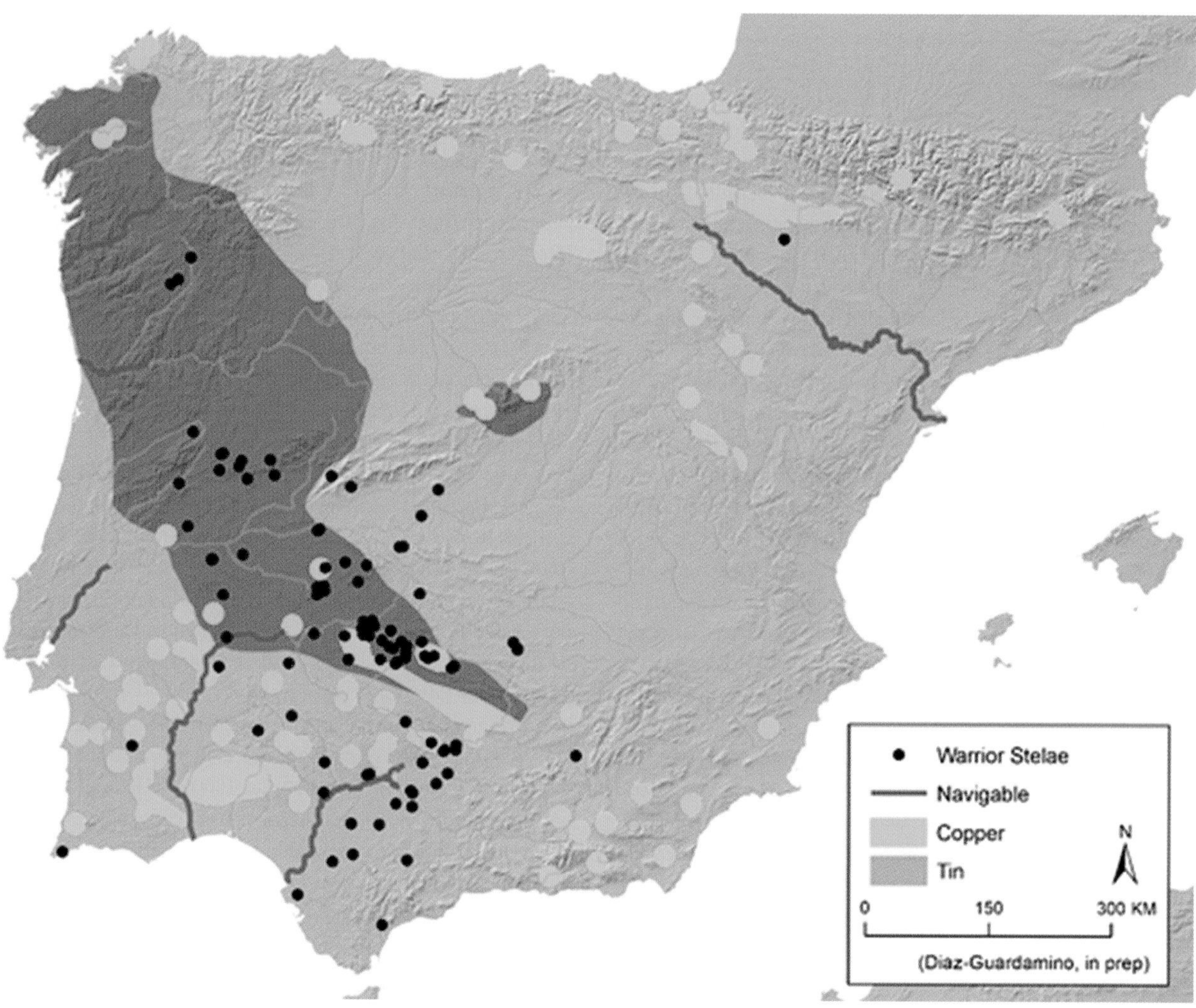

FIGURE 11.3. *Deposits of copper and tin, findspots of Late Bronze Age "warrior" stelae, and navigable rivers in the Iberian Peninsula (map by M. Díaz-Guardamino). The densest concentration of warrior stelae is found in the Zujar and Alcudia valleys. In the Zujar valley, there is evidence of ancient mining (Las Minillas with LBA pottery and thousands of stone hammers).*

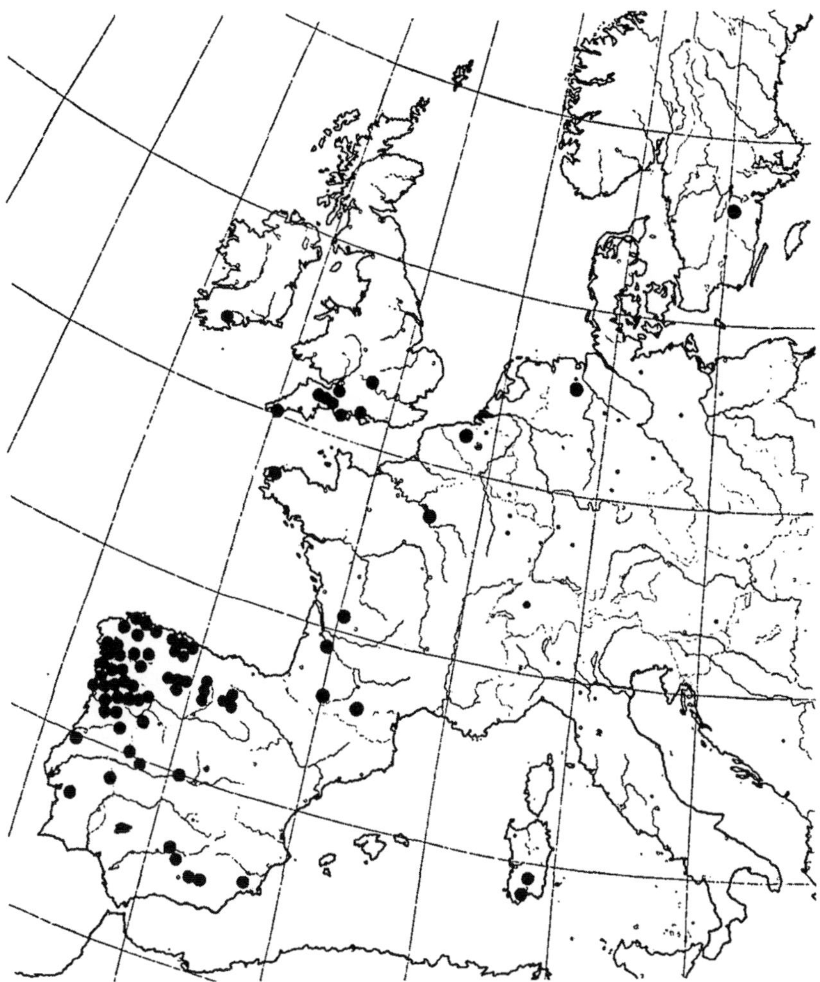

FIGURE 11.4. *Childe's 1939 map of "double-looped palstaves in western Europe," showing the findspot of the Tåkern palstave.*

typically Galician palstave from Lake Tåkern, Sweden (Nordén 1925). This type of ax, a double-looped palstave, dates between 1250 and 900 BC (Monteagudo 1977, Pl. 86, 87 & 100); it became known to Gordon Childe, who wrote the curator of Gothenburg Museum to ask about the find's circumstances (Ling & Uhnér 2015). Childe recognized the Tåkern palstave as the northernmost example of a type occurring also in southern England, western France, and Sardinia, and he published a short paper on this in *The Antiquaries Journal* (1939). That paper included a map on which Childe envisioned an Atlantic trade system (Fig. 11.4).

Further evidence for these Atlantic links includes two Herzsprung shields from Fröslunda, Western Sweden, made of copper from the Ossa-Morena massif in Extremadura. These "U-notched" Fröslunda shields are dated between ca. 1100 and 800 BC (Uckelmann 2012). Depictions of LBA Herzprung shields occur on forty-six Extremaduran Late Bronze Age stelae (Harrison 2004: 124). Most of these are of the slightly earlier V-notched type, but there are at least two representations of U-notched shields (cf. Uckelmann 2012: 129, fig. 15b). The U-notched model derives from the V-notched one. A leather V-notched shield was found at Clonbrin, County Longford, Ireland, and a wooden U-notched shield at Cloonlara, County Mayo (Harbison 1988: 140). It is likely that both types made of perishable materials were also in use elsewhere, in areas with less favorable conditions for preservation. The combined distribution of the two types is clearly Atlantic, from Iberia, via the British Isles, then to Scandinavia, where only the later U-notched shields occur (Uckelmann 2012: 50–62, 127–137, pl. 160).

There are figural categories of special interest when comparing Extremaduran and Scandinavian rock art of about 1200 to 800 BC (Fig. 11.1). In general, the same categories of weapons, shields, daggers, bows and arrows, spears, and swords figure in both corpora, but often reflect different regional types. Bi-horned warriors are a prominent shared theme among the several parallels. Their horns show formal similarities, as well as similar gestures and weapons. Similarities between depictions of bi-horned warriors in Extremaduran rock art, Nuragic Late Bronze Age figurines, and stone statues from Sardinia and the horned bronze figurines from Grevensvænge in Denmark should be seen against this background (Harrison 2004; Coles 2005; Vandkilde 2013). Even though these horned anthropomorphic representations were produced in widely separated regions, they belong to the same time frame of 1300 to 900 BC, bear witness to long-range interaction, and constitute a

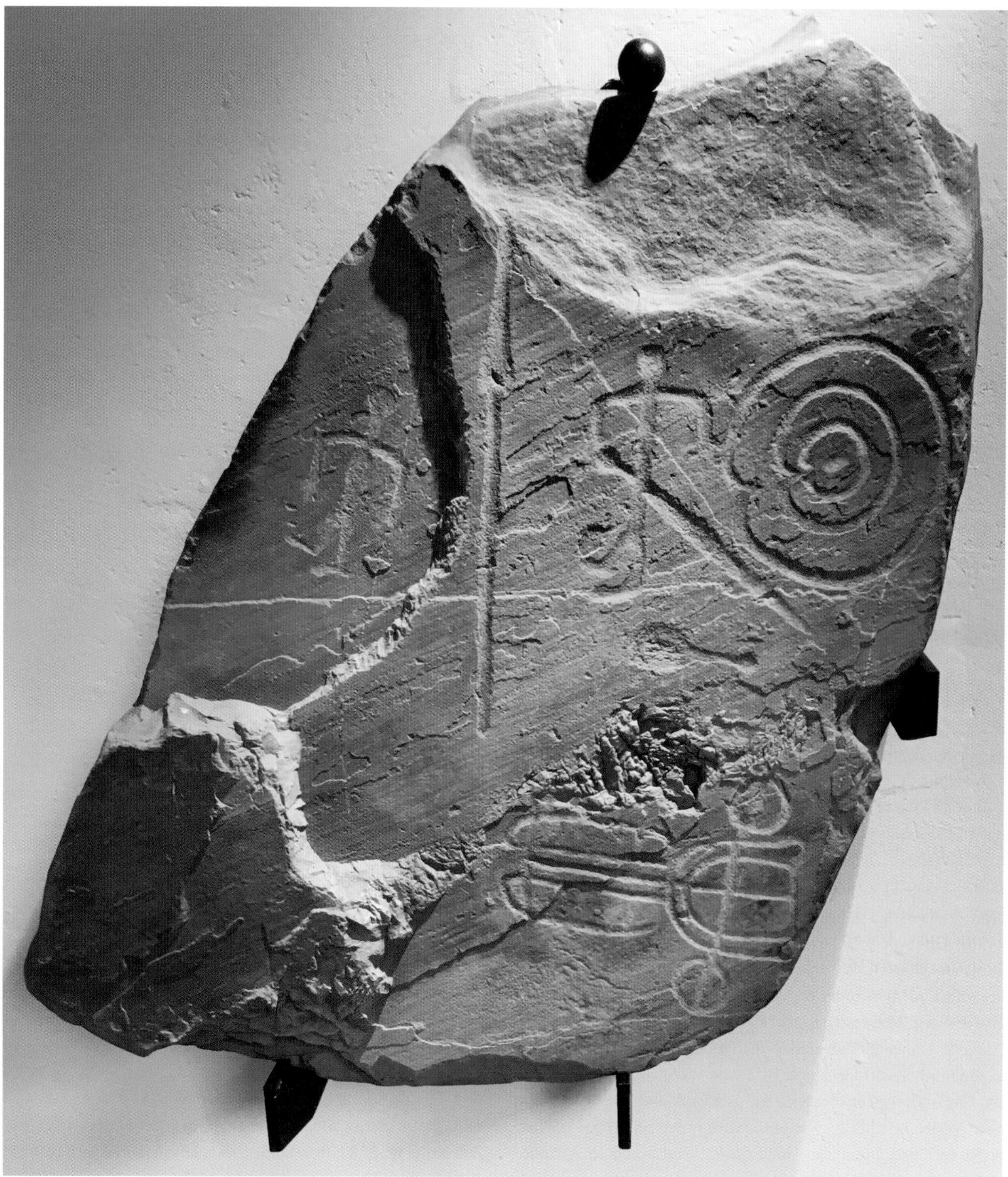

FIGURE 11.5. *Late Bronze Age stela from La Solanilla, Córdoba, Spain, showing a spear, V-notched shield, mirror, chariot with two-horse team, and warrior with sword (photo: J. Koch).*

vivid representation of pan-European warrior symbolism that could be connected with the expansion of the Urnfield culture (Harrison 2004: 60; Vandkilde 2013).

Images of chariots (Figs. 11.5 and 11.6) from the two regions also show detailed similarities (Harrison 2004; Ling & Uhnér 2015). Two-wheeled vehicles were widely used during the Bronze Age in the Near East and Eastern Mediterranean, and they were evidently known in Iberia, southern Scandinavia, and other parts of temperate Europe in the Late Bronze Age (Koch 2013a). Noting strong similarities between war-chariot depictions in Scandinavia and Iberia, Harrison (2004) and Koch (2013a) argue for direct contact. The stereotypical views of chariot frames, draft poles, and sometimes yokes and reins, as if seen from above, while the wheels and draft horses are represented turned out 90°, as if viewed from the side (see Figs. 11.5 and 11.6), is best explained as a shared tradition of

FIGURE 11.6. *Paper rubbing of a rock-art image of a chariot and two-horse team from Frännarp, Skåne, Sweden, showing the recurrent conventional representation of the horses, chariot frame, wheels, axle, spokes, yoke, and draft pole (source: D. Evers, SHFA).*

visual art, rather than a disembodied transmission of oral descriptions of heroic accoutrements independently committed to graphic representation.

Images of mirrors occur in the rock carvings of both regions, with forty-two in Iberia as the largest group in Europe (Harrison 2004, 151). Shown in masculine martial contexts, they can be understood as an expression of the warrior ideal, including male physical beauty. In our view, similar mirror depictions occur in at least three sites in Bohuslän, Western Sweden (Kville 216:1, Tossene 46:1, and Fredsjö 427:4; see Ling & Uhnér 2015). For both the Iberian and Scandinavian Bronze Age carvings of mirrors, the form of the object and its handle can be traced back to artifacts produced in the Eastern Mediterranean. Albeit in fewer numbers, the Scandinavian mirror representations are, as in Iberia, found in close association with martial motifs, such as warriors, bi-horned figures, and war canoes, and they are undoubtedly a local articulation of pan-European warrior symbolism.

11.9 Conclusion

In this chapter, we have argued that there existed strong links between Iberia and Scandinavia in the Bronze Age and that both rock art and metal sourcing provide evidence of this interaction. Recent advances in Mediterranean and Iberian archaeology show substantial contacts between Atlantic Iberia and the Mycenaeans, Cypriots, and Phoenicians (Mederos 1996; 2018; Blázquez 2011; Ruiz-Gálvez 2013), long before the full-blown Phoenician colonies and "Orientalization" of the Iberian Early Iron Age. This leaves an unexplored question to be confronted in our research: did two linear sea routes overlap in Late Bronze Age Iberia or did these become an integrated triangular network – Scandinavia–Iberia–Aegean/Levant?

In this context, it becomes relevant to reexamine the old idea of a connection between the British Isles and the Eastern Mediterranean, going back to the shaft grave period of Mycenae (1600–1450 BC), the so-called "Wessex connection" (Harding 1984; 1990; Maran 2016), driven by the demand for tin and amber from what Herodotus called "the ends of the earth," bordering the "sea beyond Europe to the north and west." A shift of focus toward the northwest at this time possibly came in response to the exhaustion or interruption of earlier Afghan sources of tin combined with rising demand for Baltic amber. Perspectives to be pursued in our future research include the roles of Scandinavia and Iberia as terminus zones in an integrated Atlantic sea route between 1300 and 900 BC, and the dual role of the Iberian Peninsula in the Late Bronze Age as both a source of metals (copper, tin, silver, and gold) and a cultural and economic crossroads between the Atlantic and Mediterranean networks. The post-Proto-Indo-European vocabulary shared by Celtic and Germanic is also consistent with other evidence for Iberian–Scandinavian contact in later prehistory, and it may be possible to draw more precise conclusions from this linguistic evidence as dating evidence and etymologies are carefully reconsidered.

In order to investigate these issues we intend to apply the following methods:

1. laser scanning and image-based modeling of rock art in the Iberian Peninsula and Scandinavia, making it possible to map the sharing and spread of specific details of ideologies, cosmologies, iconographic conventions, and artistic techniques for the period ca. 1300 to 900 BC;
2. isotopic and geochemical sourcing, to analyze extensive corpora of metal objects in Atlantic Europe traceable to Iberian ores;
3. aDNA and isotopic results for human remains will be used to assess degrees of change in populations from later prehistory to early historic times; increasingly detailed data for population movements in the Bronze Age will permit the refinement of models of the formation of the Indo-European branches and survival of non-Indo-European in Northern and Western Europe;
4. these new data will be used to investigate a novel multidisciplinary hypothesis that understands the rise and fall of Bronze Age economic activity and social complexity as running closely parallel to the diversification of Proto-Indo-European into separate languages;
5. we will seek to integrate and develop more theoretical aspects about the connections between social complexity and long-distance trade with reference to rock art, metal trade, and "secret societies."

References

Allentoft, Morten E. et al. 2015. Population genomics of Bronze Age Eurasia. *Nature* 522(7555): 167–172.

Almagro Basch, Martín. 1966. *La estelas decoradas del suroeste peninsular* (Bibliotheca Praehistoria Hispana 8). Madrid: Imprenta Fareso.

Anthony, David W. 2007. *The horse, the wheel, and language: How Bronze-Age riders from the Eurasian steppes shaped the modern world*. Princeton: Princeton University Press.

Anthony, David W. & Don Ringe. 2015. The Indo-European homeland from linguistic and archaeological perspectives. *Annual Review of Linguistics* 1: 199–219.

Anthony, David W. & D. R. Brown. 2017. Molecular archaeology and Indo-European linguistics: Impressions from new data. In: Bjarne Simmelkjær Sandgaard Hansen et al. (ed.), *Usque as radices: Indo-European studies in honour of Birgit Anette Olsen*, 25–54. Copenhagen: Museum Tusculanum Press.

Bengtsson, Boel. 2017. *Sailing rock art boats. A reassessment of seafaring abilities in Bronze Age Scandinavia and the introduction of the sail in the North*. Oxford: BAR.

Bengtsson, Lasse (ed.). 2002. Arkeologisk rapport 6. *Askum socken* (Bohuslän 3). Bengtsfors: Vitlycke Museum.

(ed.). 2009. Arkeologisk rapport 7. *Tossene socken*. Gothenburg: Vitlycke Museum.

Blázquez Martínez, José María. 2011. Chipre y la Península Ibérica. In: Manuel Álvarez Martí-Aguilar (ed.), *Fenicios en Tartessos: nuevas perspectivas* (BAR International Series 2245), 7–31. Oxford: Archaeopress.

Brandherm, Dirk. 2007. Algunas reflexiones sobre el bronce inicial en el noroeste peninsular. La cuestion del llamado horizonte "Montelavar." *Cuadernos de Prehistoria y Arqueología de Universidad Autónoma de Madrid* 33: 69–90.

2013. Mediterranes, Atlantisches und Kontinentales in der bronze- und ältereisenzeitlichen Stelenkunst der Iberischen Halbinsel. In: Georg Kalaitzoglou & Gundula Lüdorf (ed.), *Petasos: Festschrift für Hans Lohmann*, 131–148. Paderborn: Fink & Schöningh.

2016. Stelae, funerary practice, and group identities in the Bronze and Iron Ages of SW Iberia: A moyenne durée perspective. In: John T. Koch, Barry Cunliffe, Catriona D. Gibson, & Kerri Cleary (ed.), *Celtic from the West 3. Atlantic Europe in the Metal Ages. Questions of shared language* (Celtic Studies Publications 19), 179–216. Oxford: Oxbow Books.

Burgess, Colin & Brendan O'Connor. 2008. Iberia, the Atlantic Bronze Age and the Mediterranean. In: Sebastián Celestino Pérez et al. (ed.), *Contacto cultural entre el Mediterráneo y el Atlántico (siglos XII–VIII ANE), La precolonización a debate* (Serie Arqueológica 11), 41–58. Madrid: Escuela Española de Historia y Arqueología en Roma CSIC.

Cassidy, Lara M. et al. 2016. Neolithic and Bronze Age migration to Ireland and establishment of the insular Atlantic genome. *PNAS* 113(2): 368–373.

Childe, V. Gordon. 1939. Notes: About the distribution in Atlantic Europe and Scandinavia of the double looped Galician Axe. *The Antiquaries Journal* 19: 321–323.

Cleary, Kerri & Catriona Gibson. 2019. Connectivity in Atlantic Europe during the Bronze Age (2800–800 BC). In: Barry Cunliffe & John T. Koch (ed.), *Exploring Celtic origins: New ways forward in archaeology, linguistics, and genetics* (Celtic Studies Publications 22), 80–116. Oxford: Oxbow Books.

Coles, John M. 2005. *Shadows of a northern past: Rock carvings of Bohuslän and Østfold*. Oxford: Oxbow Books.

Cunliffe, Barry. 2001. *Facing the Ocean. The Atlantic and its Peoples 8000 BC–AD 1500*. Oxford: Oxford University Press.

2010. Celticization from the West. The contribution of archaeology. In: Barry Cunliffe & John T. Koch (ed.), *Celtic from the West. Alternative perspectives from archaeology, genetics, language and literature* (Celtic Studies Publications 15), 13–38. Oxford: Oxbow Books.

2013. *Britain begins*. Oxford: Oxford University Press.

2019. Setting the scene. In: Barry Cunliffe & John T. Koch (ed.), *Exploring Celtic Origins: New ways forward in archaeology, linguistics, and genetics* (Celtic Studies Publications 22), 1–17. Oxford: Oxbow Books.

de Barros Damgaard, Peter et al. 2018. The first horse herders and the impact of early Bronze Age steppe expansions into Asia. *Science* 10.1126/science.aar7711.

Díaz-Guardamino Uribe, Marta. 2010. *Las estelas decoradas en la Prehistoria de la Península Ibérica*. Madrid: Universidad Complutense de Madrid.

Díaz-Guardamino Uribe, Marta, & D. W. Wheatley. 2013. Rock art and digital technologies. The application of Reflectance Transformation Imaging (RTI) and 3D laser scanning to the study of Late Bronze Age Iberian stelae. *Menga: Revista de prehistoria de Andalucía* 4: 187–203.

Earle, Timothy. 2002. *Bronze Age economics*. Boulder (CO): Westview Press.

2015. The political economy and metal trade in Bronze Age Europe. Understanding regional variability in terms of comparative advantages and articulations. *European Journal of Archaeology* 18(4): 633–657.

Enright, Michael J. 1996. *Lady with a mead cup. Ritual, prophecy and lordship in the European warband from La Tène to the Viking Age*. Blackrock: Four Courts.

Eogan, George. 1995. Ideas, people and things. Ireland and the external world during the Late Bronze Age. In: John Waddell & Elizabeth Shee Twohig (ed.), *Ireland in the Bronze Age. Proceedings of the Dublin conference, April 1995*, 128–135. Dublin: Stationery Office.

Falileyev, Alexander et al. 2010. *Dictionary of Continental Celtic place-names. A Celtic companion to the Barrington Atlas of the Greek and Roman World*. Aberystwyth: CMCS.

Fitzpatrick, Andrew P. 2013. The arrival of the Bell Beaker set in Britain and Ireland. In: John T. Koch & Barry Cunliffe (ed.), *Celtic from the West 2. Rethinking the Bronze Age and the arrival of Indo-European in Atlantic Europe* (Celtic Studies Publications 16), 41–70. Oxford: Oxbow Books.

Fredsjö, Åke. 1981. *Hällristningar Kville härad i Bohuslän, Kville socken*. Gothenburg: Fornminnesförening i Göteborg.

Garrett, Andrew. 2006. Convergence in the formation of Indo-European subgroups. Phylogeny and chronology. In: Peter Forster & Colin Renfrew (ed.), *Phylogenetic methods and the prehistory of languages*, 139–151. Cambridge: McDonald Institute for Archaeological Research.

Gimbutas, Marija. 1970. Proto-Indo-European culture: The Kurgan culture during the 5th to the 3rd millennia BC. In: G. Cardona, H. M. Koenigswald, & A. Senn (ed.), *Indo-European and Indo-Europeans*, 155–198. Philadelphia: University of Pennsylvania Press.

Haak, Wolfgang et al. 2015. Massive migration from the steppe was a source for Indo-European languages in Europe. *Nature* 522: 207–211.

Harbison, Peter. 1988. *Pre-Christian Ireland: From the first settlers to the early Celts*. London: Thames and Hudson.

Harding, Anthony. 1990. The Wessex connection. Developments and perspectives. In: Peter Schauer (ed.), *Orientalisch-ägäische Einflüsse inder europäischen Bronzezeit. Ergebnisse eines Kolloquiums (1985)* (Monographien RGZM 15), 139–154. Mainz: Zabern.

2000. *European societies in the Bronze Age*. Cambridge: Cambridge University Press.

2013. World systems, cores, and peripheries in prehistoric Europe. *European Journal of Archaeology* 16(3): 378–400.

Harrison, Richard J. 2004. *Symbols and warriors: Images of the European Bronze Age*. Bristol: Western Academic & Specialist Press.

Harrison, Richard J. & Volker Heyd. 2007. The transformation of Europe in the third millennium BC. The example of "Le Petit Chasseur I + III" (Sion, Valais, Switzerland). *Prähistorische Zeitschrift* 82: 129–214.

Hayden, Brian. 2018. *The power of ritual in prehistory: Secret societies and origins of social complexity*. Cambridge: Cambridge University Press.

Herodotus = Aubrey de Sélincourt (trans.). 1972. *Herodotus: The histories*, rev. ed. Harmondsworth: Penguin. First published 1954.

Horn, Christian. 2014. *Studien zu den europäischen Stabdolchen* (Universitätsforschungen zur Prähistorischen Archäologie 246). Bonn: Habelt.

Horn, Christian & Richard Potter. 2017. Transforming the rocks: Time and rock art in Bohuslän, Sweden. *European Journal of Archaeology* 63: 1–24.

Hyllested, Adam. 2010. The precursors of Celtic and Germanic. In: Stephanie W. Jamison et al. (ed.), *Proceedings of the 21st Annual UCLA Indo-European Conference*, 107–128. Bremen: Hempen.

Isaac, Graham. R. 2007. *Studies in Celtic sound changes and their chronology*. Innsbruck: Institut für Sprachen und Literaturen der Universität Innsbruck.

Kaul, Flemming. 2013. The Nordic razor and the Mycenaean lifestyle. *Antiquity* 87(336): 461–472.

Kienlin, Tobias L. 2012. Patterns of change, or perceptions deceived? Comments on the interpretation of Late Neolithic and Bronze Age tell settlement in the Carpathian Basin. In: Tobias Kienlin & Andreas Zimmermann (ed.), *Beyond elites. Alternatives to hierarchical systems in modelling social formations*, 251–310. Bonn: Habelt.

Koch, John T. 2013a. Out of the flow and ebb of the European Bronze Age. Heroes, Tartessos, and Celtic. In: John T. Koch & Barry Cunliffe (ed.), *Celtic from the West 2. Rethinking the Bronze Age and the arrival of Indo-European in Atlantic Europe* (Celtic Studies Publications 16), 101–146. Oxford: Oxbow Books.

2013b. *Tartessian. Celtic in the South-west at the dawn of history* (Celtic Studies Publications 13). Aberystwyth: Celtic Studies Publications.

2013c. Prologue. Ha C1a ≠ PC (the earliest Hallstatt Iron Age cannot equal Proto-Celtic). In: John T. Koch & Barry Cunliffe (ed.), *Celtic from the West 2. Rethinking the Bronze Age and the arrival of Indo-European in Atlantic Europe* (Celtic Studies Publications 16), 1–16. Oxford: Oxbow Books.

2016. Phoenicians in the West and break-up of the Atlantic Bronze Age. In: John T. Koch, Barry Cunliffe, Catriona D. Gibson, & Kerri Cleary (ed.), *Celtic from the West 3. Atlantic Europe in the Metal Ages. Questions of shared language* (Celtic Studies Publications 19), 431–476. Oxford: Oxbow Books.

2019a. Rock art and Celto-Germanic vocabulary: Shared iconography and words as reflections of Bronze Age contact. *Adoranten* 2019: 80–95.

2019b. *Common ground and progress on the Celtic of the South-western (S.W.) inscriptions*. Aberystwyth: Centre for Advanced Welsh and Celtic Studies.

2020. *Celto-Germanic: Later prehistory and Post-Proto-Indo-European vocabulary in the North and West*. Aberystwyth: Centre for Advanced Welsh and Celtic Studies.

Koch, John T., with Fernando Fernández Palacios. 2019. A case of identity theft? Archaeogenetics, Beaker People, and Celtic origins. In: Barry Cunliffe & John T. Koch (ed.), *Exploring Celtic origins: New ways forward in archaeology, linguistics, and genetics* (Celtic Studies Publications 22), 38–79. Oxford: Oxbow Books.

Koch, John T., with Raimund Karl, Antone Minard, & Simon Ó Faoláin. 2007. *An atlas for Celtic studies. Archaeology and names in ancient Europe and early medieval Ireland, Britain, and Brittany* (Celtic Studies Publications 12). Oxford: Oxbow Books.

Kristiansen, Kristian. 1998. *Europe before history*. Cambridge: Cambridge University Press.

2007. The rules of the game, decentralised complexity and power structures. In: Sheila Kohring & Stephanie Wynne-Jones (ed.), *Socializing complexity. Structure interaction and power in archaeological discourse*, 60–75. Oxford: Oxbow Books.

2014. Towards a new paradigm? The third science revolution and its possible consequences in archaeology. *Current Swedish Archaeology* 22, 11–34.

2017. When language meets archaeology. From Proto-Indo-European to Proto-Germanic in northern Europe. In: Bjarne Simmelkjær Sandgaard Hansen et al. (ed.), *Usque as radices: Indo-European studies in honour of Birgit Anette Olsen*, 427–438. Copenhagen: Museum Tusculanum Press.

2018. Warfare and the political economy: Bronze Age Europe 1500–1100 BC. In: Christian Horn & Kristian Kristiansen (ed.), *Warfare in Bronze Age society*, 23–46. Cambridge: Cambridge University Press.

Kristiansen, Kristian & Paulina Suchowska-Ducke. 2015. Connected histories. The dynamics of Bronze Age interaction and trade 1500–1100 BC. *Proceedings of the Prehistoric Society* 81, 361–382.

Kristiansen, Kristian & Timothy Earle. 2015. Neolithic versus Bronze Age social formations. A political economy approach. In: Kristian Kristiansen et al. (ed.), *Paradigm found. Archaeological theory – present, past and future. Essays in honour of Evžen Neustupný*, 236–249. Oxford: Oxbow Books.

Kroonen, Guus. 2013. *Etymological dictionary of Proto-Germanic* (Leiden Indo-European Etymological Dictionary Series 11). Leiden & Boston: Brill.

Lazaridis, Iosif. 2018. The evolutionary history of human populations in Europe. *Current Opinion in Genetics & Development* 53: 21–27.

Lévi-Strauss, Claude. 1964. *Mythologiques*. Part 1. Le cru et le cuit. Paris: Plon.

vander Linden, Marc. 2007. What linked the Bell Beakers in third millennium BC Europe? *Antiquity* 81(312): 343–352.

Ling, Johan & Claes Uhnér. 2015. Rock art and metal trade. *Adoranten* 2014: 23–43.

Ling, Johan & Michael Rowlands. 2013. Structure from the North content from the South. Rock art, metal trade and cosmopolitical codes. In: Emmanuel Anati (ed.), *Art as a source of history, XXV Valcamonica Symposium Capo di Ponte, September 20–26, 2013*, 187–196. Capo di Ponte: Edizioni del Centro.

Ling, Johan & Ulf Bertilsson. 2017. Biography of the Fossum panel. *Adoranten* 2016: 58–72.

Ling, Johan et al. 2013. Moving metals or indigenous mining? Provenancing Scandinavian Bronze Age artefacts by lead isotopes and trace elements. *Journal of Archaeological Science* 40(1): 291–304.

2014. Moving metals II. Provenancing Scandinavian Bronze Age artefacts by lead isotope and elemental analyses. *Journal of Archaeological Science* 41(1): 106–112.

Ling, Johan, Richard Chacon, & Yolande Chacon. 2018. Rock art, secret societies, long-distance exchange, and warfare in Bronze Age Scandinavia. In: A. Dolfini, R. Crellin, C. Horn, & M. Uckelmannn (ed.), *Prehistoric warfare and violence: Quantitative and qualitative approaches*, 149–174. New York: Springer.

Ling, Johan, Timothy Earle, & Kristian Kristiansen. 2018. Maritime mode of production. Raiding and trading in seafaring chiefdoms. *Current Anthropology* 59(5): 488–524.

Mallory, James P. 1989. *In search of the Indo-Europeans: Language, archaeology and myth*. London: Thames and Hudson.

2013. The Indo-Europeanization of Atlantic Europe. In: John T. Koch & Barry Cunliffe (ed.), *Celtic from the West 2. Rethinking the Bronze Age and the arrival of Indo-European in Atlantic Europe* (Celtic Studies Publications 16), 17–40. Oxford: Oxbow Books.

Mallory, James P. & Douglas Q. Adams. 2006. *The Oxford introduction to Proto-Indo-European and the Proto-Indo-European world*. Oxford: Oxford University Press.

Maran, Joseph. 2004. Wessex und Mykene. Zur Deutung des Bernsteins in der Schachtgräberzeit Südgriechenlands. In: Bernhard Hänsel & Etela Studeníkova (ed.), *Zwischen Karpaten und Ägais. Neolithikum und Ältere Bronzezeit. Gedenkschrift für Viera Nemejcová-Pavúková*, 47–65. Rahden: Leidorf.

2016. Bright as the sun. The appropriation of amber objects in Mycenaean Greece. In: Hans Peter Hahn & Hadas Weiss (ed.), *Mobility, meaning and the transformation of things*, 147–169. Oxford: Oxbow Books.

Martiniano, Rui et al. 2017. The population genomics of archaeological transition in west Iberia. Investigation of ancient substructure using imputation and haplotype-based methods. *PLoS Genet* 13(7): e1006852.

Matasović, Ranko. 2009. *Etymological dictionary of Proto-Celtic* (Leiden Indo-European Etymological Dictionary Series). Leiden & Boston: Brill.

McCone, Kim R. 1996. *Towards a relative chronology of ancient and medieval Celtic sound change* (Maynooth Studies in Celtic Linguistics 1). Maynooth: St Patrick's College.

McKinley, Jacqueline I. et al. 2013. Dead sea connections. A Bronze Age and Iron Age ritual site on the Isle of Thanet. In: John T. Koch & Barry Cunliffe (ed.), *Celtic from the West 2. Rethinking the Bronze Age and the arrival of Indo-European in Atlantic Europe* (Celtic Studies Publications 16), 157–183. Oxford: Oxbow Books.

2015. *Cliffs End Farm, Isle of Thanet, Kent*. Oxford: Oxbow Books.

Mederos Martín, Alfredo. 1996. La conexión levantino-chipriota. Indicios de comercio atlántico con el Mediterráneo oriental durante el Bronce Final (1150–950 AC). *Trabajos de prehistoria* 53(2): 95–115.

Melheim, Lena & Johan Ling. 2017. Taking the stranger on board. In: Peter Skoglund, Johan Ling, & Ulf Bertilsson (ed.), *North meets south. Theoretical aspects on the northern and southern rock art traditions in Scandinavia*, 59–86. Oxford: Oxbow Books.

Melheim, Lena et al. 2018. Moving metals III. Possible origins for copper in Bronze Age Denmark based on lead isotopes and geochemistry. *Journal of Archaeological Science* 96: 85–105.

Milcent, Pierre-Yves. 2012. *Le temps des élites en Gaule atlantique. Chronologie des mobiliers et rythmes de constitution des dépots métalliques dans le contexte européen (XIIIe–VIIe av. J.-C.)*. Rennes: Presses Universitaires de Rennes.

Monteagudo, Luis. 1977. *Die Beile auf der Iberischen Halbinsel*. Munich: C.H. Beck'sche Verlagsbuchhandlung.

Murillo-Barroso, Mercedes & Marcos Martinón-Torres. 2012. Amber sources and trade in the prehistory of the Iberian Peninsula. *European Journal of Archaeology* 15(2): 187–216.

Narasimhan, Vagheesh M. et al. 2018. The formation of human populations in South and Central Asia. *Science* 365(6457).

Needham, Stuart P. 1996. Chronology and periodisation in the British Bronze Age. *Acta Archaeologica* 67: 121–140.

2016. The lost cultures of the halberd bearers: A non-Beaker ideology in later 3rd millennium Atlantic Europe. In: John T. Koch, Barry Cunliffe, Catriona D. Gibson, & Kerri Cleary (ed.), *Celtic from the West 3. Atlantic Europe in the Metal Ages. Questions of shared language* (Celtic Studies Publications 19), 40–81. Oxford: Oxbow Books.

Van de Noort, Robert. 2011. *North Sea archaeologies. A maritime biography, 10,000 BC to AD 1500*. Oxford: Oxford University Press.

Nordén, Arthur. 1925. *Östergötlands bronsålder: Med omkr. 500 textbilder och 141 pl.* Linköping: H. Carlsons bokhandel.

Nørgaard, Heide W. et al. 2019. Provenance studies on metal artefacts of the Danish Bronze Age: The archaeological and chemical evidence of metal trade 2100–1600 BC. Paper read at the 15th Nordic Bronze Age Symposium, Lund, June 2019.

O'Brien, William. 2004. *Ross Island. Mining, metal and society in early Ireland* (Bronze Age Studies 6). Galway: National University of Ireland.

2016. Language shift and political context in Bronze Age Ireland: Some implications of hillfort chronology. In: John T. Koch, Barry Cunliffe, Catriona D. Gibson, & Kerri Cleary (ed.), *Celtic from the West 3. Atlantic Europe in the Metal Ages. Questions of shared language* (Celtic Studies Publications 19), 219–246. Oxford: Oxbow Books.

O'Brien, William & James O'Driscoll. 2017. *Hillforts, warfare and society in Bronze Age Ireland*. Oxford: Archaeopress.

Odriozola, Carlos P. et al. 2017. Amber, beads and social interaction in the Late Prehistory of the Iberian Peninsula: An update. *Archaeological and Anthropological Sciences*, 1–29.

Olalde, Iñigo et al. 2018. The Beaker phenomenon and the genomic transformation of Northwest Europe. *Nature* 555: 190–196.

2019. The genomic history of the Iberian Peninsula over the past 8000 years. *Science* 363: 1230–1234.

Pare, Christopher F. E. 2000. Bronze and the Bronze Age. In: C. F. E. Pare (ed.), *Metals make the world go round. Supply and circulation of metals in Bronze Age Europe*, 1–37. Oxford: Oxbow Books.

Patterson, Nick et al. 2021. Large-scale migration into Britain during the Middle to Late Bronze Age. *Nature* 601: 588–594.

Radivojević, Miljana et al. 2018. The provenance, use, and circulation of metals in the European Bronze Age: The state of debate. *Journal of Archaeological Research* 27: 1–55.

Ringe, Don. 2017. *A linguistic history of English. From Proto-Indo-European to Proto-Germanic*. Oxford: Oxford University Press. First published 2006.

Ringe, Don, T. Warnow, & A. Taylor 2002. Indo-European and computational cladistics. *Transactions of the Philological Society* 100(1): 59–129.

Ruiz-Gálvez Priego, Marisa. 2013. *Con el fenicio en los talones: Los inicios de la Edad del hierro en la cuenca del Mediterráneo*. Barcelona: Bellaterra.

Schleicher, August. 1861/1862. *Compendium der vergleichenden Grammatik der indogermanischen Sprachen. (Kurzer Abriss der indogermanischen Ursprache, des Altindischen, Altiranischen, Altgriechischen, Altitalischen, Altkeltischen, Altslawischen, Litauischen und Altdeutschen.)*. 2 vols. Weimar: H. Boehlau. Reprinted by Minerva GmbH, Wissenschaftlicher Verlag.

Schrijver, Peter. 2016. Sound change: The Italo-Celtic linguistic unity, and the Italian homeland of Celtic. In: John T. Koch, Barry Cunliffe, Catriona D. Gibson & Kerri Cleary (ed.), *Celtic from the West 3. Atlantic Europe in the Metal Ages. Questions of shared language* (Celtic Studies Publications 19), 489–502. Oxford: Oxbow Books.

Schulz Paulsson, Bettina. 2017. *Time and stone. The emergence and development of megaliths and megalithic societies in Europe*. Oxford: Archaeopress.

2019. Radiocarbon dates and Bayesian modeling support maritime diffusion model for megaliths in Europe. *PNAS* 116(9): 3460–3465.

Sherratt, Andrew. 1993. What would a Bronze-Age world system look like? Relations between temperate Europe and the Mediterranean in later prehistory. *Journal of European Archaeology* 1(2): 1–57.

Sherratt, Susan. 2003. The Mediterranean economy. "Globalisation" at the end of the second millennium BCE. In: William G. Dever & Seymour Gitin (ed.), *Symbiosis, symbolism, and the power of the past. Canaan, ancient Israel, and their neighbours from the Late Bronze Age through Roman Palaestina*, 37–62. Winona Lake (IN): Eisenbrauns.

2009. The Aegean and the wider world. Some thoughts on a world-system perspective. In: William A. Parkinson & Michael L. Galaty (ed.), *Archaic state interaction. The Eastern Mediterranean in the Bronze Age*, 81–107. Santa Fe (NM): School for Advanced Research Press.

Thrane, H. 1990. The Mycenaean fascination: A northerners' view. In: T. Bader (ed.), *Orientalisch-ägäische Einflüsse in der europäischen Bronzezeit: Ergebnisse eines Kolloquiums*, 165–179. Bonn: Habelt.

Uckelmann, Marion. 2012. *Die Schilde der Bronzezeit in Nord-, West- und Zentraleuropa*. Stuttgart: Franz Steiner Verlag.

Untermann, Jürgen (with Dagmar S. Wodtko). 1997. *Monumenta Linguarum Hispanicarum*. Vol. 4. Die tartessischen, keltiberischen und lusitanischen Inschriften. Wiesbaden: Reichert.

de Vaan, M. 2008. *Etymological dictionary of Latin and the other Italic languages*. Leiden, Brill.

Valdiosera, Cristina et al. 2018. Four millennia of Iberian biomolecular prehistory illustrate the impact of prehistoric migrations at the far end of Eurasia. *PNAS* 115(13): 3428–3433.

Vandkilde, Helle et al. (ed.). 2006. *Warfare and society. Archaeological and social anthropological perspectives*. Aarhus: Aarhus University Press.

Vandkilde, Helle. 2013. Bronze Age voyaging and cosmologies in the making. The helmets from Viksø revisited. In Sophie Bergerbrant & Serena Sabatini (ed.), *Counterpoint. Essays in archaeology and heritage studies in honour of Professor Kristian Kristiansen*, 165–177. Oxford: Archaeopress.

2016. Bronzization. The Bronze Age as pre-modern globalization. *Praehistorische Zeitschrift* 91(1): 103–123.

Ventris, Michael & John Chadwick. 2008. *Documents in Mycenaean Greek*, 2nd ed. Cambridge: Cambridge University Press.

Witzel, Michael. 2019. Early "Aryans" and their neighbors outside and inside India. *Journal of Biosciences* 44: 58.

12 WITH THE BACK TO THE OCEAN: THE CELTIC MARITIME VOCABULARY*

DAVID STIFTER

12.1 Methodology

The aim of this chapter is to establish the semantic field of maritime vocabulary of the Celtic languages, especially that part of the maritime vocabulary that can be reconstructed for Proto-Celtic, the common ancestor of all Celtic languages, and for the prehistoric stages of the Insular Celtic languages. The approach taken in this study is to analyse the relevant lexemes etymologically, and to assess the findings from the point of view of linguistic archaeology. Linguistic archaeology seeks to extract as much information as possible from the synchronic and diachronically reconstructable semantics and morphology of words in order to make inferences about the environment and living conditions of the language's speakers from a prehistoric and early historic perspective. Maritime vocabulary, which is the focus of this study, includes all elements of the lexicon that refer to the topographical, biological, and economic environment of the sea and the shore, and to human interaction with them.

Such an investigation, in particular with an eye to the earliest reconstructable vocabulary of Celtic, poses several methodological challenges for the researcher. The first, and most fundamental, has to do with chronology. The earliest surviving written evidence for Celtic languages dates roughly to the middle of the first millennium BC, but it is very scanty in nature. Information about Celtic languages does not abound until the second half of the first millennium AD. The attested Celtic languages are therefore "Iron Age" languages[1] by their very nature, and consequently they do not allow any direct insight into the Bronze Age of the third and second millennia BC. Pre- or Proto-Celtic, the stage of the language that can be reconstructed as ancestral to all attested Celtic languages, cannot be projected further back than ca. 1000 BC, or the final centuries of the second millennium BC at the oldest.

The second challenge has to do with the very unequal attestation of the Celtic languages in quantitative and qualitative respects. For practical purposes, the known Celtic languages can be grouped into four subbranches: Celtiberian, Gaulish (incl. Lepontic), British, and Goidelic or Irish. The precise genetic relationships between the four are more difficult to assess. Compared to the others, the archaic morphology and syntax of Celtiberian suggests that it branched off first, leaving the other three branches to develop as "Core Celtic" for some time. Within Core Celtic, British and Goidelic – which descriptively can be grouped together as "Insular Celtic" – share a number of structural features that are unusual in the wider European context. Whether they also share a lot of vocabulary to the exclusion of Gaulish is impossible to say with certainty because of the fragmentary attestation of the latter. Any apparent lack of a cognate in Gaulish may simply be due to the chances of survival in the small number of surviving sources. Both the time depth and the level of attestation are therefore very unevenly balanced between the four branches. The small Celtiberian lexicon contains no items of maritime vocabulary at all. Gaulish has only eight items of very general meaning, whereas examples are abundant in Goidelic and British. The vast majority of Celtic maritime vocabulary is therefore by its nature skewed toward Core Celtic, and within Core Celtic, it is skewed toward Insular Celtic. Any item claimed as Proto-Celtic needs to be specifically justified.

12.1.1 Etymological Layering

The third methodological challenge arises from the fact that, as may be expected a priori for any natural language, Celtic maritime vocabulary is made up of several different etymological layers. This is to say that the relevant words, even those within a single language, usually go back to several very different sources and have entered the languages at very different periods. The following types can be distinguished:

* This article was written as part of the Chronologicon Hibernicum project, which has received funding from the European Research Council (ERC) under the European Union's Horizon 2020 research and innovation program (grant agreement no. 647351). I am grateful to Deborah Hayden, Guus Kroonen, Elliott Lash, Brian Ó Catháin, Éamon Ó Ciosáin, Aonghas Ó hAlmhain, and Michaela Stifter for suggestions and comments. All disclaimers apply. I owe the title of the article to Patrick Sims-Williams.

[1] A common word for 'iron', namely **ī̆sarno-*, can be reconstructed for Celtic. This word was subsequently borrowed into Proto-Germanic; cf. Van Sluis, Jørgensen, & Kroonen, this volume.

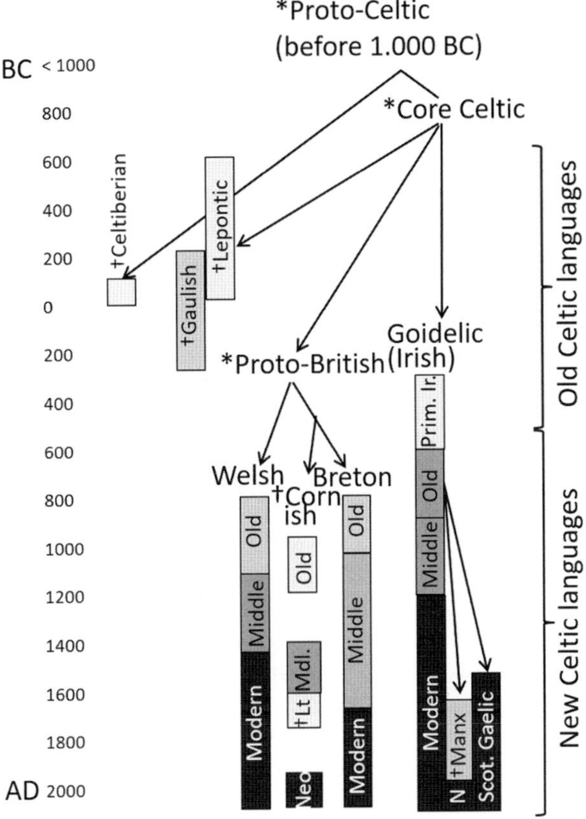

FIG. 12.1. Phylogeny of the Celtic languages.

1. inherited words that go back to Proto-Indo-European;
2. words that have been created productively within Celtic;
   2a. derived from inherited Proto-Indo-European roots using inherited Indo-European morphology;
   2b. metaphorical or descriptive use of existing words for new concepts;
3. loans from other languages;
   3a. loans from other Celtic languages;
   3b. historic loans from Latin, Norse, English, French, etc.;
   3c. historic calques based on other languages;
   3d. prehistoric loans from unknown languages;
4. words that are based on iconic principles, such as onomatopoeia.

Some explanations:

1. Inherited words that go back to Proto-Indo-European can usually be easily recognized. When a word in a given Celtic language can be derived from an established Proto-Indo-European ancestor form by regular sound laws (provided all relevant sound laws are known), it is by default regarded as directly inherited. However, a source for potential errors lurks in this procedure. It ignores the possibility of an early loan from another Indo-European, or Celtic, language where the word in question happened to have such a phonological shape, so that no formal difference can be detected from an authentically inherited word. Since there is no way of formally distinguishing between the two scenarios, this is an inherent aporia.
2. Then there are words that have been created productively within Celtic, during the Proto-Celtic stage or in the centuries when the Celtic languages started to crystallize as separate entities. When such formations involve morphology that is specific to Celtic, they are easy to recognize. However, when no telltale Celtic morphemes are used, but new words are built from inherited Indo-European roots using inherited Indo-European morphemes, the only linguistic criterion that distinguishes them from inherited words is that newly created words will have no exact correspondences in other branches of Indo-European (with minor allowances being made for words that differ only in ablaut grade but derive from the same reconstructable accent-ablaut paradigm). One material criterion for identifying such words is when they refer to items in the physical world that were not known to speakers of Proto-Indo-European, a salient example being iron. Again, there is an inherent weakness in the methodology: if an inherited word has been lost in all other branches of Indo-European, but happens to survive only in Celtic, it is impossible to tell the difference from words that were only created in Celtic. Likewise, if a word is independently created from identical inherited roots with identical inherited suffixes in two separate branches of Indo-European, the result cannot be distinguished from authentically inherited words.
3. Loans from other languages, especially from languages that are known, are for the most part easy to identify as foreign elements within Celtic. If they are borrowed from other Indo-European languages, such words do not display the effects of the established Celtic sound changes that inherited words ought to have, and/or they do not follow the phonotactics of Celtic – that is to say, they show sound combinations that would be impossible for inherited Celtic words, and/or they show morphology that is absent from the native rules of word formation. The most important known languages to provide borrowings into Celtic languages are Latin and varieties of Norse, English, and Gallo-Romance, especially French, which are usually very easy to identify. It is also very probable that unknown languages, now lost, were the sources of borrowings. These languages may have acted as substrates, adstrates, or superstrates of Celtic. Words can also be borrowed from one language into another within the Celtic branch. *Mutatis mutandis*, in these cases, the same conditions and identifying features apply as in cases of borrowing from outside of Celtic. Words of type 3a, borrowings among Celtic languages, can only be identified if the words contain sound changes that distinguish the donor from the recipient language. Where the phonological and morphological shapes of words are identical or near-similar, they are unidentifiable on purely formal grounds.
4. Finally, the lexicon can contain iconic formations. Words with a high degree of iconicity, be it sound iconicity (e.g., names that imitate the sounds of animals) or morphological iconicity (e.g. reduplication), can be difficult to assign to any particular chronological layer, since their formation or reformation can be psychologically motivated at any stage.

Even though words from all these classes would merit a close study, practical limitations do not permit more than an investigation into words from classes 1, 2a, and 3d here. When words occur with more or less exact formal correspondences in more than one subbranch of Celtic, but in no other related language, one can speak of *Sondergleichungen*, i.e. exclusive cognates within Celtic. They may have been created in Celtic (types 2 and 4), but they may also have been borrowed from another language exclusively into Celtic (type 3).

12.1.2 The Nature of Loans

Loans may be borrowings from known languages, in which case they can be easily recognized when compared to the donor language. When words are borrowed from languages that have since vanished without written record, identifying a potential loan becomes more difficult and, to a certain degree, a circular task. Arguments in favor of a word being a loan from another language include unusual sounds and sound combinations and atypical or nontransparent morphology, but the decision to classify a word as a loan from an unknown language ultimately rests on a scholar's instinct for determining the otherness of its sound and shape.

A note of caution has to be sounded as to the conclusions that can be drawn from borrowings. An individual fact of borrowing does not as such prove that the speakers of the language had no previous knowledge of the real-life items designated by the borrowed words. For instance, in the British Celtic languages, the inherited word for 'fish', PC **φei̯sko-* < PIE **pei̯(k̂)sko-*, which is reflected in Old Irish *íasc*, was replaced by the Latin loan *piscis*, namely W *pysg*, OCorn. *pisc*, Bret. *pesk* 'fish (pl.)'. One would hardly assume that British lacked a generic term for that large class of animals or that the British were even unfamiliar with such animals before the Romans came. Incidentally, the inherited word survives in the name of the river *Wysg* (Engl. *Usk*), whose name may derive from its abundance of fish. Therefore, it is not possible in any specific, isolated case to draw the conclusion that the speakers of the language were unfamiliar with a specific item of the physical world. It is only the aggregate number and the thematic clustering of such formations that supports the notion that the physical environment of the speech community had changed. Likewise, the lack of an Indo-European etymology for a word is not in itself proof of a loan, since it is an *argumentum ex silentio*. For instance, the word could have been lost in all Indo-European languages except for Celtic. However, for practical reasons, as a shorthand for the cumulative evidence of the other criteria, this conclusion will be drawn in many cases.

In a similar vein, caution is also needed in drawing conclusions about changes in habitat based on the retention of inherited vocabulary. Lexical items can stay the same, but their reference, i.e. their meaning, can shift to other physical realities, or the memory of a physical reality can be retained together with the inherited lexical item, despite a complete change in habitat. For instance, Old Irish retains the western Indo-European word for 'snake', *naithir* < **nh₁trik-*, with reference to the *serpentes* suborder of *reptiles*, even though there are, famously, no snakes in Ireland.

Another reason for caution when dealing with loanwords is that they may not always be immediately recognizable as such, for example when they have undergone sporadic deformations in their shape. The word for 'crab' in the British Celtic languages, i.e. W *cranc*, MBret. *crancg*, NBret. *krank*, probably goes back to Lat. *cancer*, with rare rhotic metathesis; cf. OCorn. *cancher* glossing Lat. *cancer*.[2]

In several cases, the arguments for a word to have originated in a loan from another, sometimes unknown, language will rest on unusual phonotactics. Unusual phonotactics is not commonly treated as a distinctive criterion for identifying loanwords in its own right but is silently subsumed under phonology. I would like to make this procedure more explicit. Deviant phonotactics, i.e. combinations of sounds that cannot be reconciled with what diachronic phonology and morphology allow inherited words to look like in Celtic, needs to be appreciated as a category of its own. Foreign phonology refers to single sounds, while phonotactics refers to diachronic or synchronic groups of sounds. A straightforward example of the former is ModIr. *portán* 'crab', whose initial *p* is irreconcilable with an inherited word – since Celtic lost all traces of word-initial Indo-European **p*, and because Irish, unlike British and Gaulish, did not develop a new word-initial phoneme *p* by language-internal means. An example of the latter, i.e., of unusual phonotactics, is NIr. *gúgán* 'whelk'. The mechanical pre-Irish reconstruction of this is **gūggo-*. Apart from the fact that this cannot be connected with any known lexical root from Celtic or Indo-European, there is no preform in Proto-Celtic that could yield a long *ú* followed by an unlenited voiced stop. **gg* can only continue **nk*, but both **unk* and hypothetical **ūnk* would have resulted in short **uc* in Old Irish and **ug* in Modern Irish. Sounds need not only occur in clusters, but can also appear disjunctively spread over different parts of the word to qualify for unusual phonotactics. For instance, on the surface, NIr. *langa* 'sea tangle' looks like a *i̯o/ā*-stem, but a mechanically reconstructed preform **langii̯o/ā-* is excluded, as this should have led to ***linge*. A loan looks more likely.

Occasionally, there are borderline cases where it is difficult to say whether a single segment or a cluster of segments is involved. The synchronic reason why a loan may be suspected for OIr. *bratán* 'salmon' is the single sound [d]. From a diachronic perspective, this reflects geminate **dd*, which in turn must continue a group of two sounds, namely either **zd* or **nt*. Since the latter would have caused a preceding **a* to become lengthened and raised to **ē*, there must have been a cluster of sounds involved in this case – as the expected effect on the preceding vowel is absent.

The Insular Celtic languages contribute the majority of lexemes investigated in this article. Therefore, the concept of Insular Celtic employed here warrants a definition. Insular Celtic is used in this chapter in a purely descriptive, geographic sense, with reference to those subbranches of Celtic that developed in the Western European archipelago. The term Proto-Insular Celtic indicates that a common preform underlies words in both the Goidelic and the British languages. Pending further research on the subgrouping of Celtic, the use of "Insular Celtic" here does not imply a preference between the following alternatives, namely whether Insular Celtic should be viewed as a common genetic node of Goidelic and British, which of course is a distinct possibility, or an areal *Sprachbund*. In accordance with what has been stated above, correspondences in Insular Celtic could be common retentions from Proto-Celtic, common innovations at the Insular Celtic level, common or individual borrowings from third languages,

[2] The alternative is to operate from a common Italo-Celtic preform **krankero-* (*uel sim.*) that underwent different dissimilations in the two branches.

or borrowings from one Insular Celtic language into another in such a way that their borrowed character cannot be recognized.

12.1.3 Collection

The unequal attestation of material and the varying quality of this material creates another methodological challenge for assessing maritime vocabulary from a pan-Celtic perspective. No relevant material survives from Celtiberian and Lepontic at all, and only a few words are attested or can be reconstructed for Gaulish. These have been gleaned from Delamarre 2003. A rich stream of data starts to flow in only with medieval Irish, from the seventh or eighth century AD. The medieval Irish data has been systematically extracted from eDIL (ver. 2015, with additions from ver. 2019) via thematic searches of the English definitions and translations, e.g., searches for 'sea', 'shell', and related concepts. Citations are normally restricted to Old Irish; younger stages of the Gaelic languages are only cited when they add information that is not already encapsulated in Old Irish; words of doubtful status, especially those belonging to the genre of *bélrae na filed* 'language of the poets', have been ignored. The sources for modern Gaelic languages are Dinneen (1927) and Dwelly (1911), but no systematic search has been carried out on them. Medieval and Modern Welsh material has been extracted from GPC by conducting similar searches of the English definitions; additionally, Falileyev 2000 has been consulted for Old Welsh. Medieval and Modern Breton material has been extracted from Favereau 2016 through a similar procedure, using French. Medieval Breton data has also been obtained from the short etymological sections at the beginning of the GPC headwords, as has the Cornish material.

However, despite the respectable size of these lexicons, especially eDIL, GPC, and Favereau (2016), none of these dictionaries can claim to exhaustively cover the entire maritime lexicon that exists or existed in these languages. The dictionaries for the medieval languages are limited by what was recorded in the written sources that they draw from. Since the extant documentation of medieval Celtic languages is little concerned with maritime life, it is evident that much of the vocabulary that must have existed at the time has gone unrecorded. The situation is better for the modern languages, especially in the twentieth century. A more systematic search of Dinneen (1927) and Dwelly (1911) than was possible within the limits of the present study will probably produce additional material.

The modern dialects in particular may contain more relevant vocabulary, but that material has its own challenges. Some of the latter-day material is accessible in specialized studies, be they studies of local dialects or thematic collections. My work was aided by using collections and specialist dictionaries for flora and fauna (Mac an Iomaire 1938; An Roinn Oideachais 1978; Çınar 2010; RM 2018). In the case of Breton, the collection of Nyberg 1996 has proved to be of some help. However, the nomenclature is sometimes contradictory between the dictionaries. Among the terms first recorded only in the twentieth century, there is not only no standard orthography for some of them, but even the word forms deviate drastically from one geographical region to another. Having undergone local phonological changes, their etymologies, which might be perfectly straightforward if earlier attestations were available, have often become nontransparent.

The collection encompasses terms referring to maritime topography, to plants and animals living in the sea, and to words connected with the technology and with economic activities at sea. Words for beach flora have been ignored because such vocabulary seems to consist mostly of generic plant names that refer to inland and maritime vegetation at the same time.

12.1.4 Arrangement of entries

The headwords are grouped according to natural semantic classes. Headwords will be given in reconstructed form first. The reconstruction will usually be to the earliest formally possible or plausible stage. Protoforms of words that are attested only in the Insular Celtic (IC) languages are given the label "Proto-Insular-Celtic" (PIC). Only if there is good reason to project such words further back in time, to Core Celtic (CC) or to Proto-Celtic (PC), will this be done. Such reasons could include types of word formation that are unlikely to have remained productive after the Proto-Celtic period. The term "pre-Celtic" is reserved for reconstructions that are thought to have been inherited from a precursor state of Proto-Celtic, but which, due to the lack of exact cognates in other Indo-European languages, cannot be projected back to the Indo-European protolanguage with confidence. These may be words that came into being in the two or three millennia between the breakup of the Indo-European protolanguage and the emergence of a protolanguage with distinctly Celtic traits. Nevertheless, the phonological system of Proto-Indo-European will be used for such reconstructions. For words that are attested only in a single branch, e.g., Irish, the reconstruction will be that of the stage immediately preceding the attested language, e.g., pre-Irish.

The headwords are followed by attestations from the individual Celtic languages. Words that probably go back to Gaulish, but survive only as loans into Latin, are termed Gallo-Latin. With regard to Proto-Indo-European reconstructions, extra-Celtic cognates will be cited only where they help to make a specific point. Those interested in the Indo-European cognates of the discussed items are referred to the standard Indo-Europeanist handbooks (IEW, LIV, NIL, LIPP, etc.).

The following abbreviations are used:

Bret. Breton, *Corn.* Cornish, *Gaul.* Gaulish, *Germ.* German, *Goth.* Gothic, *Gr.* Ancient Greek, *IC* Insular Celtic, *InsLat.* Insular Middle Latin, *It.-Clt.* Italo-Celtic, *Lat.* Latin, *LCorn.* Late Cornish, *Lith.* Lithuanian, *MBret.* Middle Breton, *MCorn.* Middle Cornish, *MIr.* Middle Irish, *MLat.* Middle Latin, *MW* Middle Welsh, *NBret.* Modern ("New") Breton, *NIr.* Modern ("New") Irish, *NW* Modern ("New") Welsh, *OBret.* Old Breton, *OBrit.* Old British, *OCorn.* Old Cornish, *OCS* Old Church Slavonic, *OE* Old English, *OFr.* Old French, *OIr.* Old Irish,

ON Old Norse, *PC* Proto-Celtic, *PIC* Proto-Insular Celtic, *PIE* Proto-Indo-European, *pre-Clt.* Pre-Celtic, *ScGael.* Scottish Gaelic, *W* Welsh.

12.2 Topography

There is a rich array of terms for aspects of the sea and the ocean, especially in Irish. Not included in the list below are manifestly late borrowings from Latin, such as *ocían* 'ocean' or *port* 'place, spot, bank, shore, haven'.

12.2.1 PC **mori-* 'sea' < PIE **mori-*

OIr. *muir* (i, n), MW *mor*, W *môr*, OCorn., MCorn., MBret., NBret. *mor* 'sea'. Gaul. and OBrit. *mori-* occurs in several compounds (*Armorica* 'land before the sea', *Moridunum* 'sea fort', *moritix* 'seagoer = sailor'; cf. item 2.4.9a) and derivatives (*Morini*); Endlicher's Glossary contains the entry *Aremorici; antemarini· quia are; ante· more, mare, morici· marini·*, where the Gaulish names and expressions *Aremorici*, *are* 'before, in front of', *more* 'sea' (with the Latinized ending *-e* for *-i*), and *morici* 'sea people' are glossed by the corresponding Latin words (Blom 2011: 167). The Gaulish ethnonym *Morini* can most straightforwardly be understood as 'sea folk', but it is conceivable that it was also used as a professional term for 'sailors'. Pliny the Elder (*Nat. hist.* 4.95) reports the indigenous name *morimarusa*, which he glosses as *mortuum mare* 'dead sea', for a part of the North Sea. Although he attributes the name to the Germanic Cimbri, the first element, *mori*, looks more Celtic than Germanic (where it would be **mari*). The Celtic words refer unambiguously to the 'sea'. Celtic therefore adds nothing to the question of whether the Proto-Indo-European word **mori-* originally referred to a large, stagnant inland body of water rather than to the sea at large (cf. Mallory & Adams 1997: 503–504; Mallory & Adams 2006: 127). Of the many derivatives and compounds of the word, I only wish to mention a few from Irish that look sufficiently old, i.e., at least Old Irish or pre-Old Irish, or that shed some interesting light on the human view of and interaction with the sea: OIr. *muiresc*, ModIr. *murrasc* < 'low-lying coastland, seaboard' < **muir-ṡesc*, a compound with *sesc* 'dry, barren' < **sisk$^{u̯}$o-*; *murbrucht* 'tidal wave, sea burst', a compound with *brúcht* 'a burst'; *murbach*, *muirbech* 'breakwater, level strip of land along the seacoast', a compound either with **bou̯go-*, a nominal formation of the verb *bongaid* 'to break' < **b^{h}eu̯g^h-* 'to bow' (LIV 85–86) or < **b^{h}eu̯g-* 'to be of use' (LIV 84–85), or with **bego-* 'breaking' < **b^{h}eg-* 'to break' (LIV 66–67); *murrech* 'a large seabird, sea raven' < *muir-ḟiäch*, a compound with *fiäch* 'raven'; *murlúaith* 'sea ashes, salt obtained by evaporation (?)', a compound with *lúaith* 'ashes'. Finally, *muirin*, *muirnech* 'bent grass, seagrass' looks like a derivative **morin(āk)o-* or **morīn(āk)o-* 'pertaining to the sea', which makes for an equation with either Gaul. *Morini*, mentioned above, or W *merin* 'sea, arm of sea, wave' < **morīno-*.

12.2.2 PC **rei̯no-* 'expanse of water, flow' < pre-Clt. *$h_3$rei̯H-no-*

Gaul. *Rēnos*/*Rīnos* 'Rhine', OIr. *rían* (o, m) 'ocean'. The underlying PIE root is **$h_3$rei̯H-* 'to surge, wave'. Gaul. *Rēnos*, or perhaps *Rīnos*, the name for the river Rhine, is indirectly transmitted through Latin and Germanic, and as part of personal names. Lat. *Renus* is first attested around the middle of the first century BC; the Germanic forms (e.g. Germ. *Rhein*, Dutch *Rijn*) presuppose Proto-Germanic **rīnaz*, probably borrowed from Celtic **rei̯nos* before the Germanic sound change **ei̯* > **ī*. Gaul. **rīnos* is continued by OFr. *rin* 'watercourse' (unless it is a loan from Germanic). Delamarre (2003: 257) mentions various minor rivers of the same name in France, Italy, Germany. The Gaulish meanings can be combined with that of OIr. *rían* 'ocean' under the original meaning '(great) body of (flowing) water', i.e. the ocean that flows around the inhabited world, or a large river that acts as a natural border.

12.2.3 PC **sālo-* 'salty water' < PIE **seh$_2$lo-* 'salty one'

OIr. *sál* (o, m) and *sáile* (i̯o, m) 'sea' continue PC **sālo-* < PIE **seh$_2$lo-* 'salty one' (cf. Alb. *gjollë* 'salt trough for animals' < **sālā*, Hamp 1996: 87), a thematic *vr̥ddhi* derivative of **sh$_2$el-* 'salt', and its derivative, PC **sālii̯o-*, respectively. PC **salii̯ā*, the preform of W *heledd* 'salt marsh, brine', is a probably younger, functionally equivalent formation with the productive suffix *-ii̯o-*, derived from the invariant stem **sal-* 'salt', which replaced the more archaic formation that involved ablaut. These words must not be confused with the metonymic use of W, Bret. *hal* 'salt' for the 'sea'.

12.2.4 PC **li-*/*lī-* (**φli-*/*φlī-*) 'to flow' < PIE **lei̯H-* 'to pour' and **pleh$_1$-* 'to become full'

A group of terms referring to the movement of large bodies of water can be linked to a Celtic root **li-* or **lī-*. It is likely that this continues two different PIE verbal roots, namely 2. **lei̯H-* 'to pour' (LIV 405–406) and **pleh$_1$-* 'to become full' (LIV 482–483). Since both led to the shape **lī-* in some contexts in Celtic, a certain amount of confusion between them may have occurred. In the following words, it is not entirely clear from which root they derive in each case. The PIE root **lei̯H-* 'to pour' is possibly attested in the Welsh compound verb *dillyddaf* 'to flow, run, pour' (Schumacher 2004: 451–452), unless it is denominative from a noun that is similar in formation to the ones discussed under 4d below. On the other hand, OIr. *do·lin* (S3b) 'to flow' is linked to **pleh$_1$-* 'to become full' by McCone (1991: 18, 21, 34–35). It is tempting to derive Celtic **lindV-* 'pond' and **lindV-* 'liquid, ale' from this root as well (Stifter 2018b: 37 fn. 13), although the morphology and the derivational processes are unclear.

4A PIC *LIRO- 'OCEAN' < PRE-CLT. *LIH-RO-
OIr. *ler* (o), OW pl. *lirou*, W *llŷr* 'sea, ocean'. The short *i of *liro- is due to laryngeal loss (Zair 2012: 140). A related, but not identical formation, is OIr. *lir* (u?) 'diarrhea' (or *lír*?).

4B PIC *LĪI̯ANT- 'FLOW, FLOOD' < PRE-CLT. *LIH-I̯N̥T-
OIr. *lië* (i̯o, n) 'flood', W *lliant* 'flood, flow, sea'. The formant *-nt- is diachronically that of the present participle of the verbal root *lei̯H-. Because of the formal similarity in the nominative singular, the word has been transferred to the *i̯o*-stems in Old Irish.

4C PIC *LĪMU- 'FLOW' < PRE-CLT. *LIH-MU-
W *lli*, *llif* 'stream, flow, deluge, sea', MCorn. *lyf*, NBret. *liñv* 'flooding'. Welsh and Cornish are ambiguous, but Breton *ñv* unequivocally continues PC *m, not *b. The formation is the verbal abstract of the root *lei̯H- (Schumacher 2004: 451–452).

4D PIC *TO-LIH-(I̯)O- 'FLOOD'? OR *TO-ΦLI-I̯O-?
OIr. *tuile* (o, n) 'flood' serves as the verbal noun of *do·lin* 'to flow', which derives from the PIE root *$pleh_1$- 'to become full' (LIV 482–483), according to McCone (1991: 18, 21, 34–35; cf. LEIA T-171). Stüber (2015: 409–411) thinks that *tuile* continues Primitive Irish *to-lii̯o-, where *lii̯o- (< PC *φlii̯o-) has been formed from the verbal root of *do·lin* (PC *φli-ni-) by analogy with other roots of the structure *Ci-, which show nasal formations in the present stem, e.g. *bii̯o- 'strike' beside *bi-na- 'to strike'. In this case, the formation must have occurred after the Proto-Celtic period, since PC *to-φlii̯o- would have resulted in OIr. ***tuible*. *Mutatis mutandis*, similar arguments can be made for OIr. *tólae* (i̯o, n) 'flood, inundation', which could be from *to-uds-liH-(i̯)o- (thus LEIA T-102) or from *to-uds-(φ)lii̯o- (Stüber 2015: 409), and for W *dillydd* 'flow' < *dī-eks-lii̯o- (*uel sim.*; cf. Schumacher 2004: 451). Alternatively, the relationship between verb and verbal noun could be viewed as suppletive and owing to the superficial similarity between the two roots in Celtic: the verb goes back to *$pleh_1$-, whereas the verbal noun continues *lei̯H-.

4E **DĪ-LIH-I̯ON- 'DELUGE'?
OIr. *díliu* (n, f) 'deluge, flood, waters of the ocean' could conceivably go back to another such formation from the root *lei̯H-, but in view of the similar W *dilyw*, *diliw* 'deluge', for which this preform is excluded, it is better regarded as a loan from Lat. *dīluuium* 'flood, deluge'.

4F PC *ΦLANU̯O- 'FLOOD' < PRE-CLT. *$PL̥H_1$-N-U̯O-
W *llanw* 'tide, flow, flood, influx', OBret. *lanu*, MBret. *lano*, *lanv*, *lanu*, NBret. *lanv* 'flood'. This word is undoubtedly derived from the root *$pleh_1$- 'to become full'. If the reconstruction *φlanu̯o- < *$pl̥h_1$-n-u̯o- is correct, it supports the rule postulated by Zair (2012: 87) that sequences of the structure *CR̥HC(C)- yielded PC *CRaC(C)- if the first consonant was not a plosive (the corollary being that the laryngeal vocalized only after PIE *p had become PC *φ), and if the laryngeal was followed by two consonants, namely *nu̯. This contrasts with the treatment of the closely related *$pl̥h_1$no- > *φlāno- 'full', where a single consonant followed the laryngeal.

12.2.5 PC **tetrāg-* 'sea, tide?'

OIr. *tethra*, gen. *tethrach* (k) 'sea'. This rare word occurs as a poetic term for the 'sea', as well as the name of a king of the Fomoiri, a supernatural race of monsters with a connection to the sea. These two independent facts, as well as its apparent etymological relationship with words for 'shore' (see item 10 below, with a discussion of the irregular phonological development of the presumed Indo-European root), support the notion that *tethra* is an old term for the 'sea', and not just a metaphorically applied word of originally unrelated semantics. If the suggested morphological analysis is correct, *tethra* is formally remarkable in several respects: it is a rare example of a reduplicated noun, and the inflectional stem is formed directly from the root without any additional suffix, an archaic morphological type. The combination of these features gives the word the flavor of some antiquity. The reduplication may have been taken over from the verbal system for some expressive effect. Because of the very divergent meaning, a connection with the homonym OIr. *tethra* 'scald crow (?)', Gr. τέτραξ 'a type of wild bird' is unlikely, unless the common denominator is 'agitation' (see Stifter forthc.).

12.2.6 PC **trei̯aton-* 'sea?' < PIE **trei̯Ht-(H)on-?*

OIr. *triäth*, gen. *trethan* (n), a poetic word for the '(agitated) sea', can be compared with the Greek mythological name Τρῖτων 'god of the sea, son of Poseidon and Amphitrite' (Zair 2012: 240). Beside the *n*-stem *triäth*, there is a masculine *o*-stem noun *trethan* with the same meaning, which was either abstracted very early from the oblique cases of *triäth* through paradigmatic split, or is a thematic derivative of it, viz. PC *trei̯atono-.

Another group of names for the sea derive from metaphorical expressions, perhaps originating in poetry, that refer to its dangerous, threatening aspects, or that evoke the soundscape of the ocean.

12.2.7 PIC **u̯orgiu̯i̯ā-?*, **u̯ergiu̯i̯ā-?* 'raging ocean?'

OIr. *foirrge*, *fairrge* (i̯ā, f) 'ocean', OBrit./Gaul. Ὠκεανός Οὐεργιούιος 'Vergivian ocean = western ocean' in Ptolemy's *Geographica*. The status of the Modern Welsh hapax *y Môr Werydd* 'the Irish Channel', only attested in 1719, is doubtful. It could be an erudite cambricization of Οὐεργιού(ι)ος, or it could be a corruption, with loss of the initial vowel, of *Iwerydd* 'Irish'. Previously (Stifter 2018: 226–228), I have argued that, if the geographical name transmitted by Ptolemy is related to the OIr. word, the best starting point is a PC adjective *$\underset{\circ}{u}$er-gi$\underset{\circ}{u}$i$\underset{\circ}{i}$o- 'furious'; cf. OIr. *ferg* < PIE *$\underset{\circ}{u}$erHĝeh₂ 'fury' (Zair 2012: 186–187). In Insular Celtic or in Irish, the *e* of the initial syllable must then have been replaced analogically by *o*, as if the noun were a compound with the preverb *$\underset{\circ}{u}$or ← PC *$\underset{\circ}{u}$er < PIE **uper*. An alternative explanation, which sees in *fairrge* a variant of *fairsinge* 'width, extent' (i.e. 'the vast extent (of the ocean)') < **u̯or-eχs-angu-i̯ā* ← **uper-eĝʰs-h₂n̥ĝu-*, is formally less satisfying (cf. Stifter ibid.).

12.2.8 pre-Ir. **bou̯koni̯ā-* 'the roaring one'?

Ir. *bóchna* (i̯ā?, f) 'sea, ocean' can be compared with the Welsh verb *bugaf, bugadaf* 'to roar' < **bou̯k-*. IEW 97 includes this word tentatively under the onomatopoetic root **b(e)u-*, **bʰ(e)u-* for muffled sounds. ScGael. *bochnadh* 'sea, narrow sea, strait' seems to belong here as well, but has a short *o*.

12.2.9 PIC **u̯ai̯lo-kū* 'wolfhound'

W *gweilgi* 'sea, ocean, flood' is a compound of PC **u̯ai̯lo-* 'wolf (wailer?)' + **kū*, gen. **konos* 'dog'; cf. OIr. *fáelchú* (n, m) 'wolf'. The use for the 'sea' of a word that originally must have meant 'wolf' is undoubtedly due to metaphor.

It is not clear in all respects whether, and which, fine semantic differences existed among the words above, especially among those for the 'sea' in general, but the distinctions may have been of a minor nature, especially among the more rarely used terms. What is clear is that there are stylistic differences between them. In Old Irish, *muir* is the most neutral term that can occur in all genres, whereas the other words are chiefly encountered in poetry or in rhetorical style. In poetry, these words can even be combined for special effect. In line 271 of the Poems of Blathmac, *nachad·báid rían romro lir* '(lit.) that the sea of the great sea of the ocean did not drown it', three of the expressions, *rían*, *romuir* (*ro-* intensive prefix + *muir*), and *ler*, are included in a single nominal phrase, apparently to create an effect of hyperbole that is impossible to render appropriately in English. *Rían* receives the epithet *trethanbras* 'sea-big' in line 244; and the poet uses the compound *lermuir* 'ocean sea' twice (lines 516, 770). On the other hand, in line 947, *beth tírmai trethan, ler, lind* 'ocean, sea, pond will be dry', *trethan* and *ler* appear to be contrasted with each other, as well as with the clearly separate *lind* 'pond'.

12.2.10 PC **trag-/trāg-* 'to flow, to ebb?' < pre-Clt. **treh₂gʰ-* << PIE **dʰreh₂gʰ-* 'to become agitated'?

The Celtic evidence allows us to set up a verbal root for the movement of tidal waters. As a verbal root, it occurs in OIr. *trágaid, tráigid* (S1?) 'to ebb, recede'. The strong inflection, e.g. the reduplicated preterite *tethraig, tethragtar*, and the reduplicated future *tethrais*, attest to an old primary verb. *Pace* Schumacher (2004: 635–636), forms beside the preterite stem are attested. Schumacher (2004: 636) connects the root with that of Lat. *trahō, -ere* 'to pull' and sets up a common PIE ancestor root **treHgʰ/ĝʰ-* or **tragʰ/ĝʰ-* 'to drag away' (not in LIV). He explicitly rejects the alternative explanation according to which these verbs go back to the PIE roots **dʰreh₂gʰ-* 'to become agitated' (LIV 154–155) or **dʰregʰ/ĝʰ-* 'to drag, pull' (LIV 154). Even though the phonological development of the initial stop from PIE **dʰreh₂gʰ-* to PC **trag-/trāg-* is irregular, it is the solution preferred here because it builds on an established PIE root, and the semantic development from 'coming into agitation' to the 'movement of tidal waters' seems acceptable. Similar sporadic fluctuations in the voicedness of initial stops are known from other etyma, e.g. PIE **ĝʰengʰ-* > PC **keng-* 'to go, step', PIE **dn̥ĝʰu̯eh₂-* → **tangᵘāt-* 'tongue'; cf. also PC *treget-* 'foot', which may be connected with PIE **dʰregʰ/ĝʰ-* 'to drag, pull'. Finally, even a connection with the PIE root **treh₃g/ĝ-* 'to gnaw away' (LIV 647) is conceivable if the motivating factor is the eroding force of the tides.

10a PIC **TRĀGI-*, **TRAGI̯O-* 'EBB TIDE'

OIr. *tráig* (i, m+f) 'shore, ebb tide' continues **trāgi-*; MW *trei*, NW *trai*, OBret. *tre*, MBret. *tré, tref*, NBret. *tre(c'h)* 'ebb tide' continue **tragi̯o-*. Despite their outward similarity, the Irish and the British words show different formations and different ablaut grades of the root.

10b PIC **TRAXTU-* 'SHORE, BEACH' < PRE-CLT. **TRH₂GʰTU-*

OIr. *tracht* (u, n) 'strand, shore', W *traeth*, OCorn. *trait* 'sand', LCorn. *treath* 'sand, beach', OBret. *cundraid* 'ebb tide', NBret. *traezh* 'sand, beach'. Formally, **traχtu-* is an abstract noun from the verbal root **trag-/trāg-* 'to flow, to ebb'. Accordingly, it must have referred specifically to that part of the coast that is subject to flooding. In contrast to the modern view of the seaside, the concept of the 'beach' in the Proto-Insular-Celtic world view is not the area in front of the sea where one spreads out towels to get a tan or from which one walks into the water for a swim. Such an area would simply be 'land'. 'Beach', on the other hand, is that part of the sea that is left uncovered by the ebb, but which is submerged during high tide and which is only of limited economic use.[3] Alternatively, these words could be a loan from Lat. *tractus* 'area' (cf. Irslinger 2002: 156), but the good etymological and morphological connection with the words for 'ebbing' renders this suggestion unattractive.

[3] Cf. "Seulement la plage, où on ne va jamais parce qu'elle est coupée de brise-lames et qu'il existe des trous de vase" (George Simenon, *Le port de brumes*, Paris: 1932 [repr. *Maigret en Normandie*, Le Livre de Poche 2012: 78]). Things cast up on the shore are of some economic value for Early Irish society, and laws regulate who has a claim on what (Kelly 1988: 107–108).

12.2.11 pre-Ir. **kladdāko-* 'stony shore'?

NIr. *cladach* (o, m) 'stony shore', ScG *cladach* 'shore, stony beach'. This word is only attested in the modern Gaelic languages. Irish intervocalic [d] is unusual phonotactically and indicates a borrowing. A connection with OIr. *clad* [klað] 'ditch, trench' is unlikely on phonological and semantic grounds. The wider semantic family in Ir., e.g. NIr. *cladar* 'heap of stones, stony place', *cladán* 'fence-like pile of stones', etc., suggests that *cladach* is a collective of 'stones', maybe from an unattested simplex NIr. **clad*, OIr. **clat* 'stone'. May one speculate as to whether this is a loan from a lost British language, i.e. Brit. **klad* < **kalad* (for the syncope of the first syllable, cf. W *crydd* 'shoemaker' < **cerydd*) < **kaleto-* 'hard' (cf. OIr. *calad*, W *caled*, B *kaled* 'hard'), with vowel assimilation? Ultimately, nothing certain can be said and this word must be regarded as being of unknown origin.

12.2.12 PIC **φrobertii̯ā-* 'spring tide' < pre-Clt. **pro-b^{h}er-t-*

OIr. *robartae*, W *rhyferthi* 'torrent, flood tide', *rhyferthwy* 'torrent, deluge', OBret. *rebirthi*, NBret. *reverzhi* 'spring tide'. For the meaning 'to flow' of the PC root **ber-* < PIE **b^{h}er-* 'to carry', cf. W *beraf*, MBr. *beraff* 'to flow', or OIr. *indber* 'river mouth'. OIr. *robartae* etc. exclude a derivation from the root **b^{h}erh$_2$-* 'to move fast' (LIV 81) unless sporadic loss of laryngeals is invoked (Schumacher 2004: 222–223).

12.2.13 PIC **tunnā-* 'wave' < pre-Clt. **tuh$_2$-s-neh$_2$-*? or < pre-Clt. **tu-n-d-neh$_2$-*?

OIr. *tonn* (ā, f), OW pl. *tonnou*, W *ton*, LCorn. *ton*, OBret. *tonn*, Bret. *tonn* 'wave'. All Insular Celtic languages possess a homophonous and homomorphous word meaning 'skin, surface' (and extended meanings thereof). GPC suggests different etymologies for the two words, but a single etymon is possible. The etymology is uncertain. At least two or three explanations are conceivable. First, PC **tunnā* 'wave' could go back to a pre-Clt. formation **tuh$_2$-s-neh$_2$* 'swelling' from the PIE root **teu̯h$_2$-* 'to swell' (LIV 639–640). In this case, laryngeal loss would have occurred (Zair 2012: 155). Second, the preform could be **tu-n-d-neh$_2$* from the PIE root **(s)teu̯d-* 'to push', with a nasal infix taken over from the verbal inflection (cf. Stifter 2018: 38). If the OIr. acc. sg. *toinn* (Poems of Blathmac 669, 909) is old and not due to analogy with the nominative, either etymology would be impossible, since the pre-Ir. acc.sg. **tunnen* would be expected to result in **tuinn*. Finally, the word could be connected with Lith. *tvãnas* 'flood', Latv. *tvans*, *tvana* 'steam, haze' < PIE **tu̯ono-*. However, since this cannot explain the geminate *nn* of the Celtic word, it is the least convincing option.

12.2.14 PIC **kaφno-* < West PIE **kh$_2$p-no-* 'harbor'

OIr. *cúan* (o, m) 'haven, harbor'. This word is related to Germanic **hafnaz* 'harbor; pot' < '*receptacle'; cf. Engl. *haven*, Germ. *Hafen* 'haven', *Häfen* 'pot', a nominal formation from the PIE root **keh$_2$p-* 'to take, grab' (LIV 344–345; see also the chapter by Van Sluis, Jørgensen, & Kroonen in this volume). The meaning 'harbor' must be a metaphorical use of 'pot', with reference to the topographical appearance of harbors. It is formally conceivable that W *cafn* 'vat, trough, primitive boat' and Bret. *kaon*, *kan* 'canal, channel, valley' belong here as well (Stifter forthc. b), if PC **aφn* developed into British **aβn*, for which there is neither evidence in favor nor against. However, an alternative explanation is possible. W *cafn* could come from **kab^{h}no-*, from the root **(s)kab^h-* 'to scratch' (LIV 549), referring originally to a vessel that has been carved out of wood, i.e. a 'dugout'.

12.2.15 PIC **enistī-* 'island' < pre-Clt. **h$_1$eni-sth$_2$-ih$_2$-* 'standing inside'

OIr. *inis*, W *ynys*, LCorn. *enys*, OBret. *inis*, MBret. *enes*, NBret. *enez*, Gwen. *iniz* 'island'. Alleged Gaul. cognates of the basis **enista* (Delamarre 2017: 260) occur only in personal names and are accordingly doubtful. Delamarre (2017: 257–260) argues that Proto-Celtic made a distinction between river islands (cf. Engl. *eyot*, *ait*) and offshore islands (cf. Engl. *island*, *isle*). For the former, he suggests that the compound PIE **h$_1$enter-h$_2$p-h$_3$on-* > PC **entarabon-* (*uel sim.*) 'between the waters/rivers' or short PIE **h$_1$n̥tro-* > PC **antro-* was used; for the latter, pre-Clt. **h$_1$eni-sth$_2$-ih$_2$-* > PC **enistī* 'which stands in (the sea)' was used. Lat. *insula* 'island' < **en-sal-o-* 'being in the salty water' furnishes a rough typological parallel for the formation of **enistī-*. However, if this distinction between the two types of islands was ever a sharp one at all, it was not maintained consistently. OIr. *Étar*, the continuation of **antro-*, refers to a (half-)island in the sea off Ireland (today Howth, Co. Dublin), whereas many inland places are called *Inis* in Ireland (e.g., numerous *Ennis*, *Inish*, *Inch*). These names usually refer to slightly raised spots historically surrounded by wetlands or marshes. De Vaan (2008: 306) is skeptical of both the Latin and the Celtic etymologies and tentatively assigns the words, together with Gr. νῆσος 'island', to borrowings from an unknown language.

12.2.16 pre-Ir. **gai̯to/ā-* 'estuary'?

OIr. *gáeth* (?) 'sea, stream, estuary'. Perhaps it occurs in the Ogam name GATTEAGLAN, which Ziegler (1994: 183) interprets as 'having clean water'. Of unclear origin (cf. Irslinger 2000: 306).

12.2.17 PIC **tabernV-* 'sea'?

Ir. *tabairn*, *tabrainn* 'sea' is chiefly found in glossaries. It has a potential, but very uncertain parallel in OW *tauern*, in the boundary clause for Llandeilo Fawr (Book of Llandaf f. 51ra 9, charter 77), *if* this is a river name. One could attempt to identify the middle sequence with the Celtic root **ber-* 'to flow' (Schumacher 2004: 222–223), but the rest of the formation remains obscure. Even more doubtful is a connection with the ancient river name *Taber* (var. *Tader*) in the Iberian Peninsula (today *río Segura*) and the river *Zaber* < **taber-* (?) in Germany. Place names such as Fr. *Tavernay*, Belg. *Taverneux*, and Ital. *Tavernago* < **tabernāko-* are most likely based on Lat. *taberna* 'tavern', as is German *Zabern*.

12.2.18 Pre-Ir. **(ambi-)bato-* 'sea'? < pre-Clt. *h$_2$m̥b^{h}i-g^{u}h$_2$-to-?

OIr. *bath* (var. *baath*; perhaps *báth*?) 'sea' and *imbath* 'ocean' occur chiefly in glossaries, where they serve to explain each other. In fact, the ostensible simplex *bath* could be a construct of medieval glossators, extrapolated through etymological decomposition from *imbath*. The Old Irish etymological lexicon *Sanas Cormaic* 753 offers a definition: *immbath .i. ocian .i. bath muir, ut est muir iter Ēirinn 7 Albain, uel aliud quodcumque mare nad·timchella imac[h]ūairt ut Mare Terrenum. imbath immoro .i. immuir .i. muir imma·timc[h]ellae imac[h]ūairt, is é do occian duit-si ón.* "*Imbath*, that is, ocean, namely *bath* is 'sea', like the sea between Ireland and Britain, or any other sea that does not go around (in a circle), like the Tyrrhenian Sea. *Imbath*, however, is 'around-sea', that is, a sea that goes around (in a circle); that's your ocean." If this explanation can be given any credence, it would be conceivable to analyze *imbath* as a compound verbal noun PC **ambi-bato-*, as if from pre-Celtic *h$_2$m̥b^{h}i-g^{u}h$_2$-to- 'going around (?)', from the PIE root *g^{u}eh$_2$- 'to step, tread' (LIV 205). Ultimately, this has to remain speculation.

12.3 Flora

With regard to plants whose habitats are in coastal and maritime regions, only names for algae and seaweed warrant inclusion in this survey. The names for all other types of plants appear to be nonspecific, that is to say, they are either names that can also be found with reference to nonmaritime wetlands, or they are generic plant names without connection to wet habitats, or they are transparently descriptive or metaphoric names. The only floral vocabulary that is exclusively restricted to a maritime environment is that of seaweed and algae. Seaweed was of great economic importance for Celtic littoral communities in the context of a much wider northwest European material culture (Nyberg & Ar Gall 1996). The vocabulary is accordingly rich and comparatively well documented, especially in Irish and Breton. Here, only those terms will be studied that can be reasonably believed to go back to Proto-Celtic or Proto-Insular Celtic. The terminology for the practices and implements used in the gathering of seaweed, which are described for medieval Ireland by Kelly (1998: 304–305, 312–315) and which are particularly well documented for Breton (Nyberg & Ar Gall 1996: 149, 153–157), will not be investigated either. This subset of vocabulary typically consists of generic terms without an original connection to maritime environments.

The attestation of Irish terminology in early medieval sources is very sparse, and accordingly little is found in eDIL. The dictionaries of the modern languages, including specialized dictionaries for flora, contain an abundance of words, but the spelling and the phonology of the words can differ substantially between the sources. Occasionally, words are only first recorded in dialectal collections of the second half of the twentieth century (e.g., *ruálach* 'sea lace'). Even if the original word formation of these terms may have been regular and transparent, in the form in which we have them now, they can be challenging to analyze etymologically. For instance, there are no old attestations of ModIr. *riseach*, *ríseach* 'sea thongs, *Chorda filum*'. Since its deeper history is unclear, it can only be speculated whether, perhaps, *riseach/ríseach* is connected to the very rare Irish word *réise* 'finger; span, handbreadth', and is so called for its appearance? Alternations such as ModIr. *slobán* ~ *spogán* 'green alga, *Cladophora*' or ModIr. *coirleach* ~ *coirleagannach* ~ *coilleaganach* ~ *cál leannógach* 'strap wrack (oarweed), *Laminaria digitata*' serve as an illustration of another dilemma into which the researcher is plunged. Without old attestations, the direction of changes between the variants is difficult to assess. Which is the more archaic term, *cál leannógach* or *coirleach*? Or are both 'distortions' of yet another third variant that happens not to be recorded? *Cál leannógach* is readily understandable as 'cloak-like (?) cauliflower'. This could be an instance of metonymic, folk-taxonomic nomenclature, but it could also have arisen through folk etymology in an effort to rationalize obscure *coirleach*, which allows no surface analysis. This possibility is strongly suggested by the fact that the adjective *leannógach*, which may be derived from *leann* 'cloak', does not otherwise seem to exist in the language. Because of the inherent difficulty of names of this type, they will not be investigated here (for a fuller list of them, see Nyberg 1993: 109–110). In yet other cases, names for seaweeds are transparently descriptive in the synchronic language or are metaphoric usages of lexemes belonging to other fields of the lexicon. Such terms have also not been included in this collection.

12.3.1 PIC **dolisko-* 'edible seaweed' < pre-Clt. *d^{h}olH-i-sko-

OIr. *duilesc* (o, m) 'edible seaweed, dillisk, dulse', W *delysg* 'edible seaweed, dulse'. Bret. *tellesk* 'seaweed' is evidently related, but the initial voiceless dental has no explanation. The etymon is PIE *d^{h}olH-i- 'leaf'; cf. OIr. *duilne* (i̯ā, f; with a singulative suffix), W *dail*, Corn., MBret. *del* 'leaf/leaves', Lat. *folium* 'leaf', to which the suffix **-sko-* has been added. **-sko-* is an inherited adjectival suffix, but it may have had developed other functions in Celtic, too. For example, in another floral term, OIr. *géscae* (i̯o, m) '(secondary) branch' beside *géc* (ā, f) 'branch', the suffix agglomeration *-scae* < **-skii̯o-* may have diminutive force. See Section 12.4 for more examples of **-sk-*.

12.3.2 PIC **u̯immon-* '(edible) seaweed' < pre-Clt. **u̯ip-s-mon-*

OIr. *femm* (n, f?), *femmach* (o, m), *femman* (f), *femnach* (ā, f), *femmar* (m) 'various (edible?) seaweeds', W *gwymon* 'seaweed, edible seaweed', Corn. *gumman*, OBret. *gueimmonou*, *gumouo*, MBret. *goumon*, NBret. *gouemon*, Fr. *goémon* 'seaweed'. This etymon allows for several formal reconstructions, but semantically it is most attractive to treat it as an agent noun **u̯ip-smon-* from the PIE root **u̯ei̯p-* 'to swing, oscillate' (LIV 671; Stifter 1998: 205 fn. 6). The most basic form in Old Irish is the *n*-stem *femm*, from which a range of derivatives were created by the addition of various suffixes, perhaps to distinguish between different types of seaweed. In Modern Irish, *feamainn* is usually followed by various adjectives or nouns for the same purpose. The morphology of this word, i.e. its inflection as an *n*-stem, is a strong argument in favor of the word's antiquity.

12.3.3 PIC **u̯itriko-* or **u̯iterāko-* 'dulse, edible seaweed'? < pre-Clt. **u̯i*h_1*tr-/u̯i*h_1*ti-*?

OIr. *fithrech*, *fithrach*, ScG *fithreach*, *fithriach* 'dulse, edible seaweed'. In medieval Irish, this word is only attested in obscure poetry and in glossaries. It does not seem to occur in Modern Irish.[4] The word can be analyzed through the lens of inherited morphology, namely as a formation from the PIE root **u̯ie*h_1*-* 'to enwrap' (LIV 695), perhaps involving an agentive noun in *-ter-/-tor-* as an intermediate stage, for instance **u̯i(*h_1*)t(e)r-*. Under this analysis, loss of the laryngeal must be assumed (cf. Zair 2012: 132–160 for the ambiguous Celtic evidence for laryngeal loss in this phonetic context). The original meaning may have been 'wrapping (plant)' or 'pliable (plant)', which seems acceptable as a semantic motivation for a type of seaweed. In Latin, a word for a creeper plant, *uītis* 'grapevine', is derived from the same root. The latter's preform, **u̯i*h_1*ti-*, could conceivably also form the basis from which *fithrech* was derived via an intermediate stage, **u̯iti-rVko-*. The root **u̯ie*h_1*-* underlies words for 'twigs' or 'flexible branches' in various other Indo-European languages (IEW 1120–1121).

12.3.4 PIC **slibVkko-* 'laver, nori, sloke, an edible seaweed'

ModIr. *sleabhac*, *sleabhcán* 'an edible seaweed'. First attested 1400 in a medical text (Nic Dhonnchadha 2019: 30). Etymologically a connection with words such as OIr. *slíab* 'moor, mountain' < **slei̯bos* and *slemuin* 'smooth' < **slibno-* suggests itself, i.e. from the root **slei̯b-* 'slippery, smooth' and referring to the slimy nature of the plant. The unlenited *-c* may have developed secondarily within Irish. Borrowed into English as *sloke* or *slawk*.

12.3.5 PIC **stlamo-* 'green herb' < pre-Clt. **stlH-mo-*

This etymon is only reflected in Bret. *stlañv* 'aquatic moss, green herb on shores', *stlañvach* (*-vesk*) 'seaweed'. The noun is derived from the PIE root **stelH-* 'wide' (Schrijver 1995: 440). The semantic motivation for the etymology is the broad leaves of the plant. See Falileyev & Owen (2005: 51–52) for the wider family of words, which also refer to leafy plants on the land.

12.3.6 PIC **attīno-/*aktīno-*?

The generic Modern Breton word for 'seaweed', which has supplanted MBret. *gouemon* in this function, is *bezhin*. Like NIr. *feamain*, it is common as a base noun followed by various attributes to refer to specific types of seaweed. The word is apparently cognate with OBret. *ethin*, W *aeth*, *eithin*, MCorn. *eythinen*, and OIr. *aitten*, the name of the land-based plant 'furze, gorse' (Deshayes 2003: 107–108). **aktīno-*, the assumed preform of the latter, looks like a formation of the Celtic root **ak-* 'pointed, acute, spiky' < PIE ***h_2*ek̂-* 'to be/become/make sharp' (LIV 261) + the Insular Celtic floral and arboreal suffix **-tīno-*. While this etymology makes good sense for the gorse, it is less intuitive for seaweed. Furthermore, the origin of the initial *b-* of *bezhin* is unclear. With an eye only on Irish, without taking the British evidence into consideration, O'Brien (1956: 177) has suggested a dialectal phenomenon of Goidelic in the sporadic development of OIr. *aitten* < **aktīno-*.

12.3.7 Pre-Ir. **langa-*? 'sea tangle'

ModIr. *langa* 'sea tangle', *langach* 'sea tangle (perhaps collective)' is only attested from the seventeenth century. Its origin is obscure; maybe it is a loan from the Old Norse adjective *langr* 'long'; cf. the loanword *langa* 'ling (a fish)' from Old Norse *langa*.

12.4 Fauna

Many sea animals, especially the large mammals, are referred to as the maritime equivalents of land animals in Insular Celtic. For instance, porcine expressions are common: *mucc mara* 'pig of the sea', *torc na tuinne* 'boar of the wave', or *torc trethain* 'boar of the sea' for 'porpoise' are calques on Lat. *porcus marinus*. W *morwch*, *mor-hwch*, *morfoch*, OCorn. *morhoch*, OBret. *mormoch*, MBret. *morhouch*, NBret. *morhouc'h* 'sea

[4] Given that it is found in Old Irish in the poem *Fil and griän Glinne Ai*, whose place of composition has been suspected to be Bangor (Co. Down), its distribution may have been dialectally confined to northeast Gaelic (cf. Stifter 2015: 54–55).

pig' refer to the 'dolphin' or 'porpoise'. A very doubtful case is MIr. *ruiseda* or *ruisenda*, the name of a sea monster, which could be related to the hapax *ruisne* 'piglet'. Both could be adjectival formations from the stem *ruis-* 'red'. Even the most generic terms occur, such as the Old Irish noun phrase *míl mór* 'big animal', and the British compounds W *morfil*, OCorn. *moruil*, Bret. *morvil* 'sea animal', all for 'whale'. The perfect formal correspondence between OIr. *muirbran*, W *morfran*, OBret. *morbran*, NBret. *morvran* 'cormorant' suggests that this transparent compound of **mori-* 'sea' and **brano-* 'raven' goes back at least to the Insular Celtic period. This list does not claim completeness. It does not illustrate a specifically Celtic practice either, since such expressions are found in other languages too, as, for instance, English *sea lion* or German *Seehund* exemplify. Their use can be interpreted in two ways: as instances of associative naming because of unfamiliarity with the animals in question, or as loan translations from other languages in situations of language contact. As a curious fact, several OIr. names for 'sea monsters' follow this pattern as well: *muirṡelche* 'sea turtle', *muirdris*, *muirdúchu* 'siren', *muirgelt* 'sea lunatic' are all compounds consisting of the first element *muir* 'sea' followed by a more or less clear second element. OIr. *muirmoru* 'siren' is considered to be a loan from W *morforwyn* (Bauer 2015: 134–136). The hapax *suire* 'siren', here only mentioned for completeness' sake, is obscure.

More interesting for the purposes of this study is another group of animal names that appear not to be of inherited origin. The number of etymologically difficult or outright obscure terms for fish and shellfish, especially in Irish, is staggering. Many of them display either unusual phonotactics, or the correspondences with manifest cognates are not "by the book." All evidence for this group of words comes from Insular Celtic. Consequently, it is impossible to say whether these are loanwords that entered the language at the Proto-Celtic stage, or only after Celtic languages had established themselves on the Western Archipelago. One question that deserves particular attention is whether some of these words are structurally compatible with the substratum language of northwest Europe postulated by Schrijver 1997. For instance, the word for 'wolf; transferred: whale', **bled-* (or rather **bleδ-*), bears a superficial structural resemblance to Schrijver's proposed substratum word **baəδ-* 'boar'.

What are the most conspicuous phonological features of the present collection? Several of the "foreign" lexemes end in **-sk*, as if this were a suffix. One of the possible preforms of W *mwyalch*, OCorn. *moelh*, NBret. *moualc'h* 'blackbird' could have been **mesalska-* (Schrijver 1997: 307), in which case *-sk* would also appear in one of the items of Schrijver's hypothetical substrate language.[5] The suffix *-sk* occurs also in the non-maritime lexeme *blesc* 'she-wolf', and apparently also in **tasko̯-* 'badger', if this is analyzed as a variant of **tazgo-* (cf. the OIr. personal name *Tadg*), namely **tazg-sk-i̯o-*. On the other hand, **-sk-* is also an adjectival suffix with a well-known Indo-European pedigree, and its occurrence has been noted in *duilesc* 'seaweed' above, a word with a perfectly Indo-European derivation. It cannot be excluded that the collected material reflects two or more different **-sk* suffixes with different origins.[6]

Many Irish terms contain an intervocalic voiced stop after a short vowel. According to the established rules of Irish historical phonology, this stop cannot always be due to the sequence of nasal + voiceless stop, which would have resulted in compensatory lengthening of some preceding vowels, but presupposes a geminate voiced stop. However, geminate voiced stops are exceedingly rare in inherited Celtic or Indo-European words (cf. Stifter forthc.). An alternative source for Irish intervocalic voiced stops could be borrowings from an early variety of British Celtic that may once have been spoken in Ireland but has since disappeared.

Having said all this, it must be stressed that not all words for which no convincing Celtic or Indo-European etymology can be found exhibit unusual phonotactics. In those cases, their etymological isolation is the main indicator of a loan from a substrate language. Words that are manifestly borrowed from well-attested European languages will be ignored, even such words as *rasmóel* and *rosualt*, which are evidently folk-etymological deformations of Old Norse *hrosshvalr* 'walrus'. Kelly (1998: 282–298) describes the details of fishing, collecting shellfish, and hunting marine mammals in medieval Ireland.

12.4.1 PC **bledā-* 'wolf?'

OIr. *bled* (ā, f) 'whale, sea monster', cognate with MW *bleidd*, NW *blaidd*, OCorn. *bleit*, MCorn. *blyth*, OBret. *bleit*, NBret. *blei(z)* 'wolf' < **bled-i̯o-*; perhaps also the basis of French place names (Delamarre 2003: 79). OIr. *blesc* 'harlot < *she-wolf' < **bled-skā* presupposes the meaning 'wolf' also for the prehistory of Irish. Also in the compounds *bledmíl*, *bledmall* 'sea animal = sea monster, whale'. The meaning 'wolf' must be primary and was then secondarily applied to a maritime animal according to the principle stated at the beginning of the section. The transferred use of the same etymon is also found in the modern British languages, e.g. Bret. *morvleiz* 'sea wolf = shark', W *morflaidd* 'sea wolf = bass, sea wolf; wolffish, sea cat, catfish; shark' or *blaidd a dŵr* 'wolf of the water = pike'. The origin of the word is unknown. A connection with Gr. φάλλαινα, Lat. *ballaena* 'whale' is formally difficult, as is the idea of a taboo deformation of the root **meld-* 'soft' (Delamarre 2003: 79). Guus Kroonen (personal communication) tentatively suspects a prehistoric *Wanderwort* for a mythical animal, which he compares with Goth. *ulbandus*, OE *olfend(a)* 'camel', and a plethora of Slavic and Baltic words (e.g., OCS *velьb(l)ǫdь* 'camel', Lith. *velbliūdas* 'camel; whale', Old Prussian *weloblundis* 'mule'), ultimately derived from

[5] The substratum origin of the word for 'blackbird' is disputed. Guus Kroonen (pers. comm.) reminds me of a Germanic bird name with the suffixal extension *-*sk*-, viz. OE *þræsce* 'thrush' < Proto-Germanic **þra(st)skōn-* vs. ON *þrǫstr* < **þrastu-* (Kroonen 2013: 545).

[6] Post-OIr. *trosc* 'cod' is a loan from Old Norse *þorskr*, in any case.

Gothic. These words can hardly be separated from Gr. ἐλέφας 'elephant', which in turn is suspected of being a borrowing from a Near Eastern language, e.g. Semitic. However, the similarities with **bledā-* may only be superficial.

12.4.2 pre-Ir. **blo.āko-* 'whale'?

OIr. *bloach* 'whale' is a rare word. The spelling *bloach* indicates a hiatus, i.e. disyllabic *bloäch*. The hiatus in this position could be variously due to the loss of **s*, **φ*, **i̯*, or **u̯*. The variant *blodach* could be influenced by *bled*. *Blaoch* in a glossary in the seventeenth-century manuscript Egerton 158 is probably due to orthographic hypercorrection and does not prove an old diphthong in *áe* or *óe*. Of unknown origin; it is formally difficult to derive it directly, i.e. via inheritance, from any of the Indo-European roots of the shape **bʰelH-* or **bʰleH-*, or with Gr. φάλλαινα 'whale'.

12.4.3 pre-Ir. **parno-* 'whale'?

OIr. *parn* 'whale' is attested once in a glossary, where it is explained by the equally obscure *bloach*. The initial *p-* points to a loan and is reminiscent of the substrate layer postulated by Schrijver (2000, 2005). Of unknown origin.

12.4.4 pre-Ir., pre-Brit. **rōno-* 'seal'

Ogam Irish RO/N̦[A]/N̦N, OIr. *rón* (o, m) 'seal', MW *moelrawn*, NW *moelrhon* 'seal; porpoise; dolphin', MCorn. *ruen*, Bret. *reunig* 'seal'.[7] Despite the great similarity between the Irish and the British words, they cannot be inherited from a common ancestor. OIr. *ó* and Brit. **ɔ̄*, reflected in MW *aw*, NW *o*, MCorn. *ue*, Bret. *eu*, do not correspond to each other in a regular fashion. The word may have been borrowed from one branch into the other, but the direction of borrowing is unclear, and the admissable time frame would be very tight. Furthermore, nothing is gained for the ultimate etymology of the word, because it does not find an internal explanation in either branch of Celtic. It is hardly the same word as W *rhawn* 'coarse animal hair'.

A loan from OE *hran*, *hron* 'small kind of whale, mussel' has been proposed in the past (cf. Bauer 2015: 48–50), but this is virtually impossible, even ignoring the phonological problems involved. The Ogam stone CIIC 145 from Arraglen, on which the name RO/N̦[A]/N̦N is found, has been dated on linguistic grounds to approximately the second half of sixth century (McManus 1991: 96–97). The corresponding OIr. name *Rónán* (o, m) 'little seal' is first mentioned in the *Annals of Ulster* in the year 624. This very early date is virtually inconceivable for a loan directly from Old English into Irish – such loans are extremely rare overall before the late Middle Irish period. Otherwise, one would have to assume that this word had been borrowed by speakers of a British language from Old English and then been passed on to Irish in rapid succession, where it became popular so quickly that it entered anthroponomastics even in the furthest reaches of the island within a generation. All this would have happened within the brief period between the arrival of the Anglo-Saxons in Britain during the fifth century and the second half of the sixth century, when the Arraglen stone was erected, and all this against the backdrop of the less-than-amicable relationships between the involved population groups during that period. It is further to be noted that the origin of *hran*, *hron* in Old English, which has no Germanic etymology, is in itself obscure. Further afield, Lith. *rúonis*, *rùinis* 'seal' of unknown etymology, shows an uncanny resemblance (Guus Kroonen, personal communication). On the whole, independent borrowings of these words from an unknown northwest European source into the various language groups seem most likely.

[7] The British-Celtic 'associative' word for 'seal' is W *morlo*, Bret. *leue-mor* 'sea calf'.

12.4.5 Pre-Ir. **gei̯rii̯o-* 'seal'?

Ir. *géire* is once attested in a poem enumerating obscure vocabulary. It is introduced as *menn mairci mur* 'the small one of the seahorse'. eDIL tentatively defines it as 'sea calf, seal (?)'. Obscure.

12.4.6 Pre-Ir. **maluko-* or **moluko-* 'seal'?

Ir. *mulach* 'sea calf, seal'. The pre-Irish reconstruction **ma/oluko-* is merely mechanical. The comparison with the glossary term *mulba*, explained as *rónmhuir* 'sea abounding in seals', points to a common element *mul-*, of which *mulach* would be an adjectival formation; the function of *-ba* in *mulba* is obscure. This *mul-* could be identical with the generic noun *mul* 'globular mass, lump'. Ultimately obscure.

12.4.7 PC **esok-*, **esāk-* 'salmon'

Gallo-Lat. *esox*, OIr. *éo*, gen. *iäch* (k, m), MW *ehawc*, W *eog*, MBret. *eheuc*, Bret. *eog*, OCorn. *ehoc*, borrowed into Basque as *izokin*. The suffix appears in two ablaut variants: as short **o* in Gallo-Latin and the Basque loanword, on the one hand (**esok-*), and as long **ā* in the British evidence on the other (**esāk-* < **esōk-*? cf. Schrijver 1997: 298–299 fn. 12). The OIr. nom.sg. *éo* also presupposes a form with short vowel; its rounded off-glide can most easily be explained from *o*; the length and quality in the Irish oblique cases is indeterminable. The further etymology of this word is unknown. Although the ablaut behavior of the suffix appears to conform with Indo-European inflectional patterns, it cannot be linked to any PIE root. Ultimately of unknown origin. The salmon has multiple other names in Irish (*bratán*, *éicne*, *erc*, *magar*, *maigre*, *mugna*, *orc*).

12.4.8 pre-Ir. **braddo-* 'salmon'?

Only attested in OIr. *bratán* (o, m) '(young?) salmon, fish', ModIr. *bradán* 'salmon'. Either from **bradd-*, of unknown origin, or synchronically derived from OIr. *brat* 'plundering, spoil', perhaps in the sense of 'a good catch' (cf. Kelly 1998: 293–294).

12.4.9 pre-Ir. **magero-* 'spawn, young fish'?

OIr. *magar* (o, m) 'spawn, fry, young fish', *maigre* (i̯o, m) 'salmon'. The initial *ma-* is reminiscent of W *maran* (see below), which, however, is itself unclear; nor are the two words otherwise formally compatible with each other. A connection with the Celtic root **mak-* 'to raise, nourish, augment' (Schumacher 2004: 466–470) < PIE **meh*$_2$*k̂-* 'to become/make long' (Kümmel 2011) is excluded because of the voiced *g*. At the most, one could speculate about a derivation from **mag-*, the Celtic representative of the PIE root **meĝ-* 'big' (LIV 468–478, esp. 476 fn. 29). Kelly (1998: 294) thinks that *maigre*, being derived from *magar* 'spawn', originally meant the 'egg-bearing female' of the salmon. Ultimately of unclear origin, but note the similarity of the initial syllable to that of item 13, **maguni̯o-*, below.

12.4.10 PC **φorko-* 'speckled (animal), salmon' < PIE **pork̂o-* 'having speckles'

OIr. *orc* (o?, m?) 'salmon'. Unless it is just a metaphorical use of *orc* 'piglet' (with identical etymology), it is an inherited term for a speckled animal with many parallels in other Indo-European languages. Formally, it seems to be a thematic derivative of an ablauting paradigm, PIE **pork̂-/perk̂-* 'speckle'; cf. also the following item. Lat. *porcus* 'a fish with spiked fins' and the Ligurian river name *Porcobera* 'salmon-carrying (?)' near Genoa are exact cognates. Perhaps this name also underlies the place name Lat. *Orcades*, OIr. *Insi Orc* 'Orkney'.

12.4.11 PC **φerko-* 'speckled (animal), salmon' < PIE **perk̂o-* 'having speckles'

OIr. *erc* (?) 'salmon'. Unless it is a specialized use of the OIr. adjective *erc* 'speckled', it is an inherited term for a speckled animal with many parallels in other Indo-European languages. Formally, it seems to be a thematic derivative of an ablauting paradigm, PIE **pork̂-/perk̂-* 'speckle'; cf. also the preceding item. Gr. πέρκη, Lat. *perca* 'perch' is an exact cognate.

12.4.12 PC **ankini̯o-/ankeni̯o-* 'salmon?' < pre-Clt. **h_2(e)nk/k̂-e/in-*

OIr. *éicne* (i̯o, m) 'salmon' allows for two equally viable reconstructions. The word could refer to the salmon as a 'hooked' fish, i.e. PC **ankini̯o-* or **ankeni̯o-*, from the PIE root **$h_2$enk-* 'to bend' (LIV 268). Or it could be a derivative from OIr. *éicen* 'necessity, compulsion, force' in the sense of 'forceful fish', with a Proto-Celtic reconstruction formally identical to the preceding instance, but from the PIE root **$h_2$enk̂-* 'to apportion' (LIV 268). In any case, it can be formally explained as an inherited word.

12.4.13 PC **maguni̯o-* 'salmon?'

MIr. *mugna* (i̯o?, m?) 'salmon' is probably a derivative of OIr. *mug* (u, m) 'male slave, servant' < PC **magu-* < PIE **mag*^{h}*u-* 'boy, young man', perhaps originally referring to a young stage in the development of the salmon. The name has a cognate in the Gaul. personal name *Magunus*. Note, however, the similarity of the initial syllable to that of **magero-*, in Section 12.4.9.

12.4.14 pre-Ir. **gisso-/gissu-* 'pike'?

Only attested in NIr. *giosán*, *geasán* 'pike'. Of unknown origin.

12.4.15 pre-Ir. **tarkono-*?

Only attested in NIr. *tarcon* 'some kind of fish'. The spelling of the vowel in the second syllable does not comply with the orthographic rules of Irish. Of unknown origin.

12.4.16 PIC **skaddo-* 'herring'

OIr. *scatán* (o, m) 'herring', W *ysgadan/sgadan* 'herring'; cf. OE *sceadd* 'shad', ON *skaddr*, Norw. dial. *skadd* 'a small whitefish' without the suffixal *-an-*. Unless the languages have borrowed from each other, the [d] that occurs in all three is best explained as due to a loan from another, unknown source. Schrijver (2005: 141–143) has considered a loan from a substrate language. Of unknown origin.

12.4.17 pre-Brit. **marano-* 'salmon'?

W *maran* '(young) salmon, mackerel, various kinds of sea animal'. The initial *ma-* is reminiscent of OIr. *magar* (see above). Of unknown origin.

12.4.18 PC **esko-ang^{u}on-*? 'eel' << PIE **h_2(e)ng^{uh}i-* 'snake'

OIr. *escung* (n, f?), MIr. *esconga* for OIr. *escongu** (n, f?) looks like a compound of *esc-* + a descendent of PC **ang^{u}-V-* < PIE **$h_2$eng^{uh}i-* 'snake'. The first element *esc-* could be the same as the rare OIr. word *esc* 'water', in which case the meaning of the compound would be 'water snake'. Formally, it could also continue PC **φisko-* < **pik̑sko-* 'fish', i.e., the animal would be called 'fish snake'. Gender and stem class of the word are fluid, but an original paradigm nom. *escung*, gen. *escongan* furnishes the best starting point from which the attested forms and inflections can be derived through analogy within Irish. Beside *escong*, the variants *escmug* and *esmong* are also found.

12.4.19 pre-Ir., pre-Brit. **ki/īmmuχo-*, **gimmuχo-* 'lobster'

NIr. *gliomach*, *giomach*, W *cimwch*, *ceimwch*, *gimwch*. A borrowing from one language into the other is conceivable. It would require the fewest extra assumptions if one reckons with the borrowing of W *gimwch* into the Gaelic languages at a comparatively late, post-Old Irish date. This would not explain the origins of the word in Welsh, however. Of unknown origin.

12.4.20 pre-Ir. **porto-* 'crab'?

MIr. *partán* (o, m), NIr. *portán*. Schrijver (2000) considers it as a borrowing from a pre-Celtic language in Ireland. Alternatively, it could be synchronically derived from OIr. *port* 'place, spot; bank, shore; port'. Of unknown origin.

12.4.21 PC **barinīko-* 'rock crustacean = limpet, barnacle'

MIr. *bairnech* (o, m), W *brennig*, sing. *brenigen*, LCorn. *brennik*, sing. *brenigan*, *bernîgan*, NBret. *brennig*, *brinnig*, *bernig*, sing. *brinikenn*; cf. also OFr. *bernaque*, Fr. *barnache* < MLat. *barneca* 'limpet' < Gaul. **barinī/ākā*; derived from PC **barinā* 'rock, rocky region', itself perhaps a nominal formation from the PIE root **b^{h}erH-* 'to treat with a sharp tool'. The British forms display either metathesis or syncope of the first syllable.

12.4.22 pre-Ir. **ai̯skā-* 'shell'

OIr. *áesc* (?) 'shell, *clasendix*',[8] later *fáesc*, ModIr. *faoisce* 'shell, shellfish', *faoisceán*, *féascán* 'crab, shellfish, mussel' with inorganic *f-*. Of unknown origin. It has no discernible connection with Lat. *aesculus* 'oak' < PIE **$h_2$ei̯g-* 'oak'. The shape of the word is reminiscent of OIr. *blóesc* (ā, f) 'integument' (applied to eggshells, nutshells, husks, pods), ModIr. *blaosc*, *plaosc*, W *blisg*, *plisg* 'shells, husks, pods', of equally unknown origin and for which Greene (1975: 175) has suspected a pre-Celtic loan. Heiermeier (1955: 70–106), who was not aware of OIr. *blóesc*, embarked on wide-ranging speculations on the basis of *plaosc*. The ostensible "ablaut" relationship between OIr. *blóesc* and W *blisg* is reminiscent of that between OIr. *fáecha* (n, f), *fáechan* (o, m) and W *gwichiad* (see items 23 and 24 below). In Welsh, the cluster *-sg* occurs also in other words for 'shell, husk': W *ballasg*, *masgl* (Bret. *maskl* 'marc, pomace'). In W *gwisg* 'clothes, garment, covering, armor; husk, hull, bark', OCorn. *guisc*, Bret. *gwisk* 'clothes' < PIE **u̯ēsko-*, *-sg* is old and inherited.

[8] A *clasendix* is a shell such as a conch shell that is used to blow signals.

12.4.23 pre-Ir. **u̯oi̯kVi̯/u̯on-*, **u̯ai̯kVi̯/u̯on-* 'sea snail'?

OIr. *fáecha* (n, f), *fáechan* (o, m) 'sea snail, periwinkle', later also *fáechóc* (ā, f). The few attested forms suggest that the word was originally an *n*-stem that transitioned to an *o*-stem. The word is only found in manuscripts from the Modern Irish period, where the diphthong of the first syllable is spelled *-áe-* or *-ao-*. This allows for the possibility that the etymon had the diphthong **oi̯*, viz. OIr. **fóechu*, originally. In that case, and given its old inflection as an *n*-stem, it would be possible to connect the word with the PIE roots **u̯ieh$_1$-* 'to wrap, wind' or **u̯iek^{u}-* 'to wrap', which would yield an acceptable semantic explanation as 'winder' or 'winding animal'. It would also allow one to relate this word to the following item in Section 12.4.24 via ablaut variation. Note also the item in Section 12.4.25, which could presuppose a British word that corresponds much more closely to the postulated **fóechu*.

12.4.24 pre-Brit. **u̯īkko-* or **u̯īkso-* 'periwinkle'?

W *gwichiad*, *-en*, *-an*, *-yn*, LCorn. *gwihan* 'periwinkle'. Brit. *i* continues Proto-Celtic **ī* or **ū*, of which the latter possibility is not further considered here. Although there is no exact correspondence, the root structure **u̯Vik-* looks similar to the preceding item 12.4.23 and could stand in some kind of ablaut relationship to it. If the root **u̯ieh$_1$-* 'to wrap, wind' is involved, one could speculate that the Irish form continues **u̯oi̯h$_1$kii̯on-* (with loss of the laryngeal), whereas the British would continue something like **u̯ih$_1$kk(i̯)o-* or **u̯ih$_1$ks(i̯)o-*. Compare also item 12.4.25.

12.4.25 pre-Ir. **gūggo-* 'whelk'?

NIr. *gúgán* 'whelk, *Buccinum undatum*'. **gūgg-* looks like a borrowing from a reflex of the regular "British" treatment of **u̯oi̯kVi̯/u̯-* above, i.e. the initial **u̯* reflected by **gw*, which was then reduced to *g* before the rounded vowel; the middle **k* reflected by its British-style lenition *g*; and Brit. **ū̆*, the regular outcome of PC **oi̯*, substituted by Ir. *ū*; but this could all be coincidence. Cf. also the entry *grúgam* 'a kind of bivalve shellfish' in Dinneen's dictionary of Irish, which may be a regional variant of the present item. Of unknown origin.

12.4.26 pre-Ir. **giruddo-* or **geruddo-* 'periwinkle'?

The preform is a mechanical reconstruction based on OIr. *giritán* (o, m), NIr. *gioradán* 'periwinkle'. In a further step of internal reconstruction, this could go back to Proto-Celtic **ger-unto-*; the suffix **-unto-* has parallels in the place names *Aguntum* (East Tyrol) and *Carnuntum* (Lower Austria), if these are Celtic. Of unknown origin.

12.4.27 pre-Ir. **gru-* 'cockle'?

Only attested in NIr. *gruán* 'cockle, *Cardium edule*'. If the word was first put to writing in the late modern period, a voiced fricative such as *dh*, *gh*, *bh*, or *mh* could have been lost after the *u*. Cf. also the entry *grúgam* 'a kind of bivalve shellfish' in Dinneen's dictionary of Irish. Of unknown origin.

12.4.28 PIC or PC? **roṷkkā-* 'husk, cloak'

NIr. *ruacán*, *rócán* 'cockle, *Cardium edule*', W *rhuch* 'bran, husk; cloak'. The Ir. hapax *rucht* (u, m?) < **ruktu-*, glossed as 'tunic', is probably also related. The meaning of the Insular Celtic words, which seem to refer to a hard husk or shell, are hard to square with Pokorny's (IEW 874) reconstruction of a word for 'web, textile' with possible congeners in Germanic, e.g. OE *roc*, ON *rokkr* 'upper garment, robe', Germ. *Rock* 'coat' (cf. Kroonen 2013: 250–251, who demonstrates that the Germanic words go back to a different preform, namely Proto-Germanic **hrukka-*). The Indo-European-looking ablaut relationship between **roṷkkā* and **ruktu-* and the word formation of the latter speak against a loan from a non-Indo-European source, but the prehistory and the further relationships of the items remain unclear.

12.4.29 pre-Ir. **sliggii̯o-* or **sleggii̯o-* 'shell'?

Only found in OIr. *slice* (i̯o) '(oyster)shell'. The name of the Irish town *Sligo*, ModIr. *Sligeach*, comes from the adjective OIr. *slicech* 'having shells, full of shells'. In a further step of internal reconstruction, **sliggii̯o-* could continue **slinkii̯o-*, which Hamp (1996: 87) proposes without further explanation. A connection with W *llyngyr*, MBret. *lencquernenn*, NBret. *lenkern* 'parasitic worms, tapeworms', MBret. *lencr*, NBret. *lenkr* 'sliding', from the PIE root **slenk*$^{\text{u̯}}$- 'to slide, glide' (LIV 567; **slenk-*, **sleng-* in IEW 961) is formally and semantically difficult. Pre-Ir. **slinkii̯o-* would have to continue **slīnk*$^{\text{u̯}}$*ii̯o-* from the lengthened grade **slēnk*$^{\text{u̯}}$-, since full grade **slenk*$^{\text{u̯}}$- would have yielded ***sléice*. Ultimately of unknown origin.

12.4.30 PIC **krokeno-* 'shell(fish)'

ScGael. *creachann* 'scallop', *creachag* 'cockle, scalloped shell', W *cragen*, *crogen* 'shell, shellfish', OCorn. *crogen*, Bret. *krogenn*, pl. *kregin* 'shellfish'. Although unattested in Irish, the Scottish Gaelic evidence necessitates the existence of the word already in the earlier stages of Goidelic. If the word had been borrowed from a British language after the spread of Gaelic to Scotland in the sixth century, British internal [g] would be expected to be echoed in the Gaelic word. The vocalism of *creachann* appears to continue a preform with a different vocalism, viz. **krekono-*, perhaps with vowel metathesis, or it arose under the influence of OIr. *crech* 'plunder'. One can speculate about a formation from the root **krek-* 'to jut out', attested in Germanic **hregan-* (Kroonen 2013: 244). Less likely, for formal and semantic reasons, is a connection with **kreh*$_1$*k-* 'fish roe' (Kroonen 2013: 250) or a relationship with PC **karrekā* 'rock' (cf. OW *carrecc*, *cerricc*, W *carreg*, Corn. *carrag*, Bret. *karreg* 'rock').

12.4.31 Ir. *máerach* '(edible part of a) shellfish'

Ir. *máerach* (ā, f) '(edible part of a) shellfish' seems to be a collective in *-ach* derived from *máer* (o, m) 'steward', which itself is a loan from Lat. *maior*. The semantic motivation for this name, first attested in 1400 (Nic Dhonnchadha 2019: 30), is unclear.

12.5 Technology and Economy

It will come as a surprise to find that there is very little vocabulary that can be reconstructed, either for Celtic in general, or for the island-based Insular Celtic languages, for the technology and economy that is by necessity associated with a life at and by the sea. Only words for the most basic concepts can be recovered, which, however, are for the most part inherited from the ancestor language and which therefore do not shed light on any specifically Celtic modes of naval activities. What is completely lacking is terminology for navigation, i.e. for finding one's way on the open sea, especially at night. Up until very recent times, a vernacular terminology for the night sky must have existed among fishermen in Celtic-speaking communities, but to my knowledge this has never been collected or recorded systematically and is probably for the most part irrecoverably lost. The archaeology of coastal communities in Ireland is treated in O'Sullivan and Breen (2007).

12.5.1 PC *$n\bar{a}\underset{\frown}{u}\bar{a}$-, *$n\bar{a}\underset{\frown}{u}\bar{\imath}$-, *$n\bar{a}\underset{\frown}{u}s$? 'boat' < PIE *$neh_2u$- 'boat'

Gallo-Lat. *nausum** (attested as a hapax dative and ablative *nauso* in Ausonius' *Epistularum liber* 22), Early OIr. *náu*, gen. *náue*, later *nó*, gen. *nóë* (ā, f) 'boat', W *noe* 'wooden vessel, trough', Bret. *new* 'nave, wooden trough'. The Proto-Indo-European inflection as a 'diphthongal stem' (see NIL 515–519 for the complex details) may be reflected in Gallo-Lat. *nausum**, if this represents a thematic formation built directly on the old nominative singular, i.e. *$n\bar{a}\underset{\frown}{u}so$- or *$na\underset{\frown}{u}so$- ← PC *$n\bar{a}\underset{\frown}{u}s$ < nom.sg. PIE *neh_2us. Alternatively, Ausonius' vocable has been interpreted as a loan from Greek ναῦς into Latin (cf. NIL 518 fn. 8), and from there into the local speech of Gaul. The Insular Celtic languages continue various thematic derivatives from the stem **nāu-*, which in British have lost all connection with maritime transport (cf. Schrijver 1995: 299–300). Even though intervocalic **s* would have been lost in the Insular Celtic languages, it is unlikely that the attested words continue *$n\bar{a}\underset{\frown}{u}so$- or *$na\underset{\frown}{u}so$-, i.e. the possible preform of the Gaulish word, since the genitive singular of this should have resulted in ***nuë* in Old Irish (Qiu 2019: 362–365).

12.5.2 PC **longā-* 'boat, ship'

Gaul. *longo-* in compounds, OIr. *long* (ā, f), W *llong* 'boat, ship', OBret. pl. *-locou* (?), Bret. placename *Traou Long*, perhaps 'valley of the ships'. Delamarre (2017: 225–232) relates several Gaulish personal and place names to this etymon, among them, most tantalizingly, a shipbuilder called *Longidienus*. It has also been suggested that Cisalpine Gaul. *lokan* 'urn (?)' (PG·1.2 Todi) reflects this word, if the spelling represents /longan/, the accusative of **longā-* (McCone 1993). The common semantic denominator of 'boat' and 'urn' would be 'vessel'. However, *lokan* could also stand for the accusative of PC **logā-* 'lying place, burial ground' < PIE *$lo\hat{g}^heh_2$- 'act of lying on the ground' (cf. Germ. *Lage*). Delamarre (2017: 230–231) derives **longā* from the PIE adjective *$h_1leng^{uh}\acute{u}$- 'light(weight), swift', designating a 'swift boat'. Another possibility is to connect it with the ethnonym *Lingones* (Delamarre ibid.), a name that can hardly be separated from the OIr. verb *lingid* (S1) 'to jump', the root of which is set up as PC **φleng-e/o-*, PIE *$(s)preng^h$- by Schumacher (2004: 522). Finally, if the Gaulish personal and place names in *longo-* are unrelated to 'ship' and the sole evidence for the word is Insular Celtic, it could be argued that it is a loan from Lat. *nauis longa* 'long ship', but see the comments on **longestā-* (12.5.3) below. While there is no dearth of etymological possibilities for PC **longā*, I do not dare to give preference to any one of them.

12.5.3 PIC **longestā-* 'fleet'

OIr. *longas*, gen. *loingse* (ā, f) 'fleet, shipping; exile', W *llynges* 'navy, fleet'. The word is derived from the word for 'ship' via the addition of the abstract or collective suffix *-*estā-*. Schrijver's (1995: 28) reconstruction **lo/ungissā* is excluded by the Irish word. The close correspondence between the Irish and the Welsh words speaks for its great age and – indirectly – for the great age of Clt. **longā-*, thereby challenging the basis for a loan from Latin.

12.5.4 pre-Clt. **koruko-* 'light hide boat'

InsLat. *curucus*, OIr. *curach*, hypercorrect *caurach* (o, m), W *corwg*, *cwrwg* 'coracle'. A coracle is a light, versatile, hide-covered boat. The word is related with *corium*, the Latin word for 'leather' < PIE *$(s)kor(h_2)o$- 'that which is cut off = hide'. The suffix of Gr. κώρυκος 'leather satchel' looks deceptively similar, but the difference in the length of the first vowel between Celtic and Greek is unexplained. Beekes (2010: 816) believes that the Greek word is a loan from a pre-Indo-European language.

12.5.5 PIC **φlestro-* 'vessel, boat' < pre-Clt. *$ple\hat{k}stro$- 'wickerwork?'

OIr. *lestar* (o, n), OW *lestir*, W *llestr*, OCorn. *lester*, *luu listri* 'navy', MCorn. *lester*, Bret. *lestr* 'vessel, boat'. It is unclear if the use of this word for boats is primary or a secondary application of a word that originally referred to a container. The word can be analyzed as a derivative of the PIE root *$ple\hat{k}$- 'to plait' (LIV 486), namely *$ple\hat{k}$-s-tro-* in the sense of 'plaited tool > wickerwork'. This resulted in PC **φlestro-* (see Stifter 2017: 1191–1192 for the development of complex consonant clusters with medial *s*). Under the assumption that PC *-*str-* was retained as such in Irish (Stifter 2005: 170), the Irish and British words go back to a common preform, and there is no need to assume a borrowing from British into Irish. Alternatively, the word has been reconstructed as **les-tro-* 'tool for collecting' (from the PIE root **les-* 'to collect, gather up', LIV 413), or as **lent-tro-*, related to Lat. *linter* 'trough, vat, small boat' (VKG i 81). However, the oldest form of the latter is *lunter*, which excludes the suggested preform.

12.5.6 PC **siglo-* 'sail'

OIr. *séol* (o, n), OW *huil*, W *hwyl* 'sail'. This is further related to Germanic **se/igla-* 'sail', either as a very early loan or as a Celtic-Germanic isogloss. While the word is traditionally derived from the PIE root **sekH-* 'to cut, separate' (LIV 524) in the sense of 'cut piece of cloth', Schrijver (1995: 357) and Kroonen (2013: 430–431) dispute this explanation. Kroonen suggests a link with Gallo-Lat. *sagum* 'coarse woolen cloak' and Lith. *sãgė* 'shawl, warp' instead. However, this cannot explain the vocalism of PC **siglo-*. See also Chapter 13 by Van Sluis, Jørgensen, & Kroonen in this volume. Of unclear etymology.

12.5.7 PIC *branesā-*? 'prow'

OIr. _braine_ (f?), OW _bréni_, W _breni_ 'prow', OCorn. _brenniat_ 'man on the prow'. While the Irish and the British words are patently related, a reliable etymology is lacking so far. If the words are exact equations, the correspondence between the OIr. ending _-e_ and Brit. _-i_ can only be explained via a Celtic suffix *_-esā-_ (Schrijver 1995: 393). The first part is obscure. It is reminiscent of PC *_brano-_ 'raven', so perhaps the designation derives metaphorically from a prominent part of the raven, viz. its beak. If the geminate _nn_ of the Old Cornish word can be taken seriously, it would rule out the connection with the bird. LEIA (B-77) rejects various suggested connections with words in other Indo-European languages, namely with Lat. _frōns_ 'forehead, front' or with ON _brandr_ 'board at the ship's stem', all of which are etymologically obscure themselves (cf. De Vaan 2008: 244). A purely mechanical reconstruction of possible preforms of *_branesā-_ yields pre-Clt. *_g^{u}/b^{h}r̥Hn-es-_.

12.5.8 pre-Ir. *erostu-? 'stern'

Only attested in OIr. _eros_, _erus_ (u, m?), later also _erais_ (f) 'poop, stern'. The gender fluctuates: while in the earliest attestations, the word behaves like a masculine or neuter noun, in later Irish, its behavior agrees with that of feminine nouns. The rounded vowel in the second syllable of the earliest attestations points to a _u_-stem, although no decisive forms are attested. A possible etymology, which must remain speculative, is to operate with the reconstruction *_$h_1$eros-sth$_2$-u-_ 'standing up at the back', a compound of PIE *_$h_1$ers-_ 'hind part' and the root *_steh$_2$-_ 'to stand'.

12.5.9 PC *mori-tei̯g- 'to navigate, travel the sea' < PIE *mori- 'sea' + *(s)teig^h- 'to step, stride'

This compound arose from the univerbation of the Proto-Celtic idiom of verb *_tei̯g-_ 'to go' + object *_mori-_ 'sea' < PIE *_(s)teig^h-_ 'to step, stride' (LIV 593–594) + *_mori-_ 'sea'. It survives in various derivatives and in two ablaut grades of the second compound member. Since no trace of such a compound can be found in Irish, it is possible that it is a specifically Gallo-British isogloss.

A PC *MORITIG- 'SAILOR'

The second element of Gaul. _moritix_, _moritex_ 'sailor' is the root noun of PC *_tei̯g-_ 'to go'. The attested variation between _i_ and _e_ in the vocalism of the final syllable is best explained as the common fluctuation between unstressed short _i_ and _e_ in Gaulish, perhaps under Vulgar Latin influence. This would then point to the root noun being in the zero grade *_-tig-_, as is expected for Celtic root nouns of the structure *_CEI̯C-_ and *_CERC-_. Another possible, but morphologically less well motivated, explanation for the vowel alternation is to operate with a full grade of the root noun, i.e. *_-tēg-_ < *_-tei̯g-_, with sporadic Late Gaulish raising of _ē_ > _ī_.

B PC *MORITEI̯GE/O- 'TO NAVIGATE, TRAVEL THE SEA'

The verb is reflected in W _mordwyaf_, verbal noun _mordwyo_, and MBret. _mordeiff_, NBret. _mordeiñ_, _merdeiñ_ 'to voyage on the sea'.

C PIC *MORITEI̯GO- 'VOYAGE ON THE SEA'

Nominal formations derived from the verbal stem show the _e_-grade of the root. W _mordwy_ 'sea, flood, sea journey' continues *_mori-tei̯g-o-_, The agent noun MW _mordwyad_, OBret. _mortoiat_, NBret. _mordead_, _merdead_ 'sailor' < *_mori-tei̯g-ati-_ is derived from it.

12.5.10 PC *rā- 'to row' << PIE *h_1reh_1- 'to row'

Several verbal and nominal formations in the Celtic languages are built on the inherited Indo-European root for 'rowing'. The root vowel _ā_ in Celtic continues the _o_-grade of the generalized iterative formation. See also Chapter 13 by Van Sluis, Jørgensen, & Kroonen in this volume.

10A PC *RĀI̯E/O- 'TO ROW'

OIr. _ráïd_ (H1) 'to row' continues PIE *_h_1roh_1i̯e/o-_. Its verbal noun is _rám_ (u, m) < *_rāmu-_. Its compound _imm·rá_, verbal noun _immram_ (u, m) 'rowing around' is the common word for 'sea-voyaging, navigation' in Old Irish.

10B PIC *RĀMI̯O- 'OAR, IMPLEMENT FOR ROWING'

OIr. _rámae_ (i̯o, m) 'oar; spade', W _rhaw_, LCorn. _rêv_, OBret. pl. _roiau_, MBret. _reuf_, NBret. _reuñv_ 'shovel, spade'. In British, the word must have lost its inherited meaning very early, and a new word for 'oar' was borrowed from Lat. _rēmus_ < *_$h_1reh_1$mo-_, namely OW _(dluith-)ruim_, W _rhwyf_, OCorn. _ruif_, MBret. _reuff_, _roeuff_, NBret. _roeñv_. OBret. _roiau_ glosses Lat. _soffosoria_ (= _suffusoria_) 'pitchers', which must be a mistake for _fossoria_ 'digging implements', required by the context.

12.5.11 PC *φlou̯- 'to move, float'? < PIE *pleu̯- 'to swim, float' (LIV 487)

Another inherited root with a large number of reflexes in almost all branches of Celtic, which in turn form the bases of further language-internal derivatives.

11A PC *ΦLOU̯E/O- OR *ΦLOU̯EI̯E/O- 'TO MOVE, FLOAT'

OIr. *luïthir* (H3) 'to move, fly'. The primary verb survives only in Irish. Synchronically, it has lost all connection with navigation on water, but has become a general term for movement of any kind. The verbal formation is either a thematic present **pleu̯e/o-* 'to float' or a causative **plou̯ei̯e/o-* 'to make float'.

11B PC *ΦLOU̯Ī- 'RUDDER, HELM' < PRE-CLT. *PLEU̯IH$_2$-

OIr. *luí*, gen. sg. *lue*, gen. pl. *luae*, dat. sg. *luith*/*luid* (ī, f) 'steering oar, rudder', OW pl. *liuou*, W *llyw* 'rudder, helm', OCorn. *leu* 'key', LCorn. *lew* 'rudder', OBret. *-leu* '-ruler?' can be combined under the reconstruction PC **φlou̯ī-*. The outcome of the reconstruction **φluu̯ī-*, favored by Schrijver (1995: 291, 338–339; after Cowgill 1985: 23), would probably be the same, but has the disadvantage of requiring a morphologically awkward pre-Celtic antecedent **pluih$_2$-*. OIr. *luí* could continue the reconstructed form directly, as is borne out by the attested forms of the genitive singular and plural. The once-attested dental-stem dative singular *luith*/*luid* could either be a nonce formation influenced by agentive dental stems such as *fili*, gen. *filed* 'poet', or it is evidence for a separate, but otherwise lost noun that continues a preform **φlou̯et-* or **φlou̯īt-*, or even **φloui̯i̯ati-* (cf. Hamp 1997).

11C PC *ΦLOU̯I̯O- 'STEERSMAN, HELMSMAN'

Gaul. theonym *Suleuiae* 'the well-steering ones?', W *llywydd* 'ruler, steersman', OCorn. *leuuit* 'steersman', LCorn. place name *Treloweth*. OIr. *luäm* 'pilot, steersman' < **φlou̯i̯amon-*, NBret. *levial* 'to direct', *levier* 'steersman, leader' can in theory all be analyzed as secondary formations based on **φluu̯i̯o-* to which synchronically productive agentive suffixes were added for morphological recharacterization.

12.6 Interpretation

The raw data allows for a variety of interpretations. And not only do the data that have been brought together in the over eighty items above tell us something, but the items that are not there are also revealing by their absence. Languages do not exist independently of the people who speak them. Looked at from the point of view of Proto-Celtic around 1000 BC, i.e. in the late Bronze Age, the most striking aspect of the word list is the dearth of vocabulary that relates to a maritime habitat. Taken at face value, the data can be read as speaking of a land-based population with little concern for the sea and its ecosystem (cf. 12.5 Technology and Economy). The role of the sea in subsistence also seems to have been limited. On the basis of the vocabulary that can be reconstructed for Proto-Celtic, one would not want to place its speech community on or near the sea. This agrees with traditional accounts of Celtic glottogenesis that place the Proto-Celtic speech communities somewhere in the area of eastern France and western Germany. Also following the traditional account, the spread of the Celtic languages over a much wider area must have been mediated through the physical movement of Celtic-speaking groups. Languages do not travel by themselves. Speakers of early Celtic languages must by necessity have crossed the sea by rowing (**rāi̯e/o-*) and sailing (**siglo-*) to arrive in Britain and in Ireland, maybe during the second half of the first millennium BC. Linking this with the results of the present investigation, they must have done so partly in light craft (**φlestro-*, **koruko-*) that were probably better suited for rivers, less so for the high sea, and, having reached those islands, one cannot avoid the impression that the new settlers burned their boats (**nāu̯ā-*) upon arrival and continued their mostly land-centered ways of living. No need was felt to challenge the sea again. In British Celtic, some of the most fundamental terms for seafaring (PC **nāu̯ā-* 'boat', **rāmi̯o-* 'oar') lost their primary meanings in favor of entirely different land-based concepts, and words for the original activities had to be borrowed from other languages later on.

When confronted with the Atlantic seafront, especially in Ireland, the tidal changes and the irascibility of the ocean seem to have left a deep impression (cf. 12.2 Topography). The only maritime plants of importance were various kinds of algae and seaweed (cf. 12.3 Flora). Seeing that their names display a rather archaic character, they could already have formed part of the earliest habitats of Celtic speech communities. Where the sea was exploited as a food source, mostly for shellfish, the terminology of the antecedent population was adopted, or land-based terminology was metaphorically carried over to larger sea animals (cf. 12.4 Fauna). The previous populations seem to have left their strongest imprint in the astonishing number of borrowings from unidentified languages that refer to sea animals. Some of these words form part of, or are reminiscent of, O'Rahilly's Ivernic word list of substrate words in Irish (O'Rahilly 1935: 4–5, 27 fn. 2). The only animal with which they seem to have been firmly familiar is the salmon, or at least a fish with a similar appearance.

Of course, alternative narratives could be developed. One could, for instance, toy with a scenario where Celtic speech communities started out as thoroughly seafaring people. In such a scenario, it must then be assumed that as soon as Celtic population groups finally arrived in a truly maritime environment, namely the Western Archipelago, they gave up seafaring and removed most of the associated terminology from their language almost immediately (while, in the case of Irish, at the same time retaining words for 'serpent' or 'bear', which certainly had no *signifié* in their new habitat). Only later, after coming into contact with superior seafaring populations like the Romans, the Norse, or the modern English and French, was the maritime lexicon replenished with loans and loan translations.

Of these two models, I find the first more economical than the second, since the latter requires comparatively counterintuitive assumptions. What the reconstructable vocabulary of the Celtic languages says about the history of their speakers is that the Atlantic seaboards and seaways are unlikely to have been their natural environment, but that their lives were rather spent with their backs to the ocean.

4. Appendix – Chronological Layers of the Maritime Lexicon in the Celtic Languages

	topography	**flora**	**fauna**	**technology/economy**
inherited from PIE	**mori-* **sālo-* **trei̯Ht(H)on-*		**perk̂o-* **pork̂o-*	**neh$_2$u-* **h$_1$reh$_1$-* **pleu̯-*
pre-Celtic	**rei̯no-* **plh$_1$nu̯o-* **treh$_2$g^h-* **trh$_2$g^{h}tu-* **tuh$_2$sneh$_2$-/tundneh$_2$-* **kh$_2$pno-* **h$_1$enisth$_2$ih$_2$-* **h$_2$m̥b^{h}i-g^{u}h$_2$to-*	**d^{h}olHisko-* **u̯ipsmon-* **u̯ih$_1$ti-/*u̯ih$_1$ter-* **stlHmo-* **slibVkko-*	**anke/ini̯o-* **esko-ang^{u}on-*	**koruko-* **plek̂stro-*
Proto-Celtic	**tetrāg-*		**barinīko-* **maguni̯o-*	**longā-* **siglo-* **mori-tei̯g-* **moritig-* **φlou̯ī-* **φlou̯i̯o-*
Proto-Celtic loans			**bledā-* **esok-/*esāk-*	
Proto-Insular Celtic	**liro-* **līi̯ant-* **līmu-* **to-liH-(i̯)o-* **u̯orgiu̯i̯ā-* **trāgi-/tragi̯o-* **φrobertii̯ā-* **tabernV-?*	**attīno-/aktīno-*	**rou̯kkā-* **krokeno-/krekono-*	**longestā-* **branesā-* **erostu-* **rāmi̯o-*
Pre-Insular Celtic loans or unclear origin	**kladdāko-* **gai̯to/ā-*		**blo.āko-* **parno-* **rōno-* **gei̯rii̯o-* **ma/oluko-* **braddo-* **magero-* **gisso-/gissu-* **tarkon-* **skaddo-* **marano-* **ki/īmmuχo-* **porto-* **ai̯skā-* **u̯o/ai̯kVi̯/u̯on-* **u̯īkko-/u̯īkso-* **gūggo-* **giruddo-/geruddo-* **gru-* **sliggii̯o-/sleggii̯o-*	
historical loans		*langa?*	*máerach*	

References

An Roinn Oideachais. 1978. *Ainmneacha Plandaí agus Ainmhithe. Flora and fauna nomenclature*. Dublin: Oifig an tSoláthair.

Bauer, Bernhard. 2015. *Intra-Celtic loanwords*. PhD diss., University of Vienna.

Beekes, Robert. 2010. *Etymological dictionary of Greek*. With the assistance of Lucien van Beek (Leiden Indo-European Etymological Dictionary Series 10). Leiden: Brill.

Blom, Alderik. 2011. Endlicher's glossary. *Études Celtiques* 37: 159–181.

Çınar, Ümüt. 2010. Bretonca Balık Adları. Breton fish names. Accessed July 13, 2021. www.academia.edu/36642557/Breton_Fish_Names.

Cowgill, Warren. 1985. PIE **duu̯o* "2" in Germanic and Celtic, and the nom.-acc. dual of non-neuter *o*-stems. *Münchener Studien zur Sprachwissenschaft* 46: 13–28.

de Bernardo Stempel, Patrizia. 1999. *Nominale Wortbildung des älteren Irischen. Stammbildung und Derivation* (Buchreihe der Zeitschrift für celtische Philologie 15). Tübingen: Niemeyer.

Delamarre, Xavier. 2003. *Dictionnaire de la langue gauloise. Une approche linguistique du vieux-celtique continental*. Paris: Éditions errance.

2017. *Les noms de Gaulois*. Paris: Les Cent Chemins.

Deshayes, Albert. 2003. *Dictionnaire étymologique du breton*. Douarnenez: Le Chasse-Marée.

de Vaan, Michiel. 2008. *Etymological dictionary of Latin and the other Italic languages* (Leiden Indo-European Etymological Dictionary Series 7). Leiden: Brill.

Dinneen, Pádraig S. 1927. *Foclóir Gaedhilge agus Béarla. An Irish-English dictionary, being a thesaurus of the words, phrases and idioms of the Modern Irish language. New edition, revised and greatly enlarged*. Dublin: Irish Texts Society.

Dwelly, Edward. 1911. *Faclair Gaidhlig gu Beurla le Dealbhan. The illustrated Gaelic-English dictionary*. Glasgow: Gairm Publications.

eDIL 2015 = *An electronic dictionary of the Irish language, based on the contributions to a dictionary of the Irish language (Dublin: Royal Irish Academy, 1913–1976)*. Accessed July 13, 2021. http://edil.qub.ac.uk/.

Falileyev, Alexander. 2000. *Etymological glossary of Old Welsh* (Buchreihe der Zeitschrift für celtische Philologie 18). Tübingen: Niemeyer.

Falileyev, Alexander, & Morfydd E. Owen. 2005. *The Leiden leechbook. A study of the earliest Neo-Brittonic medical compilation*. With two appendices contributed by Helen McKee (Innsbrucker Beiträge zur Kulturwissenschaft Sonderheft 122), Innsbruck: Institut für Sprachen und Literaturen der Universität Innsbruck.

Favereau, Francis. 2016. *Geriadur Bras*. Morlaix: Skol Vreizh. http://geriadurbrasfavereau. monsite-orange.fr/index.html.

GPC 2014 = *Geiriadur Prifysgol Cymru Online*. Aberystwyth: University of Wales Centre for Advanced Welsh & Celtic Studies. http://geiriadur.ac.uk/gpc/gpc.html.

Greene, David. 1975. Varia III. 1. Ceciderunt ab oculis eius tamquam scamae. *Ériu* 26: 175–178.

Hamp, Eric P. 1996. Varia. *Études Celtiques* 32: 87–90.

1997. Varia. *Études Celtiques* 33: 81–82.

Heiermeier, Anne. 1955. *Indogermanische Etymologien des Keltischen*. Heft 2. Würzburg: Institut für Keltologie und Irlandkunde.

Irslinger, Britta Sofie. 2002. *Abstrakta mit Dentalsuffixen im Altirischen*. Heidelberg: Winter.

Kelly, Fergus. 1988. *A guide to early Irish law* (Early Irish Law Series 3). Dublin: Dublin Institute for Advanced Studies.

1998. *Early Irish farming* (Early Irish Law Series 4). Dublin: Dublin Institute for Advanced Studies.

Kroonen, Guus. 2013. *Etymological dictionary of Proto-Germanic* (Leiden Indo-European Etymological Dictionaries 11). Leiden & Boston: Brill.

Kümmel, Martin. 2011–. Addenda und Corrigenda zu LIV². Accessed July 13, 2021. http://www.martinkuemmel.de/liv2add.html.

LEIA = Joseph Vendryes et al. 1959. *Lexique étymologique de l'irlandais ancien*. Vols. A, B, C, D, M N O P, R S, T U. Paris & Dublin: Centre National de la Recherche Scientifique & Dublin Institute for Advanced Studies.

LIV = Helmut Rix, Martin Kümmel, Thomas Zehnder, Reiner Lipp, & Brigitte Schirmer (ed.). 2001. *Lexikon der indogermanischen Verben. 2., erw. und verb. Aufl.* Wiesbaden: Reichert.

Mac an Iomaire, Séamus, & Tomás Ó Máille. 1938. *Cladaigh Chonamara*. Dublin: Oifig an tSoláthair.

Mallory, James P., & Douglas Q. Adams (ed.). 1997. *Encyclopedia of Indo-European culture*. London & Chicago: Fitzroy Dearborn.

2006. *The Oxford introduction to Proto-Indo-European and the Proto-Indo-European world*. Oxford: Oxford University Press.

McCone, Kim. 1991. *The Indo-European origins of the Old Irish nasal presents, subjunctives and futures* (Innsbrucker Beiträge zur Sprachwissenschaft 66). Innsbruck: Institut für Sprachwissenschaft.

1993. Zisalpinisch-gallisch *uenia* und *lokan*. In: Frank Heidermanns, Helmut Rix, & Elmar Seebold (ed.), *Sprachen und Schriften des antiken Mittelmeerraums. Festschrift für Jürgen Untermann zum 65. Geburtstag* (Innsbrucker Beiträge zur Sprachwissenschaft 78), 243–249. Innsbruck: Institut für Sprachwissenschaft der Universität Innsbruck.

McManus, Damian. 1991. *A guide to ogam* (Maynooth Monographs 4). Maynooth: An Sagart.

Nic Dhonnchadha, Aoibheann. 2019. Some words from "Almusór" (1400). *Ossory, Laois and Leinster* 7: 14–31.

Nyberg, Harri. 1993. Celtic ideas of plants. In: Hannu-Pekka Huttunen & Riita Latvio (ed.), *Entering the arena. Presenting Celtic studies in Finland. Papers read at the seminar "Celtic studies, what are they?," held at the University of Turku, Finland, 18th to 19th of September, 1992* (Etiäinen 2), 85–114. Turku: Department of Cultural Studies, University of Turku & The Finnish Society for Celtic Studies.

Nyberg, Harri, & Erwan Ar Gall. 1996. Traditional material culture and regulations concerning the use of seaweeds in Celtic areas. In: Anders Ahlqvist, Glyn Welden Banks, Riita Latvio, Harri Nyberg, & Tom Sjöblom (ed.), *Celtica helsingiensia. Proceedings from a symposium on Celtic studies.* (Commentationes humanarum litterarum Societatis Scientiarum Fennicae 107), 149–178. Helsinki: Societas Scientiarum Fennica.

O'Brien, Micheal A. 1956. Etymologies and notes. *Celtica* 3: 168–184.

O'Rahilly, Thomas F. 1935. *The Goidels and their predecessors* (Sir John Rhŷs Memorial Lecture British Academy 1935). London: Humphrey Milford.

O'Sullivan, Aidan, & Colin Breen. 2007. *Maritime Ireland. An archaeology of coastal communities*. Stroud: Tempus.

Qiu, Fangzhe. 2019. *Aue* 'descendant' and its descendants. *Indogermanische Forschungen* 124: 343–374.

RM (unidentified). 2018. Molluscs species names. Accessed July 13, 2021. www.nature.scot/sites/default/files/2018-05/Molluscs%20consultation%20-%20species%20names.pdf.

Schrijver, Peter. 1995. *Studies in British Celtic historical phonology* (Leiden Studies in Indo-European 5). Amsterdam & Atlanta: Rodopi.

1997. Animal, vegetable and mineral: Some Western European substratum words. In: Alexander Lubotsky (ed.), *Sound law and analogy. Papers in honor of Robert S. P. Beekes on the occasion of his 60th birthday* (Leiden Studies in Indo-European 9), 293–316. Amsterdam: Rodopi.

2000. Varia V. Non-Indo-European surviving in Ireland in the first millenium AD. *Ériu* 51: 195–199.

2005. Varia I. More on non-Indo-European surviving in Ireland in the first millennium AD. *Ériu* 55: 137–144.

Schumacher, Stefan. 2004. *Die keltischen Primärverben. Ein vergleichendes, etymologisches und morphologisches Lexikon.* Unter Mitarbeit von Britta Schulze-Thulin und Caroline aan de Wiel (Innsbrucker Beiträge zur Sprachwissenschaft 110). Innsbruck: Institut für Sprachwissenschaft.

Stifter, David. 2004. Study in red. *Die Sprache* 40(2): 202–223.

2005. Zur Bedeutung und Etymologie von altirisch *sirem*. *Die Sprache* 45: 160–189.

2015. The language of the poems of Blathmac. In: Pádraig Ó Riain (ed.), *The poems of Blathmac son of Cú Brettan: Reassessments* (Irish Texts Society Subsidiary Series 27), 47–103. London: Irish Texts Society.

2017. The phonology of Celtic. In: Jared S. Klein, Brian Joseph, & Matthias Fritz (ed.), *Handbook of comparative and historical Indo-European linguistics. An international handbook* (Handbücher zur Sprach- und Kommunikationswissenschaft 41/2), 1188–1202. Berlin & New York: Walter de Gruyter.

2018. An early Irish poetic formula. In: Pamela O'Neill & Anders Ahlqvist (ed.), *Fír Fesso: A Festschrift for Neil McLeod* (Sydney Series in Celtic Studies 17), 223–232. Sydney: University of Sydney.

2018b. The stars look very different today. *Ériu* 68: 29–54.

forthc. The gravyty of dark matter. An edition of *Fil and griän Glinne Aí*. In: Chantal Kobel (ed.), *Obscurity*. Dublin: Dublin Institute for Advanced Studies.

forthc. b. Die Behandlung von Gruppen von Labiallaut und *n* im Keltischen.

forthc. c. The rise of gemination in Celtic. *Open Research Europe*.

Stüber, Karin. 2015. *Die Verbalabstrakta des Altirischen*. 2 vols. (Münchner Forschungen zur historischen Sprachwissenschaft 15). Bremen: Hempen.

Zair, Nicholas. 2012. *The reflexes of the Proto-Indo-European laryngeals in Celtic* (Brill's Studies in Indo-European Languages and Linguistics 7). Leiden & Boston: Brill.

Ziegler, Sabine. 1994. *Die Sprache der altirischen Ogam-Inschriften* (Historische Sprachforschung Ergänzungsheft 36). Göttingen: Vandenhoeck & Ruprecht.

13 EUROPEAN PREHISTORY BETWEEN CELTIC AND GERMANIC: THE CELTO-GERMANIC ISOGLOSSES REVISITED*

PAULUS VAN SLUIS, ANDERS RICHARDT JØRGENSEN, AND GUUS KROONEN

13.1 Introduction

Recent advances in the field of palaeogenomics have revealed that at the onset of the Late Neolithic, Europe was characterized by a major cultural and genetic transformation triggered by multiple population movements from the Pontic–Caspian steppe. Corded Ware populations show a large-scale introduction of Yamnaya steppe ancestry across the entire archaeological horizon (Allentoft et al. 2015; Haak et al. 2015; Malmström 2019). The emergence of the Bell Beaker burial identity in the early third millennium BCE was similarly accompanied by a dramatic genetic turnover, at least in Northwestern Europe (Olalde et al. 2018). These population changes call for the integration of genetic evidence into existing models for the linguistic Indo-Europeanization of Europe (cf. Kristiansen et al. 2017).

In spite of these advances in the debate on the Indo-European dispersal, many key linguistic questions remain, most notably those on the movements and contact of prehistoric groups in the millennia that followed. Here we focus on Western Europe, where the Celtic and Germanic languages historically formed some of the most prominent subgroups of the Indo-European language family. Germanic and Celtic are not traditionally considered monophyletic or even closely related Indo-European subgroups, and most likely arrived in their historical locations through independent dispersals from the Indo-European homeland. In spite of this distant relationship, a considerable amount of lexical stock has nevertheless been identified as exclusive to these two branches, being suggestive of a partially shared prehistory separate from the other Indo-European subgroups. This linguistic problem has been recognized since the early days of Indo-European studies (Ebel 1861; Kluge 1913: 5–6) and revisited multiple times since then (see Section 2.1). However, due to the highly complex evolution of the surviving Celtic languages and the lack of a linguistic methodology for the absolute dating of prehistoric lexical change, no consensus currently exists on either the exact extent of the lexical evidence for Celto-Germanic language contact, or the timing and linguistic processes by which it accrued.

Several linguistic mechanisms may be hypothesized to account for these Celto-Germanicisms.

13.1.1 Mechanism 1: A Celto-Germanic Subnode

One way to account for uniquely Celtic and Germanic lexical commonalities is to posit a period of shared linguistic evolution. This scenario revolves around the question of when exactly the unity between those Proto-Indo-European dialects that evolved into Celtic and Germanic was disrupted. Celtic is known to share a number of post-PIE linguistic innovations with Italic, with which it may have formed a subunit until well after the migration from the Pontic–Caspian steppe (cf. Schrijver 2016). No such subunit has been hypothesized for Celtic and Germanic, however, because sound laws and morphological developments uniquely shared between Celtic and Germanic are incomparable in number compared to Italo-Celtic. It is nevertheless possible that the Celto-Germanic isoglosses contain lexical elements – inherited archaisms or shared innovations – from the PIE dialectal period that have so far been overlooked.

13.1.2 Mechanism 2: Mutual Contact

In addition to vertically transmitted features, lexical material may have been exchanged from one branch to another horizontally in the period following the breakup of Indo-European and the intrusions of Celtic and Germanic into Europe. The presumed *in situ* evolution of these branches over the millennia leading up to the attested Celtic and Germanic languages are likely to have entailed multiple periods of contact where goods, customs, ideas, and vocabulary may have been exchanged. The

* This study has received funding from the European Research Council under the European Union's Horizon 2020 research and innovation program (grant nº 716732), the Independent Research Fund Denmark (grant nº 9037-00086B) and the Riksbankens Jubileumsfond (grant nº M19-0625:1). We further express our gratitude to Marijn van Putten, David Stifter, and Anthony Jakob for providing feedback on important aspects of this chapter.

second question that we therefore address in this study is to what extent the Celto-Germanic isoglosses are due to secondary, post-settlement contact between speakers of Germanic and Celtic in Europe.

A key question in exploring the prehistoric contact between Celtic and Germanic is where and when in Europe such contact could have taken place. Obviously, this question cannot be answered without addressing the debates on the periodizations and locations of the Celtic and Germanic linguistic homelands, which due to a lack of written sources cannot be established with the help of direct evidence. If indeed Celtic and Germanic developed in Europe following the Yamnaya expansion, several hypotheses are at hand.

Germanic is generally considered to have been in place in Northern Europe in the Iron Age, and plausibly already during the Nordic Bronze Age (cf. Mallory 1989: 84–87). A further hypothesis is that it developed from an Indo-European dialect that arrived in Northern Europe with the Corded Ware in the first quarter of the third millennium BCE (Mallory 1989: 108; Schm 130; Iversen & Kroonen 2017).

There are various hypotheses on where and when Proto-Celtic was spoken. Direct attestation of Celtic languages dates to the first millennium BCE, but already in this millennium, Celtic languages are attested from Iberia to Central Europe, so a mechanism by which it spread across Europe must also be identified. The traditional hypothesis identifies Proto-Celtic with the Hallstatt and La Tène cultures found in Western and Central Europe in the Late Bronze Age and Iron Age. Celtic speakers then migrated from Central Europe into the Iberian Peninsula and the British Isles as these material cultures spread.

Current archaeological evidence does not support a major settlement of a foreign population during the La Tène period, however, and Mallory (2016), among others, argues that other mechanisms than mass migration must be found to account for the spread of Celtic across Europe. He connects its spread with social practices such as guest–host relationships, feasting, and fosterage found in socially stratified Celtic-speaking communities. The spread of hillforts and sword warfare, i.e. a warrior culture, from Atlantic Europe to the British Isles in the Middle to Late Bronze Age is proposed to serve as an archaeological correlate for these mechanisms. Amid the lack of unambiguous archaeological evidence for an intrusive population associated with hillforts, however, Mallory's argumentation in favor of a language shift has faced the same criticism as the traditional hypothesis (O'Brien 2016).

Under the "Celtic from the West" hypothesis, the Proto-Celtic language community was situated both earlier in time and further to the west. Under this hypothesis, Indo-European dialects were spoken along the Atlantic coast at least as early as the Bell Beaker period, either because Indo-European spread to the Atlantic with Neolithic farmers, or because people associated with the spread of the Bell Beaker package adopted Indo-European from their steppe-derived Corded Ware neighbors. The spread of Celtic then entailed a process of dialect leveling among Indo-European speakers over the course of the Bronze Age. The archaeological vector for this dialect leveling was the Atlantic Bronze Age. Under this hypothesis, Celtic emerged – as a lingua franca used among Indo-European speakers for trade along the Atlantic coast – through a process of dialect leveling,[1] and the Hallstatt and La Tène cultures may still have served as vectors of later expansion of Celtic into the Balkans (Cunliffe & Koch 2019; Sims-Williams 2020).

While both a Central European and an Atlantic homeland of Proto-Celtic allow for Celtic-Germanic language contact, the expected location and nature of this contact differs. Under the traditional hypothesis, as well as that of Mallory, Celtic and Germanic prehistoric language contact was land-based, in what is now Germany (cf. Stifter, Chapter 12 in this volume). Under the Celtic from the West hypothesis, a sea-based vector of contact around the North Sea is more likely. These contact scenarios should yield different types of shared vocabulary. In this study, we will not just review the evidence for prehistoric Celtic-Germanic language contact from a purely linguistic perspective, but additionally, use the results to review the aforementioned perspectives on the hypothetical locations of the Proto-Celtic language community.

Several second- and first-millennium BCE archaeological vectors may be relevant. The Bell Beaker phenomenon reached all the way north to Jutland and represented a second layer of potentially Indo-European-speaking communities following the Corded Ware incursions, so it may have served as the vector for the earlier strata of Celto-Germanic vocabulary. Somewhat later vectors of contact may be between either the Atlantic Bronze Age or the Urnfield culture on the one hand, and the Nordic Bronze Age on the other. The final vector of prehistoric language contact may have been between Hallstatt/La Tène and the final Nordic Bronze Age.

13.1.3 Mechanism 3: Shared Contact with Non-IE Languages

Finally, a remaining explanation for vocabulary shared exclusively by Celtic and Germanic is that both of these Indo-European subgroups were subjected to linguistic influences from non-Indo-European language(s) spoken in Europe before the steppe incursions. This question in turn ties back in with the Celtic homeland problem, as well as with one of the most important archaeological debates of the past decades: the origin and nature of the Bell Beaker package. While in the traditional view, the early-third-millennium spread of this package, consisting of characteristic reversed bell beakers, copper daggers, and stone wrist guards, was taken to represent the expansion of a distinct ethnocultural unity, the "Bell Beaker folk," later archaeology emphasized a mechanism of cultural diffusion without large-scale mobility of people.

This century-old debate has, however, now been decided by a comprehensive genetic study on individuals selected from

[1] However, language spread through use as a lingua franca for trade would be expected to exhibit significant grammatical simplification, which is not found (Mallory 2016: 393).

Bell Beaker burial contexts from all across Europe (Olalde et al. 2018). The result of this study was that the two explanations for the spread of the Bell Beaker cultural package are in fact complementary. Whereas individuals from Southern Europe, especially the Iberian Peninsula, cluster with Neolithic populations, individuals from Northern Europe carry a strong steppe signal, with Y-chromosomal lineages peaking around 90% in Britain and the Netherlands. This contrast between cultural homogeneity versus genetic heterogeneity has decisively demonstrated that the spread of the Bell Beaker package did not involve a detectable population movement in the south but was indeed coupled with a large-scale population turnover in the north. One possible explanation is that incoming steppe males adopted cultural traditions from local populations through mechanisms of cultural adaptation while largely keeping their original genetic profile. Another is that the Bell Beaker package at least partly stems from derived steppe traditions, most notably the large beakers resembling the ceramics of the Corded Ware, which were transmitted to non-steppe populations in Europe.

Whatever the case may be, the observable contact between highly divergent genetic groups in Western Europe may indicate language contact between Indo-European and non-Indo-European languages. Such contact would indeed appear to offer one possible scenario for the emergence of shared Celtic-Germanic vocabulary not inherited from the common linguistic parent. Although the estimated date of Proto-Celtic, around 1500 BCE, postdates the Bell Beaker period by almost a millennium, and as such precludes the possibility that Proto-Celtic was proliferated through this cultural phenomenon, Celtic may still have developed from a more primitive Indo-European subdialect spoken by Bell Beaker-associated steppe groups. Moreover, as the Bell Beaker horizon also partly encompassed Northern Europe, including parts of South Norway and Jutland, it is conceivable that certain linguistic features spread from the south to the future Germanic-speaking area through the same horizon. The third major mechanism we therefore explore in this study is whether there are Celto-Germanicisms that can be positively attributed to a non-Indo-European language and result from contact between steppe and Late Neolithic groups in the Western European Bell Beaker zone.

13.2 Methodology

13.2.1 Compilation of the Corpus

To address the key questions above, we collected all roots, derivations, and semantic innovations that, within the Indo-European language family, are unique to Germanic and Celtic. We call words of this type Celto-Germanic *isoglosses* or simply Celto-Germanicisms (CG).

In order to compile the corpus, we first review the lexical Celto-Germanicisms posited in previous studies. These include Lane (L), Krahe (Kr), Porzig (Pr), Polomé (Pl), Schmidt (Schm), Schumacher (Schu), Hyllested (H), and Koch (Ko).[2] We also review the Celto-Germanic status of words discussed by Schrijver (1997), who specifically discusses substrate words found only in Celtic and Germanic. Moreover, some authors have written on Celtic-Germanic contact more generally, such as Birkhan (1970), Schumacher (Schu), and Stifter (2009), and the lexical correspondences there are also considered. Some etymological dictionaries also identify Celto-Germanicisms, either explicitly or by implication when only Celtic and Germanic are mentioned (IEW; EDPC; EDPG); the more plausible of these suggestions are considered in this study. Finally, we propose a number of new Celto-Germanicisms ourselves.

In order to ensure the robustness of the results, we have excluded irrelevant and methodologically problematic evidence. We only consider Celto-Germanicisms up to the period when Proto-Germanic diverged into separate dialects around the start of the common era, as later loans do not inform us about the shared linguistic prehistory of the two branches. Words that exclusively or primarily exist as personal names, place names, etc. in at least one of the branches are not discussed either, because the original meanings of these formations are often irrecoverable or at least not directly attested. Finally, we have not evaluated morphosyntactic and phonological innovations unique to Celtic and Germanic (cf. Hill 2002; Hill 2012; Schu).

13.2.2 Etymological Scrutiny

During the past century, a vast number of Celto-Germanicisms has been posited, as shown by the impressive body of literature given above. However, despite an extensive period of linguistic research, the reliability of the corpus is still highly variable. One major reason for this is the fact that the philology of Celtic languages is highly demanding. Another reason lies in the complex evolutions of the languages themselves, as the phonologies of Goidelic and British both underwent thorough restructurings in the early medieval period. As a consequence, the reconstruction of the Proto-Celtic form of words is not always feasible, or at least not to the extent that a single proto-form can be established.[3] In order to establish the reliability of the corpus of isoglosses, we therefore subjected them to systematic etymological scrutiny, during which we divided the isoglosses into *compelling*, *doubtful*, and *rejected* isoglosses (see appendix).

During our investigation, we rejected a large number of isoglosses. One major reason for rejecting proposed Celto-Germanicisms was basic formal incongruence: i.e., the formal

[2] Koch (2020) has not been included, because this work appeared only after we finished the etymological scrutiny.

[3] This situation is further complicated by the extensive dark age between the reconstructed Indo-European protolanguage, estimated to have been spoken in the late fourth millennium BCE, and reconstructed Proto-Celtic and Proto-Germanic, starting at approximately 1500 and 500 BCE, respectively.

correspondence simply did not hold up to scrutiny.[4] Other important grounds on which we rejected isoglosses were philological errors, cognates outside C and G having been overlooked (nonexclusive isoglosses), or the presence of convincing alternative etymologies. These rejections led to a considerable reduction of the corpus.

The *doubtful* category contains instances where an isogloss or loanword has an equally convincing alternative etymology. Doubtful instances also include possibly independent innovations: morphological isoglosses where the shared derivation is so productive that it may well have occurred independently in both branches, or semantic isoglosses where the shared semantic development is potentially trivial. Other doubtful instances are formally speculative: they contain words that are too short to exclude chance resemblance, or they require poorly understood sound laws or derivations. Some doubtful instances are such because they constitute an imperfect formal or semantic match that is nevertheless striking. A few instances are doubtful because the evidence is poor, i.e. some of the words are poorly attested, or the transmission of the material to the present day may have introduced a bias in interpretation.

The remaining *compelling* Celto-Germanicisms are unlikely to be trivial or due to chance. It is exclusively on these isoglosses that we base our further analysis.

13.2.3 Typological Classification

We found that the resulting corpus of compelling isoglosses can be satisfactorily described with the help of four typological labels. Consequently, all Celto-Germanicisms have received at least one label, but in numerous cases, the nature of the evidence required the use of more than one label.

- RT = root isoglosses: uniquely shared roots attested in the different branches with dissimilar suffixes or nonidentical ablaut patterns;
- MO = morphological isoglosses: uniquely shared formations whose roots are identifiable through cognates in at least one other Indo-European branch;
- SM = semantic isoglosses: formations found in at least one other Indo-European branch, but with a uniquely shared meaning;
- LX = lexical isoglosses: uniquely shared but otherwise etymologically isolated lexemes with no demonstrable derivational structure.

Practically speaking, lexical isoglosses are the broadest type that is typically applied when the formation of the isogloss in question resists further analysis, e.g. when no deeper etymology is at hand and when no morpheme boundaries can positively be identified. In absence of any external connections, the LX type cannot logically be associated with any semantic innovations, which excludes combination with the SM type. The latter type can, however, be combined with root isoglosses or uniquely shared formations of the RT and MO types.

13.2.4 Etymological Classification

The typological subdivision enabled us to further interpret the compelling isoglosses, and in most cases it was possible to establish the linguistic processes that led to the Celto-Germanicism.

- IE = Indo-Europeanisms:
  - IE = etymologically nonisolated, but derivationally isolated isoglosses;
  - IE(?) = derivationally nonisolated, but semantically isolated isoglosses;
  - IE? = etymologically isolated isoglosses that do not violate PIE phonotactics;
- L = undefined loans: loanwords that may belong to any of the following categories:
  - 3L = third-party loans: loanwords from unknown sources, e.g. substrate words or *Wanderwörter;*
  - ML = mutual loans: loanwords that originate in Celtic or Germanic, but whose direction of borrowing cannot be established;
  - CGL = Celtic to Germanic loans;
  - GCL = Germanic to Celtic loans.

13.2.5 Temporal Stratification

In addition to a formal categorization, we provide a relative periodization for the time frame in which a given CG could have plausibly arisen. The strategy for establishing the relative chronology is based on the order of the sound changes that can be demonstrated for the prehistoric stages of Celtic and Germanic. The temporal strata are schematically represented in Figure 13.1 and defined as follows:

- Stratum 0: Proto-Indo-European. This stratum starts with the earliest phase of linguistic unity of all Indo-European branches, including the early offshoots Anatolian and Tocharian, and ends with the fragmentation of the late Indo-European dialect continuum, in our case specifically with the departure of Celtic and Germanic.
- Stratum I: Fragmented Indo-European. In this stratum, the Proto-Indo-European dialects have broken off from the original dialect continuum, but they still lack evidence of the major sound laws that allow for their characterization as specifically Celtic or Germanic.
- Stratum II. This stratum contains borrowings after the sound changes leading up to Proto-Celtic, e.g. PIE **ē* > PC **ī*, PIE **p* > PC **ϕ* (> **0*), PIE **sn* > PC **nn*.
- Stratum III. This stratum contains borrowings after the major consonant shifts leading up to Proto-Germanic, i.e. Grimm's law, Verner's law, and Kluge's law. Somewhere during this stratum, the vocalic changes Pre-G **o* > PG **a* and Pre-G **ā* > PG **ō* also take place.
- Stratum IV: Fragmented Germanic. This stratum started with the breakup of Proto-Germanic into separate dialects. Any language

[4] Formal incongruencies are permissible in words independently suspected to be borrowed from a third language, i.e. substrate borrowings and *Wanderwörter*. However, identification of these words comes with constraints of its own (Schrijver 1997: 296).

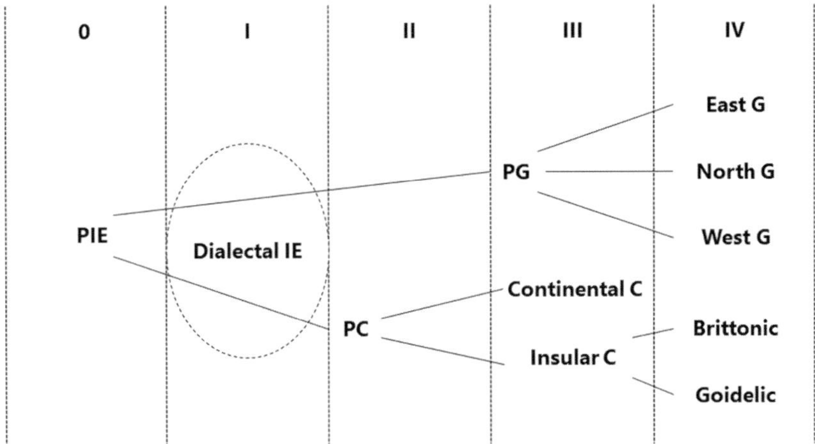

FIGURE 13.1. Schematic representation of the main temporal strata of Celtic and Germanic.

contact that happened during this phase falls outside of the temporal scope of this study, i.e. lexical exchange between individual Germanic and Celtic dialects and languages.

The precision with which the exchange of a Celto-Germanicism can be dated differs from word to word. Some words lack the phonemes that have undergone particular sound changes, in which case the adoption of these words cannot be dated relatively to these sound changes. For example, the difference between Stratum II and III is defined with respect to the Germanic consonant shifts mainly affecting stop consonants. When a word with no stop consonants therefore enters Germanic, this event cannot be dated relatively to these consonant shifts, and a range of strata must be given.

Moreover, this stratification is only possible when the Celto-Germanicism concerns the shared retention or transfer of lexical material. That is, the exchange of a Celto-Germanicism can only be dated when the sound of a word is exchanged. This excludes semantic isoglosses, i.e. instances in which a meaning is uniquely shared, but the formation itself is not unique. A semantic innovation may result from shared inheritance, dialectal affiliation, or from later horizontal transfer, but sound laws cannot arbitrate on this matter. Morphological isoglosses are similarly undateable using sound laws: a morphological isogloss can come into being through shared inheritance or later calquing, and the correct scenario cannot be decided with sound laws. It may generally be assumed that morphological and semantic isoglosses are early rather than late, because sound laws obscure the cognacy between roots and formations, making calquing less likely over time.

13.3 Results

13.3.1 Linguistic Classification

In this section, we provide a classification of the shared Celto-Germanic lexicon on the basis of formal, semantic, and temporal criteria. Our full analysis is too detailed to include here, but can be found in the appendix. In this section, it suffices to offer a concise presentation of the evidence, which we have divided into three main classes: (1) morphologically isolated Celto-Germanicisms; (2) semantically isolated Celto-Germanicisms; and (3) etymologically isolated Celto-Germanicisms.

13.3.1.1 Morphologically Isolated Celto-Germanicisms

The first group of CG we discuss comprises the uniquely shared formations whose roots are identifiable through cognates in at least one other Indo-European branch. The material is clustered according to its perceived age.

One clear cluster of Indo-Europeanisms consists of pure *archaisms*, which we define as lexemes whose creation is unlikely to postdate Proto-Indo-European. This cluster contains exclusively Celto-Germanic formations that display archaic IE derivational patterns such as reduplication, *tudáti* formations, or nasal infixes. In addition, they are based on roots that are well attested in the other branches, as a result of which their PIE origins are beyond a reasonable doubt.

- COVER – PC **tog-ī-* (OIr. *tuigithir* 'covers') ~ PG **þakjan-* (ON *þekja*, OE *þeccan*, OS *bi-thekkia*, OHG *decken* 'to cover') < **tog-eie-*. An old causative-iterative formation vs. Lat. *tegere* 'to cover' < **teg-e-*.
- FAT – PC **tegu-* (MIr. *tiug* 'thick, dense, solid', W *tew*, B *tev* 'fat') ~ PG **þeku-* (ON *þykkr*, OE *þicce*, OHG *dicki* 'fat, thick') < ?PIE **te*$^{(}$*ǵ*$^{)}$*-u-*, probably related to **teg-* 'to cover', but the formation appears to conserve a more primary meaning, i.e. 'to tighten, make tight'; cf. G *dicht machen* 'to seal, close' (< "to make dense/tight").
- FEAR – PC **āg-ī-* (OIr. *-ágadar* 'fears') ~ PG **agan-*, pres. **ōg-* (Go. *ogan* 'to fear') < **h_2e-h_2(o)ǵ^h-*, in C and G continued by an archaic reduplicated present probably continuing a PIE perfect.
- FIGHT – PC **uik-o-* (OIr. *fichid*, W *amwyn* 'to fight, contend, seize') ~ PG **wihan-* (Go. *waihan**, *weihan*, ON *vega*, OE *wīgan*, OHG *wīgan* 'to fight, do battle') < PIE **uik-e-*, a *tudáti*-type verbal formation, moribund in G.

- ROW – PC _*rā-_ (OIr. _ráïd_ 'rows') ~ PG _*rōan-_ (ON _róa_, OE _rōwan_ 'to row') < _*$h_1$roh$_1$-e-_, and _o_-grade (iterative) present with an archaic reduplicated preterite in both branches.
- STICK – PC _*gli-na-_ (OIr. _glenaid_ 'adheres, cleaves', W _glynu_, MB _englenaff_ 'to adhere, stick, bind') ~ PG _*klinan-_ (OHG _klenan_ 'to baste, stick together') < _*ǵli-n-H-_, a nasal infix present.

Another old cluster consists of isoglosses that are also derivationally isolated, but with less archaic derivational patterns. These may have been created in dialectal Indo-European or in some cases even later; it indeed cannot be excluded that some of these formations arose independently in the separate daughter languages. On the other hand, it is still possible that some of them were simply inherited from PIE, i.e. are vestiges of lexemes that were lost in the other branches.

- FATHOM – PC _*ϕatamV-_ (W _edef_, pl. _adafedd_ 'thread, yarn'), secondarily with palatalization in Goidelic, as if from _*ϕatimā_ (ScG _aitheamh_ 'fathom') ~ PG _*faþma-_ (ON _faðmr_, OE _fæðm_, OHG _fadam_, _fadum_ 'fathom', OS _fathmos_ 'two stretched arms') < _*p(o)th$_2$-mV-_, to PIE _*peth$_2$-_ 'to spread'.
- FLOOR – PC _*ϕlāro-_ (OIr. _lár_ 'ground, surface, middle', MW _llawr_, B _leur_ 'floor, ground') ~ PG _*flōra-_ (ON _flórr_ 'floor of a cowshed', OE _flōr_ 'floor', OHG _fluor_ 'field') < _*pleh$_2$-ro-_ to PIE 'flat; to spread'; also a semantic isogloss.
- HARBOR – PC _*kauno-_ (MIr. _cúan_ 'harbor, bay') ~ PG _*hafnō-_ (ON _hǫfn_, OE _hæfen_, MLG _havene_ 'harbor, bay') < _*kh$_2$p-no/eh$_2$-_, to PIE _*keh$_2$p-_ 'to seize'. Since the root has given rise to four different formations in G, it appears native to this branch; cf. MHG _habe_ f. 'harbor, haven, sea', Swi. G. _Hab_ f. 'harbor' < _*kh$_2$p-éh$_2$-_, ON _haf_, OE _hæf_, OFri. _hef_ 'sea, lake' < _*kh$_2$p-o-_, and ON _hóp_ 'small bay' < _*ke/oh$_2$p-nó-_.
- LEFT – PC _*kl(e)io-_ (OIr. _clé_ 'left (side); malign', W _cledd_, B _kleiz_, Co. _cledh_ 'left (hand)') ~ PG _*hlī̆(j)a-_ (Go. _hleiduma_ comp. 'left') < _*ḱl(e)i-(i)o-_, to PIE _*ḱlei-_ 'to lean, be slanted'.
- SIEVE – PC _*sītlo-/ā_ (W _hidl_, MB _sizl_ 'sieve') ~ PG _*sēþla-_ (ON _sáld_ 'sieve, riddle') < _*seh$_1$-tlo-_, an instrument noun to PIE _*seh$_1$-_ 'to sift', otherwise lost in both branches.
- THROAT – PC _*brāgant-_ (OIr. _brágae_, MW _breuant_ 'neck, throat') ~ PG _*k(w)ragan(þ)-_ (ON _kragi_, MHG _krage_, E _craw_ 'throat, collar') < _*g^{w}rōg^h-(o)nt-_; cf. Gr. βρόχω* 'to gulp down' < _*g^{w}rog^h-_.
- THIRST? – PC _*tartu-_ (OIr. _tart_ 'dryness, thirst', W _tarth_ 'steam') ~ PG _*þurstu-_ (OE _þurst_, _þyrst_, OS _thurst_, OHG _durst_ 'thirst') < _*trs-tu-_, to PIE _*ters-_ 'to be dry'.
- UTTERANCE? – PC _*iexti-_ (OIr. _icht_ 'people, tribe', W _iaith_, B _yezh_, MCo. _yēth_ 'language') ~ PG _*jehti-_ (OHG _jiht_ 'confession; praise', OFri. _jecht_ 'confession') < _*iek-ti-_; cf. Lat. _iocus_ 'joke' < _*iok-o-_.

This cluster also contains some potential pseudo-Indo-Europeanisms, i.e. isoglosses that technically can be projected back into (dialectal) Proto-Indo-European, but in which case mutual borrowing or calquing in strata I to III cannot be excluded. Still, all of these isoglosses have convincing Indo-European etymologies, which could mean that they actually were inherited from PIE in both branches.

- DISTANT COUSIN – PC _*kom-neϕot-_ (MW _keifn_, W _caifn_ 'third or distant cousin', MB _quifniant_ 'distant cousin') ~ PG _*ga-nefan-_ (OE _ge-nefa_ 'nephew; son of a cousin') < _*kom-nepot-_, a compound of _*kom_ 'joint' and PIE _*nepot-_ 'cousin, grandchild'.
- FIERCE – PC _*abro-_ (MIr. _abar-_, _amar-_, W _afr-_ 'very') ~ PG _*abra-_ (Go. _abrs_ 'great, severe', ON _afar-_ 'very, exceedingly') < CG _*ab^{h}ro-_ or _*apró-_, perhaps from PIE _*h$_2$ep-ró-_; cf. Skt. _ápara-_ 'posterior, later; extreme, strange' < _*h$_2$ep-ero-_. It could be an early shared innovation or mutual borrowing at any stage.
- INHERITANCE – PC _*orbio-_ (OIr. _orbae_ 'inheritance, legacy') ~ PG _*arbja-_ (Go. _arbi_, OE _ierfe_, OFri. _erve_ 'inheritance, patrimony', ON _erfi_ 'ritual burial celebration') < _*h$_3$erb^h-io-_, to PIE _*h$_3$erb^h-_; cf. Hitt. _ḫarp-_ 'to change allegiance, status'.
- LAW – PC _*rextu-_ (OIr. _recht_, W _cyf-raith_, MB _reiz_ 'law, justice') ~ PG _*rehtu-_ (ON _réttr_ 'justice, law') < _*h$_3$reǵ-tu-_, to PIE _*h$_3$reǵ-e-_ 'to straighten'.
- MANE – PC _*mongo-/ā_ (OIr. _mong_, W _mwng_, OB. _mogou_ 'mane, hair', MB. _moe_) ~ PG _*mankan-_ (ON _makki_, Elfd. _maunke_, Da. _manke_ 'mane'). Possibly derived, in either C or G or a shared pre-stage, from PIE _*mon-i-_ 'mane, neck', although the suffix _*-g-_ is obscure.
- NUMBER – PC _*rīmā_ (OIr. _rím_, W _rhif_ 'number') ~ PG _*rīma-_ (ON _rím_ 'number', ON _rím_ 'computation', OHG _rīm_ 'account, series, number') < _*h$_2$riH-mo-/eh$_2$-_, to PIE _*h$_2$reiH-_ 'to fit, fix'.

13.3.1.2 Semantically Isolated Celto-Germanicisms

Another category found within the corpus encompasses potential semantic isoglosses. Here we have selected formations not restricted to C and G that exhibit exclusively CG semantics. All of these formations can technically be made to comply with the phonotactic and derivational rules of the protolanguage and can arguably be shown to have a derivational base in PIE.

In some cases, both the formation and meaning are unique to CG, in which case we can speak of a full lexical isogloss. However, we have not included such formally isolated semantic isoglosses here, because their unique meanings may have resulted from the very process by which these formations were derived, by which principle they cannot with certainty be regarded as semantic innovations.

We find that semantic isoglosses are notoriously difficult to analyze. A major concern is that it is often problematic to objectively determine whether a shared CG shift in meaning is significant and therefore shared, or in fact trivial and independent. As trivial shifts can have plausibly occurred in C and G independently, these Celto-Germanicisms could represent semantically nonexclusive isoglosses, in which case we have labeled them with a question mark.

- AXE – PC _*beiatli-_ (OIr. _biail_, W _bwyall_, MCo. _bool_, MB _bouhazl_ 'axe' ~ PG _*bīþla-_ (ON _bíldr_ 'knife for bloodletting', MDu. _bijl_, OHG _bīhal_ 'axe') < _*b^h(e)iH-tl-_; cf. Slavic _*bidlo_ 'hammer, pole'.
- BESTOW? – PC _*link^w-o-_ (OIr. _léicid_ 'leaves, lets, allows, grants') ~ PG _*līhwan-_ (Go. _leihvan_ 'to loan', ON _ljá_ 'to lend; to give, grant', OE _lēon_, OS _far-līhan_, MDu. _lien_, OHG _līhan_ 'to lend') < _*li-n-k^w-_; cf. Skt. _riṇákti_ 'leaves'.
- CHOOSE? – PC _*gus-o-_ (OIr. _do-goa_ 'chooses, selects, elects') ~ PG _*keusan-_ (Go. _kiusan_ 'to put to a test, prove by trial', ON _kjósa_, OE _cēosan_, OHG _kiosan_ 'to choose, elect, examine') < _*ǵ(e)us-_; cf. Gr. γεύομαι 'to taste'.

- COAL – PC *goulo- (MIr. *gúal* 'coal') < *ǵoulH-o- ~ PG *kula- (ON *kol*, OE *col*, OHG *kol* 'coal') < *ǵulH-o-; cf. Skt *jválati* 'burns'.
- FORTIFICATION? – PC *brig- (OIr. *brí* 'hill'), *brigā (W, MB, Co. *bre* 'hill', Gaul. place names in *-briga* 'hillfort') ~ PG *burg- (Go. *baurgs* 'fortified place; city', ON *borg* 'town, citadel; small hill', OE *burg*, OHG *burg* 'city') < *b^{h}r̥ǵ^h-; cf. Av. *bərəz-* 'mountain'. Possibly independent; cf. the Insular Celtic meaning.
- LOUSE – PC *lu(u/s)ā (W *llau*, B *laou*, Co. *low* 'lice') ~ PG *lūs- (OE *lūs*, ON *lús*, OHG, MDu. *lūs* 'louse') < *luH(s)-; cf. ToA *lu*, pl. *lwā*, B *luwo*, pl. *lwāsa* 'animal' < *luH-(s)-. The semantic shift does appear significant but is possibly more indicative of an early Tocharian split-off rather than an exclusively Celto-Germanic subnode.
- ONE-EYED? – PC *kaiko- (OIr. *cáech* 'one-eyed', W *coeg-ddall* 'half-blind', OCo. *cuic* 'one-eyed') ~ PG *haiha- (Go. *haihs* 'one-eyed') < *keh$_2$iko-; cf. Lat. *caecus* 'blind'. Possibly trivial; cf. Skt. *kekara-* 'squint-eyed'.
- SPEAK? – PC *rād-ī- (OIr. *ráidid*, W *adrodd* 'to speak') ~ PG *rodjan- (Go. *rodjan* 'to speak', ON *rœða* 'to speak, converse') < *(H)roh$_1$d^h-eie-; cf. Lith. *ródyti* 'to show, indicate'. Possibly trivial; cf. Lat. *dīcere* 'to talk, speak' < *deiḱ- 'to show'.
- YEW – PC *iuo- (OIr. *eó* 'stem, shaft, yew tree', W *yw*, B *ivin*, OCo. *hiuin* 'yew, yew wood') ~ PG *īwa/ō- (ON *ýr*, OE *īw*, *ēow*, OHG *īwa* 'yew') < *h$_1$eiH-u-; cf. Gr. ὄα, ὄη 'elderberry tree, mountain ash', Lith. *ievà*, Latv. *iẽva* 'bird cherry'. This isogloss appears strong because the formal incongruence excludes mutual borrowing. The semantic shift to 'yew' must be posterior to the migration into the natural range of this tree, which is limited to Western and Central Europe.

Again, some of the relevant material contains possible pseudo-Indo-Europeanisms, i.e., isoglosses that show a uniquely shared semantic innovation that could theoretically go back to dialectal Indo-European, but which alternatively may be a mirage, i.e., a result of post-split, mutual borrowing.

- FREE – PC *ɸriio- (W *rhydd*, OCo. *rid* 'free') ~ PG *frī̆(j)a- (Go. *freis*, OE *frēo*, OHG *frī*, ON *frjals* 'free') < *priH-o-; cf. Skt. *priya-* 'dear'. The isogloss may have arisen due to a Stratum I (before the loss of PIE *p in C) CGL in view of the original semantics being preserved within G; cf. Go. *frijon* 'to love', *frijonds* 'friend'.
- MEDICINE – PC *lub-ī (OIr. *luib* 'wort, plant; healing herb, remedy') ~ PG *lubja- (Go. *lubja-leisei* 'witchcraft', ON *lyf* 'medicine, healing herb', OE *lyb* 'medicine, drug, potion').
- OATH – PC *oito- (OIr. *óeth* 'oath', W *an-udon* 'perjury') ~ PG *aiþa- (Go. *aiþs*, OE *āð*, ON *eiðr*, OHG *eid* 'oath'). If related to Gr. οἶτος 'fate, destiny' (< 'course'?) < *h$_1$oi-to-, the semantic change to 'going under oath'[5] is more likely to have occurred in C, as G preserves this formation with more primary semantics in ON *eið* 'isthmus'. This makes it a possible Stratum I or II C to G loan.
- PHANTOM – PC *skāxslo- (OIr. *scál* 'phantom, giant, hero', MW *yscawl* 'young hero, warrior') ~ PG *skōhsla- (Go. *skohsl* 'evil spirit, demon'). The meaning 'phantom' can possibly be derived from OIr. *scuichid* 'to move, to stir' < PC *skok-ī-, pret. *skōk-, making it a likely borrowing from C to G, although the date of borrowing cannot be established.
- RIDE – PC *reid- (Gaul. *rēda* 'wagon', OIr. *réidid* 'rides', W *rhwydd* 'easy, quick') ~ PG *rīdan- (ON *ríða*, OE *rīdan*, OFri. *rīdan*, OS *rīdan* 'to ride, drive') < *Hreid^h-e-; cf. Lith. *riedė́ti* (*riedù*) 'to roll'. Since the original semantic range is largely preserved in G (cf. ON *ríða* 'to ride; to reel, stagger; to rise', OE *rīdan* 'to ride; to move, rock'), the specific meaning 'to ride' may have developed within this branch, and spread from there to C.
- WOOD – PC *uidu- (OIr. *fid*, W *gwŷdd*, B *gwez*, OCo. *guid-en* 'trees, wood') ~ PG *widu- (ON *viðr*, OE *widu*, *wudu*, OHG *witu* 'wood') < *(h$_1$)ui-d^h(h$_1$)-u-; cf. Skt. *vidhú-* 'isolated', Lith. *vidùs*, Latv. *vidus* 'interior, middle'. Although the semantic change from 'middle' to 'wood' may plausibly have happened in dialectal PIE, at a stage when originally nomadic groups became more sedentary, strictly speaking, a Stratum III loan in either direction cannot be excluded on formal grounds.

13.3.1.3 Etymologically Isolated Celto-Germanicisms

Especially remarkable is the existence of a set of verbal roots that conform to the PIE root structure, and sometimes even display the effects of PIE sound changes, but lack any cognates outside C and G. In most of these cases, mutual borrowing is unlikely or at least not demonstrable because the two branches make use of dissimilar suffixes and ablaut patterns. This seems to imply that these isoglosses represent roots that were lost in the other branches, or roots that were present in only part of the original PIE dialect continuum.

- DARE – PC *n(e/a)nti- (OIr. *néit* 'battle') ~ PG *ninþan- (OHG *gi-nindan* 'to dare'), *nanþjan- (Go. *ana-nanþjan* 'to dare, take courage', ON *nenna* 'to be willing', OE *nēðan* 'to have courage, dare').
- DEBT – PC *dlig-o- (OIr. *dligid* 'is entitled to, is owed', W *dylyaf* 'to be obliged, owe, ought', B *dleout* 'should') ~ PG *dulga- (Go. *dulgs* 'debt') < PIE *d^{h}l̥(ǵ)^h-. In both branches, *l̥ is vocalized regularly.
- QUARREL – PC *bāg-ī- (OIr. *bág* 'boast, threat, fight', *báigid* 'boasts'), *bāgio- (MW *bei* 'fault, transgression') ~ PG *bēg- (OHG *bāgan* (pret. *biag*) 'to quarrel', ON *bágr* 'contest, resistance', *bægjast* 'to quarrel, strive'). The seeming ablaut *b^{h}eh$_1$g^h- ~ *b^{h}oh$_1$g^h- is suggestive of an archaism, but it may also be a late borrowing with Germanic /ē/ = [æ:] being borrowed as Celtic /ā/ or Celtic /ā/ being borrowed as the lowered continuant of Germanic /ē/, North-West Germanic [a:].
- SEEP – PC *leg-o- (OIr. *legaid* 'melts, dissolves', W *llaith*, B *leizh* 'damp', W *dadlaith* 'to melt') ~ PG *lekan- (ON *leka*, OHG *lehhan* 'to leak') < ?PIE *le(ǵ)-.
- VOW – PC *lugio- (OIr. *lugae*, *luige*, W *llw* 'oath') ~ PG *leugō- (Go. *liuga* 'marriage'), *lugōn- (OFri. *logia* 'to arrange, allot') < ?PIE *leu(ǵ)^h-.

In addition, we can discern a small cluster of nominal formations that too consists of isoglosses that are borderline Indo-European. They cannot plausibly be considered mutual borrowings, but the roots from which they are derived lack an evident Indo-European etymology, although in most of the cases proposals have been made.

- FRUIT – PC *agronā (W *aeron* 'berries') ~ PG *akrana- (Go. *akran* 'fruit', ON *akarn*, OE *æcern*, MHG *ackeran* 'acorn'). The origin of the element *agr- is unclear: it could be PIE *h$_2$eǵro- 'field; wild', but the semantic link is not compelling. The suffix *-on- is productive for fruits and berries in G.

[5] Cf. Sw. *gå ed* 'to swear'.

- SKIN – PC **sekio-* (OIr. *seiche* 'skin, hide') ~ PG **segja-* (ON *sigg* 'hard skin') < ?PIE **sek-io-*. Sometimes derived from the root **sek-* 'to cut', but this is uncertain. The word is unlikely to be a Stratum II CGL loan in view of the occurrence of Verner's law in G, which points to oxytone accentuation.
- WILD – PC **gʷelti-* (MIr. *geilt* 'panicked person, lunatic', W *gwyllt*, 'wild, mad') ~ PG **welþja-* (Go. *wilþeis*, ON *villr*, OE *wild*, OHG *wildi* 'wild, uncultivated') < **gʷʰel-ti-*. The root **gʷʰel-* is obscure, but in view of the regular development of **gʷʰ* in both C and G, this is hardly a borrowing.

Finally, there is another cluster of pseudo-Indo-Europeanisms, viz. isoglosses that can technically be projected back into the protolanguage, perhaps even as archaisms, but which may equally well have come about through borrowing from each other or from a third, unknown source. However, as these cases lack the specifically Celtic, Germanic, or non-Indo-European features that we use in our diagnostics, we must accept that no further classification is feasible at this point.

- CUT – PC **snad-o-* (OIr. *snaidid* 'cuts, chips, hews, carves', W *naddu* 'to chip, cut') ~ PG **snadwō-* (OHG *snatta* 'weal, scar').
- HORSE 1 – PC **marko-* (MIr. *marc*, W *march*, B *marc'h*, OCo. *march*, Gaul. *markan* (acc. sg.) 'horse') ~ PG **marha-* (ON *marr*, OE *mearh*, OFri. *mar*, OHG *marh*, *marah* 'horse, stallion').
- MALICIOUS – PC **elko-* (OIr. *elc* 'mischievous, bad') ~ PG **elhja-* (ON *illr* 'ill, evil, bad, mean') < ?PIE **(h$_1$)elk-*.
- RIDGE – PC **roino-* (OIr. *róen* 'way, path', OB *runt*, B *run* 'mound, plateau', MCo. *runyow* 'hills') ~ PG **raina-* (ON *rein* 'strip of land', MHG *rein* 'border wall, edge of a field').
- SAIL – PC **siglo-* (OIr. *séol*, W *hwyl* 'sail, covering') ~ PG **sigla-* (ON *segl*, OE *segel*, OS *segal*, OHG *segal*, *segil* 'sail, canvas').
- SECRET – PC **rūnā/o-* (OIr. *rún* 'secret', W *rhin* 'spell, enchantment') ~ PG **rūnō-* (Go. *runa* 'secret', OE *rūn*, OS *rūna* 'whisper, secret', ON *rún* 'rune, secret').
- SLAUGHTER – PC **boduo-* (OIr. *Bodb*, *Badb* 'war-goddess; hooded crow') ~ PG **badwa/ō-* (OE *beadu*, ON *bǫð* 'battle, war').
- TIP 1 – PC **brozdo-* (OIr. *brot* 'goad, spike') ~ PG **brazda-* (Icel. *bradd* 'edge', OE *breard* 'brim, margin', OHG *brart* 'edge'), **bruzda-* (ON *broddr* 'spike', OE *brord* 'point, grass shoot').

13.3.1.4 Non-Indo-European Celto-Germanicisms

An intriguing subset consists of demonstrably non-Indo-European lexical elements. These elements are identifiable as such because no cognates are found in other Indo-European languages, including the Asian branches. More importantly, their PC and PG forms resist unification into a single proto-form, which precludes both inheritance from PIE and mutual borrowing. As a result, independent borrowing from a third, unknown source is left as a plausible explanation. A striking fact of the demonstrably non-IE Celto-Germanic isoglosses in this category is that they fall within the usual semantic fields that are cross-linguistically liable to substrate borrowing, such as local flora and fauna.

- BADGER – PC **tazgo-*, **tasko-* (MIr. PN *Tadg*, Gaul. PN *Tascos*, Fr. dial. *taisse*, Sp. *tejón* 'badger') ~ PG **þahsu-* (MDu. *das*, MHG *dahs* 'badger').
- CLOVER – PC **semmVr-* (OIr. *semar* 'clover, shamrock') ~ PG **smēran-* (Icel. *smári* 'clover'), **smērjōn-* (Icel., Far. *smæra*, Nw., Da. *smære*, Sw. dial. *smäre* 'clover').
- COPSE – PC **kʷresti(o)-* (W *prys(g)* 'copse, grove' (>> ScG *preas* 'bush, shrub, thicket')) ~ PG **h(w)ursti-* (OE *hyrst*, OS *hyrst*, OHG *hurst* 'crest, copse'). OCS *xvrastije*, Ru. *xvórost* 'brushwood, bush' < PSl. **xvorstъ* can be compared as well.
- HEDGE – PC **kagio-* (W *cae*, B *kae*, Co. *ke*, Gaul. (Endlicher) *caio* 'hedge, fence') ~ PG **hagja-* (ON *heggr* 'bird cherry'), **hagjō-* (OE *hecg*, OHG *heckia*, *heggia* 'hedge, fence'). A connection to the European root **ḱagʰ-* 'to hold' is possible, but this requires the semantic shift 'to hold' > 'enclosure' > 'hedge'.
- HOLLY – PC **kolinno-* (Ir. *cuilenn*, W *celyn*, MB *quelennenn* (sglt.) 'holly') < **kolis-n-* ~ PG **hulisa-* (MDu. *huls*, OHG *hulis*, *huls* 'holly') < **kulis-*. Formally irregular, but closer to each other than to the Celto-Germanic forms are Basque *gorosti*, Sard. *golosti*, *colostri*, Gr. κήλαστρος, and Arm. *kostli*.
- LARK – PC **alaudā* (Gaul. **alauda* > Lat. *alauda* 'lark') ~ PG **laiwiz-akōn-* (OE *lāwrice*, WFri. *ljurk*, OHG *lērahha* 'lark').
- OATS – PC **korkio-* (MIr. *corca*, *coirce*, W *ceirch*, B *kerc'h* 'oats', OCo. *bara keirch* gl. *panis avena*) ~ PG **hagran-* (OSw. *hagri*, Nw. dial. *hagre* 'oats'), **hagrja-* (Da. *hejre* 'brome grass').
- PINE – PC **gisusto-* (OIr. *giús*, ScG *giuthas*, MoIr. *giumhas*, *giúis* 'fir tree, pine') ~ PG **kizna-* (OE *cēn* 'pine tree, spruce', MLG *kēn* 'pine cone, pinewood', OHG *kien* 'pine tree, pinewood torch').
- RUSHES – PC / PG **sem-* (OIr. *sim(a)* 'stalk, stem', *simin(n)*, *seimen(n/d)* 'rush, reed') / (OS *semith*, OHG *semida* 'rushes, reed', G *Simse* '(bul)rush') ~ PC / PG **seb-* (MIr. *sibin(n)*, *sifin(n)* 'rush, reed' / ON *sef*, MHG *sebede* 'rush, reed').
- SHOOT – PC **slattā* (MIr. *slat* 'stalk, stem, branch', W *llath* 'rod, staff', B *lazh* 'pole, rod') ~ PG **laþ(þ)a/ōn-*, **latta(n)-* (OE *lætt*, ME *laþþe*, MoE *lath*, *lat*, MDu. *latte* 'lath', OHG *lad(d)a/o*, *lat(t)a/o* 'lath, shoot').
- SILVER – Celtib. *silabur* 'silver, money' ~ PG **silubra-* (Go. *silubr*, ON *silfr*, *sylfr*, OE *seolfor*, OHG *silabar* 'silver'). An old *Wanderwort* in view of B *zilhar*, Semitic **ṣarp-*. The Basque word seems to point to **silpar-* and Celtiberian to PC **silabur-*. PG **silubra-* is ambiguous, continuing either **silupró-* (with Verner's law) or **silubʰro-*.
- SLOPE – PC **glendos-* (OIr. *glend*, W *glyn* 'glen, valley', MB *glenn* 'land'), **glandā* (W *glan*, B *glann*, Co. *glan* 'shore') ~ PG **klinta-* (ON *klettr* 'rock, cliff', MLG *klint* 'shore'), **klanta-* (Nw. dial. *klant* 'cliff; peak', Sw. dial. *klant* 'cliff'). The shared root **glend-* violates PIE root constraints, making an ultimate non-IE origin likely.
- WILDERNESS – PC **kaito-* (W *coed*, B *koad*, MCo. *coys* 'wood') ~ PG **haiþī-* (Go. *haiþi* 'open field', ON *heiðr* 'heath, moor', OE *hǣð*, MLG *hēde* 'heather'), ?**haiþa-* (dial. early MoE *hothe*).

Although some of the non-Indo-European elements are restricted to Celtic and Germanic (BADGER, LARK), others have a potentially wider distribution, which links them to the Neolithic linguistic landscape that existed prior to the Indo-European expansion. Of these, COPSE, PINE, HOLLY, and CLOVER are especially noteworthy. CG **kʷr(e)sti-*, in combination with PC **kʷrenno-*, potentially exhibits an alternation between *n-* and *st*-suffixes, which is also found in other pre-Indo-European dendronyms across Europe. Two such other tree names are in fact CG isoglosses as well. The doublet PINE (**gisusto-* ~ **kizna-*) appears to be based on a stem **gis-*, followed by an *st*-suffix in Celtic and a *n*-suffix in Germanic. For HOLLY (**kolinno-*|**hulis-*), irregular lexical correspondents are found across Europe, viz. Gr. κήλαστρος, Arm. *kostłi*, Sard. *golosti*, *colostri*, and Basque *gorostri*. These forms can in turn be contrasted with the Celto-Germanic doublet PC **kolinno-* (< **kolis(t)-no-*?) ~ PG **hulis-* (< **kulis-*), which stands out within the wider European cluster because they can both contain the formally more comparable stem **kVlis(t)-*. Finally, the CLOVER isogloss, technically reconstructable as the formally irregular doublet G **smēr-* : C **semmar-*, should be mentioned here.

13.3.1.5 Mutual Celto-Germanic Loanwords

The final class of Celto-Germanicisms consists of lexical elements that can be demonstrated to have been borrowed either from Celtic to Germanic, or – far less often – from Germanic into Celtic.

Stratum II loans can be detected because they participate in known sound changes in both Celtic and Germanic. For Celtic, these are the merger of aspirated and nonaspirated voiced stops as well as the raising of the vowel **ē* to **ī*, and for Germanic, the sound shifts of Grimm's, Verner's, and Kluge's law as well as the vocalic changes **o* > **a* and **ā* > **ō*.

- ENCLOSURE – PC **dūno-* (OIr. *dún*, *W din*, OB *din* 'fort') ~ PG **tūna-* (ON *tún* 'enclosure, home field, town', OE *tūn* 'yard; town', OFri. *tūn* 'fence, enclosure', MLG *tūn* 'fence'). The intra-Goidelic etymological link with OIr. *doé* 'wall, mound' < **d^huH-io-* may point to a C origin for this word (unless this is etymologically related to OIr. *doé* 'shoulder').
- HAYSTACK 2 – PC **dassi-* (OIr. *daiss*, W *das* 'heap, stack') ~ PG **tassa-* (Mdu. *tas*, *tasse*, MLG *tas* 'haystack'). PC **dassi-* may continue **dh₂-sti-*, from PIE **deh₂-* 'to cut', meaning that G borrowed this word after C **-st-* > **-ts-/-ss-*, but before the consonant shifts.
- JESTER – PC **drūto-* (OIr. *drúth* 'jester, buffoon, vagrant; courtesan, harlot') ~ PG **trūþa-* (ON *trúðr* 'juggler', OE *trúð* 'trumpet player, actor, buffoon'). Borrowed by G before Grimm's law. The native G form is continued by PG **drūda-*; cf. OHG *trūt*, NHG *traut* 'dear, beloved' < **d^hruH-tó-*; cf. OIr. *drúth* 'extravagant, wanton', Lith. *drū̃tas* 'thick, strong, deep (of voice)'.
- LEECH – PC **leCVgi-* (OIr. *lïaig*, gen. *lego*, *lega* 'leech, doctor, physician') ~ PG **lēkja-* (Go. *lekeis*, ON *lækir*, OE *lǣce* 'doctor', ODu. *lake*, OHG *lāhhi*, *lāchi* 'leech'). Generally assumed to be a C to G loan, although the C word admittedly does not have an etymology.
- LEATHER – PC **ϕle/itro-* (OIr. *lethar*, W *lledr*, MB *lezr* 'leather') ~ PG **le/iþra-* (ON *leðr*, OE *leðer*, OHG *ledar* 'leather'). The C word can be from **ϕlitro-* < PIE **pl-tro-* if we assume generalized lowering of the vowel in the collective **ϕlitrā* in Brittonic, for which compare the neuter gender of G **le/iþra-*.
- KING – PC **rīg-* (OIr. *rí*, W *rhi* 'king', Gaul. PN *Catu-rix*, Celtib. PN *Teiuo-reikis*) ~ PG **rīk-* (Go. *reiks* 'king').

Stratum III loans postdate the Germanic sound shifts, but they may participate in the vocalic changes **o* > **a* and **ā* > **ō*. PC **nn* from earlier **sn* appears to have been substituted by G with a single *n*, despite the fact that geminates must already have been present in G in this phase.

- BADGER(HOUND) – PC **brokko-* (MIr. *brocc*, W *broch*, MB *broc'h*, OCo. *broch* 'badger') ~ PG **brakkan-* (OHG *bracko* 'hound').
- BREAST(PLATE) – PC **brunnio-* (OIr. *bruinne* 'breast', W *brynn* 'hill') ~ PG **brunjōn-* (Go. *brunjo* 'breastplate', ON *brynja*, OE *byrne*, OS *brunnia*, OHG *brunja* 'coat of mail'). Demonstrably Celtic in view of the change **-sn-* > **-nn-*, borrowed as single *n* in G.
- BREECHES – PC **brākā* (Gallo-Lat. *brācae*, *brācēs*, Gallo-Gr. pl. βράκας 'trousers, breeches') ~ PG **brōk-* (ON *brōk* 'leg of a pair of breeches', pl. *brœkr* 'breeches', OE *brōc* 'behind, breech', OFri. *brēk*, OHG *bruoh* 'trousers'). Early loans are often borrowed as root nouns in G, which favors a C origin for this word.
- BRISTLE – PC **granno-* (MIr. *grend*, MW *grann* 'beard, chin, cheek', Provençal *gren* 'mustache' < Gaul.) ~ PG **granō-* (ON *grǫn* 'hair of the beard; spruce', OE *granu* 'mustache', OHG *grana* 'hair of the beard'). Given the single *n* in G as opposed to C *nn* (cf. BREAST(PLATE)), more likely to have transferred from C to G than the other way around.
- HILLTOP – PC **dūno-* (OIr. *dún*, *W din*, OB *din*, Co. *dyn* 'fort') ~ PG **dūna-* (OE *dūn* 'hill', E *down* 'rolling hill, dune', Du. *duin* 'dune') < **d^huH-no-*; cf. OIr. *doé* 'wall, mound' < **d^huH-io-*.
- HOSTAGE – PC **geisslo-* (OIr. *gíall* 'hostage', W *gwystl*, B *gouestl* 'surety, hostage, pledge') ~ PG **gīsla-* (ON *gísl*, OE *gīsel*, OFri. *jēsel-*, OS *gīsal*). Native in C in view of the ablauting OIr. *gell*, *gill* 'pledge' < PC **gisslo-*.
- IRON – PC **īsarno-* (Gaul. PN *Isarnus*, OIr. *ïarn*, W *haearn*, B *houarn* 'iron') ~ PG **īsarna-* (Go. *eisarn*, ON *ísarn*, OE *īsern*, *īsen*, *īren* 'iron'). Borrowed by G from C (or a third source?), as inherited unstressed **-rn-* should have yielded PG **-rr-* by regular assimilation of the *n* and subsequent shortening in unstressed syllables.
- LEAD – PC **ϕloudio-* (MIr. *lúaide* 'lead') ~ PG **lauda-* (OE *lēad*, OFri. *lād*, Du. *lood* 'lead').
- SERVANT – PC **ambaxto-* (Gaul. *ambaktos*, *ambactus* 'vassal', W *amaeth* 'farmer') ~ **ambahta-* (Go. *andbahts*, OHG *ambaht* 'servant, representative'), **ambahtō-* (ON *ambátt* 'bondwoman').

Some G to C loanwords can be identified with relative certainty. There are at least seven candidates, almost all from Stratum III, when the major sound shifts as well as the change **o* > **a* had taken place. Proto-Celtic had already broken up by Stratum III, yet a Proto-Celtic form is nevertheless reconstructible for these borrowings. These reconstructions, while anachronistic, demonstrate that Celtic was phonologically stable in the period when Germanic underwent its major consonant shifts.

- BOY – PC **magu-* (OIr. *mug* 'slave, servant', W *meu-dwy* 'hermit < servant of god', MCorn. *maw* 'lad', B *mau* 'happy, active') ~ PG **magu-* (Go. *magus* 'boy', OE *magu* 'child, son'). In view of PG **mag-aþi-* 'girl' (Go. *magaþs*, OE *mæg(e)ð*, OHG *magad*), the *u*-stem appears to have been created in G.
- CROOKED – PC **krumbo-* (MIr. *cromm*, W *crwm*, B *kromm*, Co. *crom* 'bent, curved, crooked') ~ PG **krum(b/p)a-* (OE *crump*, OS *krumb*, OHG *krumpf* 'bent, crooked'). Probably native in G given the clear link with the verb **krimpan-* 'to shrink'.
- FORK – PC **gablo/ā-* (OIr. *gabul* 'fork; forked beam, rafter; thighs', W *gafl* 'fork; lap, groin', B *gaol* 'fork, bifurcation;

crotch') ~ PG *gablō- (OHG *gabala*, OE *geafol* 'fork'). Probably from G in view of the possible etymological identity with ON *gafl* 'gable' < PIE *$^{(}$ǵ$^{)h}$ob^{h}h$_2$-l-; cf. Go. *gibla* 'gable, pinnacle', ToA *śpāl* 'head', Gr. κεφαλή 'head, top' < PIE *$^{(}$ǵ$^{)h}$eb^{h}h$_2$-l-.

- HAYSTACK 1 – PC *krouko- (MIr. *crúach* 'stack (of corn), rick, heap, hill', W *crug* 'hillock, cairn, heap', B *krug* 'haystack', OCo. *cruc* gl. *collis*) ~ PG *hrauka- (ON *hrauk*, OE *hrēac* 'stack, haycock, rick'). The word has some pedigree in G, as shown by Verner and Kluge variants, e.g. PG *hrūha- (ON *hró* 'hillock'), *hrūgōn- (ON *hrúga* 'pile'). Likely borrowed after *kn > *kk and simplification of geminates in overlong syllables in G, but before the change *o to *a. This scenario presupposes sound substitution, whereby PG [xr] was adopted as C *kr-.
- HE-GOAT – PC *bukko- (OIr. *boc*, W *bwch*, B *bouc'h*, OCo. *boch* 'he-goat') ~ PG *bukka(n)- (ON *bokkr*, *bukkr*, OE *bucca*, OHG *bock* 'he-goat'). Since gemination is regular and expected in G *n*-stems through Kluge's law, while in C the equivalent Stokes' law is much more speculative, assuming a G to C loan seems reasonable.
- SAVOR – PC *suek- (W *chweg*, B *c'hwek* 'sweet') ~ PG *swekan- (OS *suecid* gl. *olet*, OHG *swehhan* 'to gush, smell (bad)'), *swak(k)u-, *swak(k)ja- (OE *swecc*, *swæcc* '(sweet) taste or smell', OS *suec* 'smell'). Germanic has a related verbal root meaning 'to smell', the strong verb suggesting a G origin; a precise donor form is not securely attested in G, however.
- SPEAR – PC *gaiso- (Gallo-Gr. γαῖσον, Gallo-Lat. *gaesum*, OIr. *gae*, W *gwayw* 'spear, javelin') ~ PG *gaiza- (OE *gār*, OHG *gēr*, ON *geirr* 'dart, spear'). If this word is related to Skt. *heṣá-* 'missile' < *ǵ^{h}ois-ó-, PC *gaiso- must be from PG in view of the regular development *o > *a.
- TIP 2 – PC *brazdo- (W *brath* 'bite, prick, stinging') ~ PG *brazda- (Icel. *bradd* 'edge', OE *breard* 'brim, margin', OHG *brart* 'edge').

Finally, it should be acknowledged that many of the aforementioned pseudo-Indo-Europeanisms may in fact be Celto-Germanic loans. However, since the (mutual?) borrowing of these words may have taken place early in Stratum II or even in Stratum I, when the phonologies of C and G would still have been largely compatible, it cannot be determined at this point whether these isoglosses were horizontally or vertically transmitted.

13.3.2 Linguistic Palaeontology

Here we provide a discussion as to how the linguistic evidence of the Celto-Germanic isoglosses can be correlated with the archaeological record.

13.3.2.1 Flora and Fauna

Native flora and fauna form a striking cluster within the Celto-Germanicisms: BADGER, CLOVER, COPSE, HOLLY, LARK, PINE, RUSH, SHOOT, and YEW. None of these isoglosses except YEW are in compliance with the known sound changes, meaning that no Indo-European form can be reconstructed, and that they may rather have arisen through independent borrowing by C and G from a third language, of which we otherwise have no evidence. These loans appear to be early on average, dating to either Stratum I or II, which implies that they are a reflection of the earliest cultural exchanges and linguistic contact between incoming Indo-European and local-non-Indo-European groups (cf. Iversen & Kroonen 2017).

Although the details of the different isoglosses vary, the general picture that these terms for flora and fauna offer is one of linguistic contact. The different Indo-European dialects that later evolved into C and G adopted similar words from previous populations that were culturally more embedded in the natural environment of Western Europe (cf. also WILDERNESS and SLOPE). The practice of coppicing, i.e., the repeated yearly cutting of stems (cf. STALK?) from the same stump, is known from the Neolithic onwards (Noble 2017: 132). HOLLY and RUSHES are known sources of hay, i.e., winter fodder for animals (Robinson 1986: 281). The call of the LARK is heard around the beginning of spring and may have aided early farmers in following an agricultural calendar. Other species may simply have been absent in the steppe ecozone from which the Indo-European languages dispersed, such as the BADGER and HOLLY, which could have provided the motivation for adopting a nonnative term into the lexicon. The word for YEW (*iwo-|*īwa/ō-) can actually be reconstructed for PIE, but its cognates mean 'berry' or 'bird cherry' in the other IE languages. The uniquely CG semantic shift to YEW can similarly be understood from the fact that this species has a Western European natural range, as shown in Figure 13.2.

13.3.2.2 Farmstead Life

Three CG isoglosses are related to haymaking: HAYSTACK 1 (*krouko-|*hrauka-), HAYSTACK 2 (*dassi-|*tassa-), and FORK (*gablo-/ā|*gablō-). Indirect evidence of hay meadows in Northwestern Europe from the Iron Age and the Roman period includes scythes suitable for mowing, buildings that could be used to stable animals, and increased animal size, which may reflect improved feeding and housing through winter (Hodgson et al. 1999: 261). More direct evidence comes from plant macrofossils and pollen. For example, plants with an intermediate canopy height thrive in hay meadows, because these plants are best suited to a period of abandonment followed by the hay harvest. The Iron Age saw an increase in this type of plants (Hodgson et al. 1999: 266; French 2017).

It is conceivable that the shared Celto-Germanic vocabulary relating to haystacks represents the transfer of this technology from one language community to another in the Iron Age. The linguistic details indicate that the exchange of HAYSTACK 2 in the early first millennium BCE predates Stratum III.

The invention of haymaking marked a profound change, both economically and socially. The number of animals that can be kept is constrained by the availability of grazing and fodder. By preparing hay for winter when little grazing material is available, more cattle can be kept per unit of land. However, in order to produce hay with it, one must physically fence off the land in such a way that animals do not graze on it, and a social mechanism was required to control who had access to pasture or meadow. This, in turn, could play a role in shaping and strengthening social inequalities (Hodgson 1999: 261).

The earliest evidence for land division predates the BA. Stone boundary walls dating to the Neolithic are found across

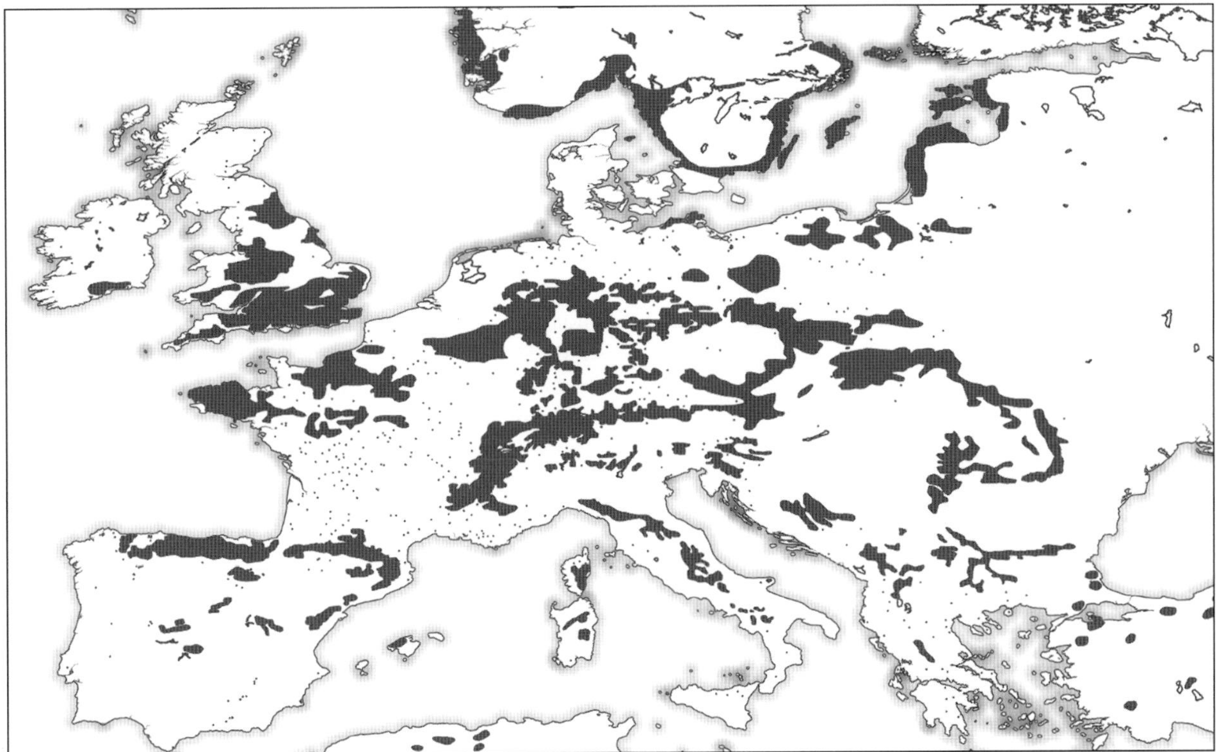

FIGURE 13.2. Distribution range of the common yew (*Taxus baccata*). Data from Caudullo et al. (2017) CC-BY

large tracts of land in western Ireland. Further east, such boundaries both become scarcer and appear later, but this may be a feature of more intensive land use rather at later dates than an actual spread in eastward direction. Still, the evidence for second- and first-millennia BCE fields is much more common than earlier instances (Johnston 2013: 316–318). More intensively managed landscapes through the creation of field systems occurred in Atlantic Europe toward the middle of the second millennium BCE (Cleary & Gibson 2019: 81–82). The comparative scarcity of field boundaries in the Early Bronze Age compared to the LBA and IA means that the adoption of this technology by C and G language communities clearly postdates the Indo-Europeanization of Northwestern Europe. The isogloss RIDGE (at the edge of a field) (**roino-*|**raina-*) may have referred to a ridge or elevated path along the field boundary of the so-called "Celtic" fields. Excavation of a field boundary ditch at Fengate in England has uncovered blackthorn leaves with a right-angled bend carbon-dated to 2500 BCE; this bend has been argued to have been caused by hedge trimming (Pryor 2010: 89). Remains of thorny vegetation in an Oxfordshire site dating to the Late Bronze Age or Early Iron Age were found near a ditch with postholes marking a fence, suggesting a prehistoric hedge. In spite of this, it is not known when hedges started to be used extensively (Wright 2016: 27, 199). The isogloss HEDGE (**kagio-*|**hagja/ō-*) possibly reflects shared land management practices. This, in turn, implies that the concept of a hedge entered Celtic and Germanic in Western Europe. Due to a lack of linguistic diagnostic features, the period when this word entered Celtic or Germanic cannot accurately be established: the strata I to early III apply.

The Celto-Germanicism ENCLOSURE (**dūno-*|**tūna-*) is a clear Stratum II loan from C into G. G **tūna-* 'enclosure, fence' exhibits a meaning that only partially reflects the combined semantic range of W *din* 'city, fort(ress), stronghold' and OIr. *dún* 'fort, fortified place, dwelling, residence'. It is therefore possible that G preserves a more primary meaning, in which case the meaning 'fort' must have evolved in C after the borrowing into Germanic, i.e., during the surge of hillforts in LBA or the rise of Celtic *oppida* in the IA. The latter scenario is potentially supported by the much later, second borrowing of C **dūno-* into (W)G, where **dūna-* still means '(unfortified) hill' (cf. OE *dūn*, E *down*), resulting in the Stratum III (or IV) isogloss HILLTOP. It cannot be excluded, however, that the meaning 'hill' evolved from 'hillfort' secondarily, in British Celtic, through semantic bleaching, i.e., after the hillforts had fallen into disuse. Chalcolithic fort sites are found in Iberia, but only a part of them continued to be occupied into the Bronze Age, and in Central Europe, the building of hill forts almost completely disappeared in the Middle Bronze Age. Hill forts as defended settlements only became widespread again in LBA Europe, particularly in the Urnfield period. The earliest hill forts in Britain also date to the BA (Thorpe 2013: 239–240). Palisaded and ditched enclosure settlements became more common in Atlantic Europe near the turn of the first millennium BCE (Cleary & Gibson 2019: 83).

13.3.2.3 Societal and Legal Organization

The Celto-Germanic isoglosses contain a small cluster of Stratum I or II loanwords from C to G that are associated with societal and legal organization, pointing to a BA/EIA cultural exchange. These are KING (**rīg-*|**rīk-*), JESTER (**drūto-*|**trūþa-*), FREE (**ϕriio-*|**frī̆(j)a-*), OATH (**oito-*|**aiþa-*), and LEECH (**leCVgi-*|**lēkja-*). One way to observe social stratification in the archaeological record is through luxury goods in graves: the presence of many luxury goods in a single grave indicates that single individuals were able to accumulate considerable wealth and prestige. It is tempting to connect these isoglosses with the rise of elite burials (*Fürstengräber*) in the LBA/EIA Hallstatt Culture of Central Europe, which are thought to mark a rise in social inequality. The JESTER isogloss may be associated with an otherwise undocumented institution of entertainers at halls of local KINGs. The presence of elite burials in the Low Countries several hundreds of kilometers to the north, with evidence of grave goods being imported from Southern Germany and Upper Austria (Van der Vaart-Verschoof 2017: 17), provides a potential vector for the introduction of these terms into early G.

Other such terms with societal and legal connotations are more difficult to date due to the absence of linguistically decisive diagnostic features: LAW (**rextu-*|**rehtu-*), SERVANT (**ambaxto-*|**ambahta-*), INHERITANCE (**orbio-*|**arbja-*), HOSTAGE (**geisslo-*|**gīsla-*), VOW (**lugio-*|**leugō-*). If these Celto-Germanicisms likewise arose by borrowing from C into G, Strata I and III are possible windows. Since no unambiguous Stratum I loans are extant in the entire corpus, however, Stratum III appears the more economical choice.

13.3.2.4 Equestrianism

Celto-Germanicisms related to horsemanship consist of HORSE 1 (**marko-*|**marha-*), MANE (**mongo-*|**mankan-*), RIDE (**reid-o-*|**rīdan-*), and possibly HORSE 2 (**kanxsikā-*|**hanh/gista-*). These isoglosses may have been associated with the spread of changes in equestrian practices, such as the introduction of new horse breeds and the introduction of (new techniques in) horse riding (Fages et al. 2019). Unfortunately, no exact dating can be established for these linguistic features other than that they postdate the PIE period and predate Stratum III, which positions them in the M/LBA. The oldest undisputed archaeological evidence for horse riding appears in the same period.

Roman authors refer to OATS (**korkio-*|**hagran-*) as a food crop for horses (McClatchie 2018). An agricultural innovation possibly associated with horsekeeping is therefore the domestication of this species. Remains of oats are found in EBA settlements, but only single finds are reported, and these settlements often also contain common wild oats beside common oats (Stika & Heiss 2013: 362). The earliest evidence for cultivated oats is found across Germany from the LBA (McClatchie 2018). This period and location fit our isogloss, which can be dated to Stratum II at the latest. The spread of this word between C and G may consequently have been well associated with the adoption of the crop in West-Central Europe.

13.3.2.5 Maritime Vocabulary

A possible early isogloss is ROW (**rā-*|**rōan-*), which has the appearance of a PIE archaism. Since rowing is an unspecific cultural marker, we will refrain from discussing it here.

A culturally significant nautical innovation was the introduction of sails. It is therefore likely that the Celto-Germanicism SAIL (**siglo-*|**sigla-*) arose by contact between C and G following the diffusion of sailing technology across the North Atlantic. The direction of borrowing cannot be established on linguistic grounds, but one scenario that can be excluded with certainty is a Stratum II Celtic to Germanic loan, as Celtic **siglo-* should have yielded PG ***sikla-*.

From the archaeological perspective, a Germanic to Celtic loan is unlikely. There is little evidence for sails in the prehistoric Germanic-speaking world. Direct archaeological evidence, pictorial records, or written references are lacking until well into the Middle Ages. Tacitus moreover explicitly mentions that the Suiones at the southern Baltic coast did use sails (Thier 2011: 187).[6] Evidence for sails in the Iron Age Celtic-speaking world is more direct. Examples include a boat model in first-century BCE Northern Ireland, Caesar's report of sailing craft in Armorica, and a pre-Roman coin from first-century CE Canterbury. Roman-era sailing ships in Northwestern Europe appear to be developments of native Celtic shipbuilding traditions (Thier 2011: 187–188). Taking the archaeological and the linguistic evidence together, the only remaining scenario for the exchange of the word for 'sail' is a Stratum III IA loan from Celtic to Germanic.

Another intriguing Celto-Germanicism is HARBOR (**kauno-*|**hafna-*). It may initially have referred to a natural inlet only, and usage of this word to denote a manmade structure probably postdates the initial exchange of this word. On linguistic grounds, the isogloss cannot possibly have been exchanged after the complete loss of PIE **p* in Celtic in order to correspond to PG **f*. Since the word is etymologically more rooted in Germanic than in Celtic, a relatively straightforward hypothesis is that it was borrowed by Celtic from Pre-Germanic **kapno-* in Stratum I or II. A suitable archaeological context consistent with the linguistic evidence for exchange of this maritime word is contact between the Atlantic and the Nordic Bronze Age. Alternatively, the word could have been borrowed into Celtic as the Urnfield culture spread toward the North Sea.

13.3.2.6 Metallurgy

The adoption of iron metallurgy can by its very definition be associated with the start of the Iron Age. For Proto-Indo-European, no word for 'iron' can be reconstructed, as the spread of iron-smelting techniques to Central Europe postdated the disintegration of the protolanguage by roughly two

[6] More circumstantial evidence for earlier use of sails consists of stone settings shaped like ships in Scandinavian graves from the Bronze Age. A ship suitable for rowing has a higher length-width ratio than a ship suitable for sailing, and considerable variation in this ratio is found (Artursson 2013).

millennia (cf. Gnesin 2016). A wide set of non-Indo-European words entered the different linguistic subgroups at various postmigration stages, usually as a *Wanderwörter* accompanying the diffusion of the technology across Europe. The CG isogloss IRON (**ī̆sarno-*|**īsarna-*) has no convincing Indo-European etymology, but likely arose by borrowing of the word from C into G at Stratum III. A potentially suitable archaeological context for such linguistic contact is found in the so-called "Schmiedegräber" in the core of the Jastorf culture and Nienburg group where, in the La Tène period, burials appear with iron ore, slags, anvils, and even complete sets of blacksmith tools (Brumlich 2005). The appearance of these burials has been interpreted as a reflection of the rise of a La Tène-icized "caste" of blacksmiths. If indeed the language contact between Celtic and Germanic can be attributed to these craftsmen, they may have either spoken Proto-Celtic themselves or mediated the terminology from Celtic-speaking specialists further to the south.

Another innovation associated with iron metallurgy finds a potential lexical reflection in the isogloss BREAST(PLATE) (**brunnio-*|**brunjō-*), which can be connected with the technique of making mail shirts often credited to the Celts. The oldest archaeological mail shirts occur in a La Tène context dated to ca. 300 BCE in Ciumești, Romania (Rusu 1969: 267–269). Mail shirts may have developed from older ring mail, a fragment of which has been found in a Hallstatt grave from eighth-century BCE Bohemia, and which is usually made of iron coils (Williams 1980). Linguistically, the borrowing of PC **brunnio-* as PG **brunjō-* must postdate the PC change of **-sn-* to **-nn-* as well as the PG sound shifts, which makes it a Stratum III IA borrowing.

LEAD (**(ϕ)loudio-*|**lauda-*) represents another metallurgical Celto-Germanicism. The exclusively West Germanic, but possibly Proto-Germanic **lauda-* is clearly a loan from Proto-Celtic **(ϕ)loudio-* that cannot predate Stratum III.[7] Since lead is not naturally available in Scandinavia (cf. Johannsen 2016), the appearance of an originally non-Germanic term is to be expected.

The linguistic history of the word for SILVER (Celtib. *silabur*|**silubra-*) is complex and difficult to disentangle (cf. Mallory & Huld 1984). The word is not a Celto-Germanicism strictly speaking, as it occurs in various other IE and non-IE languages in West Eurasia and North Africa. Still, the Celtiberian and PG forms are somewhat similar and might therefore be considered as belonging to a separate subcluster within the wider set of corresponding forms. With formally irreconcilable attestations ranging from Baltic (Lith. *sidãbras*), Slavic (**sьrěbro*), Basque *zil(h)ar* (< **zilpar*), Berber (**ẓrĭp-*/**ẓrŭp-*), and perhaps even Semitic (Akk. *ṣarp-*, Arab. poet. *ṣarīf*), it is clear that the word petered through multiple languages and cultures as a *Wanderwort*, and cannot possibly be correlated with the spread of Indo-European (Boutkan & Kossmann 2001). This additionally follows from the fact that PIE itself had an entirely different word for 'silver' that is continued by YAv. *ərəzata-*, Arm. *arcat*ᶜ, Lat. *argentum*, Celtib. *arkatobezom* 'silver mine', OIr. *argat*, MW *aryant* < **h₂rǵ-nt-ó-*. Interestingly, the preservation of this word in Celtic suggests that there was a continuous tradition for silver metallurgy within this language community between the PIE stage and the historical period. Germanic and Balto-Slavic, on the other hand, lost the PIE word, probably because they first migrated out of the "silver sphere" in the third millennium BCE, and readopted the metal together, perhaps, with the Atlantic *Wanderwort* when it became known in North Europe from the second millennium BCE (Johannsen 2016; see Figure 13.3). The timing of the borrowing event into Germanic can on linguistic grounds be set to either Stratum I or III. Given the fact that the Insular Celtic languages did not participate in this borrowing, it is tempting to assume that the *Wanderwort* spread from the West Mediterranean along the Atlantic coast to Germanic before the Celtic expansion to the British Isles. In this scenario, the Celtic expansion would be relatively late (LBA/IA), and as such incompatible with the much earlier Bell Beaker phenomenon. Of course, the Bell Beakers are a priori an unlikely cultural vector because they did not seem to have known this metal in the first place.[8]

13.4 Conclusions

13.4.1 The Linguistic Mechanisms behind the CG Isoglosses

In this study, we explored three mechanisms that may have given rise to the corpus of Celto-Germanic isoglosses that has puzzled linguists for over a century: (1) a monophyletic stage for both branches, i.e. a Celtic-Germanic subnode; (2) shared mutual contact; and (3) contact with other, potentially non-Indo-European languages.

13.4.1.1 Mechanism 1: Monophyleticity

The majority of the Celto-Germanic isoglosses cannot be ascribed to any shared linguistic past beyond the PIE dialectal stage, as they are often associated with cultural (ideological, technological) innovations that postdate the dissolution of the Proto-Indo-European linguistic unity.

We have found little evidence for a period of shared linguistic evolution. Some of the Celto-Germanic isoglosses that are derivationally isolated are potential archaisms, such as COVER (**tog-ī-*|**þakjan-*), FAT (**tegu-*|**þeku-*), FEAR (**āg-ī-*|**ōgan-*), FIGHT (**uik-o-*|**wihan-*), ROW (**rā-*|**rōan-*), and STICK (**gli-na-*|**klinan-*), which show archaic PIE morphology or semantics. Given the clear IE origin of these formations, it is not certain that they can be used as evidence for a shared Celto-Germanic subnode beyond the PIE stage.

[7] The common Germanic word for 'lead' was **blīwa-* (ON *blý*, OS *blī*, OHG *blīo*), possibly an ancient *Wanderwort*.

[8] A more suitable vector for the spread of silver along the Atlantic and Mediterranean could be the El Argar culture (ca. 2200–1550 BCE), in which silver is circulating from 2000 BCE and appears to have been one of the main materials used to express wealth (Lull et al. 2014).

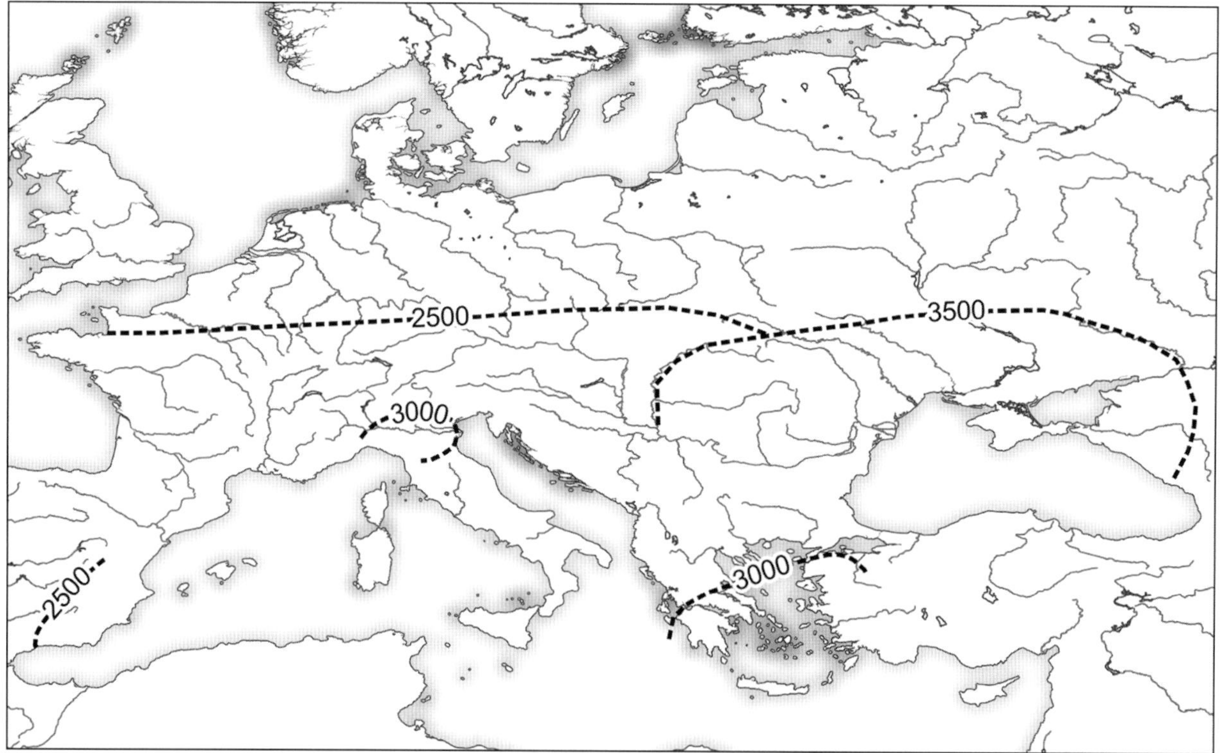

FIGURE 13.3. The spread of silver in Europe. Map data from Mallory and Huld (1984).

Some derivationally isolated isoglosses appear more innovative. These are THIRST? (*tartu-|*þurstu-), FATHOM (*ϕatamV-|*faþma-), LEFT (*kl(e)io-|*hlija-), SIEVE (*sītlo-|*sēþla-), DISTANT COUSIN (*kom-neϕot-|*ga-nefan-), THROAT (*brāgant-|*k(w)ragan(þ)-), and UTTERANCE (*iexti-|*jehti-). Still, since all of these formations make use of PIE elements, it is difficult to determine to what extent these formations represent additional archaisms or mere independent innovations. LEFT is probably the most convincing candidate for a real shared innovation, especially in view of the specific semantics.

A similar dilemma is posed by etymologically isolated isoglosses. Since they have no cognates outside C and G, but at the same time do not violate PIE phonotactics, it often seems impossible to determine whether they represent archaisms or late IE dialectalisms. Many of these isoglosses consist of obscure verbal roots: DARE (*n(e/a)nti-|*ninþan-), DEBT (*dlig-o-|*dulga-), SEEP (*lek-o-|*lekan-), VOW (*lugio-|*leugō-). In addition, there are some purely nominal formations that appear etymologically isolated, but at the same time cannot be identified with certainty as (non-IE) loans: FRUIT (*agronā|*akran-), HAYSTACK 1 (*krouko-|*hrauka-), SKIN (*sekio-|*segja-), WILD (*g^welti-|*welþja-).

Semantically isolated formations have likewise proven hard to analyze, as determining whether a CG shift in meaning results from shared or independent innovations remains intuitive. Potentially significant semantic shifts are found in AXE (*beiatli-|*bīþla-), COAL (*goulo-|*kula-), LOUSE (*lu(u/s)ā|*lūs-), WOOD (*uidu-|*widu-), and YEW (*iuo-|*īwa/ō-), the shifts in BESTOW, CHOOSE, FORTIFICATION, ONE-EYED, and SPEAK appearing more trivial.

Finally, we identified a large number of what we call pseudo-Indo-Europeanisms, i.e., isoglosses that can technically be projected back into the protolanguage, but which may equally have come about through mutual borrowing or from a third, unknown source due to a lack of any distinctively IE or non-IE features.

In conclusion, it should be clear that the evidence for a shared Celto-Germanic subnode is exceedingly limited in comparison to, for instance, the evidence for Italo-Celtic, Balto-Slavic or Indo-Iranian. Celtic and Germanic may have evolved from dialects that were located not too distantly from each other in the original Indo-European dialect continuum. It can even be surmised that C and G arose from groups that were part of the westward Yamnaya expansion toward the Balkans and the Carpathian Basin. It is intriguing to see, at any rate, that some of the isoglosses we encounter appear to be linked to potentially shared adaptations to a more sedentary way of life. Here we mention the semantic shift of PIE *$(h_1)ui$-$d^h(h_1)$-u- 'isolated, middle' to WOOD (*uidu-|*widu-), which is understandable from the perspective of inhabitants of settlements with uncultivated lands between them, but not from that of mobile steppe pastoralists. Furthermore, the shift from PIE *$h_1(e)iH$-u- 'berry; bird cherry' to YEW (*iuo-|*īwa/ō-) can only have taken place in an area where this tree species has its natural range, which is Western Europe.[9] The easiest way to account for such isoglosses is to assume that they reflect some kind of shared dialectal

[9] The fact that the formation displays ablaut seems to prove that this shift took place at an early stage.

development when the Yamnaya culture was expanding from the Don-Volga region to the west. Across the board, however, the number of reliable Celto-Germanic isoglosses does not appear significantly more numerous than that of any two branches of the Indo-European family, so no post-IE Celto-Germanic subclade can be postulated.

13.4.1.2 Mechanism 2: Mutual Contact

In Section 13.3.1.5 we have outlined the numerous identifiable mutual loans between C and G, and provided them with archaeological backgrounds in Section 13.3.2. It is clear from this that a large part of the CG borrowing events took place in the M/LBA and IA. Only one borrowing with an ultimate IE source, i.e. FREE, can be plausibly dated to Stratum I, i.e. the preceding period directly following the divergence from the IE protolanguage as a result of one or several movements toward Europe.[10] A question that presents itself is whether some of the remaining isoglosses – the many pseudo-Indo-Europeanisms such as BOY, MANE, MEDICINE, OATH, RIDE, WOOD, HORSE 1 & 2, SLAUGHTER, RIDGE, SECRET, TIP 1 – can be dated to the EBA or preceding period. The fact is, however, that many of these isoglosses are not just etymologically ambiguous in that they may be IE archaisms – dialectalisms as well as mutual loans – but also chronologically ambiguous, being datable to multiple strata, typically I/II or I/III. Given the amount of evidence that we have analyzed, and since late M/LBA and IA contact is well established, the default explanation for these pseudo-Indo-Europeanisms should be that they are late (Strata II–III) rather than old (Stratum I). There is, in other words, no compelling evidence for the claim that there were intimate linguistic contacts between C and G in the period directly following the departure from the IE language community until the demonstrable linguistic exchange that started from the BA. Admittedly, it is more difficult to identify loanwords the further one goes back in time, as the languages were more similar the closer they were in time to the PIE parent language. Nevertheless, no support can be offered either for the existence of such contacts during or within the third-millennium BCE Bell Beaker network, which connected the precursors of Celtic and Germanic as well as potential non-IE groups along the Atlantic coast under the Celtic from the West hypothesis.

The Bell Beaker maritime network is not the only archaeological context for which the diffusion of linguistic features between these early IE groups can be hypothesized. For the earliest possible Celtic and Germanic contacts, the remarkably persistent coexistence of Bell Beaker and Corded Ware burial customs east of the late-third-millennium Harz mountains provides an equally if not more attractive geographic setting. Here the Corded Ware, after a sustained period of separation, merged into the Bell Beaker culture, which was directly succeeded by the syncretic Únětice culture (Meller 2019), famed for the Nebra sky disk. Since the genomic evidence shows that the Yamnaya pastoralist components of the Corded Ware and Bell Beaker groups arrived from the Pontic–Caspian steppe by separate migrations (Allentoft et al. 2015; Olalde et al. 2018), the pre-Únětice mixed cultural setting likely formed a linguistic convergence zone for originally divergent Indo-European dialects. However, the scarcity of compelling evidence for Stratum I contact again does not warrant the identification of these dialects as C and G, despite the setting being uniquely suitable for the horizontal exchange of cultural and linguistic features: as with the Atlantic Bell Beakers, the time depth appears unnecessarily great. We may instead assume that some of the shared features of the combined North-West Indo-European languages, Germanic, Balto-Slavic, Italic, and Celtic, which previously have been interpreted as evidence for a post-Indo-European shared sub-clade (cf. Oettinger 1997; 1999), were exchanged at this stage.

13.4.1.3 Mechanism 3: Shared Contact with Non-Indo-European Languages

As argued above, a modest amount of lexemes suspected to be non-Indo-European have entered C and G. These words are largely limited to the landscape features WILDERNESS (**kaito-*|**haiþī-*) and SLOPE (**glendos-*|**klinta-*) and indigenous flora and fauna including BADGER, CLOVER, COPSE, HOLLY, LARK, PINE, RUSH, and SHOOT. On the basis of linguistic criteria, the isoglosses CLOVER, COPSE, HOLLY, and PINE must be dated to Stratum I or II, which corresponds to the period between the disintegration of the PIE language community and the formation of the descendant subgroups in their different locations in Europe. Interestingly, the three non-IE dendronyms that we identified among these isoglosses all make use of an *st*-suffix that alternates with an *n*-suffix. This non-IE derivational pattern is best explained by assuming that the areas where Indo-European speakers ancestral to Celtic and Germanic settled were populated by speakers of (dialects of) the same substrate language. This scenario has important implications for the possible areas where Celtic and Germanic prehistoric language communities were located. The easiest way to account for the possibility that one substrate language or at least closely related dialects of this substrate language transferred words to both Celtic and Germanic is that the prehistoric Celtic and Germanic language communities resided not too distantly from each other.

13.4.2 On the Celtic Homeland

The Celto-Germanic lexicon may be used to weigh the possibility of an Atlantic origin of Celtic against a Central European origin. Under the "Celtic from the West" hypothesis, in which the Bell Beaker phenomenon plays a central role, Proto-Celtic emerged as a Bronze Age lingua franca of Indo-European-speaking traders during the Atlantic Bronze Age. This sea-based connectivity also reached Scandinavia, and this contact with Scandinavia is how Celtic and Germanic exchanged vocabulary. Hypotheses connecting Proto-Celtic with the

[10] One scenario in which an early Stratum II CGL can be imagined for FREE is by assuming sound substitution of PC *ϕ- to pre-PG **p*-.

Urnfield and Hallstatt/La Tène cultures imply land-based contact in Germany as the source of the Celto-Germanicisms.

Archaeological evidence for sea-based connectivity should coincide with an exchange of maritime lexicon. The Celto-Germanic lexicon contains the isoglosses ROW, HARBOR, and SAIL and possibly MAST. However, ROW (**rā-*|**rōan-*) could be an Indo-European archaism, or alternatively a late Indo-European dialectalism formed just prior to the migration to Western Europe. The combined archaeological and linguistic analysis of the isogloss SAIL (**siglo-*|**sigla-*) points to an IA loanword from C to G, sails only becoming common in Scandinavia during the same period. HARBOR (**kauno-*|**hafna-*) is clearly of earlier date, i.e., Stratum I or early II, but if it is a mutual loanword, it is most likely to be a G loanword into C, which would be more understandable if Celtic prior to its expansion was a landlocked language. There is nothing in the shared maritime vocabulary, in other words, that suggests a linguistic spread ensuing from the maritime expansion of the mid-third-millennium BCE Bell Beaker identity.

Other parts of the vocabulary confirm this picture. The fact that C and G share the word for OATS (**korkio-*|**hagran-*) probably indicates they were close to where the plant was domesticated in Central Europe in the LBA. The *Wanderwort* SILVER is shared by Celtiberian and Germanic, but not by Insular Celtic. This may be taken as an indication that the spread of the West Mediterranean word along the Atlantic coast to Scandinavia predated the Celtic settlement of the British Isles, which again would be easily understandable if Proto-Celtic was still located on the mainland during that time. The isogloss ENCLOSURE (**dūno-*|**tūna-*) further constitutes a clear association of Celtic with the LBA hilltop-defended sites, and not with the late Celtic phenomenon of the La Tène *oppida*, as the latter period would be too late for a C loanword to be affected by the G mid-first-millennium BCE sound shift from **d* to **t*. These archaeolinguistic indications all point to a Central European location for Proto-Celtic or at least for the Proto-Celtic that can be reconstructed on the basis of the evidence offered by the Insular Celtic languages, and late second- or early first-millennium expansion to the British Isles.

Finally, the shared non-Indo-European vocabulary can be adduced to approximate the pre-Celtic center of dispersal. According to one model, this subcluster of isoglosses could have been absorbed by C and G through the culturally, but not necessarily linguistically and demonstrably not genetically uniform Bell Beaker phenomenon, which straddled a south-to-north continuum between Neolithic farmers and Yamnaya pastoralists (Olalde et al. 2018). A linguistically diverse but culturally homogenous sphere would after all offer highly suitable conditions for the diffusion of non-Indo-European features into Indo-European dialects (and *vice versa*). However, we are not able to find indications for such a scenario in the non-Indo-European elements from our corpus of isoglosses. The isogloss HOLLY (**kolinno-*|**hulisa-*) rather demonstrates that C and G formed a northern substrate cluster as opposed to a related but more divergent Mediterranean cluster consisting of Gr. κήλαστρος, Arm. *kostli*, Sard. *colostri*, and Basque *gorostri*. The isoglosses COPSE (**kʷresti-*|**hursti-*) and PINE (**gisusto-*|**kizna-*) make use of the same non-IE derivational components as the ones found in HOLLY, but they too are isolated to North Europe, the only additional link consisting of Proto-Slavic **xvórstъ* 'brushwood, osier'. Scanty as the evidence for non-IE elements remains, the elements that can be identified do not clearly exhibit any direct links to the pre-Indo-European West Mediterranean linguistic landscape (including Basque), and as such offer no direct support for a Bell Beaker-associated linguistic diffusion of non-Indo-European features from Southwest to Northwest and Central Europe. Rather, these features were absorbed in Northern Europe during the period when the different Indo-European dialects that would ultimately develop into C and G settled among local European groups, i.e., Stratum I in our chronology. We may surmise that the impact of any non-IE languages spoken within the Bell Beaker horizon was limited outside Southern Europe, or if any Indo-European dialects were impacted, that they were later superseded by other Indo-European groups.

13.4.3 Tentative Chronology of the Strata

Finally, one may tentatively assign an absolute chronology to the linguistic strata by comparing the words exchanged for various cultural and technological innovations with the archaeological record, as one may assume that a word was exchanged when the corresponding concept was exchanged between the language communities. Words whose exchange appears likely in Stratum I include HOLLY and FREE. The likely adoption of originally non-IE vocabulary for the Western European natural environment makes it attractive to date this stratum to the first contact with non-Indo-European speakers in this area in the Early Bronze Age. Celto-Germanicisms positively attributable to this stratum are scarce. Vocabulary positively identifiable to Stratum II includes KING, LEATHER, ENCLOSURE, LEECH, and JESTER. On the basis of these words, one may identify a shared shift toward more stratified and sedentary societies. These shifts are well attested in the Middle to Late Bronze Age. It follows that the sound laws leading up to Proto-Celtic, e.g. PIE **ē* > PC **ī*, PIE **p* > PC **ϕ*, may be dated to this period at the latest. Stratum III borrowings such as BREAST(-PLATE), IRON, LEAD, and SAIL must postdate these Iron Age inventions, so the Germanic consonant shifts that define Stratum III can be dated to the beginning of the Iron Age.

Linguistic Abbreviations

Arm.: Armenian, Av.: Avestan, B: Breton, Celtib.: Celtiberian, CG: Celto-Germanic, Celto-Germanicism, Co.: Cornish, dial.: dialectal, Dor.: Doric, Du.: Dutch, G: German, Gaul.: Gaulish, Go.: Gothic, Gr.: Greek, Hes.: Hesychius, Hitt.: Hittite, Icel.: Icelandic, IE: Indo-European, Ir.: Irish, Lat.: Latin, Latv.: Latvian, Lith.: Lithuanian, MB: Middle Breton, MCo.: Middle Cornish, MDu.: Middle Dutch, ME: Middle English, MFr.: Middle French, MHG: Middle High German, MIr.: Middle Irish, MLG: Middle Low German, MW: Middle Welsh, N: Norse, NFri.: North Frisian, Nw.: Norwegian, OB: Old Breton, OCo.: Old Cornish, OCS: Old Church Slavonic, OE: Old English,

OFr.: Old French, OFri.: Old Frisian, OHG: Old High German, OIcel.: Old Icelandic, OIr.: Old Irish, OLFra.: Old Low Franconian, ON: Old Norse, OPr.: Old Prussian, OS: Old Saxon, OSw.: Old Swedish, OW: Old Welsh, PBr.: Proto-Brittonic, PC: Proto-Celtic, PG: Proto-Germanic, PIE: Proto-Indo-European, PIt.: Proto-Italic, Prim.: Primitive, PSl.: Proto-Slavic, Ru.: Russian, ScG: Scottish Gaelic, SCr.: Serbo-Croatian, Skt.: Sanskrit, Sw.: Swedish, To: Tocharian, W: Welsh, WFri. West Frisian

Archaeological Abbreviations

EBA: Early Bronze Age, MBA: Middle Bronze Age, LBA: Late Bronze Age, IA: Iron Age

References

Adams, Douglas Q. 2013. *A dictionary of Tocharian B, revised and greatly enlarged* (Leiden Studies in Indo-European 10). Amsterdam; New York: Rodopi.

ALEW = Wolfgang Hock, Rainer Fecht, Anna Helene Feulner, Eugen Hill, & Dagmar S. Wodtko. 2019. *Altlitauisches etymologisches Wörterbuch (ALEW)*.

Allentoft, Morten E., Martin Sikora, Karl-Göran Sjögren, Simon Rasmussen, Morten Rasmussen, Jesper Stenderup, Peter B. Damgaard, et al. 2015. Population genomics of Bronze Age Eurasia. *Nature* 522(7555): 167–172.

Artursson, M. 2013. Ships in stone: Ship-like stone settings, war canoes and sailing ships in Bronze Age southern Scandinavia. In: S. Bergerbrant & S. Sabatini (ed.), *Counterpoint: Essays in Archaeology and Heritage Studies in Honour of Professor Kristian Kristiansen* (British Archaeological Reports International Series), 499–504. Oxford: Oxford University Press.

Birkhan, Helmut. 1967. Das gallische Namenelement **cassi-* und die germanisch-keltische Kontaktzone. In: Meid, Wolfgang (ed.) *Beiträge zur Indogermanistik und Keltologie: Julius Pokorny zum 80. Geburtstag gewidmet* (Innsbrucker Beiträge zur Kulturwissenschaft 13), 115–45. Innsbruck: Sprachwissenschaftliches Institut der Universität Innsbruck.

1970. *Germanen und Kelten bis zum Ausgang der Römerzeit: der Aussagewert von Wörtern und Sachen für die frühesten Keltisch-Germanischen Kulturbeziehungen* (Österreichische Akademie der Wissenschiften, philosophisch-historische Klasse: Sitzungsberichte 272). Vienna: Kommissionsverlag der Österreichischen Akademie der Wissenschaften.

1999. Ein Strauß nicht durchwegs bekömmlicher Kräuter aus dem keltischen und germanischen Altertum: Wort- und Sachkundliches zu einigen Pflanzen. In: Anreiter, P., Erszebét, J. (ed.), *Studia celtica et indogermanica: Festschrift für Wolfgang Meid zum 70. Geburtstag*, 43–52. Budapest: Archaeolingua.

2012. Keltisches in germanischen Runennamen? In: A. Bammesberger, A. & G. Waxenberger (ed.), *Das fuþark und seine einzelsprachlichen Weiterentwicklungen: Akten der Tagung in Eichstätt vom 20. bis 24. Juli 2003* (Ergänzungsbände zum Reallexikon der germanischen Altertumskunde), 80–100. Berlin: De Gruyter.

Bjorvand, Harald, & Frederik O. Lindeman. 2000. *Våre arveord: Etymologisk ordbok*. Oslo: Novus Forlag.

Blöndal Magnússon, Á. 1989. *Íslensk Orðsifjabók*. Reykjavik: Orðabók Háskólans.

Bomhard, Allan. 2014. Hittite *pa-ak-nu-*. *Journal of Indo-European Studies* 42: 291–93.

Boutkan, Dirk. F. H. 2003. On Gothic *magaþ* ~ Old Frisian *megith* and the form of some North European substratum words in Germanic. *Amsterdamer Beiträge zur älteren Germanistik* 58: 11–28.

Boutkan, Dirk F. H., & Maarten G. Kossmann. 2001. On the etymology of "silver." *NOWELE : North-Western European Language Evolution* 38: 3–15.

Brumlich, Markolf. 2005. Schmiedegräber der älteren vorrömischen Eisenzeit in Norddeutschland. *Ethnogr.-Arch. Zeitschr.* 46(2): 189–220.

Caudullo, G., Welk, E., San-Miguel-Ayanz, J. 2017. Chorological maps for the main European woody species. *Data in Brief* 12: 662–666.

Cheung, Johnny. 2007. *Etymological dictionary of the Iranian verb* (Leiden Indo-European Etymological Dictionary Series 2). Leiden: Brill.

Cleary, Kerry, & Catriona Gibson. 2019. Connectivity in Atlantic Europe during the Bronze Age (2800-800 BC). In: B. Cunliffe & J. T. Koch (ed.), *Exploring Celtic origins: New ways forward in archaeology, linguistics, and genetics* (Celtic Studies Publications XXII), 80–116. Oxford: Oxbow Books.

Cunliffe, Barry, & John T. Koch. (ed.). 2019. *Exploring Celtic origins: New ways forward in archaeology, linguistics, and genetics* (Celtic Studies Publications 22). Oxford: Oxbow Books.

de Bernardo Stempel, Patrizia. 2001. Gotisch *in-weitiþ guþ* und gallisch *ande-díon uēdiíu-mi* (Chamalières, Z. 1). *Historische Sprachforschung/Historical Linguistics* 114: 164–170.

De Bhaldraithe, Tomás. 1981. Varia I. *Ériu* 32: 149–152.

Demiraj, Bardhyl. 1997. *Albanische Etymologien* (Leiden Studies in Indo-European 7). Amsterdam: Rodopi.

Dinneen, Patrick S. 1904. *Foclóir Gaedhilge agus Béarla. An Irish-English dictionary.* Dublin: Irish Text Society.

Ebel, H. 1861. Die stellung des celtischen. *Beiträge zur vergleichenden Sprachforschung* 2: 137–194.

EDHIL = Alwin Kloekhorst. 2007. *Etymological dictionary of the Hittite inherited lexicon* (Leiden Indo-European Etymological Dictionary Series 5). Leiden: Brill.

eDIL = 2019. *An electronic dictionary of the Irish language.* Accessed July 29, 2021. www.dil.ie.

EDLI = Michiel de Vaan. 2008. *Etymological dictionary of Latin and the other Italic languages* (Leiden Indo-European Etymological Dictionary Series 7). Leiden: Brill.

EDPC = Ranko Matasović. 2009. *Etymological dictionary of Proto-Celtic* (Leiden Indo-European Etymological Dictionary Series 9). Leiden; Boston: Brill.

EDPG = Guus Kroonen. 2013. *Etymological dictionary of Proto-Germanic* (Leiden Indo-European Etymological Dictionary Series 11). Leiden: Brill.

Fages, Antoine, et al. 2019. Tracking five millennia of horse management with extensive ancient genome time series. *Cell* 177(6): 1419–1435.e31.

Falileyev, Alexander. 2000. *Etymological glossary of Old Welsh* (Buchreihe der Zeitschrift für celtische Philologie 18). Tübingen: Niemeyer.

Fleuriot, Léon. 1964. *Dictionnaire des gloses en vieux breton* (Collection linguistique 62). Paris: Klincksieck.

Fraenkel, Ernst. 1962–1965. *Litauisches etymologisches Wörterbuch*. Heidelberg: Universitätsverlag Winter.

French, Katherine E. 2017. Palaeoecology and GIS modeling reveal historic grasslands as "hotspots" of biodiversity and plant genetic resources. *Journal of Ethnobiology* 37: 581–600.

Gnesin, G. G., 2016. Iron Age: Origin and evolution of ferrous metallurgy. *Powder Metallurgy and Metal Ceramics* 55: 114–123.

Haak, Wolfgang, Iosif Lazaridis, Nick Patterson, Nadin Rohland, Swapan Mallick, Bastien Llamas, et al. 2015. Massive migration from the steppe was a source for Indo-European languages in Europe. *Nature* 522: 207–211.

Heidermanns, Frank. 1993. *Etymologisches Wörterbuch der germanischen Primäradjektive* (Studia Linguistica Germanica 33). Berlin: De Gruyter.

Heinertz, N. Otto. 1915. Friesisches. *Indogermanische Forschungen* 35: 304–335.

Hellquist, Elof. 1922. *Svensk etymologisk Ordbok*. Lund: Gleerup.

Hill, Eugen. 2002. Ein germanisch-keltisches Suffix für Nominalabstrakta. *Münchener Studien zur Sprachwissenschaft* 62: 39–70.

2012. Die Entwicklung von **u* vor unsilbischem **i* in den indogermanischen Sprachen Nord- und Mitteleuropas: die Stammsuppletion bei u-adjektiven und das Präsens von "sein." *NOWELE* 64/65: 5–36.

Hodgson, J. G., P. Halstead, P. J. Wilson, & S. Davis. 1999. Functional interpretation of archaeobotanical data: Making hay in the archaeological record. *Veget. Hist. Archaebot.* 8: 261–271.

Hyllested, Adam. 2010. The precursors of Celtic and Germanic. In: S. W. Jamison, H. C. Melchert, B. H. Vine, & A. Mercado (ed.), *Proceedings of the 21st Annual UCLA Indo-European Conference: Los Angeles, October 30th and 31st, 2009*, 107–28. Bremen: Hempen.

Hyllested, Adam. 2014. *Word exchange at the gates of Europe: Five millenia of language contact*. PhD diss., University of Copenhagen.

IEW = Julius Pokorny. 1959. *Indogermanisches etymologisches Wörterbuch*. Bern: A. Francke.

Irslinger, Britta. 2002. *Abstrakta mit Dentalsuffixen im Altirischen*. Heidelberg: Universitätsverlag Winter.

Iversen, Rune, & Guus Kroonen. 2017. Talking Neolithic: Linguistic and archaeological perspectives on how Indo-European was implemented in southern Scandinavia. *American Journal of Archaeology* 121: 511–525.

Jackson, Kenneth Hurlstone. 1953. *Language and History in Early Britain: A chronological survey of the Brittonic languages, first to twelfth century A.D.* Edinburgh: Edinburgh University Press.

Johannsen, Jens Winter. 2016. Heavy metal: Lead in Bronze Age Scandinavia. *Fornvännen* 111: 153–161.

Johnston, Robert. 2013. Bronze Age fields and land division. In: H. Fokkens & A. F. Harding (ed.), *The Oxford Handbook of the European Bronze Age*, 311–327. Oxford: Oxford University Press.

Jørgensen, Anders Richardt. 2006. Etymologies to go: Some further reflexes of Celtic **keng-*. *Keltische Forschungen* 1: 59–71.

Kluge, Friedrich. 1913. *Urgermanisch: Vorgeschichte der altgermanischen Dialekte*. Strassburg: Verlag von Karl J. Trübner.

Ko = John T. Koch. 2018. Rock art and Celto-Germanic vocabulary: Shared iconography and words as reflections of Bronze Age contact. *Adoranten*: 1–16.

Koch, John T. 2020. *Celto-Germanic: Later prehistory and Post-Proto-Indo-European vocabulary in the north and west.* Aberystwyth: Canolfan Uwchefrydiau Cymreig a Cheltaidd Prifysgol Cymru.

KPV = Stefan Schumacher. 2004. *Die keltischen Primärverben: ein vergleichendes, etymologisches und morphologisches Lexikon*. Innsbruck: Innsbrucker Beiträge zur Sprachwissenschaft.

Kr = Hans Krahe. 1954. *Sprache und Vorzeit*. Heidelberg: Quelle & Meyer.

Kristiansen, Kristian, et al. 2017. Re-theorising mobility and the formation of culture and language among the Corded Ware Culture in Europe. *Antiquity* 91(356): 334–347.

Kroonen, Guus. 2011. *The Proto-Germanic n-stems. A study in diachronic morphophonology* (Leiden Studies in Indo-European 18). Amsterdam: Rodopi.

2012. Non-Indo-European root nouns in Germanic: Evidence in support of the Agricultural Substrate. In: Riho Grünthal & Petri Kallio (ed.), *A linguistic map of prehistoric Northern Europe*, 239–260. Helsinki: Société Finno-Ougrienne.

L = Geo. S. Lane. 1933. The Germano-Celtic Vocabulary. *Language* 9: 244–246.

LEIA = Joseph Vendryes, Édouard Bachallery, & Pierre-Yves Lambert. 1959–1996. *Lexique étymologique de l'irlandais ancien*. Dublin: Dublin Institute for Advanced Studies.

Lidén, Evald. 1891. Etymologien. *Beiträge zur Geschichte der deutschen Sprache und Literatur* 15: 507–522.

LIV² = Helmut Rix, Martin Kümmel, Thomas Zehnder, Reiner Lipp, & Briggite Schirmer. 2001. *Lexikon der indogermanischen Verben*, 2nd ed. Wiesbaden: Dr. Ludweig Reichert Verlag.

Lubotsky, Alexander M. 1988. *On the system of nominal accentuation in Sanskrit and Indo-European* (Memoirs of the Kern Institute 4). Leiden: Brill.

Lühr, Rosemarie. 1988. *Expressivität und Lautgesetz im Germanischen* (Monographien zur Sprachwissenschaft 15). Heidelberg: Universitätsverlag Winter.

Lull, Vicente, Roberto Micó, Christina Rihuete Herrada, & Roberto Risch. 2014. The social value of silver in El Argar. In: Harald Meller, Roberto Risch, & Ernst Pernicka (ed.), *Metalle der Macht – frühes Gold und Silber* (Tagungen des Landesmuseums für Vorgeschichte Halle 11/2), 557–576. Halle: Landesamt für Denkmalpflege und Archäologie Sachsen-Anhalt, Landesmuseum für Vorgeschichte.

Mallory, James P. 1989. *In search of the Indo-Europeans: Language, archaeology and myth*. London: Thames & Hudson.

2016. Archaeology and language shift in Atlantic Europe. In: John T. Koch & Barry W. Cunliffe (ed.), *Celtic from the West 3: Atlantic Europe in the Metal Ages: Questions of Shared Language* (Celtic Studies Publications 19), 387–406. Oxford: Oxbow Books.

Mallory, James P., & Martin Huld. 1984. Proto-Indo-European 'silver'. *Zeitschrift für vergleichende Sprachforschung* 97(1): 1–12.

Marstrander, Carl. 1910. Hibernica. *Zeitschrift für celtische Philologie* 7: 357–418.

1915. *Bidrag til det norske sprogs historie i Irland* (Skrifter Norske videnskaps-akademi i Oslo. II-Hist.-filos. klasse 5). Kristiania: I kommission hos J. Dybwad.

McClatchie, Meriel. 2018. Barley, rye, and oats. In: Sandra L. López Varela (ed.), *The Encyclopedia of Archaeological Sciences*, 1–4. Hoboken (NJ): John Wiley & Sons.

McManus, Damian. 1991. *A guide to Ogam*. Maynooth: An Sagart.

Meller, Harald. 2019. Princes, armies, sanctuaries: The emergence of complex authority in the central German Únětice culture. *Acta Archaeologica* 90: 39–79.

Neumann, Günter. 1961. Hethitische Etymologien. III. *Zeitschrift für vergleichende Sprachforschung* 77: 76–81.

Noble, Gordon. 2017. *Woodland in the Neolithic of Northern Europe: The forest as ancestor*. Cambridge: Cambridge University Press.

O'Brien, William. 2016. Language shift and political context in Bronze Age Ireland: Some implications of hill fort chronology. In: John T. Koch & Barry Cunliffe (ed.), *Celtic from the West 3: Atlantic Europe in the metal ages: Questions of shared language* (Celtic Studies Publications 19), 219–246. Oxford: Oxbow Books.

Oettinger, Norbert. 1997. Grundsätzliche Überlegungen Zum Nordwest-Indogermanischen. *Incontri Linguistici* 20: 93–111.

1999. Zum nordwest-indogermanischen Lexikon (mit einer Bemerkung zum hethitischen Genitiv auf -*l*). In: P. Anreiter & J. Erszebét (ed.), *Studia celtica et indogermanica: Festschrift für Wolfgang Meid zum 70. Geburtstag*, 261–267. Budapest: Archaeolingua.

Olalde, Iñigo, Selina Brace, Morten E. Allentoft, Ian Armit, Kristian Kristiansen, Thomas Booth, et al. 2018. The Beaker phenomenon and the genomic transformation of northwest Europe. *Nature* 555(7695): 190–196.

Orel, Vladimir. 1998. *Albanian etymological dictionary*. Leiden: Brill.

Panaino, Antonio. 2016. Later Avestan *mayauua-* (?) and the (mis) adventures of a "pseudo-ascetic." In: C. Redard (ed.), *Des Contrées Avestiques à Mahabad, via Bisotun. Etudes Offertes En Hommage à Pierre Lecoq*, 167–186. Neuchâtel: Recherches et Publications.

Pedersen, Holger. 1913. *Vergleichende Grammatik der keltischen Sprachen II*. Göttingen: Vandenhoeck und Ruprecht.

Pl = Edgar C. Polomé. 1983. Celto-Germanic isoglosses (revisited). *Journal of Indo-European Studies* 11: 281–298.

Pr = Walter Porzig. 1974. *Die Gliederung des indogermanischen Sprachgebiets*. Heidelberg: Universitätsverlag Winter.

Pronk-Tiethoff, Saskia Elisabeth. 2012. *The Germanic loanwords in Proto-Slavic: Origin and accentuation*. PhD diss., Leiden University.

Pryor, Francis. 2010. *The making of the British landscape: How we have transformed the land, from prehistory to today*. London: Penguin.

Riecke, Jörg. 1996. *Die schwachen jan-Verben des Althochdeutschen: Ein Gliederungsversuch* (Studien zum Althochdeutschen 32). Göttingen: Vandenhoeck & Ruprecht.

Robinson, Patrick. 1986. Trees as fodder crops. In: M. G. R. Cannell & J. E. Jackson (ed.), *Attributes of trees as crop plants*, 281–296. Penicuik: Institute of Terrestrial Ecology, NERC.

Rübekeil, Ludwig. 2001. Einige Bemerkungen zur Wortfamilie um germ. **hatis-*. In: B. Brogyányi (ed.), *Germanisches Altertum und christliches Mittelalter: Festschrift für Heinz Klingenberg zum 65. Geburtstag*, 239–294. Hamburg: Kovač.

Rusu, Mircea. 1969. Das keltische Fürstengrab von Ciumeşti in Rumänien. *Germania* 50: 267–300.

Sahlgren, G. F. Jöran. 1953. Ortnamnet *Nymden* och lat. *nemus*. *Namn och Bygd: Tidskrift för nordisk ortnamnsforskning* 41: 46–50.

SBCHP = Peter C. H. Schrijver. 1995. *Studies in British Celtic historical phonology* (Leiden Studies in Indo-European 5). Amsterdam: Rodopi.

Schm = Karl Horst Schmidt. 1991. The Celts and the ethnogenesis of the Germanic people. *Historische Sprachforschung/ Historical Linguistics* 104: 129–152.

Schrijver, Peter C. H. 1997. Animal, vegetable and mineral: Some Western European substratum words. In: A. Lubotsky (ed.), *Sound law and analogy* (Leiden Studies in Indo-European 9), 293–314. Amsterdam: Rodopi.

2003. The etymology of Welsh *chwith* and the semantics and morphology of PIE **$k(^w)sweib^h$-*. In: Paul Russell (ed.), *Yr Hen Iaith: Studies in Early Welsh*, 1–24. Aberystwyth: Celtic Studies Publications.

2004. Apes, dwarfs, rivers and Indo-European internal derivation. In: Adam Hyllested & Jens Elmegård Rasmussen (ed.), *Per aspera ad asteriscos: Studia Indogermanica in honorem Jens Elmegård Rasmussen sexagenarii Idibus Martiis anno MMIV*, 507–511. Innsbruck: Institut für Sprachen und Literaturen der Universität Innsbruck.

2016. Sound change, the Italo-Celtic linguistic unity, and the Italian homeland of Celtic. In: John T. Koch & Barry Cunliffe (ed.), *Celtic from the West 3: Atlantic Europe in the metal ages: Questions of shared language* (Celtic Studies Publications 19), 489–502. Oxford: Oxbow Books.

Schu = Stefan Schumacher. 2007. Die Deutschen und die Nachbarstämme: Lexikalische und strukturelle Sprachkontaktphänomene entlang der keltisch-germanischen Übergangszone. *Keltische Forschungen* 2: 167–208.

Seebold, Elmar. 1970. *Vergleichendes und etymologisches Wörterbuch der germanischen starken Verben* (Janua Linguarum Series Practica 85). The Hague: Mouton.

Sims-Williams, Patrick., 2020. An alternative to "Celtic from the East" and "Celtic from the West." *Cambridge Archaeological Journal* 30(3): 1–19.

Stifter, David. 1998. Study in red. *Die Sprache: Zeitschrift für Sprachwissenschaft* 40: 202–223.

2009. The Proto-Germanic shift **ā*>**ō* and early Germanic linguistic contacts. *Historische Sprachforschung/Historical Linguistics* 122: 268–83.

2011. Lack of syncope and other *nichtlautgesetzlich* vowel developments in OIr. consonant-stem nouns. Animacy rearing its head in morphology? In: Thomas Krisch & Thomas Lindner (ed.), *Indogermanistik und Linguistik im Dialog. Akten der XIII. Fachtagung der Indogermanischen Gesellschaft vom 21. bis 27. September 2008 in Salzburg*, 556–565. Wiesbaden: Reichert Verlag.

2015. The language of the poems of blathmac. In: Pádraig Ó Riain (ed.), *The poems of Blathmac son of Cú Brettan: Reassessments* (Irish Texts Society Subsidiary Series 27), 47–103. London: Irish Texts Society.

2018. The stars look very different today. *Ériu* 68: 29–54.

Stika, Hans-Peter, & Andreas G. Heiss. 2013. Plant cultivation in the Bronze Age. In: H. Fokkens & A. F. Harding (ed.), *The Oxford handbook of the European Bronze Age*, 348–369. Oxford: Oxford University Press.

Stokes, Whitley. 1901. Irish etymologies. *Zeitschrift für celtische Philologie* 3: 467–473.

Thier, Katrin. 2011. Language and technology: Some examples from seafaring (Germanic and Celtic). *Transactions of the Philological Society* 109: 186–199.

Thorpe, Nick. 2013. Warfare in the European Bronze Age. In: H. Fokkens & A. F. Harding (ed.), *The Oxford handbook of the European Bronze Age*, 234–247. Oxford: Oxford University Press.

Trautmann, Reinhold. 1923. *Baltisch-Slavisches Wörterbuch*. Göttingen: Vandenhoeck & Ruprecht.

Van der Vaart-Verschoof, Sasja. 2017. *Fragmenting the chieftain: A practice-based study of Early Iron Age Hallstatt C elite burials in the Low Countries* (Papers on Archaeology of the Leiden Museum of Antiquities 15A). Leiden: Sidestone Press.

Van Windekens, Albert Joris. 1941. *Lexique étymologique des dialectes tokhariens* (Bibliothèque du Muséon 11). Louvain: Bureaux du Muséon.

Wadstein, Elis. 1895. Bidrag till tolkning och belysning av skalde- ock Edda-dikter. *Arkiv för nordisk filologi* 11: 64–92.

Williams, Alan R., 1980. The manufacture of mail in medieval Europe: A technical note. *Gladius* 15: 105–134.

Wissmann, Wilhelm. 1961. Ahd. *seffo. Zeitschrift für vergleichende Sprachforschung auf dem Gebiete der Indogermanischen Sprachen* 77: 81.

Wright, John. 2016. *A natural history of the hedgerow: And ditches, dykes and dry stone walls*. London: Profile Books.

Zair, N. 2013. Lat. glārea '*gravel*.' *Historische Sprachforschung/ Historical Linguistics* 126: 280–286.

13.6 Appendix

13.6.1 Onomastic Material

Onomastic material discussed in previous articles not discussed here comprises the following instances: the British tribal name *Coriono-tōtae* and ON *Herjann* (epithet of *Óðinn*) < PG **harjana-* '?army commander' (H3), PC **nerto-* 'strength' and the Germanic theonyms *Nerthus*, ON *Njǫrðr* (H10), the Celto-Lat. place-name *Hercynia* Silva and PG **fergunja-* 'mountain' (L251), names formed as PC **uiro-kʷū* (OIr. *Ferchú*) and PG **wera-wulfa-* 'werewolf' (H9, Koch 13), PC **magos-* 'field' and Austrian place-name *Mach-land* (L253), Gaul. place name *Vesontio* and PG **wisund-* (L253), the *-bona* and *-lanum* suffix in e.g. the place names *Bonn*, *Milan* (Kr126), river names such as the *Rhine*, *Meuse*, *Waal*, *Glane*, *Main*, *Danube* and river names ending in *-apa* (Kr128–131, Schmidt 1991 145), OIr. *fili* 'seer, diviner' and the name of a Germanic seer *Veleda* (Kr139).

13.6.2 Compelling Celto-Germanicisms

AXE

PC: **beiatli-* (OIr. *bíail*, W *bwyall*, MCo. *boell*, MB *bouhazl* 'axe')
PG: **bīþla-* (ON *bíldr* 'knife for bloodletting', MDu. *bijl*, OHG *bīhal* 'axe')
REF: EDPG 66, Ko9
Isogloss typology: SM
Interpretation: IE(?) (0)

An instrumental noun to the PIE verbal root **bʰeiH-* 'to strike', cf. OIr. *benaid* 'to strike, hit', MB *benaff* 'to cut' < **bʰi-neH-*, OCS *biti* 'to beat', Icel. *bjá* 'to fight, struggle' < **bʰ(e)iH-*. This formation is rather trivial and shared with Slavic **bidlo* 'hammer, pole', which makes the isogloss formally nonexclusive, but the specific meaning 'knife, axe' is uniquely CG. Borrowing between the branches can be excluded given the vocalization of the laryngeal in C as opposed to G.

BADGER

PC: **tazgo-*, **tasko-* (MIr. PN *Tadg* (king with badger as totem), Gaul. PN *Tascos*, Fr. dial. *taisse*, Sp. *tejón* 'badger')
PG: **þahsu-* (MDu. *das*, MHG *dahs* 'badger')
REF: EDPC 372, EDPG 531
Isogloss typology: LX
Interpretation: 3L (I-II)

A CG **tasC-* may be reconstructed; the multiple reflexes of medial consonant cluster in **-sk-/-zg-/-ks-* may point to a substrate borrowing; a dissimilation against the initial **t-* in Goidelic proposed by EDPC is ad hoc.

BADGER(HOUND)

PC: **brokko-* (MIr. *brocc*, W *broch*, MB *broc'h*, OCo. *broch* 'badger')
PG: **brakkan-* (OHG *bracko* 'hound')
REF: IEW 108-109, EDPC 80, EDPG 74
Isogloss typology: LX
Interpretation: CGL (III)

The *n*-stem in Germanic may be understood as an agent suffix, so the original meaning in Germanic appears to have been 'badger-er, badger-hound', which is paralleled by German *Dachshund*, lit. 'badger-dog'. If the Germanic word was borrowed from Celtic, it may have happened after the major consonant shifts, but before the change **o* > **a*.

BOY

PC: **magu-* (OIr. *mug* 'slave, servant', W *meu-dwy* 'hermit < servant of God', MCorn. *maw* 'lad', B *mau* 'happy, active')
PG: **magu-* (Go. *magus* 'boy', OE *magu* 'child, son')
REF: L259, Kr135–136, Boutkan 2003, EDPC 274, H39, EDPG 347, Panaino 2016, Ko13
Isogloss typology: MO
Interpretation: GCL (III)

A Celto-Germanic **magʰ-u-* may be reconstructed. Prim. Ir. *MAQQI*, OIr. *macc* 'son, boy' and W, B, Co. *map*, *mab* 'son' may be related, although the root-final consonant differs; they project back to PC **makkʷo-* and **makʷo-/*maggʷo-*, respectively. The combination of matching semantics and differing root-final consonants might be indicative of borrowing from a substrate language. However, in view of PG **mag-aþi-* 'girl' (Go. *magaþs*, OE *mæg(e)ð*, OHG *magad*) the *u*-stem appears to have been created in G, and therefore native in this branch. OIr. *maccdacht* 'young full-grown', OCo. *mahtheid* 'virgo', W *machdaith*, B *matez* 'servant-girl' are unrelated; the OIr. consists of *macc* 'son, boy' derived with adjectivalizing *-dae* and the abstract suffix *-acht*, while the Brittonic forms are rather compounds of PC **makko-* 'surety' and **tixtā* '(female) who travels', cf. OIr. *techt* 'messenger'. The Av. hapax *maγava-* 'unmarried' is corrupt.

BREAST(PLATE)

PC: **brunnio-* (OIr. *bruinne* 'breast', W *brynn* 'hill')
PG: **brunjōn-* (Go. *brunjo* 'breastplate', ON *brynja*, OE *byrne*, OS *brunnia*, OHG *brunja* 'coat of mail')
REF: L264, EDPG 80
Isogloss typology: MO
Interpretation: CGL (III)

The Celtic is from PIE **bʰrus-n-io-* and borrowing into Germanic must follow PIE **-sn-* > *-nn-* in Celtic. Internally in Celtic, it is derived from PC **brusū* > OIr. *brú*, gen.sg. **brus-n-os* > **brunnos* > OIr. *bronn* 'belly, womb'. For the mismatch between C *-nn-* and Germanic *-n-*, cf. PC **granno-* and PG **granō-*.

BREECHES

PC: **brākā* (Gallo-Lat. *brācae*, *brācēs*, Gallo-Gr. pl. βράκας 'trousers, breeches')
PG: **brōk-* (ON *brōk* 'leg of a pair of breeches', pl. *brœkr* 'breeches', OE *brōc* 'behind, breech', OFri. *brēk* OHG *bruoh* 'trousers')
REF: L264, Kr141, Pl284, Schm143, Stifter 2009 275-277, Kroonen 2012, EDPG 74
Isogloss typology: LX
Interpretation: L (III)

The consonantism suggests borrowing after Grimm's law, although the direction of the borrowing is difficult to establish. Early loanwords are sometimes borrowed as root nouns in G, which may tip the balance in favor of a C origin. The word is unattested in Insular Celtic, however.

BRISTLE

PC: **granno-* (MIr. *grenn*, MW *grann* 'beard, chin, cheek', Provençal *gren* 'mustache' < Gaul.)
PG: **granō-* (Go. (Isidor, *Origines* XIX.23.7) *granos* '?', ON *grǫn* 'hair of the beard; spruce', OE *granu* 'mustache', OHG *grana* 'hair of the beard')
REF: IEW 440, H91
Isogloss typology: LX
Interpretation: CGL (III)

An almost complete formal and semantic match. Celtic and Germanic only differ in the length of the nasal, which could be a feature of borrowing, cf. PC **brunnio-* >> PG **brunjō-* 'breast plate' after the C change *-*sn*- > *-*nn*- and the PG sound shifts.

CLOVER

PC: **semmVr-* (OIr. *semar* 'clover, shamrock')
PG: **smēran-* (Icel. *smári* 'clover'), **smērjōn-* (Icel., Far. *smæra*, Nw., Da. *smære*, Sw. dial. *smäre* 'clover')
REF: Schrijver 1997, 304, EDPG 457
Isogloss typology: LX
Interpretation: 3L (I)

A single CG proto-form cannot be reconstructed, but the precise semantic match and the identical consonantal skeleton nevertheless make a connection compelling. The variation in vowel placement between Celtic **sVm-* and Germanic **smV-r* requires an explanation. In Proto-Indo-European terms a doublet can be reconstructed as **semh*$_1$*-r-* vs **smeh*$_1$*-r-*, but the implied *Schwebeablaut* remains problematic, which makes this isogloss a candidate for a shared loan from a third language. A root **smh*$_1$*r* bears a remarkable resemblance to Georgian *sam-q'ura*, which synchronically can be analyzed as a compound of *sam* 'three' + *q'ur* 'ear, handle' (cf. Lat. *trifolium* 'three-leaf'). This resemblance, however, may be coincidental.

COAL

PC: **goulo-* (MIr. *gúal* 'coal')
PG: **kula-* (ON *kol*, OE *col*, OHG *kol* 'coal')
REF: L252, EDPC 165, H93, EDPG 309, Stifter 2018, Ko8
Isogloss typology: SM
Interpretation: IE(?) (0)

Both the C and G formations can be related to the PIE root **ǵuelH-* 'to burn', cf. Skt *jválati* 'burns', but they uniquely show the meaning 'coal'. The Celtic vocalism is unexpected, but may represent a secondary full grade. Stifter, on the other hand, suggests a reduplicated formation PC **guglo-* or **goglo-* from the root **g*^{h}*leh*$_3$*-* 'to glow', which is incompatible with PG **kula-*.

COPSE

PC: **k*^{w}*resti(o)-* (W *prys(g)* 'copse, grove' (>> ScG *preas* 'bush, shrub, thicket'))
PG: **h(w)ursti-* (OE *hyrst*, OS *hyrst*, OHG *hurst* 'crest, copse')
REF: IEW 633, EDPC 181
Isogloss typology: LX
Interpretation: 3L (I-II)

A CG **k*^{w}*r(e)sti-* may be posited. If the PSl. **xvorstъ*, OCS *xvrastije*, Ru. *xvórost* 'brushwood, bush' is somehow connected, it would be a non-Indo-European loanword with a wider distribution than just Celtic and Germanic. A further connection may exist within Celtic: PC **k*^{w}*renno-* < **k*^{w}*res-no-*(?), cf. Gaul. *prenne*, OIr. *crann*, W, B *prenn*, Co. *pren* 'tree, wood'.

COVER

PC: **tog-ī-* (OIr. *tuigithir* 'covers')
PG: **þakjan-* (ON *þekja*, OE *þeccan*, OS *bi-thekkia*, OHG *decken* 'to cover')
REF: L263, IEW 1013-1014, EDPC 376, EDPG 531-532
Isogloss typology: MO
Interpretation: IE (0)

Celtic and Germanic uniquely share a formation **tog-eie-* of the PIE root **(s)teg-*, cf. Lat. *tegere* 'to cover'. This may be a causative-iterative formation inherited from PIE. Assuming independent creations seems less likely in view of the isolation of the verbal root in C and G.

CROOKED

PC: **krumbo-* (MIr. *cromm*, W *crwm*, B *kromm*, Co. *crom* 'bent, curved, crooked')
PG: **krum(b/p)a-* (OE *crump*, OS *krumb*, OHG *krumpf* 'bent, crooked')
REF: EDPC 227, EDPG 307
Isogloss typology: MO
Interpretation: GCL (III-IV)

The Celtic words are probably borrowed from Germanic and not vice versa, because the Germanic adjective may belong in a cluster with PG **krimpan-* 'to shrink'. Formally, the borrowing may have been post-PG, but the widespread distribution within Celtic makes prehistoric borrowing likely.

CUT

PC: **snad-o-* (OIr. *snaidid* 'cuts, chips, hews, carves', W *naddu* 'to chip, cut')
PG: **snadwō-* (OHG *snatta* 'weal, scar')
REF: L262, IEW 972-973, KPV 594-5, EDPC 348, H62
Isogloss typology: RT
Interpretation: IE? (0), L (I)

A CG *snad^h- may be reconstructed. The G suffix *-wō- looks archaic, making late borrowing into Germanic unlikely, as does the difference in usage as a verb and noun in C and G, respectively.

DARE

PC: *n(e/a)nti- (OIr. *néit* 'battle')
PG: *ninþan- (OHG *gi-nindan* 'to dare'), *nanþjan- (Go. *ana-nanþjan* 'to dare, take courage', ON *nenna* 'to be willing', OE *nēðan* 'to have courage, dare')
REF: L248, EPDC 283, H40, EDPG 383, 391
Isogloss typology: RT/MO
Interpretation: IE? (0)

A CG root *nent- may be adduced. The root connection with ToA *nati* 'might, strength', ToB *nete* 'power' is uncertain and hinges on the CG root being reduplicated *ne-nt. Even then, a morphological Celto-Germanicism remains.

DEBT

PC: *dlig-o- (OIr. *dligid* 'is entitled to, is owed', W *dylyaf* 'to be obliged, owe, ought', B *dleout* 'should')
PG: *dulga- (Go. *dulgs* 'debt')
REF: L245, Kr136, KPV 281-3, EDPC 101, Pronk-Tiethoff 2012, 142, EDPG 108
Isogloss typology: RT
Interpretation: IE? (0), L (I)

A CG root *d^hlg^h- may be reconstructed, whose root structure conforms to Indo-European root constraints. Despite its lexical isolation, it must be old in view of the regularity of vocalization of the resonant in both branches. Outside of Germanic and Celtic, the word is found in Slavic, cf. OCS *dlъgъ*, Ru. *dolg*, SCr. *dûg* 'debt'. However, the Slavic word appears to have been borrowed from Germanic in view of dial. Bulgarian *dălg, dlăg* 'debt', which must go back to a borrowed PSl. *dъlgъ with a back yer (an inherited front yer would be expected to yield an occasional palatal reflex in South Slavic, as it does in PSl. *dьlgъ 'long' > Bulgarian *dlek, dlik* beside *dălg, dlăg*). The Slavic accent paradigm, C instead of expected A, may be due to adoption of the word by Slavic as a mobile *u*-stem. B *dellit* 'to merit' adduced by Lane is unrelated.

DISTANT COUSIN

PC: *kom-neɸot- (MW *keifn*, W *caifn* 'third or distant cousin', MB *quifniant* 'distant cousin'), *kom-neɸtī- (W *cyfnither*, MB *queniteru* 'first cousin (female)')
PG: *ga-nefan- (OE *ge-nefa* 'nephew; son of a cousin')
Isogloss typology: MO
Interpretation: IE (0), L (I)

A CG compound *kom-nepot- may be reconstructed. However, since the prefix *kom- may have been productive in kinship terms, cf. Lat. *con-sobrīnus* 'mother's sister's son, cousin' < *kom-suesr-iHno-, independent formation in Celtic and Germanic cannot be excluded.

ENCLOSURE

PC: *dūno- (OIr. *dún*, *W din*, OB *din*, Co. *dyn* 'fort')
PG: *tūna- (ON *tún* 'enclosure, home field, town', OE *tūn* 'yard; town', OFri. *tūn* 'fence, enclosure', MLG *tūn* 'fence')
REF: L247, Kr124, 140, IEW 261-267, Pl283, EDPC 108, H51, EDPG 526, Ko12
Isogloss typology: MO
Interpretation: CGL (II)

The C is from PIE *d^huH-no(s)-, which is perhaps related to Lat. *fūnus, -eris* 'burial' < ?'mound'. It was probably borrowed from Celtic into Germanic before the G consonant shifts. G probably preserves the original semantics, which means the meaning 'fort' must have arisen late within Celtic.

FAT

PC: *tegu- (MIr. *tiug* 'thick, dense, solid', W *tew*, B *tev* 'fat')
PG: *þeku- (ON *þykkr*, OE *þicce*, OHG *dicki* 'fat, thick')
REF: L263, IEW 1013-1014, EDPC 377, EDPG 537
Isogloss typology: MO
Interpretation: IE? (0)

A shared and possibly archaic formation *tegu- may be posited, a formally and semantically perfect isogloss consisting of a *u*-stem adjective exclusively found in Celtic and Germanic. It has been suggested that the meaning 'dense, thick' developed from 'to cover' in view of the potential formal link with *teg- 'to cover'. However, in view of semantic parallels such as G *dicht machen* 'to seal, close', the meaning 'dense, tight' may be archaic.

FATHOM

PC: *ɸatamV- (W *edef*, pl. *adafedd* 'thread, yarn', and with secondary palatalization, ScG *aitheamh* 'fathom')
PG: *faþma- (ON *faðmr*, OE *fæðm*, OHG *fadam, fadum* 'fathom', OS *fathmos* 'two stretched arms')
REF: L248, IEW 824-825, Bjorvand & Lindeman 2000, 248-249, H84, EDPG 132
Isogloss typology: MO
Interpretation: IE (0)

The Welsh paradigm of *edef*, pl. *adafedd* points to PC *ɸatamī, pl. *ɸatamiịās, although some remodeling of the *i*-affection in the singular must be proposed; the expected MW form is **edeif. ScG *aitheamh* points to PC *ɸatimā if taken at face value, but it is possible that that the palatalization is secondary. Hence a common PC form *ɸatamV- may be reconstructed. This may be compared to PG *faþma- < *poth_2-mV-, to PIE *peth_2- 'to spread (the arms)'. For the meaning 'thread' in W, cf. G *Faden*.

FEAR

PC: *āg-ī- (OIr. *-ágadar* 'fears')
PG: *agan-, 3sg. pret.-pres.*ōge (Go. *ogan* 'to fear')
REF: L257, KPV 206-10, LIV² 257, EDPC 26, EDPG 3
Isogloss typology: MO
Interpretation: IE (0)

Both branches continue a reduplicated perfect form of *$h_2$eg^h- with the shared meaning 'fear' as opposed to e.g., Gr. ἄχνυμαι 'I am sad'. It is uncertain whether the shared reduplication is significant: reduplication is the expected form of perfects in PIE, so this may well be archaic. The assumption of an archaism is further supported by the Germanic verb being a preterite-present, an otherwise moribund category.

FIERCE

PC: *abro- (MIr. abar-, amar-, W afr- 'very')
PG: *abra- (Go. abrs 'great, severe', ON afar- 'very, exceedingly')
REF: L258, IEW 2, EDPG 1
Isogloss typology: LX
Interpretation: IE? (0), CGL (I/III), GCL (I-III)

A CG *ab^{h}ro- or *apró- may be reconstructed, perhaps from PIE *$h_2$ep-ró- (cf. Skt. ápara- 'posterior, later; extreme, strange' < *$h_2$ep-ero-). This could be an early shared innovation or borrowing at any stage. The word is attested as a free lexeme only in Germanic, which could mean it may have spread from here. The connection, as suggested by Lane, between the Germanic and Ir. óbar, úabar 'vanity', W ofer 'worthless, vain', B euver 'bland' < PC *aubero- is formally impossible.

FIGHT

PC: *uik-o- (OIr. fichid, W amwyn 'to fight, contend, seize')
PG: *wihan- (Go. waihan*, weihan, ON vega, OE wīgan, OHG wīgan 'to fight, do battle')
REF: L247, Kr136, IEW 1128, KPV 683-8, LIV² 670, EDPC 421, H35, EDPG 586, Ko10
Isogloss typology: MO
Interpretation: IE (0)

Celtic and Germanic uniquely share a zero-grade thematic present of the PIE stem *ueik-. This so-called tudáti-verbal type is moribund in Germanic, so the CG formation is likely to be archaic. The meaning 'to fight' is Celto-Germanic, but Lat. vincō 'win, conquer' appears close enough to dismiss a semantic isogloss, especially in light of W amwyn, which may mean 'to seize' as well as 'to fight'.

FLOOR

PC: *ϕlāro- (OIr. lár 'ground, surface, middle', MW llawr, B leur 'floor, ground')
PG: *flōra- (ON flórr 'floor of a cowshed', OE flōr 'floor', OHG fluor 'field')
REF: L250, Kr140, IEW 805-807, Pr119, EDPC 132, H82, EDPG 148, Ko12
Isogloss typology: MO/SM
Interpretation: IE (0), L (I)

Celtic and Germanic uniquely expand the PIE root *pleh$_2$- 'flat; to spread' with *-ro- to create the meaning 'floor'.

FORK

PC: *gablo/ā- (OIr. gabul 'fork; forked beam, rafter; thighs', W gafl 'fork; lap, groin', B gaol 'fork, bifurcation; crotch')
PG: *gablō- (OHG gabala, OE geafol 'fork')
REF: L249, IEW 409, Lubotsky 1988, 142, EDPC 147, H81
Isogloss typology: MO
Interpretation: CGL (I, III), GCL (III)

On the one hand, PC *gablo/ā- can technically be derived from the European root *g^{h}ab^h- or *g^{h}Hb^h- 'to grasp' with an l-suffix, which would imply that it was native in that branch and borrowed by G. This root is comparatively well attested in Celtic in e.g., PC *gab-i- 'to grasp, take hold of'. On the other hand, it is not certain that PG *gabla- 'fork' can be separated from ON gafl 'gable, gable-end' < *gabla- and the closely related Go. gibla 'gable, pinnacle' (etc.) < *geblō-, which derive from PIE *ǵ$^{(\prime)h}$eb^{h}h$_2$-l-, cf. ToA śpāl 'head', Gr. κεφαλή 'head, top'. The original meaning could, for instance, have been 'pitched beam'. This would rather suggest that the borrowing occurred in the opposite direction (after G *o > a).

FREE

PC: *ϕriio- (W rhydd, OCo. rid 'free')
PG: *frī̆(j)a- (Go. freis, OE frēo, OHG frī 'free')
REF: L246, Kr136, Pr119, Pl282, Schm143, Schu177, EDPC 141, H30, EDPG 155, Ko12
Isogloss typology: SM
Interpretation: IE(?), CGL (I)

CG semantic shift to 'free' from PIE *priH-o- 'dear'; the original meaning is found in Skt priyá- 'dear'. Since G preserves the original meaning in the cluster of *frī̆(j)ōn- 'to love', *frī̆(j)ōnd- 'friend' (see FRIEND), while the word is isolated in Celtic, it seems more likely that the semantic shift took place in C than in G. This could point to an early borrowing from C to G at a stage when C had not yet lost the initial labial (Stratum I or early II).

FRUIT

PC: *agronā (W aeron 'berries')
PG: *akrana- (Go. akran 'fruit', ON akarn, OE æcern, MHG ackeran 'acorn')
REF: EDPC 27, EDPG 18
Isogloss typology: MO
Interpretation: IE? (0), L (I-II)

The shared formation *agrono/eh$_2$- seems to consist of an unknown element *agr- (PIE *h_2eǵ-ro- 'field; wild'?) and a suffix *-on-. This suffix appears to have enjoyed some productivity in G berry and tree fruit names, cf. ON aldin 'acorn' < *aldana-. In C we may see an originally neuter plural of the same suffix (*-on-eh$_2$-) in collective use, cf. Go. ahana 'chaff', Lat. agna f. 'ear of grain, straw' < *h_2eḱ-on-eh$_2$-. Lith. úoga, Russ. jágoda 'strawberry' may have a root connection to these words, but represent dissimilar formations. The formation is further reminiscent of PC *agrīnio- (OIr. áirne, W eirin, B irin 'sloe(s)').

HARBOR

PC: *kauno- (MIr. cúan 'harbor, bay')
PG: *hafnō- (ON hǫfn, OE hæfen, MLG havene 'harbor, bay')
REF: L254, Pr120, EDPC 197, H36, EDPG 196, 240, Ko8, Stifter (this volume)
Isogloss typology: MO/LX
Interpretation: IE? (0), L (I)

A CG formation *k(a/o)p-no/eh$_2$- may be reconstructed. This may be a shared derivational innovation, provided that the connection with PIE *keh$_2$p- 'to take' is accepted, but the semantic link is unclear. Within G it is possible to connect ON haf, OE hæf, OFri. hef 'sea, lake' < *kh$_2$p-o-, MHG habe 'harbor, haven, sea', Swi. G. Hab 'harbor' < *kh$_2$p-éh$_2$- and ON hóp 'small bay' < *ke/oh$_2$p-nó-), which makes it appear native at least within this branch.

HAYSTACK 1

PC: **krouko*- (?Lus. top. *crougo-/crouco-*, MIr. *crúach* 'stack (of corn), rick, heap, hill', W *crug* 'hillock, cairn, heap', B *krug* 'haystack', OCo. *cruc* gl. *collis*)
PG: **hrauka*- (ON *hrauk*, OE *hrēac* 'stack, haycock, rick')
REF: L260, IEW 938, EDPC 226, Kroonen 2011, 268-270, EDPG 243
Isogloss typology: MO
Interpretation: GCL (III)

The various ablaut grades and Verner and Kluge variants in PG **hrūha*- (ON *hró* 'hillock'), **hrūgōn*- (ON *hrúga* 'pile'), **hrukan*- (ON *hroki* 'pile'), and **hrukka*- (MDu. *rock* 'haystack') show that the word has some pedigree in this branch. It therefore appears borrowed into C with [xr] adopted as C **kr*-, but there is only a narrow time window during which borrowing of **hrauka*- could have resulted in PC **krouko*-, i.e., after the sound shifts (including the simplification of geminates in overlong syllables), but before the change **o* > **a*. A further connection with Lat. *crux* 'tree, frame, cross' is semantically unconvincing.

HAYSTACK 2

PC: **dassi*- (OIr. *daiss*, W *das* 'heap, stack')
PG: **tassa*- (MDu. *tas*, *tasse*, MLG *tas* 'haystack')
REF: Falileyev 2000, 40, Kroonen 2011, 227-228
Isogloss typology: MO/SM
Interpretation: CGL (II)

A CG **dassV*- may be posited. It is possible to derive both from a PIE root **deH*-, cf. Skt. *dā́ti* 'mows, cuts off (plants)'. It is possible that PC **dassi*- continues **dh₂-sti*-, and that G borrowed this word after C *-*st*- > *-*ss*-. ON *des* 'haystack' is probably a borrowing from Old Irish.

HEDGE

PC: **kagio*- (W *cae*, B *kae*, Co. *ke*, Gaul. (Endlicher) *caio* 'hedge, fence')
PG: **hagja*- (ON *heggr* 'bird cherry'), **hagjō*- (OE *hecg*, OHG *heckia*, *heggia* 'hedge, fence')
REF: L249, IEW 518, EDLI 99, 123, EDPC 184, H33, EDPG 198
Isogloss typology: LX/MO
Interpretation: L (I), GCL (II)

A Celto-Germanic shared formation **kag^h-io/eh$_2$*- with a Celto-Germanic meaning 'hedge' may be inferred, which may be related to the verbal root **kag^h*- as found in W *cael* 'to get', Oscan *kahad* 'takes'.[11] In G this base is derivationally more deeply rooted than in C, cf. PG **haga(n)*- 'enclosure; hedge' (ON *hagi*, OE *haga*, OS *hago*, OHG *hag*), but borrowing from G into C is phonologically problematic. Lat. *caulae* 'railing or lattice barrier', if from **kag^h-ela* (with diminutive suffix?), is compatible with the latter variant, but the connection is formally less straightforward than the one with C. A further possible connection is Alb. *thanë* 'cornel; winter stall for sheep' < **ḱa/o(C)-neh$_2$*-, which is formally and semantically close to PG **hag(V)na*- 'briar, fencing'. If correct, it would give the CG formation a non-exclusively CG derivational base, but the root-final consonant of the Albanian form is obscured by the contiguous nasal.

[11] In Celtic the root has been connected to W *caer* 'fortress', B *kêr* 'town', but these words may be borrowings from Lat. *castrum* 'fort' (SBCHP 447-8).

HE-GOAT

PC: **bukko*- (OIr. *boc*, W *bwch*, B *bouc'h*, OCo. *boch* 'he-goat')
PG: **bukka(n)*- (ON *bokkr*, *bukkr*, OE *bucca*, OHG *bock* 'he-goat')
REF: L264, Schu174–175, EPDC 83, EDPG 82
Isogloss typology: MO
Interpretation: GCL (III)

The Germanic is inflected as an *n*-stem and may go back to PIE **b^{h}uǵ-ōn*, gen. **b^{h}uǵ-n-ós*, cf. YAv. *būza*- 'he-goat' < **b^{h}uǵ-o*-. The Celtic must have been borrowed from Germanic after the operation of Kluge's law.

HILLTOP

PC: **dūno*- (OIr. *dún*, *W din*, OB *din*, Co. *dyn* 'fort')
PG: **dūna*- (OE *dūn* 'hill', E *down* 'rolling hill, dune', Du. *duin* 'dune')
REF: IEW 261-267
Isogloss typology: MO
Interpretation: CGL (III-IV)

A shared **d^{h}uH-no*- may be adduced. IEW connects this formation with a root **d^{h}ueh$_2$*- 'to blow', but OIr. *doé* 'wall, mound' < **d^{h}uH-io*- provides a better intra-Celtic etymology. In view of ON *dúnn* 'feather down' being the native G outcome of a PIE **d^{h}uh$_2$-no*-, it is likely that (W)G **dūna*- was borrowed from Celtic in Stratum III or IV. Stratum I borrowing is formally possible, but fails to account for its restriction to West Germanic. For an earlier borrowing, see PC **dūno*- ~ PG **tūna*- 'enclosure'.

HOLLY

PC: **kolinno*- (Ir. *cuilenn*, W *celyn*, MB *quelennenn* (sglt.) 'holly')
PG: **hulisa*- (MDu. *huls*, OHG *hulis*, *huls* 'holly')
REF: EDPC 213, H19, EDPG 253
Isogloss typology: MO
Interpretation: 3L (I)

H proposes that PC and PG share a PIE root **kel*-, which shifted in meaning from 'sharp, prickly' to 'holly'. EDPG suggests a substrate origin, which is supported by words found in the Mediterranean: Basque *gorosti*, Sard. *golosti*, *colostri*, Gr. κήλαστρος, Arm. *kostłi*. The geminate in PC *-*nn*- may be from *-*sn*- (the geminate *-*nn*- is confirmed by Middle Breton). In that case, the Celtic and Germanic forms uniquely share the element *-*is*- as opposed to -*Vst(r)*- in the South European languages.

HORSE 1

PC: **marko*- (MIr. *marc*, W *march*, B *marc'h*, OCo. *march*, Gaul. *markan* (acc. sg.) 'horse')
PG: **marha*- (ON *marr*, OE *mearh*, OFri. *mar*, OHG *marh*, *marah* 'horse, stallion')

REF: L253, Kr140, IEW 700, Pl284, EDPC 257, H74, EDPG 354, Ko8
Isogloss typology: LX
Interpretation: L (I-II)

A word **marko-* may be reconstructed. It is uniquely shared between Celtic and Germanic within IE.

HOSTAGE

PC: **geisslo-* (OIr. *giall* 'hostage', W *gwystl*, B *gouestl* 'surety, hostage, pledge')
PG: **gīsla-* (ON *gisl*, OE *gīsel*, OFri. *jēsel-*, OS *gīsal*)
REF: L248, IEW 426-427, Pl283, Schm140, EDPC 159, H50, EDPG 179, Ko13
Isogloss typology: MO
Interpretation: CGL (I, III)

A CG **g^{h}eisslo-* may be reconstructed, perhaps from PIE **ǵ^{h}eid^h-tlo-*, from PIE **ǵ^{h}eid^h-* 'to desire'. Celtic also has the word in the zero grade: OIr. *gell*, *gill* 'pledge' (< PC **gisslo-*), meaning the word is likely to be Celtic in origin if borrowed into Germanic.

INHERITANCE

PC: **orbio-* (OIr. *orbae* 'inheritance, legacy')
PG: **arbja-* (Go. *arbi*, OE *ierfe*, OFri. *erve* 'inheritance, patrimony', ON *erfi* 'ritual burial celebration')
REF: L246, Kr136, IEW 781-782, Pr121, Pl283, Schm143, EDHIL 311, EDPC 299, H23, EDPG 33, Ko12
Isogloss typology: MO
Interpretation: IE (I), ML (I), GCL (II)

From the PIE root **h$_3$erb^h-* 'to change allegiance, status', cf. Hitt. *ḫarp-* 'id'. The formation **h$_3$orb^h-io-* is CG. Germanic and Celtic also share a morphologically and semantically identical formation **h$_3$orb^h-o-* in OIr. *orb* 'heir; patrimony' < PC **orbo* and ON **arfr* < PG **arba-* 'inheritance, patrimony'. The meaning 'inheritance, heir' is also Celto-Germanic.

IRON

PC: **ī̆sarno-* (Gaul. PN *Isarnus*, OIr. *ïarn*, W *haearn*, B *houarn* 'iron')
PG: **īsarna-* (Go. *eisarn*, ON *ísarn*, OE *īsern*, *īsen*, *īren* 'iron')
REF: L264, Kr122, Pl284, Lühr 1988, Schm140, EDPC 172, Kroonen 2011, EDPG 271, Ko8
Isogloss typology: LX
Interpretation: CGL (III)

This word entered Germanic after the consonant shifts; borrowing at an earlier time would give PG **īsara-* < pre-PG **īsarra-* < **īsarno-*. It has been suggested that the word was derived from the PIE word for 'blood', cf. Hitt. *ēšḫar*, gen. *išḫanāš*, ToA *ysār*, B *yasar*, Gr. ἔαρ, gen. -ρος < **h$_1$esh$_2$-r/n-*, but this lexeme does not otherwise survive in Celtic, making this etymology speculative. An ancient *Wanderwort* with unknown origins is likely in view of the semantics.

JESTER

PC: **drūto-* (OIr. *drúth* 'jester, buffoon, vagrant; courtesan, harlot), **drūto-* (OIr. *drúth* (adj.) 'wanton, unchaste')
PG: **trūþa-* (ON *trúðr* 'juggler', OE *trúð* 'trumpet player, actor, buffoon')
REF: L261, EDPG 523, 524, Ko13
Isogloss typology: MO
Interpretation: CGL (II)

A borrowing from PC **drūto-* < PIE **d^{h}ruHto-* (see Dear among the rejected CGs) to Germanic following the Celtic merger of voiced stops and voiced aspirates but preceding the Germanic consonant shifts.

KING

PC: **rīg-* (OIr. *rí*, W *rhi* 'king', Gaul. PN *Catu-rix*, Celtib. PN *Teiuo-reikis*)
PG: **rīk-* (Go. *reiks* 'king')
REF: L264, Kr137, Pl283, Schm142, EDPC 310, EDPG 333, Ko11
Isogloss typology: MO
Interpretation: CGL (II)

The Celtic is from PIE **h$_3$rēǵ-s*, so borrowing from Celtic to Germanic postdates PIE **ē* > *ī* in Celtic but predates the Germanic consonant shifts. Proto-Celtic also has **rīgiiom* 'kingship', and Proto-Germanic also has the derivatives **rīk(j)a-* 'rich', and **rīkja-* 'realm', which may have been borrowed along with the base form, or it may have formed independently.

LARK

PC: **alaudā* (Gaul. **alauda-* > Lat. *alauda* 'lark')
PG: **laiwiz-akōn-* (OE *lāwrice*, WFri. *ljurk*, OHG *lērahha* 'lark')
REF: Schrijver 1997, 309-310, EDPG 324
Isogloss typology: LX
Interpretation: 3L (III)

The correspondence between Celtic intervocalic **d* [ð] and Germanic **z* suggests that the word entered Celtic after phonetic lenition of voiced stops and after Verner's law, as Germanic had no **z* before then. A substrate origin is likely because of the alternation between forms with and without the "*a*-prefix."

LAW

PC: **rextu-* (OIr. *recht*, W *cyf-raith*, MB *reiz* 'law, justice')
PG: **rehtu-* (ON *réttr* 'justice, law')
REF: L246, IEW 854-857, Pr122, Schu177, EDPC 310, H86, Ko11–12
Isogloss typology: MO/SM
Interpretation: IE(?) (0), ML (I-III)

CG derivation of PIE **h$_3$reǵ-* 'to straighten, direct' with **-tu-* and semantic shift from 'straight, direct' to 'law, justice'. This semantic shift has a parallel in Lat. *dīrēctus* 'laid straight, upright' to French *droit* 'right, entitlement, law', which may indicate that the semantic shift from 'straight' to 'just' is trivial. Nevertheless, the combination of a shared derivation and a shared semantic development appears to make for a compelling isogloss.

LEAD

PC: **ϕloudio-* (MIr. *lúaide* 'lead')
PG: **lauda-* (OE *lēad*, OFri. *lād*, Du. *lood* 'lead')

REF: L264, Kr140, IEW 837, Fraenkel 1962-1965, 378, Birkhan 1970, 147-152, Pl284, EDLI 339, 474, EDPC 135, EDPG 328
Isogloss typology: LX
Interpretation: CGL (III-IV)

The Celtic word can be etymologically connected with Lat. *plumbum* 'lead', in which case it would be a prehistoric *Wanderwort*, cf. possibly also Proto-Berber **būldūn* 'lead'. Alternatively, derivation from the PIE root **pleu-* 'to flow' is possible, but a formation **plou-d^ho-* hinges on the assumption of an ad hoc suffixation in **d^h*. In either scenario, the Germanic word must have been borrowed from Celtic after Celtic loss of PIE **p*. Within Germanic, the word is exclusively attested in West Germanic, which could point to borrowing in the period between PG and PWG. However, since the word may have been lost in North Germanic and remained unattested in Gothic, it cannot be excluded that the borrowing occurred prior to the Proto-Germanic split, in which case it would be attractive to assume adoption before to the PG change **o* > **a*.

LEATHER

PC: **ϕle/itro-* (OIr. *lethar*, W *lledr*, MB *lezr* 'leather')
PG: **le/iþra-* (ON *leðr*, OE *leðer*, OHG *ledar* 'leather')
REF: L264, Kr140, Schm145, EDPC 134, EDPG 332
Isogloss typology: MO
Interpretation: CGL (II)

The Celtic appears to be a derivative of PIE **pel-* 'to skin' with the abstract or instrumental *tro*-suffix. The word is likely to have been loaned into Germanic after Celtic loss of *p, but before the Germanic sound shifts. The *e*-vocalism of the Celtic reflexes may be accounted for by assuming a zero-grade neuter PIE **pl-tro-* > PC **ϕlitrom;* evidence for an original neuter comes from the fact that the word is overwhelmingly neuter in Germanic. In British Celtic the lowering occurring in the collective **ϕlitrā* must then have been generalized to the singular.

LEECH

PC: **leCVgi-* (OIr. *líaig*, gen. *lego*, *lega* 'leech, doctor, physician')
PG: **lēkja-* (Go. *lekeis*, ON *lækir*, OE *lǣce* 'doctor', ODu. *lake*, OHG *lāhhi*, *lāchi* 'leech')
REF: L264, Pl283, EDPG 321
Isogloss typology: LX
Interpretation: CGL (II)

A Pre-Grimm borrowing from Celtic to Germanic. The Old Irish was disyllabic, meaning a now-lost consonant must be reconstructed, which was likely **ϕ* or **i̯*. For PG, a form **le.egi-* would be optimal.

LEFT

PC: **kl(e)io-* (OIr. *clé* 'left (side); malign', W *cledd*, B *kleiz*, Co. *cledh* 'left (hand)')
PG: **hlī̆(j)a-* (Go. *hleiduma* comp. 'left')
REF: L260, IEW 600-602, EDPC 207
Isogloss typology: MO/SM
Interpretation: IE(?) (0)

The PIE root **ḱlei-* 'to lean, be slanted' only has the meaning 'left (side, hand)' in Celtic and Germanic. The comparative suffix **-duman-* (< PIE *-tmHo-*) is infrequent in Germanic, which suggests that both the formation and its meaning are old.

LOUSE

PC: **lu(u/s)ā* (W *llau*, B *laou*, Co. *low* 'lice')
PG: **lūs-* (OE *lūs*, ON *lús*, OHG, MDu. *lūs* 'louse')
REF: L253, IEW 692, EDPC 250
Isogloss typology: SM
Interpretation: IE(?)

Celtic and Germanic are compatible with a shared root **luH(s)-* 'louse'. The connection with ToA *lu*, pl. *lwā*, B *luwo*, pl. *lwāsa* 'animal' is not semantically evident, but if correct, Celtic and Germanic would still share a semantic innovation 'animal > louse'. This innovation may have occurred already in late Proto-Indo-European, however, i.e., after the departure of the Tocharian branch.

MALICIOUS

PC: **elko-* (OIr. *elc* 'mischievous, bad')
PG: **elhja-* (ON *illr* 'ill, evil, bad, mean' (>> Finnish *elkiä* 'mean, malicious'))
REF: L262, IEW 307, EDPG 117
Isogloss typology: LX/SM
Interpretation: IE (0), ML (I-II)

Both forms may continue a possibly archaic CG root **(h₁)elk-* 'bad'. A relation with **h₁e/olk-* 'to be hungry', cf. OHG *ilki* gl. *fames vel stridor dentium*, Lith. *álkti*, Latv. *al̃kt* 'to be hungry' is semantically tenuous. Even if accepted, it would still leave a semantic isogloss between Celtic and Germanic.

MANE

PC: **mong-o-/ā* (OIr. *mong*, W *mwng*, OB. *mogou* 'mane, hair', MB. *moe*)
PG: **mankan-* (ON *makki*, Elfd. *maunke*, Da. *manke* 'mane')
REF: L257, IEW 747-748, EDPC 275, H77, EDPG 353
Isogloss typology: LX/MO
Interpretation: IE (0), (M)L (I-II)

A CG **mong-* may be reconstructed. This is typically treated as a derivative of PIE **mon-* 'neck' with a velar suffix **g*. However, such a suffix is not otherwise attested, leaving the ultimate origin of the word uncertain.

MEDICINE

PC: **lub-ī* (OIr. *luib* 'wort, plant; healing herb, remedy', W *llu-arth*, MB *lu-orz*, MCo. *low-arth* 'garden')
PG: **lubja-* (Go. *lubja-leisei* 'witchcraft', ON *lyf* 'medicine, healing herb', OE *lyb* 'medicine, drug, potion')
REF: L250, Kr140–141, Pl283, EDPC 246, H21, EDPG 341
Isogloss typology: MO/SM
Interpretation: IE? (0), CGL (I, III), GCL (I-II)

A CG **(H)lub^h-i-* can be reconstructed with the meaning 'herb, medicine'. Further connection with Ru. *lub* 'bark', Go. *lauf(s)* 'foliage' < **(H)loub^h-o-* and Lat. *liber* 'bark; book' < **(H)lub^h-ro-* is formally possible.

NUMBER

PC: **rīmā* (OIr. *rím*, W *rhif* 'number')
PG: **rīma-* (ON *rím* 'number', ON *rím* 'computation', OHG *rīm* 'account, series, number')
REF: L258, EDPC 313, H13, EDPG 413, Ko8
Isogloss typology: MO
Interpretation: IE (0), ML (I-III)

A CG formation **h₂riH-m(o-/eh₂)* may be reconstructed, from **h₂reiH-* 'to fit, fix', cf. with a different suffix Gr. ἀριθμός 'number, payment'. However, it cannot be excluded that this isogloss arose as a result of mutual borrowing, in which case the formation would have to be native to only one branch.

OATH

PC: **oito-* (OIr. *óeth* 'oath', W *an-udon* 'perjury')
PG: **aiþa-* (Go. *aiþs*, OE *āð*, ON *eiðr*, OHG *eid* 'oath')
REF: L246, Pl283, Schm143, Schu176–177, EDPC 305, H2, EDPG 15
Isogloss typology: SM
Interpretation: IE(?) (0), CGL (I-II)

A CG **oito-* 'oath' may be reconstructed. This formation has previously been derived from the PIE root **h₁ei-* 'to go' (cf. Sw. *ed-gång*). This is just one possibility, but if correct, Gr. οἶτος 'fate, destiny' (< "course"?) would be morphologically parallel, making the development to 'oath' a semantic isogloss. On the other hand, given the preservation of a more primary meaning in the PG parallel formation **aiþ/da-* 'isthmus' (cf. ON *eið*), it could perhaps be argued that this semantic shift is more likely to have occurred in Celtic. This would be an argument for postulating a CGL.

OATS

PC: **korkio-* (OIr. *corcae*, MIr. *corca*, *coirce*, W *ceirch*, B *kerc'h* 'oats', OCo. *bara keirch* gl. *panis avena*)
PG: **hagran-* (OSw. *hagri*, Nw. dial. *hagre* 'oats'), **hagrja-* (Da. *hejre* 'brome grass')
REF: L252, EDPC 216, EDPG 199
Isogloss typology: LX
Interpretation: 3L (I-II)

A CG **kork-* or **kokr-* may be reconstructed. To explain the variants, a form **korkrio-* has been posited, but the alternation between **kr* and **rk* may also indicate adoption from a third language. If connected, the similar-looking but formally irreconcilable Fi. *kattara* 'brome' may be a parallel substrate borrowing.

PHANTOM

PC: **skāxslo-* (OIr. *scál* 'phantom, giant, hero', MW *yscawl* 'young hero, warrior')
PG: **skōhsla-* (Go. *skohsl* 'evil spirit, demon')
REF: EDPC 340, H17, Ko14
Isogloss typology: MO
Interpretation: ML (I-III)

A CG formation **skōkslo-* may be adduced, which may be a derivation of the PIE root **skek-* 'jump' with an instrument noun suffix. The original meaning may have been "startler" or "vanisher," for which cf. OIr. *scuichid*, perf. *scáich* 'to move, vanish', W *ysgogi* 'to move, tremble'. The peculiar ablaut grade and suffix **-slo-* (for usual **-tlo-*) finds a parallel in OIr. *tál* 'adze' from PIE **teḱ-* 'to build'.

PINE

PC: **gisusto-* (OIr. *giús*, ScG *giuthas*, MoIr. *giumhas*, *giúis* 'fir tree, pine')
PG: **kizna-* (OE *cēn* 'pine tree, spruce', MLG *kēn* 'pine cone, pinewood', OHG *kien* 'pine tree, pinewood torch')
REF: EDPG 289
Isogloss typology: LX
Interpretation: 3L (I-II)

A CG **gis-* may be reconstructed. The Germanic may be segmented as pre-PG **gis-nó-*, where the second element may perhaps be the **-no-* suffix often found in plants and trees (cf. PC **kolis-no-* 'holly'). The Goidelic vocalism appears identical to OIr. *sïur*, MoIr. *siúr*, ScG *piuthar* 'sister' < PC **suesūr*, suggesting a lost medial **s* or **p*, but the lost medial consonant cannot be established with certainty. The inferred *st*-suffix is obscure, but also found in other non-Indo-European dendronyms, cf. Basque *gorosti* 'holly' vs. the aforementioned **kolis-no-* and PC **kʷresti-* ~ PG **h(w)ursti* 'copse' vs. PS **kʷres-no-* 'tree'.

QUARREL

PC: **bāg-ī-* (OIr. *bág* 'boast, threat, fight', *báigid* 'boasts'), **bāgio-* (MW *bei* 'fault, transgression')
PG: **bēg-* (OHG *bāgan* (pret. *biag*) 'to quarrel', ON *bágr* 'contest, resistance', *bægjast* 'to quarrel, strive')
REF: L246, Van Windekens 1941, 85, EDHIL 618, Bomhard 2014, H45
Isogloss typology: RT/LX
Interpretation: IE? (0), ML (III-IV)

There are three plausible explanations for this lexical correspondence: (1) An IE archaism with ablaut **bʰeh₁gʰ-* / **bʰoh₁gʰ-*, (2) a loanword from early Germanic **bēg-* with Germanic /ē/ = [æ:] being borrowed as Celtic /ā/, (3) a Celtic loanword into (North-West) Germanic with Celt. /ā/ being borrowed as the lowered continuant of Germ. /ē/, North-West Germanic [a:]. None of the involved vocalic loan substitutions have any parallels, however, which could favor inheritance of a root in both branches. Cognacy with Hitt. *paknu-ᶻⁱ* 'to defame, slander' (< **bʰh₁ǵʰ-neu-*?) or ToB *pakwāre* 'evil, bad' (< **bʰoh₁ǵʰ-uōro-*?) is possible but less certain and the often-adduced Latv. *buôžus* (*buôzties*) 'to become angry' could perhaps ultimately go back to Low German *bōs* 'angry'.

RIDE

PC: **reid-* (Gaul. *rēda* 'wagon', OIr. *réidid* 'rides', W *rhwydd* 'easy, quick')
PG: **rīdan-* (ON *ríða*, OE *rīdan*, OFri. *rīdan*, OS *rīdan* 'ride, drive')
REF: L255, Kr140, Pr120, LIV² 502, EDPC 307, H68, EDPG 412, Ko9
Isogloss typology: SM
Interpretation: IE(?), GCL (I-II)

Germanic and Celtic reflexes of **(H)reid^h-* share the meaning 'to ride', which may have developed from a more original meaning 'to move unsteadily', cf. Lith. *riedė́ti* (*riedù*) 'to roll', with the original range of meanings preserved in ON *ríða* 'to ride; to reel, stagger; to rise', OE *rīdan* 'to ride; to move, rock'. Since the verb is less polysemous in Celtic, it seems unlikely that Germanic borrowed the verb from that language at any point in time, but the reverse borrowing is more difficult to reject.

RIDGE

PC: **roino-* (OIr. *róen* 'way, path', OB *runt*, B *run* 'mound, plateau', MCo. *runyow* 'hills')
PG: **raina-* (ON *rein* 'strip of land', MHG *rein* 'border wall, edge of a field')
REF: L253, Kr140, IEW 857-859, EDPC 316, H87, EDPG 403
Isogloss typology: LX
Interpretation: IE? (0), L (I-III)

A CG **roino-* may be reconstructed. The original meaning may have been '(walkable) ridge at edge of field', which then developed into 'path', 'mound', 'strip of land, boundary'. A root connection to PIE **(H)rei-* 'to scratch, cut' suggested by IEW is speculative.

ROW

PC: **rā-* (OIr. *ráïd* 'rows')
PG: **rōan-* (ON *róa*, OE *rōwan* 'to row')
REF: L254, IEW 338, KPV 529-30, LIV^2 251, EDPC 306, EDPG 414, Ko7
Isogloss typology: MO (0)
Interpretation: IE (0)

Celtic and Germanic uniquely continue an *o*-grade formation to the PIE root *$h_1$reh$_1$-* 'to row', cf. e.g. Lith. *ìrti*, Latv. *ir̃t* < *$h_1$rh$_1$-*. According to LIV^2, these are independent innovations based on a reduplicated perfect *$h_1$re-$h_1$roh$_1$-* (cf. OIr. *rer(a)is*, ON *rera*), but it is alternatively possible to reconstruct a primary *o*-grade iterative verb (type **molh$_1$-* 'to grind') for Proto-Indo-European. That would make it either an archaism or an early, shared innovation.

RUSHES

PC: **sem-* (OIr. *sim(a)* 'stalk, stem', *simin(n)*, *seimen(n/d)* 'rushes, reed'), **seb-* (*sibin(n)*, *sifin(n)* 'rushes, reed')
PG: **sem-* (OS *semith*, OHG *semida* 'rushes, reed', G *Simse* '(bul)rush'), **seb-* (ON *sef*, MHG *sebede* 'rushes, reed')
REF: EDPG 432, Stifter 2015, 101
Isogloss typology: LX
Interpretation: 3L (I-III)

A CG **sem-*, **seb^h-* may be reconstructed. The reconstruction of both the Celtic and the Germanic forms are problematic in that both branches have an irregular alternation between root-final *m* and *b* and in both branches this root is sometimes but not always suffixed with a poorly understood suffix. The OIr. *-in(n)* suffix may be analyzed as a diminutive suffix, but if the suffix was originally *-ind*, it may be compared to the suffix in G *Simse* < PG **semĭ̄t-* (OS *semith*, OHG *semida* seem to contain the **-eþ-* suffix denoting groups of trees and plants). The vacillation between *b* and *m* found in both branches as well as the poorly understood suffixes could point to a shared substrate origin (for an additional potential link, cf. Hitt. *šumanza-* '(bul)rush' < **sm-nt-io-*). Stifter proposes an internal Irish account for the variation between *b* and *m*.

SAIL

PC: **siglo-* (OIr. *séol*, W *hwyl* 'sail, covering')
PG: **sigla-* (ON *segl*, OE *segel*, OS *segal*, OHG *segal*, *segil* 'sail, canvas')
REF: L264, Kr141, Schm143, SBCHP 357, Thier 2011, 187-190, EDPG 430, Ko7
Isogloss typology: LX
Interpretation: IE? (0), ML (I, III), GCL (II)

A C **siglo-* must be reconstructed, as **seglo-* would yield W ***hail*, cf. PC **u-reg-n-* > W *dyrain* 'to rise'. This is mirrored by PG **se/igla-*, leaving only **sig^{h}lo-* as Celto-Germanic isogloss. This reconstruction is incompatible with the traditionally compared PIE root **sek-* 'to cut', which through Verner's law could have resulted in PG **segla-*. As a result, it seems impossible to establish the direction of borrowing on linguistic grounds.

SAVOR

PC: **suek-* (W *chweg*, B *c'hwek* 'sweet'), **suekk-* (W *chwech* (?) 'sweet')
PG: **swekan-* (OS *suecid* gl. *olet*, OHG *swehhan* 'to gush, smell (bad)'), ?**swak(k)u-*, **swak(k)ja-* (OE *swecc*, *swæcc* '(sweet) taste or smell', OS *suec* 'smell'), **swak(k)jan-* (OE *sweccan* 'to smell'), **swēkjōn-* (Icel. *svækja* 'sweltering heat; drizzle; heavy air')
REF: L258, IEW 1043, Seebold 1970, 487, EDPC 364, H88
Isogloss typology: LX
Interpretation: GCL (III)

PG **swek-* perhaps from an earlier obscure element **sueg-*, may be reconstructed. The root looks native in Germanic in view of the strong verbs and its productivity. Within Celtic, a related verb is not found and it is restricted to Brittonic. This points to borrowing from Germanic to Celtic after the consonant shifts, as does the un-Celtic-looking variation between word-final single and geminate consonants. MW *chweith* 'taste, savor' < PC **suex-to/tu-/tā* also seems related to *chweg*. If it is, then a connection between *chweith* and PIE **suek^w-* 'sap, juice' must be abandoned (*contra* EDPC). The Germanic semantics ranging from 'to gush, drizzle' to 'to smell' are paralleled by ON *rjúka* 'to smoke, steam', Du. *ruiken* 'to smell'.

SECRET

PC: **rūnā/o-* (OIr. *rún* 'secret', W *rhin* 'spell, enchantment')
PG: **rūnō-* (Go. *runa* 'secret', OE *rūn*, OS *rūna* 'whisper, secret', ON *rún* 'rune, secret')
REF: L260, Kr139, IEW 867, EDPC 316, H5, Ko13
Isogloss typology: LX
Interpretation: IE? (0), ML (I-III)

A CG formation **rūnā-* (**HruH-neh$_2$-*?) may be reconstructed. Further parallel formations are found in OHG *gi-rūni*, MHG *ge-riuni*, MoG *Geraune* 'whisperings' < **ga-rūn(j)a-* and MIr. *comrún*, *cobrún*, W *cyfrin*, MB *queffrin* '(joint) secret' < *kom-rūno-*. A connection with PIE **h₃reuH-* 'to roar' (cf. Lat. *rūmor*) is semantically weak.

SEEP

PC: **leg-o-* (OIr. *legaid* 'melts, dissolves', W *llaith*, B *leiz* 'damp', W *dadlaith* 'to melt')
PG: **lekan-* (ON *leka*, OHG *lehhan* 'to leak')
REF: L261, KPV 449, IEW 657, LIV² 397, EDPG 331
Isogloss typology: RT
Interpretation: IE? (0), L (I-II)

A possibly archaic CG root **le(ǵ)-* 'to seep' may be reconstructed. A further connection with Arm. *lič* 'lake' seems more speculative because of the formal and semantic differences.

SERVANT

PC: **ambaxto-* (Gaul. *ambaktos*, *ambactus* 'vassal', W *amaeth* 'farmer')
PG: **ambahta-* (Go. *andbahts*, OHG *ambaht* 'servant, representative', ON fem. *ambátt* 'bondwoman')
REF: L263, Kr137, Pl283, Schm142, EDPC 32, EDPG 24, Ko13
Isogloss typology: MO
Interpretation: CGL (III)

The Celtic is from PC **ambi-* + **ax-to-* 'one sent around', so the direction of borrowing was from Celtic to Germanic.

SHOOT

PC: **slattā* (MIr. *slat* 'stalk, stem, branch', W *llath* 'rod, staff', B *lazh* 'pole, rod')
PG: **laþ(þ)a/ōn-*, **latta(n)-* (OE *lætt*, ME *laþþe*, MoE *lath*, *lat*, MDu. *latte* 'lath', OHG *lad(d)a/o*, *lat(t)a/o* 'lath, shoot')
REF: Kroonen 2011, 214, EDPC 345
Isogloss typology: LX
Interpretation: ML/3L (I-II)

A CG **(s)lat(t)-* may be reconstructed. The forms do not match up precisely, as there is no trace of initial **s-* in Germanic. The Germanic appears to go back to an original *n*-stem, i.e. nom. **laþō*, gen. **lattaz* < pre-PG **lat-ōn*, **lat-n-os*, which can explain the geminated forms by Kluge's law. A borrowing from Germanic to Celtic would explain the Celtic geminate. However, the initial *s-* in Irish complicates this scenario.

SLAUGHTER

PC: **boduo-* (OIr. *Bodb*, *Badb* 'war-goddess; hooded crow')
PG: **badwa/ō-* (OE *beadu*, ON *bǫð* 'battle, war')
REF: L246, IEW 113, Pl284, H37, Ko10
Isogloss typology: MO/LX
Interpretation: IE? (0), CGL (I, III), GCL (I-III)

Although the OIr. is best attested as a specific theonym, it simply means 'vulture, carrion-crow' in MoIr. The connection with PG **badwō-* is suggestive of a uniquely CG battle deity associated with the slain. This association technically allows for derivation from the root PIE **bʰedʰ-* 'to poke, dig', but the semantics are non-compelling.

SLOPE

PC: **glendos-* (OIr. *glenn*, W *glyn* 'glen, valley', MB *glenn* 'land'), **glandnā* (W *glan*, B *glann*, Co. *glan* 'shore')
PG: **klinta-* (ON *klettr* 'rock, cliff', MLG *klint* 'shore'), **klanta-* (Nw. dial. *klant* 'cliff; peak', Sw. dial. *klant* 'cliff')
REF: EDPC 160
Isogloss typology: LX
Interpretation: 3L (I-II)

CG **glend-* may be reconstructed. According to David Stifter (p.c.) there are two Celtic formations from this 'root', namely **glendos-* (the source of W *glyn*, MB *glenn*) and **glannā* < **glandnā* < **gl̥nd-nā* (W *glan*, Old British *glanna* in place names), of which OIr. *glenn* appears to be a hybrid. Borrowing from a third language appears likely because the root contains two plain voiced stops in PIE terms, which violates PIE root constraints.

SIEVE

PC: **sītlo-/ā* (W *hidl*, MB, *sizl* 'sieve')
PG: **sēþla-* (ON *sáld* 'sieve, riddle')
REF: L250, EDPC 338, H83, EDPG 430
Isogloss typology: MO
Interpretation: IE (0)

From PIE **seh₁-tlo-*, an instrumental noun to PIE **seh₁-* 'to sift'. The formation must be fairly old, as the base verb does not survive in Germanic.

SILVER

PC: Celtib. *silabur* 'silver, money'
PG: **silubra-* (Go. *silubr*, ON *silfr*, *sylfr*, OE *seolfor*, OHG *silabar* 'silver')
REF: Mallory & Huld 1984, Boutkan & Kossmann 2001, EDPG 436, Ko8
Isogloss typology: LX (I, III)
Interpretation: 3L (I, III)

A non-IE *Wanderwort* that appears to have come to Germanic via Celtic, cf. Basque *zilhar*, Proto-Semitic **ṣarp-* 'silver'. Within Indo-European it is also found in Balto-Slavic, cf. OCS *sьrebro*, Lith. *sidābras* 'silver', but these forms are slightly more divergent.

SKIN

PC: **sekio-* (OIr. *seiche* 'skin, hide')
PG: **segja-* (ON *sigg* 'hard skin')
REF: L257, EPDC 331, Stifter 2011, 558, EDPG 430
Isogloss typology: MO/SM
Interpretation: IE?

Celtic and Germanic may uniquely share an archaic formation **sek-ió-* with the meaning '(animal) skin', possibly derived from PIE **seḱ-* 'cut'. The Irish is inflected as a *t*-stem. However, as noted by Stifter, this type enjoys some productivity and may have replaced an older *io*-stem.

SPEAR

PC: **gaiso-* (Gallo-Gr. γαῖσον, Gallo-Lat. *gaesum*, OIr. *gae*, W *gwayw* 'spear, javelin')

PG: **gaiza-* (OE *gār*, OHG *gēr*, ON *geirr* 'dart, spear')
REF: L248, IEW 410, EDPC 155, H29, EDPG 164, Ko9
Isogloss typology: MO
Interpretation: GCL (III)

A PIE formation **ǵʰois-ó-* may be reconstructed for PG **gaiza-* and Skt. *heṣá-* 'some weapon', from a root **ǵʰeis-* also found in Skt. *hinásti* 'wounds' < **ǵʰi-n-es-* (with no laryngeal). The Germanic word was borrowed into Celtic after Germanic **o* > **a*. If this is correct, Gr. χαῖος 'shepherd's staff', which is semantically more remote, cannot be related because of its vocalism.

STICK

PC: **gli-na-* (OIr. *glenaid* 'adheres, cleaves', W *glynu*, MB *englenaff* 'to adhere, stick, bind')
PG: **klinan-* (OHG *klenan* 'to baste, stick together')
REF: L261, KPV 337-339, IEW 362-363, LIV² 290
Isogloss typology: MO
Interpretation: IE (0)

A PIE root **gleiH-* 'to smear, stick' is attested as a nasal present **gli-ne-H-* in Celtic and Germanic only. This nasal infix must have been inserted before the loss of the laryngeals, which makes this a likely archaism inherited from Proto-Indo-European.

THROAT

PC: **brāgant-* (OIr. *brágae*, MW *breuant* 'neck, throat')
PG: **k(w)ragan(þ)-* (ON *kragi*, MHG *krage*, E *craw* 'throat, collar')
REF: IEW 474-6, EDPC 72, EDPG 301
Isogloss typology: MO/SM
Interpretation: IE (0), L (I)

Celtic and Germanic appear to be formed to a verbal root **gʷrogʰ-* 'to gulp', cf. Gr. βρόχω* 'to gulp down' < **gʷrogʰ-*, although this root is not otherwise attested in either Celtic or Germanic. Both formations may be unified into a common proto-form **gʷrŏ̄gʰ-ont-* (with expected loss of **þ* in absolute *Auslaut* in Germanic), although an unexplainable difference in vowel length remains. The semantic shift from 'to gulp' to 'throat' seems trivial, cf. Gr. βρόγχος 'windpipe, throat', but is nevertheless shared by Celtic and Germanic.

TIP 1

PC: **brozdo-* (OIr. *brot* 'goad, spike')
PG: **brazda-* (Icel. *bradd* 'edge', OE *breard* 'brim, margin', OHG *brart* 'edge'), **bruzda-* (ON *broddr* 'spike', OE *brord* 'point, grass shoot')
REF: EDPG 54, 74, 77, 81
Isogloss typology: LX
Interpretation: IE? (0), ML (I), GCL (II)

The variety in vocalism presents a problem in positing a shared common form (cf. TIP 2). Reanalyzed ablaut may account for the variation in Germanic, cf. ON *barð* 'brim, prow, beard', OE *beard* 'beard' < PG **barzda-* (whence probably Lith. *barzdà*, Latv. *bārda*, OCS *brada* 'beard'). The intra-Celtic alternation between vocalism in *a* (see TIP 2) and *o* (in OIr. *brot*) is more difficult to account for. Perhaps the Celtic forms are borrowings from different Germanic forms in **a* and **u*, or Germanic **a* could be interpreted as both **a* and **o* in Celtic.

TIP 2

PC: **brazdo-* (W *brath* 'bite, prick; cut, wound')
PG: **brazda-* (Icel. *bradd* 'edge', OE *breard* 'brim, margin', OHG *brart* 'edge')
REF: EDPG 54, 74, 77, 81
Isogloss typology: RT
Interpretation: GCL (III)

It appears that Celtic **brazdo-* was borrowed from PG **brazda-*.

VOW

PC: **lugio-* (OIr. *lugae*, *luige*, W *llw* 'oath')
PG: **leugō-* (Go. *liuga* 'marriage'), **lugōn-* (OFri. *logia* 'to arrange, allot')
REF: L245, Kr134–135, Pr121, Pl281–282, EDPC 247, EDPG 333, Ko13
Isogloss typology: RT
Interpretation: IE? (0), ML (I)

A CG root **leugʰ-* may be reconstructed. Although the phonotactics of this root do not preclude an IE origin, the lack of cognates in the other branches is unfavorable. Recent borrowing is unlikely because identical formations are lacking.

WILD

PC: **gʷelti-* (MIr. *geilt* 'panicked person, lunatic', W *gwyllt*, 'wild, mad')
PG: **welþja-* (Go. *wilþeis*, ON *villr*, OE *wild*, OHG *wildi* 'wild, uncultivated')
REF: L261, IEW 1139-1140, EDPC 146, H46, EDPG 579
Isogloss typology: RT/MO
Interpretation: IE? (0)

A CG adjective **gʷʰel-ti-* may be reconstructed. Given the regular development of PIE **gʷʰ* in both branches, it seems likely that the root was inherited from PIE.

WILDERNESS

PC: **kaito-* (W *coed*, B *koad*, MCo. *coys* 'wood')
PG: **haiþī-* (Go. *haiþi* 'open field', ON *heiðr* 'heath, moor', OE *hǣð*, MLG *hēde* 'heather'), ?**haiþa-* (dial. early MoE *hothe*)
Isogloss typology: LX
Interpretation: 3L (I-II)
REF: L252, EDPC 198, H95, EDPG 202

A CG lexical element **kait-* may be reconstructed that is found in no other IE branch. Within G the *ī*-stem has parallels in other feminine terrain names such as ON *elfr* 'river' < **albī-*, ON *eyrr* 'shoal' < **aurī-* and ON *mýrr* 'swamp' < **meuzī-*.

WOOD

PC: **uidu-* (OIr. *fid*, W *gwŷdd*, B *gwez*, OCo. *guid-en* 'trees, wood')
PG: **widu-* (ON *viðr*, OE *widu*, *wiodu*, *wudu*, OHG *witu* 'wood')
REF: L252, Kr140, ALEW 1423, EDPC 420, EDPG 585
Isogloss typology: SM

Interpretation: IE(?), CGL (I, III), GCL (I-II)

A PIE formation *(h_1)ui-d^hh_1-u-* 'put apart' may be reconstructed. This formation may be parsed as containing *(h_1)ui-* 'apart' and *d^heh_1-* 'to put', implying an original meaning 'put apart', with a Celto-Germanic semantic shift to 'wood'. This exact formation is also found in Skt. *vidhú-* 'isolated', Lith. *vidùs*, Latv. *vidus* 'interior, middle'.

YEW

PC: **iuo-* (OIr. *eó* 'stem, shaft, yew-tree', W *yw*, B *ivin*, OCo. *hiuin* 'yew, yew-wood')
PG: **īwa/ō-* (ON *ýr*, OE *īw*, *ēow*, OHG *īwa* 'yew')
REF: L252, EDPC 173, EDPG 271
Isogloss typology: SM
Interpretation: IE?

The European languages show different reflexes of a word with different ablaut grades: 1) **$h_1$eiH-u-* (PG **īwa/ō-*), 2) **h_1iH-u-* (PC **iuo-*), 3) **$h_1$oiH-ueh_2-* (Gr. ὄα, ὄη 'elderberry tree, mountain ash', Lith. *ievà*, Latv. *iẽva* 'bird cherry'). However, the specific meaning 'yew' is Celto-Germanic.

13.6.3 Doubtful Celto-Germanicisms

BATTLE

PC: **keldāko-* or **kellāko-* (MIr. *cellach* 'strife, contention')
PG: **helþī-* (OE *hild* 'war, battle', OHG *hiltia*, ON *hildr* 'battle')
REF: L247, EDPC 199, H31
Isogloss typology: SM
Interpretation: IE(?)

Derivatives of PIE **kelh_2-* or **keld-* 'to strike' meaning 'battle' may be found in CG, but the exact formations differ. This semantic shift is likely also trivial, cf. OCS *klati* 'to kill' < **kolh_2-*.

BESTOW

PC: **link^w-o-* (OIr. *léicid* 'leaves, lets, allows, grants')
PG: **līhwan-* (Go. *leiƕan* 'to loan', ON *ljá* 'to lend; to give, grant', OE *lēon*, OS *far-līhan*, MDu. *lien*, OHG *līhan* 'to lend')
REF: Pr121, KPV 454-6, EDPG 336
Isogloss typology: SM
Interpretation: IE(?)

A CG semantic innovation of the PIE root **leik^w-* 'to leave, abandon, release' to 'to loan, bestow, grant, allow' may be adduced. However, the related Skt. *riṇákti* has a rather close range of meanings, including 'leaves', but also 'gives up, lets go, sells'.

BREAK

PC: **brest-* (OIr. *bres* 'fight, blow', *brissid* 'breaks', B, Co. *bresel* 'war')
PG: **brestan-* (ON *bresta* 'to break', OE *berstan* 'to burst', OS *brestan* 'burst, break')
REF: EDPC 76, EDPG 75
Isogloss typology: LX
Interpretation: IE? (0) ML (I), ML(III)

If related, a CG **b^hrest-* 'to break' may be reconstructed. However, the Celtic material allows for many reconstructions; an alternative reconstruction to PIE **b^hrd^h-(t)-* allows comparison with Gr. πέρθω 'to destroy, devastate'.

BRIGHT

PC: **ber(x)to/ā* (W *berth* 'beautiful, splendid, rich, bright; wealth, treasure', MB *berz*, MoB *berzh* 'power, authority')
PG: **berhta/ō* (Go. *bairhts* 'bright, clear, manifest, evident', ON *bjartr* 'bright, shining; illustrious', OE *beorht*, OS *berht*, OHG *beraht*, MHG *berht* 'bright, shining')
REF: IEW 139-140, EDPG 61
Isogloss typology: MO
Interpretation: IE (0), ML (I), GCL (II), ML (III)

Celtic and Germanic potentially share a unique formation **b^herh_1ǵ-to/eh_2* to the root **b^herh_1ǵ-* 'to shine, white', but the Celtic may alternatively be connected to other roots such as **b^her-* 'to carry', or **b^herǵ^h-* 'to be high, hill'; both of these alternatives have semantically attractive comparanda within Celtic, e.g. W *aberth* 'offering', W *braint* 'privilege; value'.

CHOOSE?

PC: **gus-o-* (OIr. *do-goa* 'chooses, selects, elects')
PG: **keusan-* (Go. *kiusan* 'to put to a test, prove by trial', ON *kjósa*, OE *cēosan*, OHG *kiosan* 'to choose, elect, examine')
REF: L258, Pr122, KPV 356-361, EDHIL 497, EDPC 169, EDPG 286
Isogloss typology: SM
Interpretation: IE(?)

The CG meaning 'to choose' contrasts with Skt. *juṣate* 'enjoys', Gr. γεύομαι 'to taste', Lat. *gustō* 'to taste', all from PIE **ǵeus-* 'to taste'. The original meaning is preserved in Gothic, which may mean that the semantic shift to 'to choose' occurred independently. It is also possible that languages other than Celtic and Germanic underwent a semantic shift from 'to try' toward 'to taste', leaving a CG archaism.

CLAY

PC: **ūrā/i-* (OIr. *ú(i)r* 'mold, earth, clay, soil')
PG: **ūra-* (Du. *oer* << LG *ūr* 'ferriferous sand, bog iron')
REF: EDPG 561
Isogloss typology: LX
Interpretation: IE? (0), L (I-IV)

If related CG **ūr-* may be an isogloss or loanword of any age. However, the cognates are too short to exclude chance resemblance.

CREAM

PC: **ϕlouVno-* (OIr. *löon*, *löan*, *lón* 'fat, provisions, food')
PG: **flauma(n)-* (OHG *floum* 'cream, raw leaf-lard', LG *Flom (en)* 'belly fat')
REF: L262
Isogloss typology: MO/SM
Interpretation: IE(?)

CG semantic expansion of PIE **pleu-* 'to swim, float, flow' to the meaning 'cream, fat, lard'. However, it is trivial to derive 'cream' from a verb meaning 'to float', because cream naturally floats on top of the milk from which it is extracted. Lard may similarly be rendered by cooking offal in water and allowing the fat to float to the top. Celtic and Germanic may share a *mn*-stem, cf. PG **reuman-*, **rauma(n)-* 'cream'. This requires that **m* was lost in Celtic in the vicinity of the root-final labial, as it was in Av. *raoγna-* 'butter' < **Hroug$^{(h)}$-mno-*. However, OIr. *löon* was disyllabic, implying that this loss of **m* was after the Celtic vocalization of syllabic **m* to **am*, or that Celtic received an unexplained root extension in a laryngeal.

DARK

PC: **dergo-* (OIr. *derg* 'red')
PG: **derka-* (OE *deorc* 'dark')
REF: L258, IEW 251, EDPC 95, EDPG 93
Isogloss typology: MO
Interpretation: IE (0)

Celtic and Germanic share an adjective **d^{h}erg-o-*. Due to their divergent meanings, however, it is uncertain that the two adjectives are etymologically related. Germanic has semantically more attractive cognates in ToA *tärkär*, ToB *tarkär* 'cloud' < **d^{h}rg-ru-* and Lith. *dargà* 'bad weather' < **d^{h}org-eh$_2$-*. The appurtenance of the Celtic word to this root is less certain; even if it shares the root connection, the dissimilar semantics imply that usage as an adjective is independent.

DIRT

PC: **korkāko-* (MIr. *corcach* 'moor')
PG: **hurhwa-* (ON *horr* 'mucus', OE *horh, horg, horu* 'spit', OS *horu* 'mud', OHG *horo* 'dirt, mud, manure')
REF: IEW 573-574, EDPG 258
Isogloss typology: RT
Interpretation: IE? (0)

Perhaps a CG **k(o)rk* was expanded with **-uo-* in Germanic and **-āko-* in Celtic. However, the original meaning in Germanic is not secure. If the original meaning in Germanic was 'spit', then the isogloss may be rejected in favor of a sound-symbolic origin.

EVIL

PC: **uϕelo-* (OIr. *fel* 'evil')
PG: **ubila-* (Go. *ubils*, OE *yfel*, OS *ubil*, OHG *ubil* 'evil, bad')
REF: IEW 1106-1107, EDPC 396, H65, EDPG 557
Isogloss typology: MO
Interpretation: IE (0), ML (I)

Celtic and Germanic uniquely share a formation **h$_2$up(h$_1$)-elo-* 'evil' from the PIE root **h$_2$uep(h$_1$)-* 'to treat badly' or perhaps **upo-* 'under, below'. The isogloss is doubtful because OIr. *fel* is only found in glossaries and may be back-formed from *felbas* 'sorcery', which may in turn be analyzed as a compound of *fell* 'treacherous deed' and *fis* 'knowledge'. However, the single *-l* in *fel* and *felbas* remains unexplained in the latter scenario.

FAULT

PC: **loxtu-* (OIr. *locht* 'shame, fault, offense')
PG: **lahan-* (Icel. *lá*, OE *lēan*, 'blame', OS *lahan*, OHG *lahan* 'blame, prohibit')
REF: H67, EDPG 322
Isogloss typology: RT
Interpretation: IE? (0)

If related, a CG root **lok-* may be posited. This isogloss is not compelling, however, because OIr. *locht* can also be explained as having split off from OIr. *lucht* 'charge' by generalization of the lowered root vowel in gen. sg. *lochtae*. The root vowel of *lucht* cannot be reconciled with the Germanic.

FIBULA

PC: **delgos-* (OIr. *delg* 'thorn, peg, spike, brooch fastening the mantle', W *dala* 'sting, bite')
PG: **dalka-* (OE *dalc, dolc* 'clasp, buckle, brooch', ON *dalkr* 'cloak-pin')
REF: L249, EDPC 94, LIV^2 113-114
Isogloss typology: SM
Interpretation: IE(?)

With Lith. *dilgéti* (*dìlga, -jo*) 'to sting, ache, itch' < **d$^{(h)}$lg-* and additional Baltic comparanda, there appears to be a shared root **d$^{(h)}$elg-* 'to sting', which in Celtic and Germanic acquired the meaning 'cloak-pin' or 'brooch'. A *caveat* is that this is only one out of a range of meanings in Irish and Welsh appears to preserve the older meaning 'sting'. This could indicate that the meaning 'brooch' developed independently in Irish and Germanic.

FORTIFICATION

PC: **brig-* (OIr. *brí* 'hill'), **brigā* (W, MB, Co. *bre* 'hill', Gaul. toponymical *-briga* 'hillfort')
PG: **burg-* (Go. *baurgs* 'fortified place; city', ON *borg* 'town, citadel; small hill', OE *burg*, OHG *burg* 'city')
REF: L251, Kr125, IEW 140-141, EDPC 77, EDPG 85, Ko12
Isogloss typology: SM
Interpretation: IE(?)

PC **brig(ā)* '(fortified) hill' and PG **burg-* 'fortified place, town' continue a zero-grade root noun of PIE **b^{h}erǵ^h-* 'to be high, hill' (cf. Av. *bərəz-* 'mountain') and uniquely expand the meaning with 'fortified hill, settlement'. However, this meaning is only inferred from Continental Celtic toponyms, as Insular Celtic reflexes retain the bare meaning 'hill'. The evidence for the meaning 'hillfort' in Continental Celtic may be skewed by the fact that place names for built-up places are more likely to be transmitted in our sources than bare hills.

FRIEND

PC: **karant-* (OIr. *cara*, W *car* 'friend', B *kar* 'parent', OCo. *car* gl. *amicus*)
PG: **frī̆(j)ōnd-* (Go. *frijonds*, ON *frændi*, OE *frēond*, OHG *friunt* 'friend')
REF: IEW 515, 844, Schu178, EDPC 190, EDPG 155
Isogloss typology: MO/SM
Interpretation: IE

Both Celtic and Germanic have a nominalized present participle of the verb 'to love' in the meaning 'friend', however the base verb differs. If these forms are related, it must be a calque from Germanic to Celtic because nominalized present participles are common in the former and not the latter, cf. PG

$*f\bar{\breve{\imath}}$(j)and- 'enemy'. However, the isogloss is judged as doubtful because nominalized present participles are not completely unparalleled in Celtic, cf. OIr. *cana* 'poet, chanter', *náma(e)* 'enemy'. The derivational parallelism may therefore be coincidental, cf. Oss. *lymæn* | *limæn* 'friend, lover' < PIr. **friiamna-* 'the beloved one'.

HAIR

PC: **dog^{w}lo-* (MIr. *dúal* 'native, fitting; lock, tress, plait, fold'), **dog^{w}lio-* (W *dull* 'manner, method, arrangement, pattern, line; plait, fold', B *duilh* 'handful, bundle, bale of straw')
PG: **tagla-* (Go. *tagl*, ON *tagl*, OE *tægl* '(horse's) hair', OHG *zagal* 'tail, sting, penis')
REF: L256, EDPC 102, H78, EDPG 504, Hyllested 2014, 143-4
Isogloss typology: LX
Interpretation: IE (0), ML (I-II)

If related, and assumed that the C reflex of PIE *$*g^{wh}$* merged with **u* in this position, a CG isogloss **dog^{wh}lo-* may be reconstructed. The hitherto accepted proto-form **doklo-* must be rejected in view of the Brittonic evidence, cf. PC **moniklo-* > W *mwnwgl* 'neck' for the development of PC **-kl-*; therefore Skt. *daśā* 'fringe' cannot be cognate with the Celtic. The comparison is semantically imperfect: in Celtic it appears to have meant 'arrangement (e.g. of hair, thread); mode' originally, whereas the Germanic meaning is simply 'hair'.

HIDE

PC: **skanto-* (B *skant* 'scales')
PG: **skinþa-* (ON *skinn* 'skin', OS *biscindian* 'to skin, flay', OHG *scindan*, *scintan* 'to skin, flay, peel off')
REF: L257, IEW 929-930
Isogloss typology: RT/LX
Interpretation: IE? (0), L (I)

If related, a CG **sken-* 'skin, to peel' may be reconstructed. The isogloss is non-compelling: the Celtic word is restricted to Breton and the semantic connection is imperfect. Alternatively, Lat. *scandula* 'shingle (for a roof)' > MFr. *escande* 'shingle' might be the source of the Breton, but this would require a semantic shift from 'shingle' to 'scale'.

HORSE 2

PC: **kankist-ikā* or **kanx-s-ikā* (W *caseg*, B *kazeg* 'mare')
PG: **hanhista-* (ON *hestr* 'stallion, horse'), **hangista-* (OE *hengest*, *hengst*, OFri. *hengst*, *hangst*, *hingst*, ODu. *hingest*, OHG *hengist* 'gelding, horse')
REF: Pedersen 1913, 29, IEW 522-523, Pl284, Jørgensen 2006, 64-66, H76, EDPG 209, Ko9
Isogloss typology: SM/MO
Interpretation: CGL (I-II)

Pedersen and IEW reconcile the Germanic and Celtic by assuming a CG formation **kankisto-*. This form is directly continued by Germanic with Verner alternation. The Celtic would be a derivative **kankist-ikā*. However, this form can only yield the attested Celtic forms by assuming an irregular early syncope to **kankstikā*, and even then the medial consonant cluster would probably yield **-st-*, not **-s-* in British Celtic. Assuming that **kankist-ikā* went through regular syncope at a later date is also problematic, as post-syncope clusters containing a nasal and *s* generally retain the nasal, so the expected outcome would be e.g. W ***can(g)seg*, cf. PC **ammV(n)-sterā* > W *amser* 'time'. A shared proto-form **kankisto-* therefore comes at the cost of assuming one or more ad hoc sound laws. Jørgensen's etymology derives the Brittonic forms from PC **keng-* 'to go, step' through a formation **kanx-s-ikā*. Here, the expansion in **-s-* may be compared to the **-s-* in **kanx-s-man* 'step', from the same root, and **-ikā* denotes a feminine noun derived from the adjectivalizing **-iko-*. This pre-form **kanx-s-ikā* is then equated by Koch to PG **hangista-* ~ **hanhista-*, where the Germanic presumably goes back to pre-PG **kank-* followed by a superlative suffix. While this equation through a shared pre-form **kank-* is formally possible, it has a number of disadvantages. For Celtic, such a pre-form cannot be reconciled with the root **keng-*, and the segmentation of the Celtic as **kanx-s-ikā* becomes arbitrary in absence of this root connection. For Germanic, segmentation into pre-PG **kank-isto-* implies a superlative suffix, but this suffix implies that the word was originally an adjective, but no trace of usage as an adjective exists.

INGOT

PC: **tin(n)V-* (OIr. *tinne* 'ingot, bar, rod of metal')
PG: **tina-* (ON *tin*, OE *tin*, OS *tin*, OHG *zin* 'tin')
REF: McManus 1991, 37, EDPG 517
Isogloss typology: LX
Interpretation: ML (III-IV)

Within Germanic, the word appears connected with an ablauting variant **taina-*, cf. MHG *zein(e)* and MLG *tēn*, which besides 'twig, rod' also means 'ingot, bar of metal'. OIr. *tinne* has been analyzed as a derivative of *tind* 'brilliant' or *tend* 'strong', but this derivation is rather more speculative because no single formation meaning both 'strong' and 'bar, ingot' is found. The geminate *-nn-* in OIr. *tinne* may be analyzed as from a singulative **tin-inio-*, giving the meaning 'single item made of *tin*'; alternatively, the double **-nn-* in Celtic was original, and Germanic borrowed it as a single **-n-*, as in e.g., PC **granno-* ~ PG **granō-* 'beard'. A correspondence between Germanic **t-* and Celtic **t-* implies a loanword one way or another, and because the Germanic has the more plausible intra-Germanic connections, Germanic to Celtic is the more likely direction of borrowing. However, the language-internal etymologies in both branches make chance resemblance equally likely. It is also possible that the Irish is a Stratum IV borrowing from OE *tin* 'tin' or *tinn* 'beam, rafter'.

LABOR

PC: **ϕidu-* (OIr. *idu* 'pain, pangs (of childbirth)')
PG: **fitan-* / **fetan-* (Go. *fitan* 'to be in labor')
REF: L256, IEW 830, EDHIL 420, EDPC 127
Isogloss typology: RT
Interpretation: IE? (0)

A CG root **ped-* may be proposed on the basis of these forms. However, OIr. *idu* may also be connected to Arm. *erkn* 'pains of childbirth', Gr. ὀδύνη 'pain' < PIE *$*h_1ed u\bar{o}n$*. A direct reflex of this root should have given OIr. ***idb*, however, the final vocalism may have been restored on the basis of oblique forms *h_1*dun*-.

LEPROUS

PC: **tru(d)sko*- (OIr. *trosc* 'leprous, leper', W *trwsgl*, 'awkward, crude, rash', Co. *trosgan*, B *trouskenn* 'scab')
PG: **þrūt(s)*- (Go. *þruts-fill*, OE *þrūst-fell* 'leprosy')
REF: L257, IEW 1096-1097, EDPC 391, H28
Isogloss typology: SM
Interpretation: IE?

Derivatives of PIE **treud*- 'to push, thrust' may mean 'leprosy' in both C and G. However, the derivations meaning 'leprosy' differ, and the long vowel in G is likely the result of secondary ablaut, implying that the G derivative meaning 'leprosy' is rather late and likely independent from the Celtic.

MEMBRANE

PC: **kenno*- (OIr. *cenn*, W *cen*, B *kenn* 'skin, membrane, dandruff')
PG: **hin(d)nō(n)*- (ON *hinna*, OE *hion(ne)* 'thin skin, membrane'), **hindō*- (Far. *hind* 'membrane')
REF: L256, IEW 567, EDPG 226
Isogloss typology: LX
Interpretation: IE? (0) L (I)

If related, a Celto-Germanic *n*-stem **kent-on*- may be reconstructed, where an oblique case form, e.g., gen. **kent-n-es*, was generalized in Celtic. In lack of any good parallels, it is unclear, however, whether *-*ntn*- gives *-*nn*- in Celtic. The appurtenance of the formally identical Lat. *centō* 'blanket, patched cloth' is less certain in view of the semantic difference. For Celtic, an alternative reconstruction to PC **kisnā* is possible, which could then be related to Lith. *šikšnà* 'hide, leather, belt' < **ḱis-neh*$_2$-, but this requires that the medial *k* is intrusive in Lithuanian.

ONE-EYED

PC: **kaiko*- (OIr. *cáech* 'one-eyed', W *coeg-ddall* 'half-blind', OCo. *cuic* 'one-eyed')
PG: **haiha*- (Go. *haihs* 'one-eyed')
REF: L256, IEW 519-520, H55
Isogloss typology: SM
Interpretation: IE(?)

The meaning 'one-eyed' versus 'blind' is shared in Celtic and Germanic, cf. Lat. *caecus* 'blind'. However, the original meaning may have been 'one-eyed' (cf. Skt. *kekara*- 'squint-eyed'), and the semantic shift is trivial in either direction.

PLEASANT

PC: **tek-o/ā*- (W *teg*, B *tek* 'pretty', MCo. *tek* 'fair, pretty'), **an-teki*-, (OIr. *étig* 'unnatural, unseemly')
PG: **þakkja*- (ON *þekkr* 'pleasant', OHG (Hl. 25) *dechisto* (superl.) 'dearest')
REF: L263, Lühr 1988, 232, EDPG 532
Isogloss typology: LX
Interpretation: ML (I-II)

A CG adjective **tek*- 'fair, pleasant' may be adduced; however, the ON form is ambiguous, because it can also be analyzed as continuing **þanki*-, i.e., a gerund to PG **þankōn*- 'to thank'. OHG *dechisto* is a hapax, which taken at face value points to **tok-ní*- through Kluge's law. However, an OHG hapax alone is too small a base for assuming a compelling CG isogloss.

POLE

PC: **mazdio*- (MIr. *maide* 'post, stick, bundle')
PG: **masta*- (OE *mæst*, OS *mast*, OHG *mast* 'mast, pole, stick')
REF: IEW 701-702, EDPC 260, EDPG 357, Ko7
Isogloss typology: LX
Interpretation: 3L (I-II)

If uniquely related, CG **mazd(i)o*- may be reconstructed. The status of this isogloss depends on whether Lat. *mālus* 'mast, pole, beam' is related. The Latin connection can be maintained by either reconstructing a shared proto-form **mazd-slo*- or by assuming an irregular development of earlier Lat. **mādus* to *mālus*.

POOL

PC: **lindV*- (Gaul. *linda* 'beverages', OIr. *lind* 'liquid; pool, lake', W *llyn* 'drink; lake')
PG: ?**linda*- (ON, Far. (poet.) *lind* 'spring, source', ?OFri. *lind* 'lake', ?MHG *lünde* 'wave')
REF: L253, IEW 675, Kr140, H92, Ko8
Isogloss typology: LX
Interpretation: IE? (0), ML (III, IV), GCL (II)

If the connection between the Celtic and Germanic forms is accepted, a common root **lend*^{h}- may be reconstructed. However, the Old Frisian attestation is uncertain, and MHG *lünde* 'wave', if not rather connected to OFr. *onde*, *l'onde* '(the) wave', would presuppose an unrelated formation **lunþjō*-. In addition, there is a possibility that the West Norse words were borrowed from Celtic. In view of these objections, the Celto-Germanicism remains a possibility at best.

QUICK

PC: **ɸeimi*- (OIr. *éim* 'prompt, quick, timely')
PG: **fīma*- (ON *fimr* 'nimble')
REF: L261, Blöndal 1989, 175
Isogloss typology: RT/LX
Interpretation: IE? (0), L (I)

The isogloss presupposes a CG root **p(e)i*- suffixed with *-*mo*- and *-*mi*-, but the evidence for such a root is slim: it is not certain that the Celtic form had **p*- and otherwise only *-*ei*- is left to compare. The paucity of the phonological material makes the isogloss conjectural even if no formal or semantic objections can otherwise be made.

RAVE

PC: **uāti*- (Gaul. οὐάτεις (pl.), OIr. *fáith* 'prophet, seer'), **uātu*- (OIr. *fáth* 'prophecy', W *gwawd* 'song')
PG: **wōda*- (Go. *wods* 'possessed', ON *óðr* 'frantic, furious, OE *wōd* 'insane'), **wōdi*- (OHG *wuot*, MDu. *woet* 'rage'), **wōþa/ō*- (ON *óðr* 'mind, song', OE *wōð* 'sound, voice')
REF: Kr139, EDPC 404, H12, EDPG 592, Ko13
Isogloss typology: RT
Interpretation: IE? (0)

The various formations in both branches allow reconstruction of a CG root *(H)ueh$_2$- or *(H)ueh$_3$-, and the variety of formations implies the word has considerable pedigree in both branches. The use of a *ti*-suffix in animate nouns is reminiscent of *g^hos-ti- 'guest'. The Celto-Germanicism is doubtful because Lat. *uātēs* 'foreteller, seer' may be cognate, but may also be a borrowing from Celtic.

ROCK

PC: **krak-ī-*, **krek-ī-* (W *craig* 'rock'), **karrikā* (W *carreg*, B *karrek* 'stone')
PG: **hargu-* (ON *hǫrgr* 'pile of rocks, sanctuary', OE *hearg* 'pagan temple, idol', OHG *harug* 'grove), **harha(n)-* (Elfd. *ar* m. 'bedrock', Nw. *har(e)*'cliff, rocky bottom', Du. dial. *hare* 'hillock')
REF: EDPG 211
Isogloss typology: LX
Interpretation: 3L (I-II)

A CG **kVr(r)Vk-* may be reconstructed, but Celtic **-ra/re-* ~ **-arri-* versus Germanic **-ar-* provide an imperfect formal match, and the correspondence of a consonant skeleton only makes a non-IE ultimate source possible. Semantically, the match is also imperfect in that the word refers to a single rock in Celtic versus a whole mound in Germanic. MIr. *crec*, *crac*, Sc.G *creag* 'crag, rock' may be borrowed from Welsh.

ROPE

PC: **kom-uorko-* or PBr. **kom-uarko-* (W *cywarch*, OB *coarcholion* gl. *canabina*, B *kouarc'h* 'hemp')
PG: **werka-* (WFri. *wurk*, MDu. *werc*, OHG *wer(i)h* 'string of hemp, rope')
REF: L249, IEW 1155, EDPG 580
Isogloss typology: RT/LX
Interpretation: IE? (0), GCL (III-IV)

The Germanic forms appear derived from **wergan-*, **wurgjan-* 'to strangle', where the final **k* can be the result of Kluge's law **werka-* < **werkka-* < PIE *$uer\acute{g}^h$-nó-. An *o*-grade PG **warka-* could be the source of W *cywarch*, B *kouarc'h*, but such an *o*-grade reflex is not actually attested, and even then the date of borrowing may well be post-PG. Alternatively PG **werka-* could be unrelated to **wergan-*, **wurgjan-* and a CG root **uerk-* 'hemp' was continued in the *o*-grade in Brittonic while PG **werka-* continues **uerk-nó-*. Both scenarios are doubtful because they presume that the Brittonic forms were prefixed with **kom-*, but this segmentation with a prefix may not be correct.

SEDIMENT

PC: **grāuā* (W *gro* 'pebbles, gravel, sand', OCo. *grou* 'sand')
PG: **gruwwa-* (Icel. *grugg* 'sediment')
REF: IEW 460, Zair 2013, EDPG 193
Isogloss typology: LX
Interpretation: IE (0), L (I)

Celtic and Germanic appear to have two different formations *$g^{(h)}$rHu-eh$_2$- and *g^hru(H)-o- with similar meanings, but the implied laryngeal metathesis complicates the comparison. A connection with PIE root *g^hreh$_1$u- (cf. Lith. *griáuti* 'to tear down' and *griū́ti* 'to collapse') is possible. However, the Celtic formation has more convincingly been connected to the root **ǵrH-* as in **ǵrH-no-* 'grain, kernel', cf. OIr. *grán*, Lat. *grānum*, Go. *kaurn* and **ǵrH-ro-*, cf. Lat. *glārea* 'gravel' (< **grārea*).

SLAY

PC: **slak-kV-* (OIr. *slacc* 'sword'), **slak-to-* (MIr. *slachta* 'hit')
PG: **slahan-* (Go. *slahan*, ON *slá*, OE *slēan*, OHG *slahan* 'to beat, slay')
REF: L248, H42, EDPC 345, EDPG 452
Isogloss typology: RT
Interpretation: L (I)

A CG root **slak-* can be adduced. The OIr. hapax *slacc* and its derivatives may alternatively have an intra-Celtic connection in PC **slad-* 'to hit, slay', cf. OIr. *slaidid* 'strikes, slays', destroying the Celto-Germanicism. This would require derivation with suffix **-kV-* for *slacc*, and then *slachta* would have to be derived from *slacc*. However, this derivation is poorly understood, because suffixes in **-kV-* are usually found in nouns derived from prepositions, cf. OIr. *aicce* 'nearness, fosterage', W *ach* 'beside, lineage' < PC **ad-* 'to'. The geminate in *slacc* also requires a derivation with **-kV-* if the CG root **slak-* is to be maintained.

SPEAK

PC: **rād-ī-* (OIr. *ráidid*, W *adrodd* 'to speak')
PG: **rōdjan-* (Go. *rodjan* 'to speak', ON *rœða* 'to speak, converse')
REF: L258, Kr140, Pr122, EDPC 305, H79, EDPG 415
Isogloss typology: SM
Interpretation: IE(?)

Celtic and Germanic uniquely use causative formations of the PIE root *(H)reh$_1$d^h- 'to take care of, arrange' with the meaning 'to tell, speak'. However, Lith. *ródyti* 'to show, indicate, demonstrate' is rather close in meaning, as telling is merely a particular form of indicating.

SPLIT

PC: **sɸlissi-* (OIr. *slis* 'shaving(s), splinter(s)')
PG: **splītan-* (MDu. *spliten*, MHG *splīzen* 'to split')
REF: L262, IEW 1000, EDPG 468
Isogloss typology: RT
Interpretation: IE? (0)

A CG root **spleid-* 'to split' has been argued to be continued as **splid-ti-* in Celtic and as **spleid-e-* in Germanic. If so, the occurrence of dental assibilation in the Celtic form implies that the root is exceedingly archaic, so this word may be a shared archaism. David Stifter (p.c.) instead proposes a connection with Ir. *sligid* 'cuts, fells', i.e. PC **sli(x)-sti-* 'cuttings' > *sliss*.

SPRUCE

PC: **ɸ(o)uxtākā* (OIr. *ochtach* 'pine, ridge-pole')
PG: **feuhtjōn-* (OHG *fiuhta* 'spruce')
REF: Pedersen 1913, 44, Birkhan 1970, 524, Pr118, EDPG 139
Isogloss typology: MO
Interpretation: IE

Celtic and Germanic uniquely expand the PIE root **peuḱ-* 'to stab' with **-t-*. The ablaut grades differ in Celtic and Germanic, but the Celtic may go back to a full grade by assuming a secondary shortening analogous to OIr. *ochtrach* 'dung mound' < **óchtrach*. The isogloss is not compelling because OIr. *ochtach* can also be derived from PC **oux(s)tākā*, and be related to OIr. *óchtar, úachtar* 'upper part, top' < PC **oux(s)tero-*. The semantic shift would be parallel to OIcel. *þǫll* 'pine', if it is from PIE **telh₂-* 'to raise up'.

STEEP

PC: **sterto-* (W *serth* 'steep, slanted, obscene', *syrthio* 'to fall', B *serzh* 'steep, vertical', *serzhañ* 'to sail upwind')
PG: **sterþ/dja-* (OIc. *stirðr* 'stiff'), **sturþ/dō* (Icel. *storð* 'grass, green stem')
REF: IEW 1022-1027, Blöndal 1989, 962, 967
Isogloss typology: LX
Interpretation: IE (0), ML (I-II)

If related, a CG **stert(i)o-* 'steep, stiff' may be reconstructed. The connection is uncertain because the Germanic is also compatible with a root **sterdʰ-*, which allows for a connection with Gr. στόρθη Hes., στόρθυγξ 'point' instead of the Celtic.

STEP

PC: **keng-* (OIr. *cingid*, W *rhy-gyng* 'tread, step, amble')
PG: **hinkan-* (OE *hincian*, MDu. *hinken*, OHG *hinkan* 'limp, hobble')
REF: EDPC 200, EDPG 226
Isogloss typology: RT
Interpretation: IE? (0), ML (I-II)

CG **keng-* may be reconstructed. All other possible cognates have initial **s-*, cf. Pāli *khañjati* 'to limp' (< Skt. ?**skañjati*) and Gr. σκάζω 'id.', but this may be a case of *s*-mobile.

STRENGTH

PC: **trexsno-* (OIr. *trén* 'brave, strong'), superlative **trexsamo-* (OIr. *tressam*, W *trechaf*)
PG: **þrakja-* (OE *þrece* 'force, oppression', OS *wāpan-threki* 'ability with arms', ON *þrekr* 'strength, bravery')
REF: L248, IEW 1076, 1090, LIV² 632, EDPC 389, H32, Ko10
Isogloss typology: RT
Interpretation: IE? (0)

A CG **treg-* would connect these forms, but the root-final consonant is unsure for Celtic, which leaves some alternative connections open. The Celtic forms may alternatively be connected to PIE **tergʷ-* 'threaten, scare', cf. Skt. *tarjati* 'threatens, reviles', Lat. *torvus* 'grim, fierce', Hitt. *tarkuuant-* 'looking angrily'. A connection with **tergʷ-* would have the advantage that it appears to have an intra-Celtic cognate in W *tarfu* 'to disturb, trouble, scare', but it would require the assumption that the Celtic underwent *Schwebeablaut*, but such ablaut is paralleled by other root extensions in **s*, cf. **h₂euǵ-*, **h₂uéǵs-* 'to grow'. Ru. *trógatь* 'to touch', Latv. *treksne* 'thrust' are semantically distant and require root-final **gʰ* which may be connected to the Celtic, but not to the Germanic.

STRIPE

PC: **streibā* (OIr. *sríab* 'stripe, line')
PG: **strīpa/ōn-* (Far. *strípa*, Nw., MDu. *stripe*, MHG *strīfe* 'stripe')
REF: L262, IEW 1028-1029, EDPG 485
Isogloss typology: LX
Interpretation: IE? (0), ML (I-II)

If CG, **s(t)reib-* may be reconstructed. The connection is speculative because the Germanic may also be from any other labial stop through Kluge's law followed by shortening of overlong syllables. Evidence that the root-final **p* is secondary can be adduced from the possibly related MLG *streven* 'to stretch, strive', MHG *streben* 'to get up, resist, strive' < PG **stribōn-* < pre-PG **stribʰ-*. A root-final **bʰ* is compatible with the Celtic, but also invites comparison with the semantically imperfectly matching Gr. στριφνός 'dense, solid, firm'. The Celtic may alternatively be derived from PIE **streig-ueh₂-*, cf. Lat. *striga* 'strip, row' < **strig-eh₂-*.

STRIVE

PC: **(ɸ)leid-o-* (W *llwyddo* 'to succeed'), **(ɸ)loid-ī-* (MIr. *laídid* 'exhorts, incites')
PG: **flītan-* (OE *flītan* 'to contend, strive, scold', OHG *flīzan* 'to attempt, try hard')
REF: IEW 666, KPV 521-522, EDPC 133, H49, EDPG 147
Isogloss typology: RT
Interpretation: IE? (0), ML (I)

If related, a Celto-Germanic root **pleid-* 'to strive, succeed' may be reconstructed. MIr. *laídid* 'exhorts, incites' < **(ɸ)loid-ī-* would then be a causative formation, unless it is a denominal verb based on OIr. *loíd* '(type of) poem, song' (David Stifter, p.c.). This root and its formations are possibly archaic. However, the Celtic may also go back to PC **leid-*, a reflex of PIE **leid-* 'to push, play, let go', cf. Gr. Hes. λίνδεσθαι 'to contend', Lat. *lūdō* 'to play' and Lith. *léisti* 'to let, publish, send, urge'. Because PIE **p-* is lost without a trace in this position in Celtic, the matter cannot be decided with certainty.

SUFFERING

PC: **aglitā* (W *aeled* 'pain, suffering, grief')
PG: **agliþō-* (Go. *agliþa* 'tribulation')
REF: L257, IEW 7-8, EDPC 27, H57, LIV² 257, EDPG 4
Isogloss typology: MO
Interpretation: GCL (I-II)

Both C and G appear to continue *t*-expansions of PIE **h₂egʰ-leh₂-* (Skt. *aghrā-* 'evil', YAv. *aγrā-* 'name of an illness', Go. *aglo* 'tribulation'). However, these expansions must be independent in PC **aglātu-* (MIr. *álad* 'wound', W *aelawd* 'grief, affliction'), as they appear to be derivations in **-tu-*, while the Germanic (highly productive) derivation in **-iþō* < **-i-tā* is secondary from **agl-jan-*, cf. G *agljan* 'to hurt'. A pre-PG **aglitā* provides a suitable parallel formation or donor form for W *aeled*, but it requires the assumption that the W masculine noun was originally feminine.

SWIFT

PC: **kribV-* (OIr. *crib*, *crim* 'quickly, swiftly')
PG: **hrappa-* (Icel. *hrapa* 'to fall down', Nw. *rapa* 'crash down', MDu. *rap*, 'swift, fierce')

REF: Blöndal 1989 366, EDPG 243
Isogloss typology: LX
Interpretation: 3L (I)

This isogloss presumes a CG root *kreb(ʰ)- that is continued in the zero grade in Celtic, and in the *o*-grade in Germanic. This root violates PIE root constraints and is therefore unlikely to be of Proto-Indo-European age. The spelling *crim* is also attested in OIr., which, if original, would remove the isogloss and allow for a connection with W *cryf*, B *kreñv* 'strong' instead.

SWIRL

PC: **s(t)rit-antī* (OIr. *srithit* 'stream (of milk, blood)')
PG: **streþan-* (OHG *stredan* 'to seethe, swirl'), **straþma-* (MHG *stradem* 'swirl'), **struþla-* (NHG *Strudel* 'whirl, vortex')
REF: IEW 1001-1002, EDPG 484
Isogloss typology: RT
Interpretation: IE? (0), L (I)

A CG root **s(t)re(i)t-* 'to flow' may be posited, but the precise formation of OIr. *srithit* is unclear, making the root connection uncertain as well. OCo. *stret*, MCo. *streyth* 'stream, brook' must be read as containing a final /ð/ < PC **d*, so they are unrelated.

TESTICLES

PC: **kallio-* (W *caill*, B *kell* 'testicle'), **kallu-* (OIr. *caull* 'testicle'), **kalluko-* (OIr. *cullach* 'boar, stallion', MB *callouch* 'uncastrated')
PG: **skalla(n)-* (OE *sceallan*, MHG *schellen*, OFri. *skall* 'testicle(s)'), **skelhan-* (OHG *scel(ah)o*, OLFra. *skelo*, MLG *schele* 'stallion' (whence NHG *be-schälen* 'to cover (a mare)')
REF: L256, IEW 292
Isogloss typology: RT
Interpretation: L (I-II)

A CG root **(s)kal-* may be reconstructed. However, another possibility is that the Celtic is word is related to Gr. κήλων, -ωνος, Dor. κάλων 'stallion, male ass' (< "having testicles"?), through a shared root **ḱ(e)h₂l-*. This root would be incompatible with PG **skelhan-* on account of the latter's *e*-vocalism.

THIRST

PC: **tartu-* (OIr. *tart* 'dryness, thirst', W *tarth* 'steam')
PG: **þurstu-* (OE *þurst*, *þyrst*, OS *thurst*, OHG *durst* 'thirst')
REF: L259, EDPC 371, EDPG 553
Isogloss typology: MO
Interpretation: IE (0)

Celtic and Germanic share a *tu*-derivation to the PIE root **ters-* 'dry', but it is unclear whether this represents a PIE archaism or could be due to independent innovations. The semantic shift of 'dryness' to 'thirst' is trivial and shared with e.g., Avestan *taršna-* 'thirst'.

TROOP

PC: **drungo-* (OIr. *drong* 'troop', MW *dronn* 'multitude', Gallo-Lat. *drungos* 'group of enemies')
PG: **druhta-* (Go. *driugan* 'to serve as a soldier', OE *dryht* 'companion', OHG *truht* 'troop', ON *drótt* 'company, following')
REF: L247, IEW 255, H34
Isogloss typology: SM
Interpretation: IE(?)

A semantic isogloss has been proposed on the basis of a shared development of a military sense to the root **dʰreugʰ-*, which in Balto-Slavic just means 'friend', cf. OCS *drugъ*, Lith. *draũgas*. It is not certain that the Celtic form goes back to this root, however. As no nasal present is associated with this root in Celtic, the form **drungo-* would require a rare metathesis of pre-PC **drug-no-* to **drungo-* ("Thurneysen's law"), which is otherwise only found in PIE **bʰudʰ-no-* 'bottom' > PC **bundo-* (cf. Skt. *budhná-* vs MIr. *bond*, *bonn*) and perhaps PIE **tud-no-* 'broken' > PC **tundo-* (Skt. *tudná-* vs W *twn*). Another possible objection to assuming a Celto-Germanicism is the fact that the Balto-Slavic meaning 'friend' itself may have developed from (the then primary meaning) 'military ally'.

TROUBLE

PC: **saitro-* (OIr. *saethar* 'work, labor'), **saitu-* (OIr. *sáeth* 'trouble', W *hoed* 'pain')
PG: **saira-* (OE *sārig* 'sorry', OHG *serō* 'painfully', ON *sárr* 'painful', *sár* 'wound')
REF: IEW 877, H63
Isogloss typology: SM
Interpretation: IE(?)

Reflexes of PIE **seh₂i-* 'to rage, be in pain' may mean 'pain' in Celtic and Germanic only, cf. Lat. *saevus* 'wild', W *hoyw* 'lively', Hitt. *šāi-zi* 'to become sullen, angry'. However, the range of meanings and formations is wide in both branches, so this semantic development, which anyway seems trivial, may well be independent in each branch.

TUB

PC: **drukontio-* (OIr. *drochta* 'tub, vessel')
PG: **truga-* (OE, ON *trog*, OHG *troc* 'trough')
REF: Stokes 1901, 468-469, IEW 214-217, H75
Isogloss typology: SM
Interpretation: IE(?)

A derivation of PIE **dreu-* 'tree' in *-*kó-* is attractive for the Germanic, but a PC derivative **druxtio-* as has been suggested would require an irregular loss of the thematic vowel in *-*ko-*. An alternative **drukontio-* could yield the attested form, leaving a root connection and a semantic isogloss. OIr. *droichet* 'bridge, causeway' is unrelated, and must be a compound of *droch* 'wheel' and *sét* 'path'.

UTTERANCE

PC: **iexti-* (OIr. *icht* 'people, tribe', W *iaith*, B *yezh*, MCo. *yēth* 'language')
PG: **jehti-* (OHG *jiht* 'confession; praise', OFri. *jecht* 'confession')
REF: L257, Kr140, IEW 503-504, SBCHP 106-107, 268, EDPC 435, H85, EDPG 272
Isogloss typology: MO
Interpretation: IE (0)

Celtic and Germanic uniquely expand the PIE root **iek-* 'to speak' with *-*ti-*. OIr. *icht* may either be an *i*-stem or a *u*-stem; the cluster *-cht-* resists palatalization, so the distinction between a PC *-*tu-* and a *-*ti*- suffix is neutralized. For W *iaith*, B *yezh*, both suffixes are impossible: the sound law Brittonic **ie* > *ia* applied regularly, so a suffix that caused *i*-affection to this secondary stem vowel **a* must be postulated. Short **i* did not cause *i*-affection of **a* in Brittonic, but the yod in *io*-stems did, as did long **ī* < PC **ī*, **ū*. The suffix most consistent with either of the Irish options would be a secondary thematization of a *-*ti*- suffix, giving PBr. **iextio*-. The combined evidence of Brittonic and Goidelic therefore makes PC derivation in *-*ti*- more likely than any alternative; derivation in *-*tu*- would only work if this word were an exception to Brittonnic **ie* > *ia*. The Celto-Germanicism could be due to shared inheritance from PIE or to independent innovations to the inherited root **iek*-.

WIRE

PC: **uiriā*- (Celtib. *viriae* 'arm-ornament'), **ueiro*- (MIr. *fíar*, W *gŵyr*, B *gwar* 'curved')
PG: **wīra*- (OE *wīr*, ON *vírr* 'ornament of wire')
REF: L251, Kr140, Birkhan 1970, 152-155, Pl284, EDPC 414
Isogloss typology: MO/SM
Interpretation: IE(?)

Although the Germanic word is usually described as a borrowing from Celtic, this Celto-Germanicism is doubtful because *viriae* and *viriolae* 'arm-ornaments' are only indirectly attested in Pliny the Elder's *Natural History* (Book 33, 12), which describes these words as Celtic. Only if Pliny correctly identified these words as Celtic, a Celto-Germanic connection to PG **wīra*- 'ornament of wire' may be adduced. However, the Insular Celtic languages provide no semantic match to Pliny's words. Similarly, OHG *wiara* < PG **wiara*- could be a post-PG Stratum IV borrowing from a Gaulish equivalent of **weiriā*, but no such word is attested from any Celtic language. The only possible cognate, the adjective **weiro*- 'curved', is found in Insular Celtic, but it is uncertain that it is etymologically relevant to *viriae*. Even these PG **wīra*- and PC **weiro*- do not technically constitute a morphological isogloss in the form of a formation **ueih₁-ro*- (< PIE **ueih₁*- 'to turn') because G has a noun and C an adjective.

WRINKLE

PC: **grunko*- (OIr. *gruc* 'wrinkle')
PG: **kreukan*-, **krūkan*- (MDu. *crōken* 'to wrinkle, break, tear', ME *crowke* 'to bow', Nw. *krjuka* 'to cringe, crawl')
REF: IEW 389, EDPG 304
Isogloss typology: RT
Interpretation: IE? (0)

A CG root **gruk*- would connect these forms, but the meaning 'wrinkle' appears to be secondary to 'to be bent' in Germanic, so the comparison is semantically imperfect. OIr. *gruc* is moreover compatible with many other proto-forms, e.g. PC **gʷriggu*-.

13.6.4 Rejected Celto-Germanicisms

About

REF: L260, IEW 34-35, EDPC 32, EDPG 352

PC **ambi* 'about' is cognate with PG **umbi* 'about', but further cognates exist elsewhere in Indo-European, e.g. Gr. ἀμφί 'for, about'.

Angelica

REF: Dinneen 1904, L252, Marstrander 1910, IEW 262, Birkhan 1999, Pl284, H20

Ir. *cuinneog* 'angelica' has been connected with ON *hvǫnn* 'angelica'. This connection would require a Celtic-Germanic **kʷos-n*- that had a derivative **kʷonn-iā* early on in Celtic, and later received a diminutive suffix *-og* in Irish. No further reflexes of this **kʷonn*- are found in Celtic. *Cuinneog* may also mean 'churn, bucket', and it was borrowed into Welsh as *cunnog* 'bucket', where Ir. /u/ followed by a palatal consonant was adopted as Welsh /ʉ/ (cf. W *drum*, *trum* 'crest, peak' < OIr. *druimm*).[12] The meaning 'churn, bucket' must be older: it is the only meaning found in Welsh, and it is found in Irish from the Middle Ages onwards, while meaning 'angelica' is first attested in Dinneen's dictionary. Moreover, the meaning 'angelica' is often found only in compounds, e.g. ScG *cuinneag* 'bucket', *cuinneag-mhidhe* 'angelica', so it is likely a later derivation motivated by its hollow stem.

Anger, quarrel

REF: L247, EDPG 527

A CG semantic isogloss between MIr. *drenn* 'quarrel, combat' and PG **tur(z)na*- (OE, OS *torn*, OS *torn*, Du. *toorn*, OHG *zorn* 'anger, rage') has been proposed as containing PIE **derh₂*- 'to split' in the meaning 'anger, conflict', cf. Skr. *dīrṇa*- 'split'. However *drenn* cannot be formally reconciled with this root: a pre-form **drh₂-no*- would be expected to yield PC **drāno*- > MIr. ***drán* while a pre-form **drh₂-sno*- would yield PC ***dranno*- > MIr. ***drann* (cf. OIr. *flann* 'blood red' < **wlanno*- < PIE **u̯lH-sno*-).

Apple

REF: L251, IEW 1-2, EDPG 31

PC **abVl*- 'apple' is cognate with PG **apla*- 'apple', but this formation has cognates in Balto-Slavic, e.g. Lith. *obuolỹs* 'apple'.

Army

REF: L247, Kr136, IEW 615-616

PC **korio*- 'troop' may be connected to PG **harja*- 'army', but cognates are found in e.g. Lith. *kãrias* 'army'. Even if the latter is borrowed from Germanic, the *io*-stem of this root is also found as a derivational base in the Gr. personal name Κοίρανος.

Awl

REF: IEW 18-22, EDPG 44

The PIE root *h₂ek*- 'sharp' has been posited to contain a CG derivation in *-*uol*- in W *ebill* 'piercer, pin' and PG **awala*- 'awl', but this derivation leaves the Welsh vocalism and the

[12] Shared inheritance may be excluded because Irish *u* should correspond to Welsh *w*, and Welsh *u* should correspond to Irish *ó*, *úa* or *oí*.

fortis _ll_ unexplained. Whatever the exact derivation of the Welsh, it is unlikely to be closer in derivation or meaning to the Germanic than to VLat. _*acūcla_ 'needle' (OFr. _aguille_, Span. _aguja_).

Axle

REF: IEW 6, H71, Ko9

Formations of PIE _*h$_2$eḱs-i-_ with _*-l-_ in PC _*axsilā_, PG _ahsula-_ 'axle' have been argued to constitute a morphological CG isogloss, but Lat. _āla_, dim. _axilla_ 'armpit; wing' has the same formation. The meaning 'axle' is archaic, cf. Gr. ἄξων, Lat. _axis_, Skt. _ákṣa-_ 'axle'.

Bag

REF: L255, IEW 125-126, EDPC 70, EDPG 49

PC _*bolgo-_ 'sack, bag, stomach' and PG _*balgi-_ 'skin bag' both continue the PIE root _*b^{h}elǵ^h-_ 'to swell' and some reflexes in both branches have the meaning 'belly', cf. OE _belg_, WFri. _bealch_, W _bola_. However the wide range of meanings necessitates a shared IE proto-form meaning 'swollen object, bag', a meaning shared with other cognates, cf. Ru. _bólozen_ 'callus, bump', Av. _barəziš_ 'pad, pillow'.

Bald

REF: EDPC 260

PC _*mailo-_ 'bald' cannot be connected to PG _*maitan-_ 'to hew, cut' through a supposed shared root _*mai-_, because the Germanic, along with the related verbs _*mittōn-_ 'to cut' and _*maidjan-_ 'to hurt', requires an earlier PG _*maiþan-_, with the _*þ_ as part of the verbal stem. There is no trace of a dental in Celtic, so the forms can only be compared after arbitrary segmentation.

Battle

REF: L246–247, Kr136, IEW 534, Schm140, EDHIL 466

PC _*katu-_ 'battle' can be connected to PG _*haþu-_ 'battle', but IE cognates are numerous, e.g. Hitt. _kattu-_ 'enmity, strife' < _*kh$_3$-tu-_, Gr. κότος 'spite, anger' < _*kh$_3$-(e)to-_.

Bellow

REF: L258, IEW 255-256

MIr. _dresacht_ 'creaking noise' cannot be related to LG _drunsan_ 'to bellow' because the first _e_ in the MIr. form is short, showing that the stem did not contain an _n_. Gallo-Lat. _drensō_ 'to cry (of swans)' is not absolutely certain to be Gaulish in origin. All the forms may be sound-symbolic in origin, but there is no indication that forms were shared between Celtic and Germanic.

Berry

REF: IEW 105, EDPC 58, EDPG 54

The MIr. glossary word _basc_ 'red' has been connected to OE _basu_ 'purple' < PG _*baswa-_. However, the _wa_-suffix is productive in Germanic chromonyms, making it more likely that _*baswa-_ was derived from _*bas/zja-_ 'berry', cf. Go. _-basi_, ON _ber_, OHG _beri_, within Germanic itself, and that the meaning 'purple' also arose secondarily, i.e. from 'berry-colored'.

Boar

REF: Jackson 1953, 324-330, Schrijver 1997, 304, EDPG 48

W _baedd_, OCo. _bahet_ '(wild and domesticated) boar' as well as PG _*baiza-_ 'id.' have been argued to constitute borrowings from an unknown substrate language. However, the British Celtic forms may have been borrowed from West Germanic instead after British monophthongization of PC _*ai_ > _*ɛ̄_, but before rhotacism in Germanic. Jackson dates this monophthongization to the first century CE. This date is most likely post-Proto-Germanic, which means it is outside the scope of this study.

Booty

REF: L246, Kr136, Schm140, IEW 163, EDPC 72, H48

PC _*boudi-_ 'booty, victory' appears related to ON _býta_ 'to deal out', MLG _būte_, MHG _biute_ 'booty', but the relationship cannot be one of a shared root. The ON must be borrowed from West Germanic, and the West Germanic requires a vowel _*ū_, which would imply a PIE _*uH_, but a laryngeal cannot be reconciled with the Celtic forms. A borrowing from Celtic to Proto-Germanic would be expected to yield PG _*au_, cf. PG _*lauda-_ 'lead' < PC _*loud-_, so it is equally unattractive. Therefore the word can be borrowed from Gaulish into a West Germanic dialect. Gaul. _ou_ may have been heard as _ū_ in West Germanic which lacked an _ou_-diphthong, or Gaul. _ou_ had shifted to _*ū_ in parallel with Brittonic. This borrowed form then underwent the High German Consonant Shift whereby the _d_ became a _t_; this High German form was then borrowed into Low German and from there into other Germanic languages.

Branch

REF: L256, Blöndal 1989 529, EDPC 66

A formation _*g^{w}istis_ is proposed to be unique to W _bys_ 'finger' B _biz_ 'finger', MIr. _biss ega_ 'icicle' and ON _kvistr_ m. 'branch'. However, _kvistr_ is a _u_-stem and may have undergone a change of _*tw_ > _*kw_, in view of ME _twist_ 'bifurcation, branch of a tree', in which case it must go back to PG _*twistu-_ by dissimilation. The cognate set of ON _kvisl_ 'branch, fork' vs. OE _twisla_ 'fork of river, road' and OHG _zwisila_ 'twig' offers a parallel for this change.

Break

REF: L260, IEW 171, H54

The PIE root _*b^{h}reus-_ has reflexes in OIr. _bronnaid_ 'spends, consumes, injures, damages', OIr. _bruïd_ 'breaks in pieces, smashes, crushes' W _briw_ 'wound, shreds; shattered' as well as OE _brȳsan_ 'to bruise, break to pieces' and OHG _brōsma_ 'crumb', but the archaic meaning 'to break, shatter' is well-preserved in both branches and is shared with Lat. _frustum_ 'fragment' as well as with Shughni _viraỷ-_ 'to break' (M. Kümmel, _Addenda und Corrigenda zu LIV^2_). The rise of the meaning 'to wound' therefore appears independent in both branches.

Breast

REF: L256, De Bhaldraithe 1981, 151, EDPG 76

MIr. *brúasach* has been connected with PG **breusta*-in the meaning 'strong-breasted', giving a shared proto-form **bʰreus-to-*. However, the OIr. *brúasach* rather means 'thick-lipped', cf. ModIr. (dial.) *bruas* '(thick) lip'. Hence the semantic connection is too weak to maintain the comparison.

Bridge

REF: L253, IEW 173, EDPC 79, EDPG 81

Gaul. *briva* top. 'bridge', *brio* gl. *ponte* (Endlicher glossary) and PG **bru(w)ī-*, **brujjō-* 'bridge' both appear to continue PIE **(h₃)bʰruH-* in the meaning 'bridge', but this meaning is shared with Slavic, cf. Slovenian *brv* 'foot-bridge'.

Bring

REF: L254, IEW 168, EDPC 76, EDPG 77

W *hebrwng* 'to bring', OCo. *hebrenchiat* 'leader', MCo. *hembronk* 'leads', B *ambroug* 'escort' with PG **bringan-* 'to bring' have been suggested to constitute a shared a contamination of PIE roots **bʰer-* 'to bring' and **h₂neḱ-* 'to reach'. However the Brittonic forms may rather be parsed as W *heb-r-yng* < PC **sekʷV-ro-enk-*, leaving no similarity. Similarly, the Germanic strong verb may have evolved from the univerbation of **pro* + **Henḱ-*, for which cf. OAv. *fra̧štā* 3sg.aor.med. < **pro-Henḱ-* may be adduced as a parallel.

Broom

REF: IEW 104-105, H80

PC **banatlo* 'broom-plant, broom' and PG **bōnjan-* 'to decorate, scrub, polish' are considered CG expansions of **bʰeh₂-* 'to shine' with *-*n*-. However, in Celtic the semantic and morphological connection with this root is uncertain. Even if it is correct, the G verb is most probably a secondary factitive formation to an adjective **bōna-* 'shining' < **bʰe/oh₂-no-*. Expansions with *-*n*- also appear in other branches, cf. Gr. φαίνω 'to shine', Arm. *banam* 'to open, reveal'.

Cauldron

REF: L249, IEW 642, LEIA C-74, EDPG 265

PC **kʷar-io-* (Ir. *coire*, W *pair*, Co. *pêr* 'cauldron') has been compared to PG **hwera-* (ON *hverr* 'kettle'), as well as their respective expansions with *-*n*-: MIr. *cern* 'dish', ON *hverna* 'pan, basin'. However the root is probably Indo-European, cf. Skt. *carú-* 'kettle, pot' < **kʷer-u-*. The extension with *-*n*- is also found in OCS *črěnъ* 'frying pan', and MIr. *cern* can be a borrowing from Latin.

Cavalry

REF: Kr140, LEIA R-2, H69, Ko9

A morphological isogloss between PC **ekʷo-reido-* (OIr. *echrad* 'steeds; cavalcade', Gaul. PN *Epo-rēdo-rīx*, W *ebrwydd* 'swift') and PG **ehwa-raidō-* (OE *ēo-red* 'cavalry, band, troop', OS *eo-rid-folc* 'cavalry', ON PN *Jó-reiðr*) must be rejected on the grounds that their ablaut grades differ, so their formation must be independent.

Clever

REF: L257, IEW 358, Heidermanns 1993, 336

A direct connection between OIr. *glicc* 'acute, shrewd, skilled' and MDu. *cloec* 'smart, brave', MLG *klōk* 'fine, dainty; cunning, wise' (whence MHG *kluoc*, NHG *klug*) < **klōka-* is unlikely, because the Germanic adjective is more likely to be related to OHG *klecken* 'to suffice, be of use, succeed' < **klakjan-*. The semantic shift toward 'cunning, wise' appears peripheral within Germanic and therefore late.

Club

REF: Marstrander 1915, 95, L262

An isogloss has been proposed for PC **lorgo-* (MIr. *lorg*, W *llory* 'staff, stick, club', OCo. *lorch* gl. *baculus*) and ON *lurkr* 'club, bludgeon'. However the Germanic word is not found outside of Nordic, and may be explained as a borrowing from Irish. The *u*-vocalism in ON *lurkr* may be accounted for by assuming an Old Irish oblique case form as the source, e.g. gen. sg. *luirg*, cf. ScG *luirg*.

Command

REF: IEW 150-152, Pr122, EDPC 83, EDPG 61

PIE **bʰeudʰ-* 'to be awake, aware' has undergone a semantic shift to 'to notify, warn, command' in Celtic and Germanic, cf. OIr. *ad-boind* 'proclaims, gives notice', MIr. *robud*, W *rhybudd* 'warning' and Go. *biudan* 'to command, offer', ON *bjóða*, OE *bēodan* OS *biodan* 'to offer'. However, the same semantic range is also found in Baltic, cf. Lith. *baũsti* 'to incite, move, compel'.

Conceal

REF: L262, H44

OIr. *for-múigthe*, *formúchta* 'smothered, concealed' is compared with OHG *mūhhen* 'lie in ambush for' and ME *micher* 'thief', among others. However, the Irish verb *for-múcha* is clearly derived from *múchaid* 'covers, suffocates, extinguishes' (cf. B. *migañ* 'to snuff') and the meaning 'conceal' is most likely secondary within Irish. Furthermore, the root-final consonants are incompatible, Celtic requiring older **k*, Germanic older **g*.

Covering

REF: L264, IEW 690-691, Blöndal 1989 583

OIr. *lumman* 'cloak, mantle' is close to D *lomme* (whence Icel. *lumma*, Sw. dial. *lomme* and NFri. *lomm* 'pocket'), whence the assumption of a Celto-Germanic isogloss. An objection consists of the fact that in Germanic the word is restricted to Nordic, which makes it more likely to be a medieval loanword, possibly from Irish. The lack of Irish final *-n* in the Nordic languages may be the result of reanalysis as the definite article.

Alternatively, in view of the imperfect semantic match, we may be dealing with a chance resemblance.

Crooked

REF: IEW 601-602, H66, Orel 1998, 364, LIV² 332

OIr. *cloen* 'crooked, sloping; unfair, evil' from PC **kloino-* and Go. *hlain(s*)* 'hill', Icel. *hlein(n)* 'part of the loom; rest', Far. *leinur* m. 'side post of the (upright) loom', Nw. dial. *lein* f. 'steep slope; side; part of the loom', from PG **hlaina-* 'hill' both continue the PIE root **ḱlei-* 'to tip, incline, lean' with a *-*no*-suffix. However, at least the *no*-stem noun has potential parallels in Ossetic (I) *asin*, (D) *asinæ* 'stairs, ladder' < Proto-Iranian **ā-srainā-* and Alb. *qye* m. 'peak, summit' < PAlb. **klaina-*.

Curds

REF: L250, IEW 406, Irslinger 2002, 144, EDPG 306

A connection between OIr. *gruth* 'curds, cheese' and Nw. *krodde* 'dregs, boiled cheese' and ME *crudde*, *curde* 'curds' has been suggested. However it is preferable to reconstruct OIr. *gruth* as PC **g*^{w}*ritu-* < PIE **g*^{wh}*r̥-tu-*, cf. Skt. *ghr̥tá-* 'ghee'. This root cannot be connected to the Germanic forms, which may in turn be derivatives of **kruttōn-*, **kruddōn-* 'to pack, become dense', which is in turn derived from **kreudan-*, **krūdan-* 'to press, push forward'.

Dark

REF: IEW 247-248, EDPC 95, EDPG 96

A connection between PG **dimma-* 'dark', cf. ON *dimmr*, OE *dimm* 'dark,' and MIr. *deime* 'darkness' must be rejected because the PG appears to go back to a pre-PG **d*^{h}*émb*^{h}*-no-*, cf. Elfd. *dimba* 'to fume, dust'. MIr. *deime* appears to have a single lenited **m* which cannot go back to an earlier **mb* < **mb*^{h}.

Dear

REF: L261, EDPC 106

OIr. *drúth* 'extravagant, wanton, harlot' < PC **drūto-* appears cognate with OE, OS *drút* 'friend, beloved one', OHG *trút*, NHG *traut* 'dear, beloved' < PG **drūda-*. W *drud* 'dear, daring, rash, fool' must be borrowed from Goidelic in an early stratum to account for the vocalism, whereas B *druz* 'fat, fit, fertile' must be borrowed from early OFr. **dryð(ə)* (OFr. *dru* 'fat'), itself presumably from Gaul. **drūto-*. The formation **d*^{h}*ruH-to-* appears shared with Lith. *drū̃tas* 'thick, strong, deep (of voice)'.

Death

REF: Trautmann 1923, 285, IEW 1022-1027, LEIA U-31, H22,

A CG semantic shift PIE **sterb*^{h}*-* 'to be stiff' to 'to die' has been proposed for OIr. *ussarb* 'death' and OHG *sterbo*, OE *steorfa* 'plague'. However the meaning 'to die' is also found in the related Ru. *stérbnutь* 'to stiffen, die', which shows that the proposed semantic shift is either trivial or archaic.

Destruction

REF: IEW 545-547, EDPC 212, H59, EDPG 205

PC **kollo-* 'destruction, loss' (W *coll*) and PG **halta-* 'lame, limping' (Go. *halts*, etc.) are argued to contain a Celtic-Germanic isogloss whereby PIE **keld-* 'to strike, cut' is uniquely continued by a formation **koldo-*. However, **koldo-* is not the only possible source of PC **kollo-* and the poor semantic match does not warrant positing a unique root. Also, the formations are not strictly identical: Celtic would have to be a noun, i.e. PIE **kóld-o-*, and the Germanic is an adjective, i.e. PIE **kold-ó-*.

Die

REF: L255, IEW 471, KPV 211-2, EDPC 53, EDPG 316

A semantic isogloss between OIr. *at-baill* 'dies' and PG **kwelan-* 'to suffer' must be rejected because the OIr. contains a synchronically meaningless neuter infixed pronoun. A connection with PIE **g*^{w}*elh*$_{1}$*-* 'throw', (cf. Gr. βάλλω 'throw') is therefore preferable, because it allows for the reconstruction of an originally euphemistic 'throws it (out)' > 'dies'. Even if a root connection between Celtic and Germanic exists, the isogloss is not exclusive in view of Lith. *gãlas* 'end, butt, tip, finish, distance, death', Latv. *gãlas* 'end, tip, top, room, misery, death', OPr. EV *golis* 'death', and OPr. Cat. *gallan* 'death' < **g*^{w}*olH-o-*.

Disease

REF: Demiraj 1997, 198; H16

PC **klamo-* (OIr. *clam* 'leprous', W *claf*) has been connected with PG **skalmō* (OHG *scelm*, *scelmo*, *scalmo* 'pest, plague, dying off of cattle', MLG *schelm* 'cadaver', ON *skelmis-drep* 'plague, murrain'). However the Germanic forms are better reconstructed as **skel-man-*, an *mn*-stem, and with the more common **e*, not **a*. Perhaps the G formation is rather related to Alb. *helm* m. 'poison, toxin; venom, bane; sorrow' < PAlb. **skalma-*, **skalmi-* or PIE **skelh*$_{1}$*-* 'to dry up, wither', cf. Gr. σκληρός 'dry, withered' < **sklh*$_{1}$*-ró-*, σκελετός 'mummy, skeleton' < **skelh*$_{1}$*-eto-*.

Dregs, draff

REF: L249, IEW 251-252

A connection between MIr. *drab* 'draff', Ir. *drabh*, *dramh* 'refuse' and PG **drabiz-* 'dregs' has been suggested, but MIr. *drab* appears to be a ghost word, while Ir. *drabh*, *dramh* may be a loanword from English.

Drink

REF: L261, LIV²: 405-406, EDPC 241, EDPG 340,

PC **lītu-* (OIr. *líth*, B *lid* 'feast, rite', W *llid* 'anger, ferocity, passion') and PG **līþu-* (Go. *leiþu*, ON *líð*, OE *līð*, OFri. *līth*, OHG *līd* 'strong drink') both continue PIE **liH-tu-*, but this formation is also found in Lith. dial. *lytùs*, Latv. *lîts* 'rain'. The original verbs are found in Balto-Slavic, e.g. Lith. *líeti* (*lejù*), Latv. *liêt* 'to pour', OCS *-li* 'poured'; these verbs show that

Lith. dial. *lytùs*, Latv. *lîts* must originally have meant 'pouring'. This meaning is rather close to Germanic 'drink', while the Celtic meaning 'feast; anger' is more distantly removed from both the Balto-Slavic and the Germanic. This leaves no Celto-Germanic morphological or semantic isogloss. In fact, the semantic distance makes it uncertain whether the Celtic forms belong to this root at all.

Drive 1

REF: L254, IEW 392-393

W *gyrru* 'to drive (cattle)' has been connected to OE *cierran* 'to turn, go', MHG *kerren* 'to turn' through an alleged root **gers-*. It is true that the OE and MHG words can continue PG **karzjan-* < **gors-eie-*, but then they would have to be disconnected from ON *keyra* 'to drive, ride' < **kaizwjan-*, cf. Nw. *keis* 'turn, corner'.

Drive 2

REF: L261, EDPG 103

PG **drīban-* 'to drive' may be connected to Ir. *drip* 'bustle', ScG *drip* 'hurry, confusion' if one accepts that PIE **-bʰ-n-* developed into PC **pp*. However, **pp* is not reconstructable for PC and the Goidelic words are attested so late that the similarity is likely to be accidental.

Drop

REF: L261, IEW 274-275, LEIA D-202, H94, EDPG 105

OIr., MoIr. *drúcht* 'dew, drop' has been reconstructed to PC **druxtu-* < **drup-tu-*, which has been compared to PG **drup(p)an-* 'drop'. However, OIr. *drúcht* has a long *ú*, which would have to be secondary to allow for a formal match.

Enemy

REF: IEW 795, H41, EDPG 123

OIr. *oech* 'enemy' and PG **faiha-* (OE *fāh*, *fāg* 'guilty, outlawed, hostile', OHG *fēhida* 'hate, enmity', Go. *faih* 'deceit') possibly continue the PIE root **peiḱ-* 'hostile' in the *o*-grade, but the Celtic is a noun while the Germanic may be an adjective. An *o*-grade adjective of this root is also found in Lith. *paĩkas* 'foolish'. OIr. *oech* is only attested in glossaries in the Old Irish period, and these glossary entries might be back-formations of OIr. *oígi* 'stranger', making the root connection uncertain.

Eye

REF: L263, IEW 775-777, EDPG 41

MIr. *úag* 'hole' has been connected to PG **augōn-* 'eye', but this connection would come at the unacceptable cost of abandoning a connection between the Germanic word and PIE **h₃okʷ-* 'eye'.

Fall

REF: L254, IEW 542

W *cwyddo* 'fall' and PG **hittjan-* 'hit' do not constitute an isogloss, because Lat. *caedo* 'cut, fell' may be plausibly related to either word.

Fat

REF: IEW 970-971, Adams 2013, 731-732, EDPG 458

PIE **smeru-* is shared between PC **smeru-* 'marrow' and PG **smerwa-* 'butter, grease', but also with TB *ṣmare* 'smooth; oil'.

Fever

REF: EDPC 225, H27, EDPG 248

PC **kritu-* 'trembling' (W *cryd* 'trembling, fever') and PG **hrīþan-* 'fever' (OS *hrido*, OHG *rīdo*) have been argued to uniquely share a lexeme. However, both continue PIE **kreh₁(i)-* 'to sieve, separate', cf. Lat. *crībrum* 'sieve'. The basic meaning 'to sieve, shake' is still found in both branches, cf. W *crynu* 'to shake', *gogrynu* 'to sift', OHG *redan* 'to sift' (< **hriþan-*), and while the meaning 'fever' is old in Germanic, it is restricted to Welsh in Celtic.

First

REF: L260, IEW 563-564, EDPC 201

PC **kentu-* 'first, lately' has been compared to Go. *hindumists* 'hindmost'. However, the latter is an internally Germanic formation built on the unrelated directional **hinē* 'from here' < **ḱi-neh₁* (with the suffix **-duman-* < **-tmH-o-*). The Celtic form rather belongs to Lat. *re-cens*, *-tis* 'new, recent, lately', containing the PIE root **k(e)n-* 'young', cf. Gr. καινός 'new, fresh' < **kn-io-*.

Fish

REF: Hellquist 1922, 21, L252, EDPC 119, EDPG 38

PC **esok-* 'salmon' looks somewhat similar OHG *asco* 'grayling', but a shared proto-form cannot be reconstructed. The ultimate origin of the Celtic is unknown and may well be of substrate origin (cf. Stifter, this volume). OHG *asco* may be derived from PG **askō-* 'ashes' or **aska-* 'ash tree'; a parallel instance of a fish-name derived from a tree-name is Sw. *asp* 'asp' from its homophone meaning 'aspen'.

Flower

REF: L251, IEW 122, EDPC 67, EDPG 70

PC **blātu-* 'flower, blossom' (OIr. *bláth*, W *blawd*) has been connected to PG **blōdi-* 'bloom' (OE *blēd* 'shoot, branch, flower, fruit', OHG *bluot* 'blossom, blossoming'). However the root connection must be PIE through the root **bʰleh₃-* 'to blossom, flower', cf. Lat. *flōs* 'flower'. Moreover, the formations are different: Celtic has a derivation in **-tu-* versus Germanic **-ti-*.

Ford

REF: L255, Kr125, IEW 816-817, EDPC 141, EDPG 160

PC **ɸritu-* 'ford' is semantically and formally identical to PG **furdu-* 'ford', both from PIE **pr-tu-*. However, the same formation is also present in the semantically close Av. *pərətu-*, *pəšu-* 'gangway, passage, ford, bridge'.

Forehead

REF: L256, IEW 48-50, Adams 2013, 49

OIr. *étan* 'forehead' is related to ON *enni*, OHG *andi*, *endi* 'forehead' < PIE *h_2*ent-*. Here a shared Celto-Germanic semantic shift from 'front' to 'forehead' has been assumed, but this meaning is also found in Anatolian, cf. Hitt. *ḫant-* 'front, forehead', Hieroglyphic Luwian *hant-* 'face, forehead' and Tocharian, ToA *ānt*, ToB *ānte* 'surface, forehead'.

Fortification

REF: SBCHP 447, 454, EDPC 194

OE *heaðor* 'restraint, confinement' has been connected to OIr. *caithir* 'fort, enclosure, settlement'. However, the semantic match is unconvincing, and Ir. *caithir* may anyway be borrowed from Lat. *castrum* 'fort', as was W *caer* 'fortress', W *ker* 'town'.

Frighten

REF: L257

OIr. *fo-botha* 'frighten' appears similar to OS *under-badon* 'to oppress, frighten', but prototonic forms of the former verb in *-fubth-* show that the root contains **u*, not **o*, making it formally irreconcilable with the latter (David Stifter, p.c.). Moreover, the Old Saxon may have an intra-Germanic connection in Nw. *bada* 'to weigh down, press; to knead', which could be related to Skt. *bā́dhate* 'presses, troubles, opposes' < **b^heHd^h-*. The laryngeal and the root-final **-d^h-* would also eliminate OIr. *fo-botha* as a potential cognate.

Furrow

REF: L250, IEW 821, EDPG 160

PC **ϕrikā* 'furrow' (Gallo-Lat. *rica*, cf. Cat. *rega*, OFr. *roie*) and PG **furh-* 'furrow' (ON *for*, OE *furh*, OHG *furuh*) identically continue the zero grade of the PIE root **perḱ-*, but so does Lat. *porca* 'ridge between furrows' < **p(o)rḱ-eh_2-*.

Genitalia

REF: L255, Birkhan 2012

PC **buzdo-* 'penis' has been connected to the OE Runic name *peorð*, whose meaning is not directly attested. The meaning 'vulva' is inferred on the basis of a kenning by Lane, but 'pear tree' has been suggested as well by Birkhan. Either way, the connection with PC **buzdo-* seems impossible.

Ghost

REF: L259, H4

OIr. *air-drech* 'ghost' has been connected to ON *draugr* 'ghost', assuming that they uniquely share a semantic development of PIE **d^hroug^h-o-* 'lie, deceit' toward 'ghost'. However the *-drech* in the OIr. form is more likely to be from *drech* 'vision'. This leaves no shared etymology for *air-drech* and *draugr*.

Goblin

REF: L259, LEIA B62–63, H18

MIr. *boccánach*, W *bwg*, *bwga* 'ghost, hobgoblin', *bwgan* 'bogey, ghost' appears similar to Swabian *bockelman*, English *bogey*. However the Middle Irish appears derived from *boc* 'he-goat', whereas W *bwg*, *bwga* is attested only from the seventeenth century onwards, and is in all likelihood borrowed from ME *bugge* 'bogey, hobgoblin; scarecrow'.

Good

REF: L257

OIr. *remor* 'thick, fat' has been connected to MHG *frum* 'capable, good', but the Germanic is more likely from PG **fruman-* 'former, first', with a semantic shift which is paralleled by the range of meanings found in English *prime* 'first, most important, excellent'.

Green

REF: L258, IEW 429-434, EDPG 180

PC **glasto-* 'blue, green, gray' and PG **glasa-*, **glaza-* 'glass' have been connected. However, the Celtic and Germanic words are clearly different formations and the semantic gap points to derivation from two different roots, i.e. PIE **ǵ^{h}elh$_3$-* 'green' and **ǵ^{h}leh$_1$-* 'to glow'.

Grudge

REF: L248, IEW 760, EDPC 291, Adams 2013, 291, H38

PC **nītu-* (OIr. *níth* 'battle, fury, anger'), **neitV-* (W *nwyd* 'temperament') and PG **nīþa-* (Go. *neiþ* 'jealousy', ON *níð* 'libel', OE *nīþ* 'envy', OHG *nīd* 'battle-rage, hate') are most likely etymologically related, but this root is not exclusively shared between C and G, cf. ToB *ñ(y)ātse* 'danger, plague, distress' < **niH-tio-*. A connection with Lat. *nīteo* 'to be radiant, shine' suggested by IEW is semantically unconvincing.

Gull

REF: Schrijver 1997, 305, EDPG 349

PG **maiwa-* and a Gaul. **maw-* have been suggested to be loanwords from a common substrate. However the Gaulish is only indirectly attested in Gallo-Romance, e.g. French *moue* 'gull' < **mawa-*. This Gallo-Rom. **mawa-* may simply be borrowed directly from Germanic, either because the word is borrowed from a Germanic dialect with PG **ai* > *ā* or due to limitations of Gallo-Romance phonology. A borrowing from Germanic to Romance would remove the need for an unattested Gaulish word without any Insular Celtic cognates.

Guts

REF: L256, IEW 344, EDPC 115

OIr. *inathar* 'guts' and OCo. *enederen* gl. *exstum* have been considered cognate to PG **ēþrō-*, **ēdrō-* 'vein, rivulet', however another cognate is Gr. ἦτρον 'abdomen', which would make the isogloss a nonexclusive.

Hand, fist, clutch

REF: Heinertz 1915, 319-322, L256

MIr. *glacc* f. 'hand, grasp' < **glakkā* has been connected to OE *clyccean* 'to grasp, seize' < **klukjan-*, Sw. *klyka* 'crutch', OFri. *kletsie* 'spear' < **klūkjan-*/**kleukjōn-* (whence possibly PSl. **kljuka*, cf. Ru. *kljuká* 'crutch', SCr. *kljȕka* 'hook, door-knob'). However the vocalism of these forms precludes a shared proto-form and no scenario for borrowing presents itself. As a last resort, one could assume independent borrowings from an unknown source, but there is nothing else in favor of this.

Harrow

REF: L250, IEW 18-22, EDPG 4

PC **oketā* 'harrow' has been argued form a morphological isogloss with OHG *egida*, OE *egede* 'harrow', but Lat. *occa* 'id' may also continue **oketā-* (through metathesized **otekā-*). In addition, if the PG forms go back to **ageþjō-* rather than **agiþō-* (allegedly regular from **h_2oḱeteh$_2$-*), they would formally correspond to Baltic rather than Celtic, cf. OPr. *aketes*, Lith. *akėčios* 'harrow'.

Hatred

REF: L257, Birkhan 1967, Rübekeil 2001, H64

Celtic and Germanic derivatives of PIE **ḱeh$_2$d-* 'uneasiness, displeasure' have been suggested uniquely to mean 'hatred' in these branches. However some Celtic descendants have broader meaning, e.g. W *cawdd* 'anger, wrath', B *keuz* 'regret, anguish' and Oscan gen.sg. *cadeis* 'hostility' is within the range of meanings assumed to be specific to Celtic and Germanic.

Heap

REF: L251, IEW 140-141, EDPG 60

W *bera* 'rick, heap, stack' and PG **berga-* 'mountain' may both continue PIE **b^{h}erǵ^h-* 'high', but reflexes of this root are also found in Arm. *barjr*, Hitt. *parku-*, Skt. *bṛhánt-* 'high'. Use as a noun is also found in Arm. *berj* 'height'.

Heron

REF: Schrijver 1997, EDPG 241

PBr. **kraxar-* has been reconstructed based on MW *crehyr*, B *querhair* 'heron' and has been identified along with PG **hraigran-* (OE *hrāgra*, OS *hēgro*, OHG *reigar*, *heigar*), **higran-* (ON *hegri*, OSw. *hægher*) 'heron' as a loanword from a common substrate language. However the Vannetais dialect in which *querhair* is found has a number of instances of **ð* > *r*, which makes a connection with the usual Breton word for heron, *kerc'heiz* < **kerxɪð* more economical. Without the Breton cognate, there is no reason to consider MW *crehyr* the original form among a wide range of variants including *grehyr*, *cryr*, and *gryr*, some of which are attested as early as *crehyr*. Although a substrate origin cannot be rejected, it is likely that *crehyr* is of onomatopoetic origin.

Hill

REF: L252, IEW 287-289, EDPG 518

OIr. *dind* 'hill, height' has been connected to ON *tindr* 'spike, mountain peak', OE *tind*, MHG *zint* 'tine, prong', OHG *zinna* 'pinnacle', but it is preferable to derive the Germanic from PIE **h$_3$dent-*, a full-grade formation of the PIE word for 'tooth'. The Celtic word requires PIE **-nd-* or **-nd^h-* rather than **-nt-*, so a connection with the word for 'tooth' would have to be sacrificed for the isogloss to work.

Ice

REF: L251, IEW 503, EDPC 435, EDPG 273

PC **iegi-* 'ice' is cognate to PG **jekan-* 'ice', but further cognates include Lith. *yžià* 'ice-floe' and Hitt. *eka-* 'cold, frost, ice', all from PIE **ieǵ-*.

Kindle

REF: L260, IEW 179-181, EDPC 171, EDPG 508

OIr. *ad-annai* 'kindles, lights' and PG **tandjan-* 'to kindle' (Go. *tandjan*, ON *tenda*, OE *on-tendan*) have been derived from a similar univerbation of (in pre-laryngealistic terms) the prefix **ad-* and a further non-attested root **and^h-* 'to burn'. However, PG **tandjan-* is to be analyzed as a causative to **tind(n)an-* (cf. MHG *zinden*, *zinnen*) 'to burn' with *e*-vocalism, meaning that its *a* must continue **o* rather than **a*.

Kindred

REF: L259, Kr135, Schm140, EDPC 413, EDPG 579

PC **ueniā* (OIr. *fine* 'kindred, progeny; kinsperson') has a root connection to PG **weni-* (ON *vinr*, OE *wine*, OFri. *wine*, OHG *wini* 'friend') through PIE **uenh$_1$-* 'to love', cf. Skt. *vánate* 'to love'. However, the formations are dissimilar: **uenh$_1$-ieh$_2$* and **uenh$_1$-i-* respectively. The semantic development from 'to love' to 'loved one' are trivial and do not warrant a Celto-Germanicism, cf. Skt. *vanitā*, YAv. *vaṇtā* 'loved one, spouse'.

Land

REF: L253, IEW 675, EDPC 232, EDPG 326

PC: **landā* 'open land' (< **lnd^h-*) and PG **landa-* 'land' (< **lond^h-*) are cognate, but so is OPr. *lindan* 'valley' (< **lnd^h-*).

Light

REF: EDPC 339, EDPG 263, 438

OHG *scamm*, ON *skammr* 'short' is unlikely to be cognate with MIr. *scaim* 'lungs', W *ysgafn* 'light' *ysgyfaint* 'lungs', B *skañv*, Co. *scaff* 'light'. The *a*-vocalism in the Celtic may be explained by a pre-PC root **sKemH-*, which in the zero grade would yield PC **skam-*. This root is incompatible with PG **skamma-*, which may instead be from pre-PG **skabma-*, to **skaban-* 'to shave, cut off'.

Long

REF: IEW 891, EDPC 338, EDPG 435, 437

A morphological isogloss between PC **siti-* 'length' and PG **sīda-* 'long' and PG **sīþu-* 'late' cannot be upheld because the

Celtic continues a zero-grade formation of the PIE root *$seh_1(i)$- 'to let go, send' while the Germanic continues the full grade. The full grade is shared with Lat. *sētius* 'later'.

Look

REF: L256

Lane compares OCo. *lagat*, B *lagad* 'eyes' to OHG *luogēn* 'to peer', OS *lōcōn*, OE *lōcian* 'to see'. However, it is commonly accepted that the Celtic forms, including W *llygad*, are derived from PIE **leuk-* 'bright'. The Germanic forms go back to PG **lōg-*, **lōkk-*, which cannot easily be reconciled with this PIE root.

Lust

REF: L258, IEW 845, Fleuriot 1964, 220

OB *rogedou* 'orgies', W *rhewydd* 'wantonness, lust' and PG **freka-* 'avaricious' have been connected. However the Old Breton word is a misreading of *imrogalou* gl. *orgiis*. W *rhewydd* 'lust' alone cannot be plausibly connected to the Germanic word; it appears to require a medial **u* or *$*g^{wh}$*, which is incompatible with the Germanic **k*. The Germanic may be connected to Pol. *pragnąć* 'to yearn for', Czech *prahnouti* 'to covet' < *$*preg^{(w)}$-*.

Magic

REF: L259, EDPC 352, H1, EDPG 421, Ko13

PC **soito-* 'magic' (W *hud*) is cognate with PG **saida-* 'bond; magic, charm' (ON *seiðr* 'bond; magic', and the strong verb *síða* 'to work charms'), but also with Lithuanian *saĩtas* 'bond; magic'. The formation **s(H)oi-to-* may be Indo-European, cf. Skt. *sétu-* 'bond, fetter', with more primary semantics. B *hud*, which is frequently brought up in this context, is in all likelihood introduced from Welsh by lexicographers.

Mantle, tunic

REF: L250, IEW 874, EDPC 315, EDPG 250

W *rhuch* 'layer, film, bran; (rough) garment, cloak, mantle' cannot be cognate with OE *roc*, OS *hrok*, OHG *rock* 'robe, skirt, coat' < PG **hrukka-*, cf. Old French *froc* 'frock', where PG **hr-* was borrowed as *fr-*. The British word cannot be related to this Germanic formation in any period before the breakup of Proto-Germanic (following IEW). It may be borrowed from a West Germanic dialect in a similar timeframe as the French, although the vocalism with *u* is unexpected in this scenario. MIr. *rucht* 'tunic' is a glossary word whose final *t* is unclear.

Milk

REF: L256, IEW 722-723

OIr. *mlicht*, W *blith* 'milk' (PIE **$h_2$mlǵ-ti-*) has a root connection to ON *mjaltr* 'giving milk' (PIE **$h_2$melǵ-to-*), but the formations are dissimilar. Celtic and Germanic form a noun from the PIE root **$h_2$melǵ-* 'to milk', OIr. *melg* 'milk' and PG **meluk-* 'milk'. However deriving a **-to-*stem in Germanic and a **-ti-*stem in Celtic from a verbal root is trivial.

Mis-

REF: L262, LEIA M-46

OIr. negative and pejorative prefix *mis(s)-* has been connected to ON, OE, OS negative prefix *mis-*, OHG *missa-*, *missi-*. However, while the Germanic is from PIE **mith$_2$-to-*, cf. Skt. *mithita-* 'having become hostile' and OIr. *mis-* is only found in a few doubtful examples usually before consonants, the usual form being *mí-*. This suggests that the OIr. must be reconstructed to a root-final **s*, not **ss*, and that it is incompatible with the G.

Monkey

REF: L264, IEW 2-3, Schrijver 2004, H11, EDPG 31

PC **abanko-* (OIr. *abac* 'dwarf-like water-creature', W *afanc* 'beaver') is most likely unrelated to PG **apan-* 'monkey, ape'. (ON *api*, OE *apa*, OS *apo*, OHG *affo* 'monkey, ape'). The Insular Celtic material may be parsed as **aban-ko-*, a derivative of **abon-* 'river', explaining the meaning 'water-creature' as from 'pertaining to the water'. The Germanic word has no association with water, and is therefore more likely an early adoption of a *Wanderwort* meaning 'monkey', cf. Gr. κῆβος, κῆπος, Hebrew *qōf*, Akkadian *uqūpu*, *iqūpu*, *aqūpu*. The appurtenance of the Hesychian ἀβράνας (perhaps for *ἀββάνας), which is glossed as a 'long-tailed monkey' among the Celts, is uncertain as it must be emended to resemble the Insular Celtic material, and even then provides an imperfect formal match.

Mortal

REF: IEW 260-361, H26

PC **doueno-* < OIr. pl. *dóini*, *doíni* 'men' has been compared to PG **dewana-* > Go. *diwans* 'mortal', cf. OHG *touwen*, OS *dōian*, ON *deyja* 'to die'. However, OIr. *doíni* may rather be derived from PC **gdon-en-* with a later *i*-stem ending, which also explains why it is suppletive to the singular *duine*.

Mound

REF: IEW 1160-1162, H25, EDPG 601

PC **uer-to-* > OIr. *fert* 'mound; esp. a mound over a burial-place' and its derivatives *fertae* 'burial mound', W *gwerthyr* 'fort', *gweryd* 'earth, soil; grave' has been compared with OE *weorð* 'place', *weard* 'guarding', ON *varða*, *varði* 'milestone' < **(H)uor-to/ti-*, *vǫrðr* 'warden' < **(H)uor-tu-*. The isogloss is supposed to lie in the uniquely shared morphology, but the ablaut is different and the application of the *to*-suffix is trivial. The Celtic forms are better connected with PG **wurþi-* 'mound, elevation' < PIE **$h_2$ur-ti-*, which is further cognate with Skt. *vr̥ti-* 'enclosure', ToA *wärt* 'forest'.

Move 1

REF: L254, IEW 1046, Schrijver 2003, 20, H90

W *chwyfio* 'to move', *chwyf* 'motion' has been connected with PG **swimman-* 'swim', but the Welsh is better connected to OIr. *scibid* 'moves'. PG **swimman-* has also been connected to OIr. *to-seinn* 'pursues, drives, hunts', verbal noun *tafann*, following Pokorny's reconstruction **suem-d-n-*, but the *d*-suffix appears ad hoc.

Move 2

REF: L262, IEW 853; Cheung 2007, 184

OIr. *reb* 'sport, game', *rebrad* 'trick, feat' and MHG *reben* 'to move, stir', MLG *reven* 'to talk nonsense', may be related, but the semantics are too weak to warrant an isogloss. Moreover, there is a potential cognate in Proto-Iranian **Hrab/f-* 'to go', cf. Persian *raftan* 'to go', Middle Parthian *raf-* 'to engage, fight'.

Nourisher

REF: IEW 26-27, EDPC 31, EDPG 21

PC **altro-* (OIr. *com-altar* 'joint fosterage', *mí-altar* 'bad fosterage') and PG **aldra-* (ON *aldr*, OE *aldor*, OS *aldar*, OHG *altar*, *aldar* 'age, lifetime') demonstrate the extension of the verb **$h_2$el-* with the instrumental suffix **-tro-*. However, while the meaning PC **altro-* can be derived from that of Lat. *alere*, OIr. *alt* 'to nourish, raise', the meaning of PG **aldra-* 'age, lifetime' rather follows from the semantically divergent **alan-* 'to grow up'. This incongruity points to independent derivation in each of the two branches.

Obscene

REF: L262, IEW 911

A connection between W *serth* 'steep, slanted; obscene' and ON *serða* 'to sodomize', MHG *serten* 'to violate' must be rejected because the Welsh meaning 'obscene' is secondary to 'steep, slanted', as can be observed by comparison with its verbal derivative *syrthio* 'to fall' and the B *serzh* 'steep'.

Plain, moor

REF: L253

Ir. *macha* 'plain, enclosure for milking cows' has been connected with ON *mór* 'moor' through an earlier **mākos*. However the ON word is in reality rather related to PG **mari* 'sea'.

Poem

REF: H8

PC **daunā* > MIr. *dúan* 'poem' may be connected PG **tafna-* > ON *tafn* 'sacrificial animal', and they may continue an identical PIE formation **dh_2p-n-*. However, the same formation is also found in Arm. *tawn* 'feast', Lat. *damnum* 'cost', Gr. δαπάνη 'cost'.

Praise

REF: De Bernardo Stempel 2001, H6, KPV 369-371

Gaul. *ande-díon uediíu-mi* 'I praise a god' and Go. *in-weitan guþ* 'to praise god' have been proposed to share a formation whereby PIE **ueid-* 'see' is combined with semantically similar preverbs to form the meaning 'praise (a god)'. However, this parallel hinges on the analysis of *andedíon uediíumi* as having tmesis, whereby the preverb *ande* and the verb *uēdiíumi* are separated by *díon* 'god'. An alternative interpretation whereby *andedíon* is interpreted as a single noun followed by a simplex verb would remove the Celtic-Germanic isogloss. Moreover, PIE **g^{wh}* probably gives **w-* in Gaulish, so it is preferable to connect *uediíu-mi* to PIE **$g^{wh}ed^h$-io*, because this verb is found elsewhere in Celtic, in e.g. OIr. *guidid*. De Bernardo Stempel rejects the connection with *guidid* because she analyses *guidid* as being in the o-grade, however the vocalism of *guidid* is better explained as the result of raising and rounding in Goidelic: PIE **$g^{wh}ed^h$-ie-* > PC. **g^wed-i-* > **g^wiði-* > **guð'i-* > Ir. *guid-*.

Protection

REF: L259, IEW 740-741, EDPC 276, EDPG 375

OIr. *muin* 'love, protection, patronage' and *muinter* 'family-group' have been connected to OE *mund*, OHG *munt* 'protection'. However, OIr. *muin* in the meaning of 'protection' appears to be specialized use of *muin* 'upper back below the neck', cf. W *mynydd* 'mountain' < **monii̯o-*. The Germanic forms, on the other hand, go back to the unrelated **mundō-* 'hand', cf. ON *mund*, and perhaps Lat. *manus* 'hand'. OIr. *muinter* is from VLat. *monisterium* 'monastery, church'.

Pupil

REF: L264, Kr141, Wissmann 1961, Riecke 1996, 285, Stifter 2009, 273-274, 122

Otherwise unattested Gaulish derivatives of **sek^w-* 'to follow' have been proposed as the sources of Go. *siponeis* 'pupil, disciple' and the hapax OHG *seffo* Prud. gl. *satelles*. However the derivation required to arrive to the Gaulish donor form (**sepānios*) that could be adopted as Go. *siponeis* is unparalleled as well as unattested, leaving the assumption of a Celtic origin speculative at best. OHG *seffo* does not necessarily constitute a Celtic loan either and can alternatively continue an *n*-stem to PG **safjan-* 'to perceive' or **sapjan-*, cf. MHG *sepfen* 'to join, ally oneself with' (cf. Riecke).

Reach

REF: L263, IEW 1057-1058, LEIA T41–42, EDPG 536

OIr. *techtaid* 'to own' and B *tizhout* 'to reach, overtake' have been connected with PG **þegjan-* 'to request'. However, the semantic distance is considerable and the Germanic word has a preferable cognate in Lith. *tenkù*, *tèkti* 'to reach for, suffice' through a root **tek-*. In addition, it is highly likely that the Celtic forms are instead derived from the root **$steig^h$-* (LEIA), cf. OCS *po-stignǫti* 'to attain, catch up with, grasp'.

Ready

REF: L262, IEW 861, H70

The PIE root **(H)$reid^h$-* 'to drive' is continued as *i*-stem adjectives meaning 'ready' in Celtic and Germanic. However the meaning 'ready' is also found in Latv. *raids* and usage as an *i*-stem is rather trivial.

Reject, bud

REF: L261, IEW 169, EDPG 76, 81

OIr. *fris-brudi* 'rejects, refuses' < **brud-ī-* and PG **breutan-* 'to break open, bud' (ON *brjóta*, OE *brēotan*) cannot be reconciled to a single root. The variant OE *brēoðan* 'to break' implies that the primary root was **bʰreut-* in pre-PG, and that the root-final consonantism of **breutan-* is secondary from a geminate *-*tt-* (Kluge's law), probably adopted from the iterative **bruttōn-*. PC **brud-ī-* requires PIE root-final *-*d-* or -*dʰ-*. The semantic connection is furthermore tenuous at best.

Right

REF: L261, IEW 189-191, EDPC 97

The *-*uo-* suffix in PC **dexs(i)uo-* 'right' and PG **tehswō(n)-* 'right' has been suggested to be CG, but Gr. δεξιός 'right (side)' < **deḱsiuo-* (cf. Myc. PN *de-ki-si-wo*, Pamphyl. δεξιϝος) is formed identically.

Ring, clasp

REF: L250, IEW 758, EDPC 282, EDPG 235

OIr. *nasc* 'ring', *naiscid* 'binds, fastens' and OHG *nusca* 'clasp' (whence OFr. *nouche*, MoE *ouche*) have been inferred as CG cognates. However, OIr. *nasc* 'ring' is deverbal from *naiscid* (B *naskañ* 'to tether'), cf. the corresponding verbal noun *naidm*, and derives from the PIE root **neHd-* 'to tie'. The Germanic forms, on the other hand, are possibly derived from **hneudan-* 'to rivet' (implying PG **hnudsk(j)ōn-*), which cannot be cognate with **neHd-* for evidentformal reasons.

Road

REF: L255, Kr140, IEW 908, SBCHP 29, EDPC 330, H73, EDPG 437

PC **sentu-* 'road' (OIr. *sét*), PG **sinþa-* (OE *sīð* 'journey, way, course') have been mentioned as a potential isogloss, but ToA *ṣont* 'road' provides a perfect morphological and semantic match with the Celtic.

Rock

REF: IEW 678, 683, EDPC 134, 242, EDPG 325

PG **lajō-* 'rock, slate' (OFri. *laie*, MDu. *leye* 'slate', OS *leia*, MHG *leie* 'rock') cannot be cognate with or borrowed from PC **ɸlikkā* 'stone' (OIr. *lecc* 'slab', W *llech*, B *lec'h* 'slate'). A connection with OIr. *lía*, acc. *liaic* 'stone' is equally problematic: it is a disyllabic *nk*-stem, suggesting PC **leɸank-*, possibly with a root connection to Lat. *lapis*, gen. *-idis*, Gr. λέπας 'stone', or perhaps PC **līuank-*, cf. Gr. λᾶας 'stone'.

Roof

REF: L250, Kr140, IEW 1013-1014, EDPC 376, 382, EDPG 531

PC **togo-* 'roof' and Germanic **þaka-* 'roof' identically continue an *o*-grade thematic stem **togo-* of the PIE root **(s)teg-* 'to cover', as opposed to e.g. Lat. *tectum* 'roof', but Lith. *stógas* 'roof' also continues the *o*-grade, albeit with *s*-mobile.

Rushes, twig

REF: L252, IEW 174

A deep Celtic-Germanic connection between W *brwyn*, OCo. *brunn-en*, B *broenn* 'rushes' and OE *brogn(e)* 'twig, bush', Nw. *brogn* 'raspberry shrub' is unlikely. The Norwegian connection must be rejected because it appears cherry-picked from a cluster whose variants are irreconcilable with the Celtic: *bragn* is also found, and a connection with Standard Nw. *bringe-bær* 'raspberry' separates it even further from the Celtic. OE *brogn(e)* may be a borrowing from Brittonic in the early first millennium CE.

Sacred grove

REF: L260, Kr139, Sahlgren 1953, EDPC 288, H7 Ko14

A Celto-Germanic morphological isogloss between PC **nemeto-* (Gaul. νεμητον, OIr. *nemed* 'sacred grove, sanctuary') and *nimidas* 'sacred grove', a hapax attested in the *Indiculus superstitionum et paganiarum*. This *nimidas* may be Old Saxon or Old Low Franconian, but could ultimately be a West Germanic loan from Gaulish and hence fall outside the scope of this study. The Swedish farm name *Nymden*, whose original meaning is unclear, does not necessarily belong here.

Settlement

REF: L250, IEW 1090, Pl283, EDPC 338, EDPG 553, Ko12

PC **trebā* 'settlement' is cognate with and semantically identical to PG **þurpa-* 'settlement'. It is noted that in other languages (cf. Lith. *trobà* 'house') it refers to a single building, while Celtic and Germanic share a semantic extension to settlements of more than one building. However, the primary meaning of the Celtic appears to be 'farm with surrounding buildings', the ablaut grades differ between Celtic and Germanic, and the shift from 'farm' to 'village' is trivial, cf. Lat. *villa* 'country house, farm' to French *ville* 'town'.

Shadow

REF: L262, IEW 957

PC **skāto-* 'shadow' (< **ske/oh₃-to-*) has been considered a semantic isogloss with PG **skadu-* 'shadow' (< **skh₃-tú-*), and contrasted with Gr. σκότος (< **skh₃-(e)to-*) 'darkness', but the semantic difference seems trivial. Moreover, the Celtic and Germanic forms go back to two separate formations.

Shake

REF: L253, IEW 152-153

MIr. *bocaid* 'softens, shakes', from MIr. *boc*, MoIr. *bog* 'soft' < **bo/uggo-*, has been compared to OE *cwacian* 'to tremble', *cweccan* 'to turn, shake' < **kwak(ō)jan-*. However this is semantically unconvincing, because the meaning 'to shake' is derived from 'soft' in Goidelic. The Germanic verbs may be sound-symbolic in origin and may not go back to Proto-Germanic being only attested in English.

Shape, manner

REF: L260, IEW 522, 597

A CG *o*-grade and derivation in **-tu-* of the PIE root **ḱek-* 'to help, be able' have been proposed for OIr. *cucht* 'shape, form, color' and ON *hǫ́ttr* 'habit, mode, manner, meter' < **hahtu-*. However this morphology would have resulted in OIr. ***cocht*, because raising of *o* to *u* does not occur before *-cht*, cf. OIr. *ocht* 'eight' < PC **oxtū-*. The Irish requires a root with **u* in it instead, e.g. **ḱeuk-* 'to shine'.

Shield

REF: L247, H52

OIr. *clíab* 'basket, wicker frame' and ON *hlíf* 'shield, protection', OHG *līpen, līppen* 'to protect', Go. *hleibjan* 'to take good care of' are formally reconcilable as a shared root, but this is semantically far-fetched both in Celtic and in Germanic. A proposed older meaning of *clíab* as 'shield (of wickerwork)' is not based on any further evidence, and the meaning 'shield' in Germanic appears derived from 'to protect, to take care of', and not the other way around.

Shining

REF: L259, IEW 429-434

A CG expansion of PIE **ǵʰel-* 'to shine' in **ǵʰlus-(tu-)* is proposed for OIr. *glus* 'light' and ON *glys* 'finery', MHG *glosten, glosen* 'to glow, shine'. However, OIr. *glus* outside compounds is only attested in glossaries, and must be back-formed from compounds such as *íarnglús* 'afterglow, elderniness', *soglus* 'bright light'. The second member of these compounds is most likely a derivative in **-stu-* of OIr. *glé* 'clear, bright', which is unrelated to the Germanic word.

Shirt

REF: Kr142, Schm143, Schu176

OCo. *heuis* gl. *colobium*, B *hiñviz* 'shirt' are borrowed from early reflexes of PG **hamiþja-* 'shirt' (OS *hemithi*, OHG *hemidi*, OE *hemede*), but this borrowing most likely postdates Proto-Germanic, and therefore falls outside of the scope of this study. It was borrowed as Lat. *camisia* 'shirt' around the same period.

Slave

REF: L246, IEW 527-528

The semantic shift of PC **kaxto-* and PG **hafta-* from 'grasped, seized' to 'slave, prisoner, captive' has been described as Celto-Germanic. The Latin term with the most similar meaning would be *captīvus*, rather than the exact cognate *captus* 'grasped, seized'. However *captus* may also refer to prisoners and captives. Moreover, W *caeth* used as an adjective may mean 'tight, close, strict' in addition to 'bond, captive' and thus preserves the original meaning 'grasped'.

Slender

REF: L262, IEW 1047, EDPC 358, H89

OIr. *seng* 'slender' < PC **su(a/e)ngo-* and MHG, MLG *swanc* 'slender' < PG **swanka-* have been argued to contain a CG root **sueng-* 'to bend'. However, Skt. *svájate*, 'embraces', fut. *svaṅkṣyate* must also be from **sueng-*. The meaning 'slender' is shared, but this innovation is trivial from the perspective of the original meaning 'to bend', because bendable objects are by definition slender. The Irish word does not need to derive from **suengo-*, but could equally well begin with **s-*, **sp-*, or **st-*. It is only the suggested etymology that supports a reconstruction with **su -*. A different root connection incompatible with Germanic could be with PC **stung-o-* 'to bend', which in the full grade would give **stuengo-* > OIr. *seng*.

Snare, sling

REF: L248, IEW 1062, Blöndal 1989, 1181, EDPC 377, H53

PG **þelman-* (OE *þelma* 'trap', Icel. *þjálmi* 'snare') is formed identically to Gr. τελαμών 'leather strap', both from a PIE root **telh₂-* 'to bear, endure' expanded with **-mn-*. This word is probably not related to OIr. *teilm, tailm* 'sling' < PC **telmi-*, because the root-final laryngeal would vocalize giving OIr. ***talaim*. B *talm* 'sling', W *telm* 'snare, trap' contain an *-lm-* cluster that cannot be inherited from PIE **lm*, so they must be borrowed from OIr., or perhaps from OE *þelma* 'trap'.

Sneak

REF: L255, IEW 974, EDPC 349

Ir. *snighid* 'creeps, crawls' has been connected to PG **snīgan-* 'to crawl, creep'. However the Irish primarily means 'to pour down, flow, drip'. Its ancestor OIr. *snigid* 'drips, flows' does not carry the semantics 'creep, crawl' at all, and is from PIE **sneigʷʰ-* 'to snow'.

Soap

REF: Kr142, IEW 894, Birkhan 1970, 248-250, EDLI 550

PG **saipwōn-, saipjōn-* 'soap' has been argued to have been borrowed into Celtic because Pliny the Elder's *Natural History* (Book 28, 51) describes *sāpō* 'soap' as an invention from the Gallic provinces. However, no descendant of *sāpō* is continued in Insular Celtic, so Lat. *sāpō* is best considered a loanword from Germanic. W *sebon* 'soap' may be a borrowing from Old Low Franconian or primitive Old Frisian, which underwent PG **ai* > **ē*.

Soft

REF: L261, IEW 661-662

MIr. *lían* 'soft' and ON *linr* 'soft, gentle, weak', MHG *līn*, gen. *-wes* 'tepid, exhausted, bad' and Bavarian *len* 'soft, exhausted, unsalted' < **lĭnwa-* appear similar. However, the (rare) Irish word may be a borrowing from Lat. *lēnis* 'soft'. Even if it is inherited from PIE, it has a perfect cognate in Lith. *leĩnas* 'lithe, slender, flexible' < **leino-*.

Spear

REF: L248, IEW 681-682, H43

W *llost* 'tail, spear', B *lost* 'tail', Ir. *loss* 'end, tail' has been connected with ON *ljóstr* 'fish-spear', *ljósta* 'to strike', but the meaning 'tail' rather than 'spear' is primary in Celtic and therefore presumably older; the transferred sense 'spear' is only found in Welsh. The Celtic forms are masculine in Irish and Breton and feminine in Breton, so a reconstruction to masculine PC **losto-* rather than feminine **lustā* is to be preferred. This masculine proto-form is formally irreconcilable with the Germanic forms, which build on a root **leust-*.

Speckled

REF: Marstrander 1910, 371-373, L251, IEW 28, 30-31, EDLI 24

Ir. and ScG *ala* 'speckled; trout' (Kerry?), MIr. *alad* 'speckled, piebald', ScG *àladh* 'speckled, variegated' < PC **alado-* and OHG *alant*, *alunt* 'ide', ON *ǫlunn* 'mackerel' < PG **alunþa-* have been alleged to contain a CG semantic shift of a root *h_2*el-* 'to burn' > 'be speckled', and perhaps thence to 'speckled fish'. However, the meaning 'trout' is apparently restricted to dialectal modern Irish, and clearly developed from 'variegated'. A semantic shift to 'speckled' is otherwise unattested in Germanic, cf. Sw. dial. (Småland, Kalmar län) *ala* 'to smolder', and the existence of a PIE root **al-* (*h_2*el-*) 'to burn' is itself doubtful.

Steep

REF: IEW 170-171, EDPG 74

A connection between PG **branta-* 'high, steep' and W *bryn* 'hill' has been suggested, but the Welsh word is rather connected to OIr. *bruinne* 'breast' < Pre-PC. **brusnio-* (cf. W *bron* 'breast; hill-side, slope'), which means it is incompatible with the Germanic.

Stem

REF: L262–263, LEIA TU-25, IEW 1004-1010

OIr. *tamon* 'stump, tree trunk' and OHG *stam*, ON *stafn* 'stem' both continue PIE *(s)*th*$_2$*-mn-* from root *(s)*teh*$_2$*-* 'to stand'. However the formation is found in many languages, e.g. Lat. *stāmen* 'warp (of loom)', and the semantics look archaic in view of ToA *ṣtām*, B *stām* 'tree'. OIr. *tamon* can also be derived from **temh*$_1$*-no-* 'cut-off thing'.

Stream

REF: L252, IEW 161, EDPG 140-141, eDIL

OIr. *búal* 'water; healing' is compatible with a reconstruction PC **boglā* 'stream', which may then be compared to PG **bakja-* 'creek'. However the OIr. appears to be a glossary word back-formed to *búalad* 'bathing, healing, curing', itself a verbal noun of *búailid* 'strikes' with semantic narrowing, as eDIL suggests. A third possibility is that OIr. *búal* was somehow back-formed to *fúal* 'urine, foul water'. Even if *búal* were related to PG **bakja-*, ORu. *bagъno* 'mud, marsh' provides a potential non-Celtic cognate (*pace* IEW). Alternatively, the Germanic word has been derived from **b*^{h}*og*^{w}*-io-*, i.e. a *io*-stem to the PIE root **b*^{h}*eg*^{w}*-* 'to run'.

Strike, wound

REF: L248, IEW 491-493, H58, H61, EDPG 599

PC **g*^{w}*an-o-* 'to strike' and PG **wunda-* 'wound' have been considered lexemes restricted to Celtic and Germanic. However both go back to the PIE root **g*^{wh}*en-* 'to strike', cf. Hittite *ku̯enzi* 'id.'.

Tale, poet

REF: Lidén 1891, 507-508, Wadstein, 1895, L258, IEW 897-898, Blöndal 1989, 826, H14

OIr. *scél* 'tale', W *chwedl* 'saying, fable' and (late) ON *skáld* have been adduced to hypothesize a shared element PC **sk*^{w}*etlo-* ~ PG **sk*^{w}*ētlo-* (the latter with *vṛddhi*) derived from the PIE root **sek*^{w}*-* followed by the abstract suffix **-etlo-*. However, despite secondary derivations such as *skældinn* 'skilled in poetry', the long vowel of *skáld* is probably secondary due to the regular twelfth-century lengthening of back vowels before *-lC-*, which renders this analysis formally problematic. The older form *skăld* can alternatively be a derivation of the PG strong verb **skeldan-* 'to announce, reproach'; this derivation seems preferable because it has intra-Germanic cognates in OHG *skelto*, MHG *schelte* 'blamer, criticizer, satirist'.

Talk

REF: L257, IEW 831, EDPC 231

A connection between OIr. *labar* 'talkative', OIr. *labraithir* 'to speak', W *llafar* 'loud, talkative', W *llefaru* 'to speak' and LG *flappen* 'to gossip', ME *flappen* 'to hit' has been proposed, but a sound-symbolic origin is to be preferred. Since these types of words are constantly reinvented, one cannot base an isogloss on them, cf. Du. *babbelen* 'to chatter', Swiss German *plapperen* 'to attempt to speak (as a baby)'.

Thunder

REF: IEW 1021, EDPC 384

PC **tonaro-* > **torano-* 'thunder' and PG **þunra-* 'thunder' identically continue formations of PIE *(s)*tenH-* 'thunder' expanded with **-r-*, but this appears shared with MoP *tundar* 'thunder'.

Tip 3

REF: EDPG 141, Stifter 2018, fn. 10

OIr. *ind*, *inn* 'end, tip, top' and PG **fin(n)ōn-* (OSw. *fina* 'fin', MDu. *vinne* 'fin, wing, prickle, awn') could point to a CG **pinno-*. However there is a single early attestation of *ind* in the Milan Glosses (45d19), which requires a PC reconstruction with **-nd-*, removing the isogloss.

Top

REF: L260, IEW 96-97, EDPC 54

OIr. _benn_ 'peak, horn' and MW _bann_ 'beacon, peak, top', B _bann_ 'peak' may go back to PC *_ban(d)nā_. The Gaulish reflex of this root is borrowed into Occitan _bano_ 'horn'. Even if the Celtic is formally compatible with OE _pintel_ 'penis', the semantics do not convince. MLG _pinne_ 'pin' is most likely from Lat. _penna_ 'feather'.

Tower

REF: Kr141, Pl283

Gaul. _celicnon_ '?temple' and Go. _kelikn_ 'tower, upper room' may be a borrowing from Gaulish into Gothic, but this borrowing, if accepted, most likely postdates the Proto-Germanic period in view of the restriction to both Gothic and Gaulish. The Gothic word has been compared to MP _kl'k_ 'fortress' and derived forms in Georgian, Armenian and Ossetic.

Tree 1

REF: L253, IEW 873, Stifter 1998

OIr. _rúaim_ 'water alder, alder tree' and OHG _ruzboum_, _ruost_, MoHG _rüster_ 'elm' do not constitute an isogloss. The Irish is most likely related to OIr. _rúam_ 'red dye' < PIE *h_1reud^h-_smon-_ from *h_1reud^h- 'to redden', and the Germanic word has a different suffix and appears to have PG *-_ō_-.

Tree 2

REF: IEW 697, Neumann 1961, 77f., EDPC 369

OCo. _glas-tannen_, MBr. _glastannenn_ 'green oak' has been connected to OS _danna_ 'pine', OHG _tanna_ 'fir wood'. However, the initial consonants, PC *_t_- vs. PG *_d_- cannot be reconciled and the meanings 'oak' vs. 'fir, pine' are also dissimilar. A proposed PIE *_(s)d_^{h}- giving PC *_st_ followed by loss of *_s_- in Celtic is ad hoc, because there is no evidence of such an _s_-mobile. In the absence of such an _s_-mobile, the Hitt. hapax _tanau_- 'some kind of tree' may be related to either Celtic or Germanic, but not both. A connection with Skt. _dhánuṣ_- 'bow', YAv. _ϑanuuarə_, _ϑanuuan_- 'bow' is formally compatible with the Germanic reflexes, but not the Celtic. The only way to save the isogloss would be to divorce it from the proposed IE cognates, and assume a substrate origin.

Tribe

REF: L259, IEW 503-504, EDPC 435, EDPG 9

OIr. _icht_ 'tribe, progeny' appears similar to PG *_aihti_- 'property, family', but the Irish may be connected within Celtic with W _iaith_, MB _yez_ 'language', which is in turn connected with the PIE root *_iek_- 'to speak, utter'. The Germanic form, on the other hand, cannot be derived from this root.

Twig

REF: IEW 412-413, EDPG 172

OIr. _gat_ 'withe, osier', OIr. _gas_ 'sprig, shoot, twig' allow for reconstruction of PC *_gazdo_-, *_gasto_-, which in turn looks similar to Go. _gazds_ 'sting, goad', ON _gaddr_ 'goad, spike' < PG *_gazda_-. However Lat. _hasta_ 'spear' may also be connected.

Urine

REF: L257

B _staot_ 'urine' and MHG, MLG, MDu. _stal_ 'horse piss', MHG, MLG, MDu. _stallen_ 'to piss (of horses)' are clearly connected, but not as a Celto-Germanic isogloss. B _staot_ < *_stalt_ (with the regular change of *_alt_ > _aot_) was likely borrowed from OFr. _estal_ 'urine', even though the final _t_ remains unexplained. This _estal_, in turn, was probably borrowed from Old Low Franconian *_stall_, for which see the aforementioned West Germanic forms. Ir. _stalladh_ 'warm or stale drink' cannot be inherited because PC *_st_- regularly becomes _s_- in Goidelic.

Uterus

REF: L256

OW _gumbelauc_ 'womb' and B _gwamm_ 'woman' (jocular) have been connected to PG *_wambō_- 'womb, belly'. The OW appears to be a ghost word and the Breton word meant '(newly-)married woman; prostitute' in Middle Breton, hence it provides a poor semantic match. Even if the Germanic and Breton words are related, the existence of Skt. _gabhá_- 'vagina' < *$g^{wh}mb^h$-_o_- shows that this lexeme is not specific to Celtic and Germanic.

Vessel

REF: L249, IEW 351, H96, EDPG 280

PG *_kannō_ 'can, jug' has been connected to MIr. _gann_ 'vessel, jug, pitcher', but _gann_ is only attested in glossaries and may well be a sideform of OIr. _cann_, _canna_ 'can, vessel' < OE _canne_ or Lat. _panna_.

Wagon

REF: L254, IEW 1118-1120, Pr120, H72, Ko9, EDPG 565

A Celto-Germanic formation of the PIE root *_ueǵ_^{h}- 'to move, carry, drive' with *-_no_- in PC *_uegno_- (OIr. _fén_ 'wagon') and PG *_wagna_- (ON _vagn_, OHG _wagan_ 'wagon') has been proposed. However, ToA _wkäṃ_, ToB _yakne_ 'way, manner' continue an identical formation, and a semantic isogloss may be rejected on the basis of e.g. Gr. ὄχος 'carriage'. OIr. _fén_ 'wagon' may moreover be from PC *_ued-no_, from PIE *_ued_^{h}- 'to lead'. This root is better attested in Celtic in e.g. OIr. _feidid_ 'brings, leads'. The oft-quoted W _gwain_ is a ghost word back-formed from _certwain_ 'wagon', an OE loanword.

Whirl

REF: L254, IEW 1050-1051

W _chwerfu_ 'to whirl' and _chwerfan_ 'whorl, pulley' has been compared to PG *_swerban_- 'to wipe, sweep, swerve', but _chwerfu_ appears to be a ghost word not found outside dictionaries, and _chwerfan_ is borrowed from OE _hweorfa_, obl. -_an_ m. 'joint, whorl'.

Wild

REF: IEW 1123-1142, H47

A uniquely shared root is proposed for PC **ueidu-* 'wild' and PG **waiþa-* 'hunt'. However, the proto-forms to not match because of the different dentals. The Germanic word goes back to PIE **uoih$_1$-to-*, see PIE **ueih$_1$-* 'to strive for', cf. Skt. *véti* 'turns toward, pursues'. The Celtic word is probably derived from **uidu-* 'wood' (q.v.).

Wisdom

REF: Irslinger 2002, 412ff., H15, EDPG 163

OIr. *gáes* 'intelligence' and PG **gaista-* 'supernatural spirit' appear superficially similar, however the Irish may be synchronically derived from *gáeth* 'intelligent', cf. *báes* 'folly' < *báeth* 'foolish'. This means that there is no guarantee that the Irish formation goes back far enough to warrant a Celto-Germanicism. Moreover, EDPG reconstructs pre-PG **ǵ^{h}ois-do-* for **gaista-*, cf. Av. *zōižda-* 'terrible', which would have yielded an unattested OIr. ***gáet*.

Withered

REF: IEW 578, LEIA C-236-237, KPV 420-422, H24

PC **krīno-* (OIr. *crín* 'enfeebled, decrepit, withered', W *crin* 'withered, brittle', B *krin* 'dry, miserly') and PG **hraiwa-* (ON *hrœ*, OE *hrǣ(w)*, *hrā(w)*, OFri. *hrē-* 'corpse, remains'), have been argued to contain a Germano-Celtic extension of PIE **kerh$_2$-* 'to break' to **ḱr(e/o)iH-*. However the Celtic most likely is from **ḱrih$_1$-no-*, derived from **ḱreh$_1$(i)-* 'to shake'.

Wound 1

REF: IEW 618, 933, EDPC 222, H60, EDPG 242

PC **kre(n)xtu-* 'wound, scar' (MIr. *crécht*, W *craith*) has a cognate in Lith. *krèkti* 'to coagulate', so a uniquely CG connection with ON *skrá* 'scroll' or ON *hrekja* 'to drive away, worry, damage' would have to be based on a morphological or semantic similarity, which is not found.

Wound 2

REF: IEW 559-563, H56, EDPG 236

PC **knidā* 'wound' (OIr. *cned* 'wound'), PG **hnītan-* 'to wound, poke, butt' (cf. OIcel. *hnīta* 'to butt'), both from PIE **ḱneid-*, have been identified as containing a semantic isogloss with the meaning 'wound', as opposed to Gr. κνίζω 'to scratch, tickle, provoke'. However the meaning 'to gash' is also found in Greek, and the range of meanings in Germanic is so broad that a chance resemblance with Celtic is likely.

Part IV The Bronze Age Chariot and Wool Horizons

14 RELATIVE AND ABSOLUTE CHRONOLOGIES OF THE CHARIOT COMPLEX IN NORTHERN EURASIA AND EARLY INDO-EUROPEAN MIGRATIONS

IGOR V. CHECHUSHKOV AND ANDREY EPIMAKHOV

14.1 Introduction

Linking the distribution of wheeled transport to the evolution of language is a strategy often employed to locate the Indo-European (IE) motherland and trace the formation of various Indo-European languages in different parts of the Old World. The underlying assumption is that archaeological assemblages that are separate in space but similar in appearance represent people speaking dialects of the same language. The chronology, sources, and spatiality of the IE migrations, however, remain topics of heated discussion. Specifically, researchers disagree on which early archaeological phenomenon represents the source of early IE migration (Grigoriyev 2002; Anthony 2007; Allentoft et al. 2015; Klejn et al. 2017).

In this chapter, we examine the most prominent type of early wheeled transport, namely, the two-wheeled horse-drawn chariot. We accept the proposition that the horse chariot has a strong association with speakers of the Indo-European languages, and thus its origin and distribution may be employed to solve the IE riddle (Kuzmina 2007). A chariot is a two-wheeled vehicle drawn by a team of bridled horses, technically consisting of a draft pole and spoked wheels. As a complex technology, the chariot represents a new stage in technological and social development, related to the formation of military leadership during long-distance migration. In northern Eurasia, the material evidence for the chariot complex includes the buried remains of two-wheeled vehicles, accompanied by horses, cheekpieces, and combat arms (Chechushkov & Epimakhov 2018; Chechushkov et al. 2018). Further research on the chariot complex aims to illuminate the sources and direction of the IE migration within the Eurasian landmass and to deepen our understanding of related social processes.

Today, archaeological work has allowed us to outline the overall territory of the chariot complex within the Eastern European and Central Asian steppes, but the chronology of its diffusion remains unassessed. The contradictions between regional chronological schemes keep us from a comprehensive understanding of the historical processes that caused the invention and distribution of the horse chariot throughout northern Eurasia. In conjunction, there is also a lack of understanding of the early IE migrations within this part of the Old World: despite advances in palaeo-DNA studies, we still need to assess just how fast the IE people moved and the principal directions in which they traveled. In the remainder of this paper, we will examine the relative and absolute chronologies of the Eurasian chariot complex to clarify its origins and expansions. The analytical foundation is the comparative study of material culture and examination of the radiocarbon evidence. Our analysis covers 800 years within the Middle and Late Bronze Age (ca. 4300–3500 BP), during which the horse-drawn chariot was invented, developed, and then started its journey across northern Eurasia.

To give a synopsis, the modeling of radiocarbon dates and analysis support the previous notion of the steppe chariots as the earliest known in the world (Anthony 2007). The forerunner of the chariot concept originated in the Eastern European steppes, then spread eastward. In the Southern Urals, the chariot concept reached its apex ca. 4000 to 3950 BP. The Sintashta society became the primary center of chariot development, from which the complex propagated in all directions. It seems logical to assume that long-distance migration caused the original invention, but the further spread could be due to networking and intergroup and intercultural connections. The analysis also highlights the existing difficulties and unsolved issues. We conclude that the exclusive focus on assessing the chronology of archaeological cultures – rather than dating individual assemblages for comparative purposes – as well as the lack of radiocarbon dating for the Middle Bronze Age complexes from the Don–Volga interfluve limit our understanding of the early IE migrations. Data collection is crucial for further analysis.

14.2 Cultural Background and Relative Chronology

To understand how the horse chariot was developed in the steppes, we first need to consider the relative chronology and cultural background of the Bronze Age, including the chariot's precursors and early practices of horse utilization.

The relative chronology of the Bronze Age steppe consists of three consecutive periods: the Early (ca. 5600–4450 BP), Middle (ca. 4450–3950 BP), and Late Bronze Age (ca. 3950–3450 BP). Kurgan stratigraphy provided the initial evidence for the relative chronology of Bronze Age cultures. Gorotsov (1927) demonstrated stratigraphically that the Pit Grave culture was followed by the Catacomb Grave and then by the Timber Grave (Srubnaya) complexes in Eastern Europe. There is no such evidence, however, in the Southern Urals, where the Catacomb phenomenon hardly existed, and the Pit Grave culture is followed by Late Bronze Age cultures (Morgunova 2014). Moreover, Gorotsov's scheme has since been updated with evidence that in some areas, the cultural traditions coexisted.

Chernykh (1992) conducted a typological and chemical analysis of metal artifacts that allowed this relative chronology to be refined. He found that each period of the Bronze Age is characterized by uniform technologies and traditions of copper metallurgy, present across vast areas. The upper and lower limits of phases are not necessarily simultaneous in various regions but are staggered based on the spread and adoption of technologies, stagnation processes, multilineal cultural processes, etc. This last notion is also supported by radiocarbon dating, which demonstrates the significant overlap between the measurements from the Pit Grave and Catacomb sites (Chernykh 2008). The Early and Middle phases of the Bronze Age correspond to the development and diffusion of the so-called Circumpontic Metallurgical Province: the phenomenon that integrates the technological and morphological standards of metalworking, particular categories, and forms of tools and weapons, as well as the use of copper-arsenic alloys. The Late Bronze Age corresponds to the formation and spread of the Western Asian Metallurgical Province, which differs sharply from the former by relying on new sources of metal in Asia and the production of tin bronzes (Chernykh 2008: 79–85).

Complex pastoralism dominated the steppe subsistence system throughout the Bronze Age, but a certain amount of wild fauna and plants, as indicated by the Mikhailovskoye III settlement (Korobkova & Shaposhnikova 2005: 256–257), also contributed to the diet. The specific ecological niches also caused significant variability in caloric intake from different sources, herd composition, degree of mobility and traveling distances, and seasonality. Horse herding and breeding could already be practiced in Early Bronze Age Eastern Europe. For instance, faunal remains comprised of up to 70% horse bones from the early Pit Grave settlement of Repin suggest that the horse constituted a major source of meat. Inhabitants of the Mikhailovskoye I settlement could have practiced horse breeding as well, with an assemblage containing up to 7% horse bones. While this evidence does not point to breeding, horse bones from the Neolithic settlements of Mullino II, Ivanovo, Davlekanovo, Vilovatovo, Varfolomeyevka, and Rakushechnyy Yar and unambiguous evidence from the Khvalynsk and Syezhee cemeteries, as well as Srednyi Stog II, Dereivka, and other habitation sites, suggest that the horse played an important role in subsistence from the Neolithic/Chalcolithic period, ca. 8000 to 5600 BP (Naumov 2002; Dergachev 2007; Agapov 2010, etc.). Altogether, these facts allow us to assume that Early Bronze Age Eastern Europeans could at least attempt to control horse breeding and sporadically use it to perform work.

Wheeled transport emerged in the Eurasian steppes during the time of the Early Bronze Age Pit Grave and Novotitorovskaya cultures (ca. 5600–4200 BP). The Pit Grave burials were the earliest in the steppe to be accompanied by either complete four-wheeled wagons or their wheels. The wagons and wheels were constructed of heavy planks, so it is accepted that they were pulled by bovines and used as both a means of transport, and as mobile homes. Currently, we lack direct evidence to attest the use of draft horses at that time, but there are possible metal cheekpieces (Munchaev 1973) and metal bovine nose rings from the Maikop culture sites of the Caucasus (Kantarovich et al. 2013).

Various archaeological cultures characterize the Middle Bronze Age (ca. 4450–3950 BP) west of the Volga River, including the Catacomb culture and its derivatives. The elaborate burials of the Catacomb culture, especially those with numerous four-wheeled wagons, can be associated with high-status people, possibly chiefs and warlords of local communities (Cherednichenko & Pustovalov 1991). During this period, the first two-wheeled vehicles in the steppes appeared and were buried in the cemeteries of Tyagunova Mogila, Izhevka (Pustovalov 2000), and Bolshoi Ipatovskyi Kurgan (Korenevskiy et al. 2007), all located in the Black Sea region. These carts have small (up to 60 cm diameter), single-piece disk wheels with an integral nave rotating independently on the axle. They can thus be seen as forerunners of an actual chariot, similar to those vehicles known in the Near East at this time. It is unclear whether the Catacomb people utilized domestic horses for transportation, but horse remains at the seasonal settlement Rykan-3 (Gak et al. 2019) and the undoubted presence of horses as ritual offerings in the burials suggest their great importance (Andreeva 2009; Shishlina et al. 2014). Finally, clay models that are interpreted by some archaeologists as representations of two-wheeled carts are worth mentioning in this context (for a detailed critique, see Izbitser 2017).

In the post-Catacomb period, evidence for two- and four-wheeled vehicles almost vanishes from ritual contexts. There are two cases of four-wheeled vehicles (the Aktove and Sadovyi cemeteries of the Coțofeni culture), as well as Babino culture clay models that possibly represent the wheel (Litvinenko 2016). There is no direct evidence that would demonstrate the methods of bridling draft animals. Due to the lack of materials, however, it remains unclear exactly what happened on the eastern periphery of the Middle Bronze Age cultures (east of the Volga) between ca. 4250 and 4050 BP, and our analysis in the next section aims to reconstruct the hypothetical scenario that covers this gap.

The transition to the Late Bronze Age (ca. 4050–3650 BP) is the time when the use of horse chariots emerged in the steppes between the Don and Irtysh rivers. The actual artifacts are associated with such archaeological developments as Sintashta-Petrovka, Potapovka, and Abashevo-Pokrovka, and the Sintashta sites have yielded the most famous chariot finds

(Gening 1977). This period demonstrates the increase in social complexity related to the emergence of military leadership; both the chariot complex and new types of combat arms support this notion. In stark contrast to the preceding periods, there is also a complete embodiment of "the chariot myth," including the sacrifice of teamed horses and the organization of burial space to represent the chariot ride to the Afterlife.

There are thirty-one known cases of actual chariots, but cheekpieces are spread widely across the ecumene of the Late Bronze Age cultures. Brownrigg (2006) and Chechushkov et al. (2018) have concluded that patterns of use-wear indicate that shield-like antler cheekpieces were used to exercise control over harnessed horses. Given the fact that this class of cheekpieces always occurs in the Sintashta-Petrovka chariot graves, we suggest that shield-like cheekpieces were primarily developed in the transition period to be used with the teamed chariot horses. In our view, in this period the warrior elites started to play a leading role in expanding the pastoral groups across the Eurasian steppes, resulting in the formation of the Sintashta phenomenon and, later, the Srubnaya and Andronovo horizons.

The Timber Grave (Srubnaya) and Andronovo cultures are massive cultural entities of the Late Bronze Age (ca. 3650–3450 BP), the former covering the area from the Dnieper to the Ural River and the latter stretching east of the Ural Mountains. Both phenomena are characterized by many features of the preceding times, augmented by innovations. For instance, the Andronovo people continued to rely on livestock breeding, hunting, and gathering, while the Srubnaya people attempted to practice some plant cultivation (Ryabogina & Ivanov 2011). The mining of copper ore reached an almost industrial scale in such settlements as Gorny, which is believed to be a specialized metallurgical center where metal was produced for trade (Chernykh 2002). On the other hand, signs of combat leadership vanished from the mortuary practices, suggesting the simplification of the social structure.

Chariots are not known in the Timber Grave and Andronovo material, but there are finds of teamed horses, in some cases bridled with studded cheekpieces, and ceramic vessels with images of two-wheeled vehicles on them (Zaharova 2000). Moreover, numerous petroglyphs depicting chariot technology are widespread throughout the Andronovo territory (Novozhenov 2012). Although petroglyphs on open-air natural rock surfaces are obviously hard to date, the occurrence of similar carvings on stone grave stelae within some Andronovo culture cemeteries (such as the Tamgaly Cemetery and the Samara Cemetery in Sary Arka, Kazakhstan) provide a level of chronological control.

The plate-like cheekpieces of this period signify changes in horse utilization, since they are made in a simplified fashion and from cheaper material, and the majority of them are found in domestic, not ritual contexts. Moreover, Chechushkov et al. (2018) have experimentally demonstrated that the plate-like cheekpieces could be used for both riding and driving, but use-wear patterns suggest that the majority of them were used for riding. Perhaps the use of chariots was limited to the early phase of the Srubnaya-Andronovo period, while at a later period, cheekpieces served for horseback riding for transportation and herding instead of chariotry. In this case, horseback riding may have become important in warfare earlier than the Iron Age, even beginning as early as the Srubnaya period of the Late Bronze Age, the precursor of the IE-speaking Cimmerians and the Scythians.

In the remainder of this chapter, we will examine the facts of absolute chronology to assess the timing and direction of the chariot complex diffusion.

14.3 Absolute Chronology

Here we apply a Bayesian approach in order to test whether the relative chronology discussed above complies with the available series of radiocarbon dates. We isolated a total of twenty-nine measurements for calibration with OxCal 4.3 (intCal13) (Ramsey 2009; Reimer et al. 2013). Specifically, we chose radiocarbon dates that came from closed archaeological complexes (i.e., graves) and contained evidence for either vehicles or cheekpieces. If more than one measurement was obtained from the complex, the dates were combined (with the R_Combine command in OxCal) and tested to determine whether they agree with each other. In some cases, measurements from the same contexts fail the chi-square test, so we disregard those that do not agree with the larger series of radiometric observations yielded by parental archaeological assemblages. For instance, the majority of measurements from the Krivoe Ozero Cemetery cluster around 3500 BP. At the same time, two radiocarbon measurements from Grave 1 (kurgan 9) yielded the ages 3740±50 and 3700±60 BP, while two others have the ages 3580±50 and 3525 ±50 BP. So, in addition to the fact that the two earlier dates contradict the larger series, they also contradict two other measurements, both of which were obtained from the same specimens, respectively. As a result, the combined pairs fail the chi-square test, and the two earliest are disregarded from further consideration as outliers.

In total, twenty-four measurements were brought together to model the chronology of the Eurasian chariot complex (Table 14.1).

The Bayesian sequence model consists of four successive phases. The isolation of chronological phase 1 (metaphorically called "The Age of Two-Wheelers") serves to establish the initial point in time and space where the idea of two-wheeled carts first appeared in the steppes and from which it spread. Chronological phase 2 ("The Dawn of the Chariot") combines the data on the earliest evidence of the chariot complex, including the simplest forms of shield-like cheekpieces, which were probably used to bridle harnessed horses. Chronological phase 3 ("The Age of Heroes") defines the time when chariots were in wide use in northern Eurasia. This is the period when the Sintashta-Petrovka development occupied the territory of the southern Trans-Urals and diffused to the territory of present-day northern Kazakhstan, while the sites of the Pokrovka and Potapovka developments occupied the Don–Volga interfluve. The differentiation between phase 2 and phase 3 are justified by

TABLE 14.1. Chronology of chariotry of Northern Eurasia. Radiocarbon measurements.

#	Site	Lab code	Radiocarbon determination	Cultural interpretation	Finds*	Reference
1	Bolshoi Ipatovskiy, G. 32	GrA-13660	3850±40	Catacomb	v	Korenevskiy et al. 2007
2	Bolshoi Ipatovskiy, G. 32	GIN 10147	3770±40	Catacomb	v	Korenevskiy et al. 2007
3	Sintashta Cemetery, SM, g. 28	Ki-657	3760±120	Sintashta	v	Hanks et al. 2007
3	Dubovyi Gai, g. 4	IGRAN-3251	2025–1944 (calibrated interval only)	Abashevo-Pokrovka	cp	Zeleneyev and Yudin. 2010
4	Lipetskiy Kurgan, g. 2	KIA-46737	3698±25	Abashevo-Pokrovka	cp	Shishlina and Fernandes 2016
5	Sintashta Cemetery, SM, g. 19	Vil-?	3620±60	Sintashta	v/cp	Hanks et al. 2007
6	Rozdestveno 1, Kurgan 4, g. 1	Le-10486	3590±40	Abashevo-Pokrovka	cp	Shishlina et al. 2015
7	Krivoe Ozero, Kurgan 9, g. 1	AA-9874a	3580±50	Sintashta	v	Anthony and Vinogradov 1995
8	Kamennyi Ambar 5 Cemetery, Kurgan 2, g. 6	OxA-12530	3572±50	Sintashta	v/cp	Hanks et al. 2007
9	Utevka VI Cemetery, Kurgan 6, g. 6	OxA-4264	3565±80	Potapovka	v	Kuznetsov 2006
10	Sintashta Cemetery, SM, g. 19	Ki-654	3560±180	Sintashta	v/cp	Hanks et al. 2007
11	Sintashta Cemetery, SM, g. 19	Ki-864	3560±180	Sintashta	v/cp	Hanks et al. 2007
12	Kamennyi Ambar 5 Cemetery, Kurgan 2, g. 8	OxA-12531	3549±29	Sintashta	v/cp	Hanks et al. 2007
13	Potapovka, Kurgan 3. g. 4	AA-47807	3536±57	Potapovka	cp	Kuznetsov 2006
14	Rozdestveno 1, Kurgan 4, g. 1	Poz-66115	3530±35	Abashevo-Pokrovka	cp	Shishlina et al. 2015
15	Krivoe Ozero, Kurgan 9, g. 1	AA-9875b	3525±50	Sintashta	v	Anthony and Vinogradov 1995
16	Novoil'inovskiy 2, Kurgan 5, RO1a	AA109587	3514±30	Petrovka	cp	Usmanova et al. 2018
17	Utevka VI Cemetery, Kurgan 6, g. 4	OxA-4262	3510±80	Potapovka	v	Kuznetsov 2006
18	Rozdestveno 1, Kurgan 4, g. 1	Poz-66057	3495±35	Abashevo-Pokrovka	cp	Shishlina et al. 2015
19	Utevka VI Cemetery, Kurgan 6, g. 6	OxA-4263	3470±80	Potapovka	cp	Kuznetsov 2006
20	Potapovka, Kurgan 3, g. 4	GIN-11873	3450±90	Potapovka	cp	Kuznetsov 2006
21	Satan Cemetery, Kurgan 1	LOIA-2320	3420±160	Petrovka	v	Novozhenov 1989
22	Khripunovskiy Cemetery, g. 44	Le-6150	3370±25	Alakul	cp	Matveev et al. 2007
23	Sintashta Cemetery, SM, g. 5	Ki-862	3360±70	Sintashta (?)	v	Hanks et al. 2007
24	Khripunovskiy Cemetery, g. 44	SOAN-4502	3320±45	Alakul	cp	Matveev et al. 2007

* v – vehicle, cp – cheekpiece(s)

the stylistic variations in the shield-like cheekpieces that are known in the materials of both phases. Chronological phase 4, called "The Age of Riders Begins," marks the end of phase 3 as the beginning of the transition from shield-like to rod-shaped cheekpieces, which we believe to have been used primarily to bridle riding horses.

The resulting Bayesian chronological model suggests a total span of 763 radiocarbon years between the median values of

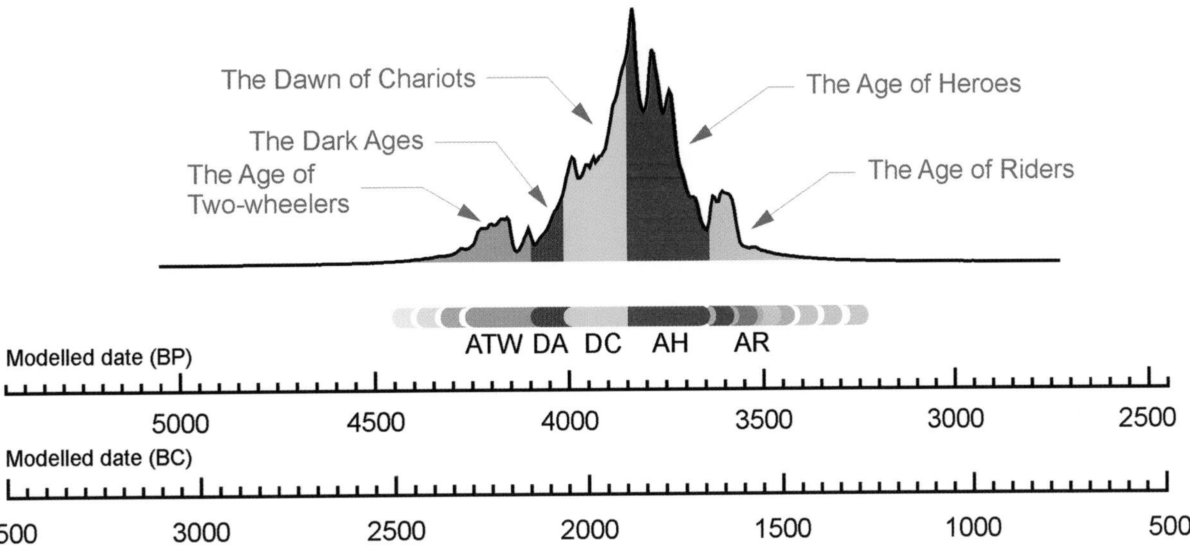

FIGURE 14.1. The Bayesian sequence model (the summed probability distribution) of the chariot complex chronology.

cal. 4274 BP and cal. 3511 BP, during which the two-wheelers initially appeared and then spread throughout northern Eurasia (Fig. 14.1).

Phase 1, "The Age of Two-Wheelers," is modeled as cal. 4230–4102 BP at 68.2%, though it could actually begin earlier. The phase is determined by two measurements from Grave 32 of the Bolshoi Ipatovskii kurgan near Stavropol, Russia, which yielded one of the earliest known two-wheeled vehicles (Korenevskiy et al. 2007). However, there are three undated two-wheelers – from Grave 27 of the Tyagunova Mogila Kurgan; Grave 23, kurgan 2 of the Rayon okislennykh otvalov Cemetery; and Grave 5, kurgan 1 of the Izhevka Cemetery – all from the Catacomb culture (Pustovalov 2000). These materials come from the geographic core of the Catacomb culture (all near the Town of Kryvyi Rih, Ukraine), and could theoretically predate Bolshoi Ipatovski's Grave 32.

The modeled sequence continues with an apparent chronological gap between phase 1 and phase 2, "The Dark Ages," covering the interval of cal. 4102–4018 BP at 68.2%. In our view, the observed gap is a result of both methodological problems and a lack of knowledge. On the one hand, there is a lack of radiocarbon dating for the Catacomb and Abashevo-Pokrovka assemblages of the Eastern European steppes. On the other hand, there are no apparent finds that would demonstrate the process of transition from two-wheeled carts to chariots, so the actual source of the Sintashta materials of phase 2 remains unknown. Perhaps, the further increase in radiocarbon measurements of some Catacomb and Abashevo complexes with two-wheelers and cheekpieces will help to resolve this problem.

Phase 2, "The Dawn of Chariots," begins around the year cal. 3954 BP and lasts until cal. 3883 BP if the median values for the opening and the closing date within the phase are taken, or between cal. 4018 BP and 3847 BP at 68.2%. This is a relatively short period when the antler cheekpieces and actual chariots appear for the first time east of the Don River, but chiefly in the southern Trans-Urals.

Phase 3, "The Age of Heroes," begins around the year cal. 3833 BP and lasts until cal. 3759 BP (both are the median years), or between cal. 3870 BP and 3669 BP at 68.2%. The chronological gap between the median values of the end of phase 2 and the beginning of phase 3 is perhaps due to the vagaries of sampling, since the error ranges of two phases do intersect. However, two important observations made at Kamenniy Ambar-5 allow us to separate the two phases: first, Grave 6 and Grave 8 yielded morphologically different cheekpieces, and the one from Grave 8 could be interpreted as a development in bridling technology and style compared to its counterpart from Grave 6. Accordingly, Grave 6 yielded the radiocarbon age of 3572±50 BP, while Grave 8 demonstrates the age 3549±29 BP. These facts allow us to suggest that the chariot complex went through consecutive developmental stages that correspond to the modeled phases 2 and 3.

Phase 4, "The Age of Riders Begins," begins around the year cal. 3604 BP (median) or 3632 BP (the upper limit of the 68.2% confidence interval) and it lasts for the rest of the Bronze Age. There are only two radiocarbon measurements to model the interval, both coming from the Cemetery of Khripunovskiy, Grave 44, which contained a tubular-bone-made cheekpiece. This type of cheekpiece is usually associated with the Late Bronze Age developments of Alakul and Srubnaya, and appears in the same contexts neither as the shield-like cheekpieces nor the two-wheelers. However, the unambiguous evidence demonstrates that people continued to use chariots even when the mounted horse started to play a more important role in warfare, even during the Early Iron Age (Valchak 2009).

In summary, the twenty-four radiocarbon measurements available to date and the resulting Bayesian model support the accepted relative chronology and allow us to establish the chronological frame and timing of the early development of the chariot complex in northern Eurasia. In accordance with the Bayesian sequence model (Fig. 14.1), the chronology of the chariot complex is the following:

- **phase 0, "The Age of Wagons":** prior cal. 4375 BP
- **phase 1, "The Age of Two-Wheelers":** cal. 4375–4100 BP (2426–2151 BCE)
- **a transitional phase, "The Dark Ages":** cal. 4100–4020 BP (2151–2071 BCE)
- **phase 2, "The Dawn of Chariots":** cal. 4020–3850 BP (2071–1901 BCE)
- **phase 3, "The Age of Heroes":** cal. 3850–3670 BP (1901–1721 BCE)
- **phase 4, "The Age of Riders Begins":** after cal. 3630 BP (1681 BCE)

It is worth noting, however, that all the radiocarbon measurements came from burial contexts, and thus represent the end of each phase. To allow for the fact that all events actually occurred during the lifetime of the buried individuals, the phases should be adjusted by at least twenty-five years.

14.4 The Timing and Directions of Diffusion

We use the method of kriging to assess the timing and direction of the chariot complex diffusion across the steppes. In principle, the mean value of each calibrated interval and the geographic coordinates of the corresponding sites are pulled together to interpolate a three-dimensional surface. This surface represents the distribution of the original radiocarbon measurements, and it also predicts the unknown values (for example, see Davison et al. 2009). The resulting contour map visually represents the diffusion process. However, the exact line locations should be understood as an approximation on the basis of the available data, not as a definite statement.

In accordance with the sequence model, Figure 14.2 demonstrates the general west-east and south-north trends of the chariot complex diffusion. The model predicts that the whole process took approximately two hundred years at an average rate of about 1,000 kilometers per century, or 10 kilometers per year (Fig. 14.2).

The origin of the two-wheeled vehicle (phase 1) is linked to the southern-western periphery of the study area (the northern Black Sea region), from which the idea spread to the north and east, first to the Lower Volga region, then crossed the Ural. This transitional period is characterized as "The Dark Ages" due to the absence of two-wheelers in the record. However, both the chronological and spatial models correspond well to the chronology and territory of the post-Catacomb Lola and Krivolukskaya archaeological cultures. The earliest series of radiocarbon measurements from the Lola cemeteries falls between 4500 and 4000 BP, predating the real chariot cultures (though the latest dates intersect with the Sintashta dates). The people of Lola share physical features with the Sintashta population, and the material assemblage is seen as a forerunner of Sintashta antiquities (Mimokhod 2011). In other words, the model's prediction corresponds with the established archaeological facts.

The spatial model demonstrates two primary centers of chariot technology, which appeared relatively quickly after the initial impulse between cal. 4000 BP and cal. 3900 BP, corresponding to phase 2, "The Dawn of Chariots." The first – and slightly earlier – center is located east of the Ural Mountains and is represented by the Sintashta chariot complex. The second center lies in the Upper Don river basin and is

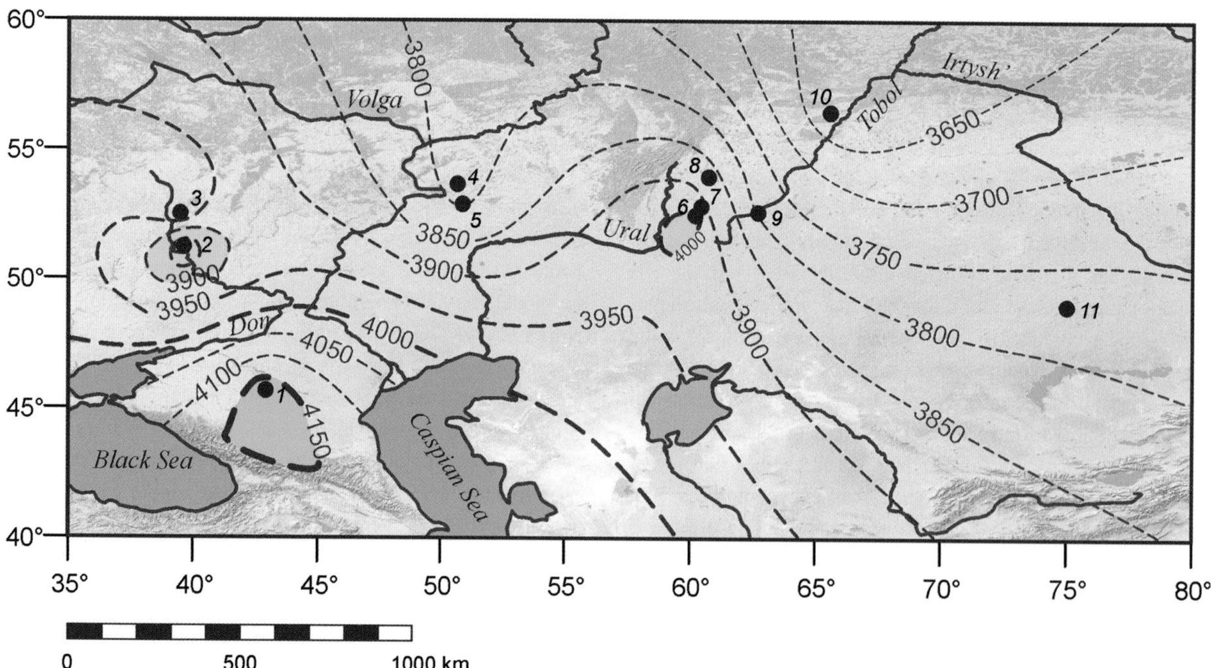

FIGURE 14.2. Map approximating the diffusion of two-wheeled vehicles and chariots in northern Eurasia.

represented by the Abashevo-Pokrovka sites. There are no finds of chariots in the Pokrovka burials, but a representative series of shield-like cheekpieces supports the notion of chariot use. The statistical analysis of Chechushkov et al. (2018) has revealed that the cheekpieces from the western and eastern flanks fundamentally share the same functional elements and served similar purposes. The stylistic differences between them can be explained by cultural heterogeneity.

The influence of the two centers drove the appearance of the chariot complex in the secondary centers, including the Upper Volga Potapovka and Utevka VI sites and the Petrovka culture sites in northern Kazakhstan, in phase 3 ("The Age of Heroes"). During this period, the chariot complex became truly widespread in the Old World. Chronologically, the period corresponds to the appearance of the horse chariot outside the Eurasian steppes, including the Near East (Littauer and Crouwel 1979).

14.5 Discussion

Our analysis has revealed the chronological and spatial patterns that explain the growth of the use of two-wheeled vehicles in the steppes. The next question is whether the patterns observed were caused by the spread of ideas and technologies through social networks or by the direct migration of knowledge carriers to new territories. The notion of migration accepted here is discussed in great detail by Anthony (1990), who defines it "as a behavior that typically performed by defined groups (often kin recruited) with specific goals, targeted on known destinations and likely to use familiar routes" (Anthony 1990: 895–896). Anthony delineates and describes short-distance and long-distance migrations, both of which concepts are useful for the following discussion.

The spatial model (Fig. 14.2) suggests that the initial process could have been relatively slow and progressive, taking place within the northern Black Sea cultural core. In general, the speed of movement of 10 km per year is consonant with the seasonal movement of pastoralists, and the closest abstract model is the wave-of-advance model of the Neolithic population advance in Europe, with the difference being that the pushing factor is pasture depletion rather than population growth (Ammerman and Cavalli-Sforza 1984). Perhaps, during this initial period, the Middle Bronze Age pastoral groups migrated short distances to the north and the east, along river valleys and seashores, in search of pasture grounds (Shishlina 2007). At that time, the two-wheeled design could spread through a social network of heterarchical communities that participated equally in the development of the technology. The case of the Bolshoi Ipatovskyi Kurgan is a particularly good example, as wood for the cart was imported from the distinct cultural area of the Caucasus Mountains, several hundred kilometers away (Korenevskyi et al. 2007).

In contrast, eastward-leading migration could have been quite rapid, as the spatial model has produced simultaneous 4000 BP contours, located both in the Lower Volga region and in the Southern Urals. The center in the Upper Don region emerged with a temporal lag of fifty radiocarbon years, suggesting the northward-leading migration was only slightly slower (Fig. 14.3). This rapid long-distance migration resembles the Anthony's migration stream model (1990), when migrants proceed toward a specific destination and earlier migrants discover and create pathways.

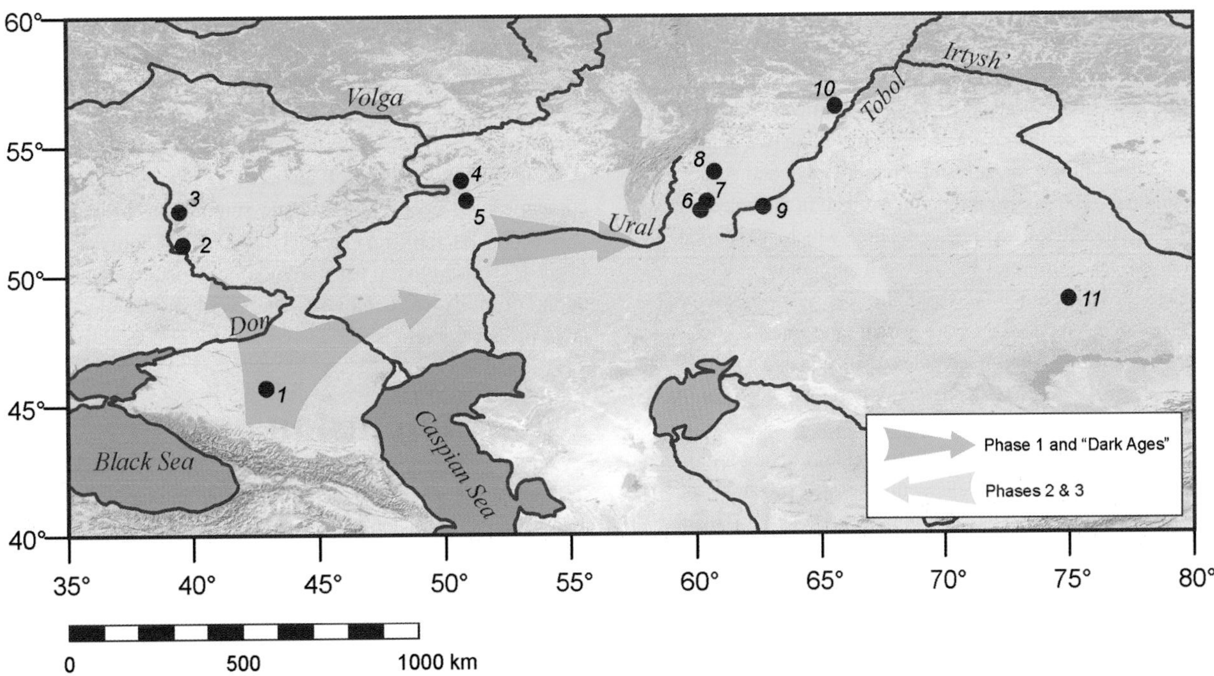

FIGURE 14.3. The principal directions of the IE migrations during the Bronze Age in northern Eurasia.

TABLE 14.2. Relative chronology of the Eurasian Bronze Age and the absolute (unadjusted) chronology of the chariot complex.

Relative	Absolute	Span of Phase
Early Bronze Age (ca. 5600–4450 BP)	**Phase 0, "The Age of Wagons"**	**>1100 years**
Middle Bronze Age (ca. 4450–3950 BP)	**Phase 1, "The Age of Two-Wheelers"** Cal. 4375–4100 BP (2426–2151 BCE)	**275 years**
	A transitional phase, "The Dark Ages" Cal. 4100–4020 BP (2151–2071 BCE)	**80 years**
Late Bronze Age (ca. 3950–3450 BP)	**Phase 2, "The Dawn of Chariots"** Cal. 4020–3850 BP (2071–1901 BCE)	**170 years**
	Phase 3, "The Age of Heroes" Cal. 3850–3670 BP (1901–1721 BCE)	**180 years**
	Phase 4, "The Age of Riders Begins" Cal. 3630 BP (1681 BCE)	**>3600 years**

The scenario presented in Figure 14.3 agrees well with the notion that the chariot complex originated during rapid long-distance migration as an integral part of the military leadership package. During the initial period of the colonization of both centers, the human groups faced conflict with hostile aboriginal groups and adverse environmental conditions in the Southern Urals, which made the families and clans aggregate under the leadership of military chiefs or "apex families" that helped newcomers (Anthony 1990: 904). Their primary benefit was to protect clans and their herds from human and animal predators and to manage internal conflicts that undoubtedly arose as a consequence of aggregation. The concept could hardly have been transferred through a network of knowledge, as it required a number of technological innovations and specialized skills and training. Initially, chariot technology could only spread spatially due to such knowledge barriers. Thus, the period of "The Dark Ages" is the most critical for understanding both the origin of the horse chariot and IE migration. Perhaps future advances in studies of the Lola culture sites and in dating the Abashevo-Pokrovka assemblages will illuminate these processes.

The proposed migratory routes to the north and the east agree well with the Late Bronze Age existence of the two contemporary cultural entities, namely, the Timber Grave and Andronovo phenomena. The eastern migration resulted in the emergence of the Sintashta-Petrovka phenomenon, which generated the Andronovo culture, and the northern migration produced the precursor of the Timber Grave culture. The vast coverage of the territory suggests demographic growth and intense social networking. Further chariot complex diffusion was due to networking and intergroup and intercultural connections, as in the initial period.

The absolute chronology of the chariot complex reconstructed above agrees well with the periodization of the Bronze Age (Table 14.2). The initial phase 1, the transitional phase, and the beginning of phase 2 fall within the Middle Bronze Age, which is consistent with the interpretation of the Catacomb and post-Catacomb Lola cultures and the early phase of the Abashevo and Sintashta developments. The end of phases 2 and 3 correspond to the beginning of the Late Bronze Age, again in agreement with Chernykh's periodization, as the later Sintashta-Petrovka, Potapovka, and Abashevo-Pokrovka material cultures are derivative of the Eurasian Metallurgical Province. The conclusion of phase 4 stretches through the Late Bronze Age, consistent with the interpretation of the Andronovo culture. This observation is of theoretical significance, as it pushes the beginning of mounted warfare back as early as 3630 BP.

In connection with linguistics, we support the proposition that the chariot complex distribution reflects the phased diffusion of IE speakers, and the events reconstructed here should correlate with the existence and split of the Proto-Indo-Iranian group. The emergence of subsequent languages could hardly be dated exclusively on the basis of linguistic reconstruction, and archaeological correlates are inevitable.

Despite the interesting conclusions on the history of the chariot complex and the early IE migrations, the analysis also reveals gaps in knowledge and methodological problems. Thus, the lack of radiocarbon dating for chariot burials on the western flank limits the potential of the analytical tools and prevents a fuller understanding, as the migratory scenario proposed above is biased by the overrepresentation of the eastern flank. Moreover, Bronze Age archaeology still follows the cognitive paradigm that is focused on the determining, delineating, characterization, and dating of archaeological cultures, and the comparison of deeply problematic summed probability intervals serves as the primary analytical tool (Chernykh 2008). Instead, in the future, we need to focus on the radiocarbon dating of individual complexes and avoid attempts to date the archaeological cultures.

14.6 Conclusion

In this chapter, we examined IE migration in conjunction with the origin and diffusion of the two-wheeled horse-drawn chariot. Employing a Bayesian analysis of twenty-four radiocarbon measurements and their plotting in geographic space, we came up with three principal conclusions. First, the concept of two-wheeled vehicles was developed in the Middle Bronze Age in the northern Black Sea region and then spread to the Eurasian steppes. Second, this period corresponds to the transformation of the Proto-Indo-Iranian language into separate dialects. Third, the chariot complex is an integral part of the military leadership package that originated during the rapid migration of the Indo-Europeans to the regions of the Upper Ural and Upper Don rivers.

Acknowledgments

The study was supported by a Russian Science Foundation grant (project No. 20-18-00402), Migration of Human Groups and Individual Mobility within the Framework of Multidisciplinary Analysis of Archaeological Information (Bronze Age of the Southern Urals). We are also grateful to Alexander Lubotsky, Gail Brownrigg, Carlos Quiles, Hsiaoyun Wu, Pavel Kuznetsov, and Carlos Aramayo for a detailed discussion of the manuscript.

References

Agapov, S. A. 2010. *Khvalynsk Copper Age cemeteries and Khvalynsk Copper Age cultures. The research of materials*. Samara: Ofort Press.

Allentoft, M. E., et al. 2015. Population genomics of Bronze Age Eurasia. *Nature 522*: 167–172.

Ammerman, A. J., & L. L. Cavalli-Sforza. 1984. *The Neolithic transition and the genetics of populations in Europe*. Princeton (NJ): Princeton University Press.

Andreeva, M. V. 2009. Traditsii i novatsii v pogrebal'nom obryade katakombn'ikh plemen severo-vostochnogo Predkavkaz'ya [Traditions and innovations in the funeral ceremony of the Catacomb tribes in northeast Ciscaucasia]. *Kratkiye soobshcheniya Instituta arheologii* 223: 101–115.

Anthony, D. W. 2007. *The horse, the wheel, and language : How Bronze-Age riders from the Eurasian steppes shaped the modern world*. Princeton (NJ): Princeton University Press.

1990. Migration in archaeology: The baby and the bathwater. *American Anthropologist* 92: 895–914.

Anthony, D. W., & N. B. Vinogradov. 1995. Birth of the chariot. *Archaeology* 48: 36–41.

Brownrigg, G. 2006. Horse control and the bit. In: S. L. Olsen, S. Grant, A. M. Choyke, & L. Bartosiewicz (eds.), *Horses and humans: The evolution of human-equine relationships*, 165–171. Oxford: Archaeopress.

Chechushkov, I. V., & A. V. Epimakhov. 2018. Eurasian Steppe chariots and social complexity during the Bronze Age. *Journal of World Prehistory* 31: 435–483.

Chechushkov, I. V., A. V. Epimakhov, & A. G. Bersenev. 2018. Early horse bridle with cheekpieces as a marker of social change: An experimental and statistical study. *Journal of Archaeological Science* 97: 125–136.

Chernykh, E. N. 1992. *Ancient metallurgy in the USSR: The Early Metal Age*. New York: Cambridge University Press.

2008. The "steppe belt" of stockbreeding cultures in Eurasia during the Early Metal Age. *Trabajos de Prehistoria* 65: 79–93.

Davison, K., P. M. Dolukhanov, G. R. Sarson, A. Shukurov, & G. I. Zaitseva. 2009. Multiple sources of the European Neolithic: Mathematical modelling constrained by radiocarbon dates. *Quaternary International* 203: 10–18.

Dergachev, V. A. 2007. *O skipetrakh, o loshadyakh, o voyne* [On scepters, horses, and war]. St. Petersburg: Nestor-Istoriya.

Gak, E. I., E. E. Antipina, E. Y. Lebedeva, & E. Kaiser. 2019. The economic pattern of the Middle Don Catacomb culture settlement of Rykan-3. *Russian Archaeology* 2: 19–34.

Gening, V. F. 1977. Mogilnik Sintashta i Problema Rannikh Indoiranskikh Plemyen [The Sintashta cemetery and the problem of Early Indo-Iranian migration]. *Soviet Archaeology* 4: 53–73.

Gorotsov, V. A. 1927. Bronzovyy vek na territorii SSSR [The Bronze Age on the territory of the USSR]. In: O. U. Shmidt (ed.) *Great Soviet encyclopedia*, 610–626. Moscow: Great Soviet Encyclopedia.

Grigoriev, S. A. 2002. *Ancient Indo-Europeans*. Chelyabinsk: RIFEI.

Hanks, B. K., A. V. Epimakhov, & C. Renfrew. 2007. Towards a refined chronology for the Bronze Age of the Southern Urals, Russia. *Antiquity* 81: 352–367.

Izbitser, E. 2017. "Arba" models and a burial with wagons from Kurgan 9 of the Tri Brata I Cemetery. In: L. B. Vishnyatsky (ed.), *Ex Ungue Leonem*, 130–138. Saint Petersburg: Nestor-Istoria.

Kantorovich, A. R., V. Y. Maslov, & V. G. Petrenko. 2013. Pogrebeniya maykopskoy kul'tury kurgana 1 mogil'nika Mar'inskaya-5 [Burials of the Maykop culture of the Maryinskaya-5 Cemetery, Kurgan 1]. In A. B. Belinskiy (ed.), *Materialy po izucheniyu istoriko-kul'turnogo naslediya Severnogo Kavkaza*, 71–108. Moscow: Pamyatniki istoricheskoy mysli.

Klejn, L. S., W. Haak, I. Lazaridis, N. Patterson, D. Reich, K. Kristiansen., K.-G. Sjögren, M. Allentoft, M. Sikora, E. Willerslev. 2017. Discussion: Are the origins of Indo-European languages explained by the migration of the Yamnaya culture to the west? *European Journal of Archaeology* 21: 1–15.

Korenevskiy, S. N., A. B. Belinskiy, & A. A. Kalmykov. 2007. *Bol'shoy Ipatovskiy kurgan na Stavropol'ye* [The Great Mound of Ipatovsk in Stavropol Region]. Moscow: Nauka.

Korobkova, G. F., & O. G. Shaposhnikova. 2005. *Poseleniye Mikhaylovka - etalonnyy pamyatnik drevneyamnoy kul'tury* [The settlement of Mikhailovka as a reference site of the Pit Grave culture]. Saint Petersburg: Evropeiskyi Dom.

Kuzmina, E. E. 2007. *The origin of the Indo-Iranians*. Leiden: Brill.

Littauer, M. A., & J. H. Crouwel. 1979. *Vehicles and ridden animals in the Ancient Near East*. Leiden & Cologne: Brill.

Litvinenko, R. O. 2016. Kolisnyy transport u pokhoval'niy paradyhmi kul'tur postkatakombnoho bloku [Wheeled transport in the burial paradigm of post-Catacomb cultures]. In: Z. P. Marina (ed.), *Arheologiya ta etnologiyaa pivdnya Shidnoi Evropi*, 129–140. Dnipro: Lira.

Matveyev, A. V., Y. N. Volkov, & Y. V. Kostomarova. 2007. Materialy novykh raskopok Khripunovskogo mogil'nika [New material on the Khripunovskiy cemetery]. In: M. P. Vokhmettzhev (ed.) *Problemy arkheologii: Ural i Zapadnaya Sibir' (k 70-letiyu T.M. Potemkinoy)*, 108–113. Kurgan: Izdatelstvo Kurganskogo Gosudarstvennogo Universiteta.

Mimokhod, R. A. 2011. Radiocarbon chronology of post-Catacomb cultural units. *Kratkie soobsheniya Instituta Arkheologii* 263, 28–53.

Morgunova, N. L. 2014. *Priuralskaya gruppa pamyatnikov v sisteme Volzhsko-Uralskogo varianta Yamnoyi kulturno-istoricheskoyi oblasti* [The South Ural group of the Volga-Ural variant of the Yamnaya cultural and historical community]. Orenburg: Izdatelstvo OGPU.

Munchaev, R. M. 1973. Bronzovyye psalii maykopskoy kul'tury i problema voznik noveniya konevodstva na Kavkaze [Maikop culture bronze cheekpieces and the problem of horse breeding in the Caucasus], In: R. M. Munchaev & V. I. Markovin (eds.), *Kavkaz i Vostochnaya Yevropa v drevnosti*, 71–77. Moscow: Nauka.

Naumov, I. N. 2002. Khronologicheskiye ramki nachal'nykh etapov rasprostraneniya domashney loshadi i navykov yeye domestikatsii v povolzhsko-donskikh stepyakh [Chronological limits of the initial stages of spreading of the horse and horse domestication practice in the Volga-Don Steppes]. *Lower Volga Archaeological Bulletin* 5: 11–23.

Pustovalov, S. Z. 2000. The "Tjagunova Mogila" burial mound and the problem of wheeled transport of the Pit Grave and Catacomb cultures epoch in Eastern Europe. *Stratum Plus* 2: 296–321.

Ramsey, B. C. 2009. Bayesian analysis of radiocarbon dates. *Radiocarbon* 51: 337–360.

Reimer, P. J., E. Bard, A. Bayliss, J. W. Beck, P. G. Blackwell, C. B. Ramsey, C. E. Buck, H. Cheng, R. L. Edwards, & M. Friedrich. 2013. IntCal13 and marine13 radiocarbon age calibration curves 0–50,000 years cal BP. *Radiocarbon* 55: 1869–1887.

Shishlina, N. I., R. Fernandez. 2016. Radiouglerodnoye datirovaniye parnykh obraztsov iz zakhoroneniy kurgana 2 Lipetskogo mogil'nika [Radiocarbon dating of paired samples from graves of Kurgan 2 of the Lipetsk Cemetery]. *Lipetskiy kurgan – pamyatnik elity dono-volzhskoy abashevskoy kul'tury: monografiya*, 53–54. Lipetsk: Novyi Vzglyad.

Shishlina, N. I., D. S. Kovalev, E. R. Ibragimova. 2014. Catacomb culture wagons of the Eurasian steppes, *Antiquity* 88: 378–394.

Shishlina, N. I., A. M. Skorobogatov, E. Kaiser, A. N. Usachuk. 2015. Radiouglerodnoye datirovaniye parnykh obraztsov iz mogil'nika Rozhdestveno: rezul'taty analiza i obsuzhdeniye [Radiocarbon dating of paired samples from the Rozhdestvensky cemetery: Analysis of results and discussion]. *Bulletin of the Samara Scientific Center of the Russian Academy of Sciences* 17, 262–72.

Usmanova, E. R., I. V. Chechushkov, P. A. Kosintsev, A. S. Suslov, & M. K. Lachkova. 2018. Loshad' v dukhovnoy kul'ture i sotsial'nom ustroystve naseleniya uralo-kazakhstanskikh stepey (po materialam mogil'nika Novoil'inovskiy II) [The horse in spiritual culture and social structure in the Ural–Kazakhstan steppes (on materials from the Novoilinovsky II cemetery)]. In: D. G. Zdanovich (ed.), *Stepnaya Evraziya v epokhu bronzy: kul'tury, idei, tekhnologii*, 198–215. Chelyabinsk: Chelyabinskiy gosudarstvennyy universitet.

Valchak, S. B. 2009. *Konskoye snaryazheniye v pervoi treti I-go tys. do n.e. na yuge Vostochnoy Evropy* [The horse harness of the first millenia BC in the south of Eastern Europe]. Moscow: Taus.

Zeleneyev, Y. A., & A. I. Yudin. 2010. Kurgan u sela Dubovyi Gai [The Kurgan near the village of Dubovyi Gai]. In: A. I. Yudin (ed.), *Arkheologicheskiye pamyatniki Saratovskogo Pravoberezh'ya: ot ranney bronzy do srednevekov'ya*, 134–155. Saratov: Izd-vo "Nauchnaya kniga."

15 INDO-EUROPEAN AND INDO-IRANIAN WAGON TERMINOLOGY AND THE DATE OF THE INDO-IRANIAN SPLIT*

ALEXANDER LUBOTSKY

15.1 The Indo-European Wheel and Wagon Terminology

In the literature (e.g., Anthony 2007: 35–37), it is often stated that we can reconstruct five words of wheel and wagon terminology for Proto-Indo-European (PIE), viz. the words for 'wheel' (2×), 'axle', 'thill', and the verb 'to convey in a vehicle':

- PIE *k^wek^wlo- 'wheel' (Skt. *cakrá-*, YAv. *caxra-*, ON *hvél*, Gr. κύκλος; Toch. B *kokale* 'wagon');
- PIE **HrotHo-* 'wheel' (Lat. *rota*, OIr. *roth*, OHG *rad*, Lith. *rãtas* 'wheel', *rataĩ* pl. 'chariot'; Skt. *rátha-* and YAv. *raϑa-* 'chariot');
- PIE *h_2*eḱs-* 'axle' (Skt. *ákṣa-*, Gr. ἄξων, Lat. *axis*, OE *eax*);
- PIE *h_2*eiHs-* 'pole, thill' (Skt. *īṣā́-*, YAv. *aēša*, Hitt. *ḫišša-*, Sln. *ojê*, Lith. *íena*; Gr. οἴαξ 'handle');
- PIE **ueǵ^h-* 'to convey in a vehicle' (Skt. *vah-*, Av. *vaz-*, Gr. (Pamph.) ϝεχέτω, Lat. *uehō*, Lith. *vežù*, OCS *vezǫ*; OHG *wegan* 'to move').

This list can be extended with at least five more terms:

- PIE **iug-* 'yoke' (Skt. *yugá-*, YAv. *yuua-*, Hitt. *iūk-*, Gr. ζυγόν, Lat. *iugum*, OS *juk*, OCS *igo*);
- PIE **ieug-* 'to yoke, harness' (Skt. *yuj-*, Av. *yuj-*, Gr. ζεύγνῡμι, Lat. *iungō*, Lith. *jùngti*);
- PIE **d^{h}ur-* 'joint, pivot of the chariot pole and the yoke' (Skt. *dhúr-* 'joint of the chariot pole and the yoke, the pole and the yoke together', Hitt. *tūri̯e/a-^{zi}* 'to harness'), possibly identical with the word for 'door', if it originally meant 'pivot';
- PIE *h_3*neb^h-* 'wheel hub' (Skt. *nábhya-*, OPr. *nabis*, OHG *naba*);
- PIE **ḱomieh$_2$-* 'yoke pin' (Skt. *śámyā-*, YAv. *simā-*, Arm. *samik'* 'pair of yoke sticks', *sametik'* 'yoke band' (unless an Iranian LW), Eng. *hame* 'horse collar', which has replaced the yoke with the pins rather recently).

The list calls for two comments. First, Anatolian attests only the terms for the yoke (Hitt. *iūk-*), for the pole (Hitt. *ḫišša-*), and for the connection of the two (Skt. *dhúr-* 'joint of the pole and the yoke', Hitt. *tūri̯e/a-^{zi}* 'to harness'). These terms, however, could also refer to the construction of sleighs or plows, which then is compatible with the idea that the Anatolians split off from the rest of the Indo-Europeans before the invention of the wheel.

Secondly, it is important that the other terms have a clear internal Indo-European etymology.

- PIE *k^wek^wlo- 'wheel' ~ PIE *$k^wel(H)$- 'to roam, move'. In the literature, it is often asserted that the verbal root originally meant 'to turn', but this can hardly be the case; cf. the meanings of Skt. *car^i-* 'to move, walk, go, wander; to perform', Av. *car-* 'to move, walk', Gr. πέλομαι 'to become, take place, be', and Lat. *colō* 'to live in, inhabit', as well as Gr. βου-κόλος m. and OIr. *bua-chail* m. 'cowherd'. We have to assume that the verbal root meant 'to roam (with cattle), to live a nomadic life', which in some languages developed into 'to live, to be'. The original meaning of *k^wek^wlo- with its reduplication was thus something like 'constantly roaming, moving'. The original four-wheeled wagons were also the mobile homes of the nomads.
- PIE **HrotHo-* 'wheel' ~ PIE **HretH-* 'to run'. Unfortunately, there is only one branch that preserves the verb, viz. OIr. *reithid* 'to run, speed', so we cannot be sure that this is the original meaning. If it was, then it is likely that **HrotHo-* was a 'runner' (cf. Gr. τροχός m. 'wheel', derived from τρέχω 'to run, hurry') and represented a lighter wheel that could be used on a two-wheeled wagon.
- PIE *h_2*eḱs-* 'axle' = 'armpit' (YAv. *aša-*, Lat. *axilla*, OE *eaxl*). The cognates show that the words for 'axle' and 'armpit' were originally identical; cf., on the one hand, Skt. *ákṣa-* 'axle' = YAv. *aša-* 'armpit' and, on the other, with an *l*-suffix, W. *echel*, ON *ǫxull* 'axle' = Lat. *āla* 'armpit, wing', *axilla*, OIc. *ǫxl*, OE *eaxl*, OHG *ahsala* 'armpit'. This means that the different suffixes in separate languages must be due to later disambiguation.
- PIE *h_3*neb^h-* 'wheel hub' = 'navel, belly button' (Skt. *nā́bhi-*, YAv. *nāfa-*, OHG *nabalo*, Gr. ὀμφαλός, Lat. *umbilīcus*). The same is true for this pair: the words were originally identical.
- PIE **ḱomieh$_2$-* 'yoke pin/peg' ~ PIE **ḱem-* 'hornless' (Skt. *śáma-* 'hornless'; ON *hind* f. 'hind, doe', Lith. *šmùlas* 'hornless, bald'; Russ. *komólyj* 'hornless'; Gr. κεμάς, -άδος f. 'young deer or dog'). As far as I know, this connection has not been made before, but it looks attractive if we assume that this term was coined by the wagon-makers who saw some resemblance between the yoke with its two pins and the head of an animal with two scurs or nub horns (Figs. 15.1 and 15.2).

* I would like to express my gratitude to David Anthony and Guus Kroonen for many discussions concerning the subject of this paper.

FIGURE 15.1. Plowing oxen in Nepal (Dr. N. Kafle).

FIGURE 15.2. A young buck with nub horns (Buck Manager).

We see that the speakers of PIE tried to find ways to describe these new inventions, either by deriving new words from verbs or by invoking parallels with the bodies of animals or humans. We further often encounter body parts in chariot terminology in the separate IE languages, even though we cannot reconstruct these terms for Proto-Indo-European. For instance, the spoke of the wheel is called a 'shank' in Greek (κνήμη), a 'rib' in Khotan Saka (*pālsu-*); the linchpin of the wheel is called a 'hip' in Sanskrit (*āṇí-*, as the broadest part of the wagon; cf. Toch. B *oñi-* 'hip', and see Pinault 2003: 138–40 for more examples, including Skt. *ratha-mukhá-* 'front part of a chariot', lit. 'mouth of a chariot', and *ratha-śīrṣá-* 'id.', lit. 'head of a chariot').[1] All this seems to prove that the Indo-Europeans had developed these innovations themselves and did not borrow them.

[1] In a paper presented at the conference "The Atharvaveda and its South Asian Contexts. 3rd Zurich International Conference on Indian Literature and Philosophy," September 26–28, 2019, Laura Massetti pointed out that the parallel between the chariot and the human body was even used, in both Vedic and Greek, to compare the work of a physician who cures the body to that of a chariot maker who mends the chariot.

15.2 Proto-Indo-Iranian (PIIr.) Chariot Terminology

Indo-Aryan and Iranian share the same word for 'battle chariot', which can be reconstructed for PIIr. as *_HratHa-_ (Skt. _rátha-_, YAv. _raθa-_, Khot. _rraha-_, etc.). This word is identical with one of the two IE words for 'wheel' discussed above.

We further have common PIIr. terms for 'charioteer', *_HratHiH-_ (Skt. _rathī́-_, OAv. _raiθī-_), and for 'chariot fighter', lit. 'standing on the chariot', *_HratHai-štaH-_ (Skt. _rathe-ṣṭhā́-_, YAv. _raθaē-štā-_). Possibly, the adjective *_HratH-iHa-_ 'belonging to the chariot' (with further specialization to 'chariot horse' in Vedic and to 'page, servant < groom' in Iranian) is of PIIr. date, but the suffix is productive, and we cannot be sure that this adjective is old. All these terms are derivatives from the word for 'chariot'. We may add here the PIIr. verb for 'to drive a chariot', PIIr. *_HiaH-_ (Skt. _yā-_ 'to drive', Av. _yāman-_ 'course') and PIIr. *_Haua-saHana-_ 'unharnessing of horses, resting place' (Skt. _avasā́na-_, OAv. _auuaŋhāna-_).

Further, there are three terms for (the straps of) the bridle or halter: PIIr. *_HraćanaH-_ (Skt. _raśanā́-_ 'cord, bridle', MP (Pahl.) _lsn /rasan/_ 'rope', and Arm. _erasan_ 'bridle', an Iranian loanword; cf. also Skt. _raśmí-_ 'rope, rein, leash' and _raśmán-_ 'bridle', derived from the same root), PIIr. *_Hiauktra-_ (Skt. _yóktra-_ 'thong, yoking cord', YAv. _°yaoxəδra-_ 'halter, bridle'), PIIr. *_Habʰi-dʰaHana-_ (Skt. _abhidhā́nī-_ 'horse halter', YAv. _zaraniiō. aiβiδāna-_ 'with a golden bridle', Sogd. (Buddh.) _βδ''nh_, _βyδ'n_ 'bridle', Khot. _byāna-_ 'id.', Khwar. _'βz'n-_ 'id.', Pash. _mlúna_ 'id.', Yi. _awlān_ 'id.', Sariq. _viδun_ 'id.', Yazg. _avδén_ 'bridle and bit'). The last word is especially interesting, as it seems to refer exclusively to horses, and the verb PIIr. *_Habʰi-dʰaH-_, literally 'to put on or against', is specifically used for bridling or haltering horses, which may indicate a new technology.

The status of the chariot makers was very high in the Indo-Iranian society, so high indeed that the poets used to compare their craft to that of the carpenters. Both in Vedic and in Avestan, we often encounter expressions like 'to carpenter a song of praise' (Skt. _mántram takṣ-_, OAv. _mąθrəm tašat̰_), 'to carpenter the speech' (Skt. _vácas- takṣ-_, YAv. _vacas-tašti-_), and a similar expression is also found in Greek (Pind.) ἐπέων ... τέκτονες 'the carpenters of words'.

At the same time, it is conspicuous that we cannot reconstruct the PIIr. terminology for certain parts of the chariot, especially for its most essential part, the spoked wheel (including 'spoke', 'felly', 'rim'). This may partly be due to the paucity of Old and Middle Iranian texts, but the fact is that Skt. _ará-_ 'spoke of a wheel', _nemí-_ 'rim (of a wheel)', and _paví-_ 'metal felly (of a wheel)' have no Iranian counterparts.

It follows that the Indo-Iranians knew the chariot and that they coined the names for the charioteer and the warrior/chariot fighter, which means that they were undoubtedly using the chariots for warfare already in PIIr. times.

It is hard to say how we must interpret the absence of detailed PIIr. terminology for the spoked wheel, because this would at any rate be an _argumentum ex silentio_. It is conceivable that the real progress leading to the sophisticated construction of the chariots was only achieved after the split, or that the technical improvements constantly triggered new names for the innovative elements.

Nevertheless, it seems reasonable to conclude that the Indo-Iranians did not stay together for a long time after the discovery of the battle chariot. Since the earliest true chariots known are from around 2000 BCE, the split must have taken place relatively soon after (see below).

15.3 Time Constraints for the Split of Proto-Indo-Iranian (PIIr.) into Two Branches

15.3.1 Proto-Indo-Iranian and the Sintashta–Petrovka Culture

There is growing consensus among both archaeologists and linguists that the Sintashta–Petrovka culture (2100–1900 BCE) in the Southern Trans-Urals was inhabited by the speakers of Proto-Indo-Iranian (cf. Anthony 2007: 408ff.; see also Epimakhov & Lubotsky in Chapter 16 in this volume). Since the first-ever light chariot that could be pulled by horses and used for warfare has been documented exactly in this archaeological culture, the terms for the charioteer and the chariot fighter discussed above cannot obviously be older than 2000 BCE.

The Sintashta–Petrovka culture was very compact in time and space, and it seems likely that its inhabitants spoke one language, but sometime around 1900 BCE, it ceased to exist and was continued by the Andronovo culture, with its huge spread to the south and the east. How can we interpret this linguistically?

15.3.2 Indo-Iranian Loanwords

As I have argued in a 2001 paper (see also Witzel 2003: 25ff.), there is a considerable layer of loanwords in Sanskrit and Iranian that must be of Proto-Indo-Iranian date. The form and the semantics of these loanwords lead to a number of important conclusions:

(a) Borrowed names for animals like camel, donkey, and tortoise show that the Indo-Iranians migrated in a southward direction.
(b) Borrowed terms for irrigation (canals and dug wells) and elaborate architecture (permanent houses with walls of brick and gravel) indicate a rich city culture.
(c) The Sanskrit and Iranian loanwords do not always match phonetically, which points to the dialectal disintegration of Proto-Indo-Iranian.
(d) Since a significant number of loanwords are of a cultic nature (gods or deities: *_ćaru̯a-_, *_indra-_, *_g$^{(h)}$andʰaru̯/bʰa-_; priests: *_atʰaru̯an-_, *_ućig-_, *_r̥ši-_ 'seer'; and *_anću-_ 'Soma plant'), we must assume that the whole Indo-Iranian Soma/Haoma cult

was borrowed, which could only be possible after a prolonged period of acculturation.[2]

(e) There are hardly any loanwords in the field of agriculture (only the word for 'bread'), which indicates that agriculture did not yet play an important role in the life of Indo-Iranians: presumably, they only used the products of the farmers, hardly tilling the land themselves.

The most likely candidate for the source of borrowing is the Bactria–Margiana Archaeological Complex (BMAC), which is the only rich city culture in the vicinity of Sintashta. It thus follows that a part of the Indo-Iranians, attracted by the riches of the BMAC, moved from Sintashta southward and started to interact with the BMAC people. Archaeologically, we can observe intensive contact between the Andronovans and the BMAC, and a recent genetic study (Narasimhan et al. 2019: 5) states, "We find no evidence of Steppe pastoralist-derived ancestry in groups at BMAC sites before 2100 BCE, but multiple outlier individuals buried at these sites show that by ~2100 to 1700 BCE, BMAC communities were regularly interacting with peoples carrying such ancestry."

Some of the Indo-Iranian borrowed terms may be directly compared with the BMAC artifacts. It is tempting to assume that the PIIr. word **gadā-* 'club, mace' refers to the characteristic mace-heads of stone and bronze abundantly found in BMAC towns, while PIIr. **u̯āćī-* 'ax, adze' may be identified with shaft-hole axes and ax-adzes of this culture (cf. also Parpola 2015).

Since it was the Indo-Aryans[3] who later moved further south, it seems attractive to assume that they were the first to establish contact with the BMAC, and developed and maintained this until the decline of the BMAC, which started in the seventeenth century BCE (for a recent discussion, see Luneau 2019). In those cases where Sanskrit and Iranian loanwords do not match phonetically (point (c) above), it is probable that the speakers of Sanskrit borrowed the word first and then transmitted it to the Iranians.

The next question is when the Indo-Aryans left Central Asia, and in order to answer this, let us look at where they went.

15.3.3 The Mitanni Aryans

The military elite of the Mitanni kingdom (of Aryan descent) was present in Syria and northern Iraq in the fourteenth century BCE and probably arrived there a few generations earlier, in the sixteenth to fifteenth century BCE. The language has a clear Indo-Aryan (rather than PIIr.) character, the most important argument being the word for 'one', Mitanni *a-i-ka-* (Sanskrit *eka-*) vs Iranian **ai-u̯a-* (for more details on this word, see now Lubotsky & Kloekhorst 2022). The point is that the formation with the suffix *-ka-* is found nowhere else and must be due to a typically Indo-Aryan innovation, whereas the Iranian suffix *-u̯a-* is also found in Greek οἶος < **Hoiu̯o-* (and in the Sanskrit particle *evá* 'thus', most probably of the same origin as Iranian **ai-u̯a-*).

15.3.4 The Arrival of Indo-Aryans in India

Archaeologically, Indo-Aryans have often been connected with the Gandhara Grave Culture in the Swat Valley (from 1600 BCE onwards), and this theory has now been corroborated by genetic evidence (Narasimhan et al. 2019). Interestingly, this evidence shows that "the source of this [= Steppe] ancestry is primarily from females in Late Bronze Age and Iron Age individuals from the Swat District" (p. 9), which is an indication of a large-scale migration, including women. As to the arrival of Steppe ancestry in the region, geneticists "estimate the date of admixture into the Late Bronze Age and Iron Age individuals from the Swat District of northernmost South Asia to be, on average, twenty-six generations before the date that they lived, corresponding to a 95% confidence interval of ~1900 to 1500 BCE" (p. 10).

Finally, it follows from the genetic studies that the Kalash, a group in northwest South Asia, speakers of a Dardic language, has the highest proportion of Steppe ancestry. It thus seems likely that they just stayed there when other Indo-Aryans moved further south, and the same was probably true for the Nuristani people, if we combine these findings with the linguistic evidence that the Nuristani languages are closely related to Indo-Aryan (I refer especially to the important 2016 article of Chlodwig Werba).

15.3.5 The Oldest Texts

We see that the Indo-Aryans move southward around the sixteenth century BCE and arrive in the Near East and in the Swat Valley almost simultaneously. It is probably not accidental that this date coincides with the decline of the BMAC: the profound changes in the economy of the BMAC forced the Indo-Aryan pastoralists to look for new markets.

The definitive split in Proto-Indo-Iranian language unity can thus be dated to the sixteenth century BCE, although dialectal differentiation must have begun earlier. This date is further compatible with the chronology of the oldest Indo-Iranian texts, the Rigveda and the Avesta.

The Rigveda is usually dated between 1200 and 1000 BCE, which seems a reasonable estimate to me, although it must be said that we can only rely on the internal chronology of the Vedic texts and some indirect evidence. For instance, as argued by Parpola in a recent article (2019), the Sanskrit word for 'mirror', *ādarśa-*, only appears in the texts since the Upaniṣads. It is likely that the mirror was introduced into India by the Persians, during the conquest of the Indus Valley by Darius in 519 to 518 BCE, which would mean that the early fifth century BCE is a *terminus post quem* for the Upaniṣads. The Upaniṣads are relatively young Vedic texts (the internal

[2] This is the reason why the route of Indo-Aryans through the Altai, as indicated on the map in Narasimhan 2019, is improbable.

[3] I use the term "Indo-Aryan" for the Indo-Iranian dialect that shows typical traits of the later Indo-Aryan languages, even though the term is unfortunate, because the "Indo-Aryans" of Central Asia and of the Mitanni kingdom were most probably never in India. The same is true, mutatis mutandis, for Iranian.

chronology being: Upaniṣads < Śrauta-Sūtras < Āraṇyakas < Brāhmaṇas < Yajurveda mantras < Atharvaveda mantras and book X of the Rigveda < the Family Books of the Rigveda), and if they were indeed composed in the fifth century BCE, the Family Books of the Rigveda must have been at least five centuries older. On the basis of geographical names mentioned in the Rigveda, we can be sure that the bulk of the hymns were composed in the Punjab.

I do not see sufficient reason for dating the Rigveda much older than 1200 BCE, although this cannot be excluded either. It is sometimes assumed (cf. Witzel 2001: 5–6) that the Atharvaveda, the second oldest Sanskrit text, must be dated between 1200 and 1000 BCE, because we there find a mention of *śyāmám áyas* 'dark metal' (presumably, iron), while the Iron Age starts in India around this time. Even if *śyāmám áyas* indeed refers to iron (it could, for instance, also be bronze), the occurrence of iron in the Atharvaveda would set only a *terminus post quem* for this text. It is therefore perfectly feasible that the Atharvaveda was, for instance, created between 900 and 800 BCE, and the Rigveda between 1200 and 1000 BCE.

It must be stressed, however, that both the Rigveda and Atharvaveda are collections of texts from various periods, with a possible difference of up to several centuries, so it is not very useful to talk about *the* date of these collections: we can only try to establish the date of their final redaction. It is thus imaginable that some of the Rigvedic hymns were composed earlier than 1200 BCE, and not yet even in the Punjab, but in Central Asia.

The oldest text in an Iranian language is the Avesta, in particular the Gāthās of Zarathuštra, which can also be dated approximately to 1000 BCE. The language of the Rigveda and that of the Avesta are quite similar, and it is even conceivable that at the time of the creation of their oldest parts, the two languages were still mutually intelligible. This means that the separation must have taken place not very long before, and the sixteenth century BCE would be quite fitting.

15.3.6 Indo-Iranian Loanwords in Uralic

Uralic has borrowed – rather extensively – from Proto-Indo-Iranian and, later, from Iranian. To my mind, the arguments in favor of Uralic loanwords from Indo-Aryan (rather than from Proto-Indo-Iranian or Iranian) presented by Asko Parpola in recent publications (most recently, Parpola 2017) are not convincing. When Indo-Aryans separated from the Iranians, they were already at the south of the BMAC and could not have had any contact with Uralic.

15.3.7 The Language of the BMAC and the Language of the Punjab

If we look at the loanwords that are found in the language of the Rigveda (for which see Kuiper 1991), we see a considerable number of agricultural terms: *lā́ṅgala-* 'plow', *sī́rā-* 'plowshare', *kīnā́ra-* and *kīnā́śa-* 'plowman', *ū́rdara-* 'granary', *khā́rī-* 'measure of grain', *khála-* 'threshing floor', *odaná-* 'rice dish', and *tílvila-* 'fertile', as well as *ṛbī́sa-* 'oven', *ulū́khala-* 'mortar', *kārotará-* 'sieve', *mū́la-* 'root', *phála-* 'fruit', *púṣpa-* 'flower', *píppala-* 'sweet fruit', *urvārukā́-* 'cucumber', etc. This layer signals a change in the lifestyle of the Indo-Aryans and the growing importance of agriculture in their subsistence.

A remarkable feature of the Rigvedic loanwords is that they are structurally very close to those found in Proto-Indo-Iranian, which we have discussed above, §15.3.2. This means that the language spoken in the BMAC and the language spoken in the Swat Valley and the Punjab were quite similar, if not identical (cf. Lubotsky 2001: 305). The similarity of the two languages is all the more surprising as the BMAC and the Indus Valley Culture do not have much in common either archaeologically or genetically, and it seems unlikely that their inhabitants spoke the same language.

It therefore seems worthwhile to seriously consider another scenario.[4] As already mentioned in §15.3.5, the southward movement of the Indo-Aryans was simultaneous with the decline of the BMAC and was probably triggered by it. In the situation of an economic and political crisis, it is only to be expected that in their movement, the Indo-Aryans were joined by a sizable group of BMAC people, who would bring their culture and agricultural lifestyle with them.

This scenario may account for the prolonged contact between the Indo-Aryans and the BMAC people in the Swat Valley and the Punjab and, consequently, for a large number of loanwords when the Indo-Aryans started to get settled and to learn agriculture. At the same time, it perfectly explains the fact that "intrusive BMAC material is subsequently found further to the south in Iran, Afghanistan and Pakistan" (Mallory & Adams 1997: 73), without the improbable assumption that the Indo-Aryans had adopted the culture of the BMAC in Central Asia, which led Mallory to postulate his famous *Kulturkugel* (Mallory 1998: 192–3). As we know from major people movements of the past, they were often multiethnic, and a joint movement of Indo-Aryans and BMAC people would not be surprising at all.

15.4 Conclusions

On the basis of linguistic evidence, we can make the following chronological inferences:

(a) Proto-Indo-European wagon terminology, shared by the Anatolians, can refer to the construction of sleighs or plows and can thus predate the invention of the wheel. All other terms have a clear internal Indo-European etymology, which is a strong indication that the Indo-Europeans had developed these innovations themselves and did not borrow them.

(b) Indo-Aryan and Iranian share not only the same word for 'battle chariot', but also the terms for 'charioteer' and for

[4] This scenario has been suggested to me by my colleague Maarten Kossmann.

'chariot fighter' (lit. 'standing on the chariot'), which means that they were already using the chariots for warfare in PIIr. times and that the split of Proto-Indo-Iranian must necessarily postdate 2000 BCE (the earliest known battle chariots of the Sintashta–Petrovka culture).

(c) Proto-Indo-Iranian loanwords show that a part of the Indo-Iranians, attracted by the riches of the BMAC, moved from Sintashta southward and started to interact with the BMAC people. At a later stage, when the BMAC started to decline (17–16th century BCE), the Indo-Aryans moved further south: both to the southwest (Mitanni) and to the southeast (the Swat Valley). It seems probable that in the latter movement, they were joined by a part of the BMAC population.

References

Anthony, David. 2007. *The horse, the wheel, and language: How Bronze-Age riders from the Eurasian steppes shaped the modern world*. Princeton: Princeton University Press.

Kuiper, F. B. J. 1991. *Aryans in the Rigveda*. Amsterdam: Rodopi.

Lubotsky, Alexander. 2001. The Indo-Iranian substratum. In: Christian Carpelan, Asko Parpola, & Petteri Koskikallio (ed.), *Early contacts between Uralic and Indo-European: Linguistic and archaeological considerations. Papers presented at an international symposium held at the Tvärminne Research Station of the University of Helsinki 8–10 January 1999* (Mémoires de la Société Finno-Ougrienne 242), 301–317. Helsinki: Suomalais-Ugrilainen Seura.

Lubotsky, Alexander, & Alwin Kloekhorst. 2022. Indo-Aryan *°(a) u̯artanna* in the Kikkuli-treatise. In: H. Fellner, M. Malzahn, M. Peyrot (ed.), *lyuke wmer ra. Indo-European Studies in honor of Georges-Jean Pinault*, 331–336. Ann Arbor, New York: Beech Stave Press.

Luneau, Élise. 2019. Climate change and the rise and fall of the Oxus Civilization in Southern Central Asia. In: L. E. Yang et al. (ed.), *Socio-environmental dynamics along the historical Silk Road*, 275–299. Heidelberg: Springer.

Mallory, James P. 1998. A European perspective on Indo-Europeans in Asia. In: Victor Mair (ed.), *The Bronze Age and Early Iron Age peoples of Eastern and Central Asia*, 175–201. Washington, DC: Institute for the Study of Man.

Mallory, James P., & Douglas Q. Adams. 1997. *Encyclopedia of Indo-European culture*. London: Fitzroy Dearborn.

Narasimhan, Vagheesh M. et al. 2019. The formation of human populations in South and Central Asia. *Science* 365: eaat7487.

Parpola, Asko. 2015. The Mohenjo-daro axe-adze, a vestige of Aryan migration into the Indus Valley? *Current World Archaeology* 74: 14–5.

2017. Finnish *vatsa* ~ Sanskrit *vatsá-* and the formation of Indo-Iranian and Uralic languages. *SUSA/JSFOu* 96: 245–286.

2019. The mirror in Vedic India: Its ancient use and its present relevance in dating texts. *Studia Orientalia Electronica* 7: 1–29.

Pinault, Georges-Jean. 2003. Sanskrit *kalyāṇa-* interprété à la lumière des contacts en Asie centrale. *Bulletin de la Société Linguistique de Paris* 98(1): 123–161.

Werba, Chlodwig. 2016. Ur(indo)arisches im Nūristānī: Zur historischen Phonologie des Indoiranischen. In: Andrew M. Byrd, Jessica DeLisi, & Mark Wenthe (ed.), *Tavet Tat Satyam: Studies in honor of Jared S. Klein on the occasion of his seventieth birthday*, 341–359. Ann Arbor & New York: Beech Stave Press.

Witzel, Michael. 2001. Autochthonous Aryans? The evidence from Old Indian and Iranian texts. *Electronic Journal of Vedic Studies* 7(3): 1–115.

2003. Linguistic evidence for cultural exchange in prehistoric Western Central Asia. *Sino-Platonic Papers* 129: 1–70.

16 FIRE AND WATER: THE BRONZE AGE OF THE SOUTHERN URALS AND THE RIGVEDA

ANDREY EPIMAKHOV AND ALEXANDER LUBOTSKY

16.1 Introduction

It does not often happen that linguistic and archaeological sources allow the creation of a coherent narrative: they are usually separated from each other in time and space and do not meet the necessary prerequisites for a comparative analysis. The archaeological facts must form a clear pattern and demonstrate the existence of a cultural stereotype; the linguistic attribution of the population to which the analyzed archaeological sites belong must be uncontroversial; and, finally, the linguistic sources must provide sufficient information about that cultural stereotype.

In our view, the tradition of constructing wells in the Late Bronze Age, which is quite widespread in the steppe and forest-steppe of Eurasia, is one of those rare examples where a successful comparative analysis is indeed possible. From around the turn of the third to second millennium BC, the wells are consistently combined with furnaces in that area. There are different variants of this unity, but it is best documented in the Sintashta and Petrovka cultures of the Southern Trans-Urals. These combined objects are likely to precede similar ones elsewhere, and it is here that the sources of this tradition and its interpretation must be sought. The numerous attempts at a rational explanation can only partially answer the question of this system's function; even if there was some technological advantage (limited at most) to these "furnace-well" constructions, their builders in the Bronze Age must have justified the system by mythology. The Indo-Iranian linguistic identity of the Sintashta culture has been adopted by the overwhelming majority of specialists, and the rich Indo-Iranian linguistic sources clearly demonstrate the idea of a close relationship between water and fire.

16.2 Sintashta Materials in the System of Archaeological Cultures of the Eurasian Bronze Age

The group of archaeological sites discussed in these pages has been systematically studied for almost fifty years, starting with Gening 1977. At present, the Sintashna culture's chronology and spread have been reliably established (Epimakhov & Krause 2013, Molodin et al. 2014), a primary interpretation of the materials has been provided, and a number of themes have been extensively elaborated, e.g., the population's life support systems, health level, etc. The conclusions of the experts are mostly based not only on archaeological observations, but also on a wide range of analytical data. Since a significant part of the data has already been published (e.g., Gening et al. 1992, Zdanovich 2002, Vinogradov 2003, Epimakhov 2005, Tkachev 2007, Krause & Koryakova 2013, Logvin & Ševnina 2013, Vinogradov & Epimakhov 2013, Kupriyanova & Zdanovich 2015, Zdanovich et al. 2020), we shall limit ourselves to a brief description of the culture's main features.

Sintashta monuments were discovered on the territory of the steppe part of the Southern Urals, within the borders of modern Russia and Kazakhstan (Epimakhov & Chuev 2011, Koryakova & Epimakhov 2014). They are of two main types: fortified settlements and burial grounds (Fig. 16.1). Next to these, there are sporadic examples of open settlements and a few ancient mine workings for the extraction of copper ore. Fortified settlements with a complex layout have only been found in the Trans-Urals and occupy a relatively compact area (approximately 300 × 400 km); many of them are accompanied by burial grounds. The burial mounds have a much wider distribution area: part of the mounds and individual burials were excavated not only in the immediate vicinity of the traces of stationary habitat, but also at a distance of hundreds of kilometers to the west, south, and east of its conditional boundaries. The burial grounds have numerous vivid manifestations of social complexity (armament, a chariot complex, abundant sacrifices of domestic animals, etc.).

All the settlements are located at a low hypsometric level (a few meters above the floodplain) on the banks of the small rivers of the Ural and Tobol basins. The structure of the settlements is characterized by several important features. The external outline of the defense system varies, as does the internal layout (Zdanovich & Batanina 2002). Some of the sites have an oval or round shape (about 140–170 m in diameter). In such cases, the inner space is almost entirely occupied by radially

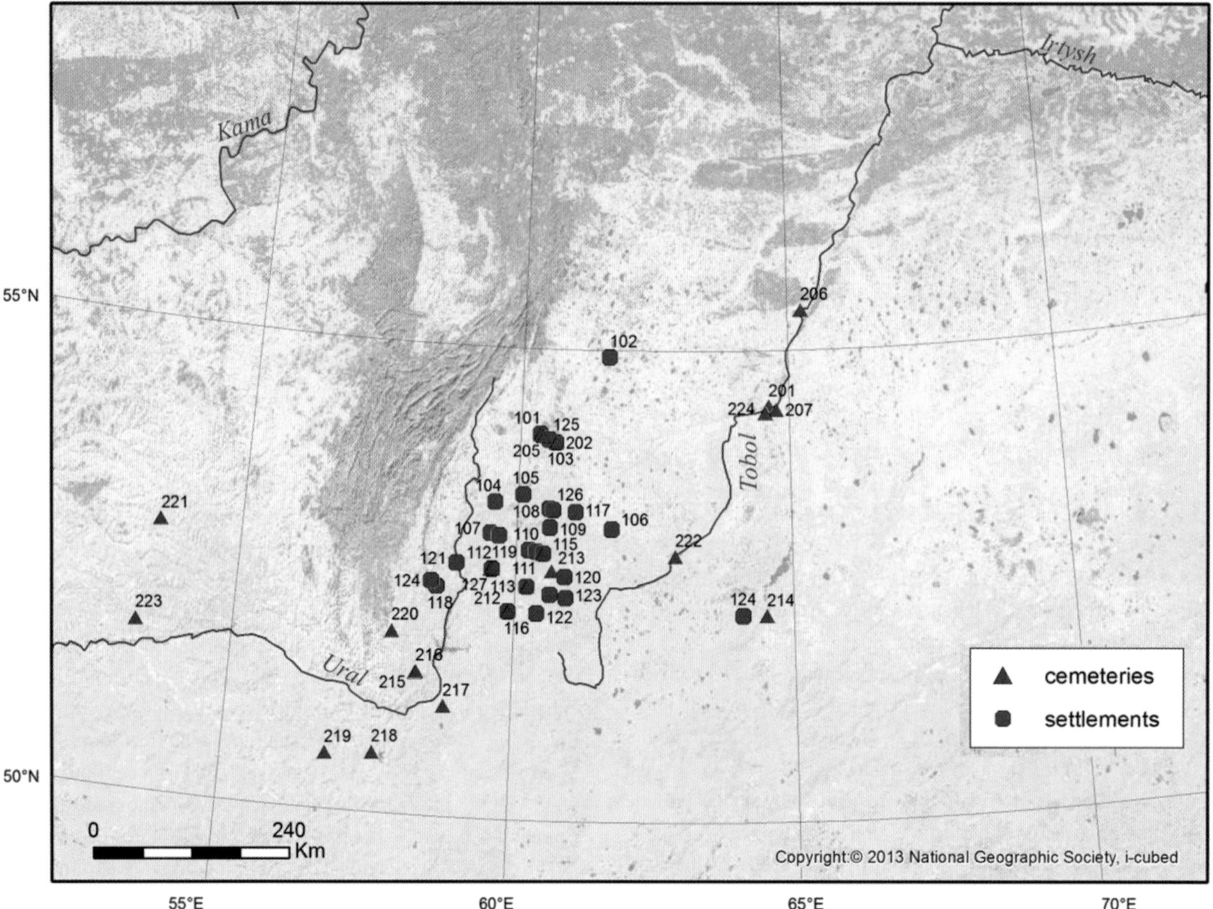

FIGURE 16.1. Sintashta sites. Map. Settlements: 101 – Stepnoe; 102 – Shibaevo I; 103 – Chernorech'e III; 104 – Bakhta; 105 – Parizh; 106 – Isenej; 107 – Kujsak; 108 – Ust'e; 109 – Rodniki; 110 – Konopljanka; 111 – Zhurumbaj; 112 – Arkaim; 113 – Sintashta; 114 – Sintashta II; 115 – Kamennyj Ambar; 116 – Alandskoe; 117 – Chekatai; 118 – Selek; 119 – Sarym-Sakly; 120 – Kamysty; 121 – Kizil'skoe; 122 – Bersuat; 123 – Andreevskoe; 124 – Ulak; 125 – Streletskoe; 126 – Zarechnoe IV; 127 – Kamennyj Brod; 124 – Semiozernoe II. Cemeteries: 201 – Ozernoe 1; 202 – Krivoe Ozero; 203 – Stepnoe M; 204 – Kamennyj Ambar-5; 205 – Stepnoe I; 206 – Carev kurgan; 207 – Ubagan I; 208 – Solnce II; 209 – Bol'shekaraganskij; 210 – Aleksandrovskij IV; 211 – Sintashta; 212 – Solonchanka Ia; 213 – Knjazhenskij; 214 – Bestamak; 215 – Ishkinovka I; 216 – Ishkinovka II; 217 – Novo-Kumakskij; 218 – Zhaman-Kargala I; 219 – Tanabergen II; 220 – Novo-Petrovka; 221 – Malojuldashevo; 222 – Halvaj 3, 5; 223 – Gerasimovskij 2; 224 – Kul'chukaj.

located buildings of rectangular or trapezoidal shape, with exits facing the inner area. The buildings form blocks with common walls, of which the outer wall is the most massive (4–5 m at the base). These sections of the walls together form the main element of the fortification. In other monuments, the results of excavations and geophysical research show a linear layout of the internal space with intermediate streets. Here, the outline of the outer wall is rectangular. The unifying element of the two variants is the similarity of their construction technology, with an absolute predominance of wooden and soil constructions (stone was rarely used, and only as an auxiliary material for covering the outer face of the defensive wall). In all cases, the settlements are surrounded by moats, the depth of which varies greatly (from 0.7–0.9 to 2.5 m). Apparently, this element mainly served for water drainage. In recent years, archaeological evidence of habitat, albeit without traces of buildings, has been found outside the fortifications, in their immediate vicinity (Chechushkov et al. 2018).

The cultural layer contains a complex of finds that is characteristic of settlements of the Bronze Age. The numerous bones of animals (almost exclusively domestic ones: cattle, small cattle, horses, and dogs) clearly illustrate the cattle-breeding specialization of the groups (Kosintzev et al. 2016). Targeted searches for traces of farming have been unsuccessful (Stobbe et al. 2016). The most abundant category of finds concerns fragments of ceramic vessels, whereas other traces of everyday activity are much less documented. However, there is evidence of local metallurgical production, processing of bone and wood, and weaving. In general, the complex of finds reflects the daily life of the settlement inhabitants. It is impossible to identify buildings or areas that deviate as far as their architecture or an unusual set of artifacts is concerned. Further, the size of the buildings within one single monument differs only slightly, the largest building reaching 180 to 200 square meters.

Important elements of the interior were the wells and heating devices of various types. The former have been found in all buildings without exception; the latter are not documented everywhere (because they are sometimes difficult to diagnose), but were probably also a universal part of the dwellings.[1]

16.3 Archaeological Manifestations of the Furnace-Well System

There is a rather extensive literature devoted to wells and furnaces, but a detailed and comprehensive study of these elements, in fact, has taken place only in the last decade (Koryakova et al. 2013, Rühl 2016, etc.). As already mentioned, wells have been found in each building. There is a fairly stable stereotype of their location: they are always located near the central axis of the building and close to the outer wall, in the one-third of the space that is farthest from the entrance.[2] Deviations from this "rule" are mainly limited to those cases where the number of wells reaches five to seven (Koryakova et al. 2013: 89, Koryakova & Kuzmina 2017). It is obvious that these numerous wells did not all function simultaneously within the same dwelling, since there are also examples of buildings with a single well. Most likely, the presence of multiple wells is due to long-term use of the building's space or to failure during construction.[3] The construction of the well is determined by its function and the technical capabilities of the builders.

The lower parts of the wells have been better investigated than the upper parts, which have been largely damaged by natural factors. In all well-documented examples, the bottom of the well was found 0.5–0.7 m below the groundwater level. The overall depth (up to 3.7 m) varied depending on the level of the aquifer. It has been reliably established that the lower part of the well (up to 1 m in diameter) had a casing of wattle or planks submerged in water. The space between the casing and the ground wall could be filled with clay mortar (or blocks), which improved the filtration of the water. A layer of coarse sand or pebbles may have served the same purpose. Thanks to the watering of the lower part, wooden details have been preserved, which are usually inaccessible for study in the conditions of the sharply continental climate of the steppe. The archaeological specifics of the upper part of the wells illustrate a variety of technical solutions. First, the form of the upper part is variable (round or subrectangular). Secondly, there are differences in the profile: along with cone-shaped stratigraphic sections, there are examples with an additional step. Finally, there is some difference in the size of well pits at the floor level of the dwelling (from 1.5 to 2.7 m). Unfortunately, there is practically no data at our disposal as to the original appearance of the wellhead, although it clearly existed, ensuring the safety of the inhabitants while also preventing littering.

It should be noted that in the filling of the wells, along with the remnants of everyday life, we find objects that were intentionally placed there.[4] The most obvious of these are traces of sacrifices. Thus, in the settlement of Kamennyi Ambar, numerous lower jaws of sheep have been extracted from the bottom of the well, some of which had been installed vertically along the walls. Interestingly, not all of them were paired. Similar examples can be cited for other settlements (Koryakova et al. 2013: 107). In addition, wooden and stone artifacts as well as pottery fragments have been found in the wells. All of this testifies to the variety of the wells' uses: along with their main function (provision of water), they could, for instance, serve as refrigerators. Given the harsh winter conditions, when ice can be more than one meter thick on small, slow-flowing rivers, and some rivers even freeze to the bottom, the problem of seasonal water supply must have been acute at times. Chemical and palynological data suggest the presence of domestic animals directly in dwellings (Rühl et al. 2016), which made the issue of water supply particularly serious.

Of course, such vital objects as wells were clearly included in mythological and ritual activity, and the same can be said of the various thermal engineering devices found in large numbers within the boundaries of the inhabited space (Grigoriev 2000: 456–470, Grigoriev 2015: 95–106). Despite significant losses due to the damage to these objects, several types stand out (Nikitin & Rusanov 2011).[5] The criteria for differentiation are the size, shape, design, and construction material of the objects (clay and stone). Another important detail is the object's location within the home. Ultimately, all these features are directly

[1] This is clearly seen not only in the excavated sites, but also in those sites for which a geomagnetic survey was performed (Fig. 16.2). Positive anomalies in the respective parts of the buildings are illustrated by calcined areas at the base of the furnaces and calcined material in the filling of the well.

[2] Most probably, this part was where the inhabitants lived most of the time, as this is where the significant finds are concentrated, and where we find the main architectural details, including internal partitions dividing the building space into zones (Fig. 16.3).

[3] This idea is inspired by the almost complete absence of organic residues in the water-filled near-bottom part of some wells. In our opinion, extraction of wooden parts from collapsing wells is hardly realistic in conditions of heavy soil and groundwater intake. Therefore, these wells were not put into operation.

[4] The distinction between these categories is not always possible and the number of deliberately placed artifacts could have been higher. Obviously, the semantics of the artifact depends heavily on the context in which it is found.

[5] Often, in the process of excavation, only areas of calcination of the soil without additional details are found. These are not necessarily traces of an open hearth (campfire). The buildings functioned for quite a long time (probably for several decades), as evidenced by signs of repairs, so part of the furnaces could break down and be transferred to new places.

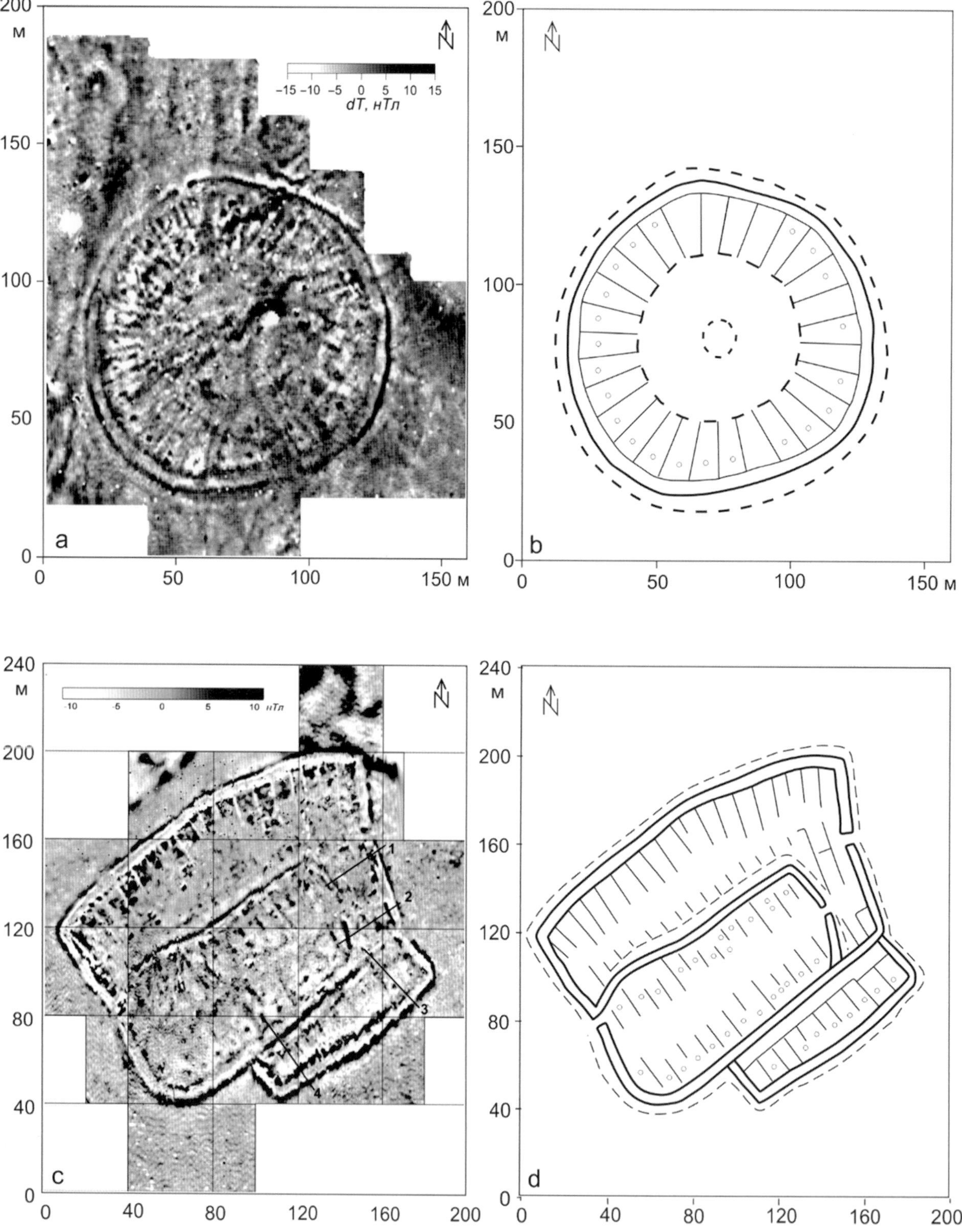

FIGURE 16.2. Sintashta fortified settlements on the basis of geomagnetic survey. Types of planning: a, b – Sarym-Sakly, c, d – Andreevskoe (after Fedorova et al. 2013; fig. 3; Noskevich et al. 2014; fig. 2).

or indirectly related to the structure's function (heating, cooking, smelting metal from ore, casting, and firing ceramics). Some of the elements cannot be unambiguously interpreted, e.g., the rectangular calcined stains with coal inclusions at the end wall, defined by the author of the excavation as a "fireplace" (Gening et al. 1992: 74–78) without any additional argumentation. Of the seven types, only two are associated with wells and will be now discussed in greater detail.

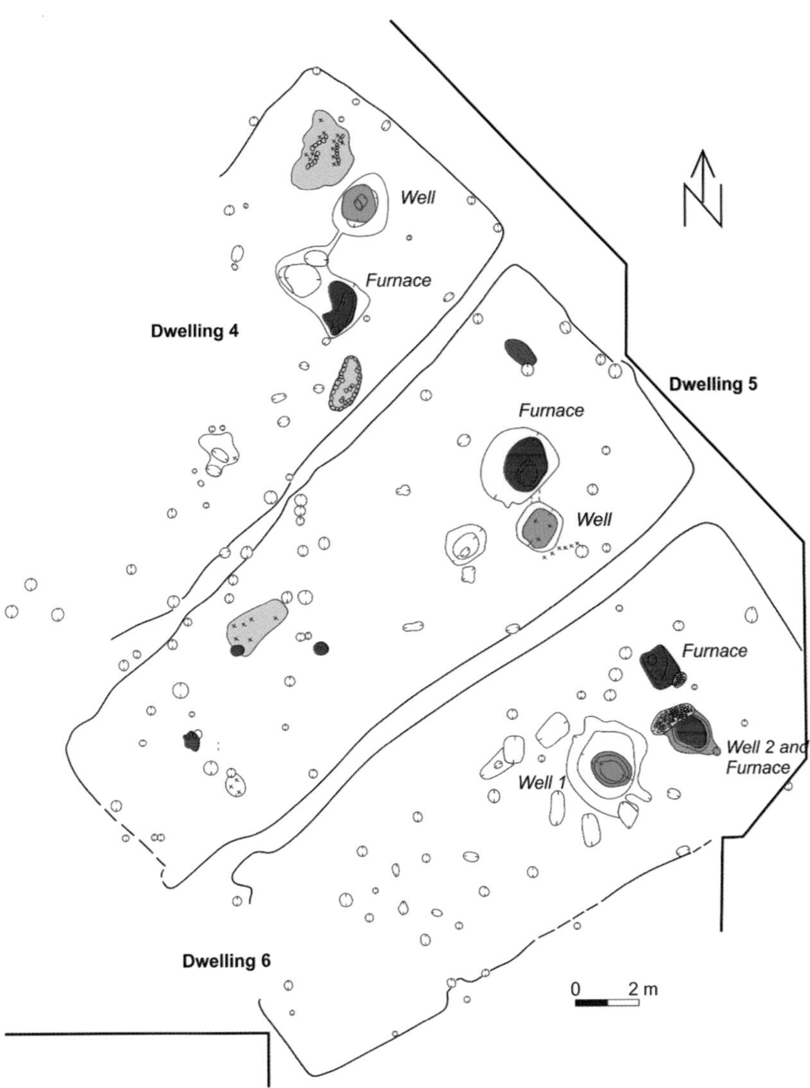

FIGURE 16.3. Sintashta settlement. Dwellings 4–6 (after Gening, Zdanovich, & Gening 1992: fig. 14).

Furnaces of the first type are connected to the well through the blower channel. As building materials, different types of clay solutions were used. For such furnaces, the diameter of the hearth can usually be determined (0.8–1 m); less often there are traces of the groove duct. The reason for this difference is the poor preservation of the floor surface near the well due to the subsidence of the soil. Experimental verification of the performance of this design has demonstrated its polyfunctionality. The inflow of air due to the temperature difference between the well and the furnace ensured that the fire in the hearth burned steadily. This technological detail made it possible to use the complex well kiln for heating, cooking food, and melting metal for pouring into molds. The latter, however, required additional air injection with the help of bellows.

The second type of furnace is also connected to the well; sometimes the duct between them is also preserved. The furnaces differ in their size and design. The diameter of the hearth is often about 30 cm, and the base is lined with small stones. On the basis of its small size (it is easier to reach and maintain the required temperature regime), it has been suggested that this type of furnace could be used in the process of smelting copper from ore (Nikitin & Rusanov 2011: 309). Traces of fire and ruined furnace constructions are often found not only near the wells, but also in their filling.

It is important to mention that the tradition of uniting wells and furnaces in the same space is also well known outside the Sintashta culture. Despite the changes in the building tradition and the abandonment of dense block construction in the subsequent period of the Late Bronze Age, a number of settlements show the relationship between wells and furnaces (Alaeva & Rassamakhin 2018). From the point of view of cultural attribution, the most famous examples come from the Alakul' and Alakul'-Fedorovka sites of the Andronovo culture. The tradition apparently survives up to the Final Bronze Age (Grigoriev 2013, Malyutina & Petrova 2018). The territory of its distribution is also impressive: the steppe and forest-steppe of Eastern Europe, the Urals, and Kazakhstan. There must have been powerful reasons for the stability and scale of the tradition. Specialists

FIGURE 16.4. Kamennyi Ambar settlement. Dwelling 2. A decommissioned well 2 and the basement of a furnace above it.

have usually focused on rational explanations, searching first of all for evidence of the use of the furnace in the field of metal production; there are many arguments for this in the form of archaeological finds and experiments. Along with this, there has been an attempt to see in the combination of well and furnace the idea of combining the elements of water and fire (Zdanovich et al. 2018: 97). From this point of view, it is telling that heat engineering devices were often placed above wells that had already been decommissioned and covered with clay (Fig. 16.4). The experience of one of the authors during the excavation of the Kamennyi Ambar settlement and the observations of other specialists (Grigoriev 2013: 97–98, Koryakova & Kuz'mina 2017: 99) show that the full conservation of a well is not a simple task: the backfill soil – less dense than the enclosing one – takes up moisture according to the capillary principle, not to mention its gradual subsidence. Accordingly, kindling and maintaining fire on a wet base was clearly more difficult than on dry areas of the floor. However, the inhabitants of the settlements apparently were not guided by purely utilitarian considerations.

The stable combination of wells and furnaces that we are interested in must have had sacred reasons as well as rational ones. If the creation of such a system may be partly justified for the purpose of metal production (Grigoriev 2015), for domestic needs it is clearly redundant. There is even less reason to search for the rational roots of the tradition of placing heating devices directly above abandoned wells. The stability of the tradition (for almost the entire 2nd millennium BC) and its spread point to its ideological roots, as is also indirectly indicated by the fact that the large furnace near the well had no narrowly specialized function.[6] This was the most popular and versatile type, the main advantage in the design being the possibility of maintaining constant fire with minimal fuel consumption (Rusanov & Kupriyanov 2003: 232).

The archaeological considerations cannot bring us further than a very general idea about the sacred fire of the hearth. To specify these ideas, we have to closely analyze the Indo-Iranian linguistic sources.

16.4 The Indo-Iranian 'Grandson of the Waters'

There is a broadly shared consensus that the Sintashta–Petrovka culture was inhabited by speakers of Proto-Indo-Iranian (cf. Anthony 2007: 408ff.), so we will have to look at the oldest Indo-Iranian texts (the Avesta for Iranian and the Rigveda for Indo-Aryan) to identify elements of the mythology or religious belief that can help us understand the archaeological findings. Evidently, we have first and foremost to consider the enigmatic Indo-Iranian deity Apām Napāt (Sanskrit Apā́ṃ Nápāt, Avestan Apąm Napāt), literally the 'Grandson of the Waters'. In the Vedas, this name most often refers to an aspect or form of Agni, the god of fire.[7] To call the god of fire the Grandson of the Waters "might seem singularly inappropriate" (Boyce 1986), which gave rise to a plethora of interpretations in the literature: Apām Napāt was taken as the sun sinking into the ocean, as lightning, as an aquatic deity, as Soma, as Varuṇa (see Findly 1979 for an overview of the older literature), or even as "oil flares on the Caspian shores" (Puhvel 1987: 279).

Because of the wildly differing approaches to this deity, it seems important to take a close look at the textual evidence to determine which aspect of fire is called the 'Grandson of the Waters' and why. Further, we must search for common features of this deity in both branches and to try to reconstruct the Indo-Iranian situation.

[6] As mentioned above, the low-volume furnaces with a floor diameter of up to 0.3–0.4 m were optimal for smelting metal from ore.

[7] He is also called *apā́ṃ gárbha* 'embryo of the waters' in a few passages.

16.5 Avestan Apąm Napāt

The Iranian evidence is relatively limited, so let us start with the Avestan deity Apąm Napāt. All we know about him has been conveniently presented by Mary Boyce in an article in *Encyclopædia Iranica*. As she indicates, "both the Avestan texts and Zoroastrian cult suggest that he is a great divinity, who has become partly overshadowed." He is mentioned in texts devoted to other divinities of water, but no hymn survives in his honor. In the Avesta, there is only one whole verse in honor of Apąm Napāt:

Yt 19.52 *bərəzaṇtəm ahurəm xšaϑrīm xšaētəm, apąm napātəm auruuaṱ. aspəm yazamaide, aršānəm zauuanō.sum, yō nərəuš daδa yō nərəuš tataša, yō upāpō yazatō, sruṱ.gaošōtəmō asti yezimnō*

'We worship the lofty, powerful Lord, the bright Apąm Napāt, who has swift horses, the male who thrives through oblations,[8] who created men, who shaped men; [we worship] the aquatic deity who better than anybody lends a listening ear when being worshipped.'

Apąm Napāt is called here an 'aquatic deity' (*upāpō yazatō*), but this does not necessarily mean that he lives *in* the water, as the Avestan adjective *upāpa-* is also used for beavers and otters, among other animals. At the same time, the passage contains several important clues for identifying Apąm Napāt (next to being an aquatic deity) as fire/sun. The fact that Apąm Napāt is called *xšaēta-* 'bright' does not say much, as this is a reasonably standard epithet for various deities and heroes, but the epithet *auruuaṱ.aspa-* 'having swift horses' in the Avesta is used exclusively of Apąm Napāt and the sun.[9] Moreover, it makes more sense to call fire 'thriving through oblations' than any other divinity. The accessibility of Apąm Napāt with his listening ear may be an indication that he is always around.

The fiery nature of Apąm Napāt and its closeness to the worshipper can also be encountered in other stray mentions of this deity scattered throughout the Avesta.

Yt 8.4 says of Tištriia 'Sirius': *yahmāṱ haca bərəzāṱ haosrauuaŋhəm, apąm nafəδraṱ haca ciϑrəm* 'from whose height [arises] (his) glory, from Apąm Napāt (his) [= Tištrya's] visible form' (translation by Panaino 1990: 30). This would mean that Apąm Napāt (as fire/sun) creates the shining form of the star Tištriia. Apąm Napāt was further a foremost helper of Tištriia and responsible for the production of pure waters (Panaino 1995: 124).

In the same text, it is said (Yt 8.34): *apąm napåsə.tā̊ āpō ... aŋ^{v}he astuuaite šōiϑrō.baxtā̊ vī.baxšaiti* 'Apąm Napāt distributes to the material world those waters assigned to dwelling places.' Apąm Napāt is thus directly related to the abodes of the people.

We further learn from the Avesta that Apąm Napāt, together with Miϑra (who is closely associated with the sun), furthers all supreme authorities of countries and pacifies those countries that are in turmoil (Yt 13.95),[10] and that Apąm Napāt, together with Miϑra and fire, is involved in the protection of *x^{v}arənah*, the symbol of sovereignty and kingship, against forces of evil.[11] In Yt 19.51, when *x^{v}arənah* escapes into the mythical lake Vourukaṣ̌a, Apąm Napāt says that he is going to get it "at the bottom of the unfathomable lake, at the bottom of the deep bays."

Finally, it is important that for the Zoroastrians, "in the divisions of the day ... the morning is set under the protection of Mithra, the afternoon under that of Apąm Napāt" (Boyce 1986). Since the names of the months and divisions of the day are normally derived from the festivals or rituals held at those periods, it seems likely that the morning was called after a ritual for the rising sun (Miϑra), and the afternoon after one for the setting sun (Apąm Napāt).

As far as the Iranian facts are concerned, we can conclude that Apąm Napāt combines the features of an aquatic deity and those of fire/sun, especially the setting sun. It is probably for this reason that Apąm Napāt says that he is going to get *x^{v}arənah* at the bottom of lake Vourukaṣ̌a. Further, he is close to the people, providing them with pure water and a listening ear.

16.6 The Hymn to Apā̃ṃ Napāt in the Rigveda (2.35)

In the Rigveda, Apā̃ṃ Napāt is mentioned ca. 30 times, but 2.35 is the only hymn that is dedicated to him. The hymn belongs to the most archaic layer of the RV and was often included in anthologies, even though much of it was considered enigmatic. On the one hand, Apā̃ṃ Napāt is the sacrificial fire at the end of the hymn, but at the beginning, he is surrounded and nurtured by the waters, which was seen as a paradox. However, with the archaeological evidence for the Indo-Iranian "furnace-well" constructions in mind, we may try to read this hymn not as a paradox, but as a poetic description of the ritual ghee libation into the fire, an original form of the later *agnihotra* ritual, an oblation into the fire to help the sun, twice daily, at each sunset and sunrise. Within the Vedic system of beliefs, the sun is just another form of the god of fire, Agni, who at sunset sinks into the ocean that is situated beneath the earth.

Because of the importance of the hymn to our understanding of the nature of Apā̃ṃ Napāt, we present it in its entirety with a few comments. The translation is mostly based on that of Jamison (Jamison & Brereton, 2014) and Geldner.

2.35.1

úpem asṛkṣi vājayúr vacasyā̃ṃ, cáno dadhīta nād̯yó gíro me |
apā̃ṃ nápād āśuhémā kuvít sá, supéśasas karati jóṣiṣad dhí ||

'I have released my eloquence in pursuit of prizes. The grandson of the rivers should take delight in my hymns. Isn't he, Apā̃ṃ Napāt, of

[8] For the interpretation of *zauuanō.sum* as 'thriving through oblations', see Kellens 1974: 102.

[9] The phrase *bərəzaṇtəm ahurəm xšaϑrīm xšaētəm apąm napātəm auruuaṱ.aspəm* is found at six different places in the Avesta, which shows that this is a standard titulature of Apąm Napāt. Sometimes it is shortened to *bərəzaṇt- ahura-*, and in the Zoroastrian literature, Apąm Napāt is usually called Burz (< *bərəzaṇt-*); see Panaino 1995.

[10] On this passage, see further Gershevitch 1959: 27–29, 59–60.

[11] As indicated by Sadovski (2018: 378), in the Avestan liturgies, Apąm Napāt occupies the place corresponding to the Vedic deity *Tanū-napāt-*, a form of Agni (fire), which again points to his fiery nature.

swift impulse? He will make [the songs] well-appreciated, since he will enjoy them.'

ā́śuhéman-, lit. 'of swift impulse', a standing epithet of Apāṃ Napāt (also found in 2.1.5, 2.31.6, and 7.47.2), is often translated as 'impelling the swift ones', i.e., that Apāṃ Napāt is a charioteer, but in RV 1.116.2 this word characterizes a horse, so it most likely refers to a horse that quickly responds to steering. Cf. also the Avestan passage Yt 19.52, discussed above, where it is said of him: *srut̰.gaošōtəmō asti yezimnō* 'who better than anybody lends a listening ear when being worshipped'.

supéśas-, lit. 'well-ornamented', here clearly expresses the desire of the poet to get good rewards for this hymn.

2.35.2

imáṃ sᵤv àsmai hr̥dá ā́ sútaṣṭam, mántraṃ vocema kuvíd asya védat |
apā́ṃ nápād asuryàsya mahnā́, víśvāniy aryó bhúvanā jajāna ||

'This well-crafted thought we would speak to him from our heart. He will surely get knowledge of it? The noble Apāṃ Napāt created all living beings by the greatness of his lordly power.'

The last line of the stanza echoes 2.40.5a *víśvāniy anyó bhúvanā jajā́na* 'the one created all living beings . . .', where it refers to Soma. Since it is often said of various gods that they have created all beings, this message is not specific and presumably only used to propitiate Apāṃ Napāt, though see the Avestan passage Yt 19.52, cited above.

2.35.3

sám anyā́ yántiy úpa yantiy anyā́ḥ, samānám ūrváṃ nadiyàḥ pr̥ṇanti |
tám ū śúciṃ śúcayo dīdivā́ṃsam, apā́ṃ nápātam pári tasthur ā́paḥ ||

'Some come together; others approach: (but) it is one and the same enclosure that the rivers fill. The pure waters have surrounded the pure, burning Apāṃ Napāt.'

ūrváṃ. The word *ūrvá-* literally means 'enclosure', a common expression being *gávya- ūrvá-* 'cow pen'. The poet is referring to the myth of releasing the waters = cows from their enclosure when they were captured there by a demon. This image would be appropriate in the case of a well, too: the waters, wherever they are, are connected with each other and fill every enclosure.

dīdivā́ṃsam. As argued in Lubotsky 2011: 122f., the perfect *dīdā́ya* does not mean 'to shine', but 'to burn'. If we take the passage literally (and why shouldn't we?), the poet sees the burning fire in front of him surrounded by waters.

śúci- 'bright, shining' often has the connotation 'clean, pure'.[12] This may be important in view of the *aponaptrīya* ritual (see below).

2.35.4

tám ásmerā yuvatáyo yúvānam, marmr̥jyámānāḥ pári yantiy ā́paḥ |
sá śukrébhiḥ śíkvabhī revád asmé, dīdā́yānidhmó ghr̥tánirṇig apsú ||

'The youthful waters, without smiling, circle around the youth while they groom him. With his gleaming, dexterous (flames), he burns richly for us without fuel, with his garment of ghee, in the waters.'

ásmerāḥ 'not smiling'. It is not quite clear what exactly this epithet seeks to express. In the Rigveda, smiling is associated with the Dawn, with young women, with lightning (cf. recently Pinault 2013: 29ff.) and can have erotic connotations. Since, in stanza 9, a lightning flash will appear above the waters, it is likely that the image refers to water in a well, which is dark and gloomy and does not shine (= smile) until illuminated by fire (see below).

The image of Apāṃ Napāt burning (as if) without fuel among the waters is repeated in 10.30.4a *yó anidhmó dī́dayad apsv àntár* 'who burns without fuel within the waters'. It perfectly fits the archaeological findings that fire in an oven connected with a well steadily burns even without extensive fuel.

2.35.5

asmaí tisró avyathiyā́ya nā́rīr, devā́ya devī́r didhiṣantiy ánnam |
kŕ̥tā ivópa hí prasarsré apsú, sá pīyū́ṣaṃ dhayati pūrvasū́nām ||

'Three women goddesses try to give food to this god so that he will not waver. He sucks the beestings of those who give birth before others, since he keeps stretching himself out into the waters like *kŕ̥tāḥ*.'

The identity of the three goddesses has always been considered unclear (see Jamison, Comm. ad loc.), but it seems attractive to assume that the poet is referring to three so-called *srúc-*, sacrificial ladles that were used for pouring ghee into the fire (Renou 1953: 171), i.e., *juhū́* ('tongue'), *upabhŕ̥t* ('support'), and *dhruvā́* ('stable, stationary'). The *juhū́* is used to offer oblations; the *upabhŕ̥t* supports the *juhū́* when it is lifted'; and the *dhruvā́* remains stationary as the oblations are scooped from it. The names of the ladles are all feminine, which explains why they are called goddesses. They form a stable triad; cf., for instance, Atharvaveda Śaunakīya 18.4.5 *juhū́r dādhāra dyā́m upabhŕ̥d antárikṣaṃ dhruvā́ dādhāra pr̥thivī́ṃ pratiṣṭhā́m* 'The *juhū́* ladle sustains the sky, the *upabhŕ̥t* ladle the atmosphere; the *dhruvā́* ladle sustains the earth, the support'.

The meaning of *kŕ̥tāḥ* is unknown, so the simile unfortunately remains obscure.

pūrvasū́- is usually translated 'who give birth for the first time', but *pū́rva-* hardly ever means 'for the first time' in the Vedic compounds, rather 'before others, in front of others'; compare *pūrva-jā́-* 'first-born (before others)' (RV), *pūrva-pā́-* 'drinking before others' (RV), *pūrva-bhā́j-* 'receiving the share before others, privileged' (RV), etc. The three sacrificial ladles are said to give birth before others as this is the first oblation.

With beestings the poet is clearly referring to the clarified butter (ghee), which is quite similar in color and texture. The stanza describes a ghee oblation.

prasarsré apsú. We take *apsú* as a locative of direction: the fire keeps stretching toward the waters, because the ghee is flowing through the channel toward the well.

2.35.6

áśvasyₐā́tra jánimāsyá ca svàr[13], *druhó riṣáḥ sampŕ̥caḥ pāhi sūrī́n* |
āmā́su pūrṣú paró apramr̥ṣyáṃ, nā́rātayo ví naśan nā́nr̥tāni ||

'Here is the birth of the horse and of this sun. Protect the patrons from deceit, from harm, from contamination (with

[12] Geldner mostly translated *śúci-* with 'rein, lauter', while Jamison and Brereton usually opt for 'blazing, gleaming', which is less fitting in contexts where waters and Soma are the carriers of this epithet.

[13] For the monosyllabic *svàr*, see Klein 1985: I, 96. This seems to be a very archaic form, testifying also to an early date of the hymn.

them)! Neither hostilities nor untruths will reach him who is not to be disregarded in the raw fortresses, (even) far away.'

As indicated by Jamison (Comm. ad loc.), the "horse" must be the sun and "this sun" Agni (fire).

ā́māsu pū́rṣú 'in the raw fortresses' can hardly refer to 'furnaces made of unbaked clay' or 'furnaces made of unfired brick', as understood in all modern translations. Furnaces made of fired brick are known only since Roman times. The raw fortresses may refer to the wells, where our fire is stretching to.

'not to be disregarded (even) far away', i.e., everybody will see the fire, even from afar, when it reaches the well. The poet is preparing the culmination, which is going to happen very soon.

2.35.7

svá ā́ dáme sudúghā yásya dhenúḥ, svadhā́m pīpāya subh$_{ú}$*v ánnam atti* |
só ^{a}*pā́ṃ nápād ūrjáyann aps*$_{ú}$*v àntár, vasudéyāya vidhaté ví bhāti* ||

'He who has a good-milking milch cow in his own house, he swells with independence; he eats good food. So Apāṃ Napāt, being nourished within the waters, radiates widely to give goods to the one who honors him.'

We may interpret this stanza as referring to a well with waters providing nourishment for the fire. Thus, when a furnace (= fire's own house) is connected with a well, fire can burn independently.

All of a sudden, the fire 'radiates widely'. Something must have happened since we saw the young, timid fire. It seems likely that at this moment, the burning ghee is approaching the well through the channel, and the fire glow becomes visible.

2.35.8

yó aps$_{ú}$*v ā́ śúcinā daív*$_{i}$*yena, ṛtā́vā́jasra urviyā́ vibhā́ti* |
vayā́ íd anyā́ bhúvanān$_{i}$*y asya, prá jāyante vīrúdhaś ca prajā́bhiḥ* ||

'He who in the waters, truthful and inexhaustible, radiates far and wide with his pure heavenly power; the other beings [= fires] are just his twigs, and the plants propagate themselves through their progeny [like this].'

The fire is now in the waters and "radiates far and wide." Presumably, the ghee has reached the well and keeps burning on the surface of the water. This is the central part of the hymn (which often contains the most important information) and describes the culmination of the ritual.

'the other beings [= fires] are just his twigs', i.e., the other fires are mere twigs of Agni (Jamison, Comm.). Here, the poet wants to stress that the fire burning in the well is identical with the sun rising from the waters.

2.35.9

apā́ṃ nápād ā́ h$_{i}$*y ásthād upásthaṃ, jihmā́nām ūrdhvó vidyútaṃ vásānaḥ | tásya jyéṣṭham mahimā́naṃ váhantīr, híraṇyavarṇāḥ pári yanti yahvī́ḥ* ||

'Since Apāṃ Napāt, clothing himself in the lightning flash, has mounted the lap of those who are horizontal, (himself) erect, the golden-hued maidens circle around him, transporting his preeminent greatness.'

This stanza becomes understandable if we envisage burning ghee falling into the well. Presumably, when ghee hits the (lap of the) waters, a flame suddenly shoots up like a lightning flash. The waters turn a golden color by reflection, while the ghee keeps burning on the water.

In this way, the ritual creates a spectacular reenactment of the sun rising from the waters. A similar spectacular "lightning" is part of the so-called *pravargya* ritual, which has been described by Jan Houben in a 2000 article.

2.35.10

híraṇyarūpaḥ sá híraṇyasaṃdṛg, apā́ṃ nápāt séd u híraṇyavarṇaḥ |
hiraṇyáyāt pári yóner niṣádyā, hiraṇyadā́ dadat$_{i}$*y ánnam asmai* ||

'Golden-formed, he has a golden appearance; and Apāṃ Napāt is golden-hued, (coming) out of a golden womb after he has settled down. The givers of gold give food to him.'

After the explosion, burning ghee is still coming from the furnace and continues burning on the surface of the water. "The givers of gold" can simply be the sacrificial ladles again, providing Apāṃ Napāt with gold, i.e., ghee (see also the next stanza). The golden womb refers to the furnace.

2.35.11

tád asyā́nīkam utá cā́ru nā́ma-, -apīc$_{i}$*yàṃ vardhate náptur apā́m* |
yám indháte yuvatáyaḥ sám itthā́, híraṇyavarṇaṃ ghṛtám ánnam asya ||

'That face of his and the dear, secret name of Apāṃ Napāt grow strong, whom the youthful women together kindle in this way: golden-hued ghee is food for him.'

This stanza identifies Apāṃ Napāt "as the secret name of Agni" (Jamison, Comm.).

2.35.12

asmaí bahūnā́m avamā́ya sákhye, yajñaír vidhema námasā havírbhiḥ |
sáṃ sā́nu mā́rjmi dídhiṣāmi bílmair, dádhām$_{i}$*y ánnaiḥ pári vanda ṛgbhíḥ* ||

'To him, the closest comrade of many, we would like to serve with sacrifices, with reverence, with oblations. I groom his back, I seek to provide (him) with wood shavings, I provide (him) with food, I extol (him) with verses.'

This is a domestic ritual, so the poet does everything himself, instead of several priests.

2.35.13

sá īṃ vṛ́ṣā janayat tā́su gárbhaṃ, sá īṃ śíśur dhayati táṃ rihanti |
só ^{a}*pā́ṃ nápād ánabhimlātavarṇo, '*$_{a}$*nyásyeveha tan*$_{ú}$*vā̀ viveṣa* ||

'As bull, he begets the embryo in these (waters). As infant, he sucks them; they lick him. That Grandson of the Waters, whose color never fades, has toiled here as if with the body of another.'

The purposely enigmatic formulation of the first half of the stanza can be understood in the sense that the fire, when just kindled (= the infant), gets support of the draft of the waters, whereas the mature fire (= the bull) throws drops of burning ghee into the waters, which can be seen as his semen. This interpretation seems to be supported by the traces of ashes in the Sintashta–Petrovka wells.

'with the body of another'. The poet is again referring to the unity of various aspects of Agni (Fire), stressing the point that the fire he kindles is actually the sun.

2.35.14

asmín padé paramé tasthivā́ṃsam, adhvasmábhir viśváhā dīdivā́ṃsam |
ā́po náptre ghṛtám ánnaṃ váhantīḥ, svayám átkaiḥ pári dīyanti yahvī́ḥ ||

'Him taking stand in this most distant place, constantly burning with not smoking (flames) – the waters bringing ghee as food to the Grandson (of the Waters), the maidens fly encircling (him) with themselves as his cloaks.'

padé paramé 'most distant place'. The interpretation of these words is controversial (Jamison & Brereton translate 'highest footprint'). If we take this expression literally, fire is now burning in the well, which was farthest from the entrance.

The first line is repeated almost verbatim in 1.72.4cd *vidán márto nemádhitā cikitvā́n, agním padé paramé tasthivā́ṃsam* || 'In the opposite position a mortal, perceiving him, found Agni standing on the highest track' (Jamison & Brereton).

Unlike in the beginning of the hymn, the waters now transport ghee because the fire is burning on the surface of the waters.

2.35.15

áyāṃsam agne sukṣitíṃ jánāya-, -áyāṃsam u maghávadbhyaḥ suvṛktím | víśvaṃ tád bhadráṃ yád ávanti devā́, bṛhád vadema vidáthe suvī́rāḥ ||

'I have proffered a good dwelling place to the people, o Agni, and I have proffered a well-twisted (hymn) to the bounteous ones. What the gods support, all that is fortunate. May we speak loftily at the ritual distribution, in possession of good heroes.'

In this final stanza, the poet states that by composing and performing his hymn to Apāṃ Napāt, he proffered a good dwelling to the people, which is an important indication that Apāṃ Napāt is directly related to dwellings. It is also evident that Apāṃ Napāt is equivalent to Agni, god of fire.

16.7 RV 2.35: Conclusions

The preceding analysis shows that the whole hymn can indeed be seen as a description of a ghee libation into the fire, which burns next to a well, thus bearing textual evidence of a "furnace-well" construction. This ghee libation has many correspondences with the later *agnihotra* ritual, performed twice daily. As argued by Bodewitz (1976: 3), "accompanying and magically maintaining the cosmic process of sunset and sunrise ... are the central functions of the agnihotra. ... The agnihotra must transport the sun, already weakened at the end of the day, through the dangerous darkness and coolness of the night. ... Therefore, the evening agnihotra is primary. It is the real offering into Agni."

In several passages in the Rigveda (2.31.6, 6.50.13, 10.149.2), Apāṃ Napāt is mentioned next to Savitar, and in 1.22.6 is even identified with him (*apā́ṃ nápātam ávase, savitā́ram úpa stuhi* 'Praise Apāṃ Napāt, Savitar, for help'). Savitar is closely related to the setting sun and his main activity takes place in the evening (cf. most recently Oberlies 2012: 159–161), since he presumably is responsible for transporting the sun to the east during the night. All this may be seen as a parallel to the Iranian situation, where Apām Napāt is associated with the afternoon.

16.8 The Vedic *aponaptrīya* Ritual

In later Vedic texts, Apāṃ Napāt is especially connected with the *aponaptrīya* ritual, an oblation consisting of mixing the water drawn from a river on the day prior to the Soma pressing with the water drawn on the morning of the pressing itself. While drawing the water, the Hotar priest recites verses from the Rigveda (hymn 10.33), where stanza 3 reads:

10.30.3

ádhvaryavo 'ₐpá itā samudrám, apā́ṃ nápātaṃ havíṣā yajadhvam | sá vo dadad ūrmím adyā́ súpūtaṃ, tásmai sómam mádhumantaṃ sunota ||

'O Adhvaryus (= priests), go to the waters, to the sea. Worship Apāṃ Napāt with your oblation. He will give you the well-purified wave today. For him press the sweet Soma.'

Here, Apāṃ Napāt is specifically invoked to make the water pure, and this function of his may be rather ancient. Characteristically, the water in the *aponaptrīya* ritual must be drawn in the evening and then again in the morning, which must be a reminiscence of the evening *agnihotra* ritual to Apāṃ Napāt.

16.9 An Indo-Iranian Reconstruction

Based on textual evidence, we can reconstruct a number of features of Apām Napāt for the common Indo-Iranian period (see Table 16.1).

The idea that Apāṃ Napāt is the setting sun, which seems essentially correct, was already expressed by Max Müller in an 1856 lecture (in print, 1868: 82), which was one of the first attempts to understand Apāṃ Napāt's nature.

TABLE 16.1. Features of Apām Napāt reconstructed for the common Indo-Iranian period.

Proto-Indo-Iranian	Avesta	Rigveda
domestic fire, close to the people	"better than anybody lends a listening ear"	"the closest comrade of many," "of swift impulse"
connected to dwelling places	distributes water to dwelling places	provides good dwelling places to the people
creator of beings	virile, creator of men	created all living beings, begets the embryo in the waters
provides pure waters	responsible for pure waters	gives the "well-purified wave" for the Soma ritual
associated with the setting sun	dives into the lake Vourukaṣ̌a; is responsible for the afternoon	associated with Savitar/the setting sun

16.10 An Indo-European Myth?

Since the work of George Dumézil (1963, 1973), it has become customary in comparative Indo-European mythology (cf. recently Oettinger 2009) to connect Apām Napāt with some myths preserved in Old Irish and Roman sources. The idea is that Roman Neptūnus and the Old Irish deity Nechtan are etymologically related to Indo-Iranian Napāt (which is contestable) and that these two divinities preside over a well with some fiery essence hidden in the waters. To combine the stories into one myth, a lot of special pleading is necessary (for a criticism, see Mallory & Adams 1997: 203–4 and, in greater detail, Jendza 2013), but even if there was such a Proto-Indo-European myth, it was only in the Indo-Iranian period that the intertwining of water and fire had acquired such an important place in religious belief.

16.11 Conclusion

Due to their specificity, archaeological facts do not always lend themselves to unambiguous interpretation. Therefore, archaeology is constantly searching for outside sources to confirm or reject its hypotheses. In the past decade, ancient DNA analysis has become such a source. Yet another potential source of information is the study of the ancient texts. In our case, the study of the hymns of the Rigveda and Avesta has shown that the "furnace-well" system of the Sintashta culture was used for the ritual (consisting of an oblation of ghee into the domestic fire) to help the sun through the night: burning ghee from the furnace reached the well and thus reenacted the rising sun. On a more profane level, the persistence of this system may be explained by the Indo-Iranian belief that the domestic fire provides pure, clean water.

The synthesis of archaeological and linguistic information in our example demonstrates that the philological study of the old texts can also profit from this collaboration: archaeology may offer a key to explaining obscure passages in the written sources. The results of the excavations make it possible to interpret the complex hymn of the Rigveda more accurately and to vividly illustrate the Indo-Iranian origin of the idea of the "Grandson of the Waters."

Acknowledgments

We are grateful to Igor Chechushkov for his help in preparing the map, Marina Epimakhova for her help in preparing the illustrations, as well as to Astrid Stobbe, Sofya Panteleeva, and Tijmen Pronk for a fruitful exchange of views. Andrey Epimakhov was supported by a grant from the Ministry of Education and Sciences of the Russian Federation No FENU-2020-0021.

References

Alaeva, I. P., & M. A. Rassomakhin. 2018. Sledy plavki medi v kolodce poselenija Chebarkul' III. In: A. M. Yuminov, E. V. Zaykova, (ed.) *Geoarheologija i arheologicheskaja mineralogija 2018*, 112–7. Miass: Institut mineralogii UrO RAN.

Anthony, David. 2007. *The horse, the wheel, and language: How Bronze-age riders from the Eurasian steppes shaped the modern world.* Princeton: Princeton University Press.

Bodewitz, Hendrik W. 1976. The daily evening and morning offering *(Agnihotra)* according to the Brāhmaṇas, Leiden: Brill.

Boyce, Mary. 1986. Apąm Napāt. In: Ehsan Yarshater (ed.), *Encyclopædia Iranica*, Vol. II, Fasc. 2, 148–150.

Chechushkov I. V., A. S. Yakimov, O. P. Bachura, Ya. Chkhuen Yn, & E. N. Goncharova. 2018. Obshchestvennoe ustrojstvo sintashtinsko-petrovskih kollektivov pozdnego bronzovogo veka i prichiny genezisa social'noj èlity (na primere poselenija Kamennyj Ambar v stepnom Zaural'e). *Stratum Plus* 2: 149–66.

Dumézil, Georges. 1963. Le puits de Nechtan, *Celtica* 6: 50–61.

1973. *Mythe et Épopée*. Vol. 3. Paris: Editions Gallimard.

Epimakhov, A. V. 2005. *Rannie kompleksnye obshchestva Severa Central'noj Evrazii (po materialam mogil'nika Kamennyj Ambar-5)*, Vol. 1. Chelyabinsk: Chelyabinskij dom pechati.

Epimakhov, A. V., & N. I. Chuev. 2011. Abashevskie i sintashtinskie pamjatniki: predvaritel'nye rezul'taty prostranstvennogo analiza. *Vestnik arheologii, antropologii i ètnografii* 2(15): 47–56.

Epimakhov, A. V., & R. Krause, 2013. Relative and absolute chronology of the Kamennyi Ambar (Olgino) settlement. In: R. Krause & L. Koryakova (ed.), *Multidisciplinary investigations of the Bronze Age settlements in the Southern Trans-Urals (Russia)*, 129–46. Bonn: Verlag Dr. Rudolf Habelt GmbH.

Fedorova, N. V., V. V. Noskevich, V. S. Ivanchenko, A. S. Bebnev, & A. V. Malikov. 2013. Geofizicheskie metody issledovanija arheologicheskih pamjatnikov Sarym-Sakly i Vorovskaja Jama (Juzhnyj Ural). *Ural'skij geofizicheskij vestnik* 2: 46–53.

Findly, Ellison Banks. 1979. "Child of the Waters": A revaluation of Vedic Apąṃ Napāt. *Numen* 26(2): 164–184.

Gening, V. F. 1977. Mogil'nik Sintashta i problema rannih indoiranskih plemen. *Sovetskaja arheologija* 4: 53–73.

Gening, V. F., G. B. Zdanovich, & V. V. Gening. 1992. *Sintashta: arheologicheskie pamjatniki arijskih plemen Uralo-Kazahstanskih stepej*. Chelyabinsk: South Ural Press.

Gershevitch, Ilya. 1959. *The Avestan hymn to Mithra*. Cambridge: Cambridge University Press.

Grigoriev, S. A. 2000. Metallurgicheskoe proizvodstvo na Juzhnom Urale v èpohu srednej bronzy. In: N. O. Ivanova (ed.), *Drevnjaja istorija Juzhnogo Zaural'ja. Kamennyj vek. Èpoha bronzy*, 443–531. Chelyabinsk: South Urals State University Press.

2013. O nekotoryh osobennostjah funkcionirovanija i interpretacii kolodcev èpohi bronzy. In: V. G. Loman (ed.), *Arheologicheskie issledovaniya stepej Evrazii*, 96–102. Karaganda: TENGRI Ltd.

2015. *Metallurgical production in Northern Eurasia in the Bronze Age*. Oxford: Archaeopress.

Houben, Jan E. M. 2000. The ritual pragmatics of a Vedic hymn: The "riddle hymn" and the Pravargya ritual. *Journal of the American Oriental Society* 120(4): 499–536.

Jamison & Brereton = Jamison, Stephanie W. & Joel P. Brereton. 2014. *The Rigveda: The earliest religious poetry of India.* Oxford: Oxford University Press.

Jamison = Jamison, Stephanie W. Rigveda Translation: Commentary. http://rigvedacommentary.alc.ucla.edu.

Jendza, Craig. 2013. Theseus the Ionian in Bacchylides 17 and Indo-Iranian Apām Napāt. *Journal of Indo-European Studies* 41: 431–457.

Kellens, Jean. 1974. *Les noms-racines de l'Avesta*. Wiesbaden: Reichelt.

Klein, Jared S. 1985. *Toward a discourse grammar of the Rigveda*. 2 vols. Heidelberg: Carl Winter.

Koryakova L. N., & S. A. Kuz'mina. 2017. Nekotorye osobennosti arhitektury ukreplennogo poselenija Kamennyj Ambar v kontekste obraza zhizni naselenija Juzhnogo Zaural'ja nachala II tys. do n. è. *Ural'skij istoricheskij vestnik* 1(54): 92–102.

Koryakova, L. N., & A. V. Epimakhov. 2014. *The Urals and Western Siberia in the Bronze and Iron Age*. Cambridge: Cambridge University Press.

Koryakova, L., R. Krause, J. Fornasier, A. Epimakhov, S. Sharapova, N. Berseneva, & S. Panteleeva. 2013. Archaeological structures of the Kamennyi Ambar settlement. In: R. Krause & L. Koryakova (ed.), *Multidisciplinary investigations of the Bronze Age settlements in the Southern Trans-Urals (Russia)*, 85–128. Bonn: Verlag Dr. Rudolf Habelt.

Kosintzev P. A., O. P. Bachura, A. Yu. Rassadnikov, & A. V. Kisagulov. 2016. Zhivotnovodstvo u naselenija Juzhnogo Zaural'ja v èpohu pozdnej bronzy. In: S. N. Udal'cov (ed.), *Dinamika sovremennyh èkosistem v golocene*, 102–4. Moscow: Tovarishchestvo nauchnyh izdanij KMK.

Krause, R., & L. Koryakova. 2013. *Multidisciplinary investigations of the Bronze Age settlements in the Southern Trans-Urals (Russia)*. Bonn: Verlag Dr. Rudolf Habelt.

Kuprijanova, E. V., & D. G. Zdanovich. 2015. *Drevnosti lesostepnogo Zaural'ja: Mogil'nik Stepnoe VII*. Chelyabinsk: Ènciklopedia.

Logvin, A., & I. Ševnina. 2013. Die Nekropole von Bestamak. In: T. Stollner & Z. Samasev (ed.), *Unbekanntes Kasachstan. Archäologie im Herzen Asiens. Katalog zur Ausstellung des Deutschen Bergbau-Museums Bochum vom 26. Januar bis zum 30. Juni 2013*, 231–44. Bochum: Deutschen Bergbau-Museum.

Lubotsky, Alexander. 2011. The origin of Sanskrit roots of the type *sīv-* "to sew," *dīv-* "to play dice," with an appendix on Vedic *i*-perfects. In: S. W. Jamison, H. C. Melchert, & B. Vine (ed.), *Proceedings of the 22nd Annual Indo-European Conference*, 105–126. Bremen: Hempen.

Mallory, James P., & Douglas Q. Adams. 1997. *Encyclopedia of Indo-European culture*. London & Chicago: Fitzroy Dearborn.

Maljutina, T. S., & L. Yu. Petrova. 2018. Kolodcy poselenija èpohi bronzy Kalmyckaja Molel'nja (Juzhnoe Zaural'e). In: A.A. Vybornov (ed.), *XXI Ural'skoe arheologicheskoe soveshchanie*, 133–5. Samara: SGSPU.

Molodin, V. I., A. V. Epimakhov, & Z. V. Marchenko. 2014. Radiouglerodnaja hronologija èpohi bronzy Urala i juga Zapadnoj Sibiri: Principy i podhody, dostizhenija i problemy. *Vestnik Novosibirskogo gosudarstvennogo universiteta. Serija: Istorija, filologija* 13(3): 136–67.

Müller, F. Max, 1868: *Chips from a German workshop*, 2nd ed., vol. 2. London: Longmans, Green.

Nikitin A. Yu., & I. A. Rusanov. 2011. Teplotehnicheskie sooruzhenija poselenija Arkaim (opyt rekonstrukcii). In: B. A. Bajtanaev (ed.), *Arheologiya Kazahstana v èpohu nezavisimosti: itogi, perspektivy. Materialy mezhdunarodnoj nauchnoj konferencii, posvjashchennoj 20-letiju Nezavisimosti Respubliki Kazahstan i 20-letiju Instituta arheologii im. A.H. Margulana KN MON RK*, Vol. 1, 307–13. Almaty.

Noskevich, V. V., N. V. Fedorova, A. S. Bebnev, A. G. Vdovin, & T. L. Mekhonoshina. 2014. Rezul'taty issledovanija geofizicheskimi metodami arheologicheskogo pamjatnika bronzovogo veka gorodishche Andreevskoe (Yuzhnyj Ural). *Ural'skij geofizicheskij vestnik* 1: 72–80.

Oberlies, Thomas. 2012. *Der Rigveda und seine Religion*. Berlin: Verlag der Weltreligionen.

Oettinger, Norbert. 2009. Zum Verhältnis von *Apąm Napāt-* and *X̌ᵛarənah-* im Avesta. In: E. Pirart & X. Tremblay (ed.), *Zarathushtra entre l'Inde et l'Iran, Études indo-iraniennes et indo-européennes offertes à Jean Kellens à l'occasion de son 65ᵉ anniversaire*, 189–96. Wiesbaden: Reichert.

Panaino, Antonio. 1990. *Tištrya. The Avestan hymn to Sirius*. Vol. 1 (Serie Orientale Roma 68.1). Rome: Istituto italiano per il Medio ed Estremo Oriente.

1995. The origin of the Pahlavi name Burz "Apąm Napāṱ": A semasiological study. *Acta Orientalia Academiae Scientiarum Hungaricae* 48 (Zsigmond Telegdi Memorial Volume): 117–126.

Pinault, Georges-Jean. 2013. Le vocabulaire et l'image du sourire dans les langues indo-européennes. In: P.-S. Filliozat & M. Zink (ed.), *Sourires d'Orient et d'Occident, Journée d'études organisée par l'Académie des Inscriptions et Belles-Lettres et la Société Asiatique (11 décembre 2009)*, 17–45. Paris: Peeters Publishers.

Puhvel, Jaan. 1987. *Comparative mythology*. Baltimore & London: John Hopkins University Press.

Renou, Louis. 1953. *Vocabulaire du rituel védique*. Paris: Klincksieck.

Rühl, L., L. N. Koryakova, R. Krause, & A. Stobbe. 2016. Wells of the fortified Bronze Age settlement Kamennyi Ambar (Chelyabinsk Oblast, Russia). In: N. P. Matveeva (ed.), *Èkologiya drevnih i tradicionnyh obshchestv*, 187–92. Tyumen: Institut problem osvoenija Severa.

Rusanov, I. A., & V. A. Kupriyanov. 2003. O funkcional'nom naznachenii kompleksa kolodec – pech' (po materialam ukreplennogo poselenija Arkaim). In: M.A. Korusenko, S. S. Tikhonov, & N. A. Tomilov (ed.), *Integracija arheologicheskih i ètnograficheskih issledovanij*, 231–2. Omsk: Nauka-Omsk.

Sadovski, Velizar. 2018. Indo-Iranian sacred texts and sacrificial practices: Structures of common heritage (Speech and performance in the Veda and Avesta, III). In: J. Braarvig & M. J. Geller (ed.), *Studies in Multilingualism, Lingua Franca and Lingua Sacra*, 357–388. Max-Planck-Gesellschaft Edition Open Access (EOA).

Stobbe A., M. Gumnior, L. Rühl, & H. Schneider. 2016. Bronze Age human-landscape interactions in the southern Transural steppe, Russia: Evidence from high-resolution palaeobotanical studies. *The Holocene* 10: 1692–1710.

Tkachev, V. V. 2007. *Stepi Juzhnogo Priural'ya i Zapadnogo Kazahstana na rubezhe epoh srednej i pozdnej bronzy*. Aktobe: Aktjubinskij oblastnoj centr istorii, ètnografii i arheologii.

Vinogradov, N. B. 2003. *Mogil'nik bronzovogo veka Krivoe Ozero v Juzhnom Zaural'e*. Chelyabinsk: South Ural Press.

Vinogradov, N. B., & A. V. Epimakhov (ed.). 2013. *Drevnee Ust'e: ukreplennoe poselenie bronzovogo veka v Juzhnom Zaural'e*. Chelyabinsk: Abris.

Zdanovich, D. G. (ed.). 2002. *Arkaim: nekropol' (po materialam kurgana 25 Bol'shekaraganskogo mogil'nika)*, Vol. 1. Chelyabinsk: South Ural Press.

Zdanovich, G. B., & I. M. Batanina. 2002. Planography of the fortified centers of the Middle Bronze Age in the Southern Trans-Urals according to aerial photography data. In: K. Jones-Blay & D. Zdanovich (ed.), *Complex societies of Central Eurasia from the 3rd to the 1st millennium BC*, vol. 2, 121–38. Washington: Institute for the Study of Man.

Zdanovich, G. B., T. S. Malyutina, & D. G. Zdanovich. 2018. Arkaim. K issledovaniju vodosnabzhenija i vodopol'zovanija v drevnej Evrazii. In: D. G. Zdanovich (ed.), *Stepnaja Evrazija v èpohu bronzy: kul'tury, idei, tehnologii*, 92–111. Chelyabinsk: Chelyabinsk State University Press.

2020. *Arkaim. The archaeology of fortified settlements*. Chelyabinsk: State University Publishing House.

17 WOOL FIBERS OF THE NORTHERN EURASIAN BRONZE AGE: THE CULTURAL AND GEOGRAPHICAL CONTEXTS

NATALIA I. SHISHLINA, POLINA S. ANKUSHEVA, OLGA V. ORFINSKAYA, AND DARIA V. KISELEVA

17.1 Introduction

The transformation of the prehistoric societies of the northern Eurasian Bronze Age is associated with the emergence and spread of not only basic production industries, i.e. agriculture and animal raising, but also related industries. Sherrat (1997) has called this a "secondary product revolution," accompanied by the implementation of innovative technologies for new products and forms of consumption. In northern Eurasia, the Middle and Late Bronze Age was a period when prehistoric societies underwent complex social and economic transformations. These changes included the introduction of new technologies of wool production and the making of wool fiber, as well as the spread of this technology. The spread of wool textiles in the third millennium BC is associated with the cultures of the South Caucasus (Kvavadze 2016) and the steppe Catacomb culture of the Lower Don region and Kalmykia (Shishlina et al. 1999; 2020). In the Late Bronze Age, at the beginning of the second millennium BC, the area where wool fibers were used included both the forest steppe and the steppe belt of the Early Srubnaya culture, as well as the forest belt of the Central Russian Pozdnyakovo culture; it extended as far as the Andronovo (Alakul, Fedorovo) world of the Trans-Ural region and North Kazakhstan (Orfinskaya & Golikov 2010; Azarov et al. 2016; Medvedeva et al. 2017) (Fig. 17.1).

The mechanisms by which this technological innovation spread are unclear. There also remain questions about the nature of the textile production. Was it a household production or a specialized one? Were the products local or imported? What was the extent of the exchange of raw material, yarn, or textile? Could resource centers for wool textile production have developed in northern Eurasia as early as the Late Bronze Age?

Geochemical methods help localize the regions where wool fiber originated. One such approach is the method of determining the $^{87}Sr/^{86}Sr$ ratio in archaeological textiles and the local baseline of bioavailable strontium, which has worked well in studies of Bronze Age Scandinavian textile (Frei et al. 2009; 2015). Isotopic composition can provide a unique isotopic signature to delineate the geochemical area associated with the origin of the animals (sheep, goats, and camels) whose wool was used as the raw material for textile-making. Participating in a food chain made of the plants, soil, surface, and groundwater of a certain region, strontium is absorbed into animal tissue; animals obtain strontium from water and grassland plants. The $^{87}Sr/^{86}Sr$ ratio correlate with the geology of the region where the grasslands were probably located. Using the isotope values of bioavailable samples from various regions, it is possible to determine the area where an archaeological find, i.e. a wool fiber, originated (Frei et al. 2009; 2015).

The objective of this study is to determine the local (or nonlocal) origin of the raw fleece material that was used to make archaeological wool textile by comparing the $^{87}Sr/^{86}Sr$ ratio in the wool fibers with the local baseline of bioavailable strontium.

17.2 Background of Eurasian Archaeological Wool

It is assumed that, starting from 2500 to 2300 cal BC, wool fibers and textile began to spread across the South Caucasus. Textiles made of wool have been uncovered in the Ananauri kurgan in Bedeni, Georgia. The plain-weave cloths were made of wool yarn or a combination of flax and wool yarn (Kalandadze & Sakhvadze 2016). Research on these finds demonstrates that the fiber was made of sheep wool (Kvavadze 2016).

While plant mats are a common find in the Catacomb graves, which date between 2600 and 2200 cal BC, wool textiles were found in such graves as well. An article of composite headwear has been found in an adult male grave at Shakhaevsky 1 (Fedorova-Davydova & Gorbenko 1974; Shishlina et al. 2005), a West Manych Catacomb burial ground located in the Lower Don region (kurgan 4, grave 32). The basic textile element of this headwear is a plaited wool band (Fig. 17.2). Bronze beads as well as beads made of gromwell (*Lithospermum gen.*) seeds were used to decorate the wool band. The tradition of using gromwell seeds for appliqués and embroidery of garments is a local steppe feature. All this suggests that the headwear was made locally and that, most likely, all the materials were from local steppes. Wool items

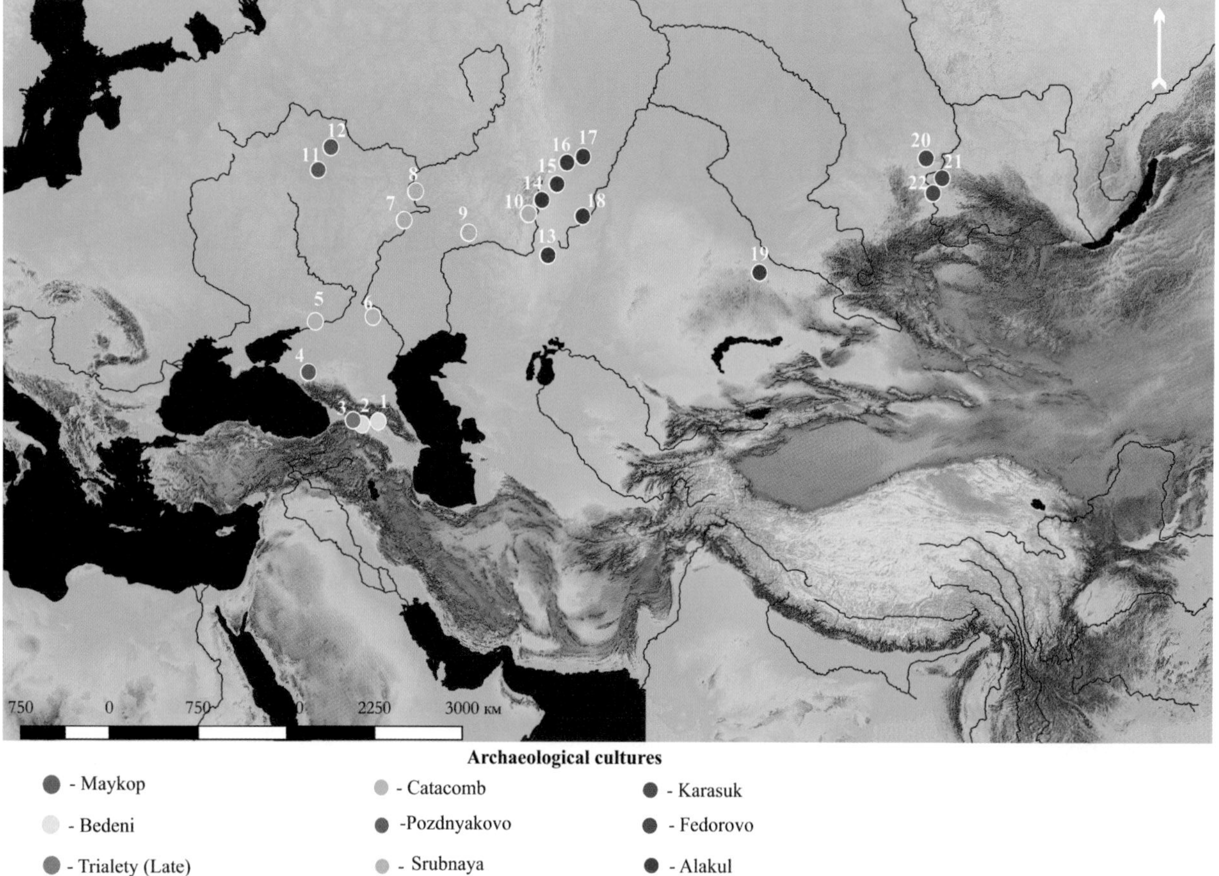

Figure 17.1. Bronze Age sites with wool textiles. 1 – Ananauri Big Kurgan 3; 2 – Bedeni; 3 – Safar-Kharaba; 4 – Tsarskaya; 5 – Shakhaevsky I; 6 – Yergueni; 7 – Alekseevsky II; 8 – Zolotaya Niva II; 9 – Gerasimovsky III; 10 – Tavlykaevsky II; 11 – Berezovy Rog; 12 – Borisoglebovsky I; 13 – Ushkattinsky I; 14 – Agapovka II; 15 – Stepnoye VII; 16 – Chernyaki II; 17 – Alakul; 18 – Lisakovsky; 19 – Tundyk; 20 – Uzhur; 21 – Ust'-Erba; 22 – Uibat.

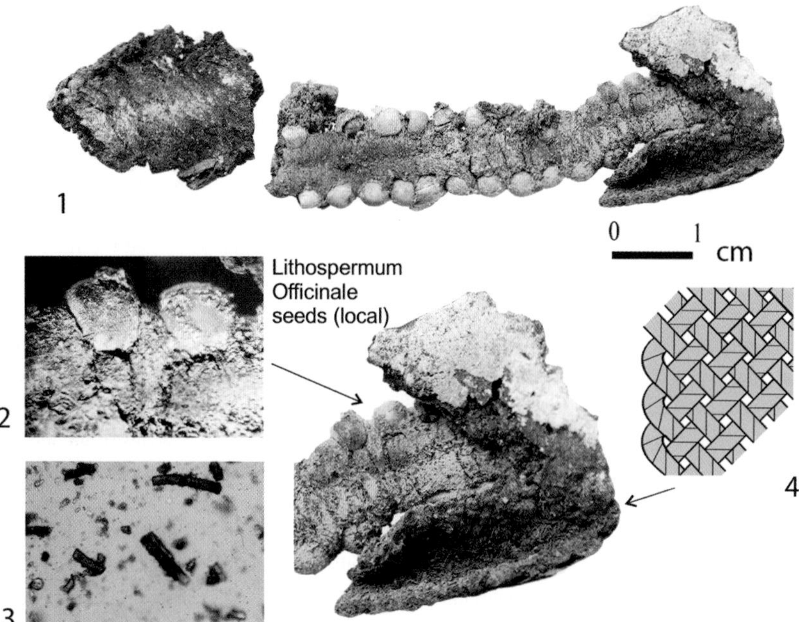

Figure 17.2. Wool textile from Shakhaevsky 1, kurgan 4, grave 32. 1 – composite cap, detail; 2 – gromwell seeds; 3 – photomicrographs of wool fibers; 4 – weave pattern of plaited wool band.

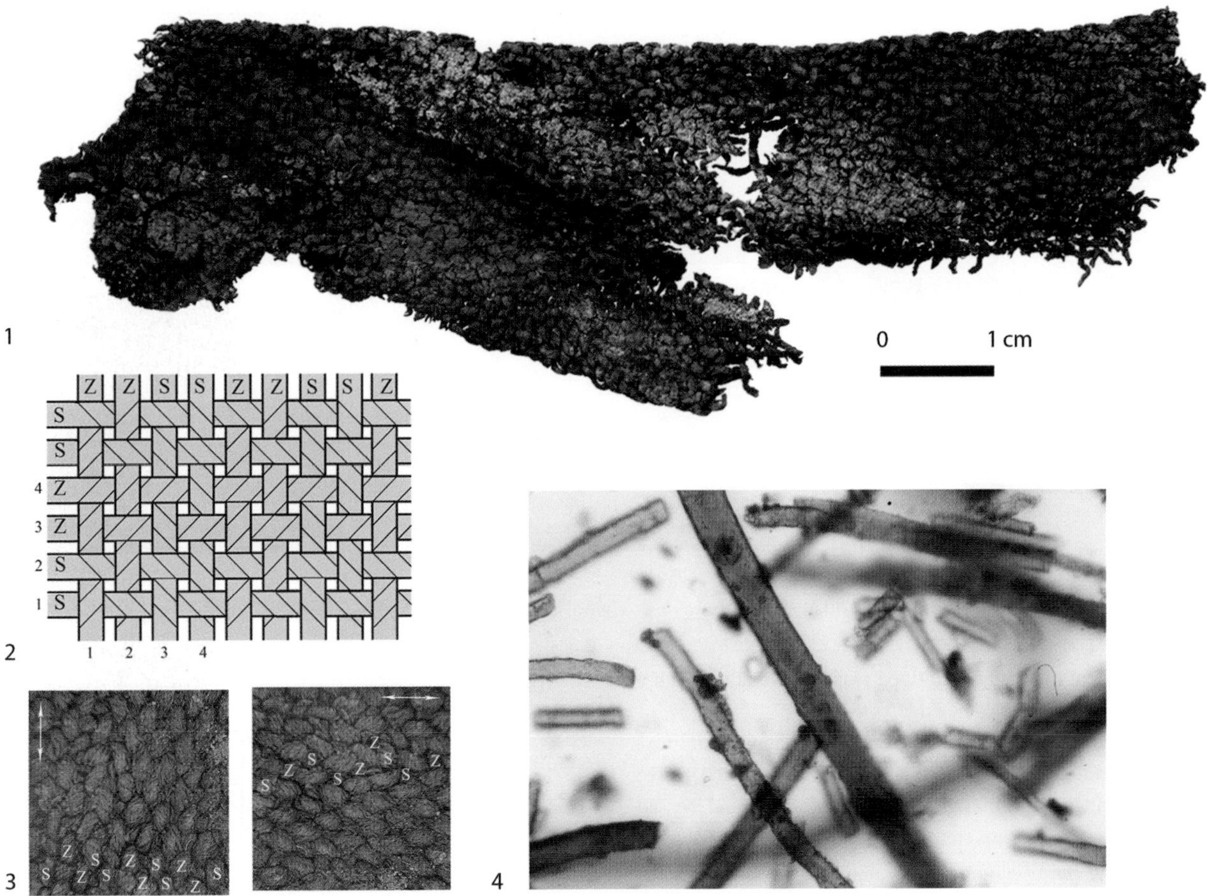

FIGURE 17.3. Wool textile from Berezovy Rog, kurgan 20. 1 – wool textile; 2 – weave scheme; 3 – wool textile fragments; 4 – photomicrographs of wool fibers.

have also been found at the Yergueni burial ground (kurgan 6, grave 3, kurgan 11), i.e. a wool band with a diagonal plain weave and a coarse plain-weave textile that had been placed at the bottom of a pot (Shishlina 1999).

As of today, we have collected the first evidence of wool in the textile production in the forest steppe and forest belts of Eastern Europe and the Urals. The wool fragments from the burial contexts date to the early second millennium BC. Numerous other fragments of wool items – however small, due to very poor preservation conditions – have been found across the entire Srubnaya–Andronovo steppe and the forest-steppe world (Shishlina et al. 2020).

Wool textiles have also appeared in the forest belt of the central Russian Plain in the Pozdnyakovo Berezovy Rog burial ground. It is found in the form of a composite box made of birch bark covered with wool textile. The seed inlay adorning the surface is made of *Lithospermum gen.*, commonly known as gromwell. The analysis of the plain-weave textile has established that it was made of wool fiber of a dark brown color (Azarov et al. 2016). Fragments of a plain-weave wool textile were found in burial 20 (Fig. 17.3).

Wool textiles were also discovered at the Alekseevsky II burial ground, attributed to the Early Srubnaya culture, in the Volga region. Female grave no. 8 has preserved a fragment of a funerary dress because this fragment had come into contact with bronze bracelets. The fragment is a plain-weave textile with sewn-on leather elements that were apparently attached to the sleeves, forming a fringe. Besides the textile, the funerary assemblage included a ball (skein) of wool yarn with bronze needles inserted into it (Medvedeva et al. 2017).

Another example of wool fibers used in dressmaking is represented by finds at Zolotaya Niva II, a Srubnaya burial ground (kurgan 1, grave 4), also located in the Volga region. (Bagautdinov & Vasilieva 2004). Fragments of a cap made of a plain-weave wool textile were located around the skull of the individual; along its edge, the cap was finished with a plaited wool band.

On the eastern edge of the Srubnaya area, wool is represented by items from the Tavlykaevsky II burial ground (Southern Ural region) (Morozov 1984). One of the finds is a fragment of wool textile preserved on a bronze temple ring that was covered in gold foil (kurgan 2, grave 1); it is a fragment of a red-brown wool band that attached the ring to a cap.

Numerous textile items made of wool have been documented at Alakul culture sites, attributed to the Andronovo culture. In the western part of this region, on the Southern Ural steppes, wool has been recorded at the Ushkatta I burial ground (kurgan 22, grave 7) (Tkachev 2016). The grave has yielded a composite textile item, apparently a fragment of a bag in which metal jewelry used to decorate a female braid was probably kept. The

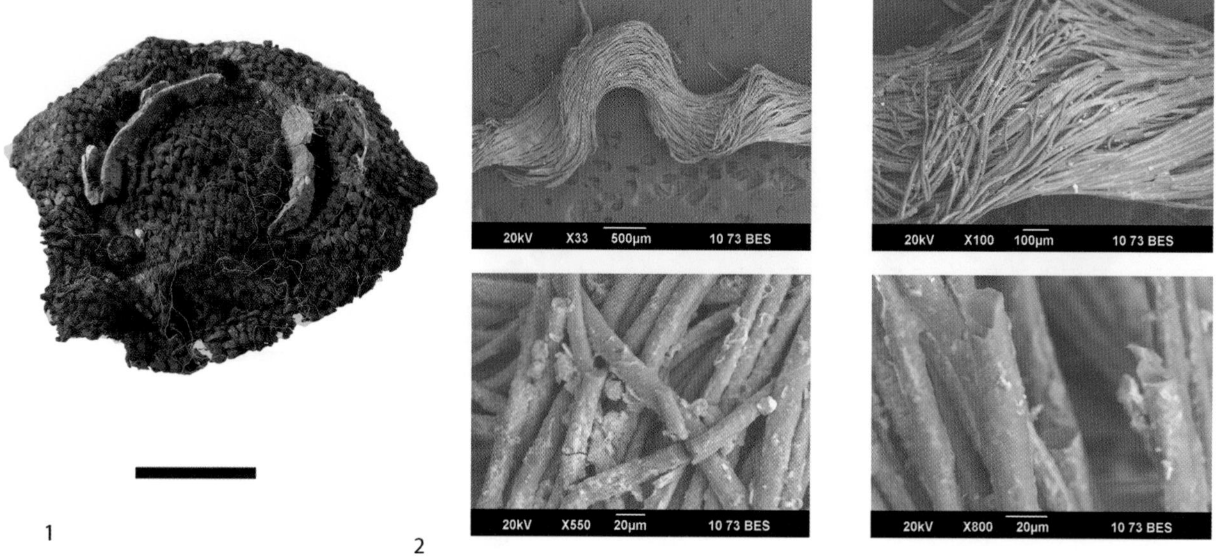

FIGURE 17.4. Wool textile from Chernyaki II, kurgan, grave. 1 – wool textile; 2 – SEM photos of wool fibers.

textile fragment consists of red-dyed plain-weave fabric with a black wool band sewn to the edge.

In the steppes of the southern Trans-Ural region, wool textiles have been discovered at the Agapovka II (kurgan 4, grave 6) and Stepnoye VII burial grounds. The skull of the deceased at Agapovka II was covered with remnants of a red wool textile. Remnants of sinew threads and red wool textile have been preserved in one of the apertures made to attach the bronze plaques. The wool textiles from Stepnoye VII (assemblage 8, grave 2) are represented by the remains of a composite item, most likely a bag (Kupriyanova 2017).

In the Trans-Ural forest steppes, wool textiles have been preserved in a number of graves at the Alakul burial ground (kurgan 27, grave 7; kurgan 23, grave 6) and the Chernyaki II burial ground. The Alakul textile items consist of different types of cords preserved inside bronze beads; plaited wool bands; embroidery threads; and a plain-weave textile (Shilov & Bogatenkova 2008). A plain-weave wool textile folded in several layers and attached to a bronze pendant has been preserved in grave 13 of Chernyaki II. The fabric itself is a fragment of a brown wool cloth (Figs. 17.4 and 17.5).

The North Kazakhstan area of the Alakul and Sargary cultures is represented by artifacts from the Lisakovsky and Alekseevsky burial grounds; some of the graves at these burial grounds have also yielded wool textiles. Fifty-five assorted wool fragments have been discovered at Alakul Lisakovsky II (kurgan 1, grave 1), including plaited items and one specimen of a gray wool textile with twined warps. The plaited items are represented by five different types of plated wool band that differ in their width and system of weaving; these items were dyed with madder; cords and embroidery threads have been found as well (Orfinskaya & Golikov, 2010). Wool fibers have also been discovered at Alakul Lisakovsky I (kurgan 1, grave 1).

At the other end of the Andronovo world, in Eastern Siberia, wool textiles have been discovered in Fedorovo burials. In particular, a wool belt and cords have been found in a stone box at the Uzhur burial ground (kurgan 47, pit 2). These items were made with diagonal plaiting and dyed orange-pink (Orfinskaya et al. 1999). A tiny fragment of a diagonal-twill

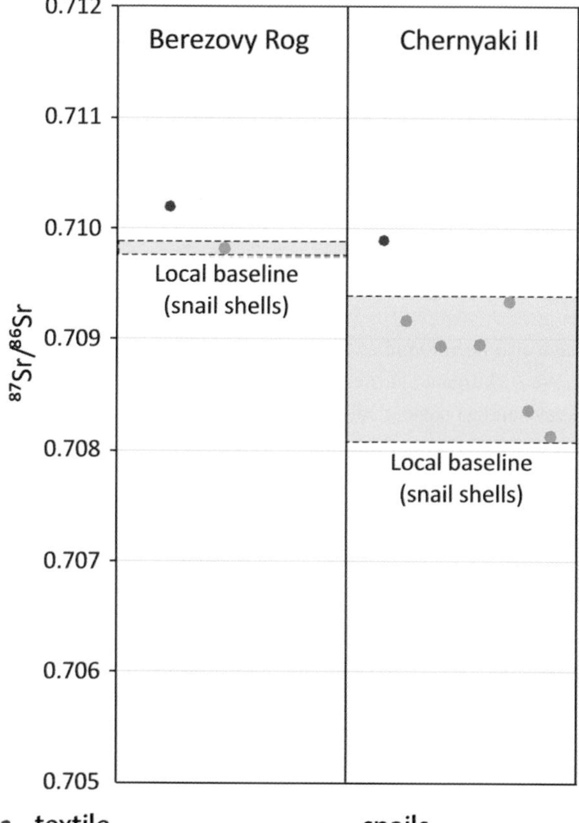

FIGURE 17.5. $^{87}Sr/^{86}Sr$ strontium isotope ratios in the bioavailable reference of snails and Bronze Age textiles from Chernyaki II and Berezovy Rog.

wool braid was also found at the Ust-Yerba burial ground (pit 1), located in Khakassia (Shishlina et al. 2019).

Therefore, in terms of chronology, geography, and cultural attribution, all these finds have substantially extended the corpus of data on the earliest Eurasian wool fibers, from the early second millennium BC.

17.3 Pilot Isotope Study of Wool Samples

Fragments of Bronze Age wool textile from the two regions – the forest belt of Eastern Europe and the forest-steppe belt of the South Trans-Ural region – characterized by different geological and geochemical environments were selected for this pilot study. Natural specimens such as snails revealed the local baseline of bioavailable strontium. To build shells, snails use lime, extracting it from plants and water, as well as hard rock and minerals in case there is a shortage of calciferous material. As an accessory element of calcium in geochemical processes, strontium is concentrated in the shells of mollusks, while its isotopic composition reflects the geochemical signature of the environment where the mollusk obtained it (Shishlina & Larionova 2013). Specimens were located along the shores of nearby lakes and rivers; when a specimen was selected, its precise position was recorded by a GPS unit.

The studied textile fragments were retrieved from two burial grounds, i.e. the Chernyaki II burial ground and the Berezovy Rog burial ground.

Chernyaki II is located in the forest-steppe belt, on the left bank of the Miass River in the Chelyabinsk region of Russia. Both at this point and further upstream, the Miass River is crossed by a large granite batholith, which shallowly intrudes across the masses of Llandovery (early Silurian) carbonaceous-siliceous schist, phyllites, and porphyritoids.

Berezovy Rog is located in the forest belt of the Ryazan region (Russia), on a sand residual outcrop of the first terrace above the floodplain of the Oka River's left bank. At this point, the Pra River cuts through aleurites, sands, and clays of the Callovian Stage of the Middle Jurassic period, clays of the Oxfordian Stage of the Late Jurassic period, and, at its confluence with the Oka River, sands, sandstones, and clays of the Valanginian and Aptian Stages of the Lower Cretaceous period. The Oka flows over these Cretaceous deposits. The Quaternary deposits consist of sands and loams of the Middle and Upper Valdai horizon of the Upper Quaternary period, as well as contemporary peat bogs.

The samples of wool and bioavailable samples (snails) were analyzed at the Institute of Geology and Geochemistry, Ural Branch of Russian Academy of Sciences, according to the protocol proposed in Frei et al. 2009 and 2015.

As the analysis of $^{87}Sr/^{86}Sr$ strontium isotope ratios demonstrates, the strontium isotopic composition of the wool textile from Berezovy Rog (0.71019) is different from the local baseline of bioavailable strontium (0.70981) as based on a sample collected near Shagara Lake, some 80 km away.

The same can be said of the second funerary assemblage. The strontium isotopic composition of the wool textile from Chernyaki II is 0.70988; this is above the $^{87}Sr/^{86}Sr$ strontium isotope ratios in the bioavailable specimens of snails collected within one kilometer of the site location (0.70895–0.70934) or near other Bronze Age sites of the forest-steppe belt of the South Trans-Ural region, i.e. the Alakul and the Stepnoye burial grounds (0.70813–0.70917).

The baseline data for local bioavailable strontium that have been used in the comparison so far delineate a rather broad geographical region. In both cases, however, the sheep whose wool was used to make the textile had presumably been grazing at some distance from the burial grounds.

It is also worth mentioning that the isotopic composition of the two wool fragments from the sites, which are located at a distance of 1300 km from each other, is rather similar. To understand this similarity, however, we would require additional data on the strontium isotopic composition of archaeological textile samples dated to the same historical period, as well as a more detailed map of the $^{87}Sr/^{86}Sr$ strontium isotope ratios in bioavailable samples from a larger geographical area.

17.4 Conclusion

Locally made wool textiles appeared in the Caucasus and the adjacent territory of the steppe Catacomb culture no earlier than the Middle Bronze Age, around 2500 to 2300 cal BC (Shishlina et al. 2020). The wool textile technology became a true innovation for Eastern Europe and the Caucasus. The presence of ruminant dung fungi, wool textiles, and felt in the Ananauri kurgan is evidence of animal raising and the local production of wool fleece (Kalandadze & Sakhvadze 2016; Kvavadze 2016). The interesting find of a cap decorated with seeds of gromwell, a typical steppe plant at Shakhaevsky in the Lower Don steppe region, also points to the local rather than nonlocal production of the composite items (Shishlina et al. 2005).

Archaeological finds from the early second millennium BC clearly demonstrate that innovative wool fibers and wool technology quickly spread from the Lower Don and Kalmyk Steppe area and the Caucasus regions to the forest-steppe, forest, and steppe areas of the Oka, Volga, South Urals, and Siberia (Shishlina et al. 2019). But does this mean that this innovative wool technology was adopted by different local populations, or that local people merely obtained these wool items through exchange? The answer requires additional data.

The pilot study on the $^{87}Sr/^{86}Sr$ strontium isotope ratios in wool textiles originating from the Bronze Age Chernyaki II and Berezovy Rog burial grounds as compared to the values for bioavailable samples demonstrate the viability of this geochemical method in identifying where wool fleece was most likely produced. In both cases, the $^{87}Sr/^{86}Sr$ values of the wool archaeological specimens exceed the $^{87}Sr/^{86}Sr$ strontium isotope ratios in bioavailable reference (snail shells) specimens reflecting the nearby geochemical areas. All this suggests that the animals (most likely sheep) whose fleece was used as the raw material grazed outside the local areas, located both near to and at a distance from the studied burial grounds. The issue of whether the raw materials (fleece) or ready-made products were local or imported requires the analysis of a larger number of wool archaeological specimens, and a more detailed regional map of background $^{87}Sr/^{86}Sr$ strontium isotope ratios in natural specimens with precise georeferencing.

Acknowledgments

This work was done with the support of RSF grants № 21-18-00026 and 22-18-00593. We would like to thank Anton Strokov for photos of the textile.

References

Azarov, Euvgeny S. et al. 2016. Issledovaniye slozhnosostavnogo izdeliya epokhi bronzy iz mogilnika Berezovy Rog metodom gazovoy khromatografii [Study of a Bronze composite item from the Berezovy Rog burial ground by means of gas chromatography]. *Kratkiye soobshcheniya Instituta arkheologii (KSIA) – Brief Communications of the Institute of Archaeology* 244: 391–407. [in Russian].

Bagautdinov, Riza S., & Irina N. Vasilieva. 2004. Zolotaya Niva I i II kurganniye gruppy [Zolotaya Niva I and II kurgan groups]. *Issues of archaeology of the Urals and the Volga Region* [Voprosy archeologii Urala I Povolzhia] 2: 181–212. Samara: Samara Pedagogical Institute. [in Russian].

Fedorova-Davydova, Eleonora A., & A. A. Gorbenko. 1974. Raskopki Shakhaevskoi kurgannoy gruppy v 1971 [Excavations of the Shakhaevsky kurgan group in 1971]. In: I. S. Kamenetsky (ed.), *Archaeological sites of the Lower Don Region* [Drevnosti Podoniya], vol. 2, 81–136. Moscow: Nauka. [in Russian]

Frei, K. M., et al. 2009. Provenance of ancient textiles: A pilot study evaluating the strontium isotope system in wool. *Archaeometry* 51: 252–76.

2015. Tracing the dynamic life story of a Bronze Age female. *Scientific Reports 5: article no. 10431.*

Kalandadze, N., & E. Sakhvadze. 2016. Textile discovered in Ananauri kurgan №3. In: Z. Makharadze, N. Kalandadze, & B. Murvanidze (ed.), *Ananauri big kurgan*, 127–136. Tbilisi: Georgian National Museum.

Kupriyanova, Elena V. 2017. Elements of the female dress and jewelry from grave 1, Stepnoye VII burial ground, as an indicator of cultural heritage traditions. *Social and Liberal Arts Sciences* 17(3): 30–37. [in Russian].

Kvavadze, E., et al. 2015. The hidden side of ritual: New palynological data from Early Bronze Age Georgia, the Southern Caucasus. *Journal of Archaeological Sciences: Report* 2: 235–245.

2016. Palynological study of organic remains from the Ananauri kurgan. In: Z. Makharadze, N. Kalandadze, & B. Murvanidze (ed), *Ananauri big kurgan*, 156–192. Tbilisi: Georgian National Museum.

Medvedeva, Polina S., et al. 2017. Drevneishiye svidetelstva tkachestva v Povolzhye (po materialam iz pamyatnikov potapovskogo tipa) [The earliest evidence of cloth-weaving in the Volga Region (artifacts from the Potapovo-type sites)]. *Stratum Plus* 2: 345–358. [in Russian].

Morozov, Yu. A. 1984. Kurganny mogilnik y s. Verkhnetavlykaevo epokhi bronzi [Bronze Age burial grounds near the village of Verkhnetavlykaevo]. In: V. I. Ivanov (ed.), *Nomadic sites of the Southern Urals: Collected papers* [Pamyatniki kochevnikov Yuzhnogo Urala: sbornik nauchnykh trudov], 117–135. Ufa: BB of USSR AS. [in Russian].

Orfinskaya, Olga V., et al. 1999. Kompleksnoye eksperimentalnoye issledovaniye terstilya Evrasiyskikh stepey [The comprehensive experimental study of Bronze Age textile items from the Eurasian steppes]. In N. I. Shishlina (ed.), *Bronze Age textiles from the Eurasian steppes* (Collected papers of the State Historical Museum 109), 58–185. Moscow: State Historical Museum. [in Russian].

Orfinskaya, Olga. V., & V. P. Golikov. 2010. Eksperimentalnoye issledovaniye tekstilnykh izdely iz raskopok mogilnika Lasakovsky II [The experimental study of textile items from the excavations of the Lisakovsky II burial ground]. In: E.R. Usmanova Bronze Age Woman's Costume. Reconstruction Experience. Application. Lisakovsk ; Karaganda : TAiS, 114–117. [in Russian].

Salnikov, K. V. 1967. *Ocherki po drevney istorii yuzhnogo Urala* [*Essays on the ancient history of the Southern Urals*]. Moscow: Nauka. [in Russian].

Sherratt, Andrew. 1997. *Economy and society in prehistoric Europe: Changing perspectives*. Princeton: Princeton University Press.

Shilov, S. N., & A. A. Bogatenkova. 2008. Pogrebeniya s zhenskimi ukrasheniyami iz Alakul'skogo mogil'nika epokhi bronzi [Burials with female jewelry at the Bronze Age Alakul burial ground]. In: E. V. Kupriyanova (ed.), *Ten' zhenshchiny: zhenskiy kostyum epokhi bronzy kak «tekst» (po materialam nekropoley Yuzhnogo Zaural'ya i Kazakhstana* [The shadow of a woman: Female dress of the Bronze Age as a "text" (based on the artifacts from necropolis of the Southern Urals and Kazakhstan], 217–235. Chelyabinsk: Avto Graf. [in Russian].

Shishlina, N. I. 1999. Tekstil epokhi bronzy Prikaspiyskikh stepey [Bronze Age textiles from the Caspian Sea maritime steppes]. In: N. I. Shishlina (ed.), *Bronze Age textiles of the Eurasian steppes* (Collected papers of the State Historical Museum 109), 7–58. Moscow: State Historical Museum. [in Russian]

Shishlina, N. I., O. Orfinskaya, & V. Golikov. 2005. Headdress from the Catacomb culture grave of the Shakhaevskaya burial ground in the Rostov Region, *Archaeological Textiles Newsletter. The University of Manchester* 40, 6–9.

Shishlina, N. I., & Y. O. Larionova. 2013. Variatsii isotopnogo sostava strontsiya v obraztsakh sovremennykh ulitok yuga Rossii: perviye resultaty [Variations in the isotopic composition of strontium in the samples of contemporary snails from the Russian South: First results]. In: A. B. Belinsky (ed.), *Materials of historical and cultural heritage studies of the North Caucasus. Archaeology, studies of local lore, museum management studies* 11, 159–168. Naslediye: Stavropol.

2019. Sherstyaniye tkani epokhi bronzi yuzhnoy Sibiri: rezultaty technologicheskogo, izotopnogo i radiouglerodnogo analiza [Bronze Age wool textiles from South Siberia: Results of technological, isotope, and 14C data]. In: L. B. Kircho (ed.), *Proceedings of the International Conference on Antiquities of Eastern Europe, Central Asia and Southern Siberia in the*

Context of Connections and Interactions in the Eurasian Cultural Space (New Data and Concepts), 257. St. Petersburg: IIMK.

2020. Bronze Age Wool Textile of the Northern Eurasia: New Radiocarbon Data. *Nanotechnologies in Russia* 15(9/10): 629–638.

Tkachev, V. V. 2016. Radiouglerodnaya khronologiya kozhumberdinskoy kulturnoi gruppy na zapadnoy periferii alakuskogo regiona [Radiocarbon chronology of the Kozhumberdy cultural group on the western periphery of the Alakul Region]. *Vestnik archeologii, antropologii I etnografii* 3: 68–78. [in Russian].

18 AN ARCHAEOLINGUISTIC APPROACH TO INDO-EUROPEAN WOOL TERMINOLOGY

BIRGIT A. OLSEN

As I have already discussed the field of Indo-European textile vocabulary on various occasions,[1] I will here concentrate on the etymological status and time horizon of the word for 'wool'. By way of introduction, it will suffice just to recapitulate a few main points.

While the use of plant fibers for clothing is several millennia older than that of wool, the corresponding vocabulary does not appear to be of Indo-European stock. Thus, the word for 'flax, linen' is **lĭnom*, in Greek λίνον (Mycenaean *ri-no*), Old Church Slavonic *lĭnŭ*, and Lithuanian *linas* (sg. 'flax fiber', pl. 'flax') as opposed to **līnom* in Latin *līnum*, Old Irish *lín*, and Gothic *lein* with a long vowel. Since a vacillation between short and long *i* is not consistent with Indo-European phonological rules, the word is generally assumed to be of foreign origin (see, e.g., Iversen/Kroonen 2017: 516 and Olsen 2018: 73).[2] The same goes for the widespread word for 'hemp' in, e.g., Greek κάνναβις, Latin *cannabis*, Russian *konoplja*, and Old English *hænep*, where the disyllabic root structure and the vocalism point to a foreign term, borrowed into Germanic before the sound shift **k* > *h*.

The vocabulary pertaining to 'sheep' and 'wool' is quite another matter. A common Indo-European word for 'sheep' is known from all branches, including Anatolian, with the sole exception of Albanian: Luwian *hāwa/i-*, Lycian *xawa*, Tocharian B (plur.) *awi*, Old Irish *oí*, Latin *ovis*, Old Norse *ær* (English *ewe*), Greek οἶς, Armenian *hoviw* 'shepherd', Vedic *ávi-*, Lithuanian *avìs*, and Old Church Slavonic (diminutive) *ovĭci* 'ewe', all pointing to a proto-form **$h_2$ou̯is* (Wodtko, Irslinger, & Schneider 2008: 335–39). In theory, it is possible that the word originally referred to wild as opposed to domesticated sheep, but this is highly unlikely, considering such factors as the inclusion of sheep in the ancient Hittite formula for counting a man's booty, e.g. NAM.RA GU$_4$ UDU KUR-*eaš āššu arha* URU*Hattuši uu̯atenun* "deportees, cattle, sheep, goods of the land I brought off to Hattusas" (Puhvel 1984: 200).

As for 'wool', at least the bulk of the non-Anatolian cognates may be united under a reconstruction **(h)u̯l̥$h_1$nah_2-*: Middle Welsh *gwlan*, Latin *lāna*, Gothic *wulla*, Vedic *ū́rṇā-*, Avestan *varənā-*, Lithuanian *vìlna*, and Old Church Slavonic *vlŭna*. Greek λῆνος, which determines the quality of the laryngeal as *-h_1-,[3] has been remodeled as a neuter *s*-stem, presumably after εἶρος, the usual word for 'wool' in the Epic language, perhaps further supported by the rare πέκος, also 'wool' (Frisk II: 117). Supplementary evidence is found in the Latin neuter *vellus* (*s*-stem) 'fleece, wool', with a possible proto-form **(h)u̯él$h_1$os* → **(h)u̯el$h_1$nos*,[4] and Armenian *gełmn* 'fleece, wool' < **(h)u̯el$h_1$mn̥*.

However, there remains one piece of potential evidence that is formally tricky, but decisive for the evaluation of the word's age, viz. Hittite **ḫulana-* 'wool', which, if related to the above-mentioned lexemes, suggests that the use of wool predated the 'first split' of the Indo-European language family, that between Anatolian and the remaining branches. An etymological connection would necessitate a modification of the reconstruction, since Hittite *ḫ-* must continue an initial **h_2-* (or, less likely, **h_3-*),[5] i.e. **h_2u̯l̥$h_1$nah_2-* for Latin *lāna* etc., **h_2u̯el$h_1$os* → **$h_2$uel$h_1$nos* for Latin *vellus*, and **h_2u̯el$h_1$mn̥* for Armenian *gełmn*. The initial laryngeal would regularly be lost in most languages outside of Anatolian, including Armenian, which has

[1] Olsen (2017) and especially (2018); Flemestad & Olsen (2017).

[2] It is uncertain whether the Celtic and/or Germanic forms are borrowed from Latin, where *līnum* might also reflect a proto-form **lei̯no-*. However, an *o*-stem with vacillation between full grade *-*ei̯*- and zero grade *-*i*- is just as problematic as a variation between short and long vowel, considering that there is not semantic justification for a vr̥ddhi formation. Another unclear formation is the Latin adjective of material *linteus* 'of linen', with an enigmatic -*t*-.

[3] Cf. Peters (1987), who points to the Hesychian gloss λείνα· ἔρια. Κύπριοι "λείνα (means) wool. (The) Cypriots." This form also proves the existence of an original *a*-stem in Greek, matching the stem formation of the other languages.

[4] In Olsen (2014), a development *-*lh*- > -*ll*- was assumed for Latin, where a proto-form **u̯elhno-* would yield **volno-* without the assimilation of *-*ln*- > -*ll*-; cf. *volnus* 'wound' from the root **u̯elh_3-* 'hit, strike' (LIV[2] 679). However, as elaborated in Olsen (2021), it seems most likely that only *-*h_2*- and *-*h_3*- triggered gemination of a preceding *-*l*-. In that case, it may be preferable to start from the corresponding verb *vellō* 'pluck', where the sequence *-*ln*- in a nasal present **(h)u̯el-ne-h_1-* (of the type *pellō* < **pel-ne-h_2-* 'beat' with analogical full grade) would regularly yield -*ll*-.

[5] **h_2-* is preferable to **h_3-*, which would probably only be preserved as *ḫ-* before a full vowel; cf. Kloekhorst (2006).

no laryngeal-based "prothetic vowel" before *-u̯-.[6] For Greek, however, one might have expected *ἀληv-, from a form with an initial *h_2- (*ὀληv- with *h_3-), so here an early loss of the first laryngeal must have taken place. Perhaps a sequence *hCR̥- is simply regularly reflected as *CəR-/*CRə- in Proto-Greek, as assumed by Peters (1980: 23; cf. also Beekes 2010: 858).

Alternatively, Pinault (2016: 244–45) hypothesizes that the original word for wool, preserved in Hittite and displaying an initial *h_2-, was re-etymologized in Proto-Greek and in post-Anatolian in general as being connected with a root *u̯el- 'wind, twist' (LIV² 675). While the structure of the root in question seems to have been more complex – i.e. *u̯elhu̯- (zero grade *u̯lhu- > *u̯luh-); cf. Armenian *gelum* 'roll' with the corresponding *-*men*-stem noun Armenian *gelumn*, Greek εἴλυμα, Latin *volūmen*[7] – a root variant *u̯el- might have been derived from forms where the root-final cluster was regularly simplified. However, Pinault's statement that the proto-form **uelnos* reshaped after this root "directly yielded" Latin *vellus* 'fleece' has the unfortunate implication that we would have to sever the otherwise obvious internal Latin connection between *vellus* and *vellō* 'pluck (out)'.[8]

Based on our non-Anatolian cognates, we may now survey the morphological ramifications of the underlying root, observing that the parallel existence of a *-*men*-stem, a secondary derivative in *-*nah₂*-, and an *s*-stem is fully compatible with the principles of Indo-European word formation. From a root *(h₂)u̯elh₁-, where the final *-h₁- is secured by Greek while the initial *h_2- depends on the evaluation of the Anatolian evidence, we would thus have the following derivatives:

*-*men*-stem:	*(h₂)u̯élh₁-mn̥ (> Armenian *gełmn*) →
*-*náh₂*-stem:	*(h₂)u̯l̥h₁-náh₂ (> Middle Welsh *gwlan*, Latin *lāna*, Gothic *wulla*, Vedic *ū́rṇā*-, Avestan *varənā*-, Lithuanian *vìlna*, Old Church Slavic *vlŭna*)
*-*s*-stem:	*(h₂)u̯élh₁-os (→ Latin *vellus*).

It is particularly noteworthy that the derivation of *(h₂)u̯l̥h₁-náh₂ from *(h₂)u̯élh₁-mn̥ must have taken place while the inherited rules of ablaut and consonant reduction of *-*mn*- > *-*n*- following a root containing a labial were still active.[9] This suggests that *(h₂)u̯l̥h₁-náh₂ 'wool' must go back to Proto-Indo-European proper, i.e. a stage including the Anatolian branch, whether or not it is actually attested in Hittite.

Our two remaining problems are now (1) the identity of the underlying root and (2) whether Hittite *ḫulana- is a cognate or not.

As often assumed, and discussed in detail by Olsen (2018 with references), Latin *vellus* is most likely internally connected with the verb *vellō* 'pluck out', especially used for hair and feathers. This connection implies that the original meaning of 'wool' is a collective 'something plucked out', suggesting that at least in post-Anatolian Indo-European, we would most likely be dealing with real, spinnable wool from the mutation of wool sheep, not just the short, rough hair of wild or early domesticated sheep.

An obvious parallel to the suggested link between the words for 'pluck' and 'wool' is found with the root *peḱ- (LIV² 467). From this we have, on the one hand, Lithuanian *pešù* 'pluck, pull out', Greek πέκω 'comb, card', and on the other, Greek πέκος and πόκος 'sheep's wool, fleece', with a further likely relation to the word for 'livestock', *péḱu, continued in Vedic *páśu*, Avestan *pasu* 'livestock', Latin *pecū* 'flock, herd', and Gothic *faíhu* 'livestock, cattle'. An original meaning 'sheep' as the animal used for 'plucking' is suggested by Hittite UDU-*uš*, acc. UDU-*um* 'sheep', presumably to be read as *pekku*-, *pikku*- (Tischler 2001: 558–59 with references). Another semantic parallel is Old Norse *reyfi* 'wool', Old English *reaf* 'fleece' (cf. Walde & Hofmann 2: 745), from the root *(h₁)reip-, which is also the basis of the verb continued in Old Norse *rīfa* 'tear', Gk. ἐρείπω 'ruin, tear down'.

As we have seen, the root for 'pluck', underlying the Indo-European word for 'wool', can be reconstructed as *(hₓ)u̯elh₁- with or without an initial laryngeal if Hittite *ḫulana- is excluded from the equation, and with *h_2-, i.e. *h₂u̯elh₁-, if the Hittite word is indeed a cognate.

In Hittite texts, the word for 'wool' is almost always written with a Sumerogram, so unfortunately the attestation is rather poor. However, a stem *ḫulana-[10] has been deduced from a sort of rebus, found in a vacillation between the two renderings of a river name ᴵᴰ*Ḫu-la-na* beside ᴵᴰSÍG-*na*, where ÍD is the Sumerogram for 'river' and SÍG that for 'wool', so that 'wool' must have been pronounced something like *ḫulana*-. The river name probably means 'the winding, twisting one' or something similar, "apparently referring to the 'meander-like' nature of many Anatolian rivers" (Puhvel 1991: 361).[11] Other attestations of the word are incomplete: dat.loc. *ḫu-u-la-[ni]* and *[ḫu-u-la]-ni* and inst.sg. SÍG-*ni-it*. The Hittite evidence is supported by Luwian SÍG-*la-ni-is*. Another unambiguously attested Hittite word for 'wool', apparently from the same root, is *ḫulii̯a*-, secured by the variants UDU.ḪI.A-*aš ḫu-li-i̯a-aš* = UDU.ḪI.A-*aš* SÍG-*aš* 'wool of sheep'.

In general, the etymological connection between the Hittite word and Latin *lāna* etc. has been taken for granted,[12] as is natural considering the combination of close formal similarity with the same sequence of consonants and full semantic identity. Oettinger (1976: 66), in a discussion of the Hittite terminology for the distaff, even considered it justified to conclude that since "*ḫulana*- [aber] eine direkte Fortsetzung des

[6] Cf. Olsen (1999: 763).

[7] Cf. Rasmussen (1989: 82–83, 99–100; 2011: 495) on the morphohonemic alternation.

[8] Cf., however, Pinault's divergent analysis (l.c. p. 249), where *h₂u̯elh₁- 'pluck off' is accepted as a possible proto-form for Latin *vellō* as well as *vellus*.

[9] Cf. Wackernagel & Debrunner 1954: § 609a: "So gehören die Instrumentale v. prathinā́ prenā́ bhūnā́ mahinā́ [. . .] zu prathimán-premán- bhūmán- mahimán- [. . .] und beruhen auf grundsprachlichem Wandel von mn zu n hinter labialem Anlaut [. . .]."

[10] Tischler (1978: 278–79); Puhvel (1991: 369); Kloekhorst (2008: 357–58); Friedrich & Kammenhuber (2010: 595–96).

[11] A similar river name, apparently from the same root, is ᴵᴰ*Ḫulai̯a*-.

[12] E.g. Puhvel (l.c.); Mallory & Adams (1997: 648–49).

urindogermanischen Wortes für 'Wolle' darstellt, sollte auch die Bedeutung 'Wolle' primär sein. Dies berechtigt zu der Annahme, daß nicht Flachs, sondern Wolle der erste Stoff war, den die Hethiter zum Spinnen verwendeten."

From a formal point of view, a revocalization of *h_2u̯l̥- > *hul- is unproblematic,[13] yet still some objections have been raised as to the details of the comparison. Thus, Kloekhorst (2008: 358), who is in opposition to the traditional etymology, argues that: "[f]irst, if Hitt. ḫulana- reflects *$h_2$ulh$_1$n-, the -a- is unexpected. It has been claimed that ḫulana- stands for / Holna-/ [...],[14] but then we should rather expect a spelling **ḫu-ul-na-. Secondly, if ḫulana- and ḫulii̯a- together with ḫulāli- ['distaff'] point to a root ḫul-, this ḫul- does not fit *$h_2$ulh$_1$-, which should have yielded **ḫull-."

Melchert (1994: 65–66) sketches the following scenario: "Hitt. ḫulana- therefore[15] reflects *$h_{2/3}$wl̥h$_1$-neh$_2$- [...] With regular loss of */h$_1$/ we would expect /Hul-na-/. Given its extreme rarity, we could read the Hittite word thus, but a pronunciation with an anaptyctic vowel is also possible, since the cluster /-ln-/ would have been virtually unique. Hittite (and probably Luvian) shows assimilation of */-ln-/ clusters ..., including from *wl̥n- in *$h_{2/3}$wl̥-ne-h$_1$- > ḫulle- 'fight'. The lack of assimilation in /Hul(a)na-/ thus requires that loss of */h$_1$/ in this environment follow assimilation of */-ln-/, to *-ll-, and finally loss of */h$_1$/ between consonants, all in PA [Proto-Anatolian]. I know of no evidence against attribution of all this to PA."

When Melchert and Kloekhorst insist that the -a- of the second syllable is unexpected as the outcome of a laryngeal in interconsonantal position (or in Melchert's wording, "between two sonorants"), this is a moot point where general agreement has not been reached.[16] Still, it must be admitted that if, for the sake of the argument, -lana- in ḫulana- were derived from *-lh$_1$no- with -a- as a reflex of the laryngeal, one would expect an intermediate stage *-lh$_1$ə$_1$no- with consonantal laryngeal + prop vowel and a laryngeal-conditioned geminate -ll-.

However, it may be asked whether the revocalization *h_2u̯l̥- > ḫul- – i.e. *$h_2$ulh$_1$n- > ḫulan-, whatever the exact origin of the -a- – would already have taken place *before* the development of this vowel, so that the laryngeal was at some point interconsonantal, as assumed by Melchert. This seems far from certain.

Obviously, it would be the most economical solution to the problem if ḫulana-, like the evidence from the other languages, could be directly derived from *h_2u̯l̥h$_1$-nah$_2$- with a "long sonorant" *-l̥h$_1$-, so our first question is what exactly to expect from such a proto-form. Assuming that the revocalization *-u̯l̥- > -ul- as an internal Anatolian phenomenon occurred *after* *-u̯l̥h$_1$- underwent its regular development, we need to know the fate of "long sonorants," i.e. sequences of the type *-CR̥HC- as opposed to *-VRHC-, in Hittite. Strange as it may seem, this appears to be unknown.

Neither Melchert in his *Anatolian Historical Phonology* (1994) nor Kimball in her *Hittite Historical Phonology* (1999) includes specific treatments of the question, though Kimball (1999: 417) does venture the idea that "[i]t is likely that medial *h$_1$ vocalized to /a/ under some conditions and to /u/ after *l or *l̥." Unfortunately, Kimball does not explicitly distinguish between postvocalic and postconsonantal position, i.e., between *l and *l̥.[17]

If we tentatively assume that laryngeals, or at least the weakly articulated *-h$_1$-, was lost without a trace in *-CR̥h$_1$C- sequences, the expected development of *h_2u̯l̥h$_1$nah$_2$- would be *ḫu̯l̥na- > *ḫulna- with revocalization of *-u̯l̥- > -ul- after the loss of the laryngeal, but before the usual development of vocalic sonorants, *R̥ > aR, i.e.:

1. *-ln- > -ll-, as per Melchert
2. *h_2u̯l̥h$_1$nah$_2$- > *ḫu̯l̥na- (laryngeal loss)
3. *h_2u̯l̥na- > *ḫulna- (revocalization)
4. perhaps, but not necessarily *ḫulna- > ḫulana- (development of anaptyctic vowel).

Similarly, the synonymous ḫulii̯a- may be derived from *h_2u̯l̥h$_1$i̯o- with regular laryngeal loss before *-i̯- (Eichner 1978: 160; Kimball 1999: 404).

Thus, it seems possible not only to unite the Anatolian and Core Indo-European word for 'wool' under a common proto-form, *h_2u̯l̥h$_1$náh$_2$-, but also to understand this form as a morphologically regular derivative, 'something plucked', from the root *h_2u̯elh$_1$-, continued in Latin *vellō* 'pluck out'.

Nevertheless, internal Hittite evidence has been adduced as an objection against such a connection. As argued by Pinault (2016: 249), "[the] common basis *ḫul- of ḫulana-, ḫuliya- and ḫulāli- cannot possibly designate the 'wool' as the product ready to be worked out in order to make clothes and other textiles. Since it is the basis of ḫulāli- 'distaff', it did not refer to the wool as already spun, but precisely as the material to be spun, hence, the wool at an anterior and raw state, to the fleece, after it had been gathered from sheep and probably cleaned and washed." According to Pinault, *ḫul- would thus be the Anatolian stem denoting the fleece, later replaced in Hittite by ^{SÍG}ēšri.

The meaning of ḫulāli- 'distaff' is well secured (Puhvel 1991: 361–63; Kloekhorst 2008: 356f–357). It is apparently derived with the suffix *-óli-, used for the formation of primarily deverbal instrument nouns (Rieken 1999: 434; Pinault 2017:

[13] Melchert (1994: 55–56) provides the comparable example *$h_{2/3}$u̯l̥-ne-h$_1$- > ḫulle- 'fight'.

[14] Cf. Melchert (1994: 65).

[15] "Therefore" refers to Peters's identification of the root-final laryngeal as *-h$_1$- (1987).

[16] Cf. the less categorical account in Kimball (1999 passim).

[17] The most striking of Kimball's examples of potential vocalization to -u- is dalūki- 'long' (1999: 420), allegedly from *dl̥h$_1$g^h- and thus allegedly matching Vedic dīrghá- 'id' (*-h$_1$-, secured by Greek ἐνδελεχής 'continuous, constant'). In Beekes's systematic survey (1988: 84), again treating vocalic and consonantal resonants indiscriminately, the development of a vowel *a* before the resonant is considered most likely ("RHC > aRC"?), though the testimony is scanty. Apart from ḫulana-, the examples given for non-initial position are tašu̯ant- 'blind' (if *tm̥hsu̯ent-) and danduki- 'mortal' (if *d^{h}n̥h$_2$-tu-), both etymologically debatable (cf. Kloekhorst [2010: 855–56] on tašu̯ant-; danduki- is unmentioned).

250) and itself the basis of the verb *ḫulaliia-* 'wind around; enwrap, entwine, encircle, surround' and the reduplicated *ḫulḫuliia-* 'entwine, embrace, wrestle, struggle'. This has led to the conclusion that a synchronic root *ḫul-* had the meaning 'roll' or the like, but there is no agreement on further implications of this. According to Puhvel (l.c.), *ḫul-* reflects "IE $*H_1wel(-H_2)$- 'wind, twist', seen in Skt. *válati*, Arm. *gelum*, Gk. εἰλέω etc.," but it is left open (l.c. 369) whether the root connection of *ḫulana-*, *ḫuliia-* is to *ḫul(a)-* 'wind' or to the root of Latin *vellus* 'fleece', *vellō* 'pluck, tear'.

Kloekhorst (2008: 358), on the other hand, concludes: "we must assume two words for wool, namely *ḫuliia-* and *ḫulana-*. Because of their formal similarity, it is likely that both are derived from a root *ḫul-* 'wool', which then possibly also underlies *ḫulāli-* 'distaff' [...] and its derivatives **ḫulāliie/a-*[zi] 'to entwine'." Finally, Pinault (2017: 251) favors an internal connection between *ḫuliia-* and *ḫulāli-*, both from **ḫul-* 'fleece', but rejects a derivation of these terms from $*h_2u̯elh_1$- 'pluck off' because the missing gemination of *-l-*. *Ḫulana-* 'wool' is deemed an archaic formation, $*h_2u̯l̥\text{-}h_1no$-, whereby the analysis becomes unnecessarily complicated. Allegedly, we are dealing with a compound of **ḫul-* 'fleece' → 'wool' + a second member related to $*h_1\acute{e}no$- "which referred to the year, and specifically the past year" (cf. e.g. Greek δίενος 'two years old'), so that *ḫulana-* would originally be 'making the year of/with fleece' → 'the yearly wool'.

Pinault's explanation has several drawbacks:

1. a root noun $*h_2ul$- 'fleece' is unknown outside of Anatolian, and even here it has allegedly been subject to lexical substitution;
2. a compound of Schindler's "double possessive" type ('having X [first member] provided with Y [second member]')[18] is not only rare, but otherwise completely missing in Anatolian, where the inventory of compounds is notoriously poor and probably not fully developed until Core Indo-European, here understood as the stage following the separation of first Anatolian, then Tocharian; and
3. the immediate, semantically attractive connection of the 'wool' word with Armenian *gełmn* 'fleece' and with Latin *vellus* 'fleece', *vellō* 'pluck' has to be abandoned.

On the other hand, it must be admitted that *ḫulāli-* 'distaff' with derivatives is impossible to reconcile semantically with a root meaning 'pluck'. From $*h_2u̯elh_1$- 'pluck', we may thus maintain the derivational chain $*h_2u̯elh_1mn̥$ 'plucking' (> Armenian *gełmn* 'fleece') → $*h_2u̯l̥h_1n\acute{a}h_2$ 'what is plucked', lexicalized as 'wool' from Hittite *ḫulana-* to Italic, Celtic, Germanic, Indo-Iranian, and Balto-Slavic, and adding the *s*-stem $*h_2u̯elh_1os$ → Latin *vellus* 'fleece' and the verb $*h_2u̯(e)l\text{-}neh_1$- → Latin *vello* 'pluck'.

A different root with the meaning 'roll' must then be the basis of Hittite *ḫulāli-* 'instrument for rolling', which is exactly what a distaff is: the wool is carded, laid out in an even layer, and rolled around a stick from which it is continuously taken to feed the spindle. More precisely, the Hittite word suggests that we are probably dealing with a root form $*h_2u̯el$- rather than the usually assumed **u̯el-* (LIV[2] 675). It is impossible to determine whether the root was simplified within Anatolian, or the more complex $*(h_2)u̯elhu̯$- is a later creation of Core Indo-European.[19] Beside *ḫulāli-*, derivatives of the same root include the denominative *ḫulaliia-* 'wind around; enwrap, entwine, encircle, surround', the reduplicated *ḫulḫulliia-* 'entwine, embrace; wrestle, struggle', and the abovementioned river name [ÍD]*Ḫu-la-na*.

Against this background, it seems the most natural solution by far that Proto-Indo-European, including Anatolian, did have a common word for 'wool', indeed one of the best-secured Indo-European etymologies, formally as well as semantically, derived by archaic morphological mechanisms from an inherited root meaning 'pluck'. This means that the early Indo-Europeans, before the first split between Anatolian and the rest of the family, must have connected 'wool' with 'plucking'.

From an archaeological point of view, it has been stressed that there is no evidence for the spinning and weaving of wool from the steppe region at an early date. One might try to sidestep this problem by hypothesizing that the original meaning of 'wool' was the unspinnable, unweavable hair of early domesticated sheep, which can only be utilized for felting, but a scenario of this kind fails to be linguistically satisfactory. It demands that 'plucking' was not really plucking but rather something like harvesting of the rough hairs of the sheep simply by running one's hands through the animal's coat at the time of shedding, and even more importantly, that 'wool' was not really wool despite the unanimous evidence to the contrary from nine branches of the Indo-European family, where one would thus have to assume independent, but identical semantic developments.

Actual 'plucking', as substantiated by the Latin verb *vellō* and the parallel root **peḱ-*, on the other hand, makes excellent sense if we are dealing with the long fibers of the sheep wool suitable for spinning and weaving. Now, according to Shishlina et al. (2003), the oldest specimens of woven wool come from the Maykop Culture (3700–3200 BC) in the Caucasus, close to the presumed Indo-European homeland and within what would seem a suitable time frame. It is unclear whether the Maykop textiles were imported or locally produced, but if the latter was the case, and if moreover it is assumed the Indo-Europeans actually did not have wool sheep, they may still have observed or known about the plucking of wool by their neighbors and created their own vocabulary for this phenomenon without necessarily having to master the technical skills themselves in the initial phase. At any rate, it is interesting that some of the characteristics of the Maykop graves, notably the wrapping of corpses in a cloth consisting of strips or bandages in several layers, also seems to be mirrored in Indo-European burial practice (cf. Olsen 2016), all pointing to a close contact between the two cultures.

[18] Cf. Schindler (1986).

[19] While Greek εἰλέω shows no sign of an initial laryngeal, this may be due to generalization from zero-grade forms, as in the word for 'wool'.

In conclusion, the linguistic evidence suggests that the Indo-Europeans at the very least knew how genuine sheep's wool was harvested and created their corresponding vocabulary accordingly, whether they practiced this harvesting themselves or merely observed the progress of their technologically more advanced neighbors.

References

Beekes, Robert. 1988. Laryngeal developments: A survey. In: Alfred Bammesberger (ed.), *Die Laryngaltheorie und die Rekonstruktion des indogermanischen Laut- und Formensystems*, 51–105. Heidelberg: Winter.

2010. *Etymological dictionary of Greek*. 2 vols. Leiden & Boston: Brill.

Eichner, Heiner. 1978. Die urindogermanische Wurzel *H_2reu 'hell machen'. *Die Sprache* 24: 144–62.

Flemestad, Peder, & Birgit Anette Olsen. 2017. Sabellic textile terminology. In: Salvatore Gaspar, Cécile Michel, & Marie-Louise Nosch (ed.), *Textile terminologies from the Orient to the Mediterranean and Europe 1000 BC–1000 AD* (Zea E-Books 56), 201–121. Lincoln (NE): University of Nebraska at Lincoln.

Friedrich, Johannes, & Annelies Kammenhuber. 2010. *Hethitisches Wörterbuch, Band III/2: Ḫ/ḫe- bis ḫu-*. Lieferung 19. Zweite, völlig neubearbeitete Auflage auf der Grundlage der edierten hethitischen Texte. Heidelberg: Winter.

Frisk, Hjalmar. 1973–79. *Griechisches etymologisches Wörterbuch*. 3 vols. Heidelberg: Winter.

Iversen, Rune & Guus Kroonen. 2017. Talking Neolithic: Linguistic and Archaeological Perspectives on How Indo-European Was Implemented in Southern Scandinavia. *American Journal of Archaeology* 121, 4: 511-25.

Kimball, Sara E. 1999. *Hittite historical phonology*. Innsbruck: Innsbrucker Studien zur Sprachwissenschaft.

Kloekhorst, Alwin. 2006. Initial laryngeals in Anatolian. *Historische Sprachforschung* 119: 77–108.

2008. *Etymological dictionary of the Hittite inherited lexicon*. Leiden & Boston: Brill.

LIV^2 = Martin Kümmel, Thomas Zehnder, Reiner Lipp, & Brigitte Schirmer (ed.). 1988. *Lexikon der indogermanischen Verben*. 2., erw. und verb. Aufl. Wiesbaden: Reichert.

Mallory, J. P. & D. Q. Adams (ed.). 1997. *Encyclopedia of Indo-European culture*. London & Chicago: Fitzroy Dearborn.

Melchert, H. Craig. 1994. *Anatolian historical phonology*. Amsterdam & Atlanta: Rodopi.

Oettinger, Norbert. 1976. *Die Militärischen Eide der Hethiter* (Studien zu den Boğazköy-Texten 22). Wiesbaden: Harrassowitz.

Olsen, Birgit Anette. 1999. *The noun in biblical Armenian* (Trends in Linguistics, Studies and Monographs 119). Berlin & New York: Mouton de Gruyter.

2014. *Latin* -ll- *and potential gemination by laryngeal. Handout from Sound of Indo-European 3*, Opava.

2016. Latin *vespillo* 'undertaker':Calvert Watkins in memoriam. *Journal of Indo-European Studies* 44(1/2): 92–100.

2017. Armenian textile terminology. In: Salvatore Gaspar, Cécile Michel, & Marie-Louise Nosch (ed.), *Textile terminologies from the Orient to the Mediterranean and Europe 1000 BC–1000 AD* (Zea E-Books 56), 188–200. Lincoln (NE): University of Nebraska at Lincoln.

2018. Notes on the Indo-European terminology of sheep, wool and textile production. In: Rune Iversen & Guus Kroonen (ed.), *Digging for words. Archaeoloinguistic case stories from the XV Nordic TAG Conference held at the University of Copenhagen 16–18 April 2015*, 66–77. Oxford: British Archaeological Reports.

2021. Latin *-ll-* and gemination by laryngeal. In: Hannes Fellner, Melanie Malzahn & Michaël Peyrot (ed.), *lyuke wmer ra: Indo-European Studies in Honor of Georges-Jean Pinault*, 226–237. Ann Arbor, New York: Beech Stave Press.

Peters, Martin. 1980. *Untersuchungen zur Vertretung der indogermanischen Laryngale im Griechischen*. Vienna: Verlag der Österreichischen Akademie der Wissenschaften.

1987. *λῆνος* aus *$h_{2/3}$u̯l̥$h_1$náh_2-. *Die Sprache* 33: 114–115.

Pinault, Georges-Jean. 2016. Hittite and Indo-European wool. In: Henning Marquardt, Silvio Reichmut, & José Virgilio García Trabazo (ed.), *Anatolica et Indogermanica. Studia linguistica in honorem Johannis Tischler septuagenarii dedicata*, 241–255. Innsbruck: Innsbrucker Studien zur Sprachwissenschaft.

Puhvel, Jaan. 1984. *Hittite etymological dictionary*. Vols. 1–2. Berlin, New York, & Amsterdam: Mouton.

1991. *Hittite etymological dictionary*. Volume 3. Words beginning with H. Berlin, New York, & Amsterdam: Mouton.

Rasmussen, Jens Elmegård. 1989. *Studien zur Morphophonemik der indogermanischen Grundsprache* (Innsbrucker Studien zur Sprachwissenschaft 55). Innsbruck: Institut für Sprachwissenschaft der Universität Innsbruck.

2011. Über Status und Entwicklung des sog. *u*-Präsens im Indogermanischen. In: Thomas Krisch & Thomas Lindner (ed.), *Indogermanistik und Linguistik im Dialog. Akten der XIII. Fachtagung der Indogermanischen Gesellschaft vom 21. bis 27. September 2008 in Salzburg*, 491–497. Wiesbaden: Reichert.

Rieken, Elisabeth. 1999. *Untersuchungen zur nominalen Stammbildung des Hethitischen* (Studien zu den Boğazköy-Texten 44). Wiesbaden: Harrassowitz.

Schindler, Jochem. 1986. Zu den homerischen ῥοδοδάκτυλος-Komposita. In: A. Etter, (ed.): *o-o-pe-ro-si. Festschrift für Ernst Risch*., 393–401. Berlin & New York: De Gruyter.

Shishlina, N. I, O. V. Orfinskaya, & V. P. Golikov. 2003. Bronze Age textiles from the North Caucasus: New evidence of fourth millenium BC fibres and fabrics. *Oxford Journal of Archaeology* 22: 331–44.

Tischler, Johann. 1978. *Hethitisches etymologisches Glossar*. Mit Beiträgen von Günter Neumann. Lieferung 2. Innsbruck: Innsbrucker Beiträge zur Sprachwissenschaft.

2001. *Hethitisches etymologisches Glossar*. Mit Beiträgen von Günter Neumann und Erich Neu. Teil II, Lieferung 11/12, P. Innsbruck: Innsbrucker Beiträge zur Sprachwissenschaft.

Wackernagel, Jakob. 1954. *Altindische Grammatik*. Band II, 2. Nominalsuffixe (von A. Debrunner). Göttingen: Vandenhoeck & Ruprecht.

Walde, A. 1938–54. *Lateinisches Etymologisches Wörterbuch* 1–2. 3. neubearbeitete Auflage von J.B. Hofmann. Heidelberg: Winter.

Wodtko, Dagmar, Britta Irslinger, & Carolin Schneider. 2008. *Nomina im Indogermanischen Lexikon*. Heidelberg: Winter.

Part V Kinship Systems, Marriage, Fosterage, Free, and Unfree

19 MOBILITY, KINSHIP, AND MARRIAGE IN INDO-EUROPEAN SOCIETY*

TIJMEN PRONK

19.1 Introduction

The purpose of this chapter is to explore one area in which comparative linguistic data can play a role in interpreting late Neolithic and early Bronze Age genetic and archaeological data from western Eurasia. The sharp rise in available samples of ancient DNA enables the establishment of kinship relations between individuals in prehistoric graveyards. It also makes it possible to establish where their ancestors came from. The analysis of strontium, oxygen, carbon, and lead isotopes in the tooth enamel of these same individuals provides information about movements during their lives. When these techniques are combined, we obtain a much better idea about who moved where and when in prehistory. Being able to establish the diet of prehistoric individuals and which diseases they may have suffered from allows archaeologists to set up hypotheses as to why some of the population movements that can be observed in the archaeological data might have taken place. Linguistics can offer a valuable contribution to the discussion of why people moved by shedding light on factors other than diet or disease; it may, for example, help to explain cases in which males appear to have migrated differently from females. In order to understand how, this chapter will take a closer look at the linguistic evidence for kinship relations and the role of gender and age in Indo-European society. At the end of the chapter, hypotheses about mobility, kinship, and marriage in early Indo-European society as based on the linguistic data will be compared to the findings of recent research into ancient DNA and isotope analysis.

* This paper would not have existed without the many fruitful discussions I had about its contents with Sasha Lubotsky. Together, we prepared and presented parts of it at the 23rd Annual Meeting of the European Association of Archaeologists in Maastricht in September 2017 and at the conference "When Archaeology Meets Linguistics and Genetics" in Gothenburg in May 2018. Any remaining errors in the paper are mine. While this paper awaited publication, Birgit Olsen (2019, 2020, and this volume) published and submitted a number of papers about some of the same topics that are discussed here. I recommend consulting these papers, which often contain additional information and sometimes slightly different interpretations.

19.2 Migration and the Spread of Indo-European Languages

Recent progress in the study of ancient DNA has had serious consequences for the questions surrounding the spread of Indo-European language across western and central Eurasia. There is now a broad consensus that the ancestor of the Indo-European languages was spoken in or along the borders of the Pontic–Caspian steppe. The spread of DNA from the Pontic–Caspian steppe to the west in the fourth millennium BCE has repeatedly and convincingly been linked to the first stages of the Indo-Europeanization of Europe. It is of great importance that the late Neolithic and Bronze Age migrations that are thought to have brought Indo-European languages from the Pontic–Caspian steppe into Central Europe are clearly visible in paternally inherited ancient Y-DNA, but not so much in maternally inherited mitochondrial DNA. This male-biased spread probably points to "ongoing male migration from the steppe over multiple generations" (Goldberg et al. 2017).[1] This is not to say that the spread of Indo-European languages did not also involve diffusion and acculturation, but the genetic data suggest that migration played a crucial role.

In the east, the situation appears to be similar. It is likely that the initial spread of Indo-European languages to the Kazakh steppe was also fueled by migration, while the subsequent southward spread of Indo-Iranian into Central Asia involved more gradual movement and diffusion (Mallory 1998). Loanwords from the language of the people from the Bactria–Margiana Archaeological Complex (BMAC) into Indo-Iranian

[1] In other geographic areas, the sex bias is less pronounced. Ancient DNA taken from individuals in Corded Ware graves in present day Poland, the Czech Republic, and the Baltic states shows greater maternal genetic affinity with the Pontic–Caspian steppe than that of individuals from present-day Germany (Juras et al. 2018). To my knowledge, there is presently no evidence for a sex bias in the eastward migrations from the Pontic–Caspian steppe by the ancestors of speakers of the Tocharian and Indo-Iranian languages.

testify to the interactions of speakers of Indo-Iranian before the Aryans moved across the Hindu Kush into the Indian subcontinent (Lubotsky 2001). One component of the ancient DNA collected from individuals from the Indus valley who were most probably speakers of early Indo-Aryan stems from the steppes (Damgaard et al. 2018; Narasimhan et al. 2019), so here, too, language spread was at least partly caused by human migration.

19.3 Proto-Indo-European[2] Society Was Patrilocal and Patrilineal

Ancient Indo-European societies were patrilocal without exception and patrilineal as a rule. There is ample linguistic evidence that this was also the case for the speakers of Proto-Indo-European. Women married into the family of their husband, leaving the family of their parents. The following linguistic features point to a patrilocal and patrilineal society:[3]

- PIE kinship terms differentiate the family of the husband (and son) much more than that of the wife:
  *suek̑uro- 'father of the husband'
  *suek̑ruh$_2$- 'mother of the husband'
  _*dh$_2$eiuer-_ '(younger) brother of the husband'
  *Hienh$_2$ter- 'wife of the husband's brother'
  *ǵlh$_2$ōu- '(unmarried) sister of the husband'[4]
  There is no comparable terminology for the family of the wife.[5]
- There was a common term for 'widow', PIE _*h$_1$uid^{h}h$_1$-(e)u-h$_2$-_, but not 'widower', suggesting a special status for women who lost their husband, but not for husbands who lost their wife. This is probably due to the exceptional legal status of the widow, who no longer had a man to act on her behalf. The word for widow derives from a PIE adjective _*h$_1$uid^{h}h$_1$-u-_ 'bereft' (Beekes 1992), which was originally a compound _*dui-d^{h}h$_1$-u-_ 'put apart, separated'. This adjective is perhaps preserved in Greek ἠΐθεος 'unmarried youth', if this Greek word is not a back-formation from the feminine form (Beekes 2010: 512). There is no linguistic evidence for levirate, the practice by which a widow marries a male member of her late husband's family, typically his brother (PIE _*dh$_2$eiuer-_), but the existence of levirate in several ancient Indo-European societies (Zimmer 2003: 121, Olsen 2019: 155) suggests that it may have been inherited.
- It is possible that it was customary for a widower to marry the sister of his late wife. This is suggested by Greek μητρυιά, Armenian _mawru_ 'stepmother', which originally meant 'mother's sister' in view of the cognate Old English _modrige_ 'mother's sister' and the morphologically parallel Sanskrit _pitr̥vyà-_ 'father's brother'.[6] It is unclear, however, whether the mother's sister only took care of the children of her late sister, or it was also customary for her to have children fathered by the husband of her late sister.
- The verb 'to wed', PIE _*ued^h-_, also meant 'to lead', which is usually interpreted as indicating that the groom led the bride away from her home and family. This is confirmed by the use of unrelated verbs meaning 'to lead', like Latin _dūcere (uxorem)_ and Greek ἄγω (γυναῖκα), in this way. The bride was given (PIE _*deh$_3$-_) to the groom by her father.
- When a marriage was agreed on, a bride-price, PIE _*h$_1$ued-no-_, was paid to the family of the bride to compensate for the loss of her services (Mallory & Adams 1997: 82–83).
- PIE _*pot-i-_ 'husband' also meant 'master'. The husband acted on behalf of the entire family; cf. Latin _potis_ 'able, possible', _suo-pte_ 'by one's own', Lithuanian _pàts_ 'self'. Benveniste (1969: 90) argued that the oldest meaning of the word _*pot-i-_ was 'self'. There is a derived feminine form PIE _*pot-nih$_2$_ 'mistress' (Sanskrit _pátnī-_, _viś-pátnī-_, Greek πότνια, δέσ-ποινα, Lithuanian _vieš-patni_), that was formed by analogy with the word _*h$_2$reh$_1$ǵ-nih$_2$_ 'wife of the chief' within core Indo-European. In Indo-Iranian, _*pot-nih$_2$_ also means 'wife'; cf. Sanskrit _sapátnī-_, Avestan _ha-paϑnī-_ 'concubine', lit. 'co-wife', but this is probably an inner-Indo-Iranian innovation. Lithuanian _patì_ 'wife' likewise arose in post-PIE times.
- The PIE feminine motion suffix _*-ih$_2$_ originally indicated appurtenance; cf. the same PIE element _*-ih$_2$_ in Sanskrit _devī́_ 'goddess' and the Latin genitive singular _deī_ 'of the god'.
- Indo-European names of females are usually derived from the names of males: from the name of the father before marriage, and that of the husband after marriage.
- In Ancient Greek, women were usually addressed with ὦ γύναι 'o woman!', while men were addressed by their name (Wackernagel 1912: 25–26).

Further evidence for patrilocality and patrilineality can be found in the textual evidence of ancient Indo-European societies, e.g. the widespread existence of special regulations for

[2] Proto-Indo-European (PIE) and Indo-European are used here in the meaning 'of people speaking an Indo-European language'. Obviously, not all speakers of Indo-European must have shared a common subset of genetic or cultural characteristics, and the genetic and cultural characteristics of certain speakers of Indo-European may well have been shared by speakers of other languages. On the other hand, for a language to keep functioning as a single entity over a longer period, all its speakers must be connected through communication, and linguistic innovations must be able to reach all speakers. The more economic, cultural, and religious features shared by the speakers of a particular language, the more likely it is that they will maintain communication. The vocabulary of a (proto-)language will therefore normally reflect a society in which the speakers shared economic, cultural, and religious habits and were probably genetically related.

[3] The Indo-European kinship system has been argued to be of the so-called Omaha III type (Friedrich 1966, 1980; Gates 1971). Although some characteristics of the Omaha III system can be reconstructed for Proto-Indo-European, other features that characterize Omaha III cannot (Szemerényi 1977: 174–183; Hettrich 1985: 457–458).

[4] Based on the Hesychian gloss γελαρος · ἀδελφοῦ γυνή. Φρυγιστί "brother's wife. In Phrygian," Benveniste (1969: 251) has suggested that the Proto-Indo-European term may have been reciprocal for the husband's sister and the brother's wife.

[5] Hettrich (1985) has argued that the restriction of the words for parents-in-law to those on the husband's side in Balto-Slavic, Greek, Indo-Iranian, and Armenian is a secondary development and that these words originally also applied to the parents of the wife. There is little support for this claim in the data.

[6] A new word for 'brother's son', Sanskrit _bhrā́tr̥vya-_, Avestan _brātruiia-_, was formed with the same suffix in Indo-Iranian. Its formation can be understood if one takes into account that if X is the brother of the father (_pitr̥vyà-_) of Y, then Y is the son of the brother (_bhrā́tr̥vya-_) of X.

the situation in which a man dies without leaving a male heir (see Zimmer 2003: 121–122).

19.4 The Stranger/Guest and Marriage

In Sanskrit, we find the word *arí-*, translated as 'stranger, guest, enemy'. The *arí-* was a stranger belonging to Vedic culture and speaking the Vedic language. It has therefore been suggested that *arí-* referred to strangers who (or whose family members) were suitable candidates for marriage in Indo-European society (Benveniste 1969: 100, 372–373). This is supported by the fact that the Vedic deity *Aryaman*, whose name is a derivative from *arí-*, was the patron of marriage. Another derivative from *arí-* is *ā́rya-* 'member of one of the three upper castes of Vedic society' (opposed to *dāsá-*, *dā́sa-* 'stranger, slave, enemy'). The Iranian equivalent of *ā́rya-* is an ethnonym referring to the Iranians themselves, e.g., in the name of the Alans < **arya-*, an Iranian people. The Indo-Iranian term and concept are most probably of Indo-European origin, because we find similar words in Hittite *arā-* 'friend', *arau̯an(n)i-* 'free (not being a slave)', Old Irish *aire* 'free man', Lithuanian *arvesnis* 'free (?)' (a hapax; Petit 2010: 180–181), and Russian *róvnyj* 'even', *rovésnik* 'peer' (Pronk 2013: 295–296). These are all derivatives from the Proto-Indo-European verbal root **$h_2$er-* 'to fit', which supports the idea that an *arí-* is a suitable male match for a young woman. A concept similar to that of *arí-*, a stranger belonging to the same culture and speaking the same language, is expressed in Greek by the word ξένος 'stranger, guest, host' (as opposed to βάρβαρος 'non-Greek stranger'), and in other European languages with the word **g^hos-tis* (Latin *hostis*, Gothic *gasts*, Old Church Slavonic *gostь*) (Benveniste 1969: 92–96). There is, however, no demonstrable connection between the European words for guest/stranger and endogamous marriage practices. The opposition between people inside and outside a larger ethnic, cultural, and/or linguistic community seems to be of Proto-Indo-European date. It is reasonable to assume, though not entirely certain, that the apparent Indo-Iranian habit of giving away one's daughter in marriage outside the direct family but within the larger community was also of Proto-Indo-European date. There is no reason to assume, however, that endogamy was absolute in Proto-Indo-European times, and it is quite possible that under certain circumstances, perhaps when the husband could not afford to pay a bride-price or when the marriage in question concerned a second or subsequent wife, it was deemed acceptable for an Indo-European male to marry a non-Indo-European female (cf. Zimmer 2003: 122–123). Whether or not the speakers of Proto-Indo-European practiced polygamy is difficult to establish. The existence of co-wives in Indo-European society is perhaps suggested by the fact that Middle Irish *airech* 'concubine' and Avestan *pairikā-* 'demonic courtesan'[7] could reflect an inherited Proto-Indo-European word (Mallory & Adams 2006: 208).

Apart from the limitation of marriage to a person from within one's own community, other kinship-related customs have been reconstructed for Proto-Indo-European. Two hypotheses about Indo-European kinship relations are based on the remarkable fact that the words for grandfather and maternal uncle derive from the same root, and the fact that there appears to have been one Indo-European word denoting both the grandson and the sister's son (nephew):

grandfather	maternal uncle	grandson	sister's son
Hitt. *ḫuḫḫa-*, CLuw. *ḫūḫa*, Lyc. *χuga-*, Lat. *avus*, Arm. *haw*, Goth. *awo* 'grandmother'	Lat. *avunculus*, OIr. *amnair*, OHG *ōheim*, OE *eam*, Lith. *avýnas*, Ru. *uj*, ?Gr. μήτρως	OE *nefa*, Alb. *nip*, Skt. *nápāt-*, Av. *napā̊*, Lat. *nepōs*, OLith. *nepuotis*	OE *nefa*, Alb. *nip*, OIr. *nia*, MW *ney*, ORu. *netii*

The hypotheses based on these forms are that (a) a preferred form of marriage was a marriage between cross-cousins and (b) there was a special relationship between a boy and his maternal uncle (the avunculate).

19.5 Cross-Cousin Marriage

We have seen above that there are indications that Proto-Indo-European society was endogamous. The more specific alleged habit of marrying one's cross-cousin proposed for Proto-Indo-European specifically relates to a marriage between the daughter of the sister of the husband's father to the son of the brother of the wife's mother.[8] From the perspective of the son, the paternal grandfather is in such cases the same person as the maternal granduncle. In Proto-Indo-European, this person would be the **$h_2$euh$_2$s* (Benveniste 1969: 223–229; see Kloekhorst 2008: 352 for the reconstruction). Because, as we have seen, the word was associated with the maternal uncle as well, Benveniste assumed a shift in meaning from 'grandfather' to any older male maternal relative.[9] This semantic shift could

[7] Avestan demonic terminology often reflects practices of Indo-Iranian society that were branded as evil by the Zoroastrians.

[8] There is an example of such cross-cousin marriage from the fragmentary Hittite royal genealogy: king Zidanta I appears to have been married to the daughter of his father's sister (Goedegebuure 2004). There are further traces of marriage within the family. In Ancient Greece, in situations when the only legal heir was a woman (the so-called ἐπίκληρος or πατροῦχος παρθένος), she was obliged to marry a relative of her father.

[9] There is a word for 'husband's brother', PIE **dh$_2$eiuer-*, but no specific word for the brother-in-law on the side of the wife (the maternal uncle of their children). It is possible that the wife's brother would have been referred to as **$h_2$euh$_2$s* by her husband as well, but there is no evidence that supports this hypothesis.

then be connected to the fact that the words for 'maternal uncle' contain additional suffixes: they are derivatives of *$h_2$euh$_2$s.[10]

Cross-cousin marriage would also be reflected in the fact that the word for 'grandson', PIE *nepōt, also means 'sister's son', an opposition that mirrors that of the 'grandfather/maternal uncle'. There is no reconstructible word for any of the cousins, including the potentially eligible cross-cousins 'paternal brother's son' and 'maternal sister's daughter', which suggests that they (or a selection of them) might simply have been referred to as 'brother' and 'sister' (Risch 1944: 117–118), a phenomenon not uncommon in kinship systems similar to the Proto-Indo-European one.

In any case, it remains unclear to what extent the various aspects of the Indo-European kinship system could be maintained by men migrating to areas where the population consisted chiefly of people not belonging to Indo-European society.

19.6 Criticism and Alternative Reconstructions

The idea that the Indo-Europeans favored cross-cousin marriages has been criticized by a number of scholars. The main objection is the lack of evidence for such a practice in the oldest Indo-European literature and in the kinship terminology (Friedrich 1966: 29; Gates 1971: 43; Beekes 1976: 45–46). Neither the specific meaning 'sister's grandson' for PIE *nepōt, nor 'maternal grand uncle' for PIE *$h_2$euh$_2$s is directly preserved (Latin *avunculus* 'maternal uncle', lit. 'little grandfather/granduncle', comes closest). These facts would imply that if cross-cousin marriages had been ever common practice, they were no longer so when Indo-European started to spread across Europe and Central Asia.

Opponents of cross-cousin marriage as an Indo-European institution have argued that the word *nepōt originally meant only 'grandson', with independent shifts to 'nephew' in Celtic, Slavic, Germanic, and Albanian (Beekes 1976: 54–55; Szemerényi 1977: 168; Hettrich 1985: 458–459). This seems unlikely, because the meaning 'sister's son' is rather specific and there is no evident connection between the grandson and the sister's son in post-Proto-Indo-European times. PIE *$h_2$euh$_2$s would originally have been an unspecified older male family member, but not the father's brother. There was a different word for the paternal uncle (father's brother): PIE *ph$_2$truiHo- (Sanskrit *pitr̥vyà-*, Old High German *fetiro*, Old Russian *stryi*, Latin *patruus*), derived from the word for father.

It turns out that there are some valid objections against positing cross-cousin marriages as a preferred type of marriage in Proto-Indo-European society. On the other hand, the fact that the reciprocal pairs grandfather–grandson and sister's son–maternal uncle are expressed with the same or similar words requires an explanation. One has to start from the grandson/sister's son, who is the same person, as the grandfather/maternal uncle are two different people. It seems that the role of the grandfather shifts to the maternal uncle at some point, either because the grandfather passes away, or because it was customary for a boy to be brought under the care of the maternal uncle at a certain age. All of this makes sense if we assume that the word that we reconstruct with the meaning 'grandfather', *$h_2$euh$_2$s, originally referred to the paterfamilias on the maternal side, i.e. either the maternal grandfather or one of his sons after his death, while the paterfamilias on the paternal side, i.e. the paternal grandfather or father, was referred to with the word for 'father' (Risch 1944: 118–121). This scenario is weakened somewhat by the fact that in those languages that preserve a reflex of *$h_2$euh$_2$s, it does not refer to the maternal or paternal grandfather only (Beekes 1976: 58).

19.7 The Avunculate

The special linguistic status of the maternal uncle and sister's son points to the existence of an avunculate, i.e., a system in which the mother's brother bears responsibility for the raising of his sister's son. Such a system is reflected in various Indo-European traditions, as shown by Bremmer (1976).[11]

There was probably one word referring to both the 'son-in-law' and the 'sister's husband', because Greek γαμβρός and Russian *zjat'* have both meanings. They appear to be derived from the Proto-Indo-European verbal root *ǵem-, but the exact reconstruction of the noun is unclear. This double meaning suggests that a woman could be given away in marriage by her brother (who would become the *avunculus* of her children), perhaps only if their father had died before she got married.

It has been suggested that the Indo-European avunculate is due to the similarity between the affectionate relationship between grandfather and grandson and that between maternal uncle and sister's son, contrasting with the severe relationship between father and son (Bremmer 1976: 71–72). A more concrete explanation could be that responsibility for (part of) the raising of a male child could shift or regularly shifted from the father's family to the mother's family, probably in the form of fosterage, which appears to have been common in Indo-European society (cf. Bremmer 1976; Olsen 2019: 150; Stockhammer, Chapter 21, this volume). This would be in line with the old idea that the 'grandson/nephew' is *ne-pot-, literally 'in-capable, not his own master' (Olsen 2019: 151). The Proto-Indo-European *$h_2$euh$_2$s would be the male relative responsible for the upbringing of a male child. The root of this noun could be identical to that of Sanskrit *ávati* 'to help, support', Latin *iuvō* 'to help, assist', Old Irish *con-ói* 'to

[10] Latin *avunculus* probably received its diminutive suffix by analogy with *homunculus* 'little man'. There is, therefore, no reason to reconstruct an *n*-stem *avō that would be comparable to the Celtic and Germanic forms (Dellbrück 1889: 488).

[11] Cf. further Barlau (1976) on Germanic, Ó Cathasaigh (1986) on early Irish literature, and Sürenhagen (1998) on kinship in the Old Hittite royal family.

protect' < PIE **HeuH-*.[12] These explanations are not completely in contradiction with cross-cousin marriage – as the avunculate is often associated with cross-cousin marriage – but there is no remaining evidence that supports the reconstruction of cross-cousin marriages for Proto-Indo-European society.

19.8 Discussion

We can conclude that in early Indo-European society, mobility into and out of the core family could be permanent or temporary and differed for men and women:

- a newlywed woman moved into the family of her husband, who was perhaps in some cases the son of her mother's brother;
- a boy could (temporarily?) move to the family of his mother to be fostered.

We can add to these practices a coming-of-age ritual for adolescent boys (PIE **$h_2$iuHones*) who would temporarily leave home in groups, the so-called *Männerbünde* (PIE **korios?*). Members of these youth bands retreated into the wilderness to live there like "animals." They were "dead" to society and were licensed to steal and carry out raids. In the rituals associated with this retreat, the young men wore clothes or masks that would characterize them as dogs or wolves.[13]

These youth bands have often been assumed to have played a role in colonization and Indo-European expansion.[14] Some of the youth bands would have explored unknown territories, looking for suitable targets to raid. Some may have chosen to settle in the newly discovered territories, or their reports back home may have stimulated a more organized colonization. From later periods, it is known that, e.g., the early Germanic war band was "from the beginning an inter-tribal association attracting warriors from other tribes to its ranks" (Greene 1998: 136). The youth bands may thus have been instrumental in exploring and colonizing new territory and in offering opportunities for youths from non-Indo-European tribes to join Indo-European society.[15]

As observed at the beginning of this chapter, elements of aDNA associated with the spread of Indo-European into Europe are predominantly found in paternally inherited ancient Y-DNA, while maternally inherited mitochondrial DNA contains a larger proportion of "local" DNA. The males who spread their DNA and Indo-European languages into Central Europe apparently often mated with local females, who themselves or whose ancestors in the not-too-distant past spoke a non-Indo-European language. Perhaps some of these non-Indo-European women in Indo-European society were taken as booty during raids by the youth bands. It seems unlikely, however, that marriages between Indo-European-speaking men and nonlocal women were predominantly the result of abduction. If marriage was seen as an indicator of group membership, it is likely that marrying off their daughters into Indo-European families was one of the ways in which non-Indo-European peoples would try to align themselves with the dominant Indo-European groups.

The linguistic data indicate that Proto-Indo-European marriage probably took place primarily between members of the same community. The genetic evidence from Corded Ware Europe suggests, however, that endogamy was at least partly abandoned for practical reasons when Indo-European males started to move out of their original communities and migrate to new territories. The genetic evidence also suggests that patrilineality remained largely unchanged during the migrations associated with the spread of Indo-European languages. The fact that at least the westward migrations were male-biased betrays a difference in societal roles between males and females. Males were clearly more mobile than females and could move more independently of other members of the family, which might confirm that the all-male youth bands of speakers of early Indo-European languages played a significant role in these migrations. Upon arrival in Europe, Steppe males mated with local females, while local males apparently became more restricted in their possibilities to father offspring. This is in accordance with the linguistic evidence that the Steppe males came from a society with a patrilineal kinship system.

In some Bronze Age settlements in the Central European area where males show predominant Steppe ancestry, there is also clear evidence for patrilocality. A large percentage of the women in these settlements were of nonlocal origin (Sjörgen et al. 2016; Knipper et al. 2017; Mittnik et al. 2019), pointing to a patrilocal society in which there was systematic mobility of women. Isotope analysis shows that the women moved away from the area where they had grown up when they were in their adolescence or later, which makes it likely that the movement was associated with marriage practices. Burial practices suggest that these women became integrated into the society of their husbands, though curiously, no offspring of the nonlocal women have been identified in the graves of the settlements. Although neither their DNA nor their material culture can show

[12] This root etymology goes back to the nineteenth century; cf. Dellbrück (1889: 482). The *Lexikon der indogermanischen Verben* (Rix 2001) reconstructs **$h_1$euH-* on the strength of the rather doubtful comparison with Hittite *iya(u)watta* 'erholt sich'. García Ramón (1996) has connected it with Latin *avēre* 'wish, take pleasure in', for which he reconstructs a causative **$h_2$ouh$_1$-éi̯o/e-*. Even if the root etymology is correct (it is explicitly rejected by the *Lexikon der indogermanischen Verben*), the semantics of the Latin verb rather point to a stative verb **He/ouH-eh$_1$-*. The full grade of the root and the absence of parallel formations elsewhere suggest that this verb is a relatively recent secondary formation, so no conclusions about the color of the laryngeal, if there was one, should be based on *avēre*.

[13] Archaeological traces of associated dog sacrifices have been suspected in Scandinavia (Gräslund 2004) and southern Russia (Brown & Anthony 2017).

[14] Sergent (2003), Kristansen et al. (2017). On *Männerbünde*, see further Falk (1986), Kershaw (2000), and McCone (1987, 2002) with references to the relevant literature.

[15] In Vedic society, youth bands were associated with horse-riding (Falk 1994). It is possible that this is a continuation of the Proto-Indo-European situation. If this is true, the spread of Indo-European languages might also be visible in ancient equine DNA. Note, however, that the silver Gundestrup cauldron, which is dated to the first centuries BCE, depicts what is usually thought to be a Celtic youth band as foot soldiers, while more mature warriors are depicted on horseback.

us which language these people spoke, it is very likely that the men spoke an Indo-European language, while, especially in the early Bronze Age, the native language of some of the women (or their recent ancestors) may well have belonged to a different language family.

The consistently patrilocal Indo-European system explains why it was so often an Indo-European language that prevailed in the genetically and linguistically diverse societies that arose as a result of the migrations of Indo-Europeans. The long-term effects of matrilocal and patrilocal systems on language transmission (and vice versa) have been shown to be significant in a recent case study of the relationship between genetics and language on Sumba and Timor (Lansing et al. 2017). This study showed that, on these islands, consistent patrilocality or matrilocality caused social communities to become speech communities.

References

Anthony, David W. & Dorcas R. Brown. 2017. The dogs of war: A Bronze Age initiation ritual in the Russian steppes. *Journal of Anthropological Archaeology* 48: 134–148.

Barlau, Stephen B. 1976. An outline of Germanic kinship. *Journal of Indo-European Linguistics* 4: 97–129.

Beekes, Robert S. P. 1976. Uncle and nephew. *Journal of Indo-European Linguistics* 4: 43–63.

1992. "Widow." *Historische Sprachforschung* 105: 171–188.

2010. *Etymological dictionary of Greek*. Leiden: Brill.

Benveniste, Émile. 1969. *Le Vocabulaire des institutions indo-européennes. Tome I : Économie, parenté, société. Tome II : Pouvoir, droit, religion*. Paris: Minuit.

Bremmer, Jan. 1976. Avunculate and fosterage. *Journal of Indo-European Linguistics* 4: 65–78.

Damgaard, P. de B. et al. 2018. The first horse herders and the impact of Early Bronze Age steppe expansions into Asia. *Science* 360: 6396.

Delbrück, Berthold. 1889. Die indogermanischen Verwandtschaftsnamen: Ein Beitrag zur vergleichenden Altertumskunde. *Abhandlungen der Königlichen Sächsischen Gesellschaft der Wissenschaften* 11, 380–606.

Falk, Harry. 1986. *Bruderschaft und Würfelspiel. Untersuchungen zur Entwicklungsgeschichte des vedischen Opfers*. Freiburg: Hedwig Falk.

1994. Das Reitpferd im vedischen Indien. In: Bernhard Hänsel & Stefan Zimmer (ed.), *Die Indogermanen und das Pferd. Akten des internationalen interdisziplinären Kolloquiums. Freie Universität Berlin, 1.–3. Juli 1992*, 91–101. Budapest: Archaeolingua.

Friedrich, Paul. 1966. Proto-Indo-European kinship. *Ethnology* 5 (1): 1–36.

1980. Review of Szemerényi 1977. *Language* 56: 186–192.

García Ramón, José Luis. 1996 Lat. *auēre* "desear," *(ad)iuuāre* "ayudar" e IE *h_2*e̯uh*$_1$- "dar preferencia, apreciar." In: Alfred Bammesberger & Friedrich Heberlein (ed.), *Akten des VIII. internationalen Kolloquiums zur lateinischen Linguistik*, 32–49. Heidelberg: Winter.

Gates, Henry Phelps. 1971. The kinship terminology of Homeric Greek. Supplement. *International Journal of American Linguistics* 37(4).

Goedegebuure, Petra. 2004. Troonsopvolging in het Oud-Hethitische Rijk: Patrilineair, matrilineair of avunkulair? *Phoenix* 50(1):5–21.

Goldberg, Amy, et al. 2017. Ancient X chromosomes reveal contrasting sex bias in Neolithic and Bronze Age Eurasian migrations. *Proceedings of the National Academy of Sciences* 114 (10): 2657–2662.

Gräslund, Anne-Sofie. 2004. Dogs in graves: A question of symbolism? In: Barbro Santillo Frizell (ed.), *Pecus: Man and animal in antiquity*, 171–180. Rome: Swedish Institute.

Greene, David H. 1998 *Language and history in the early Germanic world*. Cambridge: Cambridge University Press.

Hettrich, Heinrich. 1985. Indo-European kinship terminology in linguistics and anthropology. *Anthropological Linguistics* 27 (4): 453–480.

Juras, Anna, et al. 2018 Mitochondrial genomes reveal an east to west cline of steppe ancestry in Corded Ware populations. *Scientific Reports* 8: 11603.

Kershaw, Kris. 2000. *The one-eyed god: Odin and the (Indo-) Germanic Männerbünde*. Washington, DC: Institute for the Study of Man.

Kloekhorst, Alwin. 2008. *Etymological dictionary of the Hittite inherited lexicon*. Leiden: Brill.

Knipper, Corina, et al. 2017. Female exogamy and gene pool diversification at the transition from the Final Neolithic to the Early Bronze Age in central Europe. *Proceedings of the National Academy of Sciences* 114(38): 10083–10088.

Kristiansen, Kristian, et al. 2017 Re-theorising mobility and the formation of culture and language among the Corded Ware Culture in Europe. *Antiquity* 91(356): 334–347.

Lansing, J. Stephen, et al. 2017. Kinship structures create persistent channels for language transmission. *Proceedings of the National Academy of Sciences* 114(49): 12910-12915.

Lubotsky, Alexander. 2001. The Indo-Iranian substratum. In: Christian Carpelan, Asko Parpola, & Petteri Koskikallio (ed.), *Early contacts between Uralic and Indo-European: Linguistic and archaeological considerations. Papers presented at an international symposium held at the Tvärminne Research Station of the University of Helsinki 8–10 January 1999*, 301–317. Helsinki: Suomalais-Ugrilainen Seura.

Mallory, James P. 1998. A European perspective on Indo-Europeans in Asia. In: V. H. Mair (ed.), *The Bronze Age and Early Iron Age peoples of eastern Central Asia*, 175–201. Washington, DC & Philadelphia: Institute for the Study of Man & University of Pennsylvania Museum.

Mallory, James P., & Douglas Q. Adams (ed.). 1997. *Encyclopedia of Indo-European culture*. London: Fitzroy Dearborn.

2006. *The Oxford introduction to Proto-Indo-European and the Proto-Indo-European world*. Oxford: Oxford University Press.

McCone, Kim R. 1987. Hund, Wolf und Krieger bei den Indogermanen. In: Wolfgang Meid (ed.), *Studien zum indogermanischen Wortschatz*, 101–154. Innsbruck: IBS.

2002. Wolfsbessenheit, Nacktheit, Einäugigkeit und verwandte Aspekte des altkeltischen Männerbündes. In: Rahul Peter Das & Gerhard Meiser (ed.), *Geregeltes Ungestüm: Bruderschaft und Jugendbünde bei indogermanischen Völkern*, 43–67. Bremen: Hempen.

Mittnik, A., et al. 2019. Kinship-based social inequality in Bronze Age Europe. *Science* 366(6466): 731–734.

Narasimhan, Vagheesh M., et al. 2019. The formation of of human populations in South and Central Asia. *Science* 365 (6457).

Ó Cathasaigh, Tomás. 1986. The sister's son in early Irish literature. *Peritia* 5: 128–160.

Olsen, Birgit Anette. 2019. Aspects of family structure among the Indo-Europeans. In: Birgit Anette Olsen, Thomas Olander, & Kristian Kristiansen (ed.), *Tracing the Indo-Europeans. New evidence from archaeology and historical linguistics*, 145–163. Oxford: Oxbow.

2020. Kin, clan and community in Proto-Indo-European society. In: Benedicte Nielsen Whitehead, Birgit Anette Olsen, & Janus Bahs Jacquet (ed.), *Kin, clan and community in prehistoric Europe*, 39–180. Copenhagen: Museum Tusculanum Press.

Petit, Daniel. 2010. Suffix transfer in Baltic. *Baltistica* 45(2): 173–184.

Pronk, Tijmen. 2013. Notes on Balto-Slavic etymology: Russian *norov*, *mjat'*, *ruž'ë*, dialectal *xajat'* 'to care', *xovat'* 'to keep' and their Slavic and Baltic cognates. *Wiener Slavistisches Jahrbuch. Neue Folge* 1: 294–303.

Risch, Ernst. 1944. Betrachtungen zu den indogermanischen Verwandtschaftsnamen. *Museum Helveticum: Schweizerische Zeitschrift für klassische Altertumswissenschaft* 1(2): 115–122.

Rix, Helmut (ed.). 2001^{2}. *Lexikon der indogermanischen Verben. Die Wurzeln und ihre Primärstammbildungen*. Wiesbaden: Reichert.

Sergent, Bernard. 2003. Les troupes de jeunes hommes et l'expansion indo-européenne. *Dialogues d'histoire ancienne* 29(2): 9–27.

Sjörgen, Karl Göran et al. 2016. Diet and mobility in the Corded Ware of Central Europe. *PLoS ONE* 11(5): e0155083.

Sürenhagen, Dietrich. 1998. Verwandtschaftsbeziehungen und Erbrecht im althethitischen Königshaus vor Telipinu – ein erneuter Erklärungsversuch. *Altorientalische Forschungen* 25: 75–94.

Szemerényi, Oswald. 1977. *Studies in the kinship terminology of the Indo-European languages, with special reference to Indian, Iranian, Greek and Latin*. Leiden: Brill.

Wackernagel, Jacob. 1912. *Über einige antike Anredeformen*. Göttingen: Officina academica Dieterichiani.

Zimmer, Stefan. 2003. Glimpses of Indo-European law. In: F. J. M. Feldbrugge (ed.), *The law's beginnings*, 115–136. Leiden: Martinus Nijhoff.

20 MARRIAGE STRATEGIES AND FOSTERAGE AMONG THE INDO-EUROPEANS: A LINGUISTIC PERSPECTIVE*

BIRGIT A. OLSEN

20.1 Introduction

In recent years, it has become increasingly clear that a combination of genetics, archaeology, and historical-comparative linguistics is the only sensible way to reach a deeper and more subtle understanding of the Indo-European question. By now, there is practically general agreement that at the very least, "Indo-Tocharian,"[1] defined as the predecessor of all branches of the Indo-European family with the exception of Anatolian, originated in the Pontic–Caspian steppe. The speakers of this common language have been archaeologically connected with the Yamnaya horizon, later continued in northern Europe as the Corded Ware culture.[2]

There are probably several interrelated reasons why Indo-European-speaking populations were so successful in imposing their language and important features of their culture on the indigenous Neolithic farmers of Europe. One important element may have been the spread of the plague, since the bacteria Yersenia pestis has been found in densely populated Neolithic cultures (Rasmussen et al. 2015). However, an equally significant part of the explanation should probably be found in early Indo-European society, with its characteristic features of pastoralism, a strictly hierarchic structure, a patrilocal family pattern, and organized warbands. The potential of linguistic studies besides archaeology and genetics can hardly be overrated. We are now in a position to combine classical historical-comparative linguistics with a sociolinguistic approach, giving Indo-European studies a voice spanning thousands of years and contributing to the ongoing discussions of migrations and language change.

In the following, I will concentrate on the linguistic basis of a few defining features of Indo-European society: exogamy, marriage strategies and alliances, institutionalized fosterage, and socially conditioned language change.

20.2 Indo-European Marriages Were Exogamous

The idea that Indo-European marriages were exogamous belongs to the stock knowledge of the field, going back to Delbrück (1889). This is most clearly illustrated by the root *h_2u̯edh$_{1/2}$-*, which has the double meaning of 'lead, conduct' and 'marry' with respect to the groom, thus suggesting that brides were "led" or "conducted" into marriage; cf. e.g. Welsh *dyweddïo* 'betroth', Old English *weddian* 'marry', Lithuanian *vedù* 'lead, marry (of the man)', Old Russian *vesti ženu* '(lead →) marry a woman', Avestan *-uuadaϑa-* 'marriage' (in *xvaētuuadaϑa-* 'marriage to one's own kin'), and, with lexical substitution, Latin *uxōrem ducere* '(lead →) take a wife'.[3] The same verb is attested in Hittite *huet-* 'draw, pull, pluck, drag, move along, make march', which, since it is semantically more precise than just 'lead', probably represents the older meaning. The Hittite verb is e.g. used for dragging sheep to slaughter and marching troops.[4] With all due reservations, one may thus suspect that the bleached meaning 'lead (into marriage)', attested in the European branches and Indo-Iranian, is a common extra-Anatolian innovation, while the Anatolian evidence points to a time when brides were typically marched along, perhaps in caravans from their homestead to a new family in a distant land.[5]

Another possible linguistic indication of exogamy is the specific term for the husband's brother's wife, *(h$_1$)i̯énh$_2$ter-*, at least as secured for Core Indo-European, defined as Indo-European after the separation of first Anatolian, secondly

* For a more detailed presentation of Indo-European social vocabulary, especially kinship terminology, cf. Olsen (2020) and the general overview in Olsen (2019).

1 Terminology according to Olander (2019).

2 Cf. e.g. Anthony & Brown (2017), and the groundbreaking articles by Allentoft et al. (2015) and Haak et al. (2015).

3 Cf. also, from the same root, Lithuanian *vedẽklė*. Old Church Slavic *nevěsta* 'bride, daughter-in-law'.

4 Cf. Puhvel (1991: 343–352) for attestations.

5 In his general attempt to turn the tables, James Clackson (2007: 205–206) has objected that "it is not clear that the semantic range of these verbs really supports a patrilocal marriage pattern and does not just refer to some aspect of the marriage ceremony," even going so far as to say that this is "the only purely *linguistic* evidence against matrilocality." However, as we shall see below, this view is contradicted by the terminology for in-laws.

Tocharian;[6] cf. Vedic *yā́tar*-, Pashto *yor*, Greek pl. εἰνατέρες, Lat. pl. *ianitrices*, Old Slavic *jętry*, and probably Armenian *ner*, all with exactly the same specialized meaning. The word has no recognized etymology, but it belongs to a small group of kinship terms ending in **-(h$_2$)ter*-, also including **ph$_2$tér*- 'father', **máh$_2$ter*- 'mother', **d^{h}ugh$_2$tér*- 'daughter', and **b^{h}ráh$_2$ter*- 'brother'. Only two members of this group, 'father' and 'daughter', conform to the regular pattern of accent and ablaut,[7] both probably including the agent noun suffix **-ter*-, the father as the 'protector', the daughter less safely identified as the 'producer' or even 'milkmaid' (?).[8]

It therefore seems likely that the remaining terms in **-(h$_2$) ter*- owe their exact shape to influence from one of these archaic formations. Thus **máh$_2$ter*- 'mother' may be the result of a contamination between a nursery word **mā* or **māmā* 'mummy' and **ph$_2$tér*- 'father'. Similarly, **h$_1$i̯énh$_2$ter*- may now be analyzed as an active participle, **h$_1$i̯éh$_2$nt*- 'traveling', contaminated with the word for 'daughter', **d^{h}ugh$_2$tér*- (**h$_1$i̯eh$_2$nt*- + *-h$_2$ter*- → **h$_1$i̯énh$_2$ter*- by dissimilation/metathesis). To the young females of the family, the husband's brother's wife would thus be the 'traveler' (cf. Olsen 2020: 136–138). The underlying root **h$_1$i̯eh$_2$*- indicates long-distance travelling, by carriage or boat, on horseback or on foot, as suggested by numerous attestations of the Vedic verb *yā́ti* beside Lithuanian *jóti*, which is lexicalized in the meaning 'ride (on horseback)'. If the proposed analysis is correct, the women of an Indo-European household, with the notable exception of the wife of the head of family, are then defined as belonging to one of two categories: the (still unmarried) daughters on the one hand, and the 'travelers' or brides taken from afar on the other.

A third term, which, mechanically projected back into Proto-Indo-European, would be **ĝl̥h$_2$u*- or the like, is continued in Greek γάλως, Latin *glōs*, Old Slavic *zъlъva*, and Armenian *tal* (with initial *t*- from *taygr* 'husband's brother'), all with the meaning 'husband's sister', i.e., the daughters of the family seen from the perspective of the married women. Characteristically, this word, as opposed to all other widely attested kinship terms, withstands any morphological analysis from an Indo-European point of view and rather has the appearance of a 'Wanderwort' with similarities to Proto-Uralic **käliw* 'sister-in-law'.[9] Koivulehto (1994: 140) considers the possibility of an early loanword *from* Indo-European, but since the word is internally unanalyzable, it is more likely to have been borrowed *into* Indo-European, a precious relic of a language introduced by foreign women and referring to their sisters-in-law within the Indo-European household.

6 Sometimes also known as "Classic Indo-European." Olander (2019) introduces the term "Indo-Celtic" for this stage, assuming that Italo-Celtic was the next node to split off from the family tree after Tocharian. Obviously, the fact that a given term is attested in neither Anatolian nor Tocharian is no definite proof against its coinage in "Indo-Tocharian" or even Proto-Indo-European.

7 Regular alternating paradigms only include one "full grade" (element including the vowel **-e*-) which carries the accent, thus e.g. acc.sg. **d^{h}ugh$_2$-tér-m̥* vs. dat.sg. **d^{h}ugh$_2$-tr-éi̯* 'daughter'.

8 Cf. Olsen (2020) with references.

9 Cf. Koivulehto (1994: 140) and Bjørn (2017: 55–56).

All these details point to exogamy in a wider sense. Brides were taken not only from outside the clan, but even from foreign speech communities. In this perspective, the tenacious myth of institutionalized cross-cousin marriage seems quite out of place, and, as we shall see in the following, there is no sound basis for such an assumption.

Thus the linguistic evidence is fully compatible with the archaeological findings from Eulau (Kristiansen et al. 2017), the Lech River valley (Knipper et al.), the young women from Egtved and Skrydstrup (Frei et al. 2015; Persson 2017), and lately the beautiful holistic study by Mittnik et al. (2019), pointing to an extreme mobility of young females in the late Neolithic and Bronze Age.

20.3 Exogamous Marriages Implied Political and Military Alliances

Beyond any doubt, the conventions of marriage underwent fundamental changes throughout the long period and many ramifications of transition from the pastoral society of the Pontic–Caspian steppes to the cultures of the Indo-Iranians, Greeks, Celts, etc. Some details can be traced all the way back to Proto-Indo-European, while others can only be demonstrated for a more restricted dialect area. Even for the oldest period, it is no foregone conclusion that marriage strategies and wedding conventions were the same for all social strata. Here, it will suffice to mention some general features.

It has often been pointed out that there is no precise terminology describing a man's relatives by marriage, as opposed to the subtle distinctions made by the wife between e.g. 'husband's brother', 'husband's sister', and 'husband's brother's wife'. On the other hand, the reference to male in-laws by terms of 'binding' or 'connecting' is extremely widespread. E.g., Greek πενθερός from **b^{h}end^h*- 'bind', beside the oldest attested meaning 'father-in-law', can also be used about the 'brother-in-law' and 'son-in-law'; Vedic *bándhu*-, from the same root means, 'relative' in general, most often on the side of the woman; Lithuanian *bandžius* and Old Frisian *bōst* denote 'in-laws' in a wider sense; while Lithuanian *beñdras* is merely a 'partner, associate'.

From the synonymous root continued in Latin *ligō* 'bind', Lithuanian *laíg(u)onas* has the meaning 'wife's brother', and similarly, Hittite *ishanitar*- 'relative by marriage' is derived from the root **sh$_2$ai̯*- 'bind', as in 3.pl. *ishiyanzi* 'they bind', Vedic *ā siṣāya* = Avestan *ā-hišāiiā* 'holds captive'. Finally, the hitherto unexplained Armenian *hor* 'son-in-law' may regularly go back to **soros* 'a connecter' or 'connection' (Olsen 2020: 127–128). This combined evidence makes it reasonable to believe that alliances between in-laws were essential from the earliest period. In some cases, it even seems that intermarriage between two families could involve more than one daughter. At least, there exists a common word for men whose wives are sisters in Greek εἰλίονες: Old Norse *svilar*.

The question is now what sort of 'bindings' or alliances we should envisage. Undoubtedly, one aspect was guest friendship, for which we have ample evidence from at least Core Indo-European, also from a linguistic point of view. In particular, this includes the word for host/guest attested in Italic, Germanic, and Slavic, *g^hostis* > Latin *hostis* 'stranger; enemy'; Gothic *gasts* 'guest'; Old English *giest* 'stranger, guest'; and Old Slavic *gostь* 'guest', probably derived from the root *g^hes-* 'eat' (Vedic *ághas* 'ate'), suggesting that an important aspect of guest friendship was the banquet.[10] An extended version of the root may be found in Greek ξέν(ϝ)ος 'stranger, guest friend'.[11]

Another essential purpose of marriage alliances would have been military support. The importance of such connections may be illustrated by the following passage from the Odyssey (8.581–89):

Did some kinsman (πηός) of yours fall before Ilios, some good, true man, your daughter's husband (γαμβρός) or your wife's father (πενθερός), such as are nearest to one after one's own kin and blood? Or was it by chance some comrade (ἑταῖρος) dear to your heart, some good, true man?

Here the relative importance of the connections is clearly defined. The first in line are one's own blood relatives; then we have the relatives by marriage, and finally, the wider circle of guest friends, where it is noticeable that ἑταῖρος, like Lithuanian *svẽčias* 'guest', derives from **su̯eto-*, an extension of the reflexive pronoun **su̯e-* 'oneself, one's own'. Further cognates are Greek ἔτης 'clansman; citizen, private person' and Old Russian *svatъ* 'relative by marriage'.

The widespread use of the stem **su̯e-* for in-laws indicates that the Indo-Europeans, at least from the time of Core Indo-European, recognized their male in-laws as equals and independent individuals. Similarly, they most likely married their own daughters off to respected free men. A telling example is Old High German *gi-swio* 'sister's husband', from **sue̯i̯-(h_3)on (h_2)-*, literally 'someone of his own, with his own/separate authority'.[12] This stem is the basis of two derivatives: a feminine **su̯oi̯$h_3$niah$_2$-*, continued in Armenian *k^ceni* and the formally identical Lithuanian *svaínė*, both 'wife's sister', with the original meaning 'someone (f) under the dominance of an independent man';[13] and a masculine in Germanic **swainaz* 'someone (m) under the charge of an independent man'. Old Norse *sveinn* has the meaning 'young man, thrall, warrior', i.e., someone who somehow ranks below a master. Thus we here have a modest linguistic contribution to the understanding that in early Indo-European societies, all were not equal, and that there must have been a fundamental difference between free, independent men and those of inferior status.[14]

This brings us to the word family of **su̯eḱrúh$_2$-s* 'mother-in-law' and **su̯éḱuro-* 'father-in-law' with the derivative **su̯ēḱuró-*. Due to a preconceived idea that only the husband's blood relatives were of any significance, it has often been argued that these terms were originally only used by the wife for her husband's parents.[15] Truly, this is what we find in Greek, Armenian, and Balto-Slavic, with separate words for the wife's parents, e.g. Greek πενθερός 'wife's father', πενθερά 'wife's mother' (from **b^hend^h-*'bind'), but the other branches tell another story.

In Italic, Celtic, Germanic, Albanian, and Indo-Iranian, **su̯eḱrúh$_2$-* 'mother-in-law' is used indiscriminately for both sides of the family, sometimes even with the oldest attestations referring to the wife's mother (thus Latin *socrus*), and the same goes for the father-in-law, **su̯éḱuro-*. An important testimony is the derived adjective **su̯ēḱuró-* > Sanskrit *śvāśura-* 'pertaining to the father-in-law', lexicalized in the meaning (*'son of the father-in-law' >) 'wife's brother' in Kashmiri *hahar* and Pashai *išpairī*, and similarly, the oldest attestations of Old High German *swager* 'brother-in-law' are used for the wife's brother. Moreover, Pashto *xōṣ̌īna* < **hwasrū-aina-* 'wife's sister' is literally 'the one pertaining to the mother-in-law' (Morgenstierne 1927: 98), which evidently only makes sense if the **su̯eḱrúh$_2$-* denoted the wife's mother.

Consequently, it seems most likely that the Greek, Armenian, and Balto-Slavic usage, in which these words are restricted to the husband's family, is due to a later semantic development, which is not unnatural since in patrilocal societies, the husband's household will most often be the focal point.[16]

Clackson (2007: 205) refers to the matrilocal Laguna society of the Western Pueblos, which allegedly has a system of kinship terms typologically similar to Proto-Indo-European, with a set of terms for the husband's relatives, but no words for the wife's father etc. On this basis, he concludes that from a *linguistic* point of view, Indo-European society might have been matrilocal as well. This view, however, is contradicted by a closer analysis of kinship terms containing the reflexive stem **su̯e-*, which, as we have seen, cover all kinds of

10 Perhaps *g^hostis*, for which one would rather expect a meaning 'eating', is isolated from the compound *g^hosti-potis* (*'master of eating') > 'host'; cf. Latin **hosti-potis* > *hospes* 'host; guest', Old Slavic *gospodь* 'master'.

11 If the connection is correct, however, the morphological analysis is debatable (cf. e.g. Frisk II: 334; Beekes II: 1034). Perhaps the protoform *g^hsenu̯o-* (cf. Doric *ksenwos*) represents an *n*-stem followed by the suffix *-u̯o-*, which may have been analogically introduced from its opposite **ḱei̯u̯o-* 'domestic' (cf. Oscan *ceus*, Latin *cīvis* 'citizen', Gothic *heiwa-frauja* 'master of the house').

12 Cf. Olsen (2012) on the morphological analysis.

13 Before marriage, a young girl would be under the authority of her father; after marriage, under that of her husband.

14 Something similar is implied by the term **$h_1$leu̯d^{h}ero-* > Greek ἐλεύθερος, Latin *līber* 'free', containing the suffix of contrast *-*ero-* and from the same basic stem as German *Leute* 'people'. According to Polomé in Mallory & Adams (1997: 214), the original meaning was "*'of lawful birth', i.e. the legal position of an individual who is a full-fledged member of the ethnic community in contrast to outsiders or people subdued into servitude by war."

15 Cf. e.g. Buck (1949: 124): "used only by the wife of her husband's father or mother"; Pokorny (IEW 1043): "Mutter des Ehemannes" and "Vater des Ehemannes"; Huld and Mallory in Mallory & Adams (1997: 386–387): some branches (Italic, Celtic, Germanic, Albanian) *extend* the terms to cover both the husband's and the wife's in-laws.

16 If Graeco-Armenian was once a unity, this lexical specialization only has to have taken place twice.

independent relatives, but in particular those belonging to the wife's family.

One might expect that the linguistic evidence for a respectful relationship between the family of the groom and that of the bride would somehow be mirrored in the conventions and rituals relating to marriage. However, the question is difficult because our information must be extracted from sources of a vastly different age, and because the conventions most likely differed according to the social status of the couple. Thus, several ancient Indo-European cultures allow for cohabitation and abduction beside more formal traditions including some sort of economic exchange between the two families, be it payment of a bride-price, a dowry, or a combination of the two.

The linguistic evidence gives us reasons to believe that at least the bride-price, paid as a compensation to the bride's family, but probably also as a means of establishing a stable alliance between the two families,[17] belongs to a relatively old layer of Indo-European usage. This is substantiated by the existence of a common word for the phenomenon in several European branches of the Indo-European family: Old English *wituma* 'bride-price' (but Old High German *widamo* 'dowry'), Old Slavic *věno*, Greek ἔδνον 'bride-price'.

Another clue may be obtained by a closer view at some kinship terms. Thus, the formally difficult word for 'son-in-law', Ved. *jā́mātar-*, Avestan *zāmātar-*, Greek γαμβρός, Latin *gener* etc., has been derived from a root **ĝemh-* meaning 'buy (a wife)'; cf. Avestan *zəmanā-* 'payment, wages' beside Greek γαμέω 'marry'.[18] Additionally, Michael Janda (2020) has suggested that the word for the husband's brother, **dah₂i̯ér-*, in Latin *lēvir*,[19] Old English *tācor*, Old High German *zeihhur*, Greek δᾱήρ, Armenian *taygr*, Vedic *devár-*, Pashto *levar*, and Old Slavic *děverь*, is originally the 'distributer of gifts' (root **dah₂i̯-* 'distribute') in connection with wooing.

Overall, sporadic evidence for the payment of a bride-price is found throughout the Indo-European family, including Anatolian. Thus, Klingenschmitt (2008: 409–410) has pointed to the use of the root **kʷrei̯h₂-* 'buy' in Middle Irish *tochra* < **to-kʷrih₂o-* 'bride-price' beside Lithuanian **krienas* (gen. *krieno*) with the same meaning, indicating a lexical correspondence going back at least to Core Indo-European. Similarly, the archaic Greek word ὄαρ 'wife', as analyzed by Pinault (2013: 241, 2017: 101) and followed by Olsen (2020: 143), may be derived from a stem **u̯os-r̥* 'purchase'.

Most recently, de Lamberterie (2018), with reference to Daniel Kölligan (2014), has compared Armenian *ałǰik* 'young girl' with the Greek compound ἀλφεσίβοιος 'having the worth of (several) oxen', used as an epithet of πάρθενος 'young girl, virgin'. With a slight variation in the stem formations, both formations would contain the word for 'worth, price', **h₂(a)lgʷʰ-i-/*h₂algʷʰ-os*, and a stem derived from the noun 'cow', **gʷou̯-* (Greek βοῦς, Armenian *ku*). While this equation does not take us further back than Graeco-Armenian – if such a stage existed – the formation is still interesting, pointing back to a time when the bride-price consisted at least partly in cattle, as also attested in other Indo-European traditions,[20] and as is still the case in several present-day societies, especially in Africa.

In general, the pattern seems to be that "brideprice exists more frequently in primitive, tribal, and often nomadic societies" (Anderson 2007: 155), which would match our understanding of Proto-Indo-European society quite well.

20.4 Institutionalized Avunculate and Fosterage Does Not Go Back Further Than Core Indo-European

According to a theory going back to Émile Benveniste's studies in Indo-European society (1969: 227) and emphatically supported by Gamkrelidze & Ivanov (1995: 669–74), the Indo-Europeans practiced institutionalized cross-cousin marriage: in principle, a young man should marry a daughter of his father's sister. In this way, the paternal and the maternal line would be intimately tied together by bonds of marriage. Obviously, such a system would be incompatible with a strict principle of exogamy.

The alleged linguistic justification for Benveniste's assumption is the fact that the Indo-European word for 'grandfather', **h₂au̯h₂-s/*h₂au̯h₂-os* (e.g. Hittite *huhhas*, Latin *avus*), is the basis of several derivatives with the specific meaning 'mother's brother'; thus Latin *avunculus*, Breton *eontr*, Old Slavic *ujь*, Lithuanian *avýnas*, and Old High German *ōheim* < **awa-haima-* with the literal meaning 'belonging to grandfather's home'. If the 'grandfather' word originally had the restricted meaning of 'paternal grandfather', as has often been assumed, this apparent paradox might be solved if the **h₂au̯h₂os*, the father's father, at the same time denoted the mother's mother's brother.

It has sometimes been argued[21] that the 'skewing' of generations under common terms, in particular 'grandfather' = 'mother's brother' and 'grandson' = 'sister's son', pinpoints the Proto-Indo-European kinship system as belonging to the so-called Omaha type. However, the premises are wrong insofar as the term for 'mother's brother' is not *identical* with that for 'grandfather', just *derived* from it. Moreover, there is nothing to suggest that the **h₂au̯h₂os* would *only* have designated the

[17] Anderson (2008: 159) provides a present-day parallel: "In sub-Saharan Africa, a central purpose of the brideprice is to create an alliance between kinship groups."

[18] Cf. Tremblay (2003: 15) and further discussion of the formal details in Olsen (2020: 125–127).

[19] Perhaps with "Sabine *l*" and *-vir* by influence from *vir* 'man'.

[20] In the Old Indic *ārṣa* (priestly) marriage, the groom gives one or two pairs of kine to the bride's father, and in Irish tradition, part of the bride price typically consists in cattle.

[21] Cf. the sober account in Mallory & Adams (1997: 332–35).

'father's father'. On the contrary, we have no other word for 'mother's father', and this meaning is just more rarely attested because the focus is usually on the male lineage, which sometimes makes a specification useful, as in Latin *avus maternus* 'maternal grandfather'.[22]

Now, at least we have the ingredients for a linguistic understanding of the grandfather-uncle relationship: the 'avunculus', 'mother's brother', is simply the son of the 'avus', 'grandfather', in the meaning 'mother's father', while there seems to be no old designation for 'father's brother'.[23] The next question is *why* the mother's brother, presumably living in a different household, plays such a prominent part. At the least, the close bond between young boys and their maternal uncles is testified by numerous accounts from various European traditions, including Greek, Celtic, and Germanic;[24] cf. e.g. Tacitus' famous statement (*Germania* 20.5) that "sisters' sons are held in as much esteem by their uncles as by their fathers; indeed, some regard the relation as even more sacred and binding." The ultimate expression of this bond is fosterage in the mother's family, as expressed in the Irish law code *Senchas Már*: "the kinship of the mother or the kinship of fosterage: it happens that they are one and the same" (Bremmer 1976: 70).[25]

As mentioned above, the linguistic relationship between 'grandfather' and 'maternal uncle' somehow seems to be connected with the fact that the word for 'grandson', **né-pōt-s*,[26] in some branches takes on the meaning of 'sister's son'. This goes for Old Irish *nía* 'sister's son' (as opposed to the transparent *mac bráthar* 'brother's son'), Middle Welsh *nei* 'cousin; sister's son', and Serbo-Croatian *nȅćāk* 'sister's son'. In Old Lithuanian *nepuotìs* 'grandson' and 'nephew', Old English *nefa* 'grandson' and 'nephew, stepson', and later Latin *nepōs* 'nephew' beside Classical 'grandson', both meanings are attested. Already Delbrück (1889: 403) had realized that the terminological relationship between grandfather and mother's brother is found in exactly the same branches as those where the word for grandson merges with that for sister's son.

If the institution of fosterage within the mother's family is fully acknowledged, the reason for this striking correspondence becomes clear. The maternal uncle, the son of the **$h_2$au̯$h_2$os* on the mother's side, is the protector or even foster-father of the adolescent boy, but at the same time, from the point of view of the 'avunculus', the foster-son/sister's son becomes a member of the youngest generation, in other words a **népōts*, in his new family as he was in his paternal home. It is noteworthy that this state of affairs is only clearly demonstrable for the European branches of the Indo-European family, so at least on a linguistic basis, there is no reason to believe that the institution goes all the way back to Proto-Indo-European.

With our present conception of the Indo-European family, institutionalized fosterage is well motivated. In a patrilineal household, the presence of several sons, inevitably leading to internal strife for power, might well be a time bomb.[27] In the family of the maternal uncle, on the other hand, a boy would get not only care and protection, but presumably also the necessary military training, as we know from the well-documented institutions of *Jugendbünde* and *Männerbünde*, that would further strengthen the bonds between the two families. At least, the accounts of uncle-nephew relationships often imply warlike activities, as when the Irish hero Cú Chulain receives his weapons from his maternal uncle Conchobar.

20.5 Exogamy, Marriage Alliances, and Fosterage Are Important Factors in the Spread of Indo-European Languages

Recent investigations of traditional societies of Eastern Indonesia, described in an important paper on kinship structures and language change (Lansing et al. 2017),[28] show that matrilocality is consistent with transmission of the mother's language to the children, whereas in patrilocal societies, the father's language will prevail: "In traditional tribal societies, marriage customs channel language transmission. When women remain in their natal community and men disperse (matrilocality), children learn their mothers' language, and language correlates with maternally inherited mitochondrial DNA. For the converse kinship practice (patrilocality), language instead correlates with paternally inherited Y chromosome."

This description matches the Indo-European state of affairs perfectly. When a young bride came to stay in the patrilocal household of her husband, she must have taken with her the language of her childhood – as the other daughters-in-law, potentially coming from several different speech communities, would have done – but the only lingua franca would be the 'father-tongue' of her new home. Whether she taught her young children her own language we will never know, but communication between the children, the primary trigger of language change, would have had to be in the Indo-European tongue of the paternal clan. When, later, the boys were separated from

[22] Still, some features of the patrilineal Omaha type recur in Indo-European kinship terminology. Thus the identification between the father and his brothers (no separate word for 'father's brother') and between siblings and paternal cousins ('brother' = 'paternal cousin').

[23] Beekes (1976) and Olsen (2020: 95–104).

[24] Cf. in particular Bremmer (1976).

[25] The root **$h_2$al-* 'nourish, feed' is apparently only used for fosterage in Celtic and Italic, e.g. Old Irish *comalt* 'foster-brother', Middle Welsh *athrawon* < **altr-awon-* 'foster-uncle' (!), and Latin *alumnus* 'nursling, foster-son', a relic participle 'someone nourished'.

[26] According to the traditional interpretation 'having no power', as opposed to the **dém̥s potis* 'master of the house', ideally identical with the grandfather.

[27] Cf. the curious fact that the Vedic word for (*'father's brother's son' →) 'brother's son', *bhrā́tr̥vya-*, has the alternative meaning 'rival'.

[28] Kindly brought to my attention by Kristian Kristiansen.

their mothers and united under a military training whose structure was apparently entirely based on Indo-European practice, the situation would be the same. The language of prestige would prevail, and the mother-tongues of Europe were doomed, surviving only as substrata within lexical fields such as wildlife and agriculture where the indigenous European population had a special expertise.

References

Allentoft, Morten E., M. Sikora, K. G. Sjögren, S. Rasmussen, J. Stenderup, P. B. Damgaard, et al. 2015. Population genomics of Bronze Age Eurasia. *Nature* 522: 167–173.

Anderson, Siwan. 2008. The economics of dowry and brideprice. *Journal of Economic Perspectives* 21(4): 151–174.

Anthony, David W., & Dorcas R. Brown. 2017. Molecular archaeology and Indo-European linguistics. In: Bjarne Simmelkjær, Sandgaard Hansen, et al. (ed.), *Usque ad radices. Indo-European Studies in honour of Birgit Anette Olsen* (Copenhagen Studies in Indo-European 8), 25–54. Copenhagen: Museum Tusculanum Press.

Beekes, Robert. 1976. Uncle and nephew. *Journal of Indo-European Studies* 4(1): 43–63.

2010. *Etymological dictionary of Greek*. 2 vols. Leiden & Boston: Brill.

Benveniste, Émile. 1969. *Le vocabulaire des institutions indo-européennes. 1. Économie, parenté, societé*. Paris: Éditions de Minuit.

Bjørn, Rasmus Gudmundsen. 2017. *Foreign elements in the Proto-Indo-European vocabulary*. Master's thesis, University of Copenhagen.

Bremmer, Jan. 1976. Avunculate and fosterage. *Journal of Indo-European Studies* 4(1): 65–78.

Buck, Carl Darling. 1988 [1909]. *A dictionary of selected synonyms in the principal Indo-European languages. A contribution to the history of ideas*. Chicago & London: University of Chicago Press. First published 1909.

Clackson, James. 2007. *Indo-European linguistics: An introduction*. Cambridge: Cambridge University Press.

Delbrück, Berthold. 1889. *Die indogermanischen Verwandtschaftsnamen: ein Beitrag zur vergleichenden Altertumskunde* (Abhandlung der philologisch-historischen Classe der Königl. Sächsischen Gesellschaft der Wissenschaft, Band IX No. V). Leipzig: Hirtel.

Frei, Karin Margarita. 2015. Tracing the dynamic life story of a Bronze Age Female. *Scientific Reports* 5: 10431.

Frisk, Hjalmar. 1960–72. *Griechisches etymologisches Wörterbuch* 3 vols. Heidelberg: Winter.

Gamkrelidze, Thomas V., & Vjačeslav V. Ivanov. 1995. *Indo-European and the Indo-Europeans: A reconstruction and historical analysis of a proto-language and a proto-culture*. Vol 1. The text (Trends in Linguistics Studies and Monographs 80). Berlin & New York: Mouton de Gruyter.

Haak, Wolfgang et. al. 2015. Massive migration from the steppe was a source for Indo-European languages in Europe. *Nature* 522 (7555): 207–211.

IEW = Julius Pokorny. 1959. *Indogermanisches etymologisches Wörterbuch*. Bern: Francke.

Janda, Michael. 2020. Wooing in Indo-European culture. In: Benedicte Nielsen Whitehead, Birgit Anette Olsen, & Janus Bahs Jacquet (ed.), *Kin, clan and community in Indo-European Society* (Copenhagen Studies in Indo-European 9), 499–514. Copenhagen: Museum Tusculanum Press.

Klingenschmitt, Gert. 2008. Lit. *úošvis*. *Baltistica* 43(3): 405–430.

Knipper, Corina, et al. 2017. Female exogamy and gene pole diversification at the transition from the Final Neolithic to the Early Bronze Age in central Europe. *PNAS* 114(38): 10083–10088.

Koivulehto, Jorma. 1994. Indogermanisch–Uralisch: Lehnbeziehungen der (auch) Urverwandtschaft. In: Reinhard Sternemann (ed.), *Bopp-Symposium 1992 der Humboldt-Universität zu Berlin. Akten der Konferenz vom 24. 3.–26.3. 1992 aus Anlaß von Franz Bopps zweihundertjährigem Geburtstag am 14. 9. 1991*, 132–48. Heidelberg: Winter.

Kölligan, Daniel. 2014. *Indogermanisch und Armenisch. Studien zur historischen Grammatik des Klassisch-Armenischen*. Habilitationsschrift, Institut für Linguistik, Universität zu Köln.

Kristiansen, Kristian et al. 2017. Re-theorising mobility and the formation of culture and language among the Corded Ware Culture in Europe. *Antiquity* 91(353): 334–347.

Lamberterie, Charles de. 2018. Dérivé ou compose? L'adjectif *alkʿat* "pauvre" de l'arménien classique. Handout from the colloquium Dérivation nominale et innovations dans les langues indo-européennes anciennes, Université de Rouen, October 2018.

Lansing, J. Stephen, et al. 2017. Kinship structures create persistent channels for language transmission.

Mallory, James P., & Douglas Quentin Adams. 1997. *Encyclopedia of Indo-European culture*. London & Chicago: Fitzroy Dearborn.

Mittnik, Alissa. 2019. Kinship-based social inequality in Bronze Age Europe. *Science* 366(6466): 731–734.

Morgenstierne, Georg. 1927. *An etymological dictionary of Pashto* (Skrifter utgitt av Det Norske Videnskaps-Akademi i Oslo, II, Hist-Filos. Klasse 3). Oslo: Dybwad.

Olander, Thomas. 2019. Indo-European cladistic nomenclature. *Indogermanische Forschungen* 124: 231–244.

Olsen, Birgit Anette. 2012. A note on Indo-European in-laws. In Adam I. Cooper, Jeremy Rau, & Michael Weiss (ed.), *Multi nominis grammaticus: Studies in Classical and Indo-European linguistics in honor of Alan J. Nussbaum, on the occasion of his sixty-fifth birthday*, 213–216. Ann Arbor (MI): Beech Stave Press.

2019. Aspects of family structure among the Indo-Europeans. In: Birgit Anette Olsen, Thomas Olander, & Kristian Kristiansen (ed.), *Tracing the Indo-Europeans. New evidence from archaeology and historical linguistics*, 145–163. Oxford: Oxbow Press.

2020. Kin, clan and community in Proto-Indo-European. In: Benedicte Nielsen Whitehead, Birgit Anette Olsen, & Janus Bahs Jacquet (ed.), *Kin, clan and community in Indo-European Society* (Copenhagen Studies in Indo-European 9), 39–180. Copenhagen: Museum Tusculanum Press.

Persson, Charlotte Price. 2017. Another female Bronze Age icon is now known to have travelled across Europe. *Science Nordic*, April 10, 2017.

Pinault, Georges-Jean. 2013. The lady (almost) vanishes. In: Adam I. Cooper, Jeremy Rau, & Michael Weiss (ed.), *Multi nominis grammaticus: Studies in Classical and Indo-European linguistics in honor of Alan J. Nussbaum, on the occasion of his sixty-fifth birthday*, 240–254. Ann Arbor (MI): Beech Stave.

2017. The self-representation of the Indo-European society through kinship terms. In: Harald Bichlmeier & Andreas Opferman (ed.), *Das Menschenbild bei den Indogermanern*, 81–112. Hamburg: Baar.

Puhvel, Jaan. 1991. *Hittite etymological dictionary*. Vol. 3. Berlin & New York: Mouton de Gruyter.

Rasmussen, S., et al. 2015. Early divergent strains of Yersenia pestis in Eurasia 5,000 years ago. *Cell* 163(3): 571–82.

Tremblay, Xavier. 2003. *La déclinaison des noms de parenté indo-européens en -ter-* (Innsbrucker Beiträge zur Sprachwissenschaft 106). Innsbruck: Institut für Sprachwissenschaft der Universität Innsbruck.

21 FOSTERING WOMEN AND MOBILE CHILDREN IN FINAL NEOLITHIC AND EARLY BRONZE AGE CENTRAL EUROPE

PHILIPP W. STOCKHAMMER

Over the last several years, it has become clear that Central and Western Europe witnessed an enormous transformation during the third millennium – not only in cultural terms, as has long been clear from the appearance of the Corded Ware Complex (CWC) and the Bell Beaker Complex (BBC), but also from a genetic point of view: archaeogenetic analyses from Central Europe to the British Isles and the Iberian Peninsula have revealed genetic signatures with an origin in the western Eurasian steppe regions (Haak et al. 2015; Allentoft et al. 2015; Olalde et al. 2018; Olalde et al. 2019; Fernandes et al. 2020). Whereas early publications on this topic employed dubious vocabulary, like "Yamnaya migration," there is no doubt that the spread of genes from east to west in prehistoric times could only take place through mobile individuals. Archaeogenetic studies have also suggested a sex bias in these mobile people and that the migration process was predominantly related to male mobility (Goldberg et al. 2017). Since the publication of the scientific results for the Iberian Peninsula (Olalde et al. 2019), newspapers have even interpreted this as evidence of male hoards invading Spain and committing genocide of the local male population. There is no doubt that such simplified narratives do justice neither to archaeological theory nor to the aim of narrating a complex past in a comprehensible manner.

However, our current bioarchaeological data set has some important shortcomings and poses interpretational challenges that I would like to discuss in my contribution. Subsequently, I then dare to provide some rather speculative interpretations – speculative, because the material and scientific evidence is still too weak to fully support my hypothesis; however, they may serve as inspiration for further research. Thus, I think that it is time to instigate further debates about the mechanisms that transformed the genetic landscape during the third and early second millennium BCE. The following challenges must be addressed:

Challenge 1: The spread of steppe-related genetic signatures and its presumed male bias are insufficiently explained by the fact that two individuals of possibly different geographic origin/genetic background reproduced. It should also not be excluded that local males were killed in violent conflicts with the newcomers in larger numbers than females, although current archaeological evidence instead points to the fact that whole communities were killed, irrespective of age and/or gender (Schroeder et al. 2019). The strong genetic impact of mobile groups with ancestors in the steppes is only possible if there was a high, or at least higher, chance that children resulting from this union had a better chance of surviving until the age of fertility than children of different cultural backgrounds. Therefore, we must think simultaneously about both the spread of genetic signatures and the subsequent means of child-raising.

Challenge 2: Genetic results indicated a male bias in the spread of the steppe signature from east to west (Goldberg et al. 2017), and genetic admixture with individuals of local origins increased from east to west in the area of the Corded Ware Complex (Juras et al. 2018). Models have been proposed to reflect how first-generation male migrants procreated with women from Neolithic groups who lived in the respective regions before the arrival of the migrants (Kristiansen et al. 2017). Mobile groups of young men with predatory behaviors were proposed to have had a crucial role in taking these women from local groups as captives and producing offspring with them (Kristiansen et al. 2017; Anthony 2020; Kristiansen 2020). However, these models of (male-induced) female mobility based on rape seem to be in opposition to the results of strontium isotope analyses, which point to a stable and predominantly female mobility based on reciprocity between communities during the third and early second millennium BCE. The latter can only be explained by a long-term and stable system of exchange of marital partners through collaborative networks (Frei et al. 2015; Frei et al. 2017; Knipper et al. 2017; Mittnik et al. 2019; Sjögren et al. 2016; Sjögren et al. 2020). Evidence is growing for the existence of clearly patrilocal residential rules in different regions of Central Europe, with an increasing number of case studies from Southern Germany and beyond (Knipper et al. 2017; Mittnik et al. 2019; Sjögren et al. 2020). At the same time, the genetic signature of female individuals in the Lech valley became more and more "Neolithic" over time, whereas the male individuals did not and remained very much steppe-related (Mittnik et al. 2019). Unless one proposes a dramatic shift of marital practices from mobile young men raping local women during the early days of the Corded Ware Complex to patrilocal residential rules based on reciprocity in the subsequent millennium, these two models can hardly be combined.

Providing a possible answer to challenge 1 demands a better understanding of the factors that could enhance the number of children surviving until fertility. It forces us to shift our focus from male individuals with steppe ancestry moving through Europe and siring children to rethinking motherhood and modes of childcare in local contexts.[1]

Several factors have a positive impact on the number of children being born and reaching the relevant age, among them: first, sufficient nutrition (including extensive breastfeeding) of the children (Rebay-Salisbury 2017b; Dunne et al. 2019); second, female fertility increasing with sufficient nutrition of the women, shorter breastfeeding periods, and reduced female workloads (Eshed et al. 2004); third, sufficient caretaking for the children; and fourth, the survival of the parents (or grandparents or other close members of the social network), or at least some of them, from the children's infancy until at least the moment when the oldest sibling is able to provide sufficient nutrition and care to his/her younger siblings. Here, the woman's risk of dying during pregnancy, childbirth, or childbed (ca. 15 % of all women, according to Rebay-Salisbury 2017a: 64) needs to be taken into account, as well as the risk of death due to infectious diseases like the plague, which hit third- and second-millennium BCE societies all over Europe (Rasmussen et al. 2015; Andrades Valtueña et al. 2017). The comprehensive anthropological study of almost two hundred Bell Beaker and Early Bronze Age individuals from the Southern Bavarian Lech valley showed that most individuals died either between twenty and thirty-nine years or before the age of six (Massy 2018). Therefore, there must have been an extremely high chance that the mother or even both parents died before their youngest child reached the age of five to six years, when the mortality rate for children suddenly strongly decreases (Eshed et al. 2004).

Several possible strategies could have lowered the main risks associated with challenge 1, i.e., the death of the mother and/or the child(ren). One possibility would have been feeding children with breast milk from wet-nurses if the biological mother was not able to provide sufficient milk or died in childbed. As specialists of breast-milk production, wet-nurses would not only provide sufficient milk for the child, but, in case the biological mother survived, they could get pregnant again much earlier, as breastfeeding reduces female fertility. Therefore, wet-nurses could function as a kind of insurance, as they guaranteed optimal nutrition for the child and improved caretaking, especially in cases where other relatives could not fulfil this job due to early death, travel, workload, or young age.

A better understanding of challenge 2 requests rethinking modes of individual mobility and their institutionalization. As long as an individual is not a single genetic outlier, archaeogenetic analyses usually show mobility of ancestors based on different patterns of genetic admixture, and thus, mobility in the past with regard to the period under study. On the contrary, strontium isotope analysis offers insights into individual mobility in different phases of childhood, if the geographical distribution of the strontium isotope ratios can provide sufficient diversity to trace nonlocal and/or mobile individuals, and therefore mobility, during the period under study. Neither shorter trips during childhood nor any kind of travel during adulthood that did not result in a permanent change of residence will be visible with strontium isotope analyses, which also yields only a minimum number of mobile individuals. In consequence, the male mobility demonstrated by archaeogenetics and female mobility based on isotopic data go together very well. However, this still does not explain the diverging development of female and male admixture proportions. It is difficult to explain why male lines remained more steppe-related over time than female lines – which became more closely related to the former local Neolithic communities – when the corresponding model of long-term, stable, and transregional patrilocal networks can only be explained by the exchange of marital partners between friendly communities. Such changes in admixture call for the existence of genetically different individuals (or even populations in the broader region) who reproduced from time to time – albeit in a systematic way, as the shifting of the male and female admixture in the Lech valley cannot be explained otherwise (Mittnik et al. 2019).

The transformation of the European gene pool during the third and early second millennium BCE leaves no doubt that these are societies in which the survival of as many children as possible, as well as different kinds of mobility, played a central role. However, it is to be expected that societies develop methods for keeping children alive in cases when, e.g., the parents or other closely related family members are no longer able to fulfil this role. Archaeogenetic analyses have now provided several – albeit rare – cases from the Final Neolithic and Early Bronze Age in Southern Germany and the Iberian peninsula in which a subadult individual was buried together with an adult woman in a single grave pit, yet the individuals were biologically unrelated, meaning that the adult woman was also not the biological mother of the subadult individual (Mittnik et al. 2019; Olalde et al. 2019). If we may look at the closeness of these individuals in their joint burial as an expression of the closeness of their relation during their lifetimes, one could interpret these cases as evidence for fostering children within a family or household. The existence of fostering is further evidenced by a small number of male individuals from the Final Neolithic to Early Bronze Age Lech valley farmsteads south of present-day Augsburg: with the help of strontium isotope analysis, we identified male individuals who left the Lech valley (and also Southern Germany south of the Danube) around the age of seven years. They returned to the Lech valley as young adults, probably around the age of seventeen or slightly later, and possibly together with a female partner (Knipper et al. 2017). The continuity of such a system between 2500 and 1700 BCE would not have been possible without the existence of a reliable system of transport that enabled the safe travel of children over

[1] Projects like Katharina Rebay-Salisbury's ERC Starting Grant, The Value of Mothers to Society, have already been producing very relevant data in this line of thinking.

wide distances – at least 300 to 400 km in the case of the Lech valley – providing, e.g., guidance, food, accommodation, etc. during the trip. Moreover, a significant number of these boys must have survived in their new home for at least ten years in order to be able to return to the Lech valley afterward. Even if evidence for such fostering networks outside the Lech valley is still weak (but see Sjögren et al. 2020), it is beyond doubt that such a system could only be stable and functional if a significant number of communities participated in and/or supported the mobility of the children. Sending children to distant places to be brought up and work is well known in human history throughout space and time (Lallemand 2007; Müller-Scheeßel et al. 2015; O'Donnell 2020). The reason for sending children away to other places differs from case to case: it is possible that the adults wanted to remove the child from a dangerous environment or obtain further income and/or a future partner for him or her through the work undertaken at his or her new residence. In the Hebrew Bible, Jacob has to work on another farm in order to be able to take the daughter of his foster parents as his bride one day; from the seventeenth to nineteenth century AD, the so-called *Schwabenkinder*, children of very poor inhabitants of the Alps, were sent to Upper Swabia for work, where they would be provided with food and thus minimize their risk of death through malnutrition at home (Zimmermann, Brugger & Bereuter 2012). In the case of the Final Neolithic and Early Bronze Age, several factors could have played a role in the establishment of fostering systems: from building up transregional networks and obtaining partners to improving living conditions for children who could not be sufficiently fed otherwise. However, as our current evidence indicates that this practice was confined to male subadults, the network-and-bride option seems more probable.

Besides the evidence of fostering networks for male subadults, the rich bioarchaeological evidence from the Final Neolithic to Early Bronze Age Lech valley might provide further arguments that this society placed a particular emphasis on the successful raising of children. Through strontium isotope analysis, it has been possible to identify within every farmstead-related cemetery the existence of adult female individuals who were not born locally, but whose extraordinarily high strontium isotope ratios indicate an origin in either present-day Eastern Germany or Bohemia, where the nearest fertile soils with these specific strontium signatures are located. As both the second and third molars show a nonlocal signal, these women must have come to the Lech valley after the age of seventeen (Knipper et al. 2017). Their burials are among the richest in the Lech valley (Massy 2018). We have argued that these women not only arrived as possible marriage partners, but also brought with them advanced technological knowledge, as they originated in the area of the Únětice culture with its far better developed bronze technology (Knipper et al. 2017). Subsequently, comprehensive archaeogenetic analyses in combination with the strontium isotope analyses indicated that presumably all adult women buried in the Lech valley between 2500 and 1700 BCE came from outside the valley. However, it was surprising to see that in contrast to the other nonlocal women (who probably came from neighboring regions within Southern Germany), a significant number of women with very distant origins had no offspring in the valley (Mittnik et al. 2019). In one case, such a woman from afar was even buried together with a biologically nonrelated child (Mittnik et al. 2019).

This unexpected evidence could be explained in several ways: first, these women may indeed have had children, but their offspring were not buried in the same way as the children of the other women; second, their offspring may have been sent off through fostering networks shortly after birth, which entailed the return of children who had already died (cf. the evidence, albeit later, from Egtved, where a young woman traveled with a cremated child; Frei et al. 2015); third, these women may have been forced to abort their children in case of pregnancy; fourth, these women may never have become pregnant or, if they did, never carried the children to term.

Here, I wish to propose a new model for the significance of these women in Lech valley society, in addition to their importance as mediators of distant knowledge. In my view, it is plausible that these women had an important role as wet-nurses on the individual farmsteads. One hint for this interpretation is the abovementioned burial of the nonlocal woman with a biologically nonrelated child. Moreover, the permanent practice of breastfeeding would have reduced the fertility of the wet-nurses and shortened the period before the other women could get pregnant again after giving birth – especially when we assume two to three years as the usual period of breastfeeding of individual children (Fulminante 2015). It is interesting to note that contemporary literary sources from the Early Bronze Age urban center of Ebla in present-day Syria inform us of the importance of wet-nurses in this society. Here, women who originated from outside the urban community had an important role in feeding the children of elite families. However, the filter of available literary sources prevents us from understanding the extent of this system beyond the part of society that is mentioned in the texts. These wet-nurses also held a high status, one of them even a seal of her own, showing that their role in society was acknowledged and considered important (Biga 2000, 2016).

While I see no evidence for a link between the Early Bronze Age societies of Southern Germany and Syria in the late third millennium BCE, the textual evidence from Ebla nevertheless informs us of a contemporaneous system that should at least be taken into consideration in trying to explain the role of nonlocal women in the Lech valley, apart from their importance as mediators of technological knowledge. If their interpretation as wet-nurses is correct, these women could have become pregnant at their place of origin, but had to leave their first child there and then travel, without the child, to the Lech valley for two to three months. During this time, they would have had to continue producing milk through manual practices in order to sustain ongoing lactation. It is also possible that they became pregnant in the Lech valley for the first time, and that their child and all possible subsequent children were then sent back to their place of origin or not buried together with the other inhabitants of the respective farmstead. Moreover, manual practices even enable women to produce milk who have not been pregnant before and this is even possible after menopause. If my interpretation of this specific group of women as wet-nurses is correct, it would provide further strong evidence for a society that made a huge investment in creating a sociocultural environment that optimized the number of children born and raised, as it distinguished between those women who continuously had to give birth, but not breastfeed, and other women who were specialized in nourishing children and childcare. The significantly higher number of offspring resulting from this system might explain why the new genetic signatures had such a transformative impact.

The existence of a societal system optimized for child-raising still does not explain our second challenge, i.e., the genetic shift of female individuals toward Neolithic genetic signatures that existed in Central Europe before the emergence of the steppe-related signatures. At the same time, male offspring do not show this shift toward former Neolithic signatures, despite the female shift. From an archaeological point of view, this can most easily be explained by Final Neolithic and Early Bronze Age communities taking women from coexisting communities with roots in the Late Neolithic (Sjögren et al. 2016; Kristiansen et al. 2017; Sjögren et al. 2020). There is indeed evidence for the killing of families and/or the inhabitants of farmsteads in the archaeological evidence of the third millennium BCE (Haak et al. 2008; Schroeder et al. 2019), and there is no doubt that violence must have played a role in the course of the movement of individuals from the steppe regions toward the west. It is possible that at least some of the mothers visible in the family trees reconstructed for the Lech valley and Lower Bavaria (Mittnik et al. 2019; Sjögren et al. 2020) did not voluntarily join as marriage partners. However, we also should not exclude more peaceful modes of exchanging or acquiring marriage partners, which would better explain the long-term stability of this system. The development of the genetic admixture over time also indicates that only some of the women derived from the Neolithic-rooted communities, whereas other women (and maybe even men) must also have originated from communities with a much stronger steppe signature than in the Lech valley (cf. the corresponding evidence from Lower Bavaria: Sjögren et al. 2020). It is clear that an individual woman's role in the Lech valley community was clearly structured based on her geographical and cultural origin and that this structure remained stable over ca. 800 years.

At the beginning of my contribution, I argued for a better understanding of the complexity that led to the dramatic genetic transformation during the third millennium BCE. So far, however, only a small number of regional case studies allow for deeper insights, and it is not at all clear if these case studies are also representative of other regions or even indicate the existence of a transregional social system of mobility and fostering at least within Central Europe. Our bioarchaeological case study in the Lech valley informs us of the complexity of individual mobility: over a period of ca. 800 years, all adult women buried within the Lech valley came from outside, and their geographical and cultural place of origin determined their place and role within the Lech valley community. This stable and comprehensive system of female mobility required sufficient modes of travel and transport over vast distances. The means of travel must have been so well developed that even children of seven years were able to travel distances of 300 to 400 km. These mobile children, the burial of adult women with biologically nonrelated children, and the differentiation between women who became pregnant over and over again and women whose role was to breastfeed and take care of the biological mothers' children all point to societies where the successful raising of a large number of children was of the greatest importance. This kind of society was best qualified to exert an enormous impact on the genetic transformation of Europe.

References

Allentoft, Morten E., Martin Sikora, Karl-Göran Sjögren, Simon Rasmussen, Morten Rasmussen, Jesper Stenderup, Peter B. Damgaard, et al. 2015. Population genomics of Bronze Age Eurasia. *Nature* 522(7555): 167–172.

Andrades Valtueña, Aida, Alissa Mittnik, Felix M. Key, Wolfgang Haak, Raili Allmäe, Andrej B. Belinskij, Mantas Daubaras, et al. 2017. The Stone Age plague and its persistence in Eurasia. *Current Biology* 27(23): 3683–3691.

Anthony, David W. Forthcoming. Migration, ancient DNA, and Bronze Age pastoralists from the Eurasian Steppes. In: Megan J. Daniels (ed.), *Homo Migrans: Modelling mobility and migration in human history* (IEMA Distinguished Monograph Series). Buffalo: SUNY Press.

Biga, Maria G. 2000. Wet-nurses at Ebla: A prosopographic study. *Vicino Oriente* 12: 59–88.

2016. The role of women in work and society in the Ebla Kingdom (Syria, 24th century BC). In: Brigitte Lion & Cécile Michel (ed.), *The role of women in work and society in the ancient Near East*, 71–89. Boston & Berlin: De Gruyter.

Dunne, Julie, Katharina Rebay-Salisbury, Roderick B. Salisbury, A. Frisch, Caitlin Walton-Doyle, & Richard P. Evershed. 2019. Milk of ruminants in ceramic baby bottles from prehistoric child graves. *Nature* 574: 246–248.

Eshed, Vered, Avi Gopher, Timothy B. Gage, & Israel Hershkovitz. 2004. Has the transition to agriculture reshaped the demographic structure of prehistoric populations? New evidence from the Levant. *American Journal of Physical Anthropology* 124(4): 315–329.

Fernandes, Daniel M., Alissa Mittnik, Iñigo Olalde, Iosif Lazaridis, Olivia Cheronet, Nadin Rohland, Swapan Mallick, et al. 2020. The spread of steppe and Iranian-related ancestry in the islands of the western Mediterranean. *Nature Ecology & Evolution* 4(3): 334–345.

Frei, Karin M., Ulla Mannering, Kristian Kristiansen, Morten E. Allentoft, Andrew S. Wilson, Irene Skals, Silvana Tridico, et al. 2015. Tracing the dynamic life story of a Bronze Age female. *Scientific Reports* 5: 10431.

Frei, Karin M., Chiara Villa, Marie L. Jørkov, Morten E. Allentoft, Flemming Kaul, Per Ethelberg, Samantha S. Reiter, et al. 2017. A matter of months: High precision migration chronology of a Bronze Age female. *PLoS ONE* 12(6): e0178834.

Fulminante, Francesca. 2015. Infant feeding practices in Europe and the Mediterranean from prehistory to the Middle Ages: A comparison between the historical sources and bioarchaeology. *Childhood in the Past* 8(1): 24–47.

Goldberg, Amy, Torsten Günther, Noah A. Rosenberg, & Mattias Jakobsson. 2017. Ancient X chromosomes reveal contrasting sex bias in Neolithic and Bronze Age Eurasian migrations. *Proceedings of the National Academy of Sciences of the United States of America* 114(10): 2657–2662.

Haak, Wolfgang, Guido Brandt, Hylke N. de Jong, Christian Meyer, Robert Ganslmeier, Volker Heyd, Chris Hawkesworth, et al. 2008. Ancient DNA, strontium isotopes, and osteological analyses shed light on social and kinship organization of the Later Stone Age. *Proceedings of the National Academy of Sciences of the United States of America* 105(47): 18226–18231.

Haak, Wolfgang, Iosif Lazaridis, Nick Patterson, Nadin Rohland, Swapan Mallick, Bastien Llamas, Guido Brandt, et al. 2015. Massive migration from the steppe was a source for Indo-European languages in Europe. *Nature* 522(7555): 207–211.

Juras, Anna, Maciej Chyleński, Edvard Ehler, Helena Malmström, Danuta Żurkiewicz, Piotr Włodarczak, Stanisław Wilk, et al. 2018. Mitochondrial genomes reveal an east to west cline of steppe ancestry in Corded Ware populations. *Scientific Reports* 8(1): 11603.

Knipper, Corina, Alissa Mittnik, Ken Massy, Catharina Kociumaka, Isil Kucukkalipci, Michael Maus, Fabian Wittenborn, et al. 2017. Female exogamy and gene pool diversification at the transition from the Final Neolithic to the Early Bronze Age in Central Europe. *Proceedings of the National Academy of Sciences of the United States of America* 114(38): 10083–10088.

Kristiansen, Kristian. Forthcoming. Towards a new prehistory. Re-theorizing genes, cultures, and migratory expansions. In: Megan J. Daniels (ed.), *Homo Migrans: modelling mobility and migration in human history* (IEMA Distinguished Monograph Series). Buffalo: SUNY Press.

Kristiansen, Kristian, Morten E. Allentoft, Karin M. Frei, Rune Iversen, Niels N. Johannsen, Guus Kroonen, Łukasz Pospieszny, et al. 2017. Re-theorising mobility and the formation of culture and language among the Corded Ware Culture in Europe. *Antiquity. A Quarterly Review of Archaeology* 91 (356): 334–347.

Lallemand, Suzanne. 2007. *La circulation des enfants en société traditionnelle: Prêt, don, échange* (Anthropologie. Connaissance des hommes). Paris: Editions L'Harmattan.

Massy, Ken. 2018. *Die Gräber der Frühbronzezeit im südlichen Bayern. Untersuchungen zu den Bestattungs- und Beigabensitten sowie gräberfeldimmanenten Strukturen* (Materialhefte zur bayerischen Archäologie 107). Kallmünz: Verlag Michael Lassleben.

Mittnik, Alissa, Ken Massy, Corina Knipper, Fabian Wittenborn, Ronny Friedrich, Saskia Pfrengle, Marta Burri, et al. 2019. Kinship-based social inequality in Bronze Age Europe. *Science* 366(6466): 731–734.

Müller-Scheeßel, Nils, Gisela Grupe, & Thomas Tütken. 2015. In der Obhut von Verwandten? Die Zirkulation von Kindern und Jugendlichen in der Eisenzeit Mitteleuropas. In: Raimund Karl & Jutta Leskovar (ed.), *Interpretierte Eisenzeiten: Fallstudien, Methoden, Theorie. Tagungsbeträge der 6. Linzer Gespräche zur interpretativen Eisenzeitarchäologie* (Studien zur Kulturgeschichte von Oberösterreich 42), 9–23. Linz: Oberösterreichisches Landesmuseum.

O'Donnell, Thomas C. (ed.). 2020. *Fosterage in medieval Ireland: An emotional history* (The Early Medieval North Atlantic). Amsterdam: Amsterdam University Press.

Olalde, Iñigo, Selina Brace, Morten E. Allentoft, Ian Armit, Kristian Kristiansen, Thomas J. Booth, Nadin Rohland, et al. 2018. The Beaker phenomenon and the genomic transformation of northwest Europe. *Nature* 555(7695): 190–196.

Olalde, Iñigo, Swapan Mallick, Nick Patterson, Nadin Rohland, Vanessa Villalba-Mouco, Marina Silva, Katharina Dulias, et al. 2019. The genomic history of the Iberian Peninsula over the past 8000 years. *Science* 363(6432): 1230–1234.

Rasmussen, Simon, Morten E. Allentoft, Kasper Nielsen, Ludovic Orlando, Martin Sikora, Karl-Göran Sjögren, Anders G. Pedersen, et al. 2015. Early divergent strains of Yersinia pestis in Eurasia 5,000 years ago. *Cell* 163(3): 571–582.

Rebay-Salisbury, Katharina. 2017a. Big Mamas? Mutterschaft und sozialer Status im eisenzeitlichen Mitteleuropa. In: Christin Keller & Katja Winger (ed.), *Frauen an der Macht? Neue interdisziplinäre Ansätze zur Frauen- und Geschlechterforschung für die Eisenzeit Mitteleuropas* (Universitätsforschungen zur prähistorischen Archäologie 299), 57–73. Bonn: Habelt.

2017b. Breast is best – and are there alternatives? Feeding babies and young children in prehistoric Europe. *Mitteilungen der Anthropologischen Gesellschaft in Wien* 147: 13–29.

Schroeder, Hannes, Ashot Margaryan, Marzena Szmyt, Bertrand Theulot, Piotr Włodarczak, Simon Rasmussen, Shyam Gopalakrishnan, et al. 2019. Unraveling ancestry, kinship, and violence in a Late Neolithic mass grave. *Proceedings of the National Academy of Sciences of the United States of America* 116(22): 10705–10710.

Sjögren, Karl-Göran, Inigo Olalde, Sophie Carver, Morten E. Allentoft, Tim Knowles, Guus Kroonen, Alistair W. Pike, et al. 2020. Kinship and social organization in Copper Age Europe. A cross-disciplinary analysis of archaeology, DNA, isotopes, and anthropology from two Bell Beaker cemeteries. *Plos ONE* 15(11): e0241278.

Sjögren, Karl-Göran, T. Douglas Price, & Kristian Kristiansen. 2016. Diet and mobility in the Corded Ware of central Europe. *PLoS ONE* 11(5): e0155083.

Zimmermann, Stefan, Christine Brugger, & Elmar Bereuter (ed.). 2012. *Die Schwabenkinder: Arbeit in der Fremde vom 17. bis 20. Jahrhundert*. Ostfildern: Thorbecke Verlag.

22 HIDING IN PLAIN SIGHT? THE ENIGMA OF THE LINGUISTIC REMAINS OF PREHISTORIC SLAVERY*

BENEDICTE NIELSEN WHITEHEAD

22.1 Introduction

The present chapter discusses the linguistic evidence for slaves and slavery in Proto-Indo-European, with the Latin lexicon as its point of departure. Slavery, as such, has proven to be quite an elusive field of investigation. Archaeologists in particular have been perplexed to find that, even in historical periods for which literary sources richly document slavery as a vital institution, the archaeological evidence is meager and ambiguous. In a sense, slaves are as invisible to archaeologists as they were anonymous and socially nonexistent in the societies that they helped build and maintain. One of the keys to the archaeologist's problem is that, being possessions themselves, slaves tend not to own anything, and, given that they are not legitimate members of society, they are not likely to receive elaborate burials – to the extent that they are buried at all. However, there are other scenarios in which the material wealth of slaves was in fact similar to that of lower-class free individuals, rendering it impossible to tell the classes of free and unfree workers apart. For overviews of the complexities of slavery in the field of archaeology, see, for instance, Marshall (2016: 69) and Morris (2018).

In the following, I shall illustrate that, ironically, the historical linguist is faced with much the same challenges when it comes to reconstructing a lexicon for slaves and slavery. However, as is often the case, even silent sources can tell a story.

When embarking on an investigation of this sort, two questions arise. First: how do we define slavery? It may seem futile to attempt a universal definition of freedom and unfreedom, since all societies restrain the freedom of their members in some way, and "freedom" is obviously subject to myriad interpretations. In Section 22.1.1, I shall attempt a working definition of the term that pays due respect to the complexity of the field. Second: in the context of a study of prehistoric societies, how reliable is the evidence offered by historical linguistics? This question will be addressed in Section 22.1.2.

22.1.1 A Working Definition of Slavery

Modern English *slave* is probably associated by most people with classical Rome and Greece, as well as with early modern Brazil, the colonized Caribbean and the American South, societies that to some extent modeled themselves on the classical world. However, any definition of the institution that is based on our observations of these large-scale slaving societies is bound to be unfit to capture the types of slavery that may have existed in smaller, prehistoric societies. Since today's scholarship would probably agree that slavery in some form has been ubiquitous in all epochs of human history, and thus most probably in Proto-Indo-European society as well, we need a definition that is broad enough to capture the phenomenon in any given historical setting.

Attempts at such a definition abound; see Marshall (2016: 3–5) for a brief discussion and references. To understand the roots of slavery, I suggest that we depart – in line with Émile Benveniste (1969: 355–361), the structural linguist, and Lucien Lévy-Bruhl (1934), the social anthropologist – from a definition of freedom. Freedom, as I have already noted, is obviously an elusive and relative concept, given that every society restrains the freedom of its members in some way; some might say that each enslaves its members in some way. What is crucial for our topic is the set of rules that are in place to determine and protect, to various degrees, the rights of a society's legitimate, so-called free, members: their rights over their own physical bodies, their rights to marry and their rights over their children and possessions, their freedoms of expression and movement and so forth. Slavery comes into existence on the margins of

* The work on this topic was carried out while I was working on the research project Individual, Kin and Family in Prehistoric Europe: What Words Can Tell, expertly led by Birgit Anette Olsen, hosted by the Department of Nordic Studies and Linguistics at the University of Copenhagen and generously funded by the Velux Foundation. I would like to take the opportunity to thank Marcos Abreu de Almeida of Northwestern University for his lucid discussions of the history of slavery. Praise is also due to those involved in the peer-review process, which prompted me to rethink some of the solutions put forward in a previous version of this paper. For diligent copy-editing, I rely on Peter Machen of the Communication Factory.

most societies – and in the very midst of some – where we find individuals for whom these rules offer little or no protection. Depending on the historical context, such marginalized individuals may be foreigners, prisoners of war, victims of human trafficking, refugees or natives who have been stripped of their rights because they are criminals or debtors, or because they cannot fend for themselves due to poverty, orphanage or physical or mental impairment. Finally, they may simply have inherited their status, or lack of same.

Because of their peripheral status, such groups are vulnerable to either legal or illegal exploitation – typically, for their labor, for sex or for procreation. In broad terms, when such exploitation takes the form of ownership and total domination, it is justified to speak of slavery, even if the relationship between master and slave oftentimes carries a different label.

According to this definition, slavery is a potential by-product of every society, since the mere notion of society implies that those inside it are privileged and protected, while outsiders are not. In this sense, this definition is both a postulate about the universal and ubiquitous nature of slavery and a statement about the high likelihood of us finding slavery of some form in any society, ancient or modern, that we might choose to investigate.

22.1.2 The Value and Reliability of Linguistic Evidence: Some General Principles

The evidence that comparative linguistics offers on a given topic is in many ways similar to archaeological evidence: on the one hand, it is fragmented and random, but on the other, much of it is ordered in chronological layers, and in some cases, we can relate it to specific historical events, thus enabling us to offer relatively precise *post quem* and *ante quem* dating. Many of the insights gained from linguistic evidence are based on inference and conjecture; but these are – obviously – not random, but fact-based and subject to certain axioms and general rules.

It is quite a trivial axiom that the presence of linguistic evidence for a given concept must be taken as evidence that the speakers of that language are (in the case of a reconstructed language: were) aware of the existence of said concept. For instance, Latin *famulus* and the related Paelignian *famel* both mean 'slave'; it stands to reason that their common proto-form, Proto-Italic **famelo-*, likewise meant 'slave' (thus Untermann 2000: 262). Hence, the speakers of Proto-Italic talked about, and thus knew of, slaves.

In one of the most substantial treatments of our subject in recent times, the Indo-Europeanist Helmut Rix (1994: 38–40), who was convinced that the Proto-Italics did not practice slavery, argued that the Proto-Italic term in fact referred to a free employee. In other words, against the grain of the aforementioned axiom, he let his perception of Roman history interfere with a clear-cut etymology. This led to trouble for him, as he then needed to postulate that the term underwent the same semantic shift from 'free employee' to 'slave' independently in both Latin and Oscan. This is not impossible, but the axiom known as Occam's Razor suggests that the simplest etymology is also the more plausible one, and it is of course simpler to imagine that the Latin *famulus* 'slave' and the Umbrian *famel* 'slave' both go back to a term that meant 'slave' than it is to imagine that they go back to a form with a different meaning, but just happened to develop in a similar way in both branches of Italic.

Another universal axiom concerns the absence of evidence: the absence of linguistic evidence for a given phenomenon is not evidence of its absence in the speech community. This is highly relevant when it comes to slavery terminology, since we are in fact unable to reconstruct a single Proto-Indo-European term for 'slave' or 'slavery'. The latter observation led Rix (1994: 120ff.) to the conclusion that the Proto-Indo-Europeans did not have the sort of slavery that we know from Greece and Rome. However, although slavery in earlier epochs must necessarily have taken a different form than in Rome and Greece, this is not a conclusion that can be reached simply because there is no evidence for an inherited term for the concept of 'slave'. As I shall argue in Section 22.1.3, and as also implied in the observations on the nature of slavery made above, it is rather emblematic of this semantic field that no fixed term existed.

22.1.3 Some Observations on Slavery Vocabulary, or the Lack of Same, in Indo-European Languages

In fact, a panorama of the terminology of slavery in various Indo-European languages reveals that this part of the lexicon is inconstant and variable.[1] It also allows for some general conclusions when it comes to naming motivations. Typically, slaves are named:

1. after their ethnicity, thus:
   - Modern English *slave*, which goes back, via Late Latin *sclaueni/sclaui* (nom.pl.), to a Byzantine Greek term for a Slavic tribe, Σκλαβηνοί (nom.pl.)
   - Modern English *negro*, which, during European colonialism, had the double meaning of 'African' and 'slave'
   - Middle English *wealh* 'Welshman; slave'
2. from their function, thus:
   - Greek ἀμφίπολος 'female attendant; slave' and Sanskrit *abhicara-* 'servant' that both go back to a PIE term that simply meant 'attendant'
3. from their captured state, thus
   - Old Irish *cacht* 'slave', a borrowing from Latin *captus* 'captured'

[1] The first attempt at an overview of slavery terminology is that of Brugmann (1906); see also the brief discussion in Benveniste (1969: 355–361).

- Polish *niewolnik* 'unfree person, captive, slave'

4. after their age or gender, thus:
   - Latin *puer* 'boy; slave'
   - Sanskrit *puruṣa-* 'man, attendant, servant, friend'
   - Greek παῖς 'child; slave'.

In all these cases, the term for 'slave' has a primary meaning that does not imply slavery, so it is only from the context that we can conclude what is intended. Additionally, the classicist Rachel Zelnick-Abramovitz (2018) illustrates that both Latin and Greek sources often fail to distinguish between slaves and freemen when referring to workers. Notably, the generic term for a slave, Gk. δοῦλος, occurs but once – in the feminine δουλή – in each of the Homeric epics. Consequently, all the Homeric terms for workers, assistants, and attendants are in fact ambiguous as to whether they refer to free or unfree individuals.

This observation allows us to reconsider Émile Benveniste's exploration of how a PIE chieftain's possessions could be gauged in terms of his 'mobile wealth', which was divisible into his **pék̂u* (n.) 'cattle' and his **u̯ih$_{1}$rói̯* (n.pl. m.) 'men'.[2] Benveniste (1969: 48–49) argued that the men in question were slaves; and Calvert Watkins (1995: 211), who worked extensively on this 'Indo-European folk taxonomy of wealth', as he termed it, concurred.

If we look at this term in a little more detail, however, we can draw some interesting conclusions, and add a qualification to Benveniste's claim that, in this context, PIE **u̯ih$_{1}$ró-* refers to slaves. The stem **u̯ih$_{1}$ró-* is nowhere continued with the primary meaning of 'slave': Gothic *wair* (m.), Latin *uir* (m.) and Lithuanian *výras* (m.) are all general designations of 'a man', as is Vedic *vīrá-* (m.) 'a man', which, in addition, also designates 'a hero'. The best way to understand this is to assume that, even if there was a distinction between free and unfree members of a PIE clan, the unfree members were so integrated into the clan, and the free members in fact bound by it to such an extent, that free and unfree were perceived as a collective. In other words, the ancient folk taxonomy of wealth must have included both the free and unfree members of a man's entourage.

A very similar setup, in which free and unfree workers are merged under the same term, is described by the Roman writer Varro (*Rust.* 1.17.1–2). He remarked that when it comes to the means by which land is tilled, some divide them into three classes:

> the class of instruments which is articulate, the inarticulate, and the mute; the articulate comprising the slaves, the inarticulate comprising the cattle, and the mute comprising the vehicles.
>
> *instrumenti genus uocale et semiuocale et mutum, uocale, in quo sunt serui, semiuocale, in quo sunt boues, mutum, in quo sunt plaustra.*

The passage has often been cited in evidence that Romans perceived slaves as mere tools, not as human beings (thus also Zelnick-Abramovitz 2018, fn. 47; more references in Lewis 2013: 635). However, this interpretation has been proven wrong, most recently by the social historian and classicist Juan Lewis (2013: 636, 638), who notes that, first, the term *īnstrūmentum* does not solely refer to a 'tool' or 'utensil': being derived from the verb *īnstruere*, 'to furnish, equip', it denotes, in general, "all the means a farm . . . is furnished with in order to make it work." In support, he cites the jurist Gaius (*Dig.* 33.7.8.pr.), who explains that part of the *īnstrūmentum* is made up of

> men who work the land, and those who oversee or preside upon them, among whom are bailiffs and overseers.
>
> *homines qui agrum colunt et qui eos exercent, praepositive sunt his quorum in numero sun uilici, et monitores.*

Perhaps 'aides', 'resources' or 'auxiliary means' would have been a more fitting translation of the term.

Second, says Lewis (2013: 641), the wording "the articulate comprising the slaves," *uocale, in quo sunt serui*, does not warrant that the speaking workforce consisted only of slaves. Rather, as other scholars have pointed out before him, this is the typical way in which Varro picks one token from a list to serve as an example. The passage could, therefore, more fittingly be translated as "the articulate comprising, e.g., the slaves." The correctness of this analysis is corroborated by Varro (*LL* 1.17.2) himself, who continues the passage by observing,

> All agriculture is carried on by men – slaves, or freemen, or both.
>
> *omnes agri coluntur hominibus seruis aut liberis aut utrisque . . .*

As with the **u̯ihrói̯* in the PIE collocation, Varro's employment of *īnstrūmentī genus uocāle* thus makes no distinction between the free and unfree workforce.

This insight also helps us to understand other aspects of the Latin vocabulary pertaining to freedom and unfreedom. Latin *familia*, the ancestor of Modern English *family*, is a case in point – one in which a term for slavery is hiding in plain sight. The Latin term referred primarily to a household, consisting of the master's wife, children, slaves and sometimes his clients.[3] As such, Cicero (*Inv.* 2.148) uses it in a collocation, *familia pecūniaque* 'household and possessions', that echoes PIE **pék̂u u̯ih$_{2}$rói̯-k^{w}e*, especially as *pecūnia* 'possession' is derived from *pecu* (n.) 'cattle'.[4] Etymologically, though, *familia* is derived from *famulus* 'a slave', and the original sense of *familia* must thus have been 'a troop of slaves' or perhaps simply 'servitude'.[5] This etymology speaks volumes about the role of slaves in Roman prehistory: it tells us that they must have been an integral and natural part of a household, centuries before Rome evolved into a major slaving society.

Consider also *līberī*, the plural of Latin *līber* 'free', which became lexicalized as a designation of a free man's offspring, a usage that makes sense if we think of a free man's children in

[2] Depending on the dialect, the plural of **u̯ih$_{1}$ró-* can also take the form **u̯ih$_{1}$rṓs*.

[3] On the status of clients, see Mouritsen (2011: 42, n. 39).

[4] The phrase, whose presence in the Law of the Twelve Tables is disputed (see Warmington 1938: 447, n. c), also occurs in the anonymous *Rhetorica ad Herennium* (1.23), in a passage that cites a couple of unidentified laws.

[5] Proto-Italic **famelo-* 'slave' is of uncertain provenance, in my opinion (Nielsen Whitehead 2020: 268–276); for the more optimistic view, see Rix (1994: 48–49), who is followed by NIL, De Vaan (2008: 200–201) and Bock & al. (2015).

terms of them being part of a larger household that also included his slaves and other followers. The only *līberī* 'free individuals' of a Roman *familia* were the *pater familiās* himself, his offspring and his wife, who, however, was in the legal position of a daughter, *in fīliae locō*. Hence the double meaning of *līberī*: 'free' and 'children'.

Finally, a related case is that of the terms for 'son' and 'servant' in Celtic, reflected in Old Irish *macc* vs *mug*. Olsen (2020: 59) discusses the relationship of these two forms to various Germanic stems, namely:

1. ON *mǫgr* 'son, servant, young man'
2. OE *magu* 'child, young man, son'
3. OS *magu* 'son'

She posits a common preform, PIE *mag^h-u-*, which initially referred to a servant, but underwent a semantic shift to 'boy', then to 'son'. This development, 'servant' → 'son', would thus appear to instantiate nearly the reverse of 'man' → 'slave' that we saw above. This, too, points to the same sort of circumstances that we see in the Latin material, namely relatively fluid borders between free and unfree members of the household. In the Roman family, this set of circumstances reflects the fact that all members of the household were under the control of the same patriarchal head, whose power over his household was codified by law. In other early Indo-European cultures, other power structures may have been in place, involving the chieftains of larger clans.

We can conclude, then, that the lack of specific PIE terms for slaves and slavery is not likely to be indicative of a society without slaves. Rather, it is likely to reflect a society in which slavery was integral and ubiquitous. We should keep this in mind when we consider what the etymologies of *ancilla* (f.) and *seruus* (m.), the most frequent terms for 'female slave' and 'male slave' in Latin, might reveal about the status of slaves in Proto-Indo-European.

22.2 Lat. *ancilla* (f.) 'Female Slave'

The etymology of *ancilla* has long been established as reflecting an Italic diminutive from PIE *$h_2\eta b^h i$-$k^w olho$-*. The first member of this compound means 'around, about'. The second member (also seen in OIr. *buachill* (m.) and Gk. βούκολος < PIE *$g^w o\underline{u}$-$k^w olho$-* 'cowherd'). It is derived from PIE *$k^w elh$-*, which, as carefully laid out by Rix (1994: 17–24), means 'tend to, care for'. PIE *$h_2\eta b^h i$-$k^w olho$-* would thus refer to someone who 'tends to, cares for something or someone'.

PIE *$h_2\eta b^h i$-$k^w olho$-* is directly attested in Skt *abhicara-* (m.) 'servant', Gk. ἀμφίπολος (f.) 'attendant; female slave, mostly in the entourage of her mistress; a cultish priest or priestess', and in Latin *anculus* and *ancula*, two terms attested by Festus (18). According to him, these were ancient designations of those attending to gods and goddesses. He also notes that *anculāre* (attested in Livius Andronicus, *Trag.* 31) was an ancient synonym of *ministrāre* 'to attend, wait upon, serve':

Or they [*ancillae*] were so called because the ancients said *anculāre* for *ministrāre* 'to serve at the table', for which reason it is also said that gods and goddesses were worshipped by servants who were called *anculi* and *anculae*.

Siue ideo sic appellantur quod antiqui anculare dicebant pro ministrare, ex quo di quoque ac deae feruntur coli, quibus nomina sunt anculi et anculae.

The combined evidence of Sanskrit, Greek and Latin allows us to suggest that PIE *$h_2\eta b^h i$-$k^w olho$-* was a person who tended to the preparation and serving of food. It is fair to hypothesize that the workers in these domestic areas were mainly female and that they might also be involved in tending to more personal needs, such as wardrobe, personal hygiene and childcare. It also seems reasonable that some of these women were recruited from the underprivileged segments of the community. However, whether the term also indicated a distinction between free and unfree members is an open question that I shall pursue in more detail in the following sections.

22.3 The History of Lat. *seruus* (m.) 'A Male Slave'

As an adjective, Latin *seruus*, *-a* means 'slavish, servile'. As a noun, it refers generically to the male slave, from the earliest sources onwards. The corresponding feminine, *serua* 'female slave', is rare and need not be discussed here, since it is surely a secondary form.

Throughout the history of Latin, *seruus* remains the standard term for 'male slave' in comedy and prose, while the higher registers prefer *famulus*. There is no reason to go through the evidence for the employment of this term in literary sources; yet its employment in early law texts is interesting, since it indicates some important milestones in the evolution of Roman slaving society.

22.3.1 Lat. *seruus* in Early Legal Sources

The first attestations of *seruus* are in Rome's fundamental law code, the Law of the Twelve Tables, from which it is clear that slavery was institutionalized at that point in history, i.e., the mid-fifth century BCE. Most importantly, *Tabula* 8.3 tells us about the relative value of slaves, stipulating that breaking a freeman's bone is penalized twice as heavily as breaking that of a slave. We also learn indirectly that a freeman who failed to pay a debt could be penalized with *nexum* 'debt bondage', a status similar to slavery, but under milder conditions than those applied to slaves (*Tab.* 3.1–6). A likely less favorable option for the debtor was sale "abroad across the Tiber," *trans Tiberim peregre* (*Tab.* 3.5). This stipulation informs us, first, that slaves could be traded, and second, that Romans presumably could not be enslaved in Rome itself. To use a term that seems to have been coined by

Benveniste (1932: 440), Romans adhered to *exodouly* 'the employment of foreign slaves', a theory that was also supported by Lévy-Bruhl (1934: 19–24) around the same time.

Another indication of the preference for *exodouly* is that the *Foedus Cassianum*, by which the Roman Republic entered a peaceful union with the Latin League in 439 BCE, stipulated that Romans could no longer enslave their Latin neighbors (Stewart 2012: 3 n. 5).

The *Lex Poetelia* (326 BCE) further safeguarded a free Roman's rights in the face of slavery in that it put an end to the aforementioned *nexum*, or 'bond slavery' (Stewart 2012: 2). The historian and classicist Moses Finley (1998 [1980]) famously identified this law as a turning point: it established a Roman's inalienable right over his person and physical body and had the effect of widening the gap between slave and freeman. Since Romans could no longer be enslaved in this way, it also triggered a greater demand for foreign slaves, which boosted the slave economy and gave birth to Rome as a slaving society – one that is structurally dependent upon its slaves, to use the definition of Finley (1998 [1980]: 148–150).

In the early third century, this new order is reflected in the *Lex Aquilia*, which treats slaves on a par with cattle, and thus defines them as chattel, or fungible property, rather than, as in the Twelve Tables, persons of lesser value (Stewart 2012: 3–4).

Slavery is thus present in the earliest sources, and Romans would appear to consider it a universal institution; indeed, the jurist Gaius (*Inst.* 1.52) considered it to be rooted in the *iūs gentium* 'law of all peoples'. However, the laws also reflect that it was an evolving institution. In earlier, undocumented historical layers we expect to find what Finley (1998 [1980]: 148–150) termed a 'society with slaves', one that is not structurally dependent on slavery. This is where linguistic analysis may be able to help us out.

22.3.2 'Outlaw' or 'Guardian'? Some Etymological Proposals

The etymology of Lat. *seruus* is a longstanding enigma. Although it would appear to be roughly reconstructable as PIE **seru̯o-*, a nominal stem displaying that form, and thus a potential cognate, is only attested in Celtic and points to a completely different lexeme; compare Welsh *herwr* 'an outlaw' and Middle Irish *serbh* 'theft'. The Celtic forms would appear to continue a PIE root **ser(u̯)-* 'to seize'.

On the other hand, Latin and a couple of other languages attest to a similar-looking verbal root, PIE **ser(u̯)-*, meaning 'to observe, look out for', and attested, e.g., in Latin *seruāre* 'to observe, protect'. From this stem, we find a derived noun, **soru̯o-* 'guardian', reflected, e.g., in Gk. οὖρος 'guardian'.

Consequently, most debates revolve around the question of whether *seruus* originally denoted some sort of an outlaw and was thus a cognate of Welsh *herw*, or if it rather meant a 'lookout' and was somehow related to Gk. οὖρος. Some have evidently tried to merge PIE **ser(u̯)-* 'to seize' and **ser(u̯-)* 'to observe', which would mean that the terms for 'outlaw' and 'guardian' were ultimately related.

To assess this question from an Italic perspective, let us first consider the Latin inventory of relevant forms.

22.3.2.1 Lat. *seruīre*

The denominal verb *seruīre* means 'to serve as a slave'. Derived from *seruus* 'a slave', it is an essive in the sense that its basic meaning boils down to 'to be what the derivational base (*seruus)* denotes'. Prefixed forms of the verb derive their meanings from this semantic core; compare the following, which all occur in Plautus: *īnseruīre* 'to be submissive', *praeseruīre* 'to serve as a slave', *subseruīre* 'to aid'.

A lengthy debate revolves around the fact that, being derived from an *o/ā*-stem, *seruīre* is something of an anomaly in the fourth conjugation. As a rule, denominals derived from *o/ā*-stems follow the first conjugation; thus, e.g.:

- *arbitrāre* 'to testify' ← *arbiter* (m. *o*-st.) 'witness'
- *ancillārī* 'to serve as a (female) slave' ← *ancilla* (f. *ā*-st.) '(female) slave'
- *sānāre* 'to heal' ← *sānus* (*o/ā*-adjective) 'healthy'.

In contrast, the core of Latin fourth-conjugation denominals consists of verbs derived from *i*-stems, e.g.:

- *mentīrī* 'to lie' ← *mēns* (f. *i*-st.) 'mind'
- *grandīre* 'to grow' ← *grandis* (adj. *i*-st.) 'large'.

The derivation of *seruīre* from *seruus* thus requires an explanation.

Ernout & Meillet (1959: 620) hinted at a solution to the problem by classifying *seruīre* as "a denominal whose form gives it away as a recent formation" (*un dénominatif que sa forme dénonce comme récent*). The telltale *forme* is its fourth-conjugation morphology; thus, Ernout & Meillet (1959: 620) noted that, in line with what has just been said, a denominal verb derived from *seruus* would be expected to take the form *seruāre*. However, Latin already possessed such a verb, which meant 'to protect, keep safe, observe' and was not felt by the speakers to have any semantic affinity to *seruus*.

There was thus a need for an alternative way to create a denominal from *seruus*. Ernout & Meillet (1959: 620) asserted that "the form in *-iō* was chosen because it served to express a state" (*la forme en -i̲ō a été choisie parce qu'elle servait à exprimer un état*). In illustration, they pointed to *custōdīre* 'to guard', an essive derived from *custōs* (m.) 'a guardian', and *febrīre* ← *febris* (f.) 'fever', which is best described as a stative. There is another type of verb that follows this somewhat irregular morphological pattern, namely essives/statives that are derived from *o/ā*-adjectives denoting mental states. Compare:

- *īnsānīre* 'to be mad' ← *īnsānus* (adj.) 'mad'
- *saeuīre* 'to be wild, to rage' ← *saeuus* (adj.) 'wild'.

Theoretically, such verbs could have provided the model for the analogical creation of *seruīre*, as proposed by Ernout & Meillet (1959: 620). It may be noted, though, that essive or stative semantics is not a rule in the fourth conjugation; compare, for instance, the following factitives (verbs whose meaning boil down to 'to act by means of/by afflicting on somebody or something/to carry out that which the derivational base denotes'):

– *fīnīre* 'to limit' ← *fīnis* (f. *i*-st.) 'limit'
– *pūnīre* 'to punish' *poena* (f. *ā*-st.) 'punishment'.[6]

Therefore, it may have been even more germane to the formation of *seruīre*, as a fourth-conjugation verb, that only the first and fourth conjugations contain desubstantival verbs with the sort of agentive/essive semantics that characterize *seruīre*. Even this assumption can be challenged, however; see the discussion of *custōdīre* below, in the present section.

Ernout & Meillet's analysis of *seruīre* as a recent formation has been countered by scholars (for recent contributions, see Rix 1994: 67–76, Vine 2012: 559–564 and Meiser 2018: 746) who assert that the verb was in fact inherited from pre-Proto-Italic or even Proto-Indo-European. This is because of the presence, in Umbrian, of a verb that is only attested in the 3sg.impv. *seritu* '(he shall) save, protect'. In the detailed analysis of Rix (1994: 71–73), it was analyzed as a fourth-conjugation verb, and thus a direct cognate of *seruīre*.[7] As a common proto-form, Rix (1994: 71) posited pre-Proto-Italic **seru̯-i̯e-*, meaning 'to be a **seru̯o-*'.[8] This would imply a more complex scenario than the one proposed by Ernout & Meillet (1959: 620), and also a much older origin than implied in their analysis.

In the accounts of Rix (1994: 70) and Vine (2012: 557), the derivational base, PItal. (and supposedly PIE) **seru̯o-*, would have meant 'a guardian, lookout, protector'. Accordingly, the original sense of *seruīre* was 'to be a guardian, lookout, protector'. This meaning would be preserved in Umbrian *seritu* ('he shall protect' ← 'he shall be a protector'), and it is concluded that **seru̯o-* acquired the meaning of 'slave' at a later stage, after Latin had become an independent branch. Subsequently, the verb derived from it underwent the same semantic shift, ending up as *seruīre* 'to be a servant, to serve'.

The status of *seruīre* as an anomaly in the fourth conjugation only added to the impression that the verb had been long established, said Rix (1994: 70–71). The type of PIE formation that he proposed for **seru-i̯e-* consisted of the suffix **-i̯e-* being added to a truncated form of the thematic stem (in the case at hand, *seru̯-* ← **seru̯o-*). In Italic, this formative type was only attested in **seru̯-i̯e-*, according to Rix (1994: 69).[9] He asserted that the de-adjectival type, exemplified above by *insānīre* 'to be mad' and *saeuīre* 'be wild', was innovative (and possibly built on the analogy of *seruīre*); thus, *seruīre* stood out as an archaism that could only have been created at a stage of pre-Proto-Italic when verbs of the type **seru̯-i̯e-* could still be formed productively.

It is striking that Rix's analysis departed from a stance on the irregular nature of *seruīre* that was exactly opposite to that of Ernout & Meillet (1959: 620). As we have seen, they claimed, on the very same ground as Rix, that it must be a recent formation. Apart from the problem posed by Umbrian *seritu*, such a scenario is indeed plausible, in my opinion. This takes some of the persuasive vigor out of Rix's analysis, which was presented as absolutely compelling. As we shall see, there are further weak points.

Rix (1994: 69) added that *seruīre* displayed a further irregularity, namely that it was one of only two desubstantival essives in the fourth conjugation, the other being *custōdīre* 'to guard' ← *custōs* (m.) 'a guardian'. The latter is a consonant stem, and denominal verbs derived from such stems usually follow the same productive pattern as those derived from the *o/ā*-stems. Thus, in the normal case, we find them in the first conjugation: compare *iūdicāre* 'to be a judge, to judge', from *iūdex* (m.) 'a judge'. There are indeed a few exceptions to this rule, but they are factitives: compare verbs such as:

– *fulgurīre* 'to hurl lightning' ← *fulgur* (n.) 'lightning'
– *compedīre* 'to fetter' ← *compēs* (f.) 'a fetter'.

The fact that *custōdīre* was an essive placed it in a class that included only one other member, namely *seruīre*, Rix said.[10]

These observations prompted him to elaborate on an idea by Leumann (1977: 556), who contended that *custōdīre* was in fact modeled on *seruīre*. Rix (1994: 71) asserted that this scenario was corroborated by his reconstruction of **seru̯-i̯e-* as a Proto-Italic formation, since the age of that verb made it likely to be older than *custōdīre*, and it could thus have provided the model on which *custōdīre* was based. Crucially, this analogy would presuppose that, at the time when *custōdīre* was created, the two verbs were synonymous (Rix 1994: 72). Their shared morphological anomaly would thus be independent confirmation that *seruīre* originally meant 'to protect', with the corollary that *seruus* originally denoted a 'guardian' and was thus synonymous with *custōs*.

This account of the relationship between *custōdīre* and *seruīre* was built on unstable premises. First, the hypothesis of an analogical influence between the two words lacked any

[6] Others have speculated that *pūnīre* 'to punish' was influenced by the *i*-stem adjective *impūnis* 'unpunished', which seems rather complex to me.

[7] Rix (1994: 72) notes that, although the Umbrian form lacks the **-u̯-* seen in Lat. *seruīre,* its former presence is evidenced by the fact that only **seru̯-i̯e-* could yield **seru̯ii̯e-* > **seru̯ī-* and, thus, membership in the Latin fourth conjugation (as also implied by Meiser 2018: 746). Subsequently, **seru̯ī-* yielded **serrī-,* written <seri>. Note too that Oscan *serevkid* 'authority, supervision', abl.sg. of a neuter **i̯o*-stem reconstructed as **seru̯-ikio-,* is clearly derived from a stem or root *seru̯-* (Untermann 2000: 669). Vine (2012: 557, n. 41), furthermore, cites Martzloff (2006: 633 f.) for comparison with Pre-Samnite οσερϝια[(Ps 20; 6th/5th c.).

[8] Vine (2012: 559–560) asserts that Rix (ibid.) traced *seruus* back to a *u*-stem, which seems unfounded.

[9] There are, however, further exceptions: the enigmatic *equīre* '(of mares) to be in heat', attested in Pliny the Elder, and *catulīre* '(of cats) to be in heat', attested in Varro and Laberius. For an instance of vacillation between the first and fourth conjugation, compare *singultīre* 'to hiccup' ← *singultus* (m. *u*-st.) 'a hiccup' (Celsus+) and *singultāre* (Vergil+).

[10] Rix (1994: 70) duly noted that a further member of this class, *nūtrīre* 'to be a nurse', is not relevant here, as it would appear to be a late remake (first attested in Catullus) of regular *nūtrīcāre* (first attested in Plautus) derived from *nūtrīx*.

account of what could have motivated such an analogy: semantic similarity is not in itself a strong motivating factor. Second, there is evidence from Vedic that the PIE denominal suffix *-i̯e- was regularly added directly to consonant stems, as in:

- Ved. *bhiṣaj-yá-ti* 'is a doctor, heals' ← *bhiṣáj-* (m.) 'doctor'
- Ved. *apas-yá-ti* 'is active' ← *apás-* (adj.) 'active'.

Hence, *custōdīre* would appear to have as much of a chance of being an inherited formation as *seruīre*. As a third and more tentative point, it may also be noted that a small group of fourth-conjugation verbs seem to derive from stems in *-ia* and *-ium*. Compare:

- *fastīdīre* 'to be disgusted' ← *fastīdium* 'disgust'
- *mūnīre* 'to fortify' ← *moenia* 'defensive walls'
- and possibly a verb like *īnsānīre*, if from *īnsānia*, rather than from *īnsānus* (as also suggested by Rix 1994: 69).

This raises the question of whether *custōdīre* was rather a factitive derived from *custōdia* 'protection', which seems to agree with its transitive semantics – which, by the way, differ from the intransitive semantics of *seruīre*. This would remove *custōdīre* from the list of fourth-conjugation essives. Whatever the correct history of *custōdīre*, I see no clear evidence that it was in any way entangled with that of *seruīre*.

More recently, Vine (2012: 560) has objected that the word-formation pattern that Rix presents as pre-Proto-Italic is in fact only securely attested in Greek, as in stems like ἀγγέλλω 'to report' ← ἄγγελος 'a messenger'. The secure pattern of PIE denominals derived directly from thematic stems (i.e., without the intervention of the feminine/collective marker *-eh_2-) retain the thematic vowel. From *seru̯o-, we would thus expect a denominal *seru̯e-i̯é-, which, given our current state of knowledge, should have yielded *seruēre in Latin. In other words, it is difficult to make the claim that *seru̯-i̯e- was ever a regular form, whether in PIE or in Proto-Italic.

With this, we can proceed to consider the solution to the problem offered by Vine (2012: 563) himself. He identifies *seruīre* as the reflex of *seru̯e-i̯é, a denominal of the more securely attested type just mentioned. Relics of such a pattern have hitherto not been detected in Latin, but by proposing a Proto-Italic sound law, *-ei̯-é- > *-ii̯e-, Vine is able to suggest that verbs like *saeuīre*, *seruīre*, etc. in fact have their roots in PIE denominals in *-e-i̯é-.

Vine's contribution is part of a wider effort to detect the effects of the PIE accent in Italic, an effort that has still not gained general acceptance (see also Vine 2004, 2006). His account of verbs like *saeuīre*, *seruīre*, etc. has some obvious merits, but also leaves certain questions unanswered. The *e-i̯é- type derives primarily from substantives in Homeric Greek (see Sütterlin 1891: 60 ff. and Risch 1974: 308–309) and seemingly also in Vedic (Sütterlin 1906: 482; 498; 503 f.). In these two languages, examples such as the following prevail:

- Gk. κοσμέω 'to order' ← κόσμος (m. *o*-st.) 'order'
- Gk. οἰκέω 'inhabit' ← οἶκος (m. *o*-st.) 'house'
- Ved. *vājayánt-* (ptc.) 'competing for the prize' ← *vāja-* (m. *a*-st.) 'prize'
- Ved. *devayáti* 'serves the gods' ← *devá-* (m. *a*-st.) 'god'.

In contrast, the predominant pattern for de-adjectivals from PIE *o-/ah_2-stems would appear to have featured stems ending in *-ah_2-i̯e-, as in the Latin type *sānāre*, which presumably goes back to the same type of formation as Hit. *nēu̯ahh*^{i}- 'to renew'.[11] This gives reason to suspect that de-adjectivals like *saeuīre* are a Latin innovation, with the corollary that Vine's analysis hinges on *seruīre* as the only truly archaic form.

In essence, then, both Rix's and Vine's reconstructions of a common PItal. preform of Lat. *seruīre* and Umbrian *seritu* are marred by the same problem: in both cases, the reconstructed form is isolated and highly unusual for the Italic branch.

This is probably why Untermann (2000: 669–670) promotes the analysis of a number of scholars who analyze this verb as a durative present: Proto-Italic *ser-ē-tōd, presumably reflecting a PIE stative, *ser-eh_1-i̯e-, derived from the root *ser- 'look after, protect' (LIV: 534). As noted, Rix (1994: 69–76) objects to such an analysis, because the term is consistently spelled with the stem vowel <i>. However, according to Buck (1904: 34),

> The Imperatives of the Second Conjugation always have *i* in the Latin as against **e** in the native alphabet . . . Thus *habitu*, **habetu** : L. *habētō* . . .

Our verbal form occurs thirty times altogether in the Latin alphabet, as *seritu/serituu*, compared to a single attestation in the native alphabet, as **šeritu** (Untermann 2000: 669). For Untermann's proposal to be correct, we would thus have to assume that the latter form was an exception to the general rule postulated by Buck, which is, I think, a small price to pay if it enables us to propose a better scenario for Lat. *seruīre*.

Untermann's analysis allows us to return to Ernout & Meillet's proposal (1959: 620), according to which *seruīre* was created in Latin when *seru̯o- changed its meaning from 'lookout' to 'slave', and a new denominal verb with the meaning 'to be a slave' was needed. In the normal case, such a verb would have the form *seruāre*; however, such a verb already existed.

Rix (1994: 79) maintains that, at the relevant moment, Latin had only one other denominal verb that could have served as a model for the creation of *seruīre*. This was *custōdīre* 'to guard'. Above, I suggested, albeit tentatively, that *custōdīre* may have originated as a factitive derived from *custōdia*. This would leave us with no semantic parallels to *seruīre* if it were not for a further desubstantival essive that tends to be overlooked, namely *potīre/potīrī* 'to become a master of, take possession of'.[12] This verb is not normally listed as an essive, presumably because its derivational base, PIE *poti- (m.) 'a master', only survives in Latin in relics such as:

- *compotīre* 'make partaker of; to become partaker/master of (pass.)' ← *compos* (adj.) 'having control over' < *kom-poti- 'a fellow master'

[11] Although this type is rare in Vedic (Sütterlin 1906: 498; 503 f.).

[12] As Rix (1994: 76 n. 78) noted, the tendency for denominal essives to be deponent would appear to have set in at an early stage of Latin. The form *potīre* is only attested in Plautus; in all other texts, we find the deponent *potīrī*. However, it is quite possible that the verb was not deponent at the time when *seruīre* was coined, so the two verbs were originally parallel in that sense as well.

– *hospes* (m.) 'host, guest' < PIE *$\hat{g}^h$ósti-poti-* 'guest-lord'
– *potis* (adj.) 'able, capable'
– *posse* 'to be able' ← *potis esse*
– *potestās* 'power, ownership'.[13]

However, there can be no doubt that *potīre* and *compotīre* are entirely regular fourth-conjugation denominal essives, derived from the *i*-stem **poti-* (m.) 'a master'.[14]

What renders *potīre* interesting in our context is that it seems rather certain that there was a point in time when **poti-* 'master' and **seru̯o-* 'slave' formed an antonymic pair. This allows for the hypothesis that *seruīre* ← *seruus* was formed on the analogy of, and in semantic contrast to, *potīre* ← **potis*, still under the assumption that a new verb was needed, given that *seruāre* meant 'to observe'. As for when this analogy may have taken place, it is noteworthy that there is no evidence that **seru̯o-* denoted 'a slave' in Proto-Italic. On the contrary, the only securely reconstructed PItal. slave-term is **famelo-* (as noted in Section 22.1.2). Thus, we can establish the emergence of the Latin branch (possibly in the tenth century BCE) as a tentative *terminus post quem* for the creation of *seruīre* along the lines proposed here.

A *terminus ante quem* can be established as the point in time when **poti-* became obsolete. Elsewhere (Nielsen Whitehead 2020: 288–292), I have presented a scenario in which the political changes leading up to the foundation of the Republic also triggered certain changes in the legal vocabulary, resulting in the creation of such terms as *pater familiās* 'head of household' and *patria potestās* 'paternal power', thus instating the *pater* 'father' in the role of **potis* 'master'. As a result, **poti-* passed from use as a term for a slave master. I date this event possibly to the end of the sixth century BCE. The denominal verb *potīre* – and thus *seruīre* – must have been formed prior to this, given that it presupposes that **poti-* was still the common term for a master.

The advantages of accepting this scenario are, first, that we do not have to presuppose word-formation patterns that show no productivity in Italic, and second, that the origin of *seruīre* corresponds precisely to its attested meaning as a denominal of the word for 'slave' – all in keeping with the axiom that the simplest analysis is also most likely to be the corrct one.

The question remains whether *seruus* originally denoted an 'observer, guardian' or an 'outlaw', and whether it is related at all to *seruāre* 'to observe'. This even more tangled issue will be negotiated in the sections below.

22.3.2.2 *Lat.* seruāre *and the Etymology of* seruus

As noted, Lat. *seruāre* means 'to protect, keep safe, observe'. Prefixed forms have similar meanings: *obseruāre* 'to watch, note, heed, observe', *cōnseruāre* 'to retain, keep safe', and *reseruāre* 'to keep back, reserve'. Despite being a first-conjugation verb, it has the same function as the Umbrian verb, attested in imperative collocations such as *saluom, -a(m), -a(f) . . . seritu* 'he must keep safe', which are paralleled in Latin by the collocation *saluum, -a seruāre*, also 'to keep safe'.

In terms of its morphological history, *seruāre* is a difficult case. Though it is fairly clear that it must be a denominal verb, it is problematic in that there is no synchronic stem that it could reasonably be derived from. Formally, the only candidate is *seruus*, but there is an obvious semantic mismatch between 'slave' and 'to observe'.

Scholars who have attempted to link the two have been guided by the fact that first-declension denominals may be formed according to three formative types in Latin, each of which implies a different derivational base: namely an adjective, an agent noun, or an abstract noun (Leumann 1977: 545 §412 A541–543). Accordingly, we find the following three types of first-declension denominals:

1. de-adjectival verbs with factitive semantics, as in:
   nouuāre 'to renew' ← *nouus* (adj.) 'new'
   cantāre 'to sing' ← *cantus* (ptc.) 'sung'
2. desubstantival verbs with essive semantics, derived from terms denoting persons, as in:
   iūdicāre 'to be a judge, pass judgment' ← *iūdex* (m.) 'judge'
   ministrāre 'to attend' ← *minister* (m.) 'attendant'
3. desubstantival verbs with factitive semantics, as in:
   cūrāre 'to care for' ← *cūra* (f.) 'care'
   fūmāre 'to smoke' ← *fūmus* (m.) 'smoke'

Note that the simplest analysis is perhaps the second option, given the exstence of the agent noun *seruus*. However one chooses to analyze *seruāre*, its derivational base is **seru̯o-*, with a corresponding feminine **seru̯ah₂-* derived from a root that LIV lists as "1. **ser-* 'look after, protect'," presumably with a denominal suffix *-*u̯o-*.

22.3.2.3 *Lat.* seruus *according to Roman Etymologists*

Our verb *seruāre* has been classified along the lines of each of the three types listed above, resulting in different etymological analyses of *seruus*. To begin with the earliest proposal, late Roman etymologists asserted that *seruus* originally referred to prisoners of war who had been saved from death; see the many references in Pârvulescu (2010: 190, n. 191). This would imply derivation along the same lines as *nouus* → *nouāre* (type 1 above) and would presuppose that PItal. **seru̯o-* was an adjective that meant 'safe; saved'. This analysis is not generally accepted by modern scholarship, which leans toward the communis opinio that PIt. **seru̯o-* had the active meaning of 'observer, lookout'. Moreover, we do not know for sure that prisoners of war were the main source of slaves before the demand for foreign slaves (induced by the *Lex Poetelia* in 326 BCE; see Section 22.3.1) was met by a series of military campaigns that had the capture of slaves as one of its aims. In the present day, however, Pârvulescu (2010) has proposed an

[13] On the supposed derivation of *potestās* from **poti-*, see Nielsen Whitehead (2020: 289–290).

[14] As noted by De Vaan (2008: 492) and Vine (2012: 562), a further fourth-conjugation desubstantival essive makes a rare appearance in the supine *procītum* 'to woo', which presupposes a verb *procīre* 'to woo' ← *procus* (m.) 'suitor, wooer'. Its single attestation, in Livius Andronicus, is reported by Paulus, ex F., 282, 3. Note, however, that Livius Andronicus also employs the first-conjugation verb *procāre* 'to demand'.

analysis that is clearly inspired by this late Roman proposal; see Section 22.3.2.7.3

22.3.2.4 *Darmesteter (1875) and the Equation of Lat.* **seruus**, *Greek* οὖρος, *and Avestan* **hauruua-** *'Guardian'*

The Orientalist James Darmesteter (1875: 309–312) proposed an etymology that, for obvious reasons, is still held to be valid by most researchers today.[15] He suggested that *seruāre* belonged to type 2 above: it was derived from a lost Proto-Italic substantive **seruo̯-* that referred to a 'guardsman'. In support, he pointed to two Avestan attributes of dogs: the compound adjectives *pasuš.hauruua-* 'guarding cattle' and *uiš.hauruua-* 'guarding the village'. For the second member of these compounds, *hauruua-*, he reconstructed a primitive form **sarwa-*, which, he said, was equivalent to both the Greek οὖρος (m.) 'guardian' (from Proto-Greek **soru̯o-*) and the Latin *seruus*. The latter, consequently, must have denoted a guardian before it acquired the sense of 'slave'.

The root underlying the Greek and Avestan stems is now listed by LIV (534) as '1. **ser-*' and glossed as *aufpassen auf; beschützen* 'look after, protect'. The Greek, Avestan and Latin nouns would appear to be derived from this root with a suffix **-u̯o-*, but some scholars analyze the latter as a root enlargement, as it also occurs in a verbal form in Avestan, viz. the 3sg. pres. *ni-šhauruaiti*. Rasmussen (1989: 205), on the other hand, posited a root **serh₂u̯-*; see Section 22.3.2.7.1.

The main difficulty with Darmesteter's proposal, and one that has never been satisfactorily solved, is that, as we now know, Lat. *seruus* cannot be a direct cognate of Greek οὖρος, since the former must go back to **seru̯o-*, with an *e*-grade of the root, and the latter to **soru̯o-*, with an *o*-grade. Avestan *hauruua-* can reflect both **seru̯o-* and **soru̯o-*, but it is generally thought to belong with οὖρος and thus to reflect **soruo̯-*. This question will be tackled in Sections 22.3.3.1.1 and 22.3.31.2.

If Darmesteter's proposal sparked any debate at the time, however, it was around the likelihood that slaves would have been useful as guardians, a question that is still topical and which I shall explore in more detail in Section 22.3.4. The Indo-Europeanist Michel Bréal (1889: 172) came to Darmesteter's support, musing that, if *seruus*, in its original meaning of 'guardian', did not allude to slavery at all, it was because it was a euphemism – an honorable title given to the guardian of the master's home and his flocks in archaic times. The term was thus emblematic of the trust that the master used to have in his slaves, who were part and parcel of his *familia*: an argument that, except perhaps for its somewhat apologetic tone, is largely similar to what I have proposed above about the closeness between free and unfree members of the household (see the conclusion of Section 22.1.3).

[15] Rix (1994:61) incorrectly attributed this etymology to Wackernagel (1910: 8).

Jacob Wackernagel (1910: 8) agreed with Darmesteter, declaring that *seruus* "can, on the evidence of *seruāre*, *obseruāre*, only have meant 'protector', 'warden' originally" (*kann schon wegen servare observare ursprünglich nur „Hüter" „Wächter" bedeutet haben*). The analysis was entered into the etymological dictionaries of Bréal & Bailly (1885: 343–344), Walde & Hofmann (1938 [1906]: 706) and Pokorny (1959: I, 910).

Wackernagel (1910: 8) also noted, however, that "recently, scholars have veritably exerted themselves to misunderstand [*seruus*]" (*man sich bis neuestens förmlich Mühe gibt [servus] mißzuverstanden*). He was probably referring to a suggestion by the Celticist Joseph Loth, who was dismissive of the idea of a slave guardian.

22.3.2.5 *Loth (1905) and the Equation of seruus with Welsh* **herwr** *'Outlaw' and Middle Irish* **serbh** *'Theft'*

Referring desparingly to Darmesteter's etymology as "dear to the faint of heart" (*chère aux cœurs sensibles*), Loth (1905: 211) contended that it lent slavery in antiquity a patriarchal, idyllic character that was not realistic. Instead, he came up with a proposal that also stands strong in the present day, as it not only solves the supposed paradox of the guardian slave, but also the problematic *e*-grade in *seruus*.

Indo-European society was organized into tribes, he noted, and one of the ancient sources of slaves was outlaws, those who for one reason or another were not protected by any parentage or tribe – an argument that is also largely similar to my proposal in Section 22.1.1. The name for an 'outlaw' in Welsh is *herwr*, an agent noun derived from *herw*, meaning 'vagabondage; pillage' and having a cognate in the Middle Irish *serbh* (f.) 'theft', from which the denominative *fo-serba* 'steals' is derived (eDIL s.v. 2 *serb*).[16]

Loth asserted that these terms were better suited as matches for Latin *seruus*, which, he concluded, was originally 'an enslaved outlaw'. This terminology would thus hark back to Italo-Celtic, the putative common ancestor of Italic and Celtic.

Twenty years on, Loth's proposal was picked up by another Celticist, Joseph Vendryes (1935: 124 f.), who identified the Proto-Celtic term **seru̯o-* (n.), an abstract noun designating the status of an individual at the margins of society, i.e., 'outlawry'. The Latin word *seruus*, he said, was the very same term that had come to be applied to the individual, due to a trivial semantic shift.

A decade later, the Orientalist Jacques Duchesne-Guillemin (1946: 78) joined the debate. Going along with Loth's and Vendryes's proposal, he added Hittite *šāru-* 'booty' to the equation, noting that this item was 'close' to Latv. *sirt* 'to loot' and *siṛa* 'vagabond; vagabondage'.

[16] The GPC analyzes the form as a derivative of *herwa* 'to plunder', which seems to be inconsistent with the origin of the suffix. Thus, *-wr* goes back to *gwr* (m.) 'man'; and *herwr* is literally analyzable as 'robbery man'.

The root underlying the stems under discussion here is now listed by LIV (535) as "3. *ser- 'take, catch'"; verbal stems listed under this root are Gk. αἱρέω 'to seize' and the above-mentioned Latv. *sirt* 'to loot'. The two Celtic abstract nouns, Welsh *herw* and Middle Irish *serbh*, are reconstructed as the reflexes of a neuter/collective stem, PIE **ser-u̯om/ser-u̯ah₂*, while Old Irish *fo-serba* must reflect a denominative. If inherited, it would reflect **seru̯ah₂-i̯é-*. Watkins (1976: 118) identified Hittite *šāru-* as a *u*-stem, **sōru-*, derived from this root; thus also Kloekhorst (2006: 738–739).[17]

A welcome advantage of deriving *seruus* from the same neuter abstract noun as Welsh *herw* and Middle Irish *serbh* is that the *e*-grade would appear to be regular in neuter abstract nouns: compare, in particular, PGm. **hīwa-* < **k̑ei̯-u̯o-* (n.) 'marriage; citizen' (Kroonen 2013: 201, 227). This, however, would also be the case if the stem were derived from LIV's 1. **ser-* 'look after, protect'. What is rather intriguing about these forms is how closely they resemble Gk. οὖρος and Av. *hauruua-*: the roots are formally identical, and so are the suffixes. Only the root vocalism differs, and, of course, the meaning. This is why the Celtic and Hittite material continues to puzzle and to spark debate, as we shall see.

22.3.2.6 *Benveniste (1932) on* seruus *as an Etruscan Loanword*

Ferdinand de Saussure (1931 [1915]: 307–308) was also dismissive of Darmesteter's original idea of a term that meant 'guardian of the house' but underwent a semantic shift to 'slave'. He referred to this as "an example of the foolhardiness of yesteryear" (*un exemple des témérités d'autrefois*), contending that it is not certain that *seruuāre* and *seruus* are related at all and that the original meanings of both terms are uncertain.[18]

Similarly, Benveniste raised several objections to Darmesteter's etymology, few of which would be deemed valid today. Slavery was not a function, he said; rather, it was a condition that could not be reduced to a mere occupation (Benveniste 1932: 432). This preoccupation can be laid to rest immediately: as noted in the introduction, it is precisely typical of slavery terminology that it derives from a wide range of semantic spheres.

Benveniste (1932: 430) furthermore contended that Avestan *viš.hauruua-* and *pasuš.hauruua-*, both being adjectives used in relation to dogs, were incompatible with *seruus*, a noun referring to a man. However, much later in his life, Benveniste (1969: 355–361) famously elaborated on the theme of 'men and livestock' as an expression of mobile wealth, as has already been introduced in Section 22.1.3. He even demonstrated that Vedic *páśu* (n.), normally translated as 'livestock', sometimes referred to both men and cattle, the former being two-footed *páśu* and the latter four-footed, which seems to parallel Varro's distinction between speaking and semi-speaking types of resources on a farm. Referring to these facts, the anthropologist Tim Ingold (2000: 73) notes that,

> In those societies of the ancient world in which slavery was the dominant relation of production, the parallel between the domestic animal and the slave appears to have been self-evident.

With the qualification added by Lewis (2013: 641) that the *instrūmentī genera uocāle* surely consisted of both slaves and free workers, I think these observations should put to rest Benveniste's concerns about the same PIE word denoting both man (as in Latin *seruus*) and dog (as in Avestan *hauruua-*).

Benveniste (1932: 440) went on to propose that the etymological analysis of *seruus* should be seen in light of the Romans' preference for *exodouly*, the enslavement of foreigners, suggesting a loanword origin. Interestingly, the sixth king of Rome (who reigned from 578 to 535 BCE) was of Etruscan descent and was said to be of servile origin, hence his name *Seruius Tullius*. The Etruscan origin of this *praenōmen* would, according to Benveniste, be proven by its attestation in Etruscan epigraphy. In short, it was his assertion that the speakers of Latin borrowed the word for 'slave' from the Etruscans because they used Etruscan slaves.

Benveniste's loanword etymology was referenced by Walde & Hofmann (1938 [1906]: 527), but the idea that *Seruius*, a relatively common Latin *praenōmen*, would be of Etruscan origin does not appear to have had any significant following. For instance, even though Vendryes (1935: 124) hailed Benveniste's proposal as "a model of penetrating critique and solid construction" (*un modèle de critique pénétrante et de construction solide*) and acknowledged that "he reveals the weakness of generally accepted doctrine" (*Il y montre la faiblesse de la doctrine généralement admise*), he nonetheless proceeded to argue in favor of the aforementioned alternative proposal by Loth (1905: 211). As laid out by Rix (1994: 62–67), the epigraphic evidence for an Etruscan name has since proven illusory, and, regardless, there would be nothing rare about an Etruscan carrying a Latin name.

22.3.2.7 *Recent Proposals*

Even today, scholars are divided over the central question in this debate, namely if:

1. Loth and his followers are right in deriving Lat. *seruus*, Welsh *herw*, Middle Irish *serbh*, and Hittite *šāru-* from 3. **ser-* take, catch' in LIV (535); or
2. Darmesteter and his followers are right in deriving Latin *seruus*, Avestan *hauruua-*, and Greek οὖρος from 1. **ser-* 'look after, protect' in LIV (534); or
3. all these formations are in fact derived from one and the same root.

In addition, we are still struggling to come to terms with some difficult morphological aspects of its etymology. In the following, I shall review, as briefly as possible, some recent approaches to this topic.

[17] However, Watkins also seemed to consider *-u-* to be "part of the stem," perhaps implying a (rare neuter) root noun with *o*-grade.

[18] Benveniste (1932: 28 n. 23) cited this passage by Saussure with an unwarranted exclamation mark that rendered Saussure's rebuff even more indignant: "Voici une exemple des témérités d'autrefois : étant donnés *seruus* et *seruuāre*, on les rapproche – on n'en a peut-être pas le droit ; puis on donne au premier la signification de « gardien » pour en conclure que l'esclave a été à l'origine le gardien de la maison[!] . . ."

22.3.2.7.1 RASMUSSEN (1989) ON *SERUUS* AS THE REFLEX OF AN *S*-STEM VERBAL ABSTRACT **SERU̯OS-* 'PROTECTION'

Rasmussen (1989: 205) discussed a number of forms relevant to our topic that have not been introduced above. He did not, however, include MIr. *serbh*, Welsh *herw*, possibly because he considered them to be unrelated to the word family to which *seruus* belongs.

Rasmussen's concern was the phonological variation of so-called long-diphthong roots: roots ending in a laryngeal and one or two sonorants. On the strength of Hit. *šarhuu̯ant-* 'fetus, innards, uterus', which had not yet been brought into the equation, he posited a root *$serh_2$u̯-* 'to protect' and contended that Hit. *šarhuu̯ant-* originally meant *das Geschützte* 'what is protected.' In a meticulous treatment, he set out to demonstrate that this root would display three phonologically conditioned variants:

1. *$serh_2$u̯-*, seen in Hit. *šarhuu̯ant-* < *$serh_2$u̯-ent-*;
2. *seru̯-*, seen in Gk. οὖρος (m.) 'guardian' and Avestan *pasuš-/uiš-hauruua-* (adj.) 'guardian of cattle/the village' < *soru̯o-*, as well as in certain verbal forms, e.g., *ni-šhauruuaiti*, 3sg. active 'looks after' < *seru̯-e-*;
3. **ser-*, seen in, e.g., Avestan *harətar-* (m.) 'guardian' < **ser-tor-*; Avestan *harəθra-* (n.) 'care, guarding' **ser-tlo-* and Avestan *hārō* (nom.sg.m.) 'watching' < **sor-o-*,[19] as well as in certain verbal forms, e.g. Avestan *nī haraitē* 3sg. middle 'looks after' < **ser-e-*.

Under the first variant, *$serh_2$u̯-*, Rasmussen (1989: 98) also listed an *s*-stem, *$serh_2$u̯-os-* (n.) 'protection', which yielded Proto-Italic **serau̯-os-*. Lat. *seruus* would have emerged as a 'personification' of that stem, after being reinterpreted as an *o*-stem.

The merit of this treatment is that Rasmussen manages to account for the seemingly random occurrence of $*h_2$ and **u/u̯* in the final cluster of stems derived from the root that LIV posits as **ser-*. However, Rasmussen's 1989 work was spectacularly ignored by his peers, and, except for the tentative acceptance by Olsen (1999: 92–93; 2020: 156, n. 419) and a reference in Vine (2012: 560, n. 546), I am not aware of any contribution to the discussion of the word family under discussion here that references it.

Unfortunately, Rasmussen's analysis does not provide a compelling etymology for Lat. *seruus*, as the proposed neuter *s*-stem is unattested. Its (not entirely trivial) development into a masculine *o*-stem therefore remains hypothetical.

22.3.2.7.2 RIX (1994) ON *SERUUS* AS A 'TRANSIENT HERDER' AND 'OUTLAW'

Rix (1994: 77) proposed a derivation from 1. **ser-* 'to watch' for all the forms under discussion, except Hittite *šarhuu̯ant-* 'fetus etc.', which he left out, and *šāru-* 'booty', which he considered to be unrelated (Rix 1994: 81).

To account for the Celtic forms, Rix (1994: 83–84) departed from a neuter stem, **ser-u̯o-* 'observation; guardianship', with a corresponding collective, *$seru̯ah_2$*, both with regular and expected *e*-grade. It was his hypothesis that the neuter stem came to be used in relation to transient herdsmanship – already in PIE, as I understand it. Noting that the transient herders tended to live like outlaws, he suggested that this would explain how 'observation, care' developed the meaning of 'theft, pillage' in Celtic.

In Italic, on the other hand, **seru̯o-* (n.)/*$seru̯ah_2$* (f.) retained its original meaning and became the derivational basis of *seruāre* 'to observe'. The agent noun **soru̯o-* 'guardian' adapted its root vocalism to that of **seru̯o-/ser-u̯ah₂*, and possibly also to that of an unattested continuant of the thematic verb PIE **ser-e-*, attested in Avestan *haraiti* (3sg.prs.) 'watches'. This term underwent a semantic shift from 'observer, guardian' to 'herdsman', and then to 'slave'.

All of this is theoretically possible, but the Celtic correspondence fails to convince, since (1) we have no independent evidence for the shift from 'herding' to 'raiding' in Celtic, and (2), the existence of PIE **ser-* 'to seize' is relatively well secured by Hittite *šāru-* 'booty', Greek αἱρέω 'to seize' and Latv. *sirt* 'to loot', so deriving the Celtic forms from **ser-* 'to observe' seems unnecessarily complicated. I shall return to a discussion of Rix's scenario in Section 22.3.4, where I discuss the overlapping functions of slaves and herdsmen.

22.3.2.7.3 PÂRVULESCU (2010) ON *SERUUS* AS 'RETAINER'

In a more recent contribution, Pârvulescu (2010: 191) follows in the footsteps of the Roman etymologists mentioned in Section 22.3.2.3, while also continuing down the path taken by Loth just over a century earlier – even if, unlike Loth, Pârvulescu relates *seruus* to *seruāre*. Thus, he shares the skepticism of Saussure and Benveniste regarding the notion that *seruus* ever referred to a guardian:

> Benveniste was perfectly right and one must add that no linguistic analogy to the presupposed semantic development "guard, shepherd" > "slave" has been presented so far. The theory of *servus* as *"guard," "shepherd," or the like should be discarded . . .

Pârvulesco analyzes *seruus* as a postverbal (i.e., a noun derived from a verb without any morphological markers other than as are required for inflection), derived from *seruuāre*. As he observes, the etymologically correct meaning of *seruāre* was 'to watch etc.' Since he considers the sense of 'guardsman' irreconcilable with the notion of 'slave', he concludes that *seruus* must have been created after *seruuāre* had widened its palette of meanings. One of its many meanings is 'to keep, retain', and Pârvulescu (2010: 192) asserts that *seruus* "must have meant originally 'someone retained (for service), hired'," just like Modern English *retainer*.

The type of word-formation pattern suggested by Pârvulescu is a bit of a rarity in Latin. Gardani (2013: 60), who uses the term 'deverbal conversions' for postverbals, notes that they "do not occur particularly frequently in Latin." Furthermore, Pârvulescu (2010: 192–193) admits that they are rarely passive in Latin (i.e., the sense of 'retained' is unexpected), to

[19] This form is in fact not discussed by Rasmussen.

which I would add that only a minority of them are in fact *o*-stems.[20]

Based on this background, we would need strong evidence in favor of positing a postverbal, and such evidence is lacking. In particular, I fail to see how 'someone retained for service' is a more compelling point of departure for a noun meaning 'slave' than 'someone being observed, guarded' or indeed 'an observer, guardian'. Finally, the evidence of a semantic development from 'guard, shepherd' > 'slave' is not as slim as Pârvulescu assumes; see Section 22.3.4.

22.3.2.7.4 OLSEN (2020) ON *SERUUS* AS 'PROTECTED BOOTY'

Olsen (2020: 156–158) offers a proposal that is, to some extent, in line with the position first taken by Loth (Section 22.3.2.5): that Lat. *seruus*, Welsh *herw*, Middle Irish *serbh*, and Hittite *šāru-* all derive from 3. **ser-* 'take, catch' in LIV (535).

Thus, she includes all these stems in her analysis of Lat. *seruus*. Noting that the derivational patterns of 1. **ser-* and 3. **ser-* "are so strikingly similar that one would prefer to unite them under one heading," Olsen (2020: 157) posits a single root, **ser-*, with the original meaning 'to seize, take as booty'. This original meaning of the verb was, according to her proposal, only preserved in Anatolian, where we have Hittite *šāru-* 'booty', and in Celtic, where, as testimony to the Celts' age-old dedication to cattle raiding, we have Welsh *herw* 'outlawry' and Middle Irish *serbh* (f.) 'theft' – thus avoiding the somewhat incredible derivation of a term for 'theft' from a term from 'guardianship', as per Rix (1994: 81).

Indo-Iranian and Greek, on the other hand, bear witness to a semantic extension of the verbal root: it went from "something like 'take as booty', whence 'take into custody, include in one's flock' and finally 'herd, take care of, watch'." Unfortunately, this scenario seems to be disproven by Gk. αἱρέω 'to seize', which retains the original meaning of the root. As for Lat. *seruus*, Olsen (2020: 157) acknowledges that the semantic shift to 'guardian' would be an innovation of the Latin branch, with the corollary that it was unrelated to the same development in Indo-Iranian and Greek.

Such parallel semantic shifts tend to happen only if the development is very trivial and predictable, which is hardly the case with 'theft' → 'protection'. I think, therefore, that Loth's old proposal must be rejected.

22.3.3 A New Proposal

Clearly, there are still many unsolved problems relating to the origins of Lat. *seruus* and the many stems brought into the discussion – and the above are only the major proposals on offer. In light of the preceding discussion, I would conclude that the Celtic and Hittite material belong together as derivatives of PIE **ser-* 'to seize'. Greek οὖρος and Av. *hauruua-* must also belong together, as reflexes of PIE **sor(h₂)u̯o-* ← PIE **ser-* (or **serh₂u̯-*, with Rasmussen). As we shall see in Section 22.3.4, the semantic plausibility of this assertion can be backed up by plenty of extralinguistic evidence.

On the evidence of Latin *seruus*, it is also relatively safe to reconstruct a Proto-Italic **seru̯o-*, derived from the same root and also denoting a guardian. Exactly how this stem, with its unexpected *e*-vocalism, relates to PIE **soru̯o-* is unclear, but, as we have seen, some scholars, notably Rasmussen (1989) and Rix (1994: 80), have offered plausible – though not compelling – solutions involving intermediate neuter stems. Let us finally consider a contribution by Nussbaum (2017) that may help solve this enigma.

22.3.3.1 Nussbaum (2017) on τόμος/τομός/τομή-Stems with e-Grade

Nussbaum (2017) discusses the PIE "agentive and other derivatives of the 'τόμος-type' nouns," that is, a range of deverbal nouns displaying the *o*-grade of the root and *o*-stem inflection. He does not include Gk. οὖρος in his discussion, though this form would fall into this general class of nouns, presumably together with Av. *haurua-*. However, his approach to the general type of thematic *o*-grade nouns seems poised to cast some light on the enigmatic pair **soru̯o-* (as in Gk. οὖρος) and **seru̯o-* (as in *seruus*).

First, Nussbaum (2017: 234–239) offers a survey that illustrates that reflexes of the various types of *o*-grade nouns are not evenly distributed among the linguistic branches. For example, while they are frequent in Indo-Iranian, Greek and Germanic, they are hardly present in Italic and Celtic. Second, Nussbaum (2017: 243) observes that, contrary to universal doctrine, Germanic in particular possesses a noticeable number of stems that would fit neatly into the class under discussion, except that they display the *e*-grade of the root. Apart from that,

> such derivatives are not exactly common anywhere ... but are nevertheless reasonably and profitably seen at the core of some certainly PIE sets of forms. (Nussbaum 2017: 246)

This is interesting for our purposes, since Lat. *seruus* could potentially continue just such a stem.

The inventory of forms of the purported *e*-grade type is expectedly small in Italic and Celtic. A prominent example is Latin *indigena* (m.) 'native (literally in-born)' < PIE **endi-ĝenh₁-ah₂*. Nussbaum (2017: 247) notes that the Latin stem on its own is not a guarantee of a PIE *e*-grade, as it should have undergone syncope, but that the original *e*-grade is secured by OIr. *ingen* 'daughter', of near-identical origin: PIE **eni-ĝenh₁-ah₂*. In Greek, on the other hand, a similar type of compounds display the *o*-grade, as in πρωτό-γονος 'firstborn'.

I am less convinced by the claim that Lat. *fīdus* (*o/ā*-adj.) must necessarily reflect PIE **bʰei̯dʰ-o-* (Nussbaum 2017: 249). A more regular form, **bʰoi̯dʰ-o-*, would yield either ***fūdus* or ***foedus*, and, as noted by NIL (13, n. 8), the latter would be an unfortunate homonym of *foedus* (*o/ā*-adj.) 'foul'. Both ***fūdus* or ***foedus* would be rather dissimilar to the verb, *fīdere*, *fīsī*,

[20] The productive type consists of *a*-stems, like *secta* 'the line along which one travels' from *sectārī*, *pugna* 'battle' from *pugnāre*, or *perfuga* 'deserter' from *perfugere* (Gardani 2013: 61–62; 192–198).

fīsum 'to trust', so it is only to be expected that the noun would adopt the *ī*-vocalism of the verb.

At any rate, Nussbaum's material contains enough forms, even in Latin, to render it plausible that *seruus* reflects a perfectly regular PIE formation: **seru̯o-*. Unfortunately, this would not explain the nature of its relationship with Gk. οὖρος and Av. *hauruua-* < PIE **soru̯o-*: why would there be two parallel formations with different ablaut grades?

Although promising for our purposes, Nussbaum's contribution thus leaves an open question, which I shall attempt to answer in Section 22.3.3.2.

22.3.3.2 A Phonological Proposal: PIE **soru̯o-* > PItal. **seru̯o-*?

In view of the difficulties relating to our stem in Nussbaum's scenario, I would like to point to an intriguing feature that characterizes the remaining handful of Italic forms that Nussbaum adduces, albeit somewhat tentatively, as evidence: they all display the sequence *-er-*, just like *seruus*:[21]

- Lat. *serum* (n.) 'whey (and similar liquids)' < **sero-* is compared to Gk. ὀρός (m.) 'whey, blood serum' < **soro-* (Nussbaum 2017: 249). Despite the difference in gender, it would seem biased not to reconstruct a common origin for these two stems.
- Lat. *uerērī* 'to fear' is tentatively analyzed by LIV (687) as an indirect reflex of an essive, **u̯r̥h$_1$-i̯é-*, derived from **u̯er-* 'to watch'. However, there are phonological difficulties, and Nussbaum (2017: 249) proposes that the Latin verb may reflect a denominative stative (presumably **u̯er-eh$_1$-i̯é-*) derived from a stem **u̯eró-* 'wary; fearful', which is comparable to PGm. **wara-* (seen in, e.g., ON *varr* 'wary, aware') < PIE **u̯oro-* and Tokh. B *were*, A *war* (m.) 'smell' < **u̯oro-*. If this analysis is correct, the Latin term stands out with its *e*-vocalism.
- Lat. *uerbum* (n.) 'word' is best reconstructed, I think, as derived from the same root as Lith. *var̃das* 'name' < **(h$_2$)u̯ord^{h}ó-*.[22] A zero-grade variant is found in PGm. **wurda-*, seen in, e.g., Goth. *waurd* (n.) 'word' **(h$_2$)u̯r̥d^h-o-*, as well as in OPru. *wirds* 'id.' < **(h$_2$)u̯r̥d^h-*. Conspicuously, the *e*-grade of the root occurs only in Latin (De Vaan 2008: 664–665; Nussbaum 2017: 256–257).
- Umbrian *uerfale* (loc. or abl.sg.) 'area for taking auspices' is reconstructable as a derivative of **u̯erb^h-ah$_2$-*.[23] Hit. *u̯arpa-* (n.) 'enclosure' points to **u̯orb^{h}o-*, while Tokh. A *warpi*, B *werwiye* 'garden' point to **u̯orb^h-ii̯o-* (De Vaan 2008: 643, Pinault 2011: 175, Nussbaum 2017: 249). Again, although the Umbrian form seems to reflect the same basic lexeme as the Hittite and Tokharian ones, it alone has the *e*-grade.

Nussbaum (2017: 257–258) offers a lengthy discussion of the implications of the different ablaut grades reflected in Lat. *uerbum* and Lith. *var̃das*. It is very clear, though, that if it were not for the root vocalism, both this and the other items on Nussbaum's list would be readily accepted as direct cognates without the need to discuss intricate morphological rules and derivational chains. In this respect, it is interesting that the list of items in Italic that display *er* in an initial syllable instead of the expected *or* < PIE **or* can in fact be augmented, so it seems fair to consider a phonologically regular development of PIE **o* > PItal. *e/__ r*. Consider the following items:

- *ceruus* (m. *o*-st.) 'stag, deer' is reconstructed as **k̂er-u̯o-*, derived from **k̂er-* 'head, horn'. Other reflexes of this **u̯o*-stem display the *o*- or zero grade; thus, compare Lith. *kárvė* (f.) 'cow' < **k̂orh$_2$u-ii̯ah$_2$-*, OCS *krava* (f.) 'cow' < **k̂orh$_2$-uo-*, OPr. *sirwis* 'deer, roe, *curwis* 'ox' < **k̂r̥u̯i-*.[24] In other words, the *e*-grade of Lat. *ceruus* is an isolated phenomenon (De Vaan 2008: 111).
- *merda* (f. *a*-st.) 'excrement' is reconstructed as **merd-ah$_2$-*, derived from the root **(s)merd-* 'to stink'. However, its obvious cognates, all in Balto-Slavic, display the *o*-grade; thus, Latv. *smar̂ds* 'smell', Rus. dial. *smórod* 'stench' (De Vaan 2008: 374[25]).
- *tergēre* 'to rub clean' occurs next to the rarer synonym *tergere*, derived from a root, **terĝ$^{(u̯)}$-*, that is only preserved in Latin (LIV: 632). As De Vaan (2008: 614) remarks, *tergēre* is probably best understood as an iterative and should therefore reflect **torg-éi̯e-*. Perhaps such a form is reflected precisely in *tergēre*.

To be sure, there are counterexamples. Some of these involve words that, in PIE, displayed an initial labialized velar, *g^w-* and **g^{wh}-*, or the cluster **d^{h}u̯-* and possibly also **tu̯*, so we can postulate that the rule was blocked by the presence of a PItal. rounded obstruent:

- *uorāre* < PItal. **g^{w}or-ā-i̯e-* < PIE **g^{w}orh$_3$-ah$_3$-i̯e-*
- *formus* < PItal. **χ^{w}or-mo-* < PIE **g^{wh}or-mo-*
- *fornus* < PItal. **χ^{w}or-no-* < PIE **g^{wh}or-no-*
- *foris* 'door'< PItal. **þ^{w}or-* < PIE **d^{h}u̯or-*
- *pariēs*, *-etis* (m. *t*-st.) 'wall', if, as I would suggest, derived via a *t*-suffix from PItal. **t^{w}ori-* < PIE **tu̯or-i-* ← **tu̯er-* 'to hold', and related to Lith. *tvorà* 'fence, hedge, border wall' < **tu̯or-ah$_2$*. Here, PIE **o* would yield Lat. **a* in an open syllable, as suggested by Schrijver (1991: 460–465). This would be a unique instance of the sound change **tu̯* > **p*.

In other cases, it is possible that *-or-* represents an analogically leveled zero grade:

[21] I have left out two items from this list. Lat. *merus* 'pure, unmixed, naked' would, in Nussbaum's account, reflect < **mer-ó-* 'sparkling', with the same root as in Gk. μαρμάιρω 'flash, sparkle', also reflected in Latin *mare* (n. *i*-st), Old Irish *muir* (m.) < PIE **mori-* 'sea'. Given that that there is rather a large semantic gap between 'pure' and 'sparkling', I think more evidence is needed for this analysis to be accepted. Unlike Nussbaum (2017: 247; but see also 250), I see no reason to doubt that Lat. *ancus* reflects **h$_2$n̥k-o-*, rather than **h$_2$enko-*.

[22] For the tentative comparison with Hit. *huwarta^{hhi}-* 'to curse' and reconstruction of the root as **h$_2$u̯erd^h-* (as opposed to **h$_2$u̯ert-*; see LIV: 192), see Kroonen (2013: 600) and Kloekhorst (2007: 373).

[23] Nussbaum (2017: 249) includes Lat. *urbs* (f.) 'a city'. If related this stem could, in my opinion, reflect a root noun **u̯r̥b^h-* or an *i*-stem **u̯r̥b^h-i-* or **u̯orb^h-i-*. However, I lean more toward the analysis of Katz (2006), who reconstructs **b^{h}r̥g^h-*, thus relating this item to Gm. **burg-*, seen, e.g., in Gothic *baurgs* (f.) 'fortified town'.

[24] PGm. **heruta-*, seen, e.g., in ON *hjǫrtr* (m.) 'deer', OHG *hiruz*, *hirz*, displays the *e*-grade of the root, but has a derivational history very different from that of *ceruus*. See Kroonen (2013: 223).

[25] De Vaan (2008: 374) analyzes the Russian form as the continuant of a zero-grade formation. It is of course simpler to reconstruct one common preform for all the items.

- Lat. *mordēre, momordī, morsum* 'to bite' must reflect PIE **mord-éi̯e-*. We may think of generalization of the zero-grade form of the root, **mr̥d- > mord-*, which was regular in the weak stem of the perfect as well as in the perfect passive participle (**mr̥d-to-*).
- *torrēre torsī, tostum* 'to dry a thing by heat, parch, roast' clearly continues a causative, **tors-éi̯e-*, also reflected in Ved. (YV) *tarṣáyati* 'dries', PGm. **þarzjan*, seen, for instance, in ON *þerra* 'to (make) dry', MHG *derren* 'to wither, dry up', and possibly also in Hit. *tars-*[hhi] 'to desiccate' (LIV: 637). However, forms derived from the zero grade of the root also occur in Latin; thus, the perfect passive participle *tostum*, presumably < **tr̥s-i-to-*; the participle *torrēns* 'burning, hot', which LIV analyses as the continuant of an essive **tr̥s-h₁i̯é-*; the adjective *torridus*, which, according to the analysis of Olsen (2003), would be built precisely on the essive stem (**tr̥s-eh₁-to-*); the rare *torrēscere*, which LIV analyses as based on a fientive**tr̥s-eh₁-*, but may be derived from the verb underlying *torrēns*. Thus, one might speculate that the zero-grade forms were generalized.
- *torquēre, torsī, tortum* 'to turn (trans.), to hurl' would also appear to reflect a PIE causative, **torkʷéi̯e-*, derived from **terkʷ-*, glossed by LIV (635) as 'sich drehen'; a primary present stem is attested in Hit. *tarukzi, tarkuanzi* 'to dance'. Latin displays quite a few deverbal nouns: *torques* 'a twisted necklace', *tormentum* '(i.a.) an engine for hurling missiles', *tortor* 'a tormentor', etc. Deverbal nouns are typically derived from the same form of the verb that occurs in the perfect passive participle, which, in the case at hand, must reflect PIE **tr̥kʷ-to-*. Here, too, one might speculate on generalization of the zero-grade variant, or perhaps blocking of the rule by the root-final rounded obstruent.

To conclude, while Nussbaum has proved it plausible that PIE possessed *e*-grade variants of the PIE type commonly referred to as τόμος/τομός/τομή, there is also evidence that PItal. **seru̯o-* may in fact reflect PIE **soru̯o-*. This would be a welcome solution because (1) we would have a cognate and a reliable etymology for *seruus*; (2) we would no longer need to ponder the unexpected *e*-grade and (3) PIE would no longer have two presumably synonymous stems that only differed with respect to the root vocalism.

The phonological solution suggested here is new, and it is clear that the field needs to be more thoroughly investigated. Given that the exact conditions for the various developments of the short vowels in Italic are under constant debate, I am certain that this is not the last word on the possible reflexes of PIE **o* in Latin.

In the following, shall turn to the semantic aspect of this etymology which is, fortunately, a much more straightforward matter.

22.3.4 Semantics: From 'Guardian' to 'Slave'

In this section, I address the objections raised by various authorities who question the plausibility of a semantic shift from 'guardian' to 'slave'. First, let us consider the semantic scope of PIE **soru̯o-*, which can be assessed on the evidence of its Greek and Avestan continuants.

As we have seen in Section 22.3.2.4, the two Avestan reflexes of PIE **soru̯o-*, seen in *pasuš.hauruua-* 'guardian of cattle' and *viš.hauruua-* 'village guardian', are used in relation to dogs. If we turn to Greek, we find more attestations and a broader range of usage.

Greek οὖρος (m.) 'guardian' is attested in the *Odyssey*, where Nestor is called οὖρος Ἀχαιῶν 'guardian of the Achaeans' (*Od.* 4.311) and Eumaios is referred to as ἐπίουρος ὑῶν 'guardian of pigs' (*Od.* 13.405), and where Telemachos laments, 'I left no one behind to be a guardian [οὖρος] of my property', οὐ γὰρ ὄπισθεν οὖρον ἰὼν κατέλειπον ἐπὶ κτεάτεσσιν ἐμοῖσιν (*Od.* 15.89). Later Greek reveals similar semantics: Theocritus (8.6,25.1) combines οὖρος 'guardian' with βοῶν 'cows' (gen. pl.); furthermore, there are the compounds θυρωρός 'door-keeper' (e.g., Sappho 98) and πυλωρός 'gatekeeper' (e.g., Aeschylos *Th.* 621). The latter can be used in reference to a dog, while οἰκουρός adj. 'watching/keeping the house' is used in relation to both a dog (Aristophanes V.970) and a rooster (*Plu.* 2.998b), as well as to the sacred serpent in the Acropolis (Ar. *Lys.* 759). As a feminine substantive, οἰκουρός means 'mistress of the house, housekeeper'. The term does not necessarily denote slavery, as it is used to talk about freemen like Nestor and Telemachos, as well as about Eumaios, who was a slave, and about animals.

In support of the claim that Proto-Italic **seru̯o-* is either a direct reflex or a replacement of PIE **soru̯o-*, it may be noted that all of the tasks that, according to the Greek and Avestan evidence, may have occupied a PIE **soru̯o-* are known to have been carried out by male slaves in Rome. Slaves could serve as *pāstōrēs* 'herdsmen', *ostiāriī* 'doormen', *uīlicī* 'farm overseers' and *custōdēs* 'guards'. We shall see that there is ample evidence that keeping guard is an age-old occupation of slaves in early Indo-European societies.

Thus, we can hypothesize that PItal. **seru̯o-* was in fact synonymous with the Greek and Avestan terms for a 'guardsman' or 'lookout': οὖρος and *haurua-*, respectively. Benveniste, Saussure and Pârvulescu do not waste many words on their dismissal of the idea that a term for a guardian could evolve into a term for a slave, presumably because they find it self-evident: it seems perilous and counterproductive to entrust the safety of one's wife, children and property to a subdued outsider, perhaps a foreign captive. However, such a setup is not at all unusual from a historical perspective. See, for example, the many studies on the employment of slaves in warfare and personal protection in Brown & Morgan (2006)'s *Arming Slaves: From Classical Times to the Modern Age*. It would seem that these lines of work have always been ideal for the employment of outsiders, preferably, of course, physically strong males. Brown & Morgan (2006) point to an illustrative case of how the ultimate alien could be the perfect bodyguard:

> According to Blumenthal[26] "contemporary testimony reveals that fifteenth-century Valencians could not conceive of anyone more 'base' or 'vile' than a black male slave." Therefore, in order to

[26] This refers to Blumenthal (2000).

degrade their white enemies, white masters would order their black bodyguards to ridicule, assault, and batter their rivals or foes. Black slaves were also used to commit various crimes for their masters.

The key to this phenomenon is what the sociologist Orlando Patterson (1982) famously defined as the "natal alienation and social death" to which slaves fall victim: the fact that slavery nullifies any cultural or social roots of the enslaved individual. Neither his or her kinship ties, in either ascending or descending generations, or his/her relations with the other sex are formally recognized, since the only legally binding relations that slaves have are to their master. Even his or her children or spouse can be sold off or used for the master's sexual gratification. Patterson (1982: 10) identified the loss of honor that follows from

> the origin of his status, the indignity and all-pervasiveness of his indebtedness, his absence of any independent social existence, but most of all because he was without power except through another.

To this I would add the fact that the master protects the slave from abuse by outsiders.

These are the conditions under which a master is able to turn a slave into a loyal guardian and protector, and which justify a functional overlap between 'guardian' and 'slave'.

As noted, PIE **soru̯o-* would seem to refer generically to any sort of guardian. Rix (1994: 83), who was nevertheless adamant that the semantic shift to 'slave' was particularly tied up with herdsmanship, pointed to the practice of transhumance, the driving of cattle between summer and winter pastures. Many of the itinerant herdsmen employed in transhumance at various epochs of Roman history were slaves, and they were often involved in pillage and plunder during their many months away from home. Similar circumstances explain, in his view, the link to Welsh *herw* and the related MIr. *serbh* (n.) 'theft'.

Rix (1994: 86) even ventured to pinpoint the semantic shift from Italic 'herdsman' to Latin 'slave', linking it with certain historical developments in central Italy in the region along the Tyrrhenian Coast. The first one is incipient urbanization in the ninth to eighth centuries BCE, which would have led to the decreased popularity of herding as an occupation, and thus to a larger demand for herdsmen. The second development, which would have helped meet the demand, is a boom in industry in the seventh to sixth centuries, which presumably triggered the introduction of Greek and perhaps Phoenician slaves.

This scenario implies that Romans would have imported slavery from Greece at a point in time when, according to Mycenaean palace documents dating back to 1500 to 1200 BCE, it had been in existence in some parts of Greece for at least half a millennium (Rodriguez 1997: 312–313). This is of course not impossible: the presumed late introduction of slavery in Rome could be due to special historical circumstances in Italy, such as the late development of urban societies. Rix (1994: 83) indirectly makes such a case when noting that urbanization gradually led to Roman citizens developing a distaste for the herdsman's rough existence. But this is of course not evidence that slavery did not exist up until that point.

The evidence in favor of Rix's scenario is thus highly circumstantial, and Langslow (1997: 102–103) considered the proposal to be a "colourful example" of an *argumentum ex silentio*.[27] As far as the semantic development is concerned, Langslow (1997: 103) admitted that "doubtless there are controllable parallels for this kind of development," whereby "the standard generic term for a slave arose by semantic extension of the word for the type of worker which for a period was most extensively replaced by slave-labour," but such parallels "do not spring to mind and none is offered by R[ix]."

However, we have seen that the parallels are plentiful, and I think that the core aspect of Rix's theory – namely, that PItal. **seru̯o-* originally referred to a herdsman – is highly plausible. Despite the morphological difficulties, the etymology is indicative of some sort of guardian, and Roman society has its roots in Indo-European society, which had a strong pastoralist component. Guarding cattle has a long and prominent history in Indo-European society and its offshoots, even in Rome, where *pecūnia*, the term for 'possessions' and 'money', is derived from *pecu* 'cattle', a fact that Varro (*LL* 5.95) explains with a reference to the Romans' pastoralist past: "to the herdsmen, wealth consisted in cattle at that time" (*in pecore pecunia tum pastoribus consistebat*). If we follow this line of inquiry, it is also possible to point to at least one parallel of the proposed semantic extension, 'herdsman' → 'slave'.

The first question to pursue is whether there is any evidence of a connection between Indo-European cattle herding and slavery. On the one hand, Rix (1994: 86) rightly pointed out that the occupation was likely more prestigious before the various Indo-European societies became settled and/or urbanized; it may therefore have occupied freemen. On the other hand, though, it is an established fact that an overlap between slaves and herdsmen is common in pastoralist societies, even in recent times. Based on a cross-cultural study of 186 societies (Murdock & White 1969), Patterson (2008: 46) observed that:

> Pastoralism is the only dominant subsistence mode that has a direct and positive relationship with slavery: fully 65 per cent of all predominantly pastoral societies are slaveholding, compared with only 35 per cent of predominant fishing groups and 41 per cent of agriculturalists.

Similarly, the FAO (2001) notes:

> A key aspect of pastoral systems is the strong relationship between wealth in livestock and labour. Herds that grow beyond a certain size cannot be managed with household labour alone, and outside herders must be sought. In the twentieth century, this is generally through hired labour, but formerly it was often through slavery or vassal castes.

In line with these observations, there is ample evidence that slaves were typically employed as herdsmen in the early, individual offshoots of Indo-European culture. As far as Rome

[27] Duhoux (1996: 365) likewise cautioned that "il faut se méfier de l'argument du silence : l'institution de l'esclavage est probablement bien plus ancienne que l'époque à partir de laquelle on croit pouvoir situer les termes qui la désignent."

itself is concerned, we know that the *familia rūstica*, the household of workers at a rural farm, comprised mostly slaves, and Woodard (2013: 23–24) rightly observes that many of the herdsmen and *magistrī pecoris* 'overseers of the herds(men)' that we meet in the agricultural prose of Cato the Elder, Columella, and Varro (e.g,. *Rust.* 2.10.1–6) must be slaves. Livy (39.29.8–9) speaks of an uprising among slaves in 185 BCE that led to an investigation into a conspiracy among herdsmen – thus presupposing that slaves and herdsman were largely the same group of people. According to Plutarch (*Crassus* 9.3) and Appian (*Civ.* 1.116), the rebel Spartacus was supported by slaves and herdsmen in the Third Servile War (73–71 BCE) – which indicates that free citizens could also take up the occupation, and that it was a lowly one. In addition, free citizens seem to have been in the minority among herders at the time of Caesar, who tried to regulate the area. According to Suetonius (*Iul.* 1.42.1), he stipulated that, "those engaged in the production of flocks were to have no fewer than a third of freeborn men among their shepherds" (*ii, qui pecuariam facerent, minus tertia parte puberum ingenuorum inter pastores haberent*).

Bryce (2002: 83) says the following about the herdsman's occupation in ancient times:

> In the ancient Near Eastern as well as the Classical world, the herdsman's lot was often a harsh, lonely, and dangerous one. It was certainly not one to which a free man might aspire of his own accord, no matter how humble his status, and in fact herdsmen seem generally to have been slaves, including transported prisoners-of-war.

The Hittite law code in fact appears to employ 'herdsman' as another term for 'slave' when it stipulates (clause 35, New Hittite version) that "[i]f a herdsman takes a free woman in marriage, she will become a slave three years" (Bryce 2002: 122).

For ancient Greece, Hodkinson (2014: 575) notes that:

> Many citizens possessed a few 'house' animals; but larger herds (typically not more than 50–100 strong) were owned by wealthy landowners employing individual hired or slave herders, rather than – as recently – by independent, low-status mobile pastoralist groups.

Myrdal (2011: 302) offers some observations about Scandinavian Viking and early medieval society that echo Bryce's thoughts about the ancient Near Eastern and classical world:

> The sagas contain a number of pieces of evidence that slaves tended livestock: cattle, swine, and sheep. Sheep gained particular standing in Iceland and the shepherd was a category of slave. The same source material also shows that freemen were reluctant to take on this kind of work and that if they herded livestock, they could become the targets of verbal abuse ... But there is also evidence of the freeman's admiration of the slave for his skill as a shepherd.

Consider, finally, the semantics of OIr. *buachill* (m.) < PIE **g^{w}ou̯-k^{w}olho-* 'cowherd', also continued in Greek βούκολος 'cowherd'. According to the *eDIL*, *buachill* has four different meanings. First, 'herdsman, cowherd; herdswoman' is obviously the inherited sense; second, 'youth, boy' may have developed from it, as boys are typically employed to look after the smaller livestock. Third, 'guardian, protector (e.g., of a king)' is an unsurprising secondary development. Finally, 'servant, attendant' is a direct parallel to what is suggested here for *seruus*: that 'guardian' and/or 'herdsman' may end up as a designation of a servant or slave.

To sum it up, the term **soru̯o-* 'observer, lookout, guardsman' goes back to Proto-Indo-European. A **soru̯o-* would guard people, cattle, goods, and property. Italic possesses a form, PItal. **seru̯o-*, that is either identical or at least closely related, but has undergone a semantic shift to 'slave'. This may have been tied up with a downward shift in the prestige associated with herdsmanship in an increasingly settled and urbanized society, as noted by Rix (1994: 86), but herdsmanship may have employed the underprivileged through all epochs, as is well documented in many ancient cultures, including that of Rome.

We can now attempt an adequate response to Benveniste (1932: 432), who poses the rhetorical question:

> Why would the job of a guardian, among all the different jobs assigned to the slave, have seemed more characteristic than that of a cook or an army valet[?]
>
> *pourqoi, entre les multiples métiers imposés à l'esclave, celui de gardien aurait semblé plus caractéristique que celui de cuisinier ou de valet d'armée[?]*

As pointed out by Lévy-Bruhl (1934), Loth (1905: 211), and Benveniste (1969: 355–361) himself, the lowest social stratum of the tribal society would presumably consist of outsiders that were not kin of the head of the clan. We can think of impoverished strangers that had joined the clan for protection and housing; those who had been reared as foundlings, or who were prisoners of war; criminals, debtors, and hired men. Some of these may have worked under conditions that amounted to slavery. As such, a sort of slavery may already have been in place before slaves became a commodity that could be bought and sold, and whose conditions were codified by law. I would propose that the semantic shift from 'guardsman' to 'slave' occurred in such an environment, where the lowliest male members of the workforce were hired, aquired or sold under the general job description of 'protection' or 'guardianship'.[28] In other words, they were hired for their 'muscle' – to employ a term that is currently used to refer to a bodyguard.

We can only guess when this proposed semantic shift may have taken place. Wiedemann (1998: 228) muses, as an alternative to Rix' scenario, that "if the meaning of words like

[28] It may be noted here that one of many uncertain etymologies for the ethnonyms of the Serbs and Croats goes back to Max Vasmer, who suggested that Cr. *hrvat* reflects Ir. *hauruuatā* 'shepherd'. It is therefore an interesting coincidence, but possibly no more than that, that the unrelated Medieval name for the Slavs, Greek Σκλαβηνοί/ Latin *sclauēnī*, is at the root of the designation of 'slave' in so many European languages. I thank Adam Hyllested for pointing this out to me.

ancilla and *seruus* shifted from indicating function to indicating status in the period between the sixth and the third century B.C., it was ... rather as a result of the development of new juristic concepts such as citizenship, and the context of other changes such as the abolition of debt-bondage." However, *seruus* already referred to a slave in the Twelve Tables, authored over a decade before the *Lex Poetelia* abolished debt bondage in 326 BCE (see Section 22.3.1). Furthermore, given that Proto-Italic already had a term for a slave that was still understood in Latin itself, there seems to be no need to tie the semantic shift to any development in the juristic sphere.

An alternative turning point may have been a semantic shift in *familia*, which must originally have referred to a collective of slaves, but in historical periods included the kin of the *pater familiās*. In parallel, *familiāris* eventually became a term for a close friend. Perhaps the ancient *famulus* acquired an archaic ring as it continued to refer to a slave, while its derivative began to refer to the entire household. This might explain why *seruus* gained ground and eventually became the standard term for a slave at some point in the early history of Latin itself.

22.4 Conclusion

In the discussion of the etymologies of terms such as Latin *famulus* 'a slave', *familia* 'a household', *līberī* 'children', and Varro's *instrūmentī genus uocāle* 'sort of equipment that has a voice', I suggested that, while some of these terms confirm a differentiation between free and unfree members of the household, they all, in addition, indicate a situation in which the two groups were perceived as a collective. Moreover, when it comes to the lowest echelons of society, the discussions of terms such as Latin *ancilla* 'female slave' and *seruus* 'male slave' have revealed that certain lowly occupations could be taken up by both free and unfree individuals, thus indicating a situation in which the differentiation between the two tiers must have been of limited practical relevance, even if it was fundamental when it came to certain personal privileges.

Abbreviations

Modern handbooks

eDIL = Irish Language Dictionary (*http://www.dil.ie*)
GPC = Thomas, Bevan, & Donovan 1950
LIV = Rix et al. 2001
NIL = Wodtko et al. 2008

Classical sources

Appian
Civ. = The civil wars

Cicero
Inv. = On invention

Festus
see Paulus Diaconus

Livius Andronicus
Trag. = Tragedies: see Warmington 1936

Suetonius
Iul. = Lives of the Caesars: Julius

Varro
LL = On the Latin language
Rust. = On agriculture, see: Cato the Elder & Varro

References

Anonymous. *Rhetorica ad Herennium*. Harry Caplan (transl.) (Loeb Classical Library 403). Cambridge (MA): Harvard University Press 1953.

Appian. Vol. 3: *The civil wars*, Books 1–3.26. Horace White (transl.) (Loeb Classical Library 4). Cambridge (MA): Harvard University Press 1913.

Benveniste, Émile. 1932. Le nom de l'esclave à Rome. *Révue des Études Latines* 10(2): 429–440.

1969. *Le vocabulaire des institutions indo-européennes.* Vol. 1. Économie, parenté, société. Paris: Éditions de Minuit.

Blumenthal, Debra G. 2000. Implements of labor, instruments of honor: Muslim, Eastern and Black African slaves in fifteenth-century Valencia. PhD diss., University of Toronto.

Bock, Bettina, Stefan Lotze, Susanne Zeilfelder, & Sabine Ziegler. 2015. *Deutsche Wortfeldetymologie in europäischem Kontext.* Vol. 3. Mensch und Mitmensch. Wiesbaden: Reichert.

Bréal, Míchel. 1889. De l'importance du sens en étymologie et en grammaire. *Mémoires de la Société de Linguistique de Paris* 6: 163–175.

Bréal, Michel, & Anatole Bailly. 1885. *Dictionnaire étymologique Latin*. Paris: Hachette.

Brown, Christopher Leslie, & Philip D Morgan (ed.). 2006. *Arming slaves: From classical times to the modern age.* New Haven (CT): Yale University Press.

Brugmann, Karl. 1906. Zu den Benennungen der Personen des dienenden Standes in den indogermanischen Sprachen. *Indogermanische Forschungen* 19: 377–391.

Bryce, Trevor. 2002. *Life and society in the Hittite world.* Oxford: Oxford University Press.

Buck, Carl Darling. 1904. *A grammar of Oscan and Umbrian*. 2nd rev. ed. Boston: Ginn & Company.

Cato the Elder & Varro. *On Agriculture*. W. D. Hooper & Harrison Boyd Ash (transl.) (Loeb Classical Library 283). Cambridge (MA): Harvard University Press 1934.

Cicero. 1949. *On invention. The best kind of orator. Topics.* Translated by H. M. Hubbell. Loeb Classical Library 386. Cambridge (MA): Harvard University Press.

Darmesteter, James. 1875. Notes sur quelques expressions zendes. *Mémoires de la Société de Linguistique* 2: 300–317.

Duchesne-Guillemin, Jacques. 1946. Études hittites *Transactions of the Philological Society* 45: 73–91.

Duhoux, Yves. 1996. Review of Rix 1994. *L'Antiquité Classique* 65(1): 365.

Ernout, Alfred, & Antoine Meillet. 1959. *Dictionnaire étymologique de la langue latine*. 4th ed. Paris: Klincksieck.

FAO. 2001. *Pastoralism in the new millenium.* FAO Animal Production and Health Paper 150. Rome: Food and Agriculture Organization of the United Nations.

Finley, Moses. 1998 [1980]. *Ancient slavery and modern ideology*. Edited by Brent D. Shaw. Princeton (NJ): Marcus Wiener Publishers. First published 1980 by Viking Press.

Gaius. 1904. *Gai institutiones, or: Institutes of Roman law.* Translated by Edward Poste, E. A. Whittuck, & A. H. J. Greenidge. London: Oxford University Press.

Gardani, Francesco. 2013. *Dynamics of morphological productivity: The evolution of noun classes from Latin to Italian*. Leiden: Brill.

Hodkinson, Stephen. 2014. Pastoralism, Greek. In: Simon Hornblower, Antony Spawforth, & Esther Eidinow (ed.), *The Oxford companion to classical civilization*. 2nd ed. New York: Oxford University Press.

Ingold, Tim. 2000. *The perception of the environment: Essays on livelihood, dwelling and skill*. London: Routledge.

Katz, Joshua T. 2006. The "'*urbi et orbi*'-rule" revisited. *Journal of Indo-European Studies* 34(3–4): 319–362.

Kloekhorst, Alwin. 2006. Initial laryngeals in Anatolian. *Historische Sprachforschung* 119: 77–108.

2007. *The Hittite inherited lexicon*. Leiden: Leiden University.

Kroonen, Guus. 2013. *Etymological dictionary of Proto-Germanic*. Leiden Indo-European Etymological Dictionary Series 11. Leiden: Brill.

Langslow, David. 1997. Review of Rix 1994. *Kratylos* 42: 99–104.

Leumann, Manu. 1977. *Lateinische Grammatik*. Vol. 1. Lateinische Laut- und Formenlehre. 2nd ed. Handbuch der Altertumswissenschaft 2.2.1. Munich: C. H. Beck. First published 1926–28.

Lévy-Bruhl, Henri. 1934. *Quelques problèmes du très ancien droit romain: Essai de Solutions Sociologiques*. Paris: Les éditions Domat-Montchrestien.

Lewis, Juan. 2013. Did Varro think that slaves were tools? *Mnemosyne* 66(4–5): 634–648.

Livy. *History of Rome*. Vol. 11: Books 38–40. J. C. Yardley (transl.) (Loeb Classical Library 313). Cambridge (MA): Harvard University Press 1922.

Loth, Joseph. 1905. Contribution á la lexicographie et l'étymologie celtiques. In: H. d'Arbois de Jubainville (ed.), *Mélanges : Recueil de mémoires concernant la littérature et l'histoire celtiques dédié à M. H. d'Arbois de Jubainville à l'occassion du 78e anniversaire de sa naissance*. Paris: Ancienne Librairie Thorin et fils.

Marshall, Lydia Wilson. 2016. Introduction: The comparative archaeology of slavery. In: Lydia Wilson Marshall (ed.), *The archaeology of slavery: A comparative approach to captivity and coercion*, 1–23. Carbondale (IL): Southern Illinois University Press.

Martzloff, Vincent. 2006. *Les thèmes de présent en yod dans l'épigraphie italique et en latin archaïque*. PhD diss., Université Lumière–Lyon II.

Meiser, Gerhard. 2018. The phonology of Italic. In: Jared Klein, B. D. Joseph, Matthias Fritz, & Mark Wenthe (ed.), *Handbook of comparative and historical Indo-European linguistics 2*. Berlin: De Gruyter Mouton.

Morris, Sarah. 2018. Material evidence: Looking for slaves? The archaeological record: Greece. In: Stephen Hodkinson, Marc Kleijwegt, & Kostas Vlassopoulos (ed.), *The Oxford handbook of Greek and Roman slaveries*. Oxford: Oxford University Press Web.

Mouritsen, Henrik. 2011. *The freedman in the Roman world*. Cambridge: Cambridge University Press.

Murdock, G. P., & D. R. White. 1969. Standard cross-cultural samples. *Ethnology* 8: 329–369.

Myrdal, Janken. 2011. Milking and grinding, digging and herding: Slaves and farmwork 1000–1300. In: Bjørn Poulsen & Søren Michael Sindbæk (ed.), *Settlement and lordship in Viking and Early Medieval Scandinavia*. Turnhout: Brepols.

Nielsen Whitehead, Benedicte. 2020. Family structures in Rome: The Roman family and its free and unfree members. In: Benedicte Nielsen Whitehead, Birgit Anette Olsen, & Janus Bahs Jacquet (ed.), *Kin, clan and community in Indo-European Society* (Copenhagen Studies in Indo-European 9), 233–359. Copenhagen: Museum Tusculanum.

Nussbaum, Alan J. 2017. Agentive and other derivatives of the "τόμος-type" nouns. In: Claire Le Feuvre, Daniel Petit, & Georges-Jean Pinault (ed.), *Verbal adjectives and participles in Indo-European languages: Proceedings of the Conference of the Society for Indo-European Studies (Indogermanische Gesellschaft), Paris, 24th to 26th September 2014 = Adjectifs verbaux et participes dans les langues indo-européennes*, 233–266. Bremen: Hempen Verlag.

Olsen, Birgit Anette. 1999. *The noun in Biblical Armenian: With special emphasis on the Indo-European heritage*. Trends in Linguistics: Studies and Monographs 199. Berlin: Mouton de Gruyter.

2003. Another account of the Latin adjectives in -idus. *Historische Sprachforschung* 116(2), 234–275.

2020. Kin, clan and community in Proto-Indo-European Society. In: Benedicte Nielsen Whitehead, Birgit Anette Olsen, & Janus Bahs Jacquet (ed.), *Kin, Clan and Community in Indo-European Society* (Copenhagen Studies in Indo-European 9), 39–180. Copenhagen: Museum Tusculanum.

Pârvulescu, Adrian. 2010. Lat. *servus*. *Indogermanische Forschungen* 115: 190–197.

Patterson, Orlando. 1982. *Slavery and social death: A comparative study*. Cambridge (MA): Harvard University Press.

2008. Slavery, gender, and work in the pre-modern world and early Greece: A cross-cultural analysis. In: Enrico Dal Lago & Constantina Katsari (ed.), *Slave systems, ancient and modern*, 32–69. Cambridge: Cambridge University Press.

Paulus Diaconus. *De verborum significatu quae supersunt cum Pauli epitome. Thewrewkianis copiis usus.* Edited by Wallace M. Lindsay. Bibliotheca scriptorum Graecorum et Romanorum Teubneriana 1349. Berlin: De Gruyter 1997. First published 1913 by Teubner.

Pinault, Georges-Jean. 2011. Let us now praise famous gems. *Tocharian and Indo-European Studies* 12: 155–220.

Plutarch. 1916. *Lives*. Vol. 3. Pericles and Fabius Maximus. Nicias and Crassus. Loeb Classical Library 65. Cambridge (MA): Harvard University Press.

Pokorny, Julius. 1959. *Indogermanisches etymologisches Wörterbuch*. Vol. 1. 3rd ed. Tübingen: Francke.

Rasmussen, Jens Elmegård. 1989. *Studien zur Morphophonemik der indogermanischen Grundsprache*. Innsbrucker Beiträge zur Spachwissenschaftt 55. Innsbruck: Institut für Sprachwissenschaft der Universität Innsbruck.

Risch, Ernst. 1974. *Wortbildung der homerischen Sprache*. Berlin: De Gruyter.

Rix, Helmut. 1994. *Die Termini der Unfreiheit in den Sprachen Alt-Italiens.* Stuttgart: Franz Steiner.

Rix, Helmut, Martin Joachim Kümmel, Thomas Zehnder, Reiner Lipp, & Brigitte Schirmer. 2001. *LIV: Lexikon der indogermanischen Verben*. 2nd ed. Wiesbaden: Reichert.

Rodriguez, Junius P. 1997. *The historical encyclopedia of world slavery*. Santa Barbara (CA): ABC-CLIO.

de Saussure, Ferdinand. 1931 [1915]. *Cours de linguistique générale*. 3rd ed. Edited by Charles Bally, Charles Albert Sechehaye, & Albert Riedlinger. Paris: Payot. First published 1915.

Schrijver, Peter. 1991. *The reflexes of the Proto-Indo-European laryngeals in Latin*. Leiden Studies in Indo-European 2. Amsterdam: Rodopi.

Stewart, Roberta. 2012. *Plautus and Roman slavery*. Chichester, UK: John Wiley & Sons.

Suetonius. *Lives of the Caesars*. Vol. 1: Julius. Augustus. Tiberius. Gaius. Caligula. J.C. Rolfe (transl.) (Loeb Classical Library 31). Cambridge (MA): Harvard University Press 1914.

1914. *Lives of the Caesars*. Vol. 1. Julius. Augustus. Tiberius. Gaius. Caligula. Translated by J. C. Rolfe. Loeb Classical Library 31. Cambridge (MA): Harvard University Press.

Sütterlin, Ludwig. 1891. *Zur Geschichte der verba denominativa im Altgriechischen*. Strassburg: Karl J. Trübner.

1906. Die Denominativverba im Altindischen. *Indogermanische Forschungen* 19(1): 480–577.

Thomas, R. J., Gareth A. Bevan, & Patrick A. Donovan. 1950. *Geiriadur Prifysgol Cymru: A dictionary of the Welsh language*. Dublin: Gwasg Prifysgol Cymru.

Untermann, Jürgen. 2000. *Wörterbuch des Oskisch-Umbrischen*. Indogermanische Bibliothek, 1. Reihe: Lehr- und Handbücher. Handbuch der italischen Dialekte 3. Heidelberg: Universitätsverlag C. Winter.

De Vaan, Michiel Arnoud Cor. 2008. *Etymological dictionary of Latin and the other Italic languages*. Leiden Indo-European Etymological Dictionary Series 7. Leiden: Brill.

Varro. *On the Latin language*. Vol. 1: Books 5–7. Roland G. Kent (transl.) (Loeb Classical Library 333). Cambridge (MA): Harvard University Press 1938.

Vendryes, Joseph. 1935. A propos de lat. *seruos*. *Bulletin de la Société de Linguistique de Paris* 36: 124–130.

Vine, Brent Harmon. 2004. On PIE full grades in some zero-grade contexts: *-*tí*-, *-*tó*-. In: James Clackson & Birgit Anette Olsen (ed.), *Indo-European Word Formation*, 357–379. Copenhagen: Museum Tusculanum Press.

2006. On 'Thurneysen-Havet's law' in Latin and Italic. *Historische Sprachforschung/Historical Linguistics* 119: 211–249.

2012. PIE mobile accent in Italic: Further evidence. In: Benedicte Nielsen Whitehead, Thomas Olander, Birgit Anette Olsen, & Jens Elmegård Rasmussen (ed.), *The Sound of Indo-European: Phonetics, phonemics, and morphophonemics*, 545–575. Copenhagen Studies in Indo-European 4. Copenhagen: Museum Tusculanum.

Wackernagel, Jacob. 1910. Zur griechsichen Wortlehre. *Glotta* 2: 1–8.

Walde, Alois, & J. B. Hofmann. 1938 [1906]. *Lateinisches etymologisches Wörterbuch*. J. B. Hofmann: 3rd, revised ed. Indogermanische Bibliothek, Abt. 1, Reihe 2(1). Heidelberg: Winter. First published 1906.

Warmington, E. H. 1936. *Remains of Old Latin* 2: Livius Andronicus. Naevius. Pacuvius. Accius (Loeb Classical Library 314). Cambridge (MA): Harvard University Press.

1938. *Remains of Old Latin*. Vol. 3. Lucilius. The Twelve Tables. Loeb Classical Library 329. Cambridge (MA): Harvard University Press.

Watkins, Calvert. 1976. Varia I. *Ériu* 27: 116–122.

1995. *How to kill a dragon. Aspects of Indo-European poetics*. New York: Oxford University Press.

Wiedemann, Thomas Ernst Josef. 1998. Review of Rix 1994. *The Classical Review* 48(1): 227–228.

Wodtko, Dagmar S., Britta Irslinger, & Carolin Schneider. 2008. *Nomina im indogermanischen Lexikon*. Heidelberg: Universitätsverlag Winter.

Woodard, Roger D. 2013. *Myth, ritual, and the warrior in Roman and Indo-European antiquity*. Cambridge: Cambridge University Press.

Zelnick-Abramovitz, Rachel. 2018. Greek and Roman terminologies of slavery. In: Stephen Hodkinson, Marc Kleijwegt, & Kostas Vlassopoulos (ed.), *The Oxford handbook of Greek and Roman slaveries*. Oxford: Oxford University Press Web.

Concluding Reflections

23 NEW DIRECTIONS IN ARCHAEOGENETICS AND ARCHAEOLINGUISTICS: RECAPITULATION AND OUTLOOK

GUUS KROONEN AND KRISTIAN KRISTIANSEN

23.1 The Emergence of New Interdisciplinarity

In the past couple of years, we have witnessed how new techniques for the study of ancient biomolecules have disrupted the study of the human past and reshaped the research arena (Cappellini et al. 2018). Traditionally, only two lines of evidence have been available for human prehistory: that of prehistoric archaeology and that of historical linguistics. Now we are so fortunate as to witness these being supplemented with a third, entirely independent line of evidence, viz. palaeogenetics. The consequences of this addition can safely be called spectacular.

In the late nineteenth century, the discovery of the systematic nature of sound change unlocked a hitherto unexploitable data set on our linguistic ancestors, which gave us the methodology to reconstruct prehistoric protolanguages and – by proxy – some of the cultural features of their corresponding speech communities. Likewise, the current palaeogenomic revolution is creating an entirely new scientific record on our genetic ancestors, one that was previously unattainable and whose existence long remained covert. The breaking down of this knowledge barrier is now resulting in an explosion of new data relevant to the research agendas of archaeology and historical linguistics. During the past couple of years, we have seen how a number of major, age-old questions about European prehistory have been resolved with the help of new genetic data.

The first such debate concerned the main driving force in the spread of agriculture from Anatolia to Europe – whether it was driven by demic (Childe 1925) or cultural (Edmonson 1961) diffusion. Despite decades of research, it had not been possible for scholars to reach a consensus on the basis of the archaeological evidence alone. However, as soon as the aDNA became available, the genetic makeup of Europe's first farmers appeared to be surprisingly homogenous and consistent with a demographic expansion from Anatolia all across Europe (Skoglund et al. 2012).

A second major debate addressed with the help of aDNA was that of the age-old question of the original location of the Indo-European languages. Of the two competing main explanations, the Steppe Hypothesis and the Anatolia Hypothesis, the former had support among the wider Indo-Europeanist community, including a few archaeologists (Mallory 1995; Anthony 2007; Kristiansen 1998), while the Anatolia Hypothesis was more prevalent among the wider archaeological community. Since the early 1990s, the debate had lingered in stalemate, linguists accepting the lexical evidence for a Late Neolithic cultural context, and archaeologists rejecting that evidence. The latter argued that the only (archaeologically) known cultural transition geographically extensive enough to be able to yield the large area in which Indo-European was historically spoken was the agricultural transition (Renfrew 1987).

While the outcome of the first debate, on the spread of agricultural, initially offered support for the Anatolia Hypothesis (Skoglund et al. 2012), additional studies later revealed a second large-scale population movement, from the South Russian steppe, taking place in the third millennium BCE (Allentoft et al. 2015; Haak et al. 2015; Malmström et al. 2019). These important studies, in other words, indicated the population movement as it had been proposed by Marija Gimbutas as part of her Kurgan Hypothesis, i.e. the archaeological part of the Steppe Hypothesis. By extension, the studies confirmed that this movement indeed emanated from the area that was proposed by Otto Schrader on the basis of the lexical evidence offered by the reconstructed Indo-European protolanguage (see Chapter 1 in this volume). Once complete, the different pieces of the puzzle – of the Indo-European homeland, archaeology, linguistics, and genetics – fell into place.

As the aforementioned cases show, the breakthrough character of the new type of evidence lies, first of all, in the possibility of using it for testing hypotheses on prehistoric population movements and contacts as they have been postulated in the fields of archaeology and linguistics. However, while the new data is no doubt invaluable, the disruptive nature of the new field of palaeogenomics is even more fundamental. Since it offers a new line of evidence that is independent of the other disciplines, it offers nothing less than a test of the very methodologies by which archaeology and linguistics process their data.

Two important conclusions can be drawn from the recent genetic studies on the Indo-European languages. First of all, the genetic evidence put large-scale mobility – and its potential as a driving factor in cultural and linguistic change – back on the agenda (cf. Reiter & Frei 2019). From the latter quarter of the twentieth century, such mobility had become increasingly controversial in mainstream archaeology, but not in historical linguistics. The large area in which Indo-European languages have been spoken since the dawn of history simply makes it unthinkable, for most linguists, that anything other than a dramatic shift had taken place in Eurasia in the not-too-distant past. Nevertheless, the new genetic results took the field of Indo-European studies by surprise, as the "massive migrations from the steppe" seemed more dramatic than most Indo-Europeanists had even imagined – though "massive" here should rather be understood with reference to the scale of the genetic replacement and admixture process. The results, however, did not lead to such strong reactions as those seen in the field of archaeology (Hakenbeck 2019; Hansen 2019), since they by and large confirmed the linguistic consensus, namely that one or more large-scale population movements were driving the Indo-European dispersal.

Second, the genetic evidence provided proof that the linguistic methodology for pinpointing the original location of reconstructed protolanguages, including that of Proto-Indo-European, is robust, or at least robust enough. The methodology of linguistic palaeontology had been rejected by Colin Renfrew, who had entertainingly called the results of this line of research "a word-picture of the original homeland" (1987: 75). It is certainly true that the semantic reconstruction of the Proto-Indo-European lexicon is more probabilistic than the formal reconstruction (thus e.g. Heggarty 2006; Heggarty & Renfrew 2014), which is governed by the strict application of *sound laws*. However, this does not warrant a rejection of the methodology on the whole (Mallory 2020). After all, it can hardly be coincidental that the "word-picture" of the Indo-European homeland that was created with the help of this linguistic methodology turned out to be an almost exact match with the genetic homeland of the Yamnaya genetic expansion. One could in fact go so far as to say that the breakthrough in genetic studies was redundant to the problem of the Indo-European homeland, as this had already been answered with the help of archaeolinguistic methods (cf. Mallory 1989). Nonetheless, the results now appear to be of vital importance, as they demonstrate the robustness of the methodology and the reliability of its results to skeptics from outside linguistics, especially in archaeology. In other words, the palaeogenomic revolution did not just confirm the linguistic consensus on the Indo-European homeland question; it also offered a cross-validation of the linguistic methodology that was employed to arrive at this consensus (see Figure 23.1).

Undeniably, genetic studies are exerting a strong empirical force on the affected disciplines by evaluating the various theories and methodologies concerned with the reconstruction of the human past. Despite the initial hesitation, we can now observe a strong reorientation of the field of archaeology, in which the new tools for ancient DNA, stable isotopes, lipids, and proteins are increasingly being employed to develop complex, multifaceted models of the human past that increasingly allow or even demand integration with neighboring disciplines. Thus, the palaeogenetic revolution, or the "third science revolution" in archaeology, inevitably also drives an intellectual revolution demanding the wider theoretical and interdisciplinary integration of archaeology, genetics, and linguistics, as the previous scientific revolutions did with historical linguistics and prehistoric archaeology (Kristiansen 2014). With archaeology being ushered into a new era in which relative knowledge is increasingly replaced by absolute knowledge (Figure 23.2), the resulting empiricism promises in turn to transform the field of historical linguistics, as the new instruments for the study of ancient biomolecules offer unprecedented ways of formulating, testing, and integrating linguistic hypotheses on the kinship systems, dietary habits, locations, and movements and contacts of prehistoric speech communities.

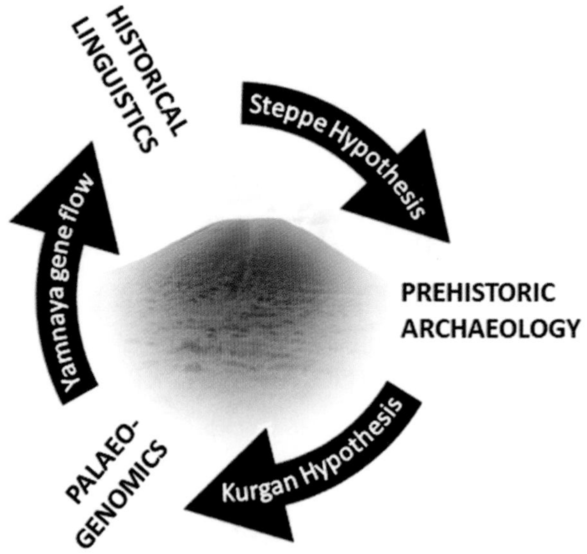

FIGURE 23.1. The interdisciplinary cross-validation of the results of the methodologies applied to the Indo-European homeland problem.

23.2 Recapitulation and Integration

The new directions and their implications become abundantly clear in the contributions to this volume, even if, or perhaps especially because, they also raise a series of new research questions.

There is now exhaustive proof that the economic foundation of the Yamnaya population was nomadism, primarily based on cattle herding (Anthony, Chapter 2 in this volume), and that this nomadism was not in any way "parasitic," i.e. reliant on contacts with agriculturalist societies. The use of wheeled wagons providing mobile homes allowed for the economic exploitation

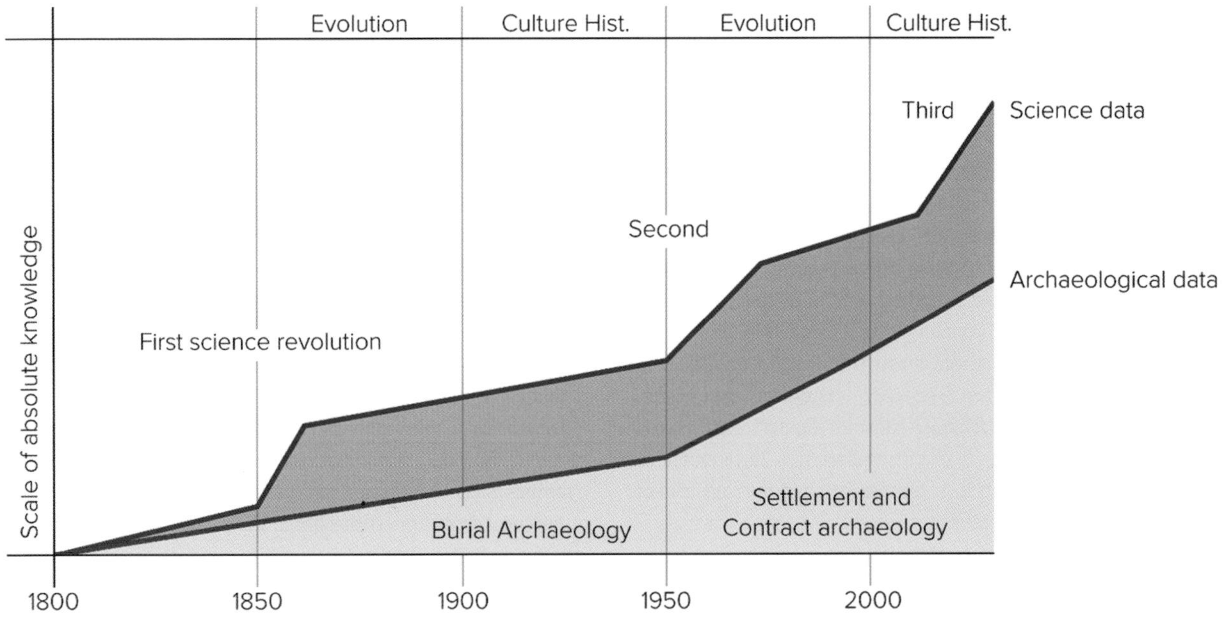

FIGURE 23.2. Diagram showing the impact of the three science revolutions in archaeology and their transformation of relative into absolute knowledge, along with the formation of archaeological Big Data.

of the vast steppe grasslands, which, through the stomachs of domesticated ruminants, was turned into a rich and reliable source of protein (Wilkin, Ventresca Miller & Fernandes et al. 2021). The rise of mobile pastoralism explains the termination of Eneolithic settlements along the major riverbanks, and the disappearance, with only few exceptions (e.g. Mikhailovka and Repin), of permanent Yamnaya settlements. Core Indo-European vocabulary for wheel and wagon technology as well as animal husbandry – including, notably, a word for 'cowherd' (Greek βουκόλος and Old Irish *búachaill*) – is largely consistent with the pastoralist lifestyle. The much-debated etymology of the Latin word for 'slave', *servus*, may in fact be understood from this context, if it originally meant 'herdsman' (Nielsen Whitehead, Chapter 22 in this volume). Many of the herdsmen involved in transhumance at various periods of Roman history were slaves. Practices of transhumance, i.e. seasonal movements of people and herds, can be demonstrated for Yamnaya groups (Shishlina 2004: 101–102; see also Chapter 3 in this volume). It is tempting to speculate that this small-scale mobility prepared Indo-European speakers for the long-distance movements, now amply documented by aDNA, that ultimately led to the large-scale dispersal of what today is one of the world's largest language families.

A more controversial aspect of the Steppe Hypothesis is the role of horse-riding in population dispersal. In Marija Gimbutas's classic formulation of this hypothesis, as well as in many of its modern manifestations, the introduction of horse-riding is seen as having been instrumental to the rise of mobile pastoralism and its expansion to Europe and Asia. Were Indo-European speakers cowboys *avant la lettre*? It is easy to imagine how steppe nomads, arriving on horseback, could have overwhelmed the more sedentary, purportedly more peaceful and matriarchal farming societies of Europe (Glob 1945: 242; Gimbutas 1956, 1994). However, the archaeological and linguistic evidence does not unequivocally support this frontierlike model of the Indo-Europeanization of Europe. Horse remains are, perhaps surprisingly, exceedingly rare at Corded Ware sites (Vandkilde 2007: 70), despite the considerable gene flow this archaeological culture received from steppe nomads. Moreover, the linguistic evidence is open to multiple interpretations. A Proto-Indo-European word for 'horse' can admittedly be reconstructed (viz. ***h_1eḱ-u(o)-*), indicating that early Indo-European speakers must have been familiar with this animal. However, it is ambiguous whether the term referred to the wild or the domesticated animal (Meid 1994: 55), as Renfrew (1989) also keenly observed, and no Proto-Indo-European word for 'horse rider' appears to be at hand. The question of mounted warfare has recently been addressed in a crossdisciplinary study (Librado et al. 2021). It reveals that, while the genetic origins of the domesticated horse can indeed be traced back to the wild populations of the Pontic–Caspian steppe, the domestication event was a long-term process, and steppe-derived horses were not introduced to Europe during the initial expansion of the Yamnaya culture. Instead, they first became dominant, across the entirety of Eurasia, a thousand years later, following the introduction of chariotry from the area south of the Ural Mountains. Genetic evidence, this time consisting of nonhuman aDNA, again turns out to be a powerful tool in evaluating archaeolinguistic hypotheses.

In conclusion, the initial Yamnaya expansion to Europe, a likely vector for the spread of a number of Indo-European dialects to this area, was probably not associated with the introduction of the genetically modern horse, nor with horse-riding.

Fascinatingly, the contrast with the spread of the Indo-Iranian languages in Asia could hardly be more striking. Here, on the other side of the Indo-European-speaking world, the dispersal of this linguistic subgroup has traditionally been connected with the introduction of chariotry (cf. Kuz'mina & Mallory 2007). A review of the Proto-Indo-Iranian lexical evidence confirms that this reconstructed language, usually dated to ±2000 BCE, indeed possessed much of the terminology associated with this highly disruptive technological advancement (Lubotsky, Chapter 15 in this volume). Terms such as **HratHiH-* 'charioteer' (Skt. *rathī́-*, OAv. *raiϑī-*) and **HratHai-štaH-* 'chariot fighter' (Skt. *rathe-ṣṭhá-*, YAv. *raϑaē-štā-*) imply that Proto-Indo-Iranian cannot have been spoken much earlier than the rise of chariotry and cannot have disintegrated much later.

This archaeolinguistic hypothesis too has been evaluated with the help of aDNA. Several important crossdisciplinary studies have jointly revealed gene flow from the steppe to South Asia during the Middle to Late Bronze Age, ca. 2300–1200 BCE (Damgaard et al. 2018; Narasimhan et al. 2019; Shinde et al. 2019). As this gene flow is consistent with the timing and geographic scope of the hypothesized introduction of Indo-Iranian, it offers a suitable proxy for the movements of its speakers. Moreover, the chariot horizon roughly coincides with the swift adoption of the genetically modern horse, as now shown by Librado et al., across Eurasia. Plausibly, late Indo-Europeans groups, including the linguistic ancestors of the Indo-Iranians, were involved in the extended domestication process of steppe horses. Conversely, the mobilization of horses for transport, both in the form of mounts and traction animals, must have greatly aided the spread of Indo-Iranians, as well as their language, to South Asia.

Again, however, a linguistic caveat is in order. As noted by Lubotsky (Chapter 15 in this volume), much of the chariot terminology is detectable in Proto-Indo-Iranian, but the word for 'spoke' is not shared by Indic and Iranian, and therefore cannot be demonstrated for the linguistic parent. This discrepancy may be due to lexical loss in Iranian, which is attested comparatively late. On the other hand, as the spoke is one of the final, defining innovations that completed the chariot, the Indo-Iranian linguistic unity may already have started fragmenting prior to the final developmental phase of this vehicle. If so, Indo-Iranian dialects must have already begun dispersing at the stage when two-wheeled vehicles still had massive wheels, a stage also indeed documented for some Sintashta graves.

In a new, highly enlightening archaeological study on this topic, it is shown that the gradual development from two-wheeled wagons to full-fledged chariots can be dated to the latter half of the third millennium BCE, and it took place between the Caucasus and Ural Mountains (Chechushkov and Epimakhov, Chapter 14 in this volume). The period in which the development was complete, ca. 2071 to 1901 BCE, thus gives us a new dating – not just for the dawn of the chariot age, but also for the time window in which the Proto-Indo-Iranian speech community must have started its linguistic diaspora. Intriguingly, the Librado et al. 2021 study is consistent with this linguistically and archaeologically refined scenario. It reveals that the genetically modern horse was already becoming more widespread in the steppe from second half of the third millennium BCE, i.e. slightly before the dawn of chariotry. Given the fit with the linguistically suitable time window, a resulting, new hypothesis could be that Indo-Iranian speakers were among the drivers of the earliest and relatively limited expansion of the domesticated horse in the East European steppe, i.e. among the literal drivers of two-wheeled, horse-pulled carts.

In summary, these new interdisciplinary breakthroughs may serve to showcase how linguistic, archaeological, and genetic hypotheses can be aligned and integrated to help answer some of the most vexed questions about the prehistory of South Asia (Bryant & Patton 2005).

Returning to Europe, it is clear that there is a great need to move beyond the traditional narratives associated with the Steppe Hypothesis, even if, or perhaps especially because, the hypothesis is increasingly becoming mainstream across different disciplines and among the general public. It is a major challenge to do so while also addressing all of the new research questions that are presenting themselves. These are especially concerned with the nature of the steppe migrations: what were the primary forces behind the Yamnaya expansion to Europe and how numerous were the migrating groups? Where did the transformation from a Yamnaya pastoral economy to a Corded Ware mixed farming/pastoral economy take place? Even if both genetic and archaeological indicators assign a relatively large role to young males as drivers of the expansion, trained and organized into warrior bands (Sjögren et al. 2016), this still does not account for the rather massive genetic replacement and admixture processes taking place in temperate Europe within a few hundred years.

Again, further integration of the different disciplines promises to enhance the ways in which these types of questions can be addressed. By applying linguistic palaeontology, aspects of kinship configurations and marital strategies can be reconstructed for various consecutive stages of the Indo-European language family, sometimes in great detail. By employing lexical evidence, two new studies on Indo-European kinship terms reveal a largely patrilocal society with institutionalized female exogamy (Pronk; Olsen, Chapter 19 and Chapter 20). With the help of the new archaeolinguistic toolkit, i.e. the combined analysis of aDNA and stable isotopes, the results of such lexical investigations can now be compared with the kinship structures documented for steppe-impacted groups in third-millennium BCE Europe (Mittnik et al. 2019). On the macrolevel, it can be demonstrated that patrilocality and patrilineality were prevalent in Europe also prior to the steppe invasions (Furtwängler et al. 2020; Haak et al., Chapter 5 in this volume), with the difference that Neolithic societies were more collective in nature. Future studies will have to show exactly how Neolithic and steppe kinship and marriage systems interacted, and how they became integrated in Corded Ware and Bell Beaker contexts. In the meantime, we can hypothesize that similarities in social practices facilitated the integration of incoming Indo-European speakers into local societies.

Fosterage, for instance, an important cultural tradition among later Indo-European-speaking groups, appears to have played an important role in the creation of kinship alliances in Late Neolithic Europe (Sjögren et al. 2020), as it did in historically known Old Germanic and Old Irish societies. For lack of a shared vocabulary, this tradition cannot be assumed with certainty for the original Proto-Indo-European society, but many of the more evolved Indo-European subgroups of Europe developed terminology for it independently. This poses a linguistic problem in that it needs to be determined when fosterage arose in this area and the motivation for its inception. Microlevel archaeogenetic studies like the one by Mittnik et al. have suggested, rather spectacularly, that this practice was already in place among Central European Bell Beaker groups. In other words, the institution of fosterage was present in the archaeological cultures that directly postdated the steppe incursions (Sjögren et al. 2020). Quite possibly, an explanation for the rise of fosterage should therefore be sought at the very interface of the mobile pastoralist and sedentary farming lifestyles; if originally nomadic groups became more sedentary after their integration with European farmers, the advantage of fosterage would be obvious, as it could be used to create and strengthen long-term alliances and long-distance networks between households. It can possibly be seen as an answer to the loss of the collective organization of sedentary farmers due to the introduction of a more individual organization based on smaller households, which may have created a need for new forms of social cohesion.

Interestingly, the reality of large-scale networks is at any rate demonstrated by the remarkable and persistent continuity of similarities in burial practices among Corded Ware groups across all of Northern Europe (Bourgeois & Kroon, Chapter 6). It is tempting to see this homogeneity as a result of the introduction of new, interregionally accepted institutions, such as, on the male side, fosterage. There is no reason only to focus on male mobility, however. New evidence for mobility based on reciprocity between communities during the third and early second millennia BCE additionally points to institutions such as female exogamy (Knipper et al. 2017; Mittnik et al. 2019; Sjögren et al. 2020). A case can further be made for the existence, in third-millennium BCE Central European Bell Beaker contexts, of mobile wet-nurses. These subadult women and accompanying children may have traveled great distances, possibly making use of the same networks as their male peers, to help foster other women's offspring (Stockhammer, Chapter 21 in this volume). Such practices would have positively impacted the mortality of the dominant societal groups, which in turn may have helped increase the genetic impact of the Yamnaya migrations. Not least, all of the aforementioned institutions must have had a strongly homogenizing effect on the cultural communities involved and also have played a role in the consolidation of one or more Indo-European dialects.

After its establishment, the Bell Beaker culture came to dominate large parts of Europe, including its Atlantic fringe. Not very surprisingly, therefore, the Bell Beaker culture also played a pivotal role in the century-old linguistic debate about the spread of Celtic to the British Isles. Interdisciplinary perspectives, especially the recent publication of relevant palaeogenomic data, have again galvanized this debate. In a large study published in 2018, Olalde, Brace, Allentoft et al. show that the Bell Beakers, while culturally homogenous, were genetically diverse. Whereas Neolithic ancestry persisted in the south, especially on the Iberian Peninsula, the arrival of the Bell Beaker phenomenon in Britain was coupled with a large-scale genetic shift to steppe ancestry within a few generations around the mid-third millennium BCE. This new data thus resolved a similarly old archaeological debate over whether the Bell Beaker identity was, in other words, propagated by a combination of cultural and demic diffusion. The study also indirectly ties in with the linguistic debate. According to some archaeologists (O'Brien, Chapter 10 in this volume), the swift introduction of Beaker metallurgy in Ireland is highly suggestive of the presence of a lingua franca, perhaps one derived from a Late Indo-European language. Could the language that spread to the British Isles with a "Beaker Folk," as has been proposed in older scholarship (Childe 1925; also cf. Hyllested 2010), and whose migrations now find new support in the contemporaneous genetic shift, have been Proto-Celtic?

Linguistically, this hypothesis confronts us with an important paradox. Upon reaching the Atlantic, migration had to come to a standstill until the maritime skills of boatbuilding and seafaring were adopted, in order to cross the English Channel and continue to Ireland. These skills were evidently at hand amid the maritime Bell Beaker horizon of the third millennium BCE, perhaps originating in Iberia and rapidly spreading all the way to Jutland (Prieto-Martinez 2012). As a result, if the northern Bell Beakers spoke Proto-Celtic, or the precursor of this, one should expect these cultural aspects to have left marks in the lexicon, whose historical distribution covered much the same territories as the Beaker complex. This question is addressed in a thorough survey by Stifter (Chapter 12 in this volume). Stifter, however, observes "a dearth of vocabulary that relates to a maritime habitat," and is consequently forced to conclude that the sea played a negligible role in the subsistence of the Proto-Celtic language community. Similarly, an overview of the shared Celtic-Germanic lexicon finds no strong evidence that maritime vocabulary was exchanged between Celtic and Germanic before the Bronze Age (Van Sluis et al., Chapter 13 in this volume). Therefore, from the linguistic perspective, the Bell Beaker maritime horizon does not appear to be a suitable fit.

There are additional linguistic counterindications for an early Celtic expansion to Britain. Lexical evidence of metalworking practices offers some clues to the locations and periodizations of the different Indo-European descendant languages (Olander; Thorsø & Wigman et al., Chapters 7 and 8 in this volume). It is well known that core Proto-Indo-European had words for copper, gold, and silver, placing it firmly in the Early Metal

Age. From the metallurgical perspective, it is therefore interesting to see that Proto-Celtic retained the Indo-European word for silver, *h_2(e)rǵ-nt-o-*, which would be an anachronism if spoken in the Bell Beaker period, as this metal became widespread in Atlantic Europe only later. It rather seems that Proto-Celtic retained the same Eastern European tradition of silver metallurgy throughout its prehistory, which distinguishes it from the Atlantic maritime Bell Beaker zone both chronologically and geographically. In fact, from the metallurgical perspective, it can even be argued that Proto-Insular Celtic was a language, or at least a relatively homogenous language community, that persisted until as late as the Iron Age. This at least appears to follow the fact that both Goidelic and British Celtic share a single term for this metal, viz. **īsarno-*.

Thus, various linguistic arguments can be offered for a much later entry of Celtic speakers to the British Isles than the dramatic appearance of steppe ancestry with the Bell Beaker burial identity. For chronologically more attractive contexts, we must rather turn to the Atlantic Bronze Age. During this period, the rise of a warrior society can be deduced from the distribution and function of Late Bronze Age hillforts in Ireland, as demonstrated by O'Brien. It has previously been argued that this societal change, which also entailed the rise of sword warfare, could have been coupled with language change (Mallory 2016). Although there is reason to be pessimistic on the archaeological side (cf. O'Brien 2016), the fact that a Proto-Celtic word for 'hillfort', i.e. **dūno-*, can be reconstructed, and is found in both mainland European and Insular British toponyms, is favorable to such a scenario. Similarly, Ling & Koch (Chapter 11 in this volume) argue for the Atlantic Bronze Age (1200–900 BCE) as the period in which Celtic was introduced to Britain and Ireland, underlining the rich archaeological evidence for long-range maritime connections between North and South Atlantic Europe. Both of these hypotheses have now received support in the form of another breakthrough genetic study, which reveals a large-scale migration from France into southern Britain at the end of the Bronze Age (Patterson et al. 2022). The genetic evidence, however, has not yet definitively resolved the long-term linguistic controversy over the original location of the Proto-Celtic homeland, i.e. whether it must be sought in Central or Southwestern Europe, although indications point to a Bohemian source population. Here, it would seem crucial to reevaluate, once more, the sparsity of Proto-Celtic maritime vocabulary: if taken at face value, this would seem to favor a relatively indifferent crossing of the channel rather than an extended cultural focus on seafaring and the Atlantic.

To summarize, we have seen in the past couple of years how some of the most prominent archaeolinguistic debates about the dispersal of the Indo-European language can be resolved by cross-testing the various hypotheses with the help of biomolecular evidence. In addition, many new research questions have presented themselves, though old questions remain. Here, we cannot avoid mentioning one of the most persistent and as yet unresolved issues, one on which there is no consensus between the disciplines: namely the question of how the Anatolian branch of Indo-European arrived in its historically attested location. As an indication of the topicality of this controversy, one has only to point to two volumes that have recently been devoted to the discussion of the Anatolian split and the Indo-Anatolian homeland (Anthony 2019; Serangeli & Olander 2019).

The classical Steppe Hypothesis is consistent with the dispersal of most of the Indo-European branches, including Tocharian, but no evidence for a masse steppe migration into Anatolia has yet been found. Proponents of the classical Steppe Hypothesis usually assume a westward entry of pre-Yamnaya steppe groups through the Bosporus (Anthony 2007; Kloekhorst, Chapter 4 in this volume). However, genetically speaking, the only major change so far detected consists of a westward gene flow of Caucasian Hunter Gather ancestry emanating from the Caucasus, ca. 5000 to 3000 BCE (Damgaard et al. 2018). So while most linguists usually interpret the presence of the Anatolian branch in Southwest Asia as the result of an intrusion from the steppe, no clear genetic proxy has surfaced so far. Until that happens, proponents of the Steppe Hypothesis are forced to resort to genetically unfalsifiable models, building on the much criticized concept of "elite dominance", in which gene flow is assumed without any consequences for the gene pool. The archaeological and genetic evidence, however, do not rule out an entirely different scenario. In what could be called a "prequel" to the steppe dispersal, some have located the split of the Indo-Anatolian protolanguage in the Caucasus region, with Proto-Indo-European moving on to the steppe, and Proto-Anatolian spreading across Anatolia. Alternative Indo-Anatolian homelands have accordingly been sought in the Caucasus, either in the south (Reich 2018; Wang, Reinhold, Kalmykov, et al. 2019) or the north, specifically in the Maykop culture (Kristiansen 2020).

From the linguistic perspective, however, the advantages of this scenario are not immediately obvious. An immediate concern is the agricultural economy of the Maykop culture, which stands in stark contrast to the almost complete lack of terms for plant domesticates in Proto-Indo-Anatolian (Kroonen et al. 2022). Arguably, a possible positive linguistic argument for placing Proto-Indo-Anatolian in the Caucasus is embodied in the Proto-Indo-European word *$h_2$ul$h_1$no-* 'wool' (Olsen, Chapter 18 in this volume), a textile that has not been found in the Pontic–Caspian steppe prior to the late third millennium BCE (Shishlina, Chapter 17 in this volume). On the other hand, this issue can be perhaps resolved by assuming that Proto-Indo-Anatolian was spoken on the northern flanks of the Caucasus, e.g., in a cultural context connected with the so-called Steppe Maykop. Moreover, the Maykop gene pool, originally pure CHG, appears to have been admixed with Anatolian farmer ancestry in the fifth millennium BCE, which disfavors a scenario in which it served as the source population of the CHG component in the Yamnaya mating network (Anthony 2019). Further genetic studies are required to determine the extent to which it is possible to identify still-undetected steppe-derived ancestry in third-millennium Anatolia, and from which side it may have arrived there. Not least, there remains the need to paint the long-due "word-picture" of the Proto-Anatolian speech community, so as to determine the extent to which their language is (or is not) compatible with the early phases of steppe pastoralism (cf. Kloekhorst, Chapter 4 in this volume). Any solution to the problem of the Anatolian dispersal would be incomplete without a comprehensive investigation of the relevant linguistic palaeontology.

23.3 Future Methodological and Interpretative Trends

In conclusion, during this initial phase of the third science revolution, we are witnessing a breakdown of the barriers between the disciplines. For a more robust scientific integration to emerge between the three disciplines, we should expect to see more advanced modeling of data from archaeology, genetics, and linguistics. We have seen already some examples in archaeogenetics, where genetic and environmental changes have been correlated over larger regions of western Eurasia through time (Racimo et al. 2020), and we should expect to see similar efforts for genetic and linguistic changes in the future (Figure 23.3). We thus propose a three-tiered research strategy, in which phase one represents more or less autonomous analytical procedures, naturally supported by a chronological foundation based on C14 and other forms of contextualized dating.

The second phase is the application of various forms of interactive mathematical modeling, which enables data from the different disciplines to be correlated and statistically weighted against each other. Again, this must be supported by digital databases of evidence (Big Data), which reformat data for use with comparable analytical platforms. High-resolution local data can, at least in theory, be analyzed in similar ways, and then brought into dialogue with the macro models. Moving from demonstrating correlations in the archaeological record to testing causal explanations in a secure, model-based framework is a giant leap that requires the development of new types of integrated modeling – ones that combine processes in the domains of linguistic, biological, cultural, and ecological data, and also link micro- and macroscale phenomena. Generative models, including Agent-Based models (ABMs), provide a general family of approaches for achieving this giant leap. It is of paramount importance to establish high chronological resolution of the different forms of evidence resulting from this phase in order to determine which comes first – social or climatic change, epidemics or migrations – in order to move from correlations to causal explanations whenever possible.

The third phase represents more qualitative and explanatory interpretations, where evidence is contextualized within a wider comparative framework of social and historical knowledge, as discussed in the introduction. By identifying prehistoric regularities in the interactions of human biology, linguistic change, social and economic organization, and demography, it will be possible to compare them to anthropological and historical models of such processes in recent times, thereby forming a more comprehensive understanding of the nature of migration, integration, and cultural change, then and now.

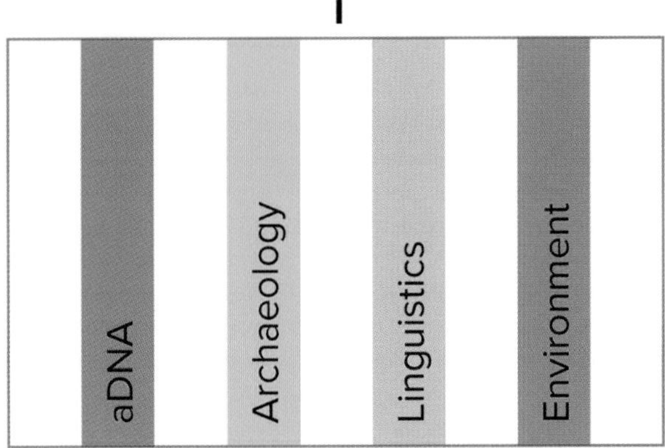

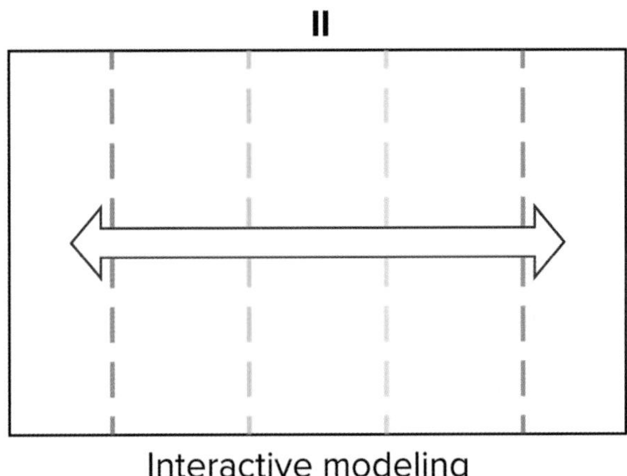

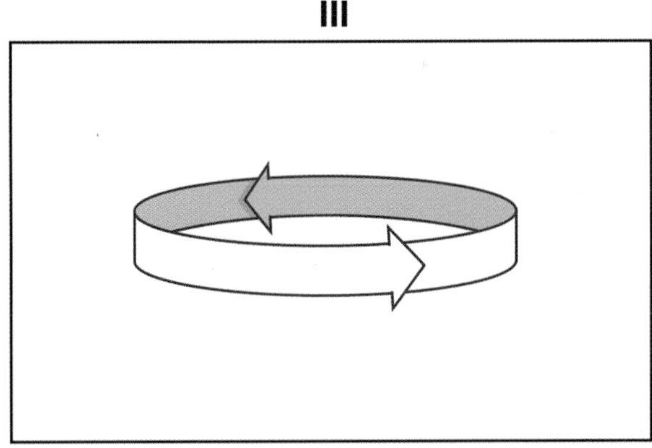

FIGURE 23.3. Model of an interdisciplinary research strategy.

It is during this phase that interpretive decisions are woven into a coherent historical narrative. However, no narrative is able to account for all types of evidence; there will always remain a "surplus," which in turn may lead to new research questions and potentially open up new avenues of interpretation. This is the never-ending research cycle, transforming empirical data into analytical evidence and, finally, historical explanation.

References

Anthony, D. W. 2007. *The horse, the wheel, and language: How Bronze-Age riders from the Eurasian steppes shaped the modern world.* Princeton: Princeton University Press.

2019. Archaeology, genetics, and language in the steppes: A comment on Bomhard. *Journal of Indo-European Studies* 47(1–2): 1–23.

Bryant, E. F. & L. L. Patton. 2005. *The Indo-Aryan controversy: Evidence and inference in Indian history.* London: Routledge.

Cappellini, E. et al. 2018. Ancient biomolecules and evolutionary inference. *Annual Review of Biochemistry* 87: 1029–1060.

Childe, V. G. 1925. *The dawn of European civilization.* London: Routledge.

Damgaard, P. de B. et al. 2018. The first horse herders and the impact of early Bronze Age steppe expansions into Asia. *Science* 360: eaar7711.

Edmonson, M. S. 1961. Neolithic diffusion rates. *Current Anthropology* 2: 71–102.

Furtwängler, A. et al. 2020. Ancient genomes reveal social and genetic structure of Late Neolithic Switzerland. *Nature Communications* 11: 1915.

Gimbutas, M. A. 1956. *The prehistory of eastern Europe.* Cambridge, Massachusetts: Peabody Museum.

1994. *Das Ende Alteuropas: der Einfall von Steppennomaden aus Südrußland und die Indogermanisierung Mitteleuropas.* Budapest: Archaeolingua.

Glob, P. V. 1945. *Studier over den jyske Enkeltgravskultur.* København: Gyldendal.

Haak, W. et al. 2015. Massive migration from the steppe was a source for Indo-European languages in Europe. *Nature* 522 (7555): 207–211.

Hakenbeck, S. E. 2019. Genetics, archaeology and the far right: an unholy trinity. *World Archaeology* 51(4): 517–527.

Hansen, S. 2019. Noch einmal: Abschied von den Indogermanen. In: S. Hansen, V. I. Molodin, & L. N. Mylnikova (ed.), *Mobility and migration: Concepts, methods, results. Materials of the V International Symposium "Mobility and Migration: Concepts, Methods, Results" (Denisova Cave (Altai, Russia), 19–24 August 2019)*, 44–60. Novosibirsk: IAET SB RAS.

Heggarty, P. 2006. Interdisciplinary indiscipline? Can phylogenetic methods meaningfully be applied to language data – and to dating languages? In: P. Forster & C. Renfrew (ed.), *Phylogenetic Methods and the Prehistory of Languages*, 183–194. Cambridge: McDonald Institute for Archaeological Research.

Heggarty, P. & C. Renfrew. 2014. Western and Central Asia: Languages. In: C. Renfrew & P. Bahn (ed.), *The Cambridge World Prehistory*, 1678–1699. Cambridge: Cambridge University Press.

Hyllested, A. 2010. The precursors of Celtic and Germanic. In: S. W. Jamison, H. C. Melchert, & B. Vine (ed.), *Proceedings of the Twenty-First Annual UCLA Indo-European Conference, Los Angeles, October 30th and 31st, 2009*, 1070–1128. Bremen: Hempen.

Knipper, C., A. Mittnik, K. Massy, C. Kociumaka, I. Kucukkalipci, M. Maus, F. Wittenborn, et al. 2017. Female exogamy and gene pool diversification at the transition from the Final Neolithic to the Early Bronze Age in Central Europe. *Proceedings of the National Academy of Sciences of the United States of America* 114(38): 10083–10088.

Koch, J. (in collaboration with R. Karl, A. Minard, & S. Ó Faolain). 2007. *An atlas of Celtic studies. Archaeology and names in ancient Europe and early medieval Ireland, Britain, and Brittany.* Oxford: Oxbow Books.

Kristiansen, K. 1998. *Europe before history.* Cambridge: Cambridge University Press.

2014. Towards a new paradigm? The Third Science Revolution and its possible consequences in archaeology. *Current Swedish Archaeology* 22: 11–71.

2020. The archaeology of Proto-Indo-European and Proto-Anatolian: Locating the split. In: M. Serangeli & T. Olander, *Dispersals and diversification: Linguistic and archaeological perspectives on the early stages of Indo-European*, 157–165. Leiden: Brill.

Kroonen, G., A. Jakob, A. I. Palmér, P. van Sluis, & A. Wigman. 2022. Indo-European cereal terminology suggests a Northwest Pontic homeland for the core Indo-European languages. *PLoS ONE* 17(10): e0275744.

Kuz'mina, E. E. & J. P. Mallory. 2007. *The origin of the Indo-Iranians.* Leiden: Brill.

Lansing, J. S., et al. 2017. Kinship structures create persistent channels for language transmission. *PNAS* 114(49): 12910–12915.

Librado, P., N. Khan, A. Fages, et al. 2021. The origins and spread of domestic horses from the Western Eurasian steppes. *Nature* 598: 634–640.

Mallory, F. 2020. The case against linguistic palaeontology. *Topoi* 40: 273–284.

Mallory, J. P. 2016. Archaeology and language shift in Atlantic Europe. In: J. T. Koch & B. W. Cunliffe (ed.), *Celtic from the West 3: Atlantic Europe in the Metal Ages: Questions of shared language* (Celtic Studies Publications 19), 387–406. Oxford: Oxbow Books.

Malmström, H. et al. 2019. The genomic ancestry of the Scandinavian Battle Axe Culture people and their relation to the broader Corded Ware horizon. *Proceedings of the Royal Society B* 286(1912).

Meid, W. 1994. Die Terminologie von Pferd und Wagen im Indogermanischen. In: B. Hänsel, S. Zimmer (ed.), *Indogermanen und das Pferd*, 53–66. Budapest: Archaeolingua Alapitvany.

Mittnik, A. et al. 2019. Kinship-based social inequality in Bronze Age Europe. *Science* 366(6466): 731–734.

Narasimhan, V. M. et al. 2019. The formation of human populations in South and Central Asia. *Science* 365(6457).

O'Brien, W. 2016. Language shift and political context in Bronze Age Ireland: Some implications of hill fort chronology. In: J. T. Koch & Barry Cunliffe (ed.), *Celtic from the West 3: Atlantic Europe in the Metal Ages: Questions of shared language* (Celtic Studies Publications 19), 219–246. Oxford: Oxbow Books.

Olalde, I., S. Brace, M. Allentoft, et al. 2018. The Beaker phenomenon and the genomic transformation of northwest Europe. *Nature* 555: 190–196.

Patterson, N. et al. 2022. Large-scale migration into Britain during the Middle to Late Bronze Age. *Nature* 601: 588–594.

Prieto-Martinez, M. P. 2012. Perceiving changes in the third millennium BC in Europe through pottery: Galicia, Brittany and Denmark as examples. In: C. Prescott and H. Glörstad (ed.), *Becoming European. The transformation of third millennium northern and western Europe*, 30–47. Oxford: Oxbow Books.

Racimo, F. et al. 2020. The spatiotemporal spread of human migrations during the European Holocene. *PNAS* 117(16): 8989–9000.

Reich, D. 2018. *Who we are and how we got here*. Oxford: Oxford University Press.

Reiter, S. S. & K. M. Frei. 2019. Interpreting past human mobility patterns: A model. *European Journal of Archaeology* 22(4): 454–469.

Renfrew, A. C. 1987. *Archaeology and language: The puzzle of Indo-European origins*. London: Pimlico.

1989. They ride horses, don't they?: Mallory on the Indo-Europeans. *Antiquity* 63: 843–847.

Serangeli, M. & T. Olander. 2019. *Dispersals and diversification offers linguistic and archaeological perspectives on the disintegration of Proto-Indo-European, the ancestor of the Indo-European language family.* Brill's Studies in Indo- European Languages & Linguistics 19. Leiden: Brill.

Shinde, V. et al. 2019. An ancient Harappan genome lacks ancestry from steppe pastoralists or Iranian farmers. *Cell* 179(3): 729–735.

Shishlina N. I. 2004. North-West Caspian Sea steppe: environment and migration crossroads of pastoral culture population during the third millennium BC. In: E. M. Scott, A. Y. Alekseev, & G. Zaitseva (ed.), *Impact of the environment on human migration in Eurasia*, 91–106. Dordrecht: Springer.

Sjögren, K.-J., T. Douglas Price, & K. Kristiansen. 2016. Diet and Mobility in the Corded Ware of Central Europe. *PloS ONE* 11 (5): e0155083.

Sjögren, K.-J. et al. 2020. Kinship and social organization in Copper Age Europe. A cross-disciplinary analysis of archaeology, DNA, isotopes, and anthropology from two Bell Beaker cemeteries. *PloS ONE* 15(11): e0241278.

Skoglund, P., et al. 2012. Origins and genetic legacy of Neolithic farmers and hunter-gatherers in Europe. *Science* 336(6080): 466–469.

Vandkilde, H. 2007. *Culture and change in Central European prehistory.* Aarhus: Aarhus University Press.

Wang, C. C., S. Reinhold, A. Kalmykov, et al. 2019. Ancient human genome-wide data from a 3000-year interval in the Caucasus corresponds with eco-geographic regions. *Nature Communications* 10(590).

Wilkin, S., A. Ventresca Miller, R. Fernandes, et al. 2021. Dairying enabled Early Bronze Age Yamnaya steppe expansions. *Nature* 598: 629–633.

Index